ISBN 978-1-5280-4097-6
PIBN 10922991

FB &c Ltd, Dalton House, 60 Windsor Avenue, London, SW19 2RR.
Company number 08720141. Registered in England and Wales.

For support please visit www.forgottenbooks.com

RECOMBINANT DNA RESEARCH
Volume 7

Documents Relating to "NIH Guidelines for Research Involving Recombinant DNA Molecules" November 1980 - August 1982

December 1982

U.S. DEPARTMENT OF HEALTH AND HUMAN SERVICES
Public Health Service National Institutes of Health

RECOMBINANT DNA RESEARCH
Volume 7

Documents Relating to
"NIH Guidelines for Research
Involving Recombinant DNA Molecules"
November 1980 - August 1982

U.S. SERVICES
Publi ...es of Health

R ESEARCH

ch

Inv ecules"

82

December 1982

Prepared by the
Office of Recombinant
DNA Activities

NIH Publication No. 83-2604

U.S. DEPARTMENT OF HEALTH AND HUMAN SERVICES
Public Health Service National Institutes of Health

PREFACE

This document is the seventh in a series constituting a "public record" of activities in regard to the NIH Guidelines for recombinant DNA research.

The first six volumes cover events from February 1975 through December 1980.

This seventh volume covers events from November 1980 through August 1982 culminating in the revised "NIH Guidelines for Research Involving Recombinant DNA Molecules" as published in the Federal Register on August 27, 1982. These appear first in this volume.

Volumes 1 through 5 in this series may be purchased from the Superintendent of Documents, U.S. Government Printing Office, Washington, D.C. 20402, or viewed in some 600 public libraries of the GPO depository system. The GPO stock number of Volume 1 is 017-004-00398-6; Volume 2, 017-040-00422-2 and (supplement: Environmental Impact Statement) 017-040-00413-3; Volume 3, 017-040-00429-0 and (appendices) 017-040-00430-3; Volume 4, 017-040-00443-5 and (appendices) 017-040-00442-7; and Volume 5, 017-040-00470-2. Volume 6 is available from the Office of Recombinant DNA Activities, National Institutes of Health, Bethesda, Maryland 20205.

CONTENTS

federal register

Friday
August 27, 1982

Part IV

Department of Health and Human Services

National Institutes of Health

Guidelines for Research Involving Recombinant DNA Molecules

DEPARTMENT OF HEALTH AND HUMAN SERVICES

National Institutes of Health

Guidelines for Research Involving Recombinant DNA Molecules

Table of Contents

I. Scope of the Guidelines

I-A. *Purpose.* The purpose of these Guidelines is to specify practices for constructing and handling (i) recombinant DNA molecules and (ii) organisms and viruses containing recombinant DNA molecules.

I-B. *Definition of Recombinant DNA Molecules.* In the context of these Guidelines, recombinant DNA molecules are defined as either (i) molecules which are constructed outside living cells by joining natural or synthetic DNA segments to DNA molecules that can replicate in a living cell, or (ii) DNA molecules that result from the replication of those described in (i) above.

Synthetic DNA segments likely to yield a potentially harmful polynucleotide or polypeptide (e.g., a toxin or a pharmacologically active agent) shall be considered as equivalent to their natural DNA counterpart. If the synthetic DNA segment is not expressed *in vivo* as a biologically active polynucleotide or polypeptide product, it is exempt from the Guidelines.

I-C. *General Applicability.* The Guidelines are applicable to all recombinant DNA research within the United States or its territories which is conducted at or sponsored by an Institution that receives any support for recombinant DNA research from NIH. This includes research performed by NIH directly.

An individual receiving support for research involving recombinant DNA must be associated with or sponsored by an Institution that can and does assume the responsibilities assigned in these Guidelines.

The Guidelines are also applicable to projects done abroad if they are supported by NIH funds. If the host country, however, has established rules for the conduct of recombinant DNA projects, then a certificate of compliance with those rules may be submitted to NIH in lieu of compliance with the NIH Guidelines. NIH reserves the right to withhold funding if the safety practices to be employed abroad are not reasonably consistent with the NIH Guidelines.

I-D. *General Definitions.* The following terms, which are used throughout the Guidelines, are defined as follows:

IV-D-1. "Institution" means any public or private entity (including Federal, State, and local government agencies).

I-D-2. "Institutional Biosafety Committee" or "IBC" means a committee that (i) meets the requirements for membership specified in Section IV-B-2, and (ii) reviews, approves, and oversees projects in accordance with the responsibilities defined in Sections IV-B-2 and IV-B-3.

I-D-3. "NIH Office of Recombinant DNA Activities" or "ORDA" means the office within NIH with responsibility for (i) reviewing and coordinating all activities of NIH related to the Guidelines, and (ii) performing other duties as defined in Section IV-C-3.

I-D-4. "Recombinant DNA Advisory Committee" or "RAC" means the public advisory committee that advises the Secretary, the Assistant Secretary for Health, and the Director of the National Institutes of Health concerning recombinant DNA research. The RAC shall be constituted as specified in Section IV-C-2.

I-D-5. "Director, NIH" or "Director" means the Director of the National Institutes of Health or any other officer or employee of NIH to whom authority has been delegated.

II. Containment

Effective biological safety programs have been operative in a variety of laboratories for many years. Considerable information, therefore, already exists for the design of physical containment facilities and the selection of laboratory procedures applicable to organisms carrying recombinant DNAs [3-16]. The existing programs rely upon mechanisms that, for convenience, can be divided into two categories: (i) a set of standard practices that are generally used in microbiological laboratories, and (ii) special procedures, equipment, and laboratory installations that provide physical barriers which are applied in varying degrees according to the estimated biohazard. Four levels of physical containment, which are designated as P1, P2, P3, and P4 are described in Appendix G. P4 provides the most stringent containment conditions, P1 the least stringent.

Experiments on recombinant DNAs, by their very nature, lend themselves to a third containment mechanism—namely, the application of highly specific biological barriers. In fact, natural barriers do exist which limit either (i) the infectivity of a *vector*, or *vehicle*, (plasmid or virus) for specific hosts or (ii) its dissemination and survival in the environment. The vectors that provide the means for replication of the recombinant DNAs and/or the host cells in which they replicate can be genetically designed to decrease by many orders of magnitude the probability of dissemination or recombinant DNAs outside the laboratory. Further details on biological containment may be found in Appendix I.

As these three means of containment are complementary, different levels of containment appropriate for experiments with different recombinants can be established by applying various combinations of the physical and biological barriers along with a constant use of the standard practices. We consider these categories of containment separately in order that such combinations can be conveniently expressed in the Guidelines.

In constructing these Guidelines, it was necessary to define boundary conditions for the different levels of physical and biological containment and for the classes of experiments to which they apply. We recognize that these definitions do not take into account all existing and anticipated information on special procedures that will allow particular experiments to be carried out under different conditions than indicated here without affecting risk. Indeed, we urge that individual investigators devise simple and more effective containment procedures and that investigators and institutional biosafety committees recommend changes in the Guidelines to permit their use.

III. Containment Guidelines for Covered Experiments

Part III discusses experiments involving recombinant DNA. These experiments have been divided into four classes:

III-A. Experiments which require specific RAC review and NIH and IBC approval before initiation of the experiment;

III-B. Experiments which require IBC approval before initiation of the experiment;

III-C. Experiments which require IBC notification at the time of initiation of the experiment;

III-D. Experiments which are exempt from the procedures of the Guidelines.

If an experiment falls into both class III-A and one of the other classes, the rules pertaining to class III-A must be followed. If an experiment falls into class III-D and into either class III-B or III-C as well, it can be considered exempt from the requirements of the Guidelines.

Changes in containment levels from those specified here may not be instituted without the express approval of the Director, NIH. (See Sections IV-C-1-b-(1), IV-C-1-b-(2), and subsections.)

III-A. *Experiments that Require RAC Review and NIH an IBC Approval Before Initiation.* Experiments in this category cannot be initiated without submission of relevant information on the proposed experiment to NIH, the publication of the proposal in the **Federal Register** for thirty days of comment, review by the RAC, and specific approval by NIH. The containment conditions for such experiments will be recommended by RAC and set by NIH at the time of approval. Such experiments also require the approval of the IBC before initiation. Specific experiments already approved in this section and the appropriate containment conditions are listed in Appendices D and F If an experiment is similar to those listed in Appendices D and F, ORDA may determine appropriate containment conditions according to case precedents under Section IV–C–1–b–(3)–(g).

III–A–1. Deliberate formation of recombinant DNAs containing genes for the biosynthesis of toxic molecules lethal for vertebrates at an LD_{50} of less than 100 nanograms per kilogram body weight (e.g., microbial toxins such as the botulinum toxins, tetanus toxin, diphtheria toxin, *Shigella dysenteriae* neurotoxin). Specific approval has been given for the cloning in *E. coli* K–12 of DNAs containing genes coding for the biosynthesis of toxic molecules which are lethal to vertebrates at 100 nanograms to 100 micrograms per kilogram body weight. Containment levels for these experiments are specified in Appendix F.

III–A–2. Deliberate release into the environment of any organism containing recombinant DNA.

III–A–3. Deliberate transfer of a drug resistance trait to microorganisms that are not known to acquire it naturally [2], if such acquisition could compromise the use of the drug to control disease agents in human or veterinary medicine or agriculture.

III–B *Experiments that Require IBC Approval Before Initiation.* Investigators performing experiments in this category must submit to their Institutional Biosafety Committee (IBC), prior to initiation of the experiments, a registration document that contains a description of: (a) the source(s) of DNA, (b) the nature of the inserted DNA sequences, (c) the hosts and vectors to be used, (d) whether a deliberate attempt will be made to obtain expression of a foreign gene, and, if so, what protein will be produced, and (e) the containment conditions specified in these Guidelines. This registration document must be dated and signed by the investigator and filed only with the local IBC. The IBC shall review all such proposals prior to initiation of the experiments. Requests for lowering of containment for experiments in this cateogry will be considered by NIH. (See Section IV–C–1–b–(3).)

III–B–1. *Experiments Using Human or Animal Pathogens (Class 2, Class 3, Class 4, or Class 5 Agents [1]) as Host-Vector Systems.*

III–B–1–a. Experiments involving the introduction of recombinant DNA into Class 2 agents can be carried out at P2 containment.

III–B–1–b. Experiments involving the introduction of recombinant DNA into Class 3 agents can be carried out at P3 containment.

III–B–1–c. Experiments involving the introduction of recombinant DNA into Class 4 agents can be carried out at P4 containment.

III–B–1–d. Containment conditions for experiments involving the introduction of recombinant DNA into Class 5 agents will be set on a case-by-case basis following ORDA review. A USDA permit is required for work with Class 5 agents [18, 20].

III–B–2. *Experiments in Which DNA from Human or Animal Pathogens (Class 2, Class 3, Class 4, or Class 5 Agents [1]) is Cloned in Nonpathogenic Prokaryotic or Lower Eukaryotic Host-Vector Systems.*

III–B–2–a. Recombinant DNA experiments in which DNA from Class 2 or Class 3 agents [1] is transferred into nonpathogenic prokaryotes or lower eukaryotes may be performed under P2 containment. Recombinant DNA experiments in which DNA from Class 4 agents is transferred into nonpathogenic prokaryotes or lower eukaryotes can be performed at P2 containment after demonstration that only a totally and irreversibly defective fraction of the agent's genome is present in a given recombinant. In the absence of such a demonstration, P4 containment should be used. Specific lowering of containment to P1 for particular experiments can be approved by the IBC. Many experiments in this category will be exempt from the Guidelines. (See Section III–D–4 and III–D–5.) Experiments involving the formation of recombinant DNAs for certain genes coding for molecules toxic for vertebrates require RAC review and NIH approval (see Section III–A–1), or must be carried out under NIH specified conditions as described in Appendix F.

III–B–2–b. Containment conditions for experiments in which DNA from Class 5 agents is transferred into nonpathogenic prokaryotes or lower eukayotes will be determined by ORDA following a case-by-case review. A USDA permit is required for work with Class 5 agents [18, 20].

III–B–3. *Experiments Involving the Use of Infectious Animal or Plant Viruses or Defective Animal or Plant Viruses in the Presence of Helper Virus in Tissue Culture Systems.*

Caution: Special care should be used in the evaluation of containment levels for experiments which are likely to either enhance the pathogenicity (e.g., insertion of a host oncogene) or to extend the host range (e.g., introduction of novel control elements) of viral vectors under conditions which permit a productive infection. In such cases, serious consideration should be given to raising the physical containment by at least one level.

Note.—Recombinant DNA molecules which contain less than two-thirds of the genome of any eukaryotic virus (all virus from a single Family [17] being considered identical [19]) may be considered defective and can be used, in the absence of helper, under the conditions specified in Section III–C.

III–B–3–a. Experiments involving the use of infectious Class 2 animal viruses [1], or defective Class 2 animal viruses in the presence of helper virus, can be carried out at P2 containment.

III–B–3–b. Experiments involving the use of infectious Class 3 animal viruses [1], or defective Class 3 animal viruses in the presence of helper virus, can be performed at P3 containment.

III–B–3–c. Experiments involving the use of infectious Class 4 viruses [1], or defective Class 4 viruses in the presence of helper virus, may be carried out under P4 containment.

III–B–3–d. Experiments involving the use of infectious Class 5 [1] viruses, or defective Class 5 viruses in the presence of helper virus will be determined on a case-by-case basis following ORDA review. A USDA permit is required for work with Class 5 pathogens [18, 20].

III–B–3–e. Experiments involving the use of infectious animal or plant viruses, or defective animal or plant viruses in the presence of helper virus, not covered by Sections III–B–3–a, III–B–3–b, III–B–3–c, or III–B–3–d may be carried out under P1 containment.

III–B–4. *Recombinant DNA Experiments Involving Whole Animals or Plants.*

III–B–4–a. DNA from any source except for greater than two-thirds of a eukaryotic viral genome may be transferred to any non-human vertebrate organism and propagated under conditions of physical containment comparable to P1 and appropriate to the organism under study [2]. It is important that the investigator demonstrate that the fraction of the viral genome being utilized does not lead to productive infection. A USDA permit is required for work with Class 5 agents [18, 20].

III–B–4–b. For all experiments involving whole animals and plants and not covered by III–B–4–a, the appropriate containment will be determined by the IBC.

III–B–5. *Experiments Involving More than 10 Liters of Culture.* The appropriate containment will be decided by the IBC. Where appropriate, the large-scale containment recommendations of the NIH should be used (45 FR 24968).

III–C. *Experiments that Require IBC Notice Simultaneously with Initiation of Experiments.* Experiments not included in Sections III–A, III–B, III–D, and subsections of these Sections are to be considered in Section III-C. All such experiments can be carried out at P1 containment. For experiments in this category, a registration document as described in Section III-B must be dated and signed by the investigator and filed with the local IBC. The IBC shall review all such proposals, but IBC review prior to initiation of the experiment is not required. (The reader should refer to the policy statement in the first two paragraphs of Section IV-A.)

For example, experiments in which all components derive from non-pathogenic prokaryotes and non-pathogenic lower eukaryotes fall under Section III-C and can be carried out at P1 containment.

Caution: *Experiments Involving Formation of Recombinant DNA Molecules Containing no more Than Two-Thirds of the Genome of any Eukaryotic Virus.* Recombinant DNA molecules containing no more than two-thirds of the genome of any eukaryotic virus (all viruses from a single Family [17] being considered identical [19]) may be propagated and maintained in cells in tissue culture using P1 containment. For such experiments, it must be shown that the cells lack helper virus for the specific Families of defective viruses being used. If helper virus is present, procedures specified under Section III-B-3 should be used. The NDA may contain fragments of the genome of viruses from more than one Family but each fragment must be less than two-thirds of a genome.

III-D. *Exempt Experiments.* The following recombinant DNA molecules are exempt from these Guidelines and no registration with the IBC is necessary.

III-D-1. Those that are not in organisms or viruses.

III-D-2. Those that consist entirely of DNA segments from a single non-chromosomal or viral DNA source, though one or more of the segments may be a synthetic equivalent.

III-D-3. Those that consist entirely of DNA from a prokaryotic host, including its indigenous plasmids or viruses, when propagated only in that host (or a closely related strain of the same species) or when transferred to another host by well established physiological means; also, those that consist entirely of DNA from an eukaryotic host, including its chloroplasts, mitochondria, or plasmids (but excluding viruses), when propagated only in that host (or a closely related strain of same species).

III-D-4. Certain specified recombinant DNA molecules that consist entirely of DNA segments from different species that exchange DNA by known physiological processes, though one or more of the segments may be a synthetic equivalent. A list of such exchangers will be prepared and periodically revised by the Director, NIH, with advice of the RAC, after appropriate notice and opportunity for public comment. (See Section IV-C-1-b-(1)-(c).) Certain classes are exempt as of publication of these Revised Guidelines. The list is in Appendix A. An updated list may be obtained from the Office of Recombinant DNA Activities, National Institutes of Health, Bethesda, Maryland 20205.

III-D-5. Other classes of recombinant DNA molecules, if the Director, NIH, with advice of the RAC, after appropriate notice and opportunity for public comment, finds that they do not present a significant risk to health or the environment. (See Section IV-C-1-b-(1)-(c).) Certain classes are exempt as of publication of these Revised Guidelines. The list is in Appendix C. An updated list may be obtained from the Office of Recombinant DNA Activities, National Institutes of Health, Bethesda, Maryland 20205.

IV. Roles and Responsibilities

IV-A. *Policy.* Safety in activities involving recombinant DNA depends on the individual conducting them. The Guidelines cannot anticipate every possible situation. Motivation and good judgement are the key essentials to protection of health and the environment.

The Guidelines are intended to help the Institution, the Institutional Biosafety Committee (IBC), the Biological Safety Officer, and the Principal Investigator determine the safeguards that should be implemented. These Guidelines will never be complete or final, since all conceivable experiments involving recombinant DNA cannot be foreseen. Therefore, *it is the responsibility of the Institution and those associated with it to adhere to the intent of the Guidelines as well as to their specifics.*

Each Institution (and the IBC acting on its behalf) is responsible for ensuring that recombinant DNA activities comply with the Guidelines. General recognition of institutional authority and responsibility properly establishes accountability for safe conduct of the research at the local level.

The following roles and responsibilities constitute an administrative framework in which safety is an essential and integral part of research involving recombinant DNA molecules. Further clarifications and interpretations of roles and responsibilities will be issued by NIH as necessary.

IV-B. *Responsibilities of the Institution.*

IV-B-1. *General Information.* Each Institution conducting or sponsoring recombinant DNA research covered by these Guidelines is responsible for ensuring that the research is carried out in full comformity with the provisions of the Guidelines. In order to fulfill this responsibility, the Institution shall:

IV-B-1-a. Establish and implement policies that provide for the safe conduct of recombinant DNA research and that ensure compliance with the Guidelines. The Institution, as part of its general responsibilities for implementing the Guidelines, may establish additional procedures, as deemed necessary, to govern the institution and its components in the discharge of it responsibilities under the Guidelines. This may include (i) statements formulated by the Institution for general implementation of the Guidelines and (ii) whatever additional precautionary steps the Institution may deem appropriate.

IV-B-1-b. Establish an Institutional Biosafety Committee (IBC) that meets the requirements set forth in Section IV-B-2 and carries out the functions detailed in Section IV-B-3.

IV-B-1-c. If the Institution is engaged in recombinant DNA research at the P3 or P4 containment level, appoint a Biological Safety Officer (BSO), who shall be a member of the IBC and carry out the duties specified in Section IV-B-4.

IV-B-1-d. Require that investigators responsible for research covered by these Guidelines comply with the provisions of Section IV-B-5, and assist investigators to do so.

IV-B-1-e. Ensure appropriate training for the IBC chairperson and members, the BSO, Principal Investigators (PIs), and laboratory staff regarding the Guidelines, their implementation, and laboratory safety. Responsibility for training IBC members may be carried out through the IBC chairperson. Responsibility for training laboratory staff may be carried out through the PI. The Institution is responsible for seeing that the PI has sufficient training, but may delegate this responsibility to the IBC.

IV-B-1-f. Determine the necessity, in connection with each project, for health surveillance of recombinant DNA research personnel, and conduct, if found appropriate, a health surveillance program for the project. [The Laboratory Safety Monograph (LSM) discusses various possible components of such a program—for example, records of agents handled, active investigation of relevant illnesses, and the maintenance of serial serum samples for monitoring serologic changes that may result from the employee's work experience. Certain medical conditions may place a laboratory worker at increased risk in any endeavor where infectious agents are handled. Examples given in the LSM include gastrointestinal disorders and treatment with steroids, immunosuppressive drugs, or antibiotics: Workers with such disorders or treatment should be evaluated to determine whether they should be engaged in research with potentially hazardous organisms during their treatment or illness. Copies of the LSM are available from ORDA.]

IV-B-1-g. Report within 30 days to ORDA any significant problems with and violations of the Guidelines and significant research-related accidents and illnesses, unless the institution determines that the PI or IBC has done so.

IV-B-2. *Membership and Procedures of the IBC.* The Institution shall establish as Institutional Biosafety Committee (IBC) whose responsibilities need not be restricted to recombinant DNA. The committee shall meet the following requirements:

IV-B-2-a. The IBC shall comprise no fewer than five members so selected that they collectively have experience and expertise in recombinant DNA technology and the capability to assess the safety of recombinant DNA research experiments and any potential risk to public health or the environment. At least two members shall not be affiliated with the Institution (apart from their membership on the IBC) and shall represent the interest of the surrounding community with respect to health and protection of the environment. Members meet this requirement if, for example, they are officials of State or local public health or environmental protection agencies, members of other local governmental bodies, or persons active in medical, occupational health, or environmental concerns in the community. The Biological Safety Officer (BSO), mandatory when research is being conducted at the P3 and P4 levels, shall be a member. (See Section IV-B-4.)

IV-B-2-b. In order to ensure the competence necessary to review recombinant DNA activities, it is recommended that (i) the IBC include persons with experties in recombinant DNA technology, biological safety, and physical containment; (ii) the IBC include, or have available as consultants, persons knowledgeable in institutional commitments and policies, applicable law, standards of professional conduct and practice, community attitudes, and the environment; and (iii) at least one member be from the laboratory technical staff.

IV-B-2-c. The Institution shall identify the committee members by name in a report to the NIH Office of Recombinant DNA Activities (ORDA) and shall include relevant background information on each member in such form and at such times as ORDA may require.

IV-B-2-d. No member of an IBC may be involved (excepted to provide information requested by the IBC) in the review or approval of a project in which he or she has been, or expects to be, engaged or has a direct financial interest.

IV-B-2-e. The Institution, who is ultimately responsible for the effectiveness of the IBC, may establish procedures that the IBC will follow in its initial and continuing review of applications, proposals, and activities. (IBC review procedures are specified in Section IV-B-3-a.)

IV-B-2-f. Institutions are encouraged to open IBC meetings to the public whenever possible, consistent with protection of privacy and proprietary interests.

IV-B-2-g. Upon request, the Institution shall make available to the public all minutes of IBC meetings and any documents submitted to or received from funding agencies which the latter are required to make available to the public. If comments are made by members of the public on IBC actions, the Institution shall forward to NIH both the comments and the IBC's response.

IV-B-3. *Functions of the IBC.* On behalf of the Institution, the IBC is responsible for:

IV-B-3-a. Reviewing for compliance with the NIH Guidelines recombinant DNA research as specified in Part III conducted at or sponsored by the Institution, and approving those research projects that it finds are in conformity with the Guidelines. This review shall include:

IV-B-3-a-(1). An independent assessment of the containment levels required by these Guidelines for the proposed research, and

IV-B-3-a-(2). An assessment of the facilities, procedures, and practices, and of the training and expertise of recombinant DNA personnel.

IV-B-3-b. Notifying the Principal Investigator (PI) of the results of their review.

IV-B-3-c. Lowering containment levels for certain experiments as specified in Sections III-B-2.

IV-B-3-d. Setting containment levels as specified in Section III-B-4-b and III-B-5.

IV-B-3-e. Reviewing periodically recombinant DNA research being conducted at the Institution, to ensure that the requirements of the Guidelines are being fulfilled.

IV-B-3-f. Adopting emergency plans covering accidental spills and personnel contamination resulting from such research.

Note.—Basic elements in developing specific procedures for dealing with major spills of potentially hazardous materials in the laboratory are detailed in the Laboratory Safety Monograph (LSM). Included are information and references on decontamination and emergency plans. NIH and the Centers for Disease Control are available to provide consultation, and direct assistance if necessary, as posted in the LSM. The Institution shall cooperate with the State and local public health departments, reporting any significant research-related illness or accident that appears to be a hazard to the public health.

IV-B-3-g. Reporting within 30 days to the appropriate institutional official and to the NIH Office of Recombinant DNA Activities (ORDA) any significant problems with or violations of the Guidelines, and any significant research-related accidents or illnesses, unless the IBC determines that the PI has done so.

IV-B-3-h. The IBC may not authorize initiation of experiments not explicitly covered by the Guidelines until NIH (with the advice of the RAC when required) establishes the containment requirement.

IV-B-3-i. Performing such other functions as may be delegated to the IBC under Section IV-B-1.

IV-B-4. *Biological Safety Officer.* The Institution shall appoint a BSO if it engages in recombinant DNA research at the P3 or P4 containment level. The officer shall be a member of the Institutional Biosafety Committee (IBC), and his or her duties shall include (but need not be limited to):

IV-B-4-a. Ensuring through periodic inspections that laboratory standards are rigorously followed;

IV-B-4-b. Reporting to the IBC and the Institution all significant problems with and violations of the Guidelines and all significant research-related accidents and illnesses of which the BSO becomes aware, unless the BSO determines that the Principal Investigator (PI) has done so;

IV-B-4-c. Developing emergency plans for dealing with accidental spills and personnel contamination, and investigating recombinant DNA research laboratory accidents;

IV-B-4-d. Providing advice on laboratory security;

IV-B-4-e. Providing technical advice to the PI and the IBC on research safety procedures.

Note.—See Laboratory Safety Monograph for additional information on the duties of the BSO.

IV-B-5. *Principal Investigator.* On behalf of the Institution, the PI is responsible for complying fully with the Guidelines in conducting any recombinant DNA research.

IV-B-5-a. *PI—General.* As part of this general responsibility, the PI shall:

IV-B-5-a-(1). Initiate or modify no recombinant DNA research requiring approval by the IBC prior to initiation (see Sections III-A and III-B) until that research, or the proposed modification thereof, has been approved by the IBC and has met all other requirements of the Guidelines;

IV-B-5-a-(2). Determine whether experiments are covered by Section III-C and follow the appropriate procedures;

IV-B-5-a-(3). Report within 30 days to the IBC and NIH (ORDA) all significant problems with and violations of the Guidelines and all significant research-related accidents and illnesses;

IV-B-5-a-(4). Report to the IBC and to NIH (ORDA) new information bearing on the Guidelines;

IV-B-5-a-(5). Be adequately trained in good microbiological techniques;

IV-B-5-a-(6). Adhere to IBC-approved emergency plans for dealing with accidental spills and personnel contamination; and

IV-B-5-a-(7). Comply with shipping requirements for recombinant DNA molecules. (See Apendix H for shipping requirements and the Laboratory Safety Monograph for technical recommendations.)

IV-B-5-b. *Submissions by the PI to NIH.* The PI shall:

IV-B-5-b-(1). Submit information to NIH (ORDA) in order to have new host-vector systems certified;

IV-B-5-b-(2). Petition NIH, with notice to the IBC, for exemptions to these Guidelines;

IV-B-5-b-(3). Petition NIH, with concurrence of the IBC, for approval to conduct experiments specified in Section III-A of the Guidelines;

IV-B-5-b-(4). Petition NIH for determination of containment for experiments requiring case-by-case review;

IV-B-5-b-(5). Petition NIH for determination of containment for experiments not covered by the Guidelines.

IV-B-5-c. *Submissions by the PI to the IBC.* The PI shall:

IV-B-5-c-(1). Make the initial determination of the required levels of physical and biological containment in accordance with the Guidelines;

IV-B-5-c-(2). Select appropriate microbiological practices and laboratory techniques to be used in the research;

IV-B-5-c-(3). Submit the initial research protocol if covered under Guidelines Sections III-A, III-B, or III-C (and also subsequent changes—e.g., changes in the source of DNA or host-vector system) to the IBC for review and approval or disapproval; and

IV-B-5-c-(4). Remain in communication with the IBC throughout the conduct of the project.

IV-B-5-d. *PI Responsibilities Prior to Initiating Research.* The PI is responsible for:

IV-B-5-d-(1). Making available to the laboratory staff copies of the protocols that describe the potential biohazards and the precautions to be taken;

IV-B-5-d-(2). Instructing and training staff in the practices and techniques required to ensure safety and in the procedures for dealing with accidents; and

IV-B-5-d-(3). Informing the staff of the reasons and provisions for any precautionary medical practices advised or requested, such as vaccinations or serum collection.

IV-B-5-e. *PI Responsibilities During the Conduct of the Research.* The PI is responsible for:

IV-B-5-e-(1). Supervising the safety performance of the staff to ensure that the required safety practices and techniques are employed;

IV-B-5-e-(2). Investigating and reporting in writing to ORDA, the Biological Safety Officer (where applicable), and the IBC any significant problems pertaining to the operation and implementation of containment practices and procedures;

IV-B-5-e-(3). Correcting work errors and conditions that may result in the release of recombinant DNA materials;

IV-B-5-e-(4). Ensuring the integrity of the physical containment (e.g., biological safety cabinets) and the biological containment (e.g., purity, and genotypic and phenotypic characteristics).

IV-C. *Responsibilities of NIH.*

IV-C-1. *Director.* The Director, NIH, is responsible for (i) establishing the NIH Guidelines for Research Involving Recombinant DNA Molecules, (ii) overseeing their implementation, and (iii) their final interpretation.

The Director has responsibilities under the Guidelines that involve the NIH Office of Recombinant DNA Activities (ORDA) and the Recombinant DNA Advisory Committee (RAC). ORDA's responsibilities under the Guidelines are administrative. Advice from the RAC is primarily scientific and technical. In certain circumstances, there is specific opportunity for public comment, with published response, before final action.

IV-C-1-a. *General Responsibilities of the Director, NIH.* The responsibilities of the Director shall include the following:

IV-C-1-a-(1). Promulgating requirements as necessary to implement the Guidelines;

IV-C-1-a-(2). Establishing and maintaining the RAC to carry out the responsibilities set forth in Section IV-C-2. The RAC's membership is specified in its charter and in Section IV-C-2;

IV-C-1-a-(3). Establishing and maintaining ORDA to carry out the responsibilities defined in Section IV-C-3; and

IV-C-1-a-(4). Maintaining the Federal Interagency Advisory Committee on Recombinant DNA Research established by the Secretary, HEW (now HHS), for advice on the coordination of all Federal programs and activities relating to recombinant DNA, including activities of the RAC. (See Appendix J.)

IV-C-1-b. *Specific Responsibilities of the Director, NIH.* In carrying out the responsibilities set forth in this Section, the Director or a designee shall weigh each proposed action, through appropriate analysis and consultation, to determine that it complies with the Guidelines and presents no significant risk to health or the environment.

IV-C-1-b-(1). *Major Actions.* To execute major actions the Director must seek the advice of the RAC and provide an opportunity for public and Federal agency comment. Specifically, the agenda of the RAC meeting citing the major actions will be published in the **Federal Register** at least 30 days before the meeting, and the Director will also publish the proposed actions in the **Federal Register** for comment at least 30 days before the meeting. In addition, the Director's proposed decision, at his discretion, may be published in the **Federal Register** for 30 days of comment before final action is taken. The Director's final decision, along with response to the comments, will be published in the **Federal Register** and the *Recombinant DNA Technical Bulletin.* The RAC and IBC chairpersons will be notified of this decision:

IV-C-1-b-(1)-(a). Changing containment levels for types of experiments that are specified in the

Guidelines when a major action is involved;

IV–C–1–b–(1)–(b). Assigning containment levels for types of experiments that are not explicitly considered in the Guidelines when a major action is involved;

IV–C–1–b–(1)–(c). Promulgating and amending a list of classes of recombinant DNA molecules to be exempt from these Guidelines because they consist entirely of DNA segments from species that exchange DNA by known physiological processes, or otherwise do not present a significant risk to health or the environment;

IV–C–1–b–(1)–(d). Permitting experiments specified by Section III–A of the Guidelines;

IV–C–1–b–(1)–(e). Certifying new host-vector systems, with the exception of minor modifications of already certified systems (the standards and procedures for certification are described in Appendix I–II–A. Minor modifications constitute, for example, those of minimal or no consequence to the properties relevant to containment); and

IV–C–1–b–(1)–(f). Adopting other changes in the Guidelines.

IV–C–1–b–(2). *Lesser Actions.* To execute lesser actions, the Director must seek the advice of the RAC. The Director's decision will be transmitted to the RAC and IBC chairpersons and published in the *Recombinant DNA Technical Bulletin:*

IV–C–1–b–(2)–(a). Interpreting and determining containment levels, upon request by ORDA;

IV–C–1–b–(b). Changing containment levels for experiments that are specified in the Guidelines (see Section III);

IV–C–1–b–(2)–(c). assigning containment levels for experiments not explicityly considered in the Guidelines;

IV–C–1–b–(2)–(d). Revising the "Classification of Etiologic Agencts" for the purpose of these Guidelines [1].

IV–C–1–b–(3). *Other Actions.* The Director's decision will be transmitted to the RAC and IBC chairpersons and published in the *Recombinant DNA Technical Bulletin:*

IV–C–1–b–(3)–(a). Interpreting the Guidelines for experiments to which the Guidelines specifically assign containment levels;

IV–C–1–b–(3)–(b). Setting containment under Section III–B–1–d and Section III–B–3–d;

IV–C–1–b–(3)–(c). Approving minor modifications of already certified host-vector systems (the standards and procedures for such modifications are described in Appendix I–II);

IV–C–1–b–(3)–(d). Decertifying already certified host-vector systems;

IV–C–1–b–(3)–(e). Adding new entries to the list of molecules toxic for vertebrates (see Appendix F);

IV–C–1–b–(3)–(f). Approving the cloning of toxin genes in host-vector systems other than *E. coli* K-12 (See Appendix F); and

IV–C–1–b–(3)–(g). Determining appropriate containment conditions for experiments according to case precedents developed under Section IV–C–1–b–(2)–(c).

IV–C–1–b–(4). The Director shall conduct, support, and assist training programs in laboratory safety for Institutional Biosafety Committee members, Biological Safety Officers, Principal Investigators, and laboratory staff.

IV–C–2. *Recombinant DNA Advisory Committee.* The NIH Recombinant DNA Advisory Committee (RAC) is responsible for carrying out specified functions cited below as well as others assigned under its charter or by the Secretary, HHS, the Assistant Secretary for Health, and the Director, NIH.

The members of the committee shall be chosen to provide, collectively, expertise in scientific fields relevant to recombinant DNA technology and biological safety—e.g., microbiology, molecular biology, virology, genetics, epidemiology, infectious diseases, the biology of enteric organisms, botany, plant pathology, ecology, and tissue culture. At least 20 percent of the members shall be persons knowledgeable in applicable law, standards of professional conduct and practice, public attitudes, the environment, public health, occupational health, or related fields. Representatives from Federal agencies shall serve as nonvoting members. Nominations for the RAC may be submitted to the NIH Office of Recombinant DNA Activities, Bethesda, Md. 20205.

All meetings of the RAC will be announced in the **Federal Register**, including tentative agenda items, 30 days in advance of the meeting, with final agendas (if modified) available at least 72 hours before the meeting. No item defined as a major action under Section IV–C–1–b–(1) may be added to an agenda after it appears in the **Federal Register.**

The RAC shall be responsible for advising the Director, NIH, on the actions listed in Section IV–C–1–b–(1) and IV–C–1–b–(2).

IV–C–3. *The Office of Recombinant DNA Activities.* ORDA shall serve as a focal point for information on recombinant DNA activities and provide advice to all within and outside NIH, including Institutions, Biological Safety Committees, Principal Investigators, Federal agencies, State and local governments, and institutions in the private sector. ORDA shall carry out such other functions as may be delegated to it by the Director, NIH, including those authorities described in Section IV–C–1–b–(3). In addition, ORDA shall be responsible for the following:

IV–C–3–a. Reviewing and approving Institutional Biosafety Committee (IBC) membership;

IV–C–3–b. Publishing in the **Federal Register:**

IV–C–3–b–(1). Announcements of Recombinant DNA Advisory Committee (RAC) meetings and agendas at least 30 days in advance;

Note.—If the agenda for an RAC meeting is modified, ORDA shall make the revised agenda available to anyone, upon request, at least 72 hous in advance of the meeting.

IV–C–3–b–(2). Proposed major actions of the type falling under Section IV–C–1–b–(1) at least 30 days prior to the RAC meeting at which they will be considered; and

IV–C–3–b–(3). The NIH Director's final decision on recommendations made by the RAC.

IV–C–3–c. Publishing the *recombinant DNA Technical Bulletin;* and

IV–C–3–d. Serving as executive secretary of the RAC.

IV–C–4. *Other NIH Components.* Other NIH components shall be responsible for certifying P4 facilities, inspecting them periodically, and inspecting other recombinant DNA facilities as deemed necessary.

IV–D. *Compliance.* As a condition for NIH funding of recombinant DNA research, Intitutions must ensure that such research conducted at or sponsored by the Institution, irrespective of the source of funding, shall comply with these Guidelines. The policies on noncompliance are as follows:

IV–D–1. All NIH-funded projects involving recombinant DNA techniques must comply with the NIH Guidelines. Noncopliance may result in: (i) Suspension, limitation, or termination of financial assistance for such projects and of NIH funds for other recombinant DNA research at the Institution, or (ii) a requirement for prior NIH approval of any or all recombinant DNA projects at the Institution.

IV–D–2. All non-NIH funded projects involving recombinant DNA techniques conducted at or sponsored by an Institution that receives NIH funds for projects involving such techniques must comply with the NIH Guidelines. Noncompliance may result in (i)

suspension, limitation, or termination of NIH funds for recombinant DNA research at the Institution, or (ii) a requirement for prior NIH approval of any or all recombinant DNA projects at the Institution.

IV-D-3. Information concerning noncompliance with the Guidelines may be brought forward by any person. It should be delivered to both NIH (ORDA) and the relevant Institution. The Institution, generally through the IBC, shall take appropriate action. Tlhe Institution shall forward a complete report of the incident to ORDA, recommending any further action indicated.

IV-D-4. In cases where NIH proposes to suspend, limit, or terminate financial assistance because of noncompliance with the Guidelines, applicable DHHS and Public Health Service Procedures shall govern.

See Appendix J for information on the Federal Interagency Advisory Committee on Recombinant DNA Research.

IV-D-5. *Voluntary Compliance.* Any individual, corporation, or institution that is not otherwise covered by the Guidelines is encouraged to conduct recombinant DNA research activities in accordance with the Guidelines, through the procedures set forth in Part VI.

V. Footnotes and References of Sections I-IV

1. The original reference to organisms as Class 1, 2, 3, 4, or 5 refers to the classification in the publication *Classification of Etiologic Agents on the Basis of Hazard,* 4th Edition, July 1974; U.S. Department of Health, Education, and Welfare, Public Health Service, Centers for Disease Control, Office of Biosafety, Atlanta, Georgia 30333.

The Director, NIH, with advice of the Recombinant DNA Advisory Committee, may revise the classification for the purposes of these Guidelines (see Section IV-C-1-b-(2)-(d)). The revised list of organisms in each class is reprinted in Appendix B to these Guidelines.

2. In Part III of the Guidelines, there are a number of places where judgments are to be made. In all these cases the principal investigator is to make the judgment on these matters as part of his responsibility to "make the initial determination of the required levels of physical and biological containment in accordance with the Guidelines" (Section IV-B-5-c-(1)). In the cases falling under Sections III-A, -B or -C, this judgment is to be reviewed and approved by the Institutional Biosafety Committee as part of its responsibility to make "an independent assessment of the containment levels required by these Guidelines for the proposed research" (Section IV-B-3-a-(1)). If the IBC wishes, any specific cases may be referred to the NIH Office of Recombinant DNA Activities as part of ORDA's functions to "provide advice to all within and outside NIH" (Section IV-C-3), and ORDA may request advice from the Recombinant DNA Advisory Committee as part of the RAC's responsibility for "interpreting and determining containment levels upon request by ORDA" (Section IV-C-1-b-(2)-(a)).

3. *Laboratory Safety at the Center for Disease Control* (Sept. 1974). U.S. Department of Health Education and Welfare Publication No. CDC 75-8118.

4. *Classification of Etiologic Agents on the Basis of Hazard.* (4th Edition, July 1974). U.S. Department of Health, Education and Welfare. Public Health Service. Centers for Disease Control, Office of Biosafety, Atlanta, Georgia 30333.

5. *National Cancer Institute Safety Standards for Research Involving Oncogenic Viruses* (Oct. 1974). U.S. Department of Health, Education and Welfare Publication No. (NIH) 75-790.

6. *National Institutes of Health Biohazards Safety Guide* (1974). U.S. Department of Health, Education, and Welfare, Public Health Service, National Institutes of Health. U.S. Government Printing Office, Stock No. 1740-00383.

7. *Biohazards in Biological Research* (1973). A. Hellman, M. N. Oxman, and R. Pollack (ed.) Cold Spring Harbor Laboratory.

8. *Handbook of Laboratory Safety* (1971). Second Edition. N. V. Steere (ed.). The Chemical Rubber Co., Cleveland.

9. Bodily, J. L. (1970). *General Adminstration of the Laboratory,* H. L. Bodily, E L. Updyke, and J. O. Mason (eds.), Diagnostic Procedures for Bacterial, Mycotic and Parasitic Infections. American Public Health Association, New York, pp. 11-28.

10. Darlow, H. M. (1969). *Safety in the Microbiological Laboratory.* In J. R. Norris and D. W. Robbins (ed.), Methods in Microbiology. Academic Press, Inc. New York pp. 169-204.

11. *The Prevention of Laboratory Acquired Infection* (1974). C. H. Collins, E. G. Hartley, and R. Pilsworth. Public Health Laboratory Service, Monograph Series No. 6.

12. *Chatigny, M. A. (1961). Protection Against Infection in the Microbiological Laboratory: Devices and Procedures.* In W. W. Umbreit (ed.). Advances in Applied Microbiology. Academic Press, New York, N.Y. 3:131-192.

13. *Design Criteria for Viral Oncology Research Facilities* (1975). U.S. Department of Health, Education, and Welfare, Public Health Service, National Institutes of Health, DHEW Publication No. (NIH) 75-891.

14. Kuehne, R. W. (1973). *Biological Containment Facility for Studying Infectious Disease.* Appl. Microbiol. 26-239-243.

15. Runkle, R. S., and G. B. Phillips (1969). *Microbial Containment Control Facilities.* Van Nostrand Reinhold, New York.

16. Chatigny, M. A., and D. I. Clinger (1969). *Contamination Control in Aerobiology.* In R. L. Dimmick and A. B. Akers (eds.). An Introduction to Experimental Aerobiology. John Wiley & Sons, New York, pp. 194-263.

17. As classified in the Third Report of the International Committee on Taxonomy of Viruses: Classification and Nomenclature of Viruses, R. E. F. Matthews, Ed. Intervirology 12 (129-296) 1979.

18. A USDA permit, required for import and interest transport of pathogens, may be obtained from the Animal and Plant Health Inspection Service, USDA, Federal Building, Hyattsville, MD 20782.

19. i.e., the total of all genomes within a Family shall not exceed two-thirds of the genome.

20. All activities, including storage of variola and whitepox are restricted to the single national facility (World Health Organization (WHO) Collaborating Center for Smallpox Research, Centers for Disease Control, in Atlanta).

VI. Voluntary Compliance

VI-A. *Basic Policy.* Individuals, corporations, and institutions not otherwise covered by the Guidelines are encouraged to do so by following the standards and procedures set forth in Parts I-IV of the Guidelines. In order to simplify discussion, references hereafter to "institutions" are intended to encompass corporations, and individuals who have no organizational affiliation. For purposes of complying with the Guidelines, an individual intending to carry out research involving recombinant DNA is encouraged to affiliate with an institution that has an Institutional Biosafety Committee approved under the Guidelines.

Since commercial organizations have special concerns, such as protection of proprietary data, some modifications and explanations of the procedures in Parts I-IV are provided below, in order to address these concerns.

VI-B. *IBC Approval.* The NIH Office of Recombinant DNA Activities (ORDA) will review the membership of an institution's Institutional Biosafety Committee (IBC) and, where it finds the IBC meets the requirements set forth in Section IV-B-2, will give its approval to the IBC membership.

It should be emphasized that employment of an IBC member solely for purposes of membership on the IBC does not itself make the member an institutionally affiliated member for purposes of Section IV-B-2-a.

Except for the unaffiliated members, a member of an IBC for an institution not otherwise covered by the Guidelines may participate in the review and approval of a project in which the member has a direct financial interest, so long as the member has not been and does not expect to be engaged in the project. Section IV-B-2-d is modified to that extent for purposes of these institutions.

VI-C. *Certification of Host-Vector Systems.* A host-vector system may be proposed for certification by the Director, NIH, in accordance with the procedures set forth in Appendix I-II-A.

In order to ensure protection for proprietary data, any public notice regarding a host-vector system which is designated by the institution as proprietary under Section VI–E–1 will be issued only after consultation with the institution as to the content of the notice.

VI–D. *Requests for Exemptions and Approvals.* Requests for exemptions or other approvals required by the Guidelines should be requested by following the procedures set forth in the appropriate sections in Parts I–IV of the Guidelines.

In order to ensure protection for proprietary data, any public notice regarding a request for an exemption or other approval which is designated by the institution as proprietary under Section VI–E–1 will be issued only after consultation with the institution as to the content of the notice.

VI–E. *Protection of Proprietary Data.* In general, the Freedom of Information Act requires Federal agencies to make their records available to the public upon request. However, this requirement does not apply to, among other things, "trade secrets and commercial and financial information obtained from a person and privileged or confidential." 18 U.S.C. 1905, in turn makes it a crime for an officer or employee of the United States or any Federal department or agency to publish, divulge, disclose, or make known "in any manner or to any extent not authorized by law any information coming to him in the course of his employment or official duties or by reason of any examination or investigation made by, or return, report or record made to or filed with, such department or agency or officer or employee thereof, which information concerns or relates to the trade secrets, [or processes . . . of any person, firm, partnership, corporation, or association." This provision applies to all employees of the Federal Government, including special Government employees. Members of the Recombinant DNA Advisory Committee are "special Government employees."

VI–E–1. In submitting information to NIH for purposes of complying voluntarily with the Guidelines, an institution may designate those items of information which the institution believes constitute trade secrets or privileged or confidential commercial or financial information.

VI–E–2. If NIH receives a request under the Freedom of Information Act for information so designated, NIH will promptly contact the institution to secure its views as to whether the information (or some portion) should be released.

VI–E–3. If the NIH decides to release this information (or some portion) in response to a Freedom of Information request or otherwise, the institution will be advised; and the actual release will not be made until the expiration of 15 days after the institution is so advised, except to the extent that earlier release, in the judgement of the Director, NIH, is necessary to protect against an imminent hazard to the public or the environment.

VI–E–4. *Presubmission Review.*

VI–E–4–a. Any institution not otherwise covered by the Guidelines, which is considering submission of data or information voluntarily to NIH, may request presubmission review of the records involved to determine whether, if the records are submitted, NIH will or will not make part or all of the records available upon request under the Freedom of Information Act.

VI–E–4–b. A request for presubmission review should be submitted to ORDA, along with the records involved. These records must be clearly marked as being the property of the institution, on loan to NIH solely for the purpose of making a determination under the Freedom of Information Act. ORDA will then seek a determination from the HHS Freedom of Information Officer, the responsible official under HHS regulations (45 CFR Part 5), as to whether the records involved (or some portion) are or are not available to members of the public under the Freedom of Information Act. Pending such a determination, the records will be kept separate from ORDA files, will be considered records of the institution and not ORDA, and will not be received as part of ORDA files. No copies will be made of the records.

VI–E–4–c. ORDA will inform the institution of the HHS Freedom of Information Officer's determination and follow the institution's instructions as to whether some or all of the records involved are to be returned to the institution or to become a part of ORDA files. If the institution instructs ORDA to return the records, no copies or summaries of the records will be made or retained by HHS, NIH, or ORDA.

VI–E–4–d. The HHS Freedom of Information Officer's determination will represent that official's judgement, as of the time of the determination, as to whether the records involved (or some portion) would be exempt from disclosure under the Freedom of Information Act, if at the time of the determination the records were in ORDA files and a request were received from them under the Act.

Appendix A.—Exemptions Under III–D–4

Section III–D–4 states that exempt from these Guidelines are "certain specified recombinant DNA molecules that consist entirely of DNA segments from different species that exchange DNA by known physiological processes, though one or more of the segments may be a synthetic equivalent. A list of such exchangers will be prepared and periodically revised by the Director, NIH, with advice of the RAC, after appropriate notice and opportunity for public comment. (See Section IV–C–1–b–(1)–(c).) Certain classes are exempt as of publication of these Revised Guidelines. The list is in Appendix A."

Under Section III–D–4 of these Guidelines are recombinant DNA molecules that are: (1) Composed entirely of DNA segments from one or more of the organisms within a sublist and (2) to be propagated in any of the organisms within a sublist. (Classification of *Bergey's Manual of Determinative Bacteriology*, eighth edition. R. E. Buchanan and N. E. Gibbons, editors. Williams and Wilkins Company: Baltimore, 1974.)

Sublist A

1. Genus *Escherichia*
2. Genus *Shigella*
3. Genus *Salmonella* (including *Arizona*)
4. Genus *Enterobacter*
5. Genus *Citrobacter* (including *Levinea*)
6. Genus *Klebsiella*
7. Genus *Erwinia*
8. *Pseudomonas aeruginosa*, *Pseudomonas putida* and *Pseudomonas flourescens*
9. *Serratia marcescens*
10. *Yersinia enterocolitica*

Sublist B

1. *Bacillus subtilis*
2. *Bacillus licheniformis*
3. *Bacillus pumilus*
4. *Bacillus globigii*
5. *Bacillus niger*
6. *Bacillus nato*
7. *Bacillus amyloliquefaciens*
8. *Bacillus aterrimus*

Sublist C

1. *Streptomyces aureofaciens*
2. *Streptomyces rimosus*
3. *Streptomyces coelicolor*

Sublist D

1. *Streptomyces griseus*
2. *Streptomyces cyaneus*
3. *Streptomyces venezuelae*

Sublist E

One way transfer of *Streptococcus mutans* or *Streptococcus lactis* DNA into *Streptococcus sanguis*.

Sublist F

1. *Streptococcus sanguis*
2. *Streptococcus pneumoniae*
3. *Streptococcus faecalis*
4. *Streptococcus pyogenes*

Appendix B.—Classification of Microorganisms on the Basis of Hazard

Appendix B-1. *Classification of Etiologic Agents.* [The original reference for this classification was the publication *"Classification of Etiological Agents on the Basis of Hazard,"* 4th edition, July 1974, U.S. Department of Health, Education, and Welfare, Public Health Service, Center for Disease Control, Office of Biosafety, Atlanta, Georgia 30333. For the purposes of these Guidelines, this list has been revised by the NIH.]

Appendix B-I-A. *Class 1 Agents.* All bacterial, parasitic, fungal, viral, rickettsial, and chlamydial agents not included in higher classes.

Appendix B-I-B. *Class 2 Agents.*

Appendix B-I-B-1. *Bacterial Agents.*

Acinetobacter calcoaceticus
Actinobacillus—all species
Aeromonas hydrophila
Arizona hinshawii—all serotypes
Bacillus anthracis
Bordetella—all species
Borrelia recurrentis, B. vincenti
Campylobacter fetus
Campylobacter jejuni
Chlamydia psittaci
Chlamydia trachomatis
Clostridium botulinum, Cl. chauvoei, Cl. haemolyticum, Cl. histolyticum, Cl. novyi, Cl. septicum, Cl. tetani
Corynebacterium diphtheriae, C. equi, C. haemolyticum, C. pseudotuberculosis, C. pyogenes, C. renale
Edwardsiella tarda
Erysipelothrix insidiosa
Escherichia coli—all enteropathogenic, enterotoxigenic, enteroinvasive and strains bearing Kl antigen
Haemophilus ducreyi, H. influenzae
Klebsiella—all species and all serotypes
Legionella pneumophila
Leptospira interrogans—all serotypes
Listeria—all species
Moraxella—all species
Mycobacteria—all species except those listed in Class 3
Mycoplasma—all species except *Mycoplasma mycoides* and *Mycoplasma agalactiae*, which are in Class 5
Neisseria gonorrhoeae, N. meningitidis
Pasteurella—all species except those listed in Class 3
Salmonella—all species and all serotypes
Shigella—all species and all serotypes
Sphaerophorus necrophorus
Staphylococcus aureus
Streptobacillus moniliformis
Streptococcus pneumoniae
Streptococcus pyogenes
Treponema carateum, T. pallidum, and *T. pertenue*
Vibrio cholerae
Vibrio parahemolyticus
Yersinia enterocolitica

Appendix B-I-B-2. *Fungal Agents.*

Actinomycetes (including *Nocardia* species and *Actinomyces* species and *Arachnia propionica*)
Blastomyces dermatitidis
Cryptococcus neoformans
Paracoccidioides braziliensis

Appendix B-I-B-3. *Parasitic Agents.*

Endamoeba histolytica
Leishmania sp.
Naegleria gruberi
Schistosoma mansoni
Toxoplasma gondii
Toxocara canis
Trichinella spiralis
Trypanosoma cruzi

Appendix B-I-B-4. *Viral, Rickettsial, and Chlamydial Agents.*

Adenoviruses—human—all types
Cache Valley virus
Coxsackie A and B viruses
Cytomegaloviruses
Echoviruses—all types
Encephalomyocarditis virus (EMC)
Flanders virus
Hart Park virus
Hepatitis-associated antigen material
Herpes viruses—except *Herpesvirus simiae (Monkey B virus)* which is in Class 4
Corona viruses
Influenza viruses—all types except A/PR8/34, which is in Class 1
Langat virus
Lymphogranuloma venereum agent.
Measles virus
Mumps virus
Parainfluenza virus—all types except Parainfluenza virus 3, SF4 strain, which is in Class 1
Polioviruses—all types, wild and attenuated
Poxviruses—all types except *Alastrim, Small-pox,* and *Whitepox*, which are Class 5 and *Monkey pox*, which depending on experiments, is in Class 3 or Class 4
Rabies virus—all strains except *Rabies street virus*, which should be classified in Class 3
Reoviruses—all types
Respiratory syncytial virus
Rhinoviruses—all types
Rubella virus
Simian viruses—all types except *Herpesvirus simiae (Monkey B virus)* and *Marburg virus*, which are in Class 4
Sindbis virus
Tensaw virus
Turlock virus
Vaccinia virus
Varicella virus
Vesicular stomatitis virus [3]
Vole rickettsia
Yellow fever virus, 17D vaccine strain

Appendix B-I-C. *Class 3 Agents.*

Appendix B-I-C-1. *Bacterial Agents.*

Bartonella—all species
Brucella—all species
Francisella tularensis
Mycobacterium avium, M. bovis, M. tuberculosis
Pasteurella multocide type *B* ("buffalo" and other foreign virulent strains) [3]
Pseudomonas mallei [3]
Pseudomonas pseudomallei [3]
Yersinia pestis

Appendix B-I-C-2. *Fungal Agents.*

Coccidioides immitis
Histoplasma capsulatum
Histoplasma capsulatum var. *duboisii*

Appendix B-I-C-3. *Parasitic Agents.*
None.

Appendix B-I-C-4. *Viral, Rickettsial, and Chlamydial Agents.*

Monkey pox, when used *in vitro* [4]
Arboviruses—all strains except those in Class 2 and 4 (*Arboviruses* indigenous to the United States are in Class 3, except those listed in Class 2. *West Nile* and *Semliki Forest* viruses may be classified up or down, depending on the conditions of use and geographical location of the laboratory.)
Dengue virus, when used for transmission or animal inoculation experiments
Lymphocytic choriomeningitis virus (LCM)
Rabies street virus
Rickettsia—all species except *Vole rickettsia* when used for transmission or animal inoculation experiments
Yellow fever virus—wild, when used *in vitro*

Appendix B-I-D. *Class 4 Agents.*

Appendix B-I-D-1. *Bacterial Agents.*
None

Appendix B-I-D-2. *Fungal Agents.*
None

Appendix B-I-D-3. *Parasitic Agents.*
None

Appendix B-I-D-4. *Viral, Rickettsial, and Chlamydial Agents.*

Ebola fever virus
Monkey pox, when used for transmission or animal inoculation experiments [4]
Hemorrhagic fever agents, including *Crimean, hemorrhagic fever, (Congo), Junin*, and *Machupo* viruses, and others as yet undefined
Herpesvirus simiae (Monkey B virus)
Lassa virus
Marburg virus
Tick-borne encephalitis virus complex, including *Russian spring-summer encephalitis, Kyasanur, forest disease, Omsk hemorrhagic fever*, and *Central European encephalitis viruses*
Venezuelan equine encephalitis virus, epidemic strains, when used for transmission or animal inoculation experiments
Yellow fever virus—wild, when used for transmission or animal inoculation experiments

Appendix B-II. *Classification of Oncogenic Viruses on the Basis of Potential Hazard [5].*

Appendix B-II-A. *Low-Risk Oncogenic Viruses.*

Rous Sarcoma
SV-40
CELO
Ad7-SV40
Polyoma
Bovine papilloma
Rat mammary tumor
Avian Leukosis
Murine Leukemia
Murine Sarcoma
Mouse mammary tumor
Rat Leukemia

Hamster Leukemia
Bovine Leukemia
Dog Sarcoma
Mason-Pfizer Monkey Virus
Marek's
Guinea Pig Herpes
Lucke (Frog)
Adenovirus
Shope Fibroma
Shope Papilloma

Appendix B-II-B. *Moderate-Risk Oncogenic Viruses.*

Ad2-SV40
FeLV
HV Saimiri
EBV
SSV-1
GaLV
HV ateles
Yaba
FeSV

Appendix B-III. *Class 5 Agents.*

Appendix B-III-A. *Animal Disease Organisms Which Are Forbidden Entry into the United States by Law.*

Foot and mouth disease virus

Appendix B-III-B. *Animal Disease Organisms and Vectors Which Are Forbidden Entry into the United States by USDA Policy.*

African horse sickness virus
African swine fever virus
Besnoitia besnoiti
Borna disease virus
Bovine infectious petechial fever
Camel pox virus
Ephemeral fever virus
Fowl plague virus
Goat pox virus
Hog cholera virus
Louping ill virus
Lumpy skin disease virus
Nairobi sheep disease virus
Newcastle disease virus (Asiatic strains)
Mycoplasma mycoides (contagious bovine pleuropneumonia)
Mycoplasma agalactiae (contagious agalactia of sheep)
Rickettsia ruminatium (heart water)
Rift valley fever virus
Rhinderpest virus
Sheep pox virus
Swine vesicular disease virus
Teschen disease virus
Trypanosoma vivax (Nagana)
Trypanosoma evansi
Theileria parva (East Coast fever)
Theileria annulata
Theileria lawrencei
Theileria bovis
Theileria hirci
Vesicular exanthema virus
Wesselsbrön disease virus
Zyonema

Appendix B-III-C. *Organisms Which May Not Be Studied in the United States Except At Specified Facilities.*

Small pox [4]
Alastrim [4]
White pox [4]

Appendix B-IV. Footnotes and References of Appendix B.

1. The original reference for this classification was the publication *Classification of Etiologic Agents on the Basis of Hazard*, 4th edition, July 1974, U.S. Department of Health, Education, and Welfare, Public Health Service, Center for Disease Control, Office of Biosafety, Atlanta, Georgia 30333. For the purposes of these Guidelines, this list has been revised by the NIH.
2. Since the publication of the classification in 1974 [1], the *Actinomycetes* have been reclassified as bacterial rather than fungal agents.
3. A USDA permit, required for import and interstate transport of pathogens, may be obtained from the Animal and Plant Health Inspection Service, USDA, Federal Building, Hyattsville, MD 20782.
4. All activities, including storage of variola and whitepox are restricted to the single national facility (World Health Organization (WHO) Collaborating Center for Smallpox Research, Center for Disease Control, in Atlanta).
5. *National Cancer Institute Safety Standards for Research Involving Oncogenic Viruses* (October 1974). U.S. Department of Health, Education, and Welfare Publication No. (NIH) 75-790.
6. U.S. Department of Agriculture, Animal and Plant Health Inspection Service.

Appendix C.—Exemptions Under III-D-5

Section III-D-5 states that exempt from these Guidelines are "Other classes of recombinant DNA molecules, if the Director, NIH, with advice of the RAC, after appropriate notice and opportunity for public comment, finds that they do not present a significant risk to health or the environment. (See Section IV-C-1-b-(1)-(c).) Certain classes are exempt as of publication of these Revised Guidelines."

The following classes of experiments are exempt under Section III-D-5 of the Guidelines: Appendix C-I. *Recombinant DNAs in Tissue Culture.* Recombinant DNA molecules derived entirely from non-viral components (that is, no component is derived from a eukaryotic virus), that are propagated and maintained in cells in tissue culture are exempt from these Guidelines with the exceptions listed below.

Exceptions

Experiments described in Section III-A which require specific RAC review and NIH approval before initiation of the experiment.

Experiments involving DNA from Class 3, 4, or 5 organisms [1] or cells known to be infected with these agents.

Experiments involving the deliberate introduction of genes coding for the biosynthesis of molecules toxic for vertebrates. (See Appendix F.)

Appendix C-II. *Experiments Involving E. coli K-12 Host-Vector Systems.* Experiments which use *E. coli* K-12 host-vector systems, with the exception of those experiments listed below, are exempt from these Guidelines provided that (a) the *E. coli* host shall not contain conjugation proficient plasmids or generalized transducing phages, and (b) lambda or lambdoid or Ff bacteriophages or nonconjugative plasmids [2] shall be used as vectors. However, experiments involving the insertion into *E. coli* K-12 of DNA from prokaryotes that exchange genetic information [3] with *E. coli* may be performed with any *E. coli* K-12 vector (e.g., conjugative plasmid). When a nonconjugative vector is used, the *E. coli* K-12 host may contain conjugation-proficient plasmids either autonomous or integrated, or generalized transducing phages.

For these exempt experiments, P1 physical containment conditions are recommended.

Exceptions

Experiments described in Section III-A which require specific RAC review and NIH approval before initiation of the experiment.

Experiments involving DNA from Class 3, 4, or 5 organisms [1] or from cells known to be infected with these agents may be conducted under containment conditions specified in Section III-B-2 with prior IBC review and approval.

Large-scale experiments (e.g., more than 10 liters of culture) require prior IBC review and approval. (See Section III-B-5.)

Experiments involving the deliberate cloning of genes coding for the biosynthesis of molecules toxic for vertebrates. (See Appendix F.)

Appendix C-III. *Experiments Involving Saccharomyces cerevisiae Host-Vector Systems.* Experiments which use *Saccharomyces cerevisiae* host-vector systems, with the exception of experiments listed below, are exempt from these Guidelines provided that laboratory strains are used.

For these exempt experiments, P1 physical containment conditions are recommended.

Exceptions

Experiments described in Section III-A which require specific RAC review and NIH approval before initiation of the experiment.

Experiments involving Class 3, 4 or 5 organisms [1] or cells known to be infected with these agents may be conducted under containment conditions specified in Section III-B-2 with prior IBC review and approval.

Large-scale experiments (e.g., more than 10 liters of culture) require prior IBC review and approval. (See Section III-B-5.)

Experiments involving the deliberate cloning of genes coding for the biosynthesis of molecules toxic for vertebrates. (See Appendix F.)

Appendix C-IV. *Experiments Involving Bacillus subtilis Host-Vector Systems.* Any asporogenic *Bacillus subtilis* strain which does not revert to a sporeformer with a frequency greater than 10^{-7} can be used for cloning DNA, with the exception of those experiments listed below. Indigenous *Bacillus* plasmids and phages, whose host-range does not include *Bacillus cereus* or *Bacillus anthracis*, may be used as vectors.

For these exempt experiments P1 physical containment conditions are recommended.

Exceptions

Experiments described in Section III-A which require specific RAC review and approval before initiation of the experiment.

Experiments involving Class 3, 4, or 5 organisms [1] or cells known to be infected with these agents may be conducted under containment conditions specified by Section III-B-2 with prior IBC review and approval.

Large-scale experiments (e.g., more than 10 liters of culture) require prior IBC review and approval. (See Section III-B-5.)

Experiments involving the deliberate cloning of genes coding for the biosynthesis of molecules toxic for vertebrates. (See Appendix F.)

Appendix C-V.—Footnotes and References of Appendix C.

1. The original reference to organisms as Class 1, 2, 3, 4, or 5 refers to the classification in the publication *Classification of Etiologic Agents on the Basis of Hazard*, 4th Edition, July 1974; U.S. Department of Health, Education, and Welfare, Public Health Service, Centers for Disease Control, Office of Biosafety, Atlanta, Georgia 30333.

The Director, NIH, with advice of the Recombinant DNA Advisory Committee, may revise the classification for the purposes of these Guidelines (see Section IV-C-1-b-(2)-(d)). The revised list of organisms in each class is reprinted in Appendix B to these Guidelines.

2. A subset of non-conjugative plasmid vectors are also poorly mobilizable (e.g., pBR322, pBR313). Where practical, these vectors should be employed.

3. Defined as observable under optimal laboratory conditions by transformation, transduction, phage infection, and/or conjugation with transfer of phage, plasmid, and/or chromosomal genetic information. Note that the definition of exchange may be less stringent than that applied to exempt organisms under Section III-D-4.

Appendix D.—Actions Taken Under the Guidelines

As noted in the subsection of Section IV-C-1-b-(1), the Director, NIH, may take certain actions with regard to the Guidelines after the issues have been considered by the RAC.

Some of the actions taken to date include the following: Appendix D-I. Permission is granted to clone Foot-and-Mouth Disease Virus in the EK1 host-vector system consisting of *E. coli* K-12 and the vector pBR322, all work to be done at the Plum Island Animal Disease Center.

Appendix D-II. Certain specified clones derived from segments of the Foot-and-Mouth Disease Virus may be transferred from Plum Island Animal Disease Center to the facilities of Genentech, Inc., of South San Francisco, California. Further development of the clones at Genetech has been approved under P1 + EK1 conditions.

Appendix D-III. The Rd strain of *Hemophilus influenzae* can be used as a host for the propagation of the cloned Tn 10 tet R gene derived from *E. coli* K-12 employing the non-conjugative *Hemophilus* plasmid, pRSF0885, under P1 conditions.

Appendix D-IV. Permission is granted to clone certain subgenomic segments of Foot-and-Mouth Disease Virus in HV1 *Bacillus subtilis* and *Saccharomyces cerevisiae* host-vector systems under P1 conditions at Genetech, Inc., South San Francisco, California.

Appendix D-V. Permission is granted to Dr. Ronald Davis of Stanford University to field test corn plants modified by recombinant DNA techniques under specified containment conditions.

Appendix D-VI. Permission is granted to clone in *E. coli* K-12, under P1 physical containment conditions, subgenomic segments of Rift Valley Fever virus subject to conditions which have been set forth by the RAC.

Appendix D-VII. Attenuated laboratory strains of *salmonella typhimurium* may be used under P1 physical containment conditions to screen for the *Saccharmoyces cerevisiae* pseudouridine synthetase gene. The plasmid YEp13 will be employed as the vector.

Appendix D-VIII. Permission is granted to transfer certain clones of subgenomic segments of Foot-and-Mouth Disease virus from Plum Island Animal Disease Center to the laboratories of Molecular Genetics, Inc., Minnetonka, Minnesota, and to work with these clones under P1 containment conditions. Approval is contingent upon review of data on infectivity testing of the clones by a working group of the RAC.

Appendix E.— Certified Host-Vector Systems

While many experiments using *E. coli* K-12, *Saccharomyces serevisiae* and *Bacillus subtilis* are currently exempt from the Guidelines under Exemption III-D-5, some derivatives of these host-vector systems were previously classified as HV1 or HV2. A listing of those systems follows.

HV1. The following plasmids are accepted as the vector components of certified *B. subtilis* HV1 systems: pUB110, pC194, pS194, pSA2100, pE194, pT127, pUB112, pC221, pC223, and pAB124. *B. subtilis* strains RUB 331 and BGSC 1S53 have been certified as the host component of HV1 systems based on these plasmids.

HV2. The asporogenic mutant derivative of *Bacillus subtilis*, ASB 298, with the following plasmids as the vector component: pUB110, pC194, pS194, pSA2100, pE194, pT127, pUB112, pC221, pC223, and pAB124.

HV2. The following sterile strains of *Saccharomyces cerevisiae*, all of which have the ste-VC9 mutation, SHY1, SHY2, SHY3, and SHY4. The following plasmids are certified for use: YIp1, YEp2, YEp4, YIp5, YEp6, YRp7, YEp20, YEp21, YEp24, YIp25, YIp26, YIp27, YIp28, YIp29, YIp30, YIp31, YIp32, and YIp33.

EK2 Plasmid Systems. The *E. coli* K-12 strain chi-1776. The following plasmids are certified for use: pSC101, pMB9, pBR313, pBR322, pDH24, pBR325, pBR327, pGL101, pHB1. The following *E. coli/S. cerevisiae* hybrid plasmids are certified as EK2 vectors when used in *E. coli* chi-1776 or in the sterile yeast strains, SHY1, SHY2, SHY3, and SHY4: YIp1, YEp2, YEp4, YIp5, YEp6, YRp7, YEp20, YEp21, YEp24, YIp25, YIp26, YIp27, YIp28, YIp29, YIp30, YIp31, YIp32, YIp33.

EK2 Bacteriophage Systems. The following are certified EK2 systems based on bacteriophage lambda:

Vector and Host

λgt *WES*.λB′—DP50*sup*F
λgt *WES*.λB*—DP50*sup*F
λgtZJ *Vir*.λB′—*E. coli* K-12
λgtALO.λB—DP50*sup*F
Charon 3A—DP50 or DP50*sup*F
Charon 4A—DP50 or DP50*sup*F
Charon 16A—DP50 or DP50*sup*F
Charon 21A—DP50*sup*F
Charon 23A—DP50 or DP50*sup*F
Charon 24A—DP50 or DP50*sup*F

E. coli K-12 strains chi-2447 and chi-2281 are certified for use with lambda vectors that are certified for use with strain DP50 or DP50supF provided that the su-strain not be used as a propagation host.

Additional certified host-vector systems.

HV1—The following specified strains of *Neurospora crassa* which have been modified to prevent aerial dispersion:

In1 (inositolless) strains 37102, 37401, 46316, 64001, and 89601.

Csp-1 strain UCLA37 and csp-2 strains FS 590, UCLA101 (these are conidial separation mutants).

Eas strain UCLA191 (an "easily wettable" mutant).

HV1—The following *Streptomyces* species: *Streptomyces coelicolor, S. lividans, S. parvulus,* and *S. griseus.* The following are accepted as vector components of certified *Streptomyces* HV1 systems: *Streptomyces* plasmids SCP2, SLP1.2, pIJ101, actinophage phi C31, and their derivatives.

HV1—*Pseudomonas putida* strain KT2440 with plasmid vectors pKT262, pKT263, and pKT264.

Appendix F.—Containment Conditions for Cloning of Genes Coding for the Biosynthesis of Molecules Toxic for Vertebrates

Appendix F-I. *General Information.* Appendix F specifies the containment to be used for the deliberate cloning of genes coding for the biosynthesis of molecules toxic for vertebrates. Cloning of genes coding for molecules toxic for vertebrates that have an LD_{50} of less than 100 nanograms per kilogram body weight (e.g., microbial toxins such as the botulinum toxins, tetanus toxin, diphtheria toxin, *Shigella dysenteriae* neurotoxin) is prohibited. No specific restrictions shall apply to the cloning of genes if the protein specified by the gene has an LD_{50} of 100 micrograms or more per kilogram of body weight. Experiments involving genes coding for toxic molecules with an LD_{50} of 100 micrograms or less per kilogram body weight shall be registered with ORDA prior to initiating the experiments. A list of toxic molecules classified as to LD_{50} is available from ORDA. Testing procedures for determining toxicity of toxic molecules not on the list are available from ORDA. The results of such tests shall be forwarded to ORDA, which will consult with an *ad hoc* working group on toxic molecules prior to inclusion of the molecule on the list. (See Section IV-C-1-b-(2)-(e).)

Appendix F-II. *Containment Conditions for Cloning of Toxic Molecule Genes in E. coli K-12.*

Appendix F-II-A. Cloning of genes coding for molecules toxic for vertebrates that have an LD_{50} in the range of 100 nanograms to 1000 nanograms per kilogram body weight (e.g., abrin, *Clostridium perfringens* epsilon toxin) may proceed under P2 + EK2 or P3 + EK1 containment conditions.

Appendix F-II-B. Cloning of genes for the biosynthesis of molecules toxic for vertebrates with an LD_{50} in the range of 1 microgram to 100 micrograms per kilogram body weight may proceed under P1 + EK1 containment conditions (e.g., *Staphylococcus aureus* alpha toxin, *Staphylococcus aureus* beta toxin, ricin, *Pseudomonas aeruginosa* exotoxin A, *Bordatella pertussis* toxin, the lethal factor of *Bacillus anthracis*, the *Pasteurella pestis* murine toxins, the oxygen-labile hemolysins such as streptolysin O, and certain neurotoxins present in snake venoms and other venoms).

Appendix F-II-C. Some enterotoxins are substantially more toxic when administered enterally than parenterally. The following enterotoxins shall be subject to P1 + EK1 containment conditions: cholera toxin, the heat labile toxin of *E. coli, Klebsiella,* and other related proteins that may be identified by neutralization with an antiserum monospecific for cholera toxin, and the heat stable toxins of *E. coli* and of *Yersinia enterocolitica.*

Appendix F-III. *Containment Conditions for Cloning of Toxic Molecule Genes in Organisms Other than E. coli K-12.* Requests involving the cloning of genes coding for modecules toxic for vertebrates in host-vector systems other than *E. coli* K-12 will be evaluated by ORDA, which will consult with the *ad hoc* working group on toxic molecules. (See Section IV-C-1-b-(3)-(f).)

Appendix F-IV. *Specific Approvals.*

Appendix F-IV-A. Permission is granted to clone the Exotoxin A gene of *Pseudomonas aeruginosa* under P1 conditions in *Pseudomonas aeruginosa.*

Appendix F-IV-B. The pyrogenic endotoxin type A (Tox A) gene of *Staphylococcus aureus* may be cloned in an HV2 *Bacillus subtilis* host-vector system under P3 containment conditions.

Appendix F-IV-C. Permission is granted to clone in *E. coli* K-12, in high containment Building 550 at the Fredrick Cancer Research Facility, restriction fragments of *Corynephage Beta* carrying the structural gene for diphtheria toxin. Laboratory practices and containment equipment are to be specified by the IBC.

Appendix F-IV-D. The genes coding for the *Staphylococcus aureus* determinants, A, B, and F, which may be implicated in toxic shock syndrome, may be cloned in *E. coli* K-12 under P2 + EK1 conditions. The *Staphylococcus aureus* strain used as the donor is to be alpha toxin minus. It is suggested that, if possible, the donor *Staphylococcus aureus* strain should lack other toxins with LD_{50}s in the range of one microgram per kilogram body weight, such as the exfoliative toxin.

Appendix F-IV-E. Fragments F-1, F-2, and F-3 of the diphtheria toxin gene (tox) may be cloned in *E. coli* K-12 under P1 + EK1 containment conditions. Fragment F-1 and fragment F-2 both contain (i) some or all of the transcriptional control elements of *tox*, (ii) the signal peptide, and (iii) fragment A (the center responsible for ADP-ribosylation of elongation factor 2). Fragment F-3 codes for most of the non-toxic fragment B of the toxin, and contains no sequences coding for any portion of the enzymatically-active fragment A moiety.

Appendix F-IV-F. The gene(s) coding for a toxin (designated LT-like) isolated from *E. coli* which is similar to the *E. coli* heat labile enterotoxin (LT) with respect to its activities and mode of action, but is not neutralized by antibodies against cholera enterotoxin or against LT from human or porcine *E. coli* strains and sequences homologous to the *E. coli* LT-like toxin gene may be cloned under P1 + EK1 conditions.

Appendix F-IV-G. Genes from *Vibrio fluvialis, Vibrio mimicus* and non 0-1 *Vibrio cholerae,* specifying virulence factors for animals, may be cloned under P1 + EK1 conditions. The virulence factors to be cloned will be selected by testing fluid induction in suckling mice and Y-1 mouse adrenal cells.

Appendix G.—Physical Containment

Appendix G-I. *Standard Practices and Training.* The first principle of containment is a strict adherence to good microbiological practices [1-10]. Consequently, all personnel directly or indirectly involved in experiments on recombinant DNAs must receive adequate instruction. (See Sections IV-B-1-e and IV-B-5-d.) This shall, as a minimum, include instructions in aseptic techniques and in the biology of the organisms used in the experiments, so that the potential biohazards can be understood and appreciated.

Any research group working with agents with a known or potential biohazard shall have an emergency plan which describes the procedures to be followed if an accident contaminates personnel or the environment. The principal investigator must ensure that everyone in the laboratory is familiar with both the potential hazards of the work and the emergency plan. (See Sections IV-B-3-d and IV-B-5-e.) If a research group is working with a known pathogen where there is an effective vaccine it should be made available to all workers. Where serological monitoring is clearly appropriate it shall be provided. (See Section IV-B-1-f.)

The "Laboratory Safety Monograph", available from ORDA, describes practices, equipment, and facilities in detail.

Appendix G-II. *Physical Containment Levels.* The objective of physical containment is to confine organisms containing recombinant DNA molecules, and thus to reduce the potential for exposure of the laboratory worker, persons outside of the laboratory, and the environment to organisms containing recombinant DNA molecules. Physical containment is achieved through the use of laboratory practices, containment equipment, and special laboratory design. Emphasis is placed on primary means of physical containment which are provided by laboratory practices and containment equipment. Special laboratory design provides a secondary means of protection against the accidental release of organisms outside the laboratory or to the environment. Special laboratory design is used primarily in facilities in which experiments of moderate to high potential hazards are performed.

Combinations of laboratory practices, containment equipment, and special laboratory design can be made to achieve different levels of physical containment. Four levels of physical containment, which are designated as P1, P2, P3, and P4, are described. It should be emphasized that the descriptions and assignments of physical containment detailed below are based on existing approaches to containment of pathogenic organisms. For example, the "Classification of Etiologic Agents on the Basis of Hazard," [2] prepared by the Centers for Disease Control, describes four general levels which roughly correspond to our descriptions for P1, P2, P3, and P4; and the National Cancer Institute describes three levels for research on oncogenic viruses which roughly correspond to our P2, P3, and P4 levels. [3]

It is recognized that several different combinations of laboratory practices, containment equipment, and special laboratory design may be appropriate for containment of specific research activities. The Guidelines, therefore, allow alternative selections of primary containment equipment within facilities that have been designed to provide P3 and P4 levels of physical containment. The selection of alternative methods of primary containment is dependent, however, on the level of biological containment provided by the host-vector system used in the experiment. Consideration will also be given by the Director, NIH, with the advice of the Recombinant DNA Advisory Committee to other combinations which achieve an equivalent level of containment. (See Section IV-C-1-b-(2)-(b).)

Appendix G-II-A. *P1 Level.*

Appendix G-II-A-1. *Laboratory Practices.*

Appendix G-II-A-1-a. Laboratory doors shall be kept closed while experiments are in progress.

Appendix G-II-A-1-b. Work surfaces shall be decontaminated daily, and immediately following spills of organisms containing recombinant DNA molecules.

Appendix G-II-A-1-c. All biological wastes shall be decontaminated before disposal. Other contaminated materials, such as glassware, animal cages, and laboratory equipment, shall be decontaminated before washing, reuse, or disposal.

Appendix G-II-A-1-d. Mechanical pipetting devices shall be used; pipetting by mouth is prohibited.

Appendix G-II-A-1-e. Eating, drinking, smoking, and storage of foods are not permitted in the laboratory area in which recombinant DNA materials are handled.

Appendix G-II-A-1-f. Persons shall wash their hands after handling organisms containing recombinant DNA molecules and when they leave the laboratory.

Appendix G-II-A-1-g. Care shall be taken in the conduct of all procedures to minimize the creation of aerosols.

Appendix G-II-A-1-h. Contaminated materials that are to be decontaminated at a site away from the laboratory shall be placed in a durable leakproof container, which is closed before removal from the laboratory.

Appendix G-II-A-1-i. An insect and rodent control program shall be instituted.

Appendix G-II-A-1-j. The use of laboratory gowns, coats, or uniforms is discretionary with the laboratory supervisor.

Appendix G-II-A-1-k. Use of the hypodermic needle and syringe shall be avoided when alternative methods are available.

Appendix G-II-A-1-l. The laboratory shall be kept neat and clean.

Appendix G-II-A-2. *Containment Equipment.* Special containment equipment is not required at the P1 level.

Appendix G-II-A-3. *Special Laboratory Design.* Special laboratory design is not required at the P1 level.

Appendix G-II-B. *P2 Level.*

Appendix G-II-B-1. *Laboratory Practices.*

Appendix G-II-B-1-a. Laboratory doors shall be kept closed while experiments are in progress.

Appendix G-II-B-1-b. Work surfaces shall be decontaminated daily, and immediately following spills of organisms containing recombinant DNA molecules.

Appendix G-II-B-1-c. All laboratory wastes shall be steam-sterilized (autoclaved) before disposal. Other contaminated materials such as glassware, animal cages, laboratory equipment, and radioactive wastes shall be decontaminated by a means demonstrated to be effective before washing, reuse, or disposal.

Appendix G-II-B-1-d. Mechanical pipetting devices shall be used; pipetting by mouth is prohibited.

Appendix G-II-B-1-e. Eating, drinking, smoking, and storage of food are not permitted in the laboratory area in which recombinant DNA materials are handled.

Appendix G-II-B-1-f. Persons shall wash their hands after handling organisms containing recombinant DNA molecules and when they leave the laboratory.

Appendix G-II-B-1-g. Care shall be exercised to minimize the creation of aerosols. For example, manipulations such as inserting a hot inoculating loop or needle into a culture, flaming an inoculation loop or needle so that it splatters, and forceful ejection of fluids from pipettes or syringes shall be avoided.

Appendix G-II-B-1-h. Contaminated materials that are to be steam sterilized (autoclaved) or decontaminated at a site away from the laboratory shall be placed in a durable leak-proof container, which is closed before removal from the laboratory.

Appendix G-II-B-1-i. Only persons who have been advised of the nature of the research being conducted shall enter the laboratory.

Appendix G-II-B-1-j. The universal biohazard sign shall be posted on all laboratory access doors when experiments requiring P2 containment are in progress. Freezers and refrigerators or other units used to store organisms containing recombinant DNA molecules shall also be posted with the universal biohazard sign.

Appendix G-II-B-1-k. An insect and rodent control program shall be instituted.

Appendix G-II-B-1-l. The use of laboratory gowns, coats, or uniforms is required. Laboratory clothing shall not be worn to the lunch room or outside of the building in which the laboratory is located.

Appendix G-II-B-1-m. Animals not related to the experiment shall not be permitted in the laboratory.

Appendix G-II-B-1-n. Use of the hypodermic needle and syringe shall be avoided when alternative methods are available.

Appendix G-II-B-1-o. The laboratory shall be kept neat and clean.

Appendix G-II-B-1-p. Experiments of lesser biohazard potential can be carried out concurrently in carefully demarcated areas of the same laboratory.

Appendix G-II-B-2. *Containment Equipment*. Biological safety cabinets [12] shall be used to contain aerosol-producing equipment, such as blenders, lyophilizers, sonicators, and centrifuges, when used to process organisms containing recombinant DNA molecules, except where equipment design provides for containment of the potential aerosol. For example, a centrifuge may be operated in the open if a sealed head or safety centrifuge cups are used.

Appendix G-II-B-3. *Special Laboratory Design*. An autoclave for sterilization of wastes and contaminated materials shall be available in the same building in which organisms containing recombinant DNA molecules are used.

Appendix G-II-C. *P3 Level*.

Appendix G-II-C-1. *Laboratory Practices*.

Appendix G-II-C-1-a. Laboratory doors shall be kept closed while experiments are in progress.

Appendix G-II-C-1-b. Work surfaces shall be decontaminated following the completion of the experimental activity, and immediately following spills of organisms containing recombinant DNA molecules.

Appendix G-II-C-1-c. All laboratory wastes shall be steam-sterilized (autoclaved) before disposal. Other contaminated materials, such as glassware, animal cages, laboratory equipment, and radioactive wastes, shall be decontaminated by a method demonstrated to be effective before washing, reuse, or disposal.

Appendix G-II-C-1-d. Mechanical pipetting devices shall be used; pipetting by mouth is prohibited.

Appendix G-II-C-1-e. Eating, drinking, smoking, and storage of food are not permitted in the laboratory area in which recombinant DNA materials are handled.

Appendix G-II-C-1-f. Persons shall wash their hands after handling organisms containing recombinant DNA molecules and when they leave the laboratory.

Appendix G-II-C-1-g. Care shall be exercised to minimize the creation of aerosols. For example, manipulations such as inserting a hot inoculating loop or needle into a culture, flaming an inoculation loop or needle so that it splatters, and forceful ejection of fluids from pipettes or syringes shall be avoided.

Appendix G-II-C-1-h. Contaminated materials that are to be steam-sterilized (autoclaved) or decontaminated at a site away from the laboratory shall be place in a durable leak-proof container, which is closed before removal from the laboratory.

Appendix G-II-C-1-i. Entry into the laboratory shall be through a controlled access area. Only persons who have been advised of the nature of the research being conducted shall enter the controlled access area. Only persons required on the basis of program or support needs shall be authorized to enter the laboratory. Such persons shall be advised of the nature of the research being conducted before entry, and shall comply with all required entry and exit procedures.

Appendix G-II-C-1-j. Persons under 16 years of age shall not enter the laboratory.

Appendix G-II-C-1-k. The universal biohazard sign shall be posted on the controlled access area door and on all laboratory doors when experiments requiring P3-level containment are in progress. Freezers and refrigerators or other units used to store organisms containing recombinant DNA molecules shall also be posted with the universal biohazard sign.

Appendix G-II-C-1-l. An insect and rodent control program shall be instituted.

Appendix G-II-C-1-m. Laboratory clothing that protects street clothing (e.g., long-sleeve solid-front or wrap-around gowns, no-button or slipover jackets) shall be worn in the laboratory. Front-button laboratory coats are unsuitable. Laboratory clothing shall not be worn outside the laboratory and shall be decontaminated before it is sent to the laundry.

Appendix G-II-C-1-n. Raincoats, overcoats, topcoats, coats, hats, caps, and such street outer-wear shall not be kept in the laboratory.

Appendix G-II-C-1-o. Gloves shall be worn when handling materials requiring P3 containment. They shall be removed aseptically immediately after the handling procedure and decontaminated.

Appendix G-II-C-1-p. Animals and plants not related to the experiment shall not be permitted in the laboratory.

Appendix G-II-C-1-q. Vacuum outlets shall be protected by filter and liquid disinfectant traps.

Appendix G-II-C-1-r. Use of hypodermic needle and syringe shall be avoided when alternative methods are available.

Appendix G-II-C-1-s. The laboratory shall be kept neat and clean.

Appendix G-II-C-1-t. If experiments involving other organisms which require lower levels of containment are to be conducted in the same laboratory concurrently with experiments requiring P3-level physical containment, they shall be conducted in accordance with all P3-level laboratory practices.

Appendix G-II-C-2. *Containment Equipment*.

Appendix G-II-C-2-a. Biological safety cabinets [12] shall be used for all equipment and manipulations that produce aerosols—e.g., pipetting, dilutions, transfer operations, plating, flaming, grinding, blending, drying, sonicating, shaking, centrifuging—where these procedures involve organisms containing recombinant DNA molecules, except where equipment design provides for containment of the potential aerosol.

Appendix G-II-C-2-b. Laboratory animals held in a P3 area shall be housed in partial-containment caging systems, such as Horsfall units [11], open cages placed in ventilated enclosures, solid-wall and -bottom cages covered by filter bonnets, or solid-wall and -bottom cages placed on holding racks equipped with ultraviolet radiation lamps and reflectors. (Note: Conventional caging systems may be used, provided that all personnel wear appropriate personal protective devices. These shall include, at a minimum, wrap-around gowns, head covers, gloves, shoe covers, and respirators. All personnel shall shower on exit from areas where these devices are required.)

Appendix G-II-C-2-c. *Alternative Selection of Containment Equipment*. Experimental procedures involving a host-vector system that provides a one-step higher level of biological containment than that specified can be conducted in the P3 laboratory using containment equipment specified for the P2 level of physical containment. Experimental procedures involving a host-vector system that provides a one-step lower level of biological containment than that specified can be conducted in the P3 laboratory using containment equipment specified for the P4 level of physical containment. Alternative combinations of containment safeguards are shown in Table I.

TABLE I.—POSSIBLE COMBINATIONS OF CONTAINMENT SAFEGUARDS

Classification of experiment		Alternate combinations of physical and biological containment			
		Physical containment			
Physical containment	Biological[1] containment	Laboratory design specified for—	Laboratory practices specified for—	Containment equipment specified for	Biological containment
P3	HV2	P3	P3	P3	HV3.
P3	HV2	P3	P3	P4	HV1.
P3	HV1	P3	P3	P3	HV1.
P3	HV1	P3	P3	P2	HV2.

[1] See Appendix I for description of biological containment.

Appendix G–II–C–3. *Special Laboratory Design.*

Appendix G–II–C–3–a. The laboratory shall be separated by a controlled access area from areas that are open to unrestricted traffic flow. A controlled access area is an anteroom, a change room, an air lock or any other double-door arrangement that separates the laboratory from areas open to unrestricted traffic flow.

Appendix G–II–C–3–b. The surfaces of walls, floors, and ceilings shall be readily cleanable. Penetrations through these surfaces shall be sealed or capable of being sealed to facilitate space decontamination.

Appendix G–II–C–3–c. A foot-, elbow-, or automatically-operated hand-washing facility shall be provided near each primary laboratory exit area.

Appendix G–II–C–3–d. Windows in the laboratory shall be sealed.

Appendix G–II–C–3–e. An autoclave for sterilization of wastes and contaminated materials shall be available in the same building (and preferably within the controlled laboratory area) in which organisms containing recombinant DNA molecules are used.

Appendix G–II–C–3–f. The laboratory shall have a ventilation system that is capable of controlling air movement. The movement of air shall be from areas of lower contamination potential to areas of higher contamination potential (i.e., from the controlled access area to the laboratory area). If the ventilation system provides positive pressure supply air, the system shall operate in a manner that prevents the reversal of the direction of air movement or shall be equipped with an alarm that would be actuated in the event that reversal in the direction of air movement were to occur. The exhaust air from the laboratory area shall not be recirculated to other areas of the building unless the exhaust air is filtered by HEPA filters or equivalent. The exhaust air from the laboratory area can be discharged to the outdoors without filtration or other means for effectively reducing an accidental aerosol burden provided that it can be dispersed clear of occupied buildings and air intakes.

Appendix G–II–C–3–g. The treated exhaust-air from Class I and Class II biological safety cabinets [12] may be discharged either to the laboratory or to the outdoors. The treated exhaust-air from a Class III cabinet shall be discharged directly to the outdoors. If the treated exhaust-air from these cabinets is to be discharged to the outdoors through a building exhaust air system, it shall be connected to this system so as to avoid any interference with the air balance of the cabinet and the building ventilation system.

Appendix G–II–D. *P4 Level.*

Appendix G–II–D–1. *Laboratory Practices.*

Appendix G–II–D–1–a. Laboratory doors shall be kept closed while experiments are in progress.

Appendix G–II–D–1–b. Work surfaces shall be decontaminated following the completion of the experimental activity and immediately following spills of organisms containing recombinant DNA molecules.

Appendix G–II–D–1–c. All laboratory wastes shall be steam-sterilized (autoclaved) before disposal. Other contaminated materials such as glassware, animal cages, laboratory equipment, and radioactive wastes shall be decontaminated by a method demonstrated to be effective before washing, reuse, or disposa.

Appendix G–II–D–1–d. Mechanical pipetting devices shall be used; pipetting by mouth is prohibited.

Appendix G–II–D–1–e. Eating, drinking, smoking, and storage of food are not permitted in the P4 facility.

Appendix G–II–D–1–f. Persons shall wash their hands after handling organisms containing recombinant DNA molecules and when they leave the laboratory.

Appendix G–II–D–1–g. Care shall be exercised to minimize the creation of aerosols. For example, manipulations such as inserting a hot inoculating loop or needle into a culture, flaming an inoculation loop or needle so that it splatters, and forceful ejection of fluids from pipettes or syringes shall be avoided.

Appendix G–II–D–1–h. Biological materials to be removed from the P4 facility in a viable or intact state shall be transferred to a nonbreakable sealed container, which is them removed from the P4 facility through a passthrough disinfectant dunk tank or fumigation chamber.

Appendix G–II–D–1–i. No materials, except for biological materials that are to remain in a viable or intact state, shall be removed from the P4 facility unless they have been steam-sterilized (autoclaved) or decontaminated by a means demonstrated to be effective as they pass out of the P4 facility. All wastes and other materials as well as equipment not damaged by high temperature or steam shall be steam sterilized in the double-door autoclave of the P4 facility. Other materials which may be damaged by temperature or steam shall be removed from the P4 facility through a passthrough fumigation chamber.

Appendix G–II–D–1–j. Materials within the Class III cabinets shall be removed from the cabinet system only after being steam-sterilized in an attached double-door autoclave or after being contained in a nonbreakable sealed container, which is then passed through a disinfectant dunk tank or a fumigation chamber.

Appendix G–II–D–1–k. Only persons whose entry into the P4 facility is required to meet program or support needs shall be authorized to enter. Before entering, such persons shall be advised of the nature of the research being conducted and shall be instructed as to the appropriate safeguards to ensure their safety. They shall comply with instructions and all other required procedures.

Appendix G–II–D–1–l. Persons under 18 years of age shall not enter the P4 facility.

Appendix G–II–D–1–m. Personnel shall enter into and exit from the P4 facility only through the clothing change and shower rooms. Personnel shall shower at each egress from the P4 facility. Air locks shall not be used for personnel entry or exit except for emergencies.

Appendix G–II–D–1–n. Street clothing shall be removed in the outer side of the clothing-change area and kept there. Complete laboratory clothing, including undergarments, head cover, shoes, and either pants and shirts or jumpsuits, shall be used by all persons who enter the P4 facility. Upon exit, personnel shall store this clothing in lockers provided for this purpose or discard it into collection hampers before entering the shower area.

Appendix G–II–D–1–o. The universal biohazard sign is required on the P4 facility access doors and on all interior doors to individual laboratory rooms where experiments are conducted. The sign shall also be posted on freezers, refrigerators, or other units used to store organisms containing recombinant DNA molecules.

Appendix G–II–D–1–p. An insect and rodent control program shall be instituted.

Appendix G–II–D–1–q. Animals and plants not related to the experiment shall not be permitted in the laboratory in which the experiment is being conducted.

Appendix G–II–D–1–r. Vacuum outlets shall be protected by filter and liquid disinfectant traps.

Appendix G–II–D–1–s. Use of the hypodermic needle and syringe shall be avoided when alternate methods are available.

Appendix G–II–D–1–t. The laboratory shall be kept neat and clean.

Appendix G–II–D–1–u. If experiments involving other organisms which require lower levels of containment are to be conducted in the P4 facility concurrently with experiments requiring P4-level containment, they shall be conducted in accordance with all P4-level laboratory practices specified in this section.

Appendix G–II–D–2. *Containment Equipment.*

Appendix G–II–D–2–a. Experimental procedures involving organisms that require P-level physical containment shall be conducted either in (i) a Class III cabinet system or in (ii) Class I or Class II cabinets that are located in a specially designed area in which all personnel are required to wear one-piece positive-pressure isolation suits.

Appendix G–II–D–2–b. Laboratory animals involved in experiments requiring P4-level physical containment shall be housed either in cages contained in Class III cabinets or in partial containment caging systems (such as Horsfall units [11], open cages placed in ventilated enclosures, or solid-wall and -bottom cages covered by filter bonnets, or solid-wall and -bottom cages placed on holding racks equipped with ultraviolet irradiation lamps and reflectors) that are located in a specially designed area in which all personnel are required to wear one-piece positive-pressure suits.

Appendix G–II–D–2–c. *Alternative Selection of Containment Equipment.* Experimental procedures involving a host-vector system that provides a one-step higher level of biological containment than that specified can be conducted in the P4 facility using containment equipment requirements specified for the P3 level of physical containment. Alternative combinations of containment safeguards are shown in Table II.

TABLE II.—POSSIBLE COMBINATIONS OF CONTAINMENT SAFEGUARDS

Classification of experiment		Alternative combinations of physical and biological containment			
		Physical containment			Biological containment
Physical containment	Biological containment[1]	Laboratory design specified for—	Laboratory practices specified for—	Containment equipment specified for—	
P4	HV1	P4	P4	P4	HV1.
P4	HV1	P4	P4[2]	P3	HV2.

[1] See Appendix I for description of biological containment.
[2] In this case gloves shall be worn, in addition to the clothing requirements specified in Appendix G-II-D-1-n.

Appendix G–II–D–3. *Special Laboratory Design.*

Appendix G–II–D–3–a. The laboratory shall be located in a restricted-access facility which is either a separate building or a clearly demarcated and isolated zone within a building. Clothing-change areas and shower rooms shall be provided for personnel entry and egress. These rooms shall be arranged so that personnel leave through the shower area to the change room. A double-door ventilated vestibule or ultraviolet air lock shall be provided for passage of materials, supplies, and equipment which are not brought into the P4 facility through the change room area.

Appendix G–II–D–3–b. Walls, floors, and ceilings of the P4 facility are constructed to form an internal shell which readily allows vapor-phase decontamination and is animal- and insect-proof. All penetrations through these structures and surfaces are sealed. (The integrity of the walls, floors, ceilings, and penetration seals should ensure adequate containment of a vapor-phase decontaminant under static pressure conditions. This requirement does not imply that these surfaces must be airtight.)

Appendix G–II–D–3–c. A foot-, elbow-, or automatically-operated handwashing facility shall be provided near the door within each laboratory in which experiments involving recombinant DNA are conducted in openface biological safety cabinets.

Appendix G–II–D–3–d. Central vacuum systems are permitted. The system, if provided, shall not serve areas outside the P4 facility. The vacuum system shall include in-line HEPA filters near each use point or service cock. The filters shall be installed so as to permit in-place decontamination and replacement. Water supply, liquid and gaseous services provided to the P4 facility shall be protected by devices that prevent backflow.

Appendix G–II–D–3–e. Drinking water fountains shall not be installed in laboratory or animal rooms of the P4 facility. Foot-operated water fountains are permitted in the corridors of the P4 facility. The water service provided to such fountains shall be protected from the water services to the laboratory areas of the P4 facility.

Appendix G–II–D–3–f. Laboratory doors shall be self-closing.

Appendix G–II–D–3–g. A double-door autoclave shall be provided for sterilization of material passing out of the P4 facility. The autoclave doors shall be interlocked so that both doors will not be open at the same time.

Appendix G–II–D–3–h. A pass-through dunk tank or fumigation chamber shall be provided for removal from the P4 facility of material and equipment that cannot be heat-sterilized.

Appendix G–II–D–3–i. All liquid effluents from the P4 facility shall be collected and decontaminated before disposal. Liquid effluents from biological safety cabinets and laboratory sinks shall be sterilized by heat. Liquid effluents from the shower and hand washing facilities may be activitated by chemical treatment. HEPA filters shall be installed in all vents from effluent drains.

Appendix G–II–D–3–j. An individual supply and exhaust-air ventilation system shall be provided. The system shall maintain pressure differentials and directional air flow as required to ensure inflow from areas outside the facility toward areas of highest potential risk within the facility. The system shall be designed to prevent the reversal of air flow. The system shall sound an alarm in the event of system malfunction.

Appendix G-II-D-3-k. Air within individual laboratories of the P4 facility may recirculated if HEPA filtered.

Appendix G-II-D-3-l. The exhaust air from the P4 facility shall be HEPA filtered and discharged to the outdoors so that it is dispersed clear of occupied buildings and air intakes. The filter chambers shall be designed to allow *in situ* decontamination before removal and to facilitate certification testing after replacement.

Appendix G-II-D-3-m. The treated exhaust-air from Class I and Class II biological safety cabinets [12] may be discharged directly to the laboratory room environment or to the outdoors. The treated exhaust-air from Class III cabinets shall be discharged to the outdoors. If the treated exhaust-air from these cabinets is to be discharged to the outdoors through the P4 facility exhaust air system, it shall be connected to this system so as to avoid any interference with the air balance of the cabinets or the facility exhaust air system.

Appendix G-II-D-3-n. As noted in Appendix G-II-D-2-a, the P4 facility may contain specially designed areas in which all personnel are required to wear one-piece positive-pressure isolation suits. Such areas shall be airtight. The exhaust-air from the suit area shall be filtered by two sets of HEPA filters installed in series, and a duplicate filtration unit and exhaust fan shall be provided. The air pressure within the suit area shall be less than that on any adjacent area. An emergency lighting system, communication systems, and power source shall be provided. A double-door autoclave shall be provided for sterilization of all waste materials to be removed from the suit area.

Personnel who enter this area shall wear a one-piece positive-pressure suit that is ventilated by a life-support system. The life-support system shall be provided with alarms and emergency backup air. Entry to this area is through an airlock fitted with airtight doors. A chemical shower area shall be provided to decontaminate the surfaces of the suit before removal.

Appendix G-III. Footnotes and References of Appendix G

1. *Laboratory Safety at the Center for Disease Control* (Sept. 1974). U.S. Department of Health Education and Welfare Publication No. CDC 75-8118.

2. *Classification of Etiologic Agents on the Basis of Hazard.* (4th Edition, July 1974). U.S. Department of Health, Education and Welfare. Public Health Service. Centers for Disease Control, Office of Biosafety, Atlanta, Georgia 30333.

3. *National Cancer Institute Safety Standards for Research Involving Oncogenic Viruses* (Oct. 1974). U.S. Department of Health, Education and Welfare Publication No. (NIH) 75-790.

4. *National Institutes of Health Biohazards Safety Guide* (1974). U.S. Department of Health, Education, and Welfare, Public Health Service, National Institutes of Health. U.S. Government Printing Office, Stock No. 1740-00383.

5. *Biohazards in Biological Research* (1973). A. Hellman, M. N. Oxman, and R. Pollack (ed.) Cold Spring Harbor Laboratory.

6. *Handbook of Laboratory Safety* (1971). Second Edition. N. V. Steere (ed.) The Chemical Rubber Co., Cleveland.

7. Bodily, J. L. (1970). *General Administration of the Laboratory*, H. L. Bodily, E. L. Updyke, and J. O. Mason (eds.), Diagnostic Procedures for Bacterial, Mycotic and Parasitic Infections. American Public Health Association, New York, pp. 11-28.

8. Darlow, H. M. (1969). *Safety in the Microbiological Laboratory*. In J. R. Norris and D. W. Robbins (ed.), Methods in Microbiology. Academic Press, Inc. New York. pp. 169-204.

9. *The Prevention of Laboratory Acquired Infection* (1974). C. H. Collins, E. G. Hartley, and R. Pilsworth. Public Health Laboratory Service, Monograph Series No. 6.

10. Chatigny, M. A. (1961). *Protection Against Infection in the Microbiological Laboratory: Devices and Procedures*. In W. W. Umbreit (ed.) Advances in Applied Microbiology. Academic Press, New York, N.Y. 3:131-192.

11. Horsfall, F. L., Jr., and J. H. Baner (1940). *Individual Isolation of Infected Animals in a Single Room*. J. Bact. 40, 569-580.

12. Biological safety cabinets referred to in this section are classified as *Class I, Class II*, or *Class III* cabinets. A *Class I* is a ventilated cabinet for personnel protection having an inward flow of air away from the operator. The exhaust air from this cabinet is filtered through a high-efficiency particulate air (HEPA) filter. This cabinet is used in three operational modes: (1) with a full-width open front, (2) with an installed front closure panel (having four 8-inch diameter openings) without gloves, and (3) with an installed front closure panel equipped with arm-length rubber gloves. The face velocity of the inward flow of air through the full-width open front is 75 feet per minute or greater.

A *Class II* cabinet is a ventilated cabinet for personnel and product protection having an open front with inward air flow for personnel protection, and HEPA filtered mass recirculated air flow for product protection. The cabinet exhaust air is filtered through a HEPA filter. The face velocity of the inward flow of air through the full-width open front is 75 feet per minute or greater. Design and performance specifications for *Class II* cabinets have been adopted by the National Sanitation Foundation, Ann Arbor, Michigan.

A *Class III* cabinet is a closed-front ventilated cabinet of gas-tight construction which provides the highest level of personnel protection of all biohazard safety cabinets. The interior of the cabinet is protected from contaminants exterior to the cabinet. The cabinet is fitted with arm-length rubber gloves and is operated under a negative pressure of at least 0.5 inches water gauge. All supply air is filtered through HEPA filters. Exhaust air is filtered through two HEPA filters or one HEPA filter and incinerator before being discharged to the outside environment.

Appendix H.—Shipment

Recombinant DNA molecules contained in an organism or virus shall be shipped only as an etiologic agent under requirements of the U.S. Public Health Service, and the U.S. Department of Transportation (§ 72.3, Part 72, Title 42, and §§ 173.386-.388, Part 173, Title 49, U.S. Code of Federal Regulations (CFR)) as specified below:

Appendix H-I. Recombinant DNA molecules contained in an organism or virus requiring P1, P2, or P3 physical containment, when offered for transportation or transported, are subject to all requirements of § 72.3(a)-(e), Part 72, Title 42 CFR, and §§ 173.386-.388, Part 173, Title 49 CFR.

Appendix H-II. Recombinant DNA molecules contained in an organism or virus requiring P4 physical containment, when offered for transportation or transported, are subject to the requirements listed above under Appendix H-I and are also subject to § 72.3(f), Part 72, Title 42 CFR.

Appendix H-III. Information on packaging and labeling of etiologic agents is shown in Figures 1, 2, and 3. Additional information on packaging and shipment is given in the "Laboratory Safety Monograph—A Supplement to the NIH Guidelines for Recombinant DNA Research," available from ORDA.

BILLING CODE 4140-01-M

PACKAGING AND LABELING OF ETIOLOGIC AGENTS

FIGURE 1

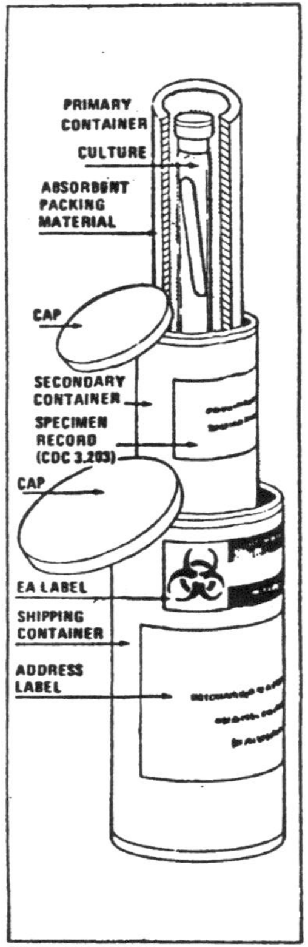

FIGURE 2

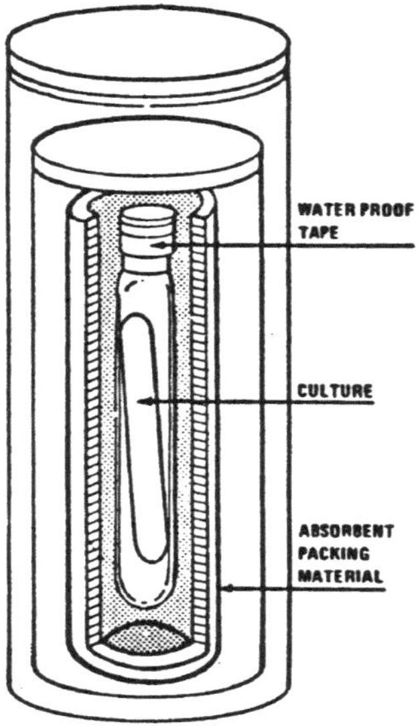

CROSS SECTION OF PROPER PACKING

The Interstate Shipment of Etiologic Agents (42 CFR, Part 72) was revised July 21, 1980 to provide for packaging and labeling requirements for etiologic agents and certain other materials shipped in interstate traffic.

Figures 1 and 2 diagram the packaging and labeling of etiologic agents in volumes of less than 50 ml. in accordance with the provisions of subparagraph 72.3 (a) of the cited regulation. Figure illustrates the color and size of the label, decribed in subparagraph 72.3 (d) (1 - 5) of the regulations, which shall be affixed to all shipments of etiologic agents.

For further information on any provision of this regulation contact:

Centers for Disease Control
Attn: Biohazards Control Office
1600 Clifton Road
Atlanta, Georgia 30333

Telephone: 404—329-3883
FTS—236-3883

FIGURE 3

ETIOLOGIC AGENTS
BIOMEDICAL MATERIAL
IN CASE OF DAMAGE OR LEAKAGE
NOTIFY DIRECTOR, CDC
ATLANTA, GEORGIA
404/633-5313

BILLING CODE 4140-01-C

Appendix I.—Biological Containment

Appendix I-I. *Levels of Biological Containment.* In consideration of biological containment, the vector (plasmid, organelle, or virus) for the recombinant DNA and the host (bacterial, plant, or animal cell) in which the vector is propagated in the laboratory will be considered together. Any combination of vector and host which is to provide biological containment must be chosen or constructed so that the following types of "escape" are minimized: (i) survival of the vector in its host outside the laboratory and (ii) transmission of the vector from the propagation host to other nonlaboratory hosts.

The following levels of biological containment (HV, or *Host-Vector*, systems) for prokaryotes will be established; specific criteria will depend on the organisms to be used.

Appendix I-I-A. *HV1.* A host-vector system which provides a moderate level of containment. *Specific systems:*

Appendix I-I-A-1. *EK1.* The host is always *E. coli* K-12 or a derivative thereof, and the vectors include nonconjugative plasmids (e.g., pSC101, ColE1, or derivatives thereof [1-7]) and variants of bacteriophage, such as lambda [8-15]. The *E. coli* K-12 hosts shall not contain conjugation-proficient plasmids, whether autonomous or integrated, or generalized tranducing phages.

Appendix I-I-A-2. *Other HV1.* Hosts and vectors shall be, at a minimum, comparable in containment to *E. coli* K-12 with a non conjugative plasmid or bacteriophage vector. The data to be considered and a mechanism for approval of such HV1 systems are described below (Appendix I-II).

Appendix I-I-B. *HV2.* These are host-vector systems shown to provide a high level of biological containment as demonstrated by data from suitable tests performed in the laboratory. Escape of the recombinant DNA either via survival of the organisms or via transmission of recombinant DNA to other organisms should be less than $1/10^8$ under specified conditions. *Specific systems:*

Appendix I-I-B-1. For EK2 host-vector systems in which the vector is a plasmid, no more than one in 10^8 host cells should be able to perpetuate a cloned DNA fragment under the specified nonpermissive laboratory conditions designed to represent the natural environment, either by survival of the original host or as a consequences of transmission of the cloned DNA fragment.

Appendix I-I-B-2. For EK2 host-vector systems in which the vector is a phage, no more than one in 10^8 phage particles should be able to perpetuate a cloned DNA fragment under the specified nonpermissive laboratory conditions designed to represent the natural environment either (i) as a prophage (in the inserted or plasmid form) in the laboratory host used for phage propagation or (ii) by surviving in natural environments and transferring a cloned DNA fragment to other hosts (or their resident prophages).

Appendix I-II. *Certification of Host-Vector Systems.*

Appendix I-II-A. *Responsibility.* HV1 systems other than *E. coli* K-12, and HV2 host-vector systems, may not be designated as such until they have been certified by the Director, NIH. Application for certification of a host-vector system is made by written application to the Office of Recombinant DNA Activities, National Institutes of Health, Bethesda, Maryland 20205.

Host-vector systems that are proposed for certification will be reviewed by the National Institutes of Health (NIH) Recombinant DNA Advisory Committee (RAC). (See Section IV-C-1-b-(1)-(e).) This will first involve review of the data on construction, properties, and testing of the proposed host-vector system by a Working Group composed of one or more members of the RAC and other persons chosen because of their expertise in evaluating such data. The Committee will then evaluate the report of the Working Group and any other available information at a regular meeting. The Director, NIH, is responsible for certification after receiving the advice of the RAC. Minor modifications of existing certified host-vector systems, where the modifications are of minimal or no consequence to the properties relevant to containment may be certified by the Director, NIH, without review by the RAC. (See Section IV-C-1-b-(3)-(c).)

When new host-vector systems are certified, notice of the certification will be sent by the Office of Recombinant DNA Activities (ORDA) to the applicant and to all Institutional Biosafety Committees (IBCs) and will be published in the *Recombinant DNA Technical Bulletin.* Copies of a list of all currently certified host-vector systems may be obtained from ORDA at any time.

The Director, NIH, may at any time rescind the certification of any host-vector system. (See Section IV-C-1-b-(3)-(d).) If certification of a host-vector system is rescinded, NIH will instruct investigators to transfer cloned DNA into a different system, or use the clones at a higher physical containment level unless NIH determines that the already constructed clones incorporate adequate biological containment.

Certification of a given system does not extend the modifications of either the host or vector component of that system. Such modified systems must be independently certified by the Director, NIH. If modifications are minor, it may only be necessary for the investigator to submit data showing that the modifications have either improved or not impaired the major phenotypic traits on which the containment of the system depends. Substantial modifications of a certified system require the submission of complete testing data.

Appendix I-II-B. *Data To Be Submitted for Certification.*

Appendix I-II-B-1. *HV1 Systems Other than E. coli K-12.* The following types of data shall be submitted, modified as appropriate for the particular system under consideration. (i) A description of the organism and vector; the strain's natural habitat and growth requirements; its physiological properties, particularly those related to its reproduction and survival and the mechanisms by which it exchanges genetic information; the range of organisms with which this organism normally exchanges genetic information and what sort of information is exchanged; and any relevant information on its pathogenicity or toxicity. (ii) A description of the history of the particular strains and vectors to be used, including data on any mutations which render this organism less able to survive or transmit genetic information. (iii) A general description of the range of experiments contemplated, with emphasis on the need for developing such an HV1 system.

Appendix I-II-B-2. *HV2 Systems.* Investigators planning to request HV2 certification for host-vector systems can obtain instructions from ORDA concerning data to be submitted [14-15]. In general, the following types of data are required: (i) Description of construction steps, with indication of source, properties, and manner of introduction of genetic traits. (ii) Quantitative data on the stability of genetic traits that contribute to the containment of the system. (iii) Data on the survival of the host-vector system under nonpermissive laboratory conditions designed to represent the relevant natural environment. (iv) Data on transmissibility of the vector and/or a cloned DNA fragment under both permissive and nonpermissive conditions. (v) Data on all other properties of the system which affect containment and utility, including information on yields of phage or plasmid molecules, ease of DNA isolation, and ease of transfection or transformation. (vi) In some cases, the investigator may be asked to submit data on survival and vector transmissibility from experiments in which the host-vector is fed to laboratory animals and human subjects. Such *in vivo* data may be required to confirm the validity of predicting *in vivo* survival on the basis of *in vitro* experiments.

Data must be submitted in writing to ORDA. Ten to twelve weeks are normally required for review and circulation of the data prior to the meeting at which such data can be considered by the RAC. Investigators are encouraged to publish their data on the construction, properties, and testing of proposed HV2 systems prior to consideration of the system by the RAC and its subcommittee. More specific instructions concerning the type of data to be submitted to NIH for proposed EK2 systems involving either plasmids or bacteriophage in *E. coli* K–12 are available from ORDA.

Appendix I–III.—Footnotes and References of Appendix I

1. Hershfield, V., H. W. Boyer, C. Yanofsky, M. A. Lovett, and D. R. Helinski (1974). *Plasmid ColEl as a Molecular Vehicle for Cloning and Amplification of DNA*. Proc. Nat. Acad. Sci. USA *71*, 3455–3459.

2. Wensink, P. C., D. J. Finnegan, J. E. Donelson, and D. S. Hogness (1974). *A System for Mapping DNA Sequences in the Chromosomes of Drosophila Melanogaster*. Cell *3*, 315–335.

3. Tanka, T., and B. Weisblum (1975). *Construction of a Colicin El–R Factor Composite Plasmid In Vitro: Means for Amplification of Deoxyribonucleic Acid*. J. Bacteriol. *121*, 354–362.

4. Armstrong, K. A., V. Hershfield, and D. R. Helinski (1977). *Gene Cloning and Containment Properties of Plasmid Col El and Its Derivatives*, Science *196*, 172–174.

5. Bolivar, F., R. L. Rodriguez, M. C. Betlach, and H. W. Boyer (1977). *Construction and Characterization of New Cloning Vehicles: I. Ampicillin-Resistant Derivative of pMB9*. Gene *2*, 75–93.

6. Cohen, S. N., A. C. W. Chang, H. Boyer, and R. Helling (1973). *Construction of Biologically Functional Bacterial Plasmids in Vitro*. Proc. Natl. Acad. Sci. USA *70*, 3240–3244.

7. Bolivar, F., R. L. Rodriguez, R. J. Greene, M. C. Batlach, H. L. Reyneker, H. W. Boyer, J. H. Crosa, and S. Falkow (1977). *Construction and Characterization of New Cloning Vehicles: II. A Multi-Purpose Cloning System*. Gene *2*, 95–113.

8. Thomas, M., J. R. Cameron, and R. W. Davis (1974). *Viable Molecular Hybrids of Bacteriophage Lambda and Eukaryotic DNA*. Proc. Nat. Acad. Sci. USA *71*, 4579–4583.

9. Murray, N. E. and K. Murray (1974). *Manipulation of Restriction Targets in Phage Lambda to Form Receptor chromosomes for DNA Fragments*. Nature *251*, 476–481.

10. Rambach, A., and P. Tiollais (1974). *Bacteriophage Having EcoRI Endonuclease Sites Only in the Non-Essential Region of the Genome*. Proc. Nat. Acad. Sci., USA *71*, 3927–3930.

11. Blattner, F. R., B. G. Williams, A. E. Bleche, K. Denniston-Thompson, H. E. Faber, L. A. Furlong, D. J. Gunwald, D. O. Kiefer, D. D. Moore, J. W. Shumm, E. L. Sheldon, and O. Smithies (1977). *Charon Phages: Safer Derivatives of Bacteriophage Lambda for DNA Cloning*. Science *196*, 163–169.

12. Donoghue, D. J., and P. A. Sharp (1977). *An Improved Lambda Vector: Construction of Model Recombinants Coding for Kanamycin Resistance*. Gene *1*, 209–227.

13. Leder, P., D. Tiemeier and L. Enquist (1977). *EK2 Derivatives of Bacteriophage Lambda Useful in the Cloning of DNA From Higher Organisms: The gt WES System*. Science *196*, 175–177.

14. Skalka, A. (1978). *Current Status of Coliphage EK2 Vectors*. Gene *3*, 29–35.

15. Szybalski, W., A. Skalka, S. Gottesman, A. Campbell, and D. Botstein (1978). *Standardized Laboratory Tests for EK2 Certification*. Gene *3*, 36–38.

Appendix J.—Federal Interagency Advisory Committee on Recombinant DNA Research

Appendix J–I. The Federal Interagency Advisory Committee on Recombinant DNA Research advises the Secretary of the Department of Health and Human Services, the Assistant Secretary for Health, and the Director, National Institutes of Health, on the coordination of those aspects of all Federal programs and activities relating to recombinant DNA research. The Committee provides for communication and exchange of information necessary to maintain adequate coordination of such programs and activities. The Committee is responsible for facilitating compliance with a uniform set of guidelines in the conduct of this research in the public and private sectors and, where warranted, to suggest administrative or legislative proposals.

The Director of the NIH, or his designee, serves as Chairman, and the Committee includes representation from all Departments and Agencies whose programs involve health functions or responsibilities as determined by the Secretary.

Departments and Agencies which have representation on this Committee, as of December 1980, are:

Department of Agriculture
Department of Commerce
Department of Defense
Department of Energy
Environmental Protection Agency
Executive Office of the President
Department of Health and Human Services
- Office of the Assistant Secretary for Health
- Centers for Disease Control
- Food and Drug Administration
- National Institutes of Health

Department of the Interior
Department of Justice
Department of Labor
National Aeronautics and Space Administration
National Science Foundation
Nuclear Regulatory Commission
Department of State
Department of Transportation
Arms Control and Disarmament Agency
Veterans Administration

At the second meeting of the Committee on November 23, 1976, all of the Federal agencies endorsed the NIH Guidelines, and Departments which support or conduct recombinant DNA research agreed to abide by the NIH Guidelines [1].

Appendix J–II. *Footnote of Appendix J*

1. Minutes of the first eight meetings of the Federal Interagency Advisory Committee on Recombinant DNA Research are reproduced in *Recombinant DNA Research, Volume 2. Documents Relating to "NIH Guidelines for Research Involving Recombinant DNA Molecules," June 1976–November 1977.*

OMB's "Mandatory Information Requirements for Federal Assistance Program Announcements" (45 FR 39592) requires a statement concerning the official government programs contained in the *Catalog of Federal Domestic Assistance*. Normally NIH lists in its announcements the number and title of affected individual programs for the guidance of the public. Because the guidance in this notice covers not only virtually every NIH program but also essentially every federal research program in which DNA recombinant molecule techniques could be used, it has been determined to be not cost effective or in the public interest to attempt to list these programs. Such a list would likely require several additional pages. In addition, NIH could not be certain that every federal program would be included as many federal agencies, as well as private organizations, both national and international, have elected to follow the NIH Guidelines. In lieu of the individual program listing, NIH invites readers to direct questions to the information address above about whether individual programs listed in the *Catalog of Federal Domestic Assistance* are affected.

NIH programs are not covered by OMB Circular A–95 because they fit the description of "programs not considered appropriate" in Section 8–(b)–(4) and (5) of that Circular.

Dated: August 18, 1982.

Richard M. Krause,
Director, National Institute of Allergy and Infectious Diseases, National Institutes of Health.

[FR Doc. 82–23306 Filed 8–26–82; 8:45 am]
BILLING CODE 4140–01–M

federal register

Friday
November 28, 1980

Part VII

Department of Health and Human Services

National Institutes of Health

Recombinant DNA Advisory Committee Meeting; Proposed Actions Under Recombinant DNA Research Guidelines

DEPARTMENT OF HEALTH AND HUMAN SERVICES

National Institutes of Health

Recombinant DNA Advisory Committee; Meeting

Pursuant to Public Law 92–463, notice is hereby given of a meeting of the Recombinant DNA Advisory Committee at the National Institutes of Health, Conference Room 10, Building 31C, 9000 Rockville Pike, Bethesda, Maryland 20205, on January 8, 1981, from 9:00 a.m. to recess at approximately 6:00 p.m., and, if necessary, on January 9, 1981, from 8:30 a.m. to 5:00 p.m. This meeting will be open to the public on January 8 from 9:00 a.m. to approximately 3:00 p.m., and on January 9 from 8:30 a.m. to adjournment to discuss:

Amendment of Guidelines
Procedures for review of minor modifications of large-scale recombinant DNA experiments
Exemptions for organisms that exchange genetic information
E. coli K-12 host-vector systems
Host-vector systems other than *E. coli* K-12
NIH risk-assessment plan
Review of protocols for required containment levels
Review of meeting of Institutional Biosafety Committee chairmen
Review of proposed evaluation of Institutional Biosafety Committees
Other matters requiring necessary action by the Committee

Attendance by the public will be limited to space available.

In accordance with provisions set forth in Section 552b(c)(4), Title 5, U.S. Code and Section 10(d) of P.L. 92–463, the meeting will be closed to the public for approximately three hours for the review, discussion and evaluation of proposal(s) from a commercial concern(s) for scale-up of recombinant DNA experiments. It is anticipated that this will occur on January 8, from approximately 3:00 p.m. until adjournment. The proposal(s) and the discussion could reveal confidential trade secrets or commercial property such as patentable material.

Dr. William J. Gartland, Jr., Executive Secretary, Recombinant DNA Advisory Committee, National Institutes of Health, Building 31, Room 4A52, telephone 301–496–6051, will provide materials to be discussed at the meeting, rosters of committee members and substantive program information. A summary of the meeting will be available at a later date.

Note.—OMB's "Mandatory Information Requirements for Federal Assistance Program Announcements" (45 FR 39592) requires a statement concerning the official government programs contained in the *Catalog of Federal Domestic Assistance*. Normally NIH lists in its announcements the number and title of affected individual programs for the guidance of the public. Because the guidance in this notice covers not only virtually every NIH program but also essentially every federal research program in which DNA recombinant molecule techniques could be used, it has been determined to be not cost effective or in the public interest to attempt to list these programs. Such a list would likely require several additional pages. In addition, NIH could not be certain that every federal program would be included as many federal agencies, as well as private organizations, both national and international, have elected to follow the NIH Guidelines. In lieu of the individual program listing, NIH invites readers to direct questions to the information address above about whether individual programs listed in the *Catalog of Federal Domestic Assistance* are affected.

NIH programs are not covered by OMB Circular A-95 because they fit the description of "programs not considered appropriate" in Section 8(b)(4) and (5) of that Circular.

Dated: November 20, 1980.

Suzanne L. Fremeau,
Committee Management Officer, National Institutes of Health.

[FR Doc. 80-37013 Filed 11-28-80; 8:45 am]
BILLING CODE 4110-08-M

Recombinant DNA Research; Proposed Actions Under Guidelines

AGENCY: National Institutes of Health, PHS, DHHS.

ACTION: Notice of Actions under NIH Guidelines for Research Involving Recombinant DNA Molecules.

SUMMARY: This notice sets forth proposed actions to be taken under the NIH Guidelines for Research Involving Recombinant DNA Molecules. Interested parties are invited to submit comments concerning these proposals. After consideration of these proposals and comments by the NIH Recombinant DNA Advisory Committee (RAC) at its January 8–9, 1981 meeting, the Director of the National Institutes of Health will issue decisions on these proposals in accord with the Guidelines.

DATE: Comments must be received by December 29, 1980.

ADDRESS: Written comments and recommendations should be submitted to the Director, Office of Recombinant DNA Activities, Building 31, Room 4A52, National Institutes of Health, Bethesda, Maryland 20205. All comments received in timely response to this notice will be considered and will be available for public inspection in the above office on weekdays between the hours of 8:30 a.m. and 5:00 p.m.

FOR FURTHER INFORMATION CONTACT: Background documentation and additional information can be obtained from Drs. Stanley Barban or Elizabeth Milewski, Office of Recombinant DNA Activities, National Institutes of Health, Bethesda, Maryland 20205, (301) 496–6051.

SUPPLEMENTARY INFORMATION: The National Institutes of Health will consider the following changes and amendments under the Guidelines for Research Involving Recombinant DNA Molecules, as well as actions under these Guidelines.

1. *Request to Include Streptococcus Faecalis and Streptococcus Sanguis in Appendix A.*

Dr. Donald Clewell of the University of Michigan has requested that *Streptococcus faecalis* and *Streptococcus sanguis* be included in a sublist of Appendix A of the Guidelines on the basis that they exchange genetic information by known physiological processes. Dr. Clewell has provided information on these species in a letter to ORDA.

2. *Proposed Containment for Experiments Involving Non-Pathogens.*

Dr. Winston Brill, RAC member, has proposed that the Guidelines be amended to permit recombinant DNA experiments involving non-pathogenic prokaryotes and lower eukaryotes under P1 containment conditions.

A. A new Section, III–O–2, would be added to the Guidelines, as follows:

"III–O–2. *Experiments Involving Non-Pathogenic Prokaryotes and Lower Eukaryotes.* Recombinant DNA experiments involving prokaryotes and lower eukaryotes, nonpathogenic [2A] for man, animals, or plants, can be conducted under P1 containment.

B. A new paragraph would be added just before Section III–O begins, as follows:

"When the reader finds that the containment level given for the same experiment is different in two different sections within Part III, he may choose which of the two levels he wishes to use for the experiment."

C. The second paragraph of Section III–B–3 would be deleted. Revised Section III–B–3 would read as follows:

"III–B–3. *Non-HV1 Systems.* Containment levels for other classes of experiments involving non-HV1 systems may be approved by the Director, NIH (See Sections IV–E–1–b–(1)–(b), IV–E–1–b–(2)–(c), and IV–E–1–b–(3)–(b)).

D. Section IV–E–1–b–2–(f) would be deleted. This Section currently reads as follows:

"IV–E–1–b–(2)–(f). Assigning containment levels for experiments in which both donor and recipient are nonpathogenic prokaryotes (see Section III-B-3)."

3. *Proposed Application Procedures for Minor Modifications of Previously Approved Large-Scale Recombinant DNA Experiments.*

A Working Group of the Recombinant DNA Advisory Committee (RAC) has requested that the following language outlining proposed procedures for minor modifications of previously approved large-scale recombinant DNA experiments be published in the **Federal Register** for public comment:

"Procedures have been developed for considering applications to grow more than ten liters of an organism containing recombinant DNA. These procedures include consideration of the request by a working group of the NIH Recombinant DNA Advisory Committee, submission of the request to the full RAC after consideration by the working group, and subsequent submission to the Director, NIH, for final review. This procedure has taken a minimum of two months. Therefore, the following procedures are proposed to expedite consideration of requests to grow more than ten liters of recombinant DNA-containing organisms when these proposals represent minor modifications of previously approved experiments. Modifications include deletion of sequences from the recombinant DNA, changes in promoters, addition of short segments not affecting the nature of the expressed products, and minor changes in the properties of the host. Changes are considered minor if they do not affect either the containment properties of the vector or the host, or the nature of products made, or add new products. Therefore, the procedures for dealing with minor modifications have the objective of determining that the change is indeed minor. To determine whether a change is minor, two levels of review will take place: (1) By ORDA, which will decide upon receipt of a request to process it as a new request or as a minor modification, and in the latter case (2) by a working group of at least two members of RAC."

The Working Group has proposed that the following language be added to the "Application Procedures for Large-Scale Recombinant DNA Experiments":

"6- Proposals that the submitter considers to represent minor modifications of already approved experiments will be handled by an expedited procedure. A request must be submitted to ORDA. This request should include the changes made, the way in which these changes were made (e.g., mutagenesis, recloning), and the nature and results of any tests done to determine that no major change has occurred (e.g., restriction enzyme analysis, tests for produced products, tests of vector mobilization).

"ORDA will determine whether the submission represents a minor modification of an approved experiment. If so, the request will be submitted promptly to a working group of at least two RAC members. If possible, these members should have been present at the RAC discussion of approval of the original experiment. If any member of the working group does not agree that the request represents a minor modification, the application will then be referred to the full RAC at its next meeting. If the working group is unanimous in concluding that the changes do not alter the organism in a way that is likely to affect containment of the organism or the vector, or the nature of the expressed product, significantly from that presented originally to RAC, recommendation for approval will be transmitted to ORDA, and, through ORDA, to the submitters. Consideration of requests by working groups should explicitly address the following issues: Is the change likely to compromise biological containment provided by the host or the vector? Does the change add to the biological activities associated with the expressed products in a way not considered by the original submission?"

4. *Request to Clone Saccharomyces Cerevisiae DNA in Tetrahymena.*

Dr. Eduardo Orias of the University of California, Santa Barbara, requests permission to clone *Saccharomyces cerevisiae* DNA in *Tetrahymena thermophila* using *S. cerevisiae/E. coli* hybrid plasmids.

5. *Proposal to Amend Item 4 of Appendix E.*

Dr. Clarence Kado of the University of California, Davis, has proposed that the fourth entry in appendix E be modified to read as follows:

"Cloned desired fragment from any non-prohibited source may be transferred into *Agrobacterium tumefaciens* containing a Ti plasmid (or derivates thereof), using a nonconjugative *E. coli* plasmid vector coupled to a fragment of the Ti plasmid and/or the orgin of replication of an *Agrobacterium* plasmid, under containment conditions that would be required for the desired DNA in HV1 systems (i.e., that specified in the subsections of Section (III-A). Transfer into plant parts or cells in culture would be permitted at the same containment level."

6. *Request for Lowering of Containment Under Entry Four of Appendix E.*

Dr. Mary-Dell Chilton of Washington University in St. Louis requests a reduction in physical containment for the manipulation in *Agrobacterium tumefaciens* of (1) the *Saccharomyces cerevisiae* alcohol dehydrogenase 1 gene cloned in pBR322, and (2) the gene coding for the maize (Zea mays) seed storage protein zein, cloned in Charon 4A. The cloned DNA and the vectors will be introduced into tobacco plants. Appendix E, entry four, currently sets containment for such experiments at P3. Dr. Chilton requests approval for these experiments under P2 physical containment. Her justification is outlined in a letter to ORDA.

7. *Request for HV1 Certification of a Schizosaccharomyces Pombe Host-Vector System and Inclusion in Section III-O.*

Dr. Benjamin D. Hall of the University of Washington requests that the fission yeast, *Schizosaccharomyces pombe*, together with yeast-*E. coli* hybrid recombinant plasmids be certified as an HV1 host-vector system. Dr. Hall in addition requests that this system be included under Section III-O. He has provided ORDA with supporting documentation.

Dated: November 20, 1980.

Donald S. Fredrickson,

Director, National Institutes of Health.

Note.—OMB's "Manadatory Information Requirements for Federal Assistance Program Announcements" (45 FR 39592) requires a statement concerning the official government programs contained in the *Catalog of Federal Domestic Assistance*. Normally NIH lists in its announcements the number and title of affected individual programs for the guidance of the public. Because the guidance in this notice covers not only virtually every NIH program but also essentially every federal research program in which DNA recombinant molecule techniques could be used, it has been determined to be not cost effective or in the public interest to attempt to list these programs. Such a list would likely require several additional pages. In addition, NIH could not be certain that every federal program would be included as many federal agencies, as well as private organizations, both national and international, have elected to follow the NIH Guidelines. In lieu of the individual program listing, NIH invites readers to direct questions to the information address above about whether individual programs listed in the *Catalog of Federal Domestic Assistance* are affected.

NIH programs are not covered by OMB Circular A-95 because they fit the description of "programs not considered appropriate" in Section 8-(b)-(4) and (5) of that Circular.

[FR Doc. 80-37014 Filed 11-26-80; 8:45 am]

BILLING CODE 4110-08-M

DEPARTMENT OF HEALTH AND HUMAN SERVICES
PUBLIC HEALTH SERVICE
NATIONAL INSTITUTES OF HEALTH

RECOMBINANT DNA ADVISORY COMMITTEE

MINUTES OF MEETING

JANUARY 8-9, 1981

TABLE OF CONTENTS

TABLE OF CONTENTS

DEPARTMENT OF HEALTH AND HUMAN SERVICES
PUBLIC HEALTH SERVICE
NATIONAL INSTITUTES OF HEALTH

RECOMBINANT DNA ADVISORY COMMITTEE

MINUTES OF MEETING[1]

JANUARY 8-9, 1981

The Recombinant DNA Advisory Committee (RAC) was convened for its twenty-first meeting at 9:00 a.m. on January 8, 1981, in Conference Room 10, Building 31C, National Institutes of Health, 9000 Rockville Pike, Bethesda, Maryland 20205. Mr. Ray Thornton (Chairman), President, Arkansas State University, presided. In accordance with Public Law 92-463, the meeting was open to the public from 9:00 a.m. to 3:00 p.m. on January 8, and from 9:00 a.m. to adjournment on January 9. The meeting was closed to the public from 3:00 p.m. to 6:00 p.m. on January 8 for the review of proposals involving proprietary information.

Committee members present for all or part of the meeting were:

Dr. Abdul Karim Ahmed; Dr. David Baltimore; Dr. Kenneth Berns; Dr. Winston Brill; Dr. Allan Campbell; Mrs. Zelma Cason; Dr. Nina Fedoroff; Dr. Richard Goldstein; Dr. Susan Gottesman; Dr. Jean Harris; Dr. King Holmes; Dr. Sheldon Krimsky; Dr. Myron Levine; Dr. Werner Maas; Dr. James Mason; Dr. Gerard McGarrity; Dr. Robert McKinney; Dr. Elena Nightingale; Dr. Ramon Pinon; Dr. John Scandalios; Dr. Luther Williams; and Dr. William J. Gartland, Jr., Executive Secretary.

A Committee roster is attached. (Attachment I)

The following non-voting members and liaison representatives were present:

Dr. Charlotte Bell, U. S. Department of Justice; Dr. Howard Berman, U. S. Veterans Administration; Dr. Donald DeVincenzi, National Aeronautics and Space Administration; Dr. George Duda, U. S. Department of Energy; Dr. Timothy J. Henry, Food and Drug Administration; Dr. Herman Lewis, National Science Foundation; Dr. Chia T. Chen, OSHA, U. S. Department of Labor; Dr. Sue Tolin, U. S. Department of Agriculture; and Dr. William J. Walsh, III, U. S. Department of State.

---

[1]The RAC is advisory to the NIH, and its recommendations should not be considered as final and accepted. The Office of Recombinant DNA Activities should be consulted for NIH policy on specific issues.

Other National Institutes of Health staff present were:

Dr. Marilyn Bach, NIAID; Dr. Stanley Barban, NIAID; Dr. W. Emmett Barkley, ORS; Mrs. Betty Butler, NIAID; Ms. Mary Donovan, NIAID; Dr. John Irwin, ORS; Dr. Richard Krause, NIAID; Dr. Elizabeth Milewski, NIAID; Dr. Stanley Nagle, NIAID; Dr. John Nutter, NIAID; Dr. Bernard Talbot, OD; and Dr. Rudolf Wanner, ORS.

Others in attendance for all or part of the meeting were:

Dr. E. A. Agostini, Pfizer, Inc.; Dr. Ray Berger, Schering-Plough Corp.; Ms. Irene Brandt, Eli Lilly & Co.; Dr. Peter Bostock, New Brunswick Scientific Co.; Dr. Jerry Callis, U. S. Department of Agriculture, Plum Island; Dr. Aileen Compton, Smith-Kline & French; Mr. L. Curley, New Brunswick Scientific Co.; Dr. Mark Finkelstein, Schering-Plough Corp.; Dr. Patrick Gage, Hoffman LaRoche, Inc.; Ms. Lizabeth Gelber, Bokon Productions; Dr. Jean Gudas, University of California, Los Angeles; Dr. Paul Hung, Abbott Research Laboratories; Dr. James Hunt, Chemapec; Dr. Dorothy Jessup, U. S. Department of Agriculture; Dr. Attila I. Kadar, Food and Drug Administration; Mr. W. H. Kampen, New Brunswick Scientific Co.; Mr. Geoffrey Karny, Office of Technology Assessment; Dr. Paul Leibowitz, Schering-Plough Corp.; Ms. Carter Leonard, Blue Sheet; Mr. Ronald Leonardi, KABI Group, Inc.; Mr. Charles Marwick, Medical World News; Dr. James McCullough, Library of Congress; Mr. Bing Miller, New Brunswick Scientific Co.; Dr. Henry Miller, Food and Drug Administration; Dr. Philip Miller, Hoffman LaRoche, Inc.; Dr. Ann Norberg, Monsanto Co.; Mr. Seth Pauker, National Institute for Occupational Safety and Health; Dr. Stephen Pijar, Food and Drug Administration; Dr. Vishva Rai, Hoffman LaRoche, Inc.; Dr. Michael Ross, Genentech, Inc.; Mr. Dan Smith, Peoples Business Commission; Mr. Charles Turbyville, Genetic Engineering Letter; Dr. Marvin Weinstein, Schering-Plough, Corp.; Dr. Susan Wright, University of Michigan; Dr. Bill Young, Genentech, Inc.; and Dr. Robert Zaugg, Teknekron, Inc.

I. CALL TO ORDER AND OPENING REMARKS

Mr. Ray Thornton, Chairman, called the meeting to order at 9:00 a.m., January 8, 1981. He introduced two newly appointed members of the committee: Dr. King Holmes of the Division of Infectious Diseases of the U.S. Public Health Service Hospital, Seattle, Washington and Dr. Robert McKinney of the Division of Safety of the National Institutes of Health (NIH).

Mr. Thornton said he had asked Dr. McKinney to serve as co-chairman, with Dr. Berns, of the newly instituted Large-Scale Review Working Group. Mr. Thornton said that any RAC member interested in serving on that working group should contact him.

Mr. Thornton announced that agenda items scheduled for Friday morning, January 9, 1981 would be considered on Thursday, January 8, 1981 if time permits.

II. MINUTES OF THE SEPTEMBER 25-26, 1980 MEETING

Dr. Harris reviewed the minutes of the September 25-26, 1980 RAC meeting (tab 978) and said she found them to be correct. She moved for adoption, which was seconded by Mrs. Cason. Dr. Susan Wright cited an exchange between herself and Dr. Maxine Singer at the September meeting concerning the composition of biohazard committees in the United Kingdom. Dr. Singer had drawn a parallel between the situation regarding recombinant DNA in the U. S. and in the U. K. Dr. Wright had said that the analogy was inaccurate because genetic engineering is regulated in the United Kingdom, i.e., the laboratories are inspected and the composition of the local Biohazards Committee is more stringently controlled. Dr. Singer replied that she had not intended to draw a parallel. Dr. Wright requested that this exchange be included in the minutes. She also requested that comments by Dr. Krimsky on the survey of California IBCs be included. She said following the report on the California IBC survey, Dr. Krimsky stated that the kind of evidence the RAC was preparing to accept in the social sciences was not of the high quality that RAC members would normally expect in their own areas of expertise. Mr. Thornton recommended that those comments be included in the minutes of the January 8-9, 1981 meeting and that the minutes of the September 24-25, 1980 meeting be approved as moved and seconded.

Dr. Maas pointed out some typographical errors in the draft minutes. The minutes, with the suggested amendments, were approved by a vote of 17 to 0.

III. MEETING OF INSTITUTIONAL BIOSAFETY COMMITTEE CHAIRPERSONS

Dr. Krause, before reporting on the IBC Chairperson's meeting (tab 977), briefly commented on the February 3-5, 1981 meeting of the U.S. - Japan Cooperative Program for Recombinant DNA Research. He said this meeting will focus on the guidelines for research, on host-vector systems, and on risk assessment studies.

Dr. Krause noted the first IBC Chairperson's Meeting had been held two years ago. Since that meeting, the Guidelines had evolved markedly with greater responsibility being delegated to the local IBC. The IBC Chairperson's Meeting sponsored by the National Institutes of Health on November 24-25, 1980, was an attempt to identify problems the IBCs might be encountering. In addition, the conference was viewed by NIAID as the first stage in a possible formal evaluation of the functioning of IBCs.

Two hundred and twelve individuals attended the meeting, including representatives from 154 IBCs. Among the participants were 21 individuals from the industrial sector and five IBC community members. Four current RAC members, Ms. King, Dr. Krimsky, Dr. Mason, and Mr. Thornton, and some former RAC members, participated. In a panel on the operation of IBCs, three IBC chairpersons, Dr. Patrick Gage of Hoffman-LaRoche, Dr. Alan Garber of Baylor College of Medicine and Dr. Melvin Chalfen of Massachusetts Institute of Technology, addressed problems which would be examined in conference workshops, and Mr. Robert Spanner evaluated IBC function from the vantage point of a community member. Three workshops subsequently addressed problems associated with (1) the IBC as a means of implementing institutional oversight, (2) health surveillance, monitoring and certification, and (3) procedures and operations. Reports from the workshop leadership teams, composed of a RAC member, an IBC chairperson and an NIH staffer, were presented at a plenary session the following morning. (A transcript of the plenary session appears under tab 977). At this session several recommendations were voted. One of these recommendations is that experiments currently covered by Section III-O should be exempted from the Guidelines.

Dr. Krause said many of the chairpersons believed much had been achieved at the meeting. As a consequence of this view, of concerns expressed for other safety issues, and of a vote taken at the IBC Chairpersons meeting, NIAID was reconsidering the IBC evaluation plan. NIH is tentatively planning to broaden the scope of the evaluation to include safety matters other than recombinant DNA issues.

Dr. Krimsky said the transcript of the plenary session (tab 977), accurately reflected the tone of the meeting. He said that one point of disagreement among the participants was on the question of whether there should be biosafety committees, or whether their functions could be performed better by some other method.

Dr. Mason commented on the health surveillance, monitoring and certification workshop. He said there had been a great deal of discussion on the cost/benefit ratio of health surveillance programs. The consensus was that if unusual medical surveillance were to be required, it should be well defined and carefully controlled in order to obtain reasonable data. No workshop participant felt there was justification for such an in-depth program; but to do less, if one really was worried, was not sensible. Most participants felt heavy stress should be placed on education in good laboratory practices and procedures for all potentially hazardous work. To single out recombinant DNA for special emphasis was unwarranted.

Dr. Baltimore asked if positive support for any part of the Guidelines had been evidenced at the meeting. Mr. Thornton replied that participants indicated that the Guidelines reflect a consensus hammered out between science and society.

Mr. Thornton then summarized his impression of the meeting. He felt most chairpersons recognized the value of IBCs, but were concerned that the focus of those efforts was recombinant DNA activities. They did not feel one area of research should be singled out for special attention. A second concern was the "paperwork burden" associated with the Guidelines. A recommendation made by the Chairpersons to exempt experiments covered by Section III-O of the Guidelines derives from this concern. Dr. Mason offered his perception that many IBC chairpersons did not like the formality associated with the review procedures and the current structure of the IBC.

Dr. Gottesman suggested three mechanisms for alleviating some of the "paperwork burden": (1) Exempt those experiments falling under Section III-O; or (2) Require P1 + EK1 containment conditions but dispense with the requirement for registration documents; or (3) Require the IBC to maintain a registry, but not to review the experiments. In the latter case, there could be a requirement for some Institutional officials, but not the full IBC to review the documents. She said she herself could not support the first option. She supported the second or third options with the understanding that large-scale (i.e., greater than 10 liters) applications still be considered as a special case.

Dr. Baltimore said he would support a motion to exempt experiments covered by Section III-O from the Guidelines, including large-scale experiments. He suggested consideration be given to changing RAC to a general advisory committee on biosafety. He felt there were many biosafety issues other than recombinant DNA which deserved consideration. Dr. Mason concurred with Dr. Baltimore's views.

Dr. McGarrity asked Dr. Barkley of the NIH Division of Safety to comment on the current status of federal guidelines on chemical carcinogens and on etiological agents. Dr. Barkley replied that the CDC guidelines on etiological agents, which are intended as a voluntary code of good practice, have been issued in draft form for comments from the scientific community.

Dr. Barkley said the Occupational Safety and Health Administration (OSHA), responsible for promulgating standards to protect American workers from exposure to chemical carcinogens, is considering the problem of carcinogen use in research laboratories. One method of addressing the problem would recognize the use of informed judgement by principal investigators. The Department of Health and Human Services (DHHS) is developing guidelines on control of carcinogens, which will apply specifically to DHHS intramural laboratories. Guidelines for the use of chemical carcinogens in NIH intramural laboratories will be issued soon.

Dr. Barkley said aspects of new regulations of the Environmental Protection Agency (EPA), particularly with respect to the Resource Conservation and Recovery Act, were also reviewed at the IBC Chairperson's meeting.

These regulations are an attempt to reduce the indiscriminate disposal of toxic chemical waste in the environment.

Dr. Berns said he found the CDC's proposed biosafety guidelines for etiological agents, with regard to some of the specific containment levels suggested, to be capricious and unscientific, and the CDC unresponsive to expressed concerns. He admitted that the guidelines may be *de jure*, voluntary, but feared they would not be voluntary, *de facto*.

Dr. Williams, while admitting that the CDC guidelines and OSHA regulations were important, urged that the RAC resist the temptation to address a variety of issues beyond its charge. Mr. Thornton supported this position.

Mr. Thornton asked for a straw vote to gauge RAC sentiment. He first asked how many RAC members preferred to maintain the *status quo* regarding Section III-O. No one favored this approach. He then asked how many favored doing something to materially reduce or eliminate the paperwork and reporting functions for experiments covered by Section III-O. Nineteen individuals supported this position. He then asked how many members felt serious consideration should be given to exempting entirely from the Guidelines, experiments currently covered by Section III-O. Ten members supported this position. Mr. Thornton asked NIH staff to prepare language on a series of options for publication in the *Federal Register* prior to the April meeting.

Dr. Campbell suggested that experiments currently covered by Section III-O be exempt from the Guidelines, but the Guidelines include a recommendation that these experiments be done under P1 containment conditions.

Dr. Krimsky asked for a clarification of the mechanism by which funds are earmarked for evaluations. Dr. Talbot replied that Congress appropriates budgetary funds for each Institute of the National Institutes of Health. A separate law specifies that up to one percent of those funds may be allocated to evaluation. A detailed review procedure within DHHS is used to allocate these funds among specific evaluation projects.

IV. UPDATE OF PROPOSED RISK ASSESSMENT PROGRAM AND REVIEW OF PAPER ON E. COLI POPULATIONS

Dr. Williams reviewed the Proposed First Annual Update of the Program to Assess Risks of Recombinant DNA Research (tab 962). Dr. Williams highlighted some of the items discussed in the plan, including the protocols that originated in the Falmouth Workshop concerning colonization by *E. coli* K-12 and transmission of genetic information from *E. coli* K-12 to the intestinal flora, and the protocol involving the *E. coli* strain HS, a good colonizer, and plasmid pBR325. The plan also discusses the results of the polyoma experiments which attempted to determine if recombinant organisms containing oncogenes would induce tumors, and includes a summary of the Pasadena Risk Assessment Workshop held on April 11-12, 1980. NIAID has awarded a contract to the University of Minnesota to develop a course on basic microbiological practices and techniques for work with hazardous agents.

Dr. Krimsky noted the statement in the plan that "no risks of recombinant DNA research have been identified that are not inherent in the microbiological and biochemical methodology used in such research." He asked whether an increase in host range resulting from a recombinant manipulation would be considered a counter-instance to that statement. Dr. Krause replied that the risk assessment plan indicates that no such case has been known to occur; it does not imply that such an event is an impossibility.

Dr. Krimsky asked if the results of EPA contracts would be available to RAC, and if these results would be integrated into future NIH risk assessment analyses. Dr. Talbot replied that EPA reports periodically to the Industrial Practices Subcommittee of the Federal Interagency Committee. Minutes of these meetings are forwarded to RAC. He noted that the United States Department of Agriculture (USDA) may also perform some risk assessment studies and the NIH will be kept abreast of those studies.

Dr. Krimsky raised a point regarding the wording in the second paragraph, third column on page 61876, dealing with colonization of the intestinal tract. After some discussion it was agreed that the word "known" should be deleted from the last clause of the paragraph, which would now read as follows: "..., even though E. coli K-12 has apparently lost those characteristics that are required for colonization of the normal intestinal tract." Other questions by Dr. Krimsky regarding the plan were answered by Dr. Krause and RAC members.

Dr. Wright suggested the risk assessment plan should be footnoted and referenced, and the identities of investigators disclosed. Dr. Wright also felt that the controversy between Rowe-Martin and Rosenberg-Simon on the interpretation of the Rowe-Martin polyoma experiments should be included in the document. Dr. Krause, Dr. Williams and Mr. Thornton noted the debate was presented to, and carefully considered by, the RAC. Dr. Baltimore said that he does not believe there is a serious controversy concerning the interpretation of the polyoma experiments; rather, there is only what he considers a twisted interpretation of those experiments by some people. Dr. Krimsky stated his understanding that any positive results in the polyoma protocols would be very important, and said that the reviewers who accepted the Rosenberg-Simon article for Nature must have seen some value in the article. [Executive Secretary's note: Nature has confirmed that the Rosenberg-Simon article appeared as a "feature article" rather than as a "scientific paper" and therefore was not formally peer reviewed]. Dr. Campbell said that what

Rosenberg and Simon judged to be positive results were what Rowe and Martin considered the controls for the experiment.

Mr. Pauker asked if studies to elucidate aspects of survival and colonization of different strains of E. coli would be undertaken. Dr. Krause pointed out that the plan states that NIAID has awarded a grant to an investigator to study the molecular mechanisms of E. coli colonization, specifically the relative importance of plasmid or chromosomal determinants on colonization. Dr. Levine said this field is very fertile and developing very rapidly.

Mr. Thornton called on Dr. Holmes to review tab 963, a paper entitled "Genetic Diversity and Structure in Escherichia coli Populations." Dr. Holmes said that in this article investigators surveyed twenty enzymes from one hundred nine clones of E. coli. In addition to the wild type isolates, twenty-four laboratory K-12 strains were studied. The genetic diversity the investigators observed led them to conclude that recombination in nature, of the genes coding for the studied proteins, is rare.

One of the E. coli isolates had been obtained from an infant in a Massachusetts hospital nursery. The twenty assayed enzymes from this strain were indistinguishable electrophoretically from the same twenty enzymes in laboratory strain E. coli K-12. Dr. Krimsky said he asked that this be discussed, as he wondered whether it might indicate that E. coli K-12 is surviving in nature. Drs. Levine, Campbell and Nightingale all said that just because the Massachusetts nursery isolate has 20 enzymes electrophoretically identical to E. coli K-12, does not at all mean that it will resemble E. coli K-12 in the parameters that are important for E. coli K-12's lack of ability to colonize. It was agreed that the data on the 20 enzymes are "a small drop in a large bucket;" very incomplete data towards establishing the similarity of the Massachusetts isolate to E. coli K-12. Further it was pointed out that the paper states the Massachusetts isolate differs in its bacteriophage sensitivities from E. coli K-12.

V. REVISED GENETIC MANIPULATION ADVISORY GROUP GUIDELINES

Dr. Gottesman began discussion of the United Kingdom's revised Genetic Manipulation Advisory Group (GMAG) guidelines for recombinant DNA experiments (tab 964). She said the British had instituted a system in which numbers are assigned for "access," "expression," and "damage." The numbers are multiplied together to obtain a final figure which determines the recommended physical containment level. She said the RAC applies similar principles when evaluating recommended containment, but in not as explicit a form. GMAG, like the RAC, has been delegating increased responsibility to local committees. She said she did not perceive any significant differences in approach between the U. S. and the British situation, which would compel the RAC to take action.

Mr. Pauker pointed out that GMAG still requires some central notification and registration. Dr. Wright said the GMAG guidelines generally required higher containment levels than the NIH Guidelines. Others said that the latest GMAG revision seemed to lead to generally lower containment levels in the U. K. as compared to the U. S.

VI. PROPOSED PROCEDURES FOR MINOR MODIFICATIONS OF PREVIOUSLY APPROVED LARGE-SCALE RECOMBINANT DNA EXPERIMENTS

A. Application Procedures for Minor Modifications of Previously Approved Large-Scale Recombinant DNA Experiments.

Dr. Gottesman began discussion of the proposed application procedures for minor modifications of previously approved large-scale recombinant DNA experiments (tabs 965, 976/3). Dr. Gottesman said that currently all large-scale experiments are reviewed by the full RAC; the proposal is an attempt to develop an expedited procedure for minor modifications of previously approved large-scale experiments. The proposal provides a procedure for determining whether a modification is minor. A request for evaluation of a minor modification would be sent to ORDA. If ORDA believes it is a minor modification, the request will be sent to a working group composed of at least two RAC members. If possible, these members should have participated in the review of the original approval. If the working group unanimously agrees that the modification is minor and that the changes do not significantly alter the organism in a way that is likely to affect containment of the organism or the vector, or the nature of the expressed product from that presented originally to RAC, recommendation for approval will be transmitted to ORDA. If the working group does not so find, the proposal would be presented to the full RAC for consideration. Dr. Gottesman moved acceptance of the proposed language. Dr. Berns seconded the motion.

Dr. Goldstein suggested that each proposal be circulated to all RAC members at the time that it is sent for review to the working group. This would provide an opportunity for all RAC members to comment. He further suggested that the decision of the working group be transmitted to all RAC members. Dr. Gottesman suggested instead that a summary of minor modifications approved between meetings using the minor modification working group procedure be provided to RAC at each RAC meeting. Dr. Goldstein accepted this proposal, and it was agreed that ORDA would provide such a summary.

Dr. Leibowitz of Schering-Plough Corporation suggested that certain minor modifications of previously approved large-scale experiments using E. coli K-12 host-vector systems might be approved by the local IBC. Dr. Gottesman said she preferred the minor modification procedure as in tab 976/3. Dr. McKinney agreed. By a vote of seventeen in favor, none opposed, the RAC accepted the proposed language (976/3).

B. Proposed Procedures for Change of Locale of Previously Approved Large-Scale Recombinant DNA Experiments.

Dr. Gartland posed the question of how to process changes of site for large-scale production using previously approved clones, i.e., a clone which had been approved for scale-up at one site would be moved to another physical facility. A second IBC might then be charged with oversight responsibilities.

Dr. Baltimore, noting that the RAC no longer reviews physical facilities, felt changes of locale were therefore not appropriate RAC considerations. It was agreed that ORDA would administratively process such proposals.

[Executive Secretary's Note: The following statement dealing with changes of facility has been added to the "Application Procedures for Large-Scale Recombinant DNA Experiments":

"7. Should a clone, previously approved for scale-up at one facility, be proposed to be moved to a second facility, the IBC with oversight responsibility at the second site shall submit to ORDA a registration document and receive ORDA approval, prior to initiating scale-up. No RAC review would be required."]

VII. PROPOSED CONTAINMENT FOR EXPERIMENTS INVOLVING NONPATHOGENS

Dr. Brill introduced the proposal (tabs 966, 973, 976/2, 980, 981, 982, 983, 984, 985, 987, and 988) to amend the Guidelines to permit use of nonpathogenic prokaryotes and nonpathogenic lower eukaryotes as donors and recipients in recombinant DNA experiments under P1 containment conditions. Specifically, it was proposed in the Federal Register on November 28, 1980, that a new Section, III-0-2, would be added to the Guidelines as follows:

"III-0-2. Experiments Involving Nonpathogenic Prokaryotes and Lower Eukaryotes. Recombinant DNA experiments involving prokaryotes and lower eukaryotes, nonpathogenic [2A] for man, animals, or plants, can be conducted under P1 containment."

Changes were also proposed in other sections of the Guidelines to accomplish this change.

In discussing the proposal, Dr. Brill suggested that this proposed language be amended as follows: (1) following the word "plants", the words "and only DNA from such sources" would be added; and (2) a requirement would be added that the experiments, and documentation that the organisms are not known pathogens, must be registered with the local IBC; and (3) containment for these experiments would be raised from P1 to P2. It was noted that Dr. Novick, in a letter, had suggested that containment be raised to P2. Dr. Brill moved acceptance of the proposal as amended. Dr. Fedoroff seconded the motion.

Dr. Goldstein asked what type of documentation would be submitted to the local IBC concerning nonpathogenicity. Dr. Brill replied that the investigator should provide evidence from the literature that the organism is not pathogenic.

Dr. Berns said that the proposed requirement for P2 had no scientific basis and moved to amend the language to require P1 containment. Drs. Brill and Fedoroff accepted Dr. Berns' amendment.

Dr. Berns then proposed an amendment which would change the word "registered" to the word "reviewed"; to Dr. Brill's amendment. Drs. Brill and Fedoroff agreed.

Mr. Thornton asked Dr. Brill to restate his proposal as amended. Dr. Brill read the following amended motion:

> "Recombinant DNA experiments involving prokaryotes or lower eukaryotes nonpathogenic to man, animals, or plants, and only DNA from such sources, can be conducted under P1 containment conditions. The experiments must be reviewed by the local IBC with documentation that the organisms are not known pathogens."

Dr. Gottesman said she could not support the proposal as: (1) It covers an enormous variety of organisms, (2) It does not restrict the type of vector to be used (e.g., conjugative plasmids would be permissible), and (3) "Nonpathogenic" may be defined differently by different IBCs. This proposal would represent a departure from current Guideline philosophy. Dr. Gottesman agreed, however, that an expedited procedure for evaluating containment for experiments involving these organisms might be desirable. She suggested that proposals involving nonpathogenic prokaryotes and nonpathogenic lower eukaryotes might be reviewed by ORDA rather than by the full RAC. ORDA could consult with experts in the field. Dr. Mason also expressed concern about the definition of nonpathogenicity, and supported the concept of ORDA review.

Dr. Gottesman moved a substitute motion to extend Section III-B-3 of the Guidelines, which currently allows recombinant DNA transfers between nonpathogenic prokaryotes at P3 containment, to include experiments with nonpathogenic lower eukaryotes. Her substitute motion would also permit requests for lowering of containment for specific experiments in this class to be approved by ORDA. RAC review would not be required. Dr. Mason seconded the substitute motion.

Dr. Brill said that the investigator would be most knowledgeable about the organism. He questioned whether ORDA review should be required. Dr. Campbell spoke in support of Dr. Brill's motion. He felt the restrictions placed on recombinant DNA research were discouraging innovation.

Mr. Thornton called the vote on Dr. Gottesman's substitute motion. The RAC voted against Dr. Gottesman's motion by a vote of six in favor, eight opposed, and two abstentions.

Dr. Nightingale suggested that "nonpathogenic" is too absolute a term; certain organisms normally not pathogenic can cause disease in compromised hosts. Other members concurred.

Dr. Baltimore said the committee, in evaluating this proposal, should face the basic question of whether recombinant DNA technology is likely to produce an organism more pathogenic than the original donor organisms.

Dr. Levine said that while many members of the committee feel it is exceedingly unlikely that recombinant DNA technology will create a new pathogen of clinical significance, disparities could arise among institutions concerning whether a given organism is, or is not, a pathogen under Dr. Brill's proposal.

Mr. Thornton then called the vote on Dr. Brill's amended proposal. By a vote of nine in favor, eight opposed, and three abstentions, the RAC accepted Dr. Brill's proposal. Dr. Goldstein and Dr. Krimsky requested to be recorded as voting against the motion.

Dr. Gottesman, in noting the closeness of the vote, again offered for consideration her substitute proposal. Her proposal was that, if Dr. Fredrickson should not accept Dr. Brill's amended proposal, the sense of the RAC was that it would be preferable to the status quo to make at least two changes in the Guidelines: (1) to extend the current situation allowing cloning between nonpathogenic prokaryotes at P3 containment to include nonpathogenic lower eukaryotes, and (2) to allow lowering containment below P3 for individual cases in this class to be approved by ORDA, rather than requiring RAC review. She moved this proposal. Dr. Goldstein seconded. Dr. Berns moved to table discussion. Dr. Campbell seconded. By a vote of eight in favor, eleven opposed and no abstentions, the motion to table Dr. Gottesman's substitute motion failed.

Mr. Thornton then called the vote on Dr. Gottesman's motion. By a vote of fourteen in favor, one opposed, and three abstentions, the RAC approved Dr. Gottesman's motion.

VIII. CLOSED SESSION

The RAC went into closed session to consider proposals from commercial concerns for scale-up of recombinant DNA experiments.

IX. PROPOSALS TO CLONE GENES OF FOOT AND MOUTH DISEASE VIRUS

Dr. Gartland introduced a request (tab 972), dated October 17, 1980, from Genentech, Inc., and the United States Department of Agriculture Plum Island Animal Disease Center concerning the cloning of the Foot and Mouth Disease Virus (FMDV) genome. An earlier proposal entitled "Cloning and Expression in *E. coli* of the VP3 Protein of Foot and Mouth Disease Virus" had been reviewed by the RAC at the December 6-7, 1979 meeting. On the recommendation of the RAC, Stage I of that proposal, the construction of clones containing cDNA segments of the FMDV genome, was approved by the NIH and announced in the Federal Register of January 17, 1980 (45 FR 3552). At that time it was noted "Dr. Campbell stated that it was the sense of the RAC that this motion constituted the 'major action' and that future recommendations of the RAC approving further stages of the experiment would be 'minor actions.'" Subsequently, permission was given (Federal Register of July 29, 1980 (45 FR 50528)) that certain clones containing cDNA copies of the FMDV genome made on Plum Island could be removed from Plum Island as they "were well characterized, lacked infectivity, and represent, in aggregate, only 75% of the FMDV genome." Dr. Gartland said request one in the October 17, 1980, proposal dealing with work in *E. coli* K-12 could be considered a "minor action" continuation of the previously reviewed proposal. However, request two of the October 17, 1980, submission dealing with proposed work in hosts other than *E. coli* could not be so considered. Dr. Gartland suggested RAC might therefore appropriately evaluate request one (but not request two) of the submission, even though the proposal (tab 972) had not been published in the Federal Register for thirty days of public comment, as the request had not been received by ORDA until December 1980.

Drs. Berns, Gottesman and Baltimore agreed that request one of the proposal could be appropriately considered at this meeting.

Dr. Baltimore, in reviewing request one of the proposal, explained that several types and subtypes of Foot and Mouth Disease Virus are endemic in the world today. He said vaccine producers must thus develop vaccines against multiple types and subtypes of the virus. He said Genentech, Inc., in the original proposal, had chosen one FMDV type as a prototype, requested and obtained NIH permission for experiments involving this type, and now is requesting permission to apply the same procedures to other FMDV serological types. Dr. Baltimore said Genentech, Inc., had agreed to abide by the conditions set by RAC. Dr. Campbell said it was appropriate that a RAC working group, but not the full RAC, review data on the infectivity of the clones before they are removed from Plum Island.

Dr. Berns suggested that, as in the previous approval, the clones allowed to leave Plum Island shall not contain, individually or collectively, more than 75% of the viral genome. Dr. Baltimore included these statements in his motion to approve request one of the proposal. Dr. Fedoroff seconded the motion.

By a vote of 20 in favor, none opposed and one abstention, the RAC recommended approval of request one of the proposal (tab 972). This action would permit cloning on Plum Island of various FMDV types in E. coli K-12. The following conditions were specified: (1) A working group of the RAC, but not the full RAC, would examine data on the infectivity of the clones produced on Plum Island before these clones were allowed to leave the Island, and (2) the clones to leave Plum Island should be well-characterized, shown to lack infectivity, and shall not contain, individually or collectively, more than 75% of the FMDV genome.

Dr. Gottesman suggested that some discussion of request two of the proposal (tab 972) was appropriate. Although no formal action could be taken at this meeting, a discussion might identify potential problems.

Dr. Baltimore said request two of the proposal (tab 972) requests permission to clone FMDV cDNA in Bacillus subtilis, Saccharomyces cerevisiae, and in eukaryotic cells in culture. He envisaged no potential hazard in cloning the VP3 protein in these host-vector systems. Dr. Ross of Genentech, Inc., said the VP3 protein has no known biological activity other than as a structural protein in the FMDV coat. Dr. Baltimore asked Dr. Ross if less than two-thirds of the SV40 genome would be used as a vector for cloning the VP3 protein. Dr. Ross replied that less than two-thirds of the SV40 genome would be used. Dr. Goldstein asked if inserting the gene for the VP3 protein into a two-third fragment of the SV40 genome could produce a viable virus with modified host range. Dr. Baltimore said that it is very unlikely that the VP3 protein could be inserted into the SV40 capsid structure.

Dr. Berns asked for a clarification of the proposal. He noted that the discussion focused on one of the FMDV capsid proteins, the VP3 protein. However, Genentech will have up to 75% of the entire viral genome, and the October 17, 1980 proposal requests permission to clone FMDV capsid proteins in general, not just VP3. Dr. Ross said that approval for just the VP3 protein would be acceptable at this time. Dr. Gottesman suggested that the proposal should be more explicit. It was also stated that additional information on the vectors to be used should be supplied.

The RAC deferred action on request two of tab 972.

X. PROPOSAL FOR APPROVAL OF SCHIZOSACCHAROMYCES POMBE FOR RECOMBINANT DNA EXPERIMENTS

Dr. Benjamin Hall of the University of Washington requested that the fission yeast, Schizosaccharomyces pombe, together with S. cerevisiae/ E. coli hybrid recombinant plasmids, be certified as an HV1 host-vector system (tabs 970, 975, 976/7). Dr. Hall in addition requested that this system be included in Section III-O of the Guidelines. Schizosaccharomyces pombe is nonpathogenic, survives poorly outside of controlled laboratory conditions, is rare in nature, and exchanges genetic information only with other closely related organisms. Dr. Campbell said the request is unusual in that the specified host is the species rather than a specific laboratory strain. He noted that the current HV1 certified hosts are at a selective disadvantage relative to their wild type counterparts. He felt the RAC should adhere to criteria specified in the Guidelines for certifying HV1 host-vector systems. On this basis he said he could not recommend approval of the request. Dr. Gottesman agreed.

Dr. Pinon agreed, but suggested that the NIH might permit certain experiments with the organism, while not certifying Schizosaccharomyces pombe as an HV1 host-vector system.

Dr. Campbell moved approval of the following motion:

"DNA from nonpathogenic prokaryotes and lower eukaryotes may be cloned into Schizosaccharomyces pombe species under P1 containment conditions."

By a vote of fourteen in favor, one opposed, and four abstentions RAC recommended the motion. Dr. Campbell then moved a second recommendation:

"DNA from higher eukaryotes may be cloned in Schizosaccharomyces pombe species under P3 containment conditions."

By a vote of fourteen in favor, none opposed, and five abstentions, RAC accepted the motion.

XI. REQUEST TO INCLUDE STREPTOCOCCUS FAECALIS AND STREPTOCOCCUS SANGUIS UNDER EXEMPTION I-E-4.

Dr. Gottesman introduced the request (tabs 967, 976/1) of Dr. Donald Clewell of the University of Michigan that Streptococcus faecalis be included along with Streptococcus sanguis in a sublist of Appendix A of the Guidelines. Dr. Gottesman noted that Appendix A currently has two sublists, E and F, both of which include Streptococcus sanguis. She suggested that Streptococcus faecalis be added to sublist F if the RAC is satisfied that the evidence demonstrates exchange in both directions between S. faecalis and S. sanguis. Dr. Campbell supported that approach, and moved approval. Dr. Fedoroff seconded the motion.

By a vote of twelve in favor, two opposed, and five abstentions, the RAC recommended that the request be approved, and that Streptococcus faecalis be added to sublist F of Appendix A.

XII. PROPOSAL FOR CONTAINMENT FOR STREPTOMYCES AND NONPATHOGENIC ACTINOMYCETES

Dr. Levine introduced three requests (tab 974) of Dr. Stanley Cohen of Stanford University to revise containment levels for recombinant DNA experiments involving the nonpathogenic free-living soil organism genus Streptomyces and other nonpathogenic Actinomycetes. Dr. Talbot pointed out that this item had not been published in the Federal Register for thirty days of public comment due to its late receipt in ORDA. He noted however that the first of the three requests was a specific instance of a much broader proposal (see item VII of these minutes) which had been published in the Federal Register, and that, therefore, the RAC could appropriately act on this. Dr. Levine read the first of Dr. Cohen's requests:

> "That all members of the nonpathogenic Actinomycetes genus Streptomyces and the plasmids native to this genus be approved as host-vector systems for the cloning under P1 conditions of DNA derived from other non-pathogenic prokaryotic organisms such as Streptomyces and other non-pathogenic Actinomycetes species, Escherichia coli K-12, Bacillus subtilis, Bacillus lichenformis, Bacillus circulans, and other non-pathogenic Bacillus species, and for the cloning of DNA derived from non-pathogenic unicellular eukaryotic microorganisms such as Saccharomyces cerevisiae and Neurospora crassa."

Dr. Levine noted that the RAC had earlier in the meeting (see item VII of these minutes) recommended P1 containment as sufficient for a large class of experiments, of which these were a small subset. He recommended approval. Dr. Maas seconded the motion.

By a vote of eighteen in favor, none opposed, and two abstentions, the RAC recommended approval of the first request of tab 974. Dr. Campbell abstained from discussing and voting on this request.

The RAC deferred action on the second and third requests of tab 974. Dr. Gottesman said that Dr. Cohen should supply additional data concerning the organisms he wishes to be certified as HV1 host-vector systems. Dr. Williams concurred.

XIII. PROPOSAL TO AMEND ITEM 4 OF APPENDIX E

Dr. Brill introduced the proposal (tabs 968, 976/5) by Dr. Clarence Kado of the University of California, Davis, to modify item 4 of Appendix E. Dr. Kado requested deletion of the specification that experiments involving *Agrobacterium tumefaciens* be performed "under containment conditions one step higher than would be required for the desired DNA in HV1 systems (i.e., one step higher physical containment than that specified in the subsections of Section III-A)."

According to Dr. Kado's proposal, item 4 of Appendix E would read as follows:

"Cloned desired fragments from any non-prohibited source may be transferred into *Agrobacterium tumefaciens* containing a Ti plasmid (or derivatives thereof), using a nonconjugative *E. coli* plasmid vector coupled to a fragment of the Ti plasmid and/or the origin of replication of an *Agrobacterium* plasmid, under containment conditions that would be required for the desired DNA in HV1 systems (i.e., that specified in the subsections of Section III-A). Transfer into plant parts or cells in culture would be permitted at the same containment level."

In support of the request, Dr. Brill said that *Agrobacterium tumefaciens*, while a pathogen, does not attack tissue which has not been injured. Expression of the Ti plasmid coded genes is diluted out as the plant grows. Furthermore, the Ti plasmid is apparently lost in meiotic segregation, and is not transmitted to progeny. He moved approval of Dr. Kado's proposal. Dr. Scandalios concurred.

Dr. Gottesman noted that the proposal would effectively designate *Agrobacterium tumefaciens* an HV1 system. She did not find this action appropriate as (1) the *Agrobacterium tumefaciens* Ti plasmid is a conjugative plasmid, and (2) although *Agrobacterium tumefaciens* is not a serious pathogen, it is, nonetheless, a pathogen. She suggested that containment conditions for certain types of experiments might appropriately be relaxed, but suggested that the RAC refrain from designating *Agrobacterium tumefaciens* a *de facto* HV1 system. She proposed to lower containment to P2 for experiments involving cloning DNA from non-pathogenic prokaryotes and plants in *Agrobacterium tumefaciens* with subsequent transfer to plants or plant tissue. Dr. Brill accepted this proposed amendment of his motion.

The motion was recommended by the RAC by a vote of seventeen in favor, none opposed, and two abstentions.

XIV. REQUEST FOR LOWERING OF CONTAINMENT UNDER ITEM 4 OF APPENDIX E

Dr. Scandalios introduced the request (tabs 969, 976/6) of Dr. Mary-Dell Chilton of Washington University in St. Louis to reduce physical containment to P2 for the manipulation in *Agrobacterium tumefaciens* of (1) the *Saccharomyces cerevisiae* alcohol dehydrogenase 1 gene and (2) the gene coding for the maize (*Zea mays*) seed storage protein, zein. The cloned DNA and the vectors will be introduced into tobacco plants. Dr. Scandalios said these experiments are currently covered by item 4 of Appendix E which specifies P3 containment conditions. He said Dr. Chilton requests a lowering of containment as the recombinant DNAs used in the manipulations are well-characterized. Dr. Scandalios recommended that the specified experiments be permitted under P1 containment conditions and so moved. Dr. Brill concurred.

By a vote of fifteen in favor, none opposed, and four abstentions, the RAC recommended Dr. Scandalios' motion.

XV. REQUEST TO CLONE SACCHAROMYCES CEREVISIAE DNA IN TETRAHYMENA

Dr. Maas began discussion of the request (tabs 979, 976/4) of Dr. Eduardo Orias of the University of California, Santa Barbara, to clone *Saccharomyces cerevisiae* DNA in *Tetrahymena thermophila* using *S. cerevisiae/E. coli* hybrid plasmids. Dr. Orias, in support of his request, noted that *Tetrahymena thermophila* is a unicellular eukaryote of no known pathogenicity. Dissemination of genetic information between members of the species by means other than eukaryotic conjugation has not been demonstrated.

Dr. Levine said this request is an example of experiments which would be covered by the new proposed mechanism concerning non-pathogenic prokaryotes and non-pathogenic lower eukaryotes (see item VII of these minutes). Dr. Maas moved acceptance of the proposal at the P1 containment level. Dr. Levine seconded the motion. By a unanimous vote of nineteen in favor, RAC recommended the action.

XVI. DRAFT PROPOSAL ON TOXINS

Dr. Maas said, in his mind, the cloning of toxin genes may be among the few real potential hazards posed by recombinant DNA experiments. Dr. Maas said an *ad hoc* group composed of Dr. Alan Bernheimer of New York University, Dr. John Collier of Yale University, Dr. Michael Gill of Tufts University, Dr. Susan Gottesman of NIH, Dr. Myron Levine of the University of Maryland, Dr. James Mason of the Utah State Department of Health, and himself had met to consider appropriate containment for recombinant DNA experiments involving genes coding for toxins.

Dr. Maas said the group had participated in two telephone conference calls and had met on January 7, 1981 to develop language for publication in the Federal Register and for subsequent consideration at the April 23-24, 1981 RAC meeting. He presented the draft language developed at the January 7, 1981 meeting (Attachment II).

Dr. Maas said the proposal could be broken down into three parts: (1) a preamble which offers the logic and reasoning behind the proposal, (2) a section outlining procedures to determine toxicity and (3) containment conditions for various potencies. He noted that for the moment the proposal dealt only with cloning in *E. coli* K-12 host-vector systems.

Dr. Maas suggested that the *ad hoc* working group might be consulted when proposals evaluating toxins are considered.

Mr. Thornton suggested that each RAC member take the opportunity to make suggestions on the draft proposal. He thanked the *ad hoc* working group for their efforts. Dr. Berns suggested that Dr. Gill might be invited as an *ad hoc* consultant to the RAC meeting at which the toxin proposal will be considered.

XVII. FUTURE MEETING DATES

Mr. Thornton directed the attention of the members to tab 961 which outlined future meeting dates of the RAC. These are April 23 and 24, 1981, September 10 and 11, 1981, and January 7 and 8, 1982.

XVIII. ADJOURNMENT

The meeting was adjourned at 12:15 p.m., January 9, 1981.

Respectively submitted,

Elizabeth A. Milewski, Ph.D.
Rapporteur

William J. Gartland, Jr., Ph.D.
Executive Secretary

20

I hereby certify that, to the best of my knowledge, the foregoing Minutes and Attachments are accurate and complete.

May 18, 1981
Date

Ray Thornton
Ray Thornton, J.D.
Chairman
Recombinant DNA Advisory Committee

RECOMBINANT DNA ADVISORY COMMITTEE

CHAIRMAN

THORNTON, Ray, J.D. (82)
President
Arkansas State University
State University, Arkansas 72467
501 972-2100

- -

AHMED, Abdul Karim, Ph.D. (82)
Senior Staff Scientist
Natural Resources Defense Council, Inc.
122 East 42nd Street
New York, New York 10017
212 949-0049

BALTIMORE, David, Ph.D. (82)
Professor of Biology
Center for Cancer Research
Massachusetts Institute of Technology
Cambridge, Massachusetts 02139
617 253-6410

BERNS, Kenneth I., Ph.D., M.D. (83)
Chairman
Department of Immunology and Medical Microbiology
University of Florida College of Medicine
Gainesville, Florida 32610
904 392-3311

BRILL, Winston J., Ph.D. (83)
Vilas Research Professor
Department of Bacteriology
University of Wisconsin
Madison, Wisconsin 53706
608 262-3567

CAMPBELL, Allan M., Ph.D. (81)
Professor
Department of Biological Sciences
Stanford University
Stanford, California 94305
415 497-1170

CASON, Zelma (81)
Supervisor
Cytopathology Laboratory
Department of Pathology
University of Mississippi Medical Center
Jackson, Mississippi 39216
601 987-5547

FEDOROFF, Nina V., Ph.D. (84)
Staff Member
Department of Embryology
Carnegie Institution of Washington
115 West University Parkway
Baltimore, Maryland 21210
301 467-1414

GOLDSTEIN, Richard, Ph.D. (82)
Associate Professor
Department of Microbiology and Molecular Genetics
Harvard Medical School
Boston, Massachusetts 02115
617 732-1911

GOTTESMAN, Susan K., Ph.D. (81)
Senior Investigator
Laboratory of Molecular Biology
National Cancer Institute
National Institutes of Health
Bethesda, Maryland 20205
301 496-2095

HARRIS, Jean L., M.D. (83)
Secretary of Human Resources
Commonwealth of Virginia
Office of Governor
Post Office Box 1475
Richmond, Virginia 23212
804 786-7765

HOLMES, King K., M.D., Ph.D. (84)
Head
Division of Infectious Diseases
U.S. Public Health Service Hospital
Seattle, Washington 98114
206 325-2997

KING, Patricia A., J.D. (82)
Deputy Assistant Attorney General
Civil Division
Department of Justice
10th & Constitution Ave., N.W.
Washington, D.C. 20530
202 724-6841

KRIMSKY, Sheldon, Ph.D. (81)
Acting Director
Program in Urban Social and Environmental Policy
Tufts University
Medford, Massachusetts 02155
617 628-5000 x726

LEVINE, Myron M., M.D. (84)
Director
Center for Vaccine Development
Division of Infectious Diseases
University of Maryland School of Medicine
Baltimore, Maryland 21201
301 528-7588

MAAS, Werner K., Ph.D. (83)
Professor
Department of Microbiology
New York University School of Medicine
New York, New York 10016
212 340-5322

MASON, James O., M.D., Dr. Ph. (83)
Executive Director
Utah State Department of Health
Post Office Box 2500
Salt Lake City, Utah 84110
801 533-6111

McGARRITY, Gerard J., Ph.D. (84)
Head
Department of Microbiology
Institute for Medical Research
Copewood Street
Camden, New Jersey 08103
609 966-7377

McKINNEY, Robert W., Ph.D. (84)
Chief, Occupational Safety and Health Branch
Division of Safety
National Institutes of Health
Bethesda, Maryland 20205
301 496-2960

NIGHTINGALE, Elena O., Ph.D., M.D. (83)
Senior Program Officer
Institute of Medicine
National Academy of Sciences
Washington, D.C. 20418
202 389-6721

NOVICK, Richard P., M.D. (81)
Member and Chief
Department of Plasmid Biology
Public Health Research Institute of the City of New York, Inc.
New York, New York 10016
212 481-0746

PARKINSON, David K., B.M., B.Ch. (81)
Associate Professor
Graduate School of Public Health
University of Pittsburgh
Pittsburgh, Pennsylvania 15261
412 624-3041

PINON, Ramon, Ph.D. (82)
Associate Professor
Department of Biology
B-022 Bonner Hall
University of California, San Diego
La Jolla, California 92093
714 452-2452

SCANDALIOS, John G., Ph.D. (84)
Head
Department of Genetics
North Carolina State University
Raleigh, North Carolina 27650
919 737-2291

WILLIAMS, Luther S., Ph.D. (81)
Professor
Department of Biology
Washington University
Campus Box 1137
St. Louis, Missouri 63130
314 889-6843

EXECUTIVE SECRETARY

GARTLAND, William J., Jr., Ph.D.
Director, Office of Recombinant DNA Activities
National Institute of Allergy and Infectious Diseases
National Institutes of Health
Bethesda, Maryland 20205
301 496-6051

RECOMBINANT DNA ADVISORY COMMITTEE

NON-VOTING REPRESENTATIVES

CENTERS FOR DISEASE CONTROL

DOWDLE, Walter R., Ph.D.
Assistant Director for Science
Centers for Disease Control
Atlanta, Georgia 30333
404 329-3701

National Institute for Occupational Safety and Health (CDC)

LEMIN, Richard A.
Director
Office of Program Planning
and Evaluation
National Institute for Occupational
Safety and Health,
Room 8A53
5600 Fishers Lane
Rockville, Maryland 20857
301 443-3680

U.S. DEPARTMENT OF AGRICULTURE

TOLIN, Sue A., Ph.D.
Science and Education Administration
Cooperative Research
U.S. Department of Agriculture
Washington, D.C. 20250
202 447-5741

FULKERSON, John F., Ph.D. (ALT)
Science and Education Administration
Cooperative Research
U.S. Department of Agriculture
Washington, D.C. 20250
202 447-5741

U.S. DEPARTMENT OF COMMERCE

GORDON, George S., Ph.D.
Analyst
Office of Environmental Affairs
U.S. Department of Commerce
Room 3425
Washington, D.C. 20230
202 377-2565

PAYNTER, O. E., Ph.D. (ALT)
Toxicologist
Office of Environmental Affairs
U.S. Department of Commerce
Room 3425
Washington, D.C. 20230
202 377-3234

U.S. DEPARTMENT OF ENERGY

DUDA, George, Ph.D.
Office of Health and
Environmental Research, EV-33
U.S. Department of Energy
Washington, D.C. 20545
202 353-3651

EDINGTON, Charles W., Ph.D. (ALT)
Deputy Director
Office of Health and Environmental
Research
U.S. Department of Energy
Washington, D.C. 20250
202 353-3251

U.S. DEPARTMENT OF THE INTERIOR

PIMENTEL, Mariano B., Ph.D.
Medical Director
U.S. Department of the Interior
Room 7045
18th & C Street, N.W.
Washington, D.C. 20240
202 343-2081

U.S. DEPARTMENT OF JUSTICE

BELL, Charlotte R., J.D.
General Litigation Section
Land and Natural Resources Division
U.S. Department of Justice
Washington, D.C. 20530
202 633-4150

U.S. DEPARTMENT OF STATE

WALSH, William J., III
Biomedical Research Liason and Health Affairs Officer
Oceans and International Environmental and Scientific Affairs
U.S. Department of State
Washington, D.C. 20520
202 632-4824

U.S. DEPARTMENT OF TRANSPORTATION

CUSHMAC, George E., Ph.D.
Chemist
Research and Special Programs Administration
U.S. Department of Transportation
Washington, D.C. 20590
202 755-4906

U.S. ENVIRONMENTAL PROTECTION AGENCY

BANKS, Darryl R., Ph.D.
Executive Assistant to the
Assistant Administrator for
Research and Development
Office of Research and Development
United States Environmental Protection Agency
RD 672, 913 West Tower
Washington, D.C. 20460
202 755-0122

FOOD AND DRUG ADMINISTRATION

HENRY, Timothy J., Ph.D.
BF, DT, HFF-156
Food and Drug Administration
200 C Street, S.W.
Washington, D.C. 20204
202 472-4690

NATIONAL AERONAUTICS AND SPACE ADMINISTRATION

DeVINCENZI, Donald L., Ph.D.
Program Manager, Planetary Biology
Code SBL-3
National Aeronautics and Space
Administration
Washington, D.C. 20546
202 755-3732

NATIONAL SCIENCE FOUNDATION

LEWIS, Herman W., Ph.D.
Senior Scientist for Recombinant DNA
Division of Physiology
Cellular and Molecular Biology
National Science Foundation
Washington, D.C. 20550
202 357-7647

HARRIMAN, Phillip, Ph.D. (ALT)
Program Director for Genetic Biology
Room 326
National Science Foundation
Washington, D.C. 20550
202 632-5985

U.S. VETERANS ADMINISTRATION

SCHULTZ, Jane S., Ph.D.
Geneticist
U.S. Veterans Administration
Medical Research Service - 151
2215 Fuller Road
Ann Arbor, Michigan 48105
313 769-7100 x696

BERMAN, Howard M. (ALT)
Health Scientist
Program Development and Review Division
U.S. Veterans Administration
810 Vermont Avenue, N.W.
Washington, D.C. 20420
202 389-5065

U.S. DEPARTMENT OF LABOR

LOGAN, David C., M.D.
Medical Officer
Office of Technical Support
Occupational Safety and Health
Room N3656
U.S. Department of Labor
Washington, D.C. 20210
202 523-9603

RECOMBINANT DNA ADVISORY COMMITTEE

LIAISON REPRESENTATIVES

JUENGST, Eric T. (Acting)
Program Specialist
Program of Science Technology
& Human Value
Mail Stop 104
National Endowment for the Humanities
Washington, D.C. 20506
202 474-0354

WEISS, Daniel L., M.D.
Assembly of Life Sciences
National Academy of Sciences
Washington, D.C. 20418
202 389-6315

IINO, Professor Tetsuo
Faculty Science
University of Tokyo
Hongo, Tokyo 113
Japan

FIRST DRAFT PRESENT TO RAC ON JANUARY 9, 1981

Cloning of Toxins

I. Preamble

Whereas it is unlikely that novel pathogens of clinical significance for man might be created by the cloning of genes for toxic proteins into new host bacteria that colonize humans or that may pass genetic information to organisms capable of colonizing humans, it is nevertheless prudent to restrict the cloning of genes for potent toxins.

The theoretical dangers stem from the habits of the new bacterial host and the toxicity of the toxin per se rather than known attributes of the organism that contributes the toxin gene(s), its ecology, virulence, amount of toxin it may synthesize in humans or elsewhere, and the possibility that it exchanges genetic information with certain other organisms in nature. Likewise, the toxins role, or otherwise, in pathogenicity of the donor organism is not necessarily of relevance.

The extent to which toxins are a danger is usually difficult to ascertain for humans. The specification thus attempts to define a level of activity below which proteins might be considered safe and specifies minimal acceptable safety tests on animals which might predict human safety levels. Because there are wide ($>10^5$ fold) differences in susceptibilities of animals to toxins, human safety may be inferred with reasonable assurance only if an agent is shown to non-potent to another primate or to several lower mammals. The specification is worded so that non-potenncy (potency) for lower animals would be over-ridden by evidence of potency (non-potency) to primates or humans.

DRAFT 1/7/81

Additional precautions may be desirable if synergy or potentiation occur as, for example those bacterial exotoxins that enhance the toxicity of endotoxin.

Toxicity Determination

A toxin shall be considered potent at a certain level if parenteral administration of a certain amount causes death, disfigurement or profound neurological effects.

a) If the human toxicity is known, this information shall be paramount.

b) If human toxicity is not known, it may be inferred pro tem from assays of toxicity to another primate (intravenous injection to at least four animals).

c) If neither human nor other primate toxicity is known, human toxicity may be inferred from 16 most sensitive of three small animals, namely mice, guinea pigs and rabbits, using intravenous injection into at least four animals of each species.

The toxin used for the tests must be of good quality without substantial denaturation or chemical alteration from its most effective form. The purity must be known sufficiently to determine the content of specific agent. If the purity is in doubt the most conservative assumption must be made. An impure toxin that appears similar in structure and action to a known toxin may be assumed pro tem to be ten times as toxic as the known toxin.

When two or more proteins act in synergy to form a toxic principle and the components are to be cloned separately under conditions that rigorously preclude the comingling of the separate clones, the toxicities of each component may be considered individually.

Restrictions

1. No specific restriction shall apply to the cloning of DNA specifying a protein if it is non-potent when administered at the level of 100 μg (or more) per kilogram of body weight.

2. Cloning of Class A, B and C toxins is, for the present, restricted to E. coli host-vector systems. Class A toxins are defined as those that are potent at the level of 1 μg - 100 μg/kg body weight. These may be cloned in EK1 P1.

   Special Case:

   Some enterotoxins are substantially more toxic when administered enterally than parenterally and must be considered separately. The following enterotoxins whose effects are confined to the stimulation of intestinal secretion that can be entirely reversed by administration of electrolyte solutions shall be subject to the rules governing Class A toxins. The heat stable toxins of E. coli (both STI & STII) and of Y. enterocolitica cholera toxin, the heat labile toxins of E. coli, Klebsiella, and other related proteins as may be identified that are neutralized by an antiserum monospecific for cholera toxin.

3. Class B toxins are those that are potent at the level of 100 ng - 1000 ng/kg body weight (examples - diphtheria toxin, Clostridium perfringens, epsilon toxin, abrin). DNA for these proteins may be cloned EK2/P2 or EK1/P3.

4. Class C toxins are potent at less than 100 ng, namely the botulinum toxins, tetanus toxin, and Shigella dysenteriae neurotoxin. Cloning of genes for these toxins is restricted but exceptions will be considered on a case-by-case basis by RAC following publication of the request in the Federal Register. It is likely that permission to proceed with some protocols involving toxins of this class will require the work to proceed in a P4 facility.

Footnote:

It is conceivable that some toxins may greatly ($\geq$100-fold) potentiate the effects of other toxins. If information on potentiation becomes available, the toxins with potentiating effects on other toxins will constitute a special situation to be considered on a case-by-case basis as a minor action.

LD_{50} or MLD/kg

1-10 ng	Man	Monkey	Mouse	Guinea Pig	Rabbit
Botulinum toxin A	10 ng		1.2 ng	(0.6 ng)	(0.5 ng)
B			1.2 ng	0.6 ng	
C		1/3 mouse		1 x mouse	1/8 mouse
D		(40 ng)	<0.4 ng	(0.1 ng)	(0.08 ng)
E proteolytically activated		(1.1 ng)	1.1 ng	(0.6 ng)	(1.1 ng)
F					
Tetanus toxin	<2.5 ng		7 ng	~2 ng	(.05-5 ng)
Shigella dysenteriae neurotoxin		(4.5 ng)	1.3 µg	>9 µg	0.9 ng
10-100 ng					
100-1000 ng					
Diphtheria toxin	≤100 ng		200 ng	160 ng	
Abrin			600 ng		
Cl. perfringens Epsilon toxin (trypsin activated)			250 ng 1 µg		
1 - 10 µg					
Staphylococcal Alpha toxin			40-60 µg		1/3 µg
Ricin			3 µg		
Pseudomonas aeruginosa exotoxin A			3 µg		
Streptolysin O			10-25 µg	as rabbit	3 µg
Cl. perfringens Theta toxin			13-16 µg		5-8 µg
Pneumolysin	0-labile hemolysins				4.4 µg
Cereolysin			40-80 µg		
Listereolysin			3-12 µg		

and presumably likewise for similar hemolysins produced by other Clostridium and Bacillus species

10 - 100 µg	Man	Monkey	Mouse	Guinea Pig	Rabbit
P. pestis murine toxins A or B			35 µg ∿50 µg		
B. pertussis toxin			<or <<60 µg, 5 µg		
B. anthracis. Lethal factor (with PA)			(Rat) <114 µg		
S. aureus Beta toxin			500 µg-5 mg	40-40 µg	3-30 µg ?
100 µg -1 mg					
Cholera Toxin (i.v.)			250 µg (less enterally)		
LT (i.v.)			presumed 250 µg		
Cl. perfringens enterotoxin			300 µg		
Cord Factor			500 µg		
1-10 mg					
Pseudomonas aeruginosa protease(s)			≥3 mg, 4 mg		
Streptococcal erythrogenic toxin (also enhances effect of endotoxin)			3.6 mg		3.5 mg
Proteus mirabilis neurotoxin S			3 mg		
10-100 mg					
Staphylococcal Gamma toxin			<50 mg ?		
Staphylococcal Delta toxin					∿40 mg
S. aureus enterotoxin A, B, C po	∿20 ng (A); < 500 ng (B)	2 µg (A); 2 µg (B)			
S. aureus enterotoxin A, B, C iv		0.1 µg			

Staph leukocidin	> 1 mg
Toxin shock toxin	
Legionella	
B. cereus enterotoxins	
ST	
C. difficile	
Streptolysin S	

federal register

Thursday
March 12, 1981

Part II

Department of Health and Human Services

National Institutes of Health

Recombinant DNA Research; Actions Under Guidelines

DEPARTMENT OF HEALTH AND HUMAN SERVICES

National Institutes of Health

Recombinant DNA Research; Actions Under Guidelines

AGENCY: National Institutes of Health, PHS, HHS.

ACTION: Notice of actions under NIH Guidelines for Research Involving Recombinant DNA Molecules.

SUMMARY: This notice sets forth actions taken by the Director, NIH, under the 1980 NIH Guidelines for Research Involving Recombinant DNA Molecules (45 FR 77384).

EFFECTIVE DATE: March 11, 1981.

FOR FURTHER INFORMATION CONTACT: Additional information can be obtained from Dr. William J. Gartland, Office of Recombinant DNA Activities (ORDA), National Institutes of Health, Bethesda, Maryland 20205. (301) 496-6051.

SUPPLEMENTARY INFORMATION: I am promulgating today several major actions under the NIH Guidelines for Research Involving Recombinant DNA Molecules. These proposed actions were published for comment in the **Federal Register** of November 28, 1980, and reviewed and recommended for approval by the Recombinant DNA Advisory Committee (RAC) at its meeting on January 8-9, 1981. In accordance with Section IV-E-1-b of the NIH Guidelines, I find that these actions comply with the Guidelines and present no significant risk to health or the environment.

Part I of this announcement provides background information on the actions. Part II provides a summary of the major actions.

I. Decisions on Actions Under Guidelines

I-A. Proposed Containment for Nonpathogens

Dr. Winston Brill, a RAC member, proposed in a letter dated November 14, 1980, that the Guidelines be amended to permit use of nonpathogenic prokaryotes and nonpathogenic lower eukaryotes as donors and recipients in recombinant DNA experiments under P1 containment conditions.

The following language was published in the November 28, 1980 **Federal Register** (45 FR 79366) for thirty days of comment:

A. A new section, III-O-2, would be added to the Guidelines, as follows:

"III-O-2. *Experiments Involving Non-Pathogenic Prokaryotes and Lower Eukaryotes.* Recombinant DNA experiments involving prokaryotes and lower eukaryotes, nonpathogenic [2A] for man, animals, or plants, can be conducted under P1 containment."

B. A new paragraph would be added just before Section III-O begins, as follows:

"When the reader finds that the containment level given for the same experiment is different in two different sections within Part III, he may choose which of the two levels he wishes to use for the experiment."

C. The second paragraph of Section III-B-3 would deleted. Revised Section III-B-3 would read as follows:

"III-B-3. *Non-HV1 Systems.* Containment levels for other classes of experiments involving non-HV1 systems may be approved by the Director, NIH. (See Sections IV-E-1-b-(1)-(b), IV-E-1-b-(2)-(c), and IV-E-1-b-(3)-(b))."

D. Section IV-E-1-b-2-(f) would be deleted. This Section currently reads as follows:

"IV-E-1-b-(2)-(f). Assigning containment levels for experiments in which both donor and recipient are non-pathogenic prokaryotes (see Section III-B-3)."

During the thirty day comment period eight letters supporting this proposal were received. Two additional letters, while supporting the proposal, recommended that containment be set at P2, rather than P1.

The RAC discussed the proposal at the January 8-9, 1981 meeting. Dr. Brill suggested that the proposed Section III-O-2 be modified in two ways: (1) following the word "plants" would be added the words, "and only DNA from such sources,"; and (2) text would be added specifying that the experiments must be reviewed with the local IBC with documentation that the organisms are not known pathogens. (Dr. Brill also initially recommended that containment for these experiments be raised from P1 to P2, but later said he was convinced by the arguments of some RAC members that P1 was appropriate).

During the ensuing discussion RAC members opposed to the motion pointed out that: (1) the proposal covers an enormous variety of organisms, (2) "nonpathogenic" may be defined differently by different IBCs and (3) no restriction is placed on the type of vectors to be used. A substitute motion was advanced by Dr. Gottesman which would provide for an expedited review procedure. Under this proposal, ORDA would review proposals involving nonpathogenic prokaryotes and lower eukaryotes on a case-by-case basis. The RAC, by a vote of six in favor, eight opposed, and two abstentions, denied this substitute motion.

The RAC continued discussion of Dr. Brill's motion. Some RAC members felt the proposal as written placed a burden of interpreting "pathogenicity" on IBCs. Nonetheless, sentiment supporting an expedited type of procedure for dealing with prokaryotic and lower eukaryotic nonpathogens was expressed. By a vote of nine in favor, eight opposed, and three abstentions, the RAC passed Dr. Brill's motion, as it had appeared in the **Federal Register**, with the two changes suggested by Dr. Brill at the meeting.

The substitute proposal which would permit ORDA to lower containment on proposals utilizing nonpathogenic prokaryotes and lower eukaryotes on a case-by-case basis, was again offered by Dr. Gottesman for consideration. The proposal was that, if Dr. Fredrickson should not accept Dr. Brill's proposal, it was the sense of the RAC that it would be preferable to the status quo to at least make two changes: (1) extend the current situation allowing cloning between nonpathogenic prokaryotes at P3 to also include lower eukaryotes; and (2) allow lowering below P3 for individual cases by ORDA rather than requiring RAC review. A motion to table this proposal failed; by a vote of eight in favor, eleven opposed. By a vote of fourteen in favor, one opposed, and three abstentions, the RAC then approved Dr. Gottesman's motion.

In deciding whether to accept the "Brill" motion, recommended by the RAC by a vote of nine in favor, eight opposed, and three abstentions, or the more conservative "Gottesman" motion, recommended by the RAC by a vote of fourteen in favor, one opposed, and three abstentions, I note that already in the Guidelines the following experiments are permitted:

1. Certain experiments with prokaryotes and lower eukaryotes are exempt from the Guidelines, under Sections I-E-3 and I-E-4.

2. Certain experiments with prokaryotes and lower eukaryotes may be done at P1 containment under Guideline Sections III-O, III-B-2 and III-C-5.

3. Certain experiments with prokaryotes and lower eukaryotes may be done at P2 containment under Guideline Sections III-A-1-a-(5) and III-A-1-b.

Dr. Brill's proposal covers an enormous number of organisms, many of which have not been well characterized. "Nonpathogenic" might be interpreted differently by different IBCs. The proposal does not require use of non-conjugative plasmids. For these reasons I am, at present, not accepting the "Brill" motion and instead I am accepting the more conservative "Gottesman" motion.

Accordingly a new section, III-O-2, is added to the Guidelines as follows:

"III-O-2. *Experiments Involving Prokaryotes Nonpathogenic for Man,*

Animals or Plants, and/or Lower Eukaryotes Nonpathogenic for Man, Animals or Plants.

Recombinant DNA experiments involving prokaryotes nonpathogenic for man, animals, or plants, and/or lower eukaryotes nonpathogenic for man, animals or plants, and only DNA from such sources, can be conducted under P3 containment (2A). Lower levels of physical containment may be assigned by ORDA on a case-by-case basis for specific donor-recipient combinations (see Section IV-E-1-b-(3)-(h))."

A new paragraph is added just before Section III-O begins, as follows:

"When the reader finds that the containment level given for the same experiment is different in two different sections within Part III, he may choose whichever of the two levels he wishes to use for the experiment."

The second paragraph of Section III-B-3 is deleted. Revised Section III-B-3 now reads as follows:

"III-B-3. *Non-HV1 Systems.* Containment levels for other classes of experiments involving non-HV1 systems may be approved by the Director, NIH. (See Sections IV-E-1-b-(1)-(b), IV-E-1-b-(2)-(c), and IV-E-1-b-(3)-(b))."

Section IV-E-1-b-(2)-(f) is deleted.

A new section IV-E-1-b-(3)-(h) is added as follows:

"IV-E-1-b-(3)-(h). Assigning containment levels for experiments in which both donor and recipient are nonpathogenic prokaryotes and/or nonpathogenic lower eukaryotes (see Section III-O-2)."

In order to clarify the relationship among Sections III-O, III-O-1, and III-O-2, the final sentence in the second paragraph under Part III is amended to read as follows:

"Prior IBC review is required for all other experiments described in the subsections of Part III, including III-O-1, III-O-2, etc."

I-B. Request for Approval of Schizosaccharomyces Pombe for Recombinant DNA Experiments

Dr. Benjamin D. Hall of the University of Washington, in letters dated November 3, 1980, and December 5, 1980, requested that the fission yeast, *Schizosaccharomyces pombe*, together with the *S. cerevisiae/E. coli* hybrid recombinant plasmids, be certified as an HV1 host-vector system. Dr. Hall further requested that this system be included under Section III-O of the Guidelines. In his submission, Dr. Hall noted that *Schizosaccharomyces pombe* is not a pathogen, it survives poorly outside of a controlled laboratory environment, it is rare in nature, and genetic exchange in the *Ascomycetes* occurs only with closely related organisms.

Dr. Hall's request was published in the November 28, 1980 **Federal Register** (45 FR 79387). No comments were received during the thirty day comment period.

The RAC, in discussing the proposal at the January 8-9, 1981 meeting, noted that specifications for HV1 certification have been defined in Section II-D-2-b of the Guidelines. It was suggested that only certain experiments be approved without certifying *S. pombe* as a general HV1 host-vector system. The RAC, therefore, recommended by a vote of fourteen in favor, one opposed and four abstentions, that DNA from non-pathogenic prokaryotes and lower eukaryotes may be cloned into *Schizosaccharomyces pombe* species under P1 containment conditions. It further recommended by a vote of fourteen in favor, none opposed and five abstentions, that DNA from higher eukaryotes may be cloned in *S. pombe* species under P3 containment conditions.

I accept these recommendations. Item 18 in Appendix E of the Guidelines is amended to read as follows:

"18· DNA from nonpathogenic prokaryotes and nonpathogenic lower eukaryotes may be cloned into *Schizosaccharomyces pombe* species under P1 containment conditions. DNA from higher eukaryotes may be cloned in *S. pombe* species under P3 containment conditions."

I-C. Request To Include Streptococcus Faecalis and Streptococcus Sanguis in Appendix A.

Dr. Donald Clewell of the University of Michigan requested in letters dated August 13, 1980 and September 10, 1980, that *Streptococcus faecalis* be included along with *Streptococcus sanguis* in a sublist of Appendix A. Recombinant DNA molecules composed entirely of DNA segments from organisms within each sublist of Appendix A are exempt from the Guidelines under Section I-E-4, which exempts "Certain specified recombinant DNA molecules that consist entirely of DNA segments from different species that exchange DNA by known physiological processes. . . ." In support of his request, Dr. Clewell submitted data indicating that exchange of genetic information between the two species occurs by natural physiological processes.

A **Federal Register** announcement of Dr. Clewell's request appeared on November 28, 1980 (45 FR 79386). No comments were received during the thirty day comment period.

The RAC discussed Dr. Clewell's proposal at the January 8-9, 1981 meeting. The RAC was satisfied that the data demonstrated two-way plasmid transfer. By a vote of twelve in favor, two opposed and five abstentions, the RAC recommended that the request be approved, and that *Streptococcus faecalis* be added to sublist F of Appendix A.

I accept this recommendation, and Appendix A, Sublist F has been amended to read as follows:

"Sublist F

1. *Streptococcus sanguis*
2. *Streptococcus pneumoniae*
3. *Streptococcus faecalis*"

I-D. Request To Clone Saccharomyces Cerevisiae DNA in Tetrahymena Thermophilia

Dr. Eduardo Orias of the University of California, Santa Barbara in a letter dated December 18, 1980 requested permission to clone *Saccharomyces cerevisiae* DNA in *Tetrahymena thermophila* using *S. cerevisiae/E. coli* hybrid plasmids.

Dr. Orias supplied data outlining the genetics and ecology of *Tetrahymena.* He noted that *Tetrahymena thermophila* is a unicellular microbial eukaryote of no known pathogenicity. Dissemination of genetic information between members of the species by means other than eukaryotic conjugation has not been demonstrated.

Dr. Orias' request appeared in the November 28, 1980 **Federal Register** (45 FR 79387). No comments were received during the thirty day comment period.

During the RAC discussion of the proposal at the January 8-9, 1981 meeting, it was noted that the proposal involves nonpathogenic organisms, and approval at the P1 level of containment was recommended by a unanimous vote of nineteen in favor.

I accept this recommendation, and a new entry has been added to Appendix E to read as follows:

"26. *Saccharomyces cerevisiae* DNA may be cloned in *Tetrahymena thermophila* using *E. coli/S. cerevisiae* hybrid plasmids under P1 containment conditions."

I-E. Proposal To Amend Item 4 of Appendix E

Entry 4 of Appendix E of the Guidelines reads as follows:

"4· Cloned desired fragments from any non-prohibited source may be transferred into *Agrobacterium tumefaciens* containing a Ti plasmid (or derivatives thereof), using a nonconjugative *E. coli* plasmid vector coupled to a fragment of the Ti plasmid and/or the origin of replication of an *Agrobacterium* plasmid, under containment conditions one step higher than would be required for the desired DNA in HV1 systems (i.e., one step higher physical containment than that specified in the subsections of Section III–A). Transfer into plant parts or cells in culture would be permitted at the same containment level (one step higher)."

Dr. Clarence Kado of the University of California, Davis, proposed in a letter dated October 2, 1980 that the fourth entry in Appendix E be modified to read as follows:

"4. Cloned desired fragments from any non-prohibited source may be transferred into *Agrobacterium tumefaciens* containing a Ti plasmid (or derivatives thereof), using a nonconjugative *E. coli* plasmid vector coupled to a fragment of the Ti plasmid and/or the origin of replication of an *Agrobacterium* plasmid, under containment conditions that would be required for the desired DNA in HV1 systems (i.e., that specified in the subsections of Section III–A). Transfer into plant parts or cells in culture would be permitted at the same containment level."

An announcement of Dr. Kado's proposed amendment was published in the **Federal Register** of November 28, 1980 (45 FR 79387). No comments were received during the thirty day comment period.

During the discussion of the proposal at the January 8–9, 1981 RAC meeting, it was noted that this proposal would effectively designate *Agrobacterium tumefaciens* an HV1 system.

It was pointed out that while *Agrobacterium tumefaciens* is a plant pathogen, plant tissue must be injured to permit infection. Further, the genetic information introduced into plant cells by the *Agrobacterium tumefaciens* Ti plasmid is not stably integrated into the plant genome and is not transmitted at meiosis into seeds. Reservations were expressed, however, about approving *A. tumefaciens* as an HV1 system. A motion to permit cloning of DNA from plants and nonpathogenic prokaryotes in *Agrobacterium tumefaciens* with subsequent transfer to plants or plant tissue under P2 containment conditions was recommended by a vote of seventeen in favor, none opposed and two abstentions.

I accept this recommendation, and entry 4 of Appendix E, is amended to read as follows:

"4. Cloned desired fragments from any non-prohibited source may be transferred into *Agrobacterium tumefaciens* containing a Ti plasmid (or derivatives thereof), using a nonconjugative *E. coli* plasmid vector coupled to a fragment of the Ti plasmid and/or the origin of replication of an *Agrobacterium* plasmid, under containment conditions one step higher than would be required for the desired DNA in HV1 systems (i.e., one step higher than that specified in the subsections of Section III–A). However, DNA from plants and nonpathogenic prokaryotes may be cloned under P2 containment conditions. Transfer into plant parts or cells in culture is permitted at the same containment level as is used for the cloning in *Agrobacterium tumefaciens*.

I–F. Request for Lowering of Containment Under Entry Four of Appendix E

Dr. Mary-Dell Chilton of Washington University in St. Louis, in a letter of September 10, 1980, requested a reduction in physical containment, to the P2 level, for the manipulation in *Agrobacterium tumefaciens* of (1) the *Saccharomyces cerevisiae* alcohol dehydrogenase 1 gene and (2) the gene coding for the maize (*Zea mays*) seed storage protein, zein. The cloned DNA and the cloning vectors will be introduced into tobacco plants. These experiments are currently covered under entry 4 of Appendix E which stipulates use of P3 containment. Dr. Chilton's proposal was published for comment in the November 28, 1980 **Federal Register** (45 FR 79387). No comments were received during the thirty day comment period.

Noting that the cloned DNA sequences to be manipulated are well characterized, the RAC at the January 8–9, 1981 meeting recommended, by a vote of fifteen in favor, none opposed and four abstentions, P1 containment conditions for the described experiments.

I accept this recommendation, and text has been added to entry 4 of Appendix E, so indicating.

I–G. Proposed Procedures for Previously Approved Large-Scale Recombinant DNA Experiments

1. *Application Procedures for Minor Modifications of Previously Approved Large-Scale Recombinant DNA Experiments.* The following procedures for handling minor modifications of previously approved large-scale recombinant DNA experiments, generated by a Working Group of the Recombinant DNA Advisory Committee (RAC), were published in the November 28, 1980 **Federal Register** (45 FR 79387):

"Procedures have been developed for considering applications to grow more than ten liters of an organism containing recombinant DNA. These procedures include consideration of the request by a working group of the NIH Recombinant DNA Advisory Committee, submission of the request to the full RAC after consideration by the working group, and subsequent submission to the Director, NIH, for final review. This procedure has taken a minimum of two months. Therefore, the following procedures are proposed to expedite consideration of requests to grow more than ten liters of recombinant DNA-containing organisms when these proposals represent minor modifications of previously approved experiments. Modifications include deletion of sequences from the recombinant DNA, changes in promoters, addition of short seqments not affecting the nature of the expressed products, and minor changes in the properties of the host. Changes are considered minor if they do not affect either the containment properties of the vector or the host, or the nature of products made, or add new products. Therefore, the procedures for dealing with minor modifications have the objective of determining that the change is indeed minor. To determine whether a change is minor, two levels of review will take place:

"(1) By ORDA, which will decide upon receipt of a request to process it as a new request or as a minor modification, and in the latter case

"(2) by a working group of at least two members of RAC.

"The Working Group has proposed that the following language be added to the 'Application Procedures for Large-Scale Recombinant DNA Experiments':

"6. Proposals that the submitter considers to represent minor modifications of already approved experiments will be handled by an expedited procedure. A request must be submitted to ORDA. This request should include the changes made, the way in which these changes were made (e.g., mutagenesis, recloning), and the nature and results of any tests done to determine that no major change has occurred (e.g., restriction enzyme analysis, tests for produced products, tests of vector mobilization).

"ORDA will determine whether the submission represents a minor modification of an approved experiment. If so, the request will be submitted promptly to a working group of at least two RAC members. If possible, these members should have been present at the RAC discussion of approval of the original experiment. If any member of the working group does not agree that the request represents a minor modification, the application will then be referred to the full RAC at its next meeting. If the working group is unanimous in concluding that the changes do not alter the organism in a way that is likely to affect containment of the organism or the vector, or the nature of the expressed product, significantly, from that presented originally to RAC, recommendation for approval will be transmitted to ORDA, and, through ORDA, to the submitters. Consideration of requests by working groups should explicitly address the following issues: Is the change likely to compromise biological containment provided by the host or the vector? Does the change add to the biological activities associated with the expressed products in a way not considered by the original submission?"

During the thirty day comment period, no comments were received.

Prior to publication in the **Federal Register**, the RAC discussed the proposal at the September 25–26, 1980 meeting; the proposed procedures were considered to be reasonable.

The RAC subsequently discussed the proposal at the January 8–9, 1981 meeting and by a vote of seventeen in favor, none opposed and one abstention, recommended approval of the proposed language.

I accept this recommendation. The complete text of the revised procedures for review of large-scale experiments appears in Part II of this announcement.

2. *Proposed Procedures for Change of Locale of Previously Approved Large-Scale Recombinant DNA Experiments.* During the discussion of proposed procedures dealing with minor modifications of previously approved large-scale recombinant DNA experiments at the January 8–9, 1981, RAC meeting, the question of how to process changes of site for large-scale production was raised. In this situation, recombinant clones, which had been approved for scale-up at one site, would be moved to another physical facility. A second IBC might then be charged with oversight responsibilities.

RAC recommended that a registration document, which would indicate compliance with the NIH Guidelines and its large-scale procedures should be filed with ORDA by the IBC of the new institution. ORDA could then give approval for large-scale growth of the clones at the new site. No RAC review would be required.

I accept this recommendation. Accordingly, the following additional language will be added to the "Application Procedures for Large-Scale Recombinant DNA Experiments":

"7· Should a clone, previously approved for scale-up at one physical facility, be proposed to be moved to a second physical facility, the IBC with oversight responsibility at the second site shall submit to ORDA a registration document and receive ORDA approval, prior to initiating scale-up. No RAC review would be required.

The complete text of the revised procedures for review of large-scale experiments appears in Part II of this announcement.

I-H. Proposals To Clone Genes of Foot and Mouth Disease Virus

The RAC at its December 6–7, 1979, meeting had reviewed a four stage proposal submitted by Dr. Howard Bachrach of the United States Department of Agriculture Plum Island Animal Disease Center and Dr. Dennis Kleid of Genentech, Inc., entitled "Cloning and Expression in *E. coli* of the VP3 protein of Foot and Mouth Disease Virus." In the **Federal Register** of January 17, 1980 (45 FR 3552), I, as Director, NIH, accepted the RAC recommendation to allow Stage I to proceed. At that time I noted, "Dr. Campbell stated that it was the sense of the RAC that this motion constituted the 'major action' and that future recommendations of the RAC approving further stages of the experiment would be 'minor actions.' "

In the **Federal Register** of July 29, 1980 (45 FR 50528), I, as Director, NIH, accepted a recommendation made by the RAC at its June 5–6, 1980, meeting that certain clones containing cDNA copies of pieces of the Foot and Mouth Disease virus, made on Plum Island under Stage I of the protocol, be allowed to be removed from Plum Island, as they "were well characterized, lacked infectivity, and represent, in aggregate, only 75% of the FMD viral genome."

On January 9, 1981, the RAC reviewed a request of October 17, 1980, from Dr. Kleid to modify Stage IV of the protocol, dealing with cloning of various FMD types. The RAC by a vote of 20 in favor, none opposed, and one abstention, recommended that this be accepted with the conditions that a working group of the RAC, but not the full RAC, would examine data on the infectivity of the clones produced on Plum Island, before they were allowed to leave Plum Island, and that such clones be well characterized, shown to lack infectivity, and shall not contain, individually or collectively, more than 75% of the viral genome.

I accept this recommendation.

I-J. Containment Levels for Recombinant DNA Experiments Involving Streptomyces and Other Non-Pathogenic Actinomycetes

Dr. Stanley Cohen of Stanford University Medical Center, in a letter dated November 18, 1980, submitted the following proposal for consideration by the RAC:

"That all members of the non-pathogenic *Actinomycetes* genus *Streptomyces* and the plasmids native to this genus be approved as host-vector systems for the cloning under P1 conditions of DNA derived from other non-pathogenic prokaryotic organisms such as *Streptomyces* and other non-pathogenic *Actinomycetes* species, *Escherichia coli* K-12, *Bacillus subtilis, Bacillus lichenformis, Bacillus circulans*, and other non-pathogenic *Bacillus* species, and for the cloning of DNA derived from non-pathogenic unicellular eukaryotic micro-organisms such as *Saccharomyces cerevisiae* and *Neurospora crassa.*"

The RAC noted that they had recommended earlier in the meeting (see I-A above) that all experiments involving nonpathogenic prokaryotes and lower eukaryotes, be allowed at P1. Dr. Cohen's request involves a subset of these. The RAC, by a vote of 18 in favor, none opposed, and two abstentions, recommended that the proposal be accepted.

I accept this recommendation, and a new entry will be added to Appendix E as follows:

"27· All members of the nonpathogenic *Actinomycetes* genus *Streptomyces* and the plasmids native to this genus are approved as host-vector systems for the cloning under P1 conditions of DNA derived from other nonpathogenic prokaryotic organisms such as *Streptomyces* and other nonpathogenic *Actinomycetes* species, *Escherichia coli* K-12, *Bacillus subtilis, Bacillus lichenformis, Bacillus circulans*, and other nonpathogenic *Bacillus* species, and for the cloning of DNA derived from nonpathogenic unicellular eukaryotic microorganisms such as *Saccharomyces cerevisiae* and *Neurospora crassa.*"

II. Summary of Actions Under Guidelines—Arranged According to Position in Guidelines

II-A. Amendment of Second Paragraph of Part III

The final sentence in the second paragraph under Part III is amended to read as follows:

"Prior IBC review is required for all other experiments described in the subsections of Part III, including III–O–1, III–O–2, etc."

II–B. Addition of New Paragraph to Part III

A new paragraph is added just before Section III–O begins, as follows:

"When the reader finds that the containment level given for the same experiment is different in two different sections within Part III, he may choose whichever of the two levels he wishes to use for the experiment."

II–C. Addition of New Section III–O–2

A new section, III–O–2, is added to the guidelines as follows:

"III–O–2. *Experiments Involving Prokaryotes Nonpathogenic for Man, Animals or Plants, and/or Lower Eukaryotes Nonpathogenic for Man, Animals or Plants.* Recombinant DNA experiments involving prokaryotes nonpathogenic for man, animals, or plants, and/or lower eukaryotes nonpathogenic for man, animals or plants, and only DNA from such sources, can be conducted under P3 containment (2A). Lower levels of physical containment may be assigned by ORDA on a case-by-case basis for specific donor-recipient combinations (see Section IV–E–1–b–(3)–(h))."

II–D. Amendment of Section III–B–3

The second paragraph of Section III–B–3 is deleted. Revised Section III–B–3, now reads as follows:

"III–B–3. *Non-HVI Systems.* Containment levels for other classes of experiments involving non-HVI systems may be approved by the Director, NIH. (See Sections IV–E–1–b–(1)–(b), IV–E–1–b–(2)–(c), IV–E–1–b–(3)–(b))."

II–E. Deletion of Section IV–E–1–b–(2)–(f)

Section IV–E–1–b–(2)–(f) is deleted.

II–F. Addition of Section IV–E–1–b–(3)–(h)

A new section IV–E–1–b–(3)–(h) is added as follows:

"IV–E–1–b–(3)–(h). Assigning containment levels for experiments in which both donor and recipient are nonpathogenic prokaryotes and/or nonpathogenic lower eukaryotes (see Section III–O–2)."

II–G. Amendment of Appendix A, Sublist F

Appendix A, Sublist F is amended to read as follows:

"Sublist F

1. *Streptococcus sanguis*
2. *Streptococcus pneumoniae*
3. *Streptococcus faecalis"*

II–H. Amendments of Appendix E

Entires 4 and 18 of Appendix E, are amended to read as follows:

"4. Cloned desired fragments from any non-prohibited source may be transferred into *Agrobacterium tumefaciens* containing a Ti plasmid (or derivatives thereof), using a nonconjugative *E. coli* plasmid vector coupled to a fragment of the Ti plasmid and/or the origin of replication of an *Agrobacterium* plasmid, under containment conditions one step higher than would be required for the desired DNA in HVl systems (i.e., one step higher than that specified in the subsections of Section III–A). However, DNA from plants and nonpathogenic prokaryotes may be cloned under P2 containment conditions; and the *Saccharomyces cerevisiae* alcohol dehydrogenase 1 gene and the gene coding for the maize (*Zea mays*) seed storage protein, zein, may be cloned under P1 conditions. Transfer into plant parts or cells in culture is permitted at the same containment level as is used for the cloning in *Agrobacterium tumefaciens*.

"18. DNA from nonpathogenic prokaryotes and nonpathogenic lower eukaryotes may be cloned into *Schizosaccharomyces pombe* species under P1 containment conditions. DNA from higher eukaryotes may be cloned in *S. pombe* species under P3 containment conditions."

The following new entries are added to Appendix E:

"26. *Saccharomyces cerevisiae* DNA may be cloned in *Tetrahymena thermophila* using *E. coli/S. cerevisiae* hybrid plasmids under P1 containment conditions."

"27. All members of the nonpathogenic *Actinomycetes* genus *Streptomyces* and the plasmids native to this genus are approved as host-vector systems for the cloning under P1 conditions of DNA derived from other nonpathogenic prokaryotic organisms such as *Streptomyces* and other nonpathogenic *Actinomycetes* species, *Escherichia coli* K-12, *Bacillus subtilis, Bacillus licheniformis, Bacillus circulans*, and other nonpathogenic *Bacillus* species, and for the cloning of DNA derived from nonpathogenic unicellular eukaryotic microorganisms such as *Saccharomyces cerevisiae* and *Neurospora crassa*."

II–I. Procedures for Review of Large-Scale Experiments

The following procedures, which are not incorporated into the Guidelines, have been adopted for the review of large-scale experiments. (They are an expansion of the procedures which appeared in the November 21, 1980 **Federal Register** (45 FR 77380)):

"Application Procedures for Large-Scale Recombinant DNA Experiments.

"1. For each research project proposing to exceed the 10-liter limit, the applicant shall file a request with the NIH Office of Recombinant DNA Activities (ORDA). The request should include the following information:

"a. The registration document submitted to the local Institutional Biosafety Committee (see Section III of the Guidelines). This should include, or have appended to it, a summary paragraph which describes the proposed project in language that is comprehensible to non-specialists.

"b. A statement of the rationale for wishing to exceed the 10-liter limit.

"c. Evidence that the recombinant DNAs to be employed in the research have been rigorously characterized and are free of harmful sequences.

"d. Specification of the P–LS level proposed to be used as defined in the NIH Physical Containment Recommendations for Large-Scale Uses of Organisms Containing Recombinant DNA Molecules (**Federal Register**, April 11, 1980).

"2. Each request submitted to ORDA shall be referred to a working group of the NIH Recombinant DNA Advisory Committee for review.

"3. Following review and approval by the working group, each request shall be submitted to the entire Recombinant DNA Advisory Committee for review.

"4. Following review and approval by the RAC, each request shall be submitted to the Director, NIH, for the final review.

"5. Applications for large-scale experiments which are submitted by institutions not receiving NIH funds for recombinant DNA research shall be kept confidential (provided the institutions so desire) in accordance with the provisions of the NIH Guidelines for Research Involving Recombinant DNA Molecules and to the extent permitted by law.

"6. Proposals that the submitter considers to represent minor modifications of already approved experiments will be handled by an expedited procedure. A request must be submitted to ORDA. This request should include the changes made, the way in which these changes were made (e.g., mutagenesis, recloning), and the nature and results of any tests done to determine that no major change has occurred (e.g., restriction enzyme analysis, tests for produced products, tests of vector mobilization). ORDA will determine whether the submission represents a minor modification of an approved experiment. If so, the request will be submitted promptly to a working group of at least two RAC members. If possible, these members should have been present at the RAC discussion of approval of the original experiment. If any member of the working group does not agree that the request represents a minor modification, the application will then be referred to the full RAC at its next meeting. If the working group is unanimous in concluding that the changes do not alter the organism in a way that is likely to affect containment of the organism or the vector, or the nature of the expressed product significantly from that presented originally to RAC, recommendation for approval will be transmitted to ORDA, and, through ORDA, to the submitters. Consideration of requests by working groups should explicitly address the following issues: Is the change likely to compromise biological containment provided by the host or the vector? Does the change add to the biological activities associated with the expressed products in a way not considered by the original submission?

"7. Should a clone, previously approved for scale-up at one facility, be proposed to be moved to a second facility, the IBC with oversight responsibility at the second site shall submit to ORDA a registration document and receive ORDA approval, prior to initiating scale-up. No RAC review would be required.

"8. These procedures may be refined or revised on the basis of discussion and action by the NIH Recombinant DNA Advisory Committee."

Additional Announcements of the Director, NIH

Section IV-E-1-b-(3)-(d) of the Guidelines gives responsibility to the Director, NIH, for "authorizing, under procedures specified by the RAC, large-scale experiments (i.e., involving more than 10 liters of culture) for recombinant DNAs that are rigorously characterized and free of harmful sequences."

Accordingly, several requests for authorization to culture, on a large-scale, recombinant DNA host-vector systems have been received and reviewed by the NIH.

I. Genentech, Inc.

On February 2, 1981, the Director, NIH, on the recommendation of the RAC, approved a request from Genentech, Inc., for the large-scale culture of EK1 host-vector systems containing plasmids coding for human leukocyte interferons.

This request was approved with the understanding that Genentech, Inc., has agreed to permit an observer, designated by NIH, to visit the facilities if NIH should choose to inspect the site.

The principal investigator is Dr. Norm S. C. Lin. The work is to be done at the P1-LS level of containment at the research and development facility at 460 Point San Bruno Boulevard, South San Francisco, California 94080.

II. Genentech, Inc.

On February 2, 1981, the Director, NIH, on the recommendation of the RAC, approved a request from Genentech, Inc., for the large-scale culture of EK1 host-vector systems containing plasmids coding for bovine growth hormone.

This request was approved with the understanding that Genentech, Inc., has agreed to permit an observer, designated by NIH, to visit the facilities should NIH choose to inspect the site.

The principal investigator is Dr. Norm S. C. Lin. The work is to be done at the P1-LS level of containment at the research facility at 460 Point San Bruno Boulevard, South San Francisco, California 94080.

III. Hoffman-LaRoche, Inc.

On February 2, 1981, the Director, NIH, on the recommendation of the RAC, approved a request from Hoffman-LaRoche, Inc., for the large-scale culture of EK1 host-vector systems containing plasmids coding for human leukocyte and fibroblast interferons.

This request was approved with the understanding that Hoffman-LaRoche, Inc., has agreed to permit an observer, designated by NIH, to visit the facilities if NIH should choose to inspect the site.

The principal investigators are Drs. Philip A. Miller and Vishra Rai. The work is to be done at the P1-LS level of containment at the research and development facilities at 340 Kingsland Avenue, Nutley, New Jersey 07110.

IV. Burns-Biotec Laboratories, Inc.

On February 20, 1981, the Director, NIH, on the recommendation of the RAC, approved a request from Burns-Biotec, Inc., a wholly owned subsidiary of Schering-Plough Corporation, for the large-scale culture of EK1 host-vector systems containing plasmids coding for human leukocyte interferon.

This request was approved with the understanding that Burns-Biotec, Inc., has agreed to permit an observer, designated by NIH, to visit the facilities if NIH should choose to inspect the site.

The principal investigator is Dr. Donald Baldwin. The work is to be performed at the P1-LS level of containment at the facilities in Elkhorn, Indiana 68022.

V. Schering-Plough Corporation

On February 20, 1981, the Director, NIH, on the recommendation of the RAC, approved a request from Schering-Plough Corporation for the large-scale culture of EK1 host-vector systems containing plasmids coding for human leukocyte interferon.

This request was approved with the understanding that Schering-Plough Corporation has agreed to permit an observer, designated by NIH, to visit the facilities if NIH should choose to inspect the site.

The principal investigator is Dr. Paul J. Leibowitz. The work is to be performed at the P1-LS level of containment at the research and development facilities in Bloomfield, New Jersey 07003.

Dated: March 4, 1981.

Donald S. Fredrickson,

Director, National Institutes of Health.

OMB's "Mandatory Information Requirements for Federal Assistance Program Announcements" (45 FR 39592) requires a statement concerning the official government programs contained in the *Catalog of Federal Domestic Assistance.* Normally NIH lists in its announcements the number and title of affected individual programs for the guidance of the public. Because the guidance in this notice covers not only virtually every NIH program but also essentially every federal research program in which DNA recombinant molecule techniques could be used, it has been determined to be not cost effective or in the public interest to attempt to list these programs. Such a list would likely require several additional pages. In addition, NIH could not be certain that every federal program would be included as many federal agencies, as well as private organizations, both national and international, have elected to follow the NIH Guidelines. In lieu of the individual program listing, NIH invites readers to direct questions to the information address above about whether individual programs listed in the *Catalog of Federal Domestic Assistance* are affected.

NIH programs are not covered by OMB Circular A-95 because they fit the description of "programs not considered appropriate" in Section 8-(b)-(4) and (5) of that Circular.

[FR Doc. 81-7543 Filed 3-11-81; 8:45 am]

BILLING CODE 4110-08-M

federal register

Friday
March 20, 1981

Part III

Department of Health and Human Services

National Institutes of Health

Recombinant DNA Advisory Committee; Meeting

DEPARTMENT OF HEALTH AND HUMAN SERVICES

National Institutes of Health

Recombinant DNA Advisory Committee; Meetings

Pursuant to Pub. L. 92-463, notice is hereby given of a meeting of the Large Scale Review Working Group sponsored by the Recombinant DNA Advisory Committee at the National Institutes of Health, Conference Room 7A24, Building 31A, 9000 Rockville Pike, Bethesda, Maryland 20205, on April 22, 1981, from 2 p.m. to 5 p.m.

The Working Group will hold an organizational meeting to institute working procedures.

Further information may be obtained from Dr. Elizabeth Milewski, Executive Secretary, Large Scale Review Working Group, NIAID, Building 31, Room 4A52, Bethesda, Maryland, telephone, (301) 496-6051.

The meeting will be open to the public. Attendance will be limited to space available.

In addition, notice is hereby given of a meeting of the Recombinant DNA Advisory Committee at the National Institutes of Health, Conference Room 10, Building 31C, 9000 Rockville Pike, Bethesda, Maryland 20205, on April 23, 1981, from 9 a.m. to recess to approximately 6 p.m., and, if necessary, on April 24, 1981, from 8:30 a.m. to 5 p.m. This meeting will be open to the public on April 23 from 9 a.m. to approximately 3 p.m., and on April 24 from 8:30 a.m. to adjournment to discuss:

Amendment of Guidelines
E. coli K-12 host-vector systems
Host-vector systems other than *E. coli* K-12
Risk-assessment
Review of protocols for required containment levels
Request for exception to a prohibition to clone genes of Foot and Mouth Disease Virus
Containment levels for cloning of toxins
Other matters requiring necessary action by the Committee.

Attendance by the public will be limited to space available.

In accordance with provisions set forth in Section 552b(c)(4), Title 5, U.S. Code and Section 10(d) of Pub. L. 92-463, the meeting will be closed to the public for approximately three hours for the review, discussion and evaluation of proposal(s) from a commercial concern(s) for scale-up of recombinant DNA experiments. It is anticipated that this will occur on April 23, from approximately 3 p.m. until adjournment. The proposal(s) and the discussion could reveal confidential trade secrets or commercial property such as patentable material.

Dr. William J. Gartland, Jr., Executive Secretary, Recombinant DNA Advisory Committee, National Institutes of Health, Building 31, Room 4A52, telephone (301) 496-6051, will provide materials to be discussed at the meeting, rosters of committee members and substantive program information. A summary of the meeting will be available at a later date.

Dated: March 9, 1981.

Thomas E. Malone, Ph.D.,
Deputy Director, NIH.

Note.—OMB's "Mandatory Information Requirements for Federal Assistance Program Announcements" (45 FR 39592) requires a statement concerning the official government programs contained in the *Catalog of Federal Domestic Assistance.* Normally NIH lists in its announcements the number and title of affected individual programs for the guidance of the public. Because the guidance in this notice covers not only virtually every NIH program but also essentially every Federal research program in which DNA recombinant molecule techniques could be used, it has been determined to be not cost effective or in the public interest to attempt to list these programs. Such a list would likely require several additional pages. In addition, NIH could not be certain that every Federal program would be included as many Federal agencies, as well as private organizations, both national and international, have elected to follow the NIH Guidelines. In lieu of the individual program listing, NIH invites readers to direct questions to the information address above about whether individual programs listed in the *Catalog of Federal Domestic Assistance* are affected.

NIH programs are not covered by OMB Circular A-95 because they fit the description of "programs not considered appropriate" in Section 8(b) (4) and (5) of that Circular.

[FR Doc. 81-8597 Filed 3-19-81; 8:45 am]

BILLING CODE 4110-08-M

federal register

Friday,
March 20, 1981

Part IV

Department of Health and Human Services

National Institutes of Health

Recombinant DNA Research; Proposed Actions Under Guidelines

DEPARTMENT OF HEALTH AND HUMAN SERVICES

Recombinant DNA Research; Proposed Actions Under Guidelines

AGENCY: National Institutes of Health, PHS, DHHS.

ACTION: Notice of actions under NIH guidelines for research involving recombinant DNA molecules.

SUMMARY: This notice sets forth proposed actions to be taken under the NIH Guidelines for Research Involving Recombinant DNA Molecules. Interested parties are invited to submit comments concerning these proposals. After consideration of these proposals and comments by the NIH Recombinant DNA Advisory Committee (RAC) at its April 23-24, 1981 meeting, the Director of the National Institutes of Health will issue decisions on these proposals in accord with the Guidelines.

DATE: Comments must be received by April 20, 1981.

ADDRESS: Written comments and recommendations should be submitted to the Director, Office of Recombinant DNA Activities, Building 31, Room 4A52, National Institutes of Health, Bethesda, Maryland 20205. All comments received in timely response to this notice will be considered and will be available for public inspection in the above office on weekdays between the hours of 8:30 a.m. and 5:00 p.m.

FOR FURTHER INFORMATION CONTACT: Background documentation and additional information can be obtained from Drs. Stanley Barban or Elizabeth Milewski, Office of Recombinant DNA Activities, National Institutes of Health, Bethesda, Maryland 20205, (301) 496-6051.

SUPPLEMENTARY INFORMATION: The National Institutes of Health will consider the following changes and amendments under the Guidelines for Research Involving Recombinant DNA Molecules, as well as actions under these Guidelines.

I. Proposed Revision of Guidelines for Recombinant DNA Experiments Involving E. Coli K-12 and Saccharomyces Cerevisiae Host-Vector Systems

Containment requirements and administrative procedures for the conduct of most recombinant DNA experiments involving EK1 *E. coli* K-12 and laboratory strain *Saccharomyces cerevisiae* host-vector systems are currently specified by Section III-O of the Guidelines. The chairpersons of Institutional Biosafety Committees, at a meeting in Washington, D.C. on November 24-25, 1980, passed by a large majority a resolution that experiments currently covered by Section III-O should be made exempt from the Guidelines. The chairpersons felt that the risks associated with these experiments are negligible, and that exemption of experiments currently covered by Section III-O would reduce paperwork by approximately 90%.

This proposal was discussed by the RAC at its meeting on January 8-9, 1981. In "straw votes" at the meeting, an overwhelming majority of RAC members favored doing something to reduce materially or eliminate the paperwork and reporting functions for experiments covered by Section III-O; about half the RAC members felt serious consideration should be given to exempting entirely from the Guidelines experiments currently covered by Section III-O. The RAC requested that a series of options be developed and published for comment in the **Federal Register**. Accordingly, the following options will be considered at the April 23-24, 1981 meeting of the RAC.

Note.—It is recognized that changes will be necessary in a number of sections of the Guidelines in order to implement whatever option is selected. Necessary editorial changes will be made by the NIH Director when a final decision on the recommendations of the RAC is promulgated.

Option A—Review by an Institutional Official of Experiments Covered by Section III-O: Under Option A, experiments currently covered under Section III-O would remain under Section III-O. However, rather than requiring IBC review of all registration documents, option A would specify that experiments covered by Section III-O could be reviewed by a designated institutional official. This official may be a member of the IBC. Large-scale experiments (e.g., more than 10 liters of culture) would continue to be reviewed by procedures specified by RAC.

Two types of experiments, currently covered under Section III-O, are treated differently from the majority of experiments under this Section. These experiments are:

(1) Experiments involving the cloning in *E. coli* K-12 of DNA from CDC Class 3 etiological agents. These experiments currently require P3 containment conditions.

(2) Experiments involving a deliberate attempt to have *E. coli* K-12 efficiently express a eukaryotic gene. This type of experiment currently requires prior review and approval by the IBC.

These cases may be handled under one of the following suboptions:

Suboption A-1-a: Under Suboption A-1-a, experiments involving DNA from CDC Class 3 etiological agents would continue to require P3 containment and continue to require review by the IBC.

Suboption A-1-b: Under Suboption A-1-b, experiments involving Class 3 agents would continue to require P3 containment, but review may be effected by a designated institutional official.

Suboption A-1-c: Under Suboption A-1-c, experiments involving Class 3 agents would require P1 containment and would be reviewed by a designated institutional official. This option would relax the requirements for these experiments to the same level as experiments with CDC Class 1 or Class 2 agents.

Suboption A-2-a: Under Suboption A-2-a, deliberate attempts to obtain expression of a eukaryotic gene in *E. coli* K-12 would continue to require prior review and approval by the IBC.

Suboption A-2-b: Under Suboption A-2-b, deliberate attempts to obtain expression of a eukaryotic gene in *E. coli* K-12 would require prior review by a designated institutional official.

Suboption A-2-c: Under Suboption A-2-c, no prior review would be required of attempts to obtain expression of a eukaryotic gene in *E. coli* K-12

Option B—Elimination of Registration Requirements for Experiments Covered by Section III-O: Under Option B, experiments currently covered under Section III-O would remain under Section III-O. However, under Option B, the current requirements for the registration and review of experiments covered by Section III-O would be eliminated. That is, under Option B, no registration or review of such experiments, by the IBC or by an institutional official, would be required. Large-scale experiments (e.g., more than 10 liters of culture) would continue to be reviewed by procedures specified by the RAC.

The following suboptions might be considered for handling the special cases of (1) cloning of DNA from CDC Class 3 agents in *E. coli* K-12, and, (2) deliberate attempts to efficiently express eukaryotic genes in *E. coli* K-12.

Suboption B-1-a: Under Suboption B-1-a, experiments involving the cloning of DNA from CDC Class 3 etiological agents in *E. coli* K-12 would continue to require P3 containment conditions and continue to require review by the IBC.

Suboption B-1-b: Under Suboption B-1-b, experiments involving the DNA of Class 3 agents would continue to require P3 containment conditions. However, no registration document would be required, nor would review by the IBC or by any institutional official be required.

Suboption B-1-c: Under Suboption B-1-c, experiments involving Class 3 agents would require P1 containment conditions. No registration document or review by the IBC or a designated official, however, would be required. The status of these experiments would then be equivalent to experiments with CDC Class 1 or Class 2 agents.

Suboption B-2-a: Under Suboption B-2-a, deliberate attempts to obtain expression of a eukaryotic gene in *E. coli* K-12 would continue to require prior review by the IBC.

Suboption B-2-b: Under Suboption B-2-b, no prior review of experiments involving deliberate attempts to obtain expression of eukaryote gene in *E. coli* K-12 would be required.

Option C—Exemption of Experiments Currently Covered by Section III-O: Under Option C, experiments currently covered by Section III-O would be removed from Section III-O. These experiments would be exempted from the Guidelines under Section I-E-5. The exemption would apply to all nonprohibited experiments which use either laboratory strains of *Saccharomyces cerevisiae* or *E. coli* K-12 as the host-vector system.

Suboption C-1-a: Under Suboption C-1-a, the exemption would apply to all nonprohibited experiments using *E. coli* K-12 as the host.

Suboption C-1-b: Under Suboption C-1-b, the exemption would be qualified with the statement that "(a) the *E. coli* host shall not contain conjugation proficient plasmids or generalized transducing phages, and (b) lambda or lambdoid or Ff bacteriophages or non-conjugative plasmids (49) shall be used as vectors." This qualification would then be qualified by the statement that experiments "involving the insertion into *E. coli* K-12 of DNA from prokaryotes that exchange genetic information (35) with *E. coli* may be performed with any *E. coli* K-12 vector (e.g., conjugative plasmid); When a non-conjugative vector is used, the *E. coli* K-12 host may contain conjugation-proficient plasmids either autonomous or integrated, or generalized transducing phages."

Suboption C-2-a: Under Suboption C-2-a, language would be added to the Guidelines to explicitly make Prohibition I-D-6 concerning large-scale applicable to these experiments.

Suboption C-2-b: Under Suboption C-2-b, Prohibition I-D-6 would not apply to those experiments. That is, experiments involving over, as well as under, 10 liters in volume would be exempt from the Guidelines.

Suboption C-3-a: Under Suboption C-3-a, the entry in Appendix C which would effect the exemption under Section I-E-5 would contain a statement that although exempt, for these experiments "Pl physical containment conditions are recommended."

Suboption C-3-b: Under Suboption C-3-b, no statement would be included recommending Pl physical containment conditions.

Suboption C-4-a: Under Suboption C-4-a, experiments involving the cloning in *E. Coli* K-12 of DNA from CDC Class 3 etiological agents would not be exempted. Rather they would continue to require P3 containment conditons and would continue to require review and approval by the IBC.

Suboption C-4-b: Under Suboption C-4-b, experiments involving the DNA of CDC Class 3 agents would not be exempted. However, containment might be specified at Pl, P2 or P3, and some form of review by either the IBC or an institutional official would be required.

Suboption C-4-c: Under Suboption C-4-c, experiments involving the cloning of CDC Class 3 agents in *E. Coli* K-12 would be exempt.

Suboption C-5-a: Under Suboption C-5-a, attempts at deliberate expression of a eukaryotic gene in *E. coli* K-12 would continue to require prior review by the IBC.

Suboption C-5-b: Under Suboption C-5-b, no prior review of experiments involving attempts at deliberate expression of a eukaryotic gene in *E. coli* K-12 would be required.

II. Proposal To Convert the NIH Guidelines Into a Code of Standard Practice and To Reduce the Recommended Containment Levels for Some Experiments

Drs. Allan Campbell and David Baltimore, RAC members, propose to convert the NIH Guidelines into a "code of standard practice" and to reduce recommended containment levels for some experiments. They propose that the Guidelines be amended as follows:

(1) Section I-A of the Guidelines would be amended to read as follows:

I-A. *Purpose.* The purpose of these Guidelines is to specify standard practices for constructing and handling (i) recombinant DNA molecules and (ii) organisms and viruses containing recombinant DNA molecules. Adherence to these standards by all laboratories using recombinant DNA is recommended.

(2) Section I-C of the Guidelies wold be eliminated.

(3) Part III of the Guidelines would be replaced with the following:

Part III discusses experiments covered by the Guidelines. The reader must first consult Part I, where listings are given of prohibited and exempt experiments.

Where there are existing recommended physical containment levels applicable to non-recombinant DNA experiments with either the host or the vector (such as those specified by the CDC Guidelines), recombinant DNA experiments should be carried out at containment levels at least as high as those recommended for non-recombinant DNA experiments. Otherwise, all non-prohibited experiments may be carried out under conditions of Pl physical containment. As a general practice, investigators should use the highest level of biological containment (HV3 HV2 HV1) which is available and appropriate for the purposes of the experiment.

Specific exceptions to the prohibitions may be approved by the Director, NIH (see Section I-D). The Director will consider requests for exceptions from individuals, institutions or corporations regardless of whether the applicant is affiliated with or supported by NIH. Such exceptions will generally be approved for specified levels of physical and biological containment.

This will be followed by a listing of those exceptions which are presently authorized and the containment levels approved for the excepted experiments.

(4) Part IV of the Guidelines would be eliminated, with the following exceptions:

(a) Those definitions listed in Part IV-C which may be needed to clarify statements made elsewhere in the Guidelines shall be retained.

(b) Those portions of Part IV-E defining the composition of RAC and prescribing rules for RAC procedures shall be retained.

(c) The following statement shall be added:

Each institution conducting or sponsoring recombinant DNA research should take responsibility for monitoring its own activities in this area. Any unusual events that might be associated with the use of recombinant DNA molecules should be reported to the Director, NIH.

(5) Section VI of the Guidelines will be eliminated, except for those portions of section VI-F relevant to the protection of proprietary information submitted in support of requests for exceptions from the prohibiitons.

The authors provide an explanaton and justification for their proposals in a letter to ORDA.

III. Containment Levels for Recombinant DNA Experiments Involving Neurospora Crassa

Dr. David Perkins of Stanford University has proposed that entry 2 in Appendix E be amended to read as follows:

Unmodified laboratory strains of *Neurospora crassa* can be used in all experiments for which HV1 *N. crassa* systems are approved, provided that only DNA from Class 1 agents is used. For agents other than Class 1, unmodified laboratory strains of *N. crassa* can be used in all experiments for which HV1 *N. crassa* systems are approved, provided that these are carried out at physical containment one level higher than required for HV1. However, if P3 containment is specified for HV1 *N. crassa*, this level is considered adequate for unmodified *N. crassa*. Care must be exercised to prevent aerial dispersal or macroconidia, in accordance with good laboratory practice.

Mutationally modified strains of *N. crassa* specified as HV1 in Appendix D can used in all experiments for which HV2 *N. crassa* systems are approved, provided that only DNA from Class 1 agents is used.

The rationale for the proposed changes is stated in a letter to ORDA.

IV. Request for Approval of Certain Streptomyces HV1 Host-Vector Systems

Dr. Stanley Cohen of Stanford University has requested that *Streptomyces coelicolor* and the related organisms with which *S. coelicolor* naturally exchanges genetic information (e.g., *S. lividans*, *S. parvulus* and *S. griseus*), using *Streptomyces* plasmids SCP2, SLP1.2, pIJ101, actinophage phiC31, and their derivatives as vectors, be approved as HV1 host-vector systems.

V. Proposed Containment for Recombinant DNA Experiments Involving the Genus Streptomyces

Dr. Stanley Cohen of Stanford University has requested that the following entry be added to Appendix E:

Experiments involving the cloning of DNA among members of the genus *Streptomyces* are permitted under P1 conditions. For these experiments, no registration document, as described in Part III, is required.

The rationale for the proposal is stated in a letter to ORDA.

VI. Containment Levels for Recombinant DNA Experiments Involving Bacillus Subtilis

Dr. Donald Dean of the Ohio State University has proposed that any *Bacillus subtilis* strain which does not revert to a sporeformer with a frequency greater than 10^7 can be used for cloning DNA from any nonprohibited source, using vectors indigenous to *B. subtilis*, under the same conditions specified by the RAC for *E. coli* K-12 and *Saccharomyces cerevisiae* host-vector systems.

Dr. Dean has further proposed that the following items be added to Appendix E:

Bacillus subtilis strains that do not carry an asporogenic mutation can be used with vectors indigenous to *B. subtilis* for the cloning of DNA from any CDC Class 1 organism under P2 conditions.

Bacillus subtilis strains that do not carry an asporogenic mutation can be used with vectors indigenous to *B. subtilis* under P1 conditions for the cloning of DNA from any Class 1 *Bacillus* species.

VII. Expression of Foot Mouth Disease Virus Capsid Proteins in Saccharomyces Cerevisiae, Bacillus Subtilis, and Mammalian Tissue Culture

Genetech, Inc. South San Francisco, California and the United States Department of Agriculture Plum Island Animal Disease Center, Greenport, New York request permission to extend their cooperative studies aimed at the eventual production of a viral subunit vaccine for Foot and Mouth Disease (FMD). They wish to expand studies aimed at the expression of the FMD capsid protein in host vector systems other than *E. coli* K-12. They propose to study the expression of FMD capsid proteins in *Saccharomyces cerevisiae*, *Bacillus subtilis*, and mammalian tissue culture systems.

VIII. Proposals Concerning Recombinant DNA Experiments With Genes Coding for Toxins

The Recombinant DNA Advisory Committee (RAC), at its September 25–26, 1980 meeting, requested that an *ad hoc* working group be formed to evaluate Section I–D–2 of the Guidelines. Section I–D–2 prohibits the "deliberate formation of recombinant DNAs containing genes for the biosynthesis of toxins potent for vertebrates (2A) (e.g., botulinum or diphtheria toxins; venons from insects, snakes, etc.)." An *ad hoc* working group on toxins composed of Drs. Werner Maas and Alan Bernheimer of New York University, Dr. john Collier of Yale University, Dr. Michael Gill of Tufts University, Dr. Myron Levine of the University of Maryland, and Dr. james Mason of the Utah State Department of Health, was subsequently convened on January 7, 1981 to recommend containment conditions for recombinant DNA experiments with genes coding for toxins. Their recommendations were discussed by the RAC at the january 8–9, 1981 meeting. The *ad hoc* working group requests that the following proposed modifications to the Guidelines be published in the **Federal Register** for thirty days of comment.

A. Section I–D–2 of Section I–D, Prohibitions, would be amended to read as follows:

I–D–2. Deliberate formation of recombinant DNAs containing genes for the biosynthesis of toxins lethal for vertebrates at an LD_{50} of less than 100 nanograms per kilogram body weight (e.g., the botulinum toxins, tetanus toxin, *Shigella dysenteriae* neurotoxin). Guidelines for the cloning of DNAs containing genes coding for the biosynthesis of toxins which are lethal to vertebrates at 100 nanograms to 100 micrograms per kilogram body weight are specified in Appendix G.

B. A new Appendix G, would be added to the Guidelines as follows:

Appendix G—Containment Conditions for Cloning of Genes Coding for the Biosynthesis of Toxins for Vertebrates.

1. General Information

Appendix G specifies the containment to be used for the cloning of genes coding for the biosynthesis of toxins for vertebrates. Cloning of genes coding for toxins for vertebrates that have an LD_{50} of less than 100 nanograms per kilogram body weight (e.g., the botulinum toxins, tetanus toxin, *Shigella dysenteriae* neurotoxin) is prohibited. No specific restrictions shall apply to the cloning of genes if the protein specified by the gene has an LD_{50} of 100 micrograms or more per kilogram of body weight. A list of toxins classified as to LD_{50} is available from ORDA. Testing procedures for determining toxicity of toxins not on the list are available from ORDA. The results of such tests shall be forwarded to ORDA, which will consult with the *ad hoc* working group on toxins prior to inclusion of the toxin on the list. (See Section IV–E–1–b–(3)–(i)).

2. Containment Conditions for Cloning of Toxin Genes in E. Coli K-12

(a) Cloning of genes coding for toxins for vertebrates that have an LD_{50} in the range of 100 nanograms to 1000 nanograms per kilogram body weight (e.g., diphtheria toxin, abrin, *Clostridium perfringens* epsilon toxin) may proceed under P2+EK2 or P3+EK1 containment conditions.

(b) Cloning of genes for the biosynthesis of toxins for vertebrates with an LD_{50} in the range of 1 microgram to 100 micrograms per kilogram body weight may proceed under Section III–O (e.g., *Staphylococcus aureus* alpha toxin, *Staphylococcus aureus* beta toxin, ricin, *Pseudomonas aeruginosa* exotoxin A, *Bordatella pertussis* toxin, the lethal factor of *Bacillus anthracis*, the *Pasteurella pestis* murine toxins, the oxygen-labile hemolysins such as streptolysin O, and certain neurotoxins present in snake venoms and other venoms).

(c) Some enterotoxins are substantially more toxic when administered enterally than parenterally. The following enterotoxins, whose effects are confined to the stimulation of intestinal secretion and whose effects can be entirely reversed by administration of electrolyte solutions, shall be subject to Section III–O. These are cholera toxin, the heat labile toxins of *E. coli*, *Klebsiella*, and other related proteins that may be identified by neutralization with an antiserum monospecific for cholera toxin, and the heat stable toxins of *E. coli* and of *Yersinia enterocolitica*.

3. Containment Conditions for Cloning of Toxins Genes in Organisms Other Than E. Coli K-12

Requests involving the cloning of genes coding for toxins for vertebrates in host-vector systems other than *E. coli* K-12 will be evaluated by ORDA, which will consult with the *ad hoc* working group on toxins. (See Section IV-E-1-b-(3)-(j)).

C. Section V, Footnote 2A would be modified to delete the words: " 'toxins potent for vertebrates' (Section I-D-2)"

D. A new Section IV-E-1-b-(3)-(i) would be added as follows: "IV-E-1-b-(3)-(i). Adding new entries to the list of toxins for vertebrates. (See Appendix G.)"

E. A new Section IV-E-1-b-(3)-(j) would be added as follows: "IV-E-1-b-(3)-(j): Approving the cloning of toxin genes in host-vector systems other than *E. coli* K-12. (See Appendix G.)"

IX. Cloning and Expression of DNA Coding for Diphtheria Toxin

Dr. John Murphy of Harvard University has proposed that the 3.9 kb Bam restriction fragment of *Corynephage Beta* which carries the structural gene of diphtheria toxin be cloned in *E. coli* K-12.

He advances the following arguments as to why these experiments should be permitted:

(1) Studies of diphtheria toxin-producing organisms would yield valuable data for risk assessment.

(2) To determine the localization of diphtheria toxin in *E. coli* and its possible secretion by *E. coli.*

(3) Mutagenesis of the tox gene would be used to elucidate (a) diphtheria toxin interaction with the eukaryotic cell toxin receptor, and (b) the mechanism of fragment A translocation into the eukaryotic cell cytosol.

X. Request for Permission to Clone the Vibrio Cholerae Enterotoxin Gene in E. Coli K-12.

Dr. J. J. Mekalanos of Harvard Medical School has requested an exemption from Section I-D-2 of the Guidelines. This section prohibits the "formation of recombinant DNAs containing genes for the biosynthesis of toxins potent for vertebrates."

Dr. Mekalanos requests the exemption based on the fact that naturally occurring transmissible plasmids, which encode a heat-labile enterotoxin (LT), exist in *E. coli*. LT has recently been shown to share a high degree of structural, antigenic and DNA sequence homology with cholera enterotoxin. In addition, both the LT and cholera enterotoxins are composed of two subunits (A and B) both of which are required for toxicity.

Dr. Mekalanos requests consideration and approval of the appropriate containment level for the experiments which will be performed in three stages, i.e., the cloning in *E. coli* K-12 of specific cholera DNA restriction enzyme fragments known to contain sequences homologous to: (1) The LT A subunit gene, (2) the LT B subunit gene, (3) the LT A and B subunit genes.

Since stage 3 experiments are anticipated to produce recombinant DNA molecules which might express active cholera enterotoxin in *E. coli* K-12 hosts, these experiments might be conducted at more stringent levels of containment than either stage 1 or 2.

Dr. Mekalanos also proposes to perform risk assessment experiments in appropriate animal models to evaluate the pathogenicity of *E. coli* K-12 recombinant clones constructed during the course of this work.

XI. Request To Clone the Genetic Determinant of the Toxic-Shock Syndrome Caused by Staphylococcus Aureus

Dr. Richard Novick of the Public Health Research Institute of the City of New York, Inc., requests permission to clone in *Staphylococcus aureus* the genetic determinant of the toxic-shock syndrome caused by *S. aureus*. Dr. Novick states that recombinant DNA techniques promise the most rapid and direct means of unraveling the biology of this determinant and of the disease in which it is implicated. He requests permission to conduct the experiments under P2 containment using *S. aureus* strain, RN450, which is non-hemolytic, non-pigmented, and lacking any detectable prophage.

XII. Request To Use an E. Coli Strain Containing a MU Phage Insertion

Dr. Daryl Holten of the University of California at Riverside, requests permission to utilize the *E. coli* K-10 strain DF 214 (or derivatives thereof), and EK plasmid vectors (e.g., pBR322, pBR325) to clone rat cDNA. Strain DF 214, a K-12 derivative, contains a Mu phage insertion in the phosphoglucose isomerase gene.

XIII. Request To Employ a Conjugative Plasmid To Transfer N. Crassa DNA

Dr. Norman Giles of the University of Georgia requests permission to use a conjugative plasmid to transfer the QA2 gene of *Neurospora crassa* among *E. coli* K-12 strains. The *N. crassa* QA2 gene would be ligated into a derivative of the mobilizable plasmid RSF2124.

Dated: March 13, 1981.

Donald S. Fredrickson,

Director, National Institutes of Health.

Note.—OMB's "Mandatory Information Requirements for Federal Assistance Program Announcements" (45 FR 39592) requires a statement concerning the official government programs contained in the *Catalog of Federal Domestic Assistance.*

Normally NIH lists in its announcements the number and title of affected individual programs for the guidance of the public. Because the guidance in this notice covers not only virtually every NIH program but also essentially every federal research program in which DNA recombinant molecule techniques could be used, it has been determined to be not cost effective or in the public interest to attempt to list these programs. Such a list would likely require several additional pages. In addition, NIH could not be certain that every federal program would be included as many federal agencies, as well as private organizations, both national and international, have elected to follow the NIH Guidelines. In lieu of the individual program listing, NIH invites readers to direct questions to the information address above about whether individual programs listed in the *Catalog of Federal Domestic Assistance* are affected.

NIH programs are not covered by OMB Circular A-95 because they fit the description of "programs not considered appropriate" in Section 8-(b)-(4) and (5) of that Circular.

[FR Doc. 81-8596 Filed 3-19-81; 8:45 am]

BILLING CODE 4110-08-M

DEPARTMENT OF HEALTH AND HUMAN SERVICES
PUBLIC HEALTH SERVICE
NATIONAL INSTITUTES OF HEALTH

RECOMBINANT DNA ADVISORY COMMITTEE
LARGE-SCALE REVIEW WORKING GROUP

MINUTES OF MEETING

APRIL 22, 1981

The Large-Scale Review Working Group was convened for its first meeting at 2:00 p.m. on April 22, 1981, in Conference Room 9, at the National Institutes of Health, 9000 Rockville Pike, Bethesda, Maryland 20205. Dr. Kenneth Berns and Dr. Robert McKinney were co-chairmen.

Working Group members present for all or part of the meeting were:

Dr. Lucille Adamson, Occupational Safety and Health Administration; Dr. Darryl R. Banks, Environmental Protection Agency; Mr. Manuel Barbeito, NIH; Dr. Kenneth Berns, University of Florida, (co-chairman); Mrs. Zelma Cason, University of Mississippi; Dr. Timothy J. Henry, Food and Drug Administration; Dr. Sheldon Krimsky, Tufts University; Dr. James Mason, Utah State Department of Health; Dr. Robert McKinney, NIH, (co-chairman); Dr. Elizabeth Milewski, NIH, (Executive Secretary); Mr. Seth Pauker, National Institute for Occupational Safety and Health; Dr. John Richardson, Centers for Disease Control; Dr. Sue Tolin, U. S. Department of Agriculture.

Other National Institutes of Health staff present were:

Dr. William Gartland, NIAID.

Others in attendance for all or part of the meeting were:

Ms. Irene Brandt, Eli Lilly & Co.; Dr. Daniel Bull, New Brunswick Scientific Co., Inc.; Mr. Charles R. Gaush, Bethesda Research Laboratories; Dr. Attila T. Kadar, Food and Drug Administration; Mr. Rihito Kimura, Georgetown University; Ms. Carter Leonard, Blue Sheet; Dr. Bing Miller, New Brunswick Scientific Co., Inc., Dr. Henry Miller, Food and Drug Administration; Mr. Ray Thornton, Arkansas State University.

The first meeting of the Large-Scale Review Working Group of the Recombinant DNA Advisory Committee (RAC) was called to order at 2:05 p.m. Wednesday, April 22, 1981. Dr. McKinney, co-chairman of the Large-Scale Review Working Group, began the meeting by requesting the members of the working group to identify themselves, their affiliations, their background and interests.

Dr. Berns, co-chairman of the Large-Scale Review Working Group, presented his views on the role of the group. He said RAC had instructed the ad hoc working group to evaluate questions dealing with large-scale procedures and facilities. He said the working group would function in a completely advisory capacity. The Large-Scale Review Working Group might also appropriately advise institutions, individuals and companies working in the area of recombinant DNA technology on physical containment standards and procedures. Dr. McKinney emphasized that while the function of the committee was to serve RAC in an advisory capacity, he hoped the working group would serve industry by providing assistance and guidance.

Dr. McKinney suggested that one issue the working group might consider is whether and/or how large-scale submissions from institutions receiving NIH funds might be handled. Dr. McKinney said he expected to see an increase in the number of universities at which scale-up of growth of recombinant organisms is permitted and expressed concern that these IBCs might lack expertise in fermentation technology. He suggested that the performance of IBCs that oversee large-scale procedures might be examined. Mr. Barbeito of the NIH Division of Safety supported this view.

Dr. McKinney said that while no prior review of physical facilities of an institution under the voluntary compliance program would be performed by the working group, the group could review facilities with the intent of advising local IBCs. He added that the group might also monitor the large-scale physical containment standards and suggest modifications if necessary.

Mr. Pauker of the National Institute for Occupational Safety and Health (NIOSH), questioned how the Large-Scale Review Working Group would relate to RAC. Dr. Berns replied that the working group was completely advisory to RAC, but pointed out that RAC itself was advisory to Dr. Fredrickson, the NIH Director. Dr. Fredrickson would make any final decisions. Dr. Banks of the Environmental Protection Agency (EPA) suggested that working group deliberations should be considered by Dr. Fredrickson as well as by RAC.

Mr. Pauker asked if the results of review of facilities would be referred back to the companies evaluated. He further asked if generalizable conclusions drawn from these reviews would be disseminated to other industrial concerns. Dr. Berns replied that the working group must decide if the dissemination of such information falls within its mandate. Dr. McKinney noted that some of the material handled by the working group would be proprietary and procedures for handling proprietary information should be considered. Mr. Pauker said he might have information, obtained through NIOSH walkthroughs, which might be pertinent to working group considerations. Dr. Berns felt conceptual information of this type might appropriately be brought before the working group.

Dr. McKinney said that the relationship between the various represented agencies and the Large-Scale Review Working Group should be discussed. Dr. Adamson of the Occupational Safety and Health Administration (OSHA) noting the relationship between NIOSH and OSHA said that, for the moment, OSHA would follow NIOSH's lead. Dr. Henry of the Food and Drug Administration (FDA) said FDA viewed the Large-Scale Review Working Group as a service to FDA and to companies in the recombinant technology area. Dr. Tolin of the United States Department of Agriculture (USDA) suggested that large-scale requests, important to agriculture, will increasingly be brought forward for consideration. She felt the composition of Large-Scale Review Working Group was appropriate to consider physical containment problems, both in industry and in agriculture.

Dr. Richardson of the Centers for Disease Control (CDC) said that CDC currently plays a secondary or a tertiary role as regards recombinant DNA technology. He views CDC as a technical resource to NIOSH, the NIH and RAC, and in one-on-one relationships, to individuals working with etiological agents. He believed CDC would continue to participate in recombinant DNA activities in this capacity. Dr. Berns noted that RAC containment levels set in deliberation are often closely related to suggested CDC levels of containment.

Dr. Krimsky, a RAC member, said the Large-Scale Review Working Group would provide an opportunity to view large-scale processes "prospectively," and an opportunity for resource people to exchange information. He viewed the working group as having four relevant goals, some of which are legitimate concerns at the local level.

(1) Procedures to validate systems, e.g., how facility effluents are treated. Such information could be transmitted to communities in which plants utilizing recombinant DNA technology are located.

(2) Environmental monitoring in plant facilities. He felt that an inventory of current procedures might be a service to newcomers to the field and the experience of seasoned firms might be useful to these newcomers.

(3) Risk assessments related to large-scale work should be performed and be available. He noted that most risk assessment to date has been performed with E. coli K-12. However, industrial trends appear to be towards use of many other organisms as host-vector systems. He said that any important risk assessments performed by EPA or NIOSH should be available to the Large-Scale Review Working Group and to RAC.

(4) Decisions of local IBCs concerning large-scale work. He said this is most difficult to conceptualize and suggested that the role and effectiveness of these IBCs in "self-monitoring" could be assessed.

Dr. Mason suggested the working group define clearly the mission of the group. Dr. Berns called the attention of the group to the motion passed by the RAC at the September 25-26, 1980 meeting:

"A large-scale review subcommittee of the RAC shall be established with the responsibility for advising the RAC on procedures and facilities design pertaining to large-scale operations, and on the performance of local IBCs in reviewing physical containment facilities."

Dr. Fredrickson wrote further in the Federal Register of November 21, 1980 (45 FR 77380):

"In accordance with the recommendation of the RAC, the Working Group will not be involved in pre-review of individual applications. To assist in its function of advising the RAC on the performance of local IBCs in reviewing physical containment facilities and on future revisions of the Large-Scale Physical Containment Recommendations, the Working Group may request information from individual companies. Since NIH is not a regulatory agency, the intent of any such information collection will be fact-finding, to help in development of general recommendations from the Working Group to the RAC, and not for purposes of regulatory actions directed at individual companies."

Dr. McKinney suggested that the working group might examine the question of medical surveillance. Mr. Pauker suggested that environmental monitoring as undertaken by companies might also be examined; he said specific questions must be asked and a large data base accumulated.

Dr. Henry of the Food and Drug Administration (FDA) suggested the working group begin a preliminary consideration of the issue of medical surveillance. Dr. Mason suggested that medical surveillance might be quite costly and questioned whether such expenditures were warranted. Dr. Richardson said a medical surveillance program might not prove too expensive if a select group of (one to three) were examined. He said disease surveillance should not be confused with an employee health care program. Mr. Pauker concurred saying that medical surveillance can be as simple as recording incidence of illness. He noted that many larger companies are currently doing this. He said both EPA and NIOSH have received requests for information in this area from companies planning to move into the area of recombinant DNA technology.

Dr. Henry suggested that the working group begin to consider how an evaluation of IBC function would be made. Dr. McKinney suggested the scope of the study be limited to IBCs dealing with large-scale procedures. He suggested the working group could request the minutes of IBC meetings. Dr. Gartland said two large-scale proposals from universities will be reviewed at the April 23-24, 1980 RAC meeting. He said nineteen industrial IBCs are currently registered with ORDA, but only four of these companies are currently performing large-scale procedures. He did not know if these industrial IBCs would be willing to submit the minutes of their proceedings to the working group for review. Mr. Pauker and Dr. Berns felt the companies would cooperate. Dr. McKinney pointed out that in all likelihood these IBC minutes would have to be treated as proprietary information. Dr. Gartland agreed. Mr. Barbeito felt the working group should examine the composition of IBCs monitoring large-scale procedures e.g., does the IBC possess the requisite expertise to review the facilities? Did the IBC examine and consider the important issues associated with large-scale fermentation technology?

Dr. Berns questioned whether an IBC survey, such as the preliminary survey of California IBCs performed by a Stanford University group, would be appropriate.

Mr. Pauker pointed out that such a survey requires specific expertise in the social sciences which he felt the working group did not possess. Dr. McKinney said he did not believe the working group should evaluate IBC function, rather he felt the working group should be a "clearing house," collating data.

Mr. Thornton asked the working group to consider how issues might be presented for consideration. Dr. Berns suggested that the Office of Recombinant DNA Activities (ORDA) would continue to be the contact point for individuals with questions relating to recombinant DNA and that ORDA would refer issues to the working group. Mr. Thornton asked how a member of the working group would present items to the group. Dr. Berns said that any member of the working group might suggest agenda items.

Dr. Berns suggested that any members with specific suggestions on agenda items should write these up and forward them to the Executive Secretary. He suggested that the next scheduled meeting of the Large-Scale Review Working Group be held on September 9, 1981, the day before the September 10-11, 1981 RAC meeting.

The meeting was adjourned at 4:00 p.m., Wednesday, April 22, 1981.

Respectively submitted,

Elizabeth Milewski

Elizabeth Milewski, Ph.D.
Executive Secretary

I hereby certify that, to the best of my knowledge, the foregoing Minutes are accurate and complete.

5/14/81
Date

Kenneth I. Berns, Ph.D.
Co-Chairman
Large-Scale Review Working Group
of the Recombinant DNA Advisory Committee

5/26/81
Date

Robert W. McKinney, Ph.D.
Co-Chairman
Large-Scale Review Working Group
of the Recombinant DNA Advisory Committee

DEPARTMENT OF HEALTH AND HUMAN SERVICES
PUBLIC HEALTH SERVICE
NATIONAL INSTITUTES OF HEALTH

RECOMBINANT DNA ADVISORY COMMITTEE

MINUTES OF MEETING

APRIL 23-24, 1981

TABLE OF CONTENTS

TABLE OF CONTENTS

DEPARTMENT OF HEALTH AND HUMAN SERVICES
PUBLIC HEALTH SERVICE
NATIONAL INSTITUTES OF HEALTH

RECOMBINANT DNA ADVISORY COMMITTEE

MINUTES OF MEETING[1]

APRIL 23-24, 1981

The Recombinant DNA Advisory Committee (RAC) was convened for its twenty-second meeting at 9:00 a.m. on April 23, 1981, in Conference Room 10, Building 31C, National Institutes of Health, 9000 Rockville Pike, Bethesda, Maryland 20205. Mr. Ray Thornton (Chairman), President, Arkansas State University, presided. In accordance with Public Law 92-463, the meeting was open to the public from 9:00 a.m. to 4:30 p.m. on April 23, and from 8:30 a.m. to adjournment at 1:25 p.m. on April 24. The meeting was closed to the public from 4:30 p.m. to 6:00 p.m. on April 23 for the review of proposals involving proprietary information.

Committee members present for all or part of the meeting were:

Dr. David Baltimore; Dr. Kenneth Berns; Dr. Winston Brill; Dr. Allan Campbell; Mrs. Zelma Cason; Dr. Nina Fedoroff; Dr. Richard Goldstein; Dr. Susan Gottesman; Dr. Jean Harris; Dr. King Holmes; Ms. Patricia King; Dr. Sheldon Krimsky; Dr. Myron Levine; Dr. Werner Maas; Dr. James Mason; Dr. Gerard McGarrity; Dr. Robert McKinney; Dr. Elena Nightingale; Dr. Richard Novick; Dr. Ramon Pinon; Dr. John Scandalios; Dr. Luther Williams; and Dr. William J. Gartland, Jr., Executive Secretary.

A Committee roster is attached. (Attachment I)

The following ad hoc consultants to the Committee were present:

Dr. Edward A. Adelberg, Yale University; Dr. D. Michael Gill, Tufts University.

The following non-voting members and liaison representatives were present:

Dr. Charlotte Bell, U.S. Department of Justice; Dr. Chia T. Chen, OSHA, U.S. Department of Labor; Dr. George Duda, U.S. Department of Energy; Dr. Timothy J. Henry, Food and Drug Administration; Dr. Herman Lewis, National Science Foundation; Mr. Seth Pauker, National Institute for Occupational Safety and Health;

---

[1]The RAC is advisory to the NIH, and its recommendations should not be considered as final and accepted. The Office of Recombinant DNA Activities should be consulted for NIH policy on specific issues.

Dr. Jane Shultz, Veterans Administration; Dr. Sue Tolin, U.S. Department of Agriculture; and Dr. William J. Walsh, III, U.S. Department of State.

Other National Institutes of Health staff present were:

Dr. Edward R. Applebaum, NICHD; Dr. Marilyn Bach, NIAID; Dr. Stanley Barban, NIAID; Mr. Manuel S. Barbeito, ORS; Dr. Pravin N. Bhatt, NIAID; Ms. Becky Connors, NIAID; Dr. Irving Delappe, NIAID; Dr. John Irwin, ORS; Ms. Kitty Kaplan, ORS; Dr. Richard Krause, NIAID; Dr. Elizabeth Milewski, NIAID; Dr. Stanley Nagle, NIAID; Dr. John Nutter, NIAID; Ms. Suzanne Pitts, ORS; Mr. Richard Riseberg, OGC; Dr. Bernard Talbot, OD; Dr. Michael H. Vodkin, NIAID; and Dr. Rudolf Wanner, ORS.

Others in attendance for all or part of the meeting were:

Ms. Claudia Baskin, Pharmaceutical Manufacture Association Newsletter; Ms. Tineke Bodde, BioScience Magazine; Ms. Irene Brandt, Eli Lilly & Co.; Dr. Daniel Bull, New Brunswick Science Co., Inc.; Dr. Jerry Callis, USDA; Dr. Aileen Compton, Smith-Kline & French; Mr. David Dickson, Nature; Dr. Peter Farley, Cetus Corporation; Dr. David Gelfand, Cetus Corporation; Dr. Patricia Guerry, Genex Corporation; Dr. Lowell Harmison, Office of Assistant Secretary for Health; Mr. Phil Hilts, Washington Post; Mr. David Holzman, Freelance Writer; Dr. Paul Hung, Abbott Research Laboratories; Dr. Evelyn Hurlburt, Johns Hopkins School of Medicine; Mr. Eric Juengst, National Endowment for the Humanities; Ms. Chris Joyce, New Scientist Magazine; Dr. Attila I. Kadar, Food and Drug Administration; Mr. Alan Kaplan, Attorney, Washington, D.C.; Mr. Geoffrey Karny, Office of Technology Assessment; Mr. B. Khosrovi, Cetus Corporation; Dr. Rihito Kimura, Georgetown University; Dr. Dennis G. Kleid, Genentech, Inc.; Dr. Michael Konrad, Cetus Corporation; Dr. Walter Laird, Food and Drug Administration; Ms. Carter Leonard, Blue Sheet; Dr. Morris A. Levine, Environmental Protection Agency; Ms. Pat Lewis, Genetic Tech News; Dr. D. S. Mabry, Pfizer, Inc.; Dr. John J. Mekalanos, Harvard Medical School; Dr. James McCullough, Library of Congress; Ms. Laura Mergher, NCSM; Dr. Henry Miller, Food and Drug Administration; Dr. Bernard J. Mlynczak, Monsanto Co.; Dr. John Murphy, Harvard Medical School; Dr. Seigo Nakajira, Hamanatsu University School of Medicine; Dr. Ann Norberg, Monsanto Co.; Dr. Stephen Pijar, Food and Drug Administration; Dr. William Pilacinski, Molecular Genetics, Inc.; Dr. John Richardson, Centers for Disease Control; Ms. Sandra Ronspies, Genentech, Inc.; Dr. Michael Ross, Genentech, Inc.; Dr. B. A. Rubin, Wyeth Laboratories; Mr. Harold Schmeck, New York Times; Mr. Vincent Simmons, Genex Corporation; Mr. Dan Smith, Peoples Business Commission; Dr. Gerald Still, U.S. Department of Agriculture; Ms. Nancy Tomich, U.S. Medicine; Mr. Jeff Treuhitt, McGraw-Hill, Inc.; Mr. Charles Turbyville, Genetic Engineering Letter; and Dr. Susan Wright, University of Michigan.

I. CALL TO ORDER AND OPENING REMARKS

Mr. Ray Thornton, Chairman, called the meeting to order at 9:00 a.m., on April 23, 1981. He introduced the two *ad hoc* consultants who would participate in the session, Dr. Edward Adelberg of Yale University and Dr. D. Michael Gill of Tufts University.

Mr. Thornton said that the terms of several RAC members would expire with the April 1981 RAC meeting. These members are: Drs. Susan Gottesman, Allan Campbell, Luther Williams, Richard Novick, David Parkinson, Sheldon Krimsky, and Ms. Zelma Cason. Mr. Thornton extended his personal appreciation and the appreciation of the committee to the retiring members.

Mr. Thornton said a risk assessment protocol had been submitted to the NIH by Dr. Malcolm Martin of the NIH. He asked the Risk Assessment Subcommittee to evaluate the proposal. Dr. Gartland said that if the subcommittee approved the protocol, it would then be forwarded to the NIH Biosafety Committee for evaluation.

II. MINUTES OF THE JANUARY 8-9, 1981 MEETING

Ms. Cason said she had reviewed the minutes (tab 1014) of the January 8-9, 1981, meeting and found them to be correct. She moved acceptance of the minutes. Dr. Harris said she also had reviewed the minutes and found them to be substantively accurate. She seconded Ms. Cason's motion. Mr. Thornton noted that several typographical errors had been called to ORDA's attention.

Dr. Berns said that a substantive phrase had been omitted from a statement attributed to him. (January 8-9, 1981 Meeting, Item III. Meeting of the Institutional Biosafety Committee Chairpersons, page 6). He asked that this phrase be added to his statement on the proposed CDC Biosafety Guidelines for Etiological Agents (additional language in italics):

> "Dr. Berns said he found the CDC's proposed biosafety guidelines for etiological agents, *with regard to some of the specific containment levels suggested*, to be capricious and unscientific, and the CDC unresponsive to expressed concerns."

Ms. Cason accepted, as an amendment, the proposed language. Mr. Thornton called for a voice vote, and the minutes of the January 8-9, 1981 meeting, as amended, were unanimously accepted.

III. REPORT FROM DIRECTOR, NIAID

Dr. Krause, the Director of National Institute of Allergy and Infectious Diseases (NIAID), said that the institute had recently been reorganized; as part of this reorganization, responsibility for risk assessment activities in recombinant DNA had been transferred from the Office of Specialized Research and Facilities to the Office of Recombinant DNA Activities.

Dr. Krause reported that as a follow-up to the recommendations of the NIAID Workshop on Recombinant DNA Risk Assessment held in Pasadena, California, a receipt date of July 1981 had been set for applications solicited to examine the fate of biologically active polypeptides in the human intestinal tract. In addition, NIAID had intensely advertised to identify a contractor to perform insulin autoimmunity studies. Only one proposal was received in response to the Request for Proposals (RFP); this proposal was rated unacceptable by the scientific review group.

Dr. Krause briefly commented on the U.S. - Japan meeting which was held in Hawaii in February 1981. He said the meeting was an outgrowth of a science and technology agreement between the U.S. and Japan. In the area of recombinant DNA that agreement entails sharing of information on Guidelines, risk assessment activities, etc. Four RAC members, Drs. Berns, Gottesman and Levine and Mr. Thornton, attended the Hawaii meeting. Dr. Krause said there will be a second meeting in November 1981 at the NIH dealing with the introduction of recombinant DNA into eukaryotic cells. He said the Japanese wish to host a subsequent meeting on yeast genetics. He acknowledged Mr. Justin Bloom of the U. S. State Department, currently Counselor for Scientific and Technological Affairs with the U. S. Embassy in Tokyo, as having been most helpful.

IV. PROPOSED REVISION OF GUIDELINES FOR RECOMBINANT DNA INVOLVING E. COLI K-12 AND S. CEREVISIAE HOST-VECTOR SYSTEMS

Mr. Thornton introduced Dr. Adelberg and asked him to initiate the discussion on this proposed revision of the Guidelines (tabs 998, 1015/I, 1017). Dr. Adelberg said he had originally proposed, at the November 1980 IBC Chairpersons' Meeting, that the paperwork associated with experiments covered by Section III-O be eliminated. He said he offered his proposal in light of the widely held view that experiments covered by Section III-O are "negligible in risk." In response to this request and the level of support it had received at the IBC Chairpersons' meeting and at the request of the RAC, ORDA had developed the language which appeared in the March 20, 1981 Federal Register (46 FR 17994). Dr. Adelberg said he would support any of the three published proposed options as all would reduce unnecessary paperwork. He said he personally favored option B as this option would eliminate paperwork but would require a P1 level of containment for Section III-O experiments.

Dr. Gottesman said that RAC, at the January 8-9, 1981 meeting, had indicated that diminishing the amount of paperwork associated with experiments covered by Section III-O was desirable. She said that currently, Section III-O covered experiments employing *E. coli* K-12 and laboratory strain *Saccharomyces cerevisiae* host-vector systems. She noted that RAC, at the April 1981 meeting, would review a request to include *B. subtilis* HV1 host-vector systems under Section III-O. Dr. Gottesman briefly reviewed the three options. She favored going as far as option A, did not favor option C, and was undecided about option B.

Dr. Krimsky said the primary goals are: (1) to reduce excessive paperwork, (2) to eliminate the collection of information of no practical use, and (3) to support good laboratory practice. Dr. Krimsky said he was not certain registration of Section III-O experiments with the IBCs was useful, but he suggested such a procedure might prove useful in investigating worker illness or to uncover inadvertent misclassifications of experiments. He supported option A.

Dr. Mason said he would support option C. He suggested that RAC has acquired enough experience to justify exempting those experiments covered by Section III-O; the exemption might be tailored to meet residual concerns through the selecting of suboptions. He moved acceptance of option C. Mr. Thornton called the vote. Ten RAC members supported the motion while ten voted against it.

Mr. Thornton cast his tie-breaking vote against the motion. Dr. Scandalios indicated at this point that he had not voted, but now wanted to support the motion, making the vote eleven in favor to ten opposed.

Dr. Gottesman said, in view of the close vote on option C, it might be helpful to Dr. Fredrickson to know the sense of the RAC in regard to changing the Guidelines at least as far as option B or option A, and suggested that the RAC cast strawvotes on these options. Mr. Thornton and Dr. Berns agreed.

Dr. Fedoroff requested further discussion of the issues. She felt registration of experiments was an important aspect of the Guidelines; option A differed significantly from options B and C in entailing a registration provision.

Citing parliamentary procedure, Dr. Baltimore said a motion should be perfected through amendments and selection of suboptions before any vote is called. Mr. Thornton agreed with Dr. Baltimore but indicated that in this case he had hoped to expedite discussion by gauging the sentiment of the RAC in straw votes; RAC would subsequently amend and perfect the language.

Ms. King said that if other RAC members wished to call attention to procedural problems, she felt obliged to indicate that the previous vote on Dr. Mason's motion contained two procedural irregularities: (1) the chair had not called for discussion before the vote, and (2) a vote (Dr. Scandalios') was noted after the RAC vote had been tallied.

Mr. Thornton made the following ruling: The chair ruled that the votes on Dr. Mason's motion were cast ten in favor, ten opposed. The chair broke the tie by casting his vote against the motion. The vote noted after the tally was not accepted. Consequently, the motion, as made, failed. Mr. Thornton said he would entertain appeals on this ruling of the chair. As no appeal was made, he said the RAC should now proceed following strict parliamentary procedure, rather than taking straw votes.

Dr. Novick moved adoption of option B with the proviso that a listing requirement be appended, but that no review be required. Dr. Fedoroff seconded the motion. Ms. King pointed out that supporters of option C could move a substitute motion at this point. She said she herself would not do so, as she would not support option C. Dr. Brill moved substitution of option C. The motion was seconded. Mr. Thornton said that the substitute motion would be considered before the original motion, but that it should be perfected before a vote to adopt would occur. In order to expedite discussion, Mr. Thornton asked Dr. Brill, as the maker of the substitute motion, to select the suboptions he would prefer under option C. Dr. Brill said he would prefer suboptions C-1-a, C-2-b, C-3-b, C-4-c, and C-5-b.

Dr. Gottesman suggested that suboption C-1-b be substituted for suboption C-1-a. She said suboption C-1-a is much broader than Section III-O of the current Guidelines; it would permit the use of all vectors including conjugation proficient plasmids and vectors. Dr. Brill accepted Dr. Gottesman's amendment.

Dr. Berns suggested that suboption C-2-a, in which large-scale experiments are not exempt, be substituted for suboption C-2-b, which would exempt large-scale experiments. Dr. Brill accepted the substitution.

Dr. Berns also suggested that suboption C-3-a be substituted for C-3-b, as he thought good microbiological procedures should be recommended. Dr. Brill accepted this substitution.

Dr. Berns further suggested an amendment to option C; cloning of CDC Class 3 agents in host-vector systems covered by Section III-O, would be exempt provided that not more than 75 percent of the genome is cloned. Dr. Baltimore asked if this provision would apply to bacteria as well as to viruses. Dr. Berns said he had made the proposal with viruses in mind. Dr. Fedoroff said the amendment did not clearly indicate whether less than 75 percent of the genome could be used to construct a library or if less than 75 percent of the genome was permissible in a single clone. Dr. Berns said he visualized his proposal as applying to a single clone or a single cell. There was no second to Dr. Berns' amendment.

Dr. Gottesman moved to substitute suboption C-4-b for suboption C-4-c. Dr. McKinney asked Dr. Adelberg how suboption C-4-b would impact on his institution. Dr. Adelberg replied that in his IBC experience, experiments involving CDC Class 3 agents constitute a very small fraction of all recombinant DNA work. Dr. McGarrity noted that suboption C-4-b requires review by either the IBC or an institutional official. He asked that the reviewing official be stipulated. Dr. Gottesman agreed and specified review by the IBC. By a vote of eleven in favor, four opposed, and five abstentions, RAC adopted suboption C-4-b.

Dr. Campbell offered an amendment to suboption C-4-b. The following sentence would be added:

"If there is any chance that the original Class 3 agent can be regenerated from the cloned DNA, the containment level shall be no lower than that appropriate for the agent itself."

Dr. Gottesman seconded the amendment. By a vote of twenty in favor, none opposed, and one abstention the amendment was adopted.

Suboption C-5-b, eliminating prior review requirements for experiments involving deliberate expression of eukaryotic genes, was discussed by the RAC. No proposal was advanced to substitute suboption C-5-a for suboption C-5-b.

Mr. Thornton said the next vote would occur on the perfected substitute motion, i.e., option C with suboptions C-1-b, C-2-a, C-3-a, C-4-b with the added Campbell sentence, and C-5-b. By a vote of thirteen in favor, eight opposed, and no abstentions the RAC substituted this perfected motion.

Mr. Thornton then called the vote on the motion. By a vote of thirteen in favor, eight opposed, and no abstentions, the RAC adopted the motion.

V. PROPOSED BIOSAFETY GUIDELINES FOR MICROBIOLOGICAL AND BIOMEDICAL LABORATORIES

Mr. Thornton introduced Dr. John Richardson of the Centers for Disease Control to brief the RAC on the status of the "Proposed Biosafety Guidelines for Microbiological and Biomedical Laboratories." Dr. Richardson said that a notice soliciting public comment had been issued in the Federal Register in October 1980. Since that announcement, approximately 300 written comments were received by the NIH and the CDC.

Most responses from industry and state health departments were supportive of the underlying philosophy, although some reservations were expressed concerning classifications of particular agents, or of recommended practices at a particular containment level. Responses from academic institutions and many clinical laboratories did not support either the philosophy of a voluntary national guideline or the classifications of many of the etiological agents or some of the work practices and facility recommendations. Many of the academic institutions and some of the clinical laboratories see the proposed guidelines as the first step in the development of federal regulations. Many academic institutions are concerned about possible premature implementations of the proposed guidelines by IBCs. Also, concern has been expressed that the time provided for public comment is insufficient.

In response to these concerns, Dr. Richardson said that public comments received after April 15 will also be considered. He said that there is no existing Public Health Service authority under which intrastate laboratory activities could be regulated, and that neither NIH or CDC is interested in assuming this task.

Dr. Richardson said that at least one revision, incorporating comments, and very likely two or more additional revised drafts will be prepared, and will be subjected to a reasonable review process. He felt that the guidelines were philosophically appropriate for the NIH and the CDC; the guidelines are only guidelines, they are voluntary and hopefully they will result in an upgrading of laboratory functions.

Dr. Richardson said the proposed guidelines were initiated with two purposes in mind:

(1) to modify the current Classification of Etiological Agents on the Basis of Hazard, and

(2) to use the guidelines as an "in-house" guidance document for CDC staff in the absence of any other document of similar nature. He pointed out that had comment on the guidelines not been solicited, the "in-house" CDC document would have become the national standard by default.

Dr. Brill said he supported the concept of guidelines for the handling of potentially dangerous organisms. He said, however, that the guidelines will become "regulations" as many institutions would require investigators to abide by them. Dr. Baltimore said that questions of legal liability ensure that the guidelines will be in a sense "regulations;" they would legally be regarded as standard practice. For this reason every recommendation in the guidelines should be carefully considered.

Dr. Levine noted that the guidelines specify containment levels for "activities involving the use or manipulation of large quantities or high concentrations of cultures or other materials known or suspected of containing the agent." He asked if "large quantities" or "high concentrations" had been defined, and if not, who would determine this. Dr. Richardson replied that the guidelines in this respect are meant to be interpretive and judgemental. CDC would never propose to set any stated quantity as representing a "large quantity" for all microorganisms. Much concern has been expressed over this aspect of the guidelines however, and attempts may be made in the revision to be more descriptive of criteria to be used in determining what constitutes a "large quantity" or "high concentration" of an agent.

VI. PROPOSAL TO CONVERT NIH GUIDELINES INTO A CODE OF STANDARD PRACTICE AND TO REDUCE RECOMMENDED CONTAINMENT LEVELS FOR SOME EXPERIMENTS

Mr. Thornton said he would recognize Dr. Nightingale who had requested an opportunity to present her views on the proposal (tabs 994, 1015/II, 1017) offered by Drs. Baltimore and Campbell.

Dr. Nightingale said it had been apparent for some time that the committee perceived a need for a reassessment of the purpose of the Guidelines. The proposal from Drs. Baltimore and Campbell is a serious attempt to meet that need, and since the proposal had been published in the Federal Register, action might be taken on it today. She said she herself doubted the wisdom of this approach. She suggested rather that a subcommittee of RAC, selected with a balance of expertise and perspective, should study the issues and present to the RAC at a future meeting an array of policy options on the existence, nature, and content of the Guidelines. Such a procedure is more likely to lead to decisions that are balanced, well-thought through and have maximum potential to be perceived as such by those not engaged in the research in question.

Dr. Campbell said he thought his proposal was an appropriate action at this time. Removing the regulatory aspects of the Guidelines is coupled to reducing the required containment levels. He stated that he would not support eliminating the regulatory aspects of the Guidelines if he believed there was some hazard worth regulating.

Dr. Campbell then discussed various aspects of the proposal. He said the proposal did not specify any containment level on the basis of the cloned segment's origin; that omission is deliberate. He and Dr. Baltimore felt that, except for the few cases covered under the prohibitions, a small segment of DNA inserted into a nonpathogenic host-vector system would not create a pathogen. Appropriate levels of containment for a pathogenic host-vector system would, on the other hand, be specified by the CDC Guidelines.

Dr. Campbell then called the committee's attention to a sentence in Part III of the proposal:

> "As a general practice, investigators should use the highest level of biological containment (HV3 > HV2 > HV1) which is available and appropriate for the purposes of the experiment."

He said he viewed the sentence as an admonition for simple prudence; where more biologically contained systems are available, and their use doesn't interfere in any way with performing the experiment, their use should be encouraged. On the other hand some feel this sentence is too strong; they say where there is no perceived hazard it is silly to be telling people to use higher containment levels.

Dr. Campbell said the proposal would eliminate most of Part IV which specifies procedures, but retain Section IV-E which defines RAC composition and procedures. Part VI of the Guidelines dealing with voluntary compliance would be eliminated, as all of the Guidelines would be voluntary, except for the sections dealing with protection of proprietary information voluntarily submitted. The prohibitions specified in the current Guidelines would still apply. He said he and Dr. Baltimore felt each prohibition should be discussed on an individual basis.

Dr. Baltimore added that he saw the maintenance of the RAC as very important. The most important RAC function would be to maintain surveillance over recombinant DNA. RAC would also continue to deal with issues surrounding the prohibitions. He hoped RAC could deal with general issues of biohazards and would aid CDC in formulating the CDC guidelines. Dr. Baltimore said the proposal would not greatly affect industry as industry has voluntarily accepted adherence to the Guidelines. Lastly, Dr. Baltimore quoted from a letter from Dr. Zinder (tab 1017). "It would be an important precedent for the NIH to dismantle the unneeded regulatory structure. If scientists are ever again to attempt to cope with potential hazard, they must see that what they believed were temporary measures can be undone."

Dr. Harris said that examination of the RAC's actions in the last two years indicates a general movement in the direction the authors propose. Although she agreed in principle with the rationale supporting the proposal, she said she felt waiving NIH and RAC responsibilities in this area is a giant leap deserving very careful evaluation and consideration. She agreed that little evidence to date supports the general public concern about potential hazards of recombinant DNA, but pointed out that public concern and distrust of bioprocessing technologies continues, particularly with those technologies which lend themselves to human genetic applications. The RAC and the NIH Guidelines both have served to inspire public trust and confidence. She said it is her strong conviction that the Guidelines have precluded precipitous regulation by local governing groups, by other federal agencies, and by Congress; regulations which, if enacted, would have stifled innovation. Premature abrogation of the Guidelines might skew future regulation and public policy.

Dr. Harris said she personally is more comfortable with the recommendation to reduce containment levels than with the proposal to convert the Guidelines to a code of standard practice. She proposed a two-stage process in which RAC would consider the recommended reduction in containment levels, while postponing consideration of converting the Guidelines into a nonregulatory code. Dr. Fedoroff and Ms. King endorsed Dr. Harris' statement.

Ms. King noted Dr. Zinder's plea that scientists "must see that what they believed were temporary measures can be undone," but also added that the public must see that if the RAC undoes the Guidelines, it does so in a responsible manner. She agreed that the Guidelines should be reassessed and reevaluated. She suggested that RAC or a RAC subcommittee should undertake such a reevaluation. She urged that public input should be solicited, and observed that a Federal Register announcement is not adequate. She felt debate with input from other sectors is important in formulating a recommendation concerning the Guidelines.

Dr. Nightingale said the process by which the status of the Guidelines would be altered will greatly influence public acceptance of that alteration. Dr. Harris said that process is of primary importance because if the public perceives the action as inappropriate, a backlash could result. She said the process will entail education of concerned citizens. Dr. Brill and Ms. King expressed the belief that there is very little public distrust of the scientific community in the area of recombinant DNA. The public is awaiting the benefits of the technology. Dr. Nightingale said the impression one receives depends on whom one talks to: she pointed to recent congressional hearings on the misbehaviour of certain scientists as evidence of a growing distrust of the scientist.

Dr. Campbell said the RAC must decide whether its function is to deal with danger or to deal with fear. He believed RAC's function is to deal with danger. He said that in his judgement, by maintaining the Guidelines as presently constituted, RAC was delivering to the public the message that a group of responsible, serious, informed people perceive a danger which should be regulated.

Ms. King said that the question of reducing containment should not be uncoupled from the issue of converting the Guidelines to a voluntary code of standard practice. She said the path which RAC has been following, one of piecemeal erosion, would eventually result in an empty facade. At some point along that path, however, deliberate discussion and consideration of the process should be undertaken. In such a discussion, the issue of reducing containment is intimately linked to the conversion of the Guidelines to a voluntary code. Dr. McKinney supported a deliberate reassessment of the Guidelines.

Dr. Gottesman said she saw the Baltimore-Campbell proposal as having three parts: (1) Elimination of the penalties from the Guidelines, which need not be coupled with other changes, would move academia into the industrial mode. (2) Other procedural changes recommended, i.e., eliminating IBCs, eliminating registration, etc. (3) Lowering of containment conditions. She said she personally would prefer to simplify some of the procedures without necessarily lowering all containment requirements to P1.

Dr. Novick summarized his opinions as follows: (1) He strongly supported the notion of prudence in biological research. (2) He felt the notion of guidelines in this area is entirely correct and appropriate. (3) At this stage in their evolution, a review and reassessment of the Guidelines was appropriate. (4) He very much wanted to see a uniform standard applied to both industry and academia.

Dr. Baltimore reiterated his views on coupling of lowering of containment to conversion of the Guidelines to a code of standard practice. If the RAC agrees on lowering of containment to P1, then the complicated regulatory edifice is unnecessary.

Dr. Holmes said that groups either exert internal control or they invite societal regulation from the greater community. He suggested that RAC learn the sentiment of the scientific community; if a substantial minority of scientists opposes deregulation and deregulation occurs, the scientific community invites societal control from without.

Dr. Susan Wright was recognized by Mr. Thornton. Dr. Wright offered the following observations. She said she has no particular ax to grind about recombinant DNA techniques, but she does have a historical perspective to which she is committed. She said there have been two serious violations of the Guidelines in the past year, and she thinks it is a reflection of the lack of concern of this committee that those items are not on the agenda before proposals to relax the Guidelines. She felt that dismantling the mechanisms that have been set up to enforce the Guidelines will signal the very small minority of scientists who pursue their research goals irresponsibly that high standards in research are no longer a concern. In addition, she felt that many scientists, perhaps the majority, would maintain that deliberate construction of hazardous organisms by recombinant DNA techniques is possible and is of concern. In view of these considerations, she felt the present system of controls, specifically the IBCs and their links to NIH, is important for the following reasons: (1). The IBCs constitute an important screening device for detecting hazards, and ensuring that experiments which entail hazards are performed under suitable conditions. (2) The IBCs serve as an important reminder to researchers that their peers and community members take the safety of their work seriously. (3) The IBCs can serve as bodies to which employees can turn if they believe that research is being improperly conducted. This last point is very important to workers who are not represented by trade unions.

Dr. Wright contended that the cost in money and time of registration of these experiments is insignificant compared to all the other paperwork that U.S. researchers are asked to undertake. The benefits in the maintenance of high standards and the avoidance of harmful experiments are very substantial and should be taken seriously in any society that is committed to the protection of the interests of all its members, not only the interests of those having the greatest access to the decision-making arenas. The history of regulation of other fields, for example, drugs, auto safety, health and safety in the workplace, shows that, in general, controls were not introduced until the social costs of accidents had become very high, really intolerable. Each potentially avoidable injury or death represents a cost in human suffering which cannot be absorbed into any cost-benefit equation. One of the original motives for the controls for recombinant DNA technology was to avoid repeating that pattern in this new field. She hoped the RAC members would maintain that commitment as they proceed to make a decision on this proposal.

Dr. Baltimore said that P1 is a much higher standard of laboratory conduct than has historically been common practice. Most RAC members appear to accept the notion that there is minimal perceptible hazard associated with recombinant DNA. The RAC should attempt to construct Guidelines reflecting that view.

Dr. Krimsky said that our society is facing an explosion of biological technology which will result in the exposure of more individuals to more types of organisms in more facilities. He felt there has been a paucity of controlled experiments to test the hypothesis that there is no risk beyond that associated with other types of biological research. That conclusion has been drawn on the available information, but not from a systematic set of experiments.

Dr. Mason said that accountability and responsibility, in the ethical, moral, and legal sense, rest ultimately with the institution and the principal investigator. Regulatory guidelines will not stop the person who is dishonest or malicious or careless. He agreed with the observation that a "piecemeal" erosion of the Guidelines was occurring. He suggested that piecemeal erosion if it continues too long without reexamination of the basic premises, can result in a loss of respect for the institution promulgating an eventually empty statement. He endorsed the Baltimore-Campbell proposal and moved that a RAC subcommittee be established with the specific mandate of evaluating that proposal and reporting back to the RAC on the implementation process. Dr. Berns seconded the motion.

Dr. Gottesman preferred that the RAC subcommittee not be tied to the Baltimore-Campbell proposal _per se_ but that it consider many options in a reevaluation of the need for changes in procedures, penalties, and containment levels of the Guidelines. Dr. Novick agreed with Dr. Gottesman. He moved that a subcommittee be instituted to review the Guidelines with respect to both general containment levels and the proposal to convert the Guidelines to a voluntary code. Dr. Gottesman seconded the motion.

Dr. Williams suggested Dr. Novick's motion be amended to direct the subcommittee to examine the Baltimore-Campbell proposal during its deliberations.

Dr. Harris, with Dr. Nightingale, offered the following substitute motion:

> "That RAC recommend to the Director, NIH, that a study group comprised of RAC members, and any others he so directs or appoints, be constituted to review the current regulations. Such review to include but not be limited to: (a) the present need for the Guidelines in their existing form and procedures, as opposed to a voluntary standard of practice, (b) the continued applicability of the present Guidelines to recombinant DNA technology, (c) the currently recommended levels of containment, (d) current processes and procedures impeding or facilitating research and/or industrial application, and (e) mechanisms for soliciting public input. Such study group to report to the RAC and the Director, NIH, its finding, conclusions and recommendations for RAC review and recommendation."

Dr. Nightingale said that the mechanisms for soliciting public comment were to include processes beyond publication in the _Federal Register_.

Dr. Goldstein asked if Dr. Harris' proposal would relieve RAC of responsibility for the reevaluation of the Guidelines. Dr. Harris replied that the initiative would remain with the RAC, but that the NIH Director might wish to expand the review group to include non-RAC members. The working group would report to RAC, which would then offer recommendations to the Director. Dr. Goldstein suggested the language be amended to indicate clearly that the working group is a RAC subcommittee. Dr. Harris agreed and substituted the following sentence:

"The Chairman of the RAC appoint a study group comprised of RAC members and others deemed appropriate."

Dr. Campbell asked whether the working group would actually solicit public comment or whether it would offer suggestions to RAC on mechanisms for soliciting comment. Dr. Harris envisaged the working group offering suggestions on mechanisms. Dr. Campbell said he would prefer the working group begin soliciting comment and suggested the motion be rephrased to state this. Dr. Harris agreed. Dr. Williams asked if comment would be solicited before recommendations are formulated. He felt it was more practical to seek input after a recommendation has been formulated.

Dr. Harris replied that she originally envisaged the working group formulating recommendations, and RAC subsequently soliciting comment. She was not, however, adverse to Dr. Campbell's proposition. Dr. McKinney suggested that RAC should not hamstring the working group with specific guidance as to how to obtain public input.

Mr. Pauker suggested that evidence supporting the premise that there is no risk in recombinant DNA manipulations beyond those due to the constituent parts, should be assembled and critically evaluated. It should also be publicly available. Dr. Goldstein supported this position and asked if Dr. Harris would add this to her motion. Dr. Harris replied that her proposal already implicitly included this change.

Dr. Williams asked if Dr. Harris would accept an amendment deleting the reference to soliciting public input. She replied she would not. Dr. Gottesman offered an amendment which would delete item (e) from its current place in Dr. Harris' proposal and instead add at the end of the proposal the sentence: "RAC will solicit public comment on this proposal."

Dr. Norberg of Monsanto Corporation pointed out that the NIH Guidelines were not regulations and questioned whether language identifying them as regulations should be included in Dr. Harris' proposal. Dr. Harris replied that she meant the Guidelines as currently constituted versus a standard code of practice, and amended the language to eliminate any reference to "regulations."

Dr. Campbell requested a clarification of the amended language proposed by Dr. Gottesman. He suggested that the last sentence should read: "Public comment will be solicited on the proposal." Drs. Gottesman and Harris agreed.

Mr. Thornton called the vote on Dr. Harris' amended substitute motion. Dr. Harris reread the motion as follows:

"The Chairman of the RAC appoint a study group composed of RAC members and any others deemed appropriate to review existing recombinant DNA Guidelines. Such review to include but not be limited to: (a) the present need for the Guidelines in their existing form and procedures, as opposed to a voluntary standard of practice; (b) continued applicability to recombinant DNA technology; (c) currently recommended levels of containment; (d) current processes and procedures impeding or facilitating research and/or industrial application. Such study group to report back to the RAC its findings, conclusions, and recommendations for RAC review and consideration. Solicitation of public input and comment beyond publication in the Federal Register will be obtained."

By a vote of fifteen in favor, four opposed, and two abstentions, the committee accepted this substitute motion. Mr. Thornton then called the vote on the motion. By a vote of nineteen in favor, two opposed, the RAC adopted the motion.

VII. PROPOSED CONTAINMENT CONDITIONS FOR FLIES

Dr. McGarrity introduced the proposal (tab 1004) from Dr. Thomas Maniatis of Harvard University to transform *Drosophila* with the *Drosophila* alcohol dehydrogenase gene. The cloned DNA (in lambda, plasmid or cosmid vectors) will be injected into either the abdomen of adult female alcohol dehydrogenase deficient flies, or into early stage alcohol dehydrogenase deficient embryos. The Guidelines allow such work to proceed at P1 containment. The Harvard IBC believes the safety measures proposed meet the requirements of P1, but asked for RAC concurrence. The containment conditions include: (1) Bottles containing flies will be disposed of by autoclaving. (2) Flies will be propagated in bottles or vials. (3) Only experienced personnel will handle the *Drosophila*. (4) All manipulations of adult flies will be performed in a cold room. The cold environment will act as an anesthetic for the flies. (5) All propagation of transformed flies will be carried out in an approved P1 laboratory.

Dr. McGarrity said the precautions to be employed appear to be adequate and recommended approval. Dr. McKinney said that installation of an air curtain on the entry to the cold room would provide an additional barrier against escape. Dr. Gottesman felt the precautions specified in the proposal were adequate and moved acceptance of the proposal. Dr. Fedoroff seconded. By a vote of nineteen in favor, none opposed, and no abstentions, the RAC recommended adoption of the proposal.

VIII. CONTAINMENT LEVELS FOR RECOMBINANT DNA EXPERIMENTS INVOLVING BACILLUS SUBTILIS

Dr. Williams initiated review of the request (tabs 1005, 1007, 1011, 1015/VI, 1016) submitted by Dr. Donald Dean of Ohio State University. Dr. Dean requested consideration of the current classification of *Bacillus subtilis* host-vector systems. Dr. Dean's request consisted of three parts:

(1) that any asporogenous *Bacillus subtilis* strain which does not revert to a sporeformer with a frequency greater than 10^{-7} can

be used for cloning DNA from any nonprohibited sources, using vectors indigenous to B. subtilis, under the same conditions specified by RAC for E. coli K-12 and S. cerevisiae host-vector systems.

(2) Bacillus subtilis strains that do not carry an asporogenous mutation can be used with vectors indigenous to B. subtilis for the cloning of DNA from any CDC Class 1 organism under P2 conditions.

(3) Bacillus subtilis strains that do not carry an asporogenic mutation can be used with vectors indigenous to B. subtilis under P1 conditions for the cloning of DNA from any Class 1 Bacillus species.

Dr. Williams said that Bacillus subtilis is probably the most extensively understood gram-positive organism, both genetically and biochemically. It is capable of both generalized and specialized transduction and has been widely used in the industrial sector in the production of an array of antibiotics. It may be particularly well suited for certain types of recombinant DNA experiments, as Bacillus strains have the capacity to secrete a variety of proteins. Bacillus subtilis is nonpathogenic and is not known to exchange genetic information with pathogens.

Dr. Williams directed the committee's attention to data comparing the survivability of B. subtilis and E. coli K-12 in soil or water samples; E. coli survives better than B. subtilis over a five day period. Additional data demonstrate that B. subtilis spores placed in a mammalian intestine rarely sporulate, and if they do the vegetative cells quickly die.

Dr. Williams recommended approval of the request. Dr. Holmes seconded the motion.

Dr. Gottesman, noting that currently certified HV1 B. subtilis host-vector systems only employ certain specified plasmids, pointed out that Dr. Dean's proposal would also permit use of phage vectors. She requested additional information concerning the proposed phage vectors. Dr. Dean replied that the host ranges of the Bacillus phages are very narrow. In his experience, transformation affords greater possibilities and avenues of genetic exchange.

Dr. Goldstein asked if B. subtilis engineered to excrete recombinant proteins is a concern. Dr. Novick replied that B. subtilis does not colonize the mammalian gastrointestinal tract. He personally did not regard the excretion of cloned proteins into soil as potentially hazardous.

Dr. Talbot requested clarification of Dr. Williams' motion. He asked if the intent was that the asporogenic B. subtilis strains would be exempted from the Guidelines as had been recommended by the RAC for E. coli K-12 and S. cerevisiae earlier in the meeting. Dr. Williams replied that he intended they would. Noting that the language of the proposal would permit the use of any "indigenous vector," Dr. Talbot questioned whether the motion is limited to those vectors listed by Dr. Dean. Dr. Williams replied that it would not be limited. Dr. Talbot said that current certification specifications for B. subtilis HV1 systems require that data demonstrating a reversion frequency to sporogeny of less than 10^{-7}, be evaluated by NIH; he questioned whether this specification was implied under Dr. Williams' motion. Dr. Williams said it was not.

Dr. Gottesman asked if in permitting use of all indigenous vectors, RAC might inadvertently authorize the use of an extremely broad host range vector which might infect Bacillus pathogens.

Dr. Dean said that his proposal could be modified to eliminate the use of phage vectors that infect CDC Class 2 Bacilli such as Bacillus anthracis. It was pointed out that Bacillus cereus also is a pathogen. Dr. Levine said that Bacillus cereus enterotoxin causes disease, particularly in Southeast Asia, where it is a major cause of enteric problems. The organism produces and excretes a potent enterotoxin which contaminates foodstuffs.

Dr. Gottesman suggested the phrase "indigenous plasmid and phage vectors, whose host-range does not include Bacillus cereus and Bacillus anthracis" be substituted for the words "vectors indigenous to B. subtilis." Dr. Williams accepted this modification of the motion.

Mr. Thornton called for the vote on the amended motion. By a vote of twelve in favor, none opposed, and five abstentions, the RAC recommended the motion.

IX. CERTIFICATE OF APPRECIATION TO MRS. BETTY BUTLER

Mr. Thornton announced that Mrs. Betty Butler, who has worked for ORDA for many years, had recently accepted another position at NIH. Mr. Thornton, calling the attention of the committee to Mrs. Butler's many years of service to the RAC, which have contributed so much to its efficient functioning, presented to her a plaque in appreciation of her services, signed by NIH Director Donald S. Fredrickson.

X. EXPRESSION OF FOOT AND MOUTH DISEASE VIRUS PROTEINS IN SACCHAROMYCES CEREVISIAE, BACILLUS SUBTILIS, AND MAMMALIAN TISSUE CULTURE

Dr. Berns said he preferred to divide the Genentech, Inc., proposal (tabs 999, 1015/VII) into four parts, each to be discussed separately.

Dr. Berns first discussed the question of removing additional clones of the Foot and Mouth Disease Virus (FMDV) genome from the Plum Island Animal Disease Center. Previous NIH approval of the project permitting clones contained in E. coli K-12 to be removed from Plum Island, stipulated that the plasmids removed from Plum Island should not separately or collectively represent more than 75% of the FMDV genome. Unfortunately, the plasmids transferred from Plum Island to the Genentech, Inc., facilities in California apparently did not contain the VP3 coding region, the VP3 protein being the predominant antigenic moiety for the virus.

The VP3 region of several FMDV serological types were subsequently cloned on Plum Island. Genentech, Inc., now requests permission to remove these additional clones to their facilities in South San Francisco. If these clones are removed, however, more than 75% of the FMDV genome will have been shipped from Plum Island. Discussion between the RAC working group on FMDV, USDA, and Genentech, Inc., led to the proposal that plasmids representing sequences to the right of base pair 6000 be returned to Plum Island, after which it would be permissible to ship from Plum Island to Genentech the plasmids of interest.

It was pointed out that the RAC recommendation at the last meeting, accepted by the NIH Director, allows the working group to approve the removal of these clones from Plum Island without obtaining full RAC concurrence. Nevertheless, Dr. Berns moved that Genentech, Inc., be granted permission to return those clones representing the extreme right portion of the genome to Plum Island, and in exchange be permitted to remove the requested clones containing the center of the FMDV genome. Dr. McGarrity seconded the motion.

The motion was adopted by a vote of sixteen in favor, none opposed, and two abstentions.

Dr. Berns proceeded to that portion of the request dealing with use of host-vector systems other than E. coli K-12. Dr. Berns said Genentech, Inc., had requested permission to clone the FMDV genome in B. subtilis host-vector systems. A discussion between the RAC working group on FMDV and representatives of Genentech, Inc., led to agreement that this would be limited to those portions of the FMDV genome lying between base pairs 500 and 4,100. He suggested that P1 conditions are adequate and so moved. Dr. McGarrity seconded the motion. By a vote of sixteen in favor, none opposed, and two abstentions, the motion was adopted.

Dr. Berns said the same type of experiment was proposed utilizing Saccharomyces cerevisiae host-vector systems. He again suggested that the experiments be permitted under P1 physical containment conditions if the subgenomic FMDV segments were restricted to those sequences which map between 500 and 4,100 of the FMDV genome. Dr. McGarrity seconded the motion. By a vote of sixteen in favor, none opposed, and two abstentions, the RAC adopted the proposal.

Dr. Berns then turned the discussion to the proposal to clone portions of the FMDV genome, using the SV40 genome as a vector, in mammalian cell culture. Dr. Berns noted that tissue culture systems are suitable "hosts" for large numbers of different types of picornaviruses. He questioned whether an adventitious recombination between a contaminating picornavirus and the hybrid SV40 - FMDV molecule might occur. Dr. Baltimore said evidence demonstrating recombination among homologous picornaviruses is marginal. He did not know of experiments in the literature looking for recombination among heterologous picornaviruses. He added that he knew of no human virus similar by nucleic acid homology to FMDV, but some rhinoviruses appear to be similar structurally to FMDV.

Dr. Goldstein asked that FMDV disease be described. Dr. Callis of the Plum Island Animal Disease Center said that the virus does not normally cause a high mortality in adult animals. FMDV causes death among young animals, but in adults causes weight loss and, as it infects secretory cells in the mammary glands, disrupts milk production. The disease spreads very, very rapidly and can infect every barnyard animal except the horse.

Dr. Callis said that FMDV can chronically infect tissue culture systems and that many types of cells in culture, including primate cells, may be infected with FMDV.

Dr. Berns said Genentech, Inc., had requested permission to perform this type of experiment at their facilities in South San Francisco. Noting that the laboratories at Plum Island were already working with whole FMDV, he moved to permit these experiments at Plum Island under P3 containment conditions. The FMDV genome between base pairs 500 and 4,100 may be cloned subject to the RAC Working Group evaluating individual experiments prior to their initiation.

Dr. Ross asked if RAC could indicate what sort of data it would require before it would allow transfer of the material from Plum Island to California for the production phase, should the tissue culture system be successful. Dr. Gottesman said that if the motion were adopted, and the work on Plum Island were successful, RAC would want to review these results before approving transfer of material to California.

Mr. Thornton called the vote on Dr. Berns' motion. By a vote of seventeen in favor, none opposed, and one abstention, RAC adopted the motion as follows:

> "Permission is granted in principle to propagate in mammalian cell culture recombinant DNA molecules consisting of segments of Foot and Mouth Disease Virus and SV40 deletion vectors under P3 conditions at the Plum Island Animal Disease Center. Approval of individual experiments is subject to review by a RAC Working Group."

XI. CLOSED SESSION

The RAC went into closed session to consider proposals from commercial concerns for scale-up of recombinant DNA experiments.

XII. CONTAINMENT LEVELS FOR RECOMBINANT DNA EXPERIMENTS INVOLVING NEUROSPORA CRASSA

Dr. Brill introduced the request (tabs 995, 1015/III) from Dr. David Perkins of Stanford University. Dr. Perkins proposed that the following language be substituted for entry 2 of Appendix E:

"Unmodified laboratory strains of Neurospora crassa can be used in all experiments for which HV1 N. crassa systems are approved, provided that only DNA from Class 1 agents is used. For agents other than Class 1, unmodified laboratory strains of N. crassa can be used in all experiments for which HV1 N. crassa systems are approved, providing that these are carried out at physical containment one level higher than required for HV1. However, if P3 containment is specified for HV1 N. crassa, this level is considered adequate for unmodified N. crassa. Care must be exercised to prevent aerial dispersion of macroconidia in accordance with good laboratory practice.

"Mutationally modified strains of N. crassa specified as HV1 in Appendix D can be used in all experiments for which HV2 N. crassa systems are approved, provided that only DNA from Class 1 agents is used."

Dr. Brill said that N. crassa is not known to be a pathogen. It is not closely associated with man or other organisms in nature. It produces no known toxins. He moved acceptance of the request. By a vote of ten in favor, none opposed, and five abstentions, the RAC adopted the motion.

XIII. REQUEST TO EMPLOY A CONJUGATIVE PLASMID TO TRANSFER NEUROSPORA CRASSA DNA

Dr. Gottesman introduced the request (tabs 1006, 1015/XIII) of Dr. Norman Giles of the University of Georgia. Dr. Giles requested permission to use a conjugative plasmid to transfer the Neurospora crassa qa-2 gene among E. coli K-12 strains. The qa-2 gene would be ligated into a derivative of the mobilizable plasmid RSF2124. The work would be performed under P2 containment conditions.

Dr. Gottesman said that although this request involved the use of a conjugative plasmid, she would support the proposal as the N. crassa qa-2 gene is a relatively well-defined DNA fragment.

Dr. Gottesman moved approval of the proposal. By a vote of seventeen in favor, none opposed, and no abstentions, RAC adopted the motion.

XIV. REQUEST TO USE AN E. COLI STRAIN CONTAINING A Mu PHAGE INSERTION

Dr. Goldstein introduced the request (tabs 1009, 1015/XII) of Dr. Darold Holten of the University of California at Riverside. Dr. Holten requested permission to utilize the E. coli K-10 strain DF214 (or derivatives thereof), and EK plasmid vectors (e.g., pBR322, pBR325) to clone rat cDNA. Strain

DF214, a K-12 derivative, contains Mu phage insertions in the phosphoglucose isomerase gene and in an unidentified location. Dr. Goldstein said the probability of the Mu lysogen transducing out the rat DNA is very low and suggested the experiment be permitted. Dr. Gottesman agreed and suggested that the initial shotgun experiments screening the rat cDNA library be conducted at P2 physical containment. After the clone of interest has been selected, work may proceed at the P1 level of containment. Dr. Goldstein moved acceptance of the proposal with Dr. Gottesman's stipulation. Dr. Novick seconded the motion.

By a vote of seventeen in favor, none opposed, and no abstentions, the RAC adopted the motion.

XV. REQUEST FOR APPROVAL OF GUIDELINE CHANGES INVOLVING STREPTOMYCES

Dr. Levine introduced the proposal (tabs 1012, 1015/IV) submitted by Dr. Stanley Cohen of Stanford University. Dr. Cohen requested that *Streptomyces coelicolor* and the related organisms with which *S. coelicolor* naturally exchanges genetic information (*S. lividans*, *S. parvulus*, and *S. griseus*) be approved as HV1 hosts. *Streptomyces* plasmids SCP2, SLP1.2, pIJ101, actinophage phi C31, and their derivatives would be used as vectors.

Dr. Levine said the *Streptomyces* are nonpathogenic; no known hazard has been associated with large-scale industrial use of the organisms. Dr. Levine moved approval of the proposal. Dr. Fedoroff seconded.

Dr. Gottesman said the proposal was vague; the strains proposed for certification are not as well defined as some of the HV1 systems approved in the past. Little data concerning known exchange mechanisms with other organisms have been included in the proposal. Furthermore, the actinophages, which are requested to be allowed as vectors, apparently have broad host ranges.

As no further comment was made, Mr. Thornton called the vote. By a vote of ten in favor, none opposed, and eight abstentions, the RAC adopted the motion.

Dr. Gottesman introduced the second proposal (tabs 1012, 1015/V) from Dr. Cohen. Dr. Cohen requested that the following entry be added to Appendix E:

> "Experiments involving the cloning of DNA among members of the genus *Streptomyces* are permitted under P1 conditions. For these experiments, no registration document, as described in Part III, is required."

Dr. Gottesman noted that entry 27 of Appendix E of the Guidelines currently permits cloning of DNA among members of the genus into nonpathogenic *Streptomyces* under P1 containment conditions. She said the request would extend this by eliminating the requirement for a registration document. She felt that this action would be premature; the working group evaluating the status of the Guidelines will be considering the need for registration documents in general. She moved to reject the request. Dr. Fedoroff seconded the motion. By a vote of fifteen in favor, none opposed, and three abstentions, RAC rejected Dr. Cohen's request.

XVI. PROPOSED LARGE SCALE EXPERIMENTS

Dr. Pinon initiated the review of a proposal (tab 1001) from Dr. Barry Nall of the University of Texas. Dr. Nall requested permission to perform large-scale fermentations of *Saccharomyces cerevisiae* strains containing recombinant DNA plasmids. The recombinant plasmid vectors consist of DNA from the *E. coli* plasmid pBR322, the yeast 2 micron circle, and yeast chromosomal DNA. The *Saccharomyces cerevisiae* cytochrome c gene will be ligated into these plasmid vectors. Dr. Pinon said the experiment is essentially self-cloning, and the sequences to be cloned are well characterized. He noted that a registration document had not been submitted and suggested approval at P1-LS containment be contingent upon submission of this document. He so moved. Dr. Williams seconded the motion. Dr. Gottesman felt P1-LS containment was not necessary and offered an amendment to substitute the words "good microbiological practice" for P1-LS. Dr. McKinney disagreed, he felt P1-LS actually represented "good microbiological practice." Mr. Thornton called the vote on Dr. Gottesman's proposed amendment. By a vote of four in favor, thirteen opposed, and three abstentions, the RAC refused the proposed amendment. Mr. Thornton then called the vote on Dr. Pinon's motion to approve the request at the P1-LS level of containment.

By a vote of nineteen in favor, none opposed, and no abstentions, the RAC adopted the motion.

Mr. Thornton then called on Dr. Campbell to begin review of the proposal (tab 1018) from Dr. Hamilton O. Smith of the Johns Hopkins University. Dr. Smith requested permission to grow large quantities of the *Hha* II restriction and modification genes from *Haemophilus haemolyticus*, in *E. coli*. Dr. Campbell said the DNA to be cloned in a pBR322 vector is a reasonably small, well-defined segment. He moved to approve cloning of the plasmid in *E. coli* at the P1-LS level of containment. By a vote of nineteen in favor, none opposed, and no abstentions, the RAC adopted the motion.

XVII. REQUEST FOR APPROVAL OF CERTAIN EXPERIMENTS INVOLVING ANABAENA AND NOSTOC

Dr. Fedoroff introduced the proposal (tab 1013) of Dr. C. Peter Wolk of Michigan State University. Dr. Wolk requested permission to (a) construct a recombinant molecule from an *E. coli* plasmid and DNA from a strain of *Anabaena*, (b) propagate that DNA in an *E. coli* K-12 strain, and (c) transfer the cloned DNA to a different *Anabaena* strain. DNA may also be derived from and/or transferred to strains of the closely related genus, *Nostoc*.

Dr. Fedoroff said the transfer of this recombinant DNA into Anabaena or Nostoc is currently permitted, under P3 containment conditions, by Section III-O-2 of the Guidelines. Dr. Wolk requested a lowering of containment to P1. Dr. Fedoroff said the request was internally inconsistent in that Dr. Wolk states that no cyanobacteria are known or suspected pathogens; however, the supporting documentation indicates that these organisms do produce toxins. She moved that RAC approve the request contingent upon ORDA receiving documentation that the strains Dr. Wolk uses will not be toxin producers.

Drs. Berns, McGarrity and McKinney felt it inappropriate to approve an incomplete, inconsistent proposal. Dr. Fedoroff withdrew her original motion, and then moved disapproval of the proposal with the request that the principal investigator submit a clearer and internally consistent proposal. By a vote of nineteen in favor, none opposed, and no abstentions, the RAC adopted the motion.

XVIII. GUIDELINES FOR RECOMBINANT DNA EXPERIMENTS WITH GENES CODING FOR TOXINS

Dr. Maas initiated the discussion of the proposed guidelines for recombinant DNA experiments with genes coding for toxins (tabs 996, 997, 1015/VIII). Dr. Maas stated that an ad hoc working group had been constituted several months ago to attempt to evaluate Section I-D-2 of the Guidelines which deals with potent toxins. The working group was composed of Drs. Werner Maas and Alan Bernheimer of New York University, Dr. John Collier of Yale University, Dr. Susan Gottesman of the NIH, Dr. Michael Gill of Tufts University, Dr. Myron Levine of the University of Maryland, and Dr. James Mason of the Utah State Department of Health. He said that the group evaluated toxins as pharmacological agents per se without consideration of other characteristics of the organism that produces the toxin.

Dr. Novick, citing recent research showing that a toxin produced by a Bacillus is functionally expressed in E. coli host-vector systems, said that the document is timely.

Dr. Levine pointed out that important vaccine development is dependent on recombinant DNA manipulations. He said the proposal under consideration will advance work in this area by clarifying the status of toxins under the Guidelines. He then deferred to Dr. Gill, an ad hoc consultant, who had been instrumental in constructing the proposal on toxins.

Dr. Gill called the committee's attention to tab 1015/VIII in the Federal Register. The proposal would modify Section I-D-2 of the Prohibitions and would add a new Appendix G to the Guidelines. Containment conditions are assigned for cloning toxins in E. coli K-12. A principal investigator wishing to use other host-vector systems would have to contact ORDA which will consult with the ad hoc working group on toxins. Toxins were divided into four groups on the basis of potency. Cloning of DNA coding for toxins with an LD_{50} of less than 100 nanograms per kilogram body weight is prohibited; cloning of genes coding for toxins with an LD_{50} of 100 nanograms to 1 microgram per kilogram may be performed at P3 + EK1 or P2 + EK2; cloning of DNAs coding for toxins with an LD_{50} of 1 microgram to 100 micrograms per kilogram may be performed at P1 + EK1. P1 + EK1 containment may be used for specified enterotoxins. DNAs coding for proteins with an LD_{50} of greater than 100 micrograms per kilogram may be handled as nontoxins under the Guidelines.

Dr. Gill said the effects of intraintestinal production of cytotoxic toxins might include (1) direct damage to the intestinal lining and (2) passage through the lining into the bloodstream. In the absence of information on the effect of E. coli elaborating toxin in the human intestine, the working group based the classification on available data from humans, primates, and small animals, generated by intravenous or parenteral administration of toxins. A listing of toxins by potency has been prepared and is available from ORDA. In addition, the working group outlined a procedure for evaluating toxins to be added to the list in the future. The procedure is also available from ORDA.

Dr. Gill outlined the types of data used to determine toxicity:

(1) Human toxicity, if known, would be paramount in fixing containment levels.

(2) If human toxicity is not known, it would be inferred from assays of toxicity to other primates.

(3) If neither human nor primate toxicity is known, it would be inferred from the LD_{50} of the most sensitive of three small animal species (mice, guinea pigs and rabbits).

Dr. Gill said that in those cases in which there is human data, man is not significantly more sensitive to the toxin than the most sensitive of three small animal species (mouse, rabbit or guinea pig).

Dr. Gill pointed out to RAC that diphtheria toxin appears to have an LD_{50} of 100 nanograms or less per kilogram body weight in humans. The working group designated P3 + EK1 containment, but Dr. Gill asked RAC to consider whether this containment was appropriate.

Dr. Levine reiterated that although the proposed classification is based on pharmacological potency, the toxin delivery system is highly important to the pathogenicity of a toxin producing organism in nature.

Dr. Nightingale asked if the toxins prohibited by the proposed classification (botulinum, tetanus, Shigella neurotoxin) would be the only prohibited toxins. Dr. Gill replied that these toxins are the only ones currently known to have an LD_{50} of 100 nanograms or less per kilogram (other than diphtheria which is right on the borderline). If other toxins are found in the future to have an LD_{50} in this range, they would be put on the list and the cloning of their gene would be prohibited.

Dr. Laird argued against prohibiting research on tetanus and botulism toxins. He said it is highly important to develop vaccines for these toxins. Dr. Gottesman said that while those toxins are placed in the prohibited category, the prohibition is not absolute, individuals may come to RAC with a case-by-case request for an exception to any prohibition.

Dr. Gottesman asked Dr. Gill which route of delivery elicits the most sensitive enterotoxin response. Dr. Gill replied that the enteral route was most effective. These toxins are the only toxins which are more toxic when administered enterally than parenterally. Dr. Gottesman asked where cholera toxin would fall in the proposed classification on the basis of enteral and parenteral LD_{50}s. Dr. Gill replied that cholera toxin would not be considered a toxin under the proposed classification when administered parenterally. The LD_{50} of cholera toxin administered enterally, would place it under Section 2-b of the proposed Appendix G, were there no Section 2-c.

Dr. Holmes praised the proposal presented by the working group but expressed several reservations. He said the premise that humans will be as sensitive as the most sensitive of three small animal species is based on data for seven toxins, as information on human toxicity for most toxins is not available. This assumption may not be true for all toxins. He was also concerned with the question of creating new ecological niches. Staphylococcal enterotoxin F, implicated in toxic shock syndrome, is not highly toxic, yet we suddenly have the appearance of this new clinically important syndrome. He questioned whether toxin producing recombinant organisms able to survive in other sites, such as vagina, respiratory tract, or wounds, might be highly hazardous. He felt additional data should be generated to address these questions. He suggested that a procedure involving case-by-case evaluation, at least at some level, as with the specific proposal involving diphtheria toxin to be reviewed by the RAC later in the meeting, was appropriate until more information was gathered.

Dr. Nightingale questioned the wisdom of discussing treatability in setting containment levels for the enterotoxins. Timing, availability of treatment, etc., affect the outcome of treatment. Drs. McGarrity and Goldstein also objected to the concept that physical containment conditions need not be as stringent if physiological remedies exist. Dr. Nightingale noted that toxins whose end point is not immediate death, such as those which cause cancer years later, are not included in the classification.

Dr. Nightingale proposed that the classification of toxins be considered in context of the upcoming total review of the Guidelines. She moved to refer consideration of the document to the working group for revision of the Guidelines. Dr. Goldstein seconded the motion.

Dr. Levine opposed the motion. He said that the classification generated by the <u>ad hoc</u> working group on toxins represented six months of work by expert toxicologists. The issue presented enormous challenges in reviewing available data, and in constructing a proposal acceptable to all members of the working group. The proposed language is the working group's best effort to come to grips with balancing potential risk versus potential benefit. He pointed out that virtually all of the points raised by RAC had been discussed and carefully evaluated by the working group. The format based on pharmacological criteria is an extremely conservative approach since many factors other than the toxin itself are of great consequence in pathogenicity. Dr. Maas supported Dr. Levine's statement. The proposal is conservative; it clarifies the issues and distinguishes between potent and nonpotent toxins. He offered a substitute motion to accept the proposal as it appeared in the Federal Register with the provision that these restrictions override all other sections of the Guidelines, e.g., exemptions, self-cloning, etc. Dr. Fedoroff seconded the motion.

Dr. Gottesman offered the following amendments to the proposal as it appeared in the Federal Register:

(1) The words "P1 + EK1" will be substituted for the words "Section III-O."

(2) Language indicating that these specifications will override other sections of the Guidelines, e.g., "exemptions" and "return to host of origin" will be added to Section I-D-2 of the Guidelines.

(3) Language describing treatability of enterotoxin effects will be deleted.

Dr. Maas accepted the proposed amendments.

Dr. Berns said he supported the proposed language in a general sense, but felt RAC must monitor toxin experiments. He said he would support the proposal if language requiring registration of toxin experiments with ORDA was incorporated.

Dr. Maas accepted this suggestion as an amendment. Dr. Adelberg urged the committee to support Dr. Maas' amended motion, as he felt Dr. Nightingale's proposal would simply postpone the discussion. Dr. McKinney also urged the committee to accept the proposal. Dr. Fedoroff complimented the working group for an extremely thoughtful, thorough treatment of a very difficult subject. Dr. Nightingale said that she supported the substitute motion.

Dr. Gill suggested a clarification in the proposed language in regard to registration with ORDA; he suggested the sentence "Experiments involving toxins that are lethal at 100 micrograms or less shall be registered with ORDA" be added to Section 1, General Information, of proposed Appendix G. Dr. Gottesman agreed, as did Dr. Maas. Dr. Williams called for the vote on the question. By a vote of fourteen in favor, three opposed, and one abstention, the call for the question carried. Mr. Thornton then called the vote on Dr. Maas' substitute motion as amended. This was to substitute the motion proposed by Dr. Maas, i.e., to accept the language in the Federal Register (1015/VIII) with four changes:

(1) "Section III-O" to be changed to "P1-EK1" in Sections 2-b and 2-c of Appendix G.

(2) The introductory text of Section 2-c of Appendix G dealing with treatability of enterotoxin effects to be eliminated.

(3) Language to be added at the end of Section I-D-2 of the Guidelines indicating that Appendix G specifications override other specifications of the Guidelines (e.g., exemptions or return to host of origin experiments).

(4) Language to be added to Section 1 of Appendix G that experiments involving toxins that are lethal at 100 micrograms or less shall be registered with ORDA.

By a vote of sixteen in favor, three opposed, and no abstentions the RAC adopted the substitute motion in place of Dr. Nightingale's previous motion to defer consideration.

Dr. Novick asked if he might offer an amendment at this point. Mr. Thornton said that technically he could rule no amendment was in order at this point in the voting process; but in an effort to permit all points of view to be heard, he would recognize Dr. Novick. Dr. Novick said he wished to add the word "prior" to the added sentence specifying registration with ORDA. Dr. Maas accepted Dr. Novick's amendment. Mr. Thornton then called the vote on the motion, i.e., to accept the language in the Federal Register (tab 1015/VIII) with the four changes listed above including the word "prior" in the fourth change. The RAC adopted the modified language by a vote of eighteen in favor, none opposed, and one abstention. Mr. Thornton expressed his appreciation to all involved in preparing the proposal.

Dr. Gill then summarized the risk assessment experiments proposed by the toxin working group (Attachment II). Mr. Thornton said he intended to refer the proposal to the Risk Assessment Subcommittee for further consideration.

XIX. REQUEST TO CLONE THE VIBRIO CHOLERAE ENTEROTOXIN GENE

Dr. Holmes initiated discussion on the proposal (tabs 1002, 1010, 1015/X) submitted by Dr. John Mekalanos of Harvard Medical School. Dr. Mekalanos requested an exemption from Section I-D-2 of the Guidelines, which prohibits the formation of recombinant DNAs containing genes for the biosynthesis of toxins potent for vertebrates. Dr. Mekalanos wishes to clone the *Vibrio cholerae* sequence coding for the biosynthesis of cholera toxin. Dr. Mekalanos requested consideration of the appropriate level to perform three experiments in *E. coli* K-12: to clone sequences coding for the (1) LT A subunit, (2) the LT B subunit, and (3) the LT A and LT B subunits. Dr. Holmes said that Dr. Mekalanos suggested experiments 1 and 2 might be performed under P2 + EK1 containment; no active LT toxin will be synthesized. Dr. Holmes said the toxin classification RAC had just adopted would indicate

P1 + EK1 containment for this type of experiment. He found P1 + EK1 adequate for experiments 1 and 2. Dr. Holmes said Dr. Mekalanos had requested P2 + EK1 containment for experiment 3, but would be ready to use P2 + EK2. Dr. Holmes felt experiment 3 could be performed under P1 + EK1 conditions as specified by the recently adopted toxin classification.

Dr. Levine viewed the request as important work. He agreed with Dr. Holmes that P1 + EK1 containment conditions were appropriate for all three experiments. Dr. Holmes moved approval of experiments 1, 2, and 3 at the P1 + EK1 level of containment. Dr. Levine seconded the motion.

Dr. Novick suggested that P2 physical containment might be more appropriate to the experiments; he expressed concern that colonization factors, permitting E. coli to attach to small bowel adhesion sites, might be picked up by E. coli making cholera toxin. Dr. Levine said recent data have demonstrated that colonization factors alone will not create a pathogen.
Dr. Novick moved an amendment to require the experiments to be performed under P2 containment conditions. He did not view P2 containment as an overwhelming burden and felt P2 would alleviate residual anxieties.
Dr. Holmes said he would accept P2 requirements for experiment 3 but felt P1 + EK1 was adequate for experiments 1 and 2.

Dr. Levine replied that P2 containment would afford little or no additional safety since Vibrio cholerae is not spread by the aerosol route. As control of aerosolization is the most significant distinction between P1 and P2 containment, he felt P1 specifications are adequate to contain the experiments. He also pointed out that the general classification of toxins just approved by the RAC permits the experiments at P1 + EK1.

Dr. Holmes said he wished to rephrase his motion to make containment conditions contingent on the Director's decision concerning the general toxin classification (Appendix G); if Dr. Fredrickson accepts the general proposal, Dr. Mekalanos may proceed with experiments 1, 2, and 3 under P1 containment conditions. Should Dr. Fredrickson not accept the proposal, the RAC recommends that Dr. Mekalanos may perform experiments 1 and 2 under P1 conditions, but must use P2 containment for experiment 3. Dr. Levine, who had seconded Dr. Holmes' original motion, did not accept the modified language; Mr. Thornton called the vote on the modified language. By a vote of three in favor, ten opposed, and three abstentions, the RAC refused the modified language. Mr. Thornton then called the vote on Dr. Holmes' original language, i.e., approval of the proposed experiments at P1 + EK1 containment. By a vote of fifteen in favor, none opposed, and one abstention, the RAC adopted the motion.

XX. CLONING AND EXPRESSION OF DNA CODING FOR DIPHTHERIA TOXIN

Dr. Holmes introduced the request (tab 1003, 1015/IX) of Dr. John Murphy of Harvard University. Dr. Murphy proposed to clone in E. coli K-12 the 3.9 kb Bam restriction fragment of Corynephage Beta which carries the diphtheria toxin structural gene. Dr. Murphy proposed to use P4 containment and to perform the experiments at Fort Detrick. If P3 containment were permitted, he would propose to perform the experiments at Sidney Farber Cancer Center in Boston or at Harvard University in Cambridge, Massachusetts. Dr. Murphy would perform risk assessment experiments, and would study toxin secretion, localization in E. coli, and the entry of toxin into eukaryotic cells.

Dr. Levine spoke of one potential future benefit of the proposed research: hormones that home to specific organs, might be linked to portions of the diphtheria toxin and the combination molecules might serve as highly specific agents in cancer chemotherapy. Dr. Levine strongly supported that portion of the request dealing with possible risk assessment studies. He noted that P3 containment conditions are specified by the general toxin classification, previously adopted by RAC; and he felt P3 was adequate containment.

Dr. Gottesman asked Dr. Gill to review the data on the potency of diphtheria toxin, which had led to its position in Appendix G in the class allowed at P3 + EK1 containment. Dr. Gill said the LD_{50} of diphtheria toxin, in the most sensitive small animal (guinea pig), is 160 nanograms per kilogram body weight. The LD_{50} in humans is estimated to be equal to or less than 100 nanograms per kilogram body weight. This figure was extrapolated from an incident in Japan in which children were inadvertently injected with diphtheria toxin rather than diphtheria toxoid. It thus falls close to the borderline of 100 nanograms per kilogram body weight, which would separate a toxin the cloning of whose gene would be prohibited from a toxin the cloning of whose gene would be allowed at P3 + EK1 in Appendix G. Dr. Gottesman said that she would support P4 containment for the proposed experiment. Dr. Levine said he could support P4 containment, but questioned whether this might conflict with the action taken earlier in the meeting on the general toxin classification. Dr. Talbot said that Dr. Fredrickson could resolve any conflict when he promulgates his decision on the recommendations from this meeting.

Dr. Levine moved acceptance of the proposal at P4 containment. Dr. Goldstein seconded the motion. Be a vote of fifteen in favor, none opposed, and one abstention, the RAC adopted the motion.

Dr. Levine suggested that if the genes are successfully cloned, an E. coli host-vector system containing the plasmid and capable of colonizing a pig might be used in an additional risk assessment experiment. The pigs should be colonized under P4 containment conditions. Dr. Murphy expressed interest in pursuing such experiments, but it was pointed out that it may not be possible to introduce a pig into the P4 line.

XXI. REQUEST TO CLONE THE GENETIC DETERMINANT OF THE TOXIC-SHOCK SYNDROME CAUSED BY STAPHYLOCOCCUS AUREUS

Dr. Mason initiated the review of a proposal (tabs 1008, 1015/XI) from Dr. Richard Novick of the Public Health Research Institute of the City of New York, Inc. Dr. Novick requested permission to clone in Staphylococcus aureus the genetic determinant of the toxic-shock syndrome caused by S. aureus. Dr. Novick stated that recombinant DNA techniques promise the most rapid and direct means of unraveling the biology of the determinant and of the disease. He requested permission to conduct the experiments under P2 containment using S. aureus strain RN 450, which is non-hemolytic, non-pigmented, and lacking any detectable prophage. Dr. Mason said he felt the work should be done but said containment should probably be assessed at the P3 level. Dr. Levine said the proposal was not sufficiently amplified; too little data had been submitted to permit a fair appraisal. Dr. Holmes agreed, he said he would like to examine additional information on the toxin and on the enfeebled S. aureus strain to be used as a host.

Dr. Novick noted that the RAC at a previous meeting had approved the cloning of the S. aureus ToxA gene in B. subtilis at P3. He admitted that the exact cause of the syndrome has not been elucidated and said he hoped to identify the toxin's role through these studies.

Dr. Nightingale said the presentation was not well-prepared. She felt that the information available on toxic-shock syndrome may not be sufficient to permit a reasonable appraisal of the proposed experiments. She requested additional data.

Dr. Maas said that currently there is a state of confusion as to which toxin is the cause of toxic shock syndrome. He felt the issues should be clarified before permission is given to begin cloning the toxin gene.

Dr. Gottesman said the previous RAC approval to clone the S. aureus Tox A gene stipulated P3 containment conditions with an HV2 Bacillus subtilis host-vector system. She questioned whether S. aureus would be a safer host-vector system than an HV2 B. subtilis host-vector system. The toxin's capacity to potentiate other toxins is also an issue. Dr. Novick said he would withdraw his proposal and attempt to provide better documentation at a future time.

XXII. ADJOURNMENT

The meeting was adjourned at 1:25 p.m. on April 24, 1981.

Respectively submitted,

Elizabeth A. Milewski
Elizabeth A. Milewski, Ph.D.
Rapporteur

William J. Gartland Jr.
William J. Gartland, Jr., Ph.D.
Executive Secretary

I hereby certify that, to the best of my knowledge, the foregoing Minutes and Attachments are accurate and complete.

September 10, 1981
Date

Ray Thornton
Ray Thornton, J.D.
Chairman
Recombinant DNA Advisory Committee

RECOMBINANT DNA ADVISORY COMMITTEE

CHAIRMAN

THORNTON, Ray, J.D. (82)
President
Arkansas State University
State University, Arkansas 72467
501 972-2100

- -

AHMED, Abdul Karim, Ph.D. (82)
Senior Staff Scientist
Natural Resources Defense Council, Inc.
122 East 42nd Street
New York, New York 10017
212 949-0049

BALTIMORE, David, Ph.D. (82)
Professor of Biology
Center for Cancer Research
Massachusetts Institute of Technology
Cambridge, Massachusetts 02139
617 253-6410

BERNS, Kenneth I., Ph.D., M.D. (83)
Chairman
Department of Immunology and Medical Microbiology
University of Florida College of Medicine
Gainesville, Florida 32610
904 392-3311

BRILL, Winston J., Ph.D. (83)
Vilas Research Professor
Department of Bacteriology
University of Wisconsin
Madison, Wisconsin 53706
608 262-3567

CAMPBELL, Allan M., Ph.D. (81)
Professor
Department of Biological Sciences
Stanford University
Stanford, California 94305
415 497-1170

CASON, Zelma (81)
Supervisor
Cytopathology Laboratory
Department of Pathology
University of Mississippi Medical Center
Jackson, Mississippi 39216
601 987-5547

FEDOROFF, Nina V., Ph.D. (84)
Staff Member
Department of Embryology
Carnegie Institution of Washington
115 West University Parkway
Baltimore, Maryland 21210
301 467-1414

GOLDSTEIN, Richard, Ph.D. (82)
Associate Professor
Department of Microbiology and Molecular Genetics
Harvard Medical School
Boston, Massachusetts 02115
617 732-1911

GOTTESMAN, Susan K., Ph.D. (81)
Senior Investigator
Laboratory of Molecular Biology
National Cancer Institute
National Institutes of Health
Bethesda, Maryland 20205
301 496-2095

HARRIS, Jean L., M.D. (83)
Secretary of Human Resources
Commonwealth of Virginia
Office of Governor
Post Office Box 1475
Richmond, Virginia 23219
804 786-7765

HOLMES, King K., M.D., Ph.D. (84)
Head
Division of Infectious Diseases
U.S. Public Health Service Hospital
Seattle, Washington 98114
206 325-2997

KING, Patricia A., J.D. (82)
Deputy Assistant Attorney General
Civil Division
Department of Justice
10th & Constitution Ave., N.W.
Washington, D.C. 20530
202 633-3333

KRIMSKY, Sheldon, Ph.D. (81)
Acting Director
Program in Urban Social
and Environmental Policy
Tufts University
Medford, Massachusetts 02155
617 628-5000 x726

LEVINE, Myron M., M.D. (84)
Director
Center for Vaccine Development
Division of Infectious Diseases
University of Maryland
School of Medicine
Baltimore, Maryland 21201
301 528-7588

MAAS, Werner K., Ph.D. (83)
Professor
Department of Microbiology
New York University
School of Medicine
New York, New York 10016
212 340-5322

MASON, James O., M.D., Dr. Ph. (83)
Executive Director
Utah State Department of
Health
Post Office Box 2500
Salt Lake City, Utah 84113
801 533-6111

McGARRITY, Gerard J., Ph.D. (84)
Head
Department of Microbiology
Institute for Medical Research
Copewood Street
Camden, New Jersey 08103
609 966-7377

McKINNEY, Robert W., Ph.D. (84)
Chief, Occupational Safety
and Health Branch
Division of Safety
National Institutes of Health
Bethesda, Maryland 20205
301 496-2960

NIGHTINGALE, Elena O., Ph.D., M.D. (83)
Senior Program Officer
Institute of Medicine
National Academy of Sciences
Washington, D.C. 20418
202 389-6168

NOVICK, Richard P., M.D. (81)
Member and Chief
Department of Plasmid Biology
Public Health Research Institute
of the City of New York, Inc.
New York, New York 10016
212 481-0746

PARKINSON, David K., B.M., B.Ch. (81)
Associate Professor
Graduate School of Public Health
University of Pittsburgh
Pittsburgh, Pennsylvania 15261
412 647-5730

PINON, Ramon, Ph.D. (82)
Associate Professor
Department of Biology
B-022 Bonner Hall
University of California, San Diego
La Jolla, California 92093
714 452-2452

SCANDALIOS, John G., Ph.D. (84)
Head
Department of Genetics
North Carolina State University
Raleigh, North Carolina 27650
919 737-2291

WILLIAMS, Luther S., Ph.D. (81)
Professor
Department of Biology
Washington University
Campus Box 1137
St. Louis, Missouri 63130
314 889-6843

EXECUTIVE SECRETARY

GARTLAND, William J., Jr., Ph.D.
Director, Office of Recombinant
DNA Activities
National Institute of Allergy
and Infectious Diseases
National Institutes of Health
Bethesda, Maryland 20205
301 496-6051

RECOMBINANT DNA ADVISORY COMMITTEE

NON-VOTING REPRESENTATIVES

CENTERS FOR DISEASE CONTROL

DOWDLE, Walter R., Ph.D.
Assistant Director for Science
Centers for Disease Control
Atlanta, Georgia 30333
404 329-3701

National Institute for Occupational Safety and Health (CDC)

LEMIN, Richard A.
Director
Office of Program Planning
and Evaluation
National Institute for Occupational
Safety and Health,
Room 8A53
5600 Fishers Lane
Rockville, Maryland 20857
301 443-3680

U.S. DEPARTMENT OF AGRICULTURE

TOLIN, Sue A., Ph.D.
Science and Education Administration
Cooperative Research
U.S. Department of Agriculture
Washington, D.C. 20250
202 447-5741

FULKERSON, John F., Ph.D. (ALT)
Science and Education Administration
Cooperative Research
U.S. Department of Agriculture
Washington, D.C. 20250
202 447-5741

U.S. DEPARTMENT OF COMMERCE

GORDON, George S., Ph.D.
Analyst
Office of Environmental Affairs
U.S. Department of Commerce
Room 3425
Washington, D.C. 20230
202 377-2565

PAYNTER, O. E., Ph.D. (ALT)
Toxicologist
Office of Environmental Affairs
U.S. Department of Commerce
Room 3425
Washington, D.C. 20230
202 377-3234

U.S. DEPARTMENT OF ENERGY

DUDA, George, Ph.D.
Office of Health and
Environmental Research, EV-33
U.S. Department of Energy
Washington, D.C. 20545
202 353-3651

EDINGTON, Charles W., Ph.D. (ALT)
Deputy Director
Office of Health and Environmental
Research
U.S. Department of Energy
Washington, D.C. 20250
202 353-3251

U.S. DEPARTMENT OF THE INTERIOR

PIMENTEL, Mariano B., Ph.D.
Medical Director
U.S. Department of the Interior
Room 7045
18th & C Street, N.W.
Washington, D.C. 20240
202 343-2081

U.S. DEPARTMENT OF JUSTICE

BELL, Charlotte R., J.D.
General Litigation Section
Land and Natural Resources
Division
U.S. Department of Justice
Washington, D.C. 20530
202 633-4150

U.S. DEPARTMENT OF STATE

WALSH, William J., III
Biomedical Research Liason
and Health Affairs Officer
Oceans and International Environmental
and Scientific Affairs
U.S. Department of State
Washington, D.C. 20520
202 632-4824

U.S. DEPARTMENT OF TRANSPORTATION

CUSHMAC, George E., Ph.D.
Chemist
Research and Special Programs
Administration
U.S. Department of Transportation
Washington, D.C. 20590
202 755-4906

U.S. ENVIRONMENTAL PROTECTION AGENCY

BANKS, Darryl R., Ph.D.
Executive Assistant to the
Assistant Administrator for
Research and Development
Office of Research and Development
United States Environmental Protection Agency
RD 672, 913 West Tower
Washington, D.C. 20460
202 755-0122

FOOD AND DRUG ADMINISTRATION

HENRY, Timothy J., Ph.D.
BF, DT, HFF-156
Food and Drug Administration
200 C Street, S.W.
Washington, D.C. 20204
202 472-4690

NATIONAL AERONAUTICS AND SPACE ADMINISTRATION

DeVINCENZI, Donald L., Ph.D.
Program Manager, Planetary Biology
Code SBL-3
National Aeronautics and Space
Administration
Washington, D.C. 20546
202 755-3732

NATIONAL SCIENCE FOUNDATION

LEWIS, Herman W., Ph.D.
Senior Scientist for Recombinant DNA
Division of Physiology
Cellular and Molecular Biology
National Science Foundation
Washington, D.C. 20550
202 357-7647

HARRIMAN, Phillip, Ph.D. (ALT)
Program Director for Genetic Biology
Room 326
National Science Foundation
Washington, D.C. 20550
202 632-5985

U.S. VETERANS ADMINISTRATION

SCHULTZ, Jane S., Ph.D.
Geneticist
U.S. Veterans Administration
Medical Research Service - 151
2215 Fuller Road
Ann Arbor, Michigan 48105
313 769-7100 x696

BERMAN, Howard M. (ALT)
Health Scientist
Program Development and Review Division
U.S. Veterans Administration
810 Vermont Avenue, N.W.
Washington, D.C. 20420
202 389-5065

U.S. DEPARTMENT OF LABOR

LOGAN, David C., M.D.
Medical Officer
Office of Technical Support
Occupational Safety and Health
Room N3656
U.S. Department of Labor
Washington, D.C. 20210
202 523-9603

RECOMBINANT DNA ADVISORY COMMITTEE

LIAISON REPRESENTATIVES

JUENGST, Eric T. (Acting)
Program Specialist
Program of Science Technology
& Human Value
Mail Stop 104
National Endowment for the Humanities
Washington, D.C. 20506
202 474-0354

WEISS, Daniel L., M.D.
Assembly of Life Sciences
National Academy of Sciences
Washington, D.C. 20418
202 389-6315

IINO, Professor Tetsuo
Faculty Science
University of Tokyo
Hongo, Tokyo 113
Japan

PROPOSED RISK ASSESSMENT

The Pharmalogical and Physiological Consequences of

Direct Intraintestinal Administration of the More Potent Toxins

With the most likely cloning host, E. coli, the principal dangers to man of cloning toxin genes appear to lie in the intraintestinal production of toxins that may (a) pass through the gut lining and cause damage elsewhere or (b) damage the gut directly, or (c) both damage the gut and, as a consequence, later pass more easily into the circulation to cause damage elsewhere. The extent to which intraintestinal toxins may create a potential danger when produced by organisms capable of colonizing humans is currently lacking and is difficult to ascertain, but may be inferred from appropriate animal tests.

Question 1: Concerning the more potent cytotoxins: how much toxin could be produced in the gut without causing death, disfigurement, profound neurological changes or severe damage to the intestine itself, and is it therefore safe to devise cloning protocols in which 50 mg., for example, of the toxin may be produced enterically.

Toxins to use: Diphtheria toxin (Perhaps repeated with abrin or ricin, but the protocol below is mostly for diphtheria toxin).

Protocol: (a) One injection of graded doses (e.g., initially 0.5%-50 mg/kg using diphtheria toxin) directly into the guts of, for diphtheria toxin - rabbits and/or guinea pigs (not mice), for abrin/ricin - mouse and/or rabbit and/or guinea pig. Determine the doses that kill.

Look histologically and grossly to determine pathologic changes due to direct action of the toxin on the gut or on viscera attributable to toxin that escaped, and hence determine cause of death. Examine 7 day survivors for other effects, namely disfigurement, profound neurological changes, or histological damage to the intestine itself. Antibody titers?

(b) Repeat (a) with injection into the various levels of the gut in order to mimic possible colonization by toxinogenic clones, namely;

i) upper gut

ii) proximal ileum

iii) distal ileum (site of uptake of B_{12} and bile salts)

iv) colon

(c) To mimic the continuous production of a toxin by a bacterial clone: Is the lethal dose much reduced by split doses? Inject sublethal doses into marked sites of the gut. Wait (2 days?) for histological damage to occur, and reinject the same doses into the same sites.

(d) Perhaps to show that any potentiation by split doses is truly caused by a rise in permeability, repeat particular experiments in (c) using diphtheria toxin for the first injection and tetanus toxin for the second injection. Is there a change in the dose-lethality curve for tetanus toxin?

<u>Question 2</u>: To further determine how much of a toxin passes out of the gut under normal and abnormal conditions.

Use tetanus toxin which has no known effect on the gut itself, yet is exquisitely toxin in the circulation. Use piglets*

(a) Dose lethality curves after direct injection of tetanus toxin into the patent gut, at the sites specified in 1 (b). Protect with tetanus antiserum iv to check that death is caused by parenteral toxin.

(b) Dose lethality curves in piglets with

i) Rotaviral diarrhea, (which damages the gut histologically)

ii) Secretory diarrhea caused by *E. coli* K88+ ent $_{LT}$
E. coli K88+ ent $_{ST}$
E. coli K88+ ent- (control)

iii) An invasive bacterial enteropathogen (*e.g.*, Yersinia, Campylobacter, Salmonella)

iv) Outflow obstruction (which causes permeability to rise). Ligate guts at various levels 2 days previously, then inject tetanus toxin above the obstructions.

(c) To learn something of the mechanism of trans-intestinal protein transport, repeat the dose-response curves of 2 (a) with

i) Chloroquin (prior to injection and every 12 h, p.o.) which blocks intestinal endocytosis

ii) Verapamil, which blocks calcium channels and hence some transport.

Question 3: The introduction of a toxin into the gut lumen may not accurately mimic the production of the same amount of toxin by an organism. Thus in the future, additional experiments may be needed to evaluate the actual risk from recombinant toxigenic organisms that colonize particular regions of the intestine.

*Because the pig is an omnivore, its gut has a flora that resembles man's more than do other animals. For example, it has relatively high E. coli count. Further, coli strains suitable for section 2 (b) are already available and characterized in piglets.

federal register

Wednesday
June 10, 1981

Part II

Department of Health and Human Services

National Institutes of Health

Recombinant DNA Research; Final Plan for a Program To Assess the Risks

DEPARTMENT OF HEALTH AND HUMAN SERVICES

National Institutes of Health

Recombinant DNA Research; Final Plan for a Program To Assess the Risks of Recombinant DNA Research

AGENCY: National Institutes of Health.

ACTION: Notice of final plan for a program to assess the risks of recombinant DNA research.

SUMMARY: This notice sets forth the first annual update of the NIH program to assess the risks of recombinant DNA research.

EFFECTIVE DATE: June 10, 1981.

FOR FURTHER INFORMATION CONTACT: Additional information may be obtained from Dr. William J. Gartland, Jr., Director, Office of Recombinant DNA Activities, NIAID, Building 31, Room 4A52, National Institutes of Health, Bethesda, Maryland 20205 (301-496-6051).

SUPPLEMENTAL INFORMATION:

I. Decision of the NIH Director to Issue the Final Plan.

The proposed first annual update was published in the **Federal Register**, Volume 45, No. 182, Wednesday, September 17, 1980, pages 61874 to 61878. A formal closing date for public comment of December 16, 1980, was established.

A. Eight correspondents submitted comments on the plan. They were divided into generic categories as follows:

1. *General Opposition to the Risk Assessment Program.*

One correspondent objected to the fact that the program failed to evaluate the risks "created by the regulations of recombinant DNA research." It was stated that risk assessment studies should be addressed to the risks created in the laboratory by the use of chemicals employed as disinfectants; by excessive use of autoclaves; by use of automatic formaldehyde atomizer guns; and other various dangers due to crowded conditions and inadequate ventilation of laboratories. The commentator suggested that the name of the program should be changed to "Program to Assess the Hpyothetical Risks of the Recombinant DNA Technique." Further, the author objected to the title of the course "Microbiological Principles and Techniques for Work With Potentially Biohazardous Agents Including Recombiant DNA" to be sponsored by the NIH.

In response to the main criticism raised, the laboratory practices and containment procedures specified in the Guidelines are those that have been widely used in containing microorganisms.

A second commentator said that there is absolutely no evidence, thus far, that indicates that recombinant DNA research is unusually risky. Further, he stated that intended programs to evaluate risks will never be able to prove that the risk is negative. The commentator concluded that "the NIH should get out of the recombinant DNA business as rapidly as possible."

As I noted in issuing the first final plan, I am required to establish that actions under the NIH Guidelines for Research Involving Recombiant DNA Molecules present no significant risks to health or the environment. While I concur with most scientists that the perception of risk from this research is certainly less now than earlier, there still remain selected areas where data are insufficient to determine risk. This plan is an attempt to satisfy this remaining need and will afford an opportunity to assess progress toward achieving the scientific objectives.

2. *Criticism of the Program and the Risk Assessment Experiments.*

One writer expressed concern that the proposed risk assessment plan update does not address "non-scientific risks," such as risks of accidents due to carelessness or arrogance, risks of sabotage, and risks of intentional misuse of recombinant DNA technology. An objection was also raised to a statement in the Plan which asserts that much information on recombinant DNA risk analysis has come from research not primarily designed to assess risks. It is the opinion of the writer that it is not good scientific practice to base policy and conclusions on research that was not designed specifically to provide information on risk.

The objective of the risk assessment program is to obtain information derived from scientific experiments relevant to the use of recombinant DNA molecules which would also be applicable to cases of accidents, carelessness, etc.

It still remains our conviction as stated in the first Final Plan that:

> The vast majority of information relevant to recombinant DNA risk analysis has already come from research not primarily designed to provide information on risk. This will undoubtedly continue to be the case. This information will be obtained chiefly from publications in the scientific literature, from persons with special scientific knowledge, and from ongoing basic biomedical research. Risk assessment analysis will require continuing review of data developed in the fields of microbiology, infectious deseases, and related biological research.

Some essential information has been, and will continue to be, derived from projects specifically designed to assess various aspects of potential risks associated with recombinant DNA experimentation. Such experiments will be supported by the Intramural and Extramural programs of NIH. Many experiments may also be conducted in the private sector or may be funded by other agencies or governments.

> The essential goal of a successful risk assessment plan will be the development of means to collect, collate, coordinate, evaluate, and disseminate data obtained from all sources.

Another commentator criticized the interpretation of the results of polyoma risk assessment experiments. The correspondent noted that positive results were obtained with regard to oncogenicity and infectivity when cloned dimeric polyoma DNA was carried in intact phage lambda particles.

The published results and interpretations derived from the polyoma DNA risk experiments have been the subject of wide reviews and discussions. The consensus of most scientists supports the conclusions of the investigators who conducted the polyoma risk assessment experiments that neither potentially infectious nor tumorigenic recombinant DNA was transferred out of the EK2 host into susceptible mice or hamster cells to produce progeny virions or tumors. Further, propagation of polyoma viral DNA as a component of a recombinant DNA molecule in *E. coli* K-12 reduces its biologic activity as an infectious unit many orders of magnitude relative to the virus.

3. *Support and General Suggestions for the Program.*

Three correspondents submitted letters supporting the Proposed Plan as published, and made some general suggestions for improvement. One commentator said that the risk assessment work has helped to allay many initial fears of this area of research. This correspondent also felt that it will be difficult to devise systematic standards for training all the workers in various areas of recombinant DNA research.

Another commentator stated that it would be prudent to provide risk assessment experiments to assess parameters of possible hazards for some of the more widely used host organisms not heretofore assessed.

One commentator stated that it was his impression that at the Pasadena Recombinant DNA Risk Assessment Workshop the question was not one of concern about antibody to insulin made by recombinant DNA, but rather to any hybrid proteins made between bacterial proteins and insulin or other peptide hormones. With regard to this comment, the central issue on this point is whether or not autoimmunity could follow administration of self proteins in any of several forms; hybrid proteins were one of the forms briefly discussed.

Another correspondent wrote that the increased responsibility given to the local Institutional Biosafety Committees will provide for more expeditious monitoring of recombinant DNA research. The commentator suggested that some effort be made to collate information eminating from ORDA memoranda, the **Federal Register**, and the Recombinant DNA Technical Bulletin. It was also suggested that thought should be given to preparing a tabular listing of a classification of microorganisms on the basis of hazard and their recommended containment levels. While these are not comments specifically on the risk-assessment plan, I wish to indicate that ORDA is exploring ways to summarize major actions of the RAC. Also, the Centers for Disease Control, in a joint effort with NIH, has published for comment "Proposed Biosafety Guidelines for Microbiological and Biomedical Laboratories."

B. The Recombinant DNA Advisory Committee considered the Proposed First Annual Update of the Risk Assessment Plan at its meetings on September 25, 1980, and January 8, 1981. At the latter meeting, Dr. Luther Williams, a RAC member, presented a summary of the program, as published in the **Federal Register** on September 17, 1980, and responded to questions. Committee members and the public were provided an opportunity to present their views, questions, criticisms, or suggestions. A RAC member raised a point regarding the wording in the second paragraph, third column of page 61876 of the **Federal Register** of September 17, 1980, dealing with colonization of the intestinal tract. It was recommended that the word "known" should be deleted from the last clause of the paragraph. This has been done, and the clause now reads as follows: ". . ., even though *E. coli* K-12 has apparently lost those characteristics that are required for colonization of the normal intestinal tract." A public commentator suggested that additional references should be added to the risk assessment plan. This has been done in this document. The RAC did not recommend any other significant changes in the plan as a result of other issues which were raised at the RAC meeting.

II. Final Plan for a Program to Assess the Risks of Recombinant DNA Research

A. *Introduction.*

With the issuance in December 1978 of revised guidelines for the conduct of recombinant DNA research, the Secretary, DHEW (now DHHS), requested that the National Institutes of Health (NIH prepare an NIH Risk Assessment Plan which, after review by the Recombinant DNA Advisory Committee (RAC) and publication in the **Federal Register** for comment, would be made final and updated annually. The present document is the first annual update.

B. *Scientific Aspects.*

We stated in the Final Plan and it is still our conviction that:

> The vast majority of information relevant to recombinant DNA risk analysis has already come from research not primarily designed to provide information on risk. This will undoubtedly continue to be the case. This information will be obtained chiefly from publications in the scientific literature, from persons with special scientific knowledge, and from ongoing basic biomedical research. Risk assessment analysis will require continuing review of data developed in the fields of microbiology, infectious diseases, and related biological research.
>
> Some essential information has been, and will continue to be, derived from projects specifically designed to assess various aspects of potential risks associated with recombinant DNA experimentation. Such experiments will be supported by the Intramural and the Extramural programs of NIH. Many experiments may also be conducted in the private sector or may be funded by other agencies or governments.
>
> The essential goal of a successful risk assessment plan will be the development of means to collect, collate, coordinate, evaluate, and disseminate data obtained from all sources.

The Scientific Aspects of the Plan noted that a number of events must occur before a laboratory microorganism becomes a possible risk to people or higher organisms outside the immediate laboratory environment. A major aspect of the risk assessment plan was to acquire and analyze information and data relevant to those elements for the three general categories of host-vector systems in use; prokaryotic, lower eukaryotic and higher eukaryotic systems. Initial emphasis was on the prokaryotic *E. coli* K-12 systems because those were, and remain, the systems predominately used by investigators, and because needed areas of investigation had already been identified. Seven areas were identified as requiring particular consideration, and progress has been made in collecting and/or analyzing data for all of them. Before considering these it is worth saying that, despite intensive study by the RAC Subcommittee on Risk Assessment and NIH staff, several conferences and workshops to consider specific issues and several experiments, no risks of recombinant DNA research have been identified that are not inherent in the microbiological and biochemical methodology used in such research. A synoptic report of progress follows and all data, reports, and other documents referred to are available on request.

1. *Prokaryotic Host-Vector Systems.*

a. Survival in the environment and the potential for selective advantage of organisms carrying recombinant DNA should they survive was cited as a matter of concern. NIAID had four contractors working on various aspects of this issue; the contracts were originally awarded to provide independent testing in the process whereby EK2 systems could possibly be elevated to EK3 status. The tests were performed in situations simulating accidental spills in the laboratory, in a model sewage treatment system, in mice and cultures simulating the mouse gastrointestinal system, in germfree mice, and finally in humans. The status of the work of all four contractors, at the time the Plan was initially published, can be found in the Recombinant DNA Technical Bulletin, Vol. 2, No. 2, July 1979. The expiration date of all contracts has now been reached and Final Reports are or soon will be available.

(1) The work of the contractor testing in "accidental spill situations" was completed shortly after publication of the Plan and was in two areas: (1) to determine whether selected strains of *E. coli*, used as hosts to propagate recombinant DNA molecules, and some phage and plasmid vectors would survive or retain their capacity to infect or transform host cells after exposure to the environments expected to occur in the event of spill or aerosolization, (2) to inventory and simulate common procedures used in recombinant DNA laboratory studies so that aerosol output potential of the procedures could be assessed.

Considerable effort was expended on quantitative descriptions of the biological characteristics of hosts and vectors of concern in current rDNA studies, and the physical dispersion aspects have been examined with particular attention to procedures unique to such laboratory work.

The data on biological survival characteristics are applicable to evaluation of potential dosage to workers or to the environments both from accidents creating massive release and from the continuing releases incidental to the labortory procedures. Evaluation of the effect of survival of the agents in the course of routine work should assist in prudent and cost-effective application of physical and biological containment. Further, it can lend emphasis to the areas in which training in "good practice" can be most productive.

This work was supported by Interagency Agreement YOI-AI-70003, Naval Biosciences Laboratory, Robert J. Heckley, principal investigator.

(2) The Survival of EK1 and EK2 Systems in Sewage Treatment Plant Models.

In an early series of studies utilizing bench scale models of wastewater treatment facilities, *E. coli* DP50*supF*, *E. coli* Chi 1776 and phage Charon 4A concentrations were shown to be reduced by at least two orders of magnitude by a conventional treatment chain (including primary settling followed by activated sludge treatment and anaerobic digestion of all sludges generated). This work was described in brief form in the *Recombinant DNA Technical Bulletin of* July 1979.

Similar results are now available for the survival of *E. coli* Chi 2656 (which carries plasmid pBR322) and for *E. coli* GF 2174 (carrying plasmid pBR325). Evidence also was sought in these studies for transfer of the plasmids to indigenous coliforms and, within the sensitivity of the methods used, such transfer was not demonstrated. Experiments favoring plasmid transfer in raw wastewater and in primary biological sludges also failed to demonstrate such mobilization.

Likewise, *E. coli* 2e01C carrying a lambda prophage (λ*cI*857*nin*5 plac5) was removed effectively by wastewater treatment; no free lambda phage was observed at any point in the treatment train.

Studies have been completed measuring the survival of an indigenous *E. coli* and *E. coli* K-12 in these treatment plant models as well. The results of experiments utilizing such genetically tagged organisms confirm an earlier report that conventional domestic wastewater treatment processes will result in at least two $\log_{10}$ reductions in concentration of indigenous EK1 and EK2 organisms. These results are similar to those obtained with the indigenous wastewater microflora. Further reduction of these host-vector populations will depend on appropriate sludge treatment and effluent disinfection.

This work was supported by Contract NO1-AI-82566, University of Texas, San Antonio, Bernard Sagik, principal investigator.

(3) The contractor who was performing tests in mice and in cultures made significant progress during the intervening year. The most notable result was the establishment of a mathematical model to study the exchange of plasmids between normal hosts and indigenous bacteria.

Plasmid transfer in continuous flow (CF) cultures of defined or natural intestinal flora occurred with similar efficiency as in pure cultures *in vitro*. One can conclude that the capacity of *E. coli* K-12 strains to function as plasmid donors or recipients was not impaired by the presence of an indigenous microflora. *E. coli* Chi 1776 donated plasmid R1drd19 with somewhat lower efficiency than a standard *E. coli* K-12 donor.

Plasmid transfer in mice harboring a defined intestinal microflora appears to have the same degree of efficiency as in the CF cultures, because the rate constants calculated on the basis of the equations are similar to those obtained in CF cultures. However, the validity of this mathematical treatment for mice is not completely certain, because the mathematical model is based on the assumption that the bacteria are freely suspended, which is not likely to be the case in the animal. Nevertheless, the data suggest that plasmid transfer efficiency in the gut should not differ profoundly from that in CF cultures. These conclusions are based on similarities of transfer rate constants as measures of donor and recipient capacity.

The actual rates of transfer are, of course, critically dependent on the concentrations of donors and recipients. The *E. coli* populations in normal mice (and in people) are so low (approx. 10^5 per ml gut content), that little plasmid transfer occurred in the mice after the initial 20 hours of the experiment, i.e., after the large inoculum of donors had passed through the animals. This was true in spite of the fact that the resident *E. coli* were artificially implanted, highly efficient recipients for the highly efficient conjugative plasmid. It is not very common to find *E. coli* of such high recipient capacity in natural gut flora. Despite the fact that the capacities of the *E. coli* strains to donate or receive the plasmid were not seriously impaired in the gut, the quantitative parameters in the normal gut are such that little actual transfer occurred once the large initial inoculum of donors had been eliminated.

From these data one may tentatively conclude that the probability for triparental transfer of a non-conjugative plasmid in the normal gut would be exceedingly small. The only circumstances in which one could imagine a realistic possibility for triparental transfer to occur, would be at times when abnormally high *E. coli* populations are present in the gut, as may be the case during fasting and other types of stress, in diarrhea, or as a consequence of antibiotic therapy.

These studies were supported by Contract NO1-AI-623518, University of Michigan, Rolf Freter, principal investigator.

(4) The major effort of the contractor who was testing in both mice and humans in the interim has been to initiate triparental mating studies using Chi 1666 (an EK1 host), the plasmid pBR322, and two additional mobilizing plasmids.

The studies are designed to determine if the presence of a mobilizing plasmid in a bacterial host cell can cause the transfer of the non-conjugative pBR322 to the indigenous microflora of either mice or humans.

Two studies have been done in mice. In both cases germ-free mice were colonized with human *E. coli* to provide an array of potential recipients and then fed the Chi 1666 containing the three plasmids. In the first study, 5×10^{9} organisms were fed once and fecal samples from the mice were pooled to facilitate assay; Chi 1666 could only be isolated during the first day of the study. In the second mouse study, the Chi 1666 containing the plasmids were fed daily for 4 days to the mice and their drinking water contained tetracycline. In this latter group the Chi 1666 survived at levels of 10^2/gram or less for the 4 days. In neither case, however, was the pBR322 mobilized to the indigenous flora.

Finally, Chi 1666 containing pBR322 and the two mobilizing plasmids was fed to 4 human subjects. More than 70 fecal samples were collected during the study and a large number of cultures and subcultures (2500) performed. The Chi 1666 survived from 3½ to 7 days and that interval corresponds well with previous data from studies in which Chi 1666 was fed to humans with and without pBR322. While the data for transfer of pBR322 await DNA:DNA colony hybridization and further confirmation, from the data already available on the two transferable plasmids, we can make certain estimates. Highly transferable pSL222-4 was found to transfer to coliforms at a frequency no higher than 8×10^{-6}. This value is 10^{-5} lower than seen when the plasmid is tested under the best laboratory conditions. Thus pBR322, which is transferable by F-like R plasmids at $10^{-5} - 10^{-8}$ would be expected to be transferred at an extremely low frequency; probably below experiemntally detectable levels. The same is presumable true of potential mobilization by the second conjugative plasmid, although the data for their mobilization of pBR322 are not readily available. We would estimate that pBR322 would be transferred at a frequency at least $10^{4} - 10^{5}$ fold less than the conjugatable plasmid, i.e., $10^{-9} - 10^{-10}$.

These studies were supported by Contract N01–AI–72529, Tufts University, Stuart Levy, principal investigator.

b. Progress on the evaluation of the transmission of vectors from *E. coli* K–12 to other bacteria in the gastrointestinal tract of animals and human beings has been made via three approaches.

(1) Data reported in section a. by two of the contractors relates directly to this question.

(2) A meeting was convened on August 30, 1979 at the NIH with the purpose of considering Falmouth Workshop Protocols I and II (Jour. Infect. Dis. *157*, 704–708, 1978) and some related issues. Dr. Stanley Falkow served as Chairman and sixteen participants and NIH staff attended.

Protocol I addressed the colonization and transmission of plasmids from *E. coli* K–12 in the gastrointestinal tract of humans to other bacterial strains in the intestinal flora. The Working Group unanimously recommended that the NIAID not initiate new studies to pursue the investigations as written in Protocol I. This judgment was based on a review of data that existed at the time of the Falmouth Workshop, a consideration of some newer published data and the results of contracts that NIAID was supporting. As written by the Falmouth Workshop Participants, the experiments were to be based on *E. coli* K–12 and this was judged to not be a fruitful experimantal model. It was a clear consensus of the Group that, based on the available data, it can be predicted that only negative results will be obtained and that limited resources could be better expended in other pursuits.

Protocol II was designed to study the transmission of plasmids from *E. coli* K–12, including Chi 1776, into the normal intestinal flora utilizing a germ-free mouse model.

The Working Group unanimously supported the view that the NIAID should not initiate new studies for the Protocol as it was written, but to rely on the contracts to supply some additional data. This judgment was based on the same reasoning and data base considered for Protocol I.

During discussion of the issues cited above it was obvious that the Working Group felt that a more beneficial use of monies would be to support the training of workers in good microbiological laboratory practices and to support research aimed at gaining a better basic scientific understanding of bacterial colonization and plasmid mobilization. Toward this last goal the Working Group strongly recommended that the NIAID support studies that could obtain quantitative data, expand scientific knowledge in an important area and which may prove useful at some future date for risk assessment. The Group felt that such studies should be performed directly in humans and employ wild type *E. coli* (not K–12). Strain HS containing pBR325 was suggested as a good initial combination, and the study should be developed to assay for both survival and transfer to the indigenous flora. [These studies are now in their early stages and being performed by an NIAID contractor at the University of Maryland Medical School.]

The full transcript of this meeting and a verbal report was made to RAC at their March 1980 meeting and the recommendations were approved by that Committee.

(3) NIAID identified two relevant grant applications, and the National Advisory Allergy and Infectious Diseases Council supported selective payment of these projects for inclusion into the risk assessment program.

One grantee (Dr. Rolf Freter, University of Michigan, AI 15279) will focus on the mechanisms that control human and animal gut flora. Of the four stated proposed aims of the research plan three relate to issues of importance to the NIH Recombinant DNA Risk Assessment Program. They are: (1) characterize and extend the application of anaerobic continuous flow cultures, (2) analyze the efficiency of plasmid and bacteriophage transfer, and (3) determine whether human microflora can be maintained in gnotobiotic mice and in anaerobic continuous flow cultures. The issue of mobilization of vector plasmids to the indigenous flora has always been a concern when considering the use of *E. coli* K–12 based host-vector systems. Most recently concern has been expressed over the potential for exchange of plasmids in the intestinal tract between the Enterobacteriaceae and the anaerobic flora, principally members of the genus Bacteroides. This project has the capacity for filling a significant void in experimental data.

A second grantee (Dr. Paul Cohen, University of Rhode Island, AI 16370) will be exploring a related issue which focuses on the molecular mechanisms of *E. coli* colonization of the intestine, specifically on the relative importance of plasmid or chromosomal determinants of colonization.

At this point in time the majority of experiments using recombinant DNA technology employ host-vector systems based on *E. coli* K–12 and its plasmids or bacteriophages. Prominent among the scenarios raised early in the debate over use of this technology was the possible colonization of the intestinal tract by host-vector systems followed by various consequences due to the elaboration of a product which would cause harm to the individual by either direct or indirect mechanisms. There now are a considerable number of studies describing the survival of various types of *E. coli* in the intestinal tracts of man and mice and they demonstrate a tremendous disparity in the survivability and colonization potential of such strains. A complete understanding of those factors that control survival and colonization may permit the development of both safer and more useful *E. coli* hosts in the future as well as perhaps provide data suggesting adjustments in the physical containment requirements of the NIH Guidelines governing use of this technology.

c. Experiments testing *E. coli* K–12 host-vector systems carrying recombinant DNA for virulence have been done by NIH scientists (Dr. Malcolm Martin and colleagues). The studies were designed to determine the pathogenicity and stability of shotgun clones of *Saccharomyces* DNA when used with both plasmid and bacteriophage vectors. In this experimental model, which utilized mice, there was no evidence that the presence of segments of the entire yeast genome altered the inherently low pathogenicity of *E. coli* K–12 in any way.

d. A Workshop was convened to consider two areas [within the NIH Program] recommended by the Risk Assessment Subcommittee of RAC. This Workshop was designed to define the scientific issues and assess the potential risks of: (a) Possible direct adverse effects of hormone-producing strains of *E. coli* K–12 and (b) The possible occurrence of autoantibodies or autoreactive cells due to the production of eukaryotic polypeptides (including hormones) by *E. coli* K-12 should they colonize higher organisms.

In the charge to the Workshop it was noted that these potential risks were under consideration because there is still debate over the degree of possible risk, even though *E. coli* K-12 has apparently lost those characteristics that are required for colonization of the normal intestinal tract.

The purpose was to decide whether the two specific possibilities are valid scientific hypotheses if such an event did occur; and if valid, to determine if sufficient experimental data already exist to make a final judgment concerning possible risk. If data were insufficient, the participants were asked to outline those types of studies necessary to develop the definitive information on these issues.

The meeting brought together 92 scientists from the fields of immunology, endocrinology, physiology, microbiology, infectious diseases and other appropriate disciplines. The Chairmen's Summary and a full transcript of the Final Plenary Session were distributed to all participants and also to the RAC for their review at the June 1980 meeting. In addition to the report of the Director, NIAID, Drs. Setlow and Campbell, members of the RAC, prepared a separate report and the RAC Risk Assessment Subcommittee alos reported their analysis of the Workshop.

NIAID plans in implementing the four prime recommendations were influenced by the RAC discussions. At this time we propose to respond to the recommendations as follows:

(1) It was recommended that experiments of the following general type should be performed: "*E. coli* cells carrying recombinant DNA and making a mammalian protein are introduced into living animals under conditions where they cause genuine infection (e.g., an abscess), with subsequent monitoring for breakdown of immune tolerance."

This subject stimulated the most discussion during the final plenary session of the Workshop. The sentiment was to acquire the data as a matter of scientific interest rather than to answer the risk assessment question. An RFP was developed to solicit proposals from interested investigators. Immunologists from the NIAID staff designed the experimental protocol for the workscope and other specifications of the study.

(2) Additional information was requested on the handling and absorption of polypeptides from the normal and pathologic colon, and the potential effects of synthetic peptides on the bowel itself.

We have confirmed that this is an issue about which there are little direct data. The Workshop participants opined that although their own calculations revealed that only extremely small amounts of hormones would be produced under the most ideal conditions, data should still be sought for potential future needs. The issue of the potential effects of synthetic peptides on the bowel itself is different from that of hormones, and that discussion was centered on interferon and its direct effect on cells.

Although this will be a difficult study to initiate because of the technical difficulties as well as the process for approval of research in human subjects, NIAID is considering solicitation of grant proposals through a Request for Applications (RFA). The study will have as its objective a determination of the fate of peptide hormones when deposited in the distal small intestine and large intestine of humans. These sites are relevant to the production of hormones by recombinant DNA technology because they represent the regions of colonization by *E. coli*.

(3) It was suggested that additional information is needed on the potential transfer of plasmids to anaerobic bacteria from *E. coli*. This recommendation differs from the findings of the *ad hoc* group convened in August 1979 which RAC reviewed at the march 1980 meeting. That expert Group noted that by studying the epidemiology of plasmids the conjugative plasmids of *E. coli* are not found within the anaerobic flora of the gut. The uniform use of nonconjugative plasmids in rDNA research further reduces the likelihood of transfer

It is likely that the requested data will be forthcoming from NIH (NIAID) supported studies on plasmids through the regular grant-supporter research programs and that new initiatives are not needed. In fact, the NIAID Advisory Council identified a grant application (AI 15279) for selective payment that addressed some aspects of this issue; this action will initiate the acquisition of the data at an early date. There is no plan to develop a RFA at this time but NIAID staff will continue to identify all appropriate incoming applications as potential sources of data.

(4) It was recommended the NIH communicate with the Centers for Disease Control (CDC) about possible types of health surveillance for workers using recombinant DNA.

A CDC representative was present at the Pasadena meeting and discussed some approaches to this issue. Furthermore, representatives of the National Institute for Occupational Safety and Health and the Occupational Safety and Health Administration were also present and therefore, are cognizant of the Workshop recommendation. All of these agencies are members of The Industrial Practices Subcommittee of The Federal Interagency Advisory Committee on Recombinant DNA Research.

e. NIH scientists have continued a further evaluation of the biological activity of polyoma virus DNA cloned in *E. coli* host-vector systems. It had been reported (Science *203:* 883–892, 1979), when the Final Plan was initially published, that polyoma DNA was noninfectious when cloned in EK2 plasmid and bacteriophage host-vector systems.

As a further step in evaluating the biologic activity of the polyoma-plasmid and polyoma-lambda recombinant DNA host-vector systems, the scientists tested the ability of the EK2 systems containing polyoma DNA to induce tumors in suckling hamsters.

These animals are highly sensitive to tumor induction by polyoma virus and in some cases even subgenomic fragments of viral DNA can induce tumors in them. The results (Science *205:* 1140–1142, 1979) indicated that inoculation of suckling hamsters with 2×10^6 live cells of *E. coli* K-12 strain Chi 1776 carrying the complete genome of polyoma virus in a recombinant plasmid, failed to induce tumors in any of 32 recipients. Also, lambda phage DNA and particles with a monomeric insert of polyoma DNA did not induce tumors. Purified recombinant plasmid DNA, as well as phage particles and DNA containing a head-to-tail dimer of polyoma DNA, showed a low degree of oncogenicity, comparable to that of polyoma DNA prepared from mouse cells. These findings support the previous conclusions, based on infectivity assays in mice, that propagation of polyoma virus DNA as a component of recombinant DNA molecules in *E. coli* K-12 reduces its biologic activity many orders of magnitude relative to the virus itself.

Currently both the infectivity and tumorigenicity experiments are being extended. In one, *E. coli* K-12 (EK1) containing recombinant plasmids consisting of two copies of polyoma virus DNA and one copy of pBR322 plasmid DNA are being incoculated into newborn hamsters and weanling mice. It is also planned to test lambdaphage lysogens (*E. coli* K-12 containing one or two copies of a lambda bacteriophage-polyoma virus DNA recombinant integrated into the bacterial chromosome) by inoculation into ppropriate animal model systems. esults will be published in the open cientific literature and will be resented in a subsequent update of the inal Plan.

f. NIH scientists are also determining ie biological activity of *E. coli* K–12 ones carrying DNA copies of an RNA imor virus. These studies involve the dministration to hamsters of bacterial reparations containing Harvey arcoma virus DNA ligated to lambda nd pBR322. These studies are still in rogress and when definitive results ave been obtained they will be iblished in the open scientific terature and will appear in a ibsequent update of the Final Plan.

g. Although they had not appeared in ie previous Final Plan, two additional IAID contract-supported projects are eripherally related to the total risk ssessement activities.

(1) RAC had suggested that a model oned DNA segment be constructed to rve as a uniform heterologous DNA gment for risk assessment studies. nis endeavor has been successfully mpleted by an investigator at the niversity of Wisconsin and employed, a source of DNA, the plasmid NR79. ie EcoRI fragment NR79–R1–G1 ntains genes encoding for loramphenicol, kanamycin and lfonamide resistance, as well as the omoters that govern these resistances. R79–R1–G1 was shown not to have an ternal EcoRI site and also not to be pable of replicating by itself or with e help of other plasmids. Experimental sults indicated that NR79–R1–G1 is not pable of autonomous replication and es not contain an origin of replication at can function in a recombinant asmid. The antibiotic resistances coded for by NR79–RI–G1 were tested d found not to be transposable, that is ne movement and insertion at a new e be a mechanism which does not volve the homologous recombination stem of the host strain.

Since the fragment is not capable of tonomous replication, plasmid pJT353, ecombinant plasmid containing t79–R1–G1 cloned into the EcoRI site pBR322, is the suggested way of opagating this fragment. Stocks of *E. li* strain KH802 containing pJT353 ve been preserved for the propagation d isolation of NR79–R1–G1. Protocols ed for the isolation of purified plasmid T353 (NR79–R1–G1 and pBR322) and rified NR79–R1–G1 fragment are ailable.

This work was supported by Contract)1–AI–92606, University of Wisconsin, bert Rownd, principal investigator.

2) A contract has been awarded to University of Minnesota, (Contract NO1–AI–02654, Donald Vesley, principal investigator) to develop a Comprehensive Course on Microbiological Principles and Techniques for Work with Potentially Biohazardous Agents Including Recombinant DNA. The Principal Investigator will work with the Board of Education and Training of the American Society for Microbiology (ASM) in developing the materials.

In 1977, the ASM undertook a study to devise standards of training for recombinant DNA research workers. A proper state of training of the laboratory workers is the first line of containment and it was their opinion that such training standards should be set by knowledgeable professionals. The product of that study was not standards but rather an outline of a body of knowledge which it was felt that any Principal Investigator should be aware of before independently embarking on recombinant DNA research. This contract will develop all necessary resources to present a course based on the ASM findings.

The plan is for the NIAID to support the development of the resource materials and once that phase is completed, the NIH Division of Safety will have the materials reproduced and distributed to the various Institutions where the NIH supports research to assist them in performing their own local training responsibilities. We will devise both a standard lecture/laboratory course and self study aides.

2. *Eukaryotic Host-Vector Systems.*

Lower eukaryotic and higher eukaryotic host/vector systems were given a lower priority in the Final Plan than prokaryotic systems.

After discussion at both the March and June 1980 meetings, the RAC recommended modifying the Guidelines to include *Saccharomyces cerevisiae* host-vector systems under Section III–0. During their consideration the RAC considered information that: (1) *S. cerevisiae* is nonpathogenic, (2) it does not implant in the intestine, (3) the dilute conditions in which it is found in nature are extremely unfavorable for mating, (4) it does not efficiently compete with wild strains of *S. cerevisiae*, and (5) it is fully sensitive to autoclaving and disinfection by standard agents.

RAC also considered the question of proper physical containment for higher eukaryotic viral vectors. The Guidelines have been modified to permit work at more relaxed levels of physical containment than previously required.

The Guidelines have been modified to permit recombinant DNA molecules containing no more than two-thirds of the genome of any eukaryotic virus (all viruses from a single Family being considered identical) to be propagated and maintained in cells in tissue culture using P1 containment. It must be shown that the cells lack helper virus for the specific families of the defective viruses being used. The DNA may contain fragments of the genomes of viruses from more than one family but each fragment must be less than two thirds of a genome.

No initiatives have been started to directly answer the issues raised in the Final Plan relative to eukaryotic host-vector systems. NIH will continue to monitor the results of free ranging research to collect useful data that can be analyzed as part of the risk assessment process.

C. *Implementation.*

The original Final Plan stated that NIAID would recruit and appoint an eminent scientist as a Special Assistant to the Director, NIAID for Risk Assessment. Attempts to recruit a person to fill this position were made including national advertising. No individual with the desired level of credentials and broad recognition by the various scientific disciplines was identified who was willing to under take this work at the NIH under the conditions we could offer. By midyear it had become evident that the probable scope and number of various activities encompassed by the Risk Assessment Plan would probably stabilize at the current level and not increase further. Consequently, the necessity for a Special Assistant was reconsidered and alternatives for satisfying the needs were evaluated. A decision was made to distribute the proposed functions of the Special Assistant to the Office of Recombinant DNA Activities and the Office of Specialized Research and Facilities, both within the NIAID. When appropriate, these offices will use *ad hoc* consultants in fulfilling the tasks originally described for the Special Assistant and for which staff and the RAC Risk Assessment Subcommittee feel that additional or specific expertise is required.

The remainder of the Implementation section of the plan remains in effect as stated. Most implementation actions have been cited earlier in this document. However, an important part of the Plan is the submission of periodic reports to the RAC. In this regard, the Director, NIAID, has reported to the RAC on activities related to risk assessment, and has provided thereby an important and continuing review of progress, and receives the advice or comment of this advisory group.

Dated: June 1, 1981.

Donald S. Fredrickson, M.D.,

Director National Institues of Health.

OMB's "Manadatory Information Requirements for Federal Assistance Program Announcements" (45 FR 39592) requires a statement concerning the official government programs contained in the *Catalog of Federal Domestic Assistance*. Normally NIH lists in its announcements the number and title of affected individual programs for the guidance of the public. Because the guidance in this notice covers not only vitually every NIH program but also essentially every federal research program in which DNA recombinant molecule techniques could be used, it has been determined to be not cost effective or in the public interest to attempt to list these programs. Such a list would likely require several additional pages. In addition, NIH could not be certain that every federal program would be included as many federal agencies, as well as private organizations, both national and international, have elected to follow the NIH Guidelines. In lieu of the individual program listing, NIH invites readers to direct questions to the inform address above about whether individual programs listed in the *Catalog of Federa Domestic Assistance* are affected.

NIH programs are not covered by OM Circular A-95 because they fit the descri of "programs not considered appropriate Section 8-(b)-(4) and (5) of that Circular.

[FR Doc. 81-16632 Filed 6-9-81; 8:45 am]

BILLING CODE 4110-08-M

federal register

Wednesday
July 1, 1981

Part II

Department of Health and Human Services

National Institutes of Health

Recombinant DNA Research; Actions Under Guidelines

DEPARTMENT OF HEALTH AND HUMAN SERVICES

National Institutes of Health

Recombinant DNA Research; Actions Under Guidelines

AGENCY: National Institutes of Health, PHS, DHHS.

ACTION: Notice of Actions under NIH Guidelines for Research Involving Recombinant DNA Molecules.

SUMMARY: This notice sets forth actions taken by the Director, NIH, under the November 1980 NIH Guidelines for Research Involving Recombinant DNA Molecules (45 FR 77384).

EFFECTIVE DATE: July 1, 1981

FOR FURTHER INFORMATION CONTACT: Additional information can be obtained from Dr. William J. Gartland, Office of Recombinant DNA Activities (ORDA), National Institutes of Health, Bethesda, Maryland 20205 (301) 496-6051.

SUPPLEMENTARY INFORMATION: I am promulgating today several major actions under the NIH Guidelines for Research Involving Recombinant DNA Molecules. These proposed actions were published for comment in the **Federal Register** of March 20, 1981, and reviewed and recommended for approval by the Recombinant DNA Advisory Committee (RAC) at its meeting on April 23-24, 1981. In accordance with Section IV-E-1-b of the NIH Guidelines, I find that these actions comply with the Guidelines and present no significant risk to health or the environment.

Following this announcement, there appears in a separate section of the **Federal Register** the revised NIH Guidelines for Research Involving Recombinant DNA Molecules. These revised Guidelines differ from the version of the Guidelines promulgated on November 21, 1980 (45 FR 77384) by incorporating within them both the changes in the Guidelines which were recommended at the RAC meeting of January 8-9, 1981, and promulgated on March 12, 1981 (46 FR 16452), and the changes in the Guidelines which were recommended at the RAC meeting of April 23-24, 1981, and which are discussed in this announcement.

I. Revision of Guidelines for Recombinant DNA Experiments Involving Escherichia Coli K-12 and Saccharomyces Cervisiae Host-Vector Systems

Containment requirements and administrative procedures for the conduct of most recombinant DNA experiments involving EKl *Escherichia coli* strain k-12 and laboratory strain *Saccharomyces cerevisiae* host-vector systems have been specified in Section III-O of the Guidelines. The chairpersons of Institutional Biosafety Committees, at a meeting in Washington, D.C. on November 24-25, 1980, passed by a large majority a resolution that experiments currently covered by Section III-O should be made exempt from the Guidelines. The chairpersons felt that the risks associated with these experiments are negligible, and that exemption of experiments currently covered by Section III-O would reduce paperwork by approximately 90%.

This proposal was discussed by the RAC at its meeting on January 8-9, 1981. In "straw votes" at the meeting, an overwhelming majority of RAC members favored doing something to reduce materially or eliminate the paperwork and reporting functions for experiments covered by Section III-0; about half the RAC members felt serious consideration should be given to exempting entirely from the Guidelines experiments currently covered by Section III-0. The RAC requested that a series of options be developed and published for comment in the **Federal Register.** Accordingly, a series of options was published for comment in the **Federal Register** of March 20, 1981 (46 FR 17994), and considered at the April 23-24, 1981 meeting of the RAC.

Three major options were published for comment. Option A would have allowed review by an institutional official rather than requiring review by the IBC of experiments currently covered by Section III-0. Option B would have eliminated the registration and review requirements for experiments currently covered under Section III-0. Option C would have exempted from the Guidelines experiments currently covered by Section III-0. Under each of these three major options a series of suboptions was proposed for alternative ways of treating certain types of experiments which were already being treated differently from the majority of experiments under Section III-0. These are experiments involving the cloning in *E. coli* K-12 of DNA from Class 3 CDC agents, and experiments involving a deliberate attempt to have *E. coli* K-12 efficiently express a eukaryotic gene. Under Option C, additional suboptions were proposed regarding biological and physical containment, and large-scale experiments (i.e., greater than 10 liters of culture).

During the 30 day comment period, only one commentator responded referring to the proposed changes ɩ "* * * an attempt to bring the Guidelines into a state of consister with present evaluations of the poɩ for hazard in recombinant DNA experiments. As I see that evaluati there is widespread agreement tha experiments involving *E. coli* K-12 *cerevisiae* host-vector systems wil generate harmful organisms. * * * commentator, who wrote after the comment period, was opposed to t proposed changes "until adequate assessment studies have been performed." The RAC discussed th proposed changes at its meeting oɩ April 23. Dr. Edward Adelberg, Chairman, Yale University Institut Biosafety Committee, summarized concerns of the chairpersons of IBɩ their meeting in November 1980. H that the chairpersons voted heavil; favor of an exemption for these experiments, but noted that any or the three proposed options would greatly reduce what was considere unnecessary paperwork. The RAC discussed in detail the various opti and suboptions.

After a series of motions and amendments, the RAC by a vote oɩ favor, 8 opposed, with no abstentiɩ passed Option C with Suboptions ɩ C-2-a, C-3-a, C-4-b as modified a meeting, and C-5-b. Under the recommendation passed by the R experiments currently covered by Section III-0 would be removed fɩ Section III-0. These experiments be exempted under Section I-E-5 exemption would apply to all nonprohibited experiments which either *E. coli* K-12 or laboratory s of *Saccharomyces cerevisiae* as t host-vector system with the follo provisos:

- The exemption would be qual with the statement that "(a) the *E.* host shall not contain conjugation proficient plasmids or generalized transducing phages, and (b) lamb lambdoid or Ff bacteriophages or conjugative plasmids (49) shall be as vectors." This qualification wo then be qualified by the statemen experiments "involving the inserti into *E. coli* K-12 of DNA from prokaryotes that exchange geneti information (35) with *E. coli* may performed with any *E. coli* K-12 ɩ (e.g., conjugative plasmid). When conjugative vector is used, the *E.* 12 host may contain conjugation-proficient plasmids either autono or integrated, or generalized tran phages."
- Language would be added to Guidelines to explicitly make

ohibition I–D–6 concerning large-scale plicable to these experiments.

- The entry in Appendix C which ould effect the exemption under ction I–E–5 would contain a statement at although exempt, for these periments "Pl physical containment nditions are recommended."
- No prior review of experiments volving attempts at deliberate pression of a eukaryotic gene in *E. li* K–12 would be required.
- Experiments involving the DNA of C Class 3 agents would not be empted. Containment might be ecified at P1, P2 or P3, and review by IBC would be required. If there is y chance that the original Class 3 ent can be regenerated from the ned DNA, the containment level shall no lower than that appropriate for agent itself.

accept these recommendations. The t recommendation dealing with Class gents is unclear as to the appropriate ysical containment level, and as to w this level is to be established. To rify this, the following language arding DNA from CDC Class 3 agents i *E. coli* K–12 is being added to pendix C:

Experiments using DNA from Class 3 anisms [1] or from cells known to be ected with these agents will be ducted at P3 containment. Lower tainment levels may be specified by H (See Section IV–E–1–b–(2)–(e)). permiments in this category require or IBC review and approval."

hese decisions regarding *E. coli* K–12 a *Saccharomyces cerevisiae* host- tor systems are being promulgated der Exemption I–E–5, and appear in pendix C of the revised Guidelines.

lthough the movement of eriments currently under Section III–0 the exempt category leaves no ries in Section III–0, I am retaining a S tion III–0 in the Guidelines. In the f ure, experiments may be placed u er Section III–0 by their listing in A endix H to the Guidelines. These e eriments may be performed at P1 p sical containment, and IBC review p r to initiation of the experiment will n be required.

II ontainment Levels for Recombinant D A Experiments Involving Bacillus S tilis

r. Donald Dean of the Ohio State U versity requested that the status of r mbinant DNA experiments i lving *Bacillus subtilis* as host-vector s ems be reevaluated. Currently, two a orogenic *B. subtilis* strains, RUB331 a BGSC 1S53 have been certified, w the plasmids pUB110, pC194, pS194, p 2100, pE194, pT127, pUB112, pC221, pC223, and pAB124, as HV1 host-vector systems.

The asporogenic mutant derivative of *B. subtilis*, ASB298, has been certified with the above plasmids as HV2 host-vector systems.

Dr. Dean proposed that any *Bacillus subtilis* strain which does not revert to a sporeformer with a frequency greater than 10^{-7} can be used for cloning DNA from any nonprohibited source, using vectors indigenous to *B. subtilis*, under the same conditions specified by the RAC for *E. coli* K–12 and *Saccharomyces cerevisiae* host-vector systems.

Dr. Dean further proposed that the following items be added to Appendix E:

"*Bacillus subtilis* strains that do not carry an asporogenic mutation can be used with vectors indigenous to *B. subtilis* for the cloning of DNA from any CDC Class 1 organism under P2 conditions."

"*Bacillus subtilis* strains that do not carry an asporogenic mutation can be used with vectors indigenous to *B. subtilis* under P1 conditions for the cloning of DNA from any Class 1 *Bacillus* species."

In support of his proposal, Dr. Dean noted that *B. subtilis* is not a pathogen and that the organism is well characterized, and a great deal is known of its genetics.

An announcement of Dr. Dean's proposal appeared in the **Federal Register** on March 20, 1981 (46 FR 17996). During the thirty day comment period seven letters supporting the proposal were received. One of the letters cited data showing that (1) *Bacillus subtilis* spores either cannot germinate, or upon germination in the ileum or colin die very quickly, and (2) the viable count of *B. subtilis* in soil or water decreases much more rapidly than that of *E. coli*.

The RAC evaluated Dr. Dean's request at the April 23–24, 1981, meeting. Noting that the **Federal Register** language would permit use of "indigenous vectors," the RAC questioned the advisability of permitting use of all *Bacillus* vectors, and recommended excluding from use as vectors any that have as hosts the pathogens, *Bacillus cereus* or *Bacillus anthracis*.

By a vote of 12 in favor, 0 opposed, with 5 abstentions, the RAC voted to recommend that any *Bacillus subtilis* strain which does not revert to a sporeformer with a frequency greater than 10^{-7} can be used for cloning DNA from any nonprohibited source at the same containment conditions as used for *E. coli* K–12 and *Saccharomyces cerevisiae* host-vector systems, using indigenous plasmid and phage vectors whose host range does not include *Bacillus anthracis* or *Bacillus cereus*.

I accept this recommendation, and this decision is being promulgated under Exemption I–E–5, and appears in Appendix C of the revised Guidelines. Information about *Bacillus subtilis* HV1 and HV2 systems has been accordingly removed from Appendix D and placed in Appendix F.

By the same vote, the RAC recommended approval of Dr. Dean's additional two specific proposals concerning *Bacillus subtilis* host-vector systems, with the limitation that *Bacillus* plasmids or phages whose host range includes *Bacillus cereus* or *Bacillus anthracis* may not be used as vectors.

I accept these recommendations and these decisions are promulgated as new entries in Appendix E of the revised Guidelines.

III. Streptomyces HV1 Host-Vector Systems

Dr. Stanley Cohen of Stanford University requested that "*Streptomyces coelicolor* and the related organisms with which *S. coelicolor* naturally exchanges genetic information (e.g., *S. lividans*, *S. parvulus*, and *S. griseus*), using *Streptomyces* plasmids SPC2, SLP1.2, pIJ101, actinophage phiC31, and their derivatives as vectors, be approved as HV1 host-vector systems."

During the 30 day comment period, no comments were received on this proposal.

The RAC reviewed this request at the April 23–24, 1981, meeting, and noted that these organisms are not pathogenic. There has been extensive experience with large-scale culture of these organisms with no known hazards.

By a vote of 10 in favor, 0 opposed, with 8 abstentions, the RAC recommended approval of this proposal. I have reviewed this recommendation, and I am certifying the four specific *Streptomyces* species cited in the proposal as HV1 host-vector systems. These host-vector systems have been added to Appendix D of the Guidelines.

IV. Guidelines for Recombinant DNA Experiments with Genes Coding for Toxins

The RAC, at its September 25–26, 1980, meeting, requested that an *ad hoc* working group be formed to evaluate Section I–D–2 of the Guidelines. Section I–D–2 prohibits the "deliberate formation of recombinant DNAs containing genes for the biosynthesis of toxins potent for vertebrates (2A) (e.g., botulimum or diphtheria toxins; venoms from insects, snakes etc.)." an *Ad hoc* Working Group on Toxins composed of Drs. Werner Maas and Alan Bernheimer of New York University, Dr. John Collier of Yale University, Dr. Michael Gill of Tufts University, Dr. Susan Gottesman of NIH, Dr. Myron Levine of the University of Maryland, and Dr. James Mason of the Utah State Department of Health, was convened to recommend containment conditions for recombinant DNA experiments with genes coding for toxins. The group conversed by telephone on November 4 and November 21, 1980, was convened at the National Institutes of Health on January 7, 1981, and participated in telephone conference calls on February 23 and March 2, 1981. The following proposal, developed by the *ad hoc* group, appeared in the **Federal Register** of March 20, 1981 (46 FR 17996):

"A. Section I-D-2 of Section I-D, Prohibitions, would be amended to read as follows:

"I-D-2. Deliberate formation of recombinant DNAs containing genes for the biosynthesis of toxins lethal for vertebrates at an LD_{50} of less than 100 nanograms per kilogram body weight (e.g., the botulinum toxins, tetanus toxin, *Shigella dysenteriae* neurotoxin). Guidelines for the cloning of DNAs containing genes coding for the biosynthesis of toxins which are lethal to vertebrates at 100 nanograms to 100 micrograms per kilogram body weight are specified in Appendix G.

B. A new Appendix G, would be added to the Guidelines as follows:

Appendix G—Containment Conditions for Cloning of Genes Coding for the Biosynthesis of Toxins for Vertebrates

1. General Information

"Appendix G specifies the containment to be used for the cloning of genes coding for the biosynthesis of toxins for vertebrates. Cloning of genes coding for toxins for vertebrates that have an LD_{50} of less than 100 nanograms per kilogram body weight (e.g., the botulinum toxins, tetanus toxin, *Shigella dysenteriae* neurotoxin) is prohibited. No specific restrictions shall apply to the cloning of genes if the protein specified by the gene has an LD_{50} of 100 micrograms or more per kilogram of body weight. A list of toxins classified as to LD_{50} is available from ORDA. Testing procedures for determining toxicity of toxins not on the list are available from ORDA. The results of such tests shall be forwarded to ORDA, which will consult with the *ad hoc* working group on toxins prior to inclusion of the toxin on the list. (See Section IV-E-1-b-(3)-(i)).

2. Containment Conditions for Cloning of Toxin Genes in E. coli K-12

(a) Cloning of genes coding for toxins for vertebrates that have an LD_{50} in the range of 100 nanograms to 1000 nanograms per kilogram body weight (e.g., diphtheria toxin, abrin, *Clostridium perfringens* epsilon toxin) may proceed under P2+EK2 or P3+EK1 containment conditions.

(b) Cloning of genes for the biosynthesis of toxins for vertebrates with an LD_{50} in the range of 1 microgram to 100 micrograms per kilogram body weight may proceed under Section III-O (e.g., *Staphylococcus aureus* alpha toxin, *Staphylococcus aureus* beta toxin, ricin, *Pseudomonas aeruginosa* exotoxin A, *Bordatella pertussis* toxin, the lethal factor of *Bacillus anthracis*, the *Pasteurella pestis* murine toxins, the oxygen-labile hemolysins such as streptolysin O, and certain neurotoxins present in snake venoms and other venoms).

(c) Some enterotoxins are substantially more toxic when administered enterally than parenterally. The following enterotoxins, whose effects are confined to the stimulation of intestinal secretion and whose effects can be entirely reversed by administration of electrolyte solutions, shall be subject to Section III-O. These are cholera toxin, the heat labile toxins of *E. coli*, *Klebsiella*, and other related proteins that may be identified by neutralization with an antiserum monospecific for cholera toxin, and the heat stable toxins of *E. coli* and of *Yersinia enterocolitica*.

3. Containment Conditions for Cloning of Toxins Genes in Organisms Other Than E. coli K-12

"Requests involving the cloning of genes coding for toxins for vertebrates in host-vector systems other than *E. coli* K-12 will be evaluated by ORDA, which will consult with the *ad hoc* working group on toxins. (See Section IV-E-1-b-(3)-(j)).

C. Section V, Footnote 2A would be modified to delete the words: 'toxins potent for vertebrates (Section I-D-2).'

D. A new Section IV-E-1-b-(3)-(i) would be added as follows: 'IV-E-1-b-(3)-(i). Adding new entries to the list of toxins for vertebrates. (See Appendix G.)'

E. A new Section IV-E-1-b-(3)-(j) would be added as follows: 'IV-E-1-b(3)-(j). Approving the cloning of toxins genes in host-vector systems other than *E. coli* K-12. (See Appendix C.)'"

During the thirty day comment period, no comments were received. However, two letters were received after the thirty day comment period. One expressed concern about experiments involving genes which control bacterial toxins recommended "against relaxation of the Guidelines." The other urged the proposed changes not be made "until adequate risk assessment studies have been performed."

Several members of the *ad hoc* Working Group on Toxins, who were members of the RAC, presented the proposal to the RAC at the April 23-24, 1981, meeting. Working group members characterized the proposal as conservative.

Noting the RAC recommendation at this meeting concerning containment conditions for *E. coli* K-12 and *Saccharomyces cerevisiae* host-vector systems currently covered under Sectio III-O of the Guidelines, *ad hoc* Working Group members recommended that language in the proposed Appendix G b amended. They said the original intent of the *ad hoc* group with regard to cloning genes for toxins with an LD_{50} in the range of 1 to 100 micrograms, as wel as for cloning enterotoxin genes, was to specify P1+EK1 containment. Thy felt i would be inappropriate to "exempt" from the Guidelines the cloning of toxin genes at this time. In response, the RAC recommended that Section 2-(b) and 2-(c) in proposed Appendix G be amende by substituting "P1+EK1" for "Section III-O."

RAC also discussed the appropriateness of the introductory language ". . . whose effects are confined to the stimulation of intestinal secretion and whose effects can be entirely reversed by administration of electrolyte solutions" in Section 2-(c) o proposed Appendix G, and recommended its deletion.

RAC also discussed the intention of the working group that Appendix G specifications override other specifications of the Guidelines (e.g., exemptions or return to host of origin experiments). RAC recommended this conservative approach at this time, an specified wording to be added at the e of Section I-D-2 indicating this.

Finally, RAC indicated a desire that the NIH be kept abreast of experiment dealing with the cloning of toxin genes and amended the proposed language t require prior registration with ORDA experiments involving the cloning of toxin genes.

After incorporating these changes, t RAC by a vote of 18 in favor, 0 oppose with 1 abstention, recommended the following amended language:

A. Section I-D-2 of Section I-D, Prohibitions, would be amended to rea as follows:

I-D-2. Deliberate formation of recombin DNAs containing genes for the biosynthesi of toxins lethal for vertebrates at an LD_{50} o less than 100 nanograms per kilogram bod weight (e.g., the botulinum toxins, tetanus toxin, *Shigella dysenteriae* neurotoxin). Guidelines for the cloning of DNAs containing genes coding for the biosynthes of toxins which are lethal to vertebrates a 100 nanograms to 100 micrograms per kilogram body weight are specified in Appendix G, which overrides other parts the Guidelines (e.g., exemptions, return to host of origin, etc.).

B. A new Appendix G, would read follows:

Appendix G—Containment Conditions for Cloning of Genes Coding for the Biosynthesis of Toxins for Vertebrates

1. General Information

Appendix G specifies the containment to be used for the cloning of genes coding for the biosynthesis of toxins for vertebrates. Cloning of genes coding for toxins for vertebrates that have an LD_{50} of less than 100 nanograms per kilogram body weight (e.g., the botulinum toxins, tetanus toxin, *Shigella dysenteriae* neurotoxin) is prohibited. No specific restrictions shall apply to the cloning of genes if the protein specified by the gene has an LD_{50} of 100 micrograms or more per kilogram of body weight. Experiments involving genes coding for toxins with an LD_{50} of 100 micrograms or less per kilogram body weight shall be registered with ORDA prior to initiating the experiments. A list of toxins classified as to LD_{50} is available from ORDA. Testing procedures for determining toxicity of toxins not on the list are available from ORDA. The results of such tests shall be forwarded to ORDA, which will consult with the *ad hoc* Working Group on toxins prior to inclusion of the toxin on the list. (See Section IV–E–1–b–(3)–(i)).

2. Containment Conditions for Cloning of Toxin Genes in E. coli K–12

(a) Cloning of genes coding for toxins for vertebrates that have an LD_{50} in the range of 100 nanograms to 1000 nanograms per kilogram body weight (e.g., diphtheria toxin, adbrin, *Clostridium perfringens* epsilon toxin) may proceed under P2+EK2 or P3+EK1 containment conditions.

(b) Cloning of genes for the biosynthesis of toxins for vertebrates with an LD_{50} in the range of 1 microgram to 100 micrograms per kilogram body weight may proceed under P1+EK1 containment conditions (e.q., *Staphylococcus aureus* alpha toxin, *Staphylococcus aureus* beta toxin, ricin, *Pseudomonas Aeruginosa* exotoxin A, *Bordatella pertussis* toxin, the lethal factor of *Bacillus anthracis*, the *Pasteurella pestis* murine toxins, the oxygen-labile hemolysins such as streptolysin O, and certain neurotoxins present in snake venoms and other venoms).

(c) Some enterotoxins are substantially more toxic when administered enterally than parenterally. The following enterotoxins shall be subject to P1+EK1 containment conditions: cholera toxin, the heat labile toxins of *E. coli*, *Klebsiella*, and other related proteins that may be identified by neutralization with an antiserum monospecific for cholera toxin, and the heat stable toxins of *E. coli* and of *Yersinia enterocolitica*.

3. Containment Conditions for Cloning of Toxins Genes in Organisms Other Than E. coli K–12

Requests involving the cloning of genes coding for toxins for vertebrates in host-vector systems other than *E. coli* K–12 will be evaluated by ORDA, which will consult with the *ad hoc* working group on toxins. (See Section IV–E–1–b–(3)–(j)).

C. Section V, Footnote 2A would be modified to delete the words: 'toxins potent for vertebrates' (Section I–D–2).

D. A new Section IV–E–1–b–(3)–(i) would be added as follows:

IV–E–1–b–(3)–(i). Adding new entries to the list of toxins for vertebrates. (See Appendix G.)

E. A new Section IV–E–1–b–(3)–(j) would be added as follows:

IV–E–1–b–(3)–(j). Approving the cloning of toxin genes in host-vector systems other than *E. coli* K–12. (See Appendix G.)

I accept these recommendations with additional modifications as stated below.

A further issue concerning cloning of toxin genes was raised by the *ad hoc* Working Group and discussed by RAC during the evaluation of a proposal from Dr. John Murphy of Harvard University, i.e., appropriate containment for cloning the diphtheria toxin gene in *E. coli* K–12 (See below, Part VI of this document). The new Section I–D–2 and Appendix G of the Guidelines uses a cutoff of LD_{50} of 100 nanograms per kilogram of body weight to separate those toxins the cloning of whose genes is prohibited under Section I–D–2 from those allowed to be cloned at P2+EK2 or P3+EK1.

Diphtheria toxin falls very close to this cut-off line. Pharmacological toxicity data for diphtheria toxin demonstrates that the LD_{50} for the most sensitive animal tested, the guinea pig, is 160 nanograms per kilogram body weight. The LD_{50} in humans is estimated to be equal to or less than 100 nanograms per kilogram body weight. This figure was extrapolated from an incident in Japan in which children were inadvertently injected with diphtheria toxin rather than diphtheria toxoid. After much discussion, RAC recommended that experiments by Dr. John Murphy involving the cloning of the gene for the biosynthesis of diphtheria toxin be conducted under P4 physical containment. The RAC realized that this recommendation results in an inconsistency between the recommendation in Appendix G concerning cloning of diphtheria toxin and the recommendation concerning Dr. Murphy's proposal. They noted that cloning the gene for diphtheria toxin could be moved to the prohibited category in general, and Dr. Murphy's proposal could be considered an exemption to the prohibition. Based upon the RAC recommendation and the data available concerning the pharmacological toxicity of diphtheria toxin, I am removing diphtheria toxin from category 2–(a) of Appendix G, "genes coding for toxins that have an LD_{50} in the range of 100 nanograms to 1000 nanograms per kilogram body weight," and placing it under section I–D–2.

Accordingly, revised Section I–D–2 will read as follows:

I–D–2. Deliberate formation of recombinant DNAs containing genes for the biosynthesis of toxins lethal for vertebrates at an LD_{50} of less than 100 nanograms per kilogram body weight (e.g., the botulinum toxins, tetanus toxin, diphtheria toxin, *Shigella dysenteride* neurotoxin). Guidelines for the cloning of DNAs containing genes coding for the biosynthesis of toxins which are lethal to vertebrates at 100 nanograms to 100 micrograms per kilogram body weight are specified in Appendix G, which overrides other parts of the Guidelines (e.g., exemptions, return to host of origin, etc.).

Section 2–(a) of Appendix G will read as follows:

(a) Cloning of genes coding for toxins for vertebrates that have an LD_{50} in the range of 100 nanograms to 1000 nanograms per kilogram body weight (e.g., abrin, *Clostridium perfringens* epsilon toxin) may proceed under P2+EK2 or P3+EK1 containment conditions.

With these modifications, I accept the RAC recommendations concerning the cloning of genes for the biosynthesis of toxins for vertebrates.

Experiments currently underway in *E. coli* K–12 host-vector systems involving genes coding for toxins with an LD_{50} of 100 micrograms or less per kilogram of body weight should be registered with ORDA within 90 days.

It is recognized that the requirements of revised Section I–D–2 and new Appendix G may result in more stringent standards for the cloning of toxin genes than interpretations under the previous Guidelines. Appendix G allows the cloning of toxin genes in *E. coli* K–12 only, and overrides other parts of the Guidelines. Under interpretations of the previous Guidelines, for example, investigators may be conducting recombinant DNA experiments with toxins not listed in Appendix G, or conducting experiments at lower containment levels than now specified in Appendix G, or using host-vector systems other than *E. coli*. K–12 as in "self cloning" experiments. Investigators currently conducting experiments that do not meet the requirements of new Appendix G and that have not already been acted upon individually by NIH must contact ORDA for a case-by-case review within 90 days. However, investigators currently conducting such experiments may continue with their ongoing projects until these projects have been evaluated by NIH.

V. Request for Permission To Clone the Vibrio Cholerae Enterotoxin Gene in E. Coli K-12

Dr. J. J. Mekalanos of Harvard Medical School requested permission to clone in *E. coli* K-12 the *Vibrio cholerae* enterotoxin gene. In support of his request, Dr. Mekalanos noted that *E. coli* elaborates a heat-labile enterotoxin (LT), which has been shown to share a high degree of structural, antigenic and DNA sequence homology with cholera toxin.

Dr. Mekalanos proposes to perform the investigation in three stages; i.e., (1) the cloning in *E. coli* K-12 of DNA restriction fragments of *V. cholerae* known to contain sequences homologous to the A subunit of the LT gene; (2) the cloning in *E. coli* K-12 of DNA restriction fragments of *V. cholerae* containing sequences homologous to the B subunit of the LT gene, and (3) the cloning in *E. coli* K-12 of restriction fragments of *V. cholerae* containing sequences homologous to both the LT A and B subunit genes.

Dr. Mekalanos' request appeared in the Federal Register of March 20, 1981 (46 FR 17997). During the thirty day comment period, no comments were received.

RAC discussed Dr. Mekalanos' request at the April 23-24, 1981 meeting. RAC reviewers indicated that P1+EKl containment would be adequate for all three stages of the proposed experiments. By a vote of 15 in favor, 0 opposed, with 1 abstention, the RAC recommended approval of the proposal at P1+EKl containment.

This recommendation is in agreement with part 2-a of Appendix G dicussed in the previous item of this decision document and is permitted under that part.

VI. Cloning and Expression of DNA Coding for Diphtheria Toxin

Dr. john Murphy of Harvard University, in a letter dated March 11, 1981, proposed to clone in *E. coli* K-12, the 3.9 kb Bam restriction fragment and/or the 8.6 kb Eco fragment of *Corynephage Beta* carrying the stuctural gene for diphtheria toxin.

Dr. Murphy advanced the following arguments in support of his proposal:

(1) Studies of diphtheria toxin-producing organisms would yield valuable data for risk assessment;

(2) The localization of diphtheria toxin in *E. coli* would be determined as well as whether the toxin might be secreted by *E. coli;*

(3) Mutagenesis of the tox gene would be used to elucidate (a) diphtheria toxin interaction with the eukaryotic cell toxin receptor, and (b) the mechanism of fragment A translocation into the eukaryotic cell cytosol.

Dr. Murphy proposed to perform the experiments under P4 conditions at the Frederick Cancer Research Center or at the NIH if the RAC recommended the P4 level of containment.

A Federal Register announcement of Dr. Murphy's requet appeared on March 20, 1981 (46 FR 17997). During the thirty day comment period, no comments were received.

The RAC discussed the proposal at the April 23-24, 1981 meeting. Members of the *ad hoc* Working Group on Toxins presented to the RAC the data gathered by the group on diphtheria toxin. The data showed that the LD_{50} in the most sensitive animal tested, the guinea pig, was 160 nanograms per kilogram body weight. The LD_{50} in humans is estimated to be equal to or less than 100 nanograms per kilogram body weight. This figure was estrapolated from an incident in Japan in which children were inadvertently injected with diphtheria toxin rather than diphtheria toxoid. By a vote of 15 in favor, 0 opposed, with 1 abstention, the RAC recommended approval of Dr. Murphy's proposal at P4 containment.

I accept this recommendation, and the following entry, number 30, is added to Appendix E:

Permission is granted to clone in *E. coli* K-12 under P4 containment conditions, restriction fragments of *Corynephage Beta* carrying the structural gene for diphtheria toxin.

VII. Proposals Involving the Expression of Foot and Mouth Disease Viral Coat Proteins in Saccharomyces Cerevisiae, Bacillus Subtilis, and Tissue Culture Systems

The RAC at its April 23-24, 1981 meeting reviewed proposed experiments jointly submitted by Genentech, Inc., South San Francisco, California, and the United States Department of Agriculture, Plum Island Animal Disease Center, Greenport, New York, to study the expression of Foot and Mouth Disease Virus (FMDV) sequences in *Bacillus subtilis, Saccharomyces cerevisiae,* and mammalian tissue culture systems, with the goal of production of a viral subunit vaccine for Foot and Mouth Disease. This proposal was an extension of their prior NIH approved proposal for the study of the expression of the capsid protein of FMDV in *E. coli* K-12.

A summary of the request was published for comment in the Federal Register of March 20, 1981 (46 FR 17996). During the 30 day comment period, no comments were received on the proposals.

The RAC recommended that the work be permitted at P1 physical containment with both the *B. subtilis* and *S. cerevisiae* aproved host-vector systems if the subgenomic FMD segments were restricted to those sequences which map between 500 and 4100 of the FMD viral genome. Separate motions to approve these experiments at P1 physical containment under the conditions set forth above were passed by votes of 16 in favor, 0 opposed, with 2 abstentions.

I accept these recommendations with the added stipulation that HV1 hostvector systems be used, as specified in the Genentech request, and an appropriate entry has been made in Appendix E.

In the RAC discussion on the proposed experiments using a SV40 virus vector for cloning the FMD capsid segments in mammalian tissue culture, concern was raised about the potential for recombination between an adventitious picornavirus in the cell culture with the SV40 and FMD viral sequences. The RAC recommended by a vote of 17 in favor, 0 opposed, with 1 abstention, that cloning of FMD capsid protein sequences employing a SV40 deletion vector in a mammalian tissue culture system at the Plum Island laboratories by approved in principle under P3 physical containment. The approval is subject to review by the Working Group of individual experiments.

I accept this recommendation, and an appropriate entry has been made in Appendix E.

VIII. Containment Levels for Recombinant DNA Experiments Involving Neurospora Crassa

Dr. David Perkins of Stanford University proposed that entry 2 in Appendix E be amended to read as follows:

Unmodified laboratory strains of *Neurospora crassa* can be used in all experiments for which HV1 *N. crassa* systems are approved, provided that only DNA from Class 1 agents is used. For agents other than Class 1, unmodified laboratory strains of *N. crassa* can be used in all experiments for which HV1 *N. crassa* system are approved, provided that these are carried out at physical containment one level higher than required for HV1. However, if P3 containment is specified for HV1 *N. crassa,* this level is considered adequate for unmodified *N. Crassa.* Care must be exercised to prevent aerial dispersal of macroconidia, in accordance with good laboratory practice.

Mutationally modified strains of *N. crassa* specified as HV1 in Appendix D can be used in all experiments for which HV2 *N. crassa* systems are approved, provided that only DNA from Class 1 agents is used.

In the submission, Dr. Perkins argued that present containment levels cannot be justified by any demonstrated hazard, especially when only Class 1 agents are involved, and that present containment levels impose a serious and unnecessary handicap on genetic analysis of *Neurospora*.

Three letters were received strongly supporting this proposal. One commentator said that it was his experience that contamination by airborne *Neurospora* conidia is not a serious problem. Another commentator stated:

> . . . Since *Neurospora crassa* is not a pest or pathogen, there is no justification for imposing more stringent containment conditions for research with Neurospora than for investigations with yeast or animal viruses. The current Guidelines are seriously hindering the use and development of Neurospora as a subject for recombinant DNA research.

The RAC recommended approval of the proposal by a vote of 10 in favor, 0 opposed, with 5 abstentions.

I accept this recommendation, and entry 2 of Appendix E has been modified to reflect this decision.

X. Request to Employ a Conjugative Plasmid To Transfer Neurospora Crassa DNA

Dr. Norman Giles of the University of Georgia in a letter dated March 18, 1981, requested permission to use a conjugative plasmid to transfer the *qa-2* gene of *Neurospora crassa* among *E. coli* K–12 strains. The *N. crassa qa–2* gene would be ligated into a derivative (pVK57) of the mobilized plasmid RSF2124.

In support of his proposal, Dr. Giles argued that (1) no *Neurospora* protein other than the *qa-2* protein (catabolic dehydroquinase) is produced in *E. coli* transformed with plasmid pVK57; no hybrid or non-functional proteins are produced, and (2) the catabolic dehydroquinase synthesized by *Neurospora* is identical to that synthesized by *E. coli*, based on heatstability, sedimentation, and amino acid composition. In addition, fragments close to the NH_2-terminal end have been sequenced and are identical in *E. coli* and *Neurospora crassa*.

A **Federal Register** announcement of Dr. Gilles' request appeared on March 20, 1981 (46 FR 17997). During the thirty day comment period, no comments were received.

The RAC discussed the request at its April 23–24, 1981 meeting. Noting that the *qa-2* fragment was relatively well-defined, RAC recommended approval of the proposal by a vote of 17 in favor, 0 opposed, with no absentions. P2 containment conditions were specified.

I accept this recommendation. A new entry, number 33, has been added to Appendix E as follows:

> A conjugative plasmid may be used to transfer among *E. coli* K–12 strains at P2 physical containment the qa-2 gene of *Neurospora crassa* ligated to a mobilizable plasmid.

X. Request To Use An E. Coli Strain Containing Mu Phage Insertions

Dr. Darold Holten of the University of California at Riverside, in a letter dated March 18, 1981, requested permission to utilize the *E. coli* strain DF214 (or derivatives thereof), and plasmid vectors (e.g., pBR322, pBR325) to clone rat cDNA. Strain DF214, a K–12 derivative, contains (1) a Mu phage insertion in the phosphoglucose isomerase gene, and (2) a Mu lysogen in an unknown location. Dr. Holten calculates the frequency of Mu lysis and transduction in DF214 to be of the order of 10^{-12} to 10^{-14}.

The **Federal Register** of March 20, 1981 (46 FR 17997) carried an announcement of Dr. Holten's proposal. No comments were received during the thirty day comment period.

The RAC discussed the proposal at the April 23–24, 1981 meeting and recommended by a vote of 17 in favor, 0 opposed, with no absentions, that the initial screening of the rat library be done at P2 containment; after the clone of interest has been purified, it may be worked with at P1 containment.

I accept this recommendation, and a new entry, item 34, will be added to Appendix E as follows:

> *E. coli* K–12 strain DF214 (or derivatives thereof) and plasmid vectors (e.g., pBR322, pBR325) may be used to clone rat cDNA under P2 conditions. After the clone of interest has been purified, it may be worked with under P1 containment.

Additional Announcements of The Director, NIH

Section IV–E–1–b–(3)–(d) of the Guidelines gives responsibility to the Director, NIH, for "authorizing, under procedures specified by the RAC, large-scale experiments (i.e., involving more than 10 liters of culture) for recombinant DNAs that are rigorously characterized and free of harmful sequences."

Accordingly, several requests for authorization to culture, on a large-scale, recombinant DNA host-vector systems have been received and reviewed by the NIH.

I. Professor Barry T. Nall

On June 16, 1981, the Director, NIH, on the recommendation of the RAC, approved a request from Professor Barry T. Nall, University of Texas Health Science Center at Houston, Houston, Texas 77025, for the large-scale culture of EK1 host-vector systems into which have been ligated recombinant DNA plasmids containing *E. coli* DNA and *Saccharomyces cerevisiae* genes for cytochrome *c*.

The principal investigator is Dr. Nall. The work is to be done at the P1–LS level.

II. Cetus Corporation

On june 16, 1981, the Director, NIH, on the recommendation of the RAC, approved requests from Cetus Corporation, 600 Bancroft Way, Berkeley, California 94710, for large-scale culture of Ek1 *E. coli* or NV1 *Bacillus subtilis* containing plasmids coding for human beta-1 fibroblast interferon.

The request was approved with the understanding that Cetus Corporation has agreed to permit an observer, designated by NIH, to visit the facilities if NIH should choose to inspect the site.

The principal investigators or Drs. Michael W. Conrad and Wolfgang H. Hanisch. The work is to be done at the P1–LS level.

III. Johns Hopkins University

On June 16, 1981, the Director, NIH, on the recommendation of the RAC, approved a request from Professor Hamilton O. Smith, Johns Hopkins University School of Medicine, Baltimore, Maryland 21205, for the large-scale culture of *E. coli* containing recombinant plasmids comprised of *E. coli* and *Haemophilus haemolyticus* DNA; the *Haemophilus* DNA consists of two of the genes that constitute the *Hha*II restriction/modification system.

Professor Smith is the principal investigator. The work is to be done at the P1–LS level.

Dated: June 22, 1981.

Donald S. Fredrickson, M.D.,

Director, National Institutes of Health.

Note.—OMB's "Mandatory Information Requirements for Federal Assistance Program Announcements" (45 FR 39592) requires a statement concerning the official government programs contained in the *Catalog of Federal Domestic Assistance*. Normally NIH lists in its announcements the number and title of affected individual programs for the guidance of the public. Because the quidance in this notice covers not only vitually every NIH program but also essentially every federal research program in which DNA recombinant molecule techniques could be used, it has been determined to be not cost effective or in the publc interest to attemp to list these program. Such a list would likely require several additional pages. In addition, NIH could not be certain that every federal program would be included as many federal agencies, as well as private organizations, both national and international, have elected to follow the NIH Guidelines. In lieu of the individual program listing, NIH invites readers to direct questions to the information address above about whether individual programs listed in the *Catalog of Federal Domestic Assistance* are affected.

NIH programs are not covered by OMB Circular A-95 because they fit the descript of "programs not considered appropriate" i Section 8-(b)-(4) and (5) of that Circular.

[FR Doc. 81-19036 Filed 6-30-81; 8:45 am]

BILLING CODE 4110-08-M

federal register

Wednesday
July 1, 1981

Part III

Department of Health and Human Services

National Institutes of Health

Guidelines for Research Involving Recombinant DNA Molecules June 1981

DEPARTMENT OF HEALTH AND HUMAN SERVICES

National Institutes of Health

Guidelines for Research Involving Recombinant DNA Molecules June 1981

These NIH guidelines supersede those of November 1980, and will be in effect until further notice.

Table of Contents

I. Scope of the Guidelines

I-A. *Purpose.* The purpose of these Guidelines is to specify practices for construction and handling (i) recombinant DNA molecules and (ii) organisms and viruses containing recombinant DNA molecules.

I-B. *Definition of Recombinant DNA Molecules.* In the context of these Guidelines, recombinant DNA molecules are defined as either (i) molecules which are constructed outside living cells by joining natural or synthetic DNA segments to DNA molecules that can replicate in a living cell, or (ii) DNA molecules that result from the replication of those described in (i) above.

I-C. *General Applicability.* See Section IV-B.

I-D. *Prohibitions.* The following experiments are not to be initiated at the present time:

I-D-1. Formation of recombinant DNAs derived from the pathogenic organisms classified (*1*) as Class 4 or 5 (*2*) or from cells known (*2A*) to be infected with such agents, regardless of the host-vector system used.

I-D-2. Deliberate formation of recombinant DNAs containing genes for the biosynthesis of toxins lethal for vertebrates at an LD_{50} of less than 100 nanograms per kilogram body weight (e.g., the botulinum toxins, tetanus toxin, diphtheria toxin, *Shigella dysenteriae* neurotoxin). Guidelines for the cloning of DNAs containing genes coding for the biosynthesis of toxins which are lethal to verebrates at 100 nanograms to 100 micrograms per kilogram body weight are specified in Appendix G, which overrides other parts of the Guidelines (e.g., exemptions, return to host of origin, etc.).

I-D-3. [Deleted]

I-D-4. Deliberate release into the environment of any organism containing recombinant DNA.

I-D-5. Deliberate transfer of a drug resistance trait to microorganisms that are not known to acquire it naturally, if such acquisition could compromise the use of a drug to control disease agents in human or veterinary medicine or agriculture. (*2A*)

I-D-6. Large-scale experiments (e.g., more than 10 liters of culture) with organisms containing recombinant DNAs, unless the recombinant DNAs are rigorously characterized and the absence of harmful sequences established (*3*). (See Section IV-E-1-b-(3)-(d).)

I-D (1-6). Experiments in Categories I-D-1 to I-D-6 may be excepted (*4*) from the prohibitions (and will at that time be assigned appropriate levels of physical and biological containment) provided that these experiments are expressly approved by the Director, National Institutes of Health (NIH), with advice of the Recombinant DNA Advisory Committee (RAC), after appropriate notice and opportunity for public comment. (See Section IV-E-1-b-(1)-(e).)

Experiments in Categories I-D-1, I-D-2, I-D-5, and experiments involving "wild type" host-vector systems are expected from the prohibitions, provided that these experiments are designed for risk-assessment purposes and are conducted within the NIH high-containment facilities located in Building 41-T on the Bethesda campus and in Building 550 located at the Frederick Cancer Research Center. The selection of laboratory practices and containment equipment for such experiments shall be approved by the Office of Recombinant DNA Activities (ORDA) following consultation with the RAC Risk Assessment Subcommittee and the NIH Biosafety Committee. ORDA shall inform RAC members of the proposed risk-assessment projects at the same time it seeks consultation from the RAC Risk Assessment Subcommittee and the NIH Biosafety Committee. If a major biohazard is detemined, the clones will be destroyed after the completion of the experiment rather than retaining them in high containment facility. Other clones that are non-hazardous or not of major hazard will be retained in the high containment.

I-E. *Exemptions.* It must be emphasized that the following exemptions (*4*) are not meant to apply to experiments described in the Sections I-D-1 to I-D-5 as being prohibited. In addition, any recombinant DNA molecules involving DNA from Class 3 organisms (*1*) or cells known to be infected with these agents, or any recombinant DNA molecules which increase the virulence and host-range of a plant pathogen beyond that which occurs by natural genetic exchange, are not exempt unless specifically so designated by NIH under Section I-E-5. Also, Appendix G overrides the exemptions for specified experiments involving genes coding for toxins.

The following recombinant DNA molecules are exempt from these Guidelines, and no registration with NIH is necessary.

I-E-1. Those that are not in organisms or viruses. (*5*)

I-E-2. Those that consist entirely of DNA segments from a single nonchromosomal or viral DNA source, though one or more of the segments may be a synthetic equivalent.

I-E-3. Those that consist entirely of DNA from a prokaryotic host, including its indigenous plasmids or viruses, when propagated only in that host (or a closely related strain of the same species) or when transferred to another host by well established physiological means; also those that consist entirely of DNA from a eukaryotic host, including its chloroplasts, mitochondria, or plasmids (but excluding viruses), when propagated only in that host (or a closely related strain of the same species).

I-E-4. Certain specified recombinant DNA molecules that consist entirely of DNA segments from different species that exchange DNA by known physiological processes, though one or more of the segments may be a synthetic equivalent. A list of such exchangers will be prepared and periodically revised by the Director, NIH, with advice of the RAC, after appropriate notice and opportunity for public comment. (See Section IV-E-1-b-(1)-(d).) Certain classes are exempt as of publication of these Revised Guidelines. The list is in Appendix A. An updated list may be obtained from the Office of Recombinant DNA Activities, National Institutes of Health, Bethesda, Maryland 20205.

I-E-5. Other classes of recombinant DNA molecules, if the Director, NIH, with advice of the RAC, after appropriate notice and opportunity for public comment, finds that they do not present a significant risk to health or the environment. (See Section IV-E-1-b-(1)-(d).) Certain classes are exempt as of publication of these Revised Guidelines. The list is in Appendix C. An updated list may be obtained from the Office of Recombinant DNA Activities; National Institutes of Health, Bethesda, Maryland, 20205.

I-F. *General Definitions.* See Section IV-C.

II. Containment

Effective biological safety programs have been operative in a variety of laboratories for many years. Considerable information, therefore, already exists for the design of physical containment facilities and the selection of laboratory procedures applicable to organisms carrying recombinant DNAs. (*6-19*) The existing programs rely upon mechanisms that, for convenience, can be divided into two categories: (i) a set of standard practices that are generally used in microbiological laboratories, and (ii) special procedures, equipment, and laboratory installations that provide physical barriers which are applied in varying degrees according to the estimated biohazard.

Experiments on recombinant DNAs, by their very nature, lend themselves to a third containment mechanism—namely, the application of highly specific biological barriers. In fact, natural barriers do exist which limit either (i) the infectivity of a *vector*, or *vehicle*, (plasmid or virus) for specific hosts or (ii) its dissemination and survival in the environment. The vectors that provide the means for replication of the recombinant DNAs and/or the host cells in which they replicate can be geneticaly designed to decrease by many orders of magnitude the probability of dissemination of recombinant DNAs outside the laboratory.

As these three means of containment are complementary, different levels of containment appropriate for experiments with different recombinants can be established by applying various combinations of the physical and biological barriers along with a constant use of the standard practices. We consider these categories of containment separately here in order that such combinations can be conveniently expressed in the Guidelines.

In constructing these Guidelines, it was necessary to define boundary conditions for the different levels of physical and biological containment and for the classes of experiments to which they apply. We recognize that these definitions do not take into account all existing and anticipated information on special procedures that will allow particular experiments to be carried out under different conditions than indicated here without affecting risk. Indeed, we urge that individual investigators devise simple and more effective containment procedures and

that investigators and institutional biosafety committees recommend changes in the Guidelines to permit their use.

II–A. *Standard Practices and Training.* The first principle of containment is a strict adherence to good microbiological practices. (*6–15*) Consequently, all personnel directly or indirectly involved in experiments on recombinant DNAs must receive adequate instruction. (see Sections IV–D–1–g, IV–D–5–d and IV–D–8–b.). This shall, as a minimum, include instructions in aseptic techniques and in the biology of the organisms used in the experiments, so that the potential biohazards can be understood and appreciated.

Any research group working with agents with a known or potential biohazard shall have an emergency plan which describes the procedures to be followed if an accident contaminates personnel or the environment. The principal investigator must ensure that everyone in the laboratory is familiar with both the potential hazards of the work and the emergency plan. (See Sections IV–D–5–e and IV–D–3–d.) If a research group is working with a known pathogen where there is an effective vaccine it should be made available to all workers. Where serological monitoring is clearly appropriate it shall be provided. (See Sections IV–D–1–h and IV–D–8–c.)

II–B *Physical Containment Levels.* The objective of physical containment is to confine organisms containing recombinant DNA molecules, and thus to reduce the potential for exposure of the laboratory worker, persons outside of the laboratory, and the environment to organisms containing recombinant DNA molecules. Physical containment is achieved through the use of laboratory practices, containment equipment, and special laboratory design. Emphasis is placed on primary means of physical containment which are provided by laboratory practices and containment equipment. Special laboratory design provides a secondary means of protection against the accidental release of organisms outside the laboratory or to the environment. Special laboratory design is used primarily in facilities in which experiments of moderate to high potential hazards are performed.

Combinations of laboratory practices, containment equipment, and special laboratory design can be made to achieve different levels of physical containment. Four levels of physical containment, which are designated as P1, P2, P3, and P4, are described. It should be emphasized that the descriptions and assignments of physical containment detailed below are based on existing approaches to containment of pathogenic organisms. For example, the "Classification of Etiologic Agents on the Basis of Hazard," (*7*) prepared by the Centers for Disease Control, describes four general levels which roughly correspond to our descriptions for P1, P2, P3, and P4; and the National Cancer Institute describes three levels for research on oncogenic viruses which roughly correspond to our P2, P3, and P4 levels. (*8*)

It is recognized that several different combinations of laboratory practices, containment equipment, and special laboratory design may be appropriate for containment of specific research activities. The Guidelines, therefore, allow alternative selections of primary containment equipment within the facilities that have been designed to provide P3 and P4 levels of physical containment. The selection of alternative methods of primary containment is dependent, however, on the level of biological containment provided by the host-vector system used in the experiment. Consideration will also be given by the Director, NIH, with the advice of the Recombinant DNA Advisory Committee to other combinations which achieve an equivalent level of containment. (See Section IV–E–1–b–(2)–(b).) Additional material on physical containment for plant host-vector systems is found in Sections III–C–3 and III–C–4.

II–B–1. *P1 Level.*

II–B–1–a. *Laboratory Practices.*

II–B–1–a–(1). Laboratory doors shall be kept closed while experiments are in progress.

II–B–1–a–(2). Work surfaces shall be decontaminated daily, and immediately following spills of organisms containing recombinant DNA molecules.

II–B–1–a–(3). All biological wastes shall be decontaminated before disposal. Other contaminated materials, such as glassware, animal cages, and laboratory equipment, shall be decontaminated before washing, reuse, or disposal.

II–B–1–a–(4). Mechanical pipetting devices shall be used; pipetting by mouth is prohibited.

II–B–1–a–(5). Eating, drinking, smoking, and storage of foods are not permitted in the laboratory area in which recombinant DNA materials are handled.

II–B–1–a–(6). Persons shall wash their hands after handling organisms containing recombinant DNA molecules and when they leave the laboratory.

II–B–1–a–(7). Care shall be taken in the conduct of all procedures to minimize the creation of aerosols.

II–B–1–a–(8). Contaminated materials that are to be decontaminated at a site away from the laboratory shall be placed in a durable leak-proof container, which is closed before removal from the laboratory.

II–B–1–a–(9). An insect and rodent control program shall be instituted.

II–B–1–a–(10). The use of laboratory gowns, coats, or uniforms is discretionary with the laboratory supervisor.

II–B–1–a–(11). Use of the hypodermic needle and syringe shall be avoided when alternative methods are available.

II–B–1–a–(12). The laboratory shall be kept neat and clean.

II–B–1–b. *Containment Equipment.* Special containment equipment is not required at the P1 level.

II–B–1–c. *Special Laboratory Design.* Special laboratory design is not required at the P1 level.

II–B–2. *P2 Level.*

II–B–2–a. *Laboratory Practices.*

II–B–2–a–(1). Laboratory doors shall be kept closed while experiments are in progress.

II–B–2–a–(2). Work surfaces shall be decontaminated daily, and immediately following spills of organisms containing recombinant DNA molecules.

II–B–2–a–(3). All laboratory wastes shall be steam-sterilized (autoclaved) before disposal. Other contaminated materials such as glassware, animal cages, laboratory equipment, and radioactive wastes shall be decontaminated by a means demonstrated to be effective before washing, reuse, or disposal.

II–B–2–a–(4). Mechanical pipetting devices shall be used; pipetting by mouth is prohibited.

II–B–2–a–(5). Eating, drinking, smoking, and storage of food are not permitted in the laboratory area in which recombinant DNA materials are handled.

II–B–2–a–(6). Persons shall wash their hands after handling organisms containing recombinant DNA molecules and when they leave the laboratory.

II–B–2–a–(7). Care shall be exercised to minimize the creation of aerosols. For example, manipulations such as inserting a hot inoculating loop or needle into a culture, flaming an inoculation loop or needle so that it splatters, and forceful ejection of fluids from pipettes or syringes shall be avoided.

II–B–2–a–(8). Contaminated materials that are to be steam sterilized (autoclaved) or decontaminated at a site away from the laboratory shall be placed in a durable leak-proof container which is closed before removal from the laboratory.

II-B-2-a-(9). Only persons who have been advised of the nature of the research being conducted shall enter the laboratory.

II-B-2-a-(10). The universal biohazard sign shall be posted on all laboratory access doors when experiments requiring P2 containment are in progress. Freezers and refrigerators or other units used to store organisms containing recombinant DNA molecules shall also be posted with the universal biohazard sign.

II-B-2-a-(11). An insect and rodent control program shall be instituted.

II-B-2-a-(12). The use of laboratory gowns, coats, or uniforms is required. Laboratory clothing shall not be worn to the lunch room or outside of the building in which the laboratory is located.

II-B-2-a-(13). Animals not related to the experiment shall not be permitted in the laboratory.

II-B-2-a-(14). Use of the hypodermic needle and syringe shall be avoided when alternative methods are available.

II-B-2-a-(15). The laboratory shall be kept neat and clean.

II-B-2-a-(16). Experiments of lesser biohazard potential can be carried out concurrently in carefully demarcated areas of the same laboratory.

II-B-2-b. *Containment Equipment.* Biological safety cabinets (*20*) shall be used to contain aerosol-producing equipment, such as blenders, lyophilizers, sonicators, and centrifuges, when used to process organisms containing recombinant DNA molecules, except where equipment design provides for containment of the potential aerosol. For example, a centrifuge may be operated in the open if a sealed head or safety centrifuge cups are used.

II-B-2-c. *Special Laboratory Design.* An autoclave for sterilization of wastes and contaminated materials shall be available in the same building in which organisms containing recombinant DNA molecules are used.

II-B-3. *P3 Level.*

II-B-3-a. *Laboratory Practices.*

II-B-3-a-(1). Laboratory doors shall be kept closed while experiments are in progress.

II-B-3-a-(2). Work surfaces shall be decontaminated following the completion of the experimental activity, and immediately following spills of organisms containing recombinant DNA molecules.

II-B-3-a-(3). All laboratory wastes shall be steam-sterilized (autoclaved) before disposal. Other contaminated materials, such as glassware, animal cages, laboratory equipment, and radioactive wastes, shall be decontaminated by a method demonstrated to be effective before washing, reuse, or disposal.

II-B-3-a-(4). Mechanical pipetting devices shall be used; pipetting by mouth is prohibited.

II-B-3-a-(5). Eating, drinking, smoking, and storage of food are not permitted in the laboratory area in which recombinant DNA materials are handled.

II-B-3-a-(6). Persons shall wash their hands after handling organisms containing recombinant DNA molecules and when they leave the laboratory.

II-B-3-a-(7). Care shall be exercised to minimize the creation of aerosols. For example, manipulations such as inserting a hot inoculating loop or needle into a culture, flaming an inoculation loop or needle so that it splatters, and forceful ejection of fluids from pipettes or syringes shall be avoided.

II-B-3-a-(8). Contaminated materials that are to be steam-sterilized (autoclaved) or decontaminated at a site away from the laboratory shall be placed in a durable leak-proof container, which is closed before removal from the laboratory.

II-B-3-a-(9). Entry into the laboratory shall be through a controlled access area. Only persons who have been advised of the nature of the research being conducted shall enter the controlled access area. Only persons required on the basis of program or support needs shall be authorized to enter the laboratory. Such persons shall be advised of the nature of the research being conducted before entry, and shall comply with all required entry and exit procedures.

II-B-3-a-(10). Persons under 16 years of age shall not enter the laboratory.

II-B-3-a-(11). The universal biohazard sign shall be posted on the controller access area door and on all laboratory doors when experiments requiring P3-level containment are in progress. Freezers and refrigerators or other units used to store organisms containing recombinant DNA molecules shall also be posted with the universal biohazard sign.

II-B-3-a-(12). An insect and rodent control program shall be instituted.

II-B-3-a-(13). Laboratory clothing that protects street clothing (e.g., long-sleeve solid-front or Wrap-around gowns, no-button or slipperover jackets) shall be worn in the laboratory. Front-button laboratory coats are unsuitable. Laboratory clothing shall not be worn outside the laboratory and shall be decontaminated before it is sent to the laundry.

II-B-3-a-(14). Raincoats, overcoats, topcoats, coats, hats, caps, and such street outer-wear shall not be kept in the laboratory.

II-B-3-a-(15). Gloves shall be worn when handling materials requiring P3 containment. They shall be removed aseptically immediately after the handling procedure and decontaminated.

II-B-3-a-(16). Animals and plants not related to the experiment shall not be permitted in the laboratory.

II-B-3-a-(17). Vacuum outlets shall be protected by filter and liquid disinfectant traps.

II-B-3-a-(18). Use of hypodermic needle and syringe shall be avoided when alternative methods are available.

II-B-3-a-(19). The laboratory shall be kept neat and clean.

II-B-3-a-(20). If experiments involving other organisms which require lower levels of containment are to be conducted in the same laboratory concurrently with experiments requiring P3-level physical containment, they shall be conductedd in accordance with all P3-level laboratory practices.

II-B-3-b. *Containment Equipment.*

II-B-3-b-(1). Biological safety cabinets (*20*) shall be used for all equipment and manipulations that produce aerosols—e.g., pipetting, dilutions, transfer operations, plating, flaming, grinding, blending, drying, sonicating, shaking, centrifuging—where these procedures involve organisms containing recombinant DNA molecules, except where equipment design provides for containment of the potential aerosol.

II-B-3-b-(2). Laboratory animals held in a P3 area shall be housed in partial-containment caging systems, such as Horsfall units (*19A*), open cages placed in ventilated enclosures, solid-wall and bottom cages covered by filter bonnets, or solid-wall and -bottom cages placed on holding racks equipped with ultraviolet radiation lamps and reflectors. (Note: Conventional caging systems may be used, provided that all personnel wear apropriate personal protective devices. These shall include, at a minumum, wrap-around gowns, head covers, gloves, shoe covers, and respirators. All personnel shall shower on exit from areas where these devices are required.)

II-B-3-b-(3). *Alternative Selection of Containment Equipment.* Experimental procedures involving a host-vector system that provides a one-step higher level of biological containment than that specified in Part III can be conducted in the P3 laboratory using containment equipment specified for the P2 level of physical containment. Experimental procedures involving a host-vector system that provides a one-step lower level of biological containment than that specified in Part III can be conducted in the P3 laboratory using containment equipment specified for the P4 level of physical containment. Alternative combinations of containment safeguards are shown in Table I.

Table I.—*Combinations of Containment Safeguards*

Classification of experiment according to guidelines		Alternate combinations of physical and biological containment			
		Physical containment			Biological containment
Physical containment	Biological[1] containment	Laboratory design specified for	Laboratory practices specified for	Containment equipment specified for	
P3	HV3	P3	P3	P3	HV3.
P3	HV3	P3	P3	P4	HV2.
P3	HV2	P3	P3	P3	HV2.
P3	HV2	P3	P3	P2	HV3.
P3	HV2	P3	P3	P4	HV1
P3	HV1	P3	P3	P3	HV1.
P3	HV1	P3	P3	P2	HV2.

[1] See Section II-D for description of biological containment.

II-B-3-c. *Special Laboratory Design.*

II-B-3-c-(1). The laboratory shall be separated by a controlled access area from areas that are open to unrestricted traffic flow. A controlled access area is an anteroom, a change room, an air lock or any other double-door arrangement that separates the laboratory from areas open to unrestricted traffic flow.

II-B-3-c-(2). The surfaces of walls, floors, and ceilings shall be readily cleanable. Penetrations through these surfaces shall be sealed or capable of being sealed to facilities space decontamination.

II-B-3-c-(3). A foot-, elbow-, or automatically-operated hand-washing facility shall be provided near each primary laboratory exit area.

II-B-3-c-(4). Windows in the laboratory shall be sealed.

II-B-3-c-(5). An autoclave for sterilization of wastes and contaminated materials shall be available in the same building (and perferably within the controlled laboratory area) in which organisms containing recombinant DNA molecules are used.

II-B-3-c-(6). The laboratory shall have a ventilation system that is capable of controlling air movement. The movement of air shall be from areas of lower contamination potential to areas of higher contamination potential (i.e., from the controlled access area to the laboratory area). If the ventilation system provides positive pressure supply air, the system shall operate in a manner that prevents the reversal of the direction of air movement or shall be equipped with an alarm that would be actuated in the event that reversal in the direction of air movement were to occur. The exhaust air from the laboratory areas shall not be recirculated to other areas of the building unless the exhaust air is filtered by HEPA filters or equivalent. The exhaust air from the laboratory area can be discharged to the outdoors without filtration or other means for effectively reducing an accidental aerosol burden provided that it can be dipersed clear of occupied buildings and air intakes.

II-B-3-c-(7). The treated exhaust-air from Class I and Class II biological safety cabinets (*20*) may be discharged either to the laboratory or to the outdoors. The treated exhaust-air from a Class III cabinet shall be discharged directly to the outdoors. If the treated exhaust-air from these cabinets is to be discharged to the outdoors through a building exhaust air system, it shall be connected to this system so as to avoid any interference with the air balance of the cabinet and the building ventilation system.

II-B-4. *P4 Level.*

II-B-4-a. *Laboratory Practices.*

II-B-4-a-(1). Laboratory doors shall be kept closed while experiments are in progress.

II-B-4-a-(2). Work surfaces shall be decontaminated following the completion of the experimental activity and immediately following spills of organisms containing recombinant DNA molecules.

II-B-4-a-(3). All laboratory wastes shall be steam-sterilized (autoclaved) before disposal. Other contaminated materials such as glassware, animal cages, laboratory equipment, and radioactive wastes shall be decontaminated by a method demonstrated to be effective before washing, reuse, or dispoal.

II-B-4-a-(4). Mechanical pipetting devices shall be used; pipetting by mouth is prohibited.

II-B-4-a-(5). Eating, drinking, smoking, and storage of food are not permitted in the P4 facility.

II-B-4-a-(6). Persons shall wash their hands after handling organisms containing recombinant DNA molecules and when they leave the laboratory.

II-B-4-a-(7). Care shall be exercised to minimize the creation of aerosols. For example, manipulations such as inserting a hot inoculating loop or needle into a culture, flaming an inoculation loop or needle so that it splatters, and forceful ejection of fluids from pipettes or syringes shall be avoided.

II-B-4-a-(8). Biological materials to be removed from the P4 facility in a viable or intact state shall be transferred to a nonbreakable sealed container, which is then removed from the P4 facility through a pass-through disinfectant dunk tank or fumigation chamber.

II-B-4-a-(9). No materials, except for biological materials that are to remain in a viable or intact state, shall be removed from the P4 facility unless they have been steam-sterilized (autoclaved) or decontaminated by a means demonstrated to be effective as they pass out of the P4 facility. All wastes and other materials as well as equipment not damaged by high temperature or stream shall be steam sterilzed in the double-door autoclave of the P4 facility. Other materials which may be damaged by temperature or steam shall be removed from the P4 facility through a pass-through fumigation chamber.

II-B-4-a-(10). Materials within the Class III cabinets shall be removed from the cabinet system only after being steam-sterilized in an attached double-door autoclave or after being contained in a nonbreakable sealed container, which is then passed through a disinfectant dunk tank or a fumigation chamber.

II-B-4-a-(11). Only persons whose entry into the P4 facility is required to meet program or support needs shall be authorized to enter. Before entering, such persons shall be advised of the nature of the research being conducted and shall be instructed as to the appropriate safeguards to ensure their safety. They shall comply with instructions and all other required procedures.

II-B-4-a-(12). Persons under 18 years of age shall not enter the P4 facility.

II-B-4-a-(13). Personnel shall enter into and exit from P4 facility only through the clothing change and shower rooms. Personnel shall shower at each egress from the P4 facility. Air locks shall not be used for personnel entry or exit except for emergencies.

II-B-4-a-(14). Street clothing shall be removed in the outer side of the clothing-change areas and kept there.

Complete laboratory clothing, including undergarments, head covers, shoes, and either pants and shirts or jumpsuits, shall be used by all persons who enter the P4 facility. Upon exit, personnel shall store this clothing in lockers provided for this purpose or discard it into collection hampers before entering the shower area.

II–B–4–a–(15). The universal biohazard sign is required on the P4 facility access doors and on all interior doors to individual laboratory rooms where experiments are conducted. The sign shall also be posted on freezers, refrigerators, or other units used to store organisms containing recombinant DNA molecules.

II–B–4–a–(16). An insect and rodent control program shall be instituted.

II–B–4–a–(17). Animals and plants not related to the experiment shall not be permitted in the laboratory in which the experiment is being conducted.

II–B–4–a–(18). Vacuum outlet shall be protected by filter and liquid disinfectant traps.

II–B–4–a–(19). Use of the hypodermic needle and syringe shall be avoided when alternate methods are available.

II–B–4–a–(20). The laboratory shall be kept neat and clean.

II–B–4–a–(21). If experiments involving other organisms which require lower levels of containment are to be conducted in the P4 facility concurrently with experiments requiring P4-level containment, they shall be conducted in accordance with all P4-level laboratory practices specified in this section.

II–B–4–b. *Containment Equipment.*

II–B–4–b–(1). Experimental procedures involving organisms that require P4-level physical containment shall be conducted either in (i) a Class III cabinet system or in (ii) Class I or Class II cabinets that are located in a specially designed area in which all personnel are required to wear one-piece positive-pressure isolation suits.

II–B–4–b–(2). Laboratory animals involved in experiments requiring P4-level physical containment shall be housed either in cages contained in Class III cabinets or in partial containment caging systems (such as Horsfall units (*19A*), open cages placed in ventilated enclosures, or solid-wall and -bottom cages covered by filter bonnets, or solid-wall and -bottom cages placed on holding racks equipped with ultraviolet irradiation lamps and reflectors) that are located in a specially designed area in which all personnel are required to wear one-piece positive-pressure suits.

II–B–4–b–(3). *Alternative Selection of Containment Equipment.* Experimental procedures involving a host-vector system that provides a one-step higher level of biological containment than that specified in Part III can be conducted in the P4 facility using containment equipment requirements specified for the P3 level of physical containment. Alternative combinations of containment safeguards are shown in Table II.

Table II.—*Combinations of Containment Safeguards*

Classification of experiment according to guidelines		Alternate combinations of physical and biological containment			
		Physical containment			Biological containment
Physical containment	Biological containment [1]	Laboratory design specified for	Laboratory practices specified for	Containment equipment specified for	
P4	HV1	P4	P4	P4	HV1.
P4	HV1	P4	P4 [2]	P3	HV2.

[1] See Section II–D for description of biological containment.
[2] In this case gloves shall be worn, in addition to the clothing requirements specified in II–B–4–a–(14).

II–B–4–c. *Special Laboratory Design.*

II–B–4–c–(1). The laboratory shall be located in a restricted-access facility which is either a separate building or a clearly demarcated and isolated zone within a building. Clothing-change areas and shower rooms shall be provided for personnel entry and egress. These rooms shall be arranged so that personnel leave through the shower area to the change room. A double-door ventilated vestibule or ultraviolet air lock shall be provided for passage of materials, supplies, and equipment which are not brought into the P4 facility through the change room area.

II–B–4–c–(2). Walls, floors, and ceilings of the P4 facility are constructed to form an internal shell which readily allows vapor-phase decontamination and is animal- and insect-proof. All penetrations through these structures and surfaces are sealed. (The integrity of the walls, floors, ceilings, and penetration seals should ensure adequate containment of a vapor-phase decontaminant under static pressure conditions. This requirement does not imply that these surfaces must be airtight.)

II–B–4–c–(3). A foot-, elbow-, or automatically-operated handwashing facility shall be provided near the door within each laboratory in which experiments involving recombinant DNA are conducted in openface biological safety cabinets.

II–B–4–c–(4). Central vacuum systems are permitted. The system, if provided, shall not serve areas outside the P4 facility. The vacuum system shall include in-line HEPA filters near each use point or service cock. The filters shall be installed so as to permit in-place decontamination and replacement. Water supply, liquid and gaseous services provided to the P4 facility shall be protected by devices that prevent backflow.

II–B–4–c–(5). Drinking water fountains shall not be installed in laboratory or animal rooms of the P4 facility. Foot-operated water fountains are permitted in the corridors of the P4 facility. The water service provided to such fountains shall be protected from the water services to the laboratory areas of the P4 facility.

II–B–4–c–(6). Laboratory doors shall be self-closing.

II–B–4–c–(7). A double-door autoclave shall be provided for sterilization of material passing out of the P4 facility. The autoclave doors shall be interlocked so that both doors will not be open at the same time.

II–B–4–c–(8). A pass-through dunk tank or fumigation chamber shall be provided for removal from the P4 facility of material and equipment that cannot be heat-sterilized.

II–B–4–c–(9). All liquid effluents from the P4 facility shall be collected and decontaminated before disposal. Liquid effluents from biological safety cabinets and laboratory sinks shall be sterilized by heat. Liquid effluents from the shower and hand washing facilities may be activated by chemical treatment. HEPA filters shall be installed in all vents from effluent drains.

II–B–4–c–(10). An individual supply and exhaust-air ventilation system shall be provided. The system shall maintain pressure differentials and directional air flow as required to ensure inflow from areas outside the facility toward areas of highest potential risk within the facility. The system shall be designed to prevent the reversal of air flow. The system shall sound an alarm in the event of system malfunction.

II–B–4–c–(11). Air within individual laboratories of the P4 facility may be recirculated if HEPA filtered.

II–B–4–c–(12). The exhaust air from the P4 facility shall be HEPA filtered and discharged to the outdoors so that it is dispersed clear of occupied buildings and air intakes. The filter chambers shall be designed to allow *in situ* decontamination before removal and to facilitate certification testing after replacement.

II-B-4-c-(13). The treated exhaust-air from Class I and Class II biological safety cabinets (*20*) may be discharged directly to the laboratory room environment or to the outdoors. The treated exhaust-air from Class III cabinets shall be discharged to the outdoors. If the treated exhaust-air from these cabinets is to be discharged to the outdoors through the P4 facility exhaust air system, it shall be connected to this system so as to avoid any interference with the air balance of the cabinets or the facility exhaust air system.

II-B-4-c-(14). As noted in Section II-B-4-b-(1), the P4 facility may contain specially designed areas in which all personnel are required to wear one-piece positive-pressure isolation suits. Such areas shall be airtight.

The exhaust-air from the suit area shall be filtered by two sets of HEPA filters installed in series, and a duplicate filtration unit and exhaust fan shall be provided. The air pressure within the suit area shall be less than that in any adjacent area. An emergency lighting system, communication systems, and power source shall be provided. A double-door autoclave shall be provided for sterilization of all waste materials to be removed from the suit area.

Personnel who enter this area shall wear a one-piece positive-pressure suit that is ventilated by a life-support system. The life-support system shall be provided with alarms and emergency backup air. Entry to this area is through an airlock fitted with airtight doors. A chemical shower area shall be provided to decontaminate the surfaces of the suit before removal.

II-C. *Shipment.* Recombinant DNA molecules contained in an organism or virus shall be shipped only as an etiologic agent under requirements of the U.S. Public Health Service, and the U.S. Department of Transportation (Section 72.25, Part 72, Title 42, and Sections 173.386-.388, Part 173, Title 49, U.S. Code of Federal Regulations (CFR)) as specified below:

II-C-1. Recombinant DNA molecules contained in an organism or virus requiring P1, P2, or P3 physical containment, when offered for transportation or transported, are subject to all requirements of Section 72.25(c) (1)-(5), Part 72, Title 42 CFR, and Sections 173.386-.388, Part 173, Title 49 CFR.

II-C-2. Recombinant DNA molecules contained in an organism or virus requiring P4 physical containment, when offered for transportation or transported, are subject to the requirements listed above under II-C-1 and are also subject to Section 72.25(c)(6), Part 72, Title 42 CFR.

II-C-3. Additional information on packaging and shipment is given in the "Laboratory Safety Monograph—A Supplement to the NIH Guidelines for Recombinant DNA Research."

II-D. *Biological Containment.*

II-D-1. *Levels of Biological Containment.* In consideration of biological containment, the vector (plasmid, organelle, or virus) for the recombinant DNA and the host (bacterial, plant, or animal cell) in which the vector is propagated in the laboratory will be considered together. Any combination of vector and host which is to provide biological containment must be chosen or constructed so that the following types of "escape" are minimized: (i) survival of the vector in its host outside the laboratory and (ii) transmission of the vector from the propagation host to other nonlaboratory hosts.

The following levels of biological containment (HV, or *Host-Vector*, systems) for prokaryotes will be established; specific criteria will depend on the organisms to be used. Eukaryotic host-vector systems are considered in Part III.

II-D-1-a. *HV1.* A host-vector system which provides a moderate level of containment. *Specific systems:*

II-D-1-a-(1). *EK1.* The host is always *E. coli* K-12 or a derivative therof, and the vectors include nonconjugative plasmids (e.g., pSC101, ColE1, or derivatives thereof) (*21-27*)) and variants of bacteriophage, such as lambda (*28-33*). The *E. coli* K-12 hosts shall not contain conjugation-proficient plasmids, whether autonomous or integrated, or generalized transducing phages, except as specified in Section III-O.

II-D-1-a-(2). *Other Prokaryotes.* Hosts and vectors shall be, at a minimum, comparable in containment to *E. coli* K-12 with a non conjugative plasmid or bacteriophage vector. The data to be considered and a mechanism for approval of such HV1 systems are described below (Section II-D-2).

II-D-1-b. *HV2.* These are host-vector systems shown to provide a high level of biological containment as demonstrated by data from suitable tests performed in the laboratory. Escape of the recombinant DNA either via survival of the organisms or via transmission of recombinant DNA to other organisms should be less than 1/10⁸ under specified conditions. *Specific systems:*

II-D-1-b-(1). For EK2 host-vector systems in which the vector is a plasmid, no more than one in 10^8 host cells should be able to perpetuate a cloned DNA fragment under the specified nonpermissive laboratory conditions designed to represent the natural environment, either by survival of the original host or as a consequence of transmission of the cloned DNA fragment.

II-D-1-b-(2). For EK2 host-vestor systems in which the vector is a phage, no more than one in 10^8 phage particles should be able to perpetuate a cloned DNA fragment under the specified nonpermissive laboratory conditions designed to represent the natural environment either (i) as a prophage (in the inserted or plasmid form) in the laboratory host used for phage propagation of (ii) by surviving in natural environments and transferring a cloned DNA fragment to other hosts (or their resident prophages).

II-D-1-c. *HV3.* These are host-vector systems in which:

II-D-1-c-(1). All HV2 criteria are met.

II-D-1-c-(2). The vector is dependent on its propagation host or is highly defective in mobilizability. Reversion to host-independence must be less than $1/10^8$ per vector genome per generation.

II-D-1-c-(3). No markers conferring resistance to antibiotics commonly used clinically or in agriculture are carried by the vector, unless expression of such markers is dependent on the propagating host or on unique laboratory-controlled conditions or is blocked by the inserted DNA.

II-D-1-c-(4). The specified containment shown by laboratory tests has been independently confirmed by specified tests in animals, including primates, and in other relevant environments.

II-D-1-c-(5). The relevant genotypic and phenotypic traits have been indepently confirmed.

II-D-2. *Certification of Host-Vector Systems.*

II-D-2-a. *Responsibility.* HV1 systems other than *E. coli* K-12, and HV2 and HV3 host-vector systems, may not be designated as such until they have been certified by the Director, NIH. Application for certification of a host-vector system is made by written application to the Office of Recombinant DNA Activities, National Institutes of Health, Bethesda, Maryland 20205.

Host-vector systems that are proposed for certification will be reviewed by the National Institutes of Health (NIH) Recombinant DNA Advisory Committee (RAC). (See Section IV-E-1-b-(1)-(c).) This will first involve review of the data on construction, properties, and testing of the proposed host-vector system by a Working Group composed of one or more members of the RAC and other persons chosen because of their expertise in evaluating such data. The Committee will then evaluate the report of the Working Group and any other available information at a regular meeting. The Director, NIH, is responsible for certification after receiving the advice of the RAC. Minor modifications of existing certified host-vector systems, where the modifications are of minimal or no consequence to the properties relevant to containment may be certified by the Director, NIH, without review by the RAC. (See Section IV-E-1-b-(3)-(f).)

When new host-vector systems are certified, notice of the certification will be sent by the Office of Recombinant DNA Activities (ORDA) to the applicant and to all Institutional Biosafety Committees (IBCs) and will be published in the *Recombinant DNA Technical Bulletin*. Copies of a list of all currently certified host-vector systems may be obtained from ORDA at any time.

The Director, NIH, may at any time rescind the certification of any host-vector system. (See Section IV-E-1-b-(3)-(i).) If certification of a host-vector system is rescinded, NIH will instruct investigators to transfer cloned DNA into a different system, or use the clones at a higher physical containment level unless NIH determines that the already constructed clones incorporate adequate biological containment.

Certification of a given system does not extend to modifications of either the host or vector component of that system. Such modified systems must be independently certified by the Director, NIH. If modifications are minor, it may only be necessary for the investigator to submit data showing that the modifications have either improved or not impaired the major phenotypic traits on which the containment of the system depends. Substantial modifications of a certified system require the submission of complete testing data.

II-D-2-b. *Data To Be Submitted for Certification.*

II-D-2-b-(1). *HV1 Systems Other than E. Coli K-12.* The following types of data shall be submitted, modified as appropriate for the particular system under consideration. (i) A description of the organism and vector; the strain's natural habitat and growth requirements; its physiological properties, particularly those related to its reproduction and survival and the mechanisms by which it exchanges genetic information; the range of organisms with which this organism normally exchanges genetic information and what sort of information is exchanged; and any relevant information on its pathogenicity or toxicity. (ii) A description of the history of the particular strains and vectors to be used, including data on any mutations which render this organism less able to survive or transmit genetic information. (iii) A general description of the range of experiments contemplated, with emphasis on the need for developing such an HV1 system.

II-D-2-b-(2). *HV2 systems.* Investigators planning to request HV2 certification for host-vector systems can obtain instructions from ORDA concerning data to be submitted (*33A, 33B*). In general, the following types of data are required: (i) Description of construction steps, with indication of source, properties, and manner of introduction of genetic traits. (ii) Quantitative data on the stability of genetic traits that contribute to the containment of the system (iii) Data on the survival of the host-vector system under nonpermissive laboratory conditions designed to represent the relevant natural environment. (iv) Data on transmissibility of the vector and/or a cloned DNA fragment under both permissive and nonpermissive conditions. (v) Data on all other properties of the system which affect containment and utility, including information on yields of phage or plasmid molecules, ease of DNA isolation, and ease of transfection or transformation. (vi) In some cases, the investigator may be asked to submit data on survival and vector transmissibility from experiments in which the host-vector is fed to laboratory animals (e.g., rodents). Such *in vivo* data may be required to confirm the validity of predicting *in vivo* survival on the basis of *in vitro* experiments.

Data must be submitted in writing to ORDA. Ten to twelve weeks are normally required for review and circulation of the data prior to the meeting at which such data can be considered by the RAC. Investigators are encouraged to publish their data on the construction, properties, and testing of proposed HV2 systems prior to consideration of the system by the RAC and its subcommittee. More specific instructions concerning the type of data to be submitted to NIH for proposed EK2 systems involving either plasmids or bacteriophage in *E. coli* K-12 are available from ORDA.

II-D-2-b-(3). *HV3 systems.* Putative HV3 systems must, as the first step in certification, be certified as HV2 systems. Systems which meet the criteria given above under II-D-1-(c)-1, II-D-1-(c)-2, and II-D-1-(c)-3 will then be recommended for HV3 testing. Tests to evaluate various HV2 host-vector systems for HV3 certification will be performed by contractors selected by NIH. These contractors will repeat tests performed by individuals proposing the HV2 system and, in addition, will conduct more extensive tests on conditions likely to be encountered in nature. The genotypic and phenotypic traits of HV2 systems will be evaluated. Tests on survival and transmissibility in and on animals, including primates, will be performed, as well as tests on survival in certain specified natural environments.

II-D-3. *Distribution of Certified Host-Vectors.* Certified HV2 and HV3 host-vector systems (plus appropriate control strains) must be obtained from the NIH or its designees, one of whom will be the investigator who developed the system. NIH shall announce the availability of the system by publication of notices in appropriate journals.

Plasmid vectors will be provided in a suitable host strain, and phage vectors will be distributed as small-volume lysates. If NIH propagates any of the host strains or phage, a sample will be sent to the investigator who developed the system or to an appropriate contractor, prior to distribution, for verification that the material is free from contamination and unchanged in phenotypic properties.

In distributing the certified HV2 and HV3 host-vector systems, NIH or its designee will (i) send out a complete description of the system; (ii) enumerate and describe the tests to be performed by the user in order to verify important phenotypic traits; (iii) remind the user that any modification of the system necessitates independent approval of the system by the NIH; and (iv) remind the user of responsibility for notifying ORDA of any discrepancies with the reported properties or any problems in the safe use of the system.

NIH may also distribute certified HV1 host-vector systems.

III. Containment Guidelines for Covered Experiments

Part III discusses experiments covered by the Guidelines. The reader must first consult Part I, where listings are given of prohibited and exempt experiments.

Containment guidelines for permissible experiments are given in Part III. For these experiments no registration with the National Institutes of Health (NIH) is necessary. However, for these experiments, prior to their initiation, investigators must submit to their Institutional Biosafety Committee

(IBC) a registration document that contains a description of (a) the source(s) of DNA, (b) the nature of the inserted DNA sequences, (c) the hosts and vectors to be used, (d) whether a deliberate attempt will be made to obtain expression of a foreign gene in the cloning vehicle and if so, what protein, and (e) the containment conditions specified by these Guidelines. This registration document must be dated and signed by the investigator and filed only with the local IBC. The IBC shall review all such proposals: IBC review prior to initiation of the experiment is not required for experiments described in Section III-O. Prior IBC review is required for all other experiments described in the subsections of Part III, including III-O-1, III-O-2, etc.

Changes from the levels specified in Part III for specific experiments (or the assignment of levels to experiments not explicitly considered here) may not be instituted without the express approval of the Director, NIH. (See Sections IV-E-1-b-(1)-(a), IV-E-1-b-(1)-(b), IV-E-1-b-(2)-(b), IV-E-1-b-(2)-(c), and IV-E-1-b-(3)-(b).)

In the classification of containment criteria for different kinds of recombinant DNAs, the stated levels of physical and biological containment are minimal for the experiments designated. The use of higher levels of biological containment (HV3>HV2>HV1) is encouraged if they are available and equally appropriate for the purposes of the experiment.

When the reader finds that the containment level given for the same experiment is different in two different sections within Part III, he may choose whichever of the two levels he wishes to use for the experiment.

III-O. *Classification of Experiments Using Certain Host-Vector Systems.* Experiments listed in Appendix H may be performed at P1 physical containment. For these experiments IBC review prior to initiation of the experiment is not required.

III-O-1. *Experiments Involving Class 3 organisms.* Experiments involving recombinant DNA from Class 3 Organisms (*1*) or from cells known to be infected with these agents may be conducted at P3 containment in *E. coli* K-12 EK1 hosts (see Appendix C). Containment levels for all other experiments with Class 3 organisms or with recombinant DNA which increases the virulence and host range of a plant pathogen beyond that which occurs by natural genetic exchange will be determined by NIH. (See Section IV-E-1-b-2-(e)).

III-O-2. *Experiments Involving Prokaryotes Nonpathogenic for Man, Animals or Plants, and/or Lower Eukaryotes Nonpathogenic for Man, Animals or Plants.* Recombinant DNA experiments evolving prokaryotes nonpathogenic for man, animals or plants, and/or lower eukaryotes nonpathogenic for man, animals or plants, and only DNA from such sources, can be conducted under P3 containment (*2A*). Lower levels of physical containment may be assigned by ORDA on a case-by-case basis for specific donor-recipient combinations (see Section IV-E-1-b-(3)-(h)).

III-A. *Classification of Experiments Using Certain HV1 and HV2 Host-Vector Systems.* Certain HV1 and HV2 host-vector systems are assigned containment levels as specified in the subsections of this Section III-A. Those so classified as of publication of these revised Guidelines are listed in Appendix D. An updated list may be obtained from the Office of Recombinant DNA Activities, National Institutes of Health, Bethesda, Maryland 20205.

III-A-1. *Shotgun Experiments.* These experiments involve the production of recombinant DNAs between the vector and portions of the specified cellular source, preferably a partially purified fraction. Care should be taken either to preclude or eliminate contaminating microorganisms before isolating the DNA.

III-A-1-a. *Eukaryotic DNA Recombinants.*

III-A-1-a-(1). *Primates.* P2 physical containment + an HV2 host-vector or P3 + HV1.

III-A-1-a-(2). *Other Mammals.* P2 physical containment + an HV2 host-vector or P3 + HV1.

III-A-1-a-(3). *Birds.* P2 physical containment + an HV2 host-vector, or P3 + HV1.

III-A-1-a-(4). *Cold-Blooded Vertebrates.* P2 physical containment + an HV1 host-vector or P1 + HV2. If the eukaryote is known to produce a potent polypeptide toxin, (*34*) the containment shall be increased to P3 + HV2.

III-A-1-a-(5). *Other Cold-Blooded Animals and Lower Eukaryotes.* This large class of eukaryotes is divided into two groups:

III-A-1-a-(5)-(a). Species that are known to produce a potent polypeptide toxin (*34*) that acts in vertebrates, or are known pathogens listed in Class 2,[1] or are known to carry such pathogens must use P3 physical containment + an HV2 host-vector. When the potent toxin is not a polypeptide and is likely not to be the product of closely linked eukaryote genes, containment may be reduced to P3+HV1 or P2+HV2. Species that produce potent toxins that affect invertebrates or plants but not vertebrates require P2+HV2 or P3+HV1. Any species that has a demonstrated capacity for carrying particular pathogenic microorganisms is included in this group, unless the organisms used as the source of DNA have been shown not to contain those agents, in which case they may be placed in the following group. (*2A*)

III-A-1-a-(5)-(b). The remainder of the species in this class including plant pathogenic or symbiotic fungi that do not produce potent toxins: P2+HV1 or P1+HV2. However, any insect in this group must be either (i) grown under laboratory conditions for at least 10 generations prior to its use as a source of DNA, or (ii) if caught in the wild, must be shown to be free of disease-causing microorganisms or must belong to a species that does not carry microorganisms causing disease in vertebrates or plants. (*2A*) If these conditions cannot be met, experiments must be done under P3+HV1 or P2+Hv2 containment.

III-A-1-a-(6). *Plants.* P2 physical containment + an HV1 host-vector, or P1+HV2. If the plant source makes a potent polypeptide toxin, (*34*) the containment must be raised to P3 physical containment + an HV2 host-vector. When the potent toxin is not a polypeptide and is likely not to be the product of closely linked plant genes, containment may be reduced to P3+HV1 or P2+HV2. (*2A*)

III-A-1-b. *Prokaryotic DNA Recombinants.* P2+HV1 or P1+HV2 for experiments with phages, plasmids and DNA from nonpathogenic prokaryotes which do not produce polypeptide toxins. (*34*) P3+HV2 for experiments with phages, plasmids and DNA from Class 2 agents. (*1*)

III-A-2-a. *Viruses of Eukaryotes* (summary given in Table III; see also exception given at asterisk at end of Appendix D).

III-A-2-a-(1). *DNA Viruses.*

III-A-2-a-(1)-(a). *Nontransforming viruses.*

III-A-2-a-(1)-(a)-(*1*). *Adeno-Associated Viruses, Minute Virus of Mice, Mouse Adenovirus (Strain FL), and Plant Viruses.* (*48*) P1 physical containment + and HV1 host-vector shall be used for DNA recombinants produced with (i) the whole viral genome, (ii) subgenomic DNA segments, or (iii) purified cDNA copies of viral mRNA. (*37*)

III-A-2-a-(1)-(a)-(*2*). *Hepatitis B.*

III-A-2-a-(1)-(a)-(*2*)-(*a*). P1 physical containment + an HV1 host-vector shall be used for purified subgenomic DNA segments. (*38*)

III-A-2-a-(1)-(a)-(*2*)-(*b*). P2 physical containment + an HV2 host-vector, or P3+HV1, shall be used for DNA recombinants produced with the whole viral genome or with subgenomic segments that have not been purified to the extent required in footnote *38*.

III-A-2-a-(1)-(a)-(*2*)-(*c*). P2 physical containment + an HV1 host-vector shall be used for DNA recombinants derived from purified cDNA copies of viral mRNA. (*37*)

III-A-2-a-(1)-(a)-(*3*). *Other Nontransforming Members of Presently Classified Viral Families. (36)*

III-A-2-a-(1)-(a)-(*3*)-(*a*). P1 physical containment + an HV1 host-vector shall be used for (i) DNA recombinants produced with purified subgenomic DNA (*38*) segments or (ii) purified cDNA copies of viral mRNA. (*37*)

III-A-2-a-(1)-(a)-(*3*)-(*b*). P1 physical containment + an HV1 host-vector shall be used for DNA recombinants produced with the whole viral genome or with subgenomic segments that have not been purified to the extent required in footnote *38*.

III-A-2-a-(1)-(b). *Transforming Viruses. (37A)*

III-A-2-a-(1)-(b)-(*1*). *Herpes Saimiri, Herpes Ateles, and Epstein Barr Virus. (39)*

III-A-2-a-(1)-(b)-(*1*)-(*a*). P1 physical containment + an HV1 host-vector shall be used for DNA recombinants produced with purified nontransforming subgenomic DNA segments. (*38*)

III-A-2-a-(1)-(b)-(*1*)-(*b*). P2 physical containment + an HV1 host-vector shall be used for (i) DNA recombinants produced with purified subgenomic DNA segments containing an entire transforming gene [38] or (ii) purified cDNA copies of viral mRNA. (*37*)

III-A-2-a-(1)-(b)-(*1*)-(*c*). P3 physical containment + an HV1 host-vector, or P2+HV2, shall be used for DNA recombinants produced with the whole viral genome or with subgenomic segments that have not been purified to the extent required in footnote *38*.

III-A-2-a-(1)-(b)-(*2*). *Other Transforming Members of Presently Classified Viral Families. (36)*

III-A-2-a-(1)-(b)-(*2*)-(*a*). P1 physical containment + an HV1 host-vector shall be used for DNA recombinants produced with purified nontransforming subgenomic DNA segments. (*38*)

III-A-2-a-(1)-(b)-(*2*)-(*b*). P2 physical containment + an HV1 host-vector shall be used for (i) DNA recombinants produced with the whole viral genome, (ii) subgenomic DNA segments containing an entire transforming gene, (iii) purified cDNA copies of viral mRNA, (*37*) or (iv) subgenomic segments that have not been purified to the extent required in footnote *38*.

III-A-2-a-(2). *DNA Transcripts of RNA Viruses.*

III-A-2-a-(2)-(a). *Retroviruses.*

III-A-2-a-(2)-(a)-(*1*). *Gibbon Ape, Woolly Monkey, Feline Leukemia and Feline Sarcoma Viruses. (39)*

III-A-2-a-(2)-(a)-(*1*)-(*a*). P1 physical containment + an HV1 host-vector shall be used for DNA recombinants produced with purified nontransforming subgenomic DNA segments. (*38*)

III-A-2-a-(2)-(a)-(*1*)-(*b*). P2 physical containment + an HV1 host-vector shall be used for DNA recombinants produced with purified subgenomic DNA segments (*38*) containing an entire transforming gene.

III-A-2-a-(2)-(a)-(*1*)-(*c*). P2 physical containment + an HV2 host-vector, or P3+HV1, shall be used for DNA recombinants produced with (i) the whole viral genome, (ii) purified cDNA copies of viral mRNA, (*37*) or (iii) subgenomic segments that have not been purified to the extent required in footnote *38*.

III-A-2-a-(2)-(a)-(*2*). *Other Members of the Family Retroviridiae. (36)*

III-A-2-a-(2)-(a)-(*2*)-(*a*). P1 physical containment + an HV1 host-vector shall be used for DNA recombinants produced with purified nontransforming subgenomic DNA segments. (*38*)

III-A-2-a-(2)-(a)-(*2*)-(*b*). P2 physical containment + HV1 host-vector shall be used for DNA recombinants produced with (i) subgenomic DNA segments containing an entire transforming gene, (ii) the whole viral genome, or (iii) purified cDNA copies of viral mRNA, (*37*) or (iv) subgenomic segments that have not been purified to the extent required in footnote *38*.

III-A-2-a-(2)-(b). *Negative Strand RNA Viruses.* P1 physical containment + an HV1 host-vector shall be used for DNA recombinants produced with (i) cDNA copies of the whole genome, (ii) subgenomic cDNA segments, or (iii) purified cDNA copies of viral genome, (ii) subgenomic cDNA segments, or (iii) purified cDNA copies of viral mRNA. (*37*)

III-A-2-a-(2)-(c). *Plus-Strand RNA Viruses.*

III-A-2-a-(2)-(c)-(*1*). *Types 1 and 2 Sabin Poliovirus Vaccine Strains and Strain 17D (Theiler) of Yellow Fever Virus.* P1 physical containment + and HV1 host-vector shall be used for DNA recombinants produced with (i) cDNA copies of the whole viral mRNA. (*37*)

III-A-2-a-(2)-(c)-(*2*). *Other Plus-Strand RNA Viruses Belonging to Presently Classified Viral Families. (36)*

III-A-2-a-(2)-(c)-(*2*)-(*a*). P1 physical containment + an HV1 host-vector shall be used for DNA recombinants produced with purified subgenomic cDNA segments. (*38*)

Table III.—*Recommended Containment for Cloning of Viral DNA or cDNA in Certain HV1 and HV2 Systems Specified in Appendix D*

[See text for full details]

Virus class	Type of viral DNA segment to be cloned: Subgenomic (*38*): Nontransforming segment	Type of viral DNA segment to be cloned: Subgenomic (*38*): Segment containing an entire transforming gene	Type of viral DNA segment to be cloned: Genomic [1]: Nonsegmented genome	Type of viral DNA segment to be cloned: Genomic [1]: Segmented genome	cDNA from viral mRNA [37]
DNA					
Nontransforming viruses:					
AVV, MVM, Mouse Adeno (strain FL).	P1+HV1		P1+HV1		P1+HV1.
Plant Viruses	P1+HV1		P1+HV1		P1+HV1.
Hepatitus B	P1+HV1 (*38*)		P2+HV2 or P3+HV1.		P2+HV1.
Other	P1+HV1 (*38*)		P1+HV1		P1+HV1.
Transforming Viruses:					
Herpes, Saimiri, H. Ateles and EBV (*39*).	P1+HV1 (*38*)	P2+HV1	P2+HV2 or P3+HV1.		P2+HV1.
Other	P1+HV1 (*38*)	P2+HV1	P2+HV1		P2+HV1.
RNA					
Retroviruses:					
Gibbon Ape, Woolly Monkey FeLV and FeSV (*39*).	P1+HV1 (*38*)	P2+HV1	P2+HV2 or P3+HV1.		P2+HV2 or P3+HV1.
Other	P1+HV1 (*38*)	P2+HV1	P2+HV1		P2+HV1.
Negative-Strand RNA	P1+HV1		P1+HV1	P1+HV1	P1+HV1.
Plus-Strand RNA:					
Types 1 and 2 Sabin Polio, 17D Yellow Fever Vaccine Strains.	P1+HV1		P1+HV1		P1+HV1.
Other	P1+HV1 (*38*)		P2+HV1		P2+HV1.

Table III.—*Recommended Containment for Cloning of Viral DNA or cDNA in Certain HV1 and HV2 Systems Specified in Appendix D*—Continued

[See text for full details]

Virus class	Type of viral DNA segment to be cloned: Subgenomic (*38*): Nontransforming segment	Subgenomic (*38*): Segment containing an entire transforming gene	Genomic [1]: Nonsegmented genome	Genomic [1]: Segmented genome	cDNA from viral mRNA (37)
Double-Stranded RNA	P1+HV1			P1+HV1	P1+HV1.
Plant Viruses+Viroids	P1+HV1		P1+HV1	P1+HV1	P1+HV1
Intracellular Viral DNA	See text	See text	See text		

[1] See exception given at asterisk at end of Appendix D.

III–A–2–a–(2)–(c)–(*2*)–(*b*). P2 physical containment + an HV1 host-vector shall be used for DNA recombinants produced with (i) cDNA copies of the whole genome, or (ii) purified cDNA copies of viral mRNA. (*37*)

III–A–2–a–(2)–(d). *Double-Stranded Segmented RNA Viruses.* P1 physical containment + an HV1 host-vector shall be used for DNA recombinants produced with (i) mixtures of subgenomic cDNA segments, (ii) a specific subgenomic cDNA segment, or (iii) purified cDNA copies of viral mRNA. (*37*)

III–A–2–a–(2)–(e). *RNA Plant Viruses and Plant Viroids.* (*48*) P1 physical containment + an HV1 host-vector shall be used for DNA recombinants produced with (i) cDNA copies of the whole viral genome, (ii) subgenomic cDNA segments, or (iii) purified cDNA copies of viral mRNA. (*37*)

III–A–2–a–(3). *Intracellular Viral DNA.* Physical and biological containment specified for shotgun experiments with eukaryotic cellular DNA [see Section III–A–(1)–(a)] shall be used for DNA recombinants produced with integrated viral DNA or viral genomes present in infected cells.

III–A–2–a–b. *Eukaryotic Organelle DNAs.* P2 physical containment + an HV1 host-vector, or P1+HV2, for mitochondrial or chloroplast DNA from eukaryotes when the organelle DNA has been obtained from isolated organelles. Otherwise, the conditions given for shotgun experiments apply.

III–A–2–c. *Prokaryotic Plasmid and Phage DNAs.* The containment levels required for shotgun experiments with DNA from prokaryotes apply to their plasmids or phages (See Section III–A–1–b.)

III–A–3. *Lowering of Containment Levels for Characterized or Purified DNA Preparations and Clones.* Many of the risks which might conceivably arise from some types of recombinant DNA experiments, particularly shotgun experiments, would result from the inadvertent cloning of a harmful sequence. Therefore, in cases where the risk of inadvertently cloning the "wrong" DNA is reduced by prior enrichment for the desired piece, or in which a clone made from a random assortment of DNAs has been purified and the absence of harmful sequences established, the containment conditions for further work may be reduced. The following section outlines the mechanisms for such reductions.

III–A–3–a. *Purified DNA Other than Plasmids, Bacteriophages, and Other Viruses.* The formation of DNA recombinants from cellular DNAs that have been purified [41] and in which the absence of harmful sequences has been established [3] can be carried out under lower containment conditions than used for the corresponding shotgun experiment. (*42*) The containment may be decreased one step in physical containment (P4, P3; P3, P2; P2, P1) while maintaining the biological containment specified for the shotgun experiment, or one step in biological containment (HV3; HV2; HV2; HV1) while maintaining the specified physical containment. The Institutional Biosafety Committee (IBC) must review such a reduction and the approval of the IBC and of the NIH must be secured before such a reduction may be put into effect. IBC approval is sufficient for such a reduction except for any lowering of containment under Section III–A–3 to levels below P1+HV1, which requires prior NIH approval. (See Section IV–E–1–b–(3)–(e).)

III–A–3–b. *Characterized Clones of DNA Recombinants.* When a cloned DNA recombinant has been rigorously characterized and the absence of harmful sequences has been established (*3*), experiments involving this recombinant DNA may be carried out under lower containment conditions. Institutional Biosafety Committees (IBCs) may give approval for a single-step reduction in physical or biological containment on receipt of evidence of characterization of a clone derived from a shotgun experiment and its probable freedom from harmful genes. IBC approval is sufficient for such a reduction except for any lowering of containment under Section III–A–3–b to levels below P1+HV1, or reduction of containment levels by more than one step, which also requires prior NIH approval. (See Section IV–E–1–b–3–(e).)

III–B. *Experiments with Prokaryotic Host-Vectors Other Than E. coli K-12.*

III–B–1. *HV1 and HV2 Systems.* Certain certified HV1 and HV2 host-vector systems appear in Appendix D. The containment levels for these systems are given in the subsections of Section III–A. Other systems in the future may be certified as HV1 and HV2. At the time of certification, the classification of containment levels for experiments using them will be assigned by NIH.

III–B–2. *Return of DNA Segments to Prokaryotic Non-HV1 Host of Origin.* Certain experiments involving those prokaryotes that exchange genetic information with *E. coli* by known physiological processes will be exempt from these Guidelines if they appear on the "list of exchangers" set forth in Appendix A (see Section I–E–4). For a prokaryote which can exchange genetic information [35] with *E. coli* under laboratory conditions but which is not on the list (Host A), the following type of experiment may be carried out under P1 conditions without Host A having been approved as an HV1 host: DNA from Host A may be inserted into a vector and propagated in *E. coli* K-12. Subsequently, this recombinant DNA may be returned to Host A by mobilization, transformation, or transduction and may then be propagated in Host A in any desired vector under P1 conditions.

For a prokaryote which does not exchange genetic information with *E. coli* (Host B), the following type of experiment may be carried out without Host B having been approved as an HV1 host: DNA from Host B may be inserted into a vector and propagated in *E. coli* K-12. Subsequently, this recombinant DNA may be returned to Host B and propagated in Host B under P1 conditions. (*43*)

III–B–3. *Non-HV1 Systems.* Containment levels for other classes of experiments involving non-HV1 systems may be approved by the Director, NIH. (See Sections IV–E–1–b–(1)–(b), IV–E–1–b–(2)–(c), and IV–E–1–b–(3)–(b).)

III–C. *Experiments with Eukaryotic Host-Vectors.*

III–C–1. *Vertebrate Host-Vector Systems. (44)* The subsections of Sections III–C–1 –a, –b, –c and –d involve the use of specific viral vectors, namely polyoma, SV40, human adenoviruses 2 and 5, and mouse adenovirus strain FL, respectively. The subsections of Section III–C–1–e involve the use of all viral vectors including the specific viral vectors considered in the subsections of Sections III–C–1 –a, –b, –c and –d, as well as any other viral vector. When the reader finds that the containment level given for a specific experiment in a subsection of Section III–C–1–e is different from the containment level given in a subsection of Section III–C–1 –a, –b, –c, or –d, he may choose which of the two containment levels he wishes to use for the experiment.

III–C–1–a. *Polyoma Virus.*

III–C–1–a–(1). *Productive Virus-Cell Interactions.*

III–C–1–a–(1)–(a). Defective or whole polyoma virus genomes, with appropriate helper, if necessary, can be used in P2 conditions to propagate DNA sequences:

III–C–1–a–(1)–(a)–(*1*). from bacteria of Class 1 or Class 2 (*1*) or their phages or plasmids, except for those that produce potent polypeptide toxins; (*34*)

III–C–1–a–(1)–(a)–(*2*). from mice;

III–C–1–a–(1)–(a)–(*3*). from eukaryotic organisms that do not produce potent polypeptide toxins, (*34*) provided that the DNA segment is >99% pure.

III–C–1–a–(1)–(b). Defective polyoma genomes, with appropriate helper, if necessary, can be used in P2 conditions for shotgun experiments to propagate DNA sequences from eukaryotic organisms that do not produce potent polypeptide toxins. (*34*)

III–C–1–a–(1)–(c). Whole virus genomes with appropriate helper, if necessary, can be used in P3 conditions for shotgun experiments to propagate DNA sequences from eukaryotic organisms that do not produce potent polypeptide toxins. (*34*)

III–C–1–a–(1)–(d). Experiments involving the use of defective polyoma virsu genomes to propagate DNA sequences from eukaryotic viruses will be evaluated by NIH on a case-by-case basis (*45*) and will be conducted under the prescribed physical and biological containment conditions. (See Section IV–E–1–b–(3)–(c).)

III–C–1–a–(2). *Nonproductive Virus-Cell Interactions.* Defective or whole polyoma virus genomes can be used as vectors in P2 conditions when production of viral particles cannot occur (e.g., transformation of nonpermissive cells or propagation of an unconditionally defective recombinant genomes in the absence of helper), provided the inserted DNA sequences are not derived from eukaryotic viruses. In the latter case, such experiments will be evaluated by NIH on a case-by-case basis (*45*) and will be conducted under the prescribed physical and biological containment conditions. (See Section IV–E–1–b–(3)–(c).)

III–C–1–b. *Simian Virus 40.*

III–C–1–b–(1). *Productive Virus-Cell Interactions.*

III–C–1–b–(1)–(a). SV40 DNA, rendered unconditionally defective by a deletion in an essential gene, with appropriate helper, can be used in P2 conditions to propagate DNA sequences from:

III–C–1–b–(1)–(a)–(*1*). Bacteria of Class 1 or Class 2, [1] or their phages or plasmids, except for those that produce potential polypeptide toxins; (*34*)

III–C–1–b–(1)–(a)–(*2*). Uninfected African green monkey kidney cell cultures.

III–C–1–b–(1)–(b). SV40 DNA, rendered unconditionally defective by a deletion in an essential gene, with an appropriate helper, can be used in P3 conditions to propagate DNA sequences from eukaryotic organisms that do not produce potent polypeptide toxins (*34*) (shotgun experiments or purified DNA).

III–C–1–b–(1)–(c). Experiments involving the use of defective SV40 genomes to propagate DNA sequences from eukaryotic viruses will be evaluated by NIH on a case-by-case basis (*45*) and will be conducted under the prescribed physical and biological containment conditions. (See Section IV–E–1–b–(3)–(c).)

III–C–1–b–(2). *Nonproductive Virus-Cell Interactions.* Defective or whole SV40 genomes can be used as vectors in P2 conditions when production of viral particles cannot occur (e.g., transformation of nonpermissive cells or propagation of an unconditionally defective recombinant genome in the absence of helper), provided the inserted DNA sequences are not derived from eukaryotic viruses. In the latter case, such experiments will be evaluated by NIH on a case-by-case basis (*45*) and will be conducted under the prescribed physical and biological containment conditions. (See Section IV–E–1–b–(3)–(c).)

III–C–1–c. *Human Adenoviruses 2 and 5.*

III–C–1–c–(1). *Productive Virus-Cell Interactions.*

III–C–1–c–(1)–(a). Human adenoviruses 2 and 5, rendered unconditionally defective by deletion of at least two essential genes, with appropriate helper, can be used in P3 conditions to propagate DNA sequences from:

III–C–1–c–(1)–(a)–(*1*). Bacteria of Class 1 or Class 2 (*1*) or their phages or plasmids except for those that produce potent polypeptide toxins; (*34*)

III–C–1–c–(1)–(a)–(*2*). Eukaryotic organisms that do not produce potent polypeptide toxins (*34*) (shotgun experiments or purified DNA).

III–C–1–c–(1)–(b) Experiments involving the use of unconditionally defective human adenovirus 2 and 5 genomes to propagate DNA sequences from eukaryotic viruses will be evaluated by NIH on a case-by-case basis (*45*) and will be conducted under the prescribed physical and biological containment conditions. (See Section IV–E–1–b–(3)–(c).)

III–C–1–c–(2). *Nonproductive Virus-Cell Interactions.* Defective or whole human adenovirus 2 and 5 genomes can be used as vectors in P2 conditions when production of viral particles cannot occur (e.g., transformation of nonpermissive cells or propagation of an unconditionally defective recombinant genome in the absence of helper), provided the inserted DNA sequences are not derived from eukaryotic viruses. In the latter case, such experiments will be evaluated by NIH on a case-by-case basis (*45*) and will be conducted under the prescribed physical and biological containment conditions. (See Section IV–E–1–b–(3)–(c).)

III–C–1–d. *Murine Adenovirus Strain FL.*

III–C–1–d–(1). Productive Virus-Cell Interactions.

III–C–1–d–(1)–(a). Unconditionally defective murine adenovirus strain FL genomes, with appropriate helper, can be used in P2 conditions to propagate DNA sequences from:

III–C–1–d–(1)–(a)–(*1*). bacteria of Class 1 or Class 2 (*1*) or their phages or plasmids except for those that produce potent polypeptide toxins; (*34*)

III–C–1–d–(1)–(a)–(*2*). eukaryotic organisms that do not produce potent polypeptide toxins (*34*) (shotgun experiments or purified DNA).

III–C–1–d–(1)–(b). Experiments involving the use of whole murine adenovirus strain FL genomes to propagate DNA sequences from prokaryotic or eukaryotic organisms will be evaluated by NIH on a case-by-case basis (*45*) and will be conducted under the prescribed physical and biological containment conditions. (See Section IV–E–1–b–(3)–(c).)

III–C–1–d–(1)–(c). Experiments involving the use of unconditionally defective murine adenovirus strain FL genomes to propagate DNA sequences from eukaryotic viruses will be evaluated by NIH on a case-by-case basis (*45*) and will be conducted under the prescribed physical and biological containment conditions. (See Section IV–E–1–b–(3)–(c).)

III–C–1–d–(2). *Nonproductive Virus-Cell Interactions.* Defective or whole murine adenovirus strain FL genomes can be used as vectors in P2 conditions when production of viral particles cannot occur (e.g., transformation of nonpermissive cells or propagation of an unconditionally defective recombinant genome in the absence of helper), provided the inserted DNA sequences are not derived from eukaryotic viruses. In the latter case, such experiments will be evaluated by NIH on a case-by-case basis (*45*) and will be conducted under the prescribed physical and biological containment conditions. (See Section IV-E-1-b-(3)-(c).)

III-C-1-e. *All Viral Vectors.*

III-C-1-e-(1). Other experiments involving eukaryotic virus vectors can be done as follows:

III-C-1-e-(1)-(a). Recombinant DNA molecules containing no more than two-thirds of the genome of any eukaryotic virus [all viruses from a single Family (*36*) being considered indentical (*50*)] may be propagated and maintained in cells in tissue culture using P1 containment. For such experiments, it must be shown that the cells lack helper virus for the specific Families of defective viruses being used. The DNA may contain fragments of the genomes of viruses from more than one Family but each fragment must be less than two-thirds of a genome.

III-C-1-e-(1)-(b). Recombinants with less than two-thirds of the genome of any eukaryotic virus may be rescued with helper virus using P2 containment if wild type strains of the virus are CDC Class 1 or 2 agents, or using P3 containment if wild type strains of the virus are CDC class 3 agents (*1*).

III-C-1-e-(2). Experiments involving the use of other whole or defective virus genomes to propagate DNA sequences from prekaryotic or eukaryotic organisms (and viruses), or as vectors to transform nonpermissive cells, will be evaluated by NIH on a case-by-case basis [45] and will be conducted under the prescribed physical and biological containment conditions. (See Section IV-E-1-b-(3)-(c).)

NIH will also reveiw on a case-by-case basis [45] all experiments involving the use of virus vectors in animals and will prescribe the physical and biological containment conditions appropriate for such studies. (See Section IV-E-1-b-(3)-(c).)

III-C-1-f. *Nonviral Vectors.* Organelle, plasmid, and chromosomal DNAs may be used as vectors. DNA recombinants formed between such vectors and host DNA, when propagated only in that host (or a closely related strain of the same species), are exempt from these Guidelines (see Section I-E). DNA recombinants formed between such vectors and nonviral DNA from cells other than the host species require only P1 physical containment for cells in culture since vertebrate cells in tissue culture inherently exhibit a very high level of containment. Recombinants involving viral DNA or experiments which require the use of the whole animals will be evaluated by NIH on a case-by-case basis.(*45*)

III-C-2. *Invertebrate Host-Vector Systems.*

III-C-2-a. *Insect Viral Vectors.* As soon as information becomes available on the host range restrictions and on the infectivity, persistence, and integration of the viral DNA in vertebrate and invertebrate cells, experiments involving the use of insect viruses to propagate DNA sequences will be evaluated by NIH on a case-by-case (*45*) and will be conducted under the recommended physical containment conditions. (See Section IV-E-1-b-(3)-(c).)

III-C-2-b. *Nonviral Vectors.* Organelle, plasmid, and chromosomal DNAs may be used as vectors. DNA recombinants formed between such vectors and host DNA, when propagated only in that host (or a closely related strain of the same species), are exempt from these Guidelines (see Section I-E). DNA recombinants formed between such vectors and DNA from cells other than the host species require P1 physical containment for invertebrate cells in culture since invertebrate cells in culture inherently exhibit a very high level of containment. Experiments which require the use of whole animals will be evaluated by NIH on a case-by-case basis. (*45*)

III-C-3. *Plant Viral Host-Vector Systems.* (*48*) The DNA plant viruses which could currently serve as vectors for cloning genes in plants and plant cell protoplasts are Cauliflower Mosaic Virus (CaMV) and its close relatives (*2A*) which have relaxed circular double-stranded DNA genomes with a molecular weight of 4.5×10^6, and Bean Golden Mosaic Virus (BGMV) and related viruses with small ($<10^6$ daltons) single-stranded DNA genomes. CaMV is spread in nature by aphids, in which it survives for a few hours. Spontaneous mutants of CaMV which lack a factor essential for aphid transmission arise frequently. BGMV is spread in nature by whiteflies, and certain other single-stranded DNA plant viruses are transmitted by leafhoppers.

The DNA plant viruses have narrow host ranges and are relatively difficult to transmit mechanically to plants. For this reason, they are most unlikely to be accidentally transmitted from spillage of purified virus preparations.

When these viruses are used as vectors in intact plants, or propagative plant parts, the plants shall be grown under P1 conditions—that is, in either a limited access greenhouse or plant growth cabinet which is insect-restrictive, preferably with positive air pressure, (*2A*) and in which an insect fumigation regime is maintained. Soil, plant pots, and unwanted infected materials shall be removed from the greenhouse or cabinet in sealed insect-proof containers and sterilized. It is not necessary to sterilize run-off water from the infected plants, as this is not a plausible route for secondary infection. When the viruses are used as vectors tissue cultures or in small plants in axenic cultures, no special containment is neccessary. Infected plant materials which have to be removed from the greenhouse or cabinet for futher research shall be maintained under insect-restrictive conditions. These measures provide an entirely adequate degree of containment.

They are similar to those required in many countries for licensed handling of "exotic" plant viruses.

The viruses or their DNA may also be useful as vectors to introduce genes into plant protoplasts. The fragility of plant protoplasts combined with the properties of the viruses provides adequate safety. Since no risk to the environment from the use of the DNA plant virus/protoplast system is envisaged, no special containment is necessary, except as described in the following paragraph.

Experiments involving the use of plant genomes to propagate DNA sequences from eukaryotic viruses will be evaluated by NIH on a case-by-case basis (*45*) and will be conducted under the prescribed physical and biological containment conditions. (See Section IV-E-1-b-(3)-(o).)

III-C-4. *Plant Host-Vector Systems Other than Viruses.* (*48*) Organelle, plasmid, and chromosomal DNAs may be used as vectors. DNA recombinants formed between such vectors and host DNA, when propagated only in that host (or a closely related strain of the same species), are exempt from these Guidelines (See Section I-E). DNA recombinants formed between such vectors and DNA from cells other than the host species require P2 physical containment. The development of host-vector systems that exhibit a high level of biological containment, such as those using protoplasts or undifferentiated cells in culture, permit (*2A*) a decrease in the physical containment to P1.

Intact plants or propagative plant parts which cannot be grown in a standard P2 laboratory because of their large size may be grown under the P1 conditions described above in Section III–C–3, except that (i) sterilization of run-off water is required where this is a plausible route for secondary infection and (ii) the standard P2 practices are adopted for microbiological work, and (iii) negative air pressure should be employed in the greenhouse or growth chamber when infectious agents are used which generate airborne propagules.

III–C–5. *Fungal or Similar Lower Eukaryotic Host-Vector Systems.*

Certain certified HV1 and HV2 host-vector systems appear in Appendix D. The containment levels for these systems are given in the subsections of Section III–A. Other systems in the future may be certified as HV1 and HV2. At the time of certification, they may be added to appendix D (and thus the containment levels for their use will be those of the subsections of Section III–A). Alternatively, at the time of their certification, another classification of containment levels for experiments using them may be assigned by NIH.

In addition to the experiments described above, the following experiments may be carried out without the eukaryotic host (Host C) having been approved as an HV1 host: DNA from Host C may be inserted into a vector and propagated in *E. coli* K-12. Subsequently, this recombinant DNA may be returned to Host C and propagated there under P1 conditions. (*43*) Containments levels for other classes of experiments involving non-HV1 systems may be expressly approved by the Director, NIH. (see Sections IV–E–1–b–(1)–(b), IV–E–1–b–(2)–(c), and IV–E–1–b–(3)–(b).)

III–C–6. *Return of DNA Segments to a Higher Eukaryotic Host of Origin.* DNA from a higher eukaryote (Host D) may be inserted into a vector and propagated in *E. coli* K-12. Subsequently, this recombinant DNA may be returned to Host D and propagated under conditions of physical containment comparable to P1 and appropriate to the organism under study. (*2A*)

III–C–7. *Transfer of Cloned DNA Segments to Eukaryotic Organisms.*

III–C–7–a. *Transfer to Non-human Vertebrates.* DNA from any nonprohibited source [Section I–D], except for greater than one quarter of a eukaryotic viral genome, which has been cloned and propagated in *E. coli* K-12, may be transferred with the *E. coli* vector used for cloning to any eukaryotic cells in culture or to any non-human vertebrate organism and propagated under conditions of physical containment comparable to P1 and appropriate to the organism under study (*2A*). Transfers to any other host will be considered by the RAC on a case-by-case basis (*45*).

III–C–7–b. *Transfer to Higher Plants.* DNA from any nonprohibited source [Section I–D] which has been cloned and propagated in *E. coli* K-12 or *S. cerevisiae*, may be transferred with the *E. coli* or *S. cerevisiae* vector used for cloning to any higher plant organisms (Angiosperms and Gymnosperms) and propagated under conditions of physical containment comparable to P1 and appropriate to the organism under study (*2A*). Intact plants or propagative plant parts may be grown under P1 conditions described under Section III–C–3. Containment must be modified to ensure that the spread of pollen, seed or other propagules is prevented. This can be accompanied by conversion to negative pressure in the growth cabinet or greenhouse or by physical entrapment by "bagging" or reproductive structures. Transfers to any other plant organisms will be considered on a case-by-case basis (*45*).

III–D. *Complementary DNAs.* Specific containment levels are given in Section III–A–2–a (see also last column of Table III) for complementary DNA (cDNA) of viral mRNA. For the other Sections of the Guidelines, where applicable, cDNAs synthesized *in vitro* are included within each of the above classifications. For example, cDNAs formed from cellular RNAs that are not purified and characterized are included under III–A–1, shotgun experiments; cDNAs formed from purified and characterized RNAs are included under III–A–3; etc.

Due to the possibility of nucleic acid contamination of enzyme preparations used in the preparation of cDNAs, the investigator must employ purified enzyme preparations that are free of viral nucleic acid.

III–E. *Synthetic DNAs.* If the synthetic DNA segment is likely to (*2A*) yield a potentially harmful polynucleotide or polypeptide (e.g., a toxin or a pharmacologically active agent), the containment conditions must be as stringent as would be used for propagating the natural DNA counterpart.

If the synthetic DNA sequence codes for a a harmless product, (*2A*) it may be propagated at the same containment level as its purified natural DNA counterpart. For example, a synthetic DNA segment which corresponds to a nonharmful gene of birds, to be propagated in *saccharomyces cerevisiae*, would require P2 physical containment plus an HV1 host-vector, or P1+HV2.

If the synthetic DNA segment is not expressed *in vivo* as a polynucleotide or polypeptide product, the organisms containing the recombinant DNA molecule are exempt (*4*) from the Guidelines.

IV. Roles and Responsibilities

IV–A. *Policy.* Safety in activities involving recombinant DNA depends on the individual conducting them. The Guidelines cannot anticipate every possible situation. Motivation and good judgement are the key essentials to protection of health and the environment.

The Guidelines are intended to help the Institution, the Institutional Biosafety Committee (IBC), the Biological Safety Officer, and the Principal Investigator determine the safeguards that should be implemented. These Guidelines will never be complete or final, since all conceivable experiments involving recombinant DNA cannot be foreseen. Therefore, it is the responsibility of the Institution and those associated with it to adhere to the *purpose* of the Guidelines as well as to their specifics.

Each Institution (and the IBC acting on its behalf) is responsible for ensuring that recombinant DNA activities comply with the Guidelines. General recognition of institutional authority and responsibility properly establishes accountability for safe conduct of the research at the local level.

The following roles and responsibilities constitute an administrative framework in which safety is an essential and integral part of research involving recombinant DNA molecules. Further clarifications and interpretations of roles and responsibilities will be issued by NIH as necessary.

IV–B. *General Applicability.* The Guidelines are applicable to all recombinant DNA research within the United States or its territories which is conducted at or sponsored by an Institution that receives any support for recombinant DNA research from NIH. This includes research performed by NIH directly.

An individual receiving support for research involving recombinant DNA must be associated with or sponsored by an Institution that can and does assume the responsibilities assigned in these Guidelines.

The Guidelines are also applicable to projects done abroad if they are supported by NIH funds. If the host country, however, has established rules for the conduct of recombinant DNA projects, then a certificate of compliance with those rules may be submitted to NIH in lieu of compliance with the NIH Guidelines. NIH reserves the right to withhold funding if the safety practices to be employed abroad are not reasonably consistent with the NIH Guidelines.

IV-C. *General Definitions.* The following terms, which are used throughout the Guidelines, are defined as follows:

IV-C-1. "DNA" means deoxyribonucleic acid.

IV-C-2. "Recombinant DNA" or "recombinant DNA molecules" means either (i) molecules which are constructed outside living cells by joining natural or synthetic DNA segments to DNA molecules that can replicate in a living cell, or (ii) DNA molecules which result from the replication of a molecule described in (i) above.

IV-C-3. [Deleted]

IV-C-4. "Institution" means any public or private entity (including Federal, State, and local government agencies).

IV-C-5. "Institutional Biosafety Committee" or "IBC" means a committee that (i) meets the requirements for membership specified in Section IV-D-2, and (ii) reviews, approves, and oversees projects in accordance with the responsibilities defined in Sections IV-D-2 and -3.

IV-C-6. "NIH Office of Recombinant DNA Activities" or "ORDA" means the office within NIH with responsibility for (i) reviewing and coordinating all activities of NIH related to the Guidelines, and (ii) performing other duties as defined in Section IV-E-3.

IV-C-7. "Recombinant DNA Advisory Committee" or "RAC" means the public advisory committee that advises the Secretary, the Assistant Secretary for Health, and the Director of the National Institutes of Health concerning recombinant DNA research. The RAC shall be constituted as specific in Section IV-E-2.

IV-C-8. "Director, NIH" or "Director" means the Director of the National Institutes of Health and any other officer or employee of NIH to whom authority has been delegated.

IV-C-9. "Federal Interagency Advisory Committee on Recombinant DNA Research" means the committee established in October 1976 to advise the Secretary, HHS, the Assistant Secretary for Health, and the Director, NIH, on the coordination of those aspects of all Federal programs and activities which relate to recombinant DNA research.

IV-C-10. "Administrative Practices Supplement" or "APS" means a publication to accompany the NIH Guidelines specifying administrative procedures for use at NIH and at Institutions.

IV-C-11. "Laboratory Safety Monograph" or "LSM" means a publication to accompany the NIH Guidelines describing practices, equipment, and facilities in detail.

IV-D. *Responsibilities of the Institution.*

IV-D-1. Each Institution conducting or sponsoring recombinant DNA research covered by these Guidelines is responsible for ensuring that the research is carried out in full conformity with the provisions of the Guidelines. In order to fulfill this responsibility, the Institution shall:

IV-D-1-a. Establish and implement policies that provide for the safe conduct of recombinant DNA research and that ensure compliance with the Guidelines. The Institution, as part of its general responsibilities for implementing the Guidelines, may establish additional procedures, as deemed necessary, to govern the Institution and its components in the discharge of its responsibilities under the Guidelines. This may include (i) statements formulated by the Institution for general implementation of the Guidelines and (ii) whatever additional precautionary steps the Institution may deem appropriate.

IV-D-1-b. Establish an Institutional Biosafety Committee (IBC) that meets the requirements set forth in Section IV-D-2 and carries out the functions detailed in Section IV-D-3.

IV-D-1-c. [Deleted]

IV-D-1-d. [Deleted]

IV-D-1-e. If the Institution is engaged in recombinant DNA research at the P3 or P4 containment level, appoint a Biological Safety Officer (BSO), who shall be a member of the IBC and carry out the duties specified in Section IV-D-4.

IV-D-1-f. Require that investigators responsible for research covered by these Guidelines comply with the provisions of Section IV-D-5, and assist investigators to do so.

ID-D-1-g. Ensure appropriate training for the IBC chairperson and members, the BSO, Principal Investigators (PIs), and laboratory staff regarding the Guidelines, their implementation, and laboratory safety. Responsibility for training IBC members may be carried out through the IBC chairperson. Responsibility for training laboratory staff may be carried out through the PI. The Institution is responsible for seeing that the PI has sufficient training, but may delegate this responsibility to the IBC.

IV-D-1-h. Determine the necessity, in connection with each project, for health surveillance of recombinant DNA research personnel, and conduct, if found appropriate, a health surveillance program for the project. [The Laboratory Safety Monograph (LSM) discusses various possible components of such a program—for example, records of agents handled, active investigation of relevant illnesses, and the maintenance of serial serum samples for monitoring serologic changes that may result from the employees' work experience. Certain medical conditions may place a laboratory worker at increased risk in any endeavor where infectious agents are handled. Examples given in the LSM include gastrointestinal disorders and treatment with steroids, immunosuppressive drugs, or antibiotics. Workers with such disorders or treatment should be evaluated to determine whether they should be engaged in research with potentially hazardous organisms during their treatment or illness.]

IV-D-1-i. Report within 30 days to ORDA any significant problems with and violations of the Guidelines and significant research-related accidents and illnesses, unless the institution determines that the PI or IBC has done so.

IV-D-2. *Membership and Procedures of the IBC.* The Institution shall establish an Institutional Biosafety Committee (IBC) meeting the following requirements:

IV-D-2-a. The IBC shall comprise no fewer than five members so selected that they collectively have experience and expertise in recombinant DNA technology and the capability to assess the safety of recombinant DNA research experiments and any potential risk to public health or the environment. At least two members (but not less than 20 percent of the membership of the committee) shall not be affiliated with the Institution (apart from their membership on the IBC) and shall represent the interest of the surrounding community with respect to health and protection of the environment. Members meet this requirement if, for example, they are officials of State or local public health or environmental protection agencies, members of other local governmental bodies, or persons active in medical, occupational health, or environmental concerns in the community. The Biological Safety Officer (BSO), mandatory when research is being conducted at the P3 and P4 levels, shall be a member (see Section IV-D-4).

IV-D-2-b. In order to ensure the professional competence necessary to review recombinant DNA activities, it is recommended that (i) the IBC include persons from disciplines relevant to recombinant DNA technology, biological safety, and engineering; (ii) the IBC include, or have available as consultants, persons knowledgeable in institutional commitments and policies, applicable law, standards of professional conduct and practice, community attitudes, and the environment; and (iii) at least one member be a nondoctoral person from a laboratory technical staff.

IV-D-2-c. The Institution shall identify the committee members by name in a report to the NIH Office of Recombinant DNA Activities (ORDA) and shall include relevant background information on each member in such form and at such times as ORDA may require. (See the Administrative Practices Supplement for further guidance.)

IV-D-2-d. No member of an IBC may be involved (except to provide information requested by the IBC) in the review or approval of a project in which he or she has been, or expects to be, engaged or has a direct financial interest.

IV-D-2-e. The Institution may establish procedures that the IBC will follow in its initial and continuing review of applications, proposals, and activities. (IBC review procedures are specified in Section IV-D-3-a.)

IV-D-2-f. Central to implementation of the Guidelines is the review of experiments by the IBC. In carrying out this responsibility, the Institution shall comply with instructions and procedures specified in the Administrative Practices Supplement.

IV-D-2-g. Institutions are encouraged to open IBC meetings to the public whenever possible, consistent with protection of privacy and proprietary interests.

IV-D-2-h. Upon request, the Institution shall make available to the public all minutes of IBC meetings and any documents submitted to or received from funding agencies which the latter are required to make available to the public (e.g., reports of Guideline violations and significant research-related accidents, and agency directives to modify projects). If comments are made by members of the public on IBC actions, the Institution shall forward to NIH both the comments and the IBC's response.

IV-D-3. *Functions of the IBC.* On behalf of the Institution, the IBC is responsible for:

IV-D-3-a. Reviewing for compliance with the NIH Guidelines all recombinant DNA research conducted at or sponsored by the Institution, and approving those research projects that it finds are in conformity with the Guidelines. This review shall include:

IV-D-3-a-(1). An independent assessment of the containment levels required by these Guidelines for the proposed research, and

IV-D-3-a-(2). An assessment of the facilities, procedures, and practices, and of the training and expertise of recombinant DNA personnel.

Note.—See Laboratory Safety Monograph (pages 187-190) for suggested guidance in conducting this review.

IV-D-3-b. Notifying the Principal Investigator (PI) of the results of their review.

IV-D-3-c. Reviewing periodically recombinant DNA research being conducted at the Institution, to ensure that the requirements of the Guidelines are being fufilled.

IV-D-3-d. Adopting emergency plans covering accidental spills and personnel contamination resulting from such research.

Note.—Basic elements in developing specific procedures for dealing with major spills of potentially hazardous materials in the laboratory are detailed in the Laboratory Safety Monograph. Included are information and references on decontamination and emergency plans. NIH and the Centers for Disease Control are available to provide consultation, and direct assistance if necessary, as posted in the LSM. The Institution shall cooperate with the State and local public health departments, reporting any significant research-related illness or accident that appears to be a hazard to the public health.

IV-D-3-e. Reporting within 30 days to the appropriate institutional official and to the NIH Office of Recombinant DNA Activities (ORDA) any significant problems with or violations of the Guidelines, and any significant research-related accidents or illnesses, unless the IBC determines that the PI has done so.

IV-D-3-f. The IBC may not authorize initiation of experiments not explicitly covered by the Guidelines until NIH, (with the advice of the RAC when required) establishes the containment requirement.

IV-D-3-g. Performing such other functions as may be delegated to the IBC under Section IV-D-1.

IV-D-4. *Biological Safety Officer.* The Institution shall appoint a BSO if it engages in recombinant DNA research at the P3 or P4 containment level. The officer shall be a member of the Institutional Biosafety Committee (IBC), and his or her duties shall include (but need not be limited to):

IV-D-4-a. Ensuring through periodic inspections that laboratory standards are rigorously followed;

IV-D-4-b. Reporting to the IBC and the Institution all significant problems with and violations of the Guidelines and all significant research-related accidents and illnesses of which the BSO becomes aware, unless the BSO determines that the Principal Investigator (PI) has done so.

IV-D-4-c. Developing emergency plans for dealing with accidental spills and personnel contamination, and investigating recombinant DNA research laboratory accidents;

IV-D-4-d. Providing advice on laboratory security;

IV-D-4-e. Providing technical advice to the PI and the IBC on research safety procedures.

Note.—See Laboratory Safety Monograph for additional information on the duties of the BSO.

IV-D-5. *Principal Investigator.* On behalf of the Institution, the PI is responsible for complying fully with the Guidelines in conducting any recombinant DNA research.

IV-D-5-a. *PI—General.* As part of this general responsibility, the PI shall:

IV-D-5-a-(1). Initiate or modify no recombinant DNA research subject to the Guidelines until that research, or the proposed modification thereof, has been approved by the Institutional Biosafety Committee (IBC) and has met all other requirements of the Guidelines and the Administrative Practices Supplement (APS).

Note.—No prior approval by the IBC is required for most experiments described in Section III-O. Modify containment and experimental protocol according to recommendations of the IBC.

IV-D-5-a-(2). Report within 30 days to the IBC and NIH (ORDA) all significant problems with and violations of the Guidelines and all significant research-related accidents and illnesses;

IV-D-5-a-(3). Report to the IBC and to NIH (ORDA) new information bearing on the Guidelines;

IV-D-5-a-(4). Be adequately trained in good microbiological techniques;

IV-D-5-a-(5). Adhere to IBC-approved emergency plans for dealing with accidental spills and personnel contamination; and

IV-D-5-a-(6). Comply with shipping requirements for recombinant DNA molecules. (See Section II-C for shipping requirements, Laboratory Safety Monograph for technical recommendations, and the APS for administrative instructions and procedures. The requesting laboratory must be in compliance with the NIH Guidelines and under appropriate review by its IBC, and the sending investigator must maintain a record of all shipments of recombinant DNA materials.)

IV-D-5-b. *Submissions by the PI to NIH.* The PI shall:

IV-D-5-b-(1). Submit information to NIH (ORDA) in order to have new host-vector systems certified;

IV-D-5-b-(2). Petition NIH, with notice to the IBC, for exemptions to these Guidelines (see Sections I-E-4 and I-E-5 and, for additional information on procedures, the APS); and

IV-D-5-b-(3). Petition, NIH, with concurrence of the IBC, for exceptions to the prohibitions under these Guidelines (see Section I-D and, for additional information on procedures, the APS).

IV-D-5-b-(4). Petition NIH for determination of containment for experiments requiring case-by-case review.

IV-D-5-b-(5). Petition NIH for determination of containment for experiments not covered by the Guidelines.

IV-D-5-c. *Submissions by the PI to the IBC.* The PI shall:

IV-D-5-c-(1). Make the initial determination of the required levels of physical and biological containment in accordance with the Guidelines;

IV-D-5-c-(2). Select appropriate microbiological practices and laboratory techniques to be used in the research;

IV-D-5-c-(3). Submit the initial research protocol (and also subsequent changes—e.g., changes in the source of DNA or host-vector system) to the IBC for review and approval or disapproval, and

IV-D-5-c-(4). Remain in communication with the IBC throughout the conduct of the project.

IV-D-5-d. *PI Responsibilities After Approval but Prior to Initiating the Research.* The PI is responsible for:

IV-D-5-d-(1). Making available to the laboratory staff copies of the approved protocols that describe the potential biohazards and the precautions to be taken;

IV-D-5-d-(2). Instructing and training staff in the practices and techniques required to ensure safety and in the procedures for dealing with accidents; and

IV-D-5-d-(3). Informing the staff of the reasons and provisions for any precautionary medical practices advised or requested, such as vaccinations or serum collection.

IV-D-5-e. *PI Responsibilities During the Conduct of the Approved Research.* The PI is responsible for:

IV-D-5-e-(1). Supervising the safety performance of the staff to ensure that the required safety practices and tehniques are employed;

IV-D-5-e-(2). Investigating and reporting in writing to ORDA, the Biological Safety Officer (where applicable), and the IBC any significant problems pertaining to the operation and implementation of containment practices and procedures;

IV-D-5-e-(3). Correcting work errors and conditions that may result in the release of recombinant DNA materials;

IV-D-5-e-(4). Ensuring the integrity of the physical containment (e.g., biological safety cabinets) and the biological containment (e.g., purity, and genotypic and phenotypic characteristics); and

IV-D-5-e-(5). *Publications.* PIs are urged to include, in all publications reporting on recombinant DNA reseach, a description of the physical and biological containment procedures employed.

IV-E. *Responsibilities of NIH.*

IV-E-1. *Director.* The Director, NIH, is responsible for (i) establishing the NIH Guidelines on recombinant DNA research, (ii) overseeing their implementation, and (iii) their final interpretation.

The Director has a number of responsibilities under the Guidelines that involve the NIH Office of Recombinant DNA Activities (ORDA) and the Recombinant DNA Advisory Committee (RAC). ORDA's responsibilities under the Guidelines are administrative. Advice from the RAC is primarily scientific and technical. In certain circumstances, there is specific opportunity for public comment, with published response, before final action.

IV-E-1-a. *General Responsibilities of the Director, NIH.* The responsibilities of the Director shall include the following:

IV-E-1-a-(1). promulgating requirements as necessary to implement the Guidelines;

IV-E-1-a-(2). Establishing and maintaining the RAC to carry out the responsibilities set forth in Section IV-E-2. The RAC's membership is specified in its charter and in Section IV-E-2;

IV-E-1-a-(3). Establishing and maintaining ORDA to carry out the responsibilities defined in Section IV-E-3; and

IV-E-1-a-(4). Maintaining the Federal Interagency Advisory Committee on Recombinant DNA Research established by the Secretary, HEW, for advice on the coordination of all Federal programs and activities relating to recombinant DNA, including activities of the RAC.

IV-E-1-b. *Specific Responsibilities of the Director, NIH.* In carrying out the responsibilities set forth in this Section, the Director shall weigh each proposed action, through appropriate analysis and consultation, to determine that it complies with the Guidelines and presents no significant risk to health or the environment.

IV-E-1-b-(1). *The Director is responsible for the following major actions* (For these, the Director must seek the advice of the RAC and provide an opportunity for public and Federal agency comment. Specifically, the agenda of the RAC meeting citing the major actions will be published in the **Federal Register** at least 30 days before the meeting, and the Director will also publish the proposed actions in the **Federal Register** for comment at least 30 days before the meeting. In addition, the Director's proposed decision, at his discretion, may be published in the **Federal Register** for 30 days of comment before final action is taken. The Director's final decision, along with response to the comments, will be published in the **Federal Register** and the *Recombinant DNA Technical Bulletin.* The RAC and IBC chairpersons will be notified of this decision):

IV-E-1-b-(1)-(a). Changing containment levels for types of experiments that are specified in the Guidelines when a major action is involved;

IV-E-1-b-(1)-(b). Assigning containment levels for types of experiments that are not explicitly considered in the Guidelines when a major action is involved;

IV-E-1-b-(1)-(c). Certifying new host-vector systems, with the exception of minor modifications of already certified systems. [The standards and procedures for certificatin are described in Section II-D-2-a. Minor modifications constitute, for example, those of minimal or no consequence to the properties relevant to containment. See the Administrative Practices Supplement (APS) for further information];

IV-E-1-b-(1)-(d). Promulgating and amending a list of classes of recombinant DNA molecules to be exempt from these Guidelines because they consist entirely of DNA segments from species that exchange DNA by known physiological processes, or otherwise do not present a significant risk to health or the environment (see Sections I-E-4 and -5 and the APS for further information);

IV-E-1-b-(1)-(e). Permitting exceptions to the prohibited

experiments in the Guidelines, in order, for example, to allow risk-assessment studies; and

IV-E-1-b-(1)-(f). Adopting other changes in the Guidelines.

IV-E-1-b-(2). *The Director is also responsible for the following lesser actions* (For these, the Director must seek the advice of the RAC. The Director's decision will be transmitted to the RAC and IBC chairpersons and published in the Recombinant DNA Technical Bulletin):

IV-E-1-b-(2)-(a). Interpreting and determining containment levels, upon request by ORDA;

IV-E-1-b-(2)-(b). Changing containment levels for experiments that are specified in the Guidelines (see Section III);

IV-E-1-b-(2)-(c). Assigning containment levels for experiments not explicitly considered in the Guidelines (see Section III);

IV-E-1-b-(2)-(d). Designating certain class 2 agents as class 1 for the purpose of these Guidelines (see Footnote 1 and Appendix B);

IV-E-1-b-(2)-(e). Assigning containment levels for experiments with recombinant DNA from Class 3 organisms (1) and assigning containment levels for experiments which increase the host-range and virulence of plant pathogens beyond that which occurs by natural genetic exchange.

IV-E-1-b-(3). *The Director is also responsible for the following actions.* (The Director's decision will be transmitted to the RAC and IBC chairpersons and published in the *Recombinant DNA Technical Bulletin):*

IV-E-1-b-(3)-(a). Interpreting the Guidelines for experiments to which the Guidelines specifically assign containment levels;

IV-E-1-b-(3)-(b). Determining appropriate containment conditions for experiments according to case precedents developed under Section IV-E-1-b-(2)-(c).

IV-E-1-b-(3)-(c). Determining appropriate containment conditions upon case-by-case analysis of experiments explicitly considered in the Guidelines but for which no containment levels have been set (see Footnote 45 in Part V; Sections III-C-1-a through -e; and Sections III-C-2 and -3);

IV-E-1-b-(3)-(d). Authorizing, under procedures specified by the RAC, large-scale experiments (i.e., involving more than 10 liters of culture) for recombinant DNAs that are rigorously characterized and free of harmful sequences (see Footnote *3* and Section I-D-6);

IV-E-1-b-(3)-(e). Lowering containment levels for characterized clones or purified DNA (see Sections III-A-3-a and -b, and Footnotes *3* and *41*);

IV-E-1-b-(3)-(f). Approving minor modifications of already certified host-vector systems. (The standards and procedures for such modifications are described in Section II-D-2); and

IV-E-1-b-(3)-(g). Decertifying already certified host-vector systems.

IV-E-1-b-(3)-(h). Assigning containment levels for experiments in which both donor and recipient are nonpathogenic prokaryotes and/or nonpathogenic lower eukaryotes (see Section III-O-2).

IV-E-1-b-(3)-(i). Adding new entries to the list of toxins for vertebrates (see Appendix G).

IV-E-1-b-(3)-(j). Approving the cloning of toxin genes in host-vector systems other than *E. coli* K-12 (see Appendix G).

IV-E-1-b-(4). The Director shall conduct, support, and assist training programs in laboratory safety for Institutional Biosafety Committee members, Biological Safety Officers, Principal Investigators, and laboratory staff.

IV-E-1-b-(5). The Director, at the end of 36 months from the time these Guidelines are promulgated, will report on the Guidelines, their administration, and the potential risks and benefits of this research. In doing so, the Director will consult with the RAC and the Federal Interagency Committee. Public comment will be solicited on the draft report and taken into account in transmitting the final report to the Assistant Secretary for Health and the Secretary, HHS.

IV-E-2. *Recombinant Advisory Committee.* The NIH Recombinant DNA Advisory Committee (RAC) is responsible for carrying out specified functions cited below as well as others assigned under its chapter or by the Secretary, HHS, the Assistant Secretary for Health, and the Director, NIH.

The members of the committee shall be chosen to provide, collectively, expertise in scientific fields relevant to recombinant DNA technology and biological safety—e.g., microbiology, molecular biology, virology, genetics, epidemiology, infectious diseases, the biology of enteric organisms, botany, plant pathology, ecology, and tissue culture. At least 20 percent of the members shall be persons knowledgeable in applicable law, standards of professional conduct and practice, public attitudes, the environment, public health, occupational health, or related fields. Representatives from Federal agencies shall serve as nonvoting members. Nominations for the RAC may be submitted to the NIH Office of Recombinant DNA Activities, Bethesda, Md. 20205.

All meetings of the RAC will be announced in the **Federal Register**, including tentative agenda items, 30 days in advance of the meeting, with final agendas (if modified) available at least 72 hours before the meeting. No item defined as a major action under Section IV-E-1-b-(1) may be added to an agenda after it appears in the **Federal Register.**

IV-E-2-a. *The RAC shall be responsible for advising the Director, NIH, on the actions listed in Section IV-E-1-b -(1) and -(2).*

IV-E-3. *The Office of Recombinant DNA Activities.* ORDA shall serve as a focal point for information on recombinant DNA activities and provide advice to all within and outside NIH, including Institutions, Biological Safety Committees, Principal Investigators, Federal agencies, State and local governments, and institutions in the private sector. ORDA shall carry out such other functions as may be delegated to it by the Director, NIH, including those authorities described in Section IV-E-1-b-(3). In addition, ORDA shall be responsible for the following:

IV-E-3-a. Review and approval of Institutional Biosafety Committee (IBC) membership;

IV-E-3-b through IV-E-3-c-(3). [Deleted]

IV-E-3-c-(4). Publish in the **Federal Register:**

IV-E-3-c-(4)-(a). Announcements of Recombinant DNA Advisory Committee (RAC) meetings and agendas 30 days in advance, with publication of the Director's proposed decision for 30 days of public and Federal agency comment followed by a published response, on any action listed in Section IV-E-1-(b)-(1); and

IV-E-3-c-(4)-(b). Announcements of RAC meetings and agendas 30 days in advance on any action listed in Section IV-E-1-b-(2).

Note.—If the agenda for an RAC meeting is modified, ORDA shall make the revised agenda available to anyone, upon request, at least 72 hours in advance of the meeting.

IV-E-3-c-(5). Publish the *Recombinant DNA Technical Bulletin:* and

IV-E-3-c-(6). Serve as executive secretary to the RAC.

IV-E-4. *Other NIH Components.* Other NIH components shall be responsible for:

IV-E-4-a. [Deleted]

IV-E-4-b. Certifying P4 facilities, inspecting them periodically, and inspecting other recombinant DNA facilities as deemed necessary; and

IV–E–4–c. Announcing and distributing certified HV2 and HV3 host-vector systems (see SECTION II–E–3).

(See Administrative Practices Supplement for additional information on the administrative procedures of ORDA and other NIH components.)

IV–F [Deleted]

IV–G. *Compliance.* As a condition for NIH funding of recombinant DNA research, Institutions must ensure that such research conducted at or sponsored by the Institution, irrespective of the source of funding, shall comply with these Guidelines. The policies on noncompliance are as follows:

IV–G–1. All NIH–funded projects involving recombinant DNA techniques must comply with the NIH Guidelines. Noncompliance may result in (i) suspension, limitation, or termination of financial assistance for such projects and of NIH funds for other recombinant DNA research at the Institution, or (ii) a requirement for prior NIH approval of any or all recombinant DNA projects at the Institution.

IV–G–2. All non–NIH funded projects involving recombinant DNA techniques conducted at or sponsored by an Institution that receives NIH funds for projects involving such techniques must comply with the NIH Guidelines. Noncompliance may result in (i) suspension, limitation, or termination of NIH funds for recombinant DNA research at the Institution, or (ii) a requirement for prior NIH approval of any or all recombinant DNA projects at the Institution.

IV–G–3. Information concerning noncompliance with the Guidelines may be brought forward by any person. It should be delivered to both NIH (ORDA) and the relevant Institution. The Institution, generally through the IBC, shall take appropriate action. The Institution shall forward a complete report of the incident to ORDA, recommending any further action indicated.

IV–G–4. In cases where NIH proposes to suspend, limit, or terminate financial assistance because of noncompliance with the Guidelines, applicable DHEW and Public Health Service procedures shall govern.

IV–G–5. *Voluntary Compliance.* Any individual, corporation, or institution that is not otherwise covered by the Guidelines is encouraged to conduct recombinant DNA research activities in accordance with the Guidelines, through the procedures set forth in Part VI.

V. Footnotes and References

(*1*) The reference to organisms as Class 1, 2, 3, 4, or 5 refers to the classification in the publication *Classification of Etiologic Agents on the Basis of Hazard,* 4th Edition, july 1974; U.S. Department of Health, Education, and Welfare, Public Health Service, Centers for Disease Control, Office of Biosafety, Atlanta, Georgia 30333. The list of organisms in each class, as given in this publication, is reprinted in Appendix B to these Guidelines.

The Director, NIH, with advice of the Recombinant DNA Advisory Committee, may designate certain of the agents which are listed as Class 2 in the *Classification of Etiologic Agents on the Basis of Hazard,* 4th Edition, july 1974, as Class 1 agents for the Purposes of these Guidelines (see Section IV–E–1–b–(2)–(d)). An updated list of such agents may be obtained from the Office of Recombinant DNA Activities (ORDA), National Institutes of Health, Bethesda, Maryland 20205.

The entire *Classification of Etiologic Agents on the Basis of Hazard* is in the process of revision.

(*2*) For experiments using Vesicular Stomatitis virus (VSV), contact the NIH Office of Recombinant DNA Activities.

(*2A*) In Parts I and III of the Guidelines, there are a number of places where judgments are to be made. These include: "cells known to be infected with such agents" (Section I–D–1); "known to acquire it naturally" (Section I–D–5); "known to produce a potent polypeptide toxin . . . or known to carry such pathogens . . . not likely to be a product of closely linked eukaryote genes . . . shown not to contain such agents" (Section III–A–1–a–(5)–(a)); "shown to be free of disease causing microorganisms" (Section III–A–1–a(5)–(b)); "close relatives" (Section III–C–3); and "produce a potent polypeptide toxin" (Footnote 34).

In all these cases the principal investigator is to make the initial judgment on these matters as part of his responsibility to "make the initial determination of the required levels of physical and biological containment in accordance with the Guidelines" (Section IV–D–7–a). In all these cases, this judgment is to be reviewed and approved by the Institutional Biosafety Committee as part of its responsibility to make "an independent assessment of the containment levels required by these Guidelines for the proposed research" (Section IV–D–3–a–(1)). If the IBC wishes, any specific cases may be referred to the NIH Office of Recombinant DNA Activities as part of ORDA's functions to "Provide advice to all within and outside NIH" (Section IV–E–3), and ORDA may request advice from the Recombinant DNA Advisory Committee as part of the RAC's responsibility for "interpreting and determining containment levels upon request by ORDA" (Section IV–E–1–b–(2)–(a)).

(*3*) The following types of data should be considered in determining whether DNA recombinants are "characterized" and the absence of harmful sequences has been established: (a) the absence of potentially harmful genes (e.g., sequences contained in indigenous tumor viruses or sequences that code for toxins, invasins, virulence factors, etc., that might potentiate the pathogenicity or communicability of the vector and/or the host or be detrimental to humans, animals, or plants); (b) the type(s) of genetic information on the cloned segment and the nature of transcriptional and translation gene products specified; (c) the relationship between the recovered and desired segment (e.g., hybridization and restriction endonuclease fragmentation analysis where applicable); (d) the genetic stability of the cloned fragment: and (e) any alterations in the biological properties of the vector and host.

(*4*) In Section I–E, "exemptions" from the Guidelines are discussed. Such experiments are not covered by the Guidelines and need not be registered with NIH. In Section I–D on "prohibitions," the possibility of "exceptions" is discussed. An "exception" means that an experiment may be expressly released from a prohibition. At that time it will be assigned an appropriate level of physical and biological containment.

(*5*) Care should be taken to inactivate recombinant DNA before disposal. Procedures for inactivating DNA can be found in the "Laboratory Safety Monograph: A Supplement to the NIH Guidelines for Recombinant DNA Research."

(*6*) *Laboratory Safety at the Center for Disease Control* (Sept. 1974). U.S. Department of Health Education and Welfare Publication No. CDC 75–8118.

(*7*) *Classification of Etiologic Agents on the Basis of Hazard.* (4th Edition, July 1974). U.S. Department of Health, Education and Welfare. Public Health Service. Centers for Disease Control, Office of Biosafety, Altanta, Georgia 30333.

(*8*) *National Cancer Institute Safety Standards for Research Involving Oncogenic Viruses* (Oct. 1974). U.S. Department of Health, Education and Welfare Publication No. (NIH) 75–790.

(*9*) *National Institutes of Health Biohazards Safety Guide* (1974). U.S. Department of Health, Education, and Welfare, Public Health.

(*10*) *Biohazards in Biological Research* (1973). A. Hellman, M. N. Oxman, and R. Pollack (ed.) Cold Spring Harbor Laboratory.

(*11*) *Handbook of Laboratory Safety* (1971). Second Edition. N. V. Steere (ed.). The Chemical Rubber Co., Cleveland.

(*12*) *Bodily, J. L. (1970). General Administration of the Laboratory,* H. L. Bodily, E. L. Updyke, and J. O. Mason (eds.), Diagnostic Procedures for Bacterial, Mycotic and Parasitic Infections. American Public Health Association, New York, pp. 11–28.

(*13*) Darlow, H. M. (1969). *Safety in the Microbiological Laboratory.* In J. R. Norris and D. W. Robbins (ed.), Methods in Microbiology. Academic Press, Inc. New York. pp. 169–204.

(*14*) *The Prevention of Laboratory Acquired Infection* (1974). C. H. Collins, E. G. Hartley, and R. Pilsworth. Public Health Laboratory Service, Monograph Series No. 6.

(*15*) Chatigny, M. A. (1961). *Protection Against Infection in the Microbiological Laboratory: Devices and Procedures.* In W. W. Umbreit (ed.). Advances in Applied Microbiology. Academic Press, New York, N.Y. 3:131–192.

(*16*) *Design Criteria for Viral Oncology Research Facilities* (1975). U.S. Department of Health, Education and Welfare, Public Health Service, National Institutes of Health, DHEW Publication No. (NIH) 75–891.

(*17*) Kuehne, R. W. (1973). *Biological Containment Facility for Studying Infectious Disease*. Appl. Microbiol. 26–239–243.

(*18*) Runkle, R. S., and Phillips (1969). *Microbial Containment Control Facilities*. Van Nostrand Reinhold, New York.

(*19*) Chatigny, M. A., and D. I. Clinger (1969). *Contamination Control in Aerobiology*. In R. L. Dimmick and A. B. Akers (eds.), An Introduction to Experimental Aerobiology. John Wiley & Sons, New York, pp. 194–263.

(*19A*) Horsfall, F. L., Jr., and J. H. Baner (1940). *Individual Isolation of Infected Animals in a Single Room*. J. Bact. *40*, 569–580.

(*20*) Biological safety cabinets referred to in this section are classified as *Class I*, *Class II*, or *Class III* cabinets. A *Class I* is a ventilated cabinet for personnel protection having an inward flow of air away from the operator. The exhaust air from this cabinet is filtered through a high-efficiency particulate air (HEPA) filter. This cabinet is used in three operational modes: (1) with a full-width open front, (2) with an installed front closure panel (having four 8-inch diameter openings) without gloves, and (3) with an installed front closure panel equipped with arm-length rubber gloves. The face velocity of the inward flow of air through the full-width open front is 75 feet per minute or greater. A *Class II* cabinet is a ventilated cabinet for personnel and product protection having an open front with inward air flow for personnel protection, and HEPA filtered mass recirculated air flow for product protection. The cabinet exhaust air is filtered through a HEPA filter. The face velocity of the inward flow of air through the full-width open front is 75 feet per minute or greater. Design and performance specifications for *Class II* cabinets have been adopted by the National Sanitation Foundation, Ann Arbor, Michigan. A *Class III* Cabinet is a closed-front ventilated cabinet of gas-tight construction which provides the highest level of personnel protection of all biohazard safety cabinets. The interior of the cabinet is protected from contaminants exterior to the cabinet. The cabinet is fitted with arm-length rubber gloves and is operated under a negative pressure of at least 0.5 inches water gauge. All supply air is filtered through HEPA filters. Exhaust air is filtered through two HEPA filters or one HEPA filter and incinerator before being discharged to the outside evironment.

(*21*) Hershfield, V., H. W. Boyer, C. Yanofsky, M. A. Lovett, and D. R. Helinski (1974). *Plasmid Col E1 as a Molecular Vehicle for Cloning and Amplification of DNA*. Proc. Nat. Acad. Sci. USA *71*, 3455–3459.

(*22*) Wensink, P. C., D. J. Finnegan, J. E. Donelson, and D. S. Hogness (1974). *A System for Mapping DNA Sequences in the Chromosomes of Drosophila Melanogaster*. Cell *3*, 315–335.

(*23*) Tanaka, T., and B. Weisblum (1975). *Construction of a Colicin E1-R Factor Composite Plasmid In Vitro: Means for Amplification of Deoxyribounucleic Acid*. J. Bacteriol. *121*, 354–362.

(*24*) Armstrong, K. A., V. Hershfield, and D. R. Helinski (1977). *Gene Cloning and Containment Properties of Plasmid Col E1 and Its Derivatives*, Science *196*, 172–174.

(*25*) Bolivar, F., R. L. Rodriguez, M. C. Betlach, and H. W. Boyer (1977). *Construction and Characterization of New Cloning Vehicles: I. Ampicillin-Resistant Derivative of pMB9*. Gene *2*, 75–93.

(*26*) Cohen, S. N., A. C. W. Chang, H. Boyer, and R. Helling (1973). *Construction of Biologically Functional Bacterial Plasmids in Vitro*. Proc. Natl. Acad. Sci. USA *70*, 3240–3244.

(*27*) Bolivar, F., R. L. Rodriguez, R. J. Greene, M. C. Batlach, H. L. Reyneker, H. W. Boyer, J. H. Crosa, and S. Falkow (1977). *Construction and Characterization of New Cloning Vehicles: II. A Multi-Purpose Cloning System*. Gene *2*, 95–113.

(*28*) Thomas, M., J. R. Cameron, and R. W. Davis (1974). *Viable Molecular Hybirds of Bacteriophage Lambda and Eukaryotic DNA*. Proc. Nat. Acad. Sci. USA *71*, 4579–4583.

(29) Murray, N. E., and K. Murray (1974). *Manipulation of Restriction Targets in Phage Lambda to Form Receptor Chromosomes for DNA Fragments*.

(30) Rambach, A., and P. Tiollais (1974). *Bacteriophage Having EcoRI Endonuclease Sites Only in Non-Essential Region of the Genome*. Proc. Nat. Acad. Sci., USA *71*, 3927–3930.

(31) Blattner, F. R., B. G. Williams, A. E. Bleche, K. Denniston-Thompson, H. E. Faber, L. A. Furlong, D. J. Gunwald, D. O. Kiefer, D. D. Moore, J. W. Shumm, E. L. Sheldon, and O. Smithies (1977). *Charon Phages: Safer Derivatives of Bacteriophage Lambda for DNA Cloning*. Science *196*, 163–169.

(32) Donoghue, D. J., and P. A. Sharp (1977). *An Improved Lambda Vector: Construction of Model Recombinants Coding for Kanamycin Resistance*, Gene *1*, 209–227.

(33) Leder, P., D. Tiemeier and L. Enquist (1977). *EK2 Derivatives of Bacteriophage Lambda Useful in the Cloning of DNA from Higher Organisms: The gt WES System*. Science *196*, 175–177.

(33A) Skalka, A. (1978). *Current Status of Coliphage EK2 Vectors*. Gene *3*, 29–35.

(33B) Szybalski, W., A. Skalka, S. Gottesman, A. Campbell, and D. Botstein (1978). *Standardized Laboratory Tests for EK2 Certification*. Gene *3*, 36–38.

(34) We are specifically concerned with the remote possibility that potent toxins could be produced by acquiring a single gene or cluster of genes. See also footnote 2A.

(35) Defined as observable under optimal laboratory conditions by transformation, transduction, phage infection, and/or conjugation with transfer of phage, plasmid, and/or chromosomal genetic information. Note that this definition of exchange may be less stringent than that applied to exempt organisms under Section 1–E–4.

(*36*) As classified in the Third Report of the International Committee on Taxonomy of Viruses: Classification and Nomenclature of Viruses, R. E. F. Matthews, Ed. Intervirology 12 (129–296) 1979. (As noted in the Prohibition Section, the use of viruses classified [1] as Class 4 or 5 is prohibited.)

(*37*) The cDNA copy of the viral mRNA must be >99% pure; otherwise as for shotgun experiments with eukaryotic cellular DNA.

(*37A*) For the purpose of these Guidelines, viruses of the families *Papovaviridae*, *Adenoviridae*, and *Herpetoviridae* (36) should be considered as "transforming" viruses. While only certain of these viruses have been associated with cell transformation *in vivo* or *in vitro*, it seems prudent to consider all members to be potentially capable of transformation. In addition, those viruses of the family *Poxviridae* that produce proliferative responses—i.e., myxoma, rabbit and squirrel fibroma, and Yaba viruses-should be considered as "transforming."

(*38*) >99% pure (i.e., less than 1% of the DNA consists of intact viral genomes); otherwise as for whole genomes.

(*39*) The viruses have been classified by NCI as "moderate-risk oncogenic viruses." See "Laboratory Safety Monograph—A Supplement to the NIH Guidelines for Recombinant DNA Research" for recommendations on handling the viruses themselves.

(*40*) [Deleted]

(*41*) The DNA preparation is defined as "purified" if the desired DNA represents at least 99% (w/w) of the total DNA in the preparation, provided that it was verified by more than one procedure.

(*42*) The lowering of the containment level when this degree of purification has been obtained is based on the fact that the total number of clones that must be examined to obtain the desired clone is markedly reduced. Thus, the probability of cloning a harmful gene could, for example, be reduced by more than 10^5-fold when a nonrepetitive gene from mammals was being sought. Furtheremore, the level of purity specified here makes it easier to establish that the desired DNA does not contain harmful genes.

(*43*) This is not permitted, of course, if it falls under any of the Prohibitions of Section I–D. Of particular concern here is prohibition I–D–5, i.e., "Deliberate transfer of a drug resistance trait to micro-organisms that are not known to acquire it naturally if such acquisition could compromise the use of a drug to control disease agents in human or veterinary medicine or agriculture."

(*44*) Because this work will be done almost exclusively in tissue culture cells, which have no capacity for propagation outside the laboratory, the primary focus for containment is the vector. It should be pointed out that risk of laboratory-acquired infection as a consequence of tissue culture manipulation is very low. Given good microbiological practices, the most likely mode of escape of recombinant DNAs from a physically contained laboratory is carriage by an infected human. Thus the vector with an inserted DNA segment should have little or no ability to replicate or spread in humans.

For use as a vector in a vertebrate host cell system, an animal viral DNA molecule should display the following properties:

(i) It should not consist of the whole genome of any agent that is infectious for humans or that replicates to a significant extent in human cells in tissue culture. If the recombinant molecule is used to transform nonpermissive cells (i.e., cells which do not produce infectious virus particles), this is not a requirement.

(i) It should be derived from a virus whose epidemiological behavior and host range are well understood.

(iii) In permissive cells, it should be defective when carrying an inserted DNA segment (i.e., propagation of the recombinant DNA as a virus must be dependent upon the presence of a complementing helper genome). In almost all cases this condition would be achieved automatically by the manipulations used to construct and propagate the recombinants. In addition, the amount of DNA encapsulated in the particles of most animal viruses is defined within fairly close limits. The insertion of sizable foreign DNA sequences, therefore, generally demands a compensatory deletion of viral sequences. It may be possible to introduce very short insertions (50–100 base pairs) without rendering the viral vector defective. In such a situation, the requirement that the viral vector be defective is not necessary, except in those cases in which the inserted DNA encodes a biologically active polypeptide.

It is desired but not required that the functional anatomy of the vector be known—that is, there should be a clear idea of the location within the molecule of;

(i) the sites at which DNA synthesis originates and terminates,

(ii) the sites that are cleaved by restriction endonucleases, and

(iii) the template regions for the major gene product.

If possible the helper virus genome should:

(i) be integrated into the genome of a stable line of host cells (a situation that would effectively limit the growth of the vector recombinant to such cell lines) or

(ii) consist of a defective genome, or an appropriate conditional lethal mutant virus, making vector and helper dependent upon each other for propagation.

However, neither of these stipulations is a requirement.

(*45*) Review by NIH on a case-by-case basis means that NIH must review and set appropriate containment conditions before the work may be undertaken. NIH actions in such case-by-case reviews will be published in the *Recombinant DNA Technical Bulletin.*

(*46*) Provided the inserted DNA sequences are not derived from eukaryotic viruses. In the latter case, such experiments will be evaluated on a case-by-case basis.

(*47*) >99% pure; otherwise as for shotgun experiments.

(*48*) A USDA permit is required for import and interstate transport of pathogens, may be obtained from the Animal and Plant Health Inspection Service, USDA, Federal Building, Hyattsville, MD 20782.

(*49*) A subset of non-conjugated plasmit vectors are also poorly mobilizable (e.g., pBR 322, pBR 313). where practical, these vectors should be employed.

(*50*) i.e., the total of all genomes within a Family shall not exceed two-thirds of the genome.

VI. Voluntary Compliance

VI–A. *Basic Policy.* Individuals, corporations, and institutions not otherwise covered by the Guidelines are encouraged to do so by following the standards and procedures set forth in Parts I–IV of the Guidelines. In order to simplify discussion, references hereafter to "institutions" are intended to encompass corporations, and individuals who have no organizational affiliation. For purposes of complying with the Guidelines, an individual intending to carry out research involving recombinant DNA is encouraged to affiliate with an institution that has an Institutional Biosafety Committee approved under the Guidelines.

Since commerical organizations have special concerns, such as protection of proprietary data, some modifications and explanations of the procedures in Parts I–IV are provided below, in order to address these concerns.

VI–B. *IBC Approval.* The NIH Office of Recombinant DNA Activities (ORDA) will review the membership of an institutional Biosafety Committee (IBC) and, where it finds the IBC meets the requirements set forth in Section IV–D–2, will give its approval to the IBC membership.

It should be emphasized that employment of an IBC member solely for purposes of membership on the IBC does not itself make the members an institutionally affiliated member for purposes of Section IV–D–2–a.

Except for the unaffiliated members, a member of an IBC for an institution not otherwise covered by the Guidelines may participate in the review and approval of a project in which the member has a direct financial interest, so long as the member has not been and does not expect to be engaged in the project. Section IV–D–2–d is modified to that extent for purposes of these institutions.

VI–C. [Deleted]

VI–D. *Certification of Host-Vector Systems.* A host-vector system may be proposed for certification by the Director, NIH, in accordance with the procedures set forth in Section II–D–2–a.

Institutions not otherwise covered by the Guidelines will not be subject to Section II–D–3 by complying with these procedures.

In order to ensure protection for proprietary data, any public notice regarding a host-vector system which is designated by the institution as proprietary under Section VI–F–1 will be issued only after consultation with the institution as to the content of the notice.

VI–E. *Requests for Exceptions, Exemptions, Approvals.* Requests for exceptions from prohibitions, exemptions, or other approvals required by the Guidelines should be requested by following the procedures set forth in the appropriate sections in Parts I–IV of the Guidelines.

In order to ensure protection for proprietary data, any public notice regarding a request for an exception, exemption, or other approval which is designated by the institution as proprietary under Section VI–F–1 will be issued only after consultation with the institution as to the content of the notice.

VI–F. *Protection of Proprietary Data.* In general, the Freedom of Information Act requires Federal agencies to make their records available to the public upon request. However, this requirement does not apply to, among other things, "trade secrets and commerial and financial information obtained from a person and privileged or confidential." 18 U.S.C. 1905, in turn makes it a crime for an officer or employee of the United States of any Federal department or agency to publish, divulge, disclose, or make known "in any manner or to any extent not authorized by law any information coming to him in the course of his employment or official duties or by reason of any examination or investigation made by, or return, report or record made to of filed with, such department or agency or officer or employee thereof, which information concerns or relates to the trade secrets, [or processes. . . of any person, firm, partnership, corporation, or association." This provision applies to all employees of the Federal Government, including Special Government employees. Member of the Recombinant DNA Advisory Committee are "special Government employees."

VI–F–1. In submitting information to NIH for purposes of complying voluntarily with the Guidelines, an institution may designate those items of information which the institution believes constitutes trade secrets or privileged or confidential commerical or financial information.

VI–F–2. If NIH receives a request under the Freedom of Information Act for information so designated, NIH will promptly contact the institution to secure its reviews as to whether the information (or some portion) should be released.

VI–F–3. If the NIH decides to release this information (or some portion in response to a Freedom of Information request or otherwise, the institution will be advised and the actual release will not be made until the expiration of 15 days after the institution is so advised, except to the extent that earlier release, in the judgement of the Director, NIH, is necessary to protect against an imminent hazard to the public or the environment.

VI-F-4. Projects should be registered in accordance with procedures specified in the Administrative Practices Supplement. The following information will usually be considered publicly available information, consistent with the need to protect proprietary data:

a. The names of the institution and principal investigator.

b. The location where the experiments will be performed.

c. The host-vector system.

d. The source of the DNA.

e. The level of physical containment.

VI-F-5-a. Any institution not otherwise covered by the Guidelines, which is considering submission of data or information voluntarily to NIH, may request presubmission review of the records involved to determine whether, if the records are submitted, NIH will or will not make part or all of the records available upon request under the Freedom of Information Act.

VI-F-5-b. A request for presubmission review should be submitted to ORDA, along with the records involved. These records must be clearly marked as being the property of the institution, on loan to NIH solely for the purpose of making a determination under the Freedom of Information Act. ORDA will then seek a determination from the HEW Freedom of Information Officer, the responsible official under HEW regulations (45 C.F.R. Part 5), as to whether the records involved (or some portion) are or are not available to members of the public under the Freedom of Information Act. Pending such a determination, the records will be kept separate from ORDA files, will be considered records of the institution and not ORDA, and will not be received as part of ORDA files. No copies will be made of the records.

VI-F-5-c. ORDA will inform the institution of the HEW Freedom of Information Officer's determination and follow the institution's instructions as to whether some or all of the records involved are to be returned to the institution or to become a part of ORDA files. If the institution instructs ORDA to return the records, no copies or summaries of the records will be made or retained by HEW, NIH, or ORDA.

VI-F-5-d. The HEW Freedom of Information Officer's determination will represent that official's judgment, as of the time of the determination, as to whether the records involved (or some portion) would be exempt from disclosure under the Freedom of Information Act, if at the time of the determination the records were in ORDA files and a request were received from them under the Act.

Appendix A.—Exemptions Under I-E-4

Section I-E-4 states that exempt from these Guidelines are "certain specified recombinant DNA molecules that consist entirely of DNA segments from different species that exchange DNA by known physiological processes, though one or more of the segments may be a synthetic equivalent. A list of such exchangers will be prepared and periodically revised by the Director, NIH, with advice of the Recombinant DNA Advisory Committee, after appropriate notice and opportunity for public comment (see Section IV-E-1-b-(1)-(d).) Certain classes are exempt as of publication of these Revised Guidelines. The list in in Appendix A."

Under exemption I-E-4 of these revised Guidelines are recombinant DNA molecules that are (1) composed entirely of DNA segments from one or more of the organisms within a sublist and (2) to be propagated in any of the organisms within a sublist. (Classification of *Bergey's Manual of Determinative Bacteriology*, eighth edition. R. E. Buchanan and N. E. Gibbons, editors. Williams and Wilkins Company: Baltimore, 1974.)

Sublist A

1. Genus *Escherichia*
2. Genus *Shigella*
3. Genus *Salmonella* (including *Arizona*)
4. Genus *Enterobacter*
5. Genus *Citrobacter* (including *Levinea*)
6. Genus *Klebsiella*
7. Genus *Erwinia*
8. *Pseudomonas aerugninosa, Pseudomonas putida* and *Pseudomonas fluorescens*
9. *Serratia marcescens*

Sublist B

1. *Bacillus subtilis*
2. *Bacillus licheniformis*
3. *Bacillus pumilus*
4. *Bacillus globigii*
5. *Bacillus niger*
6. *Bacillus nato*
7. *Bacillus amyloliquefaciens*
8. *Bacillus aterrimus*

Sublist C

1. *Streptomyces aureofaciens*
2. *Streptomyces rimosus*
3. *Streptomyces coelicolor*

Sublist D

1. *Streptomyces griseus*
2. *Streptomyces cyaneus*
3. *Streptomyces venezuelae*

Sublist E

One way transfer of *Streptococcus mutans* DNA into *Streptococcus sanguis*.

Sublist F

1. *Streptococcus sanguis*
2. *Streptococcus pneumoniae*
3. *Streptococcus faecalis*

Appendix B.—Classification of Microorganisms on the Basis of Hazard

Classification of Etiologic Agents on the Basis of Hazard (*1*)

A. Class 1 Agents

All bacterial, parasitic, fungal, viral, rickettsial, and chlamydial agents not included in higher classes.

B. Class 2 Agents

1. Bacterial Agents:

Actinobacillus—all species except *A. mallei*, which is in Class 3
Arizona hinshawii—all serotypes
Bacillus anthracis
Bordetella—all species
Borrelia recurrentis, B. vincenti
Clostridium botulinum, Cl. chauvoei, Cl. haemolyticum, Cl. histolyticum, Cl. novyi, Cl. septicum, Cl. tetani
Corynebacterium diptheriae, C. equi, C. haemolyticum, C. pseudotuberculosis C. pyogenes, C. renale
Diplococcus (Streptococcus) pneumoniae
Erysipelothrix insidiosa
Escherichia coli—all enteropathogenic serotypes
Maemophilus ducreyi, H. influenzae
Herellae vaginicola
Klebsiella—all species and all serotypes
Haemophilus ducreyi, H. influenzae
Herellae vaginicola
Klebsiella—all species and all serotypes
Leptospira interrogans—all serotypes
Listeria—all species
Mima polymorpha
Moraxella—all species
Mycobacteria—all species except those listed in Class3
Mycoplasma—all species except *Mycoplasma mycoides and Mycoplasma agalactiae*, which are in Class 5
Neisseria gonorrhoeae, N. meningitidis
Pasteurella—all species except those listed in Class 3
Salmonella—all species and all serotypes
Shigella—all species and all serotypes
Sphaerophorus necrophorus
Staphylococcus aureus
Streptobacillus moniliformis
Streptococcus pyogenes
Treponema carateum, T. pallidum, and T. pertenue
Vibrio fetus, V. comma, including biotype El Tor, and *V. parahemolyticus*

2. Fungal Agents:

***Actinomycetes* (including *Nocardia* species and *Actinomyces species and Arachnia propionica*)
Blastomyces dermatitidis
Cryptococcus neoformans
Paracoccidioides brasiliensis

3. Parasitic Agents:

Endamoeba histolytica
Leishmania sp.
Naegleria gruberi
Toxoplasma gondii
Toxocara canis
Trichinella spiralis
Trypanosoma cruzi

4. Viral, Rickettsial, and Chlamydial Agents:

Adenoviruses—human—all types
Cache Valley virus

Coxsackie A and B viruses
Cytomegaloviruses
Echoviruses—all types
Encephalomyocarditis virus (EMC)
Flanders virus
Hart Park virus
Hepatitis-associated antigen material
Herpes viruses—except *Herpesvirus simiae* (Monkey B virus) which is in Class 4
Corona viruses
Influenza viruses—all types except A/PR8/34, which is in Class 1
Langat virus
Lymphogranuloma venereum agent
Measles virus
Mumps virus
Parainfluenza virus—all types except Parainfluenza virus 3, SF4 strain, which is in Class 1
Polioviruses—all types, wild and attenuated
Poxviruses—all types except *Alastrim, Smallpox, Monkey pox, and Whitepox,* which depending on experiments, are in Class 3 or Class 4
Rabies virus—all strains except *Rabies street virus,* which should be classified in Class 3 when inoculated into carnivores
Reoviruses—all types
Rubella virus
Simian viruses—all types except *Herpesvirus simiae (Monkey B virus) and Marburg virus,* which are in Class 4
Sindbis virus
Tensaw virus
Turlock virus
Vaccinia virus
Varicella virus
Vole rickettsia
Yellow fever virus, 17D vaccine strain

C. Class 3 Agents
1. Bacterial Agents:
*Actinobacillus mallei**
Bartonella—all species
Brucella—all species
Francisella tularensis
Mycobacterium avium, M. bovis, M. tuberculosis
Pasteurella multocide type B ("buffalo" and other foreign virulent strains*)
*Pseudomonas pseudomallei**
Yersenia pestis
2. Fungal Agents:
Coccidioides immitis
Histoplasma capsulatum
Histoplasma capsulatum var. *duboisii*
3. Parasitic Agents:
Schistosoma mansoni
4. Viral, Rickettsial, and Chlamydial Agents:
****Alastrim, Smallpox, Monkey pox, and Whitepox,* when used *in vitro*
Arboviruses—all strains except those in Class 2 and 4 (Arboviruses indigenous to the United States are in Class 3, except those listed is Class 2.
West Nile and *Semliki Forest* viruses may be classified up or down, depending on the conditions of use and geographical location of the laboratory.)
Dengue virus, when used for transmission or animal inoculation experiments
Lymphocytic choriomeningitis virus (LCM)
Psittacosis-Ornithosis-Trachoma group of agents
Rabies street virus, when used in inoculations of carnivores (See Class 2)
Rickettsia—all species except *Vole rickettsia* when used for transmission or animal inoculations experiments
*Vesicular stomatitis virus**
Yellow fever virus—wild, when used *in vitro*

D. Class 4 Agents
1. Bacterial Agents: None
2. Fungal Agents: None
3. Parasitic Agents: None
4. Viral, Rickettsial, and Chlamydial Agents:
****Alastrim, Smallpox, Monkey pox, and Whitepox,* when used for transmission or animal inoculation experiments
Hemorrhagic fever agents, including *Crimean hemorrhagic fever, (Congo), Junin,* and *Machupo* viruses, and other as yet undefined
Herpesvirus simiae (Monkey B virus)
Lassa virus
Marburg virus
Tick-borne encephalitis virus complex, including *Russian spring-summer encephalitis, Kyasanur forest disease, Omsk hemorrhagic fever,* and *Central European encephalitis viruses*
Venezuelan equine encephalitis virus, epidemic strains, when used for transmission or animal inoculation experiments
Yellow fever virus—wild, when used for transmission or animal inoculation experiments

II. Classification of Oncogenic Viruses on the Basis of Potential Hazard (*2*)

A. Low-Risk Oncogenic Viruses
Rous Sarcoma
SV-40
CELO
Ad7-SV40
Polyoma
Bovine papilloma
Rat mammary tumor
Avian Leukosis
Murine Leukemia
Murine Sarcoma
Mouse mammary tumor
Rat Leukemia
Hamster Leukemia
Bovine Leukemia
Dog Sarcoma
Mason-Pfizer Monkey Virus
Marek's
Guinea Pig Herpes
Lucke (Frog)
Adenovirus
Shope Fibroma
Shope Papilloma

B. Moderate-Risk Oncogenic Viruses
Ad2-SV40
FeLV
HV Saimiri
EBV
SSV-1
GaLV
HV ateles
Yaba
FeSV

III. Animal Pathogens (*3*)

A. Animal disease organisms which are forbidden entry into the United States by Law (CDC Class 5 agents)
1. Foot and mouth disease virus

B. Animal disease organisms and vectors which are forbidden entry into the United States by USDA Policy (CDC Class 5 Agents)
African horse sickness virus
African swine fever virus
Besnoitia besnoiti
Borna disease virus
Bovine infectious petechial fever
Camel pox virus
Ephemeral fever virus
Fowl plague virus
Goat pox virus
Hog cholera virus
Louping ill virus
Lumpy skin disease virus
Nairobi sheep disease virus
Newcastle disease virus (Asiatic strains)
Mycoplasma mycoides (contagious bovine pleuropneumonia)
Mycoplasma agalactiae (contagious agalactia of sheep)
Rickettsia ruminatium (heart water)
Rift valley fever virus
Rhinderpest virus
Sheep pox virus
Swine vesicular disease virus
Teschen disease virus
Trypanosoma vivax (Nagana)
Trypanosoma evansi
Theileria parva (East Coast fever)
Theileria annulata
Theileria lawrencei
Theileria bovis
Theileria hirci
Vesicular exanthema virus
Wesselsbron disease virus
Zyonema

Footnotes and References of Appendix B

*A USDA permit, required for import and interstate commerce of pathogens, may be obtained from the Animal and Plant Health Inspection Service, USDA, Federal Building, Hyattsville, MD. 20782.

**Since the publication of the classification in 1974 [1], the *Actinomycetes* have been reclassified as bacterial rather than fungal agents.

***All activities, including storage of variola and whitepox are restricted to the single national facility (World Health Organization (WHO) Collaborating Center for Smallpox Research, Center for Disease Control, in Atlanta).

(*1*) *Classification of Etiologic Agents on the Basis of Hazard.* (4th Edition, July 1974). U.S. Department of Health, Education and Welfare, Public Health Service, Center for Disease Control, Office of Biosafety, Atlanta, Georgia 30333.

(*2*) *National Cancer Institute Safety Standards for Research Involving Oncogenic Viruses* (October 1974). U.S. Department of Health, Education, and Welfare Publication No. (NIH) 75-790.

(*3*) U.S. Department of Agriculture, Animal and Plant Health Inspection Service.

Appendix C.—Exemptions Under I-E-5

Section I-E-5 states that exempt from these Guidelines are "Other classes of recombinant DNA molecules, if the Director, NIH, with advice of the recombinant DNA Advisory Committee, after appropriate notice and opportunity for public comment, finds that they do not present a significant risk to health or the environment. (See Section IV-E-1-b-(1)-(d).) Certain classes are exempt as of publication of these Revised Guidelines."

The following classes of experiments are exempt under Section I-E-5 of the Guidelines:

1. *Recombinant DNAs in Tissue Culture.* Recombinant DNA molecules derived entirely from non-viral components (that is, no component is derived from a eukaryotic virus), that are propagated and maintained in cells in tissue culture are exempt from these Guidelines with the exceptions listed below.

Exceptions

Experiments described in Sections I-D-1 to I-D-5 as being prohibited.

Experiments involving DNA from Class 3 organisms [1] or cells known to be infected with these agents, or any recombinant DNA molecules which increase the virulence and host-range of a plant pathogen beyond that which occurs by natural genetic exchange. (See Section III-O-1.)

Experiments involving the deliberate introduction of genes coding for the biosynthesis of toxins potent for vertebrates. (See Appendix G.)

2. *Experiments Involving E. coli K-12 host-vector systems.*

Experiments which use *E. coli* K-12 host-vector systems, with the exception of those experiments listed below, are exempt from these Guidelines provided that (a) the *E. coli* host shall not contain conjugation proficient plasmids or generalized transducing phages, and (b) lambda or lambdoid or Ff bacteriophages or nonconjugative plasmids [49] shall be used as vectors. However, experiments involving the insertion into *E. coli* K-12 of DNA from prokaryotes that exchange genetic information [35] with *E. coli* may be performed with any *E. coli* K-12 vector (e.g., conjugative plasmid). When a nonconjugative vector is used, the *E. coli* K-12 host may contain conjugations-proficient plasmids either autonomous or integrated, or generalized transducing phages.

For these exempt experiments, P1 physical containment conditions are recommended.

Exceptions

Experiments described in Section I-D-1 to I-D-5 as being prohibited.

Experiments involving DNA from Class 3 organisms [1] or from cells known to be infected with these agents may be conducted at P3 containment. Lower containment levels may be specified by NIH. (See Section IV-E-1-b-(2)-(e).) Experiments in this category require prior IBC review and approval.

Experiments which increase the virulence and host range of a plant pathogen beyond that which occurs by natural genetic exchange. (See Section III-O-1.)

Prohibition I-D-6 concerning large-scale experiments (e.g., more than 10 liters of culture) applies to experiments with *E. coli* K-12 host-vector systems. The Director, NIH is responsible for authorizing, under procedures specified by the RAC, large-scale experiments using recombinant DNAs that are rigorously characterized and free of harmful sequences [3]. (See Section IV-E-1-b-(3)-(d).)

Experiments involving the deliberate cloning of genes coding for the biosynthesis of toxins potent for vertebrates. (See Appendix G.)

3. *Experiments Involving Saccharomyces cerevisiae host-vector systems.*

Experiments which use *Saccharomyces cerevisiae* host-vector systems, with the exception of experiments listed below, are exempt from these Guidelines provided that laboratory strains are used.

For these exempt experiments, P1 physical containment conditions are recommended.

Exceptions

Experiments described in Sections I-D-1 to I-D-5 as being prohibited.

Experiments involving CDC Class 3 organisms [1] or cells known to be infected with these agents, or any recombinant DNA molecules which increase the virulence and host-range of a plant pathogen beyond that which occurs by natural genetic exchange. (See Section III-O-1.)

Prohibition I-D-6 concerning large-scale experiments (e.g., more than 10 liters of culture) applies to experiments with *S. cerevisiae* host-vector systems. The Director, NIH, is responsible for authorizing, under procedures specified by RAC, large-scale experiments using recombinant DNAs that are rigorously characterized and free of harmful sequences [3]. (See Section IV-E-1-b-(3)-(d).)

Experiments involving the deliberate cloning of genes coding for the biosynthesis of toxins potent for vertebrates. (See Appendix G.)

4. *Experiments Involving Bacillus subtilis host-vector systems.*

Any asporogenic *Bacillus subtilis* strain which does not revert to a sporeformer with a frequency greater than 10^{-7} can be used for cloning DNA from any nonprohibited source, with the exception of those experiments listed below. Indigenous *Bacillus* plasmids and phages, whose host-range does not include *Bacillus cereus* or *Bacillus anthracis*, may be used as vectors.

For these exempt experiments P1 physical containment conditions are recommended.

Exceptions

Experiments described in Sections I-D-1 to I-D-5 as being prohibited.

Experiments involving CDC Class 3 organisms [1] or cells known to be infected with these agents, or any recombinant DNA molecules which increase the virulence and host-range of a plant pathogen beyond that which occurs by natural genetic exchange. (See Section III-O-1.)

Prohibition I-D-6 concerning large-scale experiments (e.g., more than 10 liters of culture) applies to experiments with *B. subtilis* host-vector systems. The Director, NIH, is responsible for authorizing, under procedures specified by RAC, large-scale experiments using recombinant DNAs that are rigorously characterized and free of harmful sequences [3]. (See Section IV-E-1-b-(3)-(d).)

Experiments involving the deliberate cloning of genes coding for the biosynthesis of toxins potent for vertebrates. (See Appendix G.)

Appendix D.—HV1 and HV2 Host-Vector Systems Assigned Containment Levels as Specified in the Subsections of Section III-A

As noted above at the beginning of Section III-A, certain HV1 and HV2 host-vector systems are assigned containment levels as specified in the subsections of Section III-A. Those so classified as of publication of these Revised Guidelines are listed below.

HV1*—The following specified strains of *Neurospora crassa* which have been modified to prevent aerial dispersion:

(1) inl (inositolless) strains 37102, 37401, 46316, 64001 and 89601.

(2) csp-1 strain UCLA37 and csp/2 strains FS 590, UCLA101 (these are conidial separation mutants).

(3) eas strain UCLA191 (an "easily wettable" mutant).

HV1—The following *Streptomyces* species: *Streptomyces coelicolor, S. lividans, S. parvulus,* and *S. griseus*. The following are accepted as vector components of certified *Streptomyces* HV1 systems: *Streptomyces* plasmids SCP2, SLP1.2, pIJ101, actinophage phi.C31, and their derivatives.

Appendix E.—Actions Taken Under the Guidelines

As noted in the subsections of Sections IV-E-1-b-(1) and IV-E-1-b-(2), the Director, NIH, may take certain actions with regard to the Guidelines after consideration by the RAC.

Some of the actions taken to date include the following:

1. The following experiment has been approved: The cloning in *B. subtilis*, under P2 conditions, of DNA dervied from *Saccharomyces cerevisiae* using EK2 plasmid vectors provided that an HV1 *B. subtilis* host is used.

2. Unmodified laboratory strains of *Neurospora crassa* can be used in all experiments for which HV1 *N. crassa* systems are approved, provided that only DNA from Class 1 agents is used. For agent other than Class 1, unmodified laboratory strains of *N. crassa* can be used in all experiments for which HV1 *N. crassa* systems are approved, provided that these are carried out at physical containment one level higher than required for HV1. However, if P3 containment is specified for HV1 *N. crassa*, this level is considered adequate for unmodified *N. crassa*. Care must be exercised to prevent aerial dispersal of macroconidia, in accordance with good laboratory practice. Mutationally modified strains of *N. crassa* specified as HV1 in Appendix D can be used in all experiments for which HV2 *N. crassa*

*These follow the assigned containment levels as specified in the subsections of Section III-A with one exception. The exception is that experiments involving complete genomes of eukaryotic viruses will require P3 + HV1 or P2 + HV2 rather than the levels given in the subsections of Section III-A.

systems are approved, provided that only DNA from Class 1 agents is used.

3. P2 physical containment shall be used for DNA recombinants produced between members of the *Actinomycetes* group except for the species which are known to be pathogenic for man, animals, or plants.

4. Cloned desired fragments from any non-prohibited source may be transferred into *Agrobacterium tumefaciens* containing a Ti plasmid (or derivatives thereof), using a nonconjugative *E. coli* plasmid vector coupled to a fragment of the Ti plasmid and/or the origin of replication of an *Agrobacterium* plasmid, under containment conditions one step higher than would be required for the desired DNA in HV1 systems (i.e. one step higher physical containment than that specified in the subsections of Section III–A). However, DNA from plants and nonpathogenic prokaryotes may be cloned under P2 containment conditions; and the *Saccharomyces cerevisiae* alcohol dehydrogenase 1 gene and the gene coding for the maize (*Zea mays*) seed storage protein, zein, may be cloned under P1 conditions. Transfer into plant parts or cells in culture is permitted at the same containment level as is used for the cloning in *Agrobacterium tumefaciens*.

5. *Bacillus subtilis* strains that do not carry an asporogenic mutation can be used as hosts specifically for the cloning of DNA dervied from *E. coli* K–12 and *Streptomyces coelicolor, S. aureofaciens, S. rimosus, S. griseus, S. cyaneus,* and *S. venezuelae*, using NIH-approved *Staphylococcus aureus* plasmids as vectors under P2 conditions.

6. *Streptomyces coelicolor, S. aureofaciens, S. rimosus, S. griseus, S. cyaneus,* and *S. venezuelae* can be used as hosts for the cloning of DNA derived from *B. subtilis, E. coli* K–12, or from *S. aureus* vectors that have been approved for use in *B. subtilis under P2 conditions, using as vectors any plasmid indigenous to Streptomyces* species or able to replicate in these hosts by natural biological mechanisms.

7. Certain cloned segments of *Anabena* DNA may be transferred into *Klebsiella* under P2 physical containment.

8. Permission is granted to clone foot-and-mouth disease virus in the EK1CV host-vector system consisting of E. coli K–12 and the vector pBR322, all work to be done at the Plum Island Animal Disease Center.

9. Permission is granted to clone the Exotoxim A gene of *Pseudomonas aeruginosa* under P1 + EK1 conditions in *Escherichia coli* K–12 and under P1 conditions in *Pseudomonas aeruginosa*.

10. Permission is granted to return to the host of origin *Helminthosporanium maydis* (race O) DNA which has been cloned in yeast strain SHY2 using the hybrid *E. coli*—yeast plasmid Y1p5. The cloned DNA may be retured to, and propagated in, *Helminthosporanium maydis* at the P2 level of physical containment.

11. Permission is granted to return *Schizophyllum commune* DNA (or yeast DNA) cloned in *Saccharomyces cerevisiae* with YR or 2 mu circle vectors to *Schizophyllum commune*. The cloned DNA may be returned to, and propagated in, *Schizophyllum commune* at the P2 level of physical containment.

12. Permission is granted to return *Wangiella dermatitidis* DNA to *Wangiella dermatitidis* using an HV2 certified *Saccharomyces/E. coli* hybrid vector. The *Wangiella dermatitidis* may be propagated at the P3 level of physical containment.

13. Certain specified clones dervied from segments of the Foot-and-Mouth Diseas Virus may be transferred from Plum Island Animal Disease Center to the facilities of Genentech, Inc., of South San Francisco, California. Further development of the clones at Genentech has been approved under P1 + EK1 conditions.

14. *Saccharomycopsis lipolytica* may be used as a host for transformation with defined *Escherichia coli/Saccharomyces cerevisiae* hybrid plasmids and the hybrid plasmids may be used for cloning *S. lipolytica* DNA in *E. coli* and returning the cloned DNA to *S. lipolytica*.

15. Conjugative plasmids or transducing phages may be employed in recombinant DNA experiments when employing *E. coli* as host when a small defined segment of Adenovirus 2 DNA is employed as linker DNA.

16. Permission is granted to introduce DNA segments from aphid transmissible strains into non-aphid transmissible strains of Cauliflower mosaic virus in order to study the factors determining aphid transmissibility.

17. Permission is granted to return *Mucor racemosus* DNA which has been cloned in *Saccharomyces cerevisiae* host-vector systems to *Mucor racemosus*. In addition, permission is granted to transform *Mucor racemosus* with *S. cerevisiae* sequences. These manipulations may be performed under P2 conditions.

18. DNA from nonpathogenic prokaryotes and nonpathogenic low eukaryotes may be cloned into *Schizosaccharomyces pombe* species under P1 containment conditions. DNA from higher eukaryotes may be cloned in *S. pombe* species under P3 containment conditions.

19. The pyrogenic endotoxin type A (Tox A) gene of *Staphylococcus aureus* may be cloned in an HV2 *Bacillus subtilis* host-vector system under P3 containment conditions.

20. A hybrid plasmid composed of, (1) *E.* Coli plasmid pBR325, (2) the origin of replication and transfer genes of *Agrobacterium tumefaciens* plasmid Ti, (3) the thiamine gene of *E. coli*, and (4) *Arabidopsis* DNA, may be transformed into *Agrobacterium tumefaciens* under P1 conditions. The *Agrobacterium tumefaciens* may subsequently be used to introduce the composite plasmid carrying *Arabidopsis* DNA and the *E. coli* thiamine gene into *Arabidopsis* plants under P1 containment conditions.

21. *Chlamydomonas reinhardi* can be used as a host for cloning defined DNA segments derived form *E. coli* and *Saccharomyces cerevisiae* using *E. coli/S. cerevisiae* hybrid vectors under P2 physical containment.

22. *Candida albicans* can be used as a host for cloning *candida albicans* DNA following propagation of the DNA in *E. coli* K–12 or in *Saccharomyces cerevisiae* employing an *E. coli/S. cerevisiae* hybrid plasmid vector or the yeast 2 micron plasmid.

23. The Rd strain of *Hemophilus influenzae* can be used as a host for the propagation of the cloned Tn 10 tet R gene derived from *E. coli* K–12 employing the non-conjugative *Haemophilus* plasmid, pRSF0885, under P1 conditions.

24. *Zymomonas mobilis* may be used as a host under P2 conditions for transformation by recombinant DNA derived from *Pseudomonas* strains that are non-pathogenic for animals or plants, and that has been cloned in an *E. coli* K–12 host.

25. Protoplasts of *Streptosporangium brasiliense* may be transformed with a hybrid plasmid containing pBR322 plus a *Streptosporangium* plasmid into which have been incorporated specified DNA segments from *Streptomyces* species or an HV1 approved *Bacillus subtilis* cloning vector.

26. *Saccharomyces cerevisiae* DNA may be cloned in *Tetrahymena thermophila* using *E. coli/S. cerevisiae* hybrid plasmids under P1 containment conditions.

27. All members of the nonpathogenic *Actinomycetes genus Streptomyces* the the plasmids native to this genus are approved as host-vector systems for the cloning under P1 conditions of DNA derived from other nonpathogenic prokaryotic organisms such as *Streptomyces* and other nonpathogenic *Actinomycetes* species, *Escherichia coli* K–12, *Bacillus subtilis, Bacillus licheniformis, Bacillus circulans*, and other nonpathogenic *Bacillus* species, and for the cloning of DNA derived from nonpathogenic unicellular eukaryotic microorganisms such as *Saccharomyces cerevisiae* and *Neurospora crassa*.

28. *Bacillus subtilis* strains that do not carry an asporogenic mutation can be used under P2 conditions for the cloning of DNA from any CDC Class 1 organism, using indigenous plasmid and phage vectors whose host range does not include *Bacillus anthracis* or *Bacillus cereus*.

29. *Bacillus subtilis* strains that do not carry an asporogenic mutation can be used under P1 conditions for the cloning of DNA from any Class 1 *Bacillus* species, using indigenous plasmid and phage vectors whose host range does not include *Bacillus anthracis* or *Bacillus cereus*.

30. Permission is granted to clone in *E. coli* K–12, under P4 containment conditions, restriction fragments of *Corynephage Beta* carrying the structural gene for diptheria toxin.

31. Permission is granted to clone certain subgenomic segments of Foot and Mouth Disease Virus in HV1 *Bacillus subtilis* and *Saccharomyces cerevisiae* host-vector systems under P1 conditions at Genentech, Inc., South San Francisco, California.

32. Permission is granted in principle to propagate in mammalian cell culture recombinant DNA molecules consisting of segments of Foot and Mouth Disease Virus and SV40 deletion vectors under P3 conditions at the Plum Island Animal Disease Center. Approval is subject to review by a RAC Working Group of individual experiments.

33. A conjugative plasmid may be used to transfer among *E. coli* K–12 strains, under P2 physical containment, the qa-2 gene of

Neurospora crassa ligated to a mobilizable plasmid.

34. *E. coli* K-12 strain DF214 (or derivatives thereof) and plasmid vectors (e.g., pBR322, pBR325) may be used to clone rat cDNA under P2 conditions. After the clone of interest has been purified, it may be worked with the under P1 containment.

Appendix F.—Certified Host-Vector Systems

While many experiments using *E. coli* K-12, *Saccharomyces cerevisiae* and *Bacillus subtilis* are currently exempt from the Guidelines under Exemption I-E-5, some derivatives of these host-vector systems were previously classified as HV1 or HV2. A listing of those systems follows.

HV1—The following plasmids are accepted as the vector components of certified *B. subtilis* HV1 systems: pUB110, pC194, pS194, pSA2100, pE194, pT127, pUB112, pC221, pC223, and pAB124. *B. subtilis* strains RUB 331 and BGSC 1S53 have been certified as the host component of HV1 systems based on these plasmids.

HV2—The asporogenic mutant derivative of *Bacillus subtilis*, ASB 298, with the following plasmids as the vector component: pUB110, pC194, pS194, pSA2100, pE194, pT127, pUB112, pC221, pC223, and pAB124.

HV2—The following sterile strains of *Saccharomyces cerevisiae*, all of which have the ste-VC9 mutation, SHY1, SHY2, SHY3, and SHY4. The following plasmids are certified for use: YIp1, YEp2, YEp4, YIp5, YEp6, YRp7, YEp20, YEp21, YEp24, YIp25, YIp26, YIp27, YIp28, YIp29, YIp30, YIp31, YIP32 and YIp33.

EK2 Plasmid Systems. The *E. coli* K-12 strain chi-1776. The following plasmids are certified for use: pSC101, pMB9, pBR313, pBR322, pDH24, pBR327, pGL101, pHB1. The following *E. coli/S. cerevisiae* hybrid plasmids are certified as EK2 vectors when used in *E. coli* chi-1776 or in the sterile yeast strains, SHY1, SHY2, SHY3, and SHY4: YIp1, YEp2, YEp4, YIp5, YEp6, YRp7, YEp20, YEp21, YEp24, YIp25, YIp26, YIp27, YIp28, YIp29, YIp30, YIp31, YIp32, YIp33.

EK2 Bacteriophage Systems. The following are certified EK2 systems based on bacteriophage lambda:

Vector	*Host*
λgt*WES*. λB′	DP50*sup*F
λgt*WES*. λB′	DP50*sup*F
λgt(Z)*vir*. λB′	*E. coli* K-12
λgtALO. λB	DP50*sup*F
Charon 3A	DP50 or DP50*sup*F
Charon 4A	DP50 or DP50*sup*F
Charon 16A	DP50 or DP50*sup*F
Charon 21A	DP50*sup*F
Charon 23A	DP50 or DP50*sup*F
Charon 24A	DP50 or DP50*sup*F

Appendix G.—Containment Conditions for Cloning of Genes Coding for the Biosynthesis of Toxins for Vertebrates

1. *General Information.* Appendix G specifies the containment to be used for the deliberate cloning of genes coding for the biosynthesis of toxins for vertebrates. Cloning of genes coding for toxins for vertebrates that have an LD_{50} of less than 100 nanograms per kilogram body weight (e.g., the botulinum toxins, tetanus toxin, diphtheria toxin, *Shigella dysenteriae* neurotoxin) is prohibited. No specific restrictions shall apply to the cloning of genes if the protein specified by the gene has an LD_{50} of 100 micrograms or more per kilogram of body weight. Experiments involving genes coding for toxins with an LD_{50} of 100 micrograms or less per kilogram body weight shall be registered with ORDA prior to initiating the experiments. A list of toxins classified as to LD_{50} is available from ORDA. Testing procedures for determining toxicity of toxins not on the list are available from ORDA. The results of such tests shall be forwarded to ORDA, which will consult with the *ad hoc* Working Group on toxins prior to inclusion of the toxin on the list. (See Section IV-E-1-b-(3)-(i).)

2. *Containment Conditions for Cloning of Toxin Genes in E. coli K-12.*

(a) Cloning of genes coding for toxins for vertebrates that have an LD_{50} in the range of 100 nanograms to 1000 nanograms per kilogram body weight (e.g., abrin, *Clostridium perfringens* epsilon toxin) may proceed under P2+EK2 or P3+EK1 containment conditions.

(b) Cloning of genes for the biosynthesis of toxins for vertebrates with an LD_{50} in the range of 1 microgram to 100 micrograms per kilogram body weight may proceed under P1+EK1 containment conditions (e.g., *Staphylococcus aureus* alpha toxin, *Staphylococcus aureus* beta toxin, ricin, *Pseudomonas aeruginosa* exotoxin A, *Bordatella pertussis* toxin, the lethal factor of *Bacillus anthracis*, the *Pasteurella pestis* murine toxins, the oxygen-labile hemolysins such as streptolysin O, and certain neurotoxins present in snake venoms and other venoms).

(c) Some enterotoxins are substantially more toxic when administered enterally then parenterally. The following enterotoxins shall be subject to P1+EK1 containment conditions: cholera toxin, the heat labile toxins of *E. coli*, *Klebsiella*, and other related proteins that may be identified by neutralization with an antiserum mono specific for cholera toxin, and the heat stable toxins of *E. coli* and of *Yersinia enterocolitica*.

3. *Containment Conditions for Cloning of Toxins Genes in Organisms Other than E. coli K-12.*

Requests involving the cloning of genes coding for toxins for vertebrates in host-vector systems other than *E. coli* K-12 will be evaluated by ORDA, which will consult with the *ad hoc* working group on toxins. (See Section IV-E-1-b-(3)-(j).)

Appendix H.—Experiments Covered by Section III-O

No experiments currently fall under Section III-O of the Guidelines.

Dated: June 22, 1981.

Donald S. Fredrickson, M.D.,

Director, National Institutes of Health.

OMB's "Mandatory Information Requirements for Federal Assistance Program Announcements" (45 FR 39592) requires a statement concerning the official government programs contained in the *Catalog of Federal Domestic Assistance*. Normally NIH lists in its announcements the number and title of affected individual programs for the guidance of the public. Because the guidance in this notice covers not only virtually every NIH program but also essentially every federal research program in which DNA recombinant molecule techniques could be used, it has been determined to be not cost effective or in the public interest to attempt to list these programs. Such a list would likely require several additional pages. In addition, NIH could not be certain that every federal program would be included as many federal agencies, as well as private organizations, both national and international, have elected to follow the NIH Guidelines. In lieu of the individual program listing, NIH invites readers to direct questions to the information address above about whether individual programs listed in the *Catalog of Federal Domestic Assistance* are affected.

NIH programs are not covered by OMB Circular A-95 because they fit the description of "programs not considered appropriate" in Section 8-(b)-(4) and (5) of that Circular.

[FR Doc. 81-19037 Filed 6-30-81; 8:45 am]

BILLING CODE 4110-03-M

federal register

Tuesday
August 4, 1981

Part III

Department of Health and Human Services

National Institutes of Health

Recombinant DNA Research; Notice of Meetings and Notice of Proposed Actions Under Guidelines

DEPARTMENT OF HEALTH AND HUMAN SERVICES

National Institutes of Health

Recombinant DNA Advisory Committee; Notice of Meetings

Pursuant to Pub. L. 92-463, notice is hereby given of a meeting of the Recombinant DNA Advisory Committee at the National Institutes of Health, Conference Room 6, Building 31C, 9000 Rockville Pike, Bethesda, Maryland 20205, on September 10, 1981, from 9:00 a.m. to recess at approximately 6:00 p.m., and, if necessary, on September 11, 1981, from 8:30 a.m. to 5:00 p.m. This meeting will be open to the public on September 10 from 9:00 a.m. to approximately 3:00 p.m., and on September 11 from 8:30 a.m. to adjournment to discuss:

Proposed major revision of Guidelines
Amendment of Guidelines
E. coli K-12 host-vector systems
Host-vector systems other than *E. coli* K-12
Risk-assessment
Review of protocols for required containment levels
Requests for exceptions to prohibitions
Other matters requiring necessary action by the Committee.

Attendance by the public will be limited to space available.

In accordance with provisions set forth in Section 552b(c)(4), Title 5, U.S. Code and Section 10(d) of Pub. L. 92-463, the meeting will be closed to the public for approximately three hours for the review, discussion and evaluation of proposal(s) from a commercial concern(s) for scale-up of recombinant DNA experiments. It is anticipated that this will occur on September 10, from approximately 3:00 p.m. until adjournment. The proposal(s) and the discussion could reveal confidential trade secrets or commercial property such as patentable material.

Dr. William J. Gartland, Jr., Executive Secretary, Recombinant DNA Advisory Committee, National Institutes of Health, Building 31, Room 4A52, telephone (301) 496-6051, will provide materials to be discussed at the meeting, rosters of committee members and substantive program information. A summary of the meeting will be available at a later date.

In addition, notice is hereby given of a meeting of the Large Scale Review Working Group sponsored by the Recombinant DNA Advisory Committee at the National Institutes of Health, Conference Room 4, Building 31A, 9000 Rockville Pike, Bethesda, Maryland 20205, on September 9, 1981, from 2:00 p.m. to 5:00 p.m. The meeting will be open to the public. Attendance will be limited to space available.

Further information may be obtained from Dr. Elizabeth Milewski, Executive Secretary, Large Scale Review Working Group, NIAID, Building 31, Room 4A52, Bethesda, Maryland, telephone, (301) 496-6051.

July 27, 1981.

Thomas E. Malone, Ph.D.,
Deputy Director, NIH.

OMB's "Mandatory Information Requirements for Federal Assistance Program Announcements" (45 FR 39592) requires a statement concerning the official government programs contained in the *Catalog of Federal Domestic Assistance*. Normally NIH lists in its announcements the number and title of affected individual programs for the guidance of the public. Because the guidance in this notice covers not only virtually every NIH program but also essentially every federal research program in which DNA recombinant molecule techniques could be used, it has been determined to be not cost effective or in the public interest to attempt to list these programs. Such a list would likely require several additional pages. In addition, NIH could not be certain that every federal program would be included, as many federal agencies, as well as private organizations, both national and international, have elected to follow the NIH Guidelines. In lieu of the individual program listing, NIH invites readers to direct questions to the information addressed above about whether individual programs listed in the *Catalog of Federal Domestic Assistance* are affected.

NIH programs are not covered by OMB Circular A-95 because they fit the description of "programs not considered appropriate" in Section 8-(b)-(4) and (5) of that Circular.

[FR Doc. 81-22141 Filed 8-3-81; 8:45 am]
BILLING CODE 4110-08-M

Recombinant DNA Research; Proposed Actions Under Guidelines

AGENCY: National Institutes of Health, PHS, HHS.

ACTION: Notice of actions under NIH Guidelines for Research Involving Recombinant DNA Molecules.

SUMMARY: This notice sets forth proposed actions to be taken under the NIH Guidelines for Research Involving Recombinant DNA Molecules. Interested parties are invited to submit comments concerning these proposals. After consideration of these proposals and comments by the NIH Recombinant DNA Advisory Committee (RAC) at its September 10-11, 1981 meeting, the Director of the National Institutes of Health will issue decisions on these proposals in accord with the Guidelines.

DATE: Comments must be received by September 3, 1981.

ADDRESS: Written comments and recommendations should be submitted to the Director, Office of Recombinant DNA Activities, Building 31, Room 4A52, National Institutes of Health, Bethesda, Maryland 20205. All comments received in timely response to this notice will be considered and will be available for public inspection in the above office on weekdays between the hours of 8:30 a.m. and 5:00 p.m.

FOR FURTHER INFORMATION CONTACT: Background documentation and additional information can be obtained from Drs. Stanley Barban or Elizabeth Milewski, Office of Recombinant DNA Activities, National Institutes of Health, Bethesda, Maryland 20205, (301) 496-6051.

SUPPLEMENTARY INFORMATION: The National Institutes of Health will consider the following changes and amendments under the Guidelines for Research Involving Recombinant DNA Molecules, as well as actions under these Guidelines.

1. *Request to Utilize Hemophilus Parainfluenzae to Clone Moloney Murine Leukemia Provirus.*

Dr. James. W. Gautsch of Scripps Clinic and Research Foundation requests permission to clone Moloney MuLV provirus and cellular flanking regions in *Hemophilus parainfluenzae*. The provirus DNA and flanking regions will be ligated into vector pRK290, a plasmid with a broad host range in gram negative bacteria. The cloned plasmid DNA will subsequently be used to infect NIH 3T3 cells.

2. *Evaluation of a Proposal Using Conjugative Plasmids to Transfer DNA between E. Coli, Vibrio Cholera, and Vibrio Harveyi.*

Dr. J. W. Hastings of Harvard University requests permission to clone *Vibrio Harveyi* DNA in *E. coli* and *Vibrio cholera*. Conjugation proficient plasmids (e.g., pRK290 derivatives) will be used to transfer the cloned *V. Harveyi* DNA between *E. coli*, *V. cholera*, and *V. Harveyi*.

3. *Request to Include Streptococcus Lactis and Streptococcus Sanguis in a Sublist of Appendix A.*

Dr. Larry McKay of the University of Minnesota has requested permission for the one way transfer of *Streptococcus lactis* DNA into *S. sanguis* strain Challis, and that these strains be included under the exemption category of Appendix A on the basis that they exchange genetic information by known physiological processes. He also requests permission to transfer a recombinant plasmid from *S. faecalis* to *S. lactis*.

4. *Request for Permission to Clone Subgenomic Segments of Rift Valley Fever Virus.*

Molecular Genetics, Inc., of Minnetonka, Minnesota in collaboration with the U.S. Army Medical Research Institute of Infectious Diseases, Fort Detrick, Md., has requested permission to clone, under P1 conditions, segments of Rift Valley Fever Virus encoding for antigenic determinants.

5. *Request to Clone Saccharomyces Cerevisiae DNA in Salmonella Typhimurium.*

Drs. Christopher Marvel and Edward Penhoet of the University of California, Berkeley, have requested permission to clone *Saccharomyces cerevisiae* DNA in *Salmonella typhimurium* using a nonmobilizable plasmid (YEpl3).

6. *Proposal To Amend Section III–B–3.*

Dr. Michael J. Ross, of Genentech, Inc., has requested the RAC to evaluate a proposal to amend Section III–B–3 of the Guidelines. Section III–B–3 currently specifies that the Director, NIH may set containment levels after a case-by-case review of certain experiments involving non-HV1 host-vector systems. The cloning of higher eukaryotic DNA into non-certified host-vector systems is cited as an example. Dr. Ross proposes a provision which would permit cloning of DNA from any nonpathogenic species into nonpathogenic lower eukaryotes at the P3 level of containment; cloning of DNA from any nonpathogenic species into nonpathogenic prokaryotes would be allowed at the P2 level of containment. Data supporting the contention that the donor and recipient are nonpathogenic would be submitted to the local IBC.

7. *Proposed Amendment of Section I–D–6.*

Dr. Irving Johnson of Eli Lilly and Company has requested that Section I–D–6 be amended to read as follows (new text in italics):

"I–D–6. Large-Scle experiments [e.g., more than 10 liters of culture] with organisms containing recombinant DNAs *other than those listed in Appendix C, Paragraphs 2, 3, and 4 of the Guidelines,* unless the recombinant DNAs are rigorously characterized and the absence of harmful sequences established (3). [See Section IV–E–1–b–(3)–(d).]

It is noted that certain other modifications of the Guidelines will be necessary in order to make them consistent with the adoption of the amendment. For instance, the text dealing with large-scale experiments in Sections 2, 3, and 4 in Appendix C would be replaced with the following revised text:

"Large-scale experiments (e.g., more than 10 liters of culture) require prior IBC review and approval."

8. *Request to include streptococcus Pyogenes on Sublist F of Appendix A.*

Dr. Joseph Ferretti of the University of Okahoma Health Sciences Center, Oklahoma City, Oklahoma, has requested that *Streptococcus pyogenes* and *streptococcus sanguis* be considered as natural exchangers of DNA under the exemption category of Section I–E–4 and included in Sublist F of Appendix A. He has submitted information concerning the evidence for exchange of genetic information between these organisms.

9. *Proposed Amendment of III–C–2a and Addition of a New Section III–C–7–c.*

Dr. Lois Miller of the University of Idaho, Moscow, Idaho, has proposed the following revision of Section III–C–2–a regarding experiments involving invertebrate viral vectors:

"III–C–2. Invertebrate Host-Vector Systems.

III–C–2–a. Invertebrate Viral Vectors. Experiments involving invertebrate virus vectors can be done as follows:

III–C–2–a–(1). Recombinant DNA molecules containing no more than two-thirds of the genome of any invertebrate virus [all viruses from a single Family (36) being considered identical (50)] may be propagated and maintained in cells in tissue culture using P1 containment. For each experiments, it must be shown that the cells lack helper virus for the specific Families of defective viruses being used. The DNA may contain fragments of the genomes of viruses from more than one Family but each fragment must be less than two-thirds of a genome.

III–C–2–a–(2). Recombinants with less than two-thirds of the genome of any invertebrate virus may be rescued with helper virus using P2 containment unless it is classified by the CDC as a class 3 agent (1) in which case P3 containment is required.

III–C–2–a–(3). Experiments involving the use of other whole or defective virus genomes to propagate DNA sequences from prokaryotic or eukaryotic organisms (and viruses), or as vectors to transform nonpermissive cells, will be evaluated by NIH on a case-by-case basis (45) and will be conducted under the prescribed physical and biological containment conditions. (See Section IV–E–1–b–(3)–(c).)

NIH will also review on a case-by-case basis (45) all experiments involving the use of virus vectors in animals and will prescribe the physical and biological containment conditions appropriate for such studies. (See Section IV–E–1–b–(3)–(c).)"

Dr. Miller also proposes that a new Section, III–C–7–c, be added to the Guidelines, as follows:

"III–C–7–c. *Transfer to Invertebrates.* DNA from any nonprohibited source [Section I–D], except for greater than one quarter of a eukaryotic viral genome, which has been cloned and propagated in *E. coli* K–12, may be transferred with the *E. coli* vector used for cloning to any eukaryotic cells in culture or to any invertebrate organism and propagated under conditions of physical containment comparable to P1 and appropriate to the organism under study (2A). Transfers to any other host will be considered by the RAC on a case-by-case basis (45)."

10. *Containment Conditions for Cloning and Expression of DNA Coding for Diphtheria Toxin.*

In the revised Guidelines issued on July 1, 1981, Dr. John Murphy of Harvard University was given permission to clone in *E. coli* K–12, under P4 containment conditions, restriction fragments of *Corynephage Beta* carrying the structural gene for diphtheria toxin. Dr. Murphy requests that he be permitted to carry out the experiments within NIH high-containment facilities with the selection of laboratory practices and containment equipment to be specified by the local biosafety committee (IBC).

11. *Development of New Host-Vector System based on Corynebacterium Glutamicum.*

Dr. Daniel Liberman of Massachusetts Institute of Technology, Cambridge, Massachusetts, has requested assignment of appropriate containment conditions for development of a new host-vector system based on the gram positive bacterium *Corynebacterium glutamicum* as host with three possible types of vectors, including hybrid plasmids.

Richard M. Krause,

Director, National Institute of Allergy and Infectious Diseases.

July 28, 1981.

OMB's "Mandatory Information Requirements for Federal Assistance Program Announcements" (45 FR 39592) requires a statement concerning the official government programs contained in the *Catalog of Federal Domestic Assistance.* Normally NIH lists in its announcements the number and title of affected individual programs for the guidance of the public. Because the guidance in this notice covers not only virtually every NIH program but also essentially every federal research program in which DNA recombinant molecule techniques could be used, it has been determined to be not cost effective or in the public interest to attempt to list these programs. Such a list would likely require several additional pages. In addition, NIH could not be certain that every federal program would be included as many federal agencies, as well as private organizations, both national and international, have elected to follow the NIH Guidelines. In lieu of the individual program listing, NIH invites readers to direct questions to the information address above about whether individual programs listed in the *Catalog of Federal Domestic Assistance* are affected.

NIH programs are not covered by OMB Circular A-95 because they fit the description of "programs not considered appropriate" in Section 8-(b)-(4) and (5) of that Circular.

[FR Doc. 81-22442 Filed 8-3-81; 8:45 am]

BILLING CODE 4110-08-M

DEPARTMENT OF HEALTH AND HUMAN SERVICES
PUBLIC HEALTH SERVICE
NATIONAL INSTITUTES OF HEALTH

RECOMBINANT DNA ADVISORY COMMITTEE
LARGE-SCALE REVIEW WORKING GROUP

MINUTES OF MEETING

SEPTEMBER 9, 1981

The Large-Scale Review Working Group was convened for its second meeting at 2:00 p.m. on September 9, 1981, in Building 31A, Conference Room 4, at the National Institutes of Health, 9000 Rockville Pike, Bethesda, Maryland 20205. Kenneth Berns and Robert McKinney were co-chairmen.

Working Group members present for all or part of the meeting were:

Manuel Barbeito, NIH; Kenneth Berns, University of Florida (Co-chairman); Timothy J. Henry, Food and Drug Administration; Morris Levin, Environmental Protection Agency; James Mason, Utah State Department of Health; Robert McKinney, NIH, (Co-chairman); Elizabeth Milewski, NIH, (Executive Secretary); Henry Miller, Bureau of Drugs, FDA; Sue Tolin, U. S. Department of Agriculture; and David West, National Institute for Occupational Safety and Health.

Others in attendance for all or part of the meeting were:

Paula Dwyer, McGraw-Hill; Charles R. Gaush, Bethesda Research Laboratories; Pat Germann, Genex Corporation; Judith Hautala, Genex Corporation; J. Hyman, Japanese Embassy; M. J. Johnson, Pall Corporation; Howard Koonse, Fort Dodge Laboratories; Carter Leonard, Blue Sheet; Max Marsh, Eli Lilly & Company; James McCullough, Library of Congress; Jim Silverman, Stauffer Chemical; and H. Tanake, Japanese Embassy.

DEPARTMENT OF HEALTH AND HUMAN SERVICES
PUBLIC HEALTH SERVICE
NATIONAL INSTITUTES OF HEALTH

RECOMBINANT DNA ADVISORY COMMITTEE
LARGE-SCALE REVIEW WORKING GROUP
MINUTES OF MEETING

SEPTEMBER 9, 1981

Dr. Kenneth Berns called the second meeting of the Large-Scale Review Working Group to order at 2:15 p.m., Wednesday, September 9, 1981. He then briefly introduced the major topic of discussion. He recalled to the group that the Recombinant DNA Advisory Committee (RAC) had discussed, at the April 23-24, 1981 meeting, a proposal by Drs. David Baltimore and Allan Campbell to convert the NIH Guidelines for Research Involving Recombinant DNA Molecules to a "code of standard practice." In response, RAC formed a working group to review the status of the NIH Guidelines and to develop recommendations concerning their status. During the summer of 1981 the Working Group for Revision of the Guidelines constructed a proposal which was to be presented to the RAC at the September 10-11, 1981 meeting. One aspect of the Working Group proposal would eliminate the prohibition against scale-up above the 10 liter limit. As the proposal has not been published for thirty days of public comment, no final action can be taken by the RAC at the September 1981 meeting. Dr. Berns said that the Large-Scale Review Working Group should nevertheless, consider the possible impact of adoption of such a proposal; RAC review of large-scale experiments would be eliminated if this proposal is accepted by RAC and adopted by the NIH.

Dr. Berns also pointed out to the Large-Scale Review Working Group that RAC would discuss at its September 10-11, 1981 meeting a proposal by Dr. Irving Johnson of Lilly Research Laboratories to modify Section I-D-6 of the Guidelines.

Section I-D-6 prohibits scale up of recombinant DNA experiments above ten liters of culture. Dr. Johnson's proposal would remove large-scale procedures involving E. coli EK1, S. cerevisiae laboratory strains and HV1 B. subtilis host-vector systems from the requirement for prior RAC review and approval; rather the Institutional Biosafety Committee (IBC) of each institution would review and approve large-scale proposals involving these host-vector systems. Dr. Berns said that RAC review of large-scale experiments would be substantially reduced if this proposed modification in the Guidelines is accepted by the RAC and approved by the Director, NIH.

Dr. Berns said that in the past, the majority of large-scale proposals reviewed by the RAC have been "voluntary submittals" from industrial firms. These reviews supported the development of large-scale methods during a period when the Federal agencies (e.g., USDA and FDA) having proximate regulatory authority have not implemented standards or guidelines for the use of recombinant DNA technology. While these agencies send liaison members to the RAC, the agencies do not exercise voting privileges; Dr. Berns said he and Dr. McKinney felt that this meeting might appropriately provide an opportunity for the agencies to discuss from their perspective, the effects of the proposed changes to the NIH Guidelines.

Dr. McKinney asked if any industrial representatives present at the meeting might explain their company's views on the NIH voluntary submission program. Mr. Silverman, a legal counsel for Stauffer Chemical Company, said his company would abide voluntarily by the NIH Guidelines because of legal considerations. Industry recognizes that local government has a great interest in this area, and dealing adequately on the Federal level would aid in interacting with local government. In addition, Stauffer Chemical Company scientists want to follow standard good practice codes; they are adamant concerning adherence to the NIH Guidelines. Industry's greatest hesitation concerning adherence is the functioning of the mechanism by which NIH will protect proprietary information. Industry is concerned about who would make a final determination of what is proprietary information, particularly in Freedom of Information (FOI) requests. Dr. Milewski explained the procedure by which confidential submissions were processed by the NIH under the Voluntary Compliance Program; Part VI of the Guidelines, Voluntary Compliance, specifies procedures to be followed in the event of an FOI request. Dr. McKinney said that the NIH review system provides industry with third party review of projects.

FDA Views

Dr. Henry of the Food and Drug Administration (FDA) said his agency favors eliminating the 10 liter limit and supports the proposal to convert the NIH Guidelines to a voluntary "code of standard practice." If such changes should occur, the FDA would continue product review using current FDA procedures, which are directed to thoroughly assessing the safety of the finished product. He said FDA possesses the authority to inspect production facilities, but not to inspect or regulate research facilities. FDA is charged with regulating the marketing of many of the products of recombinant DNA technology.

NIOSH Views

Dr. West of the National Institute for Occupational Safety and Health (NIOSH) said that the concerns of NIOSH were similar to those of the Occupational Safety and Health Administration (OSHA). He said NIOSH will evaluate recombinant DNA technology and the fermentation industry in general. At the moment, he envisaged NIOSH proceeding in the following manner: (1) field studies of recombinant DNA organisms and products will be performed by industrial hygiene experts; (2) control technology assessments will be made.

Dr. West said NIOSH is several years away from offering specific guidance to the industrial community. NIOSH will, however, continue to track developments to identify emerging problems. He said that NIOSH would be deprived of a resource in this effort should the NIH vacate their Guidelines.

Dr. Mason noted that industry complies with the NIH Guidelines voluntarily. He questioned whether the information base might, therefore, be biased and whether such a bias concerns NIOSH. Dr. West replied that he could not determine whether the information base would be biased in a voluntary submittal program. He hoped that NIOSH and industry would cooperate in the area of recombinant DNA technology; NIOSH might offer helpful suggestions to firms when these firms are setting up and tuning up their installations.
Dr. McKinney asked Dr. West if NIOSH's interests would change should the NIH Guidelines became a "code of standard practice." Dr. West said they would not. Dr. McKinney asked why NIOSH was not at the moment actively evaluating the fermentation industry. Dr. West replied that at the time NIOSH was instituted, several critical issues and obvious health concerns required NIOSH's attention. Before the advent of recombinant DNA technology, long established firms dominated the fermentation field. Most of these companies had acknowledged the existence of occupational health problems and had developed an expertise in the area. With the emergence of recombinant DNA technology, many new companies will enter the field. These companies will not have had the opportunity to develop expertise in the area of occupational health in fermentation techology, and this might be an issue of concern to NIOSH.

Dr. Marsh of Eli Lilly and Company said that Eli Lilly has forty years of experience in the fermentation industry. He felt fermentation activities are not hazardous. He suggested that many other industrial processes present clear evidence of hazard and that NIOSH must prioritize its goals to deal with these other, evident hazards. Dr. West agreed saying that while the recombinant DNA area is of interest to NIOSH, it is not currently NIOSH's top priority. He pointed out, however, that NIOSH must evaluate the area before it can rate the importance of overseeing recombinant DNA technology to NIOSH's overall mission.

Dr. McKinney said that currently companies submitting proposals to the NIH cooperate with NIOSH; he asked whether this cooperation would continue should the NIH Guidelines be abolished. Dr. West replied that NIOSH would most definitely lose a valuable resource should the Guidelines be abolished. Dr. Levin of the Environmental Protection Agency (EPA) suggested that industry would also lose a resource if the NIH no longer provides a forum for discussing and evaluating recombinant DNA issues. Dr. Berns said that industry may continue to seek advice from the NIH should NIH eliminate its prohibition against exceeding the 10 liter limit; the companies benefit when the NIH approves their submissions. Dr. Berns noted that the NIH is not currently receiving information on physical facilities; he thought this information would be the most useful type of data for NIOSH and OSHA.

Dr. West said NIOSH's activity in the recombinant DNA area are independent of NIH's decisions. He reiterated that NIH is nonetheless a convenient resource to NIOSH. In addition, NIH by its activity benefits industry by partially filling the information gap.

EPA Views

Dr. Levin said that EPA's concerns at this time are similar to those of NIOSH. He said EPA expects the fermentation industry to produce millions of tons of products over the next 20 years. EPA intends to evaluate the process and the products, and anticipates problems in the areas of worker exposure, disposal of materials, and impact on the environment.

He said NIH currently provides a forum for discussion; such a forum is an important asset in maintaining and promoting necessary interactions between industry and EPA. He felt this forum to be valuable and that it should not be lost. Dr. McKinney asked Dr. Levin if he thought EPA would formulate new standards to deal with recombinant DNA processes. Dr. Levin replied that legally all recombinant DNA processes are covered by the statutes of the Federal Insecticide, Fungicide, and Rodenticide Act (FIFRA), and of the Toxic Substances Control Act (TSCA). Dr. Tolin of the Department of Agriculture (USDA) asked Dr. Levin if EPA regulations can be applied to recombinant DNA containing organisms. Dr. Levin said he believed these organisms are covered either by FIFRA or TSCA, depending on the organism; some bacteria are considered chemicals and are covered by TSCA.

Dr. McKinney asked if EPA could cover the loss of a resource should NIH cease its activities in the recombinant DNA area. Dr. Levin said EPA is currently considering the feasibility of establishing a group to serve the function NIH currently fills, should NIH cease its activities in this area.

Dr. McKinney asked Dr. Levin if industry would have to deal with a multiplicity of agencies and information if no central information clearing house exists. Dr. Levin replied that such a situation would be inevitable, for if no central point exists, each agency must and will develop its own information and practices. Dr. Mason said it appeared that most members endorsed the idea of an "information clearing house." Dr. McKinney said that such a "clearing house" would minimize confusion during the gestation period in the industry. A "clearing house" would thus serve the public good as the industry develops.

USDA Views

Dr. Tolin of USDA said no large-scale submissions to the NIH under the Voluntary Compliance Program have yet dealt with issues of concern to USDA; most of these early submissions deal with human health products. USDA is primarily concerned with quarantine regulations, the release of organisms into the environment, and the regulation of vaccines and food products. Nonetheless, USDA feels information sharing between agencies to be most appropriate—the Federal Interagency Committee on Recombinant DNA Research and RAC are valuable in this sense to the USDA. She said USDA would cooperate with EPA in the development of processes to evaluate proposals in which recombinant DNA-containing organisms would be disseminated in the environment, should the NIH no longer provide a forum.

FDA, Bureau of Drugs Views

Dr. Miller of FDA's Bureau of Drugs said that FDA had considered linking the FDA approval process for pharmaceuticals to compliance with the NIH Guidelines; the companies would not have to prepare complete environmental impact statements if they adhere to the NIH Guidelines during development and production of pharmaceuticals. He felt that NIH acceptance of the proposal to convert the Guidelines to a "code of standard practice," would not significantly affect the FDA approval process for pharmaceuticals. FDA has found the NIH's review of large-scale proposals useful but not so useful as to justify this additional level of regulation.

Discussion of Prohibition I-D-6

Dr. Tolin suggested the group discuss in greater detail the proposal to eliminate the prohibition concerning scale-up beyond the 10 liter limit. Dr. Berns said the 10 liter limit was instituted with laboratory scale procedures in mind. Mr. Barbeito of the NIH Division of Safety said that 10 liters is the volume which can be totally contained in most standard laboratory procedures, and for this reason was selected as the upper limit for small-scale procedures. In the industrial setting, however, concerns such as protection of product purity and financial considerations force companies to employ vigorous procedures to guard against contamination. Thus, large-scale procedures in an industrial setting might logically be viewed in a different light from laboratory procedures.

Dr. McKinney pointed out that industry complies voluntarily with the 10 liter limit. The 10 liter limit is mandatory only for laboratories supported by Federal funding. Dr. Levin pointed out that those companies purchasing licensing rights under the Cohen-Boyer patent held by Stanford University and the University of California would also comply. Mr. Silverman said industry will act as if the Guidelines are regulations no matter what their status; no company wishes to run the risk of being found negligent.

Dr. McKinney asked if industry would continue to submit large-scale proposals to the NIH for review if the 10 liter limit were abolished. Dr. Marsh said Eli Lilly and Company would submit information, as industry regards RAC as a forum for discussion. Dr. McKinney asked Dr. Marsh if Eli Lilly would notify NIH of all recombinant DNA procedures, including those procedures using host-vector systems exempt from the Guidelines. Dr. Marsh replied that Eli Lilly and Company reporting procedures would comply with NIH Guideline requirements.

Mr. Silverman said Stauffer Chemical Company would probably prefer to submit information independently to each federal agency requesting information, rather than to a "central information clearing house."

Dr. Mason questioned whether the risks associated with recombinant DNA technology should be evaluated differently than those associated with other fermentation processes. Dr. Berns felt this issue revolved around the definition of meaningful medical surveillance. Until meaningful surveillance is defined, it is difficult to determine whether a company is effectively protecting the worker. He said Dr. Philip Landrigan of NIOSH had agreed to address the Large-Scale Review Group on NIOSH determinations in the area of medical surveillance.

The meeting was adjourned at 4:00 p.m.

Respectively submitted,

Elizabeth Milewski
Elizabeth Milewski, Ph.D.
Executive Secretary

I hereby certify that, to the best of my knowledge, the foregoing Minutes are accurate and complete.

12/31/81
Date

Kenneth I. Berns
Kenneth I. Berns, Ph.D.
Co-Chairman
Large-Scale Review Working Group
of the Recombinant DNA Advisory Committee

Dec 28, 1981
Date

Robert W. McKinney
Robert W. McKinney, Ph.D.
Co-Chairman
Large-Scale Review Working Group
of the Recombinant DNA Advisory Committee

DEPARTMENT OF HEALTH AND HUMAN SERVICES
PUBLIC HEALTH SERVICE
NATIONAL INSTITUTES OF HEALTH

RECOMBINANT DNA ADVISORY COMMITTEE

MINUTES OF MEETING

SEPTEMBER 10-11, 1981

TABLE OF CONTENTS

DEPARTMENT OF HEALTH AND HUMAN SERVICES
PUBLIC HEALTH SERVICE
NATIONAL INSTITUTES OF HEALTH

RECOMBINANT DNA ADVISORY COMMITTEE

MINUTES OF MEETING[1]

SEPTEMBER 10-11, 1981

The Recombinant DNA Advisory Committee (RAC) was convened for its twenty-third meeting at 9:00 a.m. on September 10, 1981, in Conference Room 6, Building 31C, National Institutes of Health, 9000 Rockville Pike, Bethesda, Maryland 20205. Ray Thornton (Chairman), President, Arkansas State University, presided. In accordance with Public Law 92-463, the meeting was open to the public from 9:00 a.m. to 4:05 p.m. on September 10, and from 8:30 a.m. to adjournment at 10:30 a.m. on September 11. The meeting was closed to the public from 4:05 p.m. to 5:50 p.m. on September 10 for the review of proposals involving proprietary information.

Committee members present for all or part of the meeting were:

Abdul Karim Ahmed; David Baltimore; Kenneth Berns; Winston Brill; L. Albert Daloz; Nina Fedoroff; Richard Goldstein; Jean Harris; King Holmes; Patricia King; Arthur Landy; Werner Maas; James Mason; Gerard McGarrity; Robert McKinney; Robert Mitchell; Elena Nightingale; Ramon Pinon; Mark Saginor; John Scandalios; Pieter Wensink; and William J. Gartland, Jr., Executive Secretary.

A Committee roster is attached. (Attachment I)

The following ad hoc consultants to the Committee were present:

Susan K. Gottesman, National Institutes of Health, and Norton Zinder, Rockefeller University.

The following non-voting members and liaison representatives were present:

Charlotte Bell, U.S. Department of Justice; Chia T. Chen, OSHA, U.S. Department of Labor; Timothy J. Henry, Food and Drug Administration; Herman Lewis, National Science Foundation; Henry Miller, Bureau of Drugs, FDA; Jane Shultz, Veterans

---

[1]The RAC is advisory to the NIH, and its recommendations should not be considered as final and accepted. The Office of Recombinant DNA Activities should be consulted for NIH policy on specific issues.

Administration; Sue Tolin, U.S. Department of Agriculture; and William J. Walsh, III, U.S. Department of State.

Other National Institutes of Health staff present were:

Stanley Barban, NIAID; W. Emmett Barkley, ORS; Becky Connors, NIAID; Irving Delappe, NIAID; Richard Krause, NIAID; Elizabeth Milewski, NIAID; Stanley Nagle, NIAID; John Nutter, NIAID; Bernard Talbot, NIAID; John Venditti, NCI; Michael H. Vodkin, NIAID; and Rudolf Wanner, ORS.

Others in attendance for all or part of the meeting were:

Robert Banks, RAND Corporation; Tineke Bodde, BioScience Magazine; Irene Brandt, Eli Lilly & Co.; Meredith Broadbent; Joel M. Dalrymple, USAMRIID; Mary Ann Danello, Amer. Assoc. for the Advancement of Science and American Society for Microbiology; Mark DeOries, Genex Corporation; David Dickson, Nature; Paula Dwyer, McGraw-Hill; Mark Finkelstein, Schering-Plough Corporation; Charles Gaush, Bethesda Research Laboratories; Pat Germann, Genex Corporation; Zsolt Harsanyi, DNA Science, Inc.; Clayton Hathaway, Monsanto Company; Judith Hautala, Genex Corporation; Leslie Henderson, University of Missouri; Holly Hexter, Higher Education Daily; Philip Hilts, Washington Post; Jerry Hunter, University of Maryland; Evelyn Hurlburt, Johns Hopkins School of Medicine; Dorothy Jessup, U.S. Department of Agriculture; J. A. Johnson, Library of Congress; M. J. Johnson, Pall Corporation; Attila I. Kadar, Food and Drug Administration; Geoffrey Karny, Office of Technology Assessment; Michael Konrad, Cetus Corporation; Howard Koonse, Fort Dodge Laboratories; Paul Leibowitz, Schering-Plough Corporation; Carter Leonard, Blue Sheet; Morris A. Levin, Environmental Protection Agency; Dan Liberman, Massachusetts Institute of Technology; Max Marsh, Eli Lilly & Company; James McCullough, Library of Congress; Kim McDonald, Chronical of Higher Education; Julia Miller, Science News; Claire Nader; Nanette Newell, Office of Technology Assessment; Norine Noonan, Science and Technology Committee, House of Representatives; Ann Norberg, Monsanto Co.; Lacy Overby, Abbott Laboratories; C. J. Peters, USAMRIID; Stephen Pijar, Food and Drug Administration; William Pilacinski, Molecular Genetics, Inc.; Michael Ross, Genentech, Inc.; Michael Ryan, Schering Corporation; John Salstein, Molecular Genetics, Inc.; Jim Silverman, Stauffer Chemical; Stephanie Soucek, National Institute for Occupational Safety & Health; Laurence Storch; J. H. Stryh, President's Commission; Donna Suchmann, Hazelton Laboratories; Charles Turbyville, NIH Week; Robert Willette, DUO Research; Susan Wright, University of Michigan; and Burke Zimmerman, George Washington University.

I. CALL TO ORDER AND OPENING REMARKS

Mr. Ray Thorton, Chairman, called the meeting to order at 9:00 a.m., September 10, 1981. He welcomed five newly appointed members: Mr. Albert Daloz of Hancock, New Hampshire; Dr. Arthur Landy of Brown University; Mr. Robert Mitchell of Norwalk, California; Dr. Mark Saginor of Los Angeles, California; and Dr. Pieter Wensink of Brandeis University. Mr. Thornton noted that two other newly appointed members, Dr. David Friedman of the University of Michigan Medical School and Dr. David Martin of the University of California, San Francisco, could not attend the September 10 and 11, 1981, meeting.

Mr. Thornton, noting the resignation of Dr. Donald S. Fredrickson as Director of the National Institutes of Health, said the community would miss his counsel and leadership. Mr. Thornton said that Dr. Fredrickson had the great ability of clearly articulating the relationship between science and public policy. Mr. Thornton said that the RAC was fortunate, however, in that it would now report to Dr. Richard Krause, the Director of the National Institute of Allergy and Infectious Diseases, who has been delegated responsibility for recombinant DNA matters. In introducing Dr. Krause, Mr. Thornton said the RAC has developed great confidence in his professional and scientific judgement.

Dr. Krause extended his welcome to the newly appointed members of the committee. He called the attention of the RAC to tab 1021, in which Dr. Fredrickson had delegated to Dr. Krause responsibility for actions under the NIH Guidelines for Research Involving Recombinant DNA Molecules.

II. MINUTES OF THE APRIL 23-24, 1981 MEETING

Dr. Mason began the review of the minutes of the April 23-24, 1981, RAC meeting by commending those responsible for the minutes. He pointed out a typographical error in Section X of those minutes. He moved approval of the minutes as written, subject to any corrections or modifications members of the Committee might wish to forward to the Executive Secretary. Dr. Scandalios concurred and seconded the motion. By a voice vote, the motion was unanimously carried.

III. PROPOSED REVISION OF THE GUIDELINES

Drs. David Baltimore and Allan Campbell, RAC members, had proposed a major revision of the Guidelines (Baltimore-Campbell proposal, Attachment II) which was considered by the RAC at its April 23-24, 1981 meeting. At the April 1981 meeting, a Working Group on Revision of the Guidelines was established to review the Baltimore-Campbell proposal as well as other approaches which might lead to a major revision of the Guidelines. The Working Group met on June 1 and July 9, 1981. The Working Group prepared a proposal for revising the Guidelines and a summary of its actions (Attachment III). In addition, the Working Group prepared a document entitled "Evaluation of the Risks Associated with Recombinant DNA Research." Two minority reports were prepared by several members of the Working Group (Attachment IV). The Working Group report (tab 1042), the minority reports, and letters of comment (tabs 1020, 1040, 1045, 1046) were distributed to RAC members prior to the September 1981 meeting.

Mr. Thornton asked Dr. Gottesman to introduce the Working Group's report. Dr. Gottesman reviewed the highlights of the report. She noted that the revision of the Guidelines promulgated on July 1, 1981, already exempts many experiments in three major host-vector systems. The Baltimore-Campbell proposal (Attachment II) would convert mandatory Guidelines to a voluntary code of good practice and would set as containment levels those appropriate for the organism being used. The Working Group considered various approaches; the majority supported a proposal (Attachment III) which adopts the containment provisions of the Baltimore-Campbell proposal but retains the mandatory aspect of the Guidelines. The proposal has not yet been published as a proposed major action in the Federal Register. The RAC may wish to modify the proposal before its formal publication in the Federal Register for public comment.

Dr. Gottesman noted that the background document discusses basic assumptions. It is difficult to imagine hazards resulting from random combinations of DNA. Furthermore, deliberate combinations will not be harmful in most cases. However, there are still some questions about certain experiments. The issue is how to deal with the latter experiments. The proposal of the Working Group would retain IBC prereview so that there is a level of review beyond the investigator. Dr. Gottesman then reviewed the main points of the Working Group proposal. The proposed containment levels are very similar to those of the Baltimore-Campbell proposal, i.e., containment would be largely based on the pathogenicity of the host. For all non-exempt experiments, at least the P1 level would be recommended. The Working Group proposal eliminates reference to biological containment in Part III of the Guidelines. The Working Group proposal also adds an admonition which reads as follows:

> "If there is clear evidence that the donor DNA will significantly change the pathogenicy of the host, the containment level appropriate to the anticipated change will be applied."

While the Baltimore-Campbell proposal would be a voluntary code of practice, the Working Group proposal retains IBC prereview of covered experiments and retains Section IV-G of the Guidelines which discusses possible penalties for failing to follow the Guidelines. However, the Working Group recommends eliminating membership requirements for IBCs currently specified in Section

IV-D of the Guidelines. While the Baltimore-Campbell proposal retains the prohibition section of the Guidelines (I-D), the Working Group proposal eliminates the prohibitions on the basis that currently prohibited experiments would be prereviewed by an IBC in their proposal. Dr. Gottesman said that she felt that the major issues for discussion are: prohibitions, prereview of covered experiments, and containment levels.

Dr. Berns noted that five Working Group members, including himself, submitted a minority report which disagrees with the Working Group's proposal to retain the mandatory nature of the Guidelines. The minority report recommends elimination of Part IV of the Guidelines.

Dr. Goldstein said that he agrees with parts of the Working Group report. He said that IBCs are still needed although a survey in California has indicated great variation in IBCs. He also said that prohibited experiments need to be more clearly considered.

Dr. Harris said that she felt that the Working Group's report is an acceptable compromise.

Ms. King said that the report suggests a direction for movement but that details need to be worked out. She said that if there are Guidelines, there should be sanctions. She said that distinguishing NIH grantees from non-grantees is not unique; she cited the situation with human experimentation. Ms. King said that she strongly favors retention of the sanctions.

Dr. Nightingale said that she supports the recommendations of the Working Group, saying that they represent a good compromise. She expressed concern about the availability of other guidelines cited in the Working Group report. In this regard, she noted the many comments received on the proposed CDC Biosafety Guidelines for Microbiological and Biomedical Laboratories. She also expressed concern that prohibition I-D-4, dealing with deliberate release into the environment, had not been dealt with. Dr. Nightingale said there is a necessity for accountability when public funds are being used. She said the RAC needs an assessment of outside perceptions and that the background document needs further work.

Dr. Zinder then addressed the RAC. He noted that he had prepared the minority reports to the Working Group's recommendations. He said that although there is a disagreement about the administrative aspects of the Guidelines, there was unanimity in the Working Group in favor of the new proposed containment levels. He noted that although inclusion of a slightly modified Part IV was recommended by the Working Group, five members have now endorsed a minority report stating that Part IV should be removed from the Guidelines. Drs. Adelberg and Zinder also signed a second minority report recommending complete elimination of the Guidelines. Dr. Zinder said that he and the scientists concerned about recombinant DNA originally proposed guidelines which would give guidance and not be enforced, rather than rules. He cited some of the history leading to the issuance of mandatory guidelines in 1976. Dr. Zinder said that if Part IV is retained in the revised Guidelines, there should be a strong justification for retaining it stated in a position paper. He said that he prefers that the Guidelines be rescinded and replaced with a simple recommendation. He said that said that if scientists are to be encouraged to speak up in the future about conjectural risks, they must be shown that when interim regulation is subsequently shown to be superfluous, it can be removed.

Dr. Baltimore said that the Baltimore-Campbell proposal was a compromise between scientific judgment that there is no justification for Guidelines being other than a code of accepted practice, and the necessity for considering political and social factors. Their proposal retained the prohibitions, which he said are one of the most noted parts of the Guidelines. It has been argued that the RAC should not consider political and social factors; however, Dr. Baltimore did not agree. He said that the prohibitions have less and less justification and that he finds no difficulty in accepting the Working Group's recommendation regarding elimination of prohibited experiments, except for elimination of the prohibition against acquisition of a drug resistance trait in those cases in which such acquisition could compromise the use of a drug to control disease agents in human or veterinary medicine or agriculture. Concerned scientists originally proposed guidelines meaning only guidance and not regulations; the RAC will have to decide the future course of the Guidelines. He noted that there apparently already is general agreement in the RAC on modifying Part III dealing with containment levels and agreement on retaining the exemptions. The issue is Part IV of the Guidelines. He said that he feels that it is anomalous to retain the current procedures section of the Guidelines. However, political and social issues need to be considered. If the Federal government pulled completely out of the issue, local governments might well overreact. The Federal government needs to provide surveillance, a forum for considering questions, and an office where inquiries can be authoritatively answered. Therefore, maintenance of the RAC, ORDA, and abbreviated guidelines are necessary. Dr. Baltimore expressed support for the original Baltimore-Campbell proposal, with some modifications based on the Working Group recommendations. Dr. Zinder said that if Guidelines are to be retained, it is for political and social reasons. However the political climate has changed. In New York State, which previously passed a law regulating recombinant DNA research, a bill has been introduced to repeal the law based on the assertion that the medical institutions which perform such research in New York State have proven to be trustworthy.

Dr. Nightingale said that she agrees with most of what Dr. Baltimore said. In order to implement sound public policy there are three basic ingredients: knowledge base, commitment of leadership, and appropriate social strategy. She said that in this case there is much agreement on the knowledge base and that there is need for change and the direction of that change. There is more disagreement on the appropriate social strategy. Having Federal involvement is one method of tempering local extremism.

Ms. King noted that the Baltimore-Campbell proposal would put industry and academia on an equal footing. She said that the RAC should consider a special meeting and public hearing on the proposed changes.

Dr. Gottesman noted that the current Guidelines are flexible and that the vast majority of experiments done today are exempt. She feels that there are scientific reasons for having a group other than the principal investigator look at the experiments still covered by the Guidelines; they should be reviewed by IBCs. She said that the critical issues in Part IV of the Guidelines are IBC prereview and compliance. She said that the Working Group's proposal does not involve an immense administrative burden.

Dr. Goldstein said that he also shares concerns about the scientific issues. He noted the number of new companies becoming involved in recombinant DNA research.

Dr. Brill stated that at a recent public meeting regarding a genetic engineering company in Madison, Wisconsin, no concerns were expressed about use of recombinant DNA technology.

Dr. McKinney said that the handling of the prohibitions is an important issue. They could perhaps be changed to cautionary advisories. He also said that citation of CDC and USDA guidelines needs to be considered. He preferred that NIH retain some form of guidance over recombinant DNA research.

With regard to the proposed revision of the CDC guidelines, Dr. Berns said that he expects great improvement in the document in the near future. He had discussed proposed revisions of the NIH Guidelines at a recent Gordon conference; most scientists there did not favor complete abolition of the Guidelines and favored instead something like the Baltimore-Campbell proposal. He also cited his local Congressman's concern about the potential for increasing public concern about recombinant DNA technology. It is important in the Guidelines revision that public confidence be maintained. Dr. Zinder said that the public trusts academic researchers, but not industry.

Dr. Gottesman stressed that under the Working Group's proposal, the IBC would make the decision on containment using the CDC document only as guidance. Dr. Goldstein said that how the IBCs use and interpret the CDC guidelines should be made more explicit, so that there are uniform standards.

Dr. McGarrity said that he is comfortable in accepting voluntary guidelines. He felt that the Working Group's background report is excellent and that perhaps an abridged version could be published for educating the general public.

Dr. Holmes said that he supports retaining the current prohibition dealing with the introduction of drug resistance traits. He said that to make the Guidelines voluntary would be a mistake and could invite legislation.

Dr. Baltimore said that the concern raised in the Boston area is not a unique situation and that activities at the Federal level are still important. He said that since there are differences in the science done at different institutions it is not suprising, and not relevant to the present discussion, that different IBCs in California operate differently. Dr. Baltimore emphasized his view that IBC prereview is a serious obstruction of science, which results in scientific momentum being lost.

Dr. McKinney pointed out that the NIH could still choose to mandate guidelines even if the RAC recommends otherwise. He suggested that reference to CDC and USDA guidelines not be incorporated into the body of the text of the revised guidelines; rather they could be cited as references.

Ms. King suggested that the RAC should structure the issues on which it wants public comment, such as treatment of prohibitions and the voluntary vs. mandatory nature of the guidelines. Dr. Talbot pointed out that the RAC could follow Ms. King's suggestion and present issues for public comment. The alternative would be for the RAC to accept the Working Group proposal, the Baltimore-Campbell proposal, or an amalgam of the two. Following the meeting, NIH staff could then develop a new version of the Guidelines based on the RAC proposal and put this out for public comment.

Dr. Harris then moved to accept the report of the Working Group so that discussion could proceed to consider the report section by section. Dr. Mason seconded the motion. There followed discussion of the effect of such a motion.

Dr. Ahmed praised the report of the Working Group. He favored publication for public comment of a series of different options. Dr. Mason expressed concern about eliminating all of the prohibitions. Dr. Saginor suggested that the RAC might first consider the Adelberg-Zinder minority proposal to abolish the Guidelines. Dr. McKinney said that he considered the Working Group's recommendations as too cursory. Dr. Gottesman responded that the Working Group had considered the issues in-depth at two meetings and had prepared a report on its evaluation of the risks associated with recombinant DNA research. The RAC could change or elaborate on the recommendations before seeking public comment. Dr. Zinder said that the recommendations of the Working Group were adopted unanimously for those concerning Part IV of the Guidelines.

Dr. Baltimore, in the interests of providing a forum for RAC discussion of the points of difference between the various proposals, moved a seven part motion as a substitute for Dr. Harris' motion:

1. Accept the first section of the Baltimore-Campbell proposal, as follows:

   "Section I-A of the NIH Guidelines will be replaced with the following:

'I-A. Purpose. The purpose of these Guidelines is to specify standard practices for constructing and handling (i) recombinant DNA molecules and (ii) organisms and viruses containing recombinant DNA molecules. Adherence to these standards by all laboratories using recombinant DNA is recommended.'"

2. Accept the second section of the Baltimore-Campbell proposal, as follows:

"Part I-C of the NIH Guidelines shall be eliminated."

3. Accept the second section of the Working Group proposal, as follows:

"Section I-D of the Guidelines, Prohibitions, would be eliminated."

4. Accept the third section of the Working Group report modified by removing references to CDC Guidelines and USDA Regulations and treating these references in a footnote, as follows:

"Part III of the Guidelines would be replaced with the following language:

'Part III discusses experiments covered by the Guidelines. The reader should first consult Part I, where exempt experiments are listed.

'Where recommended physical containment levels applicable to non-recombinant DNA experiments exist for either the host or the vector*, recombinant DNA experiments should be carried out at containment levels at least as high as those recommended for non-recombinant DNA experiments. If there is clear evidence that the donor DNA will significantly change the pathogencity of the host, the containment level appropriate to the anticipated change will be applied. Otherwise, all experiments may be carried out under conditions of P1 or P1-LS physical containment.'"

5. The following admonition would be added:

"No experiments should be performed which involve deliberate transfer of a drug resistance trait to microorganisms that are not known to acquire it naturally, if such acquisition could compromise the use of a drug to control disease agents in human or veterinary medicine or agriculture."

6. Accept the fourth section of the Baltimore-Campbell proposal, as follows:

*Such as those specified by CDC Guidelines or the USDA Quarantine Regulations.

"Part IV of the NIH Guidelines shall be eliminated, with the following exceptions:

"(a) Those definitions listed in Part IV-C which may be needed to clarify statements made elsewhere in the Guidelines shall be retained.

"(b) Those portions of Part IV-E defining the composition of RAC and prescribing rules for RAC procedures shall be retained.

"(c) The following statement shall be added:

"Each institution conducting or sponsoring recombinant DNA research should take responsibility for monitoring its own activities in this area. Any unusual events that might be associated with the use of recombinant DNA molecules should be reported to the Director, NIH."

7. Accept the fifth section of the Baltimore-Campbell proposal with deletion of the words "submitted in support of requests for exceptions from the prohibitions," as follows:

"Section VI of the Guidelines will be eliminated, except for those portions of Section VI-F relevant to the protection of proprietary information. "

Dr. Berns seconded the motion.

Dr. Saginor suggested an amendment to Dr. Harris' motion in the form of a policy statement that there is a continuing need for the RAC and applicable recombinant DNA guidelines. The purpose of the amendment was to indicate that the Adelberg-Zinder proposal is not being accepted. Dr. Harris agreed to the amendment.

Ms. King said she wanted the RAC to vote on replacing parts 1 and 6 of the Baltimore motion with wording from the Working Group proposal. It was suggested that votes be on one part at a time. Ms. King then moved to replace the first part of Dr. Baltimore's motion with the first section of the Working Group's proposal as follows:

"Section I-A of the Guidelines would be amended to read as follows:

"I-A. Purpose. The purpose of these Guidelines is to specify standard practices for constructing and handling (i) recombinant DNA molecules and (ii) organisms and viruses containing recombinant DNA molecules."

The motion was seconded by Dr. Goldstein. Ms. King stated that she favors retention of limited Guidelines that require IBC review, and she favors an oversight function for the RAC; she does not support self-regulation. Dr. Baltimore did not accept Ms. King's proposed amendment. Dr. Berns pointed out that the substitution Ms. King was proposing did not make much difference. The real point of contention in the RAC concerned part six of Dr. Baltimore's motion.

Ms. King withdrew her previous motion and then moved to delete part six of Dr. Baltimore's motion. If her motion were accepted, this would leave intact Part IV of the Guidelines. It was pointed out that the Working Group had proposed a change in Part IV dealing with IBC membership. Ms. King said that if her motion passed, then another perfecting motion could be introduced dealing with IBC membership. Dr. Harris seconded. The motion failed to carry by a vote of nine in favor, twelve opposed, and no abstentions.

Dr. Fedoroff noted that the motion as it stands would eliminate all prohibitions including the prohibition against deliberate release into the environment. Dr. Baltimore suggested that if the RAC wished, a statement regarding deliberate release could be included with the admonition on drug resistance. Dr. Berns said that in his view the recommendation that experiments be conducted under P1 containment precludes deliberate release into the environment.

Dr. Maas then moved to add the current prohibition on the cloning of certain toxins to the admonition on drug resistance. Dr. Goldstein seconded. Dr. Gottesman said that the cloning of toxins is an example of an area of concern. She noted that the RAC Working Group on Toxins recommended at the last RAC meeting prohibition of cloning of certain toxin genes and that other experiments involving cloning of toxin genes should proceed only in E. coli K-12 in the absence of special review by ORDA. Dr. Baltimore agreed to accept addition of the wording regarding toxins currently in Section I-D-2 to the admonition on drug resistance and to retain Appendix G of the current Guidelines.

Dr. Ahmed moved that a working group be appointed to study the prohibitions and report back to the RAC. Dr. Goldstein seconded the motion. Dr. Mason disagreed, noting that at the last meeting a working group had been appointed to report on revision of the guidelines. They had reported, and now the RAC was working through the proposal to prepare material for public comment. The motion failed to carry by a vote of three in favor, fourteen opposed, and three absentions.

Mr. Thornton recognized Dr. Susan Wright. She said the RAC was short-circuiting long and detailed discussions it should have on all the critical issues. She asked RAC members to acknowledge ties that they might have with genetic engineering companies. She said there should be discussion of why the working group had decided to eliminate public members on IBCs. She expressed concern about the currently prohibited experiments and large-scale experiments. She cited a report she had submitted, prepared for the Commission of the European Communities, entitled "Hazards Involved in the Industrial Use of Micro-organisms." She said that change of phenotype due to mutation and discharge of waste into the environment are important issues among many others that need to be considered before a decision is reached.

Dr. Fedoroff said that there should be flexibility to have a group look at and approve specific experiments which are otherwise admonished against. Dr. Baltimore said investigators wishing to do such experiments could come to the local IBC or the RAC to discuss conditions under which such experiments could be done.

Dr. Berns said that at a meeting of the Large Scale Review Working Group on September 9, 1981, none of the members thought that the large-scale prohibition should be retained.

Mr. Thornton recognized Ms. Claire Nader who said that the RAC should look at the assumptions behind the recommendations such as that all corporations will do the right thing, and that the technology is safe. She said that there were no experts on corporate behavior, or law enforcement, or anti-trust questions on the RAC. She said the RAC should have on it people who want to talk about risks. She criticized the way in which the RAC was proceeding.

Dr. Nightingale said that a working group on the prohibitions was appointed over a year ago and that the prohibitions have been discussed extensively before this meeting. Dr. Gottesman said that it was peculiar to be concerned about the prohibitions and at the same time recommending that the entire system become voluntary. She said that perhaps there could be a recommendation that these experiments be reviewed by the RAC.

Mr. Daloz moved that a vote be taken on Dr. Baltimore's motion, as amended. The motion to end discussion and vote failed to carry by a vote of four in favor, fourteen opposed, and three abstentions.

Dr. Ahmed said he wanted detailed procedures built into the revised Guidelines for handling the currently prohibited experiments. Dr. Baltimore said that the absence of detailed procedures pertains in the case of all nonrecombinant DNA laboratory work including that with known pathogens.

Mr. Thornton asked for a show of hands of RAC members who wished to continue discussion of this agenda item for an additional thirty minutes until approximately 3:30 p.m. The vote was eighteen in favor, one opposed.

Dr. Mason said that the RAC and the Guidelines cannot deal with scientists or industrial groups who are uninformed, dishonest, or careless. We have tried to produce guidelines that reponsible people will follow. There is no way to provide for every contingency.

Dr. Holmes moved to add current prohibition I-D-4 ("Deliberate release into the environment of any organism containing recombinant DNA.") to the admonitions regarding cloning of toxins and transfer of drug resistance traits. Dr. Landy supported inclusion of I-D-4; Dr. Berns did not support it. The motion failed to carry by a vote of eight in favor, ten opposed, and two absentions.

Dr. Baltimore's amended motion was reviewed. Dr. Talbot said that if the proposal passed, the NIH staff would prepare a version of proposed revised Guidelines based on the proposal, and that it would be put in the Federal Register for public comment, along with background describing the work of the working group and the deliberations of the RAC. NIH would actively solicit comment on the proposal beyond its publication in the Federal Register.

The question was called and the vote to substitute Dr. Baltimore's motion, as amended, for Dr. Harris' motion was fifteen in favor, three opposed, and two abstentions. Dr. Ahmed asked to be recorded as voting against the motion. The motion was as follows:

"1. Section I-A of the Guidelines would be amended to read as follows:

"I-A. Purpose. The purpose of these Guidelines is to specify standard practices for constructing and handling (i) recombinant DNA molecules and (ii) organisms and viruses containing recombinant DNA molecules. Adherence to these standards by all laboratories using recombinant DNA is recommended.

"2. Section I-C of the Guidelines would be eliminated.

"3. Section I-D of the Guidelines, Prohibitions, would be eliminated.

"4. Part III of the Guidelines would be replaced with the following language:

"Part III discusses experiments covered by the Guidelines. The reader should first consult Part I, where exempt experiments are listed.

"Where recommended physical containment levels applicable to non-recombinant DNA experiments exist for either the host or the vector*, recombinant DNA experiments should be carried out at containment levels at least as high as those recommended for non-recombinant DNA experiments. If there is clear evidence that the donor DNA will significantly change the pathogenicity of the host, the containment level appropriate to the anticipated change will be applied. Otherwise, all experiments may be carried out under conditions of P1 or P1-LS physical containment.

*Such as those specified by the CDC Guidelines or the USDA Quarantine Regulations.

"5. Material would be added to Part III, as follows:

"No experiments should be performed which involve:

"(a) Deliberate transfer of a drug resistance trait to microorganisms that are not known to acquire it naturally, if such acquisition could compromise the use of a drug to control disease agents in human or veterinary medicine or agriculture.

"(b) Deliberate formation of recombinant DNAs containing genes for the biosynthesis of toxins lethal for vertebrates at an LD_{50} of less than 100 nanograms per kilogram body weight (e.g., the botulinum toxins, tetanus toxin, diphtheria toxin, Shigella dysenteriae neurotoxin). Guidelines for the cloning of DNAs containing genes coding for the biosynthesis of toxins which are lethal to vertebrates at 100 nanograms to 100 micrograms per kilogram body weight are specified in Appendix G.

"6. Part IV of the Guidelines would be eliminated with the following exceptions:

"(a) Those definitions listed in Part IV-C which may be needed to clarify statements made elsewhere in the Guidelines shall be retained.

"(b) Those portions of Part IV-E defining the composition of RAC and prescribing rules for RAC procedures shall be retained.

"(c) The following statement shall be added:

"Each institution conducting or sponsoring recombinant DNA research should take responsibility for monitoring its own activities in this area. Any unusual events that might be associated with the use of recombinant DNA molecules should be reported to the Director, NIH.

"7. Section VI of the Guidelines will be eliminated, except for those portions of Section VI-F relevant to the protection of proprietary information."

The vote on this substitute motion was called, and the vote was sixteen in favor, three opposed, and one abstention.

Dr. Zinder requested that a motion be introduced in support of the Adelberg-Zinder proposal to eliminate the Guidelines and the RAC. No motion was introduced.

Mr. Thornton noted that RAC had approved a proposed revision of the Guidelines for publication in the Federal Register, with the understanding that the committee would subsequently review that document and any comments generated by it at the next RAC meeting.

IV. PROPOSED AMENDMENT OF SECTION III-C-2-a AND ADDITION OF NEW SECTION III-C-7-c

Mr. Thornton asked Dr. Berns to initiate discussion of the proposal (tabs 1026, 1035/9) from Dr. Lois Miller of the University of Idaho. Dr. Berns said that Dr. Miller requests a modification of Section III-C-2-a of the Guidelines. This modification would permit invertebrate viruses to be treated as animal viruses are currently treated under the NIH Guidelines. Dr. Miller also proposed that a new Section III-C-7-c be added to the Guidelines. Section III-C-7-c would read:

> "III-C-7-c. Transfer to Invertebrates. DNA from any nonprohibited source [Section I-D], except for greater than one quarter of a eukaryotic viral genome, which has been cloned and propagated in *E. coli* K-12, may be transferred with the *E. coli* vector used for cloning to any eukaryotic cells in culture or to any invertebrate organism and propagated under conditions of physical containment comparable to P1 and appropriate to the organism under study [2A]. Transfers to any other host will be considered by the RAC on a case-by-case basis [45]."

Dr. Berns asked if there are any reasons for not treating invertebrate viruses the same as animal viruses under the Guidelines. Mr. Thornton asked if containment problems for insects are of significance in relation to this proposal. Dr. Talbot said that this consideration is relevant to proposed Section III-C-7-c; this section would deal with introducing cloned DNA into insects. The proposed modification of Section III-C-2-a would affect the treatment of invertebrate viruses in tissue culture systems. Dr. Berns said he had discussed questions of containment with Dr. Tolin of the United States Department of Agriculture (USDA), who said that she saw no problem with the proposal as written.

Dr. Berns moved acceptance of the proposal to amend Section III-C-2-a and to add a new Section III-C-7-c to the Guidelines. Dr. Fedoroff seconded the motion. By a vote of eleven in favor, none opposed, and five abstentions the RAC adopted the motion.

Revised Section III-C-2 would read as follows:

> "III-C-2. Invertebrate Host-Vector Systems.
>
> "III-C-2-a. Invertebrate Viral Vectors. Experiments involving invertebrate virus vectors can be done as follows:

"III-C-2-a-(1). Recombinant DNA molecules containing no more than two-thirds of the genome of any invertebrate virus [all viruses from a single Family (36) being considered identical (50)] may be propagated and maintained in cells in tissue culture using P1 containment. For such experiments, it must be shown that the cells lack helper virus for the specific Families of defective viruses being used. The DNA may contain fragments of the genomes of viruses from more than one Family but each fragment must be less than two-thirds of a genome.

"III-C-2-a-(2). Recombinants with less than two-thirds of the genome of any invertebrate virus may be rescued with helper virus using P2 containment unless it is classified by the CDC as a class 3 agent (1) in which case P3 containment is required.

"III-C-2-a-(3). Experiments involving the use of other whole or defective virus genomes to propagate DNA sequences from prokaryotic or eukaryotic organisms (and viruses), or as vectors to transform non-permississive cells, will be evaluated by NIH on a case-by-case basis [45] and will be conducted under the prescribed physical and biological containment conditions. (See Section IV-E-1-b-(3)-(c).)"

"NIH will also review on a case-by-case basis [45] all experiments involving the use of virus vectors in animals and will prescribe the physical and biological containment conditions appropriate for such studies. (See Section IV-E-1-b-(3)-(c).)"

V. REQUEST TO CLONE SUBGENOMIC SEGMENTS OF RIFT VALLEY FEVER VIRUS

Dr. Berns introduced the request (tabs 1030, 1035/4, 1038) of Molecular Genetics, Inc., of Minnetonka, Minnesota, to clone, under P1 containment conditions, segments of the Rift Valley Fever Virus genome. The objective is to clone the segments which encode the virus' antigenic determinants. The work would be performed in collaboration with the U.S. Army Medical Research Institute of Infectious Diseases, Fort Detrick, Maryland.

Dr. Berns said Rift Valley Fever Virus is a major problem in cattle in Africa. The virus may have recently extended its range into Egypt and the Sinai Peninsula. Work with the virus in the United States is prohibited by the USDA, except under special conditions. In addition to being a significant agricultural problem, the virus may be transmitted to humans.

The virus itself is a negative stranded RNA virus. Such viruses are not infectious when purified as the complementary strand is needed to function as a messenger. The Rift Valley Fever Virus genome is segmented; the genome is composed of three separate pieces of RNA. The investigators propose to work with one of the three segments, the so-called "M" or medium sized segment which codes for those of the virus' antigenic determinants that elicit neutralizing antibodies. He said that the issues are comparable to those with the cloning of Foot and Mouth Disease Virus. However, the Rift Valley Fever Virus project provides more safeguards because the virus genome is negative stranded, segmented RNA. Dr. Berns said he felt P1 containment would be adequate for the project.

Dr. Baltimore agreed with Dr. Bern's evaluation, and added two points. He said that the proposed method of reverse transcription, the "snap-back" procedure, would ensure that the full RNA is not cloned. He cautioned, however, that Rift Valley Fever Virus is a Bunyavirus and Bunyaviruses are known to recombine within the family. He suggested that the laboratory work areas be limited to research with Rift Valley Fever Virus and that investigators not simultaneously study other Bunyaviruses. Dr. Pilacinski of Molecular Genetics, Inc., said that the company is not presently working with Bunyaviruses other than Rift Valley Fever Virus and has no plans to do so in the near future.

Dr. Baltimore moved approval of the proposal at the P1 level of containment with the stipulation that other Bunyaviruses not be studied in the same laboratory areas and that the "snap-back" procedure, as described in the protocol, be utilized to generate the DNA. Dr. Berns seconded the motion.

Mr. Thornton called the vote. By a vote of sixteen in favor, none opposed, and two abstentions, the RAC adopted the motion.

VI. STATEMENT ON THE PROPOSED REVISION OF THE GUIDELINES

Mr. Thornton asked that his statement concerning agenda item III, "Proposed Revision of the Guidelines," be distributed (Attachment V). He said that to have made this statement before consideration of the issue could have compromised his position as chairman. However, he felt it was now appropriate to distribute the statement.

VII. CLOSED SESSION

The RAC went into closed session to consider proposals involving proprietary information from commercial concerns for scale-up of recombinant DNA experiments.

VIII. PROPOSED AMENDMENT OF SECTION III-O-2

Mr. Thornton asked Dr. Talbot to discuss the proposal (tabs 1025, 1035/6) of Dr. Michael J. Ross of Genentech, Inc. Dr. Talbot said Dr. Ross had requested an amendment of Section III-B-3 of the Guidelines. Section III-B-3 currently specifies that the Director, NIH, may set containment levels, after a case-by-case review, for certain experiments involving non-HV1 prokaryotic host-vector systems. Dr. Ross proposed to amend the Section to permit the cloning of DNA from any nonpathogenic species in nonpathogenic lower eukaryotes at P3 containment and into nonpathogenic prokaryotes at the P2 level of containment.

Dr. Talbot said that modification of Section III-B-3 is not the appropriate way to make the changes Dr. Ross proposes, since Section III-B-3 deals only with prokaryotes. Dr. Talbot suggested that Section III-O-2, "Experiments Involving Prokaryotes Nonpathogenic for Man, Animals, or Plants and/or Lower Eukaryotes Nonpathogenic for Man, Animals, or Plants" could appropriately be modified to reflect Dr. Ross' intent.

Dr. Fedoroff noted that Dr. Ross' proposal would change the current Section III-O-2 in two ways: it would allow cloning of DNA from nonpathogenic higher eukaryotes; and it would lower the level for cloning in nonpathogenic prokaryotes from P3 to P2. Dr. Fedoroff moved acceptance of the proposal.

By a vote of twelve in favor, none opposed, and no abstentions the RAC adopted the motion.

Section III-O-2 would be amended to read as follows:

> "III-O-2. Experiments Involving Nonpathogenic Prokaryotic and Lower Eukaryotic Host-Vector Systems. DNA from any species nonpathogenic for man, animals, or plants may be cloned into lower eukaryotes nonpathogenic for man, animals, or plants at the P3 level of containment [2A]. DNA from any species nonpathogenic for man, animals, or plants may be cloned into prokaryotes nonpathogenic for man, animals, or plants at the P2 level of containment [2A]. Data supporting the contention that the donor and recipient are nonpathogenic must be submitted to the local IBC. Lower levels of physical containment may be assigned by ORDA on a case-by-case basis for specific donor-recipient combinations. (See Section IV-E-1-b-(3)-(h).)"

IX. PROPOSED AMENDMENT OF SECTION I-D-6

Dr. McKinney opened discussion of the proposal (tabs 1027, 1035/5) by Dr. Irving Johnson of Eli Lilly and Company to amend Section I-D-6 of the Guidelines as follows (modified language underlined):

> "I-D-6. Large-scale experiments [e.g. more than 10 liters of culture] with organisms containing recombinant DNAs other than those listed in Appendix C, Paragraphs 2, 3, and 4 of the Guidelines, unless the recombinant DNAs are rigorously characterized and the absence of harmful sequences established (3). (See Section IV-E-1-b-(3)-(d).)"

The text in Appendix C dealing with large-scale experiments in Paragraph 2 (*E. coli* K-12 host-vector systems), Paragraph 3 (*S. cerevisiae* host-vector systems), and Paragraph 4 (*B. subtilis* host-vector systems) would be replaced with the following revised text:

> "Large-scale experiments (e.g. more than 10 liters of culture) require prior IBC review and approval."

This modification would delegate authority to the IBC to review proposals and set containment for large-scale procedures when certain E. coli K-12, B. subtilis and S. cerevisiae host-vector systems are used. Large-scale procedures employing other host-vector systems would continue to be reviewed by RAC and approved by the NIH.

Dr. McKinney said that the majority of requests for exceptions to the 10 liter limit have been submitted by industry. Dr. McKinney felt that industry's response to Part VI, Voluntary Compliance, of the Guidelines has been responsible. He suggested that Dr. Johnson's proposal would serve to improve operating conditions, both at the research and industrial level, and facilitate large-scale production utilizing E. coli K-12, B. subtilis or S. cerevisiae host-vector systems. He moved adoption of the proposal.

Dr. McGarrity said he had reviewed the September 2 letter submitted to the RAC by Dr. Susan Wright as well as the attached report entitled "Hazards Involved in the Industrial Use of Microorganisms." The latter report was contracted for by the Commission of the European Communities (CEC) to evaluate the hazards involved in the industrial development, production and use of microbial cells and their products.

Dr. McGarrity addressed the criticisms Dr. Wright raised against Dr. Johnson's proposal. Dr. McGarrity agreed with Dr. Wright that the statement "the principle of the absence of increased risk with increased volume has been accepted by the RAC," as advanced by Dr. Johnson is inaccurate. He said Dr. Johnson draws a broader conclusion than is warranted from the decision at the June 1980 RAC Meeting to delete a sentence from Section I-D-6. However, he said that since June 1980 there have been many developments which indicate a modification in RAC's view. For example, in September 1980, RAC delegated the responsibility of reviewing physical facilities for large-scale experiments to the local IBCs.

In another criticism, Dr. Wright stated "that the British Genetic Manipulation Advisory Group (GMAG) is to consider in late September a proposal from the Confederation of British Industry (CBI) to weaken the British controls for large-scale work should not be used to justify the Lilly proposal." She further stated that ". . . it is not at all clear that GMAG will take the 'positive action' which Dr. Johnson anticipates." Dr. McGarrity said he agreed with Dr. Wright that the RAC should not be influenced in its decisions by possible decisions GMAG may take.

In other criticisms, Dr. Wright asserts "the fact that 'no unforeseen difficulties have been encountered' when the industry has operated under controls involving prior review cannot be used to justify the claim that no problems will arise when controls are removed." She further stated that "no comparative studies of the risks of small- and large-scale work have been carried out, and any statements comparing these risks are developed against a background of very wide uncertainty." She refers to several concerns raised in the CEC report.

Dr. McGarrity said that the CEC report raises concerns but also states that industrial fermentation processes are unlikely to be contaminated because fermentation failure is a very expensive problem. To be productive, fermentors must operate almost continuously. He said these economic facts argue for strong quality control measures in industry. Dr. McGarrity added that the authors of the CEC report were "impressed by the well documented care" taken by the industry "to ensure the wholesomeness of their products." Dr. McGarrity said that the CEC report tends to support Dr. Johnson's position rather than Dr. Wright's. Dr. McGarrity then seconded Dr. McKinney's motion for approval.

Mr. Thornton then recognized Dr. Wright. She said that the CEC report is the only report that has been written on the hazards of the industrial uses of genetic biotechnology. She said that the CEC report states: (1) that the scale of the use of microorganisms is going to expand so greatly that this area should be carefully examined, and (2) this work should be regulated. She said she was not convinced by Dr. McGarrity's arguments and said the RAC has not yet addressed several areas of serious concern.

Mr. Thornton then recognized Dr. Max Marsh of Eli Lilly and Company. Dr. Marsh noted that Dr. Wright's September 2 letter states that Dr. Johnson's proposal "would exempt large-scale work involving E. coli K-12, Saccharomyces cerevisiae, Bacillus subtilis, and any other host-vector system listed in Appendix C of the Guidelines." Dr. Marsh pointed out that Dr. Wright is incorrect in claiming this would extend to "any other host-vector system." Dr. Johnson's proposal was very specific as to the three specified host-vector systems which would be covered by this amendment.

In addition, Dr. Marsh pointed out that a continuous fermentation operation is a very complex process which is computer controlled. It is very easy with the continuous monitoring utilized to detect contamination.

Dr. Miller of FDA said that both the consuming public and the biotechnology industry would be served by this change in Section I-D-6.

Dr. Saginor said that since this proposal would delegate responsibility to IBCs, he wanted to mention for the record his concern that IBCs be kept in place, in relation to agenda item III considered earlier in the meeting.

Dr. Berns pointed out that industry currently complies with the NIH Guidelines voluntarily; there is no mandatory requirement for industrial firms to institute IBCs. Dr. McKinney concurred but added that industry is complying out of self-interest as well as public interest. In view of RAC's experience with these three host-vector systems, he said the committee should recommend Dr. Johnson's proposal.

Mr. Thornton called the vote. By a vote of eleven in favor, two opposed, and one abstention, the RAC adopted the proposal.

X. PROPOSAL TO INCLUDE STREPTOCOCCUS PYOGENES ON SUBLIST F OF APPENDIX A

Mr. Thornton asked Dr. Maas to begin discussion of the proposal (tabs 1028, 1035/8) from Dr. Joseph Ferretti of the University of Oklahoma Health Sciences Center to include *Streptococcus pyogenes* on sublist F of Appendix A. In support of his request, Dr. Ferretti submitted evidence demonstrating genetic exchange between *Streptococcus pyogenes* and *Streptococcus sanguis*. *Streptococcus sanguis* is currently included in sublist F.

Dr. Maas said the data demonstrate genetic exchange between *S. pyogenes* and *S. sanguis*. These exchanges occur primarily through transformation and conjugation with plasmids. Dr. Maas felt the request was reasonable and moved approval. Dr. Fedoroff seconded the motion.

Dr. Goldstein asked if *Streptococcus pyogenes* is implicated in rheumatic fever. Dr. Maas replied that it was. However, it was agreed that *S. pyogenes* merited inclusion on Sublist F of Appendix A on the basis of exchange data.

Mr. Thornton called for the vote on the motion. By a vote of fourteen in favor, none opposed, and no abstentions, the RAC adopted the proposal.

XI. REQUEST TO PERMIT ONE-WAY TRANSFER OF STREPTOCOCCUS LACTIS DNA INTO S. SANGUIS AND TO PERMIT TRANSFER OF A RECOMBINANT PLASMID FROM S. FAECALIS TO S. LACTIS

Dr. Fedoroff introduced the request (tabs 1029, 1035/3) of Dr. Larry McKay of the University of Minnesota for permission to transfer *Streptococcus lactis* DNA into *Streptococcus sanguis* strain Challis. Dr. McKay also requested that these strains be included in Appendix A on the basis that they exchange genetic information by known physiological processes. In addition, he requested permission to transfer a recombinant plasmid from *S. faecalis* to *S. lactis*.

Dr. Fedoroff noted that Dr. McKay wishes to reduce *S. lactis* plasmids in size with endonucleases in order to obtain the smallest functional plasmid. He would then purify the plasmid, transfer it to *Streptococcus sanguis* by transformation, transfer it by conjugation from *S. sanguis* to *S. faecalis*, and return it to *S. lactis* from *S. faecalis* by conjugation.

Dr. Fedoroff asked if organisms have been included in Appendix A of the Guidelines on the basis of data demonstrating unidirectional transformation. Dr. Gartland said organisms had been included in Appendix A on that basis.

Dr. Fedoroff, on the basis of the data submitted, moved approval of the requests as written. Dr. McGarrity seconded the motion.

Dr. Ahmed requested a clarification of the motion; he asked if S. lactis and S. sanguis would be placed on an existing sublist of Appendix A or if a new sublist would be created. Dr. Gartland asked Dr. Fedoroff whether the submitted evidence justifies including S. lactis in Sublist F of Appendix A. Dr. Fedoroff said the evidence supports one way transformation of S. sanguis by S. lactis DNA, but not the reverse. Dr. Talbot suggested, therefore, that Sublist E of Appendix A might appropriately be amended to permit transformation of S. sanguis by S. lactis DNA. A new entry could also be added to Appendix E to permit transfer of a recombinant plasmid from S. faecalis to S. lactis by conjugation. By a vote of fourteen in favor, none opposed, and no abstentions, the RAC approved these actions.

XII. REQUEST TO CLONE SACCHAROMYCES CEREVISIAE DNA IN SALMONELLA TYPHIMURIUM

Dr. Pinon introduced the request (tabs 1031, 1035/5, 1039) of Drs. Christopher Marvel and Edward Penhoet of the University of California, Berkeley, to clone Saccharomyces cerevisiae DNA in Salmonella typhimurium, using a nonmobilizable plasmid (YEp13).

Dr. Pinon noted that S. typhimurium is a CDC Class 2 etiological agent, but the investigators will employ attenuated strains. Furthermore, DNA from S. cerevisiae, a nonpathogen, will be introduced. Dr. Pinon recommended that the investigators be permitted to proceed under P1 containment conditions. Dr. Maas concurred and moved acceptance of the request. Dr. Pinon seconded the motion.

Dr. Ahmed asked why Drs. Marvel and Penhoet suggest they might be willing to employ P3 containment conditions. Dr. Landy said he did not feel willingness to employ high containment indicated the investigators have concerns on the safety of the experiments, but rather an eagerness to begin the research and a willingness to work under RAC imposed conditions.

Mr. Thornton called the question. By a vote of fourteen in favor, none opposed, and no abstentions, RAC adopted the motion to permit Drs. Marvel and Penhoet to proceed under P1 containment conditions.

XIII. REQUEST TO UTILIZE HEMOPHILUS PARAINFLUENZAE TO CLONE MOLONEY MURINE LEUKEMIA PROVIRUS

Dr. Berns began discussion of the proposal (tabs 1032, 1035/1, 1036) of Dr. James W. Gautsch of Scripps Clinic and Research Foundation to clone Moloney MuLV provirus and cellular flanking regions in Hemophilus parainfluenzae. The provirus DNA and flanking regions will be ligated into vector pRK290, a plasmid with a broad host range in gram negative bacteria. The cloned plasmid will subsequently be used to infect NIH 3T3 cells. Dr. Berns said the investigators wish to study the effect of methylation of DNA on RNA transcription.

Dr. Berns said H. parainfluenzae is part of the normal flora of the human upper respiratory tract. The investigators are thus inserting the MuLV provirus into a bacterium which could colonize a laboratory worker. He noted, however, that Moloney MuLV virus is classified by the National Cancer Institute as a low risk virus. The normal host is the mouse, and the virus is not known to function in any other organism. Should the recombinant DNA-containing H. parainfluenzae lyse in the respiratory tract of a colonized individual, the MuLV DNA would be presented to the cells of the respiratory tract as uncoated DNA, not as the whole virus. This is not the optimal manner in which to transfect cells. Dr. Berns said that he feels the risk is miniscule and recommended that the experiment be permitted at the P2 level of containment.

Dr. Goldstein asked what the host range of the MuLV virus was in tissue culture. Dr. Berns replied that MuLV is classified as an ecotropic virus, i.e., mouse-tropic. Dr. Goldstein asked how that classification was generated; was the test performed in tissue culture systems using whole virus? Dr. Berns replied that is was.

Dr. Berns moved that the experiments be permitted at the P2 level of containment. Dr. McKinney seconded the motion. By a vote of eleven in favor, none opposed, and three abstentions, the RAC adopted the motion.

XIV. DEVELOPMENT OF HOST-VECTOR SYSTEM BASED ON CORYNEBACTERIUM GLUTAMICUM

Dr. Maas introduced the request (tabs 1033, 1035/11) of Dr. Daniel Liberman of the Massachusetts Institute of Technology. Dr. Liberman requested containment conditions be established for the development of a host-vector system based on the gram positive bacterium Corynebacterium glutamicum. Corynebacterium glutamicum would be used as the host; three types of plasmids including hybrid plasmids would be tested for use as vectors. Dr. Maas said Corynebacterium glutamicum is not a pathogen and P1 containment should be adequate.
Dr. Goldstein asked if the proposed plasmid vectors carry drug resistance genes. Dr. Maas replied that some did. Dr. Goldstein pointed out that although Corynebacterium glutamicum is not a pathogen, it is related to the organism causing diphtheria.

Dr. Ahmed asked if this proposal might violate a prohibition in that drug resistance traits would be introduced into a nonpathogenic organism, which might transfer drug resistance traits to pathogens. Dr. Maas suggested that use of non-conjugative, poorly-mobilizable plasmids could be required. He said this restriction would address concerns about transfer of genetic information from Corynebacterium glutamicum to pathogenic Corynebacteria that live on the human skin. Mr. Thornton asked Dr. Liberman to comment on the effect this restriction might have on the project. Dr. Liberman thought the restriction would not seriously affect the protocol.

Dr. Maas moved approval of the proposal under P1 containment conditions provided that nonconjugative, poorly mobilizable plasmids are used as vectors. By a vote of eleven in favor, one opposed, and one abstention, RAC adopted the motion.

Dr. Liberman asked if RAC might rule in general on the use of Class 1 agents in the development of novel host-vector systems. Dr. Talbot pointed out that Dr. Liberman's request as published in the Federal Register had dealt only with Corynebacterium glutamicum; a more general statement on all Class 1 agents had not appeared in the Federal Register and thus could not be acted on. Dr. Talbot drew attention to the action adopted by RAC earlier in the meeting concerning modification of Section III-O-2, as this partially addressed Dr. Liberman's concern.

XV. PROPOSED USE OF CONJUGATIVE PLASMIDS TO TRANSFER DNA BETWEEN E. COLI, VIBRIO CHOLERA, AND VIBRIO HARVEYI

Dr. Maas initiated discussion of the request (tabs 1037, 1035/2) from Dr. J. W. Hastings of Harvard University for permission to clone Vibrio harveyi DNA in E. coli and in Vibrio cholera. Conjugation proficient plasmids (e.g., pRK290 derivatives) would be used to transfer the cloned V. harveyi DNA among E. coli, V. cholera and V. harveyi. Dr. Hastings would employ an E. coli host-vector system to select V. harveyi bioluminescence genes. He would subsequently return the bioluminescence genes to V. harveyi by first transferring the genes from E. coli to V. cholera, and then transferring the genes from V. cholera to V. harveyi. He chose this method as the frequency of plasmid transfer from E. coli to V. harveyi is very low.

Dr. Maas said V. cholera is classified by the CDC as a Class 2 etiological agent. He suggested that the experiments be permitted at P1 containment, with the exception of those experiments involving V. cholera, which would be set at P2. He so moved. Dr. McKinney seconded the motion.

Dr. McGarrity noted that V. cholera exchanges genetic information with E. coli; he questioned why V. cholera is not included in Sublist A of Appendix A. Dr. Talbot said Sublist A was originally instituted as a restrictive list and inclusion of V. cholera in Appendix A has not been requested.

Dr. McGarrity asked whether P2 containment conditions were necessary. Dr. Gottesman pointed out that the investigator would employ a mobilizable plasmid which may contain DNA homologous to the V. cholera chromosome. In such a situation concern over the possible transfer of the cholera toxin gene justifies P2 containment conditions.

By a vote of ten in favor, none opposed, and three abstentions the RAC adopted Dr. Maas' motion.

XVI. CONTAINMENT CONDITIONS FOR CLONING AND EXPRESSION OF DNA CODING FOR DIPHTHERIA TOXIN

Dr. Gartland initiated the discussion (tabs 1035/10, 1041) by recounting the history of the proposal submitted by Dr. John Murphy of Harvard Medical School. Dr. Gartland said Dr. Murphy requested that RAC, at its April 23-24, 1981 meeting (Minutes of the Meeting, page 28-29), consider a proposal to clone, in E. coli K-12, the 3.9 kb Bam restriction fragment of Corynephage Beta carrying the diphtheria toxin structural gene. At that meeting, RAC set containment for the project at P4 with the experiments to be performed in high containment Building 550 at the Frederick Cancer Research Center (FCRC). The NIH subsequently accepted this recommendation. Dr. Gartland said Dr. Murphy, in a letter dated July 11, 1981, now requested greater flexibility in the setting of containment levels. Dr. Murphy proposed that the National Institutes of Health (NIH) Institutional Biosafety Committee (IBC) be delegated authority to specify laboratory and containment practices for the work to be done in high containment Building 550 at FCRC.

Dr. McKinney said that the P3 laboratories in Building 550 are served by the same water supply, waste treatment system, and ventilation system as the P4 facility. The secondary barriers, thus, afford higher than P3 containment. They are more than adequate to contain the proposed experiments. In addition, a precedent for lowering containment when the high risk portion of the experiment is completed was set with the first risk assessment experiments performed at FCRC by Dr. Malcolm Martin. Dr. McKinney suggested RAC specify that the work be conducted in P3 laboratories in Building 550 of the Frederick Cancer Research Center under conditions specified by the local IBC.

Dr. Maas requested a clarification of the experimental protocol. Dr. Talbot said Dr. Murphy intends to use Building 550 at all times, but would not use the Class III glove boxes in all experiments. Dr. Gottesman asked whether workers, trained in P4 procedures, would assist in the experiments. Dr. McKinney replied that NIAID assigns a permanent, highly competent staff to Building 550 to assist investigators. Dr. Fedoroff seconded Dr. McKinney's motion.

By a vote of eleven in favor, none opposed, and three abstentions, the RAC recommended that permission be granted to clone in E. coli K-12, in high containment Building 550 at the Frederick Cancer Research Center, restriction fragments of Corynephage Beta carrying the structural gene for diphtheria toxin. Laboratory practices and containment equipment are to be specified by the IBC.

XVII. CONSIDERATION OF FUTURE MEETING DATES

Dr. Gartland's secretary will telephone all members of the RAC to arrange the date for a meeting in April or May 1982, subsequent to the next planned meeting in January 1982.

XVIII. ADJOURNMENT

Mr. Thornton expressed his appreciation to the committee for the fine manner in which business was conducted. He then adjourned the meeting at 10:30 a.m., September 11, 1981.

Respectively submitted,

Elizabeth Milewski

Elizabeth A. Milewski, Ph.D.
Rapporteur

William J. Gartland Jr.

William J. Gartland, Jr., Ph.D.
Executive Secretary

I hereby certify that, to the best of my knowledge, the foregoing Minutes and Attachments are accurate and complete.

4/12/82
Date

Ray Thornton

Ray Thornton, J.D.
Chairman
Recombinant DNA Advisory Committee

RECOMBINANT DNA ADVISORY COMMITTEE

CHAIRMAN

THORNTON, Ray, J.D. (82)
President
Arkansas State University
State University, Arkansas 72467
501 972-2100

- -

AHMED, Abdul Karim, Ph.D. (82)
Senior Staff Scientist
Natural Resources Defense Council, Inc.
122 East 42nd Street
New York, New York 10017
212 949-0049

BALTIMORE, David, Ph.D. (82)
Professor of Biology
Center for Cancer Research
Massachusetts Institute of Technology
Cambridge, Massachusetts 02139
617 253-6410

BERNS, Kenneth I., Ph.D., M.D. (83)
Chairman
Department of Immunology and Medical Microbiology
University of Florida College of Medicine
Gainesville, Florida 32610
904 392-3311

BRILL, Winston J., Ph.D. (83)
Vilas Research Professor
Department of Bacteriology
University of Wisconsin
Madison, Wisconsin 53706
608 262-3567

DALOZ, L. Albert (85)
R.F.D. 819
Hancock, NH 03449-0819
603 525-3788

FEDOROFF, Nina V., Ph.D. (84)
Staff Member
Department of Embryology
Carnegie Institution of Washington
115 West University Parkway
Baltimore, Maryland 21210
301 467-1414

FRIEDMAN, David, M.D. (85)
Professor of Microbiology
University of Michigan Medical School
Ann Arbor, Michigan 48109
313 763-3142

GOLDSTEIN, Richard, Ph.D. (82)
Associate Professor
Department of Microbiology and Molecular Genetics
Harvard Medical School
Boston, Massachusetts 02115
617 732-1911

HARRIS, Jean L., M.D. (83)
Secretary of Human Resources
Commonwealth of Virginia
Office of Governor
Post Office Box 1475
Richmond, Virginia 23219
804 786-7765

HOLMES, King K., M.D., Ph.D. (84)
Head
Division of Infectious Diseases
U.S. Public Health Service Hospital
Seattle, Washington 98114
206 325-2997

SEPTEMBER 1981

KING, Patricia A., J.D. (82)
Associate Professor of Law
Georgetown University Law School
600 New Jersey Avenue, N.W.
Washington D.C. 20001
202 624-8213

LANDY, Arthur, Ph.D. (85)
Professor of Medical Sciences
Brown University
Providence, Rhode Island 02912
401 863-2566

LEVINE, Myron M., M.D. (84)
Director
Center for Vaccine Development
Division of Infectious Diseases
University of Maryland
School of Medicine
Baltimore, Maryland 21201
301 528-7588

MAAS, Werner K., Ph.D. (83)
Professor
Department of Microbiology
New York University
School of Medicine
New York, New York 10016
212 340-5322

MARTIN, David W., Jr., M.D. (85)
Professor of Medicine and
Chief of Medical Genetics
University of California
Medical Center
San Francisco, California 94143
415 666-2524

MASON, James O., M.D., Dr. P.H. (83)
Executive Director
Utah State Department of
Health
Post Office Box 2500
Salt Lake City, Utah 84113
801 533-6111

MITCHELL, Robert E. (85)
Attorney at Law
13915 San Antonio Drive
Norwalk, California 90650
213 863-8736

McGARRITY, Gerard J., Ph.D. (84)
Head
Department of Microbiology
Institute for Medical Research
Copewood Street
Camden, New Jersey 08103
609 966-7377

McKINNEY, Robert W., Ph.D. (84)
Chief, Occupational Safety
and Health Branch
Division of Safety
National Institutes of Health
Bethesda, Maryland 20205
301 496-2960

NIGHTINGALE, Elena O., Ph.D., M.D. (83)
Senior Program Officer
Institute of Medicine
National Academy of Sciences
Washington, D.C. 20418
202 389-6963

PINON, Ramon, Ph.D. (82)
Associate Professor
Department of Biology
B-022 Bonner Hall
University of California, San Diego
La Jolla, California 92093
714 452-2452

SAGINOR, Mark L., M.D. (85)
Director
Metabolic Research Medical Group, Inc.
2080 Century Park East
Los Angeles, California 90067
213 553-2345

SCANDALIOS, John G., Ph.D. (84)
Head
Department of Genetics
North Carolina State University
Raleigh, North Carolina 27650
919 737-2291

WENSINK, Pieter C., Ph.D. (85)
Associate Professor of Biochemistry
Brandeis University
Waltham, Massachusetts 02254
617 647-2421

EXECUTIVE SECRETARY

GARTLAND, William J., Jr., Ph.D.
Director, Office of Recombinant
DNA Activities
National Institute of Allergy
and Infectious Diseases
National Institutes of Health
Bethesda, Maryland 20205
301 496-6051

RECOMBINANT DNA ADVISORY COMMITTEE

NON-VOTING REPRESENTATIVES

CENTERS FOR DISEASE CONTROL

DOWDLE, Walter R., Ph.D.
Assistant Director for Science
Centers for Disease Control
Atlanta, Georgia 30333
404 329-3701

National Institute for Occupational Safety and Health (CDC)

LEMIN, Richard A.
Director
Division of Criteria Documents
and Standards Development
National Institute for Occupational
Safety and Health,
5600 Fishers Lane, Room 8A53
Rockville, Maryland 20857
301 443-3680

U.S. DEPARTMENT OF AGRICULTURE

TOLIN, Sue A., Ph.D.
Science and Education Administration
Cooperative Research
U.S. Department of Agriculture
Washington, D.C. 20250
202 447-5741

FULKERSON, John F., Ph.D. (ALT)
Science and Education Administration
Cooperative Research
U.S. Department of Agriculture
Washington, D.C. 20250
202 447-5741

U.S. DEPARTMENT OF COMMERCE

GORDON, George S., Ph.D.
Analyst
Office of Environmental Affairs
U.S. Department of Commerce, Room 3425
Washington, D.C. 20230
202 377-2565

PAYNTER, O. E., Ph.D. (ALT)
Toxicologist
Office of Environmental Affairs
U.S. Department of Commerce, Room 3425
Washington, D.C. 20230
202 377-3234

U.S. DEPARTMENT OF ENERGY

DUDA, George, Ph.D.
Office of Health and
Environmental Research, EV-33
U.S. Department of Energy
Washington, D.C. 20545
202 353-3651

EDINGTON, Charles W., Ph.D. (ALT)
Deputy Director
Office of Health and Environmental
Research
U.S. Department of Energy
Washington, D.C. 20250
202 353-3251

U.S. DEPARTMENT OF THE INTERIOR

PIMENTEL, Mariano B., Ph.D.
Medical Director
U.S. Department of the Interior
Room 7045
18th & C Street, N.W.
Washington, D.C. 20240
202 343-2081

U.S. DEPARTMENT OF JUSTICE

BELL, Charlotte R., J.D.
General Litigation Section
Land and Natural Resources
Division
U.S. Department of Justice
Washington, D.C. 20530
202 633-4150

U.S. DEPARTMENT OF STATE

WALSH, William J., III
Biomedical Research Liason
and Health Affairs Officer
Oceans and International Environmental
and Scientific Affairs
U.S. Department of State
Washington, D.C. 20520
202 632-4824

U.S. DEPARTMENT OF TRANSPORTATION

CUSHMAC, George E., Ph.D.
Chemist
Research and Special Programs
Administration
U.S. Department of Transportation
Washington, D.C. 20590
202 755-4906

U.S. ENVIRONMENTAL PROTECTION AGENCY

LEVIN, Morris, Ph.D.
Director
Innovative Research Program (RD 675)
United States Environmental Protection Agency
Room 909 West Tower
401 M Street, S.W.
Washington, D.C. 20460
202 755-0644

FOOD AND DRUG ADMINISTRATION

HENRY, Timothy J., Ph.D.
BF, DT, HFF-156
Food and Drug Administration
200 C Street, S.W.
Washington, D.C. 20204
202 472-4690

Bureau of Drugs

MILLER, Henry I., M.D.
Medical Officer
Bureau of Drugs
Food and Drug Administration, Room 14B-04
5600 Fishers Lane
Rockville, Maryland 20857
301 443-3520

NATIONAL AERONAUTICS AND SPACE ADMINISTRATION

DeVINCENZI, Donald L., Ph.D.
Program Manager, Planetary Biology
Code SBL-3
National Aeronautics and Space Administration
Washington, D.C. 20546
202 755-3732

NATIONAL SCIENCE FOUNDATION

LEWIS, Herman W., Ph.D.
Senior Scientist for Recombinant DNA
Division of Physiology
Cellular and Molecular Biology
National Science Foundation
Washington, D.C. 20550
202 357-7647

HARRIMAN, Phillip, Ph.D. (ALT)
Program Director for Genetic Biology
Room 326
National Science Foundation
Washington, D.C. 20550
202 632-5985

U.S. VETERANS ADMINISTRATION

SCHULTZ, Jane S., Ph.D.
Geneticist
U.S. Veterans Administration
Medical Research Service - 151
2215 Fuller Road
Ann Arbor, Michigan 48105
313 769-7100 x696

BERMAN, Howard M. (ALT)
Health Scientist
Program Development and Review Division
U.S. Veterans Administration
810 Vermont Avenue, N.W.
Washington, D.C. 20420
202 389-5065

U.S. DEPARTMENT OF LABOR

LOGAN, David C., M.D.
Medical Officer
Office of Technical Support
Occupational Safety and Health
Room N3656
U.S. Department of Labor
Washington, D.C. 20210
202 523-9603

RECOMBINANT DNA ADVISORY COMMITTEE

LIAISON REPRESENTATIVES

JUENGST, Eric T. (Acting)
Program Specialist
Program of Science Technology
& Human Value
Mail Stop 104
National Endowment for the Humanities
Washington, D.C. 20506
202 474-0354

WEISS, Daniel L., M.D.
Assembly of Life Sciences
National Academy of Sciences
Washington, D.C. 20418
202 389-6315

IINO, Professor Tetsuo
Faculty Science
University of Tokyo
Hongo, Tokyo 113
Japan

Attachment II - Page 1

STANFORD UNIVERSITY
STANFORD, CALIFORNIA 94305

DEPARTMENT OF BIOLOGICAL SCIENCES

994

February 11, 1981

Dr. William Gartland
Office of Recombinant DNA Activities
National Institutes of Health
Bethesda, MD 20014

Dear Bill,

I enclose a proposal to be included on the agenda for the next RAC meeting. David Baltimore and I should be listed as co-authors. In my judgement, this constitutes a major action and therefore should be listed in the Federal Register.

Sincerely yours,

Allan

Allan Campbell

AMC:dp

cc: David Baltimore

Enclosure

PROPOSAL TO CONVERT THE NIH GUIDELINES INTO A NON-REGULATORY CODE OF STANDARD PRACTIVE AND TO REDUCE THE RECOMMENDED CONTAINMENT LEVELS FOR SOME EXPERIMENTS

PROPOSAL

1) Section I-A of the NIH Guidelines will be replaced with the following:

"I-A. Purpose. The purpose of these Guidelines is to specify standard practices for constructing and handling (i) recombinant DNA molecules and (ii) organisms and viruses containing recombinant DNA molecules. Adherence to these standards by all laboratories using recombinant DNA is recommended."

2) Part I-C of the NIH Guidelines shall be eliminated.

3) Part III of the Guidelines will be replaced with the following:

"Part III discusses experiments covered by the Guidelines. The reader must first consult Part I, where listings are given of prohibited and exempt experiments.

"Where there are existing recommended physical containment levels applicable to non-recombinant DNA experiments with either the host or the vector (such as those specified by the CDC Guidelines), recombinant DNA experiments should be carried out at containment levels at least as high as those recommended for non-recombinant DNA experiments. Otherwise, all non-prohibited experiments may be carried out under conditions of P1 physical containment. As a general practice, investigators should use the highest level of biological containment (HV3>HV2>HV1) which is available and appropriate for the purposes of the experiment.

"Specific exceptions to the prohibitions may be approved by the Director, NIH (Section I-D). The Director will consider requests for exceptions from individuals, institutions or corporations regardless of whether the applicant is affiliated with or supported by NIH. Such exceptions will generally be approved for specified levels of physical and biological containment."

This will be followed by a listing of those exceptions which are presently authorized and the containment levels approved for the excepted experiments.

4) Part IV of the NIH Guidelines shall be eliminated, with the following exceptions:

(a) Those definitions listed in Part IV-C which may be needed clarify statements made elsewhere in the Guidelines shall be retained.

(b) Those portions of Part IV-E defining the composition of RAC and prescribing rules for RAC procedures shall be retained.

(c) The following statement shall be added:

"Each institution conducting or sponsoring recombinant DNA research should take responsibility for monitoring its own activities in this area. Any unusual events that might be associated with the use of recombinant DNA molecules should be reported to the Director, NIH."

5) Section VI of the Guidelines will be eliminated, except for those portions of Section VI-F relevant to the protection of proprietary information submitted in support of requests for exceptions from the prohibitions.

EXPLANATION AND JUSTIFICATION

The action has two major effects:

(A) It revokes the mandatory nature of the Guidelines by eliminating those sections specifying regulatory procedures and their underlying organizational machinery. These Guidelines would then resemble the CDC Guidelines in setting standards and providing guidance rather than in regulating the performance of experiments. This purpose is accomplished by items 1, 2, 4, and 5 of the proposal.

Item 5 (elimination of most of Section VI) is included because, with the elimination of Section IV, compliance with the Guidelines will effectively become voluntary for all individuals, regardless of NIH support. Special provision for voluntary compliance by individuals and institutions not supported by NIH then becomes superfluous.

(B) It reduces the prescribed level of physical containment for most experiments to P1. This purpose is accomplished by item 3.

These two changes are justified from the following considerations: (A) Elimination of Regulatory Procedures. Opinions differ as to the wisdom of the actions and arguments which led to the adoption of the NIH Guidelines in 1976. However, there is fairly general agreement on two points: (i) The establishment of Guidelines has had some beneficial effects. In particular, it has raised the general level of awareness among investigators and institutions of the importance of considering possible hazards that might arise during microbiological research. (ii) Since 1976, neither experimental evidence nor solid theoretical arguments have been advanced to support the position that recombinant DNA research poses any danger to human health or to the integrity of the natural environment.

At this point, we doubt that the beneficial side effects of continued regulation justify the expenditure of time and money required to maintain a regulatory apparatus that has been developed to protect society from hazards that appear to be non-existent.

(B) Reduction of Recommended Containment Levels. In the absence of known or suspected hazards, it seems unjustified to single out certain classes of experiments as requiring elevated levels of physical containment. The cost, in discouraging variety and innovation and thereby limiting access to useful knowledge, is real, whereas the benefit is likely to be zero. The use of P1 containment, together with the highest available level of biological containment appropriate to the experimental purpose, will keep the probability of escape and establishment very low without interfering with the conduct of most research.

The prohibitions remain in force. Although we consider it unlikely that experiments in the prohibited categories will generate serious hazards, they represent the one area of the Guidelines which is addressed to risks whose nature can be specified, and that are in principle assessable. Restructuring of some of these categories aimed at delineating areas of real concern is desirable and is currently underway in the case of toxin genes. The results of such restructuring would be to define additional exceptions from the prohibitions, which would then appear in Part III of the Guidelines as amended by this measure.

Summary of Committee Actions, Report to RAC

At the April 1981 RAC meeting, a working group was established to consider major revisions of the recombinant DNA Guidelines. The working group, appointed by RAC chairman Ray Thornton, consists of 13 members, 9 of whom were RAC members as of June 1980 (2 have since ended their terms), 2 liaison RAC members, and 2 other scientists who have had long involvement with the recombinant DNA issue. The list of members is attached. The working group is chaired by Susan Gottesman. Two meetings were held: one on June 1, 1981, at which 8 members were present, and one on July 9, 1981, at which 11 members were present. Minutes of both meetings are available. There was a clear consensus by the working group that some major restructuring of the guidelines was appropriate. There was major disagreement about how far such a revision should go. The basic issues are: 1) Are there qualitatively unique dangers associated with Recombinant DNA research? and 2) If so, what response is necessary for guarding against such hazards; is some special procedure required? If there are not qualitatively unique dangers involved, are the remaining risks adequately addressed by already existing procedures for dealing with research dangers? If not, should one use the recombinant DNA issue to develop appropriate procedures for the more general issues?

After an analysis of the risks (detailed in the accompanying document), the following general conclusions were reached:

1) Accidental combinations of genes, rising out of "shotgun" cloning experiments or experiments where expression is not specifically

engineered, are extremely unlikely to lead to serious problems. In most organisms, the barriers to expression of foreign genes, the necessity for new enzyme activities to function as an integrated part of an existing pathway, and the selective disadvantage of carrying recombinant DNA, will interfere with such organisms establishing themselves in the environment and thus ultimately with their potential to cause harm. Therefore, for these experiments, the minimal controls associated with good laboratory practice should be sufficient. Many such experiments have already been exempted by the NIH from any special procedures.

2) A particular subset of experiments may pose some possibility of risk. In these experiments, the expression of foreign functions may have been deliberately increased, or normal functions will have been engineered to operate more efficiently. While there is no evidence that this risk is qualitatively different from the risks associated with other kinds of genetic research, the end result may be an increase in virulence, host range, or survivability of some pathogens.

Given these conclusions, the majority of those present at the July 9 meeting supported a proposal which adopts the containment provisions of the Baltimore-Campbell proposal, but retains the mandatory aspect of the guidelines. A minority preferred either a "voluntary code of practice" as stipulated in the original Baltimore-Campbell proposal, or an end to all specifications for working with recombinant DNA, apart from those stipulations of "good laboratory practice."

The text of the proposal as approved by the subcommittee, with a comparison to current (July 1, 1981) guidelines is attached. In addition, an examination of the state of our knowledge about recombinant DNA risks, to be used as a rationale for change, is attached.

We suggest the following procedures; 1) RAC consider and modify if necessary, the working group's proposal and the supporting rationale statement, 2) The modified proposal and rationale be published in the Federal Register and elsewhere, if appropriate, for public comment, 3) All comments be considered by the working group and recommendations for change, based on the comments, be made. The final version should once again be published in the Federal Register. 4) RAC take final action on the proposal. This might occur at the January 1982 RAC meeting, or possibly at the following meeting, if more time for comment is considered necessary.

Revision of the July 1, 1981 Guidelines Proposed by Working Group on Revision of the Guidelines, July 9, 1981

(1) Section I-A of the Guidelines would be amended to read as follows:

I-A. Purpose. The purpose of these Guidelines is to specify standard practices for constructing and handling (i) recombinant DNA molecules and (ii) organisms and viruses containing recombinant DNA molecules.

(2) Section I-D of the Guidelines, Prohibitions, would be eliminated.

(3) Part III of the Guidelines would be replaced with the following language:

Part III discusses experiments covered by the Guidelines. The reader should first consult Part I, where exempt experiments are listed.

Where recommended physical containment levels applicable to non-recombinant DNA experiments exist for either the host or the vector (such as those specified by the CDC Guidelines, or the USDA Quarantine Regulations), recombinant DNA experiments should be carried out at containment levels at least as high as those recommended for non-recombinant DNA experiments. If there is clear evidence that the donor DNA will significantly change the pathogenicity of the host, the containment level appropriate to the anticipated change will be applied. Otherwise, all experiments may be carried out under conditions of P1 or P1-LS physical containment.

(4) Those membership specifications of the IBC to be found in Section IV-D of Section IV of the Guidelines would be eliminated.

OUTLINE OF CURRENT NIH GUIDELINES FOR RECOMBINANT DNA RESEARCH AND PROPOSED CHANGES

	Current Guidelines: Procedures	Subcommittee Proposal	Baltimore-Campbell Proposal
I. Prohibitions (I-D)			
CDC Class 4 & 5 organisms Genes for potent toxins Release to environment Genes for drug resistance	Prohibitions take precedence over all other parts of guidelines; exceptions possible by application to RAC and *Federal Register* publication	Eliminate prohibitions as special class; handled by IBC as with other experiments	Retains prohibitions
10 liters unless well characterized and harmless	This prohibition does not take precedence over exemptions 1-4		
II. Exemptions (I-E)			
Naked DNA Rearrangements Self-cloning Exchangers Others: Tissue culture, *E. coli*, *B. subtilis* and *S. cerevisiae* HV1 systems	No special oversight required for these experiments; new additions to list by application to RAC and publication in *Federal Register*	No change	No change

	Current Guidelines: Procedures	Subcommittee Proposal	Baltimore-Campbell Proposal
III. HV1 Systems (III-A)			
Currently covers only some *N. crassa* and *Streptomyces* strains	Containment varies with source of donor DNA (P1-P3). New systems require approval by RAC and *Federal Register* publication	P1	P1
IV. All other prokaryote, lower eukaryote combinations	P3; lower by request to ORDA. Return to host of origin, P1	P1 for nonpathogens; pathogens as per CDC, etc.	P1 for nonpathogens; etc.
V. Eukaryote recipients			
non-viral vectors	P1-P2 in whole organ. (exempt in tissue culture)	P1 for non-pathogens, etc.	P1 for non-pathogens, etc.
defective viral vectors	P1-helper, P2-P3 + helper		
non-defective viral vectors	case-by-case; (P2 in most cases)	P1 for non-pathogens, etc.	P1 for non-pathogens, etc.
Procedural Changes: IBC	membership specified	no specifications for membership	voluntary system

RECOMBINANT DNA ADVISORY COMMITTEE

WORKING GROUP ON REVISION OF THE GUIDELINES

NATIONAL INSTITUTES OF HEALTH

CHAIRMAN

GOTTESMAN, SUSAN K., Ph.D.
Senior Investigator
Laboratory of Molecular Biology
National Cancer Institute
National Institutes of Health
Bethesda, Maryland 20205
301 496-2095

ADELBERG, EDWARD A., Ph.D.
Department of Human Genetics
School of Medicine
Yale University
New Haven, Connecticut 06510
203 436-0821

BERNS, KENNETH I., Ph.D., M.D.
Chairman
Department of Immunology
and Medical Microbiology
University of Florida
College of Medicine
Gainesville, Florida 32610
904 392-3311

GOLDSTEIN, RICHARD, Ph.D.
Associate Professor
Department of Microbiology
and Molecular Genetics
Harvard Medical School
Boston, Massachusetts 02115
617 732-1911

HARRIS, JEAN L., M.D.
Secretary of Human Resources
Commonwealth of Virginia
Office of Governor
Post Office Box 1475
Richmond, Virginia 23219
804 786-7765

KING, PATRICIA A., J.D.
Georgetown University
Law School
600 New Jersey Avenue, N.W.
Washington, D.C. 20001
202 624-8213

LEVINE, MYRON M., M.D.
Director
Center for Vaccine Development
Division of Infectious Diseases
University of Maryland
School of Medicine
Baltimore, Maryland 21201
301 528-7588

LEWIS, HERMAN W., Ph.D.
Senior Scientist for
Recombinant DNA
Division of Physiology
National Science Foundation
Washington, D.C. 20550
202 357-7647

MASON, JAMES O., M.D., Dr. Ph.
Executive Director
Utah State Department of
Health
Post Office Box 2500
Salt Lake City, Utah 84113
801 533-6111

NIGHTINGALE, ELENA O., Ph.D., M.D.
Senior Program Officer
Institute of Medicine
National Academy of Sciences
Washington, D.C. 20418
202 389-6963

WILLIAMS, LUTHER S., Ph.D.
Professor
Department of Biology
Washington University
Campus Box 1137
St. Louis, Missouri 63130
314 889-6843

TOLIN, SUE A., Ph.D.
Science and Education Administration
Cooperative Research
U.S. Department of Agriculture
Washington, D.C. 20250
202 447-5741

ZINDER, NORTON, Ph.D.
Professor
Rockefeller University
1230 York Avenue
New York, New York 10021
212 360-1322

EXECUTIVE SECRETARY

GARTLAND, WILLIAM J., JR., Ph.D.
Director
Office of Recombinant DNA Activities
National Institute of Allergy and Infectious Diseases
National Institutes of Health
Bethesda, Maryland 20205
301 496-6051

RECOMBINANT DNA ADVISORY COMMITTEE

AD HOC CONSULTANTS

September 10-11, 1981

GOTTESMAN, Susan K., Ph.D.
Senior Investigator
Laboratory of Molecular Biology
National Cancer Institute
National Institutes of Health
Bethesda, MD 20205
(301) 496-2095

ZINDER, Norton, Ph.D.
Professor
Rockefeller University
1230 York Avenue
New York, New York 10021
(212) 360-1322

Attachment IV - Page 1

THE ROCKEFELLER UNIVERSITY
1230 YORK AVENUE · NEW YORK, NEW YORK 10021

August 24, 1981

Dr. Elizabeth Milewski
O.R.D.A. - NIAID
National Institutes of Health
Bethesda, MD 20205

Dear Dr. Milewski:

Enclosed please find a document entitled "Further Recommendations" from a subset of the Working Group on Recombinant DNA for distribution to RAC.

Yours sincerely,

Norton D. Zinder

Norton D. Zinder

Enclosure

Further Recommendations

We the undersigned agree with the general thrust of the recommendations of the Working Group on Recombinant DNA Guidelines. In particular, we support the recommendation that those experiments, for which containment guidelines are retained, are to conform to good laboratory practice as described in the CDC and APHIS Quarantine rules. The recommendation that abolishes the category of prohibited experiments is scientifically sound in the light of current knowledge. The content of the suggested containment guidelines follows from the overall conclusion that research with recombinant DNA imposes no more risk than any other biological research. The background paper amply documents this point.

Therefore, we find no reason to retain the Administrative Guidelines (Section IV). The spirit of the Baltimore-Campbell resolution and, as titled, its major purpose, was to convert the NIH Regulations into Guidelines. Retaining pages of bureaucratic regulations for what is now perceived to require only limited oversight is a waste of time and effort, will not add to safety in any way, and will be disdained as bureaucratic capriciousness.

Edward A. Adelberg
Kenneth I. Berns
Herman W. Lewis
Sue A. Tolin
Norton D. Zinder

Given the recommendations for the containment guidelines and what would be proper for the administrative guidelines, we the undersigned conclude that special guidelines for recombinant DNA are totally unnecessary. Therefore, we further recommend that as of June 23, 1982 the NIH Guidelines cease to exist.

The arguments for their retention are primarily social and political; they do not have a scientific base (see Background Paper). It seems right, at this time, to disavow such arguments and base our conclusions solely on the scientific issues. RAC should recommend the abolition of the Guidelines. In doing so, it should prepare a strong statement of its rationale to be published in Science and Nature as well as the Federal Register. This statement should also contain as recommendation the containment guidelines for recombinant DNA experiments developed by the Working Group. Prepared as the culmination of years of consideration and analysis, such a statement would serve to inform both the scientific community and the public of the safety of research with recombinant DNA.

Edward A. Adelberg
Norton D. Zinder

Ray Thornton's Statement
September 10-11, 1981 NIH-RAC Meeting

I have a statement concerning our deliberations today. First, let me express my great confidence in Dick Krause, who has been delegated responsibility for receiving recommendations from this advisory committee. I have enjoyed many opportunities of working with him, and know his scientific and professional judgment will work to the benefit of the people affected by the actions of the National Institutes of Health.

At the same time, however, there can be no adequate statement as to how much we will all miss the wise counsel and leadership of Don Fredrickson as we continue to wrestle with the interaction of science and society. Don has a great gift of expressing clearly, as only an outstanding scientist could, his understanding of the continuing relationship between public policy and science.

Whenever either side of this relationship, the public or the scientific community, invades the province of the other or disregards the proper input of the other into decision making, the result is at best high levels of tension and frustration. At worst there may be attempts to regulate thought, as in laws regarding what theories may be taught; or just as bad, attempts to eliminate input from the public as to how scientific research should be conducted with public funds.

May I ask your indulgence as I cite the first few paragraphs of the statement I made in opening hearings on DNA research in Congress in 1977. This was at a time when legislation was being considered to prohibit or severely limit such research.

"True science always stands upon a frontier. It probes at the edges of our knowledge and our ignorance, and we accept its contributions as valuable, its continuation as a necessity. Perceived as a gradual extension of the sphere of knowledge, science is accepted and praised as both our benefactor and our servant.

"This is the science with which we are most comfortable, the science which explains how things work, which promises health, physical well-being, and material progress.

"But the boundaries of the physical and biological sciences are not so easily contained. From time to time we find or come upon a field of inquiry which fundamentally challenges our concepts of life and nature, which confronts us too directly for our collective comfort or convenience, and yet intrigues us too greatly to ignore.

"It is on this meeting ground of science and philosophy where man has made his greatest scientific advances. It is also here that science has caused its greatest strains upon our social, political, and religious institutions.

"When Galileo offered the theory that the Earth revolves around the Sun, it was bad enough to his contemporaries that he committed scientific error. It was worse that he committed heresy as well.

"Yet Galileo probed only the physical universe. As science has progressed and transformed our lives in so many ways, we have rejected many of the dogmas of an earlier day....

"... The scientific community often resolves its own conflicts more easily than our political community can even understand them....But the scientific community cannot ignore the concerns of its larger constituency, and Government cannot isolate itself from the science that it has encouraged and supported.

"Consideration of these questions brings us face to face with what I believe is one of the most fundamental issues before policymakers today: the issue of society interacting with science and the determination of the basic social responsibilities for the decision making process."

It has been a source of great personal satisfaction to me that my role as Chairman of the Science, Research, and Technology Subcommittee slowed the rush toward federal legislation, and eventually led to the acceptance by the Congress of guidelines promulgated by the NIH for the conduct of experiments funded by the public.

Except as required by local legislation, one who does not receive public money for the conduct of experiments is not affected in any way by such guidelines, unless by agreement such person accepts the guidelines on a voluntary basis. But I am unable to accept the suggestion that a person conducting research with public money stands entirely beyond the boundaries of public inquiry.

I believe the public has the right to say, and to ensure, that no public funds may be spent in an effort to construct drug resistant or toxigenic microorganisms. Certainly the public has the right to ensure that such microorganisms, if constructed, should not be released into the environment. Most would also agree that the public has the right to regulate under what conditions experiments with human subjects may be conducted.

There is, in summary, an ongoing vital connection between science and public policy.

Dr. Maxine Singer recognized this before the Congressional Committee and said:

> "Scientists today recognize their responsibility to the public that supports scientific work in the expectation that the results will have a significant positive impact on society. To describe the scientific community of the late twentieth century otherwise is to ignore or misunderstand the evidence. Dispute over the best way to exercise that responsibility must not be confused with a negation of it. The scientific community has accepted the counsel of ethicists, philosophers, and representatives of the public who have long troubled to point out this responsibility.
>
> "Scientists also accept the need to restrict certain laboratory practices in order to protect the safety and health of laboratory workers and the public. Further, we recognize the need to consider possible hazards before large scale activity is undertaken and before untoward events occur. But we differentiate between restrictions on hazardous or potentially hazardous activities and restrictions on intellectual freedom.

"For the future, scientists need to continue, together with federal and local governments, to evolve policies that offer protection from potential hazards and preserve opportunities for discovery and development of safe and desirable applications. Scientists must share their insights into the nature of living things with increasing numbers of people so that debate can be predicated on understanding rather than fear. In order to counteract the growing pessimism about the nature of knowledge, the proper separation of science from technology must be made and, in the continuing dialog, the distinct values and problems inherent in each must be carefully articulated. Finally if scientists commit themselves to their unique opportunities to serve as an early warning system, society can progress with prudence and caution as scientific knowledge grows."

In the Recombinant DNA Advisory Committee, an effort has been made to allow the public to have an input into recommendations which affect not only science, but the public as well, without unduly restricting the research which the public interest requires that we pursue.

The argument that guidelines for the conduct of publicly funded research are not needed because nothing more dangerous than now exists may be developed by this technology is beguiling, but false on two counts:

First, human experience has shown that any tool powerful enough to produce good results of sufficient importance to shake Wall Street and offer hope of treating diabetes is also powerful enough, wrongly used, to produce bad results of equal consequence.

Second, even accepting the assumption, with which I disagree, that nothing other than beneficial results may stem from this research, it does not follow that the public thereby loses its interest in having suitable guidelines for the expenditure of public funds.

Such guidelines might indeed need to be more carefully drawn, and perhaps should extend to all publicly funded research which may raise issues of the kind involved here.

Even if no additional increment of danger exists, it does not follow that dangerous or ethically or socially offensive experiments, with or without the technology involved here, should be conducted free of any guidelines except standards of good laboratory practices.

I am surprised to hear suggestions that because many of the unanswered questions relating to experiments in this field are political and social questions, that the guidelines have no further reason for existence. I doubt that the public will long remain aloof from decision making concerning the expenditure of public funds, whatever the purpose of those expenditures may be. If the possibility for interaction of science and public members as afforded by this committee is ended, some other mechanism for that input will be developed.

I believe the recommendation that the nature of the guidelines be downgraded to a simple statement of good laboratory practices, raises issues as serious - though opposite from - the ones considered by Congress several years ago.

In my view, the orderly progression of our recommendations to the Director, who has steadily eased the difficulties of performing experiments as rapidly as the consequences of that work may be evaluated, has been a useful example of the public working together with science to attain mutual goals.

I make this rather long statement in order to establish, for the record, my position with regard to the issue which the committee is considering, and to offer my views as to how we should proceed.

GPO 889-559

federal register

Friday
October 30, 1981

Part V

Department of Health and Human Services

National Institutes of Health

Recombinant DNA Research; Actions Under Guidelines

DEPARTMENT OF HEALTH AND HUMAN SERVICES

National Institutes of Health

Recombinant DNA Research; Actions Under Guidelines

AGENCY: National Institutes of Health. PHS, HHS.

ACTION: Notice of actions under NIH Guidelines for Research Involving Recombinant DNA Molecules.

SUMMARY: This notice sets forth actions taken by the Director, NIAID, by authority of the Director, NIH, under the 1981 Guidelines for Research Involving Recombinant DNA Molecules (46 FR 34462).

EFFECTIVE DATE: October 30, 1981.

FOR FURTHER INFORMATION CONTACT: Additional information can be obtained from Dr. William J. Gartland, Office of Recombinant DNA Activities (ORDA), National Institutes of Health, Bethesda, Maryland 20205 (301) 496-6051.

SUPPLEMENTARY INFORMATION: I am promulgating today several major actions under the NIH Guidelines for Research Involving Recombinant DNA Molecules. These proposed actions were published for comment in the Federal Register of August 4, 1981, and reviewed and recommended for approval by the Recombinant DNA Advisory Committee (RAC) at its meeting on September 10–11, 1981. In accordance with Section IV-E-1-b of the NIH Guidelines, I find that these actions comply with the Guidelines and present no significant risk to health or the environment.

Part I of this announcement provides background information on the actions.

Part II provides a summary of the major actions.

I. Decisions On Actions Under Guidelines

A. Modification of Section III-0-2 of the Guidelines

Dr. Michael J. Ross of Genentech, Inc., in a letter dated July 10, 1981, requested that the RAC evaluate a proposal to amend Section III-B-3 of the Guidelines. Section III-B-3 currently specifies that the Director, NIH, using a case-by-case review process, may set containment levels for certain experiments involving non-HVl host-vector systems. Dr. Ross proposed that a provision be added to this language. The provision would permit cloning of DNA from any nonpathogenic species into nonpathogenic lower eukaryotes at the P3 level of containment; closing of DNA from any nonpathogenic species into nonpathogenic prokaryotes would be allowed at the P2 level of containment. Data supporting the contention that the donor and recipient are nonpathogenic would be submitted to the local IBC.

An announcement of Dr. Ross' proposal appeared in the Federal Register of August 4, 1981 (46 FR 39771). During the thirty day comment period, no comments were received.

The RAC evaluated Dr. Ross' proposal at the September 10-11, 1981 meeting. During the discussion, it was noted that Section III-B-3 deals only with prokaryotic host-vector systems. Dr. Ross' proposal includes the cloning of DNA into nonpathogenic prokaryotes and also lower eukaryotes. It was pointed out that Section III-0-2 could be modified to accommodate the proposal including both prokaryotes and lower eukaryotes. RAC recommended approval of the proposal by a vote of twelve in favor, none opposed, with no abstentions, with NIH to modify the appropriate section of the Guidelines.

I accept this recommendation and the following wording is substituted for Section III-0-2: "III-0-2. *Experiments Involving Nonpathogenic Prokaryotic and Lower Eukaryotic Host-Vector Systems.* DNA from any species nonpathogenic for man, animal, or plants may be cloned into lower eukaryotes nonpathogenic for man, animal, or plants at the P3 level of containment [2A]. DNA from any species nonpathogenic for man, animal, or plants may be cloned into prokaryotes nonpathogenic for man, animals, or plants at the P2 level of containment [2A]. Data supporting the contention that the donor and recipient are nonpathogenic must be submitted to the local IBC. Lower levels of physical containment may be assigned by ORDA on a case-by-case basis for specific donor-recipient combinations (see Section IV-E-1-b-(3)-(b))."

B. Proposed Amendment of III-C-2-a and III-C-7-c of the Guidelines

In a letter dated April 27, 1981, Dr. Lois Miller of the Universtiy of Idaho, Moscow, Idaho, submitted a proposal to revise Section III-C-2-a and to add a new section, III-C-7-c, to the Guidelines.

The proposed revision of Section III-C-2-a which involves experiments with invertebrate viral vectors appeared as follows in the Federal Register of August 4, 1981 (46 FR 39771):

"III-C-2. Invertebrate Host-Vector Systems.

"III-C-2-a. Invertebrate Viral Vectors. Experiments involving invertebrate virus vectors can be done as follows:

"III-C-2-a-(1). Recombinant DNA molecules containing no more than two-thirds of the genome of any invertebrate virus [all viruses from a single family (36) being considered identical (50)] may be propagated and maintained in cells in tissue culture using P1 containment. For such experiments, it must be shown that the cells lack helper virus for the specific Families of defective viruses being used. The DMA may contain fragments of the genomes of viruses from more than one Family but each fragment must be less than two-thirds of a genome.

"III-C-2-a-(2). Recombinants with less than two-thirds of the genome of any invertebrate virus may be rescued with helper virus using P2 containment unless it is classified by the CDC as a class 3 agent (1) in which case P3 containment is required.

"III-C-2-a-(3). Experiments involving the use of other whole or defective virus genomes to propagate DNA sequences from prokaryotic or eukaryotic organisms (and viruses), or as vectors to transform nonpermissive cells, will be evaluated by NIH on a case-by-case basis [45] and will be conducted under the prescribed physical and biological containment conditions. (See Section IV-E-1-b-(3)-(c).)

"NIH will also review on a case-by-case basis [45] all experiments involving the use of virus vectors in animals and will prescribe the physical and biological containment conditions appropriate for such studies. (See Section IV-E-1-b-(3)-(c).)"

Dr. Miller also proposed that a new Section III-C-7-c be added to the Guidelines as follows:

"III-C-7-c. *Transfer to Invertebrates.* DNA from any non-prohibited source [Section I-D], except for greater than one quarter of a eukaryotic viral genome, which has been cloned and propagated in *E. coli* K-12, may be transferred with the *E. coli* vector used for cloning to any eukaryotic cells in culture or to any invertebrate organism and propagated under conditions of physical containment comparable to P1 and appropriate to the organism under study (2A). Transfers to any other host will be considered by the RAC on a case-by-case basis (45)."

No comments were received on these proposals. The RAC discussed the proposed changes in the Guidelines and noted that they were similar to those already pertaining to the use of vertebrate viruses as vectors. It was noted that Dr. Miller argues that employing invertebrate viral vectors poses no greater safety problems than working with vertebrate viral vectors. The RAC agreed that the suggested changes would be consistent with the current sections dealing with the use of vertebrate viral vectors.

By a vote of eleven in favor, none opposed, with five abstentions, the RAC recommended approval of Dr. Miller's proposal.

I accept this recommendation and the necessary changes and additions to the Guidelines have been made.

C. Amendment of Section I-D-6 and Appendix C of the Guidelines

Dr. Irving Johnson of Eli Lilly and Company in a letter dated July 20, 1981, requested that Section I-D-6 of the Guidelines, which prohibits certain large-scale recombinant DNA experiments, be amended to read as follows (new text in italics):

"I-D-6. Large-scale requirements [e.g., more than 10 liters of culture] with organisms conatining recombinant DNAs *other than those listed in Appendix C, Paragraphs 2, 3, and 4 of the Guidelines,* unless the recombinant DNAs are rigorously characterized and the absence of harmful sequences established (3). [See Section IV-E-1-b-(3)-(d).]"

Modifications of Appendix C would be necessitated by adoption of the proposal, and Dr. Johnson proposed modification to specify that these large-scale experiments would require IBC review and approval.

Dr. Johnson said that the RAC has already accepted the principle that no increased risk results from increased volume and that special RAC review of large-scale experiments involving host-vector systems currently exempted by Appendix C is not necessary. He submitted that large-scale fermentation expertise is found primarily in the local IBC and that responsibility for protection of workers and the environment should rest with the local IBC.

The proposal was published for public comment in the August 4, 1981, Federal Register (46 FR 39771). No comments were received on the proposal prior to the RAC meeting.

Dr. Johnson's request was discussed at the September 10-11, 1981, RAC meeting. At the meeting, Dr. Susan Wright submitted a letter opposing Dr. Johnson's proposal and submitted a report entitled "Hazards Involved in the Industrial Use of Micro-Organisms" prepared for the Commission of the European Communities.

One RAC reviewer discussed Dr. Wright's letter point by point and summarized major points in the EEC report. He stated that he believes the EEC report supports Dr. Johnson's proposal more than Dr. Wright's position. The RAC reviewers concluded that the potential environmental problems associated with the use of well-characterized organisms in large-scale recombinant DNA production processes appear to be similar to those associated with non-recombinant DNA large-scale fermentations which industry has been performing with an excellent safety record. It was pointed out that economic considerations necessitate strong quality control procedures.

RAC concluded that Dr. Johnson's proposed modification would benefit the public by facilitating the industrial development and production of useful products. Thus, by a vote of eleven in favor, two opposed, with one abstention, RAC recommended the proposal.

I accept this recommendation.

Section I-D-6 is amended to read as follows:

"I-D-6. Large-scale experiments [e.g., more than 10 liters of culture] with organisms containing recombinant DNAs other than those listed in Appendix C, Sections 2, 3, and 4 of the Guidelines, unless the recombinant DNAs are rigorously characterized and the absence of harmful sequences established. (3). [See Section IV-E-1-b-(3)-(d)]"

The text in Appendix C dealing with large-scale experiments (Sections 2, 3, and 4) will be replaced with the following:

"Large-scale experiments (e.g., more than 10 liters of culture) require prior IBC review and approval."

D. Cloning of Subgenomic Segments of Rift Valley Fever Virus

In a letter dated July 7, 1981, Dr. Charles Muscoplat of Molecular Genetics, Inc., Minnetonka, Minnesota, requested permission to clone subgenomic segments of the Rift Valley Fever Virus for the development of a vaccine. A notice concerning this request appeared in the Federal Register of August 4, 1981, (46 FR 39771). No comments were received on the proposal.

The RAC discussed this proposal at its September 10-11, 1981 meeting. It was noted that Rift Valley Fever Virus, a member of the Bunyaviridae family of viruses, is classified as a restricted agent by the Department of Agriculture since it produces a contagious disease both of cattle and sheep, and can be transmitted to man. It periodically causes disease epidemics especially in North Africa, Asia, and other parts of the world. Transmission is by insects.

Molecular Genetics, Inc., in a joint project with the U.S. Army Medical Research Institute of Infectious Diseases, proposes to clone a purified subgenomic segment. Since the virus consists of a negative, segmented single stranded RNA, cloning of the segment encoding the antigenic component poses no risk of infectivity. Further, it was noted that Molecular Genetics would be cloning the *M* segments of the RNA in an *E. coli* K-12 host-vector system only after rigorous safety testing for infectivity was performed by the Army Medical Research Institute. The RAC voted to approve the requested experiments to be performed at P1 physical containment with the restriction that the work be performed in a laboratory where no other bunyaviruses are used. In addition, it was stipulated that the "snap back" procedure be employed for generating the DNA. This assures that a complete viral genome could not be formed. The vote was sixteen in favor, none opposed, with two abstentions.

I accept this recommendation, and text has been added to Appendix E of the Guidelines indicating this action.

E. Proposed Exemption for Streptococcus Pyogenes and Streptococcus Sanguis

A request submitted by Dr. Joseph Ferretti of the University of Oklahoma Health Sciences Center that *Streptococcus pyogenes* and *Streptococcus sanguis* be considered as natural exchangers of DNA under the exemption category of Section I-E-4 and Appendix A of the Guidelines was considered by the RAC at its September 10-11, 1981 meeting. This proposal was published for comment in the Federal Register of August 4, 1981 (46 FR 39771). No comments were received on the proposal.

The evidence presented by the investigator demonstrating exchange of genetic information in both directions by natural physiological processes was considered by the RAC. On the basis of the experimental evidence, the RAC recommended by a vote of fourteen in favor, none opposed, with no abstentions that the request be approved.

I accept this recommendation and *Streptococcus pyogenes* has been added to sublist F of Appendix A.

F. Request To Include Streptococcus Lactis in a Sublist of Appendix A and to Permit Transfer of a Recombinant Plasmid From S. Faecalis to S. Lactis

Dr. Larry McKay of the University of Minnesota submitted a request for permission to allow the one way transfer of *Streptococcus lactis* DNA into *S. sanguis*, and that these strains be included in the exemption category of

Appendix A on the basis that they exchange genetic information by known physiological processes. The second part of Dr. McKay's proposal involves permission for the transfer of a recombinant plasmid from *S. faecalis* to *S. lactis*.

This proposal was published in the **Federal Register** of August 4, 1981 (46 FR 39770), and no comments were received on the proposal.

The RAC recommended approval of these requests by a vote of fourteen in favor, none opposed, with no abstentions.

I accept this recommendation. *Streptococcus lactis* has been added to Sublist E, Appendix A, as follows:

"Sublist E.

"One way transfer of *Streptococcus mutans* or *Streptococcus lactis* DNA into *Streptococcus sanguis.*"

A new entry, item 37, is added to Appendix E as follows:

"37. Permission is given to transfer a recombinant lactose plasmid from *Streptococcus faecalis* to *S. lactis* by conjugation."

G. Cloning of Saccharomyces Cerevisiae DNA in Salmonella Typhimurium

Drs. Christopher Marvel and Edward Penhoet of the University of California, Berkeley, in a letter dated July 8, 1981, requested permission to clone *Saccharomyces cerevisiae* DNA in *Salmonella typhimurium* using the plasmid, YEp13. The principal investigators wish to utilize an attenuated laboratory strain of *Salmonella typhimurium* to screen for the yeast pseudouridine synthetase gene. After screening, the selected plasmids will be maintained in an *E. coli* host.

A **Federal Register** announcement of the proposed experiments appeared on August 4, 1981 (46 FR 39771). During the comment period, no comments were received.

The RAC discussed this proposal at the September 10–11, 1981 meeting. As the *Salmonella* strains to be employed are attenuated laboratory strains, it was suggested that P1 physical containment conditions are adequate. By a vote of fourteen in favor, none opposed with no abstentions, RAC recommended that the experiments be permitted at the P1 level of containment.

I accept this recommendation and a new item, number 38, has been added to Appendix E:

"38. Attenuated laboratory strains of *Salmonella typhimurium* may be used under P1 physical containment conditions to screen for the *Saccharomyces cerevisiae* pseudouridine synthetase gene. The plasmid YEp13 will be employed as the vector."

H. Request To Utilize Haemophilus Parainfluenzae to Clone Moloney Murine Leukemia Provirus

The RAC at its September 10–11, 1981, meeting considered a proposal from Dr. James Gautsch of the Scripps Clinic and Research Foundation, La Jolla, California, to introduce Moloney MuLV proviral DNA and flanking mouse DNA into *Haemophilus parainfluenzae* employing a plasmid cloning vector with a broad host range in gram negative bacteria. The recombinant viral DNA would be subsequently used to transfect mouse cells in culture. Notice of this request appeared in the **Federal Register** of August 4, 1981 (46 FR 39770). During the comment period, no responses were received.

The RAC discussed this request at its September 10–11, 1981 meeting. It was noted that *H. parainfluenzae* is not considered a pathogen. Also, Moloney-MuLV virus can only infect mouse or rat cells, and not human cells; the virus is classified as a low-risk oncogenic virus. The RAC by a vote of eleven in favor, none opposed, with three abstentions recommended approval of the proposed experiments at the P2 level of physical containment.

I accept this recommendation and text has been added to Appendix E of the Guidelines, as follows:

"39. Permission is granted to clone in *Haemophilus parainfluenzae* Moloney murine leukemia provirus and mouse cellular flanking sequences employing the plasmid cloning vector, pRK290, under P2 containment conditions."

I. Request for Development of a New Host-Vector System Based on Corynebacterium Glutamicum

A request of Dr. Daniel Liberman, Massachusetts Institute of Technology, for an evaluation of the containment conditions for development of a new host-vector system based on a gram positive bacterium *Corynebacterium glutamicum* as host was considered by the RAC at its September 10–11, 1981 meeting. A notice of the proposal appeared in the **Federal Register** of August 4, 1981. No comments were received on the proposal.

Three possible types of vectors, including hybrid plasmids were proposed to be used with the new cloning host. It was noted during the RAC discussion that this organism is a nonpathogen and is employed in the commercial production of amino acids.

A motion to approve the request at the P1 level of containment provided that non-conjugative poorly mobilizable plasmids are used was passed by a vote of eleven in favor, one opposed, with one abstention.

I accept this recommendation and text has been added to Appendix E of the Guidelines.

J. Use of Conjugative Plasmids To Transfer DNA Between Escherichia Coli, Vibrio Cholera, and Vibrio Harveyi

Dr. J. W. Hastings of Harvard University requested permission to move *Vibrio harveyi* DNA cloned in *Escherichia coli* K-12 to *Vibrio cholera* and then to *Vibrio harveyi*. The investigator hopes to develop a system of genetic manipulation in *V. harveyi* in order to clone the luminescence gene(s).

A notice of this proposal appeared in the **Federal Register** of August 4, 1981 (46 FR 39771), for public comment. During the comment period, no comments were received.

The RAC discussed the proposal at the September 10–11, 1981 meeting. At the meeting, it was noted that the investigators hoped to enrich for an intermediate "donor" strain (*V. cholera*) which, under standard culture conditions, can mobilize plasmid DNA into *V. harveyi* at a significantly higher frequency than can be obtained by direct mating of *V. harveyi* with *E. coli*. As *Vibrio cholera* is a CDC class 2 organism, RAC felt it was appropriate to require use of P2 physical containment conditions for those experiments utilizing *V. cholera* as the intermediate "donor" strain. The other described experiments could proceed under P1 containment conditions. By a vote of ten in favor, none opposed, with three abstentions, RAC recommended that the requests be approved.

I accept this recommendation. A new item, number 41, has been added to Appendix E as follows:

"41. *Vibrio harveyi* DNA may be cloned in *Vibrio cholera*; plasmids may be used to transfer the cloned *V. harveyi* DNA between *E. coli* K-12, *V. cholera* and *V. harveyi*. P2 physical containment conditions are required for those experiments involving *V. cholera*. P1 containment conditions may be used for other phases of the project."

K. Containment Conditions for Cloning and Expression of DNA coding for Diphtheria Toxin

At the April 1981 RAC meeting, Dr. John Murphy of Harvard University was given permission to clone in *E. coli* K-12, under P4 containment conditions, restriction fragments of *Corynephage*

Beta carrying the structural gene for diphtheria toxin.

In a letter dated July 11, 1981, Dr. Murphy requested clarification on how the high containment facility located at Frederick, Mayland was to be used. Could he be permitted to carry out the experiments within the P4 facility using laboratory practices, equipment, and containment conditions specified by the NIH Biosafety Committee (IBC), which did not necessarily involve full P4 containment? Dr. Murphy's request was published for comment in the August 4, 1981 Federal Register (46 FR 39771). No comments were received on the request.

The RAC discussed the issue at its September 10–11, 1981 meeting. During the discussion, it was noted that Building 550 at the Frederick Cancer Research Center possesses full P4 containment barriers. The RAC judged that it would be appropriate for the local IBC to specify containment conditions within the facility, rather than requiring P4 containment for all phases of the work. The experiments, however, must be confined to DCRC Building 550. By a vote of eleven in favor, none opposed, with three abstentions, RAC recommended that the IBC be permitted to specify containment conditions for Dr. Murphy's experiments within Building 550 at the Frederick Cancer Research Center.

I accept this recommendation. Item 30 in Appendix E is modified as follows:

"30. Permission is granted to clone in *E. coli* K-12, in high containment building 550 at the Frederick Cancer Research Center, restriction fragments of *Corynephage Beta* carrying the structural gene for diphtheria toxin. Laboratory practices and containment equipment are to be specified by the IBC."

II. Summary of Actions Under The Guidelines

A. Modification of Section III-O-2 of the Guidelines

Section III-O-2 of the Guidelines is amended to read as follows:

"III-O-2. *Experiments Involving Nonpathogenic Prokaryotic and Lower Eukaryotic Host-Vector Systems.* DNA from any species nonpathogenic for man, animals, or plants may be cloned into lower eukaryotes nonpathogenic for man, animals, or plants at the P3 level of containment [2A]. DNA from any species nonpathogenic for man, animals, or plants may be cloned into prokaryotes nonpathogenic for man, animals, or plants at the P2 level of containment [2A]. Data supporting the contention that the donor and recipient are nonpathogenic must be submitted to the local IBC. Lower levels of physical containment may be assigned by ORDA on a case-by-case basis for specific donor-recipient combinations [see section IV-E-1-b-(3)-(h)]."

B. Modification of Section III-C-2-a and Addition of New Section III-C-7-c

Section III-C-2-a is amended to read as follows:

"III-C-2. Invertebrate Host-Vector Systems.

"III-C-2-a. Invertebrate Viral Vectors. Experiments involving invertebrate virus vectors can be done as follows:

"III-C-2-a(1). Recombinant DNA molecules containing no more than two-thirds of the genome of any invertebrate virus [all viruses from a single Family (36) being considered identical (50)] may be propagated and maintained in cells in tissue culture using P1 containment. For such experiments, it must be shown that the cells lack helper virus for the specific Families of defective viruses being used. The DNA may contain fragments of the genomes of viruses from more than one Family but each fragment must be less than two-thirds of a genome.

"III-C-2-a-(2). Recombinants with less than two-thirds of the genome of any invertebrate virus may be rescued with helper virus using P2 containment unless it is classified by the CDC as a class 3 agent (1) in which case P3 containment is required.

"III-C-2-a-(3). Experiments involving the use of other whole or defective virus genomes to propagate DNA sequences from prokaryotic or eukaryotic organisms (and viruses), or as vectors to transform nonpermissive cells, will be evaluated by NIH on a case-by-case basis [45] and will be conducted under the prescribed physical and biological containment conditions. (See Section IV-E-1-b-(3)-(c).)

'NIH will also review on a case-by-case basis [45] all experiments involving the use of virus vectors in animals and will prescribe the physical and biological containment conditions appropriate for such studies. (See Section IV-E-1-b-(3)-(c).)"

A new Section III-C-7-c is added as follows:

"III-C-7-c. *Transfer to Invertebrates.* DNA from any non-prohibited source [Section I-D], except for greater than one quarter of a eukaryotic viral genome, which has been cloned and propagated in *E. coli* K-12, may be transferred with the *E. coli* vector used for cloning to any eukaryotic cells in culture or to any invertebrate organism and propagated under conditions of physical containment comparable to P1 and appropriate to the organism under study (2A). Transfers to any other host will be considered by the RAC on a case-by-case basis (45)."

C. Amendment of Section I-D-6 of the Guidelines

Section I-D-6 is amended to read:

"I-D-6. Large-scale experiments [e.g., more than 10 liters of culture] with organisms containing recombinant DNAs other than those listed in Appendix C, Sections 2, 3, and 4 of the Guidelines, unless the recombinant DNAs are rigorously characterized and the absence of harmful sequences established (3). [See Section IV-E-1-b-(3)-(d).]"

Sections 2, 3 and 4 of Appendix C are amended to read as follows:

"2. *Experiments Involving E. coli K-12 host-vector systems.* Experiments which use *E. coli* K-12 host-vector systems, with the exception of those experiments listed below, are exempt from these Guidelines provided that (a) the *E. coli* host shall not contain conjugation proficient plasmids or generalized transducing phages, and (b) lambda or lambdoid or Ff bacterio-phages or nonconjugative plasmids [49] shall be used as vectors. However, experiments involving the insertion into *E. coli* K-12 of DNA from prokaryotes that exchange genetic information [35] with *E. coli* may be performed with any *E. coli* K-12 vector [e.g., conjugative plasmid]. When a nonconjugative vector is used, the *E. coli* K-12 host may contain conjugation-proficient plasmids either autonomous or integrated, or generalized transducing phages.

"For these exempt experiments, P1 physical containment conditions are recommended.

"*Exceptions:*

"Experiments described in Section I-D-1 to I-D-5 as being prohibited.

"Experiments involving DNA from Class 3 organisms [1] or from cells known to be infected with these agents may be conducted at P3 containment. Lower containment levels may be specified by NIH. [See Section IV-E-1-b-(2)-(e).] Experiments in this category require prior IBC review and approval.

"Experiments which increase the virulence and host range of a plant pathogen beyond that which occurs by natural genetic exchange. (See Section III-O-1.)

"Large-scale experiments (e.g., more than 10 liters of culture) require prior IBC review and approval.

"Experiments involving the deliberate cloning of genes coding for the biosynthesis of toxins potent for vertebrates. (See Appendix G.)

"3. *Experiments Involving Saccharomyces cerevisiae host-vector systems.* Experiments which use *Saccharomyces cerevisiae* host-vector systems, with the exception of experiments listed below, are exempt from these Guidelines provided that laboratory strains are used.

"For these exempt experiments, P1 physical containment conditions are recommended.

"*Exceptions.*

"Experiments described in Section I-D-1 to I-D-5 as being prohibited.

"Experiments involving CDC Class 3 organisms [1] or cells known to be infected with these agents, or any recombinant DNA molecules which increase the virulence and host-range of a plant pathogen beyond that which occurs by natural genetic exchange. (See Section III-0-1.)

"Large-scale experiments (e.g., more than 10 liters of culture) require prior IBC review and approval.

"Experiments involving the deliberate cloning of genes coding for the biosynthesis of toxins potent for vertebrates. (See Appendix G.)

"4· *Experiments Involving Bacillus subtilis host-vector systems. Any asporogenic Bacillus subtilis* strain which does not revert to a sporeformer with a frequency greater than 10^{-7} can by used for cloning DNA from any nonprohibited source, with the exception of those experiments listed below. Indigenous *Bacillus* plasmids and phages, whose host-range does not include *Bacillus cereus* or *Bacillus anthracis*, may be used as vectors.

"For these exempt experiments, P1 physical containment conditions are recommended.

"*Exceptions.*

"Experiments described in Sections I-D- to I-D-5 as being prohibited.

"Experiments involving CDC Class 3 organisms [1] or cells known to be infected with these agents, or any recombinant DNA molecules which increase the virulence and host-range of a plant pathogen beyond that which occurs by natural genetic exchange. (See Section III-0-1.)

"Large-scale experiments (e.g., more than 10 liters of culture) require prior IBC review and approval.

"Experiments involving the deliberate cloning of genes coding for the biosynthesis of toxins potent for vertebrates. (See Appendix G.)"

D. Cloning of Subgenomic Segments of Rift Valley Fever Virus

A new item, number 36, is added to Appendix E:

"36· Permission is granted to clone in *E. coli* K-12, under P1 physical containment conditions, subgenomic segments of Rift Valley Fever Virus subject to conditions which have been set forth by the RAC."

E. Addition of Streptococcus Pyogenes to Sublist F, Appendix A

Sublist F, Appendix A, is amended to read as follows:

"*Sublist F.*

"1. *Streptococcus sanguis.*

"2. *Streptococcus pneumoniae.*

"3. *Streptococcus faecalis.*

"4. *Streptococcus pyogenes.*"

F. Addition of Streptococcus Lactis to Sublist E, Appendix A, and Permission To Transfer a Recombinant Plasmid From S. Faecalis to S. Lactis

Sublist E, Appendix, is amended to read as follows:

"*Sublist E.*

"One way transfer of *Streptococcus mutans* or *Streptococcus lactis* DNA into *Streptococcus sanguis.*"

A new entry, item 37, is added to Appendix E:

"37· Permission is given to transfer a recombinant lactose plasmid from *Streptococcus faecalis* to *S. lactis* by conjugation."

G. Cloning of Saccharomyces Cerevisiae DNA in Salmonella Typhimurium

A new entry, number 38, is added to Appendix E:

"38· Attenuated laboratory strains of *Salmonella typhimurium* may be used under P1 physical containment conditions to screen for the *Saccharomyces cerevisiae* pseudouridine synthetase gene. The plasmid YEp13 will be employed as the vector."

H. Cloning Moloney MuLV Provirus and Flanking Regions in Hemophilus Parainfluenzae

A new entry, item 39, is added to Appendix E:

"39· Permission is granted to clone in *Haemophilus parainfluenzae* Moloney murine leukemia provirus and mouse cellular flanking sequences employing the plasmid vector, pRK290, under P2 containment conditions."

I. Development of a Host-Vector System Based on Corynebacterium Glatamicum

A new entry, item 40, is added to Appendix E:

"40· Permission is granted for the development, under P1 conditions, of a new host-vector system based on the use of *Corynebacterium glutamicum* as host and non-conjugative poorly mobilizable plasmids as vectors."

J. Use of Conjugative Plasmids to Transfer DNA Between E. Coli, Vibrio Cholera, and Vibrio Harveyi

A new entry, number 41, is added to Appendix E:

"41· *Vibrio harveyi* DNA may be cloned in *Vibrio cholera;* plasmids may be used to transfer the cloned *V. harveyi* DNA between *E. coli* K-12, *V. cholera*, and *V. harveyi*. P2 physical containment conditions are required for those experiments involving *V. cholera*. P1 containment conditions may be used for other phases of the project."

K. Containment Conditions for Cloning and Expression of DNA Coding for Diphtheria Toxin

Number 30 of Appendix E is modified to read as follows:

"30· Permission is granted to clone in *E. coli* K-12, in high containment Building 550 at the Frederick Cancer Research Center, restriction fragments of *Corynephage Beta* carrying the structural gene for diphtheria toxin. Laboratory practices and containment equipment are to be specified by the IBC."

Additional Announcements of the Director, NIAID

Section IV-E-1-b-(3)-(d) of the Guidelines gives responsibility to the Director, NIH or his delegate, for "authorizing, under procedures specified by the RAC, large-scale experiments (i.e., involving more than 10 liters of culture) for recombinant DNAs that are rigorously characterized and free of harmful sequences."

Accordingly, several requests for authorization to culture, on a large-scale, recombinant DNA host-vector systems have been received and reviewed by the NIH.

I. Genentech, Inc.

On October 21, 1981 the Director, NIAID, on the recommendation of the RAC, approved requests from Genentech, Inc., for the large-scale culture of:

1. *E. coli* K-12 containing plasmids coding for a human calcitonin analog,
2. *Saccharomyces cerevisiae* containing plasmids into which have been ligated cDNA coding for human leukocyte interferons A and D,
3. *E. coli* K-12 containing plasmids coding for porcine growth hormone,
4. *E. coli* K-12 containing a plasmid into which had been ligated chemically synthesized DNA and cloned cDNA coding for the VP_1 protein of Foot and Mouth Disease Virus.

The requests were approved with the understanding that Genentech, Inc., has agreed to permit an observer, designated by the NIH, to visit the facilities should NIH choose to inspect the site.

The principal investigator is Dr. Norm S.-C. Lin. The work is to be performed at the P1-LS level of containment at the research and development facility in South San Francisco, California 94080.

II. Cetus Corporation

On October 21, 1981 the Director, NIAID, on the recommendation of the RAC, approved requests from Cetus Corporation for the large scale culture of EK1 host-vector systems containing plasmids coding for human alpha-1-interferon and human proinsulin.

These requests were approved with the understanding that Cetus Corporation has agreed to permit an observer, designated by NIH, to visit the facilities if NIH should choose to inspect the site.

The principal investigator is Dr. Michael Konrad. The work is to be performed at the P1-LS level of containment at the Cetus Corporation facility in Berkeley, California 94710.

III. Schering Corporation

On October 21, 1981 the Director, NIAID, on the recommendation of the RAC, approved a request from Schering Corporation for the large scale culture of EK1 host-vector systems containing plasmids coding for human leukocyte interferons.

This request was approved with the understanding that Schering Corporation has agreed to permit an observer, designated by NIH, to visit the facilities if NIH should choose to inspect the site.

The principal investigators for the project are Drs. Paul Leibowitz and Mark Finkelstein. The work is to be performed at the P1-LS level of containment at the Schering Corporation facility in Bloomfield, New Jersey 08003.

IV. Molecular Genetics, Inc.

On October 21, 1981, the Director, NIAID, on the recommendation of the RAC, approved requests from Molecular Genetics, Inc., for the large scale culture of:

1. EK1 host-vector systems containing plasmids coding for the reverse transcriptase of the Avian Sarcoma Virus.

2. EK1 host-vector systems containing plasmids coding for bovine growth hormone.

The principal investigator for the reverse transcriptase project is Dr. John Weis. The principal investigator for the bovine growth hormone project is Dr. Richard A. Krzyzek. The work is to be performed at the P1-LS level of containment at the facility in Minnetonka, Minnesota 55343.

Dated: October 23, 1981.

Richard M. Krause,

Director, National Institute of Allergy and Infectious Diseases, National Institutes of Health.

OMB's "Mandatory Information Requirements for Federal Assistance Program Announcements" (45 FR 39592) requires a statement concerning the official government programs contained in the *Catalog of Federal Domestic Assistance*. Normally NIH lists in its announcements the number and title of affected individual programs for the guidance of the public. Because the guidance in this notice covers not only virtually every NIH program but also essentially every federal research program in which DNA recombinant molecule techniques could be used, it has been determined to be not cost effective or in the public interest to attempt to list these programs. Such a list would likely require several additional pages. In addition, NIH could not be certain that every federal program would be included as many federal agencies, as well as private organizations, both national and international, have elected to follow the NIH Guidelines. In lieu of the individual program listing, NIH invites readers to direct questions to the information address above about whether individual programs listed in the *Catalog of Federal Domestic Assistance* are affected.

Note.—NIH programs are not covered by OMB Circular A-95 because they fit the description of "programs not considered appropriate" in Section 8-(b)(-(4) and (5) of that Circular.

[FR Doc. 81-31299 Filed 10-28-81; 8:45 am]
BILLING CODE 4110-08-M

federal register

Friday
December 4, 1981

Part II

Department of Health and Human Services

National Institutes of Health

Recombinant DNA Research; Proposed Revised Guidelines

DEPARTMENT OF HEALTH AND HUMAN SERVICES

National Institutes of Health

Recombinant DNA Research: Proposed Revised Guidelines

AGENCY: National Institutes of Health, PHS, DHHS.

ACTION: Notice of proposed revision of the NIH guidelines for research involving recombinant DNA molecules.

SUMMARY: This notice sets forth a proposed revision of the 1981 NIH Guidelines for Research Involving Recombinant DNA Molecules (46 FR 34462). Interested parties are invited to submit comments concerning this proposal. This proposal and comments on it will be considered by the NIH Recombinant DNA Advisory Committee (RAC) at its next meeting.

DATE: Comments must be received by February 2, 1982.

ADDRESS: Written comments and recommendations should be submitted to the Director, Office of Recombinant DNA Activities, Building 31, Room 4A52, National Institutes of Health, Bethesda, Maryland 20205. All comments received in timely response to this notice will be considered and will be available for public inspection in the above office on weekdays between the hours of 8:30 a.m. and 5:00 p.m.

FOR FURTHER INFORMATION CONTACT: Additional information can be obtained from Drs. Stanley Barban or Elizabeth Milewski, Office of Recombinant DNA Activities, National Institutes of Health, Bethesda, Maryland 20205, (301) 496-6061.

SUPPLEMENTARY INFORMATION: I am today issuing for public comment proposed revised NIH Guidelines for Research Involving Recombinant DNA Molecules. This action is taken in accordance with Section IV-E-1-b-(1) of the NIH Guidelines. This announcement introduces the proposed revision, then gives the proposed revised Guidelines in their entirety, and then includes a series of annexes containing relevant background documents. These annexes are:

Annex A: Original proposal of Drs. David Baltimore and Allan Campbell.
Annex B: Documents prepared by Working Group on Revision of the Guidelines.
Annex C: Minority reports of working group members.
Annex D: Draft Minutes of relevant portion of September 10-11, 1981, RAC Meeting.
Annex E: Current NIH Guidelines.

The history of development of these proposed revised Guidelines is as follows. Drs. David Baltimore and Allan Campbell, RAC members, had proposed a major revision of the Guidelines (Baltimore-Campbell proposed, Annex A), which was considered by the RAC at its April 1981 meeting. At the April 1981 meeting, a Working Group on Revision of the Guidelines was established to review the Baltimore-Campbell proposal as well as other approaches which might lead to a major revision of the Guidelines. The Working Group met on June 1, 1981, and on July 9, 1981. The Working Group prepared a proposal for revising the Guidelines, a summary of its actions, and a document entitled "Evaluation of the Risks Associated with Recombinant DNA Research." These documents appear as Annex B. Two minority reports were prepared by several members of the Working Group (Annex C). The Working Group report and the minority reports were distributed to RAC members prior to the September 1981 meeting.

The RAC extensively discussed the Working Group's report and other approaches to revision of the Guidelines at its September 1981 meeting. Draft minutes of that discussion constitute Annex D. As indicated in those draft minutes, the RAC passed by a vote of 16 in favor, 3 opposed, with 1 abstention, the elements of its version of a proposed revision of the Guidelines to be published for public comment. Based upon this proposal, NIH staff prepared the proposed revised Guidelines which are published immediately following this introduction, for public comment. For comparison, the current NIH Guidelines are given in Annex E.

The proposed revised Guidelines and comments on them will be considered by the RAC at its next meeting.

The major features of the proposed revision are:

1. The Guidelines would cease to be mandatory and would become a voluntary code of standard practice. Requirements that institutions have an Institutional Biosafety Committee (IBC), that investigators obtain prior approval from the IBC before beginning certain experiments, that investigators obtain prior approval from NIH before beginning certain experiments, and the section of the Guidelines specifying that noncompliance with the Guidelines could lead to loss of NIH funds, would all be eliminated.

2. Section III of the Guidelines giving containment levels would be greatly simplified, and most experiments currently mandated at P2 or P3 containment would be recommended at P1.

3. The prohibitions section (I-D) of the Guidelines would be eliminated, although two of the previous prohibitions would be retained instead as admonishments.

Proposed Guidelines for Research Involving Recombinant DNA Molecules

October 1981.

Table of Contents

I. Scope of the Guidelines

I-A. *Purpose.* The purpose of these Guidelines is to specify practices for constructing and handling (i) recombinant DNA molecules and (ii) organisms and viruses containing recombinant DNA molecules. Adherence to those standards by all laboratories using recombinant DNA is recommended.

I-B. *Definition of Recombinant DNA Molecules.* In the context of these Guidelines, recombinant DNA molecules are defined as either (i) molecules which are constructed outside living cells by joining natural or synthetic DNA segments to DNA molecules that can replicate in a living cell, or (ii) DNA molecules that result from the replication of those described in (i) above.

I-C. [Deleted]

I-D. [Deleted]

I-E. *Exemptions.* The following recombinant DNA molecules are exempt from these Guidelines:

I-E-1. Those that are not in organisms or viruses. [5]

I-E-2. Those that consist entirely of DNA segments from a single nonchromosomal or viral DNA source, though one or more of the segments may be a synthetic equivalent.

I-E-3. Those that consist entirely of DNA from a prokaryotic host, including its indigenous plasmids or viruses, when propagated only in that host (or a closely related strain of the same species) or when transferred to another host by well established physiological means; also those that consist entirely of DNA from a eukaryotic host, including its chloroplasts, mitochondria, or plasmids (but excluding viruses), when propagated only in that host (or a closely related strain of the same species).

I-E-4. Certain specified recombinant DNA molecules that consist entirely of DNA segments from different species that exchange DNA by known physiological processes, though one or more of the segments may be a synthetic equivalent. A list of such exchangers will be prepared and periodically revised by the Director, NIH, with advice of the RAC, after appropriate notice and opportunity for public comment. (See Section IV-E-1-b-(1)-(d).) Certain classes are exempt as of publication of these Revised Guidelines. The list is in Appendix A. An updated list may be obtained from the Office of Recombinant DNA Activities, National Institutes of Health, Bethesda, Maryland 20205.

I-E-5. Other classes of recombinant DNA molecules, if the Director, NIH, with advice of the RAC, after appropriate notice and opportunity for public comment, finds that they do not present a significant risk to health or the environment. (See Section IV-E-1-b-(1)-(d).) Certain classes are exempt as of publication of these Revised Guidelines. The list is in Appendix C. An updated list may be obtained from the Office of Recombinant DNA Activities; National Institutes of Health, Bethesda, Maryland 20205.

I-F. *General Definitions.* See Section IV-C.

II. Containment

Effective biological safety programs have been operative in a variety of laboratories for many years. Considerable information, therefore, already exists for the design of physical containment facilities and the selection of laboratory procedures applicable to organisms carrying recombinant DNAs. (6-19) The existing programs rely upon mechanisms that, for convenience, can be divided into two categories: (i) A set of standard practices that are generally used in microbiological laboratories, and (ii) special procedures, equipment, and laboratory installations that provide physical barriers which are applied in varing degrees according to the estimated biohazard.

Experiments on recombinant DNAs, by their very nature, lend themselves to a third containment mechanism—namely, the application of highly specific biological barriers. In fact, natural barriers do exist which limit either (i) the infectivity of a *vector,* or *vehicle,* (plasmid or virus) for specific hosts or (ii) its dissemination and survival in the environment. The vestors that provide the means for replication of the recombinant DNAs and/or the host cells in which they replicate can be genetically designed to decrease by many orders of magnitude the probability of dissemination of recombinant DNAs outside the laboratory.

As these means of containment are complementary, different levels of containment appropriate for experiments with different recombinants can be established by apply various combinations of the physical and biological barriers along with a constant use of the standard practices. We consider these categories of containment separately here in order that such combinations can be conveniently expressed in the Guidelines.

In constructing these Guidelines, it was necessary to define boundary conditions for the different levels of physical and biological containment and for the classes of experiments to which they apply. We recognize that these definitions do not take into account all existing and anticipated information on special procedures that will allow particular experiments to be carried out under different conditions than indicated here without affecting risk. Indeed, we urge that individual investigators devise simple and more effective containment procedures and that investigators recommend changes in the Guidelines to permit their use.

II-A *Standard Practices and Training.* The first principle of containment is a strict adherence to good microbiological practices. (6-15) Consequently, all personnel directly or indirectly involved in experiments on recombinant DNAs should receive adequate instruction. This should, as a minimum, include instructions in aseptic techniques and in the biology of the organisms used in the experiments, so that the potential biohazards can be understood and appreciated.

Any research group working with agents with a known or potential biohazard should have an emergency plan which describes the procedures to be followed if an accident contaminates personnel or the environment. The principal investigator should ensure that everyone in the laboratory is familiar with both the potential hazards of the work and the emergency plan. If a research group is working with a known pathogen where there is an effective vaccine it should be made available to all workers. Where serological monitoring is clearly appropriate it should be provided.

II-B *Physical Containment Levels.* The objective of physical containment is to confine organisms containing recombinant DNA molecules, and thus to reduce the potential for exposure of the laboratory worker, persons outside of the laboratory, and the environment to organisms containing recombinant DNA molecules. Physical containment is achieved through the use of laboratory practices, containment equipment, and special laboratory design. Emphasis is placed on primary means of physical containment which are provided by laboratory practices and containment equipment. Special laboratory design provides a secondary means of protection aganist the accidental release of organisms outside the laboratory or to the environment. Special laboratory design is used primarily in facilities in which experiments of moderate to high potential hazards are performed.

Combinations of laboratory practices, containment equipment, and special laboratory design can be made to achieve different levels of physical containment. Four levels of physical containment, which are designated as P1, P2, P3, and P4, are described. It should be emphasized that the descriptions and assignments of physical containment detailed below are based on existing approaches to containment of pathogenic organisms. For example, the "Classification of Etiologic Agents on the Basis of Hazard,"[7] prepared by the Centers for Disease Control, describes four general levels which roughly correspond to our descriptions for P1, P2, P3, and P4; and the National Cancer Institute describes three levels for research on oncogenic viruses which roughly correspond to our P2, P3, and P4 levels.[8]

It is recognized that several different combinations of laboratory practices, containment equipment, and special laboratory design may be appropriate for containment of specific research activities. The Guidelines, therefore, allow alternative selections of primary containment equipment within facilities that have been designed to provide P3 and P4 levels of physical containment. The selection of alternative methods of primary containment is dependent, however, on the level of biological containment provided by the host-vector system used in the experiment. Consideration will also be given by the Director, NIH, with the advice of the Recombinant DNA Advisory Committee to other combinations which achieve an equivalent level of containment. (See Section IV-E-1-b-(2)-(b).)

Information on large-scale applications can be found in "Physical Containment Recommendations for Large-Scale Uses of Organisms Containing Recombinant DNA Molecules." Federal Register, April 11, 1980, where definitions are found of P1-LS, P2-LS, and P3-LS. Guidance is available from ORDA on physical containment levels when working with plant host-vector systems.

II-B-1. *P1 Level.*

II-B-1-a. *Laboratory Practices.*

II-B-1-a-(1). Laboratory doors shall be kept closed while experiments are in progress.

II-B-1-a-(2). Work surfaces shall be decontaminated daily, and immediately following spills of organisms containing recombinant DNA molecules.

II-B-1-a-(3). All biological wastes shall be decontaminated before disposal. Other contaminated materials, such as glassware, animal cages, and laboratory equipment, shall be decontaminated before washing, reuse, or disposal.

II-B-1-a-(4). Mechanical pipetting devices shall be used; pipetting by mouth is prohibited.

II-B-1-a-(5). Eating, drinking, smoking, and storage of foods are not permitted in the laboratory area in which recombinant DNA materials are handled.

II-B-1-a-(6). Persons shall wash their hands after handling organisms containing recombinant DNA molecules and when they leave the laboratory.

II-B-1-a-(7). Care shall be taken in the conduct of all procedures to minimize the creation of aerosols.

II-B-1-a-(8). Contaminated materials that are to be decontaminated at a site away from the laboratory shall be placed in a durable leak-proof container, which is closed before removal from the laboratory.

II-B-1-a-(9). An insect and rodent control program shall be instituted.

II-B-1-a-(10). The use of laboratory gowns, coats, or uniforms is discretionary with the laboratory supervisor.

II-B-1-a-(11). Use of the hupodermic needle and syringe shall be avoided when alternative methods are available.

II-B-1-a-(12). The laboratory shall be kept neat and clean.

II-B-1-b. *Containment Equipment.* Special containment equipment is not required at the P1 level.

II-B-1-c. *Special Laboratory Design.* Special laboratory design is not required at the P1 level.

II-B-2. *P2 Level.*

II-B-2-a. *Laboratory Practices.*

II-B-2-a-(1). Laboratory doors shall be kept closed while experiments are in progress.

II-B-2-a(2). Work surfaces shall be decontaminated daily, and immediately following spills of organisms containing recombinant DNA molecules.

II-B-2-a(3). All laboratory wastes shall be steam-sterilized (autoclaved) before disposal. Other contaiminated materials such as glassware, animal cages, laboratory equipment, and radiocative wastes shall be decontaminated by a means demonstrated to be effective before washing, reuse, or disposal.

II-B-2-a(4). Mechanical pipetting devices shall be used; pipetting by mouth is prohibited.

II-B-2-a(5). Eating, drinking, smoking, and storage of food are not permitted in the laboratory area in which recombinant DNA materials are handled.

II-B-2-a(6). Persons shall wash their hands after handling organisms containing recombinant DNA molecules and when they leave the laboratory.

II-B-2-a(7). Care shall be exercised to minimize the creation of aerosols. For example, manipulations such as inserting a hot inoculating loop or needle into a culture, flaming an inoculation loop or needle so that it splatters, and forceful ejection of fluids from pipettes or syringes shall be avoided.

II-B-2-a(8). Contaminated materials that are to be steam sterilized (autoclaved) or decontaminated at a site away from the laboratory shall be placed in a durable leak-proof container, which is closed before removal from the laboratory.

II-B-2-a(9). Only persons who have been advised of the nature of the research being conducted shall enter the laboratory.

II-B-2-a(10). The universal biohazard sign shall be posted on all laboratory access doors when experiments requiring P2 containment are in progress. Freezers and refrigerators or other units used to store organisms containing recombinant DNA molecules shall also be posted with the universal biohazard sign.

II-B-2-a(11). An insect and rodent control program shall be instituted.

II-B-2-a(12). The use of laboratory gowns, coats, or uniforms is required. Laboratory clothing shall not be worn to the lunch room or outside of the building in which the laboratory is located.

II-B-2-a(13). Animals not related to the experiment shall not be permitted in the laboratory.

II-B-2-a(14). Use of the hypodermic needle and syringe shall be avoided when alternative methods are available.

II-B-2-a(15). The laboratory shall be kept neat and clean.

II-B-2-a(16). Experiments of lesser biohazard potential can be carried out concurrently in carefully demarcated areas of the same laboratory.

II-B-2-b. *Containment Equipment.* Biological safety cabinets [20] shall be used to contain aerosol-producing equipment, such as blenders, lyophilizers, sonicators, and centrifuges, when used to process organisms containing recombinant DNA molecules, except where equipment design provides for containment of the potential aerosol. For example, a centrifuge may be operated in the open if a sealed head or safety centrifuge cups are used.

II-B-2-c. *Special Laboratory Design.* An autoclave for sterilization of wastes and contaminated materials shall be available in the same building in which organisms containing recombinant DNA molecules are used.

II-B-3. *P3 Level.*

II-B-3-a. *Laboratory Practices.*

II-B-3-a-(1). Laboratory doors shall be kept closed while experiments are in progress.

II-B-3-a-(2). Work surfaces shall be decontaminated following the completion of the experimental activity, and immediately following spills of organisms containing recombinant DNA molecules.

II-B-3-a-(3). All laboratory wastes shall be steam-sterilized (autoclaved) before disposal. Other contaminated materials, such as glassware, animal cages, laboratory equipment, and radioactive wastes, shall be decontaminated by a method demonstrated to be effective before washing, reuse, or disposal.

II-B-3-a-(4). Mechanical pipetting devices shall be used; pipetting by mouth is prohibited.

II-B-3-a-(5). Eating, drinking, smoking, and storage of food are not permitted in the laboratory area in which recombinant DNA materials are handled.

II-B-3-a-(6). Persons shall wash their hands after handling organisms containing recombinant DNA molecules and when they leave the laboratory.

II-B-3-a-(7). Care shall be exercised to minimize the creation of aerosols. For example, manipulations such as inserting a hot inoculating loop or needle into a culture, flaming an inoculation loop or needle so that it splatters, and forceful ejection of fluids from pipettes or syringes shall be avoided.

II-B-3-a-(8). Contaminated materials that are to be steam-sterilized (autoclaved) or decontaminated at a site away from the laboratory shall be placed in a durable leak-proof container, which is closed before removal from the laboratory.

II-B-3-a-(9). Entry into the laboratory shall be through a controlled access area. Only persons who have been advised of the nature of the research being conducted shall enter the controlled access area. Only persons required on the basis of program or support needs shall be authorized to enter the laboratory. Such persons shall be advised of the nature of the research being conducted before entry, and shall comply with all required entry and exit procedures.

II-B-3-a-(10). Persons under 16 years of age shall not enter the laboratory.

II-B-3-a-(11). The universal biohazard sign shall be posted on the controlled access area door and on all laboratory doors when experiments requiring P3-level containment are in progress. Freezers and refrigerators or other units used to store organisms containing recombinant DNA molecules shall also be posted with the universal biohazard sign.

II-B-3-a-(12). An insect and rodent control program shall be instituted.

II-B-3-a-(13). Laboratory clothing that protects street clothing (e.g., long-sleeve solid-front or wrap-around gowns, no-button or slipover jackets) shall be worn in the laboratory. Front-button laboratory coats are unsuitable. Laboratory clothing shall not be worn outside the laboratory and shall be decontaminated before it is sent to the laundry.

II-B-3-a-(14). Raincoats, overcoats, topcoats, coats, hats, caps, and such street outer-wear shall not be kept in the laboratory.

II-B-3-a-(15). Gloves shall be worn when handling materials requiring P3 containment. They shall be removed aseptically immediately after the handling procedure and decontaminated.

II-B-3-a-(16). Animals and plants not related to the experiment shall not be permitted in the laboratory.

II-B-3-a-(17). Vacuum outlets shall be protected by filter and liquid disinfectant traps.

II-B-3-a-(18). Use of hypodermic needle and syringe shall be avoided when alternative methods are available.

II-B-3-a-(19). The laboratory shall be kept neat and clean.

II-B-3-a-(20). If experiments involving other organisms which require lower levels of containment are to be conducted in the same laboratory concurrently with experiments requiring P3-level physical containment, they shall be conducted in accordance with all P3-level laboratory practices.

II-B-3-b. *Containment Equipment.*

II-B-3-b-(1). Biological safety cabinets[20] shall be used for all equipment and manipulations that produce aerosols—e.g., pipetting, dilutions, transfer operations, plating, flaming, grinding, blending, drying, sonicating, shaking, centrifuging—where these procedures involve organisms containing recombinant DNA molecules, except where equipment design provides for containment of the potential aerosol.

II-B-3-b-(2). Laboratory animals held in a P3 area shall be housed in partial-containment caging systems, such as Horsfall units[19A], open cages placed in ventilated enclosures, solid-wall and -bottom cages covered by filter bonnets, or solid-wall and -bottom cages placed on holding racks equipped with ultraviolet radiation lamps and reflectors.

Note.—Conventional caging systems may be used. *Provided,* That all personnel wear appropriate personal protective devices. These shall include, at a minimum, wrap-around gowns, head covers, gloves, shoe covers, and respirators. All personnel shall shower on exit from areas where these devices are required.

II-B-3-b-(3). *Alternative Selection of Containment Equipment.* Experimental procedures involving a host-vector system that provides a one-step higher level of biological containment can be conducted in the P3 laboratory using containment equipment specified for the P2 level of physical containment. Experimental procedures involving a host-vector system that provides a one-step lower level of biological containment can be conducted in the P3 laboratory using containment equipment specified for the P4 level of physical containment. Alternative combinations of containment safeguards are shown in Table I.

TABLE I.—COMBINATIONS OF CONTAINMENT SAFEGUARDS

Classification of experiment		Alternate combinations of physical and biological containment			
		Physical Containment			
Physical containment	Biological[1] containment	Laboratory design specified for—	Laboratory practices specified for—	Containment equipment specified for—	Biological containment
P3	HV3	P3	P3	P3	HV3.
P3	HV3	P3	P3	P4	HV2.
P3	HV2	P3	P3	P3	HV2.
P3	HV2	P3	P3	P2	HV3.
P3	HV2	P3	P3	P4	HV1.
P3	HV1	P3	P3	P3	HV1.
P3	HV1	P3	P3	P2	HV2.

[1] See Section II-D for description of biological containment.

II-B-3-c. *Special Laboratory Design.*

II-B-3-c(1). The laboratory shall be separated by a controlled access area from areas that are open to unrestricted traffic flow. A controlled access area is an anteroom, a change room, an air lock or any other double-door arrangement that separates the laboratory from areas open to unrestricted traffic flow.

II-B-3-c-(2). The surfaces of walls, floors, and ceilings shall be readily cleanable. Penetrations through these surfaces shall be sealed or capable of being sealed to facilitate space decontamination.

II-B-3-c-(3). A foot-, elbow-, or automatically-operated hand-washing facility shall be provided near each primary laboratory exit area.

II-B-3-c-(4). Windows in the laboratory shall be sealed.

II-B-3-c-(5). An autoclave for sterilization of wastes and contaminated materials shall be available in the same building (and preferably within the controlled laboratory area) in which organisms containing recombinant DNA molecules are used.

II-B-3-c-(6). The laboratory shall have a ventilation system that is capable of controlling air movement. The movement of air shall be from areas of lower contamination potential to areas of higher contamination potential (i.e., from the controlled access area to the laboratory area). If the ventilation system provides positive pressure supply air, the system shall operate in a manner that prevents the reversal of the direction of air movement or shall be equipped with an alarm that would actuated in the event that reversal in the direction of air movement were to occur. The exhaust air from the laboratory area shall not be recirculated to other areas of the building unless the exhaust air is filtered by HEPA filters or equivalent. The exhaust air from the laboratory area can be discharged to the outdoors without filtration or other means for effectively reducing an accidental aerosol burden provided that it can be dispersed clear of occupied buildings and air intakes.

II-B-3-c-(7). The treated exhaust-air from Class I and Class II biological safety cabinets [20] may be discharged either to the laboratory or to the outdoors. The treated exhaust-air from a Class III cabinet shall be discharged directly to the outdoors. If the treated exhaust-air from these cabinets is to be discharged to the outdoors through a building exhaust air system, it shall be connected to this system so as to avoid any interference with the air balance of the cabinet and the building ventilation system.

II-B-4. *P4 Level.*

II-B-4-a. *Laboratory Practices.*

II-B-4-a-(1). Laboratory doors shall be kept closed while experiments are in progress.

II-B-4-a-(2). Work surfaces shall be decontaminated following the completion of the experimental activity and immediately following spills of organisms containing recombinant DNA molecules.

II-B-4-a-(3). All laboratory wastes shall be steam-sterilized (autoclaved) before disposal. Other contaminated materials such as glassware, animal cages, laboratory equipment, and radioactive wastes shall be decontaminated by a method demonstrated to be effective before washing, reuse, or disposal.

II-B-4-a-(4). Mechanical pipetting devices shall be used; pipetting by mouth is prohibited.

II-B-4-a-(5). Eating, drinking, smoking, and storage of food are not permitted in the P4 facility.

II-B-4-a-(6). Persons shall wash their hands after handling organisms containing recombinant DNA molecules and when they leave the laboratory.

II-B-4-a-(7). Care shall be exercised to minimize the creation of aerosols. For example, manipulations such as inserting a hot inoculating loop or needle into a culture, flaming an inoculation loop or needle so that it splatters, and forceful ejection of fluids from pipettes or syringes shall be avoided.

II-B-4-a-(8). Biological materials to be removed from the P4 facility in a viable or intact state shall be transferred to a nonbreakable sealed container, which is then removed from the P4 facility through a pass-through disinfectant dunk tank or fumigation chamber.

II-B-4-a-(9). No materials, except for biological materials that are to remain in a viable or intact state, shall be removed from the P4 facility unless they have been steam-sterilized (autoclaved) or decontaminated by a means demonstrated to be effective as they pass out of the P4 facility. All wastes and other materials as well as equipment not damaged by high temperature or steam shall be steam-sterilized in the double-door autoclave of the P4 facility. Other materials which may be damaged by temperature or steam shall be removed from the P4 facility through a pass-through fumigation chamber.

II-B-4-a-(10). Materials within the Class III cabinets shall be removed from the cabinet system only after being steam-sterilized in an attached double-door autoclave or after being contained in a nonbreakable sealed container, which is then passed through a disinfectant dunk tank or a fumigation chamber.

II-B-4-a-(11). Only persons whose entry into the P4 facility is required to meet program or support needs shall be authorized to enter. Before entering, such persons shall be advised of the nature of the research being conducted and shall be instructed as to the appropriate safeguards to ensure their safety. They shall comply with instructions and all other required procedures.

II-B-4-a-(12). Persons under 18 years of age shall not enter the P4 facility.

II-B-4-a-(13). Personnel shall enter into and exist from the P4 facility only through the clothing change and shower rooms. Personnel shall shower at each egress from the P4 facility. Air locks shall not be used for personnel entry or exit except for emergencies.

II-B-4-a-(14). Street clothing shall be removed in the outer side of the clothing-change area and kept there. Complete laboratory clothing, including undergarments, head cover, shoes, and either pants and shirts or jumpsuits, shall be used by all persons who enter the P4 facility. Upon exit, personnel shall store this clothing in lockers provided for this purpose or discard it into collection hampers before entering the shower area.

II-B-4-a-(15). The universal biohazard sign is required on the P4 facility access doors and on all interior doors to individual laboratory rooms where experiments are conducted. The sign shall also be posted on freezers, refrigerators, or other units used to store organisms containing recombinant DNA molecules.

II-B-4-a-(16). An insect and rodent control program shall be instituted.

II-B-4-a-(17). Animals and plants not related to the experiment shall not be permitted in the laboratory in which the experiment is being conducted.

II-B-4-a-(18). Vacuum outlets shall be protected by filter and liquid disinfectant traps.

II-B-4-a-(19). Use of the hypodermic needle and syringe shall be avoided when alternate methods are available.

II-B-4-a-(20). The laboratory shall be kept neat and clean.

II-B-4-a-(21). If experiments involving other organisms which require lower levels of containment are to be conducted in the P4 facility concurrently with experiments requiring P4-level containment, they shall be conducted in accordance with all P4-level laboratory practices specified in this section.

II-B-4-b. *Containment Equipment.*

II-B-4-b-(1). Experimental procedures involving organisms that require P4-level physical containment shall be conducted either in (i) a Class III cabinet system or in (ii) Class I or Class II cabinets that are located in a specially designed area in which all personnel are required to wear one-piece positive-pressure isolation suits.

II-B-4-b-(2). Laboratory animals involved in experiments requiring P4-level physical containment shall be housed either in cages contained in Class III cabinets or in partial containment caging systems (such as Horsfall units[19A], open cages placed in ventilated enclosures, or solid-wall and -bottom cages covered by filter bonnets, or solid-wall and -bottom cages placed on holding racks equipped with ultraviolet irradiation lamps and reflectors) that are located in a specially designed area in which all personnel are required to wear one-piece positive-pressure suits.

II-B-4-b-(3). *Alternative Selection of Containment Equipment.* Experimental procedures involving a host-vector system that provides a one-step higher level of biological containment can be conducted in the P4 facility using containment equipment requirements specified for the P3 level of physical containment. Alternative combinations of containment safeguards are shown in Table II.

TABLE II.—COMBINATIONS OF CONTAINMENT SAFEGUARDS

Classification of experiment		Alternate combinations of physical and biological containment			
		Physical containment			
Physical containment	Biological [1] containment	Laboratory design specified for—	Laboratory practices specified for—	Containment equipment specified for—	Biological containment
P4	HV1	P4	P4	P4	HV1.
P4	HV1	P4	P4 [2]	P3	HV2.

[1] See Section II-D for description of biological containment.

[2] In this case gloves shall be worn, in addition to the clothing requirements specified in II-B-4-a-(14).

II-B-4-c. *Special Laboratory Design.*

II-B-4-c-(1). The laboratory shall be located in a restricted-access facility which is either a separate building or a clearly demarcated and isolated zone within a building. Clothing-change areas and shower rooms shall be provided for personnel entry and egress. These rooms shall be arranged so that personnel leave through the shower area to the change room. A double-door ventilated vestibule or ultraviolet air lock shall be provided for passage of materials, supplies, and equipment which are not brought into the P4 facility through the change room area.

II-B-4-c-(2). Walls, floors, and ceilings of the P4 facility are constructed to form an internal shell which readily allows vapor-phase decontamination and is animal- and insect-proof. All penetrations through these structures and surfaces are sealed. (The integrity of the walls, floors, ceilings, and penetration seals should ensure adequate containment of a vapor-phase decontaminant under static pressure conditions. This requirement does not imply that these surfaces must be airtight.)

II-B-4-c-(3). A foot-, elbow-, or automatically-operated handwashing facility shall be provided near the door within each laboratory in which experiments involving recombinant DNA are conducted in openface biological safety cabinets.

II-B-4-c-(4). Central vacuum systems are permitted. The system, if provided, shall not serve areas outside the P4 facility. The vacuum system shall include in-line HEPA filters near each use point or service cock. The filters shall be installed so as to permit in-place decontamination and replacement. Water supply, liquid and gaseous services provided to the P4 facility shall be protected by devices that prevent backflow.

II-B-4-c-(5). Drinking water fountains shall not be installed in laboratory or animal rooms of the P4 facility. Foot-operated water fountains are permitted in the corridors of the P4 facility. The water service provided to such fountains shall be protected from the water services to the laboratory areas of the P4 facility.

II-B-4-c-(6). Laboratory doors shall be self-closing.

II-B-4-c-(7). A double-door autoclave shall be provided for sterilization of material passing out of the P4 facility. The autoclave doors shall be interlocked so that both doors will not be open at the same time.

II-B-4-c-(8). A pass-through dunk tank or fumigation chamber shall be provided for removal from the P4 facility of material and equipment that cannot be heat-sterilized.

II-B-4-c-(9). All liquid effluents from the P4 facility shall be collected and decontaminated before disposal. Liquid effluents from biological safety cabinets and laboratory sinks shall be sterilized by heat. Liquid effluents from the shower and hand washing facilities may be activated by chemical treatment. HEPA filters shall be installed in all vents from effluent drains.

II-B-4-c-(10). An individual supply and exhaust-air ventilation system shall be provided. The system shall maintain pressure differentials and directional air flow as required to ensure inflow from areas outside the facility toward areas of highest potential risk within the facility. The system shall be designed to prevent the reversal of air flow. The system shall sound an alarm in the event of system malfunction.

II-B-4-c-(11). Air within individual laboratories of the P4 facility may be recirculated in HEPA filtered.

II-B-4-c-(12). The exhaust air from the P4 facility shall be HEPA filtered and discharged to the outdoors so that it is dispersed clear of occupied buildings and air intakes. The filter chambers shall be designed to allow *in situ* decontamination before removal and to facilitate certification testing after replacement.

II-B-4-c-(13). The treated exhaust-air from Class I and Class II biological safety cabinets[20] may be discharged directly to the laboratory room environment or to the outdoors. The treated exhaust-air from Class III cabinets shall be discharged to the outdoors. If the treated exhaust-air from these cabinets is to be discharged to the outdoors through the P4 facility exhaust air system, it shall be connected to this system so as to avoid any interference with the air balance of the cabinets or the facility exhaust air system.

II-B-4-c-(14). As noted in Section II-B-4-b-(1), the P4 facility may contain specially designed areas in which all personnel are required to wear one-piece positive-pressure isolation suits. Such areas shall be airtight. The exhaust-air from the suit area shall be filtered by two sets of HEPA filters installed in series, and a duplicate filtration unit and exhaust fan shall be provided. The air pressure within the suit area shall be less than that in any adjacent area. An emergency lighting system, communication systems, and power source shall be provided. A double-door autoclave shall be provided for sterilization of all waste materials to be removed from the suit area.

Personnel who enter this area shall wear a one-piece positive-pressure suit that is ventilated by a life-support system. The life-support system shall be provided with alarms and emergency backup air. Entry to this area is through an airlock fitted with airtight doors. A chemical shower area shall be provided to docontaminate the surfaces of the suit before removal.

II-C. *Shipment.* Recombinant DNA molecules contained in an organism or virus should be shipped only as an etiologic agent under requirements of the U.S. Public Health Service, and the U.S. Department of Transportation (§ 72.3, Part 72, Title 42, and §§ 173.386-173.388, Part 173, Title 49, U.S. Code of Federal Regulations (CFR)) as specified below:

II-C-1. Recombinant DNA molecules contained in an organism or virus requiring P1, P2, or P3 physical containment, when offered for transportation or transported, should be subject to all requirements of § 72.3(a)–(e), Part 72, Title 42 CFR, and §§ 173.386–173.388, Part 173, Title 49 CFR.

II–C–2. Recombinant DNA molecules contained in an organism or virus requiring P4 physical containment, when offered for transportation or transported, should be subject to the requirements listed above under II–C–1 and are also subject to § 72.3(f), Part 72, Title 42 CFR.

II–C–3. Additional information on packaging and shipment is given in the "Laboratory Safety Monograph—A Supplement to the NIH Guidelines for Recombinant DNA Research."

II–D. *Biological Containment.*

II–D–1. *Levels of Biological Containment.* In consideration of biological containment, the vector (plasmid, organelle, or virus) for the recombinant DNA and the host (bacterial, plant, or animal cell) in which the vector is propagated in the laboratory will be considered together. Any combination of vector and host which is to provide biological containment must be chosen or constructed so that the following types of "escape" are minimized: (i) Survival of the vector in its host outside the laboratory and (ii) transmission of the vector from the propagation host to other nonlaboratory hosts.

The following levels of biological containment (HV, or *H*ost-*V*ector, systems) for prokaryotes will be established; specific criteria will depend on the organisms to be used.

II–D–1–a. *HV1.* A host-vector system which provides a moderate level of containment. *Specific systems:*

II–D–1–a–(1). *EK1.* The host is always *E. coli* K–12 or a derivative thereof, and the vectors include nonconjugative plasmids (e.g., pSC101, ColEl, or derivatives thereof [12–27]) and variants of bacteriophage, such as lamboda [28–33]. The *E. coli* K–12 hosts shall not contain conjugation-proficient plasmids, whether autonomous or integrated, or generalized transducing phages.

II–D–1–a–(2). *Other Prokaryotes.* Hosts and vectors shall be, at a minimum, comparable in containment to *E. coli* K–12 with a non conjugative plasmid or bacteriophage vector. The data to be considered and a mechanism for approval of such HVl systems are described below (Section II–D–2).

II–D–1–b. *HV2.* These are host-vector systems shown to provide a high level of biological containment as demonstrated by data from suitable tests performed in the laboratory. Escape of the recombinant DNA either via survival of the organisms or via transmission of recombinant DNA to other organisms should be less than $1/10^8$ under specified conditions. *Specific systems:*

II–D–1–b–(1). For EK2 host-vector systems in which the vector is a plasmid, no more than one in 10^8 host cells should be able to perpetuate a cloned DNA fragment under the specified nonpermissive laboratory conditions designed to represent the natural environment, either by survival of the original host or as a consequence of transmission of the cloned DNA fragment.

II–D–1–b–(2). For EK2 host-vector systems in which the vector is a phage, no more than one in 10^8 phage particles should be able to perpetuate a cloned DNA fragment under the specified nonpermissive laboratory conditions designed to represent the natural environment either (i) as a prophage (in the inserted or plasmid form) in the laboratory host used for phage propagation or (ii) by surviving in natural environments and transferring a cloned DNA fragment to other hosts (or their resident prophages).

II–D–1–c. *HV3.* These are host-vector systems in which:

II–D–1–c–(1). All HV2 criteria are met.

II–D–1–c–(2). The vector is dependent on its propagation host or is highly defective in mobilizability. Reversion to host-independence must be less than $1/10^8$ per vector genome per generation.

II–D–1–c–(3). No markers conferring resistance to antibiotics commonly used clinically or in agriculture are carried by the vector, unless expression of such markers is dependent on the propagating host or on unique laboratory-controlled conditions or is blocked by the inserted DNA.

II–D–1–c–(4). The specified containment shown by laboratory tests has been independently confirmed by specified tests in animals, including primates, and in other relevant environments.

II–D–1–c–(5). The relevant genotypic and phenotypic traits have been independently confirmed.

II–D–2. *Certification of Host-Vector Systems.*

II–D–2–a. *Responsibility.* HV1 systems other than *E. coli* K–12, and HV2 and HV3 host-vector systems, may not be designated as such until they have been certified by the Director, NIH. Application for certification of a host-vector system is made by written application to the Office of Recombinant DNA Activities, National Institutes of Health, Bethesda, Maryland 20205.

Host-vector systems that are proposed for certification will be reviewed by the National Institutes of Health (NIH) Recombinant DNA Advisory Committee (RAC). (See Section IV–E–1–b–(1)–(c).) This will first involve review of the data on construction, properties, and testing of the proposed host-vector system by a Working Group composed of one or more members of the RAC and other persons chosen because of their expertise in evaluating such data. The Committee will then evaluate the report of the Working Group and any other available information at a regular meeting. The Director, NIH, is responsible for certification after receiving the advice of the RAC. Minor modifications of existing certified host-vector systems, where the modifications are of minimal or no consequence to the properties relevant to containment may be certified by the Director, NIH, without review by the RAC. (See Section IV–E–1–b–(3)–(f).)

When new host-vector systems are certified, notice of the certification will be sent by the Office of Recombinant DNA Activities (ORDA) to the applicant and to all Institutional Biosafety Committees (IBCs) and will be published in the *Recombinant DNA Technical Bulletin.* Copies of a list of all currently certified host-vector systems may be obtained from ORDA at any time.

The Director, NIH, may at any time rescind the certification of any host-vector system. (See Section IV–E–1–b–(3)–(g).) If certification of a host-vector system is rescinded, NIH will instruct investigators to transfer cloned DNA into a different system, or use the clones at a higher physical containment level unless NIH determines that the already constructed clones incorporate adequate biological containment.

Certification of a given system does not extend to modifications of either the host or vector component of that system. Such modified systems must be independently certified by the Director, NIH. If modifications are minor, it may only be necessary for the investigator to submit data showing that the modifications have either improved or not impaired the major phenotypic traits on which the containment of the system depends. Substantial modifications of a certified system require the submission of complete testing data.

II–D–2–b. *Data To Be Submitted for Certification.*

II–D–2–b–(1). *HV1 Systems Other than E. Coli K–12.* The following types of data shall be submitted, modified as appropriate for the particular system under consideration. (i) A description of the organism and vector; the strain's natural habitat and growth requirements; its physiological properties, particularly those related to its reproduction and survival and the mechanisms by which it exchanges genetic information; the range of organisms with which this organism normally exchanges genetic information and what sort of information is exchanged; and any relevant information on its pathogenicity or toxicity. (ii) A description of the history of the particular strains and vectors to be used, including data on any mutations which render this organism less able to survive or transmit genetic information. (iii) A general description of the range of experiments contemplated, with emphasis on the need for developing such an HV1 system.

II-D-2-b-(2). *HV2 Systems.* Investigators planning to request HV2 certification for host-vector systems can obtain instructions from ORDA concerning data to be submitted (33A, 33B). In general, the following types of data are required: (i) Description of construction steps, with indication of source, properties, and manner of introduction of genetic traits. (ii) Quantitative data on the stability of genetic traits that contribute to the containment of the system. (iii) Data on the survival of the host-vector system under nonpermissive laboratory conditions designed to represent the relevant natural environment. (iv) Data on transmissibility of the vector and/or a cloned DNA fragment under both permissive and nonpermissive conditions. (v) Data on all other properties of the system which affect containment and utility, including information on yields of phage or plasmid molecules, ease of DNA isolation, and ease of transfection or transformation. (vi) In some cases, the investigator may be asked to submit data on survival and vector transmissibility from experiments in which the host-vector is fed to laboratory animals (e.g., rodents). Such *in vivo* data may be required to confirm the validity of predicting *in vivo* survival on the basis of *in vitro* experiments.

Data must be submitted in writing to ORDA. Ten to twelve weeks are normally required for review and circulation of the data prior to the meeting at which such data can be considered by the RAC. Investigators are encouraged to publish their data on the construction, properties, and testing of proposed HV2 systems prior to consideration of the system by the RAC and its subcommittee. More specific instructions concerning the type of data to be submitted to NIH for proposed EK2 systems involving either plasmids or bacteriophage in *E. coli* K-12 are available from ORDA.

II-D-2-b-(3). *HV3 Systems.* Putative HV3 systems must, as the first step in certification, be certified as HV2 systems. Systems which meet the criteria given above under II-D-1-(c)-1, II-D-1-(c)-2, and II-D-1-(c)-3 will then be recommended for HV3 testing. Tests to evaluate various HV2 host-vector systems for HV3 certification will be performed by contractors selectd by NIH. These contractors will repeat tests performed by individuals proposing the HV2 system and, in addition, will conduct more extensive tests on conditions likely to be encountered in nature. The genotypic and phenotypic traits of HV2 systems will be evaluated. Tests on survival and transmissibility in and on animals, including primates, will be performed, as well as tests on survival in certain specified natural environments.

II-D-3. *Distribution of Certified Host-Vectors.* Certified HV2 and HV3 host-vector systems (plus appropriate control strains) must be obtained from the NIH or its designees, one of whom will be the investigator who developed the system. NIH shall announce the availability of the system by publication of notices in appropriate journals.

Plasmid vectors will be provided in a suitable host strain, and phage vectors will be distributed as small-volume lysates. If NIH propagates any of the host strains or phage, a sample will be sent to the investigator who developed the system or to an appropriate contractor, prior to distribution, for verification that the material is free from contamination and unchanged in phenotypic properties.

In distributing the certified HV2 and HV3 host-vector systems, NIH or its designee will (i) send out a complete description of the system; (ii) enumerate and describe the tests to be performed by the user in order to verify important phenotypic traits; (iii) remind the user that any modification of the system necessitates independent approval of the system by the NIH; and (iv) remind the user of responsibility for notifying ORDA of any discrepancies with the reported properties or any problems in the safe use of the system.

NIH may also distribute certified HV1 host-vector systems.

III. Containment Guidelines for Covered Experiments

Part III discusses experiments covered by the Guidelines. The reader should first consult Part I, where exempt experiments are listed.

Where recommended physical containment levels applicable to non-recombinant DNA experiments exist for either the host or the vector,* recombinant DNA experiments should be carried out at containment levels at least as high as those recommended for non-recombinant DNA experiments. If there is clear evidence that the donor DNA will significantly change the pathogenicity of the host, the containment level appropriate to the anticipated change will be applied. Otherwise, all experiments may be carried out under conditions of Pl or Pl-LS physical containment.

No experiments should be performed which involve:

(a) Deliberate transfer of a drug resistance trait to microorganisms that are not known to acquire it naturally, if such acquisition could compromise the use of a drug to control disease agents in human or veterinary medicine or agriculture.

(b) Deliberate formation of recombinant DNAs containing genes for the biosynthesis of toxins lethal for vertebrates at an LD_{50} of less than 100 nanograms per kilogram body weight (e.g., the botulinum toxins, tetanus toxin, diphtheria toxin, *Shigella dysenteriae* neurotoxin). Guidelines for the cloning of DNAs containing genes coding for the biosynthesis of toxins which are lethal to vertebrates at 100 nanograms to 100 micrograms per kilogram body weight are specified in Appendix G.

IV. Roles and Responsibilities

IV-A. [Deleted]

IV-B. [Deleted]

IV-C. *General Definitions.* The following terms are defined as follows:

IV-C-1. "DNA" means deoxyribonucleic acid.

IV-C-2. "Recombinant DNA" or "recombinant DNA molecules" means either (i) molecules which are constructed outside living cells by joining natural or synthetic DNA segments to DNA molecules that can replicate in a living cell, or (ii) DNA molecules which result from the replication of a molecule described in (i) above.

IV-C-3. [Deleted]

IV-C-4. "Institution" means any public or private entity (including Federal, State, and local government agencies).

IV-C-5. [Deleted]

IV-C-6. "NIH Office of Recombinant DNA Activities" or "ORDA" means the office within NIH with responsibility for

* Such as those specified by the CDC Guidelines, or the USDA Quarantine Regulations.

(i) reviewing and coordinating all activities of NIH related to the Guidelines, and (ii) performing other duties as defined in Section IV–E–3.

IV–C–7. "Recombinant DNA Advisory Committee" or "RAC" means the public advisory committee that advises the Secretary, the Assistant Secretary for Health, and the Director of the National Institutes of Health concerning recombinant DNA research. The RAC shall be constituted as specified in Section IV–E–2.

IV–C–8. "Director, NIH" or "Director" means the Director of the National Institutes of Health and any other officer or employee of NIH to whom authority has been delegated.

IV–C–9. [Deleted]

IV–C–10. [Deleted]

IV–C–11. "Laboratory Safety Monograph" or "LSM" means a publication to accompany the NIH Guidelines describing practices, equipment, and facilities in detail.

IV–D. *Responsibilities of the Institution.*

Each institution conducting or sponsoring recombinant DNA research should take responsibility for monitoring its own activities in this area. Any unusual events that might be associated with the use of recombinant DNA molecules should be reported to the Director, NIH.

IV–E. *Responsibilities of NIH.*

IV–E–1. *Director.* The Director, NIH, is responsible for (i) establishing the NIH Guidelines on recombinant DNA research, (ii) overseeing their implementation, and (iii) their final interpretation.

The Director has a number of responsibilities under the Guidelines that involve the NIH Office of Recombinant DNA Activities (ORDA) and the Recombinant DNA Advisory Committee (RAC). ORDA's responsibilities under the Guidelines are administrative. Advice from the RAC is primarily scientific and technical. In certain circumstances, there is specific opportunity for public comment, with published response, before final action.

IV–E–1–a. *General Responsibilities of the Director, NIH.* The responsibilities of the Director shall include the following:

IV–E–1–a–(1). Promulgating requirements as necessary to implement the Guidelines;

IV–E–1–a–(2). Establishing and maintaining the RAC to carry out the responsibilities set forth in Section IV–E–2. The RAC's membership is specified in its charter and in Section IV–E–2; and

IV–E–1–a–(3). Establishing and aintaining ORDA to carry out the responsibilities defined in Section IV–E–3.

IV–E–1–b. *Specific Responsibilities of the Director, NIH.*

IV–E–1–b–(1). *The Director is responsible for the following major actions* (For these, the Director must seek the advice of the RAC and provide an opportunity for public and Federal agency comment. Specifically, the agenda of the RAC meeting citing the major actions will be published in the **Federal Register** at least 30 days before the meeting, and the Director will also publish the proposed actions in the **Federal Register** for comment at least 30 days before the meeting. In addition, the Director's proposed decision, at his discretion, may be published in the **Federal Register** for 30 days of comment before final action is taken. The Director's final decision, along with response to the comments, will be published in the **Federal Register** and the *Recombinant DNA Technical Bulletin.* The RAC will be notified of this decision):

IV–E–1–b–(1)–(a). Changing containment levels for types of experiments that are specified in the Guidelines when a major action is involved;

IV–E–1–b–(1)–(b). Assigning containment levels for types of experiments that are not explicitly considered in the Guidelines when a major action is involved;

IV–E–1–b–(1)–(c). Certifying new host-vector systems, with the exception of minor modifications of already certified systems. (The standards and procedures for certification are described in Section II–D–2–a. Minor modifications constitute, for example, those of minimal or no consequence to the properties relevant to containment.);

IV–E–1–b–(1)–(d). Promulgating and amending a list of classes of recombinant DNA molecules to be exempt from these Guidelines because they consist entirely of DNA segments from species that exchange DNA by known physiological processes, or otherwise do not present a significant risk to health or the environment (see Sections I–E–4 and –5 for further information);

IV–E–1–b–(1)–(e). [Deleted]

IV–E–1–b–(1)–(f). Adopting other changes in the Guidelines.

IV–E–1–b–(2). *The Director is also responsible for the following lesser actions* (For these, the Director must seek the advice of the RAC. The Director's decision will be transmitted to the RAC and published in the *Recombinant DNA Technical Bulletin):*

IV–E–1–b–(2)–(a). Interpreting and determining containment levels, upon request by ORDA;

IV–E–1–b–(2)–(b). Changing containment levels for experiments that are specified in the Guidelines;

IV–E–1–b–(2)–(c). Assigning containment levels for experiments not explicitly considered in the Guidelines;

IV–E–1–b–(2)–(d). [Deleted]

IV–E–1–b–(2)–(e). [Deleted]

IV–E–1–b–(3). *The Director is also responsible for the following actions.* (The Director's decision will be transmitted to the RAC and published in the *Recombinant DNA Technical Bulletin):*

IV–E–1–b–(3)–(a). Interpreting the Guidelines for experiments to which the Guidelines specifically assign containment levels;

IV–E–1–b–(3)–(b). Determining appropriate containment conditions for experiments according to case precedents developed under Section IV–E–1–b–(2)–(c).

IV–E–1–b–(3)–(c). [Deleted]

IV–E–1–b–(3)–(d). [Deleted]

IV–E–1–b–(3)–(e). [Deleted]

IV–E–1–b–(3)–(f). Approving minor modifications of already certified host-vector systems. (The standards and procedures for such modifications are described in Section II–D–2); and

IV–E–1–b–(3)–(g). Decertifying already certified host-vector systems.

IV–E–1–b–(3)–(h). [Deleted]

IV–E–1–b–(3)–(i). Adding new entries to the list of toxins for vertebrates (see Appendix G).

IV–E–1–b–(3)–(j). Approving the cloning of toxin genes in host-vector systems other than *E. coli* K–12 (see Appendix G).

IV–E–1–b–(4). [Deleted]

IV–E–1–b–(5). [Deleted]

IV–E–2. *Recombinant DNA Advisory Committee.* The NIH Recombinant DNA Advisory Committee (RAC) is responsible for carrying out specified functions cited below as well as others assigned under its charter or by the Secretary, HHS, the Assistant Secretary for Health, and the Director, NIH.

The members of the committee shall be chosen to provide, collectively, expertise in scientific fields relevant to recombinant DNA technology and biological safety—e.g., microbiology, molecular biology, virology, genetics, epidemiology, infectious diseases, the biology of enteric organisms, botany, plant pathology, ecology, and tissue culture. At least 20 percent of the members shall be persons knowledgeable in applicable law, standards of professional conduct and practice, public attitudes, the environment, public health, occupational health, or related fields. Representatives from Federal agencies shall serve as nonvoting members. Nominations for the RAC may be submitted to the NIH Office of Recombinant DNA Activities, Bethesda, Md. 20205.

All meetings of the RAC will be announced in the **Federal Register**, including tentative agenda items, 30 days in advance of the meeting, with final agendas (if modified) available at least 72 hours before the meeting. No item defined as a major action under Section IV–E–1–b–(1) may be added to an agenda after it appears in the **Federal Register**.

IV–E–2–a. *The RAC shall be responsible for advising the Director, NIH, on the actions listed in Section IV–E–1–b–(l) and –(2).*

IV–E–3. *The Office of Recombinant DNA Activities.* ORDA shall serve as a focal point for information on recombinant DNA activities and provide advice to all within and outside NIH, including Institutions, Principal Investigators, Federal agencies, State an local governments, and institutions in the private sector. ORDA shall carry out such other functions as may be delegated to it by the Director, NIH, including those authorities described in Section IV–E–1–b–(3). In addition, ORDA shall be responsible for the following:

IV–E–3–a. through IV–E–3–c–(3). [Deleted]

IV–E–3–c–(4). Publish in the **Federal Register** announcements of RAC meetings and agendas 30 days in advance on any action listed in Section IV–E–1–b–(1) and Section IV–E–1–b–(2).

Note.—If the agenda for an RAC meeting is modified, ORDA shall make the revised agenda available to anyone, upon request, at least 72 hours in advance of the meeting.

IV–E–3–c–(5). Publish the *Recombinant DNA Technical Bulletin;* and

IV–E–3–c–(6). Serve as executive secretary to the RAC.

IV–E–4. *Other NIH Components.* Other NIH components shall be responsible for:

IV–E–4–a. [Deleted]

IV–E–4–b. [Deleted]

IV–E–4–c. Announcing and distributing certified HV2 and HV3 host-vector systems (see Section II–E–3).

IV–F. [Deleted]

IV–G. [Deleted]

V. Footnotes and References

(1)–(4) [Deleted]

(5) Care should be taken to inactivate recombinant DNA before disposal. Procedures for inactivating DNA can be found in the "Laboratory Safety Monograph: A Supplement to the NIH Guidelines for Recombinant DNA Research."

(6) *Laboratory Safety at the Center for Disease Control* (Sept. 1974). U.S. Department of Health, Education and Welfare Publication No. CDC 75–8118.

(7) *Classification of Etiological Agents on the Basis of Hazard.* (4th Edition, July 1974). U.S. Department of Health, Education and Welfare. Public Health Service. Centers for Disease Control, Office of Biosafety, Atlanta, Georgia 30333.

(8) *National Cancer Institute Safety Standards for Research Involving Oncogenic Viruses* (Oct. 1974). U.S. Department of Health, Education and Welfare Publication No. (NIH) 75–790.

(9) *National Institutes of Health Biohazards Safety Guide* (1974). U.S. Department of Health, Education, and Welfare, Public Health

(10) *Biohazards in Biological Research* (1973). A. Hellman, M. N. Oxman, and R. Pollack (ed.) Cold Spring Harbor Laboratory.

(11) *Handbook of Laboratory Safety* (1971). Second Edition. N. V Steere (ed.). The Chemical Rubber Co., Cleveland.

(12) Bodily, J. L. (1970). *General Administration of the Laboratory,* H. L. Bodily, E. L. Updyke, and J. O. Mason (eds.), Diagnostic Procedures for Bacterial Mycotic and Parasitic Infections. American Public Health Association, New York, pp. 11–28.

(13) Darlow, H. M. (1969). *Safety in the Microbiological Laboratory.* In J. R. Norris and D. W. Robbins (ed.), Methods in Microbiology. Academic Press, Inc. New York. pp. 169–204.

(14) *The Prevention of Laboratory Acquired Infection* (1974). C. H. Collins, E. G. Hartley, and R. Pilsworth. Public Health Laboratory Service, Monograph Series No. 6.

(15) Chatigny, M. A. (1961). *Protection Against Infection in the Microbiological Laboratory: Devices and Procedures.* In W. W. Umbreit (ed.). Advances in Applied Microbiology. Academic Press, New York, N.Y. 3:131–192.

(*16*) Design Criteria for Viral Oncology Research Facilities (1975). U.S. Department of Health, Education and Welfare, Public Health Service, National Institutes of Health, DHEW Publication No. (NIH) 75–891.

(*17*) Kuehne, R. W. (1973. *Biological Containment Facility for Studying Infectious Disease.* Appl. Microbiol. 26–239–243.

(*18*) Runkle, R. S., and G. B. Phillips (1969). *Microbial Containment Control Facilities.* Van Nostrand Reinhold, New York.

(*19*) Chatigny, M. A., and D. I. Clinger (1969). *Contamination Control in Aerobiology.* In R. L. Dimmick and A. B. Akers (eds.). An Introduction to Experimental Aerobiology. John Wiley & Sons, New York, pp. 194–263.

(*19A*) Horsfall, F. L., Jr., and J. H. Baner (1940). *Individual Isolation of Infected Animals in a Single Room.* J. Bact. *40,* 569–580.

(*20*) Biological safety cabinets referred to in this section are classified as *Class I, Class II,* or *Class III* cabinets. A *Class I* is a ventilated cabinet for personnel protection having an inward flow of air away from the operator. The exhaust air from this cabinet is filtered through a high-efficiency particulate air (HEPA) filter. This cabinet is used in three operational modes: (1) With a full-width open front, (2) with an installed front closure panel (having four 8-inch diameter openings) without gloves, and (3) with an installed front closure panel equipped with arm length rubber gloves. The face velocity of the inward flow of air through the full-width open front is 75 feet per minute or greater. A *Class II* cabinet is a ventilated cabinet for personnel and product protection having an open front with inward air flow for personnel protection, and HEPA filtered mass recirculated air flow for product protection. The cabinet exhaust air is filtered through a HEPA filter. The face velocity of the inward flow of air through the full-width open front is 75 feet per minute or greater. Design and performance specifications for *Class II* cabinets have been adopted by the National Sanitation Foundation, Ann Arbor, Michigan. A *Class III* cabinet is a closed front ventilated cabinet of gas-tight construction which provides the highest level of personnel protection of all biohazard safety cabinets. The interior of the cabinet is protected from contaminants exterior to the cabinet. The cabinet is fitted with arm-length rubber gloves and is operated under a negative pressure of at least 0.5 inches water gauge. All supply air is filtered through HEPA filters. Exhaust air is filtered through two HEPA filters or one HEPA filter and incinerator before being discharged to the outside environment.

(*21*) Hershfield, V., H. W Boyer, C. Yanofsky, M. A. Lovett, and D. R. Helinski (1974). *Plasmid ColEl as a Molecular Vehicle for Cloning and Amplification of DNA.* Proc. Nat. Acad. Sci. USA *71* 3455–3459.

(*22*) Wensink, P. C., D. J. Finnegan, J. E. Donelson, and D. S. Hogness (1974). *A System for Mapping DNA Sequences in the Chromosomes of Drosophila Melanogaster.* Cell *3,* 315–335.

(*23*) Tanaka, T., and B. Weisblum (1975). *Construction of a Colicin El–R Factor Composite Plasmid In Vitro: Means for Amplification of Deoxyribonucleic Acid.* J. Bacteriol. *121,* 354–362.

(*24*) Armstrong, K. A., V Hershfield, and D. R. Helinski (1977). *Gene Cloning and Containment Properties of Plasmid Col El and Its Derivatives,* Science *196,* 172–174.

(*25*) Bolivar, F., R. L. Rodriguez, M. C. Betlach, and H. W Boyer (1977). *Construction and Characterization of New Cloning Vehicles: I. Ampicillin-Resistant Derivative of pMB9.* Gene *2,* 75–93.

(*26*) Cohen, S. N., A. C. W Chang, H. Boyer, and R. Helling (1973). *Construction of Biologically Functional Bacterial Plasmids in Vitro.* Proc. Natl. Acad. Sci. USA *70,* 3240–3244.

(*27*) Bolivar, F., R. L. Rodriguez, R. J. Greene, M. C. Batlach, H. L. Reyneker, H. W. Boyer, J. H. Crosa, and S. Falkow (1977). *Construction and Characterization of New Cloning Vehicles: II A Multi-Purpose Cloning System.* Gene *2,* 95–113.

(*28*) Thomas, M., J. R. Cameron, and R. W. Davis (1974). *Viable Molecular Hybrids of Bacteriophage Lambda and Eukaryotic DNA.* Proc. Nat. Acad. Sci. USA *71,* 4579–4583.

(29) Murray, N. E., and K. Murray (1974). *Manipulation of Restriction Targets in Phage Lambda to Form Receptor Chromosomes for DNA Fragments.* Nature 251, 476–481.

(30) Rambach, A., and P. Tiollais (1974). *Bacteriophage Having EcoRI Endonuclease Sites Only in the Non-Essential Region of the Genome.* Proc. Nat. Acad. Sci., USA 71, 3927–3930.

(31) Blattner, F. R., B. G. Williams, A. E. Bleche, K. Denniston-Thompson, H. E. Faber, L. A. Furlong, D. J. Gunwald, D. O. Kiefer, D. D. Moore, J. W. Shumm, E. L. Sheldon, and O. Smithies (1977). *Charon Phages: Safer Derivatives of Bacteriophage Lambda for DNA Cloning.* Science 196, 163–169.

(32) Donoghue, D. J., and P. A. Sharp (1977). *An Improved Lambda Vector: Construction of Model Recombinants Coding for Kanamycin Resistance.* Gene 1, 209–227.

(33) Leder, P., D. Tiemeier and L. Enquist (1977). *EK2 Derivatives of Bacteriophage Lambda Useful in the Cloning of DNA from Higher Organisms: The gt WES System.* Science 196, 175–177.

(33A) Skalka, A. (1978). *Current Status of Coliphage EK2 Vectors.* Gene 3, 29–35.

(33B) Szybalski, W., A. Skalka, S. Gottesman, A. Campbell, and D. Botstein (1978). *Standardized Laboratory Tests for EK2 Certification.* Gene 3, 36–38.

(34) [Deleted]

(35) Defined as observable under optimal laboratory conditions by transformation, transduction, phage infection, and/or conjugation with transfer of phage, plasmid, and/or chromosomal genetic information. Note that this definition of exchange may be less stringent than that applied to exempt organisms under Section I–E–4.

(36–48) [Deleted]

(49) A subset of non-conjugative plasmid vectors are also poorly mobilizable (e.g., pBR322, pBR313). Where practical, these vectors should be employed.

(50) [Deleted]

VI. Voluntary Compliance

VI–A. to VI–E. [Deleted]

VI–F. *Protection of Proprietary Data.* In general, the Freedom of Information Act requires Federal agencies to make thier records available to the public upon request. However, this requirement does not apply to, among other things, "trade secrets and commercial and financial information obtained from a person and privileged or confidential." 18 U.S.C. 1905, in turn, makes it a crime for an officer or employee of the United States or any Federal department or agency to publish, divulge, disclose, or make known "in any manner or to any extent not authorized by law any information coming to him in the course of his employment or official duties or by reason of any examination or investigation made by, or return, report or record made to or filed with, such department or agency or officer or employee thereof, which information concerns or relates to the trade secrets, (or processes * * * of any person, firm, partnership, corporation, or association." This provision applies to all employees of the Federal Government, including special Government employees. Members of the Recombinant DNA Advisory Committee are "special Government employees."

VI–F–1. In submitting information to NIH for purposes of complying voluntarily with the Guidelines, an institution may designate those items of information which the institution believes constitute trade secrets or privileged or confidential commercial or financial information.

VI–F–2. If NIH receives a request under the Freedom of Information Act for information so designated, NIH will promptly contact the institution to secure its views as to whether the information (or some portion) should be released.

VI–F–3. If the NIH decides to release this information (or some portion) in response to a Freedom of Information request or otherwise, the institution will be advised; and the actual release will not be made until the expiration of 15 days after the institution is so advised, except to the extent that earlier release, in the judgment of the Director, NIH, is necessary to protect against an imminent hazard to the public or the environment.

VI–F–4. The following information will usually be considered publicly available information, consistent with the need to protect proprietary data:

a. The names of the institution and principal investigator.

b. The location where the experiments will be performed.

c. The host-vector system.

d. The source of the DNA.

e. The level of physical containment.

VI–F–5–a. Any institution, which is considering submission of data or information vountarily to NIH, may request presubmission review of the records involved to determine whether, if the records are submitted, NIH will or will not make part or all of the records available upon request under the Freedom of Information Act.

VI–F–5–b. A request for presubmission review should be submitted to ORDA, along with the records involved. These records must be clearly marked as being the property of the institution, on loan to NIH solely for the purpose of making a determination under the Freedom of Information Act. ORDA will then seek a determination from the HEW Freedom of Information Officer, the responsible official under HEW regulations (45 CFR Part 5), as to whether the records involved (or some portion) are or are not available to members of the public under the Freedom of Information Act. Pending such a determination, the records will be kept separate from ORDA files, will be considered records of the institution and not ORDA, and will not be received as part of ORDA files. No copies will be made of the records.

VI–F–5–c. ORDA will inform the institution of the HEW Freedom of Information Officer's determination and follow the institution's instructions as to whether some or all of the records involved are to be returned to the institution or to become a part of ORDA files. If the institution instructs ORDA to return the records, no copies or summaries of the records will be made or retained by HEW, NIH, or ORDA.

VI–F–5–d. The HEW Freedom of Information Officer's determination will represent that official's judgment, as of the time of the determination, as to whether the records involved (or some portion) would be exempt from disclosure under the Freedom of Information Act, if at the time of the determination the records were in ORDA files and a request were received from them under the Act.

Appendix A.—Exemptions Under I–E–4

Section I–E–4 states that exempt from these Guidelines are "certain specified recombinant DNA molecules that consist entirely of DNA segments from different species that exchange DNA by known physiological processes, though one or more of the segments may be a synthetic equivalent. A list of such exchangers will be prepared and periodically revised by the Director, NIH, with advice of the Recombinant DNA Advisory Committee, after appropriate notice and opportunity for public comment (see Section IV–E–1–b–(1)–(d).) Certain classes are exempt as of publication of these Revised Guidelines. The list is in Appendix A."

Under exemption I–E–4 of these revised Guidelines are recombinant DNA molecules that are (1) composed entirely of DNA segments from one or more of the organisms within a sublist and (2) to be propagated in any of the organisms within a sublist. (Classification of *Bergey's Manual of Determinative Bacteriology*, eighth edition. R.E. Buchanan and N.E. Gibbons, editors. Williams and Wilkins Company: Baltimore, 1974.)

Sublist A

1. Genus *Escherichia*
2. Genus *Shigella*
3. Genus *Salmonella* (including *Arizona*)
4. Genus *Enterobacter*
5. Genus *Citrobacter* (including *Levinea*)
6. Genus *Klebsiella*
7. Genus *Erwinia*

8. *Pseudomonas aeruginosa, Pseudomonas putida* and *Pseudomonas fluorescens*
9. *Serratia marcescens*

Sublist B

1. *Bacillus subtilis*
2. *Bacillus licheniformis*
3. *Bacillus pumilus*
4. *Bacillus globigii*
5. *Bacillus niger*
6. *Bacillus nato*
7. *Bacillus amyloliquefaciens*
8. *Bacillus aterrimus*

Sublist C

1. *Streptomyces aureofaciens*
2. *Streptomyces rimosus*
3. *Streptomyces coelicolor*

Sublist D

1. *Streptomyces griseus*
2. *Streptomyces cyaneus*
3. *Streptomyces venezuelae*

Sublist E

One way transfer of *Streptococcus mutans* or *Streptococcus lactis* DNA into *Streptococcus sanguis.*

Sublist F

1. *Streptococcus sanguis*
2. *Streptococcus pneumoniae*
3. *Streptococcus faecalis*
4. *Streptococcus pyogenes*

Appendix B.—Classification of Microorganisms on the Basis of Hazard

I. Classification of Etiologic Agents on the Basis of Hazard (1)

A. Class 1 Agents

All bacterial, parasitic, fungal, viral, rickettsial, and chlamydial agents not included in higher classes.

B. Class 2 Agents

1. Bacterial Agents

Actinobacillus—all species except *A. mallei*, which is in Class 3
Arizona hinshawii—all serotypes
Bacillus anthracis
Bordetella—all species
Borrelia recurrentis, B. vincenti
Clostridium botulinum,
Cl. chauvoei, Cl. haemolyticum,
Cl. histolyticum, Cl. novyi,
Cl. septicum, Cl. tetani
Corynebacterium diptheriae,
C. equi, C. haemolyticum
C. pseudotuberculosis
C. pyogenes, C. renale
Diplococcus (Streptococcus) pneumoniae
Erysipelothrix insidiosa
Escherichia coli—all enteropathogenic serotypes
Haemophilus ducreyi, H. influenzae
Herellae vaginicola
Klebsiella—all species and all serotypes
Leptospira interrogans—all serotypes
Listeria—all species
Mima poloymorpha
Moraxella—all species
Mycobacteria—all species except those listed in Class 3
Mycoplasma—all species except *Mycoplasma mycoides* and *Mycoplasma agalactiae*, which are in Class 5
Neisseria gonorrhoeae, N. meningitidis
Pasteurella—all species except those listed in Class 3
Salmonella—all species and all serotypes
Shigella—all species and all serotypes
Sphaerophorus necrophorus
Staphylococcus aureaus
Streptobacillus moniliformis
Streptococcus pyogenes
Treponema carateum, T pallidum, and T. pertenue
Vibrio fetus, V comma, including biotype El Tor, and *V parahemolyticus*

2. Fungal Agents

***Actinomycetes* (including *Nocardia* species and *Actinomyces species and Arachnia propionica)*
Blastomyces dermatitidis
Cryptococcus neoformans
Paracoccidioides brasiliensis

3. Parasitic Agents

Endomoeba histolytica
Leishmania sp.
Naegleria gruberi
Toxoplasma gondii
Toxocara canis
Trichinella spiralis
Trypanosoma cruzi

4. Viral, Rickettsial, and Chlamydial Agents

Adenoviruses—human—all types
Cache Valley virus
Coxsackie A and B viruses
Cytomegloviruses
Echoviruses—all types
Encephalomyocarditis virus (EMC)
Flanders virus
Hart Park virus
Hepatitis-associated antigen material
Herpes viruses—except *Herpesvirus simiae* (Monkey B virus) which is in Class 4
Corona viruses
Influenza viruses—all types except A/PR8/34, which is in Class 1
Langat virus
Lymhogranuloma venereum agent
Measles virus
Mumps virus
Parainfluenza virus—all types except Parainfluenza virus 3, SF4 strain, which is in Class 1
Polioviruses—all types, wild and attenuated
Poxviruses—all types except *Alastrim, Smallpox, Monkey pox, and Whitepox,* which depending on experiments, are in Class 3 or Class 4
Rabies virus—all strains except *Rabies street virus,* which should be classified in Class 3 when inoculated into carnivores
Reoviruses—all types
Respiratory syncytial virus
Rhinoviruses—all types
Rubella virus
Simian viruses—all types except *Herpesvirus simiae (Monkey B virus) and Marburg virus,* which are in Class 4
Sindbis virus
Tensaw virus
Turlock virus
Vaccinia virus
Varicella virus
Vole rickettsia
Yellow fever virus, 17D vaccine strain

C. Class 3 Agents

1. Bacterial Agents

*Actinobacillus mallei**
Bartonella—all species
Brucella—all species
Francisella tularensis
Mycobacterium avium, M. bovis, M. tuberculosis
Pasteurella multocide type B ("buffalo" and other foreign virulent strains*)
*Pseudomonas pseudomallei**
Yersenia pestis

2. Fungal Agents

Coccidioides immitis
Histoplasma capsulatum
Histoplasma capsulatum var. *duboisii*

3. Parasitic Agents

Schistosoma mansoni

4. Viral, Rickettsial, and Chlamydial Agents

****Alastrim, Smallpox, Monkey pox, and Whitepox,* when used *in vitro*
Arboviruses—all strains except those in Class 2 and 4 (Arboviruses indigenous to the United States are in Class 3, except those listed is Class 2. *West Nile* and *Semliki Forest* viruses may be classified up or down, depending on the conditions of use and geographical location of the laboratory.)
Dengue virus, when used for transmission or animal inoculation experiments
Lumphocytic choriomeningitis virus (LCM)
Psittacosis-Ornithosis-Trachoma group of agents
Rabies street virus, when used in inoculations of carnivores (See Class 2)
Rickettsi—all species except *Vole rickettsia* when used for transmission or animal inoculation experiments
*Vesicular stomatitis virus**
Yellow fever virus—wild, when used *in vitro*

D. Class 4 Agents

1: Bacterial Agents

None

2. Fungal Agents

None

3. Parasitic Agents

None

4. Viral, Rickettsial, and Chlamydial Agents

****Alastrim, Smallpox, Monkey pox, and Whitepox,* when used for transmission or animal inoculation experiments
Hemorrhagic fever agents, including *Crimean hemorrhagic fever, (Congo), Junin,* and *Machupo* viruses, and others as yet undefined
Herpesvirus simiae (Monkey B virus)
Lassa virus
Marburg virus
Tick-borne encephalitis virus complex, including *Russian spring-summer encephalitis, Kyasanur forest diesase, Omsk hemorrhagic fever,* and *Central European encephalitis viruses*
Venezuelan equine encephalitis virus, epidemic strains, when used for

transmission or animal inoculation experiments
Yellow fever virus—wild, when used for transmission or animal inoculation experiments

II. Classification of Oncogenic Viruses on the Basis of Potential Hazard (2)

A. Low-Risk Oncogenic Viruses

Rous Sarcoma
SV-40
CELO
Ad7-SV40
Polyoma
Bovine papilloma
Rat mammary tumor
Avian Leukosis
Murine Leukemia
Murine Sarcoma
Mouse mammary tumor
Rat Leukemia
Hamster Leukemia
Bovine Leukemia
Dog Sarcoma
Mason-Pfizer Monkey Virus
Marek's
Guinea Pig Herpes
Lucke (Frog)
Adenovirus
Shope Fibroma
Shope Papilloma

B. Moderate-Risk Oncogenic Viruses

Ad2-SV40
FeLV
HV Saimiri
EBV
SSV-1
GaLV
HV ateles
Yaba
FeSV

III. Animal Pathogens (3)

A. Animal disease organisms which are forbidden entry into the United States by Law (CDC Class 5 agents)

1. Foot and mouth disease virus

B. Animal disease organisms and vectors which are forbidden entry into the United States by USDA Policy (CDC Class 5 Agents)

African horse sickness virus
African swine fever virus
Besnoitia besnoiti
Borna disease virus
Bovine infectious petechial fever
Camel pox virus
Ephemeral fever virus
Fowl plague virus
Goat pox virus
Hog cholera virus
Louping ill virus
Lumpy skin disease virus
Nairobi sheep disease virus
Newcastle disease virus (Asiatic strains)
Mycoplasma mycoides (contagious bovine pleuropneumonia)
Mycoplasma agalactiae (contagious agalactia of sheep)
Rickettsia ruminatium (heart water)
Rift valley fever virus
Rhinderpest virus
Sheep pox virus
Swine vesicular disease virus
Teschen disease virus
Trypanosoma vivax (Nagana)
Trypanosoma evansi
Theileria parva (East Coast fever)
Theileria annulata
Theileria lawrencei
Theileria bovis
Theileria hirci
Vesicular exanthema virus
Wesselsbron disease virus
Zyonema

Footnotes and References of Appendix B

*A USDA permit, required for import and interstate commerce of pathogens, may be obtained from the Animal and Plant Health Inspection Service, USDA, Federal Building, Hyattsville, MD. 20782.

**Since the publication of the classification in 1974 [1], the *Actinomycetes* have been reclassified as bacterial rather than fungal agents.

***All activities, including storage of variola and whitepox are restricted to the single national facility (World Health Organization (WHO) Collaborating Center for Smallpox Research, Center for Disease Control, in Atlanta).

(1) Classification of Etiologic Agents on the Basis of Hazard. (4th Edition, July 1974). U.S. Department of Health, Education and Welfare, Public Health Service, Center for Disease Control, Office of Biosafety, Atlanta, Georgia 30333.

(2) National Cancer Institute Safety Standards for Research Involving Oncogenic Viruses. (October 1974). U.S. Department of Health, Education, and Welfare Publication No. (NIH) 75-790.

(3) U.S. Department of Agriculture, Animal and Plant Health Inspection Service.

Appendix C.—Exemptions Under I-E-5

Section I-E-5 states that exempt from these Guidelines are "Other classes of recombinant DNA molecules, if the Director, NIH, with advice of the Recombinant DNA Advisory Committee, after appropriate notice and opportunity for public comment, finds that they do not present a significant risk to health or the environment. (See Section IV-E-1-b-(1)-(d)). Certain classes are exempt as of publication of these Revised Guidelines."

The following classes of experiments are exempt under Section I-E-5 of the Guidelines:

1. *Recombinant DNAs in Tissue Culture.* Recombinant DNA molecules derived entirely from non-viral components (that is, no component is derived from a eukaryotic virus), that are propagated and maintained in cells in tissue culture are exempt from these Guidelines with the exceptions listed below.

Exceptions. Experiments, involving the deliberate introduction of genes coding for the biosynthesis of toxins potent for vertebrates. (See Appendix C.)

2. *Experiments Involving E. coli K-12 host-vector systems.* Experiments which use *E. coli* K-12 host-vector systems, with the exception of those experiments listed below, are exempt from these Guidelines provided that (a) the *E. coli* host shall not contain conjugation proficient plasmids or generalized transducing phages, and (b) lambda or lambdoid or Ff bacteriophages or nonconjugative plasmids [49] shall be used as vectors. However, experiments involving the insertion into *E. coli* K-12 of DNA from prokaryotes that exchange genetic information [35] with *E. coli* may be performed with any *E. coli* K-12 vector (e.g., conjugative plasmid). When a nonconjugative vector is used, the *E. coli* K-12 host may contain conjugation proficient plasmids either autonomous or integrated, or generalized transducing phages.

For these exempt experiments, PI physical containment conditions are recommended.

Exceptions. Experiments involving the deliberate cloning of genes coding for the biosynthesis of toxins potent for vertebrates. (See Appendix G.)

3. *Experiments Involving Saccharomyces cerevisiae host-vector systems.* Experiments which use *Saccharomyces cerevisiae* host-vector systems, with the exception of experiments listed below, are exempt from these Guidelined provided that laboratory strains are used.

For these exempt experiments, PI physical containment conditions are recommended.

Exceptions. Experiments involving the deliberate cloning of genes coding for the biosynthesis of toxins potent for vertebrates. (See Appendix G.)

4. *Experiments Involving Bacillus subtilis host-vector systems.* Any asporogenic *Bacillus subtilis* strain which does not revert to a sporeformer with a frequency greater than 10^{-7} can be used for cloning DNA from any nonprohibited source, with the exception of those experiments listed below. Indigenous *Bacillus* plasmids and phages, whose host-range does not include *Bacillus cereus* or *Bacillus anthracis*, may be used as vectors.

For these exempt experiments PI physical containment conditions are recommended.

Exceptions. Experiments involving the deliberate cloning of genes coding for the biosynthesis of toxins potent for vertebrates. (See Appendix G.)

Appendix D [Deleted]

Appendix E [Deleted]

Appendix F.—Certified Host-Vector Systems

A listing of host-vector systems previously classified as HV1 or HV2 follows.

HV1—The following plasmids are accepted as the vector components of certified *B. subtilis* HV1 systems; pUB110, pC194, pS194, pSA2100, pE194, pT127, pUB112, pC221, pC223, and pAB124. *B. subtilis* strains RUB 331 and BGSC 1S53 have been certified as the host component of HV1 systems based on these plasmids.

HV1—The following specified strains of *Neurospora crassa* which have been modified to prevent aerial dispersion:

(1) inl (inositolless) strains 37102, 37401, 46316, 64001, and 89601.

(2) csp-1 strain UCLA and csp-2 strains FS 590, UCLA101 (these are conidial separation mutants).

(3) eas strain UCLA191 (an "easily wettable" mutant).

HV1—The following *Streptomyces* species: *Streptomyces coelicolor, S. lividans, S. parvulus,* and *S. griseus.* The following are accepted as vector components of certified *Streptomyces* HV1 systems: *Streptomyces* plasmids SCP2, SLP1.2, pIJ101, actinophage phi C31, and their derivatives.

HV2—The asporogenic mutant derivative of *Bacillus subtilis,* ASB 298, with the following plasmids as the vector component: pUB110, pC194, pS194, pSA2100, pE194, pT127, pUB112, pC221, pC223, and pAB124.

HV2—The following sterile strains of *Saccharomyces cerevisiae,* all of which have the ste-VC9 mutation, SHY1, SHY2, SHY3, and SHY4. The following plasmids are certified for use: YIp1, YEp2, YEp4, YIp5, YEp6, YRp7, YEp20, YEp21, YEp24, YIp25, YIp26, YIp27, YIp28, YIp29, YIp30, YIp31, YIp32 and YIp33.

EK2 Plasmid Systems. The *E. coli* K-12 strain chi-1776. The following plasmids are certified for use: pSC101, pMB9, pBR313, pBR322, pDH24, pBR327, pGL101, pHB1. The following *E. coli/S. cerevisiae* hybrid plasmids are certified as EK2 vectors when used in *E. coli* chi-1776 or in the sterile yeast strains, SHY1, SHY2, SHY3 and SHY4: YIp1, YEp2, YEp4, YIp5, YEp6, YRp7, YEp20, YEp21, YEp24, YIp25, YIp26, YIp27, YIp28, YIp29, YIp30, YIp31, YIp32, YIp33.

EK2 Bacteriophage Systems. The following are certified EK2 systems based on bacteriophage lambda:

Vector	*Host*
λgt*WES*. λB'	DP50*sup*F
λgt*WES*. λB*	DP50*sup*F
λgt(Z)*vir*. λB'	*E. coli* K-12
λgtALO. λB	DP50*sup*F
Charon 3A	DP50 or DP50*sup*F
Charon 4A	DP50 or DP50*sup*F
Charon 16A	DP50 or DP50*sup*F
Charon 21A	DP50*sup*F
Charon 23A	DP50 or DP50*sup*F
Charon 24A	DP50 or DP50*sup*F

Appendix G—Containment Conditions for Cloning of Genes Coding for the Biosynthesis of Toxins for Vertebrates

1. *General Information.*

Appendix G specifies the containment to be used for the deliberate cloning of genes coding for the biosynthesis of toxins for vertebrates. Cloning of genes coding for toxins for vertebrates that have an LD_{50} of less than 100 nanograms per kilogram body weight (e.g., the botulinum toxins, tetanus toxin, diphtheria toxin, *Shigella dysenteriae* neurotoxin) should not be performed. No specific recommendations other than those given in Part III of the Guidelines shall apply to the cloning of genes if the protein specified by the gene has an LD_{50} of 100 micrograms or more per kilogram of body weight. Experiments involving genes coding for toxins with an LD_{50} of 100 micrograms or less per kilogram body weight should be registered with ORDA prior to initiating the experiments. A list of toxins classified as to LD_{50} is available from ORDA. Testing procedures for determining toxicity of toxins not on the list are available from ORDA. The results of such tests should be forwarded to ORDA, which will consult with the *ad hoc* Working Group on toxins prior to inclusion of the toxin on the list. (See Section IV–E–1–b–(3)–(i).)

2. *Recommended Containment Conditions for Cloning of Toxin Genes in E. coli K-12.*

(a) Cloning of genes coding for toxins for vertebrates that have an LD_{50} in the range of 100 nanograms to 1000 nanograms per kilogram body weight (e.g., abrin, *Clostridium perfringens* epsilon toxin) should proceed under P2 + EK2 or P3 + EK1 containment conditions.

(b) Cloning of genes for the biosynthesis of toxins for vertebrates with an LD_{50} in the range of 1 microgram to 100 micrograms per kilogram body weight should proceed under P1 + EK1 containment conditions (e.g., *Staphylococcus aureus* alpha toxin, *Staphylococcus aureus* beta toxin, ricin, *Pseudomonas aeruginosa* exotoxin A, *Bordatella pertussis* toxin, the lethal factor of *Bacillus anthracis,* the *Pasteurella pestis* murine toxins, the oxygen-labile hemolysins such as streptolysin O, and certain neurotoxins present in snake venoms and other venoms).

(c) Some enterotoxins are substantially more toxic when administered enterally than parenterally. The following enterotoxins should be subject to P1 + EK1 containment conditions: cholera toxin, the heat labile toxins of *E. coli, Klebsiella,* and other related proteins that may be identified by neutralization with an antiserum monospecific for cholera toxin, and the heat stable toxins of *E. coli* and of *Yersinia enterocolitica.*

3. *Containment Conditions for Cloning of Toxin Genes in Organisms Other than E. coli K-12.* Requests involving the cloning of genes coding for toxins for vertebrates in host-vector systems other than *E. coli* K-12 should be submitted to ORDA for evaluation. ORDA will consult with the *ad hoc* working group on toxins. (See Section IV–E–1–b–(3)–(j).)

Appendix H [Deleted]

Annex A.—Original Proposal of Drs. David Baltimore & Allan Campell; Proposal To Convert the NIH Guidelines Into a Non-regulatory Code of Standard Practice and To Reduce the Recommended containment Levels For Some Experiments

Proposals

(1) Section I-A of the NIH Guidelines will be replaced with the following:

"I-A. *Purpose.* The purpose of these Guidelines is to specify standard practices for constructing and handling (i) recombinant DNA molecules and (ii) organisms and viruses containing recombinant DNA molecules. Adherence to these standards by all laboratories using recombinant DNA is recommended."

(2) Part I-C of the NIH Guidelines shall be eliminated.

(3) Part III of the Guidelines will be replaced with the following:

"Part III discuss experiments covered by the Guidelines. The reader must first consult Part I, where listings are given of prohibited and exempt experiments.

"Where there are existing recommended physical containment levels applicable to non-recombinant DNA experiments with either the host or the vector (such as those specified by the CDC Guidelines), recombinant DNA experiments should be carried out at containment levels at least as high as those recommended for non-recombinant DNA experiments. Otherwise, all non-prohibited experiments may be carried out under conditions of Pl physical containment. As a general practice, investigators should use the highest level of biological containment (HV3>HV2>HV1) which is available and appropriate for the purposes of the experiment.

"Specific exceptions to the prohibitions may be approved by the Director NIH (section I-D). The Director will consider requests for exceptions from individuals, institutions or corporations regardless of whether the applicant is affiliated with or supported by NIH. Such exceptions will generally be approved for specified levels of physical and biological containment."

This will be followed by a listing of those exceptions which are presently authorized and the containment levels approved for the excepted experiments.

(4) Part VI of the NIH Guidelines shall be eliminated, with the following exceptions:

(a) Those definitions listed in Part IV-C which may be needed clarify statements made elsewhere in the Guidelines shall be retained.

(b) Those portions of Part IV-E defining the composition of RAC and prescribing rules for RAC procedures shall be retained.

(c) The following statement shall be added:

"Each institution conducting or sponsoring recombinant DNA research should take responsibility for monitoring its own activities in this area. Any unusual events that might be associated with the use of recombinant DNA molecules should be reported to the Director, NIH."

(5) Section VI of the Guidelines will be eliminated, except for those portions of section VI-F relevant to the protection of proprietary information submitted in support of requests for exceptions from the prohibitions.

Explanation and Justification

The action has two major effects:

(A) It revokes the mandatory nature of the Guidelines by eliminating those sections specifying regulatory procedures and their underlying organizational machinery. These Guidelines would then resemble the CDC Guidelines in setting standards and providing guidance rather than in regulating the performance of experiments. This purpose is accomplished by items, 1, 2, 4 and 5 of the proposal.

Item 5 (elimination of most of section VI) is included because, with the elimination of section IV, compliance with the Guidelines will effectively become voluntary for all individuals, regardless of NIH support. Special provision for voluntary compliance by individuals and institutions not supported by NIH then becomes superfluous.

(B) It reduces the prescribed level of physical containment for most experiments to P1. This purpose is accomplished by item 3.

These two changes are justified from the following considerations:

(A) *Elimination of Regulatory Procedures.* Opinions differ as to the widsom of the actions and arguments which led to the adoption of the NIH Guidelines in 1976. However, there is fairly general agreement on two points: (i) The establishment of Guidelines has had some beneficial effects. In particular, it has raised the general level of awareness among investigators and institutions of the importance of considering possible hazards that might arise during microbiological research. (ii) Since 1976, neither experimental evidence nor solid theoretical arguments have been advanced to support the position that recombinant DNA research poses any danger to human health or to the integrity of the natural environment.

At this point, we doubt that the beneficial side effects of continued regulation justify the expenditure of time and money required to maintain a regulatory apparatus that has been developed to protect society from hazards that appear to be non-existent.

(B) *Reduction of Recommended Containment Levels.* In the absence of known or suspected hazards, it seems unjustified to single out certain classes of experiments as requiring elevated levels of physical containment. The cost, in discouraging variety and innovation and thereby limiting access to useful knowledge, is real, whereas the benefit is likely to be zero. The use of P1 containment, together with the highest available level of biological containment appropriate to the experimental purpose, will keep the probability of escape and establishment very low without interfering with the conduct of most research.

The prohibitions remain in force. Although we consider it unlikely that experiments in the prohibited categories will generate serious hazards, they represent the one area of the Guidelines which is addressed to risks whose nature can be specified, and that are in principle assessable. Restructuring of some of these categories aimed at delineating areas of real concern is desirable and is currently underway in the case of toxin genes. The results of such restructuring would be to define additional exceptions from the prohibitions, which would then appear in Part III of the Guidelines as amended by this measure.

Annex B.—Documents Prepared by Working Group on Revision of the Guidelines

Summary of Committee Actions, Report to RAC

At the April 1981 RAC meeting, a working group was established to consider major revisions of the recombinant DNA Guidelines. The working group, appointed by RAC chairman Ray Thornton, consists of 13 members, 9 of whom were RAC members as of June 1980 (2 have since ended their terms), 2 liaison RAC members, and 2 other scientists who have had long involvement with the recombinant DNA issue. The list of members is attached. The working group is chaired by Susan Gottesman. Two meetings were held: one on June 1, 1981, at which 8 members were present, and one on July 9, 1981, at which 11 members were present. Minutes of both meetings are available. There was a clear consensus by the working group that some major restructuring of the guidelines was appropriate. There was major disagreement about how far such a revision should go. The basic issues are: (1) Are there qualitatively unique dangers associated with Recombinant DNA research? and (2) If so, what response is necessary for guarding against such hazards; is some special procedure required? If there are not qualitatively unique dangers involved, are the remaining risks adequately addressed by already existing procedures for dealing with research dangers? If not, should one use the recombinant DNA issue to develop appropriate procedures for the more general issues?

After an analysis of the risks (detailed in the accompanying document), the following general conclusions were reached:

(1) Accidental combinations of genes, rising out of "shotgun" cloning experiments or experiments where expression is not specifically engineered, are extremely unlikely to lead to serious problems. In most organisms, the barriers to expression of foreign genes, the necessity for new enzyme activities to function as an integrated part of an existing pathway, and the selective disadvantage of carrying recombinant DNA, will interfere with such organisms establishing themselves in the environment and thus ultimately with their potential to cause harm. Therefore, for these experiments, the minimal controls associated with good laboratory practice should be sufficient. Many such experiments have already been exempted by the NIH from any special procedures.

(2) A particular subset of experiments may pose some possibility of risk. In these experiments, the expression of foreign functions may have been deliberately increased, or normal functions will have been engineered to operate more efficiently. While there is no evidence that this risk is qualitatively

different from the risks associated with other kinds of genetic research, the end result may be an increase in virulence, host range, or survivability of some pathogens.

Given these conclusions, the majority of those present at the July 9 meeting supported a proposal which adopts the containment provisions of the Baltimore-Campbell proposal, but retains the mandatory aspect of the guidelines. A minority preferred either a "voluntary code of practice" as stipulated in the original Baltimore-Campbell proposal, or an end to all specifications for working with recombinant DNA, apart from those stipulations of "good laboratory practice."

The text of the proposal as approved by the subcommittee, with a comparison to current (July 1, 1981) guidelines is attached. In addition, an examination of the state of our knowledge about recombinant DNA risks, to be used as a rationale for change, is attached.

We suggest the following procedures; (1) RAC consider and modify if necessary, the working group's proposal and the supporting rationale statement, (2) The modified proposal and rationale be published in the Federal Register and elsewhere, if appropriate, for public comment, (3) All comments be considered by the working group and recommendations for change, based on the comments, be made. The final version should once again be published in the Federal Register. (4) RAC take final action on the proposal. This might occur at the January 1982 RAC meeting, or possibly at the following meeting, if more time for comment is considered necessary.

Recombinant DNA Advisory Committee Working Group on Revision of the Guidelines, National Institutes of Health

Chairman

Gottesman, Susan K., Ph. D., Senior Investigator, Laboratory of Molecular Biology, National Cancer Institute, National Institutes of Health, Bethesda, Maryland 20205, (301) 496-2095

Adelberg, Edward A., Ph. D., Department of Human Genetics, School of Medicine, Yale University, New Haven, Connecticut 06510, (203) 436-0821

Berns, Kenneth I., Ph. D., M.D., Chairman, Department of Immunology and Medical Microbiology, University of Florida, College of Medicine, Gainesville, Florida 32610, (904) 392-3311

Goldstein, Richard, Ph. D., Associate Professor, Department of Microbiology and Molecular Genetics, Harvard Medical School, Boston, Massachusetts 02115, (617) 732-1911

Harris, Jean L., M.D., Secretary of Human Resources, Commonwealth of Virginia, Office of Governor, Post Office Box 1475, Richmond, Virginia 23219, (804) 786-7765

King, Patricia A., J.D., Georgetown University Law School, 600 New Jersey Avenue, N.W., Washington, D.C. 20001, (202) 624-8213

Levine, Myron M., M.D., Director, Center for Vaccine Development, Division of Infectious Diseases, University of Maryland School of Medicine, Baltimore, Maryland 21201, (301) 528-7588

Lewis, Herman W., Ph. D., Senior Scientist for Recombinant DNA, Division of Physiology, National Science Foundation, Washington, D.C. 20550, (202) 357-7647

Mason, James O., M.D., Dr. Ph., Executive Director, Utah State Department of Health, Post Office Box 2500, Salt Lake City, Utah 84113, (801) 533-6111

Nightingale, Elena O., Ph. D., M.D., Senior Program Officer, Institute of Medicine, National Academy of Sciences, Washington, D.C. 20418, (202) 389-6963

Tolin, Sue A., Ph. D., Science and Education Administration, Cooperative Research, U.S. Department of Agriculture, Washington, D.C. 20250, (202) 447-5741

Williams, Luther S., Ph. D., Professor, Department of Biology, Washington University, Campus Box 1137, St. Louis, Missouri 63130, (314) 889-6843

Zinder, Norton, Ph. D., Professor, Rockefeller University, 1230 York Avenue, New York, New York 10021, (212) 360-1322

Executive Secretary

Gartland, William J., Jr., Ph. D., Director, Office of Recombinant DNA Activities, National Institute of Allergy and Infectious Diseases, National Institutes of Health, Bethesda, Maryland 20205, (301) 496-6051

Revision of the July 1, 1981 Guidelines Proposed by Working Group on Revision of the Guidelines, July 9, 1981

(1) Section I-A of the Guidelines would be amended to read as follows:

I-A. *Purpose.* The purpose of these Guidelines to specify standard practices for constructing and handling (i) recombinant DNA molecules and (ii) organisms and viruses containing recombinant DNA molecules.

(2) Section I-D of the Guidelines, *Prohibitions,* would be eliminated.

(3) Part III of the Guidelines would be replaced with the following language:

Part III discusses experiments covered by the Guidelines. The reader should first consult Part I, where exempt experiments are listed.

Where recommended physical containment levels applicable to non-recombinant DNA experiments exist for either the host or the vector (such as those specified by the CDC Guidelines, or the USDA Quarantine Regulations), recombinant DNA experiments should be carried out at containment levels at least as high as those recommended for non-recombinant DNA experiments. If there is clear evidence that the donor DNA will significantly change the pathogenicity of the host, the containment level appropriate to the anticipated change will be applied. Otherwise, all experiments may be carried out under conditions of P1 or P1-LS physical containment.

(4) Those membership specifications of the IBC to be found in Section IV-D of Section IV of the Guidelines would be eliminated.

BILLING CODE 4110-08-M

OUTLINE OF CURRENT NIH GUIDELINES FOR RECOMBINANT DNA RESEARCH AND PROPOSED CHANGES

	Current Guidelines: Procedures	Subcommittee Proposal	Baltimore-Campbell Proposal
I. Prohibitions (I-D)			
CDC Class 4 & 5 organisms Genes for potent toxins Release to environment Genes for drug resistance	Prohibitions take precedence over all other parts of guidelines; exceptions possible by application to RAC and Federal Register publication	Eliminate prohibitions as special class; handled by IBC as with other experiments	Retains prohibition
10 liters unless well characterized and harmless	This prohibition does not take precedence over exemptions 1-4		
II. Exemptions (I-E)			
Naked DNA Rearrangements Self-cloning Exchangers Others: Tissue culture, *E. coli*, *B. subtilis* and *S. cerevisiae* HV1 systems	No special oversight required for these experiments; new additions to list by application to RAC and publication in *Federal Register*	No change	No change
III. HV1 Systems (III-A)			
Currently covers only some *N. crassa* and *Streptomyces* strains	Containment varies with source of donor DNA (P1-P3). New systems require approval by RAC and *Federal Register* publication	P1	P1
IV. All other prokaryote, lower eukaryote combinations	P3; lower by request to ORDA. Return to host of origin, P1	P1 for nonpathogens; pathogens as per CDC, etc.	P1 for nonpathogens; etc.
V. Eukaryote recipients			
non-viral vectors	P1-P2 in whole organ. (exempt in tissue culture)	P1 for non-pathogens, etc.	P1 for non-pathogens, etc.
defective viral vectors	P1-helper, P2-P3 + helper		
non-defective viral vectors	case-by-case; (P2 in most cases)	P1 for non-pathogens, etc.	P1 for non-pathogens, etc.
Procedural Changes: IBC	membership specified	no specifications for membership	voluntary system

BILLING CODE 4110-08-C

Evaluation of the Risks Associated With Recombinant DNA Research

I. History and Introduction

The technique known as recombinant DNA or gene cloning was first developed in the early 1970s. It provides methods for combining pieces of DNA from essentially any source—no matter how unrelated—and reintroducing them into living cells. In practice, in order to ensure that the newly joined DNA persists in its host, small pieces of the DNA of interest are joined to a DNA (a vector) which has the capacity for self-replication in the host cell.

The development of this incredibly powerful new technique led thoughtful scientists, aware of the history of use and abuse of similar breakthroughs in the fields of chemistry and physics, to raise to their fellow scientists questions about the possible hazards of the technique. This occurred before the technique had been used enough to allow those talking about the dangers to have any expectations about what the full possibilities or complications of the experiments might be. The initial discussion raised enough concerns for scientists to ask, first, for a moratorium on some sorts of experiments, and secondly, for the development of guidelines for the use of recombinant DNA technology. The form of the initial restrictions was outlined at the meeting of 150 scientists held at Asilomar in February 1975. This document served as informal guidance to scientists working in the field until the issuance of the first NIH Recombinant DNA Guidelines in June of 1976 (**Federal Register**, July 7, 1976). The impetus to obey these Guidelines was both peer pressure and the threat of withdrawl of NIH grant funds

The original Guidelines relied on the use of physical and genetic containment procedures as safeguards for dealing with unspecified dangers. As the possibilities of the recombinant DNA technique were more fully realized, it became clear that many experiments were not mentioned in the original guidelines either because they had not been of particular concern to those who wrote the Guidelines, or because the necessary experimental techniques had not yet been developed. On the other hand, large classes of experiments, particularly those with animal viruses, had been extremely restricted. Because of a concomitant rise in public awareness and concern about the whole of recombinant DNA experimentation, NIH at this stage felt it appropriate to approve only experiments explicitly discussed in the 1976 NIH Guidelines. Scientists were frustrated that experiments they both knew how to do and knew would lead to rapid advances in subjects of major importance were blocked. In addition, they felt under attack as public scrutiny of the molecular biology field sometimes implied that no scientist could be trusted to supervise his own work and that yet stronger control would be necessary to properly guard the world against the dangers of recombinant DNA. As the original concept of care and self-policing were replaced by complex regulations and restrictions scientists perceived as inappropriate, support for the guidelines among scientists decreased dramatically.

Simultaneously, the NIH was developing the first major revision of the Guidelines to deal with inconsistencies and changing perceptions. The first major revision took more than two years from start to adoption in late 1978 (**Federal Register**, December 22, 1978). Major changes were introduced. They included: Creation of an "exempt" category for experiments considered to be innocuous, the lowering of containment requirements for experiments with animal viruses, and the delegation of more oversight authority for recombinant DNA experiments to local committees (IBCs). In addition, the new Guidelines explicitly recognized the need for a constant evolution of the Guidelines and specified a procedure for such change. That gradual evolution has continued over the last three years, and has included some fairly radical changes in the range of permitted experiments, the level of containment requirements for experiments, and the procedures for administration of the Guidelines. The trend has been to remove from most requirements, those classes of experiments for which no specific danger can be hypothesized.

At present, five years after the first Guidelines went into effect and seven years after the Asilomar Conference, the situation is as follows (**Federal Register**, July 1, 1981):

(1) The Guidelines permit a large number of experiments using the recombinant DNA technique, and interfere with and slow ongoing investigations in most areas far less than they did in 1976–1978;

(2) Many experiments, especially those in *E. coli* K-12, *Saccharomyces cerevisiae*, and *B. subtilis* host-vector systems, can be carried out at low containment, and with relatively few registration or prior approval procedures;

(3) Some recombinant DNA experiments, especially in organisms which are not as well studied as the originally used *E. coli* K-12 host, still require special permission from and discussion with an oversight committee, either at the local or national level;

(4) A great deal more experience with the limits and possibilities of the recombinant DNA technique, seven years of explicit discussion of the possibilities for harm and how these possibilities can be evaluated, as well as some NIH supported risk assessment studies have provided scientists somewhat better parameters for discussing the dangers of recombinant DNA;

(5) Experience with regulation of the recombinant DNA field over the last five years should provide some information about the effectivness of various provisions if such regulation is needed;

(6) The Guidelines have evolved into an extremely complicated, piece-meal document in response to modifications initiated by specific, single-issue requests. Most scientists experience difficulty in picking their way through this document.

(7) Administration and revision of the Guidelines continues to require scientists to expend considerable time, both as part of the RAC and the IBCs, and in the laboratory.

In response to a specific proposal by two members of the NIH Recombinant DNA Advisory Committee, that "the time for Guidelines with attached oversight procedures and penalties has passed," the RAC has designated a study group to evaluate what we now know about the possible dangers of recombinant DNA, how those dangers are met by the Guidelines as they now stand, and whether such Guidelines are still appropriate for this scientific technique. Below, we will analyze the basic assumptions and types of risk which were visualized, and what has been learned to either allay or reinforce these fears. We will then analyze the possibilities for dealing with remaining concerns, ranging from continuation of the current Guidelines through abolition of any special oversight.

II. Possible Hazards

A. Basic Assumptions

In some ways, recombinant DNA poses a unique problem. One can add new genetic information to practically any organism, and arrange matters so that new information is stably maintained and possibly expressed in the host. In addition, because we are dealing with viable, self-replicating organisms, the altered individual would not necessarily sit on the inventor's shelf, like some new and terribly explosive chemical, but might be able to establish itself in the environment and, because of its ability to replicate, magnify any harmful effect. Three assumptions are therefore involved in the decision to call recombinant DNA a unique danger; each one of these assumptions can be separately discussed and evaluated. These assumptions are:

(1) That a unique organism, never found in nature, might be constructed by recombinant DNA techniques;

(2) That such a unique organism might be able to establish itself in the environment outside the laboratory;

(3) That such an organism, established in the environment and possessing unique properties bestowed upon it by recombinant DNA techniques, might be harmful, either to man, animals, or plants.

If one could prove that any one of these three assumptions is totally false, the dire expectations of the recombinant DNA technique could be discarded and no special precautions would need to be taken. In the initial assessment, however, these assumptions seemed reasonable, in that the technique appeared to allow any organism to be mofidied in any way.

Over the last seven years, some changes in perception and in knowledge of recombinant DNA hazards have occurred:

(1) The possibilities and limits of assumption 1 are somewhat better understood in (a) the limits to which recombinant DNA can bestow new characteristics on organisms, and (b) the ways by which organisms normally exchange genetic information in anticipation of the recombinant DNA technique, thereby negating the "uniqueness" component of the assumption.

(2) A great deal of discussion in the last few years has centered on assumption 2; the whole concept of biological containment is based upon circumventing the organisms' establishment in the environment by modifying the properties of the organism. In the case of *E. coli* K-12, specific tests to asses the likelihood of establishment, with or without recombinant DNA, have been carried out (see appendix), and have suggested that such establishment is unlikely. In the more general sense, can any change made in the laboratory either intentionally or unintentionally endow an organism with a competitive advantage in a very competitive outside environment? Seven years experience with recombinant DNA has suggested that recombinant DNA is frequently not stably maintained in the host organism in the absence of selective pressures.

(3) Assumption 3, that such a unique established organism will cause harm, remains primarily one of discussion, since experiments where one might explicitly predict harm have been for the most part forbidden or discouraged. Some explicit experiments to assess risks have been performed: i.e., examination of whether *E. coli* can act as a vector to introduce viral DNA into animal cells (Israel et al., 1979, a, b; Chan et al., 1979), and whether *E. coli* manufacturing active hormones can affect the physiology of animals (Stebbing et al., 1980). Much of the other discussion involves unknowns, although understanding of the basis for pathogenicity of some organisms can help in predicting the probable effects of introducing new genetic information.

We will try to analyze (1) the kinds of information available to support or disprove each of these assumptions, (2) how these assumptions have been dealt with in past Guidelines, and (3) how they might be dealt with in the future.

The early Guidelines presumed that, since the possibility of harm could not be properly evaluated, all recombinants were potentially harmful; the Guidelines controlled the establishment of recombinant DNA containing organisms in the environment by indicating levels of physical and biological containment. More recently, the Guidelines have evolved to include the concept that only unique organisms should be of concern. This concept is the basis for the long list of exemptions in the 1978 Guideline revision. Other relaxations in the Guidelines concerning *E. coli* K-12 host-vector systems have resulted from further examination of the second assumption, as evidence accumulated on the inability of *E. coli* K-12 to establish itself in the environment.

Accidental vs. Intentional Cloning of a Harmful Segment. One other aspect of the change from early to more recent attitudes can be traced to the qualitative difference between accidental constructs of unknown recombinants and the intentional cloning of a specific gene. The early Guidelines in their concern for inadvertant combinations of potentially harmful genes, required high containment for experiments in which random pieces of DNA from one organism are inserted into a second organism (shotgun experiment). Advances in our understanding of how expression of mammalian genes (eukaryotes) differs from expression of genes in lower forms of life such as bacteria (prokaryotes), has led to a perception that the accidental altering of an organism is very unlikely to produce a harmful result. Thus, some lessening of containment for such "shotgun" experiments has seemed justified. The other concern, and probably the basis for the remaining concerns, centers on the deliberate construction of a recombinant organism expressing a foreign product. The rapidly developing techniques of recombinant DNA technology can be utilized to insure that the recombinant DNA in fact efficiently expresses a product in its new host. The organism can, in addition, be engineered to excrete the product into the outside environment. In such a case, questions about possible harm can be posed without considering assumptions on the likelihood of expression or the possibility of one DNA fragment out of many establishing itself.

1. *Uniqueness of Organisms Created by Recombinant DNA Techniques.*

A. *Limits of the techniques.*

The original assumption that DNA from essentially any source could be introduced into essentially any organism has been supported by research advances of the last six years. Methods have been developed for introducing foreign DNA stably into a variety of bacteria, yeasts, plants and animal cells. In some organisms, the nature of the vector or the growth pressures on the organism limit the amount of new information which can be introduced as recombinant DNA. For example, many viral vectors have size limits on the amount of introduced DNA; only a specific amount can be packaged into viral the coat (Blattner et al., 1977). Some bacterial plasmids become harder to maintain stably in cells as their size increases. In practice, many recombinant DNA experiments are more productive when relatively small, defined pieces of the foreign DNA of interest are used. In considering the general limits for the purposes of risk considerations, it seems fair to say that there is no limit to either the source of DNA (donor) or of the host (recipient) but that size of the donor DNA may be limited, especially where viral vectors are used.

b. *Natural exchange mechanisms.*

The earliest discussions of the recombinant DNA technique considered the well known ability of *E. coli* to exchange DNA with other organisms as a possible hazard of using the recombinant DNA technique in that host-vector system. Such exchange might disseminate recombinant DNA from an *E. coli* K-12 host to other less well characterized and less disabled hosts; therefore, use of plasmids that could not transfer readily to other hosts (nonconjugative plasmids) were specified by the Guidelines. The 1976 Guidelines did not specifically acknowledge the additional conclusion that such exchange implies: that for at least some pairs of organisms, recombinant DNA experiments may simply imitate nature in moving blocks of genes from one species to another.

A series of promiscuous plasmids that move freely among severl species of bacteria, have been found in a large series of gram negative organisms, ranging from *E. coli* through *Rhizobium* and *Pseudomonas* (Alexander & Jollick, 1977; Haas & Holloway, 1978; Baron et al., 1968). These plasmids frequently carry, in addition to genes for their own maintenance and transmission, antibiotic resistance genes and occasionally chromosomally derived genes (Olsen & Gonzalez, 1974; Holloway, 1978). Evidence of *in vivo* transfer of these plasmids from virtually any gram-negative species to any other gram-negative species has been found (Ingram et al., 1974; Smith, 1969). In laboratory experiments, chromosomal genes from a variety of organisms can be transferred by these plasmids into other species (chromosome mobilization). In some cases, such chromosomal genes can be stably recombined into the recipient chromosome. In other cases, the mobilized genes can be found stably associated with the plasmid, and, therefore, can be transferred at high efficiency to many organisms (Holloway, 1978).

Although the precise nature of this mobilization is not know, it seems to be somewhat plasmid specific. At least some plasmids can mobilize the DNA of many diverse organisms (Haas & Holloway, 1978), and many genes from any given organism can be mobilized by these plasmids. Given the ubiquity of such plasmids, the ample opportunity for exchange in the environment these organisms share, and the very long time periods available, it seems reasonable to assume that, for most gram-negative bacteria, any given gene has in fact been introduced at some time into any given recipient. This probability was explicitly recognized in the 1978 revision of the Guidelines by the inclusion of a list of "exchangers" (Federal Register, July 28, 1978). Recombinant DNA experiments between two exchangers are exempt from the Guidelines on the rationale that such a pair should have been exposed to each others DNA, and, therefore, no unique combination should be produced via recombinant DNA technology. If this principle is accepted in the broadest sense, essentially any cloning among the enterobacteriaceae, both pathogenic and non-pathogenic, would be exempted from the Guidelines.

Many gram positive bacteria take up DNA from the environment (Low & Porter, 1978). When the DNA taken up has similar sequences to the host bacteria DNA, the bacteria are capable of recombining that DNA into their own chromosome. Some of these organisms have been shown to be transformed (changed genetically) by DNA released by neighboring bacteria in the soil (Graham & Istock, 1978; Burke & Le, 1980). Therefore, such organisms exchange genetic information with other organisms by transformation; some pairs of microorganisms have been added to the exchanger list on this basis.

Similarly, bacteria may frequently encounter mammalian DNA, either from decaying matter or from intestinal cells or ingested food in the case of gut bacteria. Mammalian cells in the intestine should frequently be exposed to DNA released from resident bacteria. It is difficult in these cases to realistically estimate uptake and persistence, although mechanisms for "illegitimate recombination" do exist both in bacteria and mammalian cells (Cold Spring Harbor Symposium, 1981; Kleckner, 1981). Large pieces of non-homologous DNA can be incorporated into the mammalian genome (Scangos & Ruddle, 1981).

There have been reports of the existence of mammalian hormone-like proteins elaborated by bacteria (Koide & Maruo, 1981; LeRoith et al., 1981); this may reflect uptake and integration of mammalian DNA by bacteria sometime in the past.

In at least one case, a system for genetic transfer from bacteria to plants exists. The plant pathogen *Agrobacterium tumefaciens* transfers a specific part of its extrachromosomal DNA, implicated in plant tumor formation, stably to the infected plant cells where the DNA is expressed and stably maintained (Chilton et al., 1977). The transferred piece is derived from a large, transferable plasmid which has the capacity to enter, by conjugation, many other prokaryotes. It is not known whether other such mechanisms exist, but even this isolated example provides a mechanism for moving bacterial and perhaps other types of information into many kinds of plants.

Among animals and plants, viruses seem to be the most likely mechanism for pick up of chromosomal genes and transfer of genetic information from one host to another. In the last few years, it has become clear that many chromosomal sequences can be found in association with viral DNA (Bishop, 1981; Weinberg, 1980).

c. *Counterarguments.*

i. While exchange can be documented in the laboratory, most genes will not be transferred *in vivo* in stable association with plasmids; only the most homologous regions will recombine into the recipient chromosome. Species that do not occupy the same ecological niche are unlikely to have the opportunity for natural exchange of genetic information. Introduction of DNA via transformation will rarely lead to stable diploid formation or replacement of the original DNA with new sequences. The use of the recombinant DNA technique may increase these processes dramatically by providing a mechanism for maintaining new sequences in the absence of homology.

ii. The vectors used for recombinant DNA experiments may be engineered to exist in many copies in the cell, or other mechanisms may be used to increase expression of genes beyond that found in nature. Such optimization of expression could lead to an organism unique in its ability to produce an excess of a particular product.

2. *Dissemination.*

a. *Stability of Recombinant DNA.* Much of the discussion of the possible hazards associated with recombinant DNA in *E. coli* K-12 has centered on the inability of this organism to establish itself in the environment or disseminate recombinant DNA to other organisms. We have summarized some of these data in the Appendix, and further discussion of the data can be found in the report of a meeting in Falmouth, Massachusetts, where the epidemiological consequences of cloning in *E. coli* K-12 were discussed (Gorbach, 1978).

Some of the arguments made with respect to *E. coli* K-12 can be generalized to other systems as well. Laboratory strains, which most frequently will be used as hosts for recombinant DNA, may lose some of the characteristics which permit growth outside the laboratory. Many vectors, in being redesigned as useful vectors for recombinant DNA experiments, will lose the capacity for self-transmission. However, in a discussion of whether essentially any recombinant DNA containing organism is likely to be disseminated, we must assume that at least in some cases the host will be one not far removed from the wild environment, and that, in some cases, self-transmissible vectors will be used to carry the recombinant DNA.

Therefore, one must ask if there are

general arguments about the ability of the organism carrying recombinant DNA to compete successfully with nonrecombinant DNA organisms.

There is a great deal of anecdotal information about the difficulties that people have maintaining recombinant DNA in bacterial strains; selective pressures must be applied continuously to maintain many plasmids. Little of this type of information has been published. One such experiment, reported by Cameron and Davis (1977), examines the fate of random *E. coli* and *Saccharomyces cerevisiae* fragments cloned into a bacterial virus vector and propagated for many cycles in *E. coli*. After about 25 cycles of growth, both sets of DNAs were reduced from the original diverse population to one or two dominant types which presumably have a growth advantage over all the other types. The authors also state that none of the yeast clones outgrow the parent vector (containing no recombinant DNA information). Therefore, most recombinants grown under these conditions will be quickly lost after the host organism begins to multiply.

Evolutionary arguments suggest that an organism containing recombinant DNA information will be at a relative disadvantage; this is particularly true for complex organisms such as mammals. Ayala (1977) points out that, for developmentally advanced organisms, new information must be coadapted to the rest of the gene pool of that organism; this is almost impossible to do with new information unless the new information is simply a different form of an already present gene. If, however, the new information is very similar to that which is already present, such a variant might have arisen by natural means and the recombinant DNA containing organisms will not be unique. Chances for altering the evolution of simpler organisms, such as prokaryotes, may be somewhat greater, although short generation times and relatively economical use of DNA sequence information suggests that non-useful information will be rapidly lost. Overproduction of one or a few products would be expected to unbalance the cell's metabolism.

b. *Transmission into other potential hosts. There are three major mechanisms for transfer of recombinant DNA from the original host to other hosts encountered in the environment.*

(1) For plasmids, in particular, the conjugational mode (by mating, involving cell-to-cell contact) may be primary. Either conjugative transfer of a self-transferring plasmid or mobilization of non-conjugative plasmids may occur (Low & Porter, 1978). At least for one class of vectors frequently used for recombinant DNA, those based on the *E. coli* plasmid pBR322, it has been demonstrated *in vitro* and *in vivo* that transfer by mobilization is greatly reduced (Dougan, G., Crosa, J.H., Falkow S., 1978; Levine, M.M., Kaper, J.B., et al., unpublished data) apparently because a segment necessary for mobilization was deleted in construction of the vector (Clark & Warren, 1979). Clearly the range of possible recipients will depend on the host range of the transferring plasmids.

(2) Viral vectors, if they are intact, may readily transfer the recombinant DNA they carry to other sensitive hosts. If the host is killed in the process, the association will be only a temporary one. If the vector is defective (lacking an essential function), the function must be supplied by a helper virus for each new round of growth and infection. Therefore, if an appropriate helper is not commonly found in the environment, it is unlikely that the defective viral vector and its recombinant DNA will be disseminated.

(3) Finally, cells are capable of taking up naked foreign DNA. For bacterial systems carrying out transformation, restriction systems will frequently degrade the incoming DNA if it is from a foreign strain, thereby reducing greatly the probabilities for stable incorporation of incoming recombinant DNA. In addition, it has been found that plasmids serve as a particularly poor source of DNA for transformation into some strains (*B. subtilis*) (Canosi et al., 1978; Contente & Dubnau, 1979). Since DNA which is nonhomologous and is not competent to replicate by itself will not be recombined into the host chromosome or maintained in the cytoplasm, it may be reasonable to assume that naked recombinant DNA taken up by prokaryotes by transformation will not generate stable recombinant DNA containing organisms. In addition, at least in some environments, nucleases, pH and other environmental factors should interfere with the stability of naked recombinant DNA. In one experiment, bacterial DNA exposed to the diluted contents of rat intestine was rapidly degraded (Maturin and Curtiss, 1977). In other cases, however, *in vivo* DNA transformation has been observed, suggesting that not all DNA released into the animal tissues will be immediately destroyed (Ottolenghi-Nightingale, 1969).

Take-up of DNA by animal cells in tissue culture is not an efficient process under optimized laboratory conditions (Scangos & Ruddle, 1981). Moreover, for an effective cycle which will lead to wide-scale dissemination, the DNA would have to be stably integrated into the germ line of an intact organism. Alternatively, some constant source pool, such as infecting bacteria or viral recombinants may continue to provide a source of the DNA.

Individual plant cells, since they can be regenerated into complete plants, could disseminate DNA if it were integrated into nuclear or organelle DNA. However, this may also require a constant bacterial or viral source pool in plant cells.

3. *Harm.*

Let us assume for the moment that the organisms we have created via recombinant DNA are in fact unique, and have had the opportunity and ability to establish themselves in the environment. Will these organisms have the ability to cause harm, either to ourselves, to other animals, or to plants, microorganisms and the environment? We will consider here some general arguments about the roles recombinant DNA can play, and some of the specific cases which people have considered to be areas of concern.

a. *Breaching prokaryotic-eukaryotic barriers: evolutionary considerations.*

Prominent among the concerns expressed during the first few years of recombinant DNA technology was the fear of "breaching the barriers" to permit recombination between distantly related organisms. This concern, articulated most prominently by Sinsheimer (1975, 1976 a, b) and by Chargaff (1976), implies that the fertility barriers that evolved as organisms diverged during evolution arose to prevent the creation of new, dangerous species. Davis argues that this view "turns evolutionary principles upside down. Evolution has indeed established fertility barriers between species. But these barriers do not function to prevent the formation of *monsters* that might take over in the Darwinian struggle: They prevent wasteful matings that would produce only unbalanced *monstrosities*, unable to survive" (Davis, 1976, 1977).

In addition, information based primarily on the recombinant DNA analysis of eukaryotic genomes makes it clear that the mechanisms for processing information from DNA into protein differ greatly between many eukaryotes and prokaryotes (Breathnach & Chambon, 1981; Revel & Groner, 1978). Therefore, it is difficult to imagine that for most cases the "breaching of the brarrier" will result in much more than adding silent DNA sequences into the host cell. In the absence of any expressed function, it is difficult to hypothesize either a beneficial or harmful effect of eukaryotic DNA for a prokaryote. Therefore, experiments which do not include the intentional expression of eukaryotic DNA in prokaryotes, or prokaryotic information in eukaryotes, should be considered unlikely to express a product; any harm would have to be due to the DNA itself, and any competitive advantage for survival would likewise have to be due to the DNA itself. We will consider below those cases where the recombinant is designed to express a foreign product.

b. *Small pieces in large organisms.* Many recombinant DNA experiments involve the introduction of pieces of relatively small foreign DNA into a host. Thus, for many experiments in *E. coli*, pieces which represent no more than 0.5–1% of the recipient's genetic information are added as recombinant DNA. In most cases, this kind of new information, unless carefully integrated with information already present, will not significantly alter the ecology of the organism (Ayala, 1977). Carried further, this argument may suggest that new information introduced into a pathogen is not likely to significantly change its mechanism of pathogenicity. Information which must be processed to serve as part of a more complex biochemical pathway, as is often the case for the surface components which play an important role in bacterial pathogenesis, will be even more difficult to alter via recombinant DNA.

For more complex cells, the added DNA will represent a small part of the recipient's genome. This argument clearly does not hold as well for viral recombinants, where the added recombinant DNA information may be equal in quantity to what is already present. In addition, it may not apply if one is speaking of planned changes, such as introducing antibiotic resistance genes or causing overproduction or change in some normal cell component; i.e., increasing toxin synthesis, or altering the characteristics of a surface component of a bacterial cell such that the antigenicity of the cell will be changed.

c. *Specific Cases.*

i. *Expression of Active Peptides: Hormones, Toxins.* One major class of concerns in the discussion of the risks of recombinant DNA is based on the assumption that bacteria could be programmed to express, in large quantities, active proteins which would cause, either by themselves or through their antigenicity, some untoward reaction in their host. This issue was specifically addressed for *E. coli* hosts at a meeting sponsored by NIAID in Pasadena, California in April 1980. Since for the sake of discussion the participants assumed the "worst case" of transfer of the recombinant DNA to an established colonizing organism, some of the conclusions from that meeting can be generalized to the case of cloning in the prokaryotes which colonize the intestinal tract. Reports from that meeting have been published in the *Recombinant DNA Technical Bulletin* (Volumes 3 and 4, 1980–1981) and are summarized here.

If one assumes transfer and maintenance of a recombinant plasmid in essentially all *E. coli* of the intestinal tract one can calculate that the bacteria, at their maximum synthetic capacity, will produce in the range of 10^6 molecules/cell/generation, or about 50 micrograms a day of a product of the size of insulin. Given this number as an upper limit, one can calculate for various active peptides the maximum dosage the hose will receive and the effect on the host from these dosages. Such calculations suggest that most hormones with activities similar to insulin will not be expected to have much, if any, effect on a mammalian host, even if they are exported from the bacterial factory and absorbed from the intestine in active form. Much more active peptides or proteins, however, might be of some concern under such circumstances. If, in addition, one imagined as the host anaerobic bacteria as well as or instead of aerobes, the body dose of an expressed protein might be significantly greater.

Fifty micrograms per day, on the other hand, of the most active toxins (e.g., the botulinum toxins, *Shigella dysenteriae* neurotoxin, tetanus toxin, diphtheria toxin) is well above the intravenous lethal dose for an average man. Several other toxins, including three of plant origin (abrin, ricin and modeccin), may be lethal to man within the range of 10 to 100 micrograms. The effects of the cytotoxic toxins, intraintestinally produced, on the lining of the lower GI tract are generally unknown. They presumably might (1) damage the colonic or intestinal lining directly, (2) pass through the lumen and cause damage elsewhere, or (3) pass into the bloodstream subsequent to lumen damage. Little is known of the pharmacokinetics of toxins in the body.

Thus, these arguments suggest that for cloning of foreign proteins, only the most active kinds of peptides, at maximal levels of expression, would be likely to have some effect, if one ignores the problems of dissemination and establishment.

ii. *Expression of Cross-Reacting Antibodies.* The implication of inserting eukaryotic genetic material coding for human "self" antigens into prokaryotic microbe vectors that parasitize humans was also specifically addressed by the NIAID meeting in Pasadena, California (Workshop on Recombinant DNA Risk Assessment). When considered within the framework of microbial parasitism in its broadest perspective and against contemporary concepts of immunologic tolerance to "self" constituents and host autoreactive immune responses, the injurious potential of autoreactive immune responses elicited by "cross-reacting" infecting host-vector microbes would appear to be extraordinarily low.

This conclusion is supported by the following observations:

- Literally hundreds of cross-reactivities exist between human proteins and bacterial and viral surface proteins. Most of these cross-reacting proteins have not been implicated in autoimmune injury.
- Abundant data exists indicating that some cross-reacting systems do lead to production of autoantibodies. Most of these autoantibodies are low affinity binding antibodies which do not lead to tissue injury and clinically manifest disease. Whether low affinity or high affinity antibodies will be induced by cross-reacting systems displaying human antigens is unknown.
- Some type of regulatory restraint exists which allows "self" to be recognized by host immunocompetent cells but prohibits such cells from launching an "anti-self" immunologic attack (Paterson, 1981).

iii. *Animal Virus Cloning.* Recombinant DNA experiments involving the use of animal virus genomes fall into several possible categories:

(1) Cloning of entire or partial genomes in prokaryotes,

(2) Cloning of animal virus genomes in eukaryotic cells under conditions where the genome may replicate either autonomously or in concert with the host genome, but cannot produce an infectious particle (defective virus or non-permissive infection),

(3) Cloning of an animal virus genome in eukaryotic cells under conditions where the genome may not only be replicated but also may be matured into an infectious virus.

In all these cases, the animal virus may be considered as either "recipient" or "donor"; the difference is frequently semantic only. General considerations will be reviewed here. A more technical analysis of the issues to each class of animal virus are considered in the report of the Ascot Meeting (Federal Register, July 28, 1978).

Cloning of animal viruses is considered here with respect to the question of whether recombinant DNA experiments *per se* pose any unique hazards not associated with handling animal viruses in general. The following comments are offered in light of the consideration that all work with animal viruses poses some potential risk, unrelated to recombinant DNA, especially to investigators. It is essential to employ good laboratory techniques appropriate to the particular virus being studied.

• *Cloning of viral genomes in prokaryotes*

Our increased understanding of the differences in gene expression between prokaryotes and eukaryotes renders it difficult to imagine ways in which complete animal viral particles could be synthesized in recombinant DNA containing bacteria. Animal viruses have complex post-transcriptional modification requirements, and use host functions in processing and assembly which are not provided by a bacterial host.

• *Cloning of Viral Genomes in Eukaryotic Cells*

Because animal cells in culture are so fragile, they in themselves constitute an excellent containment system. The major potential risk would be that a recombinant DNA molecule could replicate, be encapsidated as a normal virus, and be able to propagate as a virus. There are several potential constraints on such a system, primarily the fact that there is an upper limit on the size of the genome which may be encapsidated. Under such conditions, some of the original viral genomes would most probably be deleted, rendering the recombinant virus defective. However, such a defective virus might be propogated in the presence of a helper virus. Such systems are known to exist both naturally (avian retroviruses and adeno-associated viruses) and in the laboratory (adeno-SV40 hybrid viruses, most of which are defective, but may be propogated) Recombinants might include genes from different viruses or cellular genes inserted into a viral genome. Examples of both natural types of recombinants are generated by recombination in cell culture (e.g. the adeno-SV40 hybrid viruses and the highly oncogenic types of both avian and murine retroviruses—those which have incorporated a Src gene of cellular origin). Interestingly, none of the known examples have proven particularly hazardous for experimenters to handle. Presumably a human retrovirus might be especially hazardous but this situation could obtain independently of any recombinant DNA experiments.

Recombinants between viruses which are not closely related (different Families) are likely to have such basic differences in mechanisms of replication and infection as to be unlikely to work together well enough to produce viable entities; therefore the recombinant in this case will be equivalent to, or more defective, than the parent viruses. Recombinants between viruses which are more closely related may be more likely to create new useable functions, but the close relationship may suggest that such a recombination will have already occurred naturally.

In summary recombinant DNA experiments involving animal viruses in eukaryotic cells might well lead to the construction of some viruses with properties which are novel in detail. However, there is no reason to think that these agents would be novel in terms of host range or potential virulence compared to viruses generated in other ways.

Much of the summary of animal virus recombinant DNA risks is based upon the conclusions of virologists at the EMBO meeting in Ascot, England, January 27–28 1978 (Federal Register, July 28, 1978), and at the ASM meeting in Miami Beach, Florida, April 13, 1981. Reports on these meetings are available.

B. Human Genetic Engineering

The implications of the recombinant DNA technique for inserting recombinant DNA into humans has served as a backdrop for much of the recombinant DNA debate. The guidelines as now written deal with this issue only obliquely, by requiring special RAC consideration for most such experiments. Currently, human experimentation falls under the control of human experimentation review groups (Institutional Review Boards, IRBs). If a decision to remove the recombinant DNA oversight of this technique is made, it will still be oversighted by IRBs. It is not clear that recombinant DNA *per se* poses a special problem in this area, distinct from those posed by non-recombinant transformation and genetic manipulation procedures.

III. *Costs*

Expenditures for risk assessment testing, administration of RAC, and the functioning of the Office of Recombinant DNA Activities were approximately $700,000 in the peak year of 1979. Risk assessment costs accounted for approximately one-half of that total. In all, risk assessment and vector development contracts supported by NIAID have cost over $2 million since 1976. There are also expenses associated with the functioning of Institutional Biosafety Committees, and with the oversight of physical containment facilities.

Costs in time and energy for individual scientists are difficult to estimate but continue to be significant.

IV. *Conclusions*

A. Summary Analysis of Risks

Given the above analysis of the risks associated with recombinant DNA, we have come to the following major conclusions:

(1) That accidental combinations of genes, rising out of "shotgun" cloning experiments or experiments where expression is not specifically engineered, are extremely unlikely to lead to serious problems. Both the barriers to expression of foreign genes in most organisms, the necessity for new activities to function as an integrated part of an existing pathway, and the selective disadvantage given to an organism by recombinant DNA inserts will interfere with such organisms establishing themselves in the environment and thus, ultimately with their potential to cause harm. Therefore, for these experiments, the minimal controls associated with good laboratory practice should be sufficient.

(2) A particular subset of experiments may still pose some possibility of risk. While there is no evidence that this risk is qualitatively different from the risks associated with other kinds of genetic research, the possibility for improving the virulence, host range, or survivability of some pathogens does seem to exist. In most cases, in these experiments the problems of expression of foreign functions will have been bypassed, or normal functions will have been engineered to operate more efficiently.

In many cases, even the best engineered strain will be at a major disadvantage in the environment, or will require artificial selections to maintain recombinant DNA information. The issue to be faced here, however, is (a) how serious is this risk? (b) What is the most effective, non-obtrusive mechanism for guarding against any untoward consequences of such work?

B. Possible Responses

Re-evaluation of the guidelines might in theory lead to changes in the guidelines' containment requirements, or the oversight procedures, or both. We will consider here the two extreme cases of (1) maintaining the current guidelines, or (2) totally abolishing the guidelines. The route recommended by the subcommittee will then be discussed.

1. *Maintain the Status Quo.*

a. *Advantages.* The *status quo* is not static, since the 1978 major revision of the guidelines recognized the need for constant evolution of the guidelines and provided procedures for changes which have been applied frequently in the last three years. The guidelines have been useful; their existence raised the awareness of investigators and institutions as to the importance of considering and avoiding hazards in the laboratory. If there are significant dangers associated with recombinant DNA research, the safety of this research thus for may have been due to the existence of the guidelines. Time will permit accumulation of more experience and data relevant to risk assessment so that reductions in restrictions can be derived from a greater factual base. A carefully thought-through simplification of the guidelines could be one immediate aim, while preserving the current guideline structure.

Gradual evolution of the guidelines would permit exploration of the means of dealing with possible laboratory-created biohazards so that tracking systems for such hazards in general—inclusive, but not limited to, those that might arise from recombinant DNA technology—might be established. To monitor biohazards, an expanded role for a body similar in concept to RAC might also be explored, as well as that body's relation to the IBCs. Current guidelines for good laboratory practices could be examined and possibly adapted to include recombinant DNA experiments.

b. *Disadvantages.* The current guidelines are long, cumbersome, and detailed. They are, in practice, regulations rather than guidelines. Because no guidelines or regulations can hope to anticipate, in detail, all experiments or circumstances, particularly in such a rapidly growing field, much time and effort are expended by investigators, RAC, and ORDA with requests to alter containment requirements or be granted exemptions from guidelines. The record shows that more often than not, after careful deliberation, the requests are granted.

Most scientists now conclude, after almost a decade of experience, deliberate risk assessment experimentation and theorizing, that the potential risks of recombinant DNA research have not materialized and most probably will not. While it is not possible to exclude with certainty risks to man or the ecosystem from application of recombinant DNA technology, at present these risks now appear to be much smaller than they appeared to be a few years ago.

In view of this conclusion, the current guidelines are too complex and restrictive of development of useful knowledge with direct health, agricultural, and economic benefits. They require a bureaucratic apparatus and an amount of paperwork that is viewed as excessive and excessively costly in terms of dollars and professionals' time.

2. *Abolish the Guidelines.*

a. *Advantages.* In the absence of known or suspected hazards, it appears unjustified to single out certain classes of experiments as requiring elevated levels or physical containment. Similarly unjustified is the expenditure of time and money required to maintain a regulatory apparatus that has been developed to protect society from hazards that may be non-existent. What residual uncertainties exist about such hazards can be handled more flexibly and more efficiently at the level of the individual scientist, with consultation with others as he sees fit. In some universities, the procedures for monitoring laboratory hazards will remain in force and provide a backup system for checking on the individual scientist. Other kinds of laboratory guidelines (e.g., those for working with human and animal pathogens) will still exist and will provide guidance for proper use of such organisms when recombinant DNA technology is used. Since many of the residual concerns are centered around changing the host range and pathogenicity of already existing pathogens, such appropriate containment procedures should be adequate and in line with the existing dangers.

b. *Disadvantages.* There remain some areas in which specific risks may exist. It would seem appropriate to have some mechanism for ensuring that scientists consider these risks before and during their experimentation, and that they seek some outside advice on how serious the risk may be. The current IBC structure, with ORDA and RAC as backup, provides such a structure. Its abolition will also leave the regulatory aspects of the field in chaos, and may encourage local jurisdictions, which may come to different conclusions about the degree of certainty concerning special risks, to enact less informed and less flexible guidelines and regulations for control of this field. In any case, individual determinations in many areas of the country will possibly require more time and effort of more scientists than if the same determination was made once centrally. The results will also be less uniform, encouraging pressure on local groups to keep containment low.

In the absence of a working procedure for monitoring other laboratory hazards, it seems foolhardy to abandon this mechanism even if one concludes that recombinant DNA risks are not qualitatively different from other research risks. It may be more appropriate to refine the mechanisms for tracking recombinant DNA experiments such that this mechanism can be used as a model for watching and preventing other research risks.

C. Recommendation

The Working Group on Revision of the Guidelines has proposed changes in the guidelines which (1) would significantly reduce required containment for a large class of experiments, (2) would employ other guidelines to set appropriate containment for working with pathogens containing recombinant DNA, and (3) would eliminate the prohibited class of experiments, including the large volume growth of recombinant DNA containing organisms, relegating them to the same status as other experiments. The proposal does retain, however, the requirement for IBC prereview of non-exempt experiments, and suggests that in specific cases where additional risk might be expected due to the nature of the recombinant DNA experiment itself, the containment should be adjusted accordingly. Thus, this procedure would have the effect of

(1) Supporting the notion that, for the vast majority of recombinant DNA experiments, the risks are those associated with the organisms involved. The appropriate containment for pathogens such as that specified by the proposed CDC Biosafety Guidelines for Microbiological and Biomedical Laboratories would continue to be enforced for experiments utilizing recombinant DNA.

(2) Simplifying the containment levels for the vast majority of experiments, and in most cases decreasing the required containment.

(3) Retaining flexibility in allowing change in containment in particular experiments where circumstances permit. Flexibility would reside primarily with the IBC, and, if necessary, questions could be referred to RAC.

(4) Maintaining the class of "exempt" experiments, which covers the majority of recombinant DNA experiments; new additions could be made to this class as justified.

(5) Maintaining prereview of all non-exempt experiments by the IBC. It is proposed that the requirements for the constitution of the IBC be dropped while the essential element of consultation with a group other than the principal investigator is retained.

References

(*1*) Alexander, J. L. and J. D. Jollick (1977). Transfer and Expression of *Pseudomonas* Plasmid RP1 in *Caulobacter*. J. Gen'l. Microbiology *99*, 325–331.

(*2*) Ayala, F. J. (1977). The Stability of Biological Species; in *Research with Recombinant DNA:* An Academy Forum, Washington, D.C. Natl. Acad. Sci.; 90–97.

(*3*) Baron, L. S.; P. Gemski, Jr.; E. M. Johnson; and J. A. Wohlhieter (1968). Intergenetic Bacterial Matings. Bact. Reviews *32*, 362–96.

(*4*) Bishop, J. M. (1981). Enemies Within: The Genesis of Retrovirus Oncogenes. Cell *23*, 5–6.

(*5*) Blattner, F R.; B. G. Williams; A. E. Blechl; K. Denniston-Thomason; H. E. Faber; L. A. Furlong; D. J. Grunwald; D. O. Kiefer; D. D. Moore; J. W. Schumm; E. L. Sheldon; and O. Smithies (1977). Charon Phage: Safer Derivatives of Bacteriophage for DNA Cloning. Science *196*, 161–169.

(*6*) Breathnach, R. and P. Chambon (1981). Organization and Expression of Eucaryotic Split Gene Coding for Proteins. Ann. Review Biochem. *50*, 349–83.

(*7*) Burke, W. F and T. Le Huong (1980). Characterization of a *Bacillus subtilis* Strain. Recombinant DNA Technical Bulletin Vol. 3, 1975–194.

(*8*) Cameron, J. R. and R. W Davies, (1977). The Effects of *Escherichia coli* and Yeast DNA Insertions on the Growth of Lamdba Bacteriophage. Science *196*, 212–215.

(*9*) Canosi, U., G. Morelli; and T. A. Trautner (1978). The Relationship Between Molecular Structure and Transformation Efficiency of Some *S. aureus* Plasmids Isolated from *B. subtilis*. Molec. Gen. Genet. *166*, 259–267.

(*10*) Chan, H. W.; M. A. Israel; C. F. Garon; W. P. Rowe; and M. A. Martin (1979). Molecular Cloning of Polyoma Virus DNA in *Escherichia coli:* Lambda Phage Vector System. Science *203*, 887–892.

(*11*) Chargaff, E. (1976). On the Dangers of Genetic Meddling. Science *192*, 938–940.

(*12*) Chilton, M. D.; M. H. Drummond; D. J. Merio; D. Scialig; A. L. Montoyo; M. P. Gordon; and E. W. Nester (1977). Stable Incorporation of Plasmid DNA into Higher Plant Cells: The Molecular Basis of Crown Gall Tumorigenesis. Cell *11*, 263–71.

(*13*) Clark, A. J. and G. J. Warren (1979). Conjugal Transmission of Plasmids. Ann. Review Genet. *13*, 99–125.

(*14*) Cold Spring Harbor Symposium Quant. Biol. (1981). Moveable Genetic Elements *45*.

(*15*) Contente, S. and D. Dubnau (1979). Characterization of Plasmid Transformation in *Bacillus subtilis:* Kinetic Properties and the Effect of DNA Conformation. Molec. Gen. Genet. *167*, 251–258.

(*16*) Davis, B. D. (1976). Evolution, Epidemiology, and Recombinant DNA. Science *193*, 442.

(*17*) Davis, B. D. (1977). The Recombinant DNA Scenarios: Andromeda Strain, Chimera, and Golem. Am. Scientist *65*, 547–555.

(*18*) Dougan, G., Crosa, J. H., Falkow, S. Mobilization of the *Escherichia coli* Plasmid ColEl (colicin El) and ColEl Vectors Used in Recombinant DNA Experiments. J. Infect. Dis. *137*, 676–680, 1978.

(*19*) **Federal Register** (July 7, 1976). Recombinant DNA Research Guidelines. 27902–27943.

(*20*) **Federal Register** (July 28, 1978). Recombinant DNA Research, Proposed Revised Guidelines. 33042–33178.

(*21*) **Federal Register** (July 28, 1978). Recombinant DNA Research, Proposed Revised Guidelines, Report of the U.S.-EMBO Workshop to Assess Risks for Recombinant DNA Experiments Involving the Genomes of Animal, Plant, and Insect Viruses. 33159–33169.

(*22*) **Federal Register** (December 22, 1978). Guidelines for Research Involving Recombinant DNA Molecules. 60108–60131.

(*23*) **Federal Register** (July 1, 1981). Guidelines for Research Involving Recombinant DNA Molecules. 34462–34487.

(*24*) Gorbach, S. L., ed. (1978). Risk Assessment of Recombinant DNA Experimentation with *Escherichia coli* K12. Journal of Infectious Diseases *137* 613–614.

(*25*) Graham, J. B. and C. A. Istock (1978). Genetic Exchange in *Bacillus subtilis* in Soil. Molec. Gen. Genet. *166*, 287–290.

(*26*) Haas, D. and B. W Holloway (1978). Chromosome Mobilization by the R Plasmid R68.45: A Tool in Pseudomonas Genetic. Molec. Gen. Genet. *158*, 229–237.

(*27*) Holoway, B. W (1978). Isolation and Characterization of an R' Plasmid in *Pseudomonas aeruginosa*. J. Bact. *133*, 1078–1082.

(*28*) Ingram, L. C.; J. D. Anderson; J. Arrand; and M. H. Richmond (1974). A Probable Example of R-factor Recombination in the Human Gastro-intestinal Tract. J. Med. Microbiol. *7*, 251.

(*29*) Israel, M. A.; H. W Chan; M. A. Martin; and W P. Rowe (1979a). Molecular Cloning of Polyoma Virus DNA in *Escherichia coli:* Oncogenicity Testing in Hamsters. Science *205*, 1140–1142.

(*30*) Israel, M. A.; H. W Chan; W P. Rowe; and M. A. Martin (1979b). Molecular Cloning of Polyoma Virus DNA in *Escherichia coli:* Plasmid Vector System. Science *203*, 883–887.

(*31*) Kleckner, N. (1981). Transposable Elements in Prokaryotes. Ann. Review Genet. *15*, in press.

(*32*) Koide, S. S. and T Maruo (1981). Bacterial Factor with Gonadotropin Activity. Recombinant DNA Technical Bulletin Vol. 4, 5–10.

(*33*) Le Roith, D., J. Shiloach; J. Roth; and M. A. Lesniak (1981). Insulin or a Closely Related Molecule is Native to *Escherichia coli*. J. Biol. chem. *256*, 6533–6536.

(*34*) Low, K. and D. D. Porter (1978). Modes of Gene Transfer and Recombination in Bacteria. Ann. Review Genet. *12*, 249–287.

(*35*) Maturin, L. and R. Curtiss, III (1977). Degradation of DNA by Nucleases in Intestinal Tract of Rats. Science *19*, 216–218.

(*36*) Olsen, R. H. and G. Gonzalez (1974). *Escherichia coli* Gene Transfer to Unrelated Bacteria by a Histidine Operon-RP1 Drug Resistance Plasmid Complex. Biochem. Biophys. Res. Commun. *59*, 377–385.

(*37*) Ottolenghi-Nightingale, E. (1969). Spontaneously Occurring Bacterial Transformations in Mice. J. Bac. *100*, 445–452.

(*38*) Paterson, P Y (1981). Microbial Parasitism Cross-Reactive with Host Antigens: Implications Concerning Loss of "Self" Tolerance and Development of Autoimmune Disease. Recombinant DNA Technical Bulletin, Vol. 4, No. 3, 96–107.

(*39*) Revel, M. and Y Groner (1978). Post-transcriptional and Translational Controls of Gene Expression in Eukaryotes. Ann. Review Biochem. *47* 1079–1126.

(*40*) Scangos, G. and F H. Ruddle (1981). Mechanisms and Applications of DNA-Medicated Gene Transfer in Mammalian Cells—A Review. Gene *14*, 1–10.

(*41*) Sinsheimer, R. (1975). Troubled Dawn for Genetic Engineering. New Scientist, Oct. 16, 148–151.

(*42*) Sinsheimer, R. (1976a). On Coupling Inquiry and Wisdom. Fed. Proc. *35*, 2540–2542.

(*43*) Sinsheimer, R. (1976b). Recombinant DNA—On Our Own. Biosciences *26*, 599.

(*44*) Smith, H. W (1969). Transfer of Antibiotic Resistance from Animal and Human Strains of *Escherichia coli* to Resident *E. coli* in the Alimentary Tract of Man. Lancet *1*, 1174.

(*45*) Stebbing, N., K. Olson; N. Lin; R. N. Harkins; C. Snider; M. J. Ross; F Fields; L. May; J. Fenno; D. Fodge; and G. Prender (1980). Biological Comparison of Natural and Recombinant DNA-Derived Polypeptides. Recombinant DNA Technical Bulletin, Vol. 3, No. 1, 12–21.

(*46*) Weinberg, R. A. (1980). Integrated Genomes of Animal Viruses. Ann. Review Biochem. *49*, 197–226.

(*47*) Workshop on Recombinant DNA Risk Assessment, Pasadena, California. Recombinant DNA Technical Bulletin, Vol. 4, No. 3, 98–120.

Appendix A of Annex B: Experiments with E. coli

One of the apprehensions of scientists early in the recombinant DNA era was that certain recombinant organisms (particularly *Escherichia coli*) might inadvertantly escape from the laboratory, particularly by way of inadvertant colonization of laboratory personnel. Furthermore it was feared that temporary intestinal colonization of a laboratory worker might result in exchange of genetic information from the laboratory *E. coli* strain to normal intestinal coliform flora. It was also feared by some that since some *E. coli* strains are pathogenic for man, perhaps *E. coli* K-12 should be regarded as a pathogen or "potential" pathogen.

Most of the early work with recombinant DNA involved *E. coli K-12*. Since the genetics of this strain are so well-studied, much (if not most) recombinant DNA research still involves derivatives of this strain. Thus it is pertinent to discuss "risk" relevant to working with *E. coli* K-12.

A. History and Description of D. coli K-12

E. coli K-12 was first isolated from the intestine of a patient convalescing from diphtheria in Stanford University Hospital in the 1920's. Thereafter it was stored in the laboratory as a stock strain. Presumably, at the time of initial isolation it was a smooth strain adapted to colonization of the human colon. By the term smooth is meant the fact that the strain produces a complete lipopolysaccharide O antigen on its surface with many polymeric polysaccharide side chains. Over the course of years of laboratory passage *E. coli* K-12 has become irreversibly rough. By dint of its rough state, *E. coli* K-12 has lost a major prerequisite required for successful colonization of man and animals.

1. *E. coli as a Pathogen.* It is well-recognized that within the enormous species, *E. coli*, are strains that are true pathogens for man and animals. Depending on strain and host, certain *E. coli* can cause diarrheal illiness, dysentery, urinary tract infection or meningitis. While this is true, it is now known that such pathogenicity is *not* a general or even a potential feature of all *E. coli*. Rather, a constellation of specific virulence factors must be present in certain *E. coli* for them to be able to cause disease in man (or animals) and such virulence factors tend to be stable in only a relatively small number of strains or serotypes.

For example:

A. *E. coli meningitis*— Trauma or neurosurgical intervention which breaches the integrity of the meningeal coverings of the central nervous system can result in direct contamination and nosocomial infection with many gram-negative or gram-positive organisms. In the absence of the above, for all intents and purposes, primary *E. coli* meningitis is limited to infants less than three months of age; in fact most cases occur in neonates within 28 days of birth. In the early 1970's it was discovered that the *E. coli* that cause meningitis in infants have in common a surface capsular polysaccharide, Kl, which confers virulence (*1,2*). By mid-infancy most individuals are already resistant to Kl encapsulated *E. coli*.

b. *Diarrheal Illness*—Certain *E. coli* can cause watery diarrhea. These strains, which include enterotoxigenic and enteropathogenic *E. coli*, possess a constellation of virulence properties which in tandem result in the ability to cause diarrhea. For example, enterotoxigenic *E. coli* that elaborate both heatlabile and heatstable enterotoxins usually also possess fimbrial colonization factors (adhesion pili) and such strains are usually limited to perhaps a dozen of the 164 *E. coli* O serogroups. Studies in pigs involving attempts to "create" a diarrheal pathogen by insertion of genes for adhesion pili (K88 antigen fimbriae) and enterotoxin into a K-12 strain were unsuccessful, (*3*) showing that the constellation of virulence properties of true porcine pathogens is more complex.

c. *Dysentery*—Certain strains of *E. coli* exist that are capable of causing a clinical syndrome identical to bacillary dysentery. Such strains are referred to as enteroinvasive and are limited to a very few *E. coli* O serogroups. Biochemically and serologically these strains bear many relationships to shigella.

d. *Urinary Tract Infections*—It is now recognized that the *E. coli* strains that are associated with upper urinary tract infections possess mannose resistant hemagglutinin, and fimbrial colonization factors that allow adhesion to epithelial cells of the urinary tract and prevent dislodgement by urine flow. Furthermore, it is currently recognized that urinary tract epithelial cells of certain individuals are more receptive than others to adhesion by *E. coli* strains possessing the fimbrial colonization factors.

2. *Inoculum Size and Mode of Infection*—It has been shown with volunteer studies that rather high inocula (10^6—10^{10}) and neutraliation of gastric acid (for example with $NaHCO_3$) are required to ensure colonization by enterotoxigenic *E. coli*. Volunteers with *E. coli* diarrheal disease did not transmit the infection by direct contact to uninoculated control volunteers with whom they were living in close quarters (*4*).

Volunteers challenged with enteropathogenic *E. coli* excreted large numbers of *E. coli* in thier stools and were colonized in their proximal small intestine but were not colonized in the throat (*5*).

The thrust of all these observations is that: *E. coli* enteropathogens are transmitted via large inocual contained within contaminated food and water vehicles. They are not spread by airborne or direct contact routes. In order to colonize the human gut, even with a known enteric pathogen, a large inoculum is required and modifications must be made (e.g., ingestion of $NaHCO_3$) to ensure survival of the *E. coli* through the gastric acid barrier. Thus, based on current knowledge and data it is extremely unlikely that individuals working in a recombinant DNA research laboratory could become colonized in their intestine by droplet, aerosol or contact transmission.

3. *Colonizability of Human Intestine by E. coli K-12: Summary of Feeding Studies*—Four groups have carried out studies in which high inocula (10^8—10^{10} organisms) of *E. coli* K-12 strains were fed to volunteers (*6–9*). The common observation from these studies is that *E. coli* K-12 is unable to colonize the human intestine. While counts of 10^5—10^7 K-12 organisms per gram of stool could be cultured on the first day postinfection, levels dropped to 10^2 or 10^3 by day 2 and K-12 was usually no longer detectable by day 5. In contrast, ingestion of 10^{10} organisms of a smooth non-pathogenic normal intestinal flora strain (*E. coli* HS) resulted in prolonged excretion of the organism (weeks) in high titer (10^6—10^8/gram stool), demonstrating clear-cut colonization (*8,10*).

There is only one report of apparent *in vivo* transmission of a conjugative plasmid from K-12 to normal host flora (*7*). In this instance, one day post-ingestion small numbers (10^1/gram stool) of resident coliforms were found to be carring the K-12 plasmid. The putative recombinants were detectable for only one day (*7*).

Feeding studies in volunteers have also been carried out with *E. coli* x1776, a highly defective, fastidious variant of K-12 that has been certified as host organism in EK2 levels of biological containment (*9*). x1776 was not detected in stools of volunteers following ingestion. When volunteers were fed x1776 containing plasmid pBR322, low levels of excreation, (10^1–10^2/gram for two days) were observed.

In summary, the above-mentioned feeding studies demonstrate that even after direct ingestion of large inocula, *E. coli* K-12 does not readily colonize the human intestine.

4. *Active Bacteriologic Surveillance for K-12 Colonization*—During a two year period fecal cultures were obtained every two to three days from laboratory workers handling nalidixic acid-resistant *E. coli* K-12 containing transmission-proficient R plasmids. These workers practiced no special precautions other than good microbiologic technique. Neither *E. coli* K-12 nor the R factors utilized in the laboratory were recovered from any stool culture at any time. These data demonstrate under "field conditions" that colonization of *E. coli* K-12 or acquisition by resident intestinal coliform flora of R factors used in the laboratory do not occur.

5. *"Non-Mobilizable Plasmids"*—Plasmid vectors have been created which are mobilized and transferred from bacterial cell to bacterial cell at a markedly reduced frequency than the parent strain (*12*). For example pBR322 is transferred approximately 100 thousand times less frequently than its colEl parent plasmid under comparable mating conditions. Risk assessment studies recently carried out at the Univiersity of Maryland School of Medicine under sponsorship of the National Institutes of Health have verified *in vivo* in man decreased mobilization of "nonmobilizable" plasmid vector pBR325 (*10*). Seventeen volunteers ingested 10^{10} *E. coli* HS (a smooth normal flora strain) containing plasmid pJBJK5 (a non-conjugative, mobilizable colEl variant containing tetracycline and chloramphenicol resistance genes). This strain heavily colonized the intestines of each of the 17 individuals, all of whom also ingested one gram of tetracycline daily. Normal flora recombinants containing plasmid pJBK5 were recovered from 9 to 17 volunteers. In contrast, when 15 volunteers ingested *E. coli* HS containing plasmid pBR325 (which also encodes for tetracycline resistance), although they also became heavily colonized while taking tetracyline daily, no resident flora recombinants were identified containing pBR325. These data attest to the decreased mobilizability in man of safe vector plasmids, even in the presence of antibiotic pressure modifying the environment in a way that recombinants would have enhanced survivability

References of Appendix A of Annex B

(*1*) Robbins, M.B., McCracken, G.H., Gotschlich, E.C., Orskov, F., Orskov, I., Hansen, L.A. *Escherichia coli* K-1 capsular Polysacscharide Associated with Neonatal Meningitis. 290:1216–1221, 1974.

(*2*) Sarff, L.D., McCracken, G.H., Jr., Schiffer, M.S., Glode, M.P., Robbins, J.B., Orskov, I., Orskov, F Epidemiology of *Escherichia coli* K-1 in Healthy and Diseased Newborns. Lancet I:1099–1104, 1975.

(*3*) Smith, H.W., Huggins, M.B. The Influence of Plasmid-Determined and Other Characteristics of Enteropathogenic *Escherichia coli* on their Ability to Proliferate in the Alimentary Tract of Piglets, Calves and Lambs. J. Med. Microbiol. 11:471–492, 1977

(*4*) Levine, M.M., Rennels, M.B., Cisneros, L., Hughes, T.P., Nalin, D.R., Young, C.R. Lack of Person-to-Person Transmission of Enterotoxigenic *Escherichia coli* Despite Close Contact. Am. J. Epipdemiol. 111:347–355, 1980.

(*5*) Black, R.E., Levine, M.M., et al. Unpublished data.

(*6*) Smith, H.W Survival of Orally Administered *E. coli* K-12 in Alimentary Tract of Man. Nature 255:500–502, 1975.

(*7*) Anderson, E.S. Viability of, and Transfer of a Plasmid from, *E. coli* K-12 in the Human Intestine. Nature 255–502–504, 1975.

(*8*) Formal, S.B., Hornick, R. B. Invasive *Escherichia coli*. J. Infect. Dis. 137:641–644, 1978.

(*9*) Host-Vector Systems in the Mammalian Intestine. Science 209:391–394, 1980.

(*10*) Levine, M.M., Kaper, J.B., et al. Unpublished data.

(*11*) Petrocheilou, V., Richmond, M.H. Absence of Plasmid or *Escherichia coli* K-12 Infection among Laboratory Personnel Engaged in R-Plasmid Research. Gene 2: 323–327, 1977.

(*12*) Dougan, G., Crosa, J.H., Falkow, S. Mobilization of the *Escherichia coli* Plasmid ColEl (colicin El) and ColEl Vectors Used in Recombinant DNA Experiments. J. Infect. Dis. 137:676–680, 1978.

Annex C—Minority Reports of Working Group on Revision of Recombinant DNA Guidelines

Further Recommendations

We the undersigned agree with the general thrust of the recommendations of the Working Group on Recombinant DNA Guidelines. In particular, we support the recommendation that those experiments, for which containment guidelines are retained, are to conform to good laboratory practice as described in the CDC and APHIS Quarantine rules. The recommendation that abolishes the category of prohibited experiments is scientifically sound in the light of current knowledge. The content of the suggested containment guidelines follows from the overall conclusion that research with recombinant DNA imposes no more risk than any other biological research. The background paper amply documents this point.

Therefore, we find no reason to retain the Administrative Guidelines (Section IV). The spirit of the Baltimore-Campbell resolution and, as titled, its major purpose, was to convert the NIH Regulations into Guidelines. Retaining pages of bureaucratic regulations for what is now perceived to require only limited oversight is a waste of time and effort, will not add to safety in any way and will be disdained as bureaucratic capriciousness.

Edward A. Adelberg, Kenneth I. Berns, Herman W. Lewis, Sue A. Tolin, Norton D. Zinder.

Given the recommendations for the containment guidelines and what would be proper for the administrative guidelines, we the undersigned conclude that special guidelines for recombinant DNA are totally unnecessary Therefore, we further recommend that as of June 23, 1982 the NIH Guidelines cease to exist.

The arguments for their retention are primarily social and political; they do not have a scientific base (see Background Paper). It seems right, at this time, to disavow such arguments and base our conclusions solely on the scientific issues. RAC should recommend the abolition of the Guidelines. In doing so, it should prepare a strong statement of its rationale to be published in *Science* and *Nature* as well as the **Federal Register.** This statement should also contain as recommendation the containment guidelines for recombinant DNA experiments developed by the Working Group. Prepared as the culmination of years of consideration and analysis, such a statement would serve to inform both the scientific community and the public of the safety of research with recombinant DMA:

Edward A. Adelberg, Norton D. Zinder.

Annex D—Draft Minutes of Relevant Portion of September 10–11, 1981 RAC Meeting

Drs. David Baltimore and Allan Campbell, RAC members, had proposed a major revision of the Guidelines (Baltimore-Campbell proposal) which was considered by the RAC at its April 1981 meeting. At the April 1981 meeting, a Working Group on Revision of the Guidelines was established to review the Baltimore-Campbell proposal as well as other approaches which might lead to a major revision of the Guidelines. The Working Group met on June 1, 1981, and on July 9, 1981. The Working Group prepared a proposal for revising the Guidelines, a summary of its actions, and a document entitled "Evaluation of the Risks Associated with Recombinant DNA Research." Two minority reports were prepared by several members of the Working Group. The Working Group report and the minority reports were distributed to RAC members prior to the September 1981 meeting.

Mr. Thornton asked Dr. Gottesman to introduce the Working Group's report. Dr. Gottesman reviewed the highlights of the report. She noted that the revision of the Guidelines promulgated on July 1, 1981, already exempts many experiments in three major host-vector systems. The Baltimore-Campbell proposal would convert mandatory Guidelines to a voluntary code of good practice and would set as containment levels those appropriate for the organism being used. The Working Group considered various approaches; the majority supported a proposal which adopts the containment provisions of the Baltimore-Campbell proposal but retains the mandatory aspect of the Guidelines. The proposal has not yet been published as a proposed major action in the Federal Register. The RAC may wish to modify the proposal before its formal publication in the Federal Register for public comment.

Dr. Gottesman noted that the background document discusses basic assumptions. It is difficult to imagine hazards resulting from random combinations of DNA. Furthermore, deliberate combinations will not be harmful in most cases. However, there are still some questions about certain experiments. The issue is how to deal with the latter experiments. The proposal of the Working Group would retain IBC prereview so that there is a level of review beyond the investigator.

Dr. Gottesman then reviewed the main points of the Working Group proposal. The proposed containment levels are very similar to those of the Baltimore-Campbell proposal, i.e., containment would be largely based on the pathogenicity of the host. For all non-exempt experiments, at least the P1 level would be recommended. The Working Group proposal eliminates reference to biological containment in Part III of the Guidelines. The Working Group proposal also adds in admonition which reads as follows:

If there is clear evidence that the donor DNA will significantly change the pathogenicity of the host, the containment level appropriate to the anticipated change will be applied.

While the Baltimore-Campbell proposal would be a voluntary code of practice, the Working Group proposal retains IBC prereview of covered experiments and retains Section IV-G of the Guidelines which discusses possible penalties for failing to follow the Guidelines. However, the Working Group recommends eliminating membership requirements for IBCs currently specified in Section IV-D of the Guidelines. While the Baltimore-Campbell proposal retains the prohibition section of the Guidelines (I-D), the Working Group proposal eliminates the prohibitions on the basis that currently prohibited experiments would be prereviewed by an IBC in their proposal. Dr. Gottesman said that she felt that the major issues for discussion are: prohibitions, prereview of covered experiments, and containment levels.

Dr. Berns noted that five Working Group members, including himself, submitted a minority report which disagrees with the Working Group's proposal to retain the mandatory nature of the Guidelines. The minority report recommends elimination of Part IV of the Guidelines.

Dr. Goldstein said that he agrees with parts of the Working Group report. He said that IBCs are still needed although a survey in California has indicated great variation in IBCs. He also said that prohibited experiments need to be more clearly considered.

Dr. Harris said that she felt that the Working Group's report is an acceptable compromise.

Ms. King said that the report suggests a direction for movement but that details need to be worked out. She said that if there are Guidelines, there should be sanctions. She said that distinguishing NIH grantees from non-grantees is not unique; she cited the situation with human experimentation. Ms. King said that she strongly favors retention of the sanctions.

Dr. Nightingale said that she supports the recommendations of the Working Group, saying that they represent a good compromise. She expressed concern about the availability of other guidelines cited in Working Group report. In this regard, she noted the many comments received on the proposed CDC Biosafety Guidelines for Microbiological and Biomedical Laboratories. She also expressed concern that prohibition I-D-4, dealing with deliberate release into the environment, had not been dealt with. Dr. Nightingale said there is a necessity for accountability when public funds are being used. She said the RAC needs an assessment of outside perceptions and that the background document needs further work.

Dr. Zinder then addressed the RAC. He noted that he had prepared the minority reports to the Working Group's recommendations. He said that although there is a disagreement about the administrative aspects of the Guidelines, there was unanimity in the Working Group in favor of the new proposed containment levels. He noted that although inclusion of a slightly modified Part IV was recommended by the Working Group, five members have now endorsed a minority report stating that Part IV should be removed from the Guidelines. Drs. Adelberg and Zinder also signed a second minority report recommending complete elimination of the Guidelines. Dr. Zinder said that he and the scientists concerned about recombinant DNA originally proposed guidelines which would give guidance and not be enforced, rather than rules. He cited some of the history leading to the issuance of mandatory guidelines in 1976. Dr. Zinder said that if Part IV is retained in the revised Guidelines, there should be a strong justification for retaining it stated in a position paper. He said that he prefers that the Guidelines be rescinded and replaced with a simple recommendation. He said that if scientists are to be encouraged to speak up in the future about conjectural risks, they must be shown that when interim regulation is subsequently shown to be superfluous, it can be removed.

Dr. Baltimore said the Baltimore-Campbell proposal was a compromise between scientific judgment that there is no justification for Guidelines being other than a code of accepted practice, and the necessity for considering political and social factors. Their proposal retained the prohibitions, which he said are one of the most noted parts of the Guidelines. It has been argued that the RAC should not consider political and social factors; however, Dr. Baltimore did not agree. He said that the prohibitions have less and less justification and that he finds no difficulty in accepting the Working Group's recommendation regarding elimination of prohibited experiments, except for elimination of the prohibition against acquisition of a drug resistance trait in those cases in which such acquisition could compromise the use of a drug to control disease agents in human or veterinary medicine or agriculture. Concerned scientists originally proposed guidelines meaning only guidance and not regulations; the RAC will have to decide the future course of the Guidelines. He noted that there apparently already is general agreement in the RAC on modifying Part III dealing with containment levels and agreement on retaining the exemptions. The issue is Part IV of the Guidelines. He said that he feels that it is anomalous to retain the current procedures section of the Guidelines. However, political and social issues need to be considered. If the Federal government pulled completely out of the issue, local governments might well overreact. The Federal government needs to provide surveillance, a forum for considering questions, and an office where inquiries can be authoritatively answered. Therefore, maintenance of the RAC, ORDA, and abbreviated guidelines are necessary Dr. Baltimore expressed support for the original Baltimore-Campbell proposal, with some modifications based on the Working Group recommendations. Dr. Zinder said that if Guidelines are to be retained, it is for political and social reasons. However, the political climate has changed. In New York State, which previously passed a law regulating recombinant DNA research, a bill has been introduced to repeal the law based on the assertion that the medical institutions which perform such research in New York State have proven to be trustworthy.

Dr. Nightingale said that she agrees with most of what Dr. Baltimore said. In order to implement sound public policy there are three basic ingredients: knowledge base, commitment of leadership, and appropriate social strategy. She said that in this case there is much agreement on the knowledge base and that there is need for change and the direction of that change. There is more disagreement on the appropriate social strategy. Having Federal involvement is one method of tempering local extremism.

Ms. King noted that the Baltimore-Campbell proposal would put industry and academia on an equal footing. She said that the RAC should consider a special meeting and public hearing on the proposed changes.

Dr. Gottesman noted that the current Guidelines are flexible and that the vast majority of experiments done today are exempt. She feels that there are scientific reasons for having a group other than the principal investigator look at the experiments still covered by the Guidelines; they should be reviewed by IBCs. She said that the critical issues in Part IV of the Guidelines are IBC prereview and compliance. She said that the Working Group's proposal does not involve an immense administrative burden.

Dr. Goldstein said that he also shares concerns about the scientific issues. He noted the number of new companies becoming involved in recombinant DNA research.

Dr. Brill stated that at a recent public meeting regarding a genetic engineering company in Madison, Wisconsin, no concerns were expressed about use of recombinant DNA technology.

Dr. McKinney said that the handling of the prohibitions is an important issue. They could perhaps be changed to cautionary advisories. He also said that citation of CDC and USDA guidelines needs to be considered. He preferred that NIH retain some form of guidance over recombinant DNA research.

With regard to the proposed revision of the CDC guidelines, Dr. Berns said that he expects great improvement in the document in the near future. He had discussed proposed revisions of the NIH Guidelines at a recent Gordon conference; most scientists there did not favor complete abolition of the Guidelines and favored instead something like the Baltimore-Campbell proposal. He also cited his local Congressman's concern about the potential for increasing public concern about recombinant DNA technology. It is important in the Guidelines revision that public confidence be maintained.

Dr. Zinder said that the public trusts academic researchers, but not industry.

Dr. Gottesman stressed that under the Working Group's proposal, the IBC would make the decision on containment using the CDC document only as guidance. Dr. Goldstein said that how the IBCs use and interpret the CDC guidelines should be made more explicit, so that there are uniform standards.

Dr. McGarrity said that he is comfortable in accepting voluntary guidelines. He felt that the Working Group's background report is excellent and that perhaps an abridged version could be published for educating the general public.

Dr. Holmes said that he supports retaining the current prohibition dealing with the introduction of drug resistance traits. He said that to make the Guidelines voluntary would be a mistake and could invite legislation.

Dr. Baltimore said that the concern raised in the Boston area is not a unique situation and that activities at the Federal level are still important. He said that since there are differences in the science done at different institutions it is not suprising, and not relevant to the present discussion, that different IBCs in California operate differently. Dr. Baltimore emphasized his view that IBC prereview is a serious obstruction of science, which results in scientific momentum being lost.

Dr. McKinney pointed out that the NIH could still choose to mandate guidelines even if the RAC recommends otherwise. He suggested that reference to CDC and USDA guidelines not be incorporated into the body of the text of the revised guidelines; rather they could be cited as references.

Ms. King suggested that the RAC should structure the issues on which it wants public comment, such as treatment of prohibitions and the voluntary vs. mandatory nature of the guidelines. Dr. Talbot pointed out that the RAC could follow Ms. King's suggestion and present issues for public comment. The alternative would be for the RAC to accept the Working Group proposal, the Baltimore-Campbell proposal, or an amalgam of the two. Following the meeting, NIH staff could then develop a new version of the Guidelines based on the RAC proposal and put this out for public comment.

Dr. Harris then moved to accept the report of the Working Group so that discussion could proceed to consider the report section by section. Dr. Mason seconded the motion. There followed discussion of the effect of such a motion.

Dr. Ahmed praised the report of the Working Group. He favored publication for public comment of a series of different options. Dr. Mason expressed concern about eliminating all of the prohibitions. Dr. Saginor suggested that the RAC might first consider the Adelberg-Zinder minority proposal to abolish the Guidelines. Dr. McKinney said that he considered the Working Group's recommendations as too cursory. Dr. Gottesman responded that the Working Group had considered the issues in-depth at two meetings and had prepared a report on its evalution of the risks associated with recombinant DNA research. The RAC could change or elaborate on the recommendations before seeking public comment. Dr. Zinder said that the recommendations of the Working Group were adopted unanimously except for those concerning Part IV of the Guidelines.

Dr. Baltimore, in the interests of providing a forum for RAC discussion of the points of difference between the various proposals, moved a seven part motion as a substitute for Dr. Harris' motion:

1. Accept the first section of the Baltimore-Campbell proposal, as follows:

"Section I-A of the NIH Guidelines will be replaced with the following:

'I-A. *Purpose.* The purpose of these Guidelines is to specify standard practices for constructing and handling (i) recombinant DNA molecules and (ii) organisms and viruses containing recombinant DNA molecules. Adherence to these standards by all laboratories using recombinant DNA is recommended.' "

2. Accept the second section of the Baltimore-Campbell proposal, as follows:

"Part I-C of the NIH Guidelines shall be eliminated."

3. Accept the second section of the Working Group proposal, as follows:

"Section I-D of the Guidelines, *Prohibitions*, would be eliminated."

4. Accept the third section of the Working Group report modified by removing references to CDC Guidelines and USDA Regulations and treating these references in a footnote, as follows:

"Part III of the Guidelines would be replaced with the following language:

'Part III discusses experiments covered by the Guidelines. The reader should first consult Part I, where exempt experiments are listed.

'Where recommended physical containment levels applicable to non-recombinant DNA experiments exist for either the host or the vector,* recombinant DNA experiments should be carried out at

*Such as those specified by CDC Guidelines or the USDA Quarantine Regulations.

containment levels at least as high as those recommended for non-recombinant DNA experiments. If there is clear evidence that the donor DNA will significantly change the pathogenicity of the host, the containment level appropriate to the anticipated change will be applied. Otherwise, all experiments may be carried out under conditions of P1 or P1-LS physical containment.'"

5. The following admonition would be added:

"No experiments should be performed which involve deliberate transfer of a drug resistance trait to microorganisms that are not known to acquire it naturally, if such acquisition could compromise the use of a drug to control disease agents in human or veterinary medicine or agriculture."

6. Accept the fourth section of the Baltimore-Campbell proposal, as follows:

"Part IV of the NIH Guidelines shall be eliminated, with the following exceptions:

"(a) Those definitions listed in Part IV-C which may be needed to clarify statements made elsewhere in the Guidelines shall be retained.

"(b) Those portions of Part IV-E defining the composition of RAC and prescribing rules for RAC procedures shall be retained.

"(c) The following statement shall be added:

"Each institution conducting or sponsoring recombinant DNA research should take responsbility for monitoring its own activities in this area. Any unusual events that might be associated with the use of recombinant DNA molecules should be reported to the Director, NIH."

7. Accept the fifth section of the Baltimore-Campbell proposal with deletion of the words "submitted in support of requests for exceptions from the prohibitions," as follows:

"Section VI of the Guidelines will be eliminated, except for those portions of Section VI-F relevant to the protection of proprietary information."

Dr. Berns seconded the motion.

Dr. Saginor suggested an amendment to Dr. Harris' motion in the form of a policy statement that there is a continuing need for the RAC and applicable recombinant DNA guidelines. The purpose of the amendment was to indicate that the Adelberg-Zinder proposal is not being accepted. Dr. Harris agreed to the amendment.

Ms. King said she wanted the RAC to vote on replacing parts 1 and 6 of the Baltimore motion with wording from the Working Group proposal. It was suggested that votes be on one part at a time. Ms. King then moved to replace the first part of Dr. Baltimore's motion with the first section of the Working Group's proposal as follows:

"Section I-A of the Guidelines would be amended to read as follows:

"I-A. *Purpose.* The purpose of these Guidelines is to specify standard practices for constructing and handling (i) recombinant DNA molecules and (ii) organisms and viruses containing recombinant DNA molecules."

The motion was seconded by Dr. Goldstein. Ms. King stated that she favors retention of limited Guidelines that require IBC review, and she favors an oversight function for the RAC; she does not support self-regulation. Dr. Baltimore did not accept Ms. King's proposed amedment. Dr. Berns pointed out that the substitution Ms. King was proposing did not make much difference. The real point of contention in the RAC concerned part six of Dr. Baltimore's motion.

Ms. King withdrew her previous motion and then moved to delete part six of Dr. Baltimore's motion. If her motion were accepted, this would leave intact Part IV of the Guidelines. It was pointed out that the Working Group had proposed a change in Part IV dealing with IBC membership. Ms. King said that if her motion passed, then another perfecting motion could be introduced dealing with IBC membership. Dr. Harris seconded. The motion failed to carry by a vote of nine in favor, twelve opposed, with no abstentions.

Dr. Fedoroff noted that the motion as it stands would eliminate all prohibitions including the prohibition against deliberate release into the environment. Dr. Baltimore suggested that if the RAC wished, a statement regarding deliberate release could be included with the admonition on drug resistance. Dr. Berns said that in his view the recommendation that experiments be conducted under P1 containment precludes deliberate release into the environment.

Dr. Maas then moved to add the current prohibition on the cloning of certain toxins to the admonition on drug resistance. Dr. Goldstein seconded. Dr. Gottesman said that the cloning of toxins is an example of an area of concern. She noted that the RAC Working Group on Toxins recommended at the last RAC meeting prohibition of cloning of certain toxin genes and that other experiments involving cloning of toxin genes should proceed only in *E. coli* K-12 in the absence of special review by ORDA. Dr. Baltimore agreed to accept addition of the wording regarding toxins currently in Section I-D-2 to the admonition on drug resistance and to retain Appendix G of the current Guidelines.

Dr. Ahmed moved that a working group be appointed to study the prohibitions and report back to the RAC. Dr. Goldstein seconded the motion. Dr. Mason disagreed, noting that at the last meeting a working group had been appointed to report on revision of the Guidelines. They had reported, and now the RAC was working through the proposal to prepare material for public comment. The motion failed to carry by a vote of three in favor, fourteen opposed, with three abstentions.

Mr. Thornton recognized Dr. Susan Wright. She said the RAC was short-circuiting long and detailed discussions it should have on all the critical issues. She asked RAC members to acknowledge ties that they might have with genetic engineering companies. She said there should be discussion of why the working group had decided to eliminate public members on IBCs. She expressed concern about the currently prohibited experiments and large-scale experiments. She cited a report she had submitted, prepared for the Commission of the European Communities, entitled "Hazards Involved in the Industrial Use of Micro-organisms." She said that change of phenotype due to mutation and discharge of waste into the environment are important issues among many others that need to be considered before a decision is reached.

Dr. Fedoroff said that there should be flexibility to have a group look at and approve specific experiments which are otherwise admonished against. Dr. Baltimore said investigators wishing to do such experiments could come to the local IBC or the RAC to discuss conditions under which such experiments could be done.

Dr. Berns said that at a meeting of the Large Scale Review Working Group on September 9, 1981, none of the members thought that the large-scale prohibition should be retained.

Mr. Thornton recognized Ms. Claire Nader who said that the RAC should look at the assumptions behind the recommendations such as that all corporations will do the right thing, and that the technology is safe. She said that there were no experts on corporate behavior, or law enforcement, or anti-trust questions on the RAC. She said the RAC should have on it people who want to talk about risks. She criticized the way in which the RAC was proceeding.

Dr. Nightingale said that a working group on the prohibitions was appointed over a year ago and that the prohibitions have been discussed extensively before this meeting. Dr. Gottesman said that it was peculiar to be concerned about the prohibitions and at the same time recommending that the entire system become voluntary. She said that perhaps there could be a recommendation that these experiments be reviewed by the RAC.

Mr. Daloz moved that a vote be taken on Dr. Baltimore's motion, as amended. The motion to end discussion and vote failed to carry by a vote of four in favor, fourteen opposed, with three abstentions.

Dr. Ahmed said he wanted detailed procedures built into the revised Guidelines for handling the currently prohibited experiments. Dr. Baltimore said that the absence of detailed procedures pertains in the case of all nonrecombinant DNA laboratory work including that with known pathogens.

Mr. Thornton asked for a show of hands of RAC members who wished to continue discussion of this agenda item for an additional thirty minutes until approximately 3:30 p.m. The vote was eighteen in favor, one opposed.

Dr. Mason said that the RAC and the Guidelines cannot deal with scientists or industrial groups who are uninformed, dishonest, or careless. We have tried to produce guidelines that reponsible people will follow. There is no way to provide for every contingency.

Dr. Holmes moved to add current prohibition I-D-4 ("deliberate release into the environment of any organism containing recombinant DNA.") to the admonitions regarding cloning of toxins and transfer of drug resistance traits. Dr. Landy supported inclusion of I-D-4; Dr. Berns did not support it. The motion failed to carry by a vote of eight in favor, ten opposed, with two absentions.

Dr. Baltimore's amended motion was reviewed. Dr. Talbot said that if the proposal passed, the NIH staff would prepare a version of proposed revised Guidelines based on the proposal, and that it would be put in the **Federal Register** for public comment, along with background describing the work of the working group and the deliberations of the RAC. NIH would actively solicit comment on the proposal beyond its publication in the **Federal Register**.

The question was called and the vote to substitute Dr. Baltimore's motion, as amended, for Dr. Harris' motion was fifteen in favor, three opposed, with two abstentions. Dr. Ahmed asked to be recorded as voting against the motion. The motion was as follows:

"1· Section I-A of the Guidelines would be amended to read as follows:

"I-A. Purpose. The purpose of these Guidelines is to specify standard practices for constructing and handling (i) recombinant DNA molecules and (ii) organisms and viruses containing recombinant DNA molecules. Adherence to these standards by all laboratories using recombinant DNA is recommended.

"2. Section I-C of the Guidelines would be eliminated.

"3· Section I-D of the Guidelines. *Prohibitions*, would be eliminated.

"4· Part III of the Guidelines would be replaced with the following language:

"Part III discusses experiments covered by the Guidelines. The reader should first consult Part I, where exempt experiments are listed.

"Where recommended physical containment levels applicable to non-recombinant DNA experiments exist for either the host or the vector*, recombinant DNA experiments should be carried out at containment levels at least as high as those recommended for non-recombinant DNA experiments. If there is clear evidence that the donor DNA will significantly change the pathogenicity of the host, the containment level appropriate to the anticipated change will be applied. Otherwise, all experiments may be carried out under conditions of PI or PI-LS physical containment.

"5· Material would be added to Part III, as follows:

"No experiments should be performed which involve:

"(a) Deliberate transfer of a drug resistance trait to micro-organisms that are not known to acquire it naturally, if such acquisition could compromise the use of a drug to control disease agents in human or veterinary medicine or agriculture.

"(b) Deliberate formation of recombinant DNAs containing genes for the biosynthesis of toxins lethal for vertebrates at an LD_{50} of less than 100 nanograms per kilogram body weight (e.g., the botulinum toxins, tetanus toxin, diphtheria toxin, *Shigella dysenteriae* neurotoxin). Guidelines for the cloning of DNAs containing genes coding for the biosynthesis of toxins which are lethal to vertebrates at 100 nanograms to 100 micrograms per kilogram body weight are specified in Appendix G.

"6. Part IV of the Guidelines would be eliminated with the following exceptions:

"(a) Those definitions listed in Part IV-C which may be needed to clarify statements made elsewhere in the Guidelines shall be retained.

"(b) Those portions of Part IV-E defining the composition of RAC and prescribing rules for RAC procedures shall be retained.

"(c) The following statement shall be added:

"Each institution conducting or sponsoring recombinant DNA research should take responsibility for monitoring its own activities in this area. Any unusual events that might be associated with the use of recombinant DNA molecules should be reported to the Director, NIH.

"7· Section VI of the Guidelines will be eliminated, except for those portions of Section VI-F relevant to the protection of proprietary information."

The vote on this substitute motion was called, and the vote was sixteen in favor, three opposed, with one abstention.

* Such as those specified by the CDC Guidelines or the USDA Quarantine Regulations.

Dr. Zinder requested that a motion be introduced in support of the Adelberg-Zinder proposal to eliminate the Guidelines and the RAC. No motion was introduced.

Annex E

Current Guidelines for Research Involving Recombinant DNA Molecules

October 1981.

These Guidelines are the Guidelines as published in the **Federal Register** of July 1, 1981 (46 FR 34462), with the incorporation of those changes promulgated in the **Federal Register** of October 30, 1981, Part V.

Table of Contents

I. Scope of the Guidelines

I-A. *Purpose.* The purpose of these Guidelines is to specify practices for constructing and handling (i) recombinant DNA molecules and (ii) organisms and viruses containing recombinant DNA molecules.

I-B. *Definition of Recombinant DNA Molecules.* In the context of these Guidelines, recombinant DNA molecules are defined as either (i) molecules which are constructed outside living cells by joining natural or synthetic DNA segments to DNA molecules that can replicate in a living cell, or (ii) DNA molecules that result from the replication of those described in (i) above.

I-C. *General Applicability.* See Section IV-B.

I-D. *Prohibitions.* The following experiments are not to be initiated at the present time:

I-D-1. Formation of recombinant DNAs derived from the pathogenic organisms classifed [1] as Class 4 or 5 [2] or from cells known [2A] to be infected with such agents, regardless of the host-vector system used.

I-D-2. Deliberate formation of recombinant DNAs containing genes for the biosynthesis of toxins lethal for vertebrates at an LD_{50} of less than 100 nanograms per kilogram body weight (e.g., the botulinum toxins, tetanus toxin, diphtheria toxin, *Shigella dysenteriae* neurotoxin). Guidelines for the cloning of DNAs containing genes coding for the biosynthesis of toxins which are lethal to vertebrates at 100 nanograms to 100 micrograms per kilogram body weight are specified in Appendix G, which overerides other parts of the Guidelines (e.g., exemptions, return to host of origin, etc.).

I-D-3. [Deleted].

I-D-4. Deliberate release into the environment of any organism containing recombinant DNA

I-D-5. Deliberate transfer of a drug resistance trait to microorganisms that are not known to acquire it naturally, if such acquisition could compromise the use of a drug to control disease agents in human or veterinary medicine or agriculture. [2A]

I-D-6. Large-scale experiments (e.g., more than 10 liters of culture) with organisms containing recombinant DNAs other than those listed in Appendix C, Section 2, 3, and 4 of the Guidelines, unless the recombinant DNAs are rigorously characterized and the absen^e of harmful sequences established [3]. (See Section IV-E-1-b-(3)-(d).)

I-D (1-6). Experiments in Categories I-D-1 to I-D-6 may be excepted [4] from the prohibitions (and will at that time be assigned appropriate levels of physical and biological containment) provide that these experiments are expressly approved by the Director, National Institutes of Health (NIH), with advice of the Recombinant DNA Advisory Committee (RAC), after appropriate notice and opportunity for public comment. (See Section IV-E-1-b-(1)-(e).)

Experiments in Categories I-D-1, I-D-2, I-D-5, and experiments involving "wild type" host-vector systems are excepted from the prohibitions, provided that these experiments are designed for risk-assessment purposes and are conducted within the NIH high-containment facilities located in Building 41-T on the Bethesda campus and in Building 550 located at the Frederick Cancer Research Center. The selection of laboratory practices and containment equipment for such experiments shall be approved by the Office of Recombinant DNA Activities (ORDA) following consultation with the RAC Risk Assessment Subcommittee and the NIH Biosafety Committee. ORDA shall inform RAC members of the proposed risk-assessment projects at the same time it seks consultation from the RAC Risk Assessment Subcommittee and the NIH Biosafety Committee. If a major biohazard is determined, the clones will be destroyed after the completion of the experiment rather than retaining them in the high containment facility. Other clones that are non-hazardous or not of major hazard will be retained in the high containment.

I-E. *Exemptions.* It must be emphasized that the following exemptions [4] are not meant to apply to experiments described in the Sections I-D-1 to I-D-5 as being prohibited. In addition, any recombinant DNA molecules involving DNA from Class 3 organisms [1] or cells known to be infected with these agents, or any recombinant DNA molecules which increase the virulence and host-range of a plant pathogen beyond that which occurs by natural genetic exchange, are not exempt unless specifically so designated by NIH under Section I-E-5. Also, Appendix G overrides the exemptions for specified experiments involving genes coding for toxins.

The following recombinant DNA molecules are exempt from these Guidelines, and no registration with NIH is necessary:

I-E-1. Those that are not in organisms or viruses. [5]

I-E-2. Those that consist entirely of DNA segments from a single nonchromosomal or viral DNA source, though one or more of the segments may be a synthetic equivalent.

I-E-3. Those that consist entirely of DNA from a prokaryotic host, including its indigenous plasmids or viruses, when propagated only in that host (or a closely related strain of the same species) or when transferred to another host by well established physiological means; also those that consist entirely of DNA from a eukaryotic host, including its chloroplasts, mitochondria, or plasmids (but excluding viruses), when propagated only in that host (or a closely related strain of the same species).

I-E-4. Certain specified recombinant DNA molecules that consist entirely of DNA segments from different species that exchange DNA by known physiological processes, though one or more of the segments may be a synthetic equivalent. A list of such exchanges will be prepared and periodically revised by the Director, NIH, with advice of the RAC, after appropriate notice and opportunity for public comment. (See Section IV-E-1-b-(1)-(d).) Certain classes are exempt as of publication of these Revised Guidelines. The list is in Appendix A. An updated list may be obtained from the Office of Recombinant DNA Activities, National Institutes of Health, Bethesda, Maryland 20205.

I-E-5. Other classes of recombinant DNA molecules, if the Director, NIH, with advice of the RAC, after appropriate notice and opportunity for public comment, finds that they do not present a significant risk to health or the environment. (See Section IV-E-1-b-(1)-(d).) Certain classes are exempt as of publication of these Revised Guidelines. The list is in Appendix C. An updated list may be obtained from the Office of Recombinant DNA Activities, National Institutes of Health, Bethesda, Maryland, 20205.

I-F. *General Definitions.* See Section IV-C.

II. Containment

Effective biological safety programs have been operative in a variety of laboratories for many years. Considerable information, therefore, already exists for the design of physical containment facilities and the selection of laboratory procedures applicable to organisms carrying recombinant DNAs. [6-19] The existing programs rely upon mechanisms that, for convenience, can be divided into two categories: (i) A set of standard practices that are generally used in microbiological laboratories, and (ii) special procedures, equipment, and laboratory installations that provide physical barriers which are applied in varying degrees according to the estimated biohazard.

Experiments on recombinant DNAs, by their very nature, lend themselves to a third containment mechanism—namely, the application of highly specific biological barriers. In fact, natural barriers do exist which limit either (i) the infectivity of a *vector,* or *vehicle,* (plasmid or virus) for specific hosts or (ii) its dissemination and survival in the environment. The vectors that provide the means for replication of the recombinant DNAs and/or the host cells in which they replicate can be genetically designed to decrease by many orders of magnitude the probability of dissemination of recombinant DNAs outside the laboratory.

As these three means of containment are complementary, different levels of containment appropriate for experiments with different recombinants can be established by applying various combinations of the physical and biological barriers along with a constant use of the standard practices. We consider these categories of containment separately here in order that such combinations can be conveniently expressed in the Guidelines.

In constructing these Guidelines, it was necessary to define boundary conditions for the different levels of physical and biological containment and for the classes of experiments to which they apply. We recognize that these definitions do not take into account all existing and anticipated information on special procedures that will allow particular experiments to be carried out under different conditions that indicated here without affecting risk. Indeed, we urge that individual investigators device simple and more effective containment procedures and that investigators and institutional biosafety committees recommend changes in the Guidelines to permit their use.

II-A. *Standard Practices and Training.* The first principle of containment is a strict adherence to good microbiological practices. [6-15] Consequently, all personnel directly or indirectly involved in experiments on recombinant DNAs must receive adequate instruction. (see Sections IV-D-1-g, IV-D-5-d and IV-D-8-b.). This shall, as a minimum, include instructions in aseptic techniques and in the biology of the organisms used in the experiments, so that the potential biohazards can be understood and appreciated.

Any research group working with agents with a known or potential biohazard shall have an emergency plan which describes the procedures to be followed if an accident contaminates personnel or the environment. The principal investigator must ensure that everyone in the laboratory is familiar with both the potential hazards of the work and the emergency plan. (See Sections IV-D-5-e and IV-D-3-d.) If a research group is working with a known pathogen where there is an effective vaccine it should be made available to all workers. Where serological monitoring is clearly appropriate it shall be provided. (See Sections IV-D-1-h and IV-D-8-c.)

II-B. *Physical Containment Levels.* The objective of physical containment is to confine organisms containing recombinant DNA molecules, and thus to reduce the potential for exposure of the laboratory worker, persons outside of the laboratory, and the environment to organisms containing recombinant DNA molecules. Physical containment is achieved through the use of laboratory practices, containment equipment, and special laboratory design. Emphasis is placed on primary means of physical containment which are provided by laboratory practices and containment equipment. Special laboratory design provides a secondary means of protection against the accidental release of organisms outside the laboratory or to the environment. Special laboratory design is used primarily in facilities in which experiments of moderate to high potential hazards are performed.

Combinations of laboratory practices, containment equipment, and special laboratory design can be made to achieve different levels of physical containment. Four levels of physical containment, which are designated as P1, P2, P3, and P4, are described. It should be emphasized that the descriptions and assignments of physical containment detailed below are based on existing approaches to containment of pathogenic organisms. For example, the "Classification of Etiologic Agents on the Basis of Hazard,"[7] prepared by the Centers for Disease Control, describes four general levels which roughly correspond to our descriptions for P1, P2, P3, and P4; and the National Cancer Institute describes three levels for research on oncogenic viruses which roughly correspond to our P2, P3, and P4 levels.[8]

It is recognized that several different combinations of laboratory practices, containment equipment, and special laboratory design may be appropriate for containment of specific research activities. The Guidelines, therefore, allow alternative selections of primary containment equipment within facilities that have been designed to provide P3 and P4 levels of physical containment. The selection of alternative methods of primary containment is dependent, however, on the level of biological containment provided by the host-vector system used in the experiment. Consideration will also be given by the Director, NIH, with the advice of the Recombinant DNA Advisory Committee to other combinations which achieve an equivalent level of containment. (See Section IV–E–1–b–(2)–(b).) Additional material on physical containment for plant host-vector systems is found in Sections III–C–3 and III–C–4.

II–B–1. *P1 Level.*

II–B–1–a. *Laboratory Practices.*

II–B–1–a. Laboratory doors shall be kept closed while experiments are in progress.

II–B–1–a–(2). Work surfaces shall be decontaminated daily, and immediately following spills of organisms containing recombinant DNA molecules.

II–B–1–a–(3). All biological wastes shall be decontaminated before disposal. Other contaminated materials, such as glassware, animal cages, and laboratory equipment, shall be decontaminated before washing, reuse, or disposal.

II–B–1–a–(4). Mechanical pipetting devices shall be used; pipetting by mouth is prohibited.

II–B–1–a–(5). Eating, drinking, smoking, and storage of foods are not permitted in the laboratory area in which recombinant DNA materials are handled.

II–B–1–a–(6). Persons shall wash their hands after handling organisms containing recombinant DNA molecules and when they leave the laboratory.

II–B–1–a–(7). Care shall be taken in the conduct of all procedures to minimize the creation of aerosols.

II–B–1–a–(8). Contaminated materials that are to be decontaminated at a site away from the laboratory shall be placed in a durable leak-proof container, which is closed before removal from the laboratory.

II–B–1–a–(9). An insect and rodent control program shall be instituted.

II–B–1–a–(10). The use of laboratory gowns, coats, or uniforms is discretionary with the laboratory supervisor.

II–B–1–a–(11). Use of the hypodermic needle and syringe shall be avoided when alternative methods are available.

II–B–1–a–(12). The laboratory shall be kept neat and clean.

II–B–1–b. *Containment Equipment.* Special containment equipment is not required at the P1 level.

II–B–1–c. *Special Laboratory Design.* Special laboratory design is not required at the P1 level.

II–B–2. *P2 Level.*

II–B–2–a. *Laboratory Practices.*

II–B–2–a–(1). Laboratory doors shall be kept closed while experiments are in progress.

II-B-2-a-(2). Work surfaces shall be decontaminated daily, and immediately following spills of organisms containing recombinant DNA molecules.

II-B-2-a-(3). All laboratory wastes shall be steam-sterilized (autoclaved) before disposal. Other contaminated materials such as glassware, animal cages, laboratory equipment, and radioactive wastes shall be decontaminated by a means demonstrated to be effective before washing, reuse, or disposal.

II-B-2-a-(4). Mechanical pipetting devices shall be used; pipetting by mouth is prohibited.

II-B-2-a-(5). Eating, drinking, smoking, and storage of food are not permitted in the laboratory area in which recombinant DNA materials are handled.

II-B-2-a-(6). Persons shall wash their hands after handling organisms containing recombinant DNA molecules and when they leave the laboratory.

II-B-2-a-(7). Care shall be exercised to minimize the creation of aerosols. For example, manipulations such as inserting a hot inoculating loop or needle into a culture, flaming an inoculation loop or needle so that it splatters, and forceful ejection of fluids from pipettes or syringes shall be avoided.

II-B-2-a-(8). Contaminated materials that are to be steam sterilized (autoclaved) or decontaminated at a site away from the laboratory shall be placed in a durable leak-proof container, which is closed before removal from the laboratory.

II-B-2-a-(9). Only persons who have been advised of the nature of the research being conducted shall enter the laboratory.

II-B-2-a-(10). The universal biohazard sign shall be posted on all laboratory access doors when experiments requiring P2 containment are in progress. Freezers and refrigerators or other units used to store organisms containing recombinant DNA molecules shall also be posted with the universal biohazard sign.

II-B-2-a-(11). An insect and rodent control program shall be instituted.

II-B-2-a-(12). The use of laboratory gowns, coats, or uniforms is required. Laboratory clothing shall not be worn to the lunch room or outside of the building in which the laboratory is located.

II-B-2-a-(13). Animals not related to the experiment shall not be permitted in the laboratory.

II-B-2-a-(14). Use of the hypodermic needle and syringe shall be avoided when alternative methods are available.

II-B-2-a-(15). The laboratory shall be kept neat and clean.

II-B-2-a-(16). Experiments of lesser biohazard potential can be carried out concurrently in carefully demarcated areas of the same laboratory.

II-B-2-b. *Containment Equipment.* Biological safety cabinets[20] shall be used to contain aerosol-producing equipment, such as blenders, lyophilizers, sonicators, and centrifuges, when used to process organisms containing recombinant DNA molecules, except where equipment design provides for containment of the potential aerosol. For example, a centrifuge may be operated in the open if a sealed head or safety centrifuge cups are used.

II-B-2-c. *Special Laboratory Design.* An autoclave for sterilization of wastes and contaminated materials shall be available in the same building in which organisms containing recombinant DNA molecules are used.

II-B-3. *P3 Level.*

II-B-3-a. *Laboratory Practices.*

II-B-3-a-(1). Laboratory doors shall be kept closed while experiments are in progress.

II-B-3-a-(2). Work surfaces shall be decontaminated following the completion of the experimental activity, and immediately following spills of organisms containing recombinant DNA molecules.

II-B-3-a-(3). All laboratory wastes shall be steam-sterilized (autoclaved) before disposal. Other contaminated materials, such as glassware, animal cages, laboratory equipment, and radioactive wastes, shall be decontaminated by a method demonstrated to be effective before washing, reuse, or disposal.

II-B-3-a-(4). Mechanical pipetting devices shall be used; pipetting by mouth is prohibited.

II-B-3-a-(5). Eating, drinking, smoking, and storage of food are not permitted in the laboratory area in which recombinant DNA materials are handled.

II-B-3-a-(6). Persons shall wash their hands after handling organisms containing recombinant DNA molecules and when they leave the laboratory.

II-B-3-a-(7). Care shall be exercised to minimize the creation of aerosols. For example, manipulations such as inserting a hot inoculating loop or needle into a culture, flaming an inoculation loop or needle so that it splatters, and forceful ejection of fluids from pipettes or syringes shall be avoided.

II-B-3-a-(8). Contaminated materials that are to be steam-sterilized (autoclaved) or decontaminated at a site away from the laboratory shall be placed in a durable leak-proof container, which is closed before removal from the laboratory.

II-B-3-a-(9). Entry into the laboratory shall be through a controlled access area. Only persons who have been advised of the nature of the research being conducted shall enter the controlled access area. Only persons required on the basis of program or support needs shall be authorized to enter the laboratory. Such persons shall be advised of the nature of the research being conducted before entry, and shall comply with all required entry and exit procedures.

II-B-3-a-(10). Persons under 16 years of age shall not enter the laboratory.

II-B-3-a-(11). The universal biohazard sign shall be posted on the controlled access area door and on all laboratory doors when experiments requiring P3-level containment are in progress. Freezers and refrigerators or other units used to store organisms containing recombinant DNA molecules shall also be posted with the universal biohazard sign.

II-B-3-a-(12). An insect and rodent control program shall be instituted.

II-B-3-a-(13). Laboratory clothing that protects street clothing (e.g., long-sleeve solid-front or wrap-around gowns, no-button or slipover jackets) shall be worn in the laboratory. Front-button laboratory coats are unsuitable. Laboratory clothing shall not be worn outside the laboratory and shall be decontaminated before it is sent to the laundry.

II-B-3-a-(14). Raincoats, overcoats, topcoats, coats, hats, caps, and such street outer-wear shall not be kept in the laboratory.

II-B-3-a-(15). Gloves shall be worn when handling materials requiring P3 containment. They shall be removed aseptically immediately after the handling procedure and decontaminated.

II-B-3-a-(16). Animals and plants not related to the experiment shall not be permitted in the laboratory.

II-B-3-a-(17). Vacuum outlets shall be protected by filter and liquid disinfectant traps.

II-B-3-a-(18). Use of hypodermic needle and syringe shall be avoided when alternative methods are available.

II-B-3-a-(19). The laboratory shall be kept neat and clean.

II-B-3-a-(20). If experiments involving other organisms which require lower levels of containment are to be conducted in the same laboratory concurrently with experiments requiring P3-level physical containment, they shall be conducted in accordance with all P3-level laboratory practices.

II-B-3-b. *Containment Equipment.*

II-B-3-b-(1). Biological safety cabinets [20] shall be used for all equipment and manipulations that produce aerosols—e.g., pipetting, dilutions, transfer operations, plating, flaming, grinding, blending, drying, sonicating, shaking, centrifuging—where these procedures involve organisms containing recombinant DNA molecules, except where equipment design provides for containment of the potential aerosol.

II-B-3-b-(2). Laboratory animals held in a P3 area shall be housed in partial-containment caging systems, such as Horsfall units [19A], open cages placed in ventilated enclosures, solid-wall and -bottom cases covered by filter bonnets, or solid-wall and -bottom cages placed on holding racks equipped with ultraviolet radiation lamps and reflectors.

Note.—Conventional caging systems may be used: *Provided,* That all personnel wear appropriate personal protective devices. These shall include, at a minimum, wrap-around gowns, head covers, gloves, shoe covers, and respirators. All personnel shall shower on exit from areas where these devices are required.

II-B-3-b-(3). *Alternative Selection of Containment Equipment.* Experimental procedures involving a host-vector system that provides a one-step higher level of biological containment than that specified in Part III can be conducted in the P3 laboratory using containment equipment specified for the P2 level of physical containment. Experimental procedures involving a host-vector system that provides a one-step lower level of biological containment than that specified in Part III can be conducted in the P3 laboratory using containment equipment specified for the P4 level of physical containment. Alternative combinations of containment safeguards are shown in Table I.

TABLE I.—COMBINATIONS OF CONTAINMENT SAFEGUARDS

Classification of experiment according to guidelines		Alternate combinations of physical and biological containment			
		Physical containment			
Physicial containment	Biological[1] containment	Laboratory design specified for—	Laboratory practices specified for—	Containment equipment specified for—	Biological containment
P3	HV3	P3	P3	P3	HV3.
P3	HV3	P3	P3	P4	HV2.
P3	HV2	P3	P3	P3	HV2.
P3	HV2	P3	P3	P2	HV3.
P3	HV2	P3	P3	P4	HV1.
P3	HV1	P3	P3	P3	HV1.
P3	HV1	P3	P3	P2	HV2.

[1] See Section II-D for description of biological containment.

II-B-3-c. *Special Laboratory Design.*

II-B-3-c-(1). The laboratory shall be separated by a controlled access area from areas that are open to unrestricted traffic flow. A controlled access area is an anteroom, a change room, an air lock or any other double-door arrangement that separates the laboratory from areas open to unrestricted traffic flow.

II-B-3-c-(2). The surfaces of walls, floors, and ceilings shall be readily cleanable. Penetrations through these surfaces shall be sealed or capable of being sealed to facilitate space decontamination.

II-B-3-c-(3). A foot-, elbow-, or automatically-operated hand-washing facility shall be provided near each primary laboratory exit area.

II-B-3-c-(4). Windows in the laboratory shall be sealed.

II-B-3-c-(5). An autoclave for sterilization of wastes and contaminated materials shall be available in the same building (and preferably within the controlled laboratory area) in which organisms containing recombinant DNA molecules are used.

II-B-3-c-(6). The laboratory shall have a ventilation system that is capable of controlling air movement. The movement of air shall be from areas of lower contamination potential to areas of higher contamination potential (i.e., from the controlled access area to the laboratory area). If the ventilation system provides positive pressure supply air, the system shall operate in a manner that prevents the reversal of the direction of air movement or shall be equipped with an alarm that would be actuated in the event that reversal in the direction of air movement were to occur. The exhaust air from the laboratory area shall not be recirculated to other areas of the building unless the exhaust air is filtered by HEPA filters or equivalent. The exhaust air from the laboratory area can be discharged to the outdoors without filtration or other means for effectively reducing an accidental aerosol burden provided that it can be dispersed clear of occupied buildings and air intakes.

II–B–3–c–(7). The treated exhaust-air from Class I and Class II biological safety cabinets [20] may be discharged either to the laboratory or to the outdoors. The treated exhaust-air from a Class III cabinet shall be discharged directly to the outdoors. If the treated exhaust-air from these cabinets is to be discharged to the outdoors through a building exhaust air system, it shall be connected to this system so as to avoid any interference with the air balance of the cabinet and the building ventilation system.

II–B–4. *P4 Level.*

II–B–4–a. *Laboratory Practices.*

II–B–4–a–(1). Laboratory doors shall be kept closed while experiments are in progress.

II–B–4–a–(2). Work surfaces shall be decontaminated following the completion of the experimental activity and immediately following spills of organisms containing recombinant DNA molecules.

II–B–4–a–(3). All laboratory wastes shall be steam-sterilized (autoclaved) before disposal. Other contaminated materials such as glassware, animal cages, laboratory equipment, and radioactive wastes shall be decontaminated by a method demonstrated to be effective before washing, reuse, or disposal.

II–B–4–a–(4). Mechanical pipetting devices shall be used; pipetting by mouth is prohibited.

II–B–4–a–(5). Eating, drinking, smoking, and storage of food are not permitted in the P4 facility.

II–B–4–a–(6). Persons shall wash their hands after handling organisms containing recombinant DNA molecules and when they leave the laboratory.

II–B–4–a–(7). Care shall be exercised to minimize the creation of aerosols. For example, manipulations such as inserting a hot inoculating loop or needle into a culture, flaming an inoculation loop or needle so that it splatters, and forceful ejection of fluids from pipettes or syringes shall be avoided.

II–B–4–a–(8). Biological materials to be removed from the P4 facility in a viable or intact state shall be transferred to a nonbreakable sealed container, which is then removed from the P4 facility through a pass-through disinfectant dunk tank or fumigation chamber.

II–B–4–a–(9). No materials, except for biological materials that are to remain in a viable or intact state, shall be removed from the P4 facility unless they have been steam-sterilized (autoclaved) or decontaminated by a means demonstrated to be effective as they pass out of the P4 facility. All wastes and other materials as well as equipment not damaged by high temperature or steam shall be steam sterilized in the double-door autoclave of the P4 facility. Other materials which may be damaged by temperature or steam shall be removed from the P4 facility through a pass-through fumigation chamber.

II–B–4–a–(10). Materials within the Class III cabinets shall be removed from the cabinet system only after being steam-sterilized in an attached double-door autoclave or after being contained in a nonbreakable sealed container, which is then passed through a disinfectant dunk tank or a fumigation chamber.

II–B–4–a–(11). Only persons whose entry into the P4 facility is required to meet program or support needs shall be authorized to enter. Before entering, such persons shall be advised of the nature of the research being conducted and shall be instructed as to the appropriate safeguards to ensure their safety. They shall comply with instructions and all other required procedures.

II–B–4–a–(12). Persons under 18 years of age shall not enter the P4 facility.

II–B–4–a–(13). Personnel shall enter into and exit from the P4 facility only through the clothing change and shower rooms. Personnel shall shower at each egress from the P4 facility. Air locks shall not be used for personnel entry or exit except for emergencies.

II–B–4–a–(14). Street clothing shall be removed in the outer side of the clothing-change area and kept there. Complete laboratory clothing, including undergarments, head cover, shoes, and either pants and shirts or jumpsuits, shall be used by all persons who enter the P4 facility. Upon exit, personnel shall store this clothing in lockers provided for this purpose or discard it into collection hampers before entering the shower area.

II–B–4–a–(15). The universal biohazard sign is required on the P4 facility access doors and on all interior doors to individual laboratory rooms where experiments are conducted. The sign shall also be posted on freezers, refrigerators, or other units used to store organisms containing recombinant DNA molecules.

II–B–4–a–(16). An insect and rodent control program shall be instituted.

II–B–4–a–(17). Animals and plants not related to the experiment shall not be permitted in the laboratory in which the experiment is being conducted.

II–B–4–a–(18). Vacuum outlets shall be protected by filter and liquid disinfectant traps.

II–B–4–a–(19). Use of the hypodermic needle and syringe shall be avoided when alternate methods are available.

II–B–4–a–(20). The laboratory shall be kept neat and clean.

II–B–4–a–(21). If experiments involving other organisms which require lower levels of containment are to be conducted in the P4 facility concurrently with experiments requiring P4-level containment, they shall be conducted in accordance with all P4-level laboratory practices specified in this section.

II–B–4–b. *Containment Equipment.*

II–B–4–b–(1). Experimental procedures involving organisms that require P4-level physical containment shall be conducted either in (i) a Class III cabinet system or in (ii) Class I or Class II cabinets that are located in a specially designed area in which all personnel are required to wear one-piece positive-pressure isolation suits.

II–B–4–b–(2). Laboratory animals in experiments requiring P4-level physical containment shall be housed either in cages contained in Class III cabinets or in partial containment caging systems (such as Horsfall units [19A], open cages placed in ventilated enclosures, or solid-wall and -bottom cages covered by filter bonnets, or solid-wall and -bottom cages placed on holding racks equipped with ultraviolet irradiation lamps and reflectors) that are loated in a specially designed area in which all personnel are required to wear one-piece positive-pressure suits.

II–B–4–b–(3). *Alternative Selection of Containment Equipment.* Experimental procedures involving a host-vector system that provides a one-step higher level of biological containment than that specified in Part III can be conducted in the P4 facility using containment equipment requirements specified for the P3 level of physical containment. Alternative combinations of containment safeguards are shown in Table II.

TABLE II.—COMBINATIONS OF CONTAINMENT SAFEGUARDS

Classification of experiment according to guidelines		Alternate combinations of physical and biological containment			
		Physical containment			
Physical containment	Bilogical containment [1]	Laboratory design specified for	Laboratory practices specified for	Containment equipment specified for	Biological containment
P4	HV1	P4	P4	P4	HV1.
P4	HV1	P4	P4 [2]	P3	HV2.

[1] See Section II–D for description of biological containment.
[2] In this case gloves shall be worn, in addition to the clothing requirements specified in II–B–4–a–(14).

II–B–4–c. *Special Laboratory Design.*

II–B–4–c–(1). The laboratory shall be located in a restricted-access facility which is either a separate building or a clearly demarcated and isolated zone within a building. Clothing-change areas and shower rooms shall be provided for personnel entry and egress. These rooms shall be arranged so that personnel leave through the shower area to the change room. A double-door ventilated vestibule or ultraviolet air lock shall be provided for passage of materials, supplies, and equipment which are not brought into the P4 facility through the change room area.

II–B–4–c–(2). Walls, floors, and ceilings of the P4 facility are constructed to form an internal shell which readily allows vapor-phase decontamination and is animal- and insect-proof. All penetrations through these structures and surfaces are sealed. (The integrity of the walls, floors, ceilings, and penetration seals should ensure adequate containment of a vapor-phase decontaminant under static pressure conditions. This requirement does not imply that these surfaces must be airtight.)

II–B–4–c–(3). A foot-, elbow-, or automatically-operated handwashing facility shall be provided near the door within each laboratory in which experiments involving recombinant DNA are conducted in openface biological safety cabinets.

II–B–4–c–(4). Central vacuum systems are permitted. The system, if provided, shall not serve areas outside the P4 facility. The vacuum system shall include in-line HEPA filters near each use point or service cock. The filters shall be installed so as to permit in-place decontamination and replacement. Water supply, liquid and gasous services provided to the P4 facility shall be protected by devices that prevent backflow.

II–B–4–c–(5). Drinking water foundations shall not be installed in laboratory or animal rooms of the P4 facilitiay. Foot-operated water fountains are permitted in the corridors of the P4 facility. The water service provided to such fountains shall be protected from the water services to the laboratory areas of the P4 facility.

II–B–4–c–(6). Laboratory doors shall be self-closing.

II–B–4–c–(7). A double-door autoclave shall be provided for sterilization of material passing out of the P4 facility. The autoclave doors shall be interlocked so that both doors will not be open at the same time.

II–B–4–c–(8). A pass-through dunk tank or fumigation chamber shall be provided for removal from the P4 facility of material and equipment that cannot be heat-sterilized.

II–B–4–c–(9). All liquid effluents from the P4 facility shall be collected and decontaminated before disposal. Liquid effluents from biological safety cabinets and laboratory sinks shall be sterilized by heat. Liquid effluents from the shower and hand washing facilities may be activated by chemical treatment. HEPA filters shall be installed in all vents from effluent drains.

II–B–4–c–(10). An individual supply and exhaust-air ventilation system shall be provided. The system shall maintain pressure differentials and directional air flow as required to ensure inflow from areas outside the facility toward areas of highest potential risk within the facility. The system shall be designed to prevent the reversal of air flow. The system shall sound an alarm in the event of system malfunction.

II–B–4–c–(11). Air within individual laboratories of the P4 facility may be recirculated if HEPA filtered.

II–B–4–c–(12). The exhaust air from the P4 facility shall be HEPA filtered and discharged to the outdoors so that it is dispersed clear of occupied buildings and air intakes. The filter chambers shall be designed to allow *in situ* decontamination before removal and to facilitate certification testing after replacement.

II–B–4–c–(13). The treated exhaust-air from Class I and Class II biological safety cabinets [20] may be discharged directly to the laboratory room environment or to the outdoors. The treated exhaust-air from Class III cabinets shall be discharged to the outdoors. If the treated exhaust-air from these cabinets is to be discharged to the outdoors through the P4 facility exhaust air system, it shall be connected to this system so as to avoid any interference with the air balance of the cabinets or the facility exhaust air system.

II–B–4–c–(14). As noted in Section II–B–4–b–(1), the P4 facility may contain specially designed areas in which all personnel are required to wear one-piece positive-pressure isolation suits. Such areas shall be airtight.

The exhaust-air from the suit shall be filtered by two sets of HEPA filters installed in series, and a duplicate filtration unit and exhaust fan shall be provided. The air pressure within the suit area shall be less than that in any adjacent area. An emergency lighting system, communication systems, and power source shall be provided. A double-door autoclave shall be provided for sterilization of all waste materials to be removed from the suit area.

Personnel who enter this area shall wear a one-piece positive-pressure suit that is ventilated by a life-support system. The life-support system shall be provided with alarms and emergency backup air. Entry to this area is through an airlock fitted with airtight doors. A chemical shower area shall be provided to decontaminate the surfaces of the suit before removal.

II–C. *Shipment.* Recombinant DNA molecules contained in an organism or virus shall be shipped only as an etiologic agent under requirements of the U.S. Public Health Service, and the U.S. Department of Transportation § 72.3, Part 72, Title 42, and §§ 173.386–173.388, Part 173, Title 49, U.S. Code of Federal Regulations (CFR) as specified below:

II–C–1. Recombinant DNA molecules contained in an organism or virus requiring P1, P2, or P3 physical containment, when offered for transportation or transported, are subject to all requirements of § 72.3(a)–(e), Part 72, Title 42 CFR, and §§ 173.386–173.388, Part 173, Title 49 CFR.

II–C–2. Recombinant DNA molecules contained in an organism or virus requiring P4 physical containment, when offered for transportation or transported, are subject to the requirements listed above under II–C–1 and are also subject to § 72.3(f), Part 72, Title 42 CFR.

II–C–3. Additional information on packaging and shipment is given in the "Laboratory Safety Monograph—A

Supplement to the NIH Guidelines for Recombinant DNA Research."

II-D. *Biological Containment.*

II-D-1. *Levels of Biological Containment.* In consideration of biological containment, the vector (plasmid, organelle, or virus) for the recombinant DNA and the host (bacterial, plant, or animal cell) in which the vector is propagated in the laboratory will be considered together. Any combination of vector and host which is to provide biological containment must be chosen or constructed so that the following types of "escape" are minimized: (i) Survival of the vector in its host outside the laboratory and (ii) transmission of the vector from the propagation host to other nonlaboratory hosts.

The following levels of biological containment (HV, or *H*ost-*V*ector, systems) for prokaryotes will be established; specific criteria will depend on the organisms to be used. Eukaryotic host-vector systems are considered in Part III.

II-D-1-a. *HV1.* A host-vector system which provides a moderate level of containment. *Specific systems:*

II-D-1-a-(1). *EK1.* The host is always *E. coli* K-12 or a derivative thereof, and the vectors include nonconjugative plasmids (e.g., pSC101, ColE1, or derivatives thereof[21-27]) and variants of bacteriophage, such as lambda[28-33]. The *E. coli* K-12 hosts shall not contain conjugation-proficient plasmids, whether autonomous or integrated, or generalized transducing phages, except as specified in Section III-O.

II-D-1-a-(2). *Other Prokaryotes.* Hosts and vectors shall be, at a minimum, comparable in containment to *E. coli* K-12 with a nonconjugative plasmid or bacteriophage vector. The data to be considered and a mechanism for approval of such HV1 systems are described below (Section II-D-2).

II-D-1-b. *HV2.* These are host-vector systems shown to provide a high level of biological containment as demonstrated by data from suitable tests performed in the laboratory. Escape of the recombinant DNA either via survival of the organisms or via transmission of recombinant DNA to other organisms should be less than $1/10^8$ under specified conditions. *Specific systems:*

II-D-1-b-(1). For EK2 host-vector systems in which the vector is a plasmid, no more than one in 10^8 host cells should be able to perpetuate a cloned DNA fragment under the specified nonpermissive laboratory conditions designed to represent the natural environment, either by survival of the original host or as a consequence of transmission of the cloned DNA fragment.

II-D-1-b-(2). For EK2 host-vector systems in which the vector is a phage, no more than one in 10^8 phage particles should be able to perpetuate a cloned DNA fragment under the specified nonpermissible laboratory conditions designed to represent the natural environment either (i) as a prophage (in the inserted or plasmid form) in the laboratory host used for phage propagation or (ii) by surviving in natural environments and transferring a cloned DNA fragment to other hosts (or their resident prophages).

II-D-1-c. *HV3.* These are host-vector systems in which:

II-D-1-c-(1). All HV2 criteria are met.

II-D-1-c-(2). The vector is dependent on its propagation host or is highly defective in mobilizability. Reversion to host-independence must be less than $1/10^8$ per vector genome per generation.

II-D-1-c-(3). No markers conferring resistance to antibiotics commonly used clinically or in agriculture are carried by the vector, unless expression of such markers is dependent on the propagating host or on unique laboratory-controlled conditions or is blocked by the inserted DNA.

II-D-1-c-(4). The specified containment shown by laboratory tests has been independently confirmed by specified tests in animals, including primates, and in other relevant environments.

II-D-1-c-(5). The relevant genotypic and phenotypic traits have been independently confirmed.

II-D-2. *Certification of Host-Vector Systems.*

II-D-2-a. *Responsibility.* HV1 systems other than *E. coli* K-12, and HV2 and HV3 host-vector systems, may not be designated as such until they have been certified by the Director, NIH. Application for certification of a host-vector system is made by written application to the Office of Recombinant DNA Activities, National Institutes of Health, Bethesda, Maryland 20205.

Host-vector systems that are proposed for certification will be reviewed by the National Institutes of Health (NIH) Recombinant DNA Advisory Committee (RAC). (See Section IV-E-1-b-(1).) This will first involve review of the data on construction, properties, and testing of the proposed host-vector system by a Working Group composed of one or more members of the RAC and other persons chosen because of their expertise in evaluating such data. The Committee will then evaluate the report of the Working Group and any other available informaton at a regular meeting. The Director, NIH, is responsible for certification after receiving the advice of the RAC. Minor modifications of existing certified host-vector systems, where the modifications are of minimal or no consequence to the properties relevant to containment may be certified by the Director, NIH, without review by the RAC. (See Section IV-E-1-b-(3)-(f).)

When new host-vector systems are certified, notice of the certification will be sent by the Office of Recombinant DNA Activities (ORDA) to the applicant and to all Institutional Biosafety Committees (IBCs) and will be published in the *Recombinant DNA Technical Bulletin.* Copies of a list of all currently certified host-vector systems may be obtained from ORDA at any time.

The Director, NIH, may at any time rescind the certification of any host-vector system. (See Section IV-E-1-b-(3)-(i).) If certification of a host-vector system is rescinded, NIH will instruct investigators to transfer cloned DNA into a different system, or use the clones at a higher physical containment level unless NIH determines that the already constructed clones incorporate adequate biological containment.

Certification of a given system does not extend to modifications of either the host or veetor component of that system. Such modified systems must be independently certified by the Director, NIH. If modifications are minor, it may only be necessary for the investigator to submit data showing that the modifications have either improved or not impaired the major phenotypic traits on which the containment of the system depends. Substantial modifications of a certified system require the submission of complete testing data.

II-D-2-b. *Data To be Submitted for Certification.*

II-D-2-b-(1). *HV1 Systems Other than E. Coli K-12.* The following types of data shall be submitted, modified as appropriate for the particular system under consideration. (i) A description of the organism and vector; the strain's natural habitat and growth requirements; its physiological properties, particularly those related to its reproduction and survival and the mechanisms by which it exchanges genetic information; the range of organisms with which this organism normally exchanges genetic information and what sort of information is exchanged; and any relevant information on its pathogenicity or toxicity. (ii) A description of the history of the particular strains and vectors to be used, including data on any mutations which render this organism less able to survive or transmit genetic information. (iii) A general description of the range of experiments contemplated, with emphasis on the need for developing such an HV1 system.

II-D-2-b-(2). *HV2 Systems.* Investigators planning to request HV2 certification for host-vector systems can obtain instructions from ORDA concerning data to be submitted [33A, 33B]. In general, the following types of data are required: (i) Description of construction steps, with indication of source, properties, and manner of introduction of genetic traits. (ii) Quantitative data on the stability of genetic traits that contribute to the containment of the system. (iii) Data on the survival of the host-vector system under nonpermissive laboratory conditions designed to represent the relevant natural environment. (iv) Data on transmissibility of the vector and/or a cloned DNA fragment under both permissive and nonpermissive conditions. (v) Data on all other properities of the system which affect containment and utility, including information on yields of phage or plasmid molecules, ease of DNA isolation, and ease of transfection or transformation. (vi) In some cases, the investigator may be asked to submit data on survival and vector transmissibility from experiments in which the host-vector is fed to laboratory animals (e.g., rodents). Such *in vivo* data may be required to confirm the validity of predicting *in vivo* survival on the basis of *in vitro* experiments.

Data must be submitted in writing to ORDA. Ten to twelve weeks are normally required for review and circulation of the data prior to the meeting at which such data can be considered by the RAC. Investigators are encouraged to publish their data on the construction, properties, and testing of proposed HV2 systems prior to consideration of the system by the RAC and its subcommittee. More specific instructions concerning the type of data to be submitted to NIH for proposed EK2 systems involving either plasmids or bacteriophage in *E. coli* K-12 are available from ORDA.

II-D-2-b-(3). *HV3 Systems.* Putative HV3 systems must, as the first step in certification, be certified as HV2 systems. Systems which meet the critera given above under II-D-1-(c)-1, II-D-1-(c)-2, and II-D-1-(c)-3 will then be recommended for HV3 testing. Tests to evaluate various HV2 host-vector systems for HV3 certification will be performed by contractors selected by NIH. These contractors will repeat tests performed by individuals proposing the HV2 system and, in addition, will conduct more extensive tests on conditions likely to be encountered in nature. The genotypic and phenotypic traits of HV2 systems will be evaluated. Tests on survival and transmissibility in and on animals, including primates, will be performed, as well as tests on survival in certain specified natural environments.

II-D-3. *Distribution of Certified Host-Vectors.* Certified HV2 and HV3 host-vector systems (plus appropriate control strains) must be obtained from the NIH or its designees, one of whom will be the investigator who developed the system. NIH shall announce the availability of the system by publication of notices in appropriate journals.

Plasmid vectors will be provided in a suitable host strain, and phage vectors will be distributed as small-volume lysates. If NIH propagates any of the host strains or phage, a sample will be sent to the investigator who developed the system or to an appropriate contractor, prior to distribution, for verification that the material is free from contamination and unchanged in phenotypic properties.

In distributing the certified HV2 and HV3 host-vector systems, NIH or its designee will (i) send out a complete description of the system; (ii) enumerate and describe the tests to be performed by the user in order to verify important phenotypic traits; (iii) remind the user that any modification of the system necessitates independent approval of the system by the NIH; and (iv) remind the user of responsibility for notifying ORDA of any discrepancies with the reported properties or any problems in the safe use of the system.

NIH may also distribute certified HV1 host-vector systems.

III. Containment Guidelines for Covered Experiments

Part III discusses experiments covered by the Guidelines. The reader must first consult Part I, where listings are given of prohibited and exempt experiments.

Containment guidelines for permissible experiments are given in Part III. For these experiments no registration with the National Institutes of Health (NIH) is necessary. However, for these experiments, prior to their initiation, investigators must submit to their Institutional Biosafety Committee (IBC) a registration document that contains a description of (a) the source(s) of DNA, (b) the nature of the inserted DNA sequences, (c) the hosts and vectors to be used, (d) whether a deliberate attempt will be made to obtain expression of a foreign gene in the cloning vehicle and if so, what protein, and (e) the containment conditions specified by these Guidelines. This registration document must be dated and signed by the investigator and filed only with the local IBC. The IBC shall review all such proposals: IBC review prior to initiation of the experiment is not required for experiments described in Section III-O. Prior IBC review is required for all other experiments described in the subsections of Part III, including III-O-1, III-O-2, etc.

Changes from the levels specified in Part III for specific experiments (or the assignment of levels to experiments not explicitly considered here) may not be instituted without the express approval of the Director, NIH. (See Sections IV-E-1-b-(1)-(a), IV-E-1-b-(1)-(b), IV-E-1-b-(2)-(b), IV-E-1-b-(2)-(c), IV-E-1-b-(3)-(b).)

In the classification of containment criteria for different kinds of recombinant DNAs, the stated levels of physical and biological containment are minimal for the experiments designated. The use of higher levels of biological containment (HV3 > HV2 > HV1) is encouraged if they are available and equally appropriate for the purposes of the experiment.

When the reader finds that the containment level given for the same experiment is different in two different sections within Part III, he may choose whichever of the two levels he wishes to use for the experiment.

III-O. *Classification of Experiments Using Certain Host-Vector Systems.* Experiments listed in Appendix H may be performed at P1 physical containment. For these experiments IBC review prior to initiation of the experiment is not required.

III-O-1. *Experiments Involving Class 3 Organisms.* Experiments involving recombinant DNA from Class 3 organisms [1] or from cells known to be infected with these agents may be conducted at P3 containment in *E. coli* K-12 EK1 hosts (see Appendix C). Containment levels for all other experiments with Class 3 organisms or with recombinant DNA which increases the virulence and host range of a plant pathogen beyond that which occurs by natural genetic exchange will be determined by NIH. (See Section IV-E-1-b-2-(e)).

III-O-2. *Experiments involving Nonpathogenic Prokaryotic and Lower Eukaryotic Host-Vector Systems.* DNA from any species nonpathogenic for man, animals, or plants may be cloned into lower eukaryotes nonpathogenic for man, animals, or plants at the P3 level of containment [2A]. DNA from any species nonpathogenic for man, animals, or plants may be cloned into prokaryotes nonpathogenic for man, animals, or plants at the P2 level of containment [2A]. Data supporting the contention that the donor and recipient are nonpathogenic must be submitted to the local IBC. Lower levels of physical containment may be assigned by ORDA on a case-by-case basis for specific donor-recipient combinations (see Section IV-E-1-b-(3)-(h)).

III-A. *Classification of Experiments Using Certain HV1 and HV2 Host-Vector Systems.* Certain HV1 and HV2 host-vector systems are assigned containment levels as specified in the subsections of this Section III-A. Those so classified as of publication of these revised Guidelines are listed in Appendix D. An updated list may be obtained from the Office of Recombinant DNA Activities, National Institutes of Health, Bethesda, Maryland 20205.

III-A-1. *Shotgun Experiments.* These experiments involve the production of recombinant DNAs between the vector and portions of the specified cellular source, preferably a partially purified fraction. Care should be taken either to preclude or eliminate contaminating microorganisms before isolating the DNA.

III-A-1-a . *Eukaryotic DNA Recombinants.*

III-A-1-a-(1). *Primates.* P2 physical containment+an HV2 host-vector or P3+HV1.

III-A-1-a-(2). *Other Mammals.* P2 physical containment+an HV2 host-vector or P3+HV1.

III-A-1-a-(3). *Birds.* P2 physical containment+an HV2 host-vector, or P3+HV1.

III-A-1-a-(4). *Cold-Blooded Vertebrates.* P2 physical containment+an HV1 host-vector or P1+HV2. If the eukaryote is known to produce a potent polypeptide toxin, [34] the containment shall be increased to P3+HV2.

III-A-1-a-(5). *Other Cold-Blooded Animals and Lower Eukaryotes.* This large class of eukaryotes is divided into two groups:

III-A-1-a-(5)-(a). Species that are known to produce a potent polypeptide toxin[34] that acts in vertebrates, or are known pathogens listed in Class 2,[1] or are known to carry such pathogens must use P3 physical containment+an HV2 host-vector. When the potent toxin is not a polypeptide and is likely not to be the product of closely linked eukaryote genes, containment may be reduced to P3+HV1 or P2+HV2. Species that produce potent toxins that affect invertebrates or plants but not vertebrates require P2+HV2 or P3+HV1. Any species that has a demonstrated capacity for carrying particular pathogenic microorganisms is included in this group, unless the organisms used as the source of DNA have been shown not to contain those agents, in which case they may be placed in the following group.[2A]

III-A-1-a-(5)-(b). The remainder of the species in this class including plant pathogenic or symbiotic fungi that do not produce potent toxins: P2+HV1 or P1+HV2. However, any insect in this group must be either (i) grown under laboratory conditions for at least 10 generations prior to its use as a source of DNA, or (ii) if caught in the wild, must be shown to be free of disease-causing microorganisms or must belong to a species that does not carry microorganisms causing disease in vertebrates or plants.[2A] If these conditions cannot be met, experiments must be done under P3+HV1 or P2+HV2 containment.

III-A-1-a-(6). *Plants.* P2 physical containment+an HV1 host-vector, or P1+HV2. If the plant source makes a potent polypeptide toxin,[34] the containment must be raised to P3 physical containment+an HV2 host-vector. When the potent toxin is not a polypeptide and is likely not to be the product of closely linked plant genes, containment may be reduced to P3+HV1 or P2+HV2.[2A]

III-A-1-b. *Prokaryotic DNA Recombinants.* P2+HV1 or P1+HV2 for experiments with phages, plasmids and DNA from nonpathogenic prokaryotes which do not produce polypeptide toxins.[34] P3+HV2 for experiments with phages, plasmids and DNA from Class 2 agents.[1]

III-A-2-a. *Viruses of Eukaryotes* (summary given in Table III; see also exception given at asterisk at end of Appendix D).

III-A-2-a-(1). *DNA Viruses.*

III-A-2-a-(1)-(a). *Nontransforming viruses.*

III-A-2-a(1)-(a)-(*1*). *Adeno-Associated Viruses, Minute Virus of Mice, Mouse Adenovirus (Strain FL), and Plant Viruses.[48]* P1 physical containment+and HV1 host-vector shall be used for DNA recombinants produced with (i) the whole viral genome, (ii) subgenomic DNA segments, or (iii) purified cDNA copies of viral mRNA.[37]

III-A-2-a-(1)-(a)-(*2*). *Hepatitis B.*

III-A-2-a-(1)-(a)-(*2*)-(*a*). P1 physical containment+an HV1 host-vector shall be used for purified subgenomic DNA segments.[38]

III-A-2-a-(1)-(a)-(*2*)-(*b*). P2 physical containment+an HV2 host-vector, or P3+HV1, shall be used for DNA recombinants produced with the whole viral genome or with subgenomic segments that have not been purified to the extent required in footnote 38.

III-A-2-a-(1)-(a)-(*2*)-(*c*). P2 physical containment+an HV1 Host-vector shall be used for DNA recombinants derived from purified cDNA copies of viral mRNA.[37]

III-A-2-a-(1)-(a)-(*3*). *Other Nontransforming Members of Presently Classified Viral Families.[36]*

III-A-2-a-(1)-(a)-(*3*)-(*a*). P1 physical containment+an HV1 host-vector shall be used for (i) DNA recombinants produced with purified subgenomic DNA[38] segments or (ii) purified cDNA copies of viral mRNA.[37]

III-A-2-a-(1)-(a)-(*3*)-(*b*). P1 physical containment+an HV1 host-vector shall be used for DNA recombinants produced with the whole viral genome or with subgenomic segments that have not been purified to the extent required in footnote 38.

III-A-2-a-(1)-(b). *Transforming Viruses.*[37A]

III-A-2-a-(1)-(b)-(*1*). *Herpes Saimiri, Herpes Ateles, and Epstein Barr Virus.[39]*

III-A-2-a-(1)-(b)-(*1*)-(*a*). P1 physical containment + an HV1 host-vector shall be used for DNA recombinants produced with purified nontransforming subgenomic DNA segments.[38]

III-A-2-a-(1)-(b)-(*1*)-(*b*). P2 physical containment + an HV1 host-vector shall be used for (i) DNA recombinants produced with purified subgenomic DNA segments containing an entire transforming gene [38] or (ii) purified cDNA copies of viral mRNA.[37]

III-A-2-a-(1)-(b)-(*1*)-(*c*). P3 physical containment + an HV1 host-vector, or P2 + HV2, shall be used for DNA recombinants produced with the whole viral genome or with subgenomic segments that have not been purified to the extent required in footnote 38.

III-A-2-a-(1)-(b)-(*2*). *Other Transforming Members of Presently Classified Viral Families.[36]*

III-A-2-a-(1)-(b)-(*2*)-(*a*). P1 physical containment + an HV1 host-vector shall be used for DNA recombinants produced with purified nontransforming subgenomic DNA segments.[38]

III-A-2-a-(1)-(b)-(*2*)-(*b*). P2 physical containment + an HV1 host-vector shall be used for (i) DNA recombinants produced with the whole viral genome, (ii) subgenomic DNA segments containing an entire transforming gene, (iii) purified cDNA copies of viral mRNA, [37] or (iv) subgenomic segments that have not been purified to the extent required in footnote 38.

III–A–2–a–(2). *DNA Transcripts of RNA Viruses.*

III–A–2–a–(2)–(a). *Retroviruses.*

III–A–2–a–(2)–(a)–(*1*). *Gibbon Ape, Woolly Monkey, Feline Leukemia and Feline Sarcoma Viruses. [39]*

III–A–2–a–(2)–(a)–(*1*)–(*a*). P1 physical containment + an HV1 host-vector shall be used for DNA recombinants produced with purified nontransforming subgenomic DNA segments.[38]

III–A–2–a–(2)–(a)–(*1*)–(*b*). P2 physical containment + an HV1 host-vector shall be used for DNA recombinants produced with purified subgenomic DNA segments[38] containing an entire transforming gene.

III–A–2–a–(2)–(a)–(*1*)–(*c*). P2 physical containment + an HV2 host-vector, or P3 + HV1, shall be used for DNA recombinants produced with (i) the whole viral genome, (ii) purified cDNA copies of viral mRNA,[37] or (iii) subgenomic segments that have not been purified to the extent required in footnote 38.

III–A–2–a–(2)–(a)–(*2*). *Other Members of the Family Retroviridiae.[36]*

III–A–2–a–(2)–(a)–(*2*)–(*a*). P1 physical containment + an HV1 host-vector shall be used for DNA recombinants produced with purified nontransforming subgenomic DNA segments.[38]

III–A–2–a–(2)–(a)–(*2*)–(*b*). P2 physical containment + an HV1 host-vector shall be used for DNA recombinants produced with (i) subgenomic DNA segments containing an entire transforming gene, (ii) the whole viral genome, or (iii) purified cDNA copies of viral mRNA,[37] or (iv) subgenomic segments that have not been purified to the extent required in footnote 38.

III–A–2–a–(2)–(b). *Negative Strand RNA Viruses.* P1 physical containment + an HV1 host-vector shall be used for DNA recombinants produced with (i) cDNA copies of the whole genome, (ii) subgenomic cDNA segments, or (iii) purified cDNA copies of viral mRNA.[37]

III–A–2–a–(2)–(c). *Plus-Strand RNA Viruses.*

III–A–2–a–(2)–(c)–(*1*). *Types 1 and 2 Sabin Poliovirus Vaccine Strains and Strain 17D (Theiler) of Yellow Fever Virus.* P1 physical containment + and HV1 host-vector shall be used for DNA recombinants produced with (i) cDNA copies of the whole viral genome, (ii) subgenomic cDNA segments, or (iii) purified cDNA copies of viral mRNA.[37]

III–A–2–a–(2)–(c)–(*2*). *Other Plus-Strand RNA Viruses Belonging to Presently Classified Viral Families.[36]*

III–A–2–a–(2)–(c)–(*2*)–(*a*). P1 physical containment + an HV1 host-vector shall be used for DNA recombinants produced with purified subgenomic cDNA segments.[38]

TABLE III.—RECOMMENDED CONTAINMENT FOR CLONING OF VIRAL DNA OR CDNA IN CERTAIN HV1 AND HV2 SYSTEMS SPECIFIED IN APPENDIX D

[See text for full details]

Virus class	Type of viral DNA segment to be cloned: Subgenomic[38]: Nontransforming segment	Subgenomic[38]: Segment containing an entire transforming gene	Genomic*: Nonsegmented genome	Genomic*: Segmented genome	cDNA from viral mRNA[37]
DNA:					
Nontransforming viruses:					
AAV, MVM, Mouse Adeno (Strain FL).	P1+HV1		P1+HV1		P1+HV1.
Plant Viruses	P1+HV1		P1+HV1		P1+HV1.
Hepatitis B	P1+HV1[38]		P2+HV2 or P3+HV1		P2+HV1.
Other	P1+HV1[38]		P1+HV1		P1+HV1.
Transforming Viruses:					
Herpes Saimiri, H. Ateles and EBV[39].	P1+HV1[38]	P2+HV1	P2+HV2 or P3+HV1		P2+HV1.
Other	P1+HV1[38]	P2+HV1	P2+HV1		P2+HV1.
RNA:					
Retroviruses:					
Gibbon Ape, Woolly Monkey FeLV and FeSV[39].	P1+HV1[38]	P2+HV1	P2+HV2 or P3+HV1		P2+HV2 or P3+HV1.
Other	P1+HV1[38]	P2+HV1	P2+HV1		P2+HV1.
Negative-Strand RNA	P1+HV1		P1+HV1	P1+HV1	P1+HV1.
Plus-Strand RNA:					
Types 1 and 2 Sabin Polio, 17D Yellow Fever Vaccine Strains.	P1+HV1		P1+HV1		P1+HV1.
Other	P1+HV1[38]		P2+HV1		P2+HV1.
Double-Stranded RNA	P1+HV1			P1+HV1	P1+HV1.
Plant Viruses + Viroids	P1+HV1		P1+HV1	P1+HV1	P1+HV1.
Intracellular Viral DNA	See text	See text	See text		

* See exception given at asterisk at end of Appendix D.

III–A–2–a–(2)–(c)–(*2*)–(*b*). P2 physical containment + an HV1 host-vector shall be used for DNA recombinants produced with (i) cDNA copies of the whole genome, or (ii) purified cDNA copies of viral mRNA.[37]

III–A–2–a–(2)–(d). *Double-Stranded Segmented RNA Viruses.* P1 physical containment + an HV1 host-vector shall be used for DNA recombinants produced with (i) mixtures of subgenomic cDNA segments, (ii) a specific subgenomic cDNA segment, or (iii) purified cDNA copies of viral mRNA.[37]

III–A–2–a–(2)–(e). *RNA Plant Viruses and Plant Viroids.*[48] P1 physical containment + an HV1 host-vector shall be used for DNA recombinants produced with (i) cDNA copies of the whole viral genome, (ii) subgenomic cDNA segments, or (iii) purified cDNA copies of viral mRNA.[37]

III–A–2–a–(3). *Intracellular Viral DNA.* Physical and biological containment specified for shotgun experiments with eukaryotic cellular DNA [see Section III–A–(1)–(a)] shall be used for DNA recombinants produced with integrated viral DNA or viral genomes present in infected cells.

III–A–2–b. *Eukaryotic Organelle DNAs.* P2 physical containment + an HV1 host-vector, or P1 + HV2, for mitochondrial or chloroplast DNA from eukaryotes when the organelle DNA has been obtained from isolated organelles. Otherwise, the conditions given for shotgun experiments apply.

III–A–2–c. *Prokaryotic Plasmid and Phage DNAs.* The containment levels required for shotgun experiments with DNA from prokaryotes apply to their plasmids or phages (See Section III-A-1-b.)

III-A-3. *Lowering of Containment Levels for Characterized or Purified DNA Preparations and Clones.* Many of the risks which might conceivably arise from some types of recombinant DNA experiments, particularly shotgun experiments, would result from the inadvertent cloning of a harmful sequence. Therefore, in cases where the risk of inadvertently cloning the "wrong" DNA is reduced by prior enrichment for the desired piece, or in which a clone made from a random assortment of DNAs has been purified and the absence of harmful sequences established, the containment conditions for further work may be reduced. The following section outlines the mechanisms for such reductions.

III-A-3-a. *Purified DNA Other than Plasmids, Bacteriophages, and Other Viruses.* The formation of DNA recombinants from cellular DNAs that have been purified[41] and in which the absence of harmful sequences has been established[3] can be carried out under lower containment conditions than used for the corresponding shotgun experiment.[42] The containment may be decreased one step in physical containment (P4 P3; P3 P2; P2 P1) while maintaining the biological containment specified for the shotgun experiment, or one step in biological containment (HV3 HV2; HV2 HV1) while maintaining the specified physical containment. The Institutional Biosafety Committee (IBC) must review such a reduction and the approval of the IBC and of the NIH must be secured before such a reduction may be put into effect. IBC approval is sufficient for such a reduction except for any lowering of containment under Section III-A-3-a to levels below P1+HV1, which requires prior NIH approval. (See Section IV-E-1-b-(3)-(e).)

III-A-3-b. *Characterized Clones of DNA Recombinants.* When a cloned DNA recombinant has been rigorously characterized and the absence of harmful sequences has been established[3], experiments involving this recombinant DNA may be carried out under lower containment conditions. Institutional Biosafety Committees (IBCs) may give approval for a single-step reduction in physical or biological containment on receipt of evidence of characterization of a clone derived from a shotgun experiment and its probable freedom from harmful genes. IBC approval is sufficient for such a reduction except for any lowering of containment under Section III-A-3-b to levels below P1+HV1, or reduction of containment levels by more than one step, which also requires prior NIH approval.(See Section IV-E-1-b-3-(e).)

III-B. *Experiments with Prokaryotic Host-Vectors Other Than E. coli K-12.*

III-B-1. *HV1 and HV2 Systems.* Certain certified HV1 and HV2 hostvector systems appear in Appendix D. The containment levels for these systems are given in the subsections of Section III-A. Other systems in the future may be certified as HV1 and HV2. At the time of certification, the classification of containment levels for experiments using them will be assigned by NIH.

III-B-2. *Return of DNA Segments to Prokaryotic Non-HV1 Host of Origin.* Certain experiments involving these prokaryotes that exchange genetic information with *E. coli* by known physiological processes will be exempt from these Guidelines if they appear on the "list of exchangers" set forth in Appendix A (see Section I-E-4). For a prokaryote which can exchange genetic information[35] with *E. coli* under laboratory conditions but which is not on the list (Host A), the following type of experiment may be carried out under P1 conditions without Host A having been approved as an HV1 host: DNA from Host A may be inserted into a vector and propagated in *E. coli* K-12. Subsequently, this recombinant DNA may be returned to Host A by mobilization, transformation, or transduction and may then be propagated in Host A in any desired vector under P1 conditions.

For a prokaryote which does not exchange genetic information with *E. coli* (Host B), the following type of experiment may be carried out without Host B having been approved as an HV1 host: DNA from Host B may be inserted into a vector and propagated in *E. coli* K-12. Subsequently, this recombinant DNA may be returned to Host B and propagated in Host B under P1 conditions.[43]

III-B-3. *Non-HV1 Systems.* Containment levels for other classes of experiments involving non-HV1 systems may be approved by the Director, NIH. (See Sections IV-E-1-b-(1)-(b), IV-E-1-b-(2)-(c), and IV-E-1-b-(3)-(b).)

III-C. *Experiments with Eukaryotic Host-Vectors.*

III-C-1. *Vertebrate Host-Vector Systems.[44]* The subsections of Sections III-C-1-a, -b, -c and -d involve the use of specific viral vectors, namely polyoma, SV40, human adenoviruses 2 and 5, and mouse adenovirus strain FL, respectively. The subsections of Section III-C-1-e involve the use of viral vectors including the specific viral vectors considered in the subsections of Sections III-C-1-a, -b, -c and -d, as well as any other viral vector. When the reader finds that the containment level given for a specific experiment in a subsection of Section III-C-1-e is different from the containment level given in a subsection of Section III-C-1-a, -b, -c or -d, he may choose which of the two containment levels he wishes to use for the experiment.

III-C-1-a. *Polyoma Virus.*

III-C-1-a-(1). *Productive Virus-Cell Interactions.*

III-C-1-a-(1)-(a). Defective or whole polyoma virus genomes, with appropriate helper, if necessary, can be used in P2 conditions to propagate DNA sequences:

III-C-1-a-(1)-(a)-(*1*). from bacteria of Class 1 or Class 2[1] or their phages or plasmids, except for those that produce potent polypeptide toxins;[34]

III-C-1-a-(1)-(a)-(*2*). from mice;

III-C-1-a-(1)-(a)-(*3*). from eukaryotic organisms that do not produce potent polypeptide toxins,[34] provided that the DNA segment is >99% pure.

III-C-1-a-(1)-(b). Defective polyoma genomes, with appropriate helper, if necessary, can be used in P2 conditions for shotgun experiments to propagate DNA sequences from eukaryotic organisms that do not produce potent polypeptide toxins.[34]

III-C-1-a-(1)-(c). Whole virus genomes with appropriate helper, if necessary, can be used in P3 conditions for shotgun experiments to propagate DNA sequences from eukaryotic organisms that do not produce potent polypeptide toxins.[34]

III-C-1-a-(1)-(d). Experiments involving the use of defective polyoma virus genomes to propagate DNA sequences from eukaryotic viruses will be evaluated by NIH on a case-by-case basis[45] and will be conducted under the prescribed physical and biological containment conditions. (See Section IV-E-1-b-(3)-(c).)

III-C-1-a-(2). *Nonproductive Virus-Cell Interactions.* Defective or whole polyoma virus genomes can be used as vectors in P2 conditions when production of viral particles cannot occur (e.g., transformation of nonpermissive cells or propagation of an unconditionally defective recombinant genome in the absence of helper): *Provided,* The inserted DNA sequences are not derived from eukaryotic viruses. In the latter case, such experiments will be evaluated by NIH on a case-by-case basis[45] and will be conducted under the prescribed physical and biological containment conditions. (See Section IV-E-1-b-(3)-(c).)

III-C-1-b. *Simian Virus 40.*

III-C-1-b-(1). *Productive Virus-Cell Interactions.*

III-C-1-b-(1)-(a). SV40 DNA, rendered unconditionally defective by a deletion in an essential gene, with appropriate helper, can be used in P2 conditions to propagate DNA sequences from:

III-C-1-b-(1)-(a)-(*1*). bacteria of Class 1 or Class 2,[1] or their phages or plasmids, except for those that produce potent polypeptide toxins;[34]

III-C-1-b-(1)-(a)-(*2*). uninfected African green monkey kidney cell cultures.

III-C-1-b-(1)-(b). SV40 DNA, rendered unconditionally defective by a deletion in an essential gene, with an appropriate helper, can be used in P3 conditions to propagate DNA sequences from eukaryotic organisms that do not produce potent polypeptide toxins[34] (shotgun experiments or purified DNA).

III-C-1-b-(1)-(c). Experiments involving the use of defective SV40 genomes to propagate DNA sequences from eukaryotic viruses will be evaluated by NIH on a case-by-case basis[45] and will be conducted under the prescribed physical and biological containment conditions. (See Section IV-E-1-b-(3)-(c).)

III-C-1-b-(2). *Nonproductive Virus-Cell Interactions.* Defective or whole SV40 genomes can be used as vectors in P2 conditions when production of viral particles cannot occur (e.g., transformation of nonpermissive cells or propagation of an unconditionally defective recombinant genome in the absence of helper): *Provided,* The inserted DNA sequences are not derived from eukaryotic viruses. In the latter case, such experiments will be evaluated by NIH on a case-by-case basis[45] and will be conducted under the prescribed physical and biological containment conditions. (See Section IV-E-1-b-(3)-(c).)

III-C-1-c. *Human Adenoviruses 2 and 5.*

III-C-1-c-(1). *Productive Virus-Cell Interactions.*

III-C-1-c-(1)-(a). Human adenoviruses 2 and 5, rendered unconditionally defective by deletion of at least two essential genes, with appropriate helper, can be used in P3 conditions to propagate DNA sequences from:

III-C-1-c-(1)-(a)-(*1*). bacteria of Class 1 or Class 2[1] or their phages or plasmids except for those that produce potent polypeptide toxins;[34]

III-C-1-c-(1)-(a)-(*2*). eukaryotic organisms that do not produce potent polypeptide toxins[34] (shotgun experiments or purified DNA).

III-C-1-c-(1)-(b). Experiments involving the use of unconditionally defective human adenovirus 2 and 5 genomes to propagate DNA sequences from eukaryotic viruses will be evaluated by NIH on a case-by-case basis[45] and will be conducted under the prescribed physical and biological containment conditions. (See Section IV-E-1-b-(3)-(c).)

III-C-1-c-(2). *Nonproductive Virus-Cell Interactions.* Defective or whole human adenovirus 2 and 5 genomes can be used as vectors in P2 conditions when production of viral particles cannot occur (e.g., transformation of nonpermissive cells or propagation of an unconditionally defective recombinant genome in the absence of helper); *Provided,* The inserted DNA sequences are not derived from eukaryotic viruses. In the latter case, such experiments will be evaluated by NIH on a case-by-case basis[45] and will be conducted under the prescribed physical and biological containment conditions. (See Section IV-E-1-b-(3)-(c).)

III-C-1-d. *Murine Adenovirus Strain FL.*

III-C-1-d-(1). *Productive Virus-Cell Interactions.*

III-C-1-d-(1)-(a). Unconditionally defective murine adenovirus strain FL genomes, with appropriate helper, can be used in P2 conditions to propagate DNA sequences from:

III-C-1-d-(1)-(a)-(*1*). bacteria of Class 1 or Class 2[1] or their phages or plasmids except for those that produce potent polypeptide toxins;[34]

III-C-1-d-(1)-(a)-(*2*). eukaryotic organisms that do not produce potent polypeptide toxins[34] (shotgun experiments or purified DNA).

III-C-1-d-(1)-(b). Experiments involving the use of whole murine adenovirus strain FL genomes to propagate DNA sequences from prokaryotic or eukaryotic organisms will be evaluated by NIH on a case-by-case basis[45] and will be conducted under the prescribed physical and biological containment conditions. (See Section IV-E-1-b-(3)-(c).)

III-C-1-d-(1)-(c). Experiments involving the use of unconditionally defective murine adenovirus strain FL genomes to propagate DNA sequences from eukaryotic viruses will be evaluated by NIH on a case-by-case basis[45] and will be conducted under the prescribed physical and biological containment conditions. (See Section IV-E-1-b-(3)-(c).)

III-C-1-d-(2). *Nonproductive Virus-Cell Interactions.* Defective or whole murine adenovirus strain FL genomes can be used as vectors in P2 conditions when production of viral particles cannot occur (e.g., transformation of nonpermissive cells or propagation of an unconditionally defective recombinant genome in the absence of helper); *Provided,* The inserted DNA sequences are not derived from eukaryotic viruses. In the latter case, such experiments will be evaluated by NIH on a case-by-case basis [45] and will be conducted under the prescribed physical and biological containment conditions. (See Section IV-E-1-b-(3)-(c).)

III-C-1-e. *All Viral Vectors.*

III-C-1-e-(1). Other experiments involving eukaryotic virus vectors can be done as follows:

III-C-1-(1)-(a). Recombinant DNA molecules containing no more than two-thirds of the genome of any eukaryotic virus [all viruses from a single Family (36) being considered identical (50)] may be propagated and maintained in cells in tissue culture using P1 containment: For such experiments, it must be shown that the cells lack helper virus for the specific Families of defective viruses being used. The DNA may contain fragments of the genomes of viruses from more than one Family but each fragment must be less than two-thirds of a genome.

III-C-1-e-(1)-(b). Recombinants with less than two-thirds of the genome of any eukaryotic virus may be rescued with helper virus using P2 containment if wild type strains of the virus are CDC Class 1 or 2 agents, or using P3 containment if wild type strains of the virus are CDC Class 3 agents (1).

III-C-1-e-(2). Experiments involving the use of other whole or defective virus genomes to propagate DNA sequences from prokaryotic or eukaryotic organisms (and viruses), or as vectors to transform nonpermissive cells, will be evaluated by NIH on a case-by-case basis [45] and will be conducted under the prescribed physical and biological containment conditions. (See Section IV-E-1-b-(3)-(c).)

NIH will also review on a case-by-case basis[45] all experiments involving the use of virus vectors in animals and will prescribed the physical and biological containment conditions appropriate for such studies. (See Section IV-E-1-b-(3)-(c).)

III-C-1-f. *Nonviral Vectors.* Organelle, plasmid, and chromosomal DNAs may be used as vectors. DNA recombinants formed between such vectors and host DNA, when propagated only in that host (or a closely related strain of the same species), are exempted from these Guidelines (see Section I-E). DNA recombinants formed between such vectors and nonviral DNA from cells other than the host species require only P1 physical containment for cells in culture since vertebrate cells in tissue culture inherently exhibit a very high level of containment. Recombinants involving viral DNA or experiments which require the use of the whole animals will be evaluated by NIH on a case-by-case basis.[45]

III–C–2. *Invertebrate Host-Vector Systems.*

III–C–2–a. *Inverebrate Viral Vectors.* Experiments involving invertebrate virus vectors can be done as follows:

III–C–2–a–(1). Recombinant DNA molecules containing no more than two-thirds of the genome of any invertebrate virus (all viruses from a single Family (36) being considered identical (50)) may be propagated and maintained in cells in tissue culture using P1 containment. For such experiments, it must be shown that the cells lack helper virus for the specific Families of defective viruses being used. The DNA may contain fragments of the genomes of viruses from more one Family but each fragment must be less than two-thirds of a genome.

III–C–2–a–(2). Recombinants with less than two-thirds of the genome of any invertebrate virus may be rescued with helper virus using P2 containment unless it is classified by the CDC as a class 3 agent (1) in which case P3 containment is required.

III–C–2–a–(3). Experiments involving the use of other whole or defective virus genomes to propagate DNA sequences from prokaryotic or eukaryotic organisms (and viruses), or as vectors to transform nonpermissive cells, will be evaluated by NIH on a case-by-case basis [45] and will be conducted under the prescribed physical and biological containment condtions. (See Section IV–E–1–b–(3)–(c).)

NIH will also review on a case-by-case basis [45] all experiments involving the use of virus vectors in animals and will prescribe the physical and biological containment conditions appropriate for such studies. (See Section IV–E–1–b–(3)–(c).)

III–C–2–b. *Nonviral Vectors.* Organelle, plasmid, and chromosomal DNAs may be used as vectors. DNA recombinants formed between such vectors and host DNA, when propagated only in that the host (or a closely related strain of the same species), are exempt from these Guidelines (see Section I–E). DNA recombinants formed betweên such vectors and DNA from cells other than the host species require P1 physical containment for invertebrate cells in culture inherently exhibits a very high level of containment. Experiments which require the use of whole animals will be evaluated by NIH on a case-by-case basis.[45]

III–C–3. *Plant Viral Host-Vector Systems.* [46] The DNA plant viruses which could currently serve as vectors for coloning genes in plants and plant cell protoplasts are Cauliflower Mosaic Virus (CaMV) and its close relatives [2A] which have relaxed circular double-stranded DNA genomes with a molecular weight of 4.5×10^{6}, and Bean Golden Mosaic Virus (BGMV) and related viruses with small ($>10^{6}$ daltons) single-stranded DNA genomes. CaMV is spread in nature by aphids, in which it survives for a few hours. Spontaneous mutants of CaMV which lack a factor essential for aphid transmission arise frequently. BGMV is spread in nature by whiteflies, and certain other single-stranded DNA plant viruses are transmitted by leafhoppers.

The DNA plant viruses have narrow host ranges and are relatively difficulty to transmit mechanically to plants. For this reason, they are most unlikely to be accidentally transmitted from spillage of purified virus preparations.

When these viruses are used as vectors in intact plants, or propagative plant parts, the plants shall be grown under P1 conditions—that is, in either a limited access greenhouse or plant growth cabinet which is insect-restrictive, preferably with positive air pressure, [2A] and in which an insect fumigation regime is maintained. Soil, plant pots, and unwanted infected materials shall be removed from the greenhouse or cabinet in sealed insect-proof containers and sterilized. It is not necessary to sterilize run-off water from the infected plants, as this is not a plausible route for secondary infection. When the viruses are used as vectors in tissue cultures or in small plants in axenic cultures, no special containment is necessary. Infected plant materials which have to be removed from the greenhouse or cabinet for further research shall be maintained under insect-restrictive conditions. These measures provide an entirely adequate degree of containment. They are similar to those required in many countries for licensed handling of "exotic" plant viruses.

The viruses or their DNA may also be useful as vectors to introduce genes into plant protoplasts. The fragility of plant protoplasts combined with the properties of the viruses provides adequate safety. Since no risk to the environment from the use of the DNA plant virus/protoplast system is envisaged, no special containment is necessary, except as described in the following paragraph.

Experiments involving the use of plant genomes to propagate DNA sequences from eukaryotic viruses will be evaluated by NIH on a case-by-case basis [45] and will be conducted under the prescribed physical and biological containment conditions. (See Section IV–E–1–b–(3)–(c).)

III–C–4. *Plant Host-Vector Systems Other than Viruses.* [46] Organelle, plasmid, and chromosomal DNAs may be used as vectors. DNA recombinants formed between such vectors and host DNA, when propagated only in that host (or a closely related strain of the same species), are exempt from these Guidelines (see Section I–E). DNA recombinants formed between such vectors and DNA from cells other than the host species require P2 physical containment. The development of host-vector systems that exhibit a high level of biological containment, such as those using protoplasts or undifferentiated cells in culture, permit [2A] a decrease in the physical containment to P1.

Intact plants or propagative plant parts which cannot be grown in a standard P2 laboratory because of their large size may be grown under the P1 conditions described above in Section III–C–3, except that (i) sterilization of run-off water is required where this is a plausible route for secondary infection and (ii) the standard P2 practices are adopted for microbiological work, and (iii) negative air pressure should be employed in the greenhouse or growth chamber when infectious agents are used which generate airborne propagules.

III–C–5. *Fungal or Similar Lower Eukaryotic Host-Vector Systems.* Certain certified HV1 and HV2 host-vector systems appear in Appendix D. The containment levels for these systems are given in the subsections of Section III–A. Other systems in the future may be certified as HV1 and HV2. At the time of certification, they may be added to Appendix D (and thus the containment levels for their use will be those of the subsections of Section III–A). Alternatively, at the time of their certification, another classification of containment levels for experiments using them may be assigned by NIH.

In addition to the experiments described above, the following experiments may be carried out without the eukaryotic host (Host C) having been approved as an HV1 host: DNA from Host C may be inserted into a vector and propagated in *E. coli* K–12. Subsequently, this recombinant DNA may be returned to Host C and propagated there under P1 conditions.[43]

Containment levels for other classes of experiments involving non-HV1 systems may be expressly approved by the Director, NIH. (See Sections IV-E-1-b-(1)-(b), IV-E-1-b-(2)-(c), and IV-E-1-b-(3)-(b).)

III-C-6. *Return of DNA Segments to a Higher Eukaryotic Host of Origin.* DNA from a higher eukaryote (Host D) may be inserted into a vector and propagated in *E. coli* K-12. Subsequently, this recombinant DNA may be returned to Host D and propagated under conditions of physical containment comparable to P1 and appropriate to the organism under study.[2A]

III-C-7. *Transfer of Cloned DNA Segments to Eukaryotic Organisms*

III-C-7-a. *Transfer to Non-human Vertebrates.* DNA from any nonprohibited source (Section I-D), except for greater than one quarter of a eukaryotic viral genome, which has been cloned and propagated in *E. coli* K-12, may be transferred with *E. coli* vector used for cloning to any eukaryotic cells in culture or to any non-human vertebrate organism and propagated under conditions of physical containment comparable to P1 and appropriate to the organism under study[2]. Transfers to any other host will be considered by the RAC on a case-by-case basis[45].

III-C-7-b. *Transfer to Higher Plants.* DNA from any nonprohibited source [Section I-D] which has been cloned and propagated in *E. coli* K-12 or *S. cerevisiae*, may be transferred with the *E. coli* or *S. cerevisiae* vector used for cloning to any higher plant organisms (Angiosperms and Gymnosperms) and propagated under conditions of physical containment comparable to P1 and appropriate to the organism under study [2A]. Intact plants or propagative plant parts may be grown under P1 conditions described under Section III-C-3. Containment must be modified to ensure that the spread of pollen, seed or other propagules is prevented. This can be accomplished by conversion to negative pressure in the growth cabinet or greenhouse or by physical entrapment by "bagging" of reproductive structures. Transfers to any other plant organisms will be considered on a case-by-case basis[45].

III-C-7-c. *Transfer to Invertebrates.* DNA from any nonprohibited source [Section I-D], except for greater than one quarter of a eukaryotic viral genome, which has been cloned and propagated in *E. coli* K-12, may be transferred with the *E. coli* vector used for cloning to any eukaryotic cells in culture or to any invertebrate organism and propagated under conditions of physical containment comparable to P1 and appropriate to the organism under study (2A). Transfers to any other host will be considered by the RAC on a case-by-case basis (45).

III-D. *Complementary DNAs.* Specific containment levels are given in Section III-A-2-a (see also last column of Table III) for complementary DNA (cDNA) of viral mRNA. For the other Sections of the Guidelines, where applicable, cDNAs synthesized *in vitro* are included within each of the above classifications. For example, cDNAs formed from cellular RNAs that are not purified and characterized are included under III-A-1, shotgun experiments; cDNAs formed from purified and characterized RNAs are included under III-A-3; etc.

Due to the possibility of nucleic acid contamination of enzyme preparations used in the preparation of cDNAs, the investigator must employ purified enzyme preparations that are free of viral nucleic acid.

III-E. *Synthetic DNAs.* If the synthetic DNA segment is likely to[2A] yield a potentially harmful polynucleotide or polypeptide (e.g., a toxin or a pharmacologically active agent), the containment conditions must be as stringent as would be used for propagating the natural DNA counterpart.

If the synthetic DNA sequence codes for a harmless product,[2A] it may be propagated at the same containment level as its purified natural DNA counterpart. For example, a synthetic DNA segment which corresponds to a nonharmful gene of birds, to be propagated in *Saccharomyces cerevisiae*, would require P2 physical containment plus an HV1 host-vector, or P1 + HV2.

If the synthetic DNA segment is not expressed *in vivo* as a polynucleotide or polypeptide product, the organisms containing the recombinant DNA molecule are exempt[4] from the Guidelines.

IV. Roles and Responsibilities

IV-A. *Policy.* Safety in activities involving recombinant DNA depends on the individual conducting them. The Guidelines cannot anticipate every possible situation. Motivation and good judgment are the key essentials to protection of health and the environment.

The Guidelines are intended to help the Institution, the Institutional Biosafety Committee (IBC), the Biological Safety Officer, and the Principal Investigator determine the safeguards that should be implemented. These Guidelines will never be complete or final, since all conceivable experiments involving recombinant DNA cannot be foreseen. Therefore, it is the responsibility of the Institution and those associated with it to adhere to the *purpose* of the Guidelines as well as to their specifics.

Each Institution (and the IBC acting on its behalf) is responsible for ensuring that recombinant DNA activities comply with the Guidelines. General recognition of institutional authority and responsibility properly establishes accountability for safe conduct of the research at the local level.

The following roles and responsibilities constitute an administrative framework in which safety is an essential and integral part of research involving recombinant DNA molecules. Further clarifications and interpretations of roles and responsibilities will be issued by NIH as necessary.

IV-B. *General Applicability.* The Guidelines are applicable to all recombinant DNA research within the United States or its territories which is conducted at or sponsored by an Institution that receives any support for recombinant DNA research from NIH. This includes research by NIH directly.

An individual receiving support for research involving recombinant DNA must be associated with or sponsored by an Institution that can and does assume the responsibilities assigned in these Guidelines.

The Guidelines are also applicable to projects done abroad if they are supported by NIH funds. If the host country, however, has established rules for the conduct of recombinant DNA projects, then a certificate of compliance with those rules may be submitted to NIH in lieu of compliance with the NIH Guidelines. NIH reserves the right to withhold funding if the safety practices to be employed abroad are not reasonably consistent with the NIH Guidelines.

IV-C. *General Definitions.* The following terms, which are used throughout the Guidelines, are defined as follows:

IV-C-1. "DNA" means deoxyribonucleic acid.

IV-C-2. "Recombinant DNA" or "recombinant DNA molecules" means either (i) molecules which are constructed outside living cells by joining natural or synthetic DNA segments to DNA molecules that can replicate in a living cell, or (ii) DNA molecules which result from the replication of a molecule described in (i) above.

IV-C-3. [Deleted]

IV-C-4. "Institution" means any public or private entity (including

Federal, State, and local government agencies).

IV-C-5. "Institutional Biosafety Committee" of "IBC" means a committee that (i) meets the requirements for membership specified in Section IV-D-2, and (ii) reviews, approves, and oversees projects in accordance with the responsibilities defined in Sections IV-D-2 and -3.

IV-C-6. "NIH Office of Recombinant DNA Activities" or "ORDA" means the office within NIH with responsibility for (i) reviewing and coordinating all activities of NIH related to the Guidelines, and (ii) performing other duties as defined in Section IV-E-3.

IV-C-7. "Recombinant DNA Advisory Committee" or "RAC" means the public advisory committee that advises the Secretary, the Assistant Secretary for Health, and the Director of the National Institutes of Health concerning recombinant DNA research. The RAC shall be constituted as specific in Section IV-E-2.

IV-C-8. "Director, NIH" or "Director" means the Director of the National Institutes of Health and any other officer or employee of NIH to whom authority has been delegated.

IV-C-9. "Federal Interagency Advisory Committee on Recombinant DNA Research" means the committee established in October 1976 to advise the Secretary, HHS, the Assistant Secretary of Health, and the Director, NIH, on the coordination of those aspects of all Federal programs and activities which relate to recombinant DNA research.

IV-C-10. "Administrative Practices Supplement" or "APS" means a publication to accompany the NIH Guidelines specifying administrative procedures for use at NIH and at Institutions.

IV-C-11. "Laboratory Safety Monograph" or "LSM" means a publication to accompany the NIH Guidelines describing practices, equipment, and facilities in detail.

IV-D. *Responsibilities of the Institution.*

IV-D-1. Each Institution conducting or sponsoring recombinant DNA research covered by these Guidelines is responsible for ensuring that the research is carried out in full conformity with the provisions of the Guidelines. In order to fulfill this responsibility, the Institution shall:

IV-D-1-a. Establish and implement policies that provide for the safe conduct of recombinant DNA research and that ensure compliance with the Guidelines. The Institution, as part of its general responsibilities for implementing the Guidelines, may establish additional procedures, as deemed necessary, to govern the Institution and its components in the discharge of its responsibilities under the Guidelines. This may include (i) statements formulated by the Institution for general implementation of the Guidelines and (ii) whatever additional precautionary steps the Institution may deem appropriate.

IV-D-1-b. Establish an Institutional Biosafety Committee (IBC) that meets the requirements set forth in Section IV-D-2 and carries out the functions detailed in Section IV-D-3.

IV-D-1-c. [Deleted]

IV-D-1-d. [Deleted]

IV-D-1-e. If the Institution is engaged in recombinant DNA research at the P3 or P4 containment level, appoint a Biological Safety Officer (BSO), who shall be a member of the IBC and carry out the duties specified in Section IV-D-4.

IV-D-1-f. Require that investigators responsible for research covered by these Guidelines comply with the provisions of Section IV-D-5, and assist investigators to do so.

IV-D-1-g. Ensure appropriate training for the IBC chairperson and members, the BSO, Principal Investigators (PIs), and laboratory staff regarding the Guidelines, their implementation, and laboratory safety. Responsibility for training IBC members may be carried out through the IBC chairperson. Responsibility for training laboratory staff may be carried out through the PI. The Institution is responsible for seeing that the PI has sufficient training, but may delegate this responsibility to the IBC.

IV-D-1-h. Determine the necessity, in connection with each project, for health surveillance of recombinant DNA research personnel, and conduct, if found appropriate, a health surveillance program for the project. (The Laboratory Safety Monograph (LSM) discusses various possible components of such a program—for example, records of agents handled, active investigation of relevant illnesses, and the maintenance of serial serum samples for monitoring serologic changes that may result from the employees' work experience. Certain medical conditions may place a laboratory worker at increased risk in any endeavor where infectious agents are handled. Examples given in the LSM include gastrointestinal disorders and treatment with steroids, immunosuppressive drugs, or antibiotics. Workers with such disorders or treatment should be evaluated to determine whether they should be engaged in research with potentially hazardous organisms during their treatment or illness.)

IV-D-1-i. Report within 30 days to ORDA any significant problems with and violations of the Guidelines and significant research-related accidents and illnesses, unless the institution determines that the PI or IBC has done so.

IV-D-2. *Membership and Procedures of the IBC.* The Institution shall establish an Institutional Biosafety Committee (IBC) meeting the following requirements:

IV-D-2-a. The IBC shall comprise no fewer than five members so selected that they collectively have experience and expertise in recombinant DNA technology and the capability to assess the safety of recombinant DNA research experiments and any potential risk to public health or the environment. At least two members (but not less than 20 percent of the membership of the committee) shall not be affiliated with the Institution (apart from their membership on the IBC) and shall represent the interest of the surrounding community with respect to health and protection of the environment. Members meet the requirement if, for example, they are officials of State or local public health or environmental protection agencies, members of other local governmental bodies, or persons active in medical, occupational health, or environmental concerns in the community. The Biological Safety Officer (BSO), mandatory when research is being conducted at the P3 and P4 levels, shall be a member (see Section IV-D-4).

IV-D-2-b. In order to ensure the professional competence necessary to review recombinant DNA activities, it is recommended that (i) the IBC include persons from disciplines relevant to recombinant DNA technology, biological safety, and engineering; (ii) the IBC include, or have available as consultants, persons knowledgeable in institutional commitments and policies, applicable law, standards of professional conduct and practice, community attitudes, and the environment; and (iii) at least one member be a nondoctoral person from a laboratory technical staff.

IV-D-2-c. The Institution shall identify the committee members by name in a report to the NIH Office of Recombinant DNA Activities (ORDA) and shall include relevant background information on each member in such form and at such times as ORDA may require. (See the Administrative Practices Supplement for further guidance.)

IV–D–2–d. No member of an IBC may be involved (except to provide information requested by the IBC) in the review or approval of a project in which he or she has been, or expects to be, engaged or has a direct financial interest.

IV–D–2–e. The Institution may establish procedures that the IBC will follow in its initial and continuing review of applications, proposals, and activities. (IBC review procedures are specified in Section IV–D–3–a.)

IV–D–2–f. Central to implementation of the Guidelines is the review of experiments by the IBC. In carrying out this responsibility, the Institution shall comply with instructions and procedures specified in the Administrative Practices Supplement.

IV–D–2–g. Institutions are encouraged to open IBC meetings to the public whenever possible, consistent with protection or privacy and proprietary interests.

IV–D–2–h. Upon request, the Institution shall made available to the public all minutes of IBC meetings and any documents submitted to or received from funding agencies which the latter are required to make available to the public (e.g., reports of Guideline violations and significant research-related accidents, and agency directives to modify projects). If comments are made by members of the public on IBC actions, the Institution shall forward to NIH both the comments and the IBC's response.

IV–D–3. *Functions of the IBC.* On behalf of the Institution, the IBC is responsible for:

IV–D–3–a. Reviewing for compliance with the NIH Guidelines all recombinant DNA research conducted at or sponsored by the Institution, and approving those research projects that it finds are in conformity with the Guidelines. This review shall include:

IV–D–3–a–(1). An independent assessment of the containment levels required by these Guidelines for the proposed research, and

IV–D–3–a–(2). An assessment of the facilities, procedures, and practices, and of the training and expertise of recombinant DNA personnel.

Note.—See Laboratory Safety Monograph (pages 187–190) for suggested guidance in conducting this review.

IV–D–3–b. Notifying the Principal Investigator (PI) of the results of their review.

IV–D–3–c. Reviewing periodically recombinant DNA research being conducted at the Institution, to ensure that the requirements of the Guidelines are being fulfilled.

IV–D–3–d. Adopting emergency plans covering accidental spills and personnel contamination resulting from such research.

Note.—Basic elements in developing specific procedures for dealing with major spills of potentially hazardous materials in the laboratory are detailed in the Laboratory Safety Monograph. Included are information and references on decontamination and emergency plans. NIH and the Centers for Disease Control are available to provide consultation, and direct assistance if necessary, as posted in the LSM. The Institution shall cooperate with the State and local public health departments, reporting any significant research-related illness or accident that appears to be a hazard to the public health.

IV–D–3–e. Reporting within 30 days to the appropriate institutional official and to the NIH Office of Recombinant DNA Activities (ORDA) any significant problems with or violations of the Guidelines, and any significant research-related accidents or illnesses, unless the IBC determines that the PI has done so.

IV–D–3–f. The IBC may not authorize initiation of experiments not explicitly covered by the Guidelines until NIH, (with the advice of the RAC when required) established the containment requirement.

IV–D–3–g. Performing such other functions as may be delegated to the IBC under Section IV–D–1.

IV–D–4. *Biological Safety Officer.* The Institution shall appoint a BSO if it engages in recombinant DNA research at the P3 or P4 containment level. The officer shall be a member of the Institutional Biosafety Committee (IBC), and his or her duties shall include (but need not be limited to):

IV–D–4–a. Ensuring through periodic inspections that laboratory standards are rigorously followed;

IV–D–4–b. Reporting to the IBC and the Institution all significant problems with and violations of the Guidelines and all significant research-related accidents and illnesses of which the BSO becomes aware, unless the BSO determines that the Principal Investigator (PI) has done so.

IV–D–4–c. Developing emergency plans fro dealing with accidential spills and personnel contamination, and investigating recombinant DNA research laboratory accidents;

IV–D–4–d. Providing advice on laboratory security;

IV–D–4–e. Providing technical advice to the PI and IBC on research safety procedures.

Note.—See Laboratory Safety Monograph for additional information on the duties of the BSO.

IV–D–5. *Principal Investigator.* On behalf of the Institution, the PI is responsible for complying fully with the Guidelines in conducting any recombinant DNA research.

IV–D–5–a. *PI-General.* As part of this general responsibility, the PI shall:

IV–D–5–a–(1). Initiate or modify no recombinant DNA research subject to the Guidelines until that research, or the proposed modification thereof, has been approved by the Institutional Biosafety Committee (IBC) and has met all other requirements of the Guidelines and the Administrative Practices Supplement (APS).

Note.—No prior approval by the IBC is required for most experiments described in Section III–O. Modify containment and experimental protocol according to recommendations of the IBC.

IV–D–5–a–(2). Report within 30 days to the IBC and NIH (ORDA) all significant problems with and violations of the Guidelines and all significant research-related accidents and illnesses;

IV–D–5–a–(3). Report to the IBC and to NIH (ORDA) new information bearing on the Guidelines;

IV–D–5–a–(4). Be adequately trained in good microbiological techniques;

IV–D–5–a–(5). Adhere to IBC-approved emergency plans for dealing with accidental spills and personnel contamination; and

IV–D–5–a–(6). Comply with shipping requirements for recombinant DNA molecules. (See Section II–C for shipping requirements, Laboratory Safety Monograph for technical recommendations, and the APS for administrative instructions and procedures. The requesting laboratory must be in compliance with the NIH Guidelines and under appropriate review by its IBC, and the sending investigator must maintain a record of all shipments of recombinant DNA materials.)

IV–D–5–b. *Submissions by the PI to NIH.* The PI shall:

IV–D–5–b–(1). Submit information to NIH (ORDA) in order to have new host-vector systems certified;

IV–D–5–b–(2). Petition NIH, with notice to the IBC, for exemptions to these Guidelines (see Sections I–E–4 and I–E–5 and, for additional information on procedures, the APS); and

IV–D–5–b–(3). Petition NIH, with concurrence of the IBC, for exceptions to the prohibitions under these Guidelines (see Section I–D and, for additional information on procedures, the APS).

IV–D–5–b–(4). Petition NIH for determination of containment for experiments requiring case-by-case review.

IV-D-5-b-(5). Petition NIH for determination of containment for experiments not covered by the Guidelines.

IV-D-5-c. *Submissions by the PI to the IBC.* The PI shall:

IV-D-5-c-(1). Make the initial determination of the required levels of physical and biological containment in accordance with the Guidelines;

IV-D-5-c-(2). Select appropriate microbiological practices and laboratory techniques to be used in the research;

IV-D-5-c-(3). Submit the initial research protocol (and also subsequent changes—e.g., changes in the source of DNA or host-vector system) to the IBC for review and approval or disapproval, and

IV-D-5-c-(4). Remain in communication with the IBC throughout the conduct of the project.

IV-D-5-d. *PI Responsibilities After Approval but Prior to Initiating the Research.* The PI is responsible for:

IV-D-5-d-(1). Making available to the laboratory staff copies of the approved protocols that describe the potential biohazards and the precautions to be taken;

IV-D-5-d-(2). Instructing and training staff in the practices and techniques required to ensure safety and in the procedures for dealing with accidents; and

IV-D-5-d-(3). Informing the staff of the reasons and provisions for any precautionary medical practices advised or requested, such as vaccinations or serum collection.

IV-D-5-e. *PI Responsibilities During the Conduct of the Approved Research.* The PI is responsible for:

IV-D-5-e-(1). Supervising the safety performance of the staff to ensure that the required safey practices and techniques are employed:

IV-D-5-e-(2). Investigating and reporting in writing to ORDA, the Biological Safety Officer (where applicable), and the IBC any significant problems pertaining to the operation and implementation of containment practices and procedures;

IV-D-5-e-(3). Correcting work errors and conditions that may result in the release of recombinant DNA materials;

IV-D-5-e-(4). Ensuring the integrity of the physical containment (e.g., biological safety cabinets) and the biological containment (e.g., purity, and genotypic and phenotypic characteristics); and

IV-D-5-e-(5). *Publications.* PIs are urged to include, in all publications reporting on recombinant DNA research, a description of the physical and biological containment procedures employed.

IV-E. *Responsibilities of NIH.*

IV-E-1. *Director.* The Director, NIH, is responsible for (i) establishing the NIH Guidelines on recombinant DNA research, (ii) overseeing their implementation, and (iii) their final interpretation.

The Director has a number of responsibilities under the Guidelines that involve the NIH Office of Recombinant DNA Activities (ORDA) and the Recombinant DNA Advisory Committee (RAC). ORDA's responsibilities under the Guidelines are administrative. Advice from the RAC is primarily scientific and technical. In certain circumstances, there is specific opportunity for public comment, with published response, before final action.

IV-E-1-a. *General Responsibilities of the Director, NIH.* The responsibilities of the Director shall include the following:

IV-E-1-a-(1). Promulgating requirements as necessary to implement the Guidelines.

IV-E-1-a-(2). Establishing and maintaining the RAC to carry out the responsibilities set forth in Section IV-E-2. The RAC's membership is specified in its charter and in Section IV-E-2;

IV-E-1-a-(3). Establishing and maintaining ORDA to carry out the responsibilities defined in Section IV-E-3; and

IV-E-1-a-(4). Maintaining the Federal Interagency Advisory Committee on Recombinant DNA Research established by the Secretary, HEW, for advice on the coordination of all Federal programs and activities relating to recombinant DNA, including activities of the RAC.

IV-E-1-b. *Specific Responsibilities of the Director, NIH.* In carrying out the responsibilities set forth in this Section, the Director shall weigh each proposed action, through appropriate analysis and consultation, to determine that it complies with the Guidelines and presents no significant risk to health or the environment.

IV-E-1-b-(1). *The Director is responsible for the following major actions* (For these, the Director must seek the advice of the RAC and provide an opportunity for public and Federal agency comment. Specifically, the agenda of the RAC meeting citing the major actions will be published in the **Federal Register** at least 30 days before the meeting, and the Director will also publish the proposed actions in the **Federal Register** for comment at least 30 days before the meeting. In addition, the Director's proposed decision, at his discretion, may be published in the Federal Register for 30 days for comment before final action is take. The Director's final decision, along with response to the comments, will be published in the **Federal Register** and the *Recombinant DNA Technical Bulletin.* The RAC and IBC chairpersons will be notified of this decision):

IV-E-1-b-(1)-(a). Changing containment levels for types of experiments that are specified in the Guidelines when a major action is involved;

IV-E-1-b-(1)-(b). Assigning containment levels for types of experiments that are not explicitly considered in the Guidelines when a major action is involved;

IV-E-1-b-(1)-(c). Certifying new host-vector systems, with the exception of minor modifications of already certified systems. [The standards and procedures for certification are described in Section II-D-2-a. Minor modifications constitute, for example, those of minimal or no consequence to the properties relevant to containment. See the Administrative Practices Supplement (APS) for further information];

IV-E-1-b-(1)-(d). Promulgating and amending a list of classes of recombinant DNA molecules to be exempt from these Guidelines because they consist entirely of DNA segments from species that exchange DNA by known physiological processes, or otherwise do not present a significant risk to health or the environment (see Sections I-E-4 and -5 and the APS for further information);

IV-E-1-b-(1)-(e). Permitting exceptions to the prohibited experiments in the Guidelines, in order, for example, to allow risk-assessment studies; and

IV-E-1-b-(1)-(f). Adopting other changes in the Guidelines.

IV-E-1-b-(2). *The Director is also responsible for the following lesser actions* (For these, the Director must seek the advice of the RAC. The Director's decision will be transmitted to the RAC and IBC chairpersons and published in the Recombinant DNA Technical Bulletin):

IV-E-1-b-(2)-(a). Interpreting and determining containment levels, upon request by ORDA;

IV-E-1-b-(2)-(b). Changing containment levels for experiments that are specified in the Guidelines (see Section III);

IV-E-1-b-(2)-(c). Assigning containment levels for experiments not explicitly considered in the Guidelines (see Section III);

IV-E-1-b-(2)-(d). Designating certain class 2 agents as class 1 for the purpose of these Guidelines (see Footnote 1 and Appendix B);

IV-E-1-b-(2)-(e). Assigning containment levels for experiments with recombinant DNA from Class 3 organisms[1] and assigning containment levels for experiments which increase the host-range and virulence of plant pathogens beyond that which occurs by natural genetic exchange.

IV-E-1-b-(3). *The Director is also responsible for the following actions.* (The Director's decision will be transmitted to the RAC and IBC chairpersons and published in the *Recombinant DNA Technical Bulletin):*

IV-E-1-b-(3)-(a). Interpreting the Guidelines for experiments to which the Guidelines specifically assign containment levels;

IV-E-1-b-(3)-(b). Determining appropriate containment conditions for experiments according to case precedents developed under Section IV-E-1-b-(2)-(c).

IV-E-1-b-(3)-(c). Determining appropriate containment conditions upon case-by-case analysis of experiments explicitly considered in the Guidelines but for which no containment levels have been set (see Footnote 45 in Part V; Sections III-C-1-a through -e; and Sections III-C-2 and -3);

IV-E-1-b-(3)-(d). Authorizing, under procedures specified by the RAC, large-scale experiments (i.e., involving more than 10 liters of culture) for recombinant DNAs that are rigorously characterized and free of harmful sequences (see Footnote 3 and Section I-D-6);

IV-E-1-b-(3)-(e). Lowering containment levels for characterized clones or purified DNA (see Sections III-A-3-a and -b, Footnotes 3 and 41);

IV-E-1-b-(3)-(f). Approving minor modifications of already certified host-vector systems. (The standards and procedures for such modifications are described in Section II-D-2); and

IV-E-1-b-(3)-(g). Decertifying already certified host-vector systems.

IV-E-1-b-(3)-(h). Assigning containment levels for experiments in which both donor and recipient are nonpathogenic prokaryotes and/or nonpathogenic lower eukaryotes (see Section III-O-2).

IV-E-1-b-(3)-(i). Adding new entries to the list of toxins for vertebrates (see Appendix G).

IV-E-1-b-(3)-(j). Approving the cloning of toxin genes in host-vector systems other than *E. coli* K-12 (see Appendix G).

IV-E-1-b-(4). The Director shall conduct, support, and assist training programs in laboratory safety for Institutional Biosafety Committtee members, Biological Safety Officers, Principal Investigators, and laboratory staff.

IV-E-1-b-(5). The Director, at the end of 36 months from the time these Guidelines are promulgated, will report on the Guidelines, their administration, and the potential risks and benefits of this research. In doing so, the Director will consult with the RAC and the Federal Interagency Committee. Public comment will be solicited on the draft report and taken into account in transmitting the final report to the Assistant Secretary for Health and the Secretary, HHS.

IV-E-2. *Recombinant Advisory Committee.* The NIH Recombinant DNA Advisory Committee (RAC) is responsible for carrying out specified functions cited below as well as others assigned under its charter or by the Secretary, HHS, the Assistant Secretary for Health, and the Director, NIH.

The members of the committee shall be chosen to provide, collectively expertise in scientific fields relevant to recombinant DNA technology and biological safety—e.g., microbiology, molecular biology, virology, genetics, epidemiology, infectious diseases, the biology of enteric organisms, botany, plant pathology, ecology, and tissue culture. At least 20 percent of the members shall be persons knowledgeable in applicable law, standards of professional conduct and practice, public attitudes, the environment, public health, occupational health, or related fields. Representatives from Federal agencies shall serve as nonvoting members. Nominations for the RAC may be submitted to the NIH Office of Recombinant DNA Activities, Bethesda, Md., 20205.

All meetings of the RAC will be announced in the **Federal Register**, including tentative agenda item, 30 days in advance of the meeting, with final agendas (if modified) available at least 72 hours before the meeting. No item defined as a major action under Section IV-E-1-b-(1) may be added to an agenda after it appears in the **Federal Register.**

IV-E-2-a. *The RAC shall be responsible for advising the Director, NIH, on the actions listed in Section IV-E-1-b-(1) and (2).*

IV-E-3. *The Office of Recombinant DNA Activities.* ORDA shall serve as a focal point for information on recombinant DNA activities and provide advice to all within and outside NIH, including Institutions, Biological Safety Committees, Principal Investigators, Federal agencies, State and local governments, and institutions in the private sector. ORDA shall carry out such other functions as may be delegated to it by the Director, NIH, including those authorities described in Section IV-E-1-b-(3). In addition, ORDA shall be responsible for the following:

IV-E-3-a. Review and approval of Institutional Biosafety Committee (IBC) membership;

IV-E-3-b through IV-E-3-c-(3). [Deleted]

IV-E-c-(4). Publish in the **Federal Register:**

IV-E-c-(4)-(a). Announcements of Recombinant DNA Advisory Committee (RAC) meetings and agendas 30 days in advance, with publication of the Director's proposed decision for 30 days of public and Federal agency comment followed by a published response, on any action listed in Section IV-E-1-(b)-(1); and

IV-E-3-c-(4)-(b). Announcements of RAC meetings and agendas 30 days in advance of any action listed in Section IV-E-1-b-(2).

Note.—If the agenda for an RAC meeting is modified, ORDA shall make the revised agenda available to anyone, upon request, at least 72 hours in advance of the meeting.

IV-E-3-c-(5). Publish the *Recombinant DNA Technical Bulletin;* and

IV-E-3-c-(6). Serve as executive secretary to the RAC.

IV-E-4. *Other NIH Components.* Other NIH components shall be responsible for:

IV-E-4-a. [Deleted]

IV-E-4-b. Certifying P4 facilities, inspecting them periodically, and inspecting other recombinant DNA facilities as deemed necessary; and

IV-E-4-c. Announcing and distributing certified HV2 and HV3 host-vector systems (see Section II-E-3).

(See Administrative Practices Supplement for additional information on the administrative procedures of ORDA and other NIH components.)

IV-F. [Deleted]

IV-G. *Compliance.* As a condition for NIH funding or recombinant DNA research, Institutions must ensure that such research conducted at or sponsored by the Institution, irrespective of the source of funding, shall comply with these Guidelines. The policies on noncompliance are as follows:

IV-G-1. All NIH-funded projects involving recombinant DNA techniques must comply with the NIH Guidelines. Noncompliance may result in (i) suspension, limitation, or termination of financial assistance for such projects and of NIH funds for other recombinant DNA research at the Institution, or (ii) a requirement for prior NIH approval of any or all recombinant DNA projects at the Institution.

IV–G–2. All non-NIH funded projects involving recombinant DNA techniques conducted at or sponsored by an Institution that receives NIH funds for projects involving such techniques must comply with the NIH Guidelines. Noncompliance may result in (i) suspension, limitation, or termination of NIH funds for recombinant DNA research at the Institution, or (ii) a requirement for prior NIH approval of any or all recombinant DNA projects at the Institution.

IV–G–3. Information concerning noncompliance with the Guidelines may be brought forward by any person. It should be delivered to both NIH (ORDA) and the relevant Institution. The Institution, generally through the IBC, shall take appropriate action. The Institution shall forward a complete report of the incident to ORDA, recommending any further action indicated.

IV–G–4. In cases where NIH proposes to suspend, limit, or terminate financial assistance because of noncompliance with the Guidelines, applicable DHEW and Public Health Service procedures shall govern.

IV–G–5. *Voluntary Compliance.* Any individual, corporation, or institution that is not otherwise covered by the Guidelines is encouraged to conduct recombinant DNA research activities in accordance with the Guidelines, through the procedures set forth in Part VI.

V. Footnotes and References

(*1*) The reference to organisms as Class 1, 2, 3, 4, or 5 refers to the classification in the publication *Classification of Etiologic Agents on the Basis of Hazard,* 4th Edition, July 1974; U.S. Department of Health, Education, and Welfare, Public Health Service, Centers for Disease Control, Office of Biosafety, Atlanta, Georgia 30333. The list of organisms in each class, as given in this publication, is reprinted in Appendix B to these Guidelines.

The Director, NIH, with advice of the Recombinant DNA Advisory Committee, may designate certain of the agents which are listed as Class 2 in the *Classification of Etiologic Agents on the Basis of Hazard,* 4th Edition, July 1974, as Class 1 agents for the Purposes of these Guidelines (see Section IV–E–1–b–(2)–(d)). An updated list of such agents may be obtained from the Office of Recombinant DNA Activities (ORDA), National Institutes of Health, Bethesda, Maryland 20205.

The entire *Classification of Etiologic Agents on the Basis of Hazard* is in the process of revision.

(*2*) For experiments using Vesicular Stomatitis virus (VSV), contact the NIH Office of Recombinant DNA Activities.

(*2A*) In Parts I and III of the Guidelines, there are a number of places where judgments are to be made. These include: "cells known to be infected with such agents" (Section I–D–1); "known to acquire it naturally" (Section I–D–5); "known to produce a potent polypeptide toxin * * * or known to carry such pathogens * * * not likely to be a product of closely linked eukaryote genes * * * shown not to contain such agents" (Section III–A–1–a–(5)–(a)); "shown to be free of disease causing microorganisms" (Section III–A–1–a(5)–(b)); "close relatives" (Section III–C–3); and "produce a potent polypeptide toxin" (Footnote 34).

In all these cases the principal investigator is to make the initial judgment on these matters as part of his responsibility to "make the initial determination of the required levels of physical and biological containment in accordance with the Guidelines" (Section IV–D–7–a). In all these cases, this judgment is to be reviewed and approved by the Institutional Biosafety Committee as part of its responsibility to make "an independent assessment of the containment levels required by these Guidelines for the proposed research" (Section IV–D–3–a–(1)). If the IBC wishes, any specific cases may be referred to the NIH Office of Recombinant DNA Activities as part of ORDA's functions to "provide advice to all within and outside NIH" (Section IV–E–3), and ORDA may request advice from the Recombinant DNA Advisory Committee as part of the RAC's responsibility for "interpreting and determining containment levels upon request by ORDA" (Section IV–E–1–b–(2)–(a)).

(*3*) The following types of data should be considered in determining whether DNA recombinants are "characterized" and the absence of harmful sequences has been established: (a) The absence of potentially harmful genes (e.g., sequences contained in indigenous tumor viruses or sequences that code for toxins, invasins, virulence factors, etc., that might potentiate the pathogenicity or communicability of the vector and/or the host or be detrimental to humans, animals, or plants); (b) the type(s) of genetic information on the cloned segment and the nature of transcriptional and translation gene products specified; (c) the relationship between the recovered and desired segment (e.g., hybridization and restriction endonuclease fragmentation analysis where applicable); (d) the genetic stability of the cloned fragment; and (e) any alterations in the biological properties of the vector and host.

(*4*) In Section I–E, "exemptions" from the Guidelines are discussed. Such experiments are not covered by the Guidelines and need not be registered with NIH. In Section I–D on "prohibitions," the possibility of "exceptions" is discussed. An "exception" means that an experiment may be expressly released from a prohibition. At that time it will be assigned an appropriate level of physical and biological containment.

(*5*) Care should be taken to inactivate recombinant DNA before disposal. Procedures for inactivating DNA can be found in the "Laboratory Safety Monograph: A Supplement to the NIH Guidelines for Recombinant DNA Research."

(*6*) *Laboratory Safety at the Center for Disease Control* (Sept. 1974). U.S. Department of Health Education and Welfare Publication No. CDC 75–8118.

(*7*) *Classification of Etiologic Agents on the Basis of Hazard.* (4th Edition, July 1974). U.S. Department of Health, Education and Welfare. Public Health Service. Centers for Disease Control, Office of Biosafety, Atlanta, Georgia 30333.

(*8*) *National Cancer Institute Safety Standards for Research Involving Oncogenic Viruses* (Oct. 1974). U.S. Department of Health, Education and Welfare Publication No. (NIH) 75–790.

(*9*) *National Institutes of Health Biohazards Safety Guide* (1974). U.S. Department of Health, Education, and Welfare Public Health.

(*10*) *Biohazards in Biological Research* (1973). A. Hellman, M. N. Oxman, and R. Pollack (ed.) Cold Spring Harbor Laboratory.

(*11*) *Handbook of Laboratory Safety* (1971). Second Edition. N. V. Steere (ed.). The Chemical Rubber Co, Cleveland.

(*12*) Bodily, J. L. (1970). *General Administration of the Laboratory,* H. L. Bodily, E. L. Updyke, and J. O. Mason (eds.), Diagnostic Procedures for Bacterial Mycotic and Parasitic Infections. American Public Health Association, New York, pp. 11–28.

(*13*) Darlow, H. M. (1969). *Safety in the Microbiological Laboratory.* In J. R. Norris and D. W. Robbins (ed.), Methods in Microbiology, Academic Press, Inc., New York. pp. 169–204.

(*14*) *The Prevention of Laboratory Acquired Infection* (1974). C. H. Collins, E. G. Hartley, and R. Pilsworth. Public Health Laboratory Service, Monograph Series No. 6.

(*15*) Chatigny, M. A. (1961). *Protection Against Infection in the Microbiological Laboratory: Devices and Procedures.* In W. W. Umbreit (ed.). Advances in Applied Microbiology. Academic Press, New York, N.Y. 3:131–192.

(*16*) *Design Criteria for Viral Oncology Research Facilities* (1975). U.S. Department of Health, Education and Welfare, Public Health Service, National Institutes of Health, DHEW Publication No. (NIH) 75–891.

(*17*) Kuehne, R. W. (1973). *Biological Containment Facility for Studing Infectious Disease.* Appl. Microbiol. 26–239–243.

(*18*) Runkle, R. S., and G. B. Phillips (1969). *Microbial Containment Control Facilities.* Van Nostrand Reinhold, New York.

(*19*) Chatigny, M. A., and D. I. Clinger (1969). *Contamination Control in Aerobiology.* In R. L. Dimmick and A. B. Akers (eds.). An Introduction to Experimental Aerobiology. John Wiley & Sons, New York. pp. 194–263.

(*19A*) Horsfall, F. L., Jr., and J. H. Baner (1940). *Individual Isolation of Infected Animals in a Single Room.* J. Bact. *40.* 569–580.

(*20*) Biological safety cabinets referred to in this section are classified as *Class I, Class II,* or *Class III* cabinets. A *Class I* is a ventilated cabinet for personnel protection having an inward flow of air away from the operator. The exhaust air from this cabinet is filtered through a high-efficiency particulate air (HEPA) filter. This cabinet is used in three operational modes: (1) With a full-width open front, (2) with an installed front closure panel (having four 8-inch diameter openings) without gloves, and (3) with an installed front closure panel equipped with arm-length rubber gloves. The face velocity of the inward flow of air through the full-width open front is 75 feet per minute or greater. A *Class II* cabinet is a ventilated cabinet for personnel and product protection having an open front with inward air flow for personnel protection, and HEPA filtered mass recirculated air flow for product protection. The cabinet exhaust air is filtered through a HEPA filter. The face velocity of the inward flow of air through the full-width open front is 75 feet per minute or greater. Design and performance specifications for *Class II* cabinets have been adopted by the National Sanitation Foundation, Ann Arbor, Michigan. A *Class III* cabinet is a closed-front ventilated cabinet of gas-tight construction which provides the highest level of personnel protection of all biohazard safety cabinets. The interior of the cabinet is protected from contaminants exterior to the cabinet. The cabinet is fitted with arm-length rubber gloves and is operated under a negative pressure of at least 0.5 inches water gauge. All supply air is filtered through HEPA filters. Exhaust air is filtered through two HEPA filters or one HEPA filter and incinerator before discharged to the outside environment.

(*21*) Hershfield, V., H. W. Boyer, C. Yanofsky, M. A. Lovett, and D. R. Helinski (1974). *Plasmid ColEl as a Molecular Vehicle for Cloning and Amplification of DNA.* Proc. Nat. Acad. Sci. USA *71*, 3455–3459.

(*22*) Wensink, P. C., D. J. Finnegan, J. E. Donelson, and D. S. Hogness (1974). *A System for Mapping DNA Sequences in the Chromosomes of Drosophila Melanogaster.* Cell *3*, 315–335.

(*23*) Tanaka, T., and B. Weisblum (1975). *Construction of a Colicin El-R Factor Composite Plasmid In Vitro: Means for Amplification of Deoxyribonucleic Acid.* J. Bacteriol. *121*, 354–362.

(*24*) Armstrong, K. A., V. Hershfield, and D. R. Helinski (1977). *Gene Cloning and Containment Properties of Plasmid Col El and Its Derivatives,* Science *196*, 172–174.

(*25*) Bolivar, F., R. L. Rodriguez, M. C. Betlach, and H. W. Boyer (1977). *Construction and Characterization of New Cloning Vehicles: I. Ampicillin-Resistant Derivative of pMB9.* Gene *2*, 75–93.

(*26*) Cohen, S. N., A. C. W. Chang, H. Boyer, and R. Helling (1973). *Construction of Biologically Functional Bacterial Plasmids in Vitro.* Proc. Natl. Acad. Sci. USA 70, 3240–3244.

(*27*) Bolivar, F., R. L. Rodriquez, R. J. Greene, M. C. Batlach, H. L. Reyneker, H. W. Boyer, J. H. Crosa, and S. Falkow (1977). *Construction and Characterization of New Cloning Vehicles: II. A Multi-Purpose Cloning System.* Gene *2*, 95–113.

(*28*) Thomas, M., J. R. Cameron, and R. W. Davis (1974). *Viable Molecular Hybrids of Bacteriophage Lambda and Eukaryotic DNA.* Proc. Nat. Acad. Sci. USA *71*, 4579–4583.

(*29*) Murray, N.E., and K. Murray (1974). *Manipulation of Restriction Targets in Phage Lambda to Form Receptor Chromosomes for DNA Fragments.* Nature *251*, 476–481.

(*30*) Rambach, A., and P. Tiollais (1974). *Bacteriophage Having EcoRI Endonuclease Sites Only in the Non-Essential Region of the Genome.* Proc. Nat. Acad. Sci., USA *71*, 3927–3930.

(*31*) Blattner, F. R., B. G. Williams, A. E. Bleche, K. Denniston-Thompson, H. E. Faber, L. A. Furlong, D. J. Gunwald, D. O. Kiefer, D. D. Moore, J. W. Shumm, E. L. Sheldon, and O. Smithies (1977). *Charon Phages: Safer Derivatives of Bacteriophage Lambda for DNA Cloning.* Science *196*, 163–169.

(*32*) Donoghue, D. J., and P. A. Sharp (1977). *An Improved Lambda Vector: Construction of Model Recombinants Coding for Kanamycin Resistance,* Gene *1*, 209–227.

(*33*) Leder, P., D. Tiemeier and L. Enquist (1977). *EK2 Derivatives of Bacteriophage Lambda Useful in the Cloning of DNA from Higher Organisms: The gt WES System.* Science *196*, 175–177.

(*33A*) Skalka, A. (1978). *Current Status of Coliphage EK2 Vectors.* Geen *3*, 29–35.

(*33B*) Szybalski, W., A. Skalka, S. Gottesman, A. Campbell, and D. Botstein (1978). *Standardized Laboratory Tests for EK2 Certification.* Gene *3*, 36–38.

(*34*) We are specifically concerned with the remote possibility that potent toxins could be produced by acquiring a single gene or cluster of genes. See also footnote 2A.

(*35*) Defined as observable under optimal laboratory conditions by transformation, transduction, phage infection, and/or conjugation with transfer of phage, plasmid, and/or chromosomal genetic information. Note that this definition of exchange may be less stringent than that applied to exempt organisms under Section I–E–4.

(*36*) As classified in the Third Report of the International Committee on Taxonomy of Viruses: Classification and Nomenclature of Viruses, R. E. F. Matthews, Ed. Intervirology 12 (129–296) 1979. (As noted in the Prohibition Section, the use of viruses classified[1] as Class 4 or 5 is prohibited.)

(*37*) The cDNA copy of the viral mRNA must be >99% pure; otherwise as for shotgun experiments with eukaryotic cellular DNA.

(*37A*) For the purpose of these Guidelines, viruses of the families *Papovaviridae, Adenoviridae,* and *Herpetoviridae* (36) should be considered as "transforming" viruses. While only certain of these viruses have been associated with cell transformation *in vivo* or *in vitro,* it seems prudent to consider all members to be potentially capable of transformation. In addition, those viruses of the family *Poxviridae* that produce proliferative responses—i.e., myxoma, rabbit and squirrel fibroma, and Yaba viruses—should be considered as "transforming."

(*38*) >99% pure (i.e., less than 1% of the DNA consists of intact viral genomes); otherwise as for whole genomes.

(*39*) The viruses have been classified by NCI as "moderate-risk oncogenic viruses." See "Laboratory Safety Monograph—A Supplement to the NIH Guidelines for Recombinant DNA Research" for recommendations on handling the viruses themselves.

(*40*) [Deleted]

(*41*) The DNA preparation is defined as "purified" if the desired DNA represents at least 99% (w/w) of the total DNA in the preparation, provided that it was verified by more than one procedure.

(*42*) The lowering of the containment level when this degree of purification has been obtained is based on the fact that the total number of clones that must be examined to obtain the desired clone is markedly reduced. Thus, the probability of cloning a harmful gene could, for example, be reduced by more than 10^{5}-fold when a nonrepetitive gene from mammals was being sought. Furthermore, the level of purity specified here makes it easier to establish that the desired DNA does not contain harmful genes.

(*43*) This is not permitted, of course, if it falls under any of the Prohibitions of Section I–D. Of particular concern here is prohibition I–D–5, i.e., "Deliberate transfer of a drug resistance trait to micro-organisms that are not known to acquire it naturally if such acquisition could compromise the use of a drug to control disease agents in human or veterinary medicine or agriculture."

(*44*) Because this work will be done almost exclusively in tissue culture cells, which have no capacity for propagation outside the laboratory, the primary focus for containment is the vector. It should be pointed out that risk of laboratory-acquired infection as a consequence of tissue culture manipulation is very low. Given good microbiological practices, the most likely mode of escape of recombinant DNAs from a physically contained laboratory is carriage by an infected human. Thus the vector with an inserted DNA segment should have little or no ability to replicate or spread in humans.

For use as a vector in a vertebrate host cell system, an animal viral DNA molecule should display the following properties:

(i) It should not consist of the whole genome of any agent that is infectious for humans or that replicates to a significant extent in human cells in tissue culture. If the recombinant molecule is used to transform nonpermissive cells (i.e., cells which do not produce infectious virus particles), this is not a requirement.

(ii) It should be derived from a virus whose epidemiological behavior and host range are well understood.

(iii) In permissive cells, it should be defective when carrying an inserted DNA segment (i.e., propagation of the recombinant DNA as a virus must be dependent upon the presence of a complementing helper genome). In almost all cases this condition would be achieved automatically by the manipulations used to construct and propagate the recombinants. In addition, the amount of DNA encapsidated in the particles of most animal viruses is defined within fairly close limits. The insertion of sizable foreign DNA sequences, therefore, generally demands a compensatory deletion of viral sequences. It may be possible to introduce very short insertions (50–100 base pairs) without rendering the viral vector defective. In such a situation, the requirement that the viral vector be defective is not necessary, except in those cases in which the inserted DNA encodes a biologically active polypeptide.

It is desired but not required that the functional anatomy of the vector be known—that is, fL-re sLogld be a clear idea of the location within the molecule of:

(i) The sites at which DNA synthesis originates and terminates,

(ii) The sites that are cleaved by restriction endonucleases. and

(iii) The template regions for the major gene product.

If possible the helper virus genome should:

(i) Be integrated into the genome of a stable line of host cells (a situation that would effectively limit the growth of the vector recombinant to such cell lines) or

(ii) Consist of a defective genome, or an appropriate conditional lethal mutant virus, making vector and helper dependent upon each other for propagation.

However, neither of these stipulations is a requirement.

(45) Review by NIH on a case-by-case basis means that NIH must review and set appropriate containment conditions before the work may be undertaken. NIH actions in such case-by-case reviews will be published in the *Recombinant DNA Technical Bulletin*.

(46) Provided the inserted DNA sequences are not derived from eukaryotic viruses. In the latter case, such experiments will be evaluated on a case-by-case basis.

(47) >99% pure; otherwise as for shotgun experiments.

(48) A USDA permit, required for import and interstate transport of pathogens, may be obtained from the Animal and Plant Health Inspection Service, USDA, Federal Building, Hyattsville, MD 20782.

(49) A subset of non-conjugative plasmid vectors are also poorly mobilizable (e.g., pBR322, pBR313). Where practical, these vectors should be employed.

(50) i.e., the total of all genomes within a Family shall not exceed two-thirds of the genome.

VI. Voluntary Compliance

VI-A. *Basic Policy.* Individuals, corporations, and institutions not otherwise covered by the Guidelines are encouraged to do so by following the standards and procedures set forth in Parts I-IV or the Guidelines. In order to simplify discussion, references hereafter to "institutions" are intended to encompass corporations, and individuals who have no organizational affiliation. For purposes of complying with the Guidelines, an individual intending to carry out research involving recombinant DNA is encouraged to affiliate with an institution that has an Institutional Biosafety Committee approved under the Guidelines.

Since commercial organizations have special concerns, such as protection of proprietary data, some modifications and explanations of the procedures in Parts I-IV are provided below, in order to address these concerns.

VI-B. *IBC Approval.* The NIH Office of Recombinant DNA Activities (ORDA) will review the membership of an institution's Institutional Biosafety Committee (IBC) and, where it finds the IBC meets the requirements set forth in Section IV-D-2, will give its approval to the IBC membership.

It should be emphasized that employment of an IBC member solely for purposes of membership on the IBC does not itself make the member an institutionally affiliated member for purposes of Section IV-D-2-a.

Except for the unaffiliated members, a member of an IBC for an institution not otherwise covered by the Guidelines may participate in the review and approval of a project in which the member has a direct financial interest, so long as the member has not been and does not expect to be engaged in the project. Section IV-D-2-d is modified to that extent for purposes of these institutions.

VI-C. [Deleted]

VI-D. *Certification of Host-Vector Systems.* A host-vector system may be proposed for certification by the Director, NIH, in accordance with the procedures set forth in Section II-D-2-a.

Institutions not otherwise covered by the Guidelines will not be subject to Section II-D-3 by complying with these procedures.

In order to ensure protection for proprietary data, any public notice regarding a host-vector system which is designated by the institution as proprietary under Section VI-F-1 will be issued only after consultation with the institution as to the content of the notice.

VI-E. *Requests for Exceptions, Exemptions, Approvals.* Requests for exceptions from prohibitions, exemptions, or other approvals required by the Guidelines should be requested by following the procedures set forth in the appropriate sections in Parts I-IV of the Guidelines.

In order to ensure protection for proprietary data, any public notice regarding a request for an exception, exemption, or other approval which is designated by the institution as proprietary under Section VI-F-1 will be issued only after consultation with the institution as to the content of the notice.

VI-F. *Protection of Proprietary Data.* In general, the Freedom of Information Act requires Federal agencies to make their records available to the public upon request. However, this requirement does not apply to, among other things, "trade secrets and commercial and financial information obtained from a person and privileged or confidential." 18 U.S.C. 1905, in turn makes it a crime for an officer or employee of the United States or any Federal department or agency to publish, divulge, disclose, or make known "in any manner or to any extent not authorized by law any information coming to him in the course of his employment or official duties or by reason of any examination or investigation made by, or return, report or record made to or filed with, such department or agency or officer of employee thereof, which information concerns or relates to the trade secrets, (or processes * * * of any person, firm, partnership, corporation, or association." This provision applies to all employees of the Federal Government, including special Government employees. Members of the Recombinant DNA Advisory Committee are "special Government employees."

VI-F-1. In submitting information to NIH for purposes of complying voluntarily with the Guidelines, an institution may designate those items of information which the institution believes constitute trade secrets or privileged or confidential commercial or financial information.

VI-F-2. If NIH receives a request under the Freedom of Information Act for information so designated, NIH will promptly contact the institution to secure its views as to whether the information (or some portion) should be released.

V-F-3. If the NIH decides to release this information (or some portion) in response to a Freedom of Information request or otherwise, the institution will be advised; and the actual release will not be made until the expiration of 15 days after the institution is so advised, except to the extent that earlier release, in the judgement of the Director, NIH, is necessary to protect against an imminent hazard to the public or the environment.

VI-F-4. Projects should be registered in accordance with procedures specified in the *Administrative Practices Supplement.* The following information will usually be considered publicly available information, consistent with the need to protect proprietary data:

a. The names of the institution and principal investigator.

b. The location where the experiments will be performed.

c. The host-vector system.

d. the source of the DNA.

e. The level of physical containment.

VI-F-5-a. Any institution not otherwise covered by the Guidelines, which is considering submission of data or information voluntarily to NIH, may request presubmission review of the records involved to determine whether, if the records are submitted, NIH will or will not make part or all of the records available upon request under the Freedom of Information Act.

VI-F-5-b. A request for presubmission review should be submitted to ORDA, along with the records involved. These records must be clearly marked as being the property of the institution, on loan to NIH solely for the purpose of making a determination under the Freedom of Information Act. ORDA will then seek a determination from the HEW Freedom of Information Officer, the responsible official under HEW regulations (45 CFR Part 5), as to whether the records involved (or some portion) are or are not available to members of the public under the Freedom of Information Act. Pending such a determination, the records will be kept separate from ORDA files, will be considered records of the institution and not ORDA, and will not be received as part of ORDA files. No copies will be made of the records.

VI-F-5-c. ORDA will inform the institution of the HEW Freedom of Information Officer's determination and follow the institution's instructions as to where some or all of the records involved are to be returned to the institution or to become a part of ORDA files. If the institution instructs ORDA to return the records, no copies or summaries of the records will be made or retained by HEW, NIH, or ORDA.

VI-F-5-d. The HEW Freedom of Information Officer's determination will represent the official's judgment, as of the time of the determination, as to whether the records involved (or some portion) would be exempt from disclosure under the Freedom of Information Act, if at the time of the determination the records were in ORDA files and a request were received from them under the Act.

Appendix A of Annex E.—Exemptions Under I-E-4

Section I-E-4 states that exempt from these Guidelines are "certain specified recombinant DNA molecules that consist entirely of DNA segments from different species that exchange DNA by known physiological processes, though one or more of the segments may be a synthetic equivalent. A list of such exchangers will be prepared and periodically revised by the Director, NIH, with advice of the Recombinant DNA Advisory Committee, after appropriate notice and opportunity for public comment (see Section IV-E-1-b-(1)-(d).) Certain classes are exempt as of publication of these Revised Guidelines. The list is in Appendix A."

Under exemption I-E-4 of these revised Guidelines are recombinant DNA molecules that are (1) composed entirely of DNA segments from one or more of the organisms within a sublist and (2) to be propagated in any of the organisms within a sublist. (Classification of *Bergey's Manual of Determinative Bacteriology*, eighth edition. R.E. Buchanan and N.E. Gibbons, editors. Williams and Wilkins Company: Baltimore, 1974.)

Sublist A

1. Genus *Escherichia*
2. Genus *Shigella*
3. Genus *Salmonella* (including *Arizona*)
4. Genus *Enterobacter*
5. Genus *Citrobacter* (including *Levinea*)
6. Genus *Klebsiella*
7. Genus *Erwinia*
8. *Pseudomonas aeruginosa*, *Pseudomonas putida* and *seudomonas fluorescens*
9. *Serratia marcescens*

Sublist B

1. *Bacillus subtilis*
2. *Bacillus licheniformis*
3. *Bacillus pumilus*
4. *Bacillus globigii*
5. *Bacillus niger*
6. *Bacillus nato*
7. *Bacillus amyloliquefaciens*
8 *Bacillus aterrimus*

Sublist C

1. *Streptomyces aureofaciens*
2. *Streptomyces rimosus*
3. *Streptomyces coelicolor*

Sublist D

1. *Streptomyces griseus*
2. *Streptomyces cyaneus*
3. *Streptomyces venezuelae*

Sublist E

One way transfer of *Streptococcus mutans* or *Streptococcus lactis* DNA into *Streptococcus sanguis*.

Sublist F

1. *Streptococcus sanguis*
2. *Streptococcus pneumoniae*
3. *Streptococcus faecalis*
4. *Streptococcus pyogenes*

Appendix B of Annex E.—Classification of Microorganisms on the Basis of Hazard

I. *Classification of Etiologic Agents on the Basis of Hazard (1)*

A. Class 1 Agents

All bacterial, parasitic, fungal, viral, rickettsial, and chlamydial agents not included in higher classes.

B. Class 2 Agents

1. Bacterial Agents

Actinobacillus—all species except *A. mallei*, which is in Class 3
Arizona hinshawii—all serotypes
Bacillus anthracis
Bordetella—all species
Borrelia recurrentis, *B. vincenti*
Clostridium botulinum, *Cl. chauvoei*, *Cl. haemolyticum*, *Cl. histolyticum*, *Cl. novyi*, *Cl. septicum*, *Cl. tetani*
Corynebacterium diptheriae, *C. equi*, *C. haemolyticum*, *C. pseudotuberculosis*, *C. pyogenes*, *C. renale*
Diplococcus (Streptococcus) pneumoniae
Erysipelothrix insidiosa
Escherichia coli—all enteropathogenic serotypes
Haemophilus ducreyi, *H. influenzae*
Herellae vaginicola
Klebsiella—all species and all serotypes
Leptospira interrogans—all serotypes
Listeria—all species
Mima polymorpha
Moraxella—all species
Mycobacteria—all species except those listed in Class 3
Mycoplasma—all species except *Mycoplasma mycoides* and *Mycoplasma agalactiae*, which are in Class 5
Neisseria gonorrhoeae, *N. meningitidis*
Pasteurella—all species except those listed in Class 3
Salmonella—all species and all serotypes
Shigella—all species and all serotypes
Sphaerophorus necrophorus
Staphylococcus aureus
Streptobacillus moniliformis
Streptococcus pyogenes
Treponema carateum, *T. pallidum*, and *T. pertenue*
Vibrio fetus, *V. comma*, including biotype El Tor, and *V. parahemolyticus*

2. Fungal Agents

**Actinomycetes* (including *Nocardia* species and *Actinomyces species and Arachnia propionica)*
Blastomyces dermatitidis
Cryptococcus neoformans
Paracoccidioides brasilienis

3. Parasitic Agents

Endamoeba histolytica
Leishmania sp.
Naegleria gruberi
Toxoplasma gondii
Toxocara canis
Trichinella spiralis
Trypanosoma cruzi

4. Viral, Rickettsial, and Chlamydial Agents

Adenoviruses—human—all types
Cache Valley virus
Coxsackie A and B viruses
Cytomegaloviruses
Echoviruses—all types.
Encephalomyocarditis virus (EMC)
Flanders virus
Hart Park virus
Hepatitis-associated antigen material
Herpes viruses—except *Herpesvirus simiae* (Monkey B virus) which is in Class 4
Corona viruses
Influenza viruses—all types except A/PR8/34, which is in Class 1
Langat virus
Lymphogranuloma venereum agent
Measles virus
Mumps virus

Parainfluenza virus—all types except Parainfluenza virus 3, SF4 strain, which is in Class 1
Polioviruses—all types, wild and attenuated
Poxviruses—all types except *Alastrim, Smallpox, Monkey pox, and Whitepox*, which depending on experiments, are in Class 3 or Class 4
Rabies virus—all strains except *Rabies street virus*, which should be classified in Class 3 when inoculated into carnivores
Reoviruses—all types
Respiratory syncytial virus
Rhinoviruses—all types
Rubella virus
Simian viruses—all types except *Herpesvirus simiae (Monkey B virus)* and *Marburg virus*, which are in Class 4
Sindbis virus
Tensaw virus
Turlock virus
Vaccinia virus
Varicella virus
Vole rickettsia
Yellow fever virus, 17D vaccine strain

C. Class 3 Agents

1. Bacterial Agents

*Actinobacillus mallei**
Bartonella—all species
Brucella—all species
Francisella tularensis
Mycobacterium avium, M. bovis, M. tuberculosis
Pasteurella multocide type B ("buffalo" and other foreign virulent strains*)
*Pseudomonas pseudomallei**
Yersenia pestis

2. Fungal Agents

Coccidioides immitis
Histoplasma capsulatum
Histoplasma capsulatum var. *duboisii*

3. Parasitic Agents

Schistosoma mansoni

4. Viral, Rickettsial, and Chlamydial Agents

****Alastrim, Smallpox, Monkey pox, and Whitepox*, when used *in vitro*
Arboviruses—all strains except those in Classes 2 and 4 (Arboviruses indigenous to the United States are in Class 3, except those listed in Class 2. *West Nile* and *Semliki Forest* viruses may be classified up or down, depending on the conditions of use and geographical location of the laboratory.)
Dengue virus, when used for transmission or animal inoculation experiments
Lymphocytic choriomeningitis virus (LCM)
Psittacosis-Ornithosis-Trachoma group of agents
Rabies street virus, when used in inoculations of carnivores (See Class 2)
Rickettsia—all species except *Vole rickettsia* when used for transmission or animal inoculation experiments
*Vesicular stomatitis virus**
Yellow fever virus—wild, when used *in vitro*

D. Class 4 Agents

1. Bacterial Agents

None

3. Fungal Agents

None

3. Parasitic Agents

None

Viral, Rickettsial, and Chlamydial Agents

****Alastrim, Smallpox, Monkey pox, and Whitepox*, when used for transmission or animal inoculation experiments
Hemorrhagic fever agents, including *Crimean hemorrhagic fever, (Congo), Junin*, and *Machupo* viruses, and others as yet undefined
Herpesvirus simiae (Monkey B virus)
Lassa virus
Marburg virus
Tick-borne encephalitis virus complex, including *Russian spring-summer encephalitis, Kyasanur forest disease, Omsk hemorrhagic fever*, and *Central European encephalitis viruses*
Venezuelan equine encephalitis virus, epidemic strains, when used for transmission or animal inoculation experiments
Yellow fever virus—wild, when used for transmission or animal inoculation experiments

II. Classification of Oncogenic Viruses on the Basis of Potential Hazard (2)

A. Low-Risk Oncogenic Viruses

Rous Sarcoma
SV-40
CELO
Ad7-SV40
Polyoma
Bovine papilloma
Rat mammary tumor
Avian Leukosis
Murine Leukemia
Murine Sarcoma
Mouse mammary tumor
Rat Leukemia
Hamster Leukemia
Bovine Leukemia
Dog Sarcoma
Mason-Pfizer Monkey Virus
Marek's
Guinea Pig Herpes
Lucke (Frog)
Adenovirus
Shope Fibroma
Shope Papilloma

B. Moderate-Risk Oncogenic Viruses

Ad2-SV40
FeLV
HV Saimiri
EBV
SSV-1
GaLV
HV ateles
Yaba
FeSV

III. Animal Pathogens (3)

A. Animal disease organisms which are forbidden entry into the United States by Law (CDC Class 5 agents)

1. Foot and mouth disease virus

B. Animal disease organisms and vectors which are forbidfden entry into the United States by USDA Policy (CDC Class 5 Agents)

African horse sickness virus
African swine fever virus
Besnoitia besnoiti
Borna disease virus
Bovine infectious petechial fever
Camel pox virus
Ephemeral fever virus
Fowl plague virus
Goat pox virus
Hog cholera virus
Louping ill virus
Lumpy skin disease virus
Nairobi sheep disease virus
Newcastle disease virus (Asiatic strains)
Mycoplasma mycoides (contagious bovine pleuropneumonia)
Mycoplasma agalactiae (contagious agalactia of sheep)
Rickettsia ruminatium (heart water)
Rift valley fever virus
Rhinderpest virus
Sheep pox virus
Swine vesicular disease virus
Teschen disease virus
Trypanosoma vivax (Nagana)
Trypanosoma evansi
Theileria parva (East Coast fever)
Theileria annulata
Theileria lawrencei
Theileria bovis
Theileria hirci
Vesicular exanthema virus
Wesselsbron disease virus
Zyonema

Footnotes and References of Appendix B

*A USDA permit, required for import and interstate commerce of pathogens, may be obtained from the Animal and Plant Health Inspection Service, USDA, Federal Building, Hyattsville, MD. 20782.

**Since the publication of the classification in 1974 [1], the *Actinomycetes* have been reclassified as bacterial rather than fungal agents.

***All activities, including storage of variola and whitepox are restricted to the single national facility (World Health Organization (WHO) Collaborating Center for Smallpox Research, Center for Disease Control, in Atlanta).

(1) *Classification of Etiologic Agents on the Basis of Hazard.* (4th Edition, July 1974). U.S. Department of Health, Education and Welfare, Public Health Service, Center for Disease Control, Office of Biosafety, Atlanta, Georgia 30333.

(2) *National Cancer Institute Safety Standards for Research Involving Oncogenic Viruses* (October 1974). U.S. Department of Health, Education, and Welfare Publication No. (NIH) 75-790

(3) U.S. Department of Agriculture, Animal and Plant Health Inspection Service.

Appendix C of Annex E.—Exemptions under I-E-5

Section I-E-5 states that exempt from these Guidelines are "Other classes of recombinant DNA molecules, if the Director, NIH, with advice of the Recombinant DNA Advisory Committee, after appropriate notice and opportunity for public comment, finds that they do not present a significant risk to health or the environment. (See Section IV-E-1-b-(1)-(d).) Certain classes are exempt as of publication of these Revised Guidelines."

The following classes of experiments are exempt under Section I-E-5 of the Guidelines:

1. *Recombinant DNAs in Tissue Culture.*

Recombinant DNA molecules derived entirely from non-viral components (that is, no component is derived from a eukaryotic virus), that are propagated and maintained in cells in tissue culture are exempt from these Guidelines with the exceptions listed below.

Exceptions.

Experiments described in Sections I-D-1 to I-D-5 as being prohibited.

Experiments involving DNA from Class 3 organisms [1] or cells known to be infected with these agents, or any recombinant DNA molecules which increase the virulence and host-range of a plant pathogen beyond that which occurs by natural genetic exchange. (See Section III-O-1.)

Experiments involving the deliberate introduction of genes coding for the biosynthesis of toxins potent for vertebrates. (See Appendix G.)

2. *Experiments Involving E. coli K-12 host-vector systems.*

Experiments which use *E. coli* K-12 host-vector systems, with the exception of those experiments listed below, are exempt from these Guidelines provided that (a) the *E. coli* host shall not contain conjugation proficient plasmids or generalized transducing phages, and (b) lambda or lambdoid or Ff bacteriophages or nonconjugative plasmids [49] shall be used as vectors. However, experiments involving the insertion into *E. coli* K-12 of DNA from prokaryotes that exchange genetic information [35] with *E. coli* may be performed with any *E. coli* K-12 vector (e.g., conjugative plasmid). When a nonconjugative vector is used, the *E. coli* K-12 host may contain conjugation-proficient plasmids either autonomous or integrated, or generalized transducing phages.

For these exempt experiments, P1 physical containment conditions are recommended.

Exceptions.

Experiments described in Sections I-D-1 to I-D-5 as being prohibited.

Experiments involving DNA from Class 3 organisms [1] or from cells known to be infected with these agents may be conducted at P3 containment. Lower containment levels may be specified by NIH. (See Section IV-E-1-b-(2)-(e).) Experiments in this category require prior IBC review and approval.

Experiments which increase the virulence and host range of a plant pathogen beyond that which occurs by natural genetic exchange. (See Section III-O-1.)

Large-scale experiments (e.g., more than 10 liters of culture) require prior IBC review and approval.

Experiments involving the deliberate cloning of genes coding for the biosynthesis of toxins potent for vertebrates. (See Appendix G.)

3. *Experiments Involving Saccharomyces cerevisiae host-vector systems.*

Experiments which use *Saccharomyces cerevisiae* host-vector systems, with the exception of experiments listed below, are exempt from these Guidelines provided that laboratory strains are used.

For these exempt experiments, P1 physical containment conditions are recommended.

Exceptions.

Experiments described in Sections I-D-1 to I-D-5 as being prohibited.

Experiments involving CDC Class 3 organisms [1] or cells known to be infected with these agents, or any recombinant DNA molecules which increase the virulence and host-range of a plant pathogen beyond that which occurs by natural genetic exchange. (See Section III-O-1.)

Large-scale experiments (e.g., more than 10 liters of culture) require prior IBC review and approval.

Experiments involving the deliberate cloning of genes coding for the biosynthesis of toxins potent for vertebrates. (See Appendix G.)

4. *Experiments Involving Bacillus subtilis host-vector systems.*

Any asporogenic *Bacillus subtilis* strain which does not revert to a sporeformer with a frequency greater than 10^{-7} can be used for cloning DNA from any nonprohibited source, with the exception of those experiments listed below. Indigenous *Bacillus* plasmids and phages, whose host-range does not include *Bacillus cereus* or *Bacillus anthracis*, may be used as vectors.

For these exempt experiments P1 physical containment conditions are recommended.

Exceptions.

Experiments described in Section I-D-1 to I-D-5 as being prohibited.

Experiments involving CDC Class 3 organisms [1] or cells known to be infected with these agents, or any recombinant DNA molecules which increase the virulence and host-range of a plant pathogen beyond that which occurs by natural genetic exchange. (See Section III-O-1.)

Large-scale experiments (e.g., more than 10 liters of culture) require prior IBC review and approval.

Experiments involving the deliberate cloning of genes coding for the biosynthesis of toxins potent for vertebrates. (See Appendix G.)

Appendix D of Annex E.—HV1 and HV2 Host-Vector Systems Assigned Containment Levels as Specified in the Subsections of Section III-A

As noted above at the beginning of Section III-A, certain HV1 and HV2 host-vector systems are assigned containment levels as specified in the subsections of Section III-A. Those so classified as of publication of these Revised Guidelines are listed below.

*HV1—The following specified strains of *Neurospora crassa* which have been modified to prevent aerial dispersion:

(1) inl (inositolless) strains 37102, 37401, 46316, 64001 and 89601.

(2) csp-1 strain UCLA37 and csp-2 strains FS 590, UCLA101 (these are conidial separation mutants).

(3) eas strain UCLA191 (an "easily wettable" mutant).

HV1—The following *Streptomyces* species: *Streptomyces coelicolor, S. lividans, S. parvulus,* and *S. griseus.* The following are accepted as vector components of certified *Streptomyces* HV1 systems: *Streptomyces* plasmids SCP2, SLP1.2, pIJ101, actinophage phi C31, and their derivatives.

Appendix E of Annex E.—Actions Taken Under the Guidelines

As noted in the subsections of Sections IV-E-1-b-(1) and IV-E-1-b-(2), the Director, NIH, may take certain actions with regard to the Guidelines after consideration by the RAC.

Some of the actions taken to date include the following:

1. The following experiment has been approved: The cloning in *B. subtilis,* under P2 conditions, of DNA derived from *Saccharomyces cerevisiae* using EK2 plasmid

*These follow the assigned containment levels as specified in the subsections of Section III-A with one exception. This exception is that experiments involving complete genomes of eukaryotic viruses will require P3 + HV1 or P2 + HV2 rather than the levels given in the subsections of Section III-A.

vectors provided that an HV1 *B. subtilis* host is used.

2. Unmodified laboratory strains of *Neurospora crassa* can be used in all experiments for which HV1 *N. crassa* systems are approved, provided that only DNA from Class 1 agents is used. For agents other than Class 1, unmodified laboratory strains of *N. crassa* can be used in all experiments for which HV1 *N. crassa* systems are approved, provided that these are carried out at physical containment one level higher than required for HV1. However, if P3 containment is specified for HV1 *N. crassa*, this level is considered adequate for unmodified *N. crassa*. Care must be exercised to prevent aerial dispersal of macroconidia, in accordance with good laboratory practice. Mutationally modified strains of *N. crassa* specified as HV1 in Appendix D can be used in all experiments for which HV2 *N. crassa* systems are approved, provided that only DNA from Class 1 agents is used.

3. P2 physical containment shall be used for DNA recombinants produced between members of the *Actinomycetes* group except for the species which are known to be pathogenic for man, animals, or plants.

4. Cloned desired fragments from any non-prohibited source may be transferred into *Agrobacterium tumefaciens* containing a Ti plasmid (or derivatives thereof), using a nonconjugative *E. coli* plasmid vector coupled to a fragment of the Ti plasmid and/or the origin of replication of an *Agrobacterium* plasmid, under containment conditions one step higher than would be required for the desired DNA in HV1 systems (i.e. one step higher physical containment than that specified in the subsections of Section III–A). However, DNA from plants and nonpathogenic prokaryotes may be cloned under P2 containment conditions: and the *Saccharomyces cerevisiae* alcohol dehydro-genase 1 gene and the gene coding for the maize (*Zea mays*) seed storage protein, zein, may be cloned under P1 conditions. Transfer into plant parts or cells in culture is permitted at the same containment level as is ued for the cloning in *Agrobacterium tumefaciens*.

5. *Bacillus subtilis* strains that do not carry an asporogenic mutation can be used as hosts specifically for the cloning of DNA derived from *E. coli* K-12 and *Streptomyces coelicolor, S. aureofaciens, S. rimosus, S. griseus, S. cyaneus*, and *s. venezuelae*, using NIH-approved *Staphylococcus aureau* plasmids as vectors under P2 conditions.

6. *Streptomyces coelicolor, S. auerofaciens, S. rimosus, S. griseus, S. cyaneus*, and *S. venezuelae* can be used as hosts for the cloning of DNA derived from *B. subtilis, E. coli*, K-12, or from *S. aureus* vectors that have been approved for use in *B. subtilis* under P2 conditions, using as vectors any plasmid indigenous to *Streptomyces* species or able to replicate in these hosts by natural biological mechanisms.

7. Certain cloned segments of *Anabena* DNA may be transferred into *Klebsiella* under P2 physical containment.

8. Permission is granted to clone foot-and-mouth disease virus in the EK1CV host-vector system consisting of *E. coli* K-12 and the vector pBR322, all work to be done at the Plumb Island Animal Disease Center.

9. Permission is granted to clone the Exotoxin A gene of *Pseudomonas aeruginosa* under P1 + EK1 conditions in *Escherichia coli* K-12 and under P1 conditions in *Pseudomonas aeruginosa*.

10. Permission is granted to return to the host of origin *Helminthosporanium maydis* (race O) DNA which has been cloned in yeast strain SHY2 using the hybrid *E. coli*—yeast plasmid Y1p5. The cloned DNA may be returned to, and propagated in, *Helminthosporanium maydis* at the P2 level of physical containment.

11. Permission is granted to return *Schizophyllum commune* DNA (or yeast DNA) cloned in *Saccharomyces cerevisiae* with YR or 2 mu circle vectors to *Schizophyllum commune*. The cloned DNA may be returned to, and propagated in, *Schizophyllum commune* at the P2 level of physical containment.

12. Permission is granted to return *Wangiella dermatitidis* DNA to *Wangiella dermatitidis* using an HV2 certified *Saccharomyces/E. coli* hybrid vector. The *Wangiella dermatitidis* may be propagated at the P3 level of physical containment.

13. Certain specified clones derived from segments of the Foot-and-Mouth Disease Virus may be transferred from Plum Island Animal Disease Center to the facilities of Genetech, Inc., of South San Francisco, California. Further development of the clones at Genentech has been approved under P1 + EK1 conditions.

14. *Saccharomycopsis lipolytica* may be used as a host for transformation with defined *Escherichia coli/Saccharomyces cerevisiae* hybrid plasmids and the hybrid plasmids may be used for cloning *S. lipolytica* DNA in *E. coli* and returning the cloned DNA to *S. lipolytica*.

15. Conjugative plasmids or transducing phages may be employed in recombinant DNA experiments when employing *E. coli* as host when a small defined segment of Adenovirus 2 DNA is employed as linker DNA.

16. Permission is granted to introduce DNA segments from aphid tramsmissible strains into non-aphid transmissible strains of Cauliflower mosiac virus in order to study the factors determining aphid transmissibility.

17. Permission is granted to return *Mucor racemosus* DNA which as been cloned in *Saccharomyces cerevisiae* host-vector systems to *Mucor racemosus*. In addition, permission is granted to transform *Mucor racemosus* with *S. cerevisiae* vectors with or without cloned *S. cerevisiae* sequences. These manipulations may be performed under P2 conditions.

18. DNA from nonpathogenic prokaryotes and nonpathogenic lower eukaryotes may be cloned into *Schizosaccharomyces pombe* species under P1 containment conditions. DNA from higher eukaryotes may be cloned in *S. pombe* species under P3 containment conditions.

19. The pyrogenic endotoxin type A (Tox A) gene of *Staphylococcus aureus* may be cloned in an HV2 *Bacillus subtilis* host-vector system under P3 containment conditions.

20. A hybrid plasmid composed of, (1) *E. coli* plasmid pBR325, (2) the origin of replication and transfer genes of *Agrobacterium tumefaciens* plasmid Ti, (3) the thiamine gene of *E. coli*, and (4) *Arabidopsis* DNA, may be transformed into *Agrobacterium tumefaciens* under P1 conditions. The *Agrobacterium tumefaciens* may subsequently be used to introduce the composite plasmid carrying *Arabidopsis* DNA and the *E. coli* thiamine gene into *Arabidopsis* plants under P1 containment conditions.

21. *Chlamydomonas reinhardi* can be used as a host for cloning defined DNA segments derived from *E. coli* and *Saccharomyces cerevisiae* using *E. coli/S. cerevisiae* hybrid vectors under P2 physical containment.

22. *Candida albicans* can be used as a host for cloning *Candida albicans* DNA following propagation of the DNA in *E. coli* K-12 or in *Saccharomyces cerevisiae* employing an *E. coli-S. cerevisiae* hybrid plasmid vector or the yeast 2 micron plasmid.

23. The Rd strain of *Hemophilus influenzae* can be used as a host for the propagation of the cloned Tn 10 tet R gene derived from *E. coli* K-12 employing the non-conjugative *Haemophilus* plasmid, pRSF0885, under P1 conditions.

24. *Zymomonas mobilis* may be used as a host under P2 conditions for transformation by recombinant DNA derived from *Pseudomonas* strains that are non-pathogenic for animals or plants, and that has been cloned in an *E. coli* K-12 host.

25. Protoplasts of *Streptosporangium brasiliense* may be transformed with a hybrid plasmid containing pBR322 plus a *Streptosporangium* plasmid into which have been incorporated specified DNA segments from *Streptomyces* species or an HV1 approved *Bacillus subtilis* cloning vector.

26. *Saccharomyces cerevisiae* DNA may be cloned in *Tetrahymena thermophila* using *E coli/S. cerevisiae* hybrid plasmids under P1 containment conditions.

27 All members of the nonpathogenic *Actinomycetes* genus *Streptomyces* and the plasmids native to this genus are approved as host-vector systems for the cloning under P1 conditions of DNA derived from other nonpathogenic prokaryotic organisms such as *Streptomyces* and other nonpathogenic *Actinomycetes* species, *Escherichia coli* K-12, *Bacillus subtilis, Bacillus licheniformis, Bacillus circulans*, and other nonpathogenic *Bacillus* species, and for the cloning of DNA derived from nonpathogenic unicellular eukaryotic microorganisms such as *Saccharomyces cerevisiae* and *Neurospora crassa*.

28. *Bacillus subtilis* strains that do not carry an asporogenic mutation can be used under P2 conditions for the cloning of DNA from any CDC Class 1 organism, using indigenous plasmid and phage vectors whose host range does not include *Bacillus anthracis* or *Bacillus cereus*.

29. *Bacillus subtilis* strains that do not carry an asporogenic mutation can be used under P1 conditions for the cloning of DNA from any Class 1 *Bacillus* species, using indigenous plasmid and phage vectors whose host range does not include *Bacillus anthracis* or *Bacillus cereus*.

30. Permission is granted to clone in *E. coli* K-12, in high containment Building 550 at the Frederick Cancer Research Center, restriction fragments of *Corynephage Beta* carrying the structural gene for diphtheria toxin. Laboratory practices and containment equipment are to be specified by the IBC.

31. Permission is granted to clone certain subgenomic segments of Foot and Mouth Disease Virus in HV1 *Bacillus subtilis* and *Saccharomyces cerevisiae* host-vector systems under P1 conditions at Genentech, Inc., South San Francisco, California.

32. Permission is granted in principle to propagate in mammalian cell culture recombinant DNA molecules consisting of segments of Foot and Mouth Disease Virus and SV40 deletion vectors under P3 conditions at the Plum Island Animal Disease Center. Approval is subject to review by a RAC Working Group of individual experiments.

33. A conjugative plasmid may be used to transfer among *E. coli* K-12 strains, under P2 physical containment, the qa-2 of *Neurospora crassa* ligated to a mobilizable plasmid.

34. *E. coli* K-12 strain DF214 (or derivatives thereof) and plasmid vectors (e.g., pBR322, pBR325) may be used to clone rat cDNA under P2 conditions. After the clone of interest has been purified, it may be worked with under P1 containment.

35. Permission is granted to Dr. Ronald Davis of Stanford University to field test corn plants modified by recombinant DNA techniques under specified containment conditions.

36. Permission is granted to clone in *E. coli* K-12, under P1 physical containment conditions, subgenomic segments of Rift Valley Fever Virus Subject to conditions which have been set forth by the RAC.

37. Permission is given to transfer a recombinant lactose plasmid from *Streptococcus faecalis* to *S. lactis* by conjugation.

38. Attenuated laboratory strains of *Salmonella typhimurium* may be used under P1 physical containment conditions to screen for the *Saccharomyces cerevisiae* pseudouridine synthetase gene. The plasmid YEp13 will be employed as the vector.

39. Permission is granted to clone in *Haemophilus parainfluenzae* Moloney murine leukemia provirus and mouse cellular flanking sequences employing the plasmid vector, pRK290, under P2 containment conditions.

40. Permission is granted for the development, under P1 conditions, of a new host-vector system based on the use of *Corynebacterium glutamicum* as host and non-conjugative poorly mobilizable plasmids as vectors.

41. *Vibrio harveyi* DNA may be cloned in *Vibrio cholera*; plasmids may be used to transfer the cloned *V. harveyi* DNA between *E. coli* K-12, *V. cholera*, and *V. harveyi*. P2 physical containment conditions are required for those experiments involving *V. cholera*. P1 containment conditions may be used for other phases of the project.

Appendix F of Annex E.—Certified Host-Vector Systems

While many experiments using *E. coli* K-12, *Saccharomyces cerevisiae* and *Bacillus subtilis* are currently exempt from the Guidelines under Exemption I-E-5, some derivatives of these host-vector systems were previously classified as HV1 or HV2. A listing of those systems follows.

HV1—The following plasmids are accepted as the vector components of certified *B. subtilis* HV1 systems: pUB110, pC194, pS194, pSA2100, pE194, pT127, pUB112, pC221, pC223, and pAB124. *B. subtilis* strains RUB 331 and BGSC 1553 have been certified as the host component of HV1 systems based on these plasmids.

HV2—The asporogenic mutant derivative of *Bacillus subtilis*, ASB 298, with the following plasmids as the vector component: pUB110, pC194, pS194, pSA2100, pE194, pT127, pUB112, pC221, pC223, and pAB124.

HV2—The following sterile strains of *Saccharomyces cerevisiae*, all of which have the ste-VC9 mutation, SHY1, SHY2, SHY3, and SHY4. The following plasmids are certified for use: YIp1, YEp2, YEp4, YIp5, YEp6, YRp7, YEp20, YEp21, YEp24, YIp25, YIp26, YIp27, YIp28, YIp29, YIp30, YIp31, YIp32 and YIp33.

EK2 Plasmid Systems. The *E. coli* K-12 strain chi-1776. The following plasmids are certified for use: pSC101, pMB9, pBR313, pBR322, pDH24, pBR327, pGL101, pHB1. The following *E. coli/S. cerevisiae* hybrid plasmids are certified as EK2 vectors when used in *E. coli* chi-1776 or in the sterile yeast strains, SHY1, SHY2, SHY3 and SHY4: YIp1, YEp2, YEp4, YIp5, YEp6, YRp7, YEp20, YEp21, YEp24, YIp25, YIp26, YIp27, YIp28, YIp29, YIp30, YIp31, YIp32, YIp33.

EK2 Bacteriophage Systems: The following are certified EK2 systems based on bacteriophage lambda.

Vector	*Host*
λgt*WES*. λB′	DP50*supF*
λgt*WES*. λB*	DP50*supF*
λgtZJ*vir*. λB′	*E. coli* K-12
λgtALO. λB	DP50*supF*
Charon 3A	DP50 or DP50*supF*
Charon 4A	DP50 or DP50*supF*
Charon 16A	DP50 or DP50*supF*
Charon 21A	DP50*supF*
Charon 23A	DP50 or DP50*supF*
Charon 24A	DP50 or DP50*supF*

Appendix G of Annex E.—Containment Conditions for Cloning of Genes Coding for the Biosynthesis of Toxins for Vertebrates

1. General Information

Appendix G specifies the containment to be used for the deliberate cloning of genes coding for the biosynthesis of toxins for vertebrates. Cloning of genes coding for toxins for vertebrates that have an LD_{50} of less than 100 nanograms per kilogram body weight (e.g., the botulinum toxins, tetanus toxin, diphtheria toxin, *Shigella dysenteriae* neurotoxin) is prohibited. No specific restrictions shall apply to the cloning of genes if the protein specified by the gene has an LD_{50} of 100 micrograms or more per kilogram of body weight. Experiments involving genes coding for toxins with an LD_{50} of 100 micrograms or less per kilogram body weight shall be registered with ORDA prior to initiating the experiments. A list of toxins classified as to LD_{50} is available from ORDA. Testing procedures for determining toxicity of toxins not on the list are available from ORDA. The results of such tests shall be forwarded to ORDA, which will consult with the *ad hoc* Working Group on toxins prior to inclusion of the toxin on the list. (See Section IV-E-1-b-(3)-(i).)

2. Containment Conditions for Cloning of Toxin Genes in E. coli K-12

(a) Cloning of genes coding for toxins for vertebrates that have an LD_{50} in the range of 100 nanograms to 1000 nanograms per kilogram body weight (e.g., abrin, *Clostridium perfringens* epsilon toxin) may proceed under P2 + EK2 or P3 + EK1 containment conditions.

(b) Cloning of genes for the biosynthesis of toxins for vertebrates with an LD_{50} in the range of 1 microgram to 100 micrograms per kilogram body weight may proceed under P1 + EK1 containment conditions (e.g., *Staphylococcus aureus* alpha toxin, *Staphylococcus aureus* beta toxin, ricin, *Pseudomonas aeruginosa* exotoxin A, *Bordatella pertussis* toxin, the lethal factor of *Bacillus anthracis*, the *Pasteurella pestis* murine toxins, the oxygen-labile hemolysins such as streptolysin O, and certain neurotoxins present in snake venoms and other venoms).

(c) Some enterotoxins are substantially more toxic when administered internally than parenterally. The following enterotoxins shall be subject to P1 + EK1 containment conditions: cholera toxin, the heat labile toxins of *E. coli*, *Klebsiella*, and other related proteins that may be identified by neutralization with an antiserum mono-specific for cholera toxin, and the heat stable toxins of *E. coli* and of *Yersinia enterocolitica*.

3. Containment Conditions for Cloning of Toxins Genes in Organisms Other Than E. coli K-12

Requests involving the cloning of genes coding for toxins for vertebrates in host-vector systems other than *E. coli* K-12 will be evaluated by ORDA, which will consult with the *ad hoc* working group on toxins. (See Section IV-E-1-b-(3)-(j).)

Appendix H of Annex E.—Experiments Covered by Section III-0

No experiments currently fall under Section III-0 of the Guidelines.

Note.—OMB's "Mandatory Information Requirements for Federal Assistance Program Announcements" (45 FR 39592) requires a statement concerning the official government programs contained in the *Catalog of Federal Domestic Assistance*. Normally NIH lists in its announcements the number and title of affected individual programs for the guidance of the public. Because the guidance in this notice covers not only virtually every NIH program but also essentially every federal research program in which DNA recombinant molecule techniques could be used, it has been determined to be not cost effective or in the public interest to attempt to list these programs. Such a list would likely require several additional pages. In addition, NIH could not be certain that every federal program would be included as many federal agencies, as well as private organizations, both national and international, have elected to follow the NIH Guidelines. In lieu of the individual program listing, NIH invites readers to direct questions to the information address above about whether individual programs listed in the *Catalog of Federal Domestic Assistance* are affected.

NIH programs are not covered by OMB Circular A-95 because they fit the description of "programs not considered appropriate" in Section 8-(b)-(4) and (5) of that Circular.

Dated: October 26, 1981.

Richard M. Krause,

Director, National Institute of Allergy and Infectious Diseases.

[FR Doc. 81-34469 Filed 12-3-81; 8:45 am]

BILLING CODE 4110-08-M

federal register

Monday
December 7, 1981

Part II

Department of Health and Human Services

National Institutes of Health

Recombinant DNA Research; Proposed Actions Under Guidelines

DEPARTMENT OF HEALTH AND HUMAN SERVICES

National Institutes of Health

Recombinant DNA Research; Proposed Actions Under Guidelines

AGENCY: National Institutes of Health, PHS, DHHS.

ACTION: Notice to Proposed Actions under NIH Guidelines for Research Involving Recombinant DNA Molecules.

SUMMARY: This notice sets forth proposed actions to be taken under the NIH Guidelines for Research Involving Recombinant DNA Molecules. Interested parties are invited to submit comments concerning these proposals. After consideration of these proposals and comments by the NIH Recombinant DNA Advisory Committee (RAC) at its next meeting, the Director of the National Institute of Allergy and Infectious Diseases will issue decisions on these proposals in accord with the Guidelines.

DATE: Comments must be received by February 1, 1982.

ADDRESS: Written comments and recommendations should be submitted to the Director, Office of Recombinant DNA Activities, Building 31, Room 4A52, National Institutes of Health, Bethesda, Maryland, 20205. All comments received in timely response to this notice will be considered and will be available for public inspection in the above office on weekdays between the hours of 8:30 a.m. and 5:00 p.m.

FOR FURTHER INFORMATION CONTACT: Background documentation and additional information can be obtained from Drs. Stanley Barban or Elizabeth Milewski, Office of Recombinant DNA Activities, National Institutes of Health, Bethesda, Maryland, 20205, (301) 496-6051.

SUPPLEMENTARY INFORMATION: The National Institutes of Health will consider the following changes and amendments under the Guidelines for Research Involving Recombinant DNA Molecules, as well as actions under these Guidelines.

1. Proposed Revision of Guidelines

Dr. Waclaw Szybalski, McArdle Laboratory for Cancer Research, University of Wisconsin, Madison, Wisconsin, has requested that the following sentence be added to the current NIH Guidelines:

"These are only Guidelines based on the current state of the research and on the concerns of certain individuals or groups about the hypothetical risks. Individual researchers should use their best scientific judgement and peers' advice when designing, modifying and conducting experiments, and be prepared to justify any substantial variations when requested, or in their applications and progress reports."

2. Request To Use Bacillus Megaterium in Recombinant DNA Experiments Under P1 Containment

Dr. Patricia Vary of Northern Illinois University, DeKalb, Illinois, requests permission to introduce recombinant DNA derived from *Staphylococcus aureus*, *E. coli*, and *Bacillus subtilis* into *Bacillus megaterium* under P1 conditions.

3. Proposed EK2 Host-Vector Systems

Dr. Roy Curtiss, University of Alabama, Birmingham, Alabama, requests EK2 certification of six different *E. coli* K-12 strains in conjunction with various virulent and temperate bacteriophage lambda, plasmid and cosmid vectors. Dr. Curtiss also requests that all previously approved vectors be approved as vector components of the proposed EK2 host-vector systems. Detailed information on the proposed host-vector systems has been provided by Dr. Curtiss.

4. Proposed use of EK2 Host-Vector Systems for Cloning DNA from Class 3 and 4 Etiologic Agents

Dr. Roy Curtiss, University of Alabama, Birmingham, Alabama, requests permission to use all certified EK2 host-vector systems to clone DNA fragments from Class 3 and Class 4 etiologic agents under P2 containment, and under P1 containment if the recombinant clones are shown not to express a virulence determinant that has toxic potential.

As an alternative to this general proposal, Dr. Curtiss requests permission to clone DNA from *Yersinia pestis* and *Mycobacterium leprae* into EK2 host-vector systems under P2 containment, and under P1 conditions in the absence of expression of virulence determinants by the recombinant clones.

5. Proposed Pseudomonas Putida Host-Vector System

Dr. Michael Bagdasarian of the Max-Planck Institute of Fur Molekulare Genetik, Berlin, West Germany, requests HV1 certification of a host-vector system based on *Pseudomonas putida* strain KT2440 and cloning vectors pKT262, pKT263, and pKT264.

6. Proposed Inclusion of Yersinia Enterocolitica on Sublist A, Appendix A

Dr. Guy Cornelis of the Universite Catholique de Louvain, Brussels, Belgium, requests that *Yersinia enterocolitica* be exempted from the Guidelines under Section I-E-4 and added to Sublist A, Appendix A, on the basis that this species exchanges genetic information with *E. coli*.

7. Proposal for Revision of the Guidelines

Dr. Susan Gottesman of the National Cancer Institute of the National Institutes of Health has requested that the following proposal to modify the NIH Guidelines for Research Involving Recombinant DNA Molecules be published in the **Federal Register** for comment:

I. Introduction

There seems to be a clear consensus that the guidelines require simplification, reorganization, and possible lowering of containment levels for some classes of experiments. The Recombinant DNA Advisory Committee (RAC) will be considering at its next meeting a proposal, published for comment in the **Federal Register**, to convert the NIH Recombinant DNA Guidelines into a voluntary code of practice. This proposal would change the detailed listing of containment levels to a few paragraphs of advice to the investigator. I am recommending an alternative approach to revision which retains some aspects of the current guidelines which I consider necessary for the continued orderly development of the recombinant DNA field.

(1) My proposal, as opposed to the RAC proposal, retains the requirement for IBC oversight of some experiments, and retains the current NIH compliance requirements. In addition, the record-keeping function of the IBC is retained. Since many experiments became exempt from the requirements of the Guidelines as of July 1, 1981, the remaining requirements should not be too cumbersome to either the experimenter or the IBC.

(2) My proposal simplifies the structure of the Guidelines and decreases containment for some classes of experiments. In particular, experiments involving non-pathogenic prokaryotes and lower eukaryotes could be carried out at P1 containment. Overall, containment levels would not, however, be lowered to the extent recommended in the RAC proposal.

II. Summary of Proposed Changes as Compared to Current Guidelines

A. *Prohibitions.* The word "prohibition" will no longer be applied to this class of experiments which currently require explicit RAC review and NIH approval.

1. Three of the five prohibitions (I-D-2, I-D-4, and I-D-5 in the current Guidelines) would be listed in a new section designated III-A and entitled "Experiments that require FAC review and NIH approval before initiation." These three prohibitions cover experiments involving the deliberate formation of recombinant DNAs containing genes for the biosynthesis of certain toxins lethal for vertebrates (I-D-2), the deliberate release into the environment of organisms containing recombinant DNA (I-D-4), and the deliberate transfer of a drug resistance trait to microorganisms that are not known to acquire it naturally if such acquisition could compromise the use of a drug to control disease agents in human or veterinary medicine or agriculture (I-D-5).

2. Prohibition I-D-1 in the current guidelines (formation of recombinant DNAs derived from CDC Class 4 or 5 organisms) would be deleted. Such experiments could be carried out under specific conditions set by the IBC, as described in a new section designated III-B and entitled "Experiments that require IBC approval before initiation".

3. Prohibition I-D-6 in the current Guidelines, which covers certain large-scale experiments, would be eliminated; such experiments could proceed after IBC approval (new section III-B-5). Currently the Guidelines permit certain large scale experiments involving *E. coli* K-12, *S. cerevisiae* and *B. subtilis* host-vector systems to proceed following review by the local IBC (46 FR 53983).

B. *Exemptions*. No changes in the substance of this section are proposed. The categories of exemptions now listed in Section I-E would be listed in a new Section III-D.

C. *Section II (Containment)*. All references to HV3 systems would be deleted. Such systems are not presently in use and are not required by current or proposed guidelines. Otherwise, the section would remain as is.

D. *Section III (Containment Guidelines for Covered Experiments)*. The complete text of Section III would be replaced by new text which would reorganize, simplify, and eliminate redundancy in the current Guidelines. In addition, significant lowering of containment for some classes of experiments is recommended. In the new Section III, all experiments would fall into one of four classes:

III-A. Current prohibitions; such experiments would require specific RAC review and NIH approval.

III-B. Experiments requiring prior review by the IBC. These would include the use of recombinant DNA molecules derived from or propagated in pathogens, non-defective animal virus systems, and the insertion of recombinant DNA into whole animals and plants. Many experiments which would be included in this section currently require NIH approval.

III-C. Experiments requiring notice to the IBC simultaneously with initiation of the experiment.

The proposal would change the procedure for reviewing recombinant DNA experiments involving non-pathogenic prokaryotes, lower eukaryotes, or defective animal virus systems. These experiments currently require prior review by the IBC. Under this proposal, investigators would not have to wait for IBC approval before initiating these experiments. In addition, containment requirements for experiments involving non-pathogenic prokaryotes and non-pathogenic lower eukaryotes would be relaxed.

III-D. Currently exempt experiments. No changes in the substance of this section are proposed.

E. Section IV. Changes as necessary to reflect changes in other sections of the Guidelines would be incorporated.

F. Much material currently in Appendix E would be covered or superseded by the proposed changes in the Guidelines in Section III. Appendix D would be deleted.

III. Changes in Current Guidelines to Implement Proposal

A. *Current Section I*. Section I-A, *Purpose*, would remain unchanged.

Section I-B, *Definition of Recombinant DNA Molecules*, would be modified to include a statement on synthetic DNAs, and would read as follows:

"I-B. *Definition of Recombinant DNA Molecules*. In the context of these Guidelines, recombinant DNA molecules are defined as either (i) molecules which are constructed outside living cells by joining natural or synthetic DNA segments to DNA molecules that can replicate in a living cell, or (ii) DNA molecules that result from the replication of those described in (i) above.

"Synthetic DNA segments likely to yield a potentially harmful polynucleotide or polypeptide (e.g., a toxin or a pharmacologically active agent) shall be considered as equivalent to their natural DNA counterpart. If the synthetic DNA segment is not expressed *in vivo* as a polynucleotide or polypeptide product, it is exempt from the Guidelines."

Section I-C, *General Applicability*, would remain unchanged.

Section I-D, *Prohibitions*, would be deleted. (Some of this material is included in proposed new Section III-A).

Section I-E, *Exemptions*, would be deleted. (This material would be included in proposed new Section III-D).

B. *Current Section II*. Delete current Section II-D-1-c and subsections II-D-1-c-(1) through II-D-1-c-(5), Section II-D-2-b-(3) and references to HV3 in Section II-D-3.

C. *Current Section III*. Delete and replace current Section III and all subsections of III with the following text:

"Part III discusses experiments involving recombinant DNA. These experiments have been divided into four classes:

"III-A. Experiments which require specific RAC review and NIH approval before initiation of the experiment;

"III-B. Experiments which require IBC approval before initiation of the experiment;

"III-C. Experiments which require IBC notification at the time of initiation of the experiment;

"III-D. Experiments which are exempt from the procedures of the Guidelines.

"If an experiment falls into both class III-A and one of the other classes, the rules pertaining to class III-A must be followed. If an experiment falls into class III-D and into either class III-B or III-C as well, it can be considered exempt from the requirements of the Guidelines.

"Changes in containment levels from those specified here may not be instituted without the express approval of the Director, NIH (See Sections IV-E-1-b-(1), IV-E-1-b-(2), and subsections).

"III-A. *Experiments that Require RAC Review and NIH Approval Before Initiation*. Experiments in this category cannot be initiated without submission of relevant information on the proposed experiment to NIH, the publication of the proposal in the Federal Register for thirty days of comment, review by the RAC, and specific approval by NIH. The containment conditions for such experiments will be recommended by RAC and set by NIH at the time of approval. Such experiments also require the approval of the IBC before initiation. Specific experiments already approved in this section and the appropriate containment conditions are listed in Appendices E and G.

"III-A-1. Deliberate formation of recombinant DNAs containing genes for the biosynthesis of toxins lethal for vertebrates at an LD_{50} of less than 100 nanograms per kilogram body weight (e.g., the botulinum toxins, tetanus toxin, diphtheria toxin, *Shigella dysenteriae* neurotoxin). Specific approval has been given for the cloning in *E. coli* K-12 of DNAs containing genes coding for the biosynthesis of toxins which are lethal to vertebrates at 100 nanograms to 100 micrograms per kilogram body weight. Containment levels for these experiments are specified in Appendix G.

"III-A-2. Deliberate release into the environment of any organism containing recombinant DNA.

"III-A-3. Deliberate transfer of a drug resistance trait to microorganisms that are not known to acquire it naturally, if such acquistion could compromise the use of the drug to control disease agents in human or veterinary medicine or agriculture.

"III-B. *Experiments that Require IBC Approval Before Initiation.* Investigators performing experiments in this category must submit to their Institutional Biosafety Committee (IBC), prior to initiation of the experiments, a registration document that contains a description of: (a) The source(s) of DNA, (b) the nature of the inserted DNA sequences, (c) the hosts and vectors to be used, (d) whether a deliberate attempt will be made to obtain expression of a foreign gene, and, if so, what protein will be produced, and (e) the containment conditions specified in these Guidelines. This registration document must be dated and signed by the investigator and filed only with the local IBC. The IBC shall review all such proposals prior to initiation of the experiments. Requests for lowering of containment for experiments in this category will be considered by NIH (See Section IV-E-1-b-(3)).

"III-B-1. *Experiments Using CDC Class 2, Class 3, Class 4, or Class 5 Agents* as Host-Vector Systems.*

"III-B-1-a. Experiments involving the introduction of recombinant DNA into CDC Class 2 agents can be carried out at P2 containment.

"III-B-1-b. Experiments involving the introduction of recombinant DNA into CDC Class 3 agents can be carried out at P3 containment.

"III-B-1-c. Experiments involving the introduction of recombinant DNA into CDC Class 4** or Class 5 agents can be carried out at P4 containment. A USDA permit is required for work with Class 5 agents***.

"III-B-2. *Experiments in Which DNA from CDC Class 2 or Class 3 Agents* is Cloned in Nonpathogenic Prokaryotic or Lower Eukaryotic Host-Vector Systems.*

"III-B-2-a. Recombinant DNA experiments in which DNA from CDC Class 2 or Class 3 agents* is transferred into nonpathogenic prokaryotes or lower eukaryotes may be performed under P2 containment. Specific lowering of containment to P1 for particular experiments can be approved by the IBC. Many experiments in this category will be exempt from the Guidelines (See Sections III-D-4 and III-D-5). Experiments involving the formation of recombinant DNAs for certain toxin genes requires RAC review and NIH approval (see Section III-A-1), or must be carried out under NIH specified conditions as described in Appendix G.

"III-B-2-b. Recombinant DNA experiments in which DNA from CDC Class 4** or Class 5 agents is transferred into nonpathogenic prokaryotes or lower eukaryotes can be performed at P2 containment after demonstration that only a totally and irreversibly defective fraction of the agent's viral genome is present in a given recombinant. In the absence of such a demonstration, P4 containment should be used.

Note.—A USDA permit is required for work with Class 5 pathogens***.

"III-B-3. *Experiments Involving the Use of Whole Animal or Plant Viruses or Defective Animal or Plant Viruses in the Presence of Helper Virus in Tissue Culture Systems.*

"III-B-3-a. Experiments involving the use of whole CDC Class 2 animal viruses*, or defective CDC Class 2 animal viruses* in the presence of helper virus, can be performed at P2 containment.

"III-B-3-b. Experiments involving the use of whole CDC Class 3 animal viruses*, or defective CDC Class 3 animal viruses* in the presence of helper virus, can be carried out at P3 containment.

"III-B-3-c. Experiments involving the use of whole CDC Class 4 or Class 5 animal viruses*, or defective CDC Class 4 or Class 5 animal viruses* in the presence of helper virus, may be carried out under P4 containment. A USDA permit is required for work with CDC Class 5 pathogens***.

"III-B-3-d. Experiments involving the use of whole animal or plant viruses, or defective animal or plant viruses in the presence of helper virus, not covered by Sections III-B-3-a, III-B-3-b, or III-B-3-c may be carried out under P1 containment.

"III-B-4. *Recombinant DNA Experiments Involving Whole Animals and Plants.*

"III-B-4-a. DNA from any source except for greater than one quarter of a eukaryotic viral genome may be transferred to any non-human vertebrate organism and propagated under conditions of physical containment comparable to P1 and appropriate to the organism under study (2A).

"III-B-4-b. For all experiments involving whole animals and plants and not covered by III-B-4-a, the appropriate containment will be determined by the IBC.

"III-B-5. *Experiments Involving More than 10 Liters of Culture.*

The appropriate containment will be decided by the IBC. Where appropriate, the large scale containment recommendations of the NIH should be used (45 FR 24968).

"III-C. *Experiments that Require IBC Notice Simultaneously with Initiation of Experiments.*

"For experiments in this category, a registration document as described in Section III-B must be dated and signed by the investigator and filed with the local IBC. The IBC shall review all such proposals, but IBC review prior to initiation of the experiment is not required. All experiments not included in categories III-A, III-B, III-D, and subsections of these categories are to be considered as in category III-C. All such experiments can be carried out at P1 containment. Some explicit cases are listed below.

"III-C-1. *Experiments Involving Non-Pathogenic Prokaryotes or Non-Pathogenic Lower Eukaryotic Host-Vector Systems.*

"Experiments involving non-pathogenic prokaryotes or non-pathogenic lower eukaryotes can be carried out at P1 containment.

"III-C-2. *Experiments Involving Formation of Recombinant DNA Molecules Containing no More Than Two-Thirds of the Genome of any Eukaryotic Virus.*

"Recombinant DNA molecules containing no more than two-thirds of the genome of any eukaryotic virus (all viruses from a single Family (36) being considered identical (50)) may be propagated and maintained in cells in tissue culture using P1 containment. For such experiments, it must be shown that the cells lack helper virus for the specific Families of defective viruses being used. The DNA may contain fragments of the genome of viruses from more than one Family but each fragment must be less than two-thirds of a genome.

"III-D. *Exempt Experiments.*

"The following recombinant DNA molecules are exempt from these Guidelines and no registration with the IBC is necessary.

"III-D-1. Those that are not in organisms or viruses.

"III-D-2. Those that consist entirely of DNA segments from a single nonchromosomal or viral DNA source, though one or more of the segments may be synthetic equivalent.

"III-D-3. Those that consist entirely of DNA from a prokaryotic host, including its indigenous plasmids or viruses, when propagated only in that host (or a closely related strain of the same species) or when transferred to another host by well established physiological means; also, those that consist entirely of DNA from a eukaryotic host, including its chloroplasts, mitochondria, or plasmids (but excluding viruses), when propagated only in that host (or a closely related strain of the same species).

"III-D-4. Certain specified recombinant DNA molecules that consist entirely of DNA segments from different species that exchange DNA by known physiological processes, though one or more of the segments may be a synthetic equivalent. A list of such exchangers will be prepared and periodically revised by the Director, NIH, with advice of the RAC, after appropriate notice and opportunity for public comment. (See Section IV-E-1-b-(1)-(d).) Certain classes are exempt as of publication of these Revised Guidelines. The list is in Appendix A. An updated list may be obtained from the Office of Recombinant DNA Activities, National Institutes of Health, Bethesda, Maryland 20205.

"III-D-5. Other classes of recombinant DNA molecules, if the Director, NIH, with advice of the RAC, after appropriate notice and opportunity for public comment, finds that they do not present a significant risk to health or the environment. (See Section IV-E-1-b-(1)-(d).) Certain classes are exempt as of publication of these Revised Guidelines. The list is in Appendix C. An updated list may be obtained from the Office of Recombinant DNA Activities; National Institutes of Health, Bethesda, Maryland 20205."

D. *Current Section IV, Roles and Responsibilities.* Changes as necessary to reflect changes in Parts I-III only.

E. *Current Section V. Footnotes and References.* Changes as necessary to reflect changes in Parts I-III.

F. *Current Appendices.* Delete sections subsumed by proposed guideline changes; i.e. delete Appendix D and entries 1, 2, 3, 5, 7, 10, 11, 12, 14, 15, 17, 18, 20, 22, 24, 25, 26, 27, 28, 29, 33, and 34 of Appendix E.

Footnotes

* *Classification of Etiologic Agents on the basis of Hazard.* (4th Edition, July 1974). U.S. Department of Health, Education and Welfare, Public Health Service, Centers for Disease Control, Office of Biosafety, Atlanta, Georgia 30333.

** All activities, including storage of variola and whitepox are retricted to the single national facility (World Health Organization (WHO) Collaborating Center for Smallpox Research, Center for Disease Control, in Atlanta).

*** A USDA permit, required for import and interstate commerce of pathogens, may be obtained from the Animal and Plant Health Inspection Service USDA, Federal Building, Hyattsville, MD 20782.

OMB's "Mandatory Information Requirements for Federal Assistance Program Announcements" (45 FR 39592) requires a statement concerning the official government programs contained in the *Catalog of Federal Domestic Assistance.* Normally NIH lists in its announcements the number and title of affected individual programs for the guidance of the public. Because the guidance in this notice covers not only virtually every NIH program but also essentially every federal research program in which DNA recombinant molecule techniques could be used, it has been determined to be not cost effective or in the public interest to attempt to list these programs. Such a list would likely require serveral additional pages. In addition, NIH could not be certain that every federal program would be included as many federal agencies, as well as private organizations both national and international, have elected to follow the NIH Guidelines. In lieu of the individual program listing, NIH invites readers to direct questions to the information address above about whether individual programs listed in the *Catalog of Federal Domestic Assistance* are affected.

NIH programs are not covered by OMB Circular A-95 because they fit the description of "programs not considered appropriate" in Section 8-(b)-(4) and (5) of that Circular.

Dated: November 26, 1981.

Richard M. Krause,

Director, National Institute of Allergy and Infectious Diseases, National Institutes of Health.

[FR Doc. 81-34468 Filed 12-4-81; 8:45 am]
BILLING CODE 4140-01-M

DEPARTMENT OF HEALTH & HUMAN SERVICES   Public Health Service

National Institutes of Health
Bethesda, Maryland 20205

December 18, 1981

M E M O R A N D U M

TO: Interested Parties

FROM: Director, Office of Recombinant DNA Activities

SUBJECT: Proposed Revisions of NIH Guidelines for Research Involving Recombinant DNA Molecules

Comments are invited on two proposals for a major revision of the National Institutes of Health (NIH) Guidelines for Research Involving Recombinant DNA Molecules.

The Recombinant DNA Advisory Committee (RAC) has developed a proposed revision and recommended that it be published for comment. This proposal appears in the Federal Register dated December 4, 1981.

The major features of this proposal are:

1. The Guidelines would cease to be mandatory and would become a voluntary code of standard practice. The following requirements would be eliminated: that institutions have an Institutional Biosafety Committee (IBC), that investigators obtain prior approval from the IBC before beginning certain experiments, and that investigators obtain prior approval from NIH before beginning certain experiments. The section of the Guidelines specifying that noncompliance could lead to loss of NIH funds would also be eliminated.

2. Section III of the Guidelines giving containment levels would be greatly simplified, and most experiments currently requiring P2 or P3 containment would be recommended at P1.

3. The prohibitions section (I-D) of the Guidelines would be eliminated, although two of the current prohibitions (I-D-2 and I-D-5) would be retained as admonishments.

An alternative proposal appears as item 7 in the Federal Register notice of December 7, 1981.

The major features of this proposal are:

1. The Guidelines would continue to be mandatory for institutions receiving NIH funding. Certain experiments would require prior review by NIH, certain experiments would require prior review by an IBC, and certain experiments would require notice to an IBC simultaneously with initiation of the experiment.

2. Section III of the Guidelines would be reorganized and simplified. All experiments would fall into one of four classes. Physical containment requirements for some classes of experiments would be lowered.

3. Three of five current prohibitions (I-D-2, I-D-4, and I-D-5 in the current Guidelines) would be listed in a new section that would continue to require RAC review and NIH approval before initiation. Experiments currently falling under prohibition I-D-1 and I-D-6 could proceed after IBC approval.

Copies of the above mentioned Federal Register notices as well as a summary comparing the current Guidelines with the two proposals are enclosed. Comments on these proposals should be directed to the attention of the Director, Office of Recombinant DNA Activities, National Institutes of Health, Building 31, Room 4A52, Bethesda, Maryland 20205, U.S.A.

These proposals and comments on them will be considered by the RAC at its next meeting on February 8-9, 1982.

William J. Gartland, Jr., Ph.D.

*Indicates the three major changes in the RAC Proposal

. SUMMARY OF PROPOSED CHANGES IN NIH GUIDELINES FOR RESEARCH INVOLVING RECOMBINANT DNA MOLECULES

Prepared by B. Talbot
12/8/81

Current Guideline Section	Topic	Current Guidelines	RAC Proposal (Fed. Reg. 12/4/81)	Gottesman Proposal (Fed. Reg. 12/7/81)
IV	RAC	Composition and procedures detailed for Recombinant DNA Advisory Committee (RAC).	Unchanged from current Guidelines.	Unchanged from current Guidelines.
IV	Roles and Responsibilities (Other than RAC Composition and Procedures)	Guidelines are mandatory for those receiving NIH support. Institutions must have an Institutional Biosafety Committee (IBC) with specified membership. Principal Investigators (PIs) must obtain prior approval from IBC before beginning certain experiments. PIs must obtain prior approval from NIH before beginning certain experiments. Roles and Responsibilities are specified for the Institution, the IBC, the Biological Safety Officer (BSO), the PI, and the NIH. Section IV-G of the Guidelines specifies that noncompliance can lead to loss of NIH funds.	*Guidelines cease to be mandatory and become a voluntary code of good practice. Requirements that institutions have an IBC, that investigators must obtain prior approval from the IBC before beginning certain experiments, that investigators must obtain prior approval from the NIH before beginning certain experiments, and the Section of the Guidelines specifying that noncompliance with the Guidelines could lead to loss of NIH funds, would all be eliminated. Current specified and responsibilities for the Institution, the IBC, BSO and PI would be eliminated. A new statement would be added: "Each institution conducting or sponsoring recombinant DNA research should take responsibility for monitoring its own activities in this area. Any unusual events that might be associated with the use of recombinant DNA molecules should be reported to the Director, NIH."	Unchanged from current Guidelines in all important respects. There would be minor changes in this Section of the Guidelines as necessary to reflect changes in other Sections.
I-D	Prohibitions	Five classes of experiments prohibited. Prohibitions override other Sections of the Guidelines.	*Prohibitions eliminated. Two of the current prohibitions (drug resistance traits and toxin genes) become admonishments in Part III of the Guidelines.	The term prohibition is no longer used. However, three of the current prohibitions (drug resistance traits, toxin genes, and deliberate release to the environment) appear in a new Section III-A and would require the same RAC review and NIH approval before initiation that currently hold for the prohibitions.

Current Guideline Section	Topic	Current Guidelines	RAC Proposal (Fed. Reg. 12/4/81)	Gottesman Proposal (Fed. Reg. 12/7/81)
I-E	Exemptions	Five classes of experiments exempt from the Guidelines.	Unchanged from current Guidelines.	Substance unchanged from current Guidelines. Moved to a new Section III-D.
III	Containment Levels for Covered Experiments	Experiments not otherwise prohibited or exempt are assigned a containment level (P1 to P3). All require prior IBC approval. Some require prior NIH approval. This Part of the Guidelines is very long and complex, classifying experiments into many groups and assigning a specific containment level to each.	"No prior IBC or NIH approval required. The entire current Part III of the Guidelines is replaced by an introduction, the two admonishments noted above and the following: "Where recommended physical containment levels applicable to non-recombinant DNA experiments exist for either the host or the vector, recombinant DNA experiments should be carried out at containment levels at least as high as those recommended for non-recombinant DNA experiments. If there is clear evidence that the donor DNA will significantly change the pathogenicity of the host, the containment level appropriate to the anticipated change will be applied. Otherwise, all experiments may be carried out under conditions of P1 or P1-LS physical containment."	Part III of the Guidelines is greatly simplified. As noted above, new Section III-A contains three of the current prohibitions. New Section III-D contains the current exemptions. New Section III-B specifies experiments requiring IBC approval before initiation. They are assigned containment levels, P1 to P4. (Many experiments in this Section currently require prior NIH approval.) New Section III-C to include all experiments not included in new Sections III-A, III-B or III-D. These experiments require IBC notification simultaneously with initiation of the experiment and can be carried out at P1 containment. (Experiments in this Section currently require prior IBC approval and containment level of P1 to P3.)
II	Containment	Defines physical and biological containment.	Unchanged from current Guidelines.	Unchanged from current Guidelines except for deletion of reference to HV3 systems.
	Footnotes and References	Footnotes and references.	Changes as necessary to reflect other changes in Guidelines.	Changes as necessary to reflect other changes in Guidelines.

Current Guideline Section	Topic	Current Guidelines	RAC Proposal (Fed. Reg. 12/4/81)	Gottesman Proposal (Fed. Reg. 12/7/81)
VI	Voluntary Compliance	Policy for voluntary compliance with Guidelines.	Eliminated except for those portions of Section VI-F relevant to the protection of proprietary information.	Unchanged from current Guidelines.
I-A	Purpose	"I-A. Purpose. The purpose of these Guidelines is to specify practices for constructing and handling (i) recombinant DNA molecules and (ii) organisms and viruses containing recombinant DNA molecules."	Sentence added at end, "Adherence to these standards by all laboratories using recombinant DNA is recommended."	Unchanged from current Guidelines.
I-B	Definition of Recombinant DNA Molecules	"I-B Definition of Recombinant DNA Molecules. In the context of these Guidelines, recombinant DNA molecules are defined as either (i) molecules which are constructed outside living cells by joining natural or synthetic DNA segments to DNA molecules that can replicate in a living cell, or (ii) DNA molecules that result from the replication of those described in (i) above."	Unchanged from current Guidelines.	Paragraph added at end, "Synthetic DNA segments likely to yield a potentially harmful polynucleotide or polypeptide (e.g., a toxin or a pharmacologically active agent) shall be considered as equivalent to their natural DNA counterpart. If the synthetic DNA is not expressed in vivo as a polynucleotide or polypeptide product, it is exempt from the Guidelines."
I-C	General Applicability	"I-C. General Applicability. See Section IV-B."	Eliminated.	Unchanged from current Guidelines.
Appendices	Appendices	Appendix A through H.	Changes as necessary to reflect other changes in Guidelines.	Changes as necessary to reflect other changes in Guidelines.

federal register

Wednesday
January 6, 1982

Part II

Department of Health and Human Services

National Institutes of Health

Recombinant DNA Advisory Committee Meeting; Recombinant DNA Research, Proposed Actions Under Guidelines

DEPARTMENT OF HEALTH AND HUMAN SERVICES

National Institutes of Health

Recombinant DNA Advisory Committee; Meetings

Pursuant to Pub. L. 92–463, notice is hereby given of a meeting of the Recombinant DNA Advisory Committee at the Marriott Hotel, Salon D and E, 5151 Pooks Hill Rd., Bethesda, Maryland 20014, on February 8, 1982, from 9:00 a.m. to recess at approximately 6:00 p.m., and, if necessary, on February 9, 1982, from 8:30 a.m. to 5:00 p.m. This meeting will be open to the public to discuss:

Proposed major revision of Guidelines
Amendment of Guidelines
E. coli K–12 host-vector systems
Host-vector systems other than *E. coli* K–12
Risk-assessment
Review of protocols for required containment levels
Proposed exemptions to Guidelines
Other matters requiring necessary action by the Committee

Attendance by the public will be limited to space available.

Dr. William J. Gartland, Jr., Executive Secretary, Recombinant DNA Advisory Committee, National Institutes of Health, Building 31, Room 4A52, telephone (301) 496–6051, will provide materials to be discussed at the meeting, rosters of committee members, and substantive program information. A summary of the meeting will be available at a later date.

In addition, notice is hereby given of a meeting of the Large Scale Review Working Group sponsored by the Recombinant DNA Advisory Committee at the National Institutes of Health, Building 31C, Conference Room 8, 9000 Rockville Pike, Bethesda, Maryland 20205, on February 9, 1982, after adjournment of the meeting of the Recombinant DNA Advisory Committee, from approximately 2:00 p.m. to 5:00 p.m. The meeting will be open to the public. Attendance will be limited to space available.

Further information may be obtained from Dr. Elizabeth Milewski, Executive Secretary, Large Scale Review Working Group, NIAID, Building 31, Room 4A52, Bethesda, Maryland, telephone (301) 496–6051.

Note.—OMB's "Mandatory Information Requirements for Federal Assistance Program Announcements" (45 FR 39592) requires a statement concerning the official government programs contained in the *Catalog of Federal Domestic Assistance*. Normally NIH lists in its announcements the number and title of affected individual programs for the guidance of the public. Because the guidance in this notice covers not only virtually every NIH program but also essentially every federal research program in which DNA recombinant molecule techniques could be used, it has been determined to be not cost effective or in the public interest to attempt to list these programs. Such a list would likely require several additional pages. In addition, NIH could not be certain that every federal program would be included as many federal agencies, as well as private organizations, both national and international, have elected to follow the NIH Guidelines. In lieu of the individual program listing, NIH invites readers to direct questions to the information address above about whether individual programs listed in the *Catalog of Federal Domestic Assistance* are affected.

NIH programs are not covered by OMB Circular A–95 because they fit the description of "programs not considered appropriate" in section 8–(b)–(4) and (5) of that Circular.

Dated: December 22, 1981.

Thomas E. Malone,
Deputy Director, NIH.

[FR Doc. 82–21 Filed 1–5–82; 8:45 am]
BILLING CODE 4140–01–M

Recombinant DNA Research; Proposed Actions Under Guidelines

AGENCY: National Institutes of Health, PHS, HHS.

ACTION: Notice of actions under NIH Guidelines for Research Involving Recombinant DNA Molecules.

SUMMARY: This notice sets forth proposed actions to be taken under the NIH Guidelines for Research Involving Recombinant DNA Molecules. Interested parties are invited to submit comments concerning these proposals. After consideration of these proposals and comments by the NIH Recombinant DNA Advisory Committee (RAC) at its February 8–9, 1982 meeting, the Director of the National Institutes of Health will issue decisions on these proposals in accord with the Guidelines.

DATE: Comments must be received by February 5, 1982.

ADDRESS: Written comments and recommendations should be submitted to the Director, Office of Recombinant DNA Activities, Building 31, Room 4A52, National Institutes of Health, Bethesda, Maryland 20205. All comments received in timely response to this notice will be considered and will be available for public inspection in the above office on weekdays between the hours of 8:30 a.m. and 5:00 p.m.

FOR FURTHER INFORMATION CONTACT: Background documentation and additional information can be obtained from Drs. Stanley Barban or Elizabeth Milewski, Office of Recombinant DNA Activities, National Institutes of Health, Bethesda, Maryland 20205, (301) 496–6051.

SUPPLEMENTARY INFORMATION: The National Institutes of Health will consider the following actions under the Guidelines for Research Involving Recombinant DNA Molecules.

1. Request for Permission to Clone Subgenomic Segments of Foot and Mouth Disease Virus

Molecular Genetics, Inc., of Minnetonka, Minnesota, requests approval to transfer *E. coli* K–12 cDNA clones comprising less than 75% of the entire genome of Foot and Mouth Disease Virus from the Plum Island Animal Disease Center to its research facility at 10320 Bren Road East, Minnetonka, Minnesota, and to conduct experiments with these clones under P1 containment conditions.

2. Request to Clone Plant DNA in the Cyanobacterium Anacystis Nidulans

Dr. Lawrence Bogorad of Harvard University requests permission to initiate, at P1 containment, a program involving the cloning in the cyanobacterium *Anacystis nidulans* (strain R2) of DNA from chloroplasts of various plants (initially primarily from *Zea mays*). Dr. Bogorad would employ the plasmid vector pUC104, a construct of the cyanobacterial plasmid pUC1 and the *E. coli* vector pACYC184.

Note.—OMB's "Mandatory Information Requirements for Federal Assistance Program Announcements" (45 FR 39592) requires a statement concerning the official government programs contained in the *Catalog of Federal Domestic Assistance*. Normally NIH lists in its announcements the number and title of affected individual programs for the guidance of the public. Because the guidance in this notice covers not only virtually every NIH program but also essentially every federal research program in which DNA recombinant molecule techniques could be used, it has been determined to be not cost effective or in the public interest to attempt to list these programs. Such a list would likely require several additional pages. In addition, NIH could not be certain that every federal program would be included as many federal agencies, as well as private organizations, both national and international, have elected to follow the NIH Guidelines. In lieu of the individual program listing, NIH invites readers to direct questions to the information address above about whether individual programs listed in the *Catalog of Federal Domestic Assistance* are affected.

NIH programs are not covered by OMB Circular A-95 because they fit the description of "programs not considered appropriate" in section 8-(b)-(4) and (5) of that Circular.

Dated: December 17, 1981.

Richard M. Krause,

Director, National Institute of Allergy and Infectious Diseases.

[FR Doc. 82-22 Filed 1-5-82; 8:45 am]

BILLING CODE 4140-01-M

DEPARTMENT OF HEALTH AND HUMAN SERVICES
PUBLIC HEALTH SERVICE
NATIONAL INSTITUTES OF HEALTH

RECOMBINANT DNA ADVISORY COMMITTEE

MINUTES OF MEETING

FEBRUARY 8-9, 1982

TABLE OF CONTENTS

DEPARTMENT OF HEALTH AND HUMAN SERVICES
PUBLIC HEALTH SERVICE
NATIONAL INSTITUTES OF HEALTH

RECOMBINANT DNA ADVISORY COMMITTEE

MINUTES OF MEETING[1]

FEBRUARY 8-9, 1982

The Recombinant DNA Advisory Committee (RAC) was convened for its twenty-fourth meeting at 9:00 a.m. on February 8, 1982, at the Marriott Hotel, Salon D and E, 5151 Pooks Hill Road, Bethesda, Maryland 20814. Mr. Ray Thornton (Chairman), President, Arkansas State University, presided. In accordance with Public Law 92-463, the meeting was open to the public.

Committee members present for all or part of the meeting were:

Abdul Karim Ahmed; David Baltimore; Kenneth Berns; L. Albert Daloz; Nina Fedoroff; David Friedman; Richard Goldstein; King Holmes; Patricia King; Arthur Landy; Myron Levine; Werner Maas; David Martin; James Mason; Gerard McGarrity; Robert McKinney; Robert Mitchell; Elena Nightingale; Ramon Pinon; Mark Saginor; John Scandalios; and William J. Gartland, Jr., Executive Secretary.

A Committee roster is attached. (Attachment I)

The following ad hoc consultant to the Committee was present:

Susan K. Gottesman, National Institutes of Health.

The following non-voting members and liaison representatives were present:

Howard Berman, U.S. Veterans Administration; Chia T. Chen, OSHA, U.S. Department of Labor; George Duda, Department of Energy; Timothy J. Henry, Food and Drug Administration; Herman Lewis, National Science Foundation; Henry Miller, Bureau of Drugs, FDA; Sue Tolin, U.S. Department of Agriculture; and William J. Walsh, III, U.S. Department of State.

---

[1]The RAC is advisory to the NIH, and its recommendations should not be considered as final and accepted. The Office of Recombinant DNA Activities should be consulted for NIH policy on specific issues.

<u>Other National Institutes of Health staff present were:</u>

Robert C. Backus, OD; Stanley Barban, NIAID; W. Emmett Barkley, OD; Becky Connors, NIAID; Irving Delappe, NIAID; Joan Hartman, NIAID; Elizabeth Milewski, NIAID; Stanley Nagle, NIAID; Donald Ralbovsky, OD; Monica Schaeffer, OD; Robert Schreiber, NIAID; and Bernard Talbot, NIAID.

<u>Others in attendance for all or part of the meeting were:</u>

Beth Barban; Claudia Baskin, PMA Newsletter; Robert Bazell, NBC News; Tineke Bodde, BioScience Magazine; Michael Borisov, USSR Embassy; Irene Brandt, Eli Lilly & Company; Allan Buchanan, President's Commission on Medical Ethics; Dennis Cheek, University of Baltimore; Marc Collett, Molecular Genetics, Inc.; David Collins, Department of Justice; David Dickson, Nature; James Dougherty, National Endowment for the Humanities; Paula Dwyer, McGraw Hill; Larry Elliott, National Institute for Occupational Safety and Health; John Ferrugia, CBS; Shelly Fabares; Sam Fleming, Maver School; Jeffrey Fox, Chemical and Engineering News; John Galet, Schering Plough Corporation; Charles Gaush, Bethesda Research Laboratories; Lowell Harmison, Office of Assistant Secretary for Health; Clayton Hathaway, Monsanto Company; Judith Hautala, Genex Corporation; Pamela Haynes, Government Research Corporation; T. M. Helscher, Monsanto Company; Philip Hilts, Washington Post; William Huhn, Pfizer, Inc.; Dorothy Jessop, U.S. Department of Agriculture; Irving Johnson, Eli Lilly and Company; Judith A. Johnson, Library of Congress; M. J. Johnson, Pall Corporation; Roger Johnson, Genetic Engineering Letter; Eric Juengst, National Endowment for the Humanities; Neil Jurinski, NuChem Co, Inc.; James Kaper, University of Maryland; Geoffrey Karny, Office of Technology Assessment; Rihito Kimura, Georgetown University; Warren Leary, Associated Press; S. Edward Lee, Hoffman LaRoche, Inc.; Carter Leonard, Blue Sheet; W. Lepkowski, Chemical and Engineering News; Morris A. Levin, Environmental Protection Agency; Dan Liberman, Massachusetts Institute of Technology; Charles Marwick, New Scientist; Vincent Mazzola, U.S. Department of Agriculture; James McCullough, Library of Congress; Julia Miller, Science News; Bernard Mlynczak, Monsanto Company; Claire Nader; Norine Noonan, Science and Technology Committee, House of Representatives; Stephen Pijar, Food and Drug Administration; William Pilacinski, Molecular Genetics, Inc; Michael Pimentel, University of Maryland; Harvey Price, Industrial Biotechnology Association; Daniel Rift, Princeton University; Sheila Rosenthal, Environmental Protection Agency; Sandra Ronspies, Genentech, Inc.; Perc Reeve, American Cyanamid; Renie Schapiro, President's Commission on Medical Ethics; Harold Schmeck, New York Times; Stephanie Soucek, National Institute for Occupational Safety and Health; Marjory Sun, Science Magazine; Keith Swain, New England Nuclear; Ane Talbot; Terry Vass, Genentech, Inc.; Jonathan Weiswasser, Maver School; Susan Wright, University of Michigan; and Eileen Zalisk, NOVA.

I. CALL TO ORDER AND OPENING REMARKS

Mr. Ray Thornton, Chairman, called the meeting to order at 9:00 a.m., on February 8, 1982. He introduced two new members of the Recombinant DNA Advisory Committee: Dr. David Friedman, Professor of Microbiology at the University of Michigan and Dr. David Martin, Professor of Medicine and Chief of Medical Genetics at the University of California Medical Center, San Francisco.

II. MINUTES OF THE SEPTEMBER 10-11, 1981, MEETING

Mr. Thornton asked Dr. McGarrity to comment on the minutes (tab 1061) of the September 10-11, 1981, meeting. Dr. McGarrity said the minutes accurately reflected the September meeting, and moved that they be accepted. Dr. Fedoroff seconded the motion. Dr. McKinney requested a clarification of the language in Section XVI, Containment Conditions for Cloning and Expression of DNA Coding for Diphtheria Toxin. He suggested the language should be clarified to read:

> "Dr. McKinney suggested RAC specify that the work be conducted in P3 laboratories in Building 550 of the Frederick Cancer Research Center under conditions specified by the local IBC."

Mr. Thornton called the question on the motion to accept the minutes with the clarified language. The motion was unanimously accepted.

III. RISK ASSESSMENT STUDIES

Mr. Thornton invited Dr. Levine to present the summary of recombinant DNA risk assessment studies at tab 1057. Dr. Levine said that from the early days of recombinant DNA technology there has been concern about measures used to contain genetic recombinants. Sophisticated physical containment facilities can provide containment, however, such facilities are expensive to construct and to maintain. On the other hand, a degree of biological containment can be obtained, inexpensively, by selecting "safe" poorly mobilizable plasmids as cloning vectors and by using as hosts bacterial strains that do not colonize the human intestine.

The degree to which poorly mobilizable "safe" plasmids can or cannot be transferred from bacterium to bacterium within the human intestinal milieu is a critical assessment of containability. The Falmouth Conference on Recombinant DNA in 1977 formally addressed the question of plasmid mobilizability; the conferees recommended that risk assessment studies, consisting of feeding human volunteers *E. coli* K-12 with various plasmids, be performed. In 1979, an *ad hoc* Working Group for Risk Assessment was convened at NIH. At that meeting, experts reviewed the Falmouth protocol and pointed out that it would not be feasible to evaluate plasmid transfer using *E. coli* K-12 as the host, since *E. coli* K-12 does not colonize the human intestine and is rather rapidly eliminated from the bowel. An *E. coli* K-12 strain would, thus, never reach high enough numbers in the human intestine for plasmid transfer to be detected if it occurred at low probability. The *ad hoc* Working Group suggested instead that the plasmids should be evaluated for mobilizability using as host an *E. coli* strain that readily colonizes the human intestine.

Dr. Levine said the risk assessment studies he would describe used *E. coli* strain HS-4 feeding studies to evaluate plasmid mobilizability. He said the study was to determine: (a) how well *E. coli* HS-4 colonized the human intestine; (b) whether indigenous coliforms would continue to co-habitate in the colon with HS-4; (c) whether and with what frequency a mobilizable plasmid would be transferred by triple crosses *in vivo* from HS-4 into indigenous coliforms; (d) whether and with what frequency a poorly mobilizable plasmid would be transferred by triple crosses *in vivo* from HS-4 into indigenous coliforms; and (e) whether and with what frequency a poorly mobilizable plasmid would be transferred *in vivo*, in the presence of a highly conjugative plasmid, from HS-4 into indigenous coliforms.

Dr. Levine said the experiments show that: (a) *E. coli* HS-4 very effectively colonizes the human intestine; (b) indigenous coliforms continue to cohabit the colon with HS-4 in most individuals; (c) mobilizable plasmids are transferred by triple crosses *in vivo* from HS-4 into indigenous coliforms; (d) a poorly mobilizable plasmid is not detectably transferred by triple crosses *in vivo* from HS-4 into indigenous coliforms; and (e) a poorly mobilizable plasmid transfers in the presence of a highly conjugative plasmid *in vivo* from HS-4 into indigenous coliforms.

Dr. Levine emphasized that experiment (d) described above examining whether a poorly mobilizable plasmid can be transferred *in vivo* by triple cross is the critical risk assessment study as it most resembles the potential laboratory accident. He pointed out, however, that very large numbers of organisms, in sodium bicarbonate to neutralize stomach acid, were fed to volunteers taking the antibiotic, tetracycline. The use of antacids and antibiotics is forbidden in a recombinant DNA laboratory, and the numbers of organisms administered in the study are unrealistically large in terms of what might occur in a laboratory accident. Even under these unrealistic conditions which enhance the possibility of transmission, there was no demonstrable transfer of the poorly mobilizable plasmid.

Dr. Levine said Dr. Stuart Levy of Tufts University had also performed feeding studies. Dr. Levine said Dr. Levy fed volunteers a debilitated *E. coli* K-12 strain containing a poorly mobilizable plasmid and two derepressed conjugative plasmids. The strain does not colonize, and no transfer of the plasmid to indigenous coliforms was observed. Dr. Levy's study, however, is more realistic in that it tests for plasmid transfer with a host-vector system actually used in recombinant DNA research. Dr. Martin asked if comparable studies had been performed in mice. Dr. Levine said that *E. coli* is not a major flora in the mouse and doesn't reach anywhere near the concentration per gram of fecal material that one gets in man; Dr. Levine felt that human feeding studies are the critical experiments.

IV. PROPOSED REVISION OF THE GUIDELINES

Mr. Thornton called the attention of the RAC to the major topic of the February 8-9, 1982, meeting, a discussion of two proposals (tabs 1050, 1056A, 1056B, 1056C/1, 1056C/7, 1056D, 1056E, 1056F, 1056G) to modify the the current NIH Guidelines for Research Involving Recombinant DNA Molecules.

Mr. Thornton said he would take a moment to give his personal perspective prior to resuming the role as committee chairman. He said former NIH Director, Donald Fredrickson, summarized the purposes of the Guidelines as (1) to establish a rapid, complete means of communication, (2) to assure that the Guidelines are conservative yet allow research to proceed, and (3) to permit public participation in the formulation of public policy. Mr. Thornton noted the difficulty of establishing and maintaining communication between public policy decision makers and experts in a scientific field. NIH has devised a mechanism which successfully maintains this communication, and he would not wish to abandon it.

Mr. Thornton then described the Guidelines from a lawyer's perspective. He noted that the Guidelines are not laws; he thought this is good since laws are difficult to formulate and difficult to change. Neither are they regulations; regulations are subject to formal revision procedures much more rigid than those RAC and the NIH follow in modifying the Guidelines. Neither are the Guidelines simply statements of good practice. The RAC and the NIH have been responsive to change, not as quickly perhaps as some would have preferred, but quickly enough that the advance of science has not been significantly impeded.

Mr. Thornton then recognized Dr. Baltimore who referred to the December 4, 1981, proposal which RAC had recommended for publication in the Federal Register (46 FR 59368). Dr. Baltimore said that the proposal had elicited tremendous response. He said that conversion to a voluntary code of standard practice, as described in the December 4, 1981, Federal Register, is appropriate. Although the current NIH Guidelines are not formal regulations, they have instituted an informal regulatory process. He expressed hope that the philosophy of voluntary compliance expressed in the December 4, 1981, proposal would be accepted.

Dr. Baltimore suggested that some of the concerns expressed about the December 4, 1981, proposal by correspondents could be addressed and met by modifications. Some correspondents had expressed concern that the IBCs would be dismantled. Dr. Baltimore assumed that with the language of the December 4, 1981, proposal, the IBCs would remain in place. He said he had, however, prepared an amendment, which might be added during the discussion, specifying a continuing role for IBCs.

Dr. Baltimore said that in setting P1 containment conditions, the December 4, 1981, proposal implies there could not be deliberate release of recombinant organisms into the environment. It is clear from the letters received in response to the proposal, however, that some people would prefer an explicit statement to that effect. Dr. Baltimore said that if RAC felt it was necessary, he would support an amendment to the December 4, 1981, proposal to accomplish that aim.

Finally, Dr. Baltimore suggested the language of Section I-A might be modified to include a strong statement that although voluntary, adherence to the Guidelines is strongly recommended. He said the December 4, 1981, proposal with these amendments would be responsive to comments received. He then moved the proposal appearing in the December 4, 1981, Federal Register (46 FR 59368) as an item for discussion. The motion was seconded by Dr. McGarrity.

Dr. Baltimore made an additional statement in response to certain written comments received. He said that he has never hidden his affiliation with the company, Collaborative Research, of Waltham, Massachusetts. He stressed, however, that if he were acting for the company, he would not be supporting the December 4, 1981, proposal because he said it is not in the interests of any institution in the Boston area, as it might lead to more stringent regulation at the local level. He said he supported the December 4, 1981, proposal because he believes it is correct.

Dr. Nightingale said that letters commenting on the proposals indicate many remaining concerns in both the scientific and public sectors. In her view, these concerns are not adequately addressed by the December 4, 1981, proposal even if that proposal were modified as just suggested by Dr. Baltimore.

Dr. Nightingale said that there is not a clear consensus for eliminating the mandatory nature of the Guidelines or eliminating the requirement for IBCs. She said the issue of scale-up needs further discussion. She expressed the belief that removing the mandatory nature of the Guidelines would stimulate a variety of legislative actions across the country, possibly resulting in regulatory variation from location to location. She also suggested that although the probability of an event with disastrous consequences is very small, one must acknowledge that gaps in scientific knowledge exist; if such a very rare event should occur, there could be tremendous backlash against the scientific community.

Dr. Nightingale said the December 7, 1981 (46 FR 59734, Part 7, "Gottesman"), proposal would simplify the Guidelines and remove many restrictions. Dr. Nightingale said she had a list of at least six ways in which the Gottesman proposal could be further simplified, and restrictions further removed, by the next RAC meeting. Dr. Nightingale then moved acceptance of the December 7, 1981, "Gottesman" proposal as a substitute motion with a commitment to continue to review, reorganize, simplify, and remove restrictions from the Guidelines as expeditiously as possible. Dr. Fedoroff seconded the motion.

Dr. Berns said that the current Guidelines are cumbersome and complex. The RAC has several options. The most significant issue is the mandatory nature of the Guidelines. He thought having IBCs is good, and recommended keeping the RAC. He stated a preference for readily understandable Guidelines.

Dr. Mason said RAC has acted responsibly in the process of reviewing the Guidelines. He supported the need for IBCs in both academia and industry. Indeed this type of activity should not be limited to the recombinant DNA field but should be encouraged generically. He feared that RAC, by its endorsement for publication of the December 4, 1981, proposal, did not convey to the public the importance of IBCs. Dr. Mason suggested that certain issues should be carefully scrutinized, including deliberate release of recombinant containing organisms into the environment and the cloning of genes for drug resistance and for certain toxins. Dr. Mason expressed the belief that the NIH Guidelines ultimately should and will become voluntary, but suggested they should remain mandatory for the time being for at least two reasons: (1) more information should be collected, particularly in regard to some of the areas currently prohibited; and (2) the public is not yet ready for voluntary guidelines.

Dr. Goldstein said that he could not support the December 4 proposal. He said that he supports the December 7 proposal as it simplifies the Guidelines, specifies IBCs, and maintains mandatory Guidelines. He stated that haphazard local regulations, varying from community to community, and hindering the research, will result if national oversight is not maintained. He felt the December 7, 1981, proposal does not deal adequately with large-scale work and that area should be reviewed.

Ms. King noted that at the September 8-9, 1981, RAC meeting she had not supported what became the December 4, 1981, proposal. She believes the December 7 "Gottesman" proposal is where the RAC should begin in trying to reach a final position. She expressed the belief that regulation is justified by concerns about safety. Arguments that recombinant DNA is no more dangerous than other forms of biomedical research have been advanced. This does not lead Ms. King to the conclusion that only a voluntary code of conduct is necessary. She suggested, rather, that if other research areas pose similar risk, then perhaps they too should be regulated. She favored mandatory Guidelines with sanctions and a monitoring system. The structure should not yet be dismantled nor should it be made voluntary. Otherwise a system of fragmented regulations at the state and local level might develop.

Mr. Thornton recognized Dr. Gottesman who had authored the December 7, 1981, proposal. Dr. Gottesman said her proposal is based on the assessment of risks in the document "Evaluation of the Risks Associated with Recombinant DNA" (46 FR 59385). She noted that that document had been generated by the Working Group on Revision of the Guidelines during the summer of 1981. On the basis of that evaluation, she had concluded that there are several types of experiments about which questions remain or about which so little is known that no absolute conclusion can be drawn. For these types of experiments she felt a mandatory record-keeping and oversight mechanism is appropriate.

Dr. Gottesman said her proposal requires RAC review and NIH approval for certain experiments involving toxin genes, drug resistance genes, and release into the environment. Responsibility for oversight of certain other experiments is delegated to the IBCs. The types of experiments to be reviewed and IBC review procedures might be modified by RAC. RAC may wish to permit the IBCs greater leeway in lowering containment for certain experiments. Dr. Gottesman noted that her proposal does not alter the status of currently exempt experiments.

Mr. Daloz said that specialists in general tend to develop tunnel-vision so that their own concerns become uppermost in their minds. He noted that many laws and guidelines regulate our daily lives, and that even if the NIH Guidelines were eliminated, other agencies might institute guidelines or regulations. Mr. Daloz expressed his support for the December 7, 1981, proposal; he said, in any event, the IBCs should be retained.

Dr. McKinney said he had discussed the December 4 and December 7 proposals with scientists, lawyers, and representatives of commercial organizations. He said the researchers he had spoken with are approximately evenly divided in their support of mandatory vs. voluntary Guidelines. Regarding the current prohibitions, Dr. McKinney said many people felt certain experiments should be monitored and controlled.

Dr. McKinney said that previously the RAC had extricated itself from "regulating" large-scale activities. He felt the reintroduction of the question of how to oversee large-scale work was retrogressive; RAC should address science issues and avoid reviewing large-scale activities per se.

Finally, Dr. McKinney noted that some correspondents mentioned the negative effects the Guidelines have had on research. He said the committee must also take into account the beneficial aspects of the review process; in his view the benefits far outweigh any negative aspects. He said RAC would be remiss if it eliminated oversight over recombinant DNA research before more data are accumulated.

Mr. Mitchell said he had made a rough analysis of the opinions submitted by commentators on the proposals. According to his estimate, approximately half favored the December 4 proposal; the other half favored either the current Guidelines or modest changes therein, or the December 7 proposal.

Mr. Mitchell said the press gives the impression that the recombinant DNA field is advancing very rapidly. These accounts do not support the allegation that the Guidelines have inhibited research. He suggested that should the NIH change the Guidelines substantially, RAC would find itself in an untenable position; it would forfeit the opportunity to "move" the technology on a rational basis, and uniformity of standards would be lost. Mr. Mitchell suggested that adoption of the December 4, 1981, proposal would destroy some of the scientific community's credibility. He said that should Congress ever again consider national legislation, scientists could no longer argue they were following a policy of self-regulation.

Mr. Mitchell said he had attended a panel meeting of the California legislature's Committee on Health on December 14, 1981. He said these legislators, few of whom have a scientific background, spoke in terms of public perceptions. He questioned how many of those legislators would understand the scientific arguments or attempt to comprehend technical presentations.

Mr. Mitchell said he supported the December 7 proposal as it maintains the mandatory nature of the Guidelines and the requirement for IBCs. Dr. Fedoroff said she strongly supported the December 7 proposal and urged that a mechanism for further simplification be introduced.

Dr. Saginor said that the recombinant DNA issue could easily become a political football; the Guidelines have restrained politicians from using this as an issue. He added that the RAC as a central committee providing a forum for discussion is necessary. He supported the December 7, 1981, proposal.

Dr. Irving Johnson of Eli Lilly and Company said Eli Lilly had commented favorably on both the December 4 and the December 7 proposals, although he had reservations about both proposals. He said the December 4 proposal provides no "trackability". The December 7 proposal, while it simplifies the Guidelines, perpetuates unnecessary bookkeeping. He said that Eli Lilly and Company recommends mandatory retention of IBCs which should be required to report problems to the RAC.

Dr. Johnson pointed out that representatives of regulatory agencies are on the Interagency Recombinant DNA Committee and have liaison representatives to the RAC. These representatives are there to monitor events and suggest appropriate action to their agencies. For a company involved in interstate commerce such as Eli Lilly and Company, these agencies represent regulations which are mandatory and not voluntary.

Dr. Johnson said he had attended the November 1981 hearings of the California Legislature's Committee on Health and had detected little concern over risk at that hearing. Concerns were expressed, however, over moral and ethical problems. Dr. Johnson expressed concern about again raising the issue of large-scale work and cited the safety of large-scale equipment. He proposed amending the December 4, 1981, proposal to require retention of IBCs.

Dr. McGarrity said that he has concluded that recombinant DNA research presents no hazards beyond those normally associated with microbiological research. This is not to say there are no problems in other areas of biomedical research; however, these hazards have been adequately handled. He stated that it is time to stop the discriminatory treatment of recombinant DNA research. He favored the December 4, 1981, proposal with some modifications.

Dr. Holmes said he favored retaining mandatory Guidelines and the requirement for IBCs. He rejected the argument that recombinant DNA activities should not require oversight because other areas of microbiological or biomedical research do not have special oversight. He said he would support the December 7, 1981, proposal with the addition of a recommendation that IBCs also review non-recombinant DNA research that is similar to research covered by Section III of the Guidelines.

Dr. Baltimore reiterated his belief that recombinant DNA research is no more hazardous than experiments in the mainstream of biomedical research. He felt this was the judgement of a majority of the scientific community, and that the December 4, 1981, proposal reflects this consensus. He said fear of local regulation or fear of leaving industry with no code for legal protection were not reasons for maintaining mandatory Guidelines. Adoption of the December 4, 1981, proposal would send a message to States and localities that the RAC concludes that regulations are not necessary.

Finally, Dr. Baltimore said that the CDC "Classification of Etiological Agents on the Basis of Hazard" is not appropriate for use in classifying recombinant DNA experiments.

Dr. Lewis of the National Science Foundation suggested greater flexibility in IBC specifications might be desirable. Dr. Landy said that he supported the original Baltimore-Campbell proposal, and subsequently the December 4, 1981, proposal, as the only intellectually honest recognition of the relationship between the unestablished potential risk in recombinant DNA research and known risk in other areas of research which are not regulated. In attempting to rationalize support for greater controls over recombinant DNA research than over work with known pathogens, Dr. Landy said the training, procedures, and restraints applied by the select group of investigators studying pathogens would not necessarily have been followed by all those now using recombinant DNA techniques.

Dr. Gottesman concurred with Dr. Landy's rationalization and added that investigators studying pathogens know the properties of these organisms; recombinant organisms might express unexpected properties.

Dr. Maas said he saw no logic in having guidelines for one type of experimental procedure, which is rapidly becoming a very commonly employed technique, and having no regulations for other types of more dangerous procedures, such as work with chemical carcinogens.

Dr. Gottesman said that mandatory guidelines are not necessarily synonomous with bureaucracy. She noted that the December 7, 1981, proposal no longer requires RAC review and NIH approval for large-scale procedures; rather it specifies that large-scale experiments be approved by the IBC. She said the definition of large-scale might be revised. Dr. Gottesman agreed with Dr. Baltimore that the CDC Classification of Etiological Agents is not perfect, but she said the alternative in the December 4 proposal of "use whatever you have and figure it out yourself" is not better. If RAC cannot find a better mechanism than the CDC classification, IBCs and PIs individually will not be able to make better decisions.

Ms. King said that the central issue is mandatory vs. voluntary guidelines. She said she was concerned with questions of process. She referred to Dr. Baltimore's statement that only a minority of scientists believe there may be some safety concerns with respect to recombinant DNA research. She said the public cannot ascertain whether that statement is accurate. The RAC did not cross-examine those who submitted written comments. Ms. King said RAC members should be aware of what she considers to be defects in process, and, therefore, err on the side of caution in deciding between the December 4 and December 7 proposals.

Dr. Nightingale praised the more extensive attempts to solicit comments on these proposals than had occurred in the past. As a result of this, the comments received were more varied than in the past. However, she felt it was only one small step in really assessing what the public feels. Referring back to Dr. Baltimore's statement, Dr. Nightingale said that disagreement does exist within the scientific community on whether there are unique risks of recombinant DNA research. She said that a major issue is voluntary vs. mandatory IBCs. She said that the December 7, 1981, proposal could be simplified and reorganized to make it easier to read and less cumbersome. She suggested that Section III-C could be eliminated; that the criteria for defining large-scale could be revised to emphasize inoculum size rather than volume; that Section IV could be simplified and reorganized; that the bureaucracy within IBCs could be greatly simplified; that the section dealing with whole or defective viruses could be simplified; that Sections III-B-2-a and Section III-B-2-b dealing with etiological agents could be combined; and that all work in nonpathogens could be performed at P1 containment. She viewed the December 7, 1981, proposal as a first, very positive step towards reducing complexity and restrictions.

Dr. Levine attempted to address the question of why recombinant DNA research is singled out for special consideration while other biomedical research, using inherently much more dangerous organisms, is not. He said the answer is in the historical context. Work with pathogens has had an extraordinary safety record for decades. The reason there was so much interest in control of recombinant DNA is that recombinant DNA technology became available in the 1970s, in an era of regulation. He cited procedures for research involving human subjects, which changed drastically in the early 1970s. He said he supports these constraints as they protect the public, as well as individual subjects, and they facilitate communication between the public and clinical investigators. He said being responsive to the public is very important and if a significant segment of the public is still concerned about recombinant DNA, this committee should be sensitive to that concern. He said that he would like to see something like the December 4, 1981, proposal ultimately adopted, but not immediately.

Dr. Ahmed said he wished to quote and highlight several points from the letter from the Public and Scientific Affairs Board of the American Society for Microbiology. He quoted from that letter that:

> "Our concern is for the fact that only sparse information is available for other host-vectors. With less characterized systems, new combinations may result in organisms with potentially increased pathogenicity than either the donor or the recipient.
>
> "We are not only concerned with the paucity of information but also with the lack of mechanisms for its dissemination. Many workers using modern genetic technology are not versed in pathogenic microbiology and cannot be assumed to have proper training or access to up-to-date information."

Dr. Martin said he believed as a scientist that recombinant DNA should not be singled out for special oversight. However, this position must be viewed within the historical context. He said that the state legislators and county supervisors with whom he had spoken are not primarily interested in the scientific basis for relaxation or elimination of the Guidelines, but rather in public opinion. RAC must be careful not to excite a public reaction that could result in greater bureaucratic and regulatory problems from local jurisdictions.

Dr. Saginor said he would like to propose an amendment to the December 7, 1981, proposal, should it pass, that a working group be formed to further refine, simplify, and reorganize that proposal, and that this group report to the RAC at a future meeting.

A discussion was held of the proper parliamentary procedure for the Committee to use to proceed. Mr. Thornton suggested that the Committee might vote now on Dr. Nightingale's motion to substitute the December 7 proposal for the December 4 proposal. This would result in the Committee choosing which "vehicle" it wished initially to adopt. Following this, RAC members could propose amendments to "perfect" the vehicle chosen, before the final vote on it.

Dr. Baltimore "called the question." By a vote of nineteen in favor, two opposed, and no abstentions, the RAC agreed to limit further debate and to vote on the motion to substitute the December 7, 1981, proposal for the December 4, 1981, proposal as the vehicle to be used for further amendments. Dr. Baltimore said that although, following this vote, any aspect of the winning proposal would be open for further amendments, he felt the vote should be viewed as a decision about whether "to go in the voluntary or mandatory direction." Dr. Nightingale reminded the RAC that her motion included the commitment to work towards future simplification of the Guidelines. By a vote of sixteen in favor, five opposed, and no abstentions, the RAC adopted the substitute motion, thus, choosing the Gottesman proposal as the vehicle to be placed before the Committee, open to further amendments.

Mr. Thornton recognized Dr. Susan Wright. Dr. Wright focused her comments on large-scale applications as she thought that while many other issues are being addressed, the RAC was not adequately addressing that issue. She said the primary focus of RAC has been on the hazards of research, not the hazards of industrial processes. She said that one cannot dismiss change of scale with regard to accidental release of recombinant organisms. She felt the data base on industrial hazards is very poor. She said she had heard some industrialists in other countries were considering using open fermentation tanks. If there is no oversight, companies will use whatever fermentation process they think is in their best interest. There are irresponsible companies willing to cut corners and take risks to try to gain a competitive advantage over responsible companies. Furthermore, there are no risk assessment experiments with organisms making insulin, interferon, etc. She said the committee is assuming that whatever product is being made will be harmless.

Dr. Wright said the RAC recommendation at the previous meeting to exempt from NIH review, certain large-scale experiments utilizing E. coli K-12, Saccharomyces cerevisiae and Bacillus subtilis host-vector systems was an error which produced a major gap in oversight. She urged the RAC to reconsider and re-evaluate its oversight over large-scale work.

Dr. Irving Johnson of Eli Lilly and Company said that industry has produced hundreds of gallons of the causative agents of polio, diphtheria, whooping cough, etc., with no great hazard to workers or to the environment, and in fact with great benefit to the population. Dr. Johnson said the only open vats he is aware of are in the beer brewing industry. Most industrial fermentations are generally highly contained to protect against contamination. Inocula are introduced into the growth tank through a rigid stainless steel structure. The connection does not leak and is steam sterilized.

Dr. Wright said she was not making a categorical statement about hazards, but rather about the data base. In her opinion, the data are extremely poor and incomplete, and assumptions that problems will be uncomplicated or easy to deal with are premature. These new technologies should remain under RAC review until a better data base develops.

Dr. Mason said that many industrial issues, though of concern, are beyond the scope of the RAC. Federal, state, and local authorities that make on-site inspections may wish to evaluate these issues, but RAC should not. Dr. Ahmed felt a distinction should be drawn between organism concentration and total amount in industrial processes.

Dr. Gottesman said that the December 7, 1981, proposal still requires that non-exempt large-scale procedures be reviewed by the local IBC before the project begins; P1-LS containment would still apply. It extends to all large-scale experiments the conditions approved by RAC at the previous meeting for certain large-scale experiments.

Dr. Berns questioned the language of Section I-B, Definition of Recombinant DNA Molecules, in the December 7, 1981, proposal. The relevant text of Section I-B reads as follows:

> "Synthetic DNA segments likely to yield a potentially harmful polynucleotide or polypeptide (e.g., a toxin or a pharmacologically active agent) shall be considered as equivalent to their natural DNA counterpart. If the synthetic DNA segment is not expressed *in vivo* as a polynucleotide or polypeptide product, it is exempt from the Guidelines."

Dr. Gottesman pointed out that this is a reformulation of text which appears as Section III-E of the current (July 1, 1981) Guidelines. Dr. Berns suggested the real issue is whether the synthetic fragment would produce a biologically active product; he proposed to amend the language by adding the phrase "biologically active" before the word "polynucleotide" in the last sentence. Dr. Nightingale, who had proposed the motion being considered, and Dr. Fedoroff, the seconder of the motion, accepted the amendment.

Dr. Saginor then proposed an amendment which would explicitly state that a working group be appointed to review and attempt to simplify further the Guidelines and to report to the RAC at a future meeting. Dr. Nightingale, noting this intent was part of her original motion, accepted the amendment, as did Dr. Fedoroff.

Mr. Thornton called the question on Dr. Nightingale's motion as modified by amendments. By a vote of seventeen in favor, three opposed, and no abstentions, the RAC recommended adoption of the December 7, 1981, proposal with amendments. Mr. Thornton said a working group to refine the proposal would be designated at a later date, in accordance with the motion.

Dr. McGarrity asked the committee to state for the record that RAC sees no need for additional state and local ordinances governing recombinant DNA activities. Dr. Liberman, the biological safety officer at MIT, advised against adoption of Dr. McGarrity's statement as he viewed it as counterproductive. Based on his experience as a member of the Boston Biohazards Committee, he sees growing community interest in overseeing non-recombinant biohazards as recombinant systems are being handled.

Dr. Ahmed said he thought adoption of Dr. McGarrity's statement would be viewed as arrogance on the part of the RAC, saying "our views are gospel, and don't second guess us."

Mr. Mitchell said that he is in sympathy with the motion since he is concerned about fragmentation at the state and local level. However, knowing the independence of legislative bodies, it might not be well taken. He suggested that if the statement were reworded it might be more successful. Dr. McGarrity agreed and withdrew the proposal in order that revised text could be prepared for consideration later in the meeting.

Dr. Mason spoke against Dr. McGarrity's proposal, as it runs counter to usual regulatory practice, in which states and localities may regulate as long as their requirements are at least as stringent as Federal requirements. He added that RAC's recommendation would not be binding.

Dr. Holmes made a motion that there be added to the Guidelines a statement to the effect that:

> "It is not clear that the biohazards associated with recombinant DNA are unique or different from biohazards associated with other work with pathogenic organisms; therefore, RAC encourages local Institutional Biosafety Committees to establish procedures for review of experiments not involving recombinant DNA, which, nonetheless, involve biohazards such as those addressed in Section III of the Guidelines."

Dr. Fedoroff seconded the motion. Dr. Landy suggested that a different statement be substituted for Dr. Holmes' proposed language to the effect that:

> "The Recombinant DNA Advisory Committee wants to point out the absence of demonstrated risk or danger posed by recombinant DNA research. The continuance of the Guidelines for recombinant DNA research is made with full appreciation of the fact that other areas of research in which some risk has been demonstrated are without analogous guidelines."

Dr. Landy said such a statement would make clear to the public that RAC's recommendation to maintain guidelines is not based on demonstrated risk, but on potential risk.

Dr. Ahmed asked whether NIH has the authority to expand the purview of the IBCs as in Dr. Holmes' statement. Dr. Talbot replied that such a statement could be sent to the IBCs as a recommendation.

Dr. Goldstein said that he thought Dr. Landy's proposal could "stir up a hornet's nest," regenerating the situation of previous years with recombinant DNA. Ms. King said she could not support Dr. Landy's proposal as she questioned the phrase "absence of demonstrated risk." Dr. Berns moved to table Dr. Holmes' proposal. By a vote of seventeen in favor, three opposed, and no abstentions, the proposal was tabled.

Dr. Levine called the committee's attention to the report of the Working Group on Revision of the Guidelines entitled "Evaluation of the Risks Associated with Recombinant DNA Research" and particularly Part IV-A of the report, "Summary Analysis of Risks" (46 FR 59390). He said the conclusion is that most potential recombinant DNA risks envisaged in 1975 are now considered nonexistent. Ms. King said RAC should emphasize that available data cited in that report support and justify RAC's recommendation of the December 7, 1981, proposal. She suggested the RAC might formally reaffirm the "Summary Analysis of Risks." Dr. Martin suggested this text might be used as a preamble to the introduction of the new Guidelines by the NIH Director. Dr. Holmes moved that the Director is requested to consider the "Summary Analysis of Risks" (46 FR 59390) as he determines a preamble to the revised Guidelines. Dr. Nightingale seconded the motion. She emphasized that her earlier motion for adoption of the December 7, 1981, proposal was based on the document "Evaluation of the Risks Associated with Recombinant DNA Research." She expected this document would be published as an integral part of the decision document. Dr. Mason hoped the document would note the different options considered by the RAC.

Ms. King suggested Dr. Holmes' motion be amended to call the attention of the NIH Director not just to the "Summary Analysis of Risks" (46 FR 59390) but also the motion which originally established the Working Group on Revision of the Guidelines, the Working Group's agenda, and its complete report.

Dr. Talbot asked if the motion might not be withdrawn, with the assurance that NIH staff would bring all of these items to the Director's attention without the necessity of a motion. Ms. King said she would prefer a specific motion since the Working Group report had not been formally endorsed by the RAC at the September 1981 meeting and since the RAC action today accepting the December 7, 1981, proposal is based on that report. Dr. Holmes reworded his motion to request the summary information discussed be included in the Director's preamble. Dr. Nightingale, who had seconded Dr. Holmes' earlier motion, also agreed.

Dr. Wright said that if there were to be a general statement on risks, then it should be made clear which industrial problems the RAC is not dealing with, so that no one thinks this is a global statement covering both research and industrial risks. Dr. Ahmed suggested that language be inserted indicating that the report does not address industrial scale-up. Dr. Berns noted that the NIH, on the advice of the RAC, had issued "Physical Containment Recommendations for Large-Scale Uses of Organisms Containing Recombinant DNA Molecules;" RAC, however, is no longer evaluating mechanical details in individual large-scale applications. Dr. Landy opposed Dr. Ahmed's suggestion on the introduction of a specific statement on industrial considerations as it would dilute the general policy statement.

Dr. Pinon moved to table the motion; he preferred that ORDA bring these items to the attention of the Director, NIH, without the necessity of a formal motion. By a vote of ten in favor, eight opposed, and two abstentions, the motion to table carried.

After a brief recess, Dr. Mason moved to reconsider the action in order to provide the Director with a clear indication of RAC intent. He felt the previous vote revolved about procedural issues rather than intent. By a vote of ten in favor, four opposed, and three abstentions, the motion to reconsider was adopted.

Ms. King then moved that "the RAC specifically call to the Director's attention that the action taken on the December 7, 1981, proposal results from analysis and consideration of the report entitled 'Evaluation of the Risks Associated with Recombinant DNA Research' prepared by the Working Group on Revision of the Guidelines. The vote on the December 7, 1981, proposal implements the Working Group report."

By a vote of nineteen in favor, none opposed, and one abstention, the RAC adopted Ms. King's motion as a substitute for the previous motion. Mr. Thornton then ruled that unless there were objection (which there was not), the substitute motion is adopted by unanimous consent as the recommendation of the RAC.

Following an overnight recess, Mr. Thornton called the committee to order to consider language developed by Dr. McGarrity and Mr. Mitchell regarding local and state legislation. Mr. Mitchell moved acceptance of the following language:

> "Whereas RAC has voted to recommend significant reductions in mandatory guidelines regarding recombinant DNA activity, and
>
> "Whereas RAC in establishing said reduced guidelines did so based upon collective credible scientific knowledge and experience, and
>
> "Whereas RAC believes it to be in the best interest of recombinant DNA activity to have a central arena for the dissemination of information and continuous review, and
>
> "Whereas RAC believes the existence of uniform guidelines thereby establishes certainty and clarity in the scientific community, and
>
> "Whereas RAC believes it would be detrimental to the advancement of recombinant DNA activity to have fragmentation of guidelines across the country,
>
> "Therefore, be it resolved that RAC strongly recommends that local and state governments defer to the NIH Guidelines if enacting legislation governing recombinant DNA activity, unless it clearly establishes by credible scientific evidence that unique risk in fact exists in their particular jurisdiction."

Dr. McGarrity seconded the motion. He said the RAC action taken yesterday on the December 7, 1981, proposal would significantly relax the Guidelines. When considered in the context of possible additional local legislation, Mr. Mitchell's statement expressed RAC's judgement that the NIH Guidelines are the best possible approach at this time. It would be counterproductive for RAC to strip away bureaucracy and paperwork at the national level, only to have more bureaucracy and paperwork added at the state and local level.

Dr. Miller of the FDA strongly endorsed the sense of the motion. He said, almost without exception, the mosaic of local regulations has been more draconian, much less enlightened than the NIH Guidelines, and slower to evolve.

Dr. Martin suggested that the phrase "best interests of the public" be substituted for the phrase "best interest of recombinant DNA activity." Mr. Mitchell agreed.

Dr. Nightingale requested a clarification of the word "activity" in the motion. Mr. Mitchell replied that "activity" is an all inclusive term meant to cover research, development, production, etc.

Drs. Ahmed and Goldstein supported the sentiment expressed by the motion. However, Dr. Goldstein said he would vote against the language as he felt local communities would regard it as arrogant. Mr. Mitchell said he had chosen the verb "defer" to avoid the appearance of arrogance. The language urges that any actions be based on scientific grounds, and places the burden of proof upon advocates of local action. Dr. Friedman agreed.

Dr. Ahmed asked whether addition of the phrase "in as much as possible" would soften the language of the sentence:

> ". . . therefore, be it resolved that RAC strongly recommends that local and state governments defer to the NIH Guidelines . . ."

Mr. Thornton thought the verb "defer" alone was actually softer.

Dr. Mason said he could envisage situations in which local action might be necessary because of irresponsible action by a local academic or industrial group. He hoped RAC did not intend to say that local action should not be taken in such cases. Dr. Goldstein stated that communities realize that while universities are under sanctions, industry is not. Dr. Berns said that Mr. Mitchell's language specifies that when local entities legislate, they should defer to the NIH Guidelines in the scientific component of the legislation.

Dr. Mason said that many aspects of industrial scale-up are not covered by the Guidelines, yet the proposed language implies the existence of such guidance. He questioned whether RAC might amend the language to remove such implications. Dr. McGarrity suggested the phrase "DNA activity" be modified to "DNA research activity."

Dr. Ahmed said he supported the resolution but would prefer that a statement, delineating the scope of RAC activities, be appended to the language. If the committee could not formulate such a statement today, he hoped the Director's preamble to the acceptance of the December 7, 1981, proposal would state that neither RAC nor the NIH deals with mechanical aspects of industrial scale-up activities.

Dr. Pinon requested that the word "credible" be deleted from the phrase "credible scientific evidence"; he thought the term redundant. Dr. Saginor, however, disagreed as he felt "scientific" and "credible" are not synonymous to the public.

Dr. Gottesman saw the proposed language as intending to say to local legislators "we are listening to your concerns, we believe we are responding to them, and we hope you will continue to have faith in RAC." She warned, however, that the language might lead legislators who had not previously thought of legislation to consider it. Dr. Nightingale concurred. She thought acceptance of Mr. Mitchell's statement might be counterproductive. Instead she suggested that the Director's preamble to the revised Guidelines might state that these Guidelines are based on the best available information, and it is hoped they will be applied nationally. She preferred this procedure to a motion indicating RAC's concern over possible local legislation. Dr. Holmes agreed, expressing concern that the motion appeared arrogant and would be counter-productive. Dr. Berns called for the question.

By a vote of sixteen in favor, none opposed, and no abstentions, the RAC voted to stop debate and to vote on the motion proposed by Mr. Mitchell, as amended. By a vote of six in favor, nine opposed, and one abstention, the motion offered by Mr. Mitchell was defeated.

V. REQUEST TO CLONE SUBGENOMIC SEGMENTS OF FOOT AND MOUTH DISEASE VIRUS

Dr. Berns introduced the proposal (tabs 1058, 1059, 1062/1, 1063) of Molecular Genetics, Inc., to clone subgenomic segments of the Foot and Mouth Disease Virus (FMDV) in E. coli K-12. According to U.S. law, whole FMD virus cannot be studied in the U.S. except at the Plum Island Animal Disease Center (PIADC) of the U.S. Department of Agriculture (USDA). Dr. Berns said FMDV causes a disease with serious economic consequences; it is widespread globally but has been eradicated in the U.S.

Dr. Berns said Molecular Genetics, Inc., has cloned portions of the FMDV genome in Argentina. They have characterized the clones and have sent them to Plum Island for infectivity testing. Molecular Genetics, Inc., requests permission to remove these clones to their laboratories in Minnesota. The clones represent, in aggregate, less than sixty-five percent of the FMDV genome. Dr. Berns recalled that Genentech, Inc., in collaboration with USDA had approached the NIH with a similar proposal. That project was approved by RAC and subsequently by the NIH. Genentech, Inc., had received permission to remove clones representing in aggregate seventy-five percent of the FMDV genome from Plum Island to Genentech, Inc., laboratories in California. Dr. Berns recommended approval of the Molecular Genetics, Inc., proposal.

Dr. Tolin said the USDA is waiting for RAC review of the project before testing the infectivity of the clones. She said she had reviewed the documents submitted by Molecular Genetics, Inc., and found them to be in order.

Dr. Maas asked how the FMDV strains cloned by Molecular Genetics, Inc., differed from the strains cloned by Genentech, Inc. Dr. Pilacinski said the FMDV strains cloned by Molecular Genetics, Inc., are indigenous to Argentina and Latin America.

Dr. Ahmed asked why Molecular Genetics, Inc., had requested P1 containment conditions for the work in Minnesota. Dr. Berns said that P1 conditions had been previously approved for the subgenomic FMDV clone work conducted by Genentech, Inc., in California. Dr. Goldstein asked what scale experiments Molecular Genetics anticipated. Dr. Collett said the work would be laboratory scale.

Dr. Berns moved approval of the request. Dr. McKinney seconded the motion. Dr. Talbot clarified the language of the motion: the motion would provide for review of USDA infectivity data by the FMDV Working Group of the RAC before NIH permission would be granted. This procedure had been followed in approving the Genentech, Inc., request. Dr. Goldstein inquired about the composition of this working group. Dr. Gartland said Drs. Baltimore, Berns, and Tolin currently compose the group, and additional members will be named. Dr. Goldstein said he wished that the decision of the working group be sent to the RAC. Dr. Berns agreed.

Mr. Thornton called the vote. By a vote of sixteen in favor, none opposed, and four abstentions, the motion was approved.

VI. PROPOSED INCLUSION OF YERSINIA ENTEROCOLITICA ON SUBLIST A OF APPENDIX A

Dr. Fedoroff said that tabs 1052 and 1056C/6 present a request from Dr. Guy Cornelis of the Universite Catholique de Louvain, Brussels, Belgium. Dr. Cornelis requested that *Yersinia enterocolitica* be exempted from the Guidelines under Section I-E-4 and added to Sublist A, Appendix A. Dr. Fedoroff said *Y. enterocolitica* exchanges genetic information with *E. coli* with a frequency of transfer roughly three orders of magnitude lower than seen in exchange between *E. coli* and *E. coli*. Under certain conditions, that frequency can be enhanced. Mutants which have higher exchange frequencies can also be selected.

Dr. Fedoroff asked Dr. Levine to comment on *Yersinia enterocolitica*. Dr. Levine said that some strains of *Yersinia enterocolitica* cause disease in man. The disease producing serotypes are invasive, with some producing a heat stable enterotoxin whose mechanism of action is identical to that of heat stable *E. coli* enterotoxin. In school age children, *Y. enterocolitica* is a major cause of mesenteric adenitis which leads to a pseudo-appendicitis type syndrome. In older individuals one sees hypersensitivity reactions, including erythema nodosum; in individuals of the HLAV27 allotype, chronic arthritis may develop following *Yersinia* infection.

Dr. Levine said the data demonstrate genetic exchange with E. coli in the test tube, and this exchange probably occurs in nature. On that basis, he supported the proposal. Dr. Fedoroff moved approval of the proposal. Dr. Levine seconded the motion. By a vote of eighteen in favor, none opposed, and one abstention, the RAC approved the motion.

VII. PROPOSED PSEUDOMONAS PUTIDA HOST-VECTOR SYSTEM

Dr. Maas introduced the proposal (tabs 1053, 1056C/5) of Dr. Michael Bagdasarian of the Max-Planck Institut fur Molekulare Genetik, Berlin, West Germany. Dr. Bagdasarian requested HV1 certification of a host-vector system based on Pseudomonas putida strain KT2440 and plasmid cloning vectors pKT262, pKT263 and pKT264.

Dr. Maas questioned whether it is appropriate for RAC to consider a proposal which originated with an investigator outside the U.S. Mr. Thornton replied that if the system could be widely applied in research, RAC might appropriately evaluate it for certification. Drs. Maas, Fedoroff, and McKinney said a P. putida host-vector system could be widely used.

Dr. Maas said the information provided supports the investigator's request for HV1 certification, and so moved. Dr. Berns seconded the motion, adding that a P. putida HV1 system would be very useful as genes which are not expressed in E. coli host-vector systems may be expressed in P. putida systems. Mr. Thornton called the motion. By a vote of eighteen in favor, none opposed, and one abstention, the RAC approved the motion.

VIII. PROPOSALS INVOLVING EK2 HOST-VECTOR SYSTEMS

A. Proposed EK2 Host-Vector Systems

Dr. Friedman introduced the proposal (tabs 1054, 1056C/3) of Dr. Roy Curtiss of the University of Alabama, Birmingham, Alabama. Dr. Curtiss requested EK2 certification of six different E. coli K-12 strains in conjunction with various virulent and temperate bacteriophage lambda, plasmid, and cosmid vectors. Dr. Curtiss also requested that all previously approved EK2 vectors be approved as vector components of the proposed EK2 host-vector systems.

Dr. Friedman said the proposed EK2 host-vector systems are:

(1) E. coli K-12 χ2447, and its suppressor-free sib χ2281, for use with virulent bacteriophage lambda vectors including specifically, but not limited to, Charon 4A.

(2) E. coli K-12 χ1984, and its suppressor-free sib χ2705, for use in conjunction with: virulent lambda vectors including but not limited to Charon 4A; temperate bacteriophage lambda vectors λYEQS cI857 and λZEQS cI857; plasmid cloning vector pBR322; and the cosmid cloning vectors pJC75-37, pJC75-58, pJC76, pJC77, and pHC79.

(3) E. coli χ 2001 and its suppressor-free sib χ 2363, for use in conjunction with all of the vectors enumerated in part two for χ 1984 and χ 2705 plus the cosmid vector pJC78.

Dr. Friedman said that an ad hoc working group held a telephone conference call on January 21, 1982, to discuss this request; that discussion is summarized in Attachment II. He then suggested that RAC evaluate part one of the proposal separately. He said the ad hoc working group agreed that the systems described in part one, χ 2447 and χ 2281 with the virulent bacteriophage lambda vectors, meet EK2 certification criteria. The major safety feature of these systems resides in the vectors rather than in the host; nonetheless, the hosts meet the EK2 requirements specified in the Guidelines.

Dr. Maas requested an explanation of how the suppressor-free sibs would be used. Dr. Gottesman said the suppressor-free sibs would be used to test the virus for reversion; they would not be used for propagating cloned material.

Dr. Talbot suggested that a motion be offered on the first part of the proposal. Dr. Friedman moved that strains χ2447 and χ2281 in part one of the proposal be approved for use with those lambda vectors certified for use in DP50 on the condition that the suppressor-free strain not be used as a propagation host.

Mr. Thornton called the vote. By a vote of eleven in favor, none opposed, and two abstentions, the committee approved the motion.

Dr. Friedman suggested that parts two and three of the proposal be discussed together as both have the same problems. In addition to requesting permission to utilize virulent lambda phage as vectors, Dr. Curtiss requests, in parts two and three, certification for lysogenizing lambda phage and for plasmid and cosmid vectors.

Dr. Friedman said Dr. Curtiss presented no data, as required for EK2 certification, on the lysogenizing phages or for the cosmid vectors. In order to approve plasmid vectors, data from triparental matings must be evaluated, however, Dr. Curtiss supplied no data pertinent to triparental matings in strains χ1984 and χ2705 nor for χ2001 and χ2363.

Dr. Gottesman explained the rationale behind the EK2 approval procedure. There are two considerations: (1) whether the host could establish and spread in the environment, and (2) whether the organism could disseminate recombinant DNA to secondary hosts. She explained that virulent lambda vectors containing certain mutations will not persist in the environment; the survivability of the host in the environment is then a less important consideration. For this reason virulent lambda vectors can be certified without too much data on host survivability being evaluated.

With the plasmid, cosmid and lambda lysogen vectors, whether the host establishes in the environment is a more important consideration. The data Dr. Curtiss supplied on survival for the proposed host strains are less than were evaluated for the EK2 approved host χ1776. Furthermore, Dr. Curtiss does not provide enough data on the proposed cosmid and lambda lysogen vectors. These portions of the proposal should be rejected as supporting data are lacking. Dr. Gottesman suggested that for certain plasmids, the available data may be adequate to warrant approval. The systems using virulent lambda vectors should perhaps be certified.

Dr. Friedman said the ad hoc working group did not recommend approval of those sections of the proposal dealing with lysogenizing phage vectors, plasmid, and cosmid vectors. He recommended approval of strains χ1984, χ2705, χ2001, and χ2363 when virulent lambda phages are used as vectors.

Dr. Friedman asked if the RAC had specified criteria for certification of lysogenizing lambda. Dr. Gottesman replied that they have not; no previous submissions dealing with lysogenizing phages were received. She thought the testing criteria for cosmids might be applicable to lysogenizing phages.

Dr. Levine expressed his concern over the testing criteria specified for EK2 certification. He noted that at the time the EK2 criteria were designed, no data on χ1776 survivability in man were available. When those data became available, it was discovered that χ1776, containing pBR322, survived longer in man than χ1776 without pBR322. Data generated from the mouse system did not predict this phenomenon. He suggested that another level of testing be added to the EK2 criteria: feeding experiments in man should be performed, as these yield the most pertinent data.

Dr. Talbot suggested that any redefinition of EK2 criteria should be considered by the EK2 working group which could report at the next RAC meeting. At this meeting, RAC should use current criteria to evaluate Dr. Curtiss' proposal. Mr. Thornton concurred. Dr. Levine suggested that a motion to defer consideration of parts two and three of Dr. Curtiss' proposal might be in order.

Dr. Ahmed asked if the EK2 certification criteria would be changed by the recommendation on revising the Guidelines made earlier in the meeting (Item IV above). Drs. Talbot and Gottesman replied that it would not. Dr. Martin asked if χ1776 would fall under a grandfather clause should EK2 certification criteria be changed. He wondered whether χ1776 would qualify as an EK2 host under the new criteria. Dr. Levine replied that those questions would have to be considered by the EK2 working group. One possibility would be to accept, as a maximum permissible level, the survival values of χ1776 in the human gut. Alternatively, the working group may have to deal with the possibility that χ1776 is not as debilitated in the human gut as anticipated. Dr. Liberman pointed out that other systems have been decertified, and urged that the EK2 working group reevaluate χ1776's status as an EK2 certified vector.

Dr. Gottesman suggested parts two and three of Dr. Curtiss' request should be deferred as: (1) the information provided is not adequate to evaluate the host-vector systems vis-a-vis the EK2 criteria, and (2) if the EK2 criteria is reconsidered, reconsideration would have important implications for Dr. Curtiss' proposal.

Dr. Friedman moved that the four hosts (χ1984, χ2705, χ2001, and χ2363) be accepted for use with the virulent lambda vectors on condition that the suppressor-free strains not be used as propagation hosts. Consideration of cosmid, plasmid and lysogenic lambda vectors is deferred until more information is obtained. Dr. Maas seconded the motion.

Mr. Thornton called the motion. By a vote of eleven in favor, none opposed, and four abstentions, the RAC approved the motion.

Dr. Levine said that

> "Whereas EK2 systems imply and are meant to result in a high degree of containment, and
>
> "Whereas bacterial hosts in such systems are meant to be highly defective in their ability to survive in the environment, as well as in mammalian intestine, and
>
> "Whereas the guidelines for EK2 criteria were designed before much credible scientific data on these points were available, and
>
> "Whereas data have recently come to light from human feeding experiments with EK2 hosts with and without plasmid pBR322 that demonstrated increased persistence of the host containing plasmid pBR322,"

he would move that the certification criteria for EK2 host-vector systems be reconsidered by the EK2 working group specifically to consider making human feeding studies which yield the most relevant data, one of the criteria.

Dr. Ahmed asked if the working group would report to RAC. Mr. Thornton said it would. It was stated that while many RAC members would agree to have the certification criteria reconsidered by the EK2 working group, not all would necessarily agree with Dr. Levine's "whereas" preamble. Mr. Thornton noted the "whereas" statement was merely prefatory, and not formally part of the motion. By a vote of fourteen in favor, none opposed, and four abstentions, the RAC accepted the motion.

Dr. Mason asked if the Working Group on Revision of the Guidelines would consider this motion. Dr. Talbot replied they would.

B. Proposed Use of EK2 Host-Vector Systems for Cloning DNA from Class 3 and 4 Etiologic Agents

Dr. Friedman then began discussion of a second proposal (tabs 1054, 1056C/4) from Dr. Roy Curtiss of the University of Alabama. Dr. Curtiss requested permission to use all certified EK2 host-vector sytems to clone DNA fragments from Class 3 and Class 4 etiologic agents under P2 containment conditions. P1 containment could be employed if the recombinant clones are shown not to express a virulence determinant that has toxic potential.

As an alternative, if this general proposal were not accepted by RAC, Dr. Curtiss requested permission to clone DNA from *Yersinia pestis* and *Mycobacterium leprae* into EK2 host-vector systems under P2 containment conditions. P1 conditions could be employed if virulence determinants are not expressed by the recombinant clones.

Dr. Friedman asked Dr. Gottesman how Dr. Curtiss' proposal dealing with Class 3 agents would be treated under the proposed revision of the Guidelines recommended earlier by RAC (Item IV above). Dr. Gottesman replied that in the proposed revised Guidelines experiments, in which DNA from a Class 3 etiologic agent is cloned in a nonpathogenic prokaryote, could be performed under P2 containment conditions. Under the current Guidelines, DNA from Class 3 agents may be cloned in EK1 hosts under P3 containment conditions. She suggested it would be consistent with the current Guidelines to permit the investigator to lower physical containment to P2 if biological containment is raised to EK2.

Dr. Friedman moved that DNA from Class 3 agents may be cloned in EK2 host-vector systems under P2 containment conditions; Class 4 agents, however, should be dealt with on a case-by-case basis. Dr. Maas seconded the motion. By a vote of thirteen in favor, none opposed, and two abstentions, the RAC adopted the motion.

IX. REQUEST TO USE BACILLUS MEGATERIUM IN RECOMBINANT DNA EXPERIMENTS

Dr. Holmes introduced the request (tabs 1051, 1056C/2) of Dr. Patricia Vary of Northern Illinois University for permission to introduce recombinant DNA derived from *Staphylococcus aureus*, *E. coli*, and *Bacillus subtilis* into *Bacillus megaterium* under P1 conditions. In her letter of November 24, 1981, she also requested that *B. megaterium* be classified as a genetic exchanger with B. subtilis under Section I-E-4. Dr. Holmes said the evidence supporting the request that B. megaterium be added to Appendix A, Sublist B, is weak. Dr. Gartland said that Dr. Vary had, after consulting with ORDA, withdrawn her request that B. megaterium be added to Appendix A. That part of her request was, therefore, not published in the Federal Register.

Dr. Holmes said that an issue in the Federal Register request is that the plasmids to be used are not specified. Dr. Holmes said B. megaterium is not an important pathogen in either human or veterinary medicine. It will, rarely, cause infections in compromised or immunosuppressed patients.

Dr. Berns asked if any problems could be visualized which would argue for setting containment any higher than P1. Dr. Berns said B. megaterium is only an opportunistic pathogen. Dr. Holmes pointed out that Dr. Vary could be introducing antibiotic resistance genes into B. megaterium. Dr. Levine pointed out that B. megaterium forms spores; spores are better contained under P2 conditions.

Dr. Holmes moved that the request to transfer recombinant plasmids from E. coli, B. subtilis, and S. aureus into B. megaterium be approved under P2 containment conditions. Containment is set at P2 as Dr. Vary has not specified the experiments she wishes to perform nor the plasmids to be used; however, she is encouraged to apply to her local IBC with specifics if she wishes containment lowered to P1, the local IBC is authorized to lower containment to P1 for specific experiments. Dr. Levine seconded the motion. By a vote of thirteen in favor, none opposed, and one abstention, the RAC approved the motion.

X. REQUEST TO CLONE PLANT DNA IN THE CYANOBACTERIUM ANACYSTIS NIDULANS

Dr. Scandalios introduced tabs 1055 and 1062/2, a request from Dr. Lawrence Bogorad of Harvard University for permission to initiate, at P1 containment, a program involving the cloning, in the cyanobacterium Anacystis nidulans (strain R2), of DNA from chloroplasts of various plants (initially primarily from Zea mays). Dr. Bogorad would employ the plasmid vector pUC104, a construct of the cyanobacterial plasmid pUC1 and the E. coli vector pACYC184. Dr. Scandalios said he had consulted Dr. Winston Brill by telephone on this proposal. Dr. Scandalios said neither he nor Dr. Brill could envisage any potential problems, so he would recommend that the experiments be permitted at the P1 containment level. He so moved. Dr. Levine seconded the motion. By a vote of fourteen in favor, none opposed, and no abstentions, the RAC approved the motion.

XI. <u>FUTURE MEETING DATES</u>

Mr. Thornton noted that the originally scheduled RAC meeting date of April 23-24, 1982, was probably earlier than necessary. Dr. Talbot suggested that the later part of June was most suitable and that ORDA would contact RAC members by telephone to determine the best possible date. Mr. Thornton thanked the members of the committee for their participation. He then adjourned the meeting at 11:22 a.m., February 9, 1982.

Respectively submitted,

Elizabeth A. Milewski

Elizabeth A. Milewski, Ph.D.
Rapporteur

William J. Gartland, Jr.

William J. Gartland, Jr., Ph.D.
Executive Secretary

I hereby certify that, to the best of my knowledge, the foregoing Minutes and Attachments are accurate and complete.

July 28, 1982
Date

Ray Thornton

Ray Thornton, J.D.
Chairman
Recombinant DNA Advisory Committee

RECOMBINANT DNA ADVISORY COMMITTEE

CHAIRMAN

THORNTON, Ray, J.D. (82)
President
Arkansas State University
State University, Arkansas 72467
501 972-2100

- -

AHMED, Abdul Karim, Ph.D. (82)
Senior Staff Scientist
Natural Resources Defense Council, Inc.
122 East 42nd Street
New York, New York 10017
212 949-0049

BALTIMORE, David, Ph.D. (82)
Professor of Biology
Center for Cancer Research
Massachusetts Institute of Technology
Cambridge, Massachusetts 02139
617 253-6410

BERNS, Kenneth I., Ph.D., M.D. (83)
Chairman
Department of Immunology and Medical Microbiology
University of Florida College of Medicine
Gainesville, Florida 32610
904 392-3311

BRILL, Winston J., Ph.D. (83)
Vilas Research Professor
Department of Bacteriology
University of Wisconsin
Madison, Wisconsin 53706
608 262-3567

DALOZ, L. Albert (85)
R.F.D. 819
Hancock, NH 03449-0819
603 525-3788

FEDOROFF, Nina V., Ph.D. (84)
Staff Member
Department of Embryology
Carnegie Institution of Washington
115 West University Parkway
Baltimore, Maryland 21210
301 467-1414

FRIEDMAN, David, M.D. (85)
Professor of Microbiology
University of Michigan Medical School
Ann Arbor, Michigan 48109
313 763-3142

GOLDSTEIN, Richard, Ph.D. (82)
Associate Professor
Department of Microbiology and Molecular Genetics
Harvard Medical School
Boston, Massachusetts 02115
617 732-1911

HARRIS, Jean L., M.D. (83)
Vice-President
State Marketing Programs
Control Data Corporation, HQS-130
8100 East 34th Street
Minneapolis, Minnesota 55440
612 853-6996

HOLMES, King K., M.D., Ph.D. (84)
Professor of Medicine
Adj. Professor of Microbiology, Immunology, and Epidemiology
University of Washington
Seattle, Washington 98114
206 325-2997

FEBRUARY 1982

KING, Patricia A., J.D. (82)
Associate Professor of Law
Georgetown University Law School
600 New Jersey Avenue, N.W.
Washington, D.C. 20001
202 624-8295

McGARRITY, Gerard J., Ph.D. (84)
Head
Department of Microbiolgy
Institute for Medical Research
Copewood Street
Camden, New Jersey 08103
609 966-7377

LANDY, Arthur, Ph.D. (85)
Professor of Medical Sciences
Brown University
Providence, Rhode Island 02912
401 863-2566

McKINNEY, Robert W., Ph.D. (84)
Chief, Occupational Safety
and Health Branch
Division of Safety
National Institutes of Health
Bethesda, Maryland 20205
301 496-2960

LEVINE, Myron M., M.D. (84)
Director
Center for Vaccine Development
Division of Infectious Diseases
University of Maryland
School of Medicine
Baltimore, Maryland 21201
301 528-7588

MITCHELL, Robert E. (85)
Attorney at Law
13915 San Antonio Drive
Norwalk, California 90650
213 863-8736

MAAS, Werner K., Ph.D. (83)
Professor
Department of Microbiology
New York University
School of Medicine
New York, New York 10016
212 340-5322

NIGHTINGALE, Elena O., Ph.D., M.D. (83)
Senior Program Officer
Institute of Medicine
National Academy of Sciences
Washington, D.C. 20418
202 334-2173

MARTIN, David W., Jr., M.D. (85)
Professor of Medicine and
Chief of Medical Genetics
University of California
Medical Center
San Francisco, California 94143
415 666-2524

PINON, Ramon, Ph.D. (82)
Associate Professor
Department of Biology
B-022 Bonner Hall
University of California, San Diego
La Jolla, California 92093
714 452-2452

MASON, James O., M.D., Dr. P.H. (83)
Executive Director
Utah State Department of Health
Post Office Box 2500
Salt Lake City, Utah 84113
801 533-6111

SAGINOR, Mark L., M.D. (85)
Director
Metabolic Research Medical Group, Inc.
2080 Century Park East
Los Angeles, California 90067
213 553-2345

SCANDALIOS, John G., Ph.D. (84)
Head
Department of Genetics
North Carolina State University
Raleigh, North Carolina 27650
919 737-2291

WENSINK, Pieter C., Ph.D. (85)
Associate Professor of Biochemistry
Brandeis University
Waltham, Massachusetts 02254
617 647-2421

EXECUTIVE SECRETARY

GARTLAND, William J., Jr., Ph.D.
Director, Office of Recombinant
DNA Activities
National Institute of Allergy
and Infectious Diseases
National Institutes of Health
Bethesda, Maryland 20205
301 496-6051

RECOMBINANT DNA ADVISORY COMMITTEE

NON-VOTING REPRESENTATIVES

CENTERS FOR DISEASE CONTROL

DOWDLE, Walter R., Ph.D.
Assistant Director for Science
Centers for Disease Control
Atlanta, Georgia 30333
404 329-3401

National Institute for Occupational Safety and Health (CDC)

LEMIN, Richard A.
Director
Division of Criteria Documents
and Standards Development
National Institute for Occupational
Safety and Health,
5600 Fishers Lane, Room 8A53
Rockville, Maryland 20857
301 443-3680

U.S. DEPARTMENT OF AGRICULTURE

TOLIN, Sue A., Ph.D.
Science and Education Administration
Cooperative Research
U.S. Department of Agriculture
Washington, D.C. 20250
202 447-5741

FULKERSON, John F., Ph.D. (ALT)
Science and Education Administration
Cooperative Research
U.S. Department of Agriculture
Washington, D.C. 20250
202 447-5741

U.S. DEPARTMENT OF COMMERCE

COX, John B.
Regulatory Analysis Division, Room 4512
Bureau of Industrial Economics
U.S. Department of Commerce
Washington, D.C. 20230
202 377-2565

U.S. DEPARTMENT OF ENERGY

DUDA, George, Ph.D.
Office of Health and
Environmental Research, EV-33
U.S. Department of Energy
Washington, D.C. 20545
202 353-3651

EDINGTON, Charles W., Ph.D. (ALT)
Deputy Director
Office of Health and Environmental
Research
U.S. Department of Energy
Washington, D.C. 20250
202 353-3251

U.S. DEPARTMENT OF THE INTERIOR

PIMENTEL, Mariano B., Ph.D.
Medical Director
U.S. Department of the Interior
Room 7045
18th & C Street, N.W.
Washington, D.C. 20240
202 343-2081

U.S. DEPARTMENT OF STATE

WALSH, William J., III
Biomedical Research Liason
and Health Affairs Officer
Oceans and International Environmental
and Scientific Affairs
U.S. Department of State
Washington, D.C. 20520
202 632-4824

U.S. DEPARTMENT OF TRANSPORTATION

CUSHMAC, George E., Ph.D.
Chemist
Research and Special Programs
Administration
U.S. Department of Transportation
Washington, D.C. 20590
202 426-2311

U.S. ENVIRONMENTAL PROTECTION AGENCY

LEVIN, Morris, Ph.D.
Director
Innovative Research Program (RD 675)
United States Environmental Protection Agency
Room 909 West Tower
401 M Street, S.W.
Washington, D.C. 20460
202 245-3025

FOOD AND DRUG ADMINISTRATION

HENRY, Timothy J., Ph.D.
BF, DT, HFF-156
Food and Drug Administration
200 C Street, S.W.
Washington, D.C. 20204
202 472-4690

Bureau of Drugs

MILLER, Henry I., M.D.
Medical Officer
Bureau of Drugs
Food and Drug Administration, Room 14B-04
5600 Fishers Lane
Rockville, Maryland 20857
301 443-3520

NATIONAL AERONAUTICS AND SPACE ADMINISTRATION

DeVINCENZI, Donald L., Ph.D.
Program Manager, Planetary Biology
Code SBL-3
National Aeronautics and Space Administration
Washington, D.C. 20546
202 755-3732

NATIONAL SCIENCE FOUNDATION

LEWIS, Herman W., Ph.D.
Senior Scientist for Recombinant DNA
Division of Physiology
Cellular and Molecular Biology
National Science Foundation
Washington, D.C. 20550
202 357-7647

HARRIMAN, Phillip, Ph.D. (ALT)
Executive Assistant
Directorate for Biological
Behavioral, and Social Sciences
Room 506
National Science Foundation
Washington, D.C. 20550
202 357-9854

U.S. VETERANS ADMINISTRATION

SCHULTZ, Jane S., Ph.D.
Geneticist
U.S. Veterans Administration
Medical Research Service - 151
2215 Fuller Road
Ann Arbor, Michigan 48105
313 769-7100 x696

BERMAN, Howard M. (ALT)
Health Scientist
Program Development and Review
Division
U.S. Veterans Administration
810 Vermont Avenue, N.W.
Washington, D.C. 20420
202 389-5065

U.S. DEPARTMENT OF LABOR

LOGAN, David C., M.D.
Medical Officer
Office of Technical Support
Occupational Safety and Health
Room N3656
U.S. Department of Labor
Washington, D.C. 20210
202 523-9603

RECOMBINANT DNA ADVISORY COMMITTEE

LIAISON REPRESENTATIVES

JUENGST, Eric T. (Acting)
Program Specialist
Program of Science Technology
& Human Value
Mail Stop 104
National Endowment for the Humanities
Washington, D.C. 20506
202 724-0354

WEISS, Daniel L., M.D.
Division of Medical Sciences
National Academy of Sciences
2101 Constitution Avenue, N.W.
Washington, D.C. 20418
202 334-2227

IINO, Professor Tetsuo
Department of Biology
Faculty of Science
University of Tokyo
Hongo, Tokyo 113
Japan

RECOMBINANT DNA ADVISORY COMMITTEE

AD HOC CONSULTANTS

February 8-9, 1982

GOTTESMAN, Susan K., Ph.D.
Senior Investigator
Laboratory of Molecular Biology
National Cancer Institute
National Institutes of Health
Bethesda, MD 20205
(301) 496-2095

Summary of Conference Call on Proposed EK2 Host-Vector Systems
Submitted by Dr. Roy Curtiss dated September 25, 1981

January 21, 1982

Drs. Campbell, Clewell, Friedman, Goldstein, Gottesman, Levine, Maas, and Gartland met by conference call on January 21, 1982, to discuss the submission of Dr. Roy Curtiss dated September 25, 1981.

Request 1 deals with use of su^+ and su^- derivatives of DP50 with previously approved virulent lambda vectors. It was noted that most of the containment in these systems is provided by the lambda vector and that testing data have been provided for Charon 4A. Although the testing data are for a period of 8 hours rather than 24 hours, it was felt that the strains look at least as good as DP50. With regard to survival in rats following oral administration (Table 5, page 166), it was noted that only <u>in vitro</u> data are required for testing at the EK2 level. It was the consensus of the consultants that the strains in part 1 of the request be approved for use with those lambda vectors certified for use in DP50 on the condition that the su^- strain not be used as a propagation host.

The participants then reviewed parts 2 and 3 of the request. It was noted that these proposals include requests for use of virulent and temperate lambda vectors, as well as cosmids. It was agreed that with regard to the temperate phages and cosmids, additional data are needed on how the phages are constructed, how they behave in the host, how they persist, etc. The participants requested the information provided by Dr. Pierre Tiollais on the construction and properties of the temperate lambda vectors, and information provided by Dr. John Collins on the construction and properties of the cosmid vectors. They also requested a copy of "Section 4" of a report referred to by Dr. Curtiss and information on certification of cosmid vectors (These documents were mailed to the participants on January 26). Dr. Levine suggested that testing in humans should be done. Again it was pointed out that EK2 certification has never required <u>in vivo</u> testing.

The group was divided on how to handle parts 2 and 3 of the submission. Four participants (Drs. Campbell, Clewell, Friedman, and Maas) recommended that the strains in parts 2 and 3 be approved for use with plasmids certified for use in 1776 and for use with virulent phages on the condition that su^- strains not be used as propagation hosts. Dr. Gottesman said that she would prefer to vote only on the phage vectors. Dr. Goldstein abstained. Dr. Levine abstained on the basis that he does not agree with the criteria for EK2 systems. It was agreed that further consideration is needed on the request for use of temperate phages and cosmids with these hosts.

These recommendations will be transmitted to the RAC at its meeting on February 8-9, 1982.

William J. Gartland, Jr., Ph.D.

DEPARTMENT OF HEALTH AND HUMAN SERVICES
PUBLIC HEALTH SERVICE
NATIONAL INSTITUTES OF HEALTH

RECOMBINANT DNA ADVISORY COMMITTEE
LARGE-SCALE REVIEW WORKING GROUP

MINUTES OF MEETING

FEBRUARY 9, 1982

The Large-Scale Review Working Group was convened for its third meeting at 2:00 p.m. on February 9, 1982, in Building 31C, Conference Room 8, at the National Institutes of Health, 9000 Rockville Pike, Bethesda, Maryland 20205. Kenneth Berns and Robert McKinney were co-chairmen.

Working Group members present for all or part of the meeting were:

Manuel Barbeito, NIH; Kenneth Berns, University of Florida (Co-chairman); Timothy J. Henry, Food and Drug Administration; Morris Levin, Environmental Protection Agency; David Logan, Department of Labor; James Mason, Utah State Department of Health; Robert McKinney, NIH, (Co-chairman); Elizabeth Milewski, NIH, (Executive Secretary); Henry Miller, Bureau of Drugs, FDA; John Richardson, Centers for Disease Control; and Sue Tolin, U. S. Department of Agriculture.

Others in attendance for all or part of the meeting were:

Irene Brandt, Eli Lilly and Company; Chia T. Chen, OSHA, U. S. Department of Labor; Yuan-yuan Chiu, Food and Drug Administration; George Duda, Department of Energy; Larry Elliott, National Institute for Occupational Safety and Health; John Galat, Schering-Plough Corp.; Charles R. Gaush, Bethesda Research Laboratories; E. S. Harris, National Institute for Occupational Safety and Health; T. M. Helscher, Monsanto Company; Philip Landrigan, National Institute for Occupational Safety and Health; Asger Landlykke, Genex Corporation; S. Edward Lee, Hoffman LaRoche, Inc.; Dan Liberman, Massachusetts Institute of Technology; Bernard J. Mlynczak, Monsanto Company; Harvey Price, Industrial Biotechnology Association; and Thaddeus T. Sze, Food and Drug Administration.

MINUTES OF THE MEETING, FEBRUARY 9, 1982
LARGE-SCALE REVIEW WORKING GROUP

Dr. Berns of the University of Florida called the third meeting of the Large-Scale Review Working Group to order at 2:05 p.m. on February 9, 1982. Dr. Mason of the Utah State Department of Health reviewed the minutes of the September 9, 1981 meeting of the working group. He said the minutes were substantively correct and moved approval with commendation. The minutes of the September 9 meeting were unanimously accepted.

Dr. Berns then introduced Dr. Philip Landrigan of the National Institute for Occupational Safety and Health (NIOSH). Dr. Berns said Dr. Landrigan had agreed to present to the Large-Scale Review Working Group the CDC/NIOSH draft report on Medical Surveillance for Industrial Applications of Recombinant DNA. Dr. Berns said the CDC/NIOSH report was in part a response to a RAC request to discuss medical surveillance problems.

Dr. Landrigan introduced other NIOSH representatives: Dr. Elliot Harris, the Deputy Director of NIOSH, Mr. Larry Elliott, an industrial hygenist who had participated in NIOSH's "walk-through" of six companies involved in recombinant DNA technology, and Ms. Stephanie Soucek. He also introduced Dr. John Richardson of the Centers for Disease Control (CDC).

Dr. Landrigan then distributed to the working group a revised version of the CDC/NIOSH report (Attachment I). He suggested the report was an exercise in "future forecasting", but argued that past experience might reasonably be used to predict potential hazards to workers as recombinant DNA techniques are transferred to the industrial setting. He said the CDC/NIOSH group had reviewed processes involved in the production, by recombinant DNA techniques, of pharmaceuticals and feed stock chemicals. The report examines three areas of potential hazard: (1) exposure to recombinant DNA containing microbes (2) exposure to the products of recombinant organisms and (3) exposure to reagents used in production processes. He said the study does not focus on microbial hazards as, under current applications, the likelihood of colonization or infection of workers is very small. Rather, hazardous exposure to recombinant technology products, particularly contact with biologically active molecules, is far more likely and is examined in greater detail. He cited as an example the gynecomastia developed by male workers exposed to oral contraceptives. The quantity of biologically active product that elicits a response is so minute that men wearing spacesuits have been affected. Dr. Landrigan said that in many biotechnological procedures, exposure hazard will be present throughout the process from fermentation of the organisms to packaging of the products. Indeed, packaging may be the most hazardous activity as packaging workers frequently underestimate the hazards and often do not exercise adequate caution. Allergic reactions to polypeptide products or byproducts are also considered in the report. The CDC/NIOSH document does not examine the problem of worker exposure to reagents as that concern in adequately covered in other documents.

Dr. Landrigan said NIOSH does not view the report as guidelines but as suggestions of prudent practice for the recombinant DNA industry. He said the document suggests companies using recombinant DNA technology should consider (1) a preexamination physical of workers with collection of baseline serum, (2) a periodic follow-up, (3) illness surveillance, and (4) epidemiological studies. He said the primary means of protecting worker health is careful physical containment of organisms and products. The second line of defense is biological containment, and the third is medical surveillance for a number of years sufficient to detect problems. He emphasized that workers may have little experience and training with recombinant DNA and medical surveillance of workers is simply prudent medical practice in all new technologies.

Dr. Landrigan then introduced Mr. Elliott. Mr. Elliott said the six walk-throughs in which he had participated were one or two day visits. Three of the six firms have extensive experience in fermentation technology. These firms have extensive comprehensive medical safety and health programs. Some of the firms have more extensive medical surveillance programs than that outlined in the CDC/NIOSH document. Three firms new to the field had not developed comprehensive programs; indeed one of the firms had no safety program. This firm believed that a safety program was not necessary as their employees are Ph.Ds who should have been exposed to good work practices through education. In summary, an enormous gap in sophistication in safety controls and medical surveillance exists between the three experienced companies and the three new companies. Mr. Elliott noted that five of the companies followed the NIH Physical Containment Recommendations for Large-Scale Uses of Organisms Containing Recombinant DNA Molecules (45 FR 24968). These five companies complied with the NIH Guidelines for Research Involving Recombinant DNA Molecules. The sixth company did not; they had no medical surveillance program, and did not follow the NIH Physical Containment Recommendations for Large-Scale Uses of Organisms Containing Recombinant DNA Molecules.

Dr. Mason commended the NIOSH effort in evaluating medical surveillance in recombinant DNA. He asked whether environmental surveillance e.g., air sampling, had been considered, or periodic culturing to determine if workers had been colonized by recombinant DNA containing microorganisms. Dr. Landrigan replied that NIOSH elected not to evaluate environmental surveillance as current sampling technology is not sufficiently sensitive to justify the cost. Dr. Logan of the Occupational Safety and Health Administration (OSHA) asked if periodic blood sampling of workers was recommended by the CDC/NIOSH report. Dr. Landrigan replied that the document suggests a baseline sample is necessary. The question of periodic sampling was not addressed as any measuring of serum samples must have very specific goals. Dr. Levin of the Environmental Protection Agency (EPA) asked how long the blood samples should be stored. Dr. Landrigan replied that mimimally he thought they should be stored for the period of employment. Dr. Richardson said the CDC stores its serum samples indefinitely. Drs. Mason and Levin suggested that samples should be stored for the lifetime of the individual. Dr. Landrigan said the CDC/NIOSH document was vague as to storage times to permit companies a certain latitude.

Dr. Tolin of the United States Department of Agriculture (USDA) asked if the nature of the products was considered by Dr. Landrigan's group. Dr. Landrigan replied that it was not, as all potential products of biotechnology cannot be predicted.

Dr. Levin said EPA has let two contracts to evaluate possible problems with recombinant DNA technologies. Both of those reports suggest that few if any problems will develop with established experienced firms, however, emerging firms or firms new to fermentation technology might present some difficulties. The reports suggest educational courses. Dr. Berns added that the American Society for Microbiology (ASM) has stressed the importance of education in the recombinant DNA area, including the education of industrial microbiologists.

Dr. Levin questioned whether the CDC/NIOSH report should address only recombinant DNA practices; worker safety and fermentation technology in general might be evaluated. Dr. Berns said the Large-Scale Review Working Group had requested a report dealing with recombinant DNA issues.

Dr. Miller of the FDA's Bureau of Drugs reiterated that the NIOSH report should not focus on recombinant DNA. He said singling out recombinant DNA for medical surveillance is gratuitous and baseless. He attacked the report as unnecessary and flawed. He questioned the cost effectiveness of holding large numbers of serum samples. He also questioned the advisability of evaluating inadequately explained absences from work of 48 hours or longer as suggested by the CDC/NIOSH document. Dr. Berns said the definition of the term "adequate" would determine how many absences would be investigated.

Dr. Mason again commended Dr. Landrigan and his group on their initial efforts in evaluating medical surveillance in fermentation technology using recombinant DNA technology as a model. Dr. Richardson also supported Dr. Landrigan's use of recombinant DNA technology for evaluating issues in fermentation technology.

Dr. Logan suggested that it is appropriate to consider recombinant DNA technology as a distinct subset of fermentation technology; recombinant DNA technology will produce potent products, many of which cannot be produced in any other way, and it can provide large amounts of these products. Medical surveillance is necessary in these product areas. Dr. Landrigan's report is necessary and highly appropriate.

Dr. Mason said the use of biotechnology will explode. Although the hazards associated with fermentation technology may not be new, the hazards must be considered in the context of large numbers of inexperienced workers. Dr. Miller said the situation will be analogous to that faced by FDA with generic drug producers. When generic drugs laws changed, the number of firms involved in generic production exploded; some of these firms did not meet FDA specifications and FDA has taken action. FDA clearly has the power to regulate the recombinant DNA products area. Dr. Tolin pointed out that FDA's mandate is limited, and many potential products of recombinant DNA technology may not be subject to FDA regulation.

Dr. Daniel Liberman of the Massachusetts Institute of Technology said the city of Cambridge, Massachusetts requires health surveillance of workers using recombinant DNA. In his experience, it is most important to define medical surveillance. He said the CDC/NIOSH recommendations are primarily epidemiological; such a program will protect future generations of workers but provides little or no protection to workers currently in the field. He then offered some criticisms of the CDC/NIOSH document. (1) He requested that potential and actual hazards be stated in the document. (2) He noted that it is the "hands-on" worker, i.e., the laboratory researcher, who currently is at greatest risk of exposure.

Dr. Tolin pointed out that in contrast to chemical exposure where workers may accumulate damage, the phenomenon of a threshold dosage exists in exposure to microbes. A threshold amount of organism must be administered in any one exposure to cause any effect.

Dr. Henry of the Food and Drug Administration (FDA) said that at this time he could not support the CDC/NIOSH document as written. Dr. Berns suggested that the document might be improved by stating general fermentation technology risk considerations in the introduction. Recombinant DNA technology might then be reviewed in light of these general risk considerations, and problems associated with recombinant DNA technology would be placed in a general context. Dr. Landrigan asked if such a report would be within the purview of the Large-Scale Review Working Group. Dr. Berns felt it appropriate to place problems associated with recombinant DNA technology in the context of problems associated with fermentation technology.

Dr. McKinney of the NIH Occupational Safety and Health Branch noted that the Recombinant DNA Advisory Committee (RAC) currently deals only with biological issues in large-scale processes; RAC was not considering processes, medical surveillance, etc. Rather, the Large Scale Review Working Group was formed to provide continued guidance to RAC in large-scale procedures as well as to assist in the development of the recombinant DNA industry. In light of the working group mandate, it is critical that risk information be included in any document forwarded to RAC by the Large-Scale Review Working Group; a more complete evaluation would thus be provided. It is appropriate that NIOSH provide basic guidance in medical surveillance. In addition, Dr. McKinney pointed out that reports on recombinant DNA technology serve to direct events in other areas of microbiology. These CDC/NIOSH recommendations therefore contribute to worker health and safety in microbiology in general.

Mr. Barbeito of the NIH Occupational Safety and Health Branch said the working group's mandate is to provide guidance for large scale work. He suggested that surveillance of large-scale production cannot be treated as is surveillance of laboratory research. He stated that risk increases with increasing scale. He pointed out that no comparative data exist in support of the statement that industry has a better track record in worker safety than research laboratories. Comparative data have been collected for research laboratories through the monitoring of aerosol facilities. In general, industry has not tracked employee illness. Thus, no true comparison can be made. The primary consideration in establishing medical surveillance programs in the biotechnology area is whether the costs will outweigh the benefits. For certain projects with certain organisms, the benefits will clearly outweigh the costs.

Dr. Levin requested that the redrafted CDC/NIOSH recommendations be circulated to the working group prior to the next meeting. Dr. Berns asked if time considerations would permit the document to be circulated to the working group. Dr. Milewski of the Office of Recombinant DNA Activities suggested that if the document need not be published in the _Federal Register_ before RAC consideration, the document could be reviewed by the working group prior to presenting it to the RAC in June 1982. Dr. Landrigan agreed that RAC should review the document before it is published in the _Federal Register_.

Dr. Landrigan thanked the working group for their comments on the CDC/NIOSH recommendations. Dr. Berns extended the thanks of the group to Dr. Landrigan and his co-authors.

Dr. McKinney suggested that at the next meeting the working group would offer industrial firms the opportunity to present their concerns. Mr. Barbeito asked whether the working group would address specific issues, such as information on the handling and processing of wastes, how "blow-outs" would be handled, maintenance, environmental contamination, controls preventing exposure of workers, etc. Dr. Tolin said she would like to learn how exposure to products is controlled. Dr. Berns suggested that the industrial use of robust organisms might be examined. Mr. Elliott suggested the committee would be interested in industrial viewpoints in several areas; e.g. medical surveillance, extraction of products, chemicals, etc. He suggested both industry and the working group would benefit from a question and answer period. Mr. Harvey Price of the Industrial Biotechnology Association expressed his organization's interest in participating in this forum.

The meeting was adjourned at 3:55 p.m.

Respectively submitted,

July 2, 1982
Date

Elizabeth Milewski
Elizabeth Milewski, Ph.D.
Executive Secretary

I hereby certify that, to the best of my knowledge, the foregoing Minutes are accurate and complete.

July 2, 1982
Date

Kenneth I. Berns
Kenneth I. Berns, Ph.D.
Co-Chairman
Large-Scale Review Working Group
of the Recombinant DNA Advisory Committee

July 2, 1982
Date

Robert W. McKinney
Robert W. McKinney, Ph.D.
Co-Chairman
Large Scale Review Working Group
of the Recombinant DNA Advisory Committee

Attachment I, Page 1

DEPARTMENT OF HEALTH & HUMAN SERVICES

Public Health Service
Centers for Disease Control

Memorandum

Date February 8, 1982

From Director, National Institute for Occupational Safety and Health, CDC
Director, Center for Infectious Diseases, CDC

Subject Medical Surveillance of Workers Engaged in Industrial Applications of Recombinant DNA Technology

To William Gartland, Ph.D.
Director, Office of Recombinant DNA Activities, NIH

Attached please find the Report of the CDC/NIOSH *Ad Hoc* Working Group on Medical Surveillance for Industrial Applications of Recombinant DNA.

This report was prepared by the National Institute for Occupational Safety and Health and by the Center for Infectious Diseases of the Centers for Disease Control at the request of the Subcommittee on Large-Scale Applications of the NIH Committee on Recombinant DNA Activities.

We present it to you for your review.

Elliott S. Harris
for J. Donald Millar, M.D.
Assistant Surgeon General

Walter Dowdle, Ph.D.

MEDICAL SURVEILLANCE OF BIOTECHNOLOGY WORKERS: REPORT OF THE CDC/NIOSH *AD HOC* WORKING GROUP ON MEDICAL SURVEILLANCE FOR INDUSTRIAL APPLICATIONS OF RECOMBINANT DNA

Philip J. Landrigan, M.D., M.Sc., Chairman
Mitchell L. Cohen, M.D.
Walter Dowdle, Ph.D.
Larry J. Elliott, B.S.
William E. Halperin, M.D.
J. Donald Millar, M.D.
Seth Pauker

From the Division of Surveillance, Hazard Evaluations and Field Studies, National Institute for Occupational Safety and Health, 4676 Columbia Parkway, Cincinnati, Ohio 45226.

SUMMARY

Planned industrial applications of recombinant DNA (rDNA) technologies will increase potential exposures of skilled and unskilled workers to microorganisms containing rDNA and to the products of those organisms. The health hazard of occupational exposure to recombinant organisms appears minimal, given current use of highly attenuated microbial species in rDNA applications; the hazards of microbial colonization, or infection may, however, increase with any introduction to industry of more robust microorganisms. The hazards of occupational exposure to the biologically active products of microorganisms containing rDNA appear to be more substantial; product exposures in the pharmaceutical industry have caused occupational diseases such as gynecomastia, Cushing's syndrome, and toxic hepatitis. Sensitization to peptides may produce occupational asthma.

Strict physical containment of microorganisms and their products constitutes the primary defense against occupational exposures in rDNA applications. "Biological containment", achieved through the use of attenuated species, is a second defense. Medical surveillance of workers, although inherently limited in its ability to detect disease, can provide a third level of protection. Medical surveillance programs should be highly specific; they must evaluate the particular hazards which confront an occupational group. At a minimum, medical surveillance of rDNA workers should include: (1) pre-employment examination with collection of baseline serum; (2) periodic follow-up; (3) evaluation of all illnesses; (4) epidemiologic and other longer term studies; (5) periodic evaluation of data; and (6) regular communication of results to management and workers. Establishment of medical surveillance programs for rDNA workers constitutes prudent medical practice.

INTRODUCTION

Recombinant DNA techniques have developed in the past five years from basic biological discoveries to technologies at the brink of industrial application.[1,2] In the next decade, rDNA technologies are expected to be employed in the production of enzymes, hormones, pharmaceuticals, vaccine and diagnostic antigens, improved plant strains, and a wide variety of chemical feedstocks.[3]

As these commercial applications are pursued, the number of persons engaged in work with rDNA technologies will increase exponentially. These persons will include not only professional staff, but also production workers, line supervisors, maintenance personnel, and janitors.[4] These workers will encounter several categories of potential exposures: (1) exposures to microorganisms containing rDNA; (2) exposures to the biological and chemical products of such organisms; and (3) exposures to chemical reagents used in extraction and purification of microbial products. Experience in other sectors of the biotechnology and pharmaceutical industries indicates that the products of the recombined microorganisms will pose the most serious of these potential hazards and that the hazard of occupational exposure to those biologically active products will extend throughout virtually every phase of production and packaging.

The Centers for Disease Control/National Institute for Occupational Safety and Health (CDC/NIOSH) Ad Hoc Working Group on Medical Surveillance for Industrial Applications of Recombinant DNA has considered the role that medical surveillance might play in the detection of any disease or dysfunction which might be caused by occupational exposures to microorganisms containing rDNA or their products. The Working Group recognizes that neither the extent nor the severity of any health hazards which may be associated with such exposures are known. The Group realizes further that the effectiveness of medical surveillance will inevitably be limited by such factors as the relatively small size of most groups under study, variability in individual exposures, long induction-latency from beginning of exposure to appearance of effects, and uncertainty as to the effects sought. Most importantly, the Group recognizes that medical surveillance can never replace the appropriate physical containment of recombinant microorganisms and their products as the first line of defense against exposure and disease.* Nevertheless, the Group has concluded that the medical surveillance of workers engaged in commercial applications of rDNA technologies can play a valuable auxiliary role in protecting worker health. It is therefore the opinion of the Group that the establishment of medical surveillance programs for rDNA workers constitutes prudent medical practice.

MICROBIAL HAZARDS

Under current working conditions the health hazard of exposure to microorganisms containing rDNA appears to be slight.[6,7] The majority of the

---

*The level of physical containment of microorganisms used in recombinant DNA applications must be appropriate for their level of pathogenicity.[5]

microorganisms currently used in rDNA applications are debilitated through genetic manipulation such that their ability to reproduce outside of a highly modified environment is severely curtailed. None of the organisms in current use have been shown to cause infection or disease in persons using rDNA techniques. Recent risk assessments suggest that the likelihood of infection by microorganisms containing rDNA is minimal.[6,7] Despite those reassurances, there is residual, albeit unquantified concern that workers engaged in industrial applications of rDNA technologies may be at heightened risk of colonization or infection by modified organisms.[8,9] The Working Group notes in that connection that the circumstances of potential exposure in industry will differ considerably in their scale from the usual exposures encountered in research laboratories. Also, the number of workers potentially exposed in industrial applications will be much greater than the number potentially exposed heretofore.

The primary defense against colonization or infection of workers in rDNA applications will be provided by strict physical containment of organisms containing rDNA.[5] In the development and capitalization of industrial applications of rDNA techniques, exposure control and worker protection must be given equal emphasis as process integrity and product development. Experience gained by NIOSH in other sectors of the chemical and pharmaceutical manufacturing industries indicates that preplanned maintenance is a central aspect of exposure control. Facilities for containment of recombinant organisms must periodically, in accordance with a strict timetable, be shut down for scheduled examination and repair. Procedures for evaluation of facilities and for validation of the integrity of physical containment must be developed at the outset as an integral component of facilities design.

A second defense against colonization or infection of biotechnology workers is provided by "biological containment". Such containment will be achieved through the continuing use of debilitated microorganisms. Any tendency toward reduction in levels of "biological containment" through the introduction to industry of more robust, less highly debilitated organisms must be approached with great caution and will require careful reassessment of potential health risks.

PRODUCT HAZARDS

Exposure to the biologically active products and by-products of microorganisms containing rDNA constitutes a serious class of potential hazard in the biotechnology industries. Because of the reactive nature of such products, exposure to even minute quantities may cause physiologically significant effects. Occupational exposures to products in other sectors of the biotechnology and pharmaceutical industries have produced a spectrum of illnesses, including gynecomastia (in the packaging of estrogens),[10] Cushing's syndrome (in glucocorticoid manufacture),[11] nasal polyps (in production of menthol cough drops),[12] recurrent epistaxis (in compounding of ferrous sulfate), and toxic hepatitis (following exposure to isopropanol plus carbon tetrachloride).[13] The hazards of product exposure will extend throughout the full manufacturing process from initial production to final packaging. Because of the biological activity of many products and by-products of organisms containing rDNA, prevention of any resultant health hazards will require extremely sophisticated engineering controls.

In addition to the specific hazards which may result from occupational exposures to particular products, workers in rDNA applications may also be at risk of sensitization to proteins and peptides which are generated in the course of fermentation and extraction. A high frequency of sensitization to protein enzymes has, for example, been described among workers engaged in the commercial production of enzyme detergents.[14] Asthma is the most serious health consequence of such sensitization. Dermatitis and allergic rhinitis might also be expected to occur.

PURPOSES OF MEDICAL SURVEILLANCE

Uncertainty provides the strongest argument for maintaining medical surveillance over workers engaged in industrial applications of rDNA.[15] As in the case of any newly developed technology, there is a dearth of information concerning the nature or severity of any acute or chronic health hazards which might be associated with exposure to recombinant organisms or their products. Given that lack of knowledge, the CDC/NIOSH Working Group is of the opinion that medical surveillance of such workers constitutes prudent medical practice. Such surveillance should be aimed at the early detection of sentinel disease events.[16]

NATURE OF MEDICAL SURVEILLANCE

In its essence, medical surveillance of biotechnology workers consists of periodic evaluation; regular analysis of data; and regular communication of results to workers, management, and other interested parties.[17]

The components of a medical surveillance program for recombinant DNA workers which were considered by the Working Group are as follows:

a. preemployment examination and collection of baseline serum samples for storage;
b. periodic follow-up examination;
c. follow-up evaluation of all illnesses, especially those which cause absence from work;
d. epidemiological and other longer term follow-up studies.

Preemployment Examinations - The purposes of preemployment examinations are (1) to establish a worker's health status prior to the start of work; (2) to provide baseline data for possible epidemiologic studies; and (3) to identify conditions which may place a worker at heightened risk of work-related illness. Workers with such conditions may be excluded from employment in biotechnology; fitness for employment in biotechnology must be established on an individual basis for each potential worker with any underlying medical condition. Among the conditions which may place a worker at heightened risk of illness in biotechnology are the following:[18]

- conditions which impair the non-specific defenses against infection (chronic skin, respiratory tract, and bowel disease);
- impaired immune competence;
- immunosuppression (caused, for example, by steroids, radiation therapy, alkylating agents, or antimetabolites);
- cancer;
- other chronic illnesses, such as chronic kidney disease, diabetes mellitus, or the collagen diseases;.

The collection and storage of frozen serum samples has become a widely accepted practice in the biotechnology industry. A serum sample is generally taken from each worker at the start of employment and, in some instances, periodically thereafter.[16] Serology programs will be most cost-effective when they either assess specifically the development of antigens associated with the organisms or products in a particular process or when they are simply stored in a bank and held at -70°C for future study or for reference in the event of illness.

Periodic Follow-up Examinations - Comprehensive periodic medical examinations are generally of little value in the detection of occupational disease. Any periodic examinations incorporated into a surveillance program must be specifically targeted toward evaluation of the particular hazards which may confront a particular group of workers. For example, studies of endocrine function might be devised for workers engaged in the production of peptide or steroid hormones, or appropriate evaluations of immune function might be undertaken for workers producing interferon or other immunochemicals.

Follow-up Evaluation of Illness - A biotechnology worker who develops illness or is absent from work for 48 hours without explanation should be actively evaluated. The importance of such active pursuit cannot be overemphasized. The evaluation of such illness should consider (a) whether the symptoms are in any way relatable to the microorganisms or products in the worker's place of employment, (b) whether an accident has occurred in the facility; and whether the ill worker was involved in the accident; and (c) whether any illnesses have occurred in co-workers.

Epidemiological and Other Long-Term Follow-up Studies - The likelihood that epidemiologic evaluations of workers engaged in rDNA applications will in the near term produce useful results is slight, given the relatively small numbers of exposed workers and the long induction-latency periods which may need to elapse between beginning of exposure and appearance of any disease. In the longer term, however, epidemiologic studies may be extremely useful as a health surveillance tool. Specific follow-up studies intended to evaluate specific outcomes will be the most cost-effective form of epidemiologic follow-up. Among the outcomes to be considered for long-term surveillance might be increases in cancer incidence or mortality rates, increased rates of endocrine disorders, and elevated rates of immunologic diseases. Surveillance might also be directed to the occurrence of adverse reproductive outcomes in the offspring of male or female workers. Many such studies might require the concommitant evaluation of appropriate control groups. With further development of such sophisticated biochemical indicators of genetic alteration as protein profile testing, it may be possible to couple such indices with epidemiologic follow-up studies.

The necessary foundation for any long-term studies of biotechnology workers will be the indefinite maintenance of careful records on each worker by each institution or firm engaged in biotechnology. At a minimum, such records must include the name of each worker, personal identifying information including Social Security number, results of all physical examinations and special medical tests, a complete history of work experience (including information on areas of work, specific jobs, and specific organisms, processes, and products encountered), and a record of any illnesses or of any accidents in which the worker was involved.

LIMITATIONS OF MEDICAL SURVEILLANCE

The likelihood is small that a medical surveillance program for biotechnology workers will detect any illness caused by recombined organisms or by their products. Neither the nature nor the possible time of onset of any such illness is known. Further, such illnesses may appear in only one or a few workers. Nonetheless, the detection of any occupational illness caused by recombinant organisms or by their products will have important biological and public health consequences, and should be actively sought.[16]

CONCLUDING COMMENT

Medical surveillance of workers engaged in industrial applications of rDNA will be no substitute for other mechanisms for the protection of workers in this industry. Physical containment of organisms and of their products will remain the first line of defense against occupational exposures.[5] Biological containment, resulting from use of attenuated or debilitated organisms remains a second important protection. There is however, uncertainty as to the possible health consequences of employment in the industries which are contemplating commercial application of rDNA. Medical surveillance, with all of its shortcomings, provides a means for addressing that uncertainty.

References

1. Abelson J: A revolution in biology. Science 209:1319-1321, 1980.

2. Baxter JD: Recombinant DNA and medical progress. Hospital Practice, February 1980, pp. 57-67.

3. Fox JL: Genetic engineering industry emerges. Chem Eng News, 17 March 1980, pp. 15-23.

4. Robbins AW: Statement. Hearing on Industrial Applications of Recombinant DNA Techniques. Subcommittee on Science, Technology and Space, Committee on Commerce, Science, and Transportation, U.S. Senate (96th Congress), 20 May 1980, pp. 2-13.

5. Centers for Disease Control: Proposed Biosafety Guidelines for Microbiological and Biomedical Laboratories. Atlanta: Centers for Disease Control, 1981.

6. Levy SB, Marshall B, Rowse-Eagle D, Onderdonk A: Survival of Escherichia coli host-vector systems in the mammalian intestine. Science 209:391-394, 1980.

7. National Institutes of Health: Program to Reduce the Risks of Recombinant DNA Research: Proposed First Annual Update. Federal Register 45 (192): 61874-61878, 17 September 1980.

8. Rosenberg G, Simon L: Recombinant DNA: have recent experiments assessed all the risks? Nature 282:773-774, 1979.

9. Liberman DF, Kovacic SA: Biotype determinations for monitoring of EK 1 host strains used in recombinant DNA research. J Clin Microbiol 8:99-101, 1978.

10. Harrington JM, Stein GF, Rivera RV, deMorales AV: The occupational hazards of formulating oral contraceptives - a survey of plant employees. Arch Environ Health 33:12-14, 1978.

11. Newton RW, Browning MCK, Iqbal J, Piercy N, Adamson DG: Adrenocortical suppression in workers manufacturing synthetic glucocorticoids. Brit Med J 1:73-75, 1978.

12. National Institute for Occupational Safety and Health. Health Hazard Evaluation Report (HE 77-66-531): Sucrets Department, Merck, Sharpe, and Dohme, West Point, Pennsylvania. Cincinnati: NIOSH, October 1978.

13. Centers for Disease Control: Renal failure and hepatitis from inhaled carbon tetrachloride and isopropyl alcohol - Tennessee. MMWR 24:59-60, 1975.

14. Centers for Disease Control: Sensitization of Laundry-Products Workers to Proteolytic Bacterial Enzymes - New Jersey. MMWR 30:127-128, 1981.

15. National Cancer Institute, Office of Biohazard Safety: Medical Surveillance Programs - A Review with Recommendations. Bethesda: National Cancer Institute, July 1980.

16. Rutstein DD, Berenberg W, Chalmers TC, Child CG, Fishman AP, Perrin EB: Measuring the quality of medical care - a clinical method. New Engl J Med 294:582-588, 1976.

17. Langmuir AD: The surveillance of communicable diseases of national importance. New Engl J Med 268:182, 1963.

18. Medical Research Council, Genetic Manipulation Adivsory Group: GMAG Note No. 6 - Health Monitoring. London: Medical Research Council, March 1978.

federal register

Monday
March 29, 1982

Part III

Department of Health and Human Services

National Institutes of Health

Recombinant DNA Research; Actions Under Guidelines

DEPARTMENT OF HEALTH AND HUMAN SERVICES

National Institutes of Health

Recombinant DNA Research; Actions Under Guidelines

AGENCY: National Institutes of Health, PHS, HHS.

ACTION: Notice of actions under NIH Guidelines for Research Involving Recombinant DNA Molecules.

SUMMARY: This notice sets forth actions taken by the Acting Director, NIAID, by authority of the Director, NIH, under the 1981 Guidelines for Research Involving Recombinant DNA Molecules (46 FR 34462).

EFFECTIVE DATE: March 29, 1982.

FOR FURTHER INFORMATION CONTACT: Additional information can be obtained from Dr. William J. Gartland, Office of Recombinant DNA Activities (ORDA), National Institutes of Health, Bethesda, Maryland 20205 (301) 496-6051.

SUPPLEMENTARY INFORMATION: I am promulgating today several major actions under the NIH Guidelines for Research Involving Recombinant DNA Moelcules. These proposed actions were published for comment in the **Federal Register** of December 7, 1981 (46 FR 59734), and January 6, 1982 (47 FR 732), and reviewed and recommended for approval by the Recombinant DNA Advisory Committee (RAC) at its meeting on February 8-9, 1982. In accordance with Section IV-E-1-b of the NIH Guidelines, I find that these actions comply with the Guidelines and present no significant risk to health or the environment.

Part I of this announcement provides background information on the actions. Part II provides a summary of the major actions.

The decision on the "Gottesman proposal" which was also recommended by the RAC at their February 8-9, 1982, meeting, will be issued at a later date.

I. Decisions on Actions Under Guidelines

A. *Request for Permission to Clone Subgenomic Segments of the Foot and Mouth Disease Virus.* The RAC considered a proposal submitted by Molecular Genetics, Inc. (MGI), of Minnetonka, Minnesota, to transfer *E. coli* K-12 clones comprising less than 75% of the Foot and Mouth Disease Virus (FMDV) genome from the Plum Island Animal Disease Center (PIADC) to the MGI research facility in Minnesota and to conduct experiments with these clones under P1 containment conditions. A notice of this proposal was published for 30 days comment in the **Federal Register** of January 6, 1982 (47 FR 732). No comments were received during this period. It was noted that the proposal is almost identical to one previously approved by NIH. (See **Federal Register** of January 17, 1980, pg. 1059; July 29, 1980, pg. 50528; and March 12, 1981, pg. 16455). After discussion, the RAC, by a vote of 16 in favor, none opposed, and 4 abstentions, recommended approval of the proposal contingent upon review by a working group of the RAC of data on infectivity testing of the clones, prior to their transfer from PIADC.

I accept this recommendation and text has been added to Appendix E of the Guidelines indicating this action.

B. *Request to use Bacillus Megaterium in Recombinant DNA Experiments under P1 Containment.* A request submitted by Dr. Patricia Vary of Northern Illinois University, DeKalb, Illinois, to transfer recombinant DNA segments derived from *E. coli, Bacillus subtilis,* and *Staphylococcus aureus* into *Bacillus megaterium* under P1 containment conditions was considered by the RAC at its February 8-9, 1982 meeting. A notice concerning this request appeared in the **Federal Register** of December 7, 1981 (46 FR 59734). No comments were received on the proposal.

The RAC, after discussing this proposal, recommended approval under P2 containment conditions with the stipulation that the local IBC be authorized to lower containment to P1 for specific experiments. The vote for approval of this recommendation was 13 in favor, none opposed, and 1 abstention.

I accept this recommendation and text has been added to Appendix E of the Guidelines indicating this action.

C. *Proposed Pseudomonas Putida Host-Vector System.* In response to a request from Professor Michael Bagdasarian of the Max-Plank-Institut Fur Molekulare Genetik, Berlin, West Germany, a notice was published in the **Federal Register** of December 7, 1981 (46 FR 59734). The investigator requested HV1 certification of a new host-vector system based on *Pseudomonas putida* strain KT2440 and plasmid cloning vectors pKT262, pKT263, and pKT264. During the public comment period no responses were received.

The RAC discussed this proposal at its February 8-9, 1982 meeting. It was noted that the cloning system would have broad utility. The data indicate that the plasmid vectors have been constructed to be poorly mobilizable. The data submitted meet the criteria for HV1. The RAC by a vote of 18 in favor, none opposed, and 1 abstention recommended that this system be approved as a new HV1 system.

I accept this recommendation, and appropriate text has been added to Appendix F of the Guidelines.

D. *Request to Clone Plant DNA in the Cyanobacterium Anacystis Nidulans.* In a letter dated September 24, 1981, Dr. Lawrence Bogorad of Harvard University requested permission to initiate, at P1 containment, a program involving the cloning of DNA from chloroplasts of various plants (initially primarily from *Zea mays*) in the cyanobacterium *Anacystis nidulans* strain R2. Dr. Bogorad would employ the plasmid vector pUC104, a construct of the cyanobacterial plasmid pUC1 and the *E. coli* vector pACYC184. A notice of this proposal appeared in the **Federal Register** of January 6, 1982 (47 FR 732) for public comment. No comments were received on the proposal.

The RAC discussed the proposal at the February 8-9, 1982 meeting. It was noted that neither *Anacystis nidulans* nor plant chloroplasts produce toxins. In addition, *A. nidulans* does not exchange genetic information with other cyanobacteria. By a vote of fourteen in favor, none opposed, and no abstentions, RAC recommended that the project be approved at the P1 level of containment.

I accept this recommendation and a new entry has been added to Appendix E of the Guidelines.

E. *Proposed Inclusion of Yersinia Enterocolitica on Sublist A, Appendix A.* In a letter dated September 22, 1981, Dr. Guy Cornelis of the Universite Catholique de Louvain, Brussels, Belgium requested that *Yersinia enterocolitica* be exempted from the Guidelines under the provisions of Section I-E-4 by being added to Sublist A, Appendix A, of the Guidelines. In support of this request, Dr. Cornelis supplied data indicating that *Y. enterocolitica* exchanges genetic information with *E. coli.*

Dr. Cornelis' request was published for comment in the December 7, 1981, **Federal Register** (46 FR 59734). No comments concerning the request were received.

The RAC discussed the request at the February 8-9, 1982 meeting. During the discussion, it was noted that some strains of *Y. enterocolitica* cause human disease; however, the organism is ubiquitous. The frequency of transfer of DNA between *E. coli* and *Y. enterocolitica* is three orders of magnitude lower than *E. coli—E. coli* exchange. However, exchange does occur and on this basis *Y. enterocolitica* can be included in Sublist A, Appendix A. By a vote of eighteen in favor, none opposed, and one abstention, the RAC recommended approval of the request.

I accept this recommendation and *Yersinia enterocolitica* has been added to Sublist A of Appendix A of the Guidelines.

F. *Proposed EK2 Host-Vector Systems.* In a letter dated September 25, 1981, Dr. Roy Curtiss of the University of Alabama in Birmingham, requested EK2 certification of six different *E. coli* K-12 strains in conjunction with various virulent and temperate bacteriophage lambda, plasmid, and cosmid vectors. The request was subdivided into three separate requests. The requests were published for comment in the **Federal Register** of December 7, 1981 (46 FR 59734). During the thirty day comment period, no comments were received.

Dr. Curtiss' submission was reviewed by a working group of the RAC on January 21, 1982. The working group made recommendations on the basis of data available, and requested certain additional documents. A summary of the working group conference telephone call was prepared and distributed to the full RAC.

The RAC reviewed the submission and working group report at its meeting on February 9, 1982. It was agreed that the first request posed no particular problems, and the RAC voted, by 11 in favor, none opposed, and 2 abstentions, to recommend EK2 certification of *E. coli* K-12 strains chi-2447 and chi-2281 for use with those lambda vectors that already have been certified for use with strain DP50 on the condition that the su^- strain not be used as a propagation host. I accept this recommendation and appropriate language has been added to Appendix F of the Guidelines.

The RAC then turned its attention to the second and third requests which proposed EK2 certification of four strains of *E. coli* K-12 (chi-1984, chi-2705, chi-2001, and chi-2363) in conjunction with virulent and temperate lambda vectors, plasmid vectors, and cosmid vectors. The RAC felt that there were no significant problems in considering certification of the strains specified in requests 2 and 3 with virulent lambda vectors. However, enough data were not available for the RAC to recommend their use with lysogenizing phage vectors, plasmid vectors, and cosmid vectors. The RAC voted 11 in favor, none opposed, and 4 abstentions to recommend EK2 certification of *E. coli* strains chi-1984, chi-2705, chi-2001, and chi-2363 with certified virulent lambda vectors on the condition that the su^- strains not be used as propagation hosts.

Consideration of the requests for use of other vectors with these strains was deferred. I accept these recommendations, and appropriate language has been added to Appendix F of the Guidelines.

G. *Proposed use of EK2 Host-Vector Systems for Cloning DNA from Class 3 and 4 Etiological Agents.* In a letter dated September 25, 1981, Dr. Roy Curtiss of the University of Alabama in Birmingham requested permission to use all certified EK2 host-vector systems to clone DNA fragments from CDC Class 3 and Class 4 etiological agents under P2 containment and under P1 containment if the recombinant clones are shown not to express a virulence determinant that has toxic potential.

As an alternative to this general proposal, Dr. Curtiss requested permission to clone DNA from *Yersinia pestis* and *Mycobacterium leprae* into EK2 host-vector systems under P2 containment, and under P1 conditions in the absence of expression of virulence determinants by the recombinant clones. This request was published in the December 7, 1981, **Federal Register** (46 FR 59734). During the thirty day public comment period, no comments were received.

During the RAC discussion of the proposal on February 9, 1982, it was noted that Class 3 agents can currently be worked with in EK1 systems under P3 containment conditions (Guidelines Section III-O-1). It would, therefore, be a reasonable alternative also to permit DNA from Class 3 organisms to be cloned and propagated under P2 + EK2 conditions. However, the RAC felt that recombinant DNA experiments involving Class 4 agents should be considered only on a case-by-case basis under the current Guidelines. By a vote of thirteen in favor, none opposed, and two abstentions, the RAC recommended that DNA from Class 3 etiological agents may be propagated in *E. coli* K-12 under P2 + EK2 containment conditions.

I accept this recommendation, and Section III-O-1 and Appendix C of the Guidelines have been accordingly modified.

II. Summary of Actions Under the Guidelines.

A. *Modification of Section III-O-1 and Appendix C of the Guidelines.* Section III-O-1 of the Guidelines is modified to read:

"III-O-1. *Experiments Involving Class 3 Organisms.* Experiments involving recombinant DNA from Class 3 organisms (1) or from cells known to be infected with these agents may be conducted at P3 containment in *E. coli* K-12 EK1 hosts or at P2 containment in *E. coli* K-12 EK2 hosts (see Appendix C). Containment levels for all other experiments with Class 3 organisms or with recombinant DNA which increases the virulence and host range of a plant pathogen beyond that which occurs by natural genetic exchange will be determined by NIH. (See Section IV-E-1-b-2-(e))."

In Appendix C, the second paragraph in the language detailing "exceptions" to the section "2· *Experiments Involving E. coli K-12 Host-Vector Systems*" is modified to read:

"Experiments involving DNA from Class 3 organisms (1) or from cells known to be infected with these agents may be conducted at P3 containment using *E. coli* K-12 EK1 host-vectors systems, or at P2 containment in *E. coli* K-12 EK2 host-vector systems. Lower containment levels may be specified by NIH. (See Section IV-E-1-b-(2)-(e)). Experiments in this category require prior IBC review and approval."

B. *Addition of Yersinia Enterocolitica to Sublist A, Appendix A.* Sublist A of Appendix A of the Guidelines is amended to read as follows:

1. Genus *Escherichia.*
2. Genus *Shigella.*
3. Genus *Salmonella* (including Arizona).
4. Genus *Enterobacter.*
5. Genus *Citrobacter* (including *Levinea*).
6. Genus *Klebsiella.*
7. Genus *Erwinia.*
8. *Pseudomonas aeruginosa, Pseudomonas putida* and *Pseudomonas fluorescens.*
9. *Serratia marcescens.*
10. *Yersinia enterocolitica.*

C. *Cloning of Subgenomic Segments of Foot and Mouth Disease Virus.* A net item, number 42, is added to Appendix E of the Guidelines:

"42. Permission is granted to transfer certain clones of subgenomic segments of Foot and Mouth Disease Virus from Plum Island Animal Disease Center to the laboratories of Molecular Genetics, Inc., Minnetonka, Minnesota, and to work with these clones under P1 containment conditions. Approval is contingent upon review of data on infectivity testing of the clones by a working group of the RAC."

D. *Cloning of E. Coli, Bacillus Subtilis, and Staphylococcus Aureus DNA in Bacillus Megaterium.* A new item, number 43, is added to Appendix E of the Guidelines:

"43. *Bacillus megaterium* can be used as a host for cloning DNA segments derived from *E. coli, Bacillus subtilis,* and *Staphylococcus aureus* under P2 containment conditions. Local IBCs are authorized to lower containment to P1 for specific experiments."

E. *Cloning of Plant DNA in Anacystis Nidulans.* A new item, number 44, is added to Appendix E of the Guidelines:

"44. DNA from the chloroplasts of plants may be cloned in the cyanobacterium *Anacystis nidulans* strain R-2 under P1 containment conditions using the plasmid vector pUC104."

F. *Certification of Pseudomonas Putida HV1 Host-Vector System.* The following paragraph is added under the heading "HV1" in Appendix F of the Guidelines:

"*Pseudomonas putida* strain KT2440 with plasmid vectors pKT262, pKT263, and pKT264 is certified as an HV1 host-vector system."

G. *Certification of EK2 Host-Vector Systems.* The following paragraphs are added to Appendix F of the Guidelines under the heading "EK2 Bacteriophage Systems":

"*E. coli* K-12 strains chi-2447 and chi-2281 are certified for use with lambda vectors that are certified for use with strain DP50 or DP50supF provided that the su^{0} strain not be used as a propagation host.

"*E. coli* K-12 strains chi-1984, chi-2705, chi-2001, and chi-2363 are certified for use with lambda vectors that are certified for use with strain DP50 or DP50supF provided that the su^{0} not strains be used as propagation hosts."

Note.—OMB's "Mandatory Information Requirements for Federal Assistance Program Announcements" (45 FR 39592) requires a statement concerning the official government programs contained in the *Catalog of Federal Domestic Assistance.* Normally NIH lists in its announcements the number and title of affected individual programs for the guidance of the public. Because the guidance in this notice covers not only virtually every NIH program but also essentially every federal research program in which DNA recombinant molecule techniques could be used, it had been determined to be not cost effective or in the public interest to attempt to list these programs. Such a list would likely require several additional pages. In addition, NIH could not be certain that every federal program would be included as many federal agencies, as well as private organizations, both national and international, have elected to follow the NIH Guidelines. In lieu of the individual program listing, NIH invites readers to direct questions to the information address above about whether individual programs listed in the *Catalog of Federal Domestic Assistance* are affected.

NIH programs are not covered by OMB Circular A-95 because they fit the description of "program not considered appropriate" in Section 8-(b)-(4) and (5) of that Circular.

Dated: March 16, 1982.

Bernard Talbot,

Acting Director, National Institute of Allergy and Infectious Diseases, National Institutes of Health.

[FR Doc. 82-8108 Filed 3-26-82; 8:45 am]

BILLING CODE 4140-01-M

federal register

Wednesday
April 21, 1982

Part II

Department of Health and Human Services

National Institutes of Health

Recombinant DNA Research; Actions Under Guidelines

DEPARTMENT OF HEALTH AND HUMAN SERVICES

National Institutes of Health

Recombinant DNA Research; Actions Under Guidelines

AGENCY: National Institutes of Health, Public Health Service, HHS.

ACTION: Notice of actions under NIH guidelines for research involving recombinant DNA molecules.

SUMMARY: This notice sets forth actions taken by the Acting Director, National Institute of Allergy and Infectious Diseases, by authority of the Director, National Institutes of Health, under the 1981 Guidelines for Research Invoving Recombinant DNA Molecules (46 FR 34462).

EFFECTIVE DATE: April 21, 1982.

FOR FURTHER INFORMATION CONTACT: Additional information can be obtained from Dr. William Jr. Gartland, Office of Recombinant DNA Activities (ORDA), National Institutes of Health, Bethesda, Maryland 20205 (301) 496-6051.

SUPPLEMENTARY INFORMATION: I am promulgating today a major action under the NIH Guidelines for Research Involving Recombinant DNA Molecules. This action involves a major revision of the Guidelines. In accordance with Section IV-E-1-b of the Guidelines, I find that this action complies with the Guidelines and present no significant risk to health or the environment.

The structure of this announcement is as follows:

I. Background
II. February 8-9, 1982, Meeting of Recombinant DNA Advisory Committee
III. Analysis of Correspondence Received
IV. Summary of Guideline Changes

Immediately following this announcement, there appears in a separate section of the **Federal Register** the revised NIH Guidelines for Research Involving Recombinant DNA Molecules, which are effective today.

I. Background

Drs. David Baltimore and Allan Campbell proposed a major revision of the Guidelines (Baltimore-Campbell proposal) which was published for public comment in the **Federal Register** on March 20, 1981 (46 FR 17995) and was considered by the NIH Recombinant DNA Advisory Committee (RAC) at its April 1981 meeting. At the April 1981 meeting, a Working Group on Revision of the Guidelines was established to review the Baltimore-Campbell proposal as well as other approaches which might lead to a major revision of the Guidelines. The Working Group met on June 1, 1981, and on July 9, 1981. The Working Group prepared a proposal for revising the Guidelines, a summary of its actions, and a document entitled "Evaluation of the Risks Associated with Recombinant DNA Research." Two minority reports were prepared by several members of the Working Group. The Working Group report and the minority reports were distributed to RAC members prior to the September 1981 meeting. The document entitled "Evaluation of the Risks Associated with Recombinant DNA Research" was an extensive analysis with the following headings:

I. History and Introduction
II. Possible Hazards
A. Basic Assumptions
1. Uniqueness of Organisms Created by Recombinant DNA Techniques
a. Limits of the technique
b. Natural exchange mechanisms
c. Counterarguments
2. Dissemination
a. Stability of recombinant DNA
b. Transmission into other potential hosts
3. Harm
a. Breaching prokaryotic—eukaryotic barriers: evolutionary considerations
b. Small pieces in large organisms
c. Specific cases
i. Expression of active peptides: hormones, toxins
ii. Expression of cross-reacting antibodies
iii. Animal virus cloning
B. Human Genetic Engineering
III. Costs
IV. Conclusions

A. Summary Analysis of Risks

B. Possible Responses
1. Maintain the Status Quo
2. Abolish the Guidelines
C. Recommendation

The RAC extensively discussed the Working Group's report and other approaches to revision of the Guidelines at its September 1981 meeting. The RAC passed by a vote of 16 in favor, 3 opposed, with 1 abstention, the elements of its version of a proposed revision of the Guidelines to be published for public comment. Based on these elements, NIH staff prepared the RAC version of proposed revised Guidelines (September 1981 RAC proposal) which was published for public comment in the **Federal Register** of December 4, 1981 (46 FR 59368). The relevant background documents were also published in the December 4, 1981, **Federal Register** announcement, as follow—Annex A: Original proposal of Drs. David Baltimore and Allan Campbell; Annex B: Documents prepared by Working Group on Revision of the Guidelines; Annex C: Minority reports of working group members; Annex D: Draft Minutes of relevant portion of September 10–11, 1981, RAC Meeting; and Annex E: Current NIH Guidelines. Comments were due by February 2, 1982.

The major features of the September 1981 RAC proposal were:

1. The Guidelines would cease to be mandatory and would become a voluntary code of standard practice. Requirements that institutions have an Institutional Biosafety Committee (IBC), that investigators obtain prior approval from the IBC before beginning certain experiments, that investigators obtain prior approval from NIH before beginning certain experiments, and the section of the Guidelines specifying that noncompliance with the Guidelines could lead to loss of NIH funds, would all be eliminated.

2. Section III of the Guidelines giving containment levels would be greatly simplified, and most experiments currently mandated at P2 and P3 containment would be recommended at P1.

3. The prohibitions section (I-D) of the Guidelines would be eliminated, although two of the previous prohibitions would be retained instead as admonishments.

Dr. Susan Gottesman of the National Cancer Institute of the National Institutes of Health prepared an alternative proposal (Gottesman proposal) for a major revision of the Guidelines.

The major features of this proposal were:

1. The Guidelines would continue to be mandatory for institutions receiving NIH funding. Certain experiments would continue to require prior review by NIH, certain experiments would continue to require prior review by an IBC, and certain experiments would require notice to an IBC simultaneously with initiation of the experiment.

2. Section III of the Guidelines would be reorganized and simplified. All experiments would fall into one of four classes. Physical containment requirements for some classes of experiments would be lowered.

3. Three of five prohibitions (I-D-2, I-D-4 and I-D-5 in the July 1981 Guidelines) would be listed in a new section that would continue to require RAC review and NIH approval before initiation. Experiments falling under prohibition I-D-1 and I-D-6 in the July 1981 Guidelines could proceed after IBC approval.

A summary of this (Gottesman) proposal and changes in the July 1981 Guidelines to implement the proposal were published for comment in the **Federal Register** of December 7, 1981 (46 FR 59734). Comments on this proposal were due by February 1, 1982.

ORDA and NIH staff prepared a document summarizing the two proposals (i.e., the September 1981 RAC proposal published for comment in the December 4, 1981, **Federal Register**, and the Gottesman proposal published for comment in the December 7, 1981, **Federal Register**) including a table comparing them with the July 1981 Guidelines. ORDA distributed the summary and copies of the **Federal Register** of December 4, 1981, and December 7, 1981, to over 4,300 individuals and organizations that had expressed interest in being informed about developments affecting the Guidelines and recombinant DNA research. The document invited comments on the two proposals. In addition, notices appeared in a number of periodicals inviting comments on the proposals.

II. February 8–9, 1982, Meeting of Recombinant DNA Advisory Committee

On February 8–9, 1982, the RAC reviewed the proposals for changing the Guidelines. They had been sent in advance: The December 4, 1981, **Federal Register** containing the September 1981 RAC proposal; the December 7, 1981, **Federal Register** containing the Gottesman proposal; the summary of the two proposals including the table comparing them with the July 1981 Guidelines; and all letters of comment on the proposals (a total of 86 letters) received by NIH by February 5, 1982. Part II–A of this announcement contains the draft minutes of the relevant portions of the February 8–9, 1982, RAC meeting. Part II–B of this announcement gives the response of the Acting Director, National Institute of Allergy and Infectious Diseases (NIAID), to the RAC recommendations.

II–A. Draft Minutes of Relevant Portions of February 8–9, 1982, RAC Meeting

Mr. Thornton called the attention of the RAC to the major topic of the February 8–9, 1982 meeting, a discussion of two proposals (tabs 1050, 1056A, 1056B, 1056C/1, 1056C/7, 1056D, 1056E, 1056F, 1056G) to modify the current NIH Guidelines for Research Involving Recombinant DNA molecules.

Mr. Thornton said he would take a moment to give his personal perspective prior to resuming the role as committee chairman. He said former NIH Director, Donald Fredrickson summarized the purposes of the Guidelines as (1) to establish a rapid, complete means of communication, (2) to assure that the Guidelines are conservative yet allow research to proceed, and (3) to permit public participation in the formulation of public policy. Mr. Thornton noted the difficulty of establishing and maintaining communication between public policy decision makers and experts in a scientific field. NIH has devised a mechanism which successfully maintains this communication, and he would not wish to abandon it.

Mr. Thornton then described the Guidelines from a lawyer's perspective. He noted that the Guidelines are not laws; he thought this is good since laws are difficult to formulate and difficult to change. Neither are they regulations: regulations are subject to formal revision procedures much more rigid than those RAC and the NIH follow in modifying the Guidelines. Neither are the Guidelines simply statements of good practice. The RAC and the NIH have been responsive to change, not as quickly perhaps as some would have preferred, but quickly enough that the advance of science has not been significantly impeded.

Mr. Thornton then recognized Dr. Baltimore who referred to the December 4, 1981, proposal which RAC had recommended for publication in the **Federal Register** (46 FR 59368). Dr. Baltimore said that the proposal had elicited tremendous response. He said that conversion to a voluntary code of standard practice, as described in the December 4, 1981, **Federal Register**, is appropriate. Although the current NIH Guidelines are not formal regulations, they have instituted an informal regulatory process. He expressed hope that the philosophy of voluntary compliance expressed in the December 4, 1981, proposal would be accepted.

Dr. Baltimore suggested that some of the concerns expressed about the December 4, 1981, proposal by correspondents could be addressed and met by modifications. Some correspondents had expressed concern that the IBCs would be dismantled. Dr. Baltimore assumed that with the language of the December 4, 1981, proposal, the IBCs would remain in place. He said he had, however, prepared an amendment, which might be added during the discussion, specifying a continuing role for IBCs.

Dr. Baltimore said that in setting P1 containment conditions, the December 4, 1981, proposal implies there could not be deliberate release of recombinant organisms into the environment. It is clear from the letters received in response to the proposal, however, that some people would prefer an explicit statement to that effect. Dr. Baltimore said that if RAC felt it was necessary, he would support an amendment to the December 4, 1981, proposal to accomplish that aim.

Finally, Dr. Baltimore suggested the language of Section I–A might be modified to include a strong statement that although voluntary, adherence to the Guidelines is strongly recommended. He said the December 4, 1981, proposal with these amendments would be responsive to comments received. He then moved the proposal appearing in the December 4, 1981, **Federal Register** (46 FR 59368) as an item for discussion. The motion was seconded by Dr. McGarrity.

Dr. Baltimore made an additional statement in response to certain written comments received. He said that he has never hidden his affiliation with the company, Collaborative Research, of Waltham, Massachusetts. He stressed, however, that if he were acting for the company, he would not be supporting the December 4, 1981, proposal because he said it is not in the interests of any institution in the Boston area, as it might lead to more stringent regulation at the local level. He said he supported the December 4, 1981, proposal becaue he believes it is correct.

Dr. Nightingale said that letters commenting on the proposals indicate many remaining concerns in both the scientific and public sectors. In her view, these concerns are not adequately addressed by the December 4, 1981, proposal even if that proposal were modified as just suggested by Dr. Baltimore.

Dr. Nightingale said that there is not a clear consensus for eliminating the mandatory nature of the Guidelines or eliminating the requirement for IBCs. She said the issue of scale-up needs further discussion. She expressed the belief that removing the mandatory nature of the Guidelines would stimulate a variety of legislative actions across the country, possibly resulting in regulatory variation from location to location. She also suggested that although the probability of an event with disastrous consequences is very small, one must acknowledge that gaps in scientific knowledge exist; if such a very rare event should occur, there could be tremendous backlash against the scientific community.

Dr. Nightingale said the December 7, 1981 (46 FR 59734, Part 7, "Gottesman"), proposal would simplify the Guidelines and remove many restrictions. Dr. Nightingale said she had a list of at least six ways in which the Gottesman proposal could be further simplified, and restrictions further removed, by the next RAC meeting. Dr. Nightingale then moved acceptance of the December 7,

1981, "Gottesman" propoal as a substitute motion with a commitment to continue to review, reorganize, simplify, and remove restrictions from the Guidelines as expeditiously as possible. Dr. Fedoroff seconded the motion.

Dr. Berns said that the current Guidelines are cumbersome and complex. The RAC has several options. The most significant issue is the mandatory nature of the Guidelines. He thought having IBCs is good, and recommended keeping the RAC. He stated a preference for readily understandable Guidelines.

Dr. Mason said RAC has acted responsibly in the process of reviewing the Guidelines. He supported the need for IBCs in both academia and industry. Indeed this type of activity should not be limited to the recombinant DNA field but should be encouraged generically. He feared that RAC, by its endorsement for publication of the December 4, 1981, proposal, did not convey to the public the importance of IBCs. Dr. Mason suggested that certain issues should be carefully scrutinized, including deliberate release or recombinant containing organisms into the environment and the cloning of genes for drug resistance and for certain toxins. Dr. Mason expressed the belief that the NIH Guidelines ultimately should and will become voluntary, but suggested they should remain mandatory for the time being for at least two reasons: (1) More information should be collected, particularly in regard to some of the areas currently prohibited; and (2) the public is not yet ready for voluntary guidelines.

Dr. Goldstein said that he could not support the December 4 proposal. He said that he supports the December 7 proposal as it simplifies the Guidelines, specifies IBCs, and maintains mandatory Guidelines. He stated that haphazard local regulations, varying from community to community, and hindering the research, will result if national oversight is not maintained. He felt the December 7, 1981, proposal does not deal adequately with large-scale work and that area should be reviewed.

Ms. King noted that at the September 8–9, 1981, RAC meeting she had not supported what became the December 4, 1981, proposal. She believes the December 7, "Gottesman" proposal is where the RAC should begin in trying to reach a final position. She expressed the belief that regulation is justified by concerns about safety. Arguments that recombinant DNA is no more dangerous than other forms of biomedical research have been advanced. This does not lead Ms. King to the conclusion that only a voluntary code of conduct is necessary. She suggested, rather, that if other research areas pose similar risk, then perhaps they too should be regulated. She favored mandatory Guidelines with sanctions and a monitoring system. The structure should not yet be dismantled nor should it be made voluntary. Otherwise a system of fragmented regulations at the state and local level might develop.

Mr. Thornton recognized Dr. Gottesman who had authored the December 7, 1981, proposal. Dr. Gottesman said her proposal is based on the assessment of risks in the document "Evaluation of the Risks Associated with Recombinant DNA" (46 FR 59385). She noted that that document had been generated by the Working Group on Revision of the Guidelines during the summer of 1981. On the basis of that evaluation, she had concluded that there are several types of experiments about which questions remain or about which so little is known that no absolute conclusion can be drawn. For these types of experiments she felt a mandatory record-keeping and oversight mechanism is appropriate.

Dr. Gottesman said her proposal requires RAC review and NIH approval for certain experiments involving toxin genes, drug resistance genes, and release into the environment. Responsibility for oversight of certain other experiments is delegated to the IBCs. The types of experiments to be reviewed and IBC review procedures might be modified by RAC. RAC may wish to permit the IBCs greater leeway in lowering containment for certain experiments. Dr. Gottesman noted that her proposal does not alter the status of currently exempt experiments.

Mr. Daloz said that specialists in general tend to develop tunnel-vision so that their own concerns become uppermost in their minds. He noted that many laws and guidelines regulate our daily lives, and that even if the NIH Guidelines were eliminated, other agencies might institute guidelines or regulations. Mr. Daloz expressed his support for the December 7, 1981, proposal; he said, in any event, the IBCs should be retained.

Dr. McKinney said he had discussed the December 4 and December 7 proposals with scientists, lawyers, and representatives of commercial organizations. He said the researchers he had spoken with are approximately evenly divided in their support of mandatory vs. voluntary Guidelines. Regarding the current prohibitions, Dr. McKinney said many people felt certain experiments should be monitored and controlled.

Dr. McKinney said that previously the RAC had extricated itself from "regulating" large-scale activities. He felt the reintroduction of the question of how to oversee large-scale work was retrogressive; RAC should address science issues and avoid reviewing large-scale activities *per se*. Finally, Dr. McKinney noted that some correspondents mentioned the negative effects the Guidelines have had on research. He said the committee must also take into account the beneficial aspects of the review process; in his view the benefits far outweigh any negative aspects. He said RAC would be remiss if it eliminated oversight over recombinant DNA research before more data are accumulated.

Mr. Mitchell said he had made a rough analysis of the opinions submitted by commentators on the proposals. According to his estimate, approximately half favored the December 4 proposal; the other half favored either the current Guidelines or modest changes therein, or the December 7 proposal.

Mr. Mitchell said the press gives the impression that the recombinant DNA field is advancing very rapidly. These accounts do not support the allegation that the Guidelines have inhibited research. He suggested that should the NIH change the Guidelines substantially, RAC would find itself in an untenable position; it would forfeit the opportunity to "move" the technology on a rational basis, and uniformity of standards would be lost. Mr. Mitchell suggested that adoption of the December 4, 1981, proposal would destroy some of the scientific community's credibility. He said that should Congress ever again consider national legislation, scientists could no longer argue they were following a policy of self-regulation.

Mr. Mitchell said he had attended a panel meeting of the California legislature's Committee on Health on December 14, 1981. He said these legislators, few of whom have a scientific background, spoke in terms of public perceptions. He questioned how many of those legislators would understand the scientific arguments or attempt to comprehend technical presentations.

Mr. Mitchell said he supported the December 7 proposal as it maintains the mandatory nature of the Guidelines and the requirement for IBCs. Dr. Fedoroff said she strongly suppored the December 7 proposal, and urged that a mechanism for further simplification be introduced.

Dr. Saginor said that the recombinant DNA issue could easily become a political football; the Guidelines have restrained politicians from using this as an issue. He added that the RAC as a central committee providing a forum for discussion is necessary. He supported the December 7, 1981, proposal.

Dr. Irving Johnson of Eli Lilly and Company said Eli Lilly had commented favorably on both the December 4 and the December 7 proposals, although he had reservations about both proposals. He said the December 4 proposal provides no "trackability". The December 7 proposal, while it simplifies the Guidelines, perpetuates unnecessary bookkeeping. He said that Eli Lilly and Company recommends mandatory retention of IBCs which should be required to report problems to the RAC.

Dr. Johnson pointed out that representatives of regulatory agencies are on the Interagency Recombinant DNA Committee and have liaison representatives to the RAC. These representatives are there to monitor events and suggest appropriate action to their agencies. For a company involved in interestate commerce such as Eli Lilly and Company, these agencies represent regulations which are mandatory and not voluntary.

Dr. Johnson said he had attended the November 1981 hearings of the California legislature's Committee on Health and had detected little concern over risk at that hearing. Concerns were expressed, however, over moral and ethical problems. Dr. Johnson expressed concern about again raising the issue of large-scale work and cited the safety of large-scale equipment. He proposed amending the December 4, 1981, proposal to require retention of IBCs.

Dr. McGarrity said that he has concluded that recombinant DNA research presents no hazards beyond those normally associated with microbiological research. This is not to say there are no problems in other areas of biomedical research; however, these hazards have been adequately handled. He stated that it is time to stop the discriminatory treatment of recombinant DNA research. He favored the December 4, 1981, proposal with some modifications.

Dr. Holmes said he favored retaining mandatory Guidelines and the requirement for IBCs. He rejected the argument that recombinant DNA activities should not require oversight because other areas of microbiological or biomedical research do not have special oversight. He said he would support the December 7, 1981 proposal with the addition of a recommendation that IBCs also review non-recombinant DNA research that is similar to research covered by Section III of the Guidelines.

Dr. Baltimore reiterated his belief that recombinant DNA research is no more hazardous than experiments in the mainstream of biomedical research. He felt this was the judgement of a majority of the scientific community, and that the December 4, 1981, proposal reflects this consensus. He said fear of local regulation or fear of leaving industry with no code for legal protection were not reasons for maintaining mandatory Guidelines. Adoption of the December 4, 1981, proposal would send a message to States and localities that the RAC concludes that regulations are not necessary. Finally, Dr. Baltimore said that the CDC "Classification of Etiological Agents on the Basis of Hazard" is not appropriate for use in classifying recombinant DNA experiments.

Dr. Lewis of the National Science Foundation suggested greater flexibility in IBC specifications might be desirable. Dr. Landy said that he supported the original Baltimore-Campbell proposal, and subsequently the December 4, 1981, proposal, as the only intellectually honest recognition of the relationship between the unestablished potential risk in recombinant DNA research, and known risk in other areas of research which are not regulated. In attempting to rationalize support for greater controls over recombinant DNA research than over work with known pathogens, Dr. Landy said the training, procedures and restraints applied by the select group of investigators studying pathogens would not necessarily have been followed by all those now using recombinant DNA techniques.

Dr. Gottesman concurred with Dr. Landy's rationalization and added that investigators studying pathogens know the properties of these organisms; recombinant organisms might express unexpected properties.

Dr. Maas said he saw no logic in having guidelines for one type of experimental procedure, which is rapidly becoming a very commonly employed technique, and having no regulations for other types of more dangerous procedures, such as work with chemical carcinogens.

Dr. Gottesman said that mandatory guidelines are not necessarily synonomous with bureaucracy. She noted that the December 7, 1981, proposal no longer requires RAC review and NIH approval for large-scale procedures; rather it specifies that large-scale experiments be approved by the IBC. She said the definition of large-scale might be revised. Dr. Gottesman agreed with Dr. Baltimore that the CDC Classification of Etiological Agents in not perfect, but she said the alternative in the December 4 proposal of "use whatever you have and figure it out yourself" is not better. If RAC cannot find a better mechanism than the CDC classification, IBCs and PIs individually will not be able to make better decisions.

Ms. King said that the central issue is mandatory vs. voluntary guidelines. She said she was concerned with questions of process. She referred to Dr. Baltimore's statement that only a minority of scientists believe there may be some safety concerns with respect to recombinant DNA research. She said the public cannot ascertain whether that statement is accurate. The RAC did not cross-examine those who submitted written comments. Ms. King said RAC members should be aware of what she considers to be defects in process, and therefore err on the side of caution in deciding between the December 4 and December 7 proposals.

Dr. Nightingale praised the more extensive attempts to solicit comments on these proposals than had occurred in the past. As a result of this, the comments received were more varied than in the past. However, she felt it was only one small step in really assessing what the public feels. Referring back to Dr. Baltimore's statement, Dr. Nightingale said that disagreement does exist within the scientific community on whether there are unique risks of recombinant DNA research. She said that a major issue is voluntary vs. mandatory IBCs. She said that the December 7, 1981, proposal could be simplified and reorganized to make it easier to read and less cumbersome. She suggested that Section III–C could be eliminated; that the criteria for defining large-scale could be revised to emphasize inoculum size rather than volume; that Section IV could be simplified and reorganized; that the bureaucracy within IBCs could be greatly simplified; that the section dealing with whole or defective viruses could be simplified; that Section III–B–2–a and Section III–B–2–b dealing with etiological agents could be combined; and that all work in nonpathogens could be performed at PI containment. She viewed the December 7, 1981, proposal as a first, very positive step towards reducing complexity and restrictions.

Dr. Levine attempted to address the question of why recombinant DNA research is singled out for special consideration while other biomedical research, using inherently much more dangerous organisms, is not. He said the answer is in the historical context. Work with pathogens has had an extraordinary safety record for decades. The reason there was so much interest in control of recombinant DNA is that recombinant DNA technology became available in the 1970s, in an era of regulation. He cited procedures for research involving human subjects, which changed drastically in the early 1970s. He said he supports these constraints as they protect the public, as well as individual subjects, and they facilitate communication between the public and clinical investigators. He said being responsive to the public is very important and if a significant segment of the public is still concerned about recombinant DNA, this committee should be sensitive to that concern. He said that he would like to see something like the December 4, 1981, proposal ultimately adopted, but not immediately.

Dr. Ahmed said he wished to quote and highlight several points from the letter from the Public and Scientific Affairs Board of the American Society for Microbiology. He quoted from that letter that, "Our concern is for the fact that only sparse information is available for other host-vectors. With less characterized systems, new combinations may result in organisms with potentially increased pathogenicity than either the donor or the recipient." Dr. Ahmed further quoted, "We are not only concerned with the paucity of information but also with the lack of mechanisms for its dissemination. Many workers using modern genetic technology are not versed in pathogenic microbiology and cannot be assumed to have proper training or access to up-to-date information."

Dr. Martin said he believed as a scientist that recombinant DNA should not be singled out for special oversight. However, this position must be viewed within the historical contest. He said that the State legislators and County supervisors with whom he had spoken are not primarily interested in the scientific basis for relaxation or eliminataion of the Guidelines, but rather in public opinion. RAC must be careful not to excite a public reaction that could result in greater bureaucratic and regulatory problems from local jurisdictions.

Dr. Saginor said he would like to propose an amendment to the December 7, 1981, proposal, should it pass, that a working group be formed to further refine, simplify and reorganize that proposal, and that this group report to the RAC at a future meeting.

A discussion was held of the proper parliamentary procedure for the Committee to use to proceed. Mr. Thornton suggested that the Committee might vote now on Dr. Nightingale's motion to substitute the December 7 proposal for the December 4 proposal. This would result in the Committee choosing which "vehicle" it wished initially to adopt. Following this, RAC members could propose amendments to "perfect" the vehicle chosen, before the final vote on it.

Dr. Baltimore "called the question." By a vote of nineteen in favor, two opposed, and no abstentions, the RAC agreed to limit further debate and to vote on the motion to substitute the December 7, 1981, proposal for the December 4, 1981, proposal as the vehicle to be used for further amendments. Dr. Baltimore said that although, following this vote, any aspect of the winning proposal would be open for further amendments, he felt the vote should be viewed as a decision about whether "to go in the voluntary or mandatory direction." Dr. Nightingale reminded the RAC that her motion included the commitment to work towards future simplification of the Guidelines. By a vote of sixteen in favor, five opposed, and no abstentions, the RAC adopted the substitute motion, thus choosing the Gottesman proposal as the vehicle to be placed before the Committee, open to further amendments.

Mr. Thornton recognized Dr. Susan Wright. Dr. Wright focused her comments on large-scale applications as she thought that while many other issues are being addressed, the RAC was not adequately addressing that issue. She said the primary focus of RAC has been on the hazards of research, not the hazards of industrial processes. She said that one cannot dismiss change of scale with regard to accidental release of recombinant organisms. She felt the data base on industrial hazards is very poor. She said she had heard some industrialists in other countries were considering using open fermentation tanks. If there is no oversight, companies will use whatever fermentation process they think is in their best interest. There are irresponsible companies willing to cut corners and take risks to try to gain a competitive advantage over responsible companies. Furthermore, there are no risk assessment experiments with organisms making insulin, interferon, etc. She said the committee is assuming that whatever product is being made will be harmless.

Dr. Wright said the RAC recommendation at the previous meeting to exempt from NIH review, certain large-scale experiments utilizing *E. coli* K-12, *Saccharomyces cerevisiae* and *Bacillus subtilis* host-vector systems was an error which produced a major gap in oversight. She urged the RAC to reconsider and re-evaluate its oversight over large-scale work.

Dr. Irving Johnson of Eli Lilly and Company said that industry has produced hundreds of gallons of the causative agents of polio, diphtheria, whooping cough, etc., with no great hazard to workers or to the environment, and in fact with great benefit to the population. Dr. Johnson said the only open vats he is aware of are in the beer brewing industry. Most industrial fermentations are generally highly contained to protect against contamination. Inocula are introduced into the growth tank through a rigid stainless steel structure. The connection does not leak and is steam sterilized.

Dr. Wright said she was not making a categorical statement about hazards, but rather about the data base. In her opinion, the data are extremely poor and incomplete, and assumptions that problems will be uncomplicated or easy to deal with are premature. These new technologies should remain under RAC review until a better data base develops.

Dr. Mason said that many industrial issues, though of concern, are beyond the scope of the RAC. Local, State or Federal authorities that make on-site inspections may wish to evaluate these issues, but RAC should not. Dr. Ahmed felt a distinction should be drawn between organisms concentration and total amount in industrial processes.

Dr. Gottesman said that the December 7, 1981, proposal still requires that non-exempt large-scale procedures be reviewed by the local IBC before the project begins, and PI–LS containment would still apply. It extends to all large-scale experiments the conditions approved by RAC at the previous meeting for certain large-scale experiments.

Dr. Berns questioned the language of Section I–B, *Definition of Recombinant DNA Molecules*, in the December 7, 1981, proposal. The relevant text of Section I–B reads as follows:

> Synthetic DNA segments likely to yield a potentially harmful polynucleotide or polypeptide (e.g., a toxin or a pharmacologically active agent) shall be considered as equivalent to their natural DNA counterpart. If the synthetic DNA segment is not expressed *in vivo* as a polynucleotide or polypeptide product, it is exempt from the Guidelines.

Dr. Gottesman pointed out that this is a reformulation of text which appears as Section III–E of the current (July 1, 1981) Guidelines. Dr. Berns suggested the real issue is whether the synthetic fragment would produce a biologically active product; he proposed to amend the language by adding the phrase "biologically active" before the word "polynucleotide" in the last sentence. Dr. Nightingale, who had proposed the motion being considered, and Dr. Feroroff, the seconder of the motion, accepted the amendment.

Dr. Saginor then proposed an amendment which would explicitly state that a working group be appointed to review and attempt to simplify further the Guidelines and to report to the RAC at a future meeting. Dr. Nightingale, noting this intent was part of her original motion, accepted the amendment, as did Dr. Fedoroff.

Mr. Thornton called the question on Dr. Nightingale's motion as modified by amendments. By a vote of seventeen in favor, three opposed, and no abstentions the RAC recommended adoption of the December 7, 1981, proposal with amendments. Mr. Thornton said a working group to refine the proposal would be designated at a later date, in accordance with the motion.

Dr. McGarrity asked the committee to state for the record that RAC sees no need for additional state and local ordinances governing recombinant DNA activities. Dr. Liberman, the biological safety officer at MIT, advised against adoption of Dr. McGarrity's statement as he viewed it as counter-productive. Based on his experience as a member of the Boston Biohazards Committee he sees growing community interest in overseeing non-recombinant biohazards as recombinant systems as being handled.

Dr. Ahmed said he thought adoption of Dr. McGarrity's statement would be viewed as arrogance on the part of the RAC, saying "our views are gospel, and don't second guess us."

Mr. Mitchell said that he is in sympathy with the motion since he is concerned about fragmentation at the State and local level. However, knowing the independence of legislative bodies, it might not be well taken. He suggested that if the statement were reworded it might be more successful. Dr. McGarrity agreed and withdrew the proposal in order that revised text could be prepared for consideration later in the meeting.

Dr. Mason spoke against Dr. McGarrity's proposal, as it runs counter to usual regulatory practice, in which States and localities may regulate as long as their requirements are at least as stringent as Federal requirements. He added that RAC's recommendation would not be binding.

Dr. Holmes made a motion that there be added to the Guidelines a statement to the effect that:

> It is not clear that the biohazards associated with recombinant DNA are unique or different from biohazards associated with other work with pathogenic organisms; therefore, RAC encourages local Institutional Biosafety Committees to establish procedures for review of experiments not involving recombinant DNA, which nonetheless, involve biohazards such as those addressed in Section III of the Guidelines.

Dr. Fedoroff seconded the motion. Dr. Landy suggested that a different statement be substituted for Dr. Holmes' proposed language to the effect that:

> The Recombinant DNA Advisory Committee wants to point out the absence of demonstrated risk or danger posed by recombinant DNA research The continuance of the Guidelines for recombinant DNA research is made with full appreciation of the fact that other areas of research in which some risk has been demonstrated are without analogous guidelines.

Dr. Landy said such a statement would make clear to the public that RAC's recommendation to maintain guidelines is not based on demonstrated risk, but on potential risk.

Dr. Ahmed asked whether NIH has the authority to expand the purview of the IBC's as in Dr. Holmes' statement. Dr. Talbot replied that such a statement could be sent to the IBCs as a recommendation.

Dr. Goldstein said that he thought Dr. Landy's proposal could "stir up a hornet's nest," regenerating the situation of previous years with recombinant DNA. Ms. King said she could not support Dr. Landy's proposal as she questioned the phrase "absence of demonstrated risk." Dr. Berns moved to table Dr. Holme's proposal. By a vote of seventeen in favor, three opposed, and no abstentions, the proposal was tabled.

Dr. Levine called the committee's attention to the report of the Working Group on Revision of the Guidelines entitled "Evaluation of the Risks Associated with Recombinant DNA Research" and particularly Part IV-A of the report, "Summary Analysis of Risks" (46 FR 59390). He said the conclusion is that most potential recombinant DNA risks envisaged in 1975 are now considered nonexistent. Ms. King said RAC should emphasize that available data cited in that report support and justify RAC's recommendation of the December 7, 1981, proposal. She suggested the RAC might formally reaffirm the "Summary Analysis of Risks." Dr. Martin suggested this text might be used as a preamble to the introduction of the new Guidelines by the NIH Director. Dr. Holmes moved that the Director is requested to consider the "Summary Analysis of Risks" (46 FR 59390) as he determines a preamble to the revised Guidelines. Dr. Nightingale seconded the motion. She emphasized that her earlier motion for adoption of the December 7, 1981, proposal was based on the document "Evaluation of the Risks Associated with Recombinant DNA." She expected this document would be published as an integral part of the decision document. Dr. Mason hoped the document would note the different options considered by the RAC.

Ms. King suggested Dr. Holmes' motion be amended to call the attention of the NIH Director not just the "Summary Analysis of Risks" (46 FR 59390) but also the motion which originally established the Working Group on Revision of the Guidelines, the Working Group's agenda, and its complete report.

Dr. Talbot asked if the motion might not be withdrawn, with the assurance that NIH would bring all of these items to the Director's attention without the necessity of a motion. Ms. King said she would prefer a specific motion since the Working Group report had not been formally endorsed by the RAC at the September 1981 meeting and since the RAC action today accepting the December 7, 1981, proposal is based on that report. Dr. Holmes reworded his motion to request the summary information discussed be included in the Director's preamble. Dr. Nightingale, who had seconded Dr. Holmes' earlier motion, also agreed.

Dr. Wright said that if there were to be a general statement on risks, then it should be made clear which industrial problems the RAC is not dealing with, so that no one thinks this is a global statement covering both research and industrial risks. Dr. Ahmed suggested that language be inserted indicating that the report does not address industrial scale-up. Dr. Berns noted that the NIH, on the advice of the RAC, had issued "Physical Containment Recommendations for Large-Scale Uses of Organisms Containing Recombinant DNA Molecules;" RAC, however, is no longer evaluating mechanical details in individual large-scale applications. Dr. Landy opposed Dr. Ahmed's suggestion on the introduction of a specific statement on industrial considerations as it would dilute the general policy statement.

Dr. Pinon moved to table the motion; he preferred that ORDA bring these items to the attention of the Director, NIH, without the necessity of a formal motion. By a vote of ten in favor, eight opposed, and two abstentions, the motion to table carried.

After a brief recess, Dr. Mason moved to reconsider the action in order to provide the Director with a clear indication of RAC intent. He felt the previous vote revolved about procedural issues rather than intent. By a vote of ten in favor, four opposed, and three abstentions, the motion to reconsider was adopted.

Ms. King then moved that "the RAC specifically call to the Director's attention that the action taken on the December 7, 1981, proposal results from analysis and consideration of the report entitled 'Evaluation of the Risks Associated with Recombinant DNA Research' prepared by the Working Group on Revision of the Guidelines. The vote on the December 7, 1981, proposal implements the Working Group report."

By a vote of nineteen in favor, none opposed, and one abstention, the RAC adopted Ms. King's motion as a substitute for the previous motion. Mr. Thornton then rules that unless there were objection (which there was not), the substitute motion is adopted by unanimous consent as the recommendation of the RAC.

Following an overnight recess, Mr. Thornton called the committee to order to consider language developed by Dr. McGarrity and Mr. Mitchell regarding local and state legislation. Mr. Mitchell moved acceptance of the following language:

Whereas RAC has voted to recommend significant reductions in mandatory guidelines regarding recombinant DNA activity, and

Whereas RAC in establishing said reduced guidelines did so based upon collective credible scientific knowledge and experience, and

Whereas RAC believes it to be in the best interest of recombinant DNA activity to have a central arena for the dissemination of information and continuous review, and

Whereas RAC believes the existence of uniform guidelines thereby establishes certainty and clarity in the scientific community, and

Whereas RAC believes it would be detrimental to the advancement of recombinant DNA activity to have fragmentation of guidelines across the country,

Therefore, be it resolved that RAC strongly recommends that local and state governments defer to the NIH Guidelines if enacting legislation governing recombinant DNA activity, unless it clearly establishes by credible scientific evidence that unique risk in fact exists in their particular jurisdiction.

Dr. McGarrity seconded the motion. He said the RAC action taken yesterday on the December 7, 1981, proposal would significantly relax the Guidelines. When considered in the context of possible additional local legislation, Mr. Mitchell's statement expressed RAC's judgement that the NIH Guidelines are the best possible approach at this time. It would be counterproductive for RAC to strip away bureaucracy and paperwork at the national level, only to have more bureaucracy and paperwork added at the state and local level.

Dr. Miller of the FDA strongly endorsed the sense of the motion. He said, almost without exception, the mosaic of local regulations has been more draconian and much less enlightened that the NIH Guidelines, and slower to evolve.

Dr. Martin suggested that the phrase "best interests of the public" be substituted for the phrase "best interest of recombinant DNA activity." Mr. Mitchell agreed.

Dr. Nightingale requested a clarification of the word "activity" in the motion. Mr. Mitchell replied that "activity" is an all inclusive term meant to cover research, development, production, etc.

Drs. Ahmed and Goldstein supported the sentiment expressed by the motion. However, Dr. Goldstein said he would vote against the language as he felt local communities would regard it as arrogant. Mr. Mitchell said he had chosen the verb "defer" to avoid the appearance of arrogance. The language urges that any actions be based on scientific grounds, and places the burden of proof upon advocates of local action. Dr. Friedman agreed.

Dr. Ahmed asked whether addition of the phrase "in as much as possible" would soften the language of the sentences:

* * * therefore, be it resolved that RAC strongly recommends that local and State governments defer to the NIH Guidelines * * *

Mr. Thornton thought the verb "defer" alone was actually softer.

Dr. Mason said he could envisage situations in which local action might be necessary because of irresponsible action by a local academic or industrial group. He hoped RAC did not intend to say that local action should not be taken in such cases. Dr. Goldstein stated that communities realize that while universities are under sanctions, industry is not. Dr. Berns said that Mr. Mitchell's language specifies that when local entities legislate, they should defer to the NIH Guidelines in the scientific component of the legislation.

Dr. Mason said that many aspects of industrial scale-up are not covered by the Guidelines, yet the proposed language implies the existence of such guidance. He questioned whether RAC might amend the language to remove such implications. Dr. McGarrity suggested the phrase "DNA activity" be modified to "DNA research activity."

Dr. Ahmed said he supported the resolution but would prefer that a statement, delineating the scope of RAC activities, be appended to the language. If the committee could not formulate such a statement today, he hoped the Director's preamble to the acceptance of the December 7, 1981, proposal would state that neither RAC nor the NIH deals with mechanical aspects of industrial scale-up activities.

Dr. Pinon requested that the word "credible" be deleted from the phrase "credible scientific evidence"; he thought the term redundant. Dr. Saginor, however, disagreed as he felt "scientific" and "credible" are not synonymous to the public.

Dr. Gottesman saw the proposed language as intending to say to local legislators "we are listening to your concerns, we believe we are responding to them, and we hope you will continue to have faith in RAC." She warned, however, that the language might lead legislators who had not previously thought of legislation to consider it. Dr. Nightingale concurred. She thought acceptance of Mr. Mitchell's statement might be counterproductive. Instead she suggested that the Director's preamble to the revised Guidelines might state that these Guidelines are based on the best available information and, it is hoped they will be applied nationally. She preferred this procedure to a motion indicating RAC's concern over possible local legislation. Dr. Holmes agreed, expressing concern that the motion appeard arrogant and would be counterproductive. Dr. Berns called for the question.

By a vote of sixteen in favor, none opposed, and no abstentions, the RAC voted to stop debate and to vote on the motion proposed by Mr. Mitchell, as amended. By a vote of six in favor, nine opposed, and one abstention, the motion offered by Mr. Mitchell was defeated.

II-B. Response of the Acting Director, NIAID, to the RAC Recommendations

As the deciding Federal official, having been delegated responsibility for actions relative to the NIH Guidelines, I note the following:

I was present throughout the entire February 8-9, 1982, RAC meeting (as I have been present throughout all but the first of the twenty-three meetings of the RAC.) I attest to the accuracy of the draft minutes appearing above in Part II-A of this announcement. I commend the diligence with which the RAC considered the issues, taking into careful account the many letters received.

The first of the motions passed by the RAC discussed above in Part II-A of this announcement was to recommend acceptance of the "Gottesman" proposal for revision of the Guidelines as it had appeared in the December 7, 1981, **Federal Register** with the addition of the phrase "biologically active" before the word "polynucleotide" in the last sentence of Section I-B of the Guidelines, and with the stipulation that a working group be appointed to review and attempt to further simplify the Guidelines, to report to the RAC at a future meeting.

I accept the RAC recommendation of the "Gottesman" proposal for revision of the Guidelines with the addition of the phrase "biologically active." This is discussed further in Part IV of this announcement.

The stipulation "that a working group be appointed to review and attempt to simplify further the guidelines, and to report to the RAC at a future meeting" has been accepted. Members of a new Working Group on Revision of the Guidelines have been appointed by the RAC Chairman, a first meeting is scheduled in April 1982, and it is hoped that the Working Group will have proposed revisions ready to present at the next RAC meeting on June 28, 1982.

A second motion passed by the RAC discussed above in Part II-A of this announcement was to "specifically call to the Director's attention that the action taken on the December 7, 1981, proposal results from analysis and consideration of the report entitled 'Evaluation of the Risks Associated With Recombinant DNA Research' prepared by the Working Group on Revision of the Guidelines." During the discussion prior to the adoption of this motion, there were suggestions that the entire report "Evaluation of the Risks Associated With Recombinant DNA Research" be published as an integral part of the Decision Document accompanying the Guideline revision, i.e., be published in this announcement.

I do note that the RAC action, recommending adoption of the December 7, 1981, proposal was based on analysis and consideration of the report entitled "Evaluation of the Risks Associated With Recombinant DNA Research." I commend this report and urge interested readers to consult it. I have reproduced in Part I of this announcement the headings of the Report. I do not feel, however, that it is necessary to reproduce the entire report here. It can be found on pages 59385-59394 of the **Federal Register** of December 4, 1981.

During RAC discussion of another motion, which was not approved, as discussed above in Part II-A of this announcement, Dr. Ahmed said he hoped that in the Director's preamble to the new Guidelines (i.e., in this announcement) it would be stated that neither RAC nor the NIH deals with mechanical aspects of industrial scale-up activities.

In response to this, it might be helpful to review the history and the current status of the relationship of the NIH Guidelines to industrial scale-up. The Guidelines are mandatory for institutions which receive Federal funds for recombinant DNA research. They are not mandatory for institutions which receive no Federal funds for recombinant DNA research other than in those States and localities which have local ordinances requiring all to follow the NIH Guidelines. The Guidelines promulgated today stipulate, in Section III-B-5, that experiments involving more than 10 liters of culture require prior approval by the IBC (but not NIH). They refer to the "Physical Containment Recommendations for Large-Scale Uses of Organisms Containing recombinant DNA Molecules" which NIH issued in the **Federal Register** on April 11, 1980 (45 FR 24968) and which define the containment levels P1-LS, P2-LS, and P3-LS. Previous versions of the Guidelines, in effect earlier, involved prior RAC review and NIH approval of recombinant DNA experiments over 10 liters in volume. Industry voluntarily submitted requests to go over 10 liters in volume, which were reviewed at RAC meetings in September 1979, December 1979, March 1980, June 1980, September 1980, January 1981, and April 1981. Through the September 1980 meeting the information submitted included details of the "applicant's laboratory practices, containment equipment and facilities * * *" At the request of the RAC, and as accepted by NIH in November 1980 (45 FR 77378), this was changed to no longer require such physical containment details.

During RAC discussion of another motion, which was not approved, as discussed in Part II-A of this announcement, Dr. Nightingale suggested that the Director's preamble to the revised Guidelines (i.e., this announcement) might state that the "Guidelines are based on the best available information, and it is hoped they will be applied nationally." I heartily endorse this sentiment, and hope that any State or local government, contemplating enactment of legislation governing recombinant DNA activities, will first study the documentation of the huge effort the RAC and NIH have put into establishing and modifying the NIH Guidelines, and will defer to the NIH Guidelines unless it clearly establishes by credible scientific evidence that unique risk in fact exists in their particular jurisdiction.

III. Analysis of Correspondence Received

As noted above, 86 letters were received commenting on the proposed revisions of the Guidelines between November 1981 and February 5, 1982. These 86 letters were provided to the RAC and considered at their meeting on February 8-9, 1982. Nine additional letters were received between February 8, 1982, and March 31, 1982. This Part (III) of this announcement contains an analysis of the 95 letters received. Copies of all letters received are available for inspection at the Office of recombinant DNA Activities, Building 31, Room 4A52, NIH, Bethesda, Maryland 20205. It is expected that they will be published in a Volume 7 of "Recombinant DNA Research," a series constituting a public record of documents related to the NIH Guidelines for Research Involving recombinant DNA Molecules.

Letters in Favor of Removing All Guidelines

One commentator wrote:

> I conclude that Drs. Adelberg and Zinder has the correct position: There is no scientific justification for maintaining any Guidelines in force.

Two other commentators also wrote in support of abolishing the Guidelines. This represents one end of the spectrum of views in regard to the Guidelines. The Adelberg-Zinder recommendation was reproduced in Annex C of the December 4, 1981, **Federal Register** (46 FR 59394). As noted in the minutes of the September 10-11, 1981, RAC meeting (Annex D of the December 4, 1981, **Federal Register** (46 FR 59398)):

> Dr. Zinder requested that a motion be introduced in support of the Adelberg-Zinder proposal to eliminate the Guidelines and the RAC. No motion was introduced.

I share the view of the RAC that the proposal does not merit support, at this time.

Support for the September 1981 RAC Proposal

As discussed above, the September 1981 RAC proposal (published for comment in the **Federal Register** on December 4, 1981) would have retained the Guidelines and the RAC, but would have changed the Guidelines from mandatory to voluntary, would have eliminated the requirement that each institution have an IBC, would have eliminated requirements for prior approval for certain experiments, would have eliminated the prohibitions (although two would be retained instead as admonishments), and would have lowered the containment levels of most experiments mandated at P2 or P3 to P1 recommendation.

Thirty-five commentators supported the principles of the September 1981 RAC proposal. The Chairman of one IBC which unanimously endorsed the September 1981 RAC proposal wrote:

In the Committee's view, recombinant DNA *per se* presents no hazard that is qualitatively different from the hazards associated with the pathogenicity of the hosts or vectors used. Hosts or vectors containing recombinant DNA should, therefore, be handled according to appropriate guidelines already in existence, such as the CDC guidelines for work with infectious organisms.

Another IBC Chairman, reporting the unanimous IBC endorsement of the September 1981 RAC proposal, wrote:

It is our Committee's belief that relaxation of the federal guidelines is based on careful study by RAC and ORDA and that public safety is not jeopardized.

Another IBC Chairman stated:

The adoption of these revisions proposed by the RAC will, in effect, place recombinant DNA research in the same voluntary compliance status as that research which employs any etiologic agent.

A County Health Department also endorsed the September 1981 RAC proposal. A University Vice President in reporting endorsement by the University of the RAC proposal, stated:

While we are in complete agreement that control of biological systems involving recombinant DNA should be at a level consistent with the appraised risk, we do not believe that the *de facto* regulation of recombinant DNA research, as represented by the current 'Guidelines' or by the Gottesman Proposal (FR December 7, 1981, is necessary to achieve adequate control).

A letter stated:

Based on my experience in medical microbiology and my service on the RAC, I believe that the RAC proposal described in the Federal Register is appropriate and sensible.

A foreign commentator wrote:

There seems to me to be no valid reason for mandatory regulations via guidelines of recombinant DNA research since there is no evidence that this activity is intrinsically hazardous.

Another commentator wrote:

The principle of prior review should be abandoned. It is needlessly expensive and time-consuming.

A Noble Prize winner wrote:

It makes no sense to have more stringent requirements for research that carries only vague hypothetical risks than for experiments involving known pathogenic microbes. Voluntary guidelines have worked quite well for research involving pathogens and should work equally well for microbes containing recombinant DNA * * * there is no scientific or social justification for retaining rules for recombinant DND research that inhibit creativity and waste resources.

Another Nobel Prize winner wrote:

There is widespread agreement that the risks that were once throught to be so plausible are actually remote or possible nonexistent. If that judgement is correct, and I know of no evidence to indicate otherwise, then it seems wasteful of effort and money, even counter-productive, to maintain the elaborate procedures and organizations that were set up to be guard against the hypothetical risks.

I note that the RAC carefully considered the points made in these letters; however, the RAC members were more convinced by the arguments made in support of the Gottesman proposal. I concur with this analysis.

Positions Intermediate Between the September 1981 RAC Proposal and the Gottesman Proposal

Ten letters were received supporting a position intermediate between the September 1981 RAC proposal and the Gottesman proposal.

One IBC Chairman, on behalf of his biosafety committee, wrote:

We believe the RAC proposal (Federal Register December 4, 1981) goes too far in removing certain restrictions, and that the Gottesman proposal (Federal Register December 7, 1981) is more restrictive than necessary.

The Executive Director of Industrial Biotechnology Association (IBA), writing on behalf of the Board of Directors of the IBA, commented:

We believe that the December 4 proposal by the RAC and the December 7 proposal by Dr. Susan Gottesman are each persuasive in some respects. Their best features should be combined to replace the present guidelines with a modernized version that will encourage variety and innovation to a greater extent, while retaining the confidence of both the scientific community and the general public.

The IBA proposal would combine the more stringent mandatory "Roles and Responsibilities" of the Gottesman proposal with the more lenient containment levels of the September 1981 RAC proposal. The opposite approach, combining the Gottesman proposal containment levels with the voluntary nature of the September RAC proposal, was advanced by another commentator as follows:

I have studied the two published Federal Register proposals for revising the NIH Guidelines for Research Involving Recombinant DNA and have concluded that neither proposal adequately meets the current situation * * *. As a result of this analysis I would like to propose a middle ground between the two published proposals. This takes the form of an advisory set of Guidelines based on the Gottesman proposal. In other words, the Gottesman proposal remains substantively intact, but is put in the form of recommendations or real Guidelines, rather than regulations.

A former member of the RAC wrote:

First, I enthusiastically endorse the concept of reducing both the containment requirements and the administrative review. However, as to the means of achieving the reduction, I don't find either proposal to be fully satisfactory * * *. In summary, I would like to see the regulatory aspects of the guidelines kept in place for a bare handful of experimental systems.

Another commentator wrote:

We urge the Recombinant DNA Advisory Committee to preserve those mechanisms at both the institutional and national levels which ensure continuity in judgement in determining the appropriate containment requirements when new host-vector systems are developed, or for other novel applications of this technology.

Another commentator stated:

However, while endorsing the basic tenants of the Gottesman proposal to retain some oversight of federally-supported research on recombinant DNA, some compromise between the Gottesman and Baltimore/Campbell proposals to avoid some of the unnecessary restrictions of the former would seem appropriate.

Another commentator favored RAC adoption of the Gottesman proposal now "with a *provisional* endorsement of its own proposal as an *objective* to be achieved" in the future.

I note that the RAC carefully considered the points made in these letters, but they favored supporting the December 7 proposal rather than a position intermediate between the December 7 and December 4 proposals. I concur with this analysis.

Support for the Gottesman Proposal

Thirty-two commentators favored the Gottesman proposal. One IBC Chairman reporting unanimous endorsement by the IBC stated:

The Gottesman proposal would greatly simplify the current guidelines, eliminating considerable confusion, while creating a much more usable guide for experimental scientists to follow.

Another IBC Chairman wrote:

After some discussion, the IBC reached a consensus that the current practice does not impair research activities to a significant degree * * *. The Committee therefore recommends that the Guidelines be adjusted as necessary, but not abolished completely, nor made purely voluntary.

The Chairman of the Cambridge, Massachusetts, Biohazards Committee stated:

We recognize the need to simplify the Guidelines, particularly the specification of containment levels. We do not, however, think it wise or necessary to abolish Institutional Biosafety Committees * * *. Our own perception is that the measured evolution of the Guidelines has been a model of the way new technologies can be introduced into densely populated areas with maximum safety and public reassurance.

A University Vice Chancellor wrote:

The Biosafety Committee feels strongly that whatever the federal action will be, every institution should maintain a strong review board. For reasons of consistency throughout the scientific world and across state lines and to forestall possible state legislative activities, it was agreed that mandatory controls would be preferable. In addition, the community members commented that "in an era when science is suspect in the community, evidence of institutional review is most important."

An industrial commentator wrote:

First, we would like to support the continuing evolution of the recombinant DNA guidelines as our body of knowledge concerning this technology increases * * * We believe Dr. Gottesman's proposal in general achieves these objectives, by setting reasonable standards for experiments for which sufficient information exists to do so and by assigning oversight responsibilities for certain experiments to the IBC and the NIH based on a rational assessment of potential hazard.

One member of the RAC wrote:

I believe it to be premature to do away with all mandatory aspects of the guidelines * * * The alternative proposal by Susan Gottesman constructively deals with my concerns while still doing away with much of the undesirable red tape and delays.

Another RAC member wrote:

I feel that to eliminate all mandatory aspects of the Guidelines and replace them with a voluntary code of practices is premature.

Another RAC member wrote:

I have come to the conclusion that, at least for now, we should retain the mandatory nature of the guidelines for recombinant DNA research, and the requirements for Institutional Biosafety Committees * * * My recommendation is to have a limited period of more relaxed regulations by supporting the Gottesman proposal now and immediately work to simplify the guidelines further as appropriate.

Another commentator wrote:

While decreased NIH supervision of large classes of nonhazardous experiments is certainly desirable, the RAC proposal goes rather too far, in my view, in the direction of removing controls. It would seem desirable to maintain some NIH oversight of experiments involving a degree of risk, as in Dr. Gottesman's suggested revision.

Another commentator wrote:

Part of the lesson is to avoid extremes, and that is what Dr. Gottesman's proposal tries to accomplish. I urge the RAC to adopt a final recommendation that embodies the basic philosophy expressed in her proposal.

A biological safety officer stated:

* * * some sort of organized structure for the review of recombinant DNA research activities should still be required at institutions with researchers engaged in this type of work if they are to continue to receive NIH funding.

Another commentator wrote:

I favor strongly the retention of IBC oversight and current NIH compliance requirements as advocated by Dr. Gottesman.

Another commentator wrote:

* * * it is my opinion that the RAC proposal to dismantle the Guidelines and the review process would be a major mistake. Simplification of the Guidelines might well be useful, as proposed in the Alternative Proposal.

Another commentator wrote:

The Baltimore/Campbell proposal described in the **Federal Register** would eliminate any meaningful controls of Recombinant DNA technology and would create a major hazard to the public health and safety.

A Nobel Prize winner wrote:

[I] wish now to register strong objection to the Baltimore/Campbell proposal described in the **Federal Register** of December 4, 1981, proposing that the NIH Guidelines be changed from mandatory to voluntary.

Another Nobel Prize winner wrote:

Philosophically, I am most in sympathy with the proposed guidelines in the December 4 **Federal Register**. Certainly, in hindsight, such guidelines are all that should have been present when recombinant DNA work was just beginning. However, now that we have had the history of the last years and the public concern about recombinant DNA, I question whether we can go back to essentially no regulation. I believe that we cannot and need some mechanism to protect in the future both the infant genetic engineering industry and academic work with recombinant DNA. Therefore, I support a revision like that of Dr. Gottesman described in the December 7 **Federal Register**.

As noted above in Part II–A of this announcement, the RAC at their February 8–9, 1982, meeting recommended that the Gottesman proposal be adopted. My response is given in Parts II–B and IV of this announcement.

Both the December 4 and December 7 Proposals Go Too Far

Ten commentators felt not only the December 4 proposal, but even the December 7 proposal, went too far in the direction of relaxing the Guidelines.

The Chairman to the IBC of the Harvard Medical Area, speaking for the IBC, wrote:

It is our concern that the relaxation of the NIH Guidelines would lead some local communities to regulate this activity with different standards. The impact of such an occurrence could be devastating to the scientific community and the public in the long term * * * It is our committee's opinion that a relaxation such as the ones being proposed will create many problems.

The Chairman of the IBC of the Harvard University Faculty of Arts and Sciences wrote:

Although not quite unanimous, the majority of members carried reservations concerning some of the changes being proposed. Of utmost concern was the speed with which the relaxation is being considered.

A letter on behalf of the Boston, Massachusetts, Biohazards Committee stated:

* * * we wish to indicate our strong disagreement to the three current proposals for revision of existing guidelines for RDNA research (Baltimore-Campbell, RAC, and Gottesman) which appeared in the **Federal Register** of December 4, and 7, 1981. We support the continued measured and reasonable improvement in the current guidelines, but we believe that the current proposals in their present form are not consistent with this aim.

Another commentator wrote:

I would much prefer to see the RAC carry out a full review of its policy of the last three years of progressively dismantling controls, and to decide to strengthen the guidelines * * *

Another commentator wrote:

I favor continuation of the present Guidelines with their capacity for evolution; I would accept the Gottesman revisions as the "lesser-of-two-evils" but do not endorse them.

I note that the RAC carefully considered the points made in these letters, but they were more convinced by the arguments made in support of the Gottesman proposal. I concur with this analysis.

Special Concern for Maintaining the Role of Institutional Biosafety Committees

One letter sent by the three Congressmen, all members of the Committee on Science and Technology, raised concerns about the September 1981 RAC proposal. They wrote:

It is our belief that some scientific experiments should require public review. The scientific community cannot isolate itself from the larger community that it serves and presume that an individual scientist is always capable of deciding that the degree of hazard associated with a particular experiment is acceptable to the public. Moreover, where public funds are spent, the expenditure of those funds carries with it an accountability to the public * * *. Scientists must accept (and we believe the majority do) the need to restrict certain hazardous laboratory practices to protect health and safety while realizing that these restrictions do not represent an infringement of their intellectual freedom * * *. If the Guidelines become only a voluntary code of standard practice, private firms will be more likely not to comply * * *. We would urge at the very least that the system of Institutional Biosafety Committees not be allowed to terminate.

A number of other commentators who wrote in support of the Gottesman proposal also stressed the importance of maintaining the system of IBCs. The proposal recommended by the RAC, and being promulgated today, does indeed continue to mandate the existence and functions of the IBCs. Remaining mandated in the Guidelines are Section IV-D-2, "Membership and Procedures of the IBC" and Section IV-D-3, "Functions of the IBC."

Cloning of Toxin Genes

One commentator wrote:

I see no logic for singling out toxins for special treatment in the guidelines or for dividing toxin experiments into classes dependent on LD_{50}.

The Guidelines continue to single out experiments involving the cloning of toxin genes for special treatment, and to divide such experiments into classes dependent on LD_{50}. This is done in Section III-A-1 and Appendix F of the Guidelines promulgated today. (This text is essentially identical to what was previously Section I-D-2 and Appendix G of the July 1, 1981, version of the Guidelines (46 FR 34462).) The development of these sections of the Guidelines is described in detail in the July 1, 1981. "Decision Document" (46 FR 34455). It involved the deliberation of an expert Ad Hoc Working Group on Toxins, and extensive discussion at the RAC meeting of April 23-24, 1981, prior to their acceptance by NIH Director Donald Frederickson. I believe that these provisions should continue in the current Guidelines.

Title of Section III-B-2

One commentator suggested that the title of Section III-B-2 "should be expanded to include Class 4 and Class 5 agents since these two categories are discussed under this section in subpart III.B.2.b."

This suggestion has been taken. The proposed title as it appeared in the December 7, 1981, **Federal Register** was "III-B-2. *Experiments in Which DNA from CDC Class 2 or Class 3 Agents is Cloned in Nonpathogenic Prokaryotic or Lower Eukaryotic Host-Vector Systems.*" This has been changed in the Guidelines promulgated today to also include Class 4 and Class 5 agents.

Incorrect Citation of and Conclusion from Publication

Two commentators cited a publication by Drs. Portnoy and Falkow as follows:

Unexpected surprises still do arise as was seen by * * * the converting of *E. coli* K-12 into a pathogen through the cloning of a hemolysin determinant from the wild type strain (Portnoy & Falkow, 1981, *J. Bacteriol.* *148*:877)."

* * * it has been shown that K-12 can become significantly pathogenic under certain conditions. For example, a recent report by Portnoy and Falkow (*J. Bacteriol* *148*:877, 1981) describes the acquisition of mouse lethality by K-12 as a consequence of receiving a cloned hemolysin determinant from a wild strain of *E. coli*.

Looking up the paper cited, I find the article by Portnoy and Falkow is the *Journal of Bacteriology 148*, 877-883, 1981, to be entitled "Virulence-Associated Plasmids from *Yersinia enterocolitica* and *Yersinia pestis.*" There are no experiments described in this paper which involve *E. coli* K-12, or the cloning of a hemolysin determinant. There is another paper by Dr. Stanley Falkow which does deal with the cloned hemolysin determinant in *E. coli*. This is "Haemolysin Contributes To Virulence of Extra-intestinal *E. coli* Infections" by R. A. Welch, E. P. Dellinger, B. Minshew and S. Falkow, *Nature*, 294, 665-667, 1981. Data in that paper indicate that while virulence of "wild type" *E. coli* was enhanced considerably by introduction of a DNA sequence coding for hemolysin, only a slight increase in virulence was seen when *E. coli* K-12 was used. Thus, the commentators are incorrect in citing the work as showing "The converting of *E. coli* K-12 into a pathogen through the cloning of a hemolysin determinant."

IV. Summary of Guideline Changes

Immediately following this announcement there appears in a separate section of the **Federal Register** the revised NIH Guidelines for Research Involving Recombinant DNA Molecules, which are effective today. They were derived as follows:

1. The last previous complete version of the NIH Guidelines was published in the **Federal Register** on July 1, 1981 (46 FR 34462).

2. Changes were made in the Guidelines as recommended by the RAC at its September 1981 meeting and promulgated by NIH in the **Federal Register** on October 30, 1981 (46 FR 53980).

Note.—a version of the Guidelines incorporating the October 30, 1981, changes into the July 1, 1981, Guidelines appeared as "Annex E" in the **Federal Register** of December 4, 1981 (46 FR 59398).

3. Changes were made in the Guidelines as recommended in certain actions by the RAC at its February 1982 meeting and promulgated by NIH in the **Federal Register** on March 29, 1982 (47 FR 13308).

4. As noted above in Parts II-A and II-B of this announcement, the RAC recommended, and NIH is accepting today, additional changes as stipulated in the "Gottesman" proposal which had been issued for public comment in the **Federal Register** on December 7, 1981 (46 FR 59734).

5. As noted above in Part III of this announcement, the title of Section III-B-2 is being changed, in response to a written comment received.

6. The "Gottesman" proposal requires that "changes as necessary to reflect changes in Parts I-III" of the Guidelines be made in Parts IV and V of the Guidelines. This has been done.

7. Other changes have been made. For example, in Section III-B-3 of the Guidelines, and its subsections, the term "whole" animal or plant virus has been changed to "infectius" animal or plant virus to reflect more accurately the intent of this section. Section III-C has been reorganized and edited in order to clarify the intent of this section.

Dated: April 12, 1982.

Bernard Tablot,

Acting Director, National Institute of Allergy and Infectious Diseases, National Institutes of Health.

Note.—OMB's "Mandatory Information Requirements for Federal Assistance Program Announcements" (45 FR 39592) requires a statement concerning the official government programs contained in the *Catalog of Federal Domestic Assistance*. Normally NIH lists in its announcements the number and title of affected individual programs for the guidance of the public. Because the guidance in this notice covers not only virtually every NIH program but also essentially every federal research program in which DNA recombinant molecule techniques could be used, it has been determined to be not cost effective or in the public interest to attempt to list these programs. Such a list would likely require several additional pages. In addition, NIH could not be certain that every federal program would be included as many federal agencies, as well as private organizations, both national and international, have elected to follow the NIH Guidelines. In lieu of the individual program listing, NIH invites readers to direct questions to the information address above about whether individual programs listed in the *Catalog of Federal Domestic Assistance* are affected.

NIH programs are not covered by OMB Circular A-95 because they fit the description of "programs not considered appropriate" in Section 8-(b)-(4) and (5) of the Circular.

[FR Doc. 82-10859 Filed 4-20-82; 8:45 am]

BILLING CODE 4140-01-M

federal register

Wednesday
April 21, 1982

Part III

Department of Health and Huma Services

Guidelines for Research Involving Recombinant DNA Molecules

DEPARTMENT OF HEALTH AND HUMAN SERVICES

Guidelines for Research Involving Recombinant DNA Molecules; April 1982

Table of Contents

I. Scope of the Guidelines

I-A. *Purpose.* The purpose of these Guidelines is to specify practices for constructing and handling (i) recombinant DNA molecules and (ii) organisms and viruses containing recombinant DNA molecules.

I-B. *Definition of Recombinant DNA Molecules.* In the context of these Guidelines, recombinant DNA molecules are defined as either (i) molecules which are constructed outside living cells by joining natural or synthetic DNA segments to DNA molecules that can replicate in a living cell, or (ii) DNA molecules that result from the replication of those described in (i) above.

Synthetic DNA segments likely to yield a potentially harmful polynucleotide or polypeptide (e.g., a toxin or a pharmacologically active agent) shall be considered as equivalent to their natural DNA counterpart. If the synthetic DNA segment is not expressed *in vivo* as a biologically active polynucleotide or polypeptide product, it is exempt from the Guidelines.

I-C. *General Applicability.* See Section IV-B.

I-D *General Definitions.* See Section IV-C.

II. Containment

Effective biological safety programs have been operative in a variety of laboratories for many years. Considerable information, therefore, already exists for the design of physical containment facilities and the selection of laboratory procedures applicable to organisms carrying recombinant DNAs [6–19]. The existing programs rely upon mechanisms that, for convenience, can be divided into two categories: (i) A set of standard practices that are generally used in microbiological laboratories, and (ii) special procedures, equipment, and laboratory installations that provide physical barriers which are applied in varying degrees according to the estimated biohazard.

Experiments on recombinant DNAs, by their very nature, lend themselves to a third containment mechanism—namely, the application of highly specific biological barriers. In fact, natural barriers do exist which limit either (i) the infectivity of a *vector,* or *vehicle,* (plasmid or virus) for specific hosts or (ii) its dissemination and survival in the environment. The vectors that provide the means for replication of the recombinant DNAs and/or the host cells in which they replicate can be genetically designed to decrease by many orders of magnitude the probability of dissemination of recombinant DNAs outside the laboratory.

As these three means of containment are complementary, different levels of containment appropriate for experiments with different recombinants can be established by applying various combinations of the physical and biological barriers along with a constant use of the standard practices. We consider these categories of containment separately here in order that such combinations can be conveniently expressed in the Guidelines.

In constructing these Guidelines, it was necessary to define boundary conditions for the different levels of physical and biological containment and for the classes of experiments to which they apply. We recognize that these definitions do not take into acount all existing and anticipated information on special procedures that will allow particular experiments to be carried out under different conditions than indicated here without affecting risk. Indeed, we urge that individual investigators devise simple and more effective containment procedures and that investigators and institutional biosafety committees recommend changes in the Guidelines to permit their use.

II-A. *Standard Practices and Training.* The first principle of containment is a strict adherence to good microbiological practices [6-15]. Consequently, all personnel directly or indirectly involved in experiments on recombinant DNAs must receive adequate instruction. (See Sections IV-D-1-e and IV-D-5-d.) This shall, as a minimum, include instructions in aseptic techniques and in the biology of the organisms used in the experiments, so that the potential biohazards can be understood and appreciated.

Any research group working with agents with a known or potential biohazard shall have an emergency plan which describes the procedures to be followed if an accident contaminates personnel or the environment. The principal investigator must ensure that everyone in the laboratory is familiar with both the potential hazards of the work and the emergency plan. (See Sections IV-D-3-d and IV-D-5-e.) If a research group is working with a known pathogen where there is an effective vaccine it should be made available to all workers. Where serological monitoring is clearly appropriate it shall be provided. (See Section IV-D-1-f.)

II-B. *Physical Containment Levels.* The objective of physical containment is to confine organisms containing recombinant DNA molecules, and thus to reduce the potential for exposure of the laboratory worker, persons outside of the laboratory, and the environment to organisms containing recombinant DNA molecules. Physical containment is achieved through the use of laboratory practices, containment equipment, and special laboratory design. Emphasis is placed on primary means of physical containment which are provided by laboratory practices and containment equipment. Special laboratory design provides a secondary means of protection against the accidental release of organisms outside the laboratory or to the environment. Special laboratory design is used primarily in facilities in which experiments of moderate to high potential hazards are performed.

Combinations of laboratory practices, containment equipment, and special laboratory design can be made to achieve different levels of physical containment. Four levels of physical containment, which are designated as P1, P2, P3, and P4, are described. It should be emphasized that the descriptions and assignments of physical containment detailed below are based on existing approaches to containment of pathogenic organisms. For example, the "Classification of Etiologic Agents on the Basis of Hazard," [7] prepared by the Centers for Disease Control, describes four general levels which roughly correspond to our descriptions for P1, P2, P3, and P4; and the National Cancer Institute describes three levels for research on oncogenic viruses which roughly correspond to our P2, P3, and P4 levels. [8]

It is recognized that several different combinations of laboratory practices, containment equipment, and special laboratory design may be appropriate for containment of specific research activities. The Guidelines, therefore, allow alternative selections of primary containment equipment within facilities that have been designed to provide P3 and P4 levels of physical containment. The selection of alternative methods of primary containment is dependent, however, on the level of biological containment provided by the host-vector system used in the experiment. Consideration will also be given by the Director, NIH, with the advice of the Recombinant DNA Advisory Committee to other combinations which achieve an equivalent level of containment. (See Section IV-E-1-b-(2)-(b).)

II-D-1. *Pl Level.*

II-B-1-a. *Laboratory Practices.*

II-B-1-a-(1). Laboratory doors shall be kept closed while experiments are in progress.

II-B-1-a-(2). Work surfaces shall be decontaminated daily, and immediately following spills of organisms containing recombinant DNA molecules.

II-B-1-a-(3). All biological wastes shall be decontaminated before disposal. Other contaminated materials, such as glassware, animal cages, and laboratory equipment, shall be decontaminated before washing, reuse, or disposal.

II-B-1-a-(4). Mechanical pipetting devices be used; pipetting by mouth is prohibited.

II-B-1-a-(5). Eating, drinking, smoking, and storage of foods are not permitted in the laboratory area in which recombinant DNA materials are handled.

II-B-1-a-(6). Persons shall wash their hands after handling organisms containing recombinant DNA molecules and when they leave the laboratory.

II-B-1-a-(7). Care shall be taken in the conduct of all procedures to minimize the creation of aerosols.

II-B-1-a-(8). Contaminated materials that are to be decontaminated at a site away from the laboratory shall be placed in a durable leak-proof container, which is closed before removal from the laboratory.

II-B-1-a-(9). An insect and rodent control program shall be instituted.

II-B-1-a-(10). The use of laboratory gowns, coats, or uniforms is discretionary with the laboratory supervisor.

II-B-1-a-(11). Use of the hypodermic needle and syringe shall be avoided when alternative methods are available.

II-B-1-a-(12). The laboratory shall be kept neat and clean.

II-B-1-b. *Containment Equipment.* Special containment equipment is not required at the P1 level.

II-B-1-c. *Special Laboratory Design.* Special laboratory design is not required at the P1 level.

II-B-2. *P2 Level.*

II-B-2-a. *Laboratory Practices.*

II-B-2-a-(1). Laboratory doors shall be kept closed while experiments are in progress.

II-B-2-a-(2). Work surfaces shall be decontaminated daily, and immediately following spills of organisms containing recombinant DNA molecules.

II-B-2-a-(3). All laboratory wastes shall be steam-sterilized (autoclaved) before disposal. Other contaminated materials such as glassware, animal cages, laboratory equipment, and radioactive wastes shall be decontaminated by a means demonstrated to be effective before washing, reuse, or disposal.

II-B-2-a-(4). Mechanical pipetting devices shall be used; pipetting by mouth is prohibited.

II-B-2-a-(5). Eating, drinking, smoking, and storage of food are not permitted in the laboratory area in which recombinant DNA materials are handled.

II-B-2-a-(6). Persons shall wash their hands after handling organisms containing recombinant DNA molecules and when they leave the laboratory.

II-B-2-a-(7) Care shall be exercised to minimize the creation of aerosols. For example, manipulations such as inserting a hot inoculation loop or needle into a culture, flaming an inoculating loop or needle so that it splatters, and forceful ejection of fluids from pipettes or syringes shall be avoided.

II-B-2-a-(8). Contaminated materials that are to be steam sterilized (autoclaved) or decontaminated at a site away from the laboratory shall be placed in a durable leak-proof container, which is closed before removal from the laboratory.

II-B-2-a-(9). Only persons who have been advised of the nature of the research being conducted shall enter the laboratory.

II-B-2-a-(10). The universal biohazard sign shall be posted on all laboratory access doors when experiments requiring P2 containment are in process. Freezers and refrigerators or other units used to store organisms containing recombinant DNA molecules shall also be posted with the universal biohazard sign.

II-B-2-a-(11). An insect and rodent control programs shall be instituted.

II-B-2-a-(12). The use of laboratory gowns, coats, or uniforms is required. Laboratory clothing shall not be worn to the lunch room or outside of the building in which the laboratory is located.

II-B-2-a-(13). Animals not related to the experiment shall not be permitted in the laboratory.

II-B-2-a-(14). Use of the hypodermic needle and syringe shall be avoided when alternative methods are available.

II-B-2-a-(15). The laboratory shall be kept neat and clean.

II-B-2-a-(16). Experiments of lesser biohazard potential can be carried out concurrently in carefully demarcated areas of the same laboratory.

II-B-2-b. *Containment Equipment.* Biological safety cabinets [20] shall be used to contain aerosol-producing equipment, such as blender, lyophilizers, sonicators, and centrifuges, when used to process organisms containing recombinant DNA molecules, except where equipment design provides for containment of the potential aerosol. For example, a centrifuge may be operated in the open if a sealed head or safety centrifuge cups are used.

II-B-2-c. *Special Laboratory Design.* An autoclave for sterilization of wastes and contaminated materials shall be available in the same building in which organisms containing recombinant DNA molecules are used.

II-B-3. *P3 Level.*

II-B-3-a. *Laboratory Practices.*

II-B-3-a-(1). Laboratory doors shall be kept closed while experiments are in progress.

II-B-3-a-(2). Work surfaces shall be decontaminated following the completion of the experimental activity, and immediately following spills of organisms containing recombinant DNA molecules.

II-B-3-a-(3). All laboratory wastes be steam-sterilized (autoclaved) before disposal. Other contaminated materials, such as glassware, animal cages, laboratory equipment, and radioactive wastes, shall be decontaminated by a method demonstrated to be effective before washing, reuse, or disposal.

II-B-3-a-(4). Mechanical pipetting devices shall be used; pipetting by mouth is prohibited.

II-B-3-a-(5). Eating, drinking, smoking, and storage of food are not permitted in the laboratory area in which recombinant DNA materials are handled.

II-B-3-a-(6). Persons shall wash their hands after handling organisms containing recombinant DNA molecules and when they leave the laboratory.

II-B-3-a-(7). Care shall be exercised to minimize the creation of aerosols. For example, manipulations such as inserting a hot inoculating loop or needle into a culture, flaming an inoculation loop or needle so that it splatters, and forceful ejection of fluids from pipettes or syringes shall be avoided.

II-B-3-a-(8). Contaminated materials that are to be steam-sterilized (autoclaved) or decontaminated at a site away from the laboratory shall be placed in a durable leak-proof container, which is closed before removal from the laboratory.

II-B-3-a-(9). Entry into laboratory shall be through a controlled access area. Only persons who have been advised of the nature of the research being conducted shall enter the controlled access area. Only persons required on the basis of program or support needs shall be authorized to enter the laboratory. Such persons shall be advised of the nature of the research being conducted before entry, and shall comply with all required entry and exit procedures.

II-B-3-a-(10). Persons under 16 years of age shall not enter the laboratory.

II-B-3-a-(11). The universal biohazard sign shall be posted on the controlled access area door and on all labortory doors when experiments requiring P3-level containment are in progress. Freezers and refrigerators or other units used to store organisms containing recombinant DNA molecules shall also be posted with the universal biohazard sign.

II-B-3-a-(12). An insect and rodent control program shall be instituted.

II-B-3-a-(13). Laboratory clothing that protects street clothing (e.g., long-sleeve solid-front or wrap-around gowns, no-button or slipover jackets) shall be worn in the laboratory. Front-button laboratory coats are unsuitable. Laboratory clothing shall not be worn outside the laboratory and shall be decontaminated before it is sent to the laundry.

II-B-3-a-(14). Raincoats, overcoats, topcoats, coats, hats, caps, and such street outer-wear shall not be kept in the laboratory.

II-B-3-a-(15). Gloves shall be worn when handling materials requiring P3 containment. They shall be removed aseptically immediately after the handling procedure and decontaminated.

II-B-3-a-(16). Animals and plants are not related to the experiment shall not be permitted in the laboratory.

II-B-3-a-(17). Vacuum outlets shall be protected by filter and liquid disinfectant traps.

II-B-3-a-(18). Use of hypodermic needle and syringe shall be avoided when alternative methods are available.

II-B-3-a-(19). The laboratory shall be kept neat and clean.

II-B-3-a-(20). If experiments involving other organisms which require lower levels of containment are to be conducted in the same laboratory concurrently with experiments requiring P3-level physical containment, they shall be conducted in accordance with all P3-level laboratory practices.

II-B-3-b. *Containment Equipment.*

II-B-3-b-(1). Biological safety cabinets [20] shall be used for all equipment and manipulations that produce aerosols—e.g., pipetting, dilutions, transfer operations, plating, flaming, grinding, blending, drying sonicating, shaking, centrifuging—where these procedures involve organisms containing recombinant DNA molecules, except where equipment design provides for containment of the potential aerosol.

II-B-3-b-(2). Laboratory animals held in a P3 area shall be housed in partial-containment caging systems, such as Horsfall units [19A], open cages placed in ventilated enclosures, solid-wall and -bottom cages covered by filter bonnets, or solid-wall and -bottom cages placed on holding racks equipped with ultraviolet radiation lamps and reflectors.

(Note.—Conventional caging systems may be used, provided that all personnel wear appropriate personal protective devices. These shall include, at a minimum, wrap-around gowns, head covers, gloves, shoe covers, and respirators. All personnel shall shower on exit from areas where these devices are required.)

II-B-3-b-(3). *Alternative Selection of Containment Equipment.* Experimental procedures involving a host-vector system that provides a one-step higher level of biological containment than that specified can be conducted in the P3 laboratory using containment equipment specified for the P2 level of physical containment. Experimental procedures involving a host-vector system that provides a one-step lower level of bilogical containment than that specified can be conducted in the P3 laboratory using containment equipment specified for the P4 level of physical containment. Alternative combinations of containment safeguards are shown in Table I.

TABLE I—COMBINATIONS OF CONTAINMENT SAFEGUARDS

Classification of experiment		Alternative combinations of physical and biological containment			
		Physical Containment			
Physical containment	Biological [1] containment	Laboratory design specified for—	Laboratory practices specified for—	Containment equipment specified for—	Biological containment
P3	HV2	P3	P3	P3	HV2.
P3	HV2	P3	P3	P4	HV1.
P3	HV1	P3	P3	P3	HV1.
P3	HV1	P3	P3	P2	HV2.

[1] See section II-D for description of biological containment.

II-B-3-c. *Special Laboratory Design.*

II-B-3-c-(1). The laboratory shall be separated by a controlled access area from areas that are open to unrestricted traffic flow. A controlled access area is an anteroom, a change room, an air lock or any other double-door arrangement that separates the laboratory from areas open to unrestricted traffic flow.

II-B-3-c-(2). The surfaces of walls, floors, and ceilings shall be readibly cleanible. Penetrations through these surfaces shall be sealed or capable of being sealed to facilitate space decontamination.

II-B-3-c-(3). A foot-, elbow-, or automatically-operated hand-washing facility shall be provided near each primary laboratory exit area.

II-B-3-c-(4). Windows in the laboratory shall be sealed.

II-B-3-c-(5). An autoclave for sterilization of wastes and contaminated materials shall be available in the same building (and preferably within the controlled laboratory area) in which organisms containing recombitant DNA molecules are used.

II-B-3-c-(6). The laboratory shall have a ventilation system that is capable of controlling air movement. The movement of air shall be from areas of lower contamination potential to areas of higher contamination potential (i.e., from the controlled access area to the laboratory area). If the ventilation system provides positive pressure supply air, the system shall operate in a manner that prevents the reversal of the direction of air movement or shall be equipped with an alarm that would be actuated in the event that reversal in the direction of air movement were to occur. The exhaust air from the laboratory area shall not be recirculated to other areas of the building unless the exhaust air is filtered by HEPA filters or equivalent. The exhaust air from the laboratory area can be discharged to the outdoors without filtration or other means for effectively reducing an accidental aerosol burden provided that I can be dispersed clear of occupied buildings and air intakes.

II-B-3-c-(7). The treated exhaust-air from Class I and Class II biological safety cabinets [20] may be discharged either to the laboratory or to the outdoors. The treated exhaust-air from a Class III cabinet shall be discharged directly to the outdoors. If the treated exhaust-air from these cabinets is to be discharged to the outdoors through a building exhaust air system, it shall be connected to this system so as to avoid any interference with the air balance of the cabinet and the building ventilation system.

II-B-4-4. *P4 Level.*

II-B-4-a. *Laboratory Practices.*

II-B-4-a-(1). Laboratory doors shall be kept closed while experiments are in progress.

II-B-4-a-(2). Work surfaces shall be decontaminated following the completion of the experimental activity and immediately following spills of organisms containing recombinant DNA molecules.

II-B-4-a-(3). All laboratory wastes shall be steam-sterilized (autoclaved) before disposal. Other contaminated materials such as glassware, animal cages, laboratory equipment, and radioactive wastes shall be decontaminated by a method demonstrated to be effective before washing, reuse, or disposal.

II-B-4-a-(4). Mechanical pipetting devices shall be used; pipetting by mouth is prohibited.

II-B-4-a-(5). Eating, drinking, smoking, and storage of food are not permitted in the P4 facility.

II-B-4-a-(6). Persons shall wash their hands after handling organisms containing recombinant DNA molecules and when they leave the laboratory.

II-B-4-a-(7). Care shall be exercised to minimize the creation of aerosals. For example, manipulations such as inserting a hot inoculating loop or needle into a culture, flaming an inoculation loop or needle so that it splatters, and forceful ejection of fluids from pipettes or syringes shall be avoided.

II-B-4-a-(8). Biological materials to be removed from the P4 facility in a viable or intact state shall be transferred to a nonbreakable sealed container, which is then removed from the P4 facility through a pass-through disinfectant dunk tank or fumigation chamber.

II-B-4-a-(9). No materials, except for biological materials that are to remain in a viable or intact state, shall be steam sterilized in the double-door autoclave of the P4 facility. Other materials which may be damaged by temperature or steam shall be removed from the P4 facility unless they have been steam-sterilized (autoclaved) or decontaminated by a means demonstrated to be effectve as they pass out of the P4 facility. All wastes and other materials as well as equipment not damaged by high temperature or steam shall be removed from the P4 facility through a pass-through fumigation chamber.

II-B-4-a-(10). Materials within the Class III cabinets shall be removed from the cabinet system only after being steam-sterilized in an attached double-door autoclave or after being contained in a nonbreakable sealed container, which is then passed through a disinfectant dunk tank or a fumigation chamber.

II-B-4-a-(11). Only persons whose entry into the P4 facility is required to meet program of support needs shall be authorized to enter. Before entering, such persons shall be advised of the nature of the research being conducted and shall be instructed as to the appropriate safeguards to ensure their safety. They shall comply with instructions and all other required procedures.

II-B-4-a-(12). Persons under 18 years of age shall not enter the P4 facility.

II-B-4-a-(13). Personnel shall enter into and exit from the P4 facility only through the clothing and shower rooms. Personnel shall shower at each egress from the P4 facility. Air locks shall not be used for personnel entry or exit except for emergencies.

II-B-4-a-(14). Street clothing shall be removed in the outer side of the clothing-change area and kept there. Complete laboratory clothing, including undergarments, head cover, shoes, and either pants and shirts or jumpsuits, shall be used by all persons who enter the P4 facility. Upon exit, personnel shall store this clothing in lockers provided for this purpose or discard it into collection hampers before entering the shower area.

II-B-4-a-(15). The universal biohazard sign is required on the P4 facility access doors and on all interior doors to individual laboratory rooms where experiments are conducted. The sign shall also be posted on freezers, refrigerators, or other units used to store organisms containing recombinant DNA molecules.

II-B-4-a-(16). An insect and rodent control program shall be instituted.

II-B-4-a-(17). Animals and plants not related to the experiment shall not be permitted in the laboratory in which the experiment is being conducted.

II-B-4-a-(18). Vacuum outlets shall be protected by filter and liquid disinfectant traps.

II-B-4-a-(19). Use of the hypodermic needle and syringe shall be avoided when alternate methods are available.

II-B-4-a-(20). The laboratory shall be kept neat and clean.

II-B-4-a-(21). If experiments involving other organisms which require lower levels of containment are to be conducted in the P4 facility concurrently with experiments requiring P4-level containment, they shall be conducted in accordance with all P4-level laboratory practices specified in this section.

II-B-4-b. *Containment Equipment.*

II-B-4-b-(1). Experimental procedures involving organisms that require P4-level physical containment shall be conducted either in (i) a Class III cabinet system or in (ii) Class I or Class II cabinets that are located in a specially designed area in which all personnel are required to wear one-piece positive-pressure isolation suits.

II-B-4-b-(2). Laboratory animals involved in experiments requiring P4-level physical containment shall be housed either in cages contained in Class III cabinets or in partial containment caging systems (such as Horsfall units[19A], open cages placed in ventilated enclosures, or solid-wall and -bottom cages covered by filter bonnets, or solid-wall and -bottom cages placed on holding racks equipped with ultraviolet irradiation lamps and reflectors) that are located in a specially designed area in which all personnel are required to wear one-piece positive-pressure suits.

II-B-4-b-(3). *Alternative Selection of Containment Equipment.*

Experimental procedures involving a host-vector system that provides a one-step higher level of biological containment than that specified can be conducted in the P4 facility using containment equipment requirements specified for the P3 level of physical containment. Alternative combinations of containment safeguards are shown in Table II.

TABLE II—COMBINATIONS OF CONTAINMENT SAFEGUARDS

Classification of experiment		Alternate combinations of physical and biological containment			
		Physical containment			
Physical containment	Biological[1] containment	Laboratory design specified for—	Laboratory practices specified for—	Containment equipment specified for—	Biological containment
P4	HV1	P4	P4	P4	HV1.
P4	HV1	P4	P4[2]	HV2	
			3		

[1] See section II-D for description of biological containment.
[2] In this case gloves shall be worn, in addition to the clothing requirements specified in II-B-4-a-(14).

II-B-4-c. *Special Laboratory Design.*

II-B-4-c-(1). The laboratory shall be located in a restricted-access facility which is either a separate building or a clearly demarcated and isolated zone within a building. Clothing-change areas and shower rooms shall be provided for personnel entry and egress. These rooms shall be arranged so that personnel leave through the shower area to the change room. A double-door ventilated vestibule or ultraviolet air lock shall be provided for passage of materials, supplies, and equipment which are not brought into the P4 facility through the change room area.

II-B-4-c-(2). Walls, floors, and ceilings of the P4 facility are constructed to form an internal shell which readily allows vapor-phase decontamination and is animal- and insect-proof. All penetrations through these structures and surfaces are sealed. (The integrity of the walls, floors, ceilings, and penetration seals should ensure adequate containment of a vapor-phase decontaminant under static pressure conditions. This requirement does not imply that these surfaces must be airtight.)

II-B-4-c-(3). A foot-, elbow-, or automatically-operated handwashing facility shall be provided near the door within each laboratory in which experiments involving recombinant DNA are conducted in openface biological safety cabinets.

II-B-4-c-(4). Central vacuum systems are permitted. The system, if provided, shall not serve areas outside the P4 facility. The vacuum system shall include in-line HEPA filters near each use point or service cock. The filters shall be installed so as to permit in-place decontamination and replacement. Water supply, liquid and gaseous services provided to the P4 facility shall be protected by devices that prevent backflow.

II-B-4-c-(5). Drinking water fountains shall not be installed in labortory or animal rooms of the P4 facility. Foot-operated water fountains are permitted in the corridors of the P4 facility. The water service provided to such fountains shall be protected from the water services to the laboratory areas of the P4 facility.

II-B-4-c-(6). Laboratory doors shall be self-closing.

II-B-4-c-(7). A double-door autoclave shall be provided for sterilization of material passing out of the P4 facility. The autoclave doors shall be interlocked so that both doors will not be open at the same time.

II-B-4-c-(8). A pass-through dunk tank or fumigation chamber shall be provided for removal from the P4 facility of materials and equipment that cannot be heat-sterilized.

II-B-4-c-(9). All liquid effluents from the P4 facility shall be collected and decontaminated before disposal. Liquid effluents from biological safety cabinets and laboratory sinks shall be sterilized by heat. Liquid effluents from the shower and hand washing facilities may be activited by chemical treatment. HEPA filters shall be installed in all vents from effluent drains.

II-B-4-c-(10). An individual supply and exhaust-air ventiliation system shall be provided. The system shall maintain pressure differentials and directional air flow as required to ensure inflow from areas outside the facility toward areas of highest potential risk within the facility. The system shall be designed to prevent the reversal of air flow. The system shall sound an alarm in the event of system malfunction.

II-B-4-c-(11). Air within individual laboratories of the P4 facility may be recirculated if HEPA filtered.

II-B-4-c-(12). The exhaust air from the P4 facility shall be HEPA filtered and discharged to the outdoors so that it is dispersed clear of occupied buildings and air intakes. The filter chambers shall be designed to allow *in situ* decontamination before removal and to facilitate certification testing after replacement.

II-B-4-c-(13). The treated exhaust-air from Class I and Class II biological safety cabinets[20] may be discharged directly to the labaratory room environment or to the outdoors. The treated exhaust-air from Class III cabinets shall be discharged to the outdoors. If the treated exhaust-air from these cabinets is to be discharged to the outdoors through the P4 facility exhaust air system, it shall be connected to this system so as to avoid any interference with the air balance of the cabinets or the facility exhaust air system.

II-B-4-c-(14). As noted in Section II-B-4-b-(1), the P4 facility may contain specially designed areas in which all personnel are required to wear one-piece positive-pressure isolation suits. Such areas shall be airtight. The exhaust-air from the suit area shall be filtered by two sets of HEPA filters installed in series, and a duplicate filtration unit and exhaust fan shall be provided. The air pressure within the suit area shall be less than that in any adjacent area. An emergency lighting system, communication systems, and power source shall be provided. A double-door autoclave shall be provided for sterilization of all waste materials to be removed from the suit area.

Personnel who enter this area shall wear a one-piece positive-pressure suit that is ventilated by a life-support system. The life-support system shall be provided with alarms and emergency backup air. Entry to this area is through an airlock fitted with airtight doors. A chemical shower area shall be provided to decontaminate the surfaces of the suite before removal.

II-C. *Shipment.* Recombinant DNA molecules contained in an organism or virus shall be shipped only as an etiologic agent under requirements of the U.S. Public Health Service, and the U.S. Department of Transportation (Section 72.3, Part 72, Title 42, and Sections 173.386-.388, Part 173, Title 49 U.S. Code of Federal Regulations (CFR)) as specified below:

II-C-1. Recombinant DNA molecules contained in an organism or virus reguiring Pl, P2, or P3 physical containment, when offered for transportation or transported, are subject to all requirements of Section 72.3(a)-(e), Part 72, Title 42 CFR, and Sections 173.386-.388, Part 173, Title 49 CFR.

II-C-2. Recombinant DNA molecules contained in an organism or virus requiring P4 physical containment, when offered for transportation or transported, are subject to the requirements listed above under II-C-1 and are also subject to Section 72.3(f), Part 72, Title 42 CFR.

II-C-3. Additional information on packaging and shipment is given in the "Laboratory Safety Monograph—A Supplement to the NIH Guidelines for Recombinant DNA Research."

II-D. *Biological Containment.*

II-D-1. *Levels of Biological Containment.* In consideration of biological containment, the vector (plasmid, organelle, or virus) for the recombinant DNA and the host (bacterial, plant, or animal cell) in which the vector is propagated in the laboratory will be considered together. Any combination of vector and host which is to provide biological containment must be chosen or constructed so that the following types of "escape" are minimized: (i) Survival of the vector in its host outside the laboratory and (ii) transmission of the vector from the propagation host to other nonlaboratory hosts.

The following levels of biological containment (HV, or *Host-Vector,* systems) for prokaryotes will be established; specific criteria will depend on the organisms to be used.

II-D-1-a. *HV1.* A host-vector system which provides a moderate level of containment. *Specific systems:*

II-D-1-a-(1). *EK1.* The host is always *E. coli* K-12 or a derivative thereof, and the vectors include nonconjugative plasmids (e.g., pSC101, ColEl, or derivatives thereof [21-27]) and variants of bacteriophage, such as lambda [28-33]. The *E. coli* K-12 hosts shall not contain conjugation-proficient plasmids, whether antonamous or integrated, or generalized transducing phages.

II-D-1-a-(2). *Other Prokaryotes.* Hosts and vectors shall be, at a minimum, comparable in containment to *E. coli* K-12 with a non conjugative plasmid or bacteriophage vector. The data to be considered and a mechanism for approval of such HV1 systems are described below (Section II-D-2).

II-D-1-b. *HV2.* These are host-vector systems shown to provide a high level of biological containment as demonstrated by data from suitable tests performed in the laboratory. Escape of the recombinant DNA either via survival of the organisms or via transmission of recombinant DNA to other organisms should be less than $1/10^8$ under specified conditions. *Specific systems:*

II-D-1-b-(1). For EK2 host-vector systems in which the vector is a plasmid, no more than one in 10^8 host cells should be able to perpetuate a cloned DNA fragment under the specified nonpermissive laboratory conditions designed to represent the natural environment, either by survival of the original host or as a consequence of transmission of the coloned DNA fragment.

II-D-1-b-(2). For EK2 host-vector systems in which the vector is a phage, no more than one in 10^8 phage particles should be able to perpetuate a cloned DNA fragment under the specified nonpermissive laboratory conditions designed to represent the natural environment either (i) as a prophage (in the inserted or plasmid form) in the laboratory host used for phage propagation or (ii) by surviving in natural environments and transferring a cloned DNA fragment to other hosts (or their resident prophages).

II-D-2. *Certification of Host-Vector Systems.*

II-D-2-a. *Responsibility.* HV1 systems other than *E. coli* K-12, and HV2 host-vector systems, may not be designated as such until they have been certified by the Director, NIH. Application for certification of a host-vector system is made by written application to the Office of Recombinant DNA Activities, National Institutes of Health, Bethesda, Maryland 20205.

Host-vector systems that are proposed for certification will be reviewed by the National Institutes of Health (NIH) Recombinant DNA Advisory Committee (RAC). (See Section IV-E-1-b-(1)-(c).) This will first involve review of the data on construction, properties, and testing of the proposed host-vector system by a Working Group composed of one or more members of the RAC and other persons chosen because of their expertise in evaluating such data. The Committee will then evaluate the report of the Working Group and any other available information at a regular meeting. The Director, NIH, is responsible for certification after receiving the advice of the RAC. Minor modifications of existing certified host-vector systems, where the modifications are of minimal or no consequence to the properties relevant to containment may be certified by the Director, NIH, without review by RAC. (See Section IV-E-1-b-(3)-(c).)

When new host-vector systems are certified, notice of the certification will be sent by the Office of Recombinant DNA Activities (ORDA) to the applicant and to all Institutional Biosafety Committees (IBCs) and will be published in the *Recombinant DNA Technical Bulletin.* Copies of a list of all currently certified host-vector systems may be obtained from ORDA at any time.

The Director, NIH, may at any time rescind the certification of any host-vector system. (See Section IV-E-1-b-

(3)–(d).) If certification of a host-vector system is rescinded, NIH will instruct investigators to transfer cloned DNA into a different system, or use the clones at a higher physical containment level unless NIH determines that the already constructed clones incorporate adequate biological containment.

Certification of a given system does not extend to modifications of either the host or vector component of that system. Such modified systems must be independently certified by the Director, NIH. If modifications are minor, it may only be necessary for the investigator to submit data showing that the modifications have either improved or not impaired the major phenotypic traits on which the containment of the system depends. Substantial modifications of a certified system require the submission of complete testing data.

II–D–2–b. *Data To Be Submitted for Certification.*

II–D–2–b–(1). *HV1 Systems Other than E. Coli K-12.* The following types of data shall be submitted, modified as appropriate for the particular system under consideration. (i) A description of the organism and vector; the strain's natural habitat and growth requirements; its physiological properties, particularly those related to its reproduction and survival and the mechanisms by which it exchanges genetic information; the range of organisms with which this organism normally exchanges genetic information and what sort of information is exchanged; and any relevant information on its pathogenicity or toxity. (ii) A description of the history of the particular strains and vectors to be used, including data on any mutations which render this organism less able to survive or transmit genetic information. (iii) A general description of the range of experiments contemplated, with emphasis on the need for developing such an H1L system.

II–D–2–b–(2). *HV2 Systems.* Investigators planning to request HV2 certification for host-vector systems can obtain instructions from ORDA concerning data to be submitted [33A, 33B]. In general, the following types of data are required: (i) Description of construction steps, with indication of source, properties, and manner of introduction of genetic traits. (ii) Quantitative data on the stability of genetic traits that contribute to the containment of the system. (iii) Data on the survival of the host-vector system under nonpermissive laboratory conditions designed to represent the relevant natural environment. (iv) Data on transmissibility of the vector and/or a cloned DNA fragment under both permissive and nonpermissive conditions. (v) Data on all other properties of the system which affect containment and utility, including information on yields of phage or plasmid molecules, ease of DNA isolation, and ease of transfection or tranformation. (vi) In some cases, the investigator may be asked to submit data on survival and vector transmissibility from experiments in which the host-vector is fed to laboratory animals (e.g., rodents). Such *in vivo* data may be required to confirm the validity of predicting *in vivo* survival on the basis of *in vitro* experiments.

Data must be submitted in writing to ORDA. Ten to twelve weeks are normally required for review and circulation of the data prior to the meeting at which such data can be considered by the RAC. Investigators are encouraged to publish their data on the construction, properties, and testing of proposed HV2 systems prior to consideration of the system by the RAC and its subcommittee. More specific instructions concerning the type of data to be submitted to NIH for proposed EK2 systems involving either palsmids or bacteriophage in *E. coli* K-12 are available from ORDA.

II–D–3. *Distribution of Certified Host-Vectors.* Certified HV2 host-vector systems (plus appropriate control strains) must be obtained from the NIH or its designees, one of whom will be the investigator who developed the system. NIH shall announce the availability of the system by publication of notices in appropriate journals.

Plasmid vectors will be provided in a suitable host strain, and phage vectors will be distributed as small-volume lysates. If NIH propagates any of the host strains or phage, a sample will be sent to the investigator who developed the system or to an appropriate contractor, prior to distribution, for verification that the material is free from contamination and unchanged in phenotypic properties.

In distributing the certified HV2 host-vector systems, NIH or its designee will (i) send out a complete description of the system; (ii) enumerate and describe the tests to be performed by the user in order to verify important phenotypic traits; (iii) remind the user that any modification of the system necessitates independent approval of the system by the NIH; and (iv) remind the user of responsibility for notifying ORDA of any discrepancies with the reported properties or any problems in the safe use of the system.

NIH may also distribute certified HV1 host-vector systems.

III. Containment Guidelines for Covered Experiments

Part III discusses experiments involving recombinant DNA. These experiments have been divided into four classes:

III–A. Experiments which require specific RAC review and NIH and IBC approval before initiation of the experiment;

III–B. Experiments which require IBC approval before initiation of the experiment;

III–C. Experiments which require IBC notification at the time of initiation of the experiment;

III–D. Experiments which are exempt from the procedures of the Guidelines.

IF AN EXPERIMENT FALLS INTO BOTH CLASS III–A AND ONE OF THE OTHER CLASSES, THE RULES PERTAINING TO CLASS III–A MUST BE FOLLOWED. If an experiment falls into class III–D and into either class III–B or III–C as well, it can be considered exempt from the requirements of the Guidelines.

Changes in containment levels from those specified here may not be instituted without the express approval of the Director, NIH. (See Sections IV–E–1–b–(1), IV–E–1–b–(2), and subsections.)

III–A. *Experiments that Require RAC Review and NIH and IBC Approval Before Initiation.* Experiments in this category cannot be initiated without submission of relevant information on the proposed experiment to NIH, the publication of the proposal in the **Federal Register** for thirty days of comment, review by the RAC, and specific approval by NIH. The containment conditions for such experiments will be recommended by RAC and set by NIH at the time of approval. Such experiments also require the approval of the IBC before initiation. Specific experiments already approved in this section and the appropriate containment conditions are listed in Appendices D and F.

III–A–1. Deliberate formation of recombinant DNAs containing genes for the biosynthesis of toxins lethal for vertebrates at an LD_{50} of less than 100 nanograms per kilogram body weight (e.g., the botulinum toxins, tetanus toxin, diphtheria toxin, *Shigella dysenteriae* neurotoxin). Specific approval has been given for the cloning in *E. coli* K-12 of DNAs containing genes coding for the biosynthesis of toxins which are lethal to vertebrates at 100 nanograms to 100 micrograms per kilogram body weight. Containment levels for these experiments are specified in Appendix F.

III-A-2. Deliberate release into the environment of any organism containing recombinant DNA.

III-A-3. Deliberate transfer of a drug resistance trait to microorganisms that are not known to acquire it naturally [2A], if such acquisition could compromise the use of the drug to control disease agents in human or veterinary medicine or agriculture.

III-B. *Experiments that Require IBC Approval Before Initiation.* Investigators performing experiments in this category must submit to their Institutional Biosafety Committee (IBC), prior to initiation of the experiments, a registration document that contains a description of: (a) The source(s) of DNA, (b) the nature of the inserted DNA sequences, (c) the hosts and vectors to be used, (d) whether a deliberate attempt will be made to obtain expression of a foreign gene, and, if so, what protein will be produced, and (e) the containment conditions specified in these Guidelines. This registration document must be dated and signed by the investigator and filed only with the local IBC. The IBC shall review all such proposals prior to initiation of the experiments. Requests for lowering of containment for experiments in this category will be considered by NIH. (See Section IV-E-1-b-(3).)

III-B-1. *Experiments Using CDC Class 2, Class 3, Class 4, or Class 5 Agents [1] as Host-Vector Systems.*

III-B-1-a. Experiments involving the introduction of recombinant DNA into CDC Class 2 agents can be carried out at P2 containment.

III-B-1-b. Experiments involving the introduction of recombinant DNA into CDC Class 3 agents can be carried out at P3 containment.

III-B-1-c. Experiments involving the introduction of recombinant DNA into CDC Class 4 [51] or Class 5 agents can be carried out at P4 containment. A USDA permit is required for work with Class 5 agents [48].

III-B-2. *Experiments in Which DNA from CDC Class 2, Class 3, Class 4, or Class 5 Agents [1] is Cloned in Nonpathogenic Prokaryotic or Lower Eukaryotic Host-Vector Systems.*

III-B-2-a. Recombinant DNA experiments in which DNA from CDC Class 2 or Class agents [1] is transferred into nonpathogenic prokaryotes or lower eukaryotes may be performed under P2 containment. Specific lowering of containment to P1 for particular experiments can be approved by the IBC. Many experiments in this category will be exempt from the Guidelines (See Sections III-D-4 and III-D-5). Experiments involving the formation of recombinant DNAs for certain toxin genes require RAC review and NIH approval (see Section III-A-1), or must be carried out under NIH specified conditions as described in Appendix F.

III-B-2-b. Recombinant DNA experiments in which DNA from CDC Class 4 [51] or Class 5 agents is transferred into nonpathogenic prokaryotes or lower eukaryotes can be performed at P2 containment after demonstration that only a totally and irreversibly defective fraction of the agent's viral genome is present in a given recombinant. In the absence of such a demonstration, P4 containment should be used.

Note.—A USDA permit is required for work with Class 5 pathogens [48].

III-B-3. *Experiments Involving the Use of Infectious Animal or Plant Viruses or Defective Animal or Plant Viruses in the Presence of Helper Virus in Tissue Culture Systems.*

Note: Recombinant DNA molecules which contain less than two-thirds of the genome of any eukaryotic virus (all virus from a single Family [36] being considered identical [50]) may be considered defective and can be used, in the absence of helper, under the conditions specified in Section III-C.

III-B-3-c. Experiments involving the use of infectious CDC Class 2 animal viruses [1], or defective CDC Class 2 animal viruses in the presence of helper virus, can be performed at P2 containment.

III-B-3-b. Experiments involving the use of infectious CDC Class 3 animal viruses [1], or defective CDC Class 3 animal viruses in the presence of helper virus, can be carried out at P3 containment.

III-B-3-a. Experiments involving the use of infectious CDC Class 4 or Class 5 animal virus [1], or defective CDC Class 4 or Cass 5 animal viruses in the presence of helper virus, may be carried out under P4 containment. A USDA permit is required for work with CDC Class 5 pathogens [48].

III-B-3-d. Experiments involving the use of infectious animal or plant viruses, or defective animal or plant viruses in the presence of helper virus, not covered by Sections III-B-3-a, III-B-3-b, or III-B-3-c may be carried out under P1 containment.

III-B-4. *Recombinant DNA Experiments Involving Whole Animals and Plants.*

III-B-4-a. DNA from any source except for greater than one quarter of a eukaryotic viral genome may be transferred to any non-human vertebrate organism and propagated under conditions of physical containment comparable to P1 and appropriate to the organism under study [2A].

III-B-4-b. For all experiments involving whole animals and plants and not covered by III-B-4-a, the appropriate containment will be determined by the IBC.

III-B-5. *Experiments Involving More Than 10 Liters of Culture.* The appropriate containment will be decided by the IBC. Where appropriate, the large-scale containment recommendations of the NIH should be used (45 FR 24968).

III-C. *Experiments That Require IBC Notice Simultaneously With Initiation of Experiments.* Experiments not included in Sections III-A, III-B, III-D, and subsections of these Sections are to be considered in Section III-C. All such experiments can be carried out at P1 containment. For experiments in this category, a registration document as described in Section III-B must be dated and signed by the investigator and filed with the local IBC. The IBC shall review all such proposals, but IBC review prior to initiation of the experiment is not required.

For example, experiments in which all components derive from non-pathogenic prokaryotes and non-pathogenic lower eukaryotes fall under Section III-C and can be carried out at P1 containment.

Caution: Experiments Involving Formation of Recombinant DNA Molecules Containing no more Than Two-Thirds of the Genome of any Eukaryotic Virus. Recombinant DNA molecules containing no more than two-thirds of the genome of any eukaryotic virus (all viruses from a single Family [36] being considered identical [50] may be propagated and maintained in cells in tissue culture using P1 containment. For such experiments, it must be shown that the cells lack helper virus for the specific Families of defective viruses being used. If helper virus is present, procedures specified under Section III-B-3 should be used. The DNA may contain fragments of the genome of viruses from more than one Family but each fragment must be less than two-thirds of a genome.

III-D. *Exempt Experiments.* The following recombinant DNA moleculses are exempt from these Guidelines and no registration with the IBC is necessary.

III-D-1. Those that are not in organisms or viruses.

III-D-2. Those that consist entirely of DNA segments from a single nonchromosomal or viral DNA source, though one or more of the segments may be a synthetic equivalent.

III–D–3. Those that consist entirely of DNA from a prokayotic host, including its indigenous plasmids or viruses, when propagated only in that host (or a closely related strain of the same species) or when transferred to another host by well established physiological means; also, those that consist entirely of DNA from an eukaryotic host, including its chloroplasts, mitochondria, or plasmids (but excluding viruses), when propagated only in that host (or a closely related strain of same species).

III–D–4. Certain specified recombinant DNA molecules that consist entirely of DNA segments from different species that exchange DNA by known physiological processes, though one or more of the segments may be a synthetic equivalent. A list of such exchangers will be prepared and periodically revised by the Director, NIH, with advice of the RAC, after appropriate notice and opportunity for public comment. (See Section IV–E–1–b–(1)–(d).) Certain classes are exempt as of publication of these Revised Guildelines. The list is in Appendix A. An updated list may be obtained from the Office of Recombinant DNA Activities, National Institutes of Health, Bethesda, Maryland 20205.

III–D–5. Other classes of recombinant DNA Molecules, if the Director, NIH, with advice of the RAC, after appropriate notice and opportunity for public comment, finds that they do not present a significant risk to health or the environment. (See Section IV–E–1–b–(1)–(d).) Certain classes are exempt as of publication of these Revised Guidelines. The list is in Appendix C. An updated list may be obtained from the Office of Recombinant DNA Activities, National Institutes of Health, Bethesda, Maryland 20205.

IV. Roles and Responsibilities

IV–A. *Policy.* Safety in activities involving recombinant DNA depends on the individual conducting them. The Guidelines cannot anticipate every possible situation. Motivation and good judgment are the key essentials to protection of health and the environment.

The Guidelines are intended to help the Institution, the Institutional Biosafety Committee (IBC), the Biological Safety Officer, and the Principal Investigator determine the safeguards that should be implemented. These Guidelines will never be complete or final, since all conceivable experiments involving recombinant DNA cannot be foreseen. Therfore, it is the responsibility of the Institution and those associated with it to adhere to the *purpose* of the Guidelines as well as to their specifics.

Each Institution (and the IBC acting on its behalf) is responsible for ensuring that recombinant DNA activities comply with the Guidelines. General recognition of institutional authority and responsibility properly establishes accountability for safe conduct of the research at the local level.

The following roles and responsibilities constitute an administrative framework in which safety is an essential and integral part of research involving recombinant DNA molecules. Further clarifications and interpretations of roles and responsibilities will be issued by NIH as necessary.

IV–B. *General Applicability.* The Guidelines are applicable to all recombinant DNA research within the United States or its territories which is conducted at or sponsored by an Institution that receives any support for recombinant DNA research from NIH. This includes research performed by NIH directly.

An individual receiving support for research involving recombinant DNA must be associated with or sponsored by an Institution that can and does assume the responsibilities assigned in these Guidelines.

The Guidelines are also applicable to projects done abroad if they are supported by NIH funds. If the host country however, has established rules for the conduct of recombinant DNA projects, then a certificate of compliance with those rules may be submitted to NIH in lieu of compliance with the NIH Guidelines. NIH reserves the right to withhold funding if the safety practices to be employed abroad are not reasonably consistent with the NIH Guidelines.

IV–C. *General Definitions.* The following terms, which are used throughout the Guidelines, are defined as follows:

IV–C–1. "DNA" means deoxyribonucleic acid.

IV–C–2. "Recombinant DNA" or "recombinant DNA molecules" means either (i) molecules which are constructed outside living cells by joining natural or synthetic DNA segments to DNA molecules that can replicate in a living cell, or (ii) DNA molecules which result from the replication of a molecule described in (i) above.

IV–C–3. "Institution" means any public or private entity (including Federal, State, and local government agencies).

IV–C–4. " Institutional Biosafety Committee" or "IBC" means a committee that (i) meets the requirements for membership specified in Section IV–D–2, and (ii) reviews, approves, and oversees projects in accordance with the responsibilities defined in Sections IV–D–2 and -3.

IV–C–5. "NIH Office of Recombinant DNA Activities" or "ORDA" means the office within NIH with responsibility for (i) reviewing and coordinating all activities of NIH related to the Guidelines, and (ii) performing other duties as defined in Section IV–E–3.

IV–C–6. "Recombinant DNA Advisory Committee" or "RAC" means the public advisory committee that advises the Secretary, the Assistant Secretary for Health, and the Director of the National Institutes of Health concerning recombinant DNA research. The RAC shall be constituted as specific in Section IV–E–2.

IV–C–7. "Director, NIH" or "Director" means the Director of the National Institutes of Health and any other officer or employee of NIH to whom authority has been delegated.

IV–C–8. "Federal Interagency Advisory Committee on Recombinant DNA Research" means the committee established in October 1976 to advise the Secretary, HHS, the Assistant Secretary for Health, and the Director, NIH, on the coordination of those aspects of all Federal programs and activities which relate to recombinant DNA research.

IV–C–9. "Laboratory Safety Monograph" or "LSM" means a publication describing practices, equipment, and facilities in detail.

IV–D. *Responsibilities of the Institution.*

IV–D–1. Each Institution conducting or sponsoring recombinant DNA research covered by these Guidelines is responsible for ensuring that the research is carried out in full conformity with the provisions of the Guidelines. In order to fulfill this resonsibility, the Institution shall:

IV–D–1–a. Establish and implement policies that provide for the safe conduct of recombinant DNA research and that ensure compliance with the Guidelines. The Institution, as part of its general responsibilities for implementing the Guidelines, may establish additional procedures, as deemed necessary, to govern the Institution and its components in the discharge of its responsibilities under the Guidelines. This may include (i) statements formulated by the Institution for general implementation of the Guidelines and (ii) whatever additional precautionary steps the Institution may deem appropriate.

IV-D-1-b. Establish an Institutional Biosafety Committee (IBC) that meets the requirements set forth in Section IV-D-2 and carries out the functions detailed in Section IV-D-3.

IV-D-1-c. If the Institution is engaged in recombinant DNA research at the P3 or P4 containment level, appoint a Biological Safety Officer (BSO), who shall be a member of the IBC and carry out the duties specified in Section IV-D-4.

IV-D-1-d. Require that investigators responsible for research covered by these Guidelines comply with the provisions of Section IV-D-5, and assist investigators to do so.

IV-D-1-e. Ensure appropriate training for the IBC chairperson and members, the BSO, Principal Investigators (PIs), and laboratory staff regarding the Guidelines, their implementation, and laboratory safety. Responsibility for training IBC members may be carried out through the IBC chairperson. Responsibility for training laboratory staff may be carried out through the PI. The Institution is responsible for seeing that the PI has sufficient training, but may delegate this responsibility to the IBC.

IV-D-1-f. Determine the necessity, in connection with each project, for health surveillance of recombinant DNA research personnel, and conduct, if found appropriate, a health surveillance program for the project. [The Laboratory Safety Monograph (LSM) discusses various possible components of such a program—for example, records of agents handled, active investigation of relevant illnesses, and the maintenance of serial serum samples for monitoring serologic changes that may result from the employees' work experience. Certain medical conditions may place a laboratory worker at increased risk in any endeavor where infectious agents are handled. Examples given in the LSM include gastrointestinal disorders and treatment with steroids, immunosuppressive drugs, or antibiotics. Workers with such disorders or treatment should be evaluated to determine whether they should be engaged in research with potentially hazardous organisms during their treatment or illness.]

IV-D-1-g. Report within 30 days to ORDA any significant problems with and violations of the Guidelines and significant research-related accidents and illnesses, unless the Institution determines that the PI or IBC has done so.

IV-D-2. *Membership and Procedures of the IBC.* The Institution shall establish an Institutional Biosafety Committee (IBC) meeting the following requirements:

IV-D-2-a. The IBC shall comprise no fewer than five members so selected that they collectively have experience and expertise in recombinant DNA technology and the capability to assess the safety of recombinant DNA research experiments and any potential risk to public health or the environment. At least two members (but not less than 20 percent of the membership of the committee) shall not be affiliated with the Institution (apart from their membership on the IBC) and shall represent the interest of the surrounding community with respect to health and protection of the environment. Members meet this requirement if, for example, they are officials of State or local public health or environmental protection agencies, members of other local governmental bodies, or persons active in medical, occupational health, or environmental concerns in the community. The Biological Safety Officer (BSO) mandatory when research is being conducted at the P3 and P4 levels, shall be a member (see Section IV-D-4).

IV-D-2-b. In order to ensure the professional competence necessary to review recombinant DNA activities, it is recommended that (i) the IBC include persons from disciplines relevant to recombinant DNA technology, biological safety, and engineering; (ii) the IBC include, or have available as consultants, persons knowledgeable in institutional commitments and policies, applicable law, standards of professional conduct and practice, community attitudes, and the environment; and (iii) at least one member be a nondoctoral person from a laboratory technical staff.

IV-D-2-c. The Institution shall identify the committee members by name in a report to the NIH Office of Recombinant DNA Activities (ORDA) and shall include relevant background information on each member in such form and at such times as ORDA may require.

IV-D-2-d. No member of an IBC may be involved (except to provide information requestd by the IBC) in the review or approval of a project in which he or she has been, or expects to be, engaged or has a direct financial interest.

IV-D-2-e. The Institution may establish procedures that the IBC will follow in its inital and continuing review of applications, proposals, and activities. (IBC review procedures are specified in Section IV-D-3-a.)

IV-D-2-f. Central to implementation of the Guidelines is the review of experiments by the IBC.

IV-D-2-g. Institutions are encouraged to open IBC meetings to the public whenever possible, consistent with protection of privacy and proprietary interests.

IV-D-2-h. Upon request, the Institution shall make available to the public all minutes of IBC meetings and any documents submitted to or received from funding agencies which the latter are required to make available to the public (e.g., reports of Guideline violations and significant research-related accidents, and agency directives to modify projects). If comments are made by members of the public on IBC actions, the Institution shall forward to NIH both the comments and the IBC's response.

IV-D-3. *Functions of the IBC.* On behalf of the Institution, the IBC is responsible for:

IV-D-3-a. Reviewing for compliance with the NIH Guidelines recombinant DNA research as specified in Part III conducted at or sponsored by the Institution, and approving those research projects that it finds are in conformity with the Guidelines. This review shall include:

IV-D-3-a-(1). An independent assessment of the containment levels required by these Guidelines for the proposed research, and

IV-D-3-a-(2). An assessment of the facilities, procedures, and practices, and of the training and expertise of recombinant DNA personnel.

Note.—See Laboratory Safety Monograph (pages 187-190) for suggested guidance in conducting this review.

IV-D-3-b. Notifying the Principal Investigator (PI) of the results of their review.

IV-D-3-c. Reviewing periodically recombinant DNA research being conducted at the Institution, to ensure that the requirements of the Guidelines are being fulfilled.

IV-D-3-d. Adopting emergency plans covering accidental spills and personnel contamination resulting from such research.

Note.—Basic elements in developing specific procedures for dealing with major spills of potentially hazardous materials in the laboratory are detailed in the Laboratory Safety Monograph. Included are information and references on decontamination and emergency plans. NIH and the Centers for Disease Control are available to provide consultation, and direct assistance if necessary, as posted in the LSM. The Institution shall cooperate with the State and local public health departments, reporting any significant research-related illness or accident that appears to be a hazard to the public health.

IV-D-3-e. Reporting within 30 days to the appropriate institutional official and to the NIH Office of Recombinant DNA Activities (ORDA) any significant problems with or violations of the Guidelines, and any significant research-related accidents or illnesses, unless the IBC determines that the PI has done so.

IV-D-3-f. The IBC may not authorize initiation of experiments not explicitly covered by the Guidelines until NIH (with the advice of the RAC when required) establishes the containment requirement.

IV-D-3-g. Performing such other functions as may be delegated to the IBC under Section IV-D-1.

IV-D-4. *Biological Safety Officer.* The Institution shall appoint a BSO if it engages in recombinant DNA research at the P3 or P4 containment level. The officer shall be a member of the Institutional Biosafety Committee (IBC), and his or her duties shall include (but need not be limited to):

IV-D-4-a. Ensuring through periodic inspections that laboratory standards are rigorously followed;

IV-D-4-b. Reporting to the IBC and the Institution all significant problems with and violations of the Guidelines and all significant research-related accidents and illinesses of which the BSO becomes aware, unless the BSO determines that the Principal Investigator (PI) has done so;

IV-D-4-c. Developing emergency plans for dealing with accidental spills and personnel contamination, and investigating recombinant DNA research laboratory accidents;

IV-D-4-d. Providing advice on laboratory security;

IV-D-4-e. Providing technical advice to the PI and the IBC on research safety procedures.

Note.—See Laboratory Safety Monograph for additional information on the duties of the BSO.

IV-D-5. *Principal Investigator.* On behalf of the Institution, the PI is responsible for complying fully with the Guidelines in conducting any recombinant DNA research.

IV-D-5-a. *PI—General.* As part of this general responsibility, the PI shall:

IV-D-5-a-(1). Initiate or modify no recombinant DNA research requiring approval by the IBC prior to initiation (see Sections III-A and III-B) until that research, or the proposed modification thereof, has been approved by the IBC and has met all other requirements of the Guidelines;

IV-D-5-a-(2). Report within 30 days to the IBC and NIH (ORDA) all significant problems with and violations of the Guidelines and all significant research-related accidents and illnesses;

IV-D-5-a-(3). Report to the IBC and to NIH (ORDA) new information bearing on the Guidelines;

IV-D-5-a-(4). Be adequately trained in good microbiological techniques;

IV-D-5-a-(5). Adhere to IBC-approved emergency plans for dealing with accidential spills and personnel contamination; and

IV-D-5-a-(6). Comply with shipping requirements for recombinant DNA molecules. (See Section II-C for shipping requirements and Laboratory Safety Monograph for technical recommendations.)

IV-D-5-b. *Submissions by the PI to NIH.* The PI shall:

IV-D-5-b-(1). Submit information to NIH (ORDA) in order to have new host-vector systems certified;

IV-D-5-b-(2). Petition NIH, with notice to the IBC, for exemptions to these Guidelines;

IV-D-5-b-(3). Petition NIH, with concurrence of the IBC, for approval to conduct experiments specified in Section III-A of the Guidelines;

IV-D-5-b-(4). Petition NIH for determination of containment for experiments requiring case-by-case review;

IV-D-5-b-(5). Petition NIH for determination of containment for experiments not covered by the Guidelines.

IV-D-5-c. *Submissions by the PI to the IBC.* The PI shall:

IV-D-5-c-(1). Make the initial determination of the required levels of physical and biological containment in accordance with the Guidelines;

IV-D-5-c-(2). Select appropriate microbiological practices and laboratory techniques to be used in the research;

IV-D-5-c-(3). Submit the initial research protocol if covered under Guidelines Sections III-A, III-B, or III-C (and also subsequent changes—e.g., changes in the source of DNA or host-vector system) to the IBC for review and approval or disapproval; and

IV-D-5-c-(4). Remain in communication with the IBC throughout the conduct of the project.

IV-D-5-d. *PI Responsibilities Prior to Initiating Research.* The PI is responsible for:

IV-D-5-d-(1). Making available to the laboratory staff copies of the protocols that describe the potential biohazards and the precautions to be taken;

IV-D-5-d-(2). Instructing and training staff in the practices and techniques required to ensure safety and in the procedures for dealing with accidents; and

IV-D-5-d-(3). Informing the staff of the reasons and provisions for any precautionary medical practices advised or requested, such as vaccinations or serum collection.

IV-D-5-e. *PI Responsibilities During the Condust of the Research.* The PI is responsible for:

IV-D-5-e-(1). Supervising the safety performance of the staff to ensure that the required safety practices and techniques are employed;

IV-D-5-e-(2). Investigating and reporting in writing to ORDA, the Biological Safety Officer (where applicable), and the IBC any significant problems pertaining to the operation and implementation of containment practices and procedures;

IV-D-5-e-(3). Correcting work errors and conditions that may result in the release of recombinant DNA materials;

IV-D-5-e-(4). Ensuring the integrity of the physical containment (e.g., biological safety cabinets) and the biological containment (e.g., purity, and genotypic and phenotypic characteristics); and

IV-D-5-e-(5). *Publications.* PIs are urged to include, in all publications reporting on recombinant DNA research, a description of the physical and biological containment procedures employed.

IV-E. *Responsibilities of NIH.*

IV-E-1. *Director.* The Director, NIH, is responsible for (i) establishing the NIH Guidelines for Research Involving Recombinant DNA Molecules, (ii) overseeing their implementation, and (iii) their final interpretation.

The Director has a number of responsibilities under the Guidelines that involve the NIH Office of Recombinant DNA Activities (ORDA) and the Recombinant DNA Advisory Committee (RAC). ORDA's responsibilities under the Guidelines are administrative. Advice from the RAC is primarily scientific and technical. In certain circumstances, there is specific opportunity for public comment, with published response, before final action.

IV-E-1-a. *General Responsibilities of the Director, NIH.* The responsibilities of the Director shall include the following:

IV-E-1-a-(1). Promulgating requirements as necessary to implement the Guidelines;

IV-E-1-a-(2). Establishing and maintaining the RAC to carry out the responsibilities set forth in Section IV-E-2. The RAC's membership is specified in its charter and in Section IV-E-2;

IV-E-1-a-(3). Establishing and maintaining ORDA to carry out the responsibilities defined in Section IV-E-3; and

IV-E-1-a-(4). Maintaining the Federal Interagency Advisory Committee on Recombinant DNA Research established by the Secretary, HEW, for advice on the coordination of all Federal programs and activities relating to recombinant DNA, including activities of the RAC.

IV-E-1-b. *Specific Responsibilities of the Directors, NIH.* In carrying out the responsibilities set forth in this Section, the Director shall weigh each proposed action, through appropriate analysis and consultation, to determine that is complies with the Guidelines and presents no significant risk to health or the environment.

IV-E-1-b-(1). *The Director is responsible for the following major actions.* (For these, the Director must seek the advice of the RAC and provide an opportunity for public and Federal agency comment. Specifically, the agenda of the RAC meeting citing the major actions will be published in the **Federal Register** at least 30 days before the meeting, and the Director will also publish the proposed actions in the **Federal Register** for comment at least 30 days before the meeting. In addition, the Director's proposed decision, at his discretion, may be published in the **Federal Register** for 30 days of comment before final action is taken. The Director's final decisions, along with response to the comments, will be published in the **Federal Register** and the *Recombinant DNA Technical Bulletin.* The RAC and IBC chairpersons will be notified of this decision):

IV-E-1-b-(1)-(a). Changing containment levels for types of experiments that are specified in the Guidelines when a major action is involved;

IV-E-1-b-(1)-(b). Assigning containment levels for types of experiments that are not explicity considered in the Guidelines when a major action is involved;

IV-E-1-b-(1)-(c). Certifying new host-vector systems, with the exception of minor modifications of already certified systems. (The standards and procedures for certification are described in Section II-D-2-a. Minor modifications constitute, for example, those of minimal or no consequence to the properties relevant to containment);

IV-E-1-b-(1)-(d). Promulgating and amending a list of classes of recombinant DNA molecules to be exempt from these Guidelines because they constist entirely of DNA segments from species that exchange DNA by known physiological processes, or otherwise do not present a significant risk to health or the environment;

IV-E-1-b-(1)-(e). Permitting experiments specified by Section III-A of the Guidelines; and

IV-E-1-b-(1)-(f). Adopting other changes in the Guidelines.

IV-E-1-b-(2). *The Director is also responsibile for the following lesser actions* (For these, the Director must seek the advice of the RAC. The Director's decision will be transmitted to the RAC and IBC chairpersons and published in the Recombinant DNA Technical Bulletin);

IV-E-1-b-(2)-(b). *The Director is also responsible for the following lesser actions* (For these, the Director must seek the advice of the RAC. The Director's decision will be transmitted to the RAC and IBC chairpersons and published in the Recombinant DNA Technical Bulletin):

IV-E-1-b-(2)-(a). Interpreting and determining containment levels, upon request by ORDA;

IV-E-1-b-(2)-(b). Changing containment levels for experiments that are specified in the Guidelines (see Section III);

IV-E-1-b-(2)-(c). Assigning containment levels for experiments not explicity considered in the Guidelines;

IV-E-1-b-(2)-(d). Designating certain class 2 agents as class 1 for the purpose of these Guidelines (see Footnote 1 and Appendix B);

IV-E-1-b-(3). *The Director is also responsibile for the following actions.* (The Director's decision will be transmitted to the RAC and IBC chairpersons and published in the *Recombinant DNA Technical Bulletin):*

IV-E-1-b-(3)-(a). Interpreting the Guidelines for experiments to which the Guidelines specifically assign containment levels;

IV-E-1-b-(3)-(b). Determining appropriate containment conditions for experiments according to case precedents developed under Section IV-E-1-b-(2)-(c).

IV-E-1-b-(3)-(c). Approving minor modifications of already certified host-vector systems. (The standards and procedures for such modifications are described in Section II-D-2);

IV-E-1-b-(3)-(d). Decertifying already certified host-vector systems;

IV-E-1-b-(3)-(e). Adding new entries to the list of toxins for vertebrates (see Appendix F); and

IV-E-1-b-(3)-(f). Approving the cloning of toxin genes in host-vector systems other than *E. coli* K-12 (see Appendix F).

IV-E-1-b-(4). The Director shall conduct, support, and assist training programs in laboratory safety for Institutional Biosafety Committee members, Biological Safety Officers, Principal Investigators, and laboratory staff.

IV-E-2. *Recombinant DNA Advisory Committee.* The NIH Recombinant DNA Advisory Committee (RAC) is responsible for carrying out specified functions cited below as well as others assigned under its charter or by the Secretary, HHS, the Assistant Secretary for Health, and the Director, NIH.

The members of the committee shall be chosen to provide, collectively, expertise in scientific fields relevant to recombinant DNA technology and biological safety—e.g., microbiology, molecular biology, virology, genetics, epidemiology, infectious diseases, the biology of enteric organisms, botany, plant pathology, ecology, and tissue culture. At least 20 percent of the members shall be persons knowledgeable in applicable law, standards of professional conduct and practice, public attitudes, the environment, public health, occupational health, or related fields. Representatives from Federal agencies shall serve as nonvoting members. Nominations for the RAC may be submitted to the NIH Office of Recombinant DNA Activities, Bethesda, Md. 20205.

All meetings of the RAC will be announced in the **Federal Register**, including tentative agenda items, 30 days in advance of the meeting, with final agendas (if modified) available at least 72 hours before the meeting. No item defined as a major action under Section IV-E-1-b-(1) may be added to an agenda after it appears in the **Federal Register**.

The RAC shall be responsible for advising the Director, NIH, on the actions listed in Section IV-E-1-b-(1) and -(2).

IV-E-3. *The Office of Recombinant DNA Activities.* ORDA shall serve as a focal point for information on recombinant DNA activities and provide advice to all within and outside NIH, including Institutions, Biological Safety Committees, Principal Investigators, Federal agencies, State and local governments, and institutions in the private sector. ORDA shall carry out such other functions as may be delegated to it by the Director, NIH, including those authorities described in Section IV-E-1-b-(3). In addition, ORDA shall be responsible for the following:

IV-E-3-a. Reviewing and approving Institutional Biosafety Committee (IBC) membership;

IV-E-3-b. Publishing in the **Federal Register**:

IV-E-3-b-(1). Announcements of Recombinant DNA Advisory Committee

(RAC) meetings and agendas at least 30 days in advance;

Note.—If the agenda for an RAC meeting is modified, ORDA shall make the revised agenda available to anyone, upon request, at least 72 hours in advance of the meeting.

IV–E–3–b–(2). Proposed major actions of the type falling under Section IV–E–1–b–(1) at least 30 days prior to the RAC meeting at which they will be considered; and

IV–E–3–b–(3). The NIH Director's final decision on recommendations made by the RAC.

IV–E–3–c. Publishing the *Recombinant DNA Technical Bulletin;* and

IV–E–3–d. Serving as executive secretary of the RAC.

IV–E–4. *Other NIH Components.* Other NIH components shall be responsible for:

IV–E–4–a. Certifying P4 facilities, inspecting them periodically, and inspecting other recombinant DNA facilities as deemed necessary; and

IV–E–4–b. Announcing and distributing certified HV2 host-vector systems (see Section II–D–3).

IV–F. *Compliance.* As a condition for NIH funding of recombinant DNA research, Institutions must ensure that such research conducted at or sponsored by the Institution, irrespective of the source of funding, shall comply with these Guidelines. The policies on noncompliance are as follows:

IV–F–1. All NIH-funded projects involving recombinant DNA techniques must comply with the NIH Guidelines. Noncompliance may result in (i) suspension, limitation, or termination of financial assistance for such projects and of NIH funds for other recombinant DNA research at the Institution, or (ii) a requirement for prior NIH approval of any or all recombinant DNA projects at the Institution.

IV–F–2. All non-NIH funded projects involving recombinant DNA techniques conducted at or sponsored by an Institution that receives NIH funds for projects involving such techniques must comply with the NIH Guidelines. Noncompliance may result in (i) suspension, limitation, or termination of NIH funds for recombinant DNA research at the Institution, or (ii) a requirement for prior NIH approval of any or all recombinant DNA projects at the Institution.

IV–F–3. Information concerning noncompliance with the Guildelines may be brought forward by any person. It should be delivered to both NIH (ORDA) and the relevant Institution. The Institution, generally through the IBC, shall take appropriate action. The Institution shall forward a complete report of the incident to ORDA, recommending any further action indicated.

IV–F–4. In cases where NIH proposes to suspend, limit, or terminate financial assistance because of noncompliance with the Guidelines, applicable DHEW and Public Health Service Procedures shall govern.

IV–F–5. *Voluntary Compliance.* Any individual, corporation, or institution that is not otherwise covered by the Guidelines is encouraged to conduct recombinant DNA research activities in accordance with the Guidelines, through the procedures set forth in Part VI.

V. Footnotes and References

1. The reference to organisms as Class 1, 2, 3, 4, or 5 refers to the classification in the publication *Classification of Etiologic Agents on the Basis of Hazard,* 4th Edition, july 1974; U.S. Department of Health, Education, and Welfare, Public Health Service, Centers for Disease Control, Office of Biosafety, Atlanta, Georgia 30333. The list of organisms in each class, as given in this publication, is reprinted in Appendix B to these Guidelines.

The Director, NIH, with advice of the Recombinant DNA Advisory Committee, may designate certain of the agents which are listed as Class 2 in the *Classification of Etiologic Agents on the Basis of Hazard,* 4th Edition, July 1974, as Class 1 agents for the Purposes of these Guidelines (see Section IV–E–1–b–(2)–(d)). An updated list of such agents may be obtained from the Office of Recombinant DNA Activities (ORDA), National Institutes of Health, Bethesda, Maryland 20205.

The entire *Classification of Etiologic Agents on the Basis of Hazard* is in the process of revision.

2A. In Part III of the Guidelines, there are a number of places where judgments are to be made. In all these cases the principal investigator is to make the judgment on these matters as part on his responsibility to "make the initial determination of the required levels of physical and biological containment in accordance with the Guidelines" (Section IV–D–5–c–(1)). In the cases falling under Sections III–A, –B or –C, this judgment is to be reviewed and approved by the Institutional Biosafety Committee as part of its responsibility to make "an independent assessment of the containment levels required by these Guidelines for the proposed research" (Section IV–D–3–a–(1)). If the IBC wishes, any specific cases may be referred to the NIH Office of Recombinant DNA Activities as part of ORDA's functions to "provide advice to all within and outside NIH" (Section IV–E–3), and ORDA may request advice from the Recombinant DNA Advisory Committee as part of the RAC's responsibility for "interpreting and determining containment levels upon request by ORDA" (Section IV–E–1–b–(2)–(a)).

6. *Laboratory Safety at the Center for Disease Control* (Sept. 1974). U.S. Department of Health, Education and Welfare Publication No. CDC 75–8118.

7. *Classification of Etiologic Agents on the Basis of Hazard.* (4th Edition, July 1974). U.S. Department of Health, Education and Welfare. Public Health Service. Centers for Disease Control, Office of Biosafety, Atlanta, Georgia 30333.

8. *National Cancer Institute Safety Standards for Research Involving Oncogenic Viruses* (Oct. 1974). U.S. Department of Health, Education and Welfare Publication No. (NIH) 75–790.

9. *National Institutes of Health Biohazards Safety Guide* (1974). U.S. Department of Health, Education, and Welfare, Public Health.

10. *Biohazards in Biological Research* (1973). A. Hellman, M. N. Oxman, and R. Pollack (ed.) Cold Spring Harbor Laboratory.

11. *Handbook of Laboratory Safety* (1971). Second Edition. N. V. Steere (ed.). The Chemical Rubber Co., Cleveland.

12. Bodily, J. L. (1970). *General Administration of the Laboratory,* H. L. Bodily, E. L. Updyke, and J. O. Mason (eds.), Diagnostic Procedures for Bacterial, Mycotic and Parasitic Infections. American Public Health Association, New York, pp. 11–28.

13. Darlow, H. M. (1969). *Safety in the Microbiological Laboratory.* In J. R. Norris and D. W. Robbins (ed.), Methods in Microbiology. Academic Press, Inc. New York. pp. 169–204.

14. *The Prevention of Laboratory Acquired Infection* (1974). C. H. Collins, E. G. Hartley, and R. Pilsworth. Public Health Laboratory Service, Monograph Series No. 6.

15. Chatigny, M. A. (1961). *Protection Against Infection in the Microbiological Laboratory: Devices and Procedures.* In W. W. Umbreit (ed.). Advances in Applied Microbiology. Academic Press, New York, N.Y. 3:131–192.

16. *Design Criteria for Viral Oncology Research Facilities* (1975). U.S. Department of Health, Education and Welfare, Public Health Service, National Institutes of Health, DHEW Publication No. (NIH) 75–891.

17. Kuehne, R. W. (1973). *Biological Containment Facility for Studying Infectious Disease.* Appl. Microbiol. 26–239–243.

18. Runkle, R. S., and G. B. Phillips (1969). *Microbial Containment Control Facilities.* Van Nostrand Reinhold, New York.

19. Chatigny, M. A., and D. I. Clinger (1969). *Contamination Control in Aerobiology.* In R. L. Dimmick and A. B. Akers (eds.). An Introduction to Experimental Aerobiology. John Wiley & Sons, New York, pp. 194–263.

19A. Horsfall, F. L., Jr., and J. H. Baner (1940). *Individual Isolation of Infected Animals in a Single Room.* J. Bact. *40,* 569–580.

20. Biological safety cabinets referred to in this section are classified as *Class I, Class II,* or *Class III* cabinets. A *Class I* is a ventilated cabinet for personnel protection having an inward flow of air away from the operator. The exhaust air from this cabinet is filtered through a high-efficiency particulate air (HEPA) filter. This cabinet is used in three operational modes: (1) with a full-width open front, (2) with an installed front closure panel (having four 8-inch diameter openings) without gloves, and (3) with an installed front closure panel equipped with arm-length

rubber gloves. The face velocity of the inward flow of air through the full-width open front is 75 feet per minute or greater. A *Class II* cabinet is a ventilated cabinet for personnel and product protection having an open front with inward air flow for personnel protection, and HEPA filtered mass recirculated air flow for product protection. The cabinet exhaust air is filtered through an HEPA filter. The face velocity of the inward flow of air through the full-width open front is 75 feet per minute or greater. Design and performance specifications for *Class II* cabinets have been adopted by the National Sanitation Foundation, Ann Arbor, Michigan. A *Class III* cabinet is a closed-front ventilated cabinet of gas-tight construction which provides the highest level of personnel protection of all biohazard safety cabinets. The interior of the cabinet is protected from contaminants exterior to the cabinet. The cabinet is fitted with arm-length rubber gloves and is operated under a negative pressure of at least 0.5 inch water gauge. All supply air is filtered through HEPA filters. Exhaust air is filtered through two HEPA filters or one HEPA filter and incinerator before being discharged to the outside environment.

21. Hershfield, V., H. W. Boyer, C. Yanofsky, M. A. Lovett, and D. R. Helinski (1974). *Plasmid ColEI as a Molecular Vehicle for Cloning and Amplification of DNA*. Proc. Nat. Acad. Sci. USA *71*, 3455–3459.

22. Wensink, P. C., D. J. Finnegan, J. E. Donelson, and D. S. Hogness(1974). *A System for Mapping DNA Sequences in the Chromosomes of Drosophila Melanogaster*. Cell *3*, 315–335.

23. Tanaka, T., and B. Weisblum (1975). *Construction of a Colicin El-R Factor Composite Plasmid In Vitro: Means for Amplification of Deoxyribonucleic Acid*. J. Bacteriol. *121*, 354–362.

24. Armstrong, K. A., V. Hershfield, and D. R. Helinski (1977). *Gene Cloning and Containment Properties of Plasmid Col EI and Its Derivatives*. Science *196*, 172–174.

25. Bolivar, F., R. L. Rodriguez, M. C. Bethlach, and H. W. Boyer(1977). *Construction and Characterization of New Cloning Vehicles: I. Ampicillin-Resistant Derivative of pMB9*. Gene *2*, 75–93.

26. Cohen, S. N., A. C. W. Chang, H. Boyer, and R. Helling (1973). *Construction of Biologically Functional Bacterial Plasmids in Vitro*. Proc. Natl. Acad. Sci. USA *70*, 3240–3244.

27. Bolivar, F., R. L. Rodriguez, R. J. Greene, M. C. Batlach, H. L. Reyneker, H. W. Boyer, J. H. Crosa, and S. Falkow(1977). *Construction and Characterization of New Cloning Vehicles: II. A Multi-Purpose Cloning System*. Gene *2*, 95–113.

28. Thomas, M., J. R. Cameron, and R. W. Davis (1974). *Viable Molecular Hydrids of Bacteriophage Lambda and Eukaryotic DNA*. Proc. Nat. Acad. Sci. USA *71*, 4579–4583.

29. Murray, N. E., and K. Murray (1974). *Manipulation of Restriction Targets in Phage Lambda to Form Receptor Chromosomes for DNA Fragments*. Nature *251*, 476–481.

30. Rambach, A., and P. Tiollais (1974). *Bacteriophage Having EcoRI Endonuclease Sites Only in the Non-Essential Region of the Genome*. Proc. Nat. Acad. Sci., USA *71*, 3927–3930.

31. Blattner, F. R., B. G. Williams, A. E. Bleche, K. Denniston-Thompson, H. E. Faber, L. A. Furlong, D. J. Gunwald, D. O. Kiefer, D. D. Moore, J. W. Shumm, E. L. Sheldon, and O. Smithies (1977). *Charon Phages: Safer Derivatives of Bacteriophage Lambda for DNA Cloning*. Science *196*, 163–169.

32. Donoghue, D. J., and P. A. Sharp (1977). *An Improved Lambda Vector: Construction of Model Recombinants Coding for Kanamycin Resistance*, Gene *1*, 209–227.

33. Leder, P., D. Tiemeier and L. Enquist (1977). *EK2 Derivatives of Bacteriophage Lambda Useful in the Cloning of DNA from Higher Organisms: The λgt WES System*. Science *196*, 175–177.

33A. Skalka, A. (1978). *Current Status of Coliphage λ EK2 Vectors*. Gene *3*, 29–35.

33B. Szybalski, W., A. Skalka, S. Gottesman, A. Campbell, and D. Botstein (1978). *Standardized Laboratory Tests for EK2 Certification*. Gene *3*, 36–38.

35. Defined as observable under optimal laboratory conditions by transformation, transduction, phage infection, and/or conjugation with transfer of phage, plasmid, and/or chromosomal genetic information. Note that this definition of exchange may be less stringent than that applied to exempt organisms under Section III–D–4.

36. As classified in the Third Report of the International Committee on Taxonomy of Viruses: Classification and Nomenclature of Viruses, R. E. F. Matthews, Ed. Intervirology 12 (129–296) 1979.

48. A USDA permit, required for import and interstate transport of pathogens, may be obtained from the Animal and Plant Health Inspecton Service, USDA, Federal Building, Hyattsville, MD 20782.

49. A subset of non-conjugative plasmid vectors are also poorly mobilizable (e.g., pBR 322, pBR313). Where practical, these vectors should be employed.

50. I.e., the total of all genomes within a Family shall not exceed two-thirds of the genome.

51. All activities, inlcuding storage of variloa and whitepox are restricted to the single national facility (World Health Organization (WHO) Collaborating Center for Smallpox Research, Centers for Disease Control, in Atlanta).

VI. Voluntary Compliance

VI–A. *Basic Policy.* Individuals, corporations, and institutions not otherwise covered by the Guidelines are encouraged to do so by following the standards and procedures set forth in Parts I–IV of the Guidelines. In order to simplify discussion, references hereafter to "institutions" are intended to encompass corporations, and individuals who have no organizational affiliation. For purposes of complying with the Guidelines, and individual intending to carry out research involving recombinant DNA is encouraged to affiliate with an institution that has an Institutional Biosafety Committee approved under the Guidelines.

Since commercial organizations have special concerns, such as protection of proprietary data, some modifications and explanations of the procedures in Parts I–IV are provided below, in order to address these concerns.

VI–B. *IBC Approval.* The NIH Office of Recombinant DNA Activities (ORDA) will review the membership of an institution's Institutional Biosafety Committee (IBC) and, where it finds the IBC meets the requirements set forth in Section IV–D–2, will give its approval to the IBC membership.

It should be emphasized that employment of an IBC member solely for purposes of membership on the IBC does not itself make the member an institutionally affiliated member for purposes of Section IV–D–2–a.

Except for the unaffiliated members, a member of an IBC for an institution not otherwise covered by the Guidelines may participate in the review and approval of a project in which the member has a direct financial interest, so long as the member has not been and does not expect to be engaged in the project. Section IV–D–2–d is modified to that extent for purposes of these institutions.

VI–C. *Certification of Host-Vector Systems.* A host-vector system may be proposed for certification by the Director, NIH, in accordance with the procedures set forth in Section II–D–2–a.

Institutions not otherwise covered by the Guidelines will not be subject to Section II–D–3 by complying with these procedures.

In order to ensure protection for proprietary data, any public notice regarding a host-vector system which is designated by the institution as proprietary under Section VI–E–1 will be issued only after consultation with the institution as to the content of the notice.

VI–D. *Requests for Exemptions and Approvals.* Requests for exemptions or other approvals required by the Guidelines should be requested by following the procedures set forth in the appropriate sections in Parts I–IV of the Guidelines.

In order to ensure protection for proprietary data, any public notice regarding a request for an exemption or other approval which is designated by the institution as proprietary under Section VI–E–1 will be issued only after consultation with the institution as to the content of the notice.

VI–E. *Protection of Proprietary Data.* In general, the Freedom of Information Act requires Federal agencies to make their records available to the public upon request. However, this requirement does not apply to, among other things, "trade secrets and commercial and financial information obtained from a person and privileged or confidential." 18 U.S.C. 1905, in turn makes it a crime for an officer or employee of the United States or any Federal department or agency to publish, divulge, disclose, or make known "in any manner or to any extent not authorized by law any information coming to him in the course of his employment or official duties or by reason of any examination or investigation made by, or return, report or record made to or filed with, such department or agency or officer or employee thereof, which information concerns or relates to the trade secrets, [or processes . . . of any person, firm, partnership, corporation, or association." This provision applies to all employees of the Federal Government, including special Government employees. Members of the Recombinant DNA Advisory Committee are "special Government employees."

VI-E-1. In submitting information to NIH for purposes of complying voluntarily with the Guidelines, an institution may designate those items of information which the institution believes constitute trade secrets or privileged or confidential commerical or financial information.

VI-E-2. If NIH receives a request under the Freedom of Information Act for information so designated, NIH will promptly contact the institution to secure its views as to whether the information (or some portion) should be released.

VI-E-3. If the NIH decides to release this information (or some portion) in response to a Freedom of Information request or otherwise, the institution will be advised; and the actual release will not be made until the expiration of 15 days after the institution is so advised, except to the extent that earlier release, in the judgement of the Director, NIH, is necessary to protect against an imminent hazard to the public or the environment.

VI-E-4. Presubmission Review.

VI-E-4-a. Any institution not otherwise covered by the Guidelines, which is considering submission of data or information voluntarily to NIH, may request presubmission review of the records involved to determine whether, if the records are submitted, NIH will or will not make part or all of the records available upon request under the Freedom of Information Act.

VI-E-4-b. A request for presubmission review should be submitted to ORDA, along with the records involved. These records must be clearly marked as being the property of the institution, on loan to NIH solely for the purpose of making a determination under the Freedom of Information Act. ORDA will then seek a determination from the HHS Freedom of Information Officer, the responsible official under HHS regulations (45 CFR Part 5), as to whether the records involved (or some portion) are or are not available to members of the public under the Freedom of Information Act. Pending such a determination, the records will be kept separate from ORDA files, will be considered records of the institution and not ORDA, and will not be received as part of ORDA files. No copies will be made of the records.

VI-E-4-c. ORDA will inform the institution of the HHS Freedom of Information Officer's determination and follow the institution's instructions as to whether some or all the records involved are to be returned to the institution or to become a part of ORDA files. If the institution instructs ORDA to return the records, no copies or summaries of the records will be made or retained by HHS, NIH, or ORDA.

VI-E-4-d. The HHS Freedom of Information Officer's determination will represent that official's judgement, as of the time of the determination, as to whether the records involved (or some portion) would be exempt from disclosure under the Freedom of Information Act, if at the time of the determination the records were in ORDA files and a request was received from them under the Act.

Appendix A.—Exemptions Under III-D-4

Section III-D-4 states that exemption from these Guidelines are "certain specified recombinant DNA molecules that consist entirely of DNA segments from different species that exchange DNA by known physiological processes, though one or more of the segments may be a synthetic equivalent. A list of such exchangers will be prepared and periodically revised by the Director, NIH, with advice of the RAC, after appropriate notice and opportunity for public comment. (See Section IV-E-1-b-(1)-(d).) Certain classes are exempt as of publication of these Revised Guidelines. The list is in Appendix A."

Under section III-D-4 of these Guidelines are recombinant DNA molecules that are (1) composed entirely of DNA segments from one or more of the organisms within a sublist and (2) to be propagated in any of the organisms within a sublist. (Classification of *Bergey's Manual of Determinative Bacteriology*, eighth edition. R. E. Buchanan and N. E. Gibbons, editors. Williams and Wilkins Company: Baltimore, 1974.)

Sublist A

1. Genus *Escherichia*
2. Genus *Shigella*
3. Genus *Salmonella* (including *Arizona*)
4. Genus *Enterobacter*
5. Genus *Citrobacter* (including *Levinea*)
6. Genus *Klebsiella*
7. Genus *Erwinia*
8. *Pseudomonas aeruginosa, Pseudomonas putida* and *Pseudomonas fluorescens*
9. *Serratia marcescens*
10. *Yersinia enterocolitica*

Sublist B

1. *Bacillus subtilis*
2. *Bacillus licheniformis*
3. *Bacillus pumilus*
4. *Bacillus globigii*
5. *Bacillus niger*
6. *Bacillus nato*
7. *Bacillus amyloliquefaciens*
8. *Bacillus aterrimus*

Sublist C

1. *Streptomyces aureofaciens*
2. *Streptomyces rimosus*
3. *Streptomyces coelicolor*

Sublist D

1. *Streptomyces griseus*
2. *Streptomyces cyaneus*
3. *Streptomyces venezuelae*

Sublist E

One way transfer of *Streptococcus mutans* or *Streptococcus lactis* DNA into *Streptococcus sanguis*.

Sublist F

1. *Streptococcus sanguis*
2. *Streptococcus pneumoniae*
3. *Streptococcus faecalis*
4. *Streptococcus pyogenes*

Appendix B.—Classification of Microorganisms on the Basis of Hazard

I. Classification of Etiologic Agents on the Basis of Hazard (1)

A. Class 1 Agents

All bacterial, parasitic, fungal, viral, rickettsial, and chlamydial agents not included in higher classes.

B. Class 2 Agents

1. Bacterial Agents

Actinobacillus—all species except *A. mallei*, which is in Class 3
Arizona hinshawii—all sterotypes
Bacillus anthracis
Bordetella—all species
Borrelia recurrentis, B. vincenti
Clostridium botulinum,
Cl. chauvoei, Cl. haemolyticum,
Cl. histolyticum, Cl. novyi
Cl. septicum, Cl. tetani
Corynebacterium diptheriae,
C. equi, C. haemolyticum,
C. pseudotuberculosis
C. pyogenes, C. renale
Diplococcus (Streptococcus) pneumoniae
Erysipelothrix insidiosa
Escherichia coli—all enteropathogenic serotypes
Haemophilus ducreyi, H. influenzae
Herellae vaginicola
Klebsiella—all species and all serotypes
Leptospira interrogans—all serotypes
Listeria—*all species*
Mima polymorpha
Moraxella—all species
Mycobacteria—all species except those listed in Class 3

Mycoplasma—all species except *Mycoplasma mycoides* and *Mycoplasma agalactiae*, which are in Class 5
Neisseria gonorrhoeae, N. Meningitidis
Pasteurella—all species except those listed in Class 3
Salmonella—all species and all serotypes
Shigella—all species and all serotypes
Sphaerophorus necrophorus
Staphylococcus aureus
Streptobacillus moniliformis
Streptococcus pyogenes
Treponema carateum, T. pallidum, and T. pertenue
Vibrio fetus, V. comma, including biotype El Tor, and *V. parahemolyticus*

2. Fungal Agents

***Actinomycetes* (including *Nocardia* species and *Actinomyces species and Arachnia propionica)*
Blastomyces dermatitidis
Cryptococcus neoformans
Paracoccidioides brasiliensis

3. Parasitic Agents

Endamoeba histolytica
Leishmania sp.
Naegleria gruberi
Toxoplasma gondii
Toxocara canis
Trichinella spiralis
Trypanosoma cruzi

4. Viral, Rickettsial, and Chlamydial Agents

Adenoviruses—human—all types
Cache Valley virus
Coxsackie A and B viruses
Cytomegaloviruses
Echoviruses—all types
Encephalomyocarditis virus (EMC)
Flanders virus
Hart Park virus
Hepatitis-associated antigen material
Herpes viruses—except *Herpesvirus simiae* (Monkey B virus) which is in Class 4
Corona viruses
Influenza viruses—all types except A/PR8/34, which is in Class 1
Langat virus
Lymphogranuloma venereum agent
Measles virus
Mumps virus
Parainfluenza virus—all types except Parainfluenza virus 3, SF4 strain, which is in Class 1
Poliviruses—all types, wild and attenuated
Poxviruses—all types except *Alastrim, Smallpox, Monkey pox, and Whitepox*, which depending on experiments, are in Class 3 or Class 4
Rabies virus—all strains except *Rabies street virus*, which should be classified in Class 3 when inoculated into carnivores
Reoviruses—all types
Respiratory syncytial virus
Rhinoviruses—all types
Rubella virus
Simian viruses—all types except *Herpesvirus simiae (Monkey B virus) and Marburg virus*, which are in Class 4
Sindbis virus
Tensaw virus
Turlock virus
Vaccinia virus
Varcella virus
Vole rickettsia
Yellow fever virus, 17D vaccine strain

C. Class 3 Agents

1. Bacterial Agents

*Actinobacillus mallei**
Bartonella—all species
Brucella—all species
Francisella tularensis
Mycobacterium avium, M. bovis, M. tuberculosis
Pasteurella multocide type B ("buffalo" and other foreign virulent strains*)
*Pseudenionas Pseudomallei**
Yersenia pestis

2. Fungal Agents

Coccidioides immitis
Histoplasma capsulatum
Histoplasma capsulatum var. *duboisii*

3. Parasitic Agents

Schistosoma mansoni

4. Viral, Rickettsial, and Chlamydial Agents

****Alastrim, Smallpox, Monkey pox, and Whitepox*, when used in *vitro*
Arboviruses—all strains except those in Class 2 and 4 (Arboviruses indigenous to the United States are in Class 3, except those listed in Class 2. *West Nile* and *Semliki Forest* viruses may be classified up or down, depending on the conditions of use and geographical location of the laboratory.)
Dengue virus, when used for transmission or animal inoculation experiments
Lymphocytic choriameningitis virus (LCM)
Psittacosis-Ornithosis-Trachoma group of agents
Rabies street virus, when used in inoculations of carnivores (See Class 2)
Rickettsia—all species except *Vole rickettsia* when used for transmission or animal inoculation experiments
*Vesicular stomatitis virus**
Yellow fever virus—wild, when used *in vitro*

D. Class 4 Agents

1. Bacterial Agents: None
2. Fungal Agents: None
3. Parasitic Agents: None
4. Viral, Rickettsial, and Chlamydial Agents

****Alasatrim, Smallpox, Monkey pox, and Whitepox*, when used for transmission or animal inoculation experiments
Hemorrhagic fever agents, including *Crimean hemorrhagic fever, (Congo), Junin*, and *Machupo* viruses, and others as yet undefined
Herpesvirus simiae (Monkey B virus)
Lassa virus
Marburg virus
Tick-borne encephalitis virus complex, including *Russian spring-summer encephalitis, Kyasanur forest disease, Omsk hemorrhagic fever*, and *Central European encephalitis viruses*
Venezuelan equine encephalitis virus, epidemic strains, when used for transmission or animal inoculation experiments
Yellow fever virus—wild, when used for transmission or animal inoculation experiments

II. Classification of Oncogenic Viruses on the Basis of Potential Hazard (2)

A. Low-Risk Oncogenic Viruses

Rous Sarcoma
SV-40
CELO
Ad7-SV40
Polyoma
Bovine papilloma
Rat mammary tumor
Avian Leukosis
Murine Leukemia
Murine Sarcoma
Mouse mammary tumor
Rat Leukemia
Hamster Leukemia
Bovine Leukemia
Dog Sarcoma
Mason-Pfizer Monkey Virus
Marek's
Guinea Pig Herpes
Lucke (Frog)
Adenovirus
Shope Fibroma
Shope Papilloma

B. Moderate-Risk Oncogenic Viruses

Ad2-SV40
FeLV
HV Saimiri
EBV
SSV-1
GaLV
HV ateles
Yaba
FeSV

III. Animal Pathogens (3)

A. Animal disease organisms which are forbidden entry into the United States by Law (CDC Class 5 agents)

1. Foot and mouth disease virus

B. Animal disease organisms and vectors which are forbidden entry into the United States by USDA Policy (CDC Class 5 Agents)

African horse sickness virus
African swine fever virus
Besnoitia besnoiti
Borna disease virus
Bovine infectious petechial fever
Camel pox virus
Ephemeral fever virus
Fowl plague virus
Goat pox virus
Hog cholera virus
Louping ill virus
Lumpy skin disease virus
Nairobi sheep disease virus
Newcastle disease virus (Asiatic strains)
Mycoplasma mycoides (contagious bovine pleuropneumonia)
Mycoplasma agalactiae (contagious agalactia of sheep)
Rickettsia ruminatium (heart water)
Rift valley fever virus
Rinderpest virus
Sheep pox virus
Swine vesicular disease virus
Teschen disease virus
Trypanosoma vivax (Nagana)
Trypanosoma evansi
Theileria prava (East Coast fever)
Theileria annulata
Theileria lawrencei
Theileria bovis
Theileria hirci
Vesicular exanthema virus
Wesselsbron disease virus
Zyonema

Footnotes and references of Appendix B

* A USDA permit, required for import and interstate commerce of pathogens, may be obtained from the Animal and Plant Health Inspection Service, USDA, Federal Building, Hyattsville, MD 20782.

** Since the publication of the classification in 1974 [1], the *Actinomycetes* have been reclassified as bacterial rather than fungal agents.

*** All activities, including storage of variola and whitepox are restricted to the single national facility (World Health Organization (WHO) Collaborating Center for Smallpox Research, Center for Disease Control, in Atlanta).

1. *Classification of Etiologic Agents on the Basis of Hazard.* (4th Edition, July 1974). U.S. Department of Health, Education and Welfare, Public Health Service, Center for Disease Control, Office of Biosafety, Atlanta, Georgia 30333.

2. *National Cancer Institute Safety Standards for Research Involving Oncogenic Viruses* (October 1974). U.S. Department of Health, Education, and Welfare Publication No. (NIH) 75-790.

3. U.S. Department of Agriculture, Animal and Plant Health Inspection Service.

Appendix C—Exemptions Under III-D-5

Section III-D-5 states that exempt from these Guidelines are "Other classes of recombinant DNA molecules, if the Director, NIH, with advice of the RAC, after appropriate notice and opportunity for public comment, finds that they do not present a significant risk to health or the environment. (See Section IV-E-1-b-(1)-(d)). Certain classes are exempt as of publication of these Revised Guidelines."

The following classes of experiments are exempt under Section III-D-5 of the Guidelines:

1. *Recombinant DNAs in Tissue Culture.* Recombinant DNA molecules derived entirely from non-viral components (that is, no component is derived from a eukaryotic virus), that are propagated and maintained in cells in tissue culture are exempt from these Guidelines with the exceptions listed below.

Exceptions. Experiments described in Section III-A which require specific RAC review and NIH approval before initiation of the experiment.

Experiments involving DNA from Class 3, 4, or 5 organisms [1] or cells known to be infected with these agents.

Experiments involving the deliberate introduction of genes coding for the biosynthesis of toxins potent for vertebrates. (See Appendix F.)

2. *Experiments Involving E. coli K-12 Host-Vector Systems.* Experiments which use *E. coli* K-12 host-vector systems, with the exception of those experiments listed below, are exempt from these Guidelines provided that (a) the *E. coli* host shall not contain conjugation proficient plasmids or generalized transducing phages, and (b) lambda or lambdoid or Ff bacteriophages or nonconjugative plasmids [49] shall be used as vectors. However, experiments involving the insertion into *E. coli* K-12 of DNA from prokaryotes that exchange genetic information [35] with *E. coli* may by performed with any *E. coli* K-12 vector (e.g., conjugative plasmid). When a nonconjugative vector is used, the *E. coli* K-12 host may contain conjugation-proficient plasmids either autonomous or integrated, or generalized transducing phages.

For these exempt experiments, P1 physical containment conditions are recommended.

Exceptions. Experiments described in Section III-A which require specific RAC review and NIH approval before initiation of the experiment.

Experiments involving DNA from Class 3, 4, or 5 organisms [1] or from cells known to be infected with these agents may be conducted under containment conditions specified in Section III-B-2 with prior IBC review and approval.

Large-scale experiments (e.g., more than 10 liters of culture) require prior IBC review and approval. (See Section III-B-5.)

Experiments involving the deliberate cloning of genes coding for the biosynthesis of toxins potent for vertebrates. (See Appendix F.)

3. *Experiments Involving Saccharomyces cerevisiae Host-Vector Systems.* Experiments which use *Saccharomyces cerevisiae* host-vector systems, with the exception of experiments listed below, are exempt from these Guidelines provided that laboratory strains are used.

For these exempt experiments, P1 physical containment conditions are recommended.

Exceptions. Experiments described in Section III-A which require specific RAC review and NIH approval before initiation of the experiment.

Experiments involving CDC Class 3, 4, or 5 organisms [1] or cells known to be infected with these agents may be conducted under containment conditions specified in Section III-B-2 with prior IBC review and approval.

Large-scale experiments (e.g., more than 10 liters of culture) require prior IBC review and approval. (See Section III-B-5.)

Experiments involving the deliberate cloning of genes coding for the biosynthesis of toxins potent for vertebrates. (See Appendix F.)

4. *Experiments Involving Bacillus subtilis Host Vector-Systems.* Any asporogenic *Bacillus subtilis* strain which does not revert to a sporeformer with a frequency greater than 10^{-7} can be used for cloning DNA, with the exception of those experiments listed below. Indigenous *Bacillus* plasmids and phages, whose host-range does not include *Bacillus cereus* or *Bacillus anthracis*, may be used as vectors.

For these exempt experiments P1 physical containment conditions are recommended.

Exceptions. Experiments described in Section III-A which require specific RAC review and approval before initiation of the experiment.

Experiments involving CDC Class 3, 4, or 5 organisms [1] or cells known to be infected with these agents may be conducted under containment conditions specified by Section III-B-2 with prior IBC review and approval.

Large-scale experiments (e.g., more than 10 liters of culture) require prior IBC review and approvall. (See Section III-B-5.)

Experiments involving the deliberate cloning of genes coding for the biosynthesis of toxins potent for vertebrates. (See Appendix F.)

Appendix D—Actions Taken Under The Guidelines

As noted in the subsections of Sections IV-E-1-b-(1) and IV-E-1-b-(2), the Director, NIH, may take certain actions with regard to the Guidelines after consideration by the RAC.

Some of the actions taken to date include the following:

1. Permission is granted to clone Foot-and-Mouth Disease Virus in the EKI host-vector system consisting of *E. coli* K-12 and the vector pBR322, all work to be done at the Plum Island Animal Disease Center.

2. Certain specified clones derived from segments of the Foot-and-Mouth Disease Virus may be transferred from Plum Island Animal Disease Center to the facilities of Genentech, Inc., of South San Franciso, California. Further development of the clones at Genentech has been approved under P1+EKI conditions.

3. The Rd strain of *Hemophilus influenzae* can be used as a host for the propagation of the cloned Tn 10 tet R gene derived from *E. coli* K-12 employing the non-conjugative *Haemophilus* plasmid, pRSF0885, under P1 conditions.

4. Permission is granted to clone certain subgenomic segments of Foot-and-Mouth Disease Virus in HVl *Bacillus Subtilis* and *Saccharomyces cerevisiae* host-vector systems under P1 conditions at Genentech, Inc., South San Francisco, California.

5. Permission is granted to Dr. Ronald Davis of Stanford University to field test corn plants modified by recombinant DNA techniques under specified containment conditions.

6. Permission is granted to clone in *E. coli* K-12, under P1 physical containment conditions, subgenomic segments of Rift Valley Fever Virus subject to conditions which have been set forth by the RAC.

7. Attenuated laboratory strains of *Salmonella typhimurium* may be used under P1 physical containment conditions to screen for the *Saccharomyces cerevisiae* pseudouridine synthetase gene. The plasmid YEp13 will be employed as the vector.

8. Permission is granted to transfer certain clones of subgenomic segments of Foot-and-Mouth Disease Virus from Plum Island Animal Disease Center to the laboratories of Molecular Genetics, Inc., Minnetonka, Minnesota, and to work with these clones under P1 containment conditions. Approval is contingent upon review of data on infectivity testing of the clones by a working group of the RAC.

Appendix E—Certified Host-Vector Systems

While many experiments using *E. coli* K-12, *Saccharomyces cerevisiae* and *Bacillus subtilis* are currently exempt from the Guidelines under Exemption III-D-5, some derivatives of these host-vector systems were previously classified as HV1 or HV2. A listing of those systems follows:

HV1—The following plasmids are accepted as the vector components of certified *B.*

subtilis HV1 systems: pUB110, pC194, pS194, pSA2100, pE194, pT127, pUB112, pC221, pC223, and pAB124. *B. subtilis* strains RUB 331 and BGSC 1S53 have been certified as the host component of HV1 systems based on these plasmids.

HV2—The asporogenic mutant derivative of *Bacillus subtilis*, ASB 298, with the following plasmids as the vector component: pUB110, pC194, pS194, pSA2100, pE194, pT127, pUB112, pC221, pC223, and pAB124.

HV2—The following sterile strains of *Saccharomyces cerevisiae*, all of which have the ste-VC9 mutation, SHY1, SHY2, SHY3, and SHY4. The following plasmids are certified for use: YIp1, YEp2, YEp4, YIp5, YEp6, YRp7, YEp20, YEp21, YEp24, YIp25, YIp26, YIp27, YIp28, YIp29, YIp30, YIp31, YIp32, and YIp33.

EK2 Plasmid Systems. The *E. coli* K-12 strain chi-1776. The following plasmids are certified for use: pSC101, pMB9, pBR313, pBR322, pDH24, pBR327, pGL101, pHB1. The following *E. coli/S. cerevisiae* hybrid plasmids are certified as EK2 vectors when used in *E. coli* chi-1776 or in the sterile yeast strains, SHY1, SHY2, SHY3 and SHY4: YIp1, YEp2, YEp4, YIp5, YEp6, YRp7, YEp20, YEp21, YEp24, YIp25, YIp26, YIp27, YIp28, YIp29, YIp30, YIp31, YIp32 and YIp33.

EK2 Bacteriophage Systems. The following are certified EK2 systems based on bacteriophage lambda:

Vector	Host
λgt*WES*λ*B* '	DP50*supF*
λgt*WES*λ*B*'	DP50*supF*
λgt*ZJvir*λ*B* '	T3E*coli* K-12
λgtALOλB'	DP50*supF*
Charon 3A	DP50 or DP50*supF*
Charon 4A	DP50 or DP50*supF*
Charon 16A	DP50 or DP50*supF*
Charon 21A	DP50*supF*
Charon 23A	DP50 or DP50*supF*
Charon 24A	DP50 or DP50*supF*.

E. coli K-12 strains chi-2447 and chi-2281 are certified for use with lambda vectors that are certified for use with strain DP50 or DP50supF provided that the su^{o} strain not be used as a propagation host.

' *E. coli* K-12 strains chi-1984, chi-2705, chi-2001, and chi-2363 are certified for use with lambda vectors that are certified for use with strain DP50 or SP50supF provided that the su^{o} strains not be used as propagation hosts.

Additional certified host-vector systems are as follows :

HV1—The following specified strains of *Neurospora crassa* which have been modified to prevent aerial dispersion

(1) inl (inositolless) strains 37102, 37401, 46316, 64001, and 89601.

(2) csp-1 strain UCLA37 and csp-2 strains FS 590, UCLA101 (these are conidial separation mutants).

(3) eas strain UCLA191 (an" easily wettable" mutant).

HV1—The following *Streptomyces* species: *Streptomyces coelicolor, S. lividans, S. parvulus,* and *S. griseus*. The following are accepted as vector components of certified *Streptomyces* HV1 systems: *Streptomyces* plasmids SCP2, SLP1.2, pIJ101, actinophage phi C31, and their derivatives.

HV1—*Pseudomonas putida* strain KT2440 with plasmid vectors pKT262, pKT263, and pKT264.

Appendix F—Containment Conditions for Cloning of Genes Coding for the Biosynthesis of Toxins for Vertebrates

1. *General Information.* Appendix F specifies the containment to be used for the deliberate cloning of genes coding for the biosynthesis of toxins for vertebrates. Cloning of genes coding for toxins for vertebrates that have an LD_{50} of less than 100 nanograms per kilogram body weight (e.g., the botulinum toxins, tetanus toxin, diphtheria toxin, *Shigella dysenteria* neurotoxin) is prohibited. No specific restrictions shall apply to the cloning of genes if the protein specified by the gene has an LD_{50} of 100 micrograms or more per kilogram of body weight. Experiments involving genes coding for toxins with an LD_{50} of 100 micrograms or less per kilogram body weight shall be registered with ORDA prior to initiating the experiments. A list of toxins classified as to LD_{50} is available from ORDA. Testing procedures for determining toxicity of toxins not on the list are available from ORDA. The results of such tests shall be forwarded to ORDA, which will consult with the *ad hoc* Working Group on toxins prior to inclusion of the toxin on the list. (See Section IV-E-1-b-(3)-(e).)

2. *Containment Conditions for Cloning of Toxin Genes in E. coli K-12.* (a) Cloining of genes coding for toxins for vertebrates that have an LD_{50} in the range of 100 nanograms to 1000 nanograms per kilogram body weight (e.g., abrin, *Clostridium perfringens* epsilon toxin) may proceed under P2 + EK2 or P3 + EK1 containment conditions.

(b) Cloning of genes for the biosynthesis of toxins for vertebrates with an LD_{50} in the range of 1 microgram to 100 micrograms per kilogram body weight may proceed under P1 + EK1 containment conditions (e.g., *Staphylococcus aureus* alpha toxin, *Staphylococcus aureus* beta toxin, ricin, *Pseudomonas aeruginosa* exotoxin A, *Bordatella pertussis* toxin, the lethal factor of *Bacillus anthracis*, the *Pasteurella pestis* murine toxins, the oxygen-labile hemolysins such as streptolysin O, and certain neurotoxins present in snake venoms and other venoms).

(c) Some enterotoxins are substantially more toxic when administered enterally than parenterally. The following enterotoxins shall be subject to P1 + EK1 containment conditions: cholera toxin, the heat labile toxins of *E. coli, Klebsiella,* and other related proteins that may be identified by neutralization with an antiserum mono-specific for chlorea toxin, and heat stable toxins of *E. coli* and of *Yersinia enterocolitica.*

3. *Containment Conditions for Cloning of Toxins Genes in Organisms Other than E. coli K-12.* Requests involving the cloning of genes coding for toxins for vertebrates in host-vector systems other than *E. coli* K-12 will be evaluated by ORDA, which will consult with the *ad hod* working group on toxins. (See Section IV-E-1-b-(3)-(f).)

4. *Specific Approvals.* a. Permission is granted to clone the Exotoxin A gene of *Pseudomonas aeruginosa* under P1 conditions in *Pseudomonas aeruginosa.*

b. The pyrogenic endotoxin type A (Tox A) gene of *Staphylococcus aureus* may be cloned in an HV2 *Bacillus subtilis* host-vector system under P3 containment conditions.

c. Permission is granted to clone in *E. coli* K-12, in high containment Building 550 at the Frederick Cancer Research Facility, restriction fragments of *Corynephage Beta* carrying the structural gene for diphtheria toxin. Laboratory practices and containment equipment are to be specified by the IBC.

d. The genes coding for the Staphylococcus aureus determinants, A, B, and F, which may be implicated in toxic shock syndrome, may be cloned in *E. coli* K-12 under P2 + EK1 conditions. The *Staphylococcus aureus* strain used as the donor is to be alpha toxin minus. It is suggested that, if possible, the donor *Staphylococcus aureus* strain should lack other toxins with LD_{50}s in the range of one microgram per kilogram body weight, such as the exfoliative toxin.

e. Fragments F-1 and F-2 of the diphtheria toxin gene (tox) may be cloned in *E. coli* K-12 under P1 + EK1 containment conditions. Fragment F-1 and fragment F-2 both contain (i) some or all of the transcriptional control elements of *tox*, (ii) the signal peptide, and (iii) fragment A (the center responsible for ADP-ribosylation of elongation factor 2).

f. The gene(s) coding for a toxin (designated LT-like) isolated from *E. coli* which is similar to the *E. coli* heat labile enterotoxin (LT) with respect to its activities and mode of action, but is not neutralized by antibodies against cholera enterotoxin or against LT from human or porcine *E. coli* strains and sequences homologous to the *E. coli* LT-like toxin gene may be cloned under P1 + EK1 conditions.

Dated: April 12, 1982.

Bernard Talbot,

Acting Director, National Institute of Allergy and Infectious Diseases.

Note.—OMB's "Mandatory Information Requirements for Federal Assistance Program Announcements" (45 FR 39592) requires a statement concerning the official government programs contained in the *Catalog of Federal Domestic Assistance.* Normally NIH lists in its announcements the number and title of affected individual programs for the guidance of the public. Because the guidance in this notice covers not only vitually every NIH Program but also essentially every federal research program in which DNA recombinant molecule techniques could be used, it has been determined to be not cost effective or in the public interest to attempt to list these programs. Such a list would likely require several additional pages. In addition, NIH could not be certain that every federal program would be included as many federal agencies, as well as private organizations, both national and international, have elected to follow the NIH Guidelines. In lieu of the individual program listing, NIH invites readers to direct questions to the information address above about whether individual programs listed in the *Catalog of Federal Domestic Assistance* are affected.

NIH programs are not covered by OMB Circular A-95 because they fit the description of "programs not considered appropriate" in Section 8-(b)- (4) and (5) of that Circular.

[FR Doc. 82-10860 Filed 4-20-82; 8:45 am]

BILLING CODE 4140-01-M

federal register

Wednesday
May 26, 1982

Part IV

Department of Health and Human Services

National Institutes of Health

Recombinant DNA Advisory Committee, Meeting; Recombinant DNA Research: Proposed Actions Under Guidelines

DEPARTMENT OF HEALTH AND HUMAN SERVICES

National Institutes of Health

Recombinant DNA Advisory Committee; Meeting

Pursuant to Pub. L. 92-463, notice is hereby given of a meeting of the Recombinant DNA Advisory Committee at Wilson Hall, Building, 1, National Institutes of Health, 9000 Rockville Pike, Bethesda, Maryland 20205, on June 28, 1982, from 9:00 a.m. to adjournment at approximately 6:00 p.m. This meeting will be open to the public to discuss:

Proposed major revision of the Guidelines
Amendment of Guidelines
Proposed exemptions to Guidelines
Other matters requiring necessary action by the Committee

Attendance by the public will be limited to space available.

Dr. William J. Gartland, Jr., Executive Secretary, Recombinant DNA Advisory Committee, National Institutes of Health, Building 31, Room 4A52, telephone (301) 496-6051, will provide materials to be discussed at the meeting, rosters of committee members, and substantive program information. A summary of the meeting will be available at a later date.

In addition, notice is hereby given of a meeting of the Large-Scale Review Working Group sponsored by the Recombinant DNA Advisory Committee at the National Institutes of Health, Wilson Hall, Building 1, 9000 Rockville Pike, Bethesda, Maryland 20205, on June 29, 1982, from 9:00 a.m. to 12:00 noon. The meeting will be open to the public. Attendance will be limited to space available.

Further information may be obtained from Dr. Elizabeth Milewski, Executive Secretary, Large-Scale Review Working Group, NIAID, Building 31, Room 4A52, Bethesda, Maryland, telephone (301) 496-6051.

Dated: May 19, 1982.

Betty J. Beveridge,

National Institutes of Health Committee Management Officer.

Note.—OMB's "Mandatory Information Requirements for Federal Assistance Program Announcements" (45 FR 39592) requires a statement concerning the official government programs contained in the *Catalog of Federal Domestic Assistance*. Normally NIH lists in its announcements the number and title of affected individual programs for the guidance of the public. Because the guidance in this notice covers not only virtually every NIH program but also essentially every federal research program in which DNA recombinant molecule techniques could be used, it has been determined to be not cost effective or in the public interest to attempt to list these programs. Such a list would likely require several additional pages. In addition, NIH could not be certain that every federal program would be included as many federal agencies, as well as private organizations, both national and international, have elected to follow the NIH Guidelines. In lieu of the individual program listing, NIH invites readers to direct questions to the information address above about whether individual programs listed in the *Catalog of Federal Domestic Assistance* are affected.

NIH programs are not covered by OMB Circular A-95 because they fit the description of "programs not considered appropriate" in Section 8-(b)-(4) and (5) of that Circular.

[FR Doc. 82-14374 Filed 5-25-82; 8:45 am]

BILLING CODE 4140-01-M

Recombinant DNA Research: Proposed Actions Under Guidelines

AGENCY: National Institutes of Health, PHS, HHS.

ACTION: Notice of proposed revisions of NIH guidelines for research involving recombinant DNA molecules.

SUMMARY: This notice sets forth proposed revisions of the NIH Guidelines for Research Involving Recombinant DNA Molecules. Interested parties are invited to submit comments concerning these proposals. After consideration of these proposals and comments by the NIH Recombinant DNA Advisory Committee (RAC) at its meeting on June 28-29, 1982, the Director of the National Institute of Allergy and Infectious Diseases will issue decisions on these proposals in accord with the Guidelines.

DATE: Comments must be received by June 25, 1982.

ADDRESS: Written comments and recommendations should be submitted to the Director, Office of Recombinant DNA Activities, Building 31, Room 4A52, National Institutes of Health, Bethesda, Maryland, 20205. All comments received in timely response to this notice will be considered and will be available for public inspection in the above office on weekdays between the hours of 8:30 a.m. and 5:00 p.m.

FOR FURTHER INFORMATION CONTACT: Background documentation and additional information can be obtained from Drs. Stanley Barban and Elizabeth Milewski, Office of Recombinant DNA Activities, National Institutes of Health, Bethesda, Maryland 20205, (301) 496-6051.

SUPPLEMENTARY INFORMATION: The National Institutes of Health will consider the following proposed revisions of the Guidelines for Research Involving Recombinant DNA Molecules.

I. Proposed Revision of Appendix A. Sublist F

Dr. Gary M. Dunny of the New York State College of Veterinary Medicine requests that *Streptococcus agalactiae* be added to Appendix A, Sublist F, on the basis that it exchanges genetic information with other *Streptococcus* species in Sublist F.

II. Proposed Prohibition

Dr. Richard Novick of the Public Health Research Institute of City of New York and Dr. Richard Goldstein of Harvard Medical School have proposed that a prohibition against the construction of biological weapons by molecular cloning be added to the Guidelines. The rationale for this proposal is outlined in a letter to ORDA.

III. Proposal for Revision of the Guidelines

A. Introduction

The Recombinant DNA Advisory Committee (RAC) at its February 8-9, 1982 meeting, recommended that the National Institutes of Health (NIH) accept a proposed modification (46 FR 59734) of the NIH Guidelines for Research Involving Recombinant DNA Molecules. In supporting this modification, the RAC recommended that a working group be formed to simplify further and modify the document. On April 21, 1982, the NIH promulgated the revised Guidelines (47 FR 17180).

An *ad hoc* Working Group on Revision of the Guidelines was formed and convened for a meeting on April 19, 1982. The committee addressed several issues at this meeting. The first topic was an attempt to improve the "presentation" of the Guidelines. It was felt that most of Section II, which describes physical and biological containment standards, as well as shipping, should be moved to three separate new Appendices (G, H, and I). In addition, the section describing shipment (currently II-C) should be expanded to include further information on packaging and labeling. It was noted that the current Guidelines provide little concrete guidance for shipping materials; rather, they refer the reader to other sources.

Language describing "General Applicability" and "General Definitions" should be removed from Section IV and placed in Section I.

The working group discussed the question of whether the language of Section III-A-1 and Appendix F which refers to "toxins" also applies to other pharmacologically active molecules. A correspondent questioned whether "pharmacologically active molecules" such as certain hormones should be treated as toxins. Pointing to Section I-B, second paragraph, which cites: "a toxin or a pharmacologically active agent," the working group agreed that the intent of the Guidelines is to cover these types of molecules and recommended that the language dealing with toxins in the Guidelines be amended to reflect that intent.

The working group discussed the issue of which document should be utilized to determine the pathogenic classification of an organism. The original 1976 Guidelines used the publication *Classification of Etiologic Agents on the Basis of Hazard*, 4th Edition, July 1974; U.S. Depatment of Health, Education and Welfare, Public Health Service, Center for Disease Control, as the reference source for classification of microorganisms for the purposes of the Guidelines. All subsequent revisions of the Guidelines have also used this document. At the present time, the Centers for Disease Control (CDC) and the NIH are engaged in an effort to revise the *Classification of Etiologic Agents on the Basis of Hazard*. The working group felt, however, that this revised version might not serve the purposes of the Guidelines as well as the original 1974 version. Nonetheless, the working group noted that additional pathogens should be added to the classification in the Guidelines and that the classification should be updated regularly. It was also noted that some organisms might better be treated in a manner specific for the purposes of the Guidelines. The working group recommended, therefore, that the RAC and NIH adopt for the Guidelines a revised version of the 1974 CDC classification, and that the RAC should assume responsibility for regularly updating the listing. The working group recommended that (a) the following bacteria be added to the list of Class 2 bacterial agents:

Aeromonas Hydrophila
Campylobacter fetus
Campylobacter jejuni
Edwardsiella tarda
Yersinia enterocolitica

and the listing for *Escherichia coli* be changed to refer to "all enteropathogenic, enterotoxigenic, enteroinvasive, and strains bearing Kl antigen;" (b) Vesicular stomatitis virus be listed as a Class 2 viral agent rather than a Class 3 viral agent; (c) Rabies street virus be classified as a Class 3 viral agent for all procedures; (d) Alastrim, Smallpox, and Whitepox should be listed as Class 5 viral agents rather than as Class 3 and Class 4 agents as the study of these viruses is restricted to a single national facility (WHO Collaborating Center for Smallpox Research, Centers for Disease Control) and the language dealing with Poxviruses modified accordingly; (e) Viruses classified as low risk oncogenic viruses by the National Cancer Institute Safety Standards for Research Involving Oncogenic Viruses (October 1974, U.S. Departnment of Health, Education, and Welfare Publication Number (NIH) 75-790) should be classified as Class 2 agents for the purposes of the Guidelines; and (f) Moderate-risk oncogenic viruses should be classified as Class 3 agents for the purposes of the Guidelines. Furthermore, footnotes, references, and the title of Appendix B should be modified to reflect the status of a revised Appendix B.

The working group dealt with the issue of the composition of the Institutional Biosafety Committees (IBCs). A discussion arose as to the necessity of stating in current Section IV-D-2-a that not less than 20% of the membership of the IBC shall not be affliated with the institution. It was felt that the 20% specification limits the flexibility of the university in appointing members to the IBC. The example was offered of an IBC fulfilling the 20% specification, but wishing to add an additional specialist affiliated with the university. However, non-affiliated representation would fall below 20% when this specialist is appointed and the university would have to appoint another non-affiliated member. The specification that at least two members shall not be affiliated with the institution should remain in the Guidelines to ensure community representation. It was felt that in a twenty member committee, two public members would provide adequate representation for the community. Members of the working group could not envisage IBCs larger than 20 members functioning smoothly. In addition, it was noted that ORDA reviews IBC membership for compliance and would be alert to cases in which an institution might attempt to dilute community representation by, for example, appointing a 50 member committee.

The working group also considered the language of current Section IV-D-2-b. A discussion ensued regarding representation on the IBC from the laboratory technical staff. If the term "nondoctoral" was deleted, postdoctoral associates might also be appointed to the IBC. Other members of the working group pointed out that technicians are, indeed, those most likely to be performing recombinant DNA experiments and those having the least "competitive" pressures exerted on them. Although technicians do experience certain types of pressures, many on the working group felt they would be among the best "watchpersons."

The working group also recommended a number of additional changes in the Guidelines. The recommendations of the working group, with minor modifications introduced by NIH staff, are summarized in part B of this announcement. The proposed revised Guidelines (incorporating the changes described in part B of this announcement) are given in their entirety in part C. Several additional proposed changes are given in part D.

B. Summary of Proposed Changes

Specifically, the proposed modifications would accomplish both a reorganization of the Guidelines, and a revision of the specific language of certain sections. The proposed reorganization of the Guidelines would require renumbering of several sections and minor editorial changes throughout the document to reflect this renumbering. These minor changes will not be enumerated below, but interested individuals may refer to the proposed revised Guidelines, which are reprinted *in toto* in part C. The major proposed revisions are enumerated below. Readers should note that sections which are proposed for revision are identified by their current Section numbering. The proposed modified language, however, is identified by new Section numbering when renumbering would occur in that section.

1. *Section I. Scope of the Guidelines.* a. The text from Section IV-B, *General Applicability*, would be moved to Section I-C, *General Applicability*, and be renumbered.

b. The text from Sections IV-C, *General Definitions*, would be moved to Section I-D, *General Definitions*, with the exception of Section IV-C-1, IV-C-2, and IV-C-8 which would be deleted.

Section IV-C-1 currently reads as follows:

"IV-C-1. 'DNA' means deoxyribonucleic acid."

Section IV-C-2 currently reads as follows:

"IV-C-2. 'Recombinant DNA' or 'recombinant DNA molecules' means either (i) molecules which are constructed outside living cells by joining natural or synthetic DNA segments to DNA molecules that can replicate in a living cell, or (ii) DNA molecules which result from the replication of malecules described in (i) above."

Section IV–C–8 currently reads as follows:

" 'Federal Interagency Advisory Committee on Recombinant DNA Research' means the committee established in October 1976 to advise the Secretary, HHS, the Assistant Secretary for Health, and the Directory, NIH, on the coordination of those aspects of all Federal programs and activities which related to recombinant DNA research."

Section IV–C–9, the definition of *Laboratory Safety Monograph* would be moved to Appendix G, *Physical Containment.*

The text of current Section IV–C would be renumbered to reflect its new position in I–D and the deletion of current sections IV–C–1, IV–C–2, and IV–C–8.

2. *Section II. Containment.* a. New language is added to the first paragraph of Section II, *Containment,* as follows:

"Four levels of physical containment, which are designated as P1, P2, P3, and P4 are described in Appendix G. P4 provides the most stringent containment conditions, P1 the least stringent."

b. New language is added to the second paragraph of Section II, *Containment,* as follows:

"Further details on biological containment may be found in Appendix I."

c. Section II–A, *Standard Practices and Training,* would be moved to a new Appendix G and renumbered.

d. Section II–B, *Physical Containment Levels,* would be moved to Appendix G and renumbered.

e. The title of Tables I and II in Section II–B, "Combinations of Containment Safeguards," would be changed to "Possible Combinations of Containment Safeguards." The tables would be moved to Appendix G.

f. Section II–C, *Shipment,* would be moved to a new Appendix H and renumbered. Additional information on shipping procedures would be included.

g. Section II–D, *Biological Containment,* would be moved to a new Appendix I and renumbered.

h. The language of item (vi) in the first paragraph of Section II–D–2–b–(2), *HV2 Systems,* which would become Appendix I–II–B–2, would be modified to read:

"(vi) In some cases, the investigator may be asked to submit data on survival and vector transmissibility from experiments in which the host-vector is fed to laboratory animals and human subjects. Such *in vivo* data may be required to confirm the validity of predicting *in vivo* survival on the basis of *in vitro* experiments."

i. Section II–D–3, *Distribution of Certified Host-Vectors,* would be deleted.

3. *Section III. Containment Guidelines for Covered Experiments.*

a. Section III–A would be modified to read as follows:

"III–A. *Experiments that Require RAC Review and NIH and IBC Approval Before Initiation.* Experiments in this category cannot be initiated without submission of relevant information on the proposed experiment to NIH, the publication of the proposal in the **Federal Register** for thirty days of comment, review by the RAC, and specific approval by NIH. The containment conditions for such experiments will be recommended by RAC and set by NIH at the time of approval. Such experiments also require the approval of the IBC before initiation. Specific experiments already approved in this section and the appropriate containment conditions are listed in Appendices D and F. If an experiment is similar to those listed in Appendices D and F, ORDA may determine appropriate containment conditions according to case precedents under Section IV–C–1–b–(3)–(g)."

b. Section III–A–1 would be modified to read as follows:

"III–A–1. Deliberate formation of recombinant DNAs containing genes for the biosynthesis of toxic molecules lethal for vertebrates at an LD_{50} of less than 100 nanograms per kilogram body weith (e.g., microbial toxins such as the botulinum toxins, tetanus toxin, diphtheria toxin, *Shigella dysenteriae* neuro-toxin). Specific approval has been given for the cloning in *E. coli* K-12 of DNAs containing genes coding for the biosynthesis of toxic molecules which are lethal to vertebrates at 100 nanograms to 100 micrograms per kilogram body weight. Containment levels for these experiments are specified in Appendix F."

c. The title of Section III–B–1 would be modified to read as follows:

"III–B–1. *Experiments Using Human or Animal Pathogens (Class 2, Class 3, Class 4, or Class 5 Agents [1]) as Host-Vector Systems.*"

d. Mention of CDC in Sections III–B–1–a, III–B–1–b, and III–B–1–c would be deleted.

e. Section III–B–1–c would be amended to read as follows:

"III–B–1–c. Experiments involving the introduction of recombinant DNA into Class 4 agents can be carried out at P4 containment."

f. A new Section III–B–1–d would be added as follows:

"III–B–1–d. Containment conditions for experiments involving the introduction of recombinant DNA into Class 5 agents will be set on a case-by-case basis following ORDA review. A USDA permit is required for work with Class 5 agents [18,20]"

g. The title of Section III–B–2 would be modified to read as follows:

"III–B–2. Experiments in Which DNA from Human or Animal Pathogens (Class 2, Class 3, Class 4, or Class 5 Agents [1]) is Cloned in Nonpathogenic Prokaryotic or Lower Eukaryotic Host-Vector Systems."

h. Sections III–B–2–a and III–B–2–b would be combined into a single Section III–B–2–a as follows:

"III–B–2–a. Recombinant DNA experiments in which DNA from Class 2 or Class 3 agents [1] is transferred into nonpathogenic prokaryotes or lower eukaryotes may be performed under P2 containment. Recombinant DNA experiments in which DNA from Class 4 agents is transferred into nonpathogenic prokaryotes or lower eukaryotes can be performed at P2 containment after demonstration that only a totally and irreversibly defective fraction of the agent's viral genome is present in a given recombinant. In the absence of such a demonstration, P4 containment should be used.

"Specific lowering of containment to P1 for particular experiments can be approved by the IBC. Many experiments in this category will be exempt from the Guidelines. (See Section III–D–4 and III–D–5.) Experiments involving the formation of recombinant DNAs for certain genes coding for molecules toxic for vertebrates require RAC review and NIH approval (see Section III–A–1), or must be carried out under NIH specified conditions as described in Appendix F."

i. A new Section III–B–2–b dealing with Class 5 agents would be added as follows:

"III–B–2–b. Containment conditions for experiments in which DNA from Class 5 agents is transferred into nonpathogenic prokaryotes or lower eukaryotes will be determined by ORDA following a case-by-case review. A USDA permit is required for work with Class 5 agents [18,20]."

j. A new paragraph would be added immediately after the heading of Section III–B–3 as follows:

"**Caution.**—Special care should be used in the evaluation of containment levels for experiments which are likely to either enhance the pathogenicity (e.g., insertion of a host oncogene) or to extend the host range (e.g., introduction of novel control elements) of viral vectors under conditions which permit a productive infection.

"In such cases, serious consideration should be given to raising the physical containment by at least one level."

k. Mention of the CDC would be deleted in Sections III–B–3–a, III–B–3–b, and III–B–3–c.

l. Section III–B–3–c would be modified to delete any mention of Class 5 agents as follows:

"III–B–3–c. Experiments involving the use of infectious Class 4 viruses [1], or defective Class 4 viruses in the presence of helper virus, may be carried out under P4 containment."

m. A new Section III–B–3–d would be added as follows:

"III–B–3–d. Experiments involving the use of infectious Class 5 [1] viruses, or defective Class 5 viruses in the presence of helper virus will be determined on a case-by-case basis following ORDA review. A USDA permit is required for work with Class 5 pathogens [18,20]."

n. Section III–B–4–a would be modified to read as follows:

"III–B–4–a. DNA from any source except for greater than two-thirds of a eukaryotic viral genome may be transferred to any non-human vertebrate organism and propagated under conditions of physical containment comparable to P1 and appropriate to the organism under study [2]. It is important that the investigator demonstrate that the fraction of the viral genome being utilized does not lead to productive infection."

4. *Section IV. Roles and Responsibilities.*

a. In the second paragraph of Section IV–A, *Policy,* the responsibility of the Institution would be emphasized by italicizing pertinent language, i.e.:

"The Guidelines are intended to help the Institution, the Institutional Biosafety Committee (IBC), the Biological Safety Officer, and the Principal Investigator determine the safeguards that should be inplemented. These Guidelines will never be complete or final, since all conceivable experiments involving recombinant DNA cannot be foreseen. Therefore, *it is the responsibility of the Institution and those associated with it to adhere to the purpose of the Guidelines as well as to specifics."*

b. Section IV–D, *Responsibilities of the Institution,* would be renumbered to become Section IV–B.

c. The language of Section IV–D–2, *Membership and Procedures of the IBC,* would be renumbered and modified to read as follows:

"IV–B–2. *Membership and Procedures of the IBC.* The institution shall establish an Institutional Biosafety Committee (IBC) whose responsibilities need not be restricted to recombinant DNA. The committee shall meet the following requirements * * *"

d. The requirement specifying that 20% of the IBC membership be non-affiliated with the Institution would be eliminated. Section IV–D–2–a would be renumbered and modified to read as follows:

"IV–B–2–a. The IBC shall comprise no fewer than five members so selected that they collectively have experience and expertise in recombinant DNA technology and the capability to assess the safety of recombinant DNA research experiments and any potential risk to public health or the environment. At least two members shall not be affiliated with the Institution (apart from their membership on the IBC) and shall represent the interest of the surrounding community with respect to health and protection of the environment. Members meet this requirement if, for example, they are officials of State or local public health or environmental protection agencies, members of other local governmental bodies, or persons active in medical, occupational health, or environmental concerns in the community. The Biological Safety Officer (BSO), mandatory when research is being conducted at the P3 and P4 levels, shall be a member (See Section IV–B–4.)"

e. The language of Section IV–D–2–b on professional competence and the specification on laboratory staff would be renumbered and modified to read as follows:

"IV–B–2–b. In order to ensure the competence necessary to review recombinant DNA activities, it is recommended that (i) the IBC include persons with expertise in recombinant DNA technology, biological safety, and physical containment; (ii) the IBC include, or have available as consultants, persons knowledgeable in institutional commitments ans policies, applicable law, standards of professional conduct and practice, community attitudes, and the environment; and (iii) at least one member be from the laboratory technical staff."

f. Section IV–D–2–e would be renumbered and modified to read as follows:

"IV–B–2–e. The Institution, who is ultimately responsible for the effectiveness of the IBC, may establish procedures that the IBC will follow in its initial and continuing review of applications, proposals, and activities. (IBC review procedures are specified in Section IV–B–3–a.)"

g. Section IV–D–2–f would be deleted. Section IV–D–2–f currently reads as follows:

"IV–D–2–f. Central to implementation of the Guidelines is the review of experiments by the IBC."

h. Section IV–D–2–h would be renumbered and modified to read as follows:

"IV–B–2–g. Upon request, the Institution shall make available to the public all minutes of IBC meetings and any documents submitted to or received from funding agencies which the latter are required to make available to the public. If comments are made by members of the public on IBC actions, the Institution shall forward to NIH both the comments and IBC's response."

i. Two new specifications would be added to Section IV–D–3 (renumbered IV–B–3), *Functions of the IBC,* as follows:

"IV–B–3–c. Lowering containment levels for certain experiments as specified in Sections III–B–2. IV–B–3–d. Setting containment levels as specified in III–B–4–b and III–B–5."

The Section would be renumbered to reflect these additions.

j. A new Section under IV–D–5–a (renumbered IV–B–5–a) would be added to reflect the PI's responsibility unddner Section III–C as follows:

"IV–B–5–a–(2). Determine whether experiments are covered by Section III–C and follow the appropriate procedures;"

The other Sections within IV–D–5 (renumbered IV–B–5) would be renumbered to reflect this addition.

k. Section IV–D–5–e–(5), *Publications,* would be deleted. Section IV–D–5–e–(5) currently reads as follows:

"IV–D–5–e–(5). *Publications.* PIs are urged to include, in all publications reporting on recombinant DNA research, a description of the physical and biological containment procedures employed."

l. Section IV–E, *Responsibilities of NIH,* would be renumbered to become Section IV–C.

m. The first sentence of the second paragraph of Section IV–E–1 (renumbered IV–C–1), *Director,* would be modified to read as follows:

"The Director has responsibilities under the Guidelines that involve the NIH Office of Recombinant DNA Activities (ORDA) and the Recombinant DNA Advisory Committee (RAC). ORDA's responsibilities under the Guidelines are administrative. Advice from the RAC is primarily scientific and technical. In certain circumstances, there is specific opportunity for public comment, with published response, before final action."

n. Section IV-E-1-b (renumbered IV-C-1-b), *Specific Responsibilities of the Director, NIH*, would read as follows:

"IV-C-1-b. *Specific Responsibilities of the Director, NIH.* In carrying out responsibilities set forth in this Section, the Director or a designee shall weigh each proposed action, through appropriate analysis and consultation, to determine that it complies with the Guidelines and presents no significant risk to health or the environment."

o. Section IV-E-1-b-(1) (renumbered IV-C-1-b-(1)) would be modified to read as follows:

"IV-C-1-b-(1). *Major Actions.* To execute major actions the Director must seek the advice of the RAC and provide an opportunity for public and Federal agency comment. Specifically, the agenda of the RAC meeting citing the major actions will be published in the **Federal Register** at least 30 days before the meeting, and the Director will also publish the proposed actions in the **Federal Register** for comment at least 30 days before the meeting. In addition, the Director's proposed decision, at his discretion, may be published in the **Federal Register** for 30 days of comment before final action is taken. The Director's final decision, along with response to comments will be published in the **Federal Register** and the *Recombinant DNA Technical Bulletin.* The RAC and IBC chairpersons will be notified of this decision:"

p. The order of the subsections under Section IV-E-1-b-(1) (renumbered IV-C-1-b-(1)) would be modified.

q. Section IV-E-1-b-(2) (renumbered IV-C-1-b-(2)) would be modified to read:

"IV-C-1-b-(2). *Lesser Actions.* To execute lesser actions, the Director must seek the advice of the RAC. The Director's decision will be transmitted to the RAC and the IBC chairpersons and published in the *Recombinant DNA Technical Bulletin.*"

r. Section IV-E-1-b-(2)-(d) (renumbered IV-C-1-b-(2)-(d)) would be modified to read as follows:

"IV-C-1-b-(2)-(d). Revising the 'Classification of Etiologic Agents' for the purposes of these Guidelines [1]."

s. Section IV-E-1-b-(3) (renumbered IV-C-1-b-(3)), would read as follows:

"IV-C-1-b-(3). *Other Actions.* The Director's decision will be transmitted to the RAC and IBC chairpersons and published in the *Recombinant DNA Technical Bulletin.*"

t. A new Section IV-C-1-b-(3)-(b) would be added as follows:

"IV-C-1-b-(3)-(b). Setting containment under Section III-B-1-d and Section III-B-3-d."

The order of subsections of Section IV-E-1-b-(3) (renumbered IV-C-1-b-(3)) would be modified and the subsections renumbered.

u. Section IV-E-4-b would be deleted. Section IV-E-4-b reads as follows:

"IV-E-4-b. Announcing and distributing certified HV2 host-vector systems (see Section II-D-3)."

v. Section IV-F, *Compliance*, would be renumbered to become Section IV-D.

w. A note would be added to Section IV-F-4 which would be renumbered as Section IV-D-4 as follows:

Note.—Other Federal agencies which have adopted the NIH Guidelines may have the authority to terminate funding to their grantees should these grantees not comply with the NIH Guidelines."

5. *Section V. Footnotes and References.*

a. The title of the Section would be amended to read:

"V. Footnotes and References of Sections I-IV"

b. The footnotes and references would be rearranged and renumbered. Footnotes and references applying to Appendices would be moved to relevant Appendices.

c. Reference (1) would be modified to read:

"1. The original reference to organisms as Class 1, 2, 3, 4, or 5 refers to the classification in the publication *Classification of Etiologic Agents on the Basis of Hazard*, 4th Edition, July 1974, U.S. Department of Health, Education and Welfare, Public Health Service, Center for Disease Control, Office of Biosafety, Atlanta, Georgia 30333.

"The Director, NIH, with advice of the Recombinant DNA Advisory Committee, may revise the classification for the puposes of these Guidelines (see Section IV-C-1-b-(2)-(d)). The revised list of organisms in each class is reprinted in Appendix B of these Guidelines."

6. *Section VI. Voluntary Compliance.*

a. The second paragraph of Section VI-C, *Certification of Host-Vector Systems*, would be deleted. That paragraph reads as follows:

"Institutions not otherwise covered by the Guidelines will not be subject to Section II-D-3 by complying with these procedures."

7. *Appendix B. Classification of Microorganisms on the Basis of Hazard.*

a. The title of the first heading, I, In Appendix B would be changed to read:

"*Appendix B-I. Classification of Etiologic Agents.* [The original reference for this classification was the publication *'Classification of Etiological Agents on the Basis of Hazard,'* 4th edition, July 1974, U.S. Department of Health, Education and Welfare, Public Health Service, Center for Disease Control, Office of Biosafety, Atlanta, Georgia 30333. For the purposes of these Guidelines, this list has been revised by NIH.]"

b. The following organisms would be added to the list of Class 2 bacterial agents:

"*Aeromonas hydrophila*
Campylobacter fetus
Campylobacter jejuni
Edwardsiella tarda
Yersinia enterocolita"

c. The language describing Class 2 *E. coli* would be modified to read:

"*Escherichia coli*—all enteropathogenic, enterotoxigenic, enteroinvasive and strains bearing K1 antigen."

d. Vesicular Stomatitis Virus would be added to Class 2 viral agents and deleted from Class 3 viral agents.

e. The following modifications concerning *Poxvirus* and *Rabies Virus* would be made in Class 2 viral agents:

"*Poxviruses*—all types except *Alastrim, Smallpox*, and *Whitepox*, which are Class 5 and *Monkey Pox*, which depending on experiments, is in Class 3 or Class 4.

"*Rabies virus*—all strains except *Rabies street* virus, which should be classified in Class 3."

f. *Alastrim, Smallpox*, and *Whitepox* would be reclassified from Class 3 and Class 4 agents to Class 5 agents.

g. The language including *Rabies street* virus as a Class 3 agent would read:

"*Rabies street virus*"

h. The language in Class 4 viral agents on *Monkey pox* would read:

"*Monkey pox*, when used for transmission or animal inoculation experiments [4]."

i. Descriptive language would be added to the *Classification of Oncogenic Viruses on the Basis of Potential Hazard [5]* as follows:

"Appendix B-II-A. *Low-Risk Oncogenic Viruses.* These viruses should be treated as Class 2 agents.

"Appendix B-II-B. *Moderate-Risk Oncogenic Viruses.* These viruses should be treated as Class 3 agents."

j. Class 5 Agents (Appendix B-III) would be separated into the following categories:

"Appendix B-III-A. *Animal Disease Organisms Which Are Forbidden Entry Into the United States by Law.*"

"Appendix B-III-B. *Animal Disease Organisms and Vectors Which Are*

Forbidden Entry Into the United States by USDA Policy."

"Appendix B-III-C. *Organisms Which May Not Be Studied in the United States Except at Specified Facilities."*

8. *Appendix C. Exemptions Under III-D-5.*

a. The language dealing with the introduction of genes coding for the biosynthesis of toxins in this Appendix would be modified to read:

"Experiments involving the deliberate introduction of genes coding for the biosynthesis of molecules toxic for vertebrates."

b. The abbreviation "CDC" would be deleted from this Appendix.

9. *Appendix F. Containment Conditions for Cloning of Genes Coding for the Biosynthesis of Toxins for Vertebrates.*

a. The title of Appendix F would be changed to read as follows:

"CONTAINMENT CONDITIONS FOR CLONING GENES CODING FOR THE BIOSYNTHESIS OF MOLECULES TOXIC FOR VERTEBRATES."

b. Section Appendix F-1, *General Information,* would read as follows:

Appendix F-I. *General Information.* Appendix F specifies the containment to be used for the deliberate cloning of genes coding for the biosynthesis of molecules toxic for vertebrates. Cloning of genes coding for molecules toxic for vertebrates that have an LD_{50} of less than 100 nanograms per kilogram body weight (e.g., microbial toxins such as the botulinum toxins, tetanus toxin, diphtheria toxin, *Shigella dysenteriae* neurotoxin) is prohibited. No specific restrictions shall apply to the cloning of genes if the protein specified by the gene has an LD_{50} of 100 micrograms or more per kilogram of body weight. Experiments involving genes coding for toxic molecules with an LD_{50} of 100 micrograms or less per kilogram body weight shall be registered with ORDA prior to initiating the experiments. A list of toxic molecules classified as to LD_{50} is available from ORDA. Testing procedures for determining toxicity of toxic molecules not on the list are available from ORDA. The results of such tests shall be forwarded to ORDA, which will consult with an *ad hoc* working group on toxic molecules prior to inclusion of the molecule on the list. (See Section IV-C-1-b-(2)-(e).)"

c. The title of Section Appendix F-II would read:

"Appendix F-II. *Containment Conditions for Cloning Toxic Molecule Genes in E. coli K-12."*

d. In Section Appendix F-II, the work "toxins" would be replaced by the words "molecules toxic."

e. The title of Section Appendix F-III would read:

"Containment Conditions for Cloning of Toxic Molecule Genes in Organisms Other Than E. coli K-12."

f. Appendix F-III, *Containment Conditions for Cloning of Toxic Genes in Organisms Other Than E. coli K-12* would read:

"Requests involving the cloning of genes coding for molecules toxic for vertebrates in host-vector systems other than *E. coli* K-12 will be evaluated by ORDA, which will consult with the *ad hoc* working group on toxic molecules. (See Section IV-C-1-b-(3)-(f).)"

10. *Appendix G. Physical Containment.*

a. A third paragraph would be added to new Section Appendix G-I as follows:

"The *'Laboratory Safety Monograph,'* available from ORDA, describes practices, equipment, and facilities in detail."

11. *Table of Contents.*

The table of contents would be rearranged to reflect the reorganization of the document and be expanded to better identify the position of various sections in the document.

12. *Appendices.*

All Appendices would be renumbered to reflect their status as Appendices.

C. *Proposed Revised Guidelines for Research Involving Recombinant DNA Molecules.*

Table of Contents

I. Scope of the Guidelines

I-A. *Purpose*. The purpose of these Guidelines is to specify practices for constructing and handling (i) recombinant DNA molecules and (ii) organisms and viruses containing recombinant DNA molecules.

I-B. *Definition of Recombinant DNA Molecules*. In the context of these Guidelines, recombinant DNA molecules are defined as either (i) molecules which are constructed outside living cells by joining natural or synthetic DNA segments to DNA molecules that can replicate in a living cell, or (ii) DNA molecules that result from the replication of those described in (i) above.

Synthetic DNA segments likely to yield a potentially harmful polynucleotide or polypeptide (e.g., a toxin or a pharmacologically active agent) shall be considered as equivalent to their natural DNA counterpart. If the synthetic DNA segment is not expressed *in vivo* as a biologically active polynucleotide or polypeptide product, it is exempt from the Guidelines.

I-C. *General Applicability*. The Guidelines are applicable to all recombinant DNA research within the United States or its territories which is conducted at or sponsored by an Institution that receives any support for recombinant DNA research from NIH. This includes research performed by NIH directly.

An individual receiving support for research involving recombinant DNA must be associated with or sponsored by an Institution that can and does assume the responsibilities assigned in these Guidelines.

The Guidelines are also applicable to projects done abroad if they are supported by NIH funds. If the host country, however, has established rules for the conduct of recombinant DNA projects, then a certificate of compliance with those rules may be submitted to NIH in lieu of compliance with the NIH Guidelines. NIH reserves the right to withhold funding if the safety practices to be employed abroad are not reasonably consistent with the NIH Guidelines.

I-D. *General Definitions*. The following terms, which are used throughout the Guidelines, are defined as follows:

IV-D-1. "Institution" means any public or private entity (including Federal, State, and local government agencies).

I-D-2. "Institutional Biosafety Committee" or "IBC" means a committee that (i) meets the requirements for membership specified in Section IV-B-2, and (ii) reviews, approves, and oversees projects in accordance with the responsibilities defined in Sections IV-B-2 and IV-B-3.

I-D-3. "NIH Office of Recombinant DNA Activities" or "ORDA" means the office within NIH with responsibility for (i) reviewing and coordinating all activities of NIH related to the Guidelines, and (ii) performing other duties as defined in Section IV-C-3.

I-D-4. "Recombinant DNA Advisory Committee" or "RAC" means the public advisory committee that advises the Secretary, the Assistant Secretary for Health, and the Director of the National Institutes of Health concerning recombinant DNA research. The RAC shall be constituted as specified in Section IV-C-2.

I-D-5. "Director, NIH" or "Director" means the Director of the National Institutes of Health or any other officer or employee of NIH to whom authority has been delegated.

II. Containment

Effective biological safety programs have been operative in a variety of laboratories for many years. Considerable information, therefore, already exists for the design of physical containment facilities and the selection of laboratory procedures applicable to organisms carrying recombinant DNAs [3-16]. The existing programs rely upon mechanisms that, for convenience, can be divided into two categories: (i) A set of standard practices that are generally used in microbiological laboratories, and (ii) special procedures, equipment, and laboratory installations that provide physical barriers which are applied in varying degrees according to the estimated biohazard. Four levels of physical containment, which are designated as P1, P2, P3, and P4 are described in Appendix G. P4 provides the most stringent containment conditions, P1 the least stringent.

Experiments on recombinant DNAs, by their vary nature, lend themselves to a third containment mechanism—namely, the application of highly specific biological barriers. In fact, natural barriers do exist which limit either (i) the infectivity of a *vector*, or *vehicle*, (plasmid or virus) for specific hosts or (ii) its dissemination and survival in the environment. The vectors that provide the means for replication of the recombinant DNAs and/or the host cells in which they replicate can be genetically designed to decrease by many orders of magnitude the probability of dissemination of recombinant DNAs outside the laboratory. Further details on biological containment may be found in Appendix I.

As these three means of containment are complementary, different levels of containment appropriate for experiments with different recombinants can be established by applying various combinations of the physical and biological barriers along with a constant use of the standard practices. We consider these categories of containment separately in order that such combinations can be conveniently expressed in the Guidelines.

In constructing these Guidelines, it was necessary to define boundary conditions for the different levels of physical and biological containment and for the classes of experiments to which they apply. We recognize that these definitions do not take into account all existing and anticipated information on special procedures that will allow particular experiments to be carried out under different conditions than indicated here without affecting risk. Indeed, we urge that individual investigators devise simple and more effective containment procedures and that investigators and institutional biosafety committees recommend changes in the Guidelines to permit their use.

III. Containment Guidelines for Covered Experiments

Part III discusses experiments involving recombinant DNA. These experiments have been divided into four classes:

III–A. Experiments which require specific RAC review and NIH and IBC approval before initiation of the experiment;

III–B. Experiments which require IBC approval before initiation of the experiment;

III–C. Experiments which require IBC notification at the time of initiation of the experiment;

III–D. Experiments which are exempt from the procedures of the Guidelines.

If an experiment falls into both Class III–A and one of the other clases, the rules pertaining to Class III–A must be followed. If an experiment falls into class III–D and into either class III–B or III–C as well, it can be considered exempt from the requirements of the Guidelines.

Changes in containment levels from those specified here may not be instituted without the express approval of the Director, NIH. (See Sections IV–C–1–b–(1), IV–C–1–b–(2), and subsections.)

III–A. *Experiments that Require RAC Review and NIH and IBC Approval Before Initiation.* Experiments in this category cannot be initiated without submission of relevant information on the proposed experiment to NIH, the publication of the proposal in the **Federal Register** for thirty days of comment, review by the RAC, and specific approval by NIH. The containment conditions for such experiments will be recommended by RAC and set by NIH at the time of approval. Such experiments also require the approval of the IBC before initiation. Specific experiments already approved in this section and the appropriate containment conditions are listed in Appendices D and F. If an experiment is similar to those listed in Appendices D and F, ORDA may determine appropriate containment conditions according to case precedents under Section IV–C–1–b–(3)–(g).

III–A–1. Deliberate formation of recombinant DNAs containing genes for the biosynthesis of toxic molecules lethal for vertebrates at an LD_{50} of less than 100 nanograms per kilogram body weight (e.g., microbial toxins such as the botulinum toxins, tetanus toxin, diphtheria toxin, *Shigella Dysenteriae* neurotoxin). Specific approval has been given for the cloning in *E. coli* K–12 of DNAs containing genes coding for the biosynthesis of toxic molecules which are lethal to vertebrates at 100 nanograms to 100 micrograms per kilogram body weight. Containment levels for these experiments are specified in Appdenix F.

III–A–2. Deliberate release into the environment of any organism containing recombinant DNA.

III–A–3. Deliberate transfer of a drug resistance trait to microorganisms that are not known to acquire it naturally [2], if such acquisition could compromise the use of the drug to control disease agents in human or veterinary medicine or agriculture.

III–B. *Experiments that Require IBC Approval Before Initiation.* Investigators performing experiments in this category must submit to their Institutional Biosafety Committee (IBC), prior to initiation of the experiments, a registration document that contains a description of: (a) The source(s) of DNA, (b) the nature of the inserted DNA sequences, (c) the hosts and vectors to be used, (d) whether a deliberate attempt will be made to obtain expression of a foreign gene, and, if so, what protein will be produced, and (e) the containment conditions specified in these Guidelines. This registration document must be dated and signed by the investigator and filed only with the local IBC. The IBC shall review all such proposals prior to initiation of the experiments. Requests for lowering of containment for experiments in this category will be considered by NIH. (See Section IV–C–1–b–(3).)

III–B–1. *Experiments Using Human or Animal Pathogens (Class 2, Class 3, Class 4, or Class 5 Agents [1]) as Host-Vector Systems.*

III–B–1–a. Experiments involving the introduction of recombinant DNA into Class 2 agents can be carried out at P2 containment.

III–B–1–b. Experiments involving the introduction of recombinant DNA into Class 3 agents can be carried out at P3 containment.

III–B–1–c. Experiments involving the introduction of recombinant DNA into Class 4 agents can be carried out at P4 containment.

III–B–1–d. Containment conditions for experiments involving the introduction of recombinant DNA into Class 5 agents will be set on a case-by-case basis following ORDA review. A USDA permit is required for work with Class 5 agents [18, 20].

III–B–2. *Experiments in Which DNA from Human or Animal Pathogens (Class 2, Class 3, Class 4, or Class 5 Agents [1]) is Cloned in Nonpathogenic Prokaryotic or Lower Eukaryotic Host-Vector Systems.*

III–B–2–a. Recombinant DNA experiments in which DNA from Class 2 or Class 3 agents [1] is tranferred into nonpathogenic prokaryotes or lower eukaryotes may be performed under P2 containment. Recombinant DNA experiments in which DNA from Class 4 agents is transferred into nonpathogenic prokaryotes or lower eukaryotes can be performed at P2 containment after demonstration that only a totally and irreversibly defective fraction of the agent's viral genome is present in a given recombinant. In the absence of such a demonstration, P4 containment should be used. Specific lowering of containment to P1 for particular experiments can be approved by the IBC. Many experiments in this category will be exempt from the Guidelines. (See Sections III–D–4 and III–D–5.) Experiments involving the formation of recombinant DNAs for certain genes coding for molecules toxic for vertebrates requires RAC review and NIH approval (see Section III–a–1), or must be carried out under NIH specified conditions as described in Appendix F.

III–B–2–b. Containment conditions for experiments in which DNA from Class 5 agents is transferred into nonpathogenic prokaryotes or lower eukaryotes will be determined by ORDA following a case-by-case review. A USDA permit is required for work with Class 5 agents [18, 20].

III–B–3. *Experiments Involving the Use of Infectious Animal or Plant Viruses or Defective Animal or Plant Viruses in the Presence of Helper Virus in Tissue Culture Systems.*

Caution: Special care should be used in the evaluation of containment levels for experiments which are likely to either enhance the pathogenicity (e.g., insertion of a host oncogene) or to extend the host range (e.g., introduction of novel control elements) of viral vectors under conditions which permit a productive infection. In such cases, serious consideration should be given to raising the physical containment by at least one level.

Note.—Recombinant DNA molecules which contain less than two-thirds of the genome of any eukaryotic virus (all virus from a single Family [17] being considered indentical [19]) may be considered defective and can be used, in the absence of helper, under the conditions specified in Section III–C.

III–B–3–a. Experiments involving the use of infectious Class 2 animal viruses [1], or defective Class 2 animal viruses in the presence of helper virus, can be performed at P2 containment.

III–B–3–b. Experiments involving the use of infectious Class 3 animal viruses [1], or defective Class 3 animal viruses in the presence of helper virus, can be carried out at P3 containment.

III–B–3–c. Experiments involving the use of infectious Class 4 viruses [1], or defective Class 4 viruses in the presence of helper virus, may be carried out under P4 containment.

III–B–3–d. Experiments involving the use of infectious Class 5 [1] viruses, or defective Class 5 viruses in the present of helper virus will be determined on a case-by-case basis following ORDA review. A USDA permit is required for work with Class 5 pathogens [18,20].

III–B–3–e. Experiments involving the use of infectious animal or plant viruses, or defective animal or plant viruses in the presence of helper virus, not covered by Sections III–B–3–a, III–B–3–b, III–B–3–c, or III–B–3–d may be carried out under P1 containment.

III–B–4. *Recombinant DNA Experiments Involving Whole Animals or Plants.*

III–B–4–a. DNA from any source except for greater than two-thirds of a eukaryotic viral genome may be transferred to any non-human vertebrate organism and propagated under conditions of physical containment comparable to P1 and appropriate to the organism under study [2]. It is important that the investigator demonstrate that the fraction of the viral genome being utilized does not lead to productive infection.

III–B–4–b. For all experiments involving whole animals and plants and not covered by III–B–4–a, the appropriate containment will be determined by the IBC.

–B–5. *Experiments Involving More than 10 Liters of Culture.* The appropriate containment will be decided by the IBC. Where appropriate, the large-scale containment recommendations of the NIH should be used (45 FR 24968).

III–C. *Experiments that Require IBC Notice Simultaneously with Initiation of Experiments.* Experiments not included in Sections III – A, III–B, III–D, and subsections of these Sections are to be considered in Section III–C. All such experiments can be carried out at P1 containment. For experiments in this category, a registration document as described in Section III–B must be dated and signed by the investigator and filed with the local IBC. The IBC shall review all such proposals, but IBC review prior to initiation of the experiment is not required.

For example, experiments in which all components derive from non-pathogenic prokaryotes and non-pathogenic lower eukaryotes fall under Section III–C and can be carried out at P1 containment.

Caution: Experiments Involving Formation or Recombinant DNA Molecules Containing no more Than Two-Thirds of the Genome of any Eukaryotic Virus. Recombinant DNA molecules containing no more than two-thirds of the genome of any eukaryotic virus (all viruses from a single Family [17] being considered identical [19]) may be propagated and maintained in cells in tissue culture using P1 containment. For such experiments, it must be shown that the cells lack helper virus for the specific Families of defective viruses being used. If helper virus is present, procedures specified under Section III–B–3 should be used. The DNA may contain fragments of the genome of viruses from more than one Family but each fragment must be less than two-thirds of a genome.

III–D. *Exempt Experiments.* The following recombinant DNA molecules are exempt from these Guidelines and no registration with the IBC is necessary.

III–D–1. Those that are not in organisms or viruses.

III–D–2. Those that consist entirely of DNA segments from a single nonchromosomal or viral DNA source, though one or more of the segments may be a synthetic equivalent.

III–D–3. Those that consist entirely of DNA from a prokaryotic host, including its indigenous plasmids or viruses, when propagated only in that host (or a closely related strain of the same species) or when transferred to another host by well established physiological means; also those that consist entirely of DNA from an eularyotic host, including its chloroplasts, mitochondria, or plasmids (but excluding viruses), when propagated only in that host (or a closely related strain of same species).

III–D–4. Certain specified recombinant DNA molecules that consist entirely of DNA segments from different species that exchange DNA by known physiological processes, though one or more of the segments may be a synthetic equivalent. A list of such exchangers will be prepared and periodically revised by the Director, NIH, with advice of the RAC, after appropriate notice and opportunity for public comment. (See Section IV–C–1–b–(1)–(c).) Certain classes are exempt as of publication of these Revised Guidelines. The list is in Appendix A. An updated list may be obtained from the Office of Recombinant DNA Activities, National Institutes of Health, Bethesda, Maryland 20205.

III–D–5. Other classes of recombinant DNA molecules, if the Director, NIH, with advice of the RAC, after appropriate notice and opportunity for public comment, finds that they do not present a significant risk to health or the environment. (See Section IV–C–1–b–(1)–(c).) Certain classes are exempt as of publication of these Revised Guidelines. The list is in Appendix C. An updated list may be obtained from the Office of Recombinant DNA Activities, National Institutes of Health, Bethesda, Maryland 20205.

IV. Roles and Responsibilities

IV–A. *Policy.* Safety in activities involving recombinant DNA depends on the individual conducting them. The Guidelines cannot anticipate every possible situation. Motivation and good judgment are the key essentials to protection of health and the environment.

The Guidelines are intended to help the Institution, the Institutional Biosafety Committee (IBC), the Biological Safety Officer, and the Principal Investigator determine the safeguards that should be implemented. These Guidelines will never be complete or final, since all conceivable experiments involving recombinant DNA cannot be foreseen. Therefore, *it is the responsibility of the Institution and those associated with it to adhere to the purpose of the Guidelines as well as to their specifics.*

Each Institution (and the IBC acting on its behalf) is responsible for ensuring that recombinant DNA activities comply with the Guidelines. General recognition of institutional authority and responsibility properly establishes accountability for safe conduct of the research at the local level.

The following roles and responsibilities constitute an administrative framework in which safety is an essential and integral part of research involving recombinant DNA molecules. Further clarifications and interpretations of roles and responsibilities will be issued by NIH as necessary.

IV–B. *Responsibilities of the Institution.*

IV–B–1. *General Information.* Each Institution conducting or sponsoring recombinant DNA research covered by these Guidelines is responsible for ensuring that the research is carried out in full conformity with the provisions of the Guidelines. In order to fulfill this responsibility, the Institution shall:

IV–B–1–a. Establish and implement policies that provide for the safe conduct of recombinant DHA research and that ensure compliance with the Guidelines. The Institution, as part of its general responsibilities for implementing the Guidelines, may establish additional procedures, as deemed necessary, to govern the Institution and its components in the discharge of its responsibilities under the Guidelines. This may include (i) statements formulated by the Institution for general implementation of the Guidelines and (ii) whatever additional precautionary steps the Institution may deem appropriate.

IV–B–1–b. Establish an Institutional Biosafety Committee (IBC) that meets the requirements set forth in Section IV–B–2 and carries out the functions detailed in Section IV–B–3.

IV–B–1–c. If the Institution is engaged in recombinant DNA research at the P3 or P4 containment level, appoint a Biological Safety Officer (BSO), who shall be a member of the IBC and carry out the duties specified in Section IV–B–4.

IV–B–1–d. Require that investigators responsible for research covered by these Guidelines comply with the provisions of Section IV–B–5, and assist investigators to do so.

IV–B–1–e. Ensure appropriate training for the IBC chairperson and members, the BSO, Principal Investigators (PIs), and laboratory staff regarding the Guidelines, their implementation, and laboratory safety. Responsibility for training IBC Members may be carried out through the IBC chairperson. Responsibility for training laboratory staff may be carried out through the PI. The Institution is responsible for seeing that the PI has sufficient training, but may delegate this responsibility to the IBC.

IV–B–1–f. Determine the necessity, in connection with each project, for health surveillance of recombinant DNA research personnel, and conduct, if found appropriate, a health surveillance program for the project. [The Laboratory Safety Monograph (LSM) discusses various possible components of such a program—for example, records of agents handled, active investigation of relevant illnesses, and the maintenance of serial serum samples for monitoring serologic changes that may result from the employees' work experience. Certain medical conditions may place a laboratory worker at increased risk in any endeavor where infectious agents are handled. Examples given in the LSM include gastrointestinal disorders and treatment with steriods, immunosuppressive drugs, or antibiotics. Workers with such disorders or treatment should be evaluated to determine whether they should be engaged in research with potentially hazardous organisms during their treatment or illness. Copies of the LSM are available from ORDA.]

IV–B–1–g. Report within 30 days to ORDA any significant problems with and violations of the Guidelines and significant research-related accidents and illnesses, unless the institution determines that the PI or IBC has done so.

IV–B–2. *Membership and Procedures of the IBC.* The Institution shall establish an Institutional Biosafety Committee (IBC) whose responsibilities need not be restricted to recombinant DNA. The committee shall meet the following requirements:

IV–B–2–a. The IBC shall comprise no fewer than five members so selected that they collectively have experience and expertise in recombinant DNA technology and the capability to assess the safety of recombinant DNA research experiments and any potential risk to public health or the environment. At least two members shall not be affiliated with the Institution (apart from their membership on the IBC) and shall represent the interest of the surrounding community with respect to health and protection of the environment. Members meet this requirement if, for example, they are officials of State or local public health or environmental protection agencies, members of other local governmental bodies, or persons active in medical, occupational health, or environmental concerns in the community. The Biological Safety Officer (BSO), mandatory when research is being conducted at the P3 and P4 levels, shall be a member. (See Section IV–B–4.)

IV–B–2–b. In order to ensure the competence necessary to review recombinant DNA activities, it is recommended that (i) the IBC include persons with expertise in recombinant DNA technology, biological safety, and physical containment; (ii) the IBC include, or have available as consultants, persons knowledgeable in institutional commitments and policies, applicable law, standards of professional conduct and practice, community attitudes, and the environment; and (iii) at least one member be from the laboratory technical staff.

IV–B–2–c. The Institution shall identify the committee members by name in a report to the NIH Office of Recombinant DNA Activities (ORDA) and shall include relevant background information on each member in such form and at such times as ORDA may require.

IV–B–2–d. No member of an IBC may be involved (except to provide information requested by the IBC) in the review or approval of a project in which he or she has been, or expects to be, engaged or has a direct financial interest.

IV–B–2–e. The Institution, which is ultimately responsible for the effectiveness of the IBC, may establish procedures that the IBC will follow in its initial and continuing review of applications, proposals, and activities. (IBC review procedures are specified in Section IV–B–3–a.)

IV–B–2–f. Institutions are encouraged to open IBC meetings to the public whenever possible, consistent with protection of privacy and proprietary interests.

IV–B–2–g. Upon request, the Institution shall make available to the public all minutes of IBC meetings and any documents submitted to or received from funding agencies which the latter are required to make available to the public. If comments are made by members of the public on IBC actions, the Institution shall forward to NIH both the comments and the IBC's response.

IV-B-3. *Functions of the IBC.* On behalf of the Institution, the IBC is responsible for:

IV-B-3-a. Reviewing for compliance with the NIH Guidelines recombinant DNA research as specified in Part III conducted at or sponsored by the Institution, and approving those research projects that it finds are in conformity with the Guidelines. This review shall include:

IV-B-3-a-(1). An independent assessment of the containment levels required by these Guidelines for the proposed research, and

IV-B-3-a-(2). An assessment of the facilities, procedures, and practices, and of the training and expertise of recombinant DNA personnel.

IV-B-3-b. Notifying the Principal Investigator (PI) of the results of their review.

IV-B-3-c. Lowering containment levels for certain experiments as specified in Section III-B-2.

IV-B-3-d. Setting containment levels as specified in Section III-B-4-b and III-B-5.

IV-B-3-e. Reviewing periodically recombinant DNA research being conducted at the Institution, to ensure that the requirements of the Guidelines are being fulfilled.

IV-B-3-f. Adopting emergency plans covering accidental spills and personnel contamination resulting from such research.

Note.—Basic elements in developing specific procedures for dealing with major spills of potentially hazardous materials in the laboratory are detailed in the Laboratory Safety Monograph (LSM). Included are information and references on decontamination and emergency plans. NIH and the Centers for Disease Control are available to provide consultation, and direct assistance if necessary, as posted in the LSM. The Guidelines shall cooperate with the State and local public health departments, reporting any significant research-related illness or accident that appears to be a hazard to the public health.

IV-B-3-g. Reporting within 30 days to the appropriate institutional official and to the NIH Office of Recombinant DNA Activities (ORDA) any significant problems with or violations of the Guidelines, and any significant research-related accidents or illnesses, unless the IBC determines that the PI has done so.

IV-B-3-h. The IBC may not authorize initiation of experiments not explicitly covered by the Guidelines until NIH (with the advice of the RAC when required) establishes the containment requirement.

IV-B-3-i. Performing such other functions as may be delegated to the IBC under Section IV-B-1.

IV-B-4. *Biological Safety Officer.* The Institution shall appoint a BSO if it engages in recombinant DNA research at the P3 or P4 containment level. The officer shall be a member of the Institutional Biosafety Committee (IBC), and his or her duties shall include (but need not be limited to):

IV-B-4-a. Ensuring through periodic inspections that laboratory standards are rigorously followed;

IV-B-4-b. Reporting to the IBC and the Institution all significant problems with and violations of the Guidelines and all significant research-related accidents and illnesses of which the BSO becomes aware, unless the BSO determines that the Principal Investigator (PI) has done so;

IV-B-4-c. Developing emergency plans for dealing with accidental spills and personnel contamination, and investigating recombinant DNA research laboratory accidents;

IV-B-4-d. Providing advice on laboratory security;

IV-B-4-e. Providing technical advice to the PI and the IBC on research safety procedures.

NOTE: See Laboratory Safety Monograph for additional information on the duties of the BSO.

IV-B-5. *Principal Investigator.* On behalf of the Institution, the PI is responsible for complying fully with the Guidelines in conducting any recombinant DNA research.

IV-B-5-a. *PI—General.* As part of this general responsibility, the PI shall:

IV-B-5-a-(1). Initiate or modify no recombinant DNA research requiring approval by the IBC prior to initiation (see Sections III-A and III-B) until that research, or the proposed modification thereof, has been approved by the IBC and has met all other requirements of the Guidelines;

IV-B-5-a-(2). Determine whether experiments are covered by Section III-C and follow the appropriate procedures;

IV-B-5-a-(3). Report within 30 days to the IBC and NIH (ORDA) all significant problems with and violations of the Guidelines and all significant research-related accidents and illnesses;

IV-B-5-a-(4). Report to the IBC and to NIH (ORDA) new information bearing on the Guidelines;

IV-B-5-a-(5). Be adequately trained in good microbiological techniques;

IV-B-5-a-(6). Adhere to IBC-approved emergency plans for dealing with accidental spills and personnel contamination; and

IV-B-5-a-(7). Comply with shipping requirements for recombinant DNA molecules. (See Appendix H for shipping requirements and the Laboratory Safety Monograph for technical recommendations.)

IV-B-5-b. *Submissions by the PI to NIH.* The PI shall:

IV-B-5-b-(1). Submit information to NIH (ORDA) in order to have new host-vector systems certified;

IV-B-5-b-(2). Petition NIH, with notice to the IBC, for exemptions to these Guidelines;

IV-B-5-b-(3). Petition NIH, with concurrence of the IBC, for approval to conduct experiments specified in Section III-A of the Guidelines;

IV-B-5-b-(4). Petition NIH for determination of containment for experiments requiring case-by-case review;

IV-B-5-b-(5). Petition NIH for determination of containment for experiments not covered by the Guidelines.

IV-B-5-c. *Submissions by the PI to the IBC.* The PI shall:

IV-B-5-c-(1). Make the initial determination of the required levels of physical and biological containment in accordance with the Guidelines;

IV-B-5-c-(2). Select appropriate microbiological practices and laboratory techniques to be used in the research;

IV-B-5-c-(3). Submit the initial research protocol if covered under Guidelines Section III-A, III-B, or III-C, (and also subsequent changes—e.g., changes in the source of DNA or host-vector system) to the IBC for review and approval or disapproval; and

IV-B-5-c-(4). Remain in communication with the IBC throughout the conduct of the project.

IV-B-5-d. *PI Responsibilities Prior to Initiating Research.* The PI is responsible for:

IV-B-5-d-(1). Making available to the laboratory staff copies of the protocols that describe the potential biohazards and the precautions to be taken;

IV-B-5-d-(2). Instructing and training staff in the practices and techniques required to ensure safety and in the procedures for dealing with accidents; and

IV-B-5-d-(3). Informing the staff of the reasons and provisions for any precautionary medical practices advised or requested, such as vaccinations or serum collection.

IV-B-5-e. *PI Responsibilities During the Conduct of the Research.* The PI is responsible for:

IV-B-5-e-(1). Supervising the safety performance of the staff to ensure that the required safety practices and techniques are employed;

IV-B-5-e-(2). Investigating and reporting in writing to ORDA, the Biological Safety Officer (where

applicable), and the IBC any significant problems pertaining to the operation and implementation of containment practices and procedures;

IV–B–5–e–(3). Correcting work errors and conditions that may result in the release of recombinant DNA materials;

IV–B–5–e–(4). Ensuring the integrity of the physical containment (e.g., biological safety cabinets) and the biological containment (e.g., purity, and genotypic and phenotypic characteristics).

IV–C. *Responsibilities of NIH.*

IV–C–1. *Director.* The Director, NIH, is responsible for (i) establishing the NIH Guidelines for Research Involving Recombination DNA Molecules, (ii) overseeing their implementation, and (iii) their final interpretation.

The Director has responsibilities under the Guidelines that involve the NIH Office of Recombinant DNA Activities (ORDA) and the Recombinant DNA Advisory Committee (RAC). ORDA's responsibilities under the Guidelines are administrative. Advice from the RAC is primarily scientific and technical. In certain circumstances, there is specific opportunity for public comment, with published response, before final action.

IV–C–1–a. *General Responsibilities of the Director, NIH.* The responsibilities of the Director shall include the following:

IV–C–1–a–(1). Promulgating requirements as necessary to implement the Guidelines;

IV–C–1–a–(2). Establishing and maintaining the RAC to carry out the responsibilities set forth in Section IV–C–2. The RAC's membership is specified in its charter and in Section IV–C–2;

IV–C–1–a–(3). Establishing and maintaining ORDA to carry out the responsibilities defined in Section IV–C–3; and

IV–C–1–a–(4). Maintaining the Federal Interagency Advisory Committee on Recombinant DNA Research established by the Secretary, HEW (now HHS), for advice on the coordination of all Federal programs and activities relating to recombination DNA, including activities of the RAC.

IV–C–1–b. *Specific Responsibilities of the Director, NIH.* In carrying out the responsibilities set forth in this Section, the Director or a designee shall weigh each proposed action, through appropriate analysis and consulation, to determine that it complies with the Guidelines and presents no significant risk to health or the environment.

IV–C–1–b–(1). *Major Actions.* To execute major actions the Director must seek the advice of the RAC and provide an opportunity for public and Federal agency comment. Specifically, the agenda of the RAC meeting citing the major actions will be published in the **Federal Register** at least 30 days before the meeting, and the Director will also publish the proposed actions in the **Federal Register** for comment at least 30 days before the meeting. In addition, the Director's proposed decision, at his discretion, may be published in the **Federal Register** for 30 days of comment before final action is taken. The Director's final decision, along with response to the comments, will be published in the **Federal Register** and the *Recombinant DNA Technical Bulletin.* The RAC and IBC chairpersons will be notified of this decision.

IV–C–1–b–(1)–(a). Changing containment levels for types of experiments that are specified in the Guidelines when a major action is involved;

IV–C–1–b–(1)–(b). Assigning containment levels for types of experiments that are not explicitly considered in the Guidelines when a major action is involved;

IV–C–1–b–(1)–(c). Promulgating and amending a list of classes of recombinant DNA molecules to be exempt from the Guidelines because they consist entirely of DNA segments from species that exchange DNA by known physiological processes, or otherwise do not present a significant risk to health or the environment;

IV–C–1–b–(1)–(d). Permitting experiments specified by Section III–A of the Guidelines;

IV–C–1–b–(1)–(e). Certifying new host-vector systems, with the exception of minor modifications of already certified systems (the standards and procedures for certification are described in Appendix I–II–a. Minor modifications constitute, for example, those of minimal or no consequence to the properties relevant to containment); and

IV–C–4–4. *Other NIH Components.* Other NIH components shall be responsible for certifying P4 facilities, inspecting them periodically, and inspecting other recombination DNA facilities as deemed necessary.

IV–C–1–b–(1)–(f). Adopting other changes in the Guidelines.

IV–C–1–b–(2). *Lesser Actions.* To execute lesser actions, the Director must seek the advice of the RAC. The Director's decision will be transmitted to the RAC and IBC chairpersons and published in the *Recombinant DNA Technical Bulletin:*

IV–C–1–b–(2)–(a). Interpreting and determining containment levels, upon request by ORDA;

IV–C–1–b–(2)–(b). Changing containment levels for experiments that are specified in the Guidelines (see Section III);

IV–C–1–b–(2)–(c). Assigning containment levels for experiments not explicitly considered in the Guidelines;

IV–C–1–b–(2)–(d). Revising the "Classification of Etiologic Agents" for the purpose of these Guidelines [1].

IV–C–1–b–(3). *Other Actions.* The Director's decision will be transmitted to the RAC and IBC chairpersons and published in the *Recombinant DNA Technical Bulletin:*

IV–C–1–b–(3)–(a). Interpreting the Guidelines for experiments to which the Guidelines specifically assign containment levels;

IV–C–1–b–(3)–(b). Setting containment under Section III–B–1–d and Sectin III–B–3–d;

IV–C–1–b–(3)–(c). Approving minor modifications of already certified host-vector systems (the standards and procedures for such modifications are described in Appendix I–II);

IV–C–1–b–(3)–(d). Decertifying already certified host-vector systems;

IV–C–1–b–(3–(e). Adding new entries to the list of molecules toxic for vertebrates (see Appendix F);

IV–C–1–b–(3)–(f). Approving the cloning of toxin genes in host-vector systems other than *E. coli* K-12 (See Appendix F); and

IV–C–1–b–(3)–(g). Determining appropriate containment conditions for experiments according to case precedents developed under Section IV-C-1-b-(2)-(c).

IV-C-1-b-(4). The Director shall conduct, support, and assist training programs in laboratory safety for Institutional Biosafety Committee members, Biological Safety Officers, Principal Investigators, and laboratory staff.

IV-C-2. *Recombinant DNA Advisory Committee.* The NIH Recombinant DNA Advisory Committee (RAC) is responsible for carrying out specified functions cited below as well as others assigned under its charter or by the Secretary, HHS, the Assistant Secretary for Health, and the Director, NIH.

The members of the committee shall be chosen to provide, collectively, expertise in scientific fields relevant to recoombinant DNA technology and biological safety—e.g., microbiology, molecular biology, virology, genetics, epidemiology, infectious diseases, the biology of enteric organisms, botany, plant pathology, ecology, and tissue culture. At least 20 percent of the members shall be persons knowledgeable in applicable law, standards of professional conduct and practice, public attitudes, the environment, public health, occupational health, or related fields. Representatives from Federal agencies shall serve as nonvoting members. Nominations for the RAS may be submitted to the NIH Office of Recombinant DNA Activities, Bethesda, Md. 20205.

All meetings of the RAC will be announced in the **Federal Register**, including tentative agenda items, 30 days in advance of the meeting, with final agendas (if modified) available at least 72 hours before the meeting. No item defined as a major action under Section IV-C-1-b-(1) may be added to an agenda after it appears in the **Federal Register**.

The RAC shall be responsible for advising the Director, NIH, on the actions listed in Section IV-C-1-b-(1) and IV-C-1-b-(2).

IV-C-3. *The Office of Recombinant DNA Activities.* ORDA shall serve as a focal point for information on recombinant DNA activities and provide advice to all within and outside NIH, including Institutions, Biological Safety Committees, Principal Investigators, Federal agencies, State and local governments, and institutions in the private sector. ORDA shall carry out such other functions as may be delegated to it by the Director, NIH, including those authorities described in Section IV-C-1-b-(3). In addition, ORDA shall be responsible for the following:

IV-C-3-a. Reviewing and approving Institutional Biosafety Committee (IBC) membership;

IV-C-3-b. Publishing in the **Federal Register:**

IV-C-3-b-(1). Announcements of Recombinant DNA Advisory Committee (RAC) meetings and agendas at least 30 days in advance;

NOTE: If the agenda for an RAC meeting is modified, ORDA shall make the revised agenda available to anyone, upon request, at least 72 hours in advance of the meeting.

IV-C-3-b-(2). Proposed major actions of the type falling under Section IV-C-1-b-(1) at least 30 days prior to the RAC meeting at which they will be considered; and

IV-C-3-b-(3). The NIH Director's final decision on recommendations made by the RAC.

IV-C-3-c. Publishing the *Recombinant DNA Technical Bulletin*; and

IV-C-3-d. Serving as executive secretary of the RAC.

IV-C-4. *Other NIH Components.* Other NIH components shall be responsible for certifying P4 facilities, inspecting them periodically, and inspecting other recombinant DNA facilities as deemed necessary.

IV-D. *Compliance.* As a condition for NIH funding of recombinant DNA research, Institutions must ensure that such research conducted at or sponsored by the Institution, irrespective of the source of funding, shall comply with these Guidelines. the policies on noncompliance are as follows:

IV-D-1. All NIH-funded projects involving recombinant DNA techniques must comply with the NIH Guidelines. Noncompliance may result in (i) suspension, limitation, or termination of financial assistance for such projects and of NIH funds for other recombinant DNA research at the Institution, or (ii) a requirement for prior NIH approval of any or all recombinant DNA projects at the Institution.

IV-D-2. All non-NIH funded projects involving recombinant DNA techniques conducted at or sponsored by an Institution that receives NIH funds for projects involving such techniques must comply with the NIH Guidelines. Noncompliance may result in (i) suspension, limitation, or termination of NIH funds for recombinant DNA research at the Institution, or (ii) a requirement for prior NIH approval of any or all recombinant DNA projects at the Institution.

IV-D-3. Information concerning noncompliance with the Guidelines may be brought forward by any person. It should be delivered to both NIH (ORDA) and the relevant Institution. The Institution, generally through the IBC, shall take appropriate action. The Insitution shall forward a complete report of the incident to ORDA, recommending any further action indicated.

IV-D-4. In cases where NIH proposes to suspend, limit, or terminate financial assistance because of noncompliance with the Guidelines, applicable DHHS and Public Health Service Procedures shall govern.

Note.—Other Federal agencies which have adopted the NIH Guidelines may have the authority to terminate funding to their grantees should these grantees not comply with the NIH Guidelines.

IV-D-5. *Voluntary Compliance.* Any individual, corporation, or institution that is not otherwise covered by the Guidelines is encouraged to conduct recombinant DNA research activities in accordance with the Guidelines, through the procedures set forth in Part VI.

V. Footnotes and References of Sections I-IV

1. The original reference to organisms as Class 1, 2, 3, 4, or 5 refers to the classification in the publication *Classification of Etiologic Agents on the Basis of Hazard,* 4th Edition, July 1974; U.S. Department of Health, Education, and Welfare, Public Health Service, Centers for Disease Control, Office of Biosafety, Atlanta, Georgia 30333.

The Director, NIH, with advice of the Recombinant DNA Advisory Committee, may revise the classification for the purposes of these Guidelines (see Section IV-C-1-b-(2)-(d)). The revised list of organisms in each class is reprinted in Appendix B to these Guidelines.

2. In Part III of the Guidelines, there are a number of places where judgments are to be made. In all these cases the principal investigator is to make the judgment on these matters as part of his responsibility to "make the initial determination of the required levels of physical and biological containment in accordance with the Guidelines" (Section IV-B-5-c-(1)). In the cases falling under Sections III-A, -B or -C, this judgment is to be reviewed and approved by the Institutional Biosafety Committee as part of its responsibility to make "an independent assessment of the containment levels required by these Guidelines for the proposed research" (Section IV-B-3-a-(1)). If the IBC wishes, any specific cases may be referred to the NIH Office of Recombinant DNA Activities as part of ORDA's functions to "provide advice to all within and outside NIH" (Section IV-C-3), and ORDA may request advice from the Recombinant DNA Advisory Committee as part of the RAC's responsibility for "interpreting and determining containment levels upon request by ORDA" (Section IV-C-1-b-(2)-(a)).

3. *Laboratory Safety at the Center for Disease Control* (Sept. 1974). U.S. Department of Health, Education, and Welfare Publication No. CDC 75-8118.

4. *Classification of Etiologic Agents on the Basis of Hazard.* (4th Edition, July 1974). U.S. Department of Health, Education, and Welfare. Public Health Service. Centers for Disease Control, Office of Biosafety, Atlanta, Georgia 30333.

5. *National Cancer Institute Safety Standards for Research Involving Oncogenic Viruses* (Oct. 1974). U.S. Dpeartment of Health, Education, and Welfare Publication No. (NIH) 75-790.

6. *National Institutes of Health Biohazards Safety Guide* (1974). U.S. Department of Health, Education, and Welfare, Public Health Service, National Institutes of Health. U.S. Government Printing Office, Stock No. 1740-00383.

7. *Biohazards in Biological Research* (1973). A. Hellman, M. N. Oxman, and R. Pollack (ed.) Cold Spring Harbor Laboratory.

8. *Handbook of Laboratory Safety* (9171). Second Edition. N. V. Steere (ed.). The Chemical Rubber Co., Cleveland.

9. Bodily, J. L. (1970). *General Administration of the Laboratory,* H. L. Bodily, E. L. Updyke, and J. O. Mason (eds.), Diagnostic Procedures for Bacterial, Mycotic and Parasitic Infections. American Public Health Association, New York, pp. 11-28.

10. Darlow, H. M. (1969). *Safety in the Microbiological Laboratory.* In J. R. Norris and D. W. Robbins (ed.), Methods in Microbiology. Academic Press, Inc. New York, pp. 169-204.

11. *The Prevention of Laboratory Acquired Infection* (1974). C. H. Collins, E. G. Hartley, and R. Pilsworth. Public Health Laboratory Service, Monograph Series No. 6.

12. Chatigny, M. A. (1961). *Protection Against Infection in the Microbiological Laboratory: Devices and Procedures.* In W. W. Umbreit (ed.). Advances in Applied Microbiology. Academic Press, New York, N.Y. 3:131-192.

13. *Design Criteria for Viral Oncology Research Facilities* (1975). U.S. Department of Health, Education and Welfare, Public Health Service, National Institutes of Health, DHEW Publication No. (NIH) 75-891.

14. Kuehne, R. W. (1973). *Biological Containment Facility for Studying Infectious Disease.* Appl. Microbiol. 26-239-243.

15. Runkle, R. S., and G. B. Phillips (1969). *Microbial Containment Control Facilities.* Van Nostrand Reinhold, New York.

16. Chatigny, M. A., and D. I. Clinger (1969). *Contamination Control in Aerobiology.* In R. L. Dimmick and A. B. Akers (eds.). An Introduction to Experimental Aerobiology. John Wiley & Sons, New York, pp. 194-263.

17. As classified in the Third Report of the International Committee on Taxonomy of Viruses: Classification and Nomenclature of Viruses, R. E. F. Matthews, Ed. Intervirology 12 (129-296) 1979.

18. A USDA permit, required for import and interstate transport of pathogens, may be obtained from the Animal and Plant Health Inspection Service, USDA, Federal Building, Hayttsville, MD 20782.

19. i.e., the total of all genomes within a Family shall not exceed two-thirds of the genome.

20. All activities, including storage of variola and whitepox are restricted to the single national facility (World Health Organization (WHO) Collaborating Center for Smallpox Research, Centers for Disease Control, in Atlanta).

VI. Voluntary Compliance

VI-A. *Basic Policy.* Individuals, corporations, and institutions not otherwise covered by the Guidelines are encouraged to do so by following the standards and procedures set forth in Parts I-IV of the Guidelines. In order to simplify discussion, references hereafter to "institutions" are intended to encompass corporations, and individuals who have no organizational affiliation. For purposes of complying with the Guidelines, an individual intending to carry out research involving recombinant DNA is encouraged to affiliate with an institution that has an Institutional Biosafety Committee approved under the Guidelines.

Since commercial organizations have special concerns, such as protection of proprietary data, some modifications and explanations of the procedures in Parts I-IV are provided below, in order to address these concerns.

VI-B. *IBC Approval.* The NIH Office of Recombinant DNA Activities (ORDA) will review the membership of an institution's Institutional Biosafety Committee (IBC) and, where it finds the IBC meets the requirements set forth in Section IV-B-2, will give its approval to the IBC membership.

It should be emphasized that employment of an IBC member solely for purposes of membership on the IBC does not itself make the member an institutionally affiliated member for purposes of Section IV-B-2-a.

Except for the unaffiliated members, a member of an IBC for an institution not otherwise covered by the Guidelines may participate in the review and approval of a project in which the member has a direct financial interest, so long as the member has not been and does not expect to be engaged in the project. Section IV-B-2-d is modified to that extent for purposes of these institutions.

VI-C. *Certification of Host-Vector Systems.* A host-vector system may be proposed for certification by the Director, NIH, in accordance with the procedures set forth in Appendix I-II-A.

In order to ensure protection for proprietary data, any public notice regarding a host-vector system which is designated by the institution as proprietary under Section VI-E-1 will be issued only after consultation with the institution as to the content of the notice.

VI-D. *Requests for Exemptions and Approvals.* Requests for exemptions or other approvals required by the Guidelines should be requested by following the procedures set forth in the appropriate sections in Parts I-IV of the Guidelines.

In order to ensure protection for proprietary data, any public notice regarding a request for an exemption or other approval which is designated by the institution as proprietary under Section VI-E-1 will be issued only after consultation with the institution as to the content of the notice.

VI-E. *Protection of Proprietary Data.* In general, the Freedom of Information Act requires Federal agencies to make their records available to the public upon request. However, this requirement does not apply to, among other things, "trade secrets and commercial and financial information obtained from a person and privileged or confidential." 18 U.S.C. 1905, in turn makes it a crime for an officer or employee of the United States or any Federal department or agency to publish, divulge, disclose, or make known "in any manner or to any extent not authorized by law any information coming to him in the course of his employment or official duties or by reason of any examination or investigation made by, or return, report or record made to or filed with, such department or agency or officer or employee thereof, which information concerns or relates to the trade secrets, [or processes * * * of any person, firm, partnership, corporation, or association." This provision applies to all employees of the Federal Government, including special Government employees. Members of the Recombinant DNA Advisory Committee are "special Government employees."

VI-E-1. In submitting information to NIH for purposes of complying voluntarily with the Guidelines, and institution may designate those items of information which the institution believes constitute trade secrets or privileged or confidential commercial or financial information.

VI-E-2. If NIH receives a request under the Freedom of Information Act for information so designated, NIH will promptly contact the institution to secure its views as to whether the information (or some portion) should be released.

VI-E-3. If the NIH decides to release this information (or some portion) in response to a Freedom of Information request or otherwise, the institution will be advised; and the actual release will not be made until the expiration of 15 days after the institution is so advised, except to the extent that earlier release, in the judgment of the Director, NIH, is necessary to protect against an imminent hazard to the public or the environment.

VI-E-4. *Presubmission Review.*

VI-E-4-a. Any institution not otherwise covered by the Guidelines, which is considering submission of data information voluntarily to NIH, may request presubmission review of the records involved to determine whether, if the records are submitted, NIH will or will not make part or all of the records available upon request under the Freedom of Information Act.

VI-E-4-b. A request for presubmission review should be submitted to ORDA, along with the records involved. These records must be clearly marked as being the property of the institution, on loan to NIH solely for the purpose of making a determination under the Freedom of Information Act. ORDA will then seek a determination from the HHS Freedom of Information Officer, the responsible official under HHS regulations (45 C.F.R. Part 5), as to whether the records involved (or some portion) are or are not available to members of the public under the Freedom of Information Act. Pending such a determination, the records will be kept separate from ORDA files, will be considered records of the institution and not ORDA, and will not be received as part of ORDA files. No copies will be made of the records.

VI-E-4-c. ORDA will inform the institution of the HHS Freedom of Information Officer's determination and follow the institution's instructions as to whether some or all of the records involved are to be returned to the institution or to become a part of ORDA files. If the institution instructs ORDA to return the records, no copies or summaries of the records will be made or retained by HHS, NIH, or ORDA.

VI-E-4-d. The HHS Freedom of Information Officer's determination will represent that official's judgment, as of the time of the determination, as to whether the records involved (or some portion) would be exempt.

Appendix A.—Exemptions Under III-D-4

Section III-D-4 states that exempt from these Guidelines are "certain specified recombinant DNA molecules that consist entirely of DNA segments from different species that exchange DNA by known physiological processes, though one or more of the segments may be a synthetic equivalent. A list of such exchangers will be prepared and periodically revised by the Director, NIH, with advice of the RAC, after appropriate notice and opportunity for public comment. (See Section IV-C-1-b-(1)-(c).) Certain classes are exempt as a publication of these Revised Guidelines. The list is in Appendix A."

Under Section III-D-4 of these Guidelines are recombinant DNA molecules that are (1) composed entirely of DNA segments from one or more of the organisms within a sublist and (2) to be propagated in any of the organisms within a sublist. (Classification of *Bergey's Manual of Determinative Bacteriology*, eighth edition. R. E. Buchanan and N. E. Gibbons, editors. Williams and Wilkins Company: Baltimore, 1974.)

Sublist A

1. Genus *Escherichia*
2. Genus *Shigella*
3. Genus *Salmonella* (including *Arizona*)
4. Genus *Enterobacter*
5. Genus *Citrobacter* (including *Levinea*)
6. Genus *Klebsiella*
7. Genus *Erwinia*
8. *Pseudomonas aeruginosa, Pseudomonas putida* and *Pseudomonas fluorescens*
9. *Serratia marcescens*
10. *Yersinia enterocolitica*

Sublist B

1. *Bacillus subtilis*
2. *Bacillus licheniformis*
3. *Bacillus pumilus*
4. *Bacillus globigii*
5. *Bacillus niger*
6. *Bacillus nato*
7. *Bacillus amyloiquefaciens*
8. *Bacillus aterrimus*

Sublist C

1. *Streptomyces aureofaciens*
2. *Streptomyces rimosus*
3. *Streptomyces coelicolor*

Sublist D

1. *Streptomyces griseus*
2. *Streptomyces cyaneus*
3. *Streptomyces venezuelae*

Sublist E

One way transfer of *Streptococcus mutans* or *Streptococcus lactis* DNA into *Streptococcus sanguis*

Sublist F

1. *Streptococcus sanguis*
2. *Streptococcus pneumoniae*
3. *Streptococcus faecalis*
4. *Streptococcus pyogenes*

Appendix B.—Classification of Microoganisms on the Basis of Hazard

Appendix B-I. *Classification of Etiologic Agents.* [The original reference for this classification was the publication "*Classification of Etiological Agents on the Basis of Hazard,*" 4th edition, July 1974, U.S. Department of Health, Education, and Welfare, Public Health Service, Center for Disease Control, Office of Biosafety, Atlanta, Georgia 30333. For the pusposes of these Guidelines, this list has been revised by the NIH.]

Appendix B-I-A. *Class 1 Agents.* All bacterial, parasitic, fungal, viral, rickettsial, and chlamydial agents not included in higher classes.

Appendix B-I-B. *Class 2 Agents*

Appendix B-I-B-1. *Bacterial Agents*

- *Actinobacillus*—all species except *A. mallei*, which is in Class 3
- *Aeromonas hydrophila*
- *Arizona hinshawii*—all serotypes
- *Bacillus anthracis*
- *Bordetella*—all species
- *Borrelia recurrentis, B. vincenti*
- *Campylobacter fetus*
- *Campylobacter jejuni,*
- *Clostridium botulinum,*
- *Cl. chauvoei, Cl. haemolyticum,*
- *Cl. histolyticum, cl. novyi,*
- *Cl. septicum, Cl. tetani*
- *Corynebacterium diphtheriae*
- *C. equi, C. haemolyticum,*
- *C. pseudotuberculosis,*
- *C. pyogenes, C. renale*
- *Diplococcus (Streptococcus) pneumoniae*
- *Edwardsiella tarda*
- *Erysipelothrix insidiosa*
- *Escherichia coli*—all enteropathogenic, enterotoxigenic, enteroinvasive and strains bearing Kl antigen
- *Haemophilus ducreyi, H. influenzae*
- *herellae vaginicola*
- *Klebsiella*—all species and all serotypes
- *Leptospira interrogans*—all serotypes
- *Listeria*—all species
- *Mima polymorpha*
- *Moraxella*—all species
- *Mycobacteria*—all species except those listed in Class 3
- *Mycoplasma*—all species except *Mycoplasma mycoides* and *Mycoplasma agalactiae*, which are in Class 5
- *Neisseria gonorrhoeae, N. meningitidis*
- *Pasterurella*—all species except those listed in Class 3
- *Salmonella*—all species and al serotypes
- *Shigella*—all species and all serotypes
- *Sphaerophorus necrophorus*
- *Staphylococcus aureus*
- *Streptobacillus moniliformis*
- *Stretococcus pyogenes*
- *Treponema carateum, T. pallidum,* and *T. pertenue*
- *Vibrio fetus, V. comma,* including biotype *El Tor* and *V. parahemolyticus*
- *Yersinia enterocolitica*

Appendix B-I-B-2. *Fungal Agents*

- *Actinomycetes* (including *Nocardia* species and *Actinomyces* species and *Arachnia propionica*) [2]
- *Blastomyces dermatitidis*
- *Cryptococcus neoformans*
- *Paracoccidioides braziliensis*

Appendix B-I-B-3. *Parasitic Agents*

- *Endamoeba histolytica*
- *Leishmania sp.*
- *Naegleria gruberi*
- *Toxoplasma gondii*
- *Toxocara canis*
- *Trichinella spiralis*
- *Trypanosoma cruzi*

Appendix B-I-B-4. *Viral, Rickettsial, and Chlamydial Agents*

- *Adenoviruses*—human—all types
- *Cache Valley virus*
- *Coxsackie A* and *B viruses*
- *Cytomegaloviruses*
- *Echoviruses*—all types
- *Encephalomyocarditis virus (EMC)*
- *Flanders virus*
- *Hart Park virus*
- *Hepatitis*—associated antigen material
- *Herpes viruses*—except *Herpesvirus simiae (Monkey B virus)* which is in Class 4
- *Corona viruses*

Influenza viruses—all types except A/PR8/34, which is in Class 1
Langat virus
Lymphogranuloma venereum agent
Measles virus
Mumps virus
Parainfluenza virus—all types except Parainfluenza virus 3, SF4 strain, which is in Class 1
Polioviruses—all types, wild and attenuated
Poxviruses—all types except *Alastrim, Smallpox,* and *Whitepox,* which are Class 5 and *Monkey pox,* which depending on experiments, is in Class 3 or Class 4
Rabies virus—all strains except *Rabies street* virus, which should be classified in Class 3
Reoviruses—all types
Respiratory syncytial virus
Rhinoviruses—all types
Rubella virus
Simian viruses—all types except *Herpesvirus simiae (Monkey B virus)* and *Marburg virus,* which are in Class 4
Sindbis virus
Tensaw virus
Turlock virus
Vaccinia virus
Varicella virus
Vesicular stomatitis virus [3]
Vole rickettsia
Yellow fever virus, 17D vaccine strain

Appendix B-I-C. *Class 3 Agents*

Appendix B-I-C-1. *Bacterial Agents*
Actinobacillus mallei [3]
Bartonella—all species
Brucella—all species
Francisella tularensis
Mycobacterium avium, M. bovis, M. tuberculosis
Pasteurella multocide type *B* ("buffalo" and other foreign virulent strains [3]
Pseudomonas pseudomallei [3]
Yersinia pestis

Appendix B-I-C-2. *Fungal Agents*
Coccidioides immitis
Histoplasma capsulatum
Histoplasma capsulatum var. *duboisii*

Appendix B-I-C-3. *Parasitic Agents*
Schistosoma mansoni

Appendix B-I-C-4. *Viral, Rickettsial, and Chlamydial Agents*
Monkey pox, when use *in vitro* [4]
Arboviruses—all strains except those in Class 2 and 4 *(Arboviruses* indigenous to the United States are in Class 3, except those listed in Class 2. *West Nile* and *Semliki Forest* viruses may be classified up or down, depending on the conditions of use and geographical location of the laboratory.)
Dengue virus, when used for transmission or animal inoculation experiments
Lymphocytic choriomeningitis virus (LCM)
Psittacosis-Ornithosis-Trachoma group of agents
Rabies street virus
Rickettsia—all species except *Vole rickettsia* when used for transmission or animal inoculation experiments
Yellow fever virus—wild, when used *in vitro*

Appendix B-I-D. *Class 4 Agents*

Appendix B-I-D-1. *Bacterial Agents.* None

Appendix B-I-D-2. *Fungal Agents.* None

Appendix B-I-D-3. *Parasitic Agents.* None

Appendix B-I-D-4. *Viral, Rickettsial, and Chlamydial Agents*
Monkey pox, when used for transmission or animal inoculation experiments [4]
Hemorrhagic fever agents, including *Crimean hemorrhagic fever, (Congo), Junin,* and *Machupo* viruses, and others as yet undefined
Herpesvirus simiae (Monkey B virus)
Lassa virus
Marburg virus
Tick-borne encephalitis virus complex, including *Russian spring-summer encephalitis, Kyasanur forest disease, Omsk hemorrhagic fever,* and *Central European encephalitis viruses*
Venezuelan equine encephalitis virus, epidemic strains, when used for transmission or animal inoculation experiments
Yellow fever virus—wild, when used for transmission or animal inoculation experiments

Appendix B-II. *Classification of Oncogenic Viruses on the Basis of Potential Hazard [5]*

Appendix B-II-A. *Low-Risk Oncogenic Viruses.* These viruses should be treated as Class 2 agents
Rous Sarcoma
SV-40
CELO
Ad7-SV40
Polyoma
Bovine papilloma
Rat mammary tmor
Avian Leukosis
Murine Leukemia
Murine Sarcoma
Mouse mammary tumor
Rat Leukemia
Hamster Leukemia
Bovine Leukemia
Dog Sarcoma
Mason-Pfizer Monkey Virus
Marek's
Guinea Pig Herpes
Lucke (Frog)
Adenovirus
Shope Fibroma
Shope Papilloma

Appendix B-II-B. *Moderate-Risk Oncogenic Viruses.* These viruses should be treated as Class 3 agents
Ad2-SV40
FeLV
HV Saimiri
EBV
SSV-1
GaLV
HV ateles
Yaba
FeSV

Appendix B-III. *Class 5 Agents*

Appendix B-III-A. *Animal Disease Organisms Which Are Forbidden Entry into the United States by Law*
Foot and mouth disease virus

Appendix B-III-B. *Animal Disease Organisms and Vectors Which Are Forbidden Entry into the United States by USDA Policy*
African horse sickness virus
African swine fever virus
Besnoitia besnoiti
Borna disease virus
Bovine infectious petechial fever
Camel pox virus
Ephemeral fever virus
Fowl plague virus
Goat pow virus
Hog cholera virus
Louping ill virus
Lumpy skin disease virus
Nairobi sheep disease virus
Newcastle disease virus (Asiatic strains)
Mycoplasma mycoides (contagious bovine pleuropneumonia)
Mycoplasma agalactiae (contagious agalactia of sheep)
Rickettsia ruminatium (heart water)
Rift valley fever virus
Rhinderpest virus
Sheep pox virus
Swine vesicular disease virus
Teschen disease virus
Trypanosoma vivax (Nagana)
Trypanosoma evansi
Theileria parva (East Coast fever)
Theileria annulata
Theileria lawrencei
Theileria bovis
Theileria hirci
Vesicular exanthema virus
Wesselsbron disease virus
Zyonema

Appendix B-III-C. *Organisms Which May Not Be Studied in the United States Except At Specified Facilities*
Small pox [4]
Alastrim [4]
White pox [4]

Appendix B-IV. *Footnotes and References of Appendix B*

1. The original reference for this classification was the publication *Classification of Etiologic Agents on the Basis of Hazard,* 4th edition, July 1974, U.S. Departmet of Health, Education, and Welfare, Public Health Service, Center for Disease Control, Office of Biosafety, Atlanta, Georgia 30333. For the purposes of these Guidelines, this list has been revised by the NIH.

2. Since the publication of the classification in 1974 [1], the *Actinomycetes* have been reclassified as bacterial rather than fungal agents.

3. A USDA permit, required for import and interstate transport of pathogens, may be obtained from the Animal and Plant Health Inspection Service, USDA, Federal Building, Hyattsville, MD 20782.

4. All activities, including storage of variola and whitepox are restricted to the single national facility [World Health Organization (WHO) Collaborating Center for Smallpox Research, Center for Disease Control, in Atlanta].

5. *National Cancer Institute Safety Standards for Research Ivolving Oncogenic Viruses* (October 1974). U.S. Department of Health, Education, and Welfare Publication No. (NIH) 75-790.

6. U.S. Department of Agriculture, Animal and Plant Health Inspection Service.

Appendix C.—Exemptions Under III-D-5

Section III-D-5 states that exempt from these Guidelines are "Other classes of recombinant DNA molecules, if the Director, NIH, with advice of the RAC, after appropriate notice and opportunity for public comment, finds that they do not present a significant risk to health or the envrionment. (See Section IV–C–1–b–(1)–(c).) Certain classes are exempt as of publication of these Resived Guidelines."

The following classes of experiments are exempt under Section III–D–5 of the Guidelines:

Appendix C–I. *Recombinant DNAs in Tissue Culture.* Recombinant DNA molecules derived entirely from non-viral components (that is, no component is derived from a eukaryotic virus), that are propagated and maintained in cells in tissue culture are exempt from these Guidelines with the exceptions listed below.

Exceptions. Experiments described in Section III–A which require specific RAC review and NIH approval before initiation of the experiment.

Experiments involving DNA from Class 3, 4, or 5 organisms [1] or cells known to be infected with these agents.

Experiments involving the deliberate introduction of genes coding for the biosynthesis of molecules toxic for vertebrates. (See Appendix F.)

Appendix C–II. *Experiments Involving E. coli K-12 Host-Vector Systems.* Experiments which use *E. coli* K–12 host-vector systems, with the exception of those experiments listed below, are exempt from these Guidelines provided that (a) the *E. coli* host shall not contain conjugation proficient plasmids or generalized transducing phages, and (b) lambda or lambdoid or Ff bacteriophages or nonconjugaive plasmids [2] shall be used as vectors. However, experiments involving the insertion into *E. coli* K–12 of DNA from prokaryotes that exchange genetic information [3] with *E. coli* may be performed with any *E. coli* K–12 vector (e.g., conjugative plasmid). When a nonconjugative vector is used, the *E. coli* K–12 host may contain conjugation-proficient plasmids ether autonomous or integrated, or generalized transducing phages.

For these exempt experiments, Pl physical containment conditions are recommended.

Exceptions. Experiments described in Section III–A which require a specific RAC review and NIH approval before initiation of the experiment.

Experiments involving DNA from class 3, 4, or 5 organisms [1] or from cells known to be infected with these agents may be conducted under containment conditions specified in Section III–B–2 with prior IBC review and approval.

Large-scale experiments (e.g., more than 10 liters of culture) require prior IBC review and approval. (See Section III–B–5.)

Experiments involving the deliberate cloning of genes coding for the the biosynthesis of molecules toxic for vertebrates. (See Appendix F.)

Appendix C–III. *Experiments Involving Saccharomyces cerevisiae Host-Vector Systems.* Experiments which use *Saccharomyces cerevisiae* host-vector systems, with the exception of experiments listed below, are exempt from these Guidelines provided that laboratory strains are used.

For these exempt experiments, Pl physical containment conditions are recommended.

Exemptions. Experiments described in Section III–A which require specific RAC review and NIH approval before initiation of the experiment.

Experiments involving Class 3, 4 or 5 organisms [1] or cells known to be infected with these agents may be conducted under containment conditions specified in Section III–B–2 with prior IBC review and approval.

Large-scale experiments (e.g., more than 10 liters of culture) require prior IBC review and approval. (See Section III–B–5.)

Experiments involving the deliberate cloning of genes coding for the biosynthesis of molecules toxic for vertebrates. (See Appendix F.)

Appendix C–IV. *Experiments Involving Bacillus subtilis Host-Vector Systems.* Any asporogenic *Bacillus subtilis* strain which does not revert to a sporeformer with a frequency greater than 10^{-7} can be used for cloning DNA, with the exception of those experiments listed below. Indigenous *Bacillus* plasmids and phages, whose host-range does not include *Bacillus cereus* or *Bacillus anthracis*, may be used as vectors.

For these exempt experiments Pl physical containment conditions are recommended.

Exceptions. Experiments described in Section III–A which require specific RAC review and approval before initiation of the experiment.

Experiments involving Class 3, 4, or 5 organisms [1] or cells known to be infected with these agents may be conducted under containment conditions specified by Section III–B–2 with prior IBC review and approval.

Large-scale experiments (e.g., more than 10 liters of culture) require prior IBC review and approval. (See Section III–B–5.)

Experiments involving the deliberate cloning of genes coding for the biosynthesis of molecules toxic for vertebrates. (See Appendix F.)

Appendix C–V. *Footnotes and References of Appendix C*

1. The original reference to organisms as Class 1, 2, 3, 4, or 5 refers to the calssification in the publication *Classification of Etiologic Agents on the Basis of Hazard,* 4th Edition, July 1974; U.S. Department of Health, Education, and Welfare, Public Health Service, Centers for Disease Control, Office of Biosafety, Atlanta, Georgia 30333.

The Director, NIH, with advice of the Recombinant DNA Advisory Committee, may revise the classification for the purposes of these Guidelines (see Section IV–C–1–b–(2)–(d)). The revised list of organisms in each class is reprinted in Appendix B to these Guidelines.

2.subset of non-conjugative plasmid vectors are also poorly mobilizable (e.g., pBR322, pBR313). Where practical, these vectors should be employed.

3. Defined as observable under optimal laboratory conditions by transformation, transduction, phage infection, and/or conjugation with transfer of phage, plasmid, and/or chromosomal genetic information. Note that this definition of exchange may be less stringent than that applied to exempt organisms unser Section III–D–4.

Apendix D—Actions Taken Under the guidelines

As noted in the subsections of Section IV–C–1–b–(1), the Director, NIH, may take certain actions with regard to the Guidelines after the issues have been considered by the RAC.

Some of the actions taken to date include the following:

Appendix D–I. Permission is granted to clone Foot-and-Mouth disease virus in the EK1 host-vector system consisting of *E. coli* K–12 and the vector pBR322, all work to be done at the Plum Island Animal disease Center.

Appendix D–II. Certain specified clones derived from segments of the Foot-and-Mouth disease Virus may be transferred from Plum Island Animal disease Center to the facilities of Genentech, Inc., of South San Francisco, California. Further development of the clones at Genetech has been approved under P1 + EK1 conditions.

Appendix D–III. The Rd strain of *hemophilus influenzae* can be used as a host for the propagtin of the cloned Tn 10 tet R gene derived from *E. coli* K–12 employing the non-conjugative *Haemophilus* plasmid, pRSF0885, under P1 conditions.

Appendix D–IV. Permission is granted to clone certain subgenomic segments of Foot-and-Mouth Disease Virus in HV1 *Bacillus subtilis* and *Saccharomyces cerevisiae* host-vector systems under P1 conditions at Genetech, Inc., South San Francisco, California.

Appendix D–V. Permission is granted to Dr. Ronald Davis of Stanford University to field test corn plants modified by recombinant DNA techniques under specified containment conditions.

Appendix D–VI. Permission is granted to clone in *E. coli* K–12, under P1 physical containment conditions, subgenomic segments of Rift Valley Fever Virus subject to conditions which have been set forth by the RAC.

Appendix D–VII. Attenuated laboratory strains of *Salmonella typhimurium* may be used under P1 physical containment conditions to screen for the *Saccharomyces cerevisiae* pseudouridine synthetase gene. The plasmid YEp13 will be employed as the vector.'

Appendix D–VIII. Permission is granted to transfer certain clones of subgenomic segments of Foot-and-Mouth Disease Virus from Plum Island Animal Disease Center to the laboratories of Molecular Genetics, Inc., Minnetonka, Minnesota, and to work with these clones under P1 containment conditions. Approval is contingent upon review of data on infectivity testing of the clones by a working group of the RAC.

Appendix E—Certified Host-Vector Systems

While many experiments using *E. coli* K-12, *Saccharomyces cerevisiae* and *Bacillus subtilis* are currently exempt from the Guidelines under Exemption III-D-5, some derivatives of these host-vector systems were previously classified as HV1 or HV2. A listing of those systems follows.

HV1. The following plasmids are accepted as the vector components of certified *B.*

subtilis HV1 systems: pUB110, pC194, pS194, pSA2100, pE194, pT127, pUB112, pC221, pC223, and pAB124. *B. subtilis* strains RUB 331 and BGSC 1S53 have been certified as the host component of HV1 systems based on these plasmids.

HV2. The asporogenic mutant derivative of *Bacillus subtilis*, ASB 298 with the following plasmids as the vector component: pUB110, pC194, pSA2100, pE194, pT127, pUB112, pC221, pC223, and pAB124.

HV2—The following sterile strains of *Saccharomyces cerevisiae*, all of which have the ste-VC9 mutation, SHY1, SHY2 SHY3, and SHY4. The following plasmids are certified for use: YIp1, YEp2, YEp4, YIp5, YEp6, YRp7, YEp20, YEp21, YEp24, YIp25, YIp26, YIp27, YIp28, YIp29, YIp30, YIp31, YIp32, and YIp33.

EK2 Plasmid Systems. The *E. coli* K-12 strain chi-1776. The following plasmids are certified for use: pSC101, pMB9, pBR313, pBR322, pDH24, pBR327, pGL101, pHB1. The following *E. coli/S. cerevisiae* hybrid plasmids are certified as EK2 vectors when use in *E. coli* chi-1776 or in the sterile yeast strains, SHY1, SHY2, SHY3, and SHY4: YIp1, YEp2, YEp4, YIp5, YEp6, YRp7, YEp20, YEp21, YEp24, YIp25, YIp26, YIp27, YIp28, YIp29, YIp30, YIp31 YIp32, YIp33.

EK2 Bacteriophage Systems. The following are certified EK2 systems based on bacteriophage lambda:

Vector	Host
λgt*WES*. B'	DP50*supF*
λgt*WES*. B*	DP50*supF*
λgtZJ*vir*. B'	*E. coli* K-12
λgtALO. B	DP50*supF*
Charon 3A	DP50 or DP50*supF*
Charon 4A	DP50 or DP50*supF*
Charon 16A	DP50 or DP50*supF*
Charon 21A	DP50*supF*
Charon 23A	DP50 or DP50*supF*
Charon 24A	DP50 or DP50*supF*.

E. coli K-12 strains chi-2447 and chi-2281 are certified for use with lambda vectors that are certified for use with strain DP50 or DP50supF provided that the su– strain not be used as a propagation host.

E. coli K-12 strains chi-1984, chi-2705, chi-2001, and chi-2363 are certified for use with lambda vectors that are certified for use with strain DP50 or SP50supF provided that the su– strains not be used as propagation hosts.

Additional certified host-vector systems

HV1—The following specified strains of *Neurospora crassa* which have been modified to prevent aerial dispersion:

Inl (inositolless) strains 37102, 37401, 46316, 64001, and 89601.

Csp-1 strain UCLA 37 and csp-2 strains FS 590, UCLA101 (these are conidial separation mutants).

Eas strain UCLA191 (an "easily wettable" mutant).

HV1—The following *Streptomyces* species: *Streptomyces coelicolor, S. lividans, S. parvulus,* and *S. griseus.* The following are accepted as vector components of certified *Streptomyces* HV1 systems: *Streptomyces* plasmids SCP2, SLP1.2, pIJ101, actinophage phi C31, and their derivatives.

Hv1—*Pseudomonas putida* strain KT2440 with plasmid vectors pKT262, pKT263, and PKT264.

APPENDIX F—CONTAINMENT CONDITIONS FOR CLONING OF GENES CODING FOR THE BIOSYNTHESIS OF MOLECULES TOXIC FOR VERTEBRATES

Appendix F-I. *General Information.* Appendix F specifies the containment to be used for the deliberate cloning of genes coding for the biosynthesis of molecules toxic for vertebrates. Cloning of genes coding for molecules toxic for vertebrates that have an LD_{50} of less than 100 nanograms per kilogram body weight (e.g., microbial toxins such as the botulinum toxins, tetanus toxin, diphtheria toxin, *Shigella dysenteriae* neurotoxin) is prohibited. No specific restrictions shall apply to the cloning of genes if the protein specified by the gene has an LD_{50} of 100 micrograms or more per kilogram of body weight. Experiments involving genes coding for toxic molecules with an LD_{50} of 100 micrograms or less per kilogram body weight shall be registered with ORDA prior to initiating the experiments. A list of toxic molecules classified as to LD_{50} is available from ORDA. Testing procedures for determining toxicity of toxic molecules not on the list are available from ORDA. The results of such tests shall be forwarded to ORDA, which will consult with an *ad hoc* working group on toxic molecules prior to inclusion of the molecule on the list. (See Section IV-C-1-b-(2)-(e).)

Appendix F-II. *Containment Conditions for Cloning of Toxic Molecule Genes in E. coli K-12.*

Appendix F-II-A. Cloning of genes coding for molecules toxic for vertebrates that have an LD_{50} in the range of 100 nanograms to 1000 nanograms per kilogram body weight (e.g., abrin, *Clostridium perfringens* epsilon toxin) may proceed under P2+EK2 or P3+EK1 containment conditions.

Appendix F-II-B. Coloning of genes for the biosynthesis of molecules toxic for vertebrates with an LD_{50} in the range of 1 microgram to 100 micrograms per kilogram body weight may proceed under p1+EK1 containment conditions (e.g., *Staphylococcus aureus* alpha toxin, *Staphylococcus aureus* beta toxin, ricin, *Pseudomonas aeruginosa* exotoxin A, *Bordatella pertussis* toxin, the lethal factor of *Bacillus anthracis*, the *Pasteurella pestis* murine toxins, the oxgen-labile hemolysins such as streptolysin O, and certain neurotoxins present in snake venoms and other venoms).

Appendix F-II-C. Some enterotoxins are substantially more toxic when administered enterally than parenterally. The following enterotoxins shall be subject to P1+EK1 containment conditions: cholera toxin, the heat liable toxins of *E. coli, Klebsiella,* and other related proteins that may be identified by neutralization with an antiserum monospecific for cholera toxin, and the heat stable toxins of *E. coli* and of *Yersinia enterocolitica.*

Appendix F-III. *Containment Conditions for Cloning of Toxic Molecule Genes in Organisms Other than E. coli K-12.* Requests involving the cloning of genes coding for molecules toxic for vertebrates in host-vector systems other than *E. coli* K-12 will be evaluated by ORDA, which will consult with the *ad hoc* working group on toxic molecules. (See Section IV-C-1-b-(3)-(f).)

Appendix F-IV. *Specific Approvals.*

Appendix F-IV-A. Permission is granted to clone the Exotoxin A gene of *Pseudomonas aeruginosa* under P1 conditions in *Pseudomonas aeruginosa.*

Appendix F-IV-B. The pyrogenic endotoxin type A (Tox A) gene of *Staphylococcus aureus* may be cloned in an HV2 *Bacillus subtilis* host-vector system under P3 containment conditions.

Appendix F-IV-C. Permission is granted to clone in *E. coli* K-12, in high containment Building 550 at the Frederick Cancer Research Facility, restriction fragments of *Corynephage Beta* carrying the structural gene for diphtheria toxin. Laboratory practices and containment equipment are to be specified by the IBC.

Appendix F-IV-D. The genes coding for the *Staphylococcus aureus* determinants, A, B, and F, which may be implicated in toxic shock syndrome, may be cloned in *E. coli* K-12 under P2+EK1 conditions. The *Staphylococcus aureus* strain used as the donor is to be alpha toxin minus. It is suggested that, if possible, the donor *Staphylococcus aureus* strain should lack other toxins with LD_{50}s in the range of one microgram per kilogram body weight, such as the exfoliative toxin.

Appendix F-IV-E. Fragments F-1 and F-2 of the diphtheria toxin gene (*tox*) may be cloned in *E. coli* K-12 under P1+EK1 containment conditions. Fragment F-1 and fragment F-2 both contain (i) some or all of the transcriptional control elements of *tox,* (ii) the signal peptide, and (iii) fragment A (the center responsible for ADP-ribosylation of elongation factor 2).

Appendix F-IV-F. The gene(s) coding for a toxin (designated LT-like) isolated from *E. coli* which is similar to the *E. coli* heat labile enterotoxin (LT) with respect to its activities and mode of action, but is not neutralized by antibodies against cholera enterotoxin or against LT from human or porcine *E. coli* strains and sequences homologous to the *E. coli* LT-like toxin gene may be cloned under P1+Ek1 conditions.

APPENDIX G—Physical Containment

Appendix G-I. *Standard Practices and Training.* The first principle of containment is a strict adherence to good microbiological practices [1-10]. Consequently, all personnel directly or indirectly involved in experiments on recombinant DNAs must receive adequate instruction. (See Sections IV-B-1-e and IV-B-5-d.) This shall, as a minimum, include instructions in aseptic techniques and in the biology of the organisms used in the experiments, so that the potential biohazards can be understood and appreciated.

Any research group working with agents with a known or potential biohazard shall have an emergency plan which describes the procedures to be followed if an accident contaminates personnel or the environment. The principal investigator must ensure that everyone in the laboratory is familiar with both the potential hazards of the work and the emergency plan. (See Sections IV-B-3-d and IV-B-5-e.) If a research group is working with a known pathogen where there is an effective vaccine it should be made available to all workers. Where serological monitoring is clearly appropriate it shall be provided. (See Section IV-B-1-f.)

The "Laboratory Safety Monograph", available from ORDA, describes practices, equipment, and facilities in detail.

Appendix G-II. *Physical Containment Levels.* The objective of physical containment is to confine organisms containing recombinant DNA molecules, and thus to reduce the potential for exposure of the laboratory worker, persons outside of the laboratory, and the environment to organisms containing recombinant DNA molecules. Physical containment is achieved through the use of laboratory practices, containment equipment, and special laboratory design. Emphasis is placed on primary means of physical containment which are provided by laboratory practices and containment equipment. Special laboratory design provides a secondary means of protection against the accidental release of organisms outside the laboratory or to the environment. Special laboratory design is used primarily in facilities in which experiments of moderate to high potential hazards are performed.

Combinations of laboratory practices, containment equipment, and special laboratory design can be made to achieve different levels of physical containment. Four levels of physical containment, which are designated as P1, P2, P3, and P4, are described. It should be emphasized that the descriptions and assignments of physical containment detailed below are based on existing approaches to containment of pathogenic organisms. For example, the "Classification of Etiologic Agents on the Basis of Hazard," [2] prepared by the Centers for Disease Control, describes four general levels which roughly correspond to our descriptions for P1, P2, P3, and P4; and the National Cancer Institute describes three levels for research on oncogenic viruses which roughly correspond to our P2, P3, and P4 levels. [3]

It is recognized that several different combinations of laboratory practices, containment equipment, and special laboratory design may be appropriate for containment of specific research activities. The Guidelines, therefore, allow alternative selections of primary contaiment equipment within facilities that have been designed to provide P3 and P4 levels of physical containment. The selection of alternative methods of primary containment is dependent, however, on the level of biological containment provided by the host-vector system used in the experiment. Consideration will also be given by the Director, NIH, with the advice of the Recombinant DNA Advisory Committee to other combinations which achieve an equivalent level of containment. (See Section IV-C-1-b-(2)-(b).)

Appendix G-II-A. *Pl Level.*

Appendix G-II-A-1. *Laboratory Practices.*

Appendix G-II-A-1-a. Laboratory doors shall be kept closed while experiments are in progress.

Appendix G-II-A-1-b. Work surfaces shall be decontaminated daily, and immediately following spills of organisms containing recombinant DNA molecules.

Appendix G-II-A-1-c. All biological wastes shall be decontaminated before disposal. Other contaminated materials, such as glassware, animal cages, and laboratory equipment, shall be decontaminated before washing, reuse, or disposal.

Appendix G-II-A-1-d. Mechanical pipetting devices shall be used; pipetting by mouth is prohibited.

Appendix G-II-A-1-e. Eating, drinking, smoking, and storage of foods are not permitted in the laboratory area in which recombinant DNA materials are handled.

Appendix G-II-A-1-f. Persons shall wash their hands after handling organisms containing recombinant DNA molecules and when they leave the laboratory.

Appendix G-II-A-1-g. Care shall be taken in the conduct of all procedures to minimize the creation of aerosols.

Appendix G-II-A-1-h. Contaminated materials that are to be decontaminated at a site away from the laboratory shall be placed in a durable leakproof container, which is closed before removal from the laboratory.

Appendix G-II-A-1-i. An insect and rodent control program shall be instituted.

Appendix G-II-A-1-j. The use of laboratory gowns, coats, or uniforms is discretionary with the laboratory supervisor.

Appendix G-II-A-1-k. Use of hypodermic needle and syringe shall be avoided when alternative methods are available.

Appendix G-II-A-1-l. The laboratory shall be kept neat and clean.

Appendix G-II-A-2. *Containment Equipment.* Special containment equipment is not required at the P1 level.

Appendix G-II-A-3. *Special Laboratory Design.* Special laboratory design is not required at the P1 level.

Appendix G-II-B. *P2 Level.*

Appendix G-II-B-1. *Laboratory Practices.*

Appendix G-II-B-1-a. Laboratory doors shall be kept closed while experiments are in progress.

Appendix G-II-B-1-b. Work surfaces shall be decontaminated daily, and immediately following spills of organisms containing recombinant DNA molecules.

Appendix G-II-B-1-c. All laboratory wastes shall be steam-sterilized (autoclaved) before disposal. Other contaminated materials such as glassware, animal cages, laboratory equipment, and radioactive wastes shall be decontaminated by a means demonstrated to be effective before washing, reuse, or disposal.

Appendix G-II-B-1-d. Mechanical pipetting devices shall be used; pipetting by mouth is prohibited.

Appendix G-II-B-1-e. Eating, drinking, smoking, and storage of food are not permitted in the laboratory area in which recombinant DNA materials are handled.

Appendix G-II-B-1-f. Persons shall wash their hands after handling organisms containing recombinant DNA molecules and when they leave the laboratory.

Appendix G-II-B-1-g. Care shall be exercised to minimize the creation of aerosols. For example, manipulations such as inserting a hot inoculating loop or needle into a culture, flaming an inoculation loop or needle so that it splatters, and forceful ejection of fluids from pipettes or syringes shall be avoided.

Appendix G-II-B-1-h. Contaminated materials that are to be steam sterilized (autoclaved) or decontaminated at a site away from the laboratory shall be placed in a durable leak-proof container, which is closed before removal from the laboratory.

Appendix G-II-B-1-i. Only persons who have been advised of the nature of the research being conducted shall enter the laboratory.

Appendix G-II-B-1-j. The universal biohazard sign shall be posted on all laboratory access doors when experiments requiring P2 containment are in progress. Freezers and refrigerators or other units used to store organisms containing recombinant DNA molecules shall also be posted with the universal biohazard sign.

Appendix G-II-B-1-k. An insect and rodent control program shall be instituted.

Appendix G-II-B-1-l. The use of laboratory gowns, coats, or uniforms is required. Laboratory clothing shall not be worn to the lunch room or outside of the building in which the laboratory is located.

Appendix G-II-B-1-m. Animals not related to the experiment shall not be permitted in the laboratory.

Appendix G-II-B-1-n. Use of the hypodermic needle and syringe shall be avoided when alternative methods are available.

Appendix G-II-B-1-o. The laboratory shall be kept neat and clean.

Appendix G-II-B-1-p. Experiments of lesser biohazard potential can be carried out concurrently in carefully demarcated areas of the same laboratory.

Appendix G-II-B-2. *Containment Equipment.* Biological safety cabinets [12] shall be used to contain aerosol-producing equipment, such as blenders, lyophilizers, sonicators, and centrifuges, when used to process organisms containing recombinant DNA molecules, except where equipment design provides for containment of the potential aerosol. For example, a centrifuge may be operated in the open if a sealed head or safety centrifuge cups are used.

Appendix G-II-B-3. *Special Laboratory Design.* An autoclave for sterilization of wastes and contaminated materials shall be available in the same building in which organisms containing recombinant DNA molecules are used.

Appendix G-II-C. *P3 Level.*

Appendix G-II-C-1. *Laboratory Practices.*

Appendix G-II-C-1-a. Laboratory doors shall be kept closed while experiments are in progress.

Appendix G-II-C-1-b. Work surfaces shall be decontaminated following the completion of the experimental activity, and immediately following spills of organisms containing recombinant DNA molecules.

Appendix G-II-C-1-c. All laboratory wastes shall be steam-sterilized (autoclaved) before disposal. Other contaminated materials, such as glassware, animal cages, laboratory equipment, and radioactive wastes, shall be decontaminated by a method demonstrated to be effective before washing, reuse, or disposal.

Appendix G-II-C-1-d. Mechanical pipetting devices shall be used; pipetting by mouth is prohibited.

Appendix G-II-C-1-e. Eating, drinking, smoking, and storage of food are not permitted in the laboratory area in which recombinant DNA materials are handled.

Appendix G-II-C-1-f. Persons shall wash their hands after handling organisms containing recombinant DNA molecules and when they leave the laboratory.

Appendix G-II-C-1-g. Care shall be exercised to minimize the creation of aerosols. For example, manipulations such as inserting a hot inoculating loop or needle into a culture, flaming an inoculation loop or needle so that it splatters, and forceful ejection of fluids from pipettes or syringes shall be avoided.

Appendix G-II-C-1-h. Contaminated materials that are to be steamsterilized (autoclaved) or decontaminated at a site away from the laboratory shall be placed in durable leak-proof container, which is closed before removal from the laboratory.

Appendix G-II-C-1-i. Entry into the laboratory shall be through a controlled access area. Only persons who have been advised of the nature of the research being conducted shall enter the controlled access area. Only persons required on the basis of program or support needs shall be authorized to enter the laboratory. Such persons shall be advised of the nature of the research being conducted before entry, and shall comply with all required entry and exit procedures.

Appendix G-II-C-1-j. Persons under 16 of age shall not enter the laboratory.

Appendix G-II-C-1-k. The universal biohazard sign shall be posted on the controlled access area door and on all laboratory doors when experiments requiring P3-level containment are in progress. Freezers and refrigerators or other units used to store organisms containing recombinant DNA molecules shall also be posted with the universal biohazard sign.

Appendix G-II-C-1-l. An insect and rodent control program shall be instituted.

Appendix G-II-C-1-m. Laboratory clothing that protects street clothing (e.g., long-sleeve solid-front or wrap-around gowns, no-button or slipover jackets) shall be worn in the laboratory. Front-button laboratory coats are unsuitable. Laboratory clothing shall not be worn outside the laboratory and shall be decontaminated before it is sent to the laundry.

Appendix G-II-C-1-n. Raincoats, overcoats, topcoats, coats, hats, caps, and such street outer-wear shall not be kept in the laboratory.

Appendix G-II-C-1-o. Gloves shall be worn when handling materials requiring P3 containment. They shall be removed aseptically immediately after the handling procedure and decontaminated.

Appendix G-II-C-1-p. Animals and plants not related to the experiment shall not be permitted in the laboratory.

Appendix G-II-C-1-q. Vaccum outlets shall be protected by filter and liquid disinfectant traps.

Appendix G-II-C-1-r. Use of hypodermic needle and syringe shall be avoided when alternative methods are available.

Appendix G-II-C-1-s. The laboratory shall be kept neat and clean.

Appendix G-II-C-1-t. If experiments involving other organisms which require lower levels of containment are to be conducted in the same laboratory concurrently with experiments requiring P3-level physical containment, they shall be conducted in accordance with all P3-level laboratory practices.

Appendix G-II-C-2. *Containment Equipment.*

Appendix G-II-C-2-a. Biological safety cabinets [12] shall be used for all equipment and manipulations that produce aerosols—e.g., pipetting, dilutions, transfer operations, plating, flaming, grinding, blending, drying, sonicating, shaking, centrifuging—where these procedures involve organisms containing recombinant DNA molecules, except where equipment design provides for containment of the potential aerosal.

Appendix G-II-C-2-b. Laboratory animals held in a P3 area shall be housed in partial-containment caging systems, such as Horsfall units [11], open cages placed in ventilated enclosures, solid-wall and -bottom cages covered by filter bonnets, or solid-wall and bottom cages placed on holding racks equipped with ultraviolet radiation lamps and reflectors.

Note.—Conventional caging systems may be used, provided that all personnel wear appropriate personal protective devices. These shall include, at a minimum, wrap-around gowns, head covers, gloves, shoe covers, and respirators. All personnel shall shower on exit from areas where these devices are required.

Appendix G-II-C-2-c. *Alternative Selection of Containment Equipment.* Experimental procedures involving a host-vector system that provides a one-step higher level of biological containment than that specified can be conducted in the P3 laboratory using containment equipment specified for the P2 level or physical containment. Experimental procedures involving a host-vector system that provides a one-step lower level of biological containment than that specified can be conducted in the P3 laboratory using containment equipment specified for the P4 level of physical containment. Alternative combinations of containment safeguards are shown in Table I.

TABLE I—POSSIBLE COMBINATIONS OF CONTAINMENT SAFEGUARDS

Classification of experiment		Alternate combinations of physical and biological containment			
		Physical containment			
Physical containment	Biological containment [1]	Laboratory design specified for	Laboratory practices specified for	Containment equipment specified for	Biological containment
P3	HV2	P3	P3	P3	HV2.
P3	HV2	P3	P3	P4	HV1.
P3	HV1	P3	P3	P3	HV1.
P3	HV1	P3	P3	P2	HV2.

[1] See Appendix I for description of biological containment.

Appendix G-II-C-33. *Special Laboratory Design.*

Appendix G-II-C-3-a. The laboratory shall be separated by a controlled access area from areas that are open to unrestricted traffic flow. A controlled access area is an anteroom, a change room, an air lock or any other double-door arrangement that separates the laboratory from areas open to unrestricted traffic flow.

Appendix G-II-C-3-b. The surfaces of walls, floors, and ceilings shall be readily cleanable. Penetrations through these surfaces shall be sealed or capable of being sealed to facilitate space decontamination.

Appendix G-II-C-3-c. A foot-, elbow-, or automatically-operated hand-washing facility shall be provided near each primary laboratory exit area.

Appendix G-II-C-3-d. Windows in the laboratory shall be sealed.

Appendix G-II-C-3-e. An autoclave for sterilization of wastes and contaminated materials shall be available in the same building (and preferably within the controlled laboratory area) in which organisms containing recombinant DNA molecules are used.

Appendix G-II-C-3-f. The laboratory shall have a ventilation system that is capable of controlling air movement. The movement of air shall be from areas of lower contamination potential to areas of higher contamination potential (i.e., from the controlled access area to the laboratory area). If the ventilation system provides positive pressure supply air, the system shall operate in a manner that prevents the reversal of the direction of air movement or shall be equipped with an alarm that would be actuated in the event that reversal in the direction of air movement were to occur. The exhaust air from the laboratory area shall not be recirculated to other areas of the building unless the exhaust air is filtered by HEPA filters or equivalent. The exhaust air from the laboratory area can be discharged to the outdoors without filtration or ther means for effectively reducing an accidental aerosol burden provided that it can be dispersed clear of occupied buildings and air intakes.

Appendix G-II-C-3-g. The treated exhaust-air from Class I and Class II biological safety cabinets [12] may be discharged either to the laboratory or to the outdoors. The treated exhaust-air from a Class III cabinet shall be discharged directly to the outdoors. If the treated exhaust-air from these cabinets is to be discharged to the outdoors through a building exhaust air system, it shall be connected to this system so as to avoid any interference with the air balance of the cabinet and the building ventilation system.

Appendix G-II-D. *P4 Level.*

Appendix G-II-D-1. *Laboratory Practices.*

Appendix G-II-D-1-a. Laboratory doors shall be kept closed while experiments are in progress.

Appendix G-II-D-1-b. Work surfaces shall be decontaminated following the completion of the experimental activity and immediately following spills of organisms containing recombinant DNA molecules.

Appendix G-II-D-1-c. All laboratory wastes shall be steam-sterilized (autoclaved) before disposal. Other contaminated materials such as glassware, animal cages, laboratory equipment, and radioactive wastes shall be decontaminated by a method demonstrated to be effective before washing, reuse, or disposal.

Appendix G-II-D-1-d. Mechanical pipetting devices shall be used; pipetting by mouth is prohibited.

Appendix G-II-D-1-e. Eating, drinking, smoking, and storage of food are not permitted in the P4 facility.

Appendix G-II-D-1-f. Persons shall wash their hands after handling organisms containing recombinant DNA molecules and when they leave the laboratory.

Appendix G-II-D-1-g. Care shall be exercised to minimize the creation of aerosols. For example, manipulations such as inserting a hot inoculating loop or needle into a culture, flaming an inoculation lop or needle so that it splatters, and forceful ejection of fluids from pipettes or syringes shall be avoided.

Appendix G-II-D-1-h. Biological materials to be removed from the P4 facility in a viable or intact state shall be transferred to a nonbreakable sealed container, which is then removed from the P4 facility through a pass-through disinfectant dunk tank or fumigation chamber.

Appendix G-II-D-1-i. No materials, except for biological materials that are to remain in a viable or intact state, shall be removed from the P4 facility unless they have been steam-sterilized (autoclaved) or decontaminated by a means demonstrated to be effective as they pass out of the P4 facility. All wastes and other materials as well as equipment not damaged by high temperature or steam shall be steam sterilized in the double-door autoclave of the P4 facility. Other materials which may be damaged by temperature or steam shall be removed from the P4 facility through a pass-through fumigation chamber.

Appendix G-II-D-1-j. Materials within the Class III cabinets shall be removed from the cabinet system only after being steam-sterilized in an attached double-door autoclave or after being contained in a nonbreakable sealed container, which is then passed through a disinfectant dunk tank or a fumigation chamber.

Appendix G-II-D-1-k. Only persons whose entry into the P4 facility is required to meet program or support needs shall be authorized to enter. Before entering, such persons shall be advised of the nature of the research being conducted and shall be instructed as to the appropriate safeguards to ensure their safety. They shall comply with instructions and all other required procedures.

Appendix G-II-D-1-l. Persons under 18 years of age shall not enter the P4 facility.

Appendix G-II-D-1-m. Personnel shall enter into and exit fron the P4 facility only through the clothing change and shower rooms. Personnel shall shower at each egress from the P4 facility. Air locks shall not be used for personnel entry or exit except for emergencies.

Appendix G-II-D-1-n. Street clothing shall be removed in the outer side of the clothing-change area and kept there. Complete laboratory clothing, including undergarments, head cover, shoes, and either pants and shirts or jumpsuits, shall be used by all persons who enter the P4 facility. Upon exit, personnel shall store this clothing in lockers provided for this purpose or discard it into collection hampers before entering the shower area.

Appendix G-II-D-1-o. The universal biohazard sign is required on the P4 facility access doors and on all interior doors to individual laboratory rooms where experiments are conducted. The sign shall also be posted on freezers, refrigerators, or other units used to store organisms containing recombinant DNA molecules.

Appendix G-II-D-1-p. An insect and rodent control program shall be instituted.

Appendix G-II-D-1-q. Animals and plants not related to the experiment shall not be permitted in the laboratory in which the experiment is being conducted.

Appendix G-II-D-1-r. Vacuum outlets shall be protected by filter and liquid disinfectant traps.

Appendix G-II-D-1-s. Use of the hypodermic needle and syringe shall be avoided when alternate methods are available.

Appendix G-II-D-1-t. The laboratory shall be kept neat and clean.

Appendix G-II-D-1-u. If experiments involving other organisms which require lower levels of containment are to be conducted in the P4 facility concurrently with experiments requiring P4-level containment, they shall be conducted in accordance with all P4-level laboratory practices specified in this section.

Appendix G-II-D-2. *Containment Equipment.*

Appendix G-II-D-2-a. Experimental procedures involving organisms that require P4-level physical containment shall be conducted either in (i) a Class III cabinet system or in (ii) Class I or Class II cabinets that are located in a specially designed area in which all personnel are required to wear one-piece positive-pressure isolation suits.

Appendix G-II-B-4-b. Laboratory animals involved in experiments requiring P4-level physical containment shall be housed either in cages contained in Class III cabinets or in partial containment caging systems (such as Horsfall units [11], open cages placed in ventilated enclosures, or solid-wall and-bottom cages covered by filter bonnets, or solid-wall and -bottom cages placed on holding racks equipped with ultraviolet irradiation lamps and reflectors) that are located in a specially designed area in which all personnel are required to wear one-piece positive-pressure suits.

Appendix G-II-D-2-c. *Alternative Selection of Containment Equipment.* Experimental procedures involving a host-vector system that provides a one-step higher level of biological containment than that specified can be conducted in the P4 facility using containment equipment requirements specified for the P3 level of physical containment. Alternative combinations of containment safeguards are shown in Table II.

TABLE II.—POSSIBLE COMBINATIONS OF CONTAINMENT SAFEGUARDS

Classification of experiment		Alternate combinations of physical and biological containment			
		Physical containment			
Physical containment	Biological [1] containment	Laboratory design specified for—	Laboratory practices specified for—	Containment equipment specified for—	Biological containment
P4	HV1	P4	P4	P4	HV1.
P4	HV1	P4	P4 [2]	P3	HV2.

[1] See Appendix I for description of biological containment.
[2] In this case gloves shall be worn, in addition to the clothing requirements specified in Appendix G-II-D-1-n.

Appendix G-II-D-3. *Special Laboratory Design.*

Appendix G-II-D-3-a. The laboratory shall be located in a restricted-access facility which is either a separate building or a clearly demarcated and isolated zone within a building. Clothing-change areas and shower rooms shall be provided for personnel entry and egress. These rooms shall be arranged so that personnel leave through the shower area to the change room. A double-door ventilated vestibule or ultraviolet air lock shall be provided for passage of materials, supplies, and equipment which are not brought into the P4 facility through the change room area.

Appendix G-II-D-3-b. Walls, floors, and ceilings of the P4 facility are constructed to form an internal shell which readily allows vapor-phase decontamination and is animal- and insect-proof. All penetrations through these structures and surfaces are sealed. (The integrity of the walls, floors, ceilings, and penetration seals should ensure adequate containment of a vapor-phase decontaminant under static pressure conditions. This requirement does not imply that these surfaces must be airtight.)

Appendix G-II-D-3-c. A foot-, elbow-, or automatically-operated handwashing facility shall be provided near the door within each laboratory in which experiments involving recombinant DNA are conducted in openface biological safety cabinets.

Appendix G-II-D-3-d. Central vacuum systems are permitted. The system, if provided, shall not serve areas outside the P4 facility. The vacuum system shall include in-line HEPA filters near each use point or service cock. The filters shall be installed so as to permit in-place decontamination and replacement. Water supply, liquid and gaseous services provided to the P4 facility shall be protected by devices that prevent backflow.

Appendix G-II-D-3-e. Drinking water fountains shall not be installed in laboratory or animal rooms of the P4 facility. Foot-operated water fountains are permitted in the corridors of the P4 facility. The water service provided to such fountains shall be protected from the water services to the laboratory areas of the P4 facility.

Appendix G-II-D-3-f. Laboratory doors shall be self-closing.

Appendix G-II-D-3-g. A double-door autoclave shall be provided for sterilization of material passing out of the P4 facility. The autoclave doors shall be interlocked so that both doors will not be open at the same time.

Appendix G-II-D-3-h. A pass-through dunk tank or fumigation chamber shall be provided for removal from the P4 facility of material and equipment that cannot be heat-sterilized.

Appendix G-II-D-3-i. All liquid effluents from the P4 facility shall be collected and decontaminated before disposal. Liquid effluents from biological safety cabinets and laboratory sinks shall be sterilized by heat. Liquid effluents from the shower and hand washing facilities may be activated by chemical treatment. HEPA filters shall be installed in all vents from effluent drains.

Appendix G-II-D-3-j. An individual supply and exhaust-air ventilation system shall be provided. The system shall maintain pressure differentials and directional air flow as required to ensure inflow from areas outside the facility toward areas of highest potential risk within the facility. The system shall be designed to prevent the reversal of air flow. The system shall sound an alarm in the event of system malfunction.

Appendix G-II-D-3-k. Air within individual laboratories of the P4 facility may be recirculated if HEPA filtered.

Appendix G-II-D-3-l. The exhaust air from the P4 facility shall be HEPA filtered and discharged to the outdoors so that it is dispersed clear of occupied buildings and air intakes. The filter chambers shall be designed to allow *in situ* decontamination before removal and to facilitate certification testing after replacement.

Appendix G-II-D-3-m. The treated exhaust-air from Class I and Class II biological safety cabinets [12] may be discharged directly to the laboratory room environment or to the outdoors. The treated exhaust-air from Class III cabinets shall be discharged to the outdoors. If the treated exhaust-air from these cabinets is to be discharged to the outdoors through the P4 facility exhaust air system, it shall be connected to this system so as to avoid any interference with the air balance of the cabinets or the facility exhaust air system.

Appendix G-II-D-3-n. As noted in Appendix G-II-D-2-a, the P4 facility may contain specially designed areas in which all personnel are required to wear one-piece positive-pressure isolation suits. Such areas shall be airtight. The exhaust-air from the suit area shall be filtered by two sets of HEPA filters installed in series, and a duplicate filtration unit and exhaust fan shall be provided. The air pressure within the suit area shall be less than that on any adjacent area. An emergency lighting system, communication systems, and power source shall be provided. A double-door autoclave shall be provided for sterilization of all waste materials to be removed from the suit area.

Personnel who enter this area shall wear a one-piece positive-pressure suit that is ventilated by a life-support system. The life-support system shall be provided with alarms and emergency backup air. Entry to this area is through an airlock fitted with airtight doors. A chemical shower area shall be provided to decontaminate the surfaces of the suit before removal.

Appendix G-III. *Footnotes and References of Appendix G.*

1. *Laboratory Safety at the Center for Disease Control* (Sept. 1974). U.S. Department of Health Education and Welfare Publication No. CDC 75-8118.

2. Classification of Etiologic Agents on the Basis of Hazard. (4th Edition, July 1974). U.S. Department of Health, Education and Welfare. Public Health Service. Centers for Disease Control, Office of Biosafety, Atlanta, Georgia 30333.

3. *National Cancer Institute Safety Standards for Research Involving Oncogenic Viruses* (Oct. 1974). U.S. Department of Health, Education and Welfare Publication No. (NIH) 75-790.

4. *National Institutes of Health Biohazards Safety Guide* (1974). U.S. Department of Health, Education, and Welfare, Public Health Service, National Institutes of Health. U.S. Government Printing Office, Stock No. 1740-00383.

5. *Biohazards in Biological Research* (1973). A. Hellman, M. N. Oxman, and R. Pollack (ed.) Cold Spring Harbor Laboratory.

6. *Handbook of Laboratory Safety* (1971). Second Edition. N. V. Steere (ed.). The Chemical Rubber Co., Cleveland.

7. Bodily, J. L. (1970). *General Administration of the Laboratory*, H. L. Bodily, E. L. Updyke, and J. O. Mason (eds.), Diagnostic Procedures for Bacterial, Mycotic and Parasitic Infections. American Public Health Association, New York, pp. 11-28.

8. Darlow, H. M. (1969). *Safety in the Microbiological Laboratory*. In J. R. Norris and D. W. Robbins (ed.), Methods in Microbiology. Academic Press, Inc. New York. pp. 169-204.

9. *The Prevention of Laboratory Acquired Infection* (1974). C. H. Collins, E. G. Hartley, and R. Pilsworth. Public Health Laboratory Service, Monograph Series No. 6.

10. Chatigny, M. A. (1961). *Protection Against Infection in the Microbiological Laboratory: Devices and Procedures*. In W. W. Umbreit (ed.). Advances in Applied Microbiology. Academic Press, New York, N.Y. 3:131-192.

11. Horsfall, F. L., Jr., and J. H. Baner (1940). *Individual Isolation of Infected Animals in a Single Room*. J. Bact. *40*, 569-580.

12. Biological safety cabinets referred to in this section are classified as *Class I*, *Class II*, or *Class III* cabinets. A *Class I* is a ventilated cabinet for personnel protection having an inward flow of air away from the operator. The exhaust air from this cabinet is filtered through a high-efficiency particulate air (HEPA) filter. This cabinet is used in three operational modes: (1) with a full-width open front, (2) with an installed front closure panel (having four 8-inch diameter openings) without gloves, and (3) with an installed front closure panel equipped with arm-length rubber gloves. The face velocity of the inward flow of air through the full-width open front is 75 feet per minute or greater.

A *Class II* cabinet is a ventilated cabinet for personnel and product protection having an open front with inward air flow for personnel protection, and HEPA filtered mass recirculated air flow for product protection. The cabinet exhaust air is filtered through a HEPA filter. The face velocity of the inward flow of air through the full-width open front is 75 feet per minute or greater. Design and performance specifications for *Class II* cabinets have been adopted by the National Sanitation Foundation, Ann Arbor, Michigan. A *Class III* cabinet is a closed-front ventilated cabinet of gas-tight construction which provides the highest level of personnel protection of all biohazard safety cabinets. The interior of the cabinet is protected from contaminants exterior to the cabinet. The cabinet is fitted with arm-length rubber gloves and is operated under a negative pressure of at least 0.5 inches water guage. All supply air is filtered through HEPA filters. Exhaust air is filtered through two HEPA filters or one HEPA filters. Exhaust air is filtered through two HEAP filters or one HEPA filter and incinerator before being discharged to the outside environment.

Appendix H—Shipment

Recombinant DNA molecules contained in an organixm or virus shall be shipped only as an etiologic agent under requirements of the U.S. Public Health Service, and the U.S. Department of Transportation (Section 72.3, Part 72, Title 42, and Sections 173.386-.388, Part 173, Title 49, U.S. Code of the Federal Regulations (CFR)) as specified below:

Appendix H-I. Recombinant DNA molecules contained in an organism or virus requiring P1, P2, or P3 physical containment, when offered for transportation or transported, are subject to all requirements of Section 782.3(a)-(e), Part 72, Title 42 CFR, and Sections 173.386-.388, Part 173, Title 49 CFR.

Appendix H-II. Recombinant DNA molecules contained in an organism or virus requiring P4, physical containment, when offered for transportation or transported, are subject to all requirements listed above under Appendix H-I and are also subject to Section 72.3(f), Part 72, Title 42 CFR.

Appendix H-III. Additional information on packaging and shipment is given in the "Laboratory Safety Monograph—A Supplement to the NIH Guidelines for Recombinant DNA Research," available from ORDA.

[Note.—Instructions for the packaging and labeling of etiologic agents will be printed in the revised Guidelines should that proposal be accepted by the RAC.]

Appendix I—Biological Containment

Appendix I–I. *Levels of Biological Containment.* In consideration of biological containment, the vector (plasmid, organelle, or virus) for the recombinant DNA and the host (bacterial, plant, or animal cell) in which the vector is propagated in the laboratory will be considered together. Any combination of vector and host which is to provide biological containment must be chosen or constructed so that the following types of "escape" are minimized: (i) survival of the vector in its host outside the laboratory and (ii) transmission of the vector from the propagation host to other nonlaboratory hosts.

The following levels of biological containment (HV, or *Host-Vector*, system) for prokaryotes will be establish; specific criteria will depend on the organisms to be used.

Appendix I–I–A. *HV1.* A host-vector system which provides a moderate level of containment. *Specific systems:*

Appendix I–I–A–1. *EK1.* The host is always *E. coli* K–12 or a derivative thereof, and the vectors include nonconjugative plasmids (e.g., pSC101, ColE1, or derivatives thereof [1–7]) and variants of bacteriophage, such as lambda [8–15]. The *E. coli* K–12 host shall not contain conjugation-proficient plasmids, whether autonomous or integrated, or generalized transducing phages.

Appendix I–I–A–2. *Other HV1.* Hosts and vectors shall be, at a minimum, comparable in containment to *E. coli* K–12 with a non conjugative plasmid or bacteriophage vector. The data to be considered and a mechanism for approval of such HV1 systems are described below (Appendix I–II).

Appendix I–I–B. *HV2.* These are host-vector systems shown to provide a high level of biological containment as demonstrated by data from suitable tests performed in the laboratory. Escape of the recombinant DNA either via survial of the organisms or via transmission of recombinant DNA to other organisms should be less than $1/10^8$ under specified conditions. *Specific systems:*

Appendix I–I–B–1. For EK2 host-vector systems in which the vector is a plasmid, no more than one in 10^8 host cells should be able to perpetuate a cloned DNA fragment under the specified nonpermissive laboratory conditions designed to represent the natural environment, either by survival of the original host or as a consequences of transmission of the cloned DNA fragment.

Appendix I–I–B–2. For EK2 host-vector systems in which the vector is a phage, no more than one in 10^8 phage particles should be able to perpetuate a cloned DNA fragment under the specified nonpermissive laboratory conditions designed to represent the natural environment either (i) as a prophage (in the inserted or plasmid form) in the laboratory host used for phage propagation or (ii) by surviving in natural environments and transferring a cloned DNA fragment to other hosts (or their resident prophages).

Appendix I–II. *Certification of Host-Vector Systems.*

Appendix I–II–A. *Responsibility.* HV1 systems other than *E. coli* K–12, and HV2 host-vector systems, may not be designated as such until they have been certified by the Director, NIH. Application for certification of a host-vector system is made by written application to the Office of Recombinant DNA Activities, National Institutes of Health, Bethesda, Maryland 20205.

Host-vector systems that are proposed for certification will be reviewed by the National Institutes of Health (NIH) Recombinant DNA Advisory Committee (RAC). (See Section IV–C–1–b–(1)–(e).) This will first involve review of the data on construction, properties, and testing of the proposed host-vector system by a Working Group composed of one or more members of the RAC and other persons chosen because of their expertise in evaluating such data. The Committee will then evaluate the report of the Working Group and any other available information at a regular meeting. The Director, NIH, is responsible for certification after receiving the advice of the RAC. Minor modifications of existing certified host-vector systems, where the modifications are of minimal or no consequence to the properties relevant to containment may be certified by the Director, NIH, without review by the RAC. (See Section IV–C–1–b–(3)–(c).)

When new host-vector systems are certified, notice of the certification will be sent by the Office of Recombinant DNA Activities (ORDA) to the applicant and to all Institutional Biosafety Committees (IBCs) and will be published in the *Recombinant DNA Technical Bulletin.* Copies of a list of all currently certified host-vector systems may be obtained from ORDA at any time.

The Director, NIH, may at any time rescind the certification of any host-vector system. (See Section IV–C–1–b–(3)–(d).) If certification of a host-vector system is rescinded, NIH will instruct investigators to transfer cloned DNA into a different system, or use the clones at a higher physical containment level unless NIH determines that the already constructed clones incorporate adequate biological containment.

Certification of a given system does not extend to modifications of either the host or vector component of that system. Such modified systems must be independently certified by the Director, NIH. If modifications are minor, it may only be necessary for the investigator to submit data showing that the modifications have either improved or not impaired the major phenotypic traits on which the containment of the system depends. Substantial modifications of a certified system require the submission of complete testing data.

Appendix I–II–B. *Data To Be Submitted for Certification.*

Appendix I–II–B–1. *HV1 Systems Other than E. coli K–12.* The following types of data shall be submitted, modified as appropriate for the particular system under consideration. (i) A description of the organism and vector; the strain's natural habitat and growth requirements; its physiological properties, particularly those related to its reproduction and survival and the mechanisms by which it exchanges genetic information; the range of organisms with which this organism normally exchange genetic information and what sort of information is exchanged; and any relevant information on its pathogenicity or toxicity. (ii) A description of the history of the particular strains and vectors to be used, including data on any mutations which render this organism less able to survive or transmit genetic information. (iii) A general description of the range of experiments contemplated, with emphasis on the need for developing such an HV1 system.

Appendix I–II–B–2. *HV2 Systems.* Investigators planning to request HV2 certification for host-vector systems can obtain instructions from ORDA concerning data to be submitted [14–15]. In general, the following types of data are required: (i) Description of construction steps, with indication of source, properties, and manner of introduction of genetic traits. (ii) Quantitative data on the stability of genetic traits that contribute to the containment of the system. (iii) Data on the survival of the host-vector system under nonpermissive laboratory conditions designed to represent the relevant natural environment. (iv) Data on transmissibility of the vector and/or a cloned DNA fragment under both permissive and nonpermissive conditions. (v) Data on all other properties of the system which affect containment and utility, including information on yields of phage or plasmid molecules, ease of DNA isolation, and ease of transfection or transformation. (vi) In some cases, the investigator may be asked to submit data on survival and vector transmissibility from experiments in which the host-vector is fed to laboratory animals and human subjects. Such *in vivo* data may be required to confirm the validity of predicting *in vivo* survival on the basis of *in vitro* experiments.

Data must be submitted in writing to ORDA. Ten to twelve weeks are normally required for review and circulation of the data prior to the meeting at which such data can be considered by the RAC. Investigators are encouraged to publish their data on the construction, properties, and testing of proposed HV2 systems prior to consideration of the system by the RAC and its subcommittee. More specific instructions concerning the type of data to be submitted to NIH for proposed EK2 systems involving either plasmids or bacteriophage in *E. coli* K–12 are available from ORDA.

Appendix I–III. *Footnotes and References of Appendix I.*

1. Hershfield, V., H. W., Boyer, C. Yanofsky, M. A. Lovett, and D. R. Helinski (1974). *Plasmid Col El as a Molecular Vehicle for Cloning and Amplification of DNA.* Proc. Nat. Acad. Sci. USA *71,* 3455–3459.

2. Wensink, P. C., D. J. Finnegan, J. E. Donelson, and D. S. Hogness (1974). *A System for Mapping DNA Sequences in the Chromosomes of Drosophila Melanogaster.* Cell *3,* 315–335.

3. Tanaka, T., and B. Weisblum (1975). *Construction of a Colicin El–R Factor Composite Plasmid in Vitro: Means for Amplification of Deoxyribonucleic Acid.* J. Bacteriol. *121,* 354–362.

4. Armstrong, K. A., V. Hershfield, and D. R. Helinski (1977). *Gene Cloning and Containment Properties of Plasmid Col El and Its Derivatives,* Science *196,* 172–174.

5. Bolivar, F., R. L. Rodriquez, M. C. Betlach, and H. W. Boyer (1977). *Construction and Characterization of New Cloning*

Vehicles: I. Ampicillin-Resistant Derivative of pMB9. Gene 2, 75–93.

6. Cohen, S. N., A. C. W. Chang, H. Boyer, and R. Helling (1973). *Construction of Biologically Functional Bacterial Plasmids in Vitro.* Proc. Natl. Acad. Sci. USA 70, 3240–3244.

7. Bolivar, F., R. L. Rodriquez, R. J. Greene, M. C. Batlach, H. L. Reyneker, H. W. Boyer J. H. Crosa, and S. Falkow (1977). *Construction and Characterization of New Cloning Vehicles: II. A Multi-Purpose Cloning System.* Gene 2, 95–113.

8. Thomas, M., J. R. Cameron, and R. W. Davis (1974). *Viable Molecular Hybrids of Bacteriophage Lambda and Eukaryotic DNA.* Proc. Nat. Acad. Sci. USA 71, 4579–4583.

9. Murray, N. E., and K. Murray (1974). *Manipulation of Restriction Targets in Phage Lambda to Form Receptor Chromosomes for DNA Fragments.* Nature 251, 476–481.

10. Rambach, A., and P. Tiollais (1974). *Bacteriophage Having EcoRI Endonuclease Sites Only in the Non-Essential Region of the Genome.* Proc. Nat. Acad. Sci., USA 71, 3927–3930.

11. Blattner, F. R., B. G. Williams, A. E. Bleche, K. Denniston-Thompson, H. E. Faber, L. A. Furlong, D. J. Gunwald, D. O. Kiefer, D. D. Moore, J. W. Shumm, E. L. Sheldon, and O. Smithies (1977). *Charon Phages: Safer Derivatives of Bacteriophage Lambda for DNA Cloning.* Science 196, 163–169.

12. Donoghue, D. J., and P. A. Sharp (1977). *An Improved Lambda Vector: Construction of Model Recombinants Coding for Kanamycin Resistance,* Gene 1, 209–227.

13. Leder, P., D. Tiemeier and L. Enquist (1977). *EK2 Derivatives of Bacteriophage Lambda Useful in the Cloning of DNA From Higher Organisms: The gt WES System.* Science 196, 175–177.

14. Skalka, A. (1978). *Current Status of Coliphage EK2 Vectors.* Gene 3, 29–35.

15. Szybalski, W., A. Skalka, S. Gottesman, A. Campbell, and D. Botstein (1978). *Standardized Laboratory Tests for EK2 Certification.* Gene 3, 36–38.

D. *Additional Proposals.*

1. Upon reviewing the proposed revised Guidelines, several members of the Working Group for Revision of the Guidelines requested that the language of the current Guidelines in Section III-C be evaluated by the RAC.

That language of the current Guidelines is as follows:

"III-C. *Experiments That Require IBC Notice Simultaneously With Initiation of Experiments.* Experiments not included in Sections III-A, III-B, III-D, and subsections of these Sections are to be considered in Section III-C. All such experiments can be carried out at P1 containment. For experiments in this category, a registration document as described in Section III-B must be dated and signed by the investigator and filed with the local IBC. The IBC shall review all such proposals, but the IBC review prior to initiation of the experiment is not required."

It was noted that non-exempt experiments which might merit more stringent review by RAC or by the IBC prior to initiation of the experiment might not be adequately described in Sections III-A and III-B and thus would automatically fall into Section III-C. The working group members requested that the language of that Section be evaluated at the next RAC meeting in the hope that language to alert researchers and IBCs of this possibility might be developed.

One possible suggested clarification would be to modify the sixth paragraph of Part III, *Containment Guidelines for Covered Experiments.* That paragraph currently reads: "IF AN EXPERIMENT FALLS INTO BOTH CLASS III-A AND ONE OF THE OTHER CLASSES, THE RULES PERTAINING TO CLASS III-A MUST BE FOLLOWED. If an experiment falls into Class III-D and either III-B or III-C as well, it can be considered exempt from the requirements of the Guidelines."

The proposed modification would read: "IF AN EXPERIMENT FALLS INTO BOTH CLASS III-A AND ONE OF THE OTHER CLASSES, THE RULES PERTAINING TO CLASS III-A MUST BE FOLLOWED. If an experiment falls into Class III-D and either III-B or III-C as well, it can be considered exempt from the requirements of the Guidelines. Should doubt arise as to which section covers a proposed protocol, ORDA should be contacted."

2. At the April meeting, the working group recommended deletion of several sections of the Guidelines which were not incorporated into the proposed revised Guidelines as published in Part C of this **Federal Register** document. NIH staff felt that retention of these sections would permit greater flexibility in interpreting and administering the Guidelines. Those sections which the working group suggested should be deleted but which NIH staff have not removed from the proposed revised Guidelines published in part C are:

a. Section IV-C-7 of Section IV-C, *General Definitions,* which reads: "IV-C-7. 'Director, NIH' or 'Director' means the Director of the National Institutes of Health and any other officer or employee of NIH to whom authority has been delegated."

Section IV-C-7 has been renumbered I-D-5 in the proposed revised Guidelines (Part C of this document).

b. Section IV-D-5-b and its subsections of Section IV-D-5, *Principal Investigator,* which reads:

"IV-D-5-b. *Submissions by the PI to NIH.* The PI shall:

"IV-D-5-b-(1). Submit information to NIH (ORDA) in order to have new host-vector systems certified;

"IV-D-5-b-(2). Petition NIH, with notice to the IBC, for exemptions to these Guidelines;

"IV-D-5-b-(3). Petition NIH, with concurrence of the IBC, for approval to conduct experiments specified in Section III-A of the Guidelines;

"IV-D-5-b-(4). Petition NIH for determination of containment for experiments requiring case-by-case review;

"IV-D-5-b-(5). Petition NIH for determination of containment for experiments not covered by the Guidelines."

Section IV-D-5-b has been renumbered IV-B-5-c in the proposed revised Guidelines (part C of this document).

c. Section IV-E-1-b-(1)-(a) and Section IV-E-1-b-(1)-(b) of Section IV-E-1-b, *Specific Responsibilities of the Director, NIH,* which reads:

"IV-E-1-b-(1)-(a). Changing containment levels for types of experiments that are specified in the Guidelines when a major action is involved;

"IV-E-1-b-(1)-(b). Assigning containment levels for types of experiments that are not explicitly considered in the Guidelines when a major action is involved";

Sections IV-E-1-b-(1)-(a) and IV-E-1-b-(1)-(b) have been renumbered Section IV-C-1-b-(1)-(a) and IV-C-1-b-(1)-(b) respectively in the proposed revised Guidelines (part C of this document).

d. Section IV-E-1-b-(2) and its subsection which read:

"IV-E-1-b-(2). *The Director is also responsible for the following lesser actions,* (For these, the Director must seek the advice of the RAC. The Director's decision will be transmitted to the RAC and IBC chairpersons and published in the *Recombinant DNA Technical Bulletin*):

"IV-E-1-b-(2)-(a). Interpreting and determining containment levels upon request by ORDA;

"IV-E-1-b-(2)-(b). Changing containment levels for experiments that are specified in the Guidelines (see Section III);

"IV-E-1-b-(2)-(c). Assigning containment levels for experiments not explicity considered in the Guidelines;

"IV-E-1-b-(2)-(d). Designating certain class 2 agents as class 1 for the purpose of these Guidelines (see Footnote 1 and Appendix B);"

Section IV–E–1–b–(2) has been renumbered as Section IV–C–1–b–(2) in the proposed revised Guidelines (part C of this document). In the proposed revised Guidelines, this section has been retained, but some of the text has been modified, consistent with changes made in other parts of the Guidelines.

Dated: May 19, 1982.

Richard M. Krause,

Director, National Institute of Allergy and Infectious Diseases.

Note.—OMBS's "Mandatory Information Requirements for Federal Assistance Program Announcements" (45 FR 39592) requires a statement concerning the official government programs contained in the *Catalog of Federal Domestic Assistance*. Normally NIH lists in its announcements the number and title of affected individual programs for the guidance of the public. Because the guidance in this notice covers not only virtually every NIH program but also essentially every federal research program in which DNA recombinant molecule techniques could be used, it has been determined to be not cost effective or in the public interest to attempt to list these programs. Such a list would likely require several additional pages. In addition, NIH could not be certain that every federal program would be included as many federal agencies, as well as private organizations, both national and international, have elected to follow the NIH Guidelines. In lieu of the individual program listing, NIH invites readers to direct questions to the information address above about whether individual programs listed in the *Catalog of Federal Domestic Assistance* are affected.

NIH programs are not covered by OMB Circular A–95 because they fit the description of "programs not considered appropriate" in Section 8–(b)–(4) and (5) of that Circular.

[FR Doc. 82–14375 Filed 5–25–82; 8:45 am]

BILLING CODE 4140–01–M

DEPARTMENT OF HEALTH AND HUMAN SERVICES
PUBLIC HEALTH SERVICE
NATIONAL INSTITUTES OF HEALTH

RECOMBINANT DNA ADVISORY COMMITTEE

MINUTES OF MEETING

JUNE 28, 1982

TABLE OF CONTENTS

DEPARTMENT OF HEALTH AND HUMAN SERVICES
PUBLIC HEALTH SERVICE
NATIONAL INSTITUTES OF HEALTH

RECOMBINANT DNA ADVISORY COMMITTEE

MINUTES OF MEETING[1]

JUNE 28, 1982

The Recombinant DNA Advisory Committee (RAC) was convened for its twenty-fifth meeting at 9:00 a.m. on June 28, 1982, in Wilson Hall, Building 1, National Institutes of Health, 9000 Rockville Pike, Bethesda, Maryland 20205. Mr. Ray Thornton (Chairman), President, Arkansas State University, presided. In accordance with Public Law 92-463, the meeting was open to the public.

Committee members present for all or part of the meeting were:

Abdul Karim Ahmed; David Baltimore; Kenneth Berns; Winston Brill; L. Albert Daloz; David Friedman; Richard Goldstein; Jean Harris; King Holmes; Myron Levine; David Martin; James Mason; Gerard McGarrity; Robert McKinney; Robert Mitchell; Elena Nightingale; Ramon Pinon; Mark Saginor; John Scandalios; Pieter Wensink; and William J. Gartland, Jr., Executive Secretary.

A Committee roster is attached. (Attachment I)

The following non-voting members and liaison representatives were present:

George Duda, Department of Energy; Herman Lewis, National Science Foundation; Henry Miller, National Center for Drugs and Biologics, FDA; and Sue Tolin, U.S. Department of Agriculture.

Other National Institutes of Health staff present were:

Stanley Barban, NIAID; Manuel Barbeito, OD; W. Emmett Barkley, OD; Becky Connors, NIAID; Irving Delappe, NIAID; Susan Gottesman, NCI; John Irwin, OD; Elizabeth Milewski, NIAID; John Nutter, NIAID; Robert Schreiber, NIAID; Bernard Talbot, NIAID; and Charles Wise, NIAID.

---

[1]The RAC is advisory to the NIH, and its recommendations should not be considered as final and accepted. The Office of Recombinant DNA Activities should be consulted for NIH policy on specific issues.

Others in attendance for all or part of the meeting were:

William Beisel, Department of Defense; Irene Brandt, Eli Lilly & Company; Robert Brey, Genex Corporation; Steve Budiansky, Nature Magazine; Chia T. Chen, OSHA, U.S. Department of Labor; Scott Coleridge, Millipore Corporation; Paula Dwyer, McGraw Hill; Gershon Fishbein, Genetic Engineering Letter; John Galet, Schering-Plough Corporation; Richard Geoghegan, E. I. Du Pont De Nemours and Company; Tom M. Helscher, Monsanto Company; Timothy Henry, Health Industry Manufacturing Association; Philip Hilts, Washington Post; Evelyn Hurlburt, Johns Hopkins University; Dorothy Jessop, U.S. Department of Agriculture; Judith A. Johnson, Library of Congress; Mary Jane Johnson, Pall Corporation; Attila Kader, Food and Drug Administration; Geoffrey Karny, Office of Technology Assessment; Michael Larsen, Occupational Safety & Health Administration; Carter Leonard, Blue Sheet; D. S. Mabry, Pfizer, Inc.; James McCullough, Library of Congress; James Mikulak, State Department; Mary Moore, Millipore Corporation; Harvey Price, Industrial Biotechnology Association; Rich Ring, Genentech, Inc.; Marvin Rogul, Environmental Protection Agency; Sandra Ronspies, Genentech, Inc.; Harold Schmeck, New York Times; Marjory Sun, Science Magazine; Charles Turbyville, NIH Week; Dave Wareheim, SmithKline Beckman Corporation; and Charles Weiner, Massachusetts Institute of Technology.

I. CALL TO ORDER

The Chairman, Mr. Ray Thornton, called the meeting to order at 9:00 a.m. on June 28, 1982. He asked Dr. Ahmed to review the minutes of the February 8-9, 1982, RAC meeting.

II. MINUTES OF THE FEBRUARY 8-9, 1982 MEETING

Dr. Ahmed said the draft minutes (tab 1073) of the February 8-9, 1982, RAC meeting accurately conveyed the sense of that meeting. Dr. McGarrity moved that the minutes be accepted. Dr. Ahmed seconded the motion. By a voice vote, the motion to accept the minutes of the February 8-9, 1982, meeting was unanimously carried.

III. PROPOSED PROHIBITION

Dr. Baltimore noted that the proposal (tabs 1066, 1067, 1068, 1075, 1076) advanced by Dr. Richard Goldstein of Harvard Medical School and Dr. Richard Novick of the Public Health Research Institute of New York, would amend the Guidelines to prohibit "the construction of biological weapons by molecular cloning." He said the proposal generated tremendous initial sympathy because the concept of biological warfare is horrible.

Dr. Baltimore said he felt the proposal is based on Drs. Novick and Goldstein's perception that use of recombinant DNA technology for biological warfare is not covered by the Biological Weapons Convention.[2] The Convention, which prohibits biological warfare, was signed by the United States in 1972. Dr. Baltimore said he had questioned the United States Arms Control and Disarmament Agency in 1975 as to whether the Biological Weapons Convention prohibits production of recombinant DNA molecules for the construction of biological weapons. The Arms Control and Disarmament Agency, in reply (tab 1067) to his inquiry, stated that "the use of recombinant DNA molecules for such purposes clearly falls within the scope of the Convention's provisions."

Dr. Baltimore felt it was extremely important that any action taken by RAC bolster the Biological Weapons Convention and raise no suggestion that the treaty is insufficient. He said he wished to be recorded as stating the Biological Weapons Convention prohibits the use of recombinant DNA technology to produce biological weapons. He also wished recorded his sentiment that any RAC action should support the treaty language.

---

[2]The formal name of this Convention is: Convention on the Prohibition of Development, Production, and Stockpiling of Bacteriological (Biological) and Toxin Weapons and on Their Destruction.

Dr. Baltimore noted that Mr. James George of the United States Arms Control and Disarmament Agency, in a letter of June 8, 1982 (tab 1075), had suggested alternative language to the Goldstein-Novick proposal, as follows:

> "The use of recombinant DNAs for development of microbial or other biological agents, or toxins, of types or in quantities that have no justification for prophylactic, protective or other peaceful purposes, is prohibited."

Dr. Baltimore said this suggested language, which is taken largely from the treaty, would reinforce the Biological Weapons Convention. He moved acceptance of the language proposed by Mr. George. Mr. Mitchell seconded. Dr. Harris concurred with Dr. Baltimore's opinion; she added that the discussion served a useful purpose by permitting a public expression of concern.

Dr. Baltimore then suggested an amendment to his motion: he proposed that the phrase "the use of recombinant DNA methodology for development" replace the phrase "the use of recombinant DNAs for development." Mr. Mitchell agreed.

Dr. Goldstein said he would not support Dr. Baltimore's proposal. He said he had suggested the proposed prohibition on the broadest moral and ethical grounds. He said that RAC was responsible for overseeing recombinant DNA research and, therefore, of overseeing Department of Defense (DOD) endeavors in this area. He said that in 1980 DOD spent about $16 million on their biological research program. He said that the bulk of the money was spent on defensive systems. He said that a very thin line exists between offensive and defensive studies in biological warfare.

Dr. Goldstein said the Biological Weapons Convention has no mechanism by which to monitor or enforce compliance. He recounted some alleged incidents in the Soviet Union and Cuba which, because no means of verification exist, could be interpreted as violations of the treaty. He argued that the world situation, which requires DOD to spend substantial funds on defensive systems, requires that RAC issue some firm statement prohibiting the development of biological weapons using recombinant technology.

Dr. Mason said the idea of deliberate construction and release of agents which cause disease and death is absolutely appalling. He feared, however, that the Goldstein-Novick amendment might create the presumption that the 1972 Biological Weapons Convention does not apply to recombinant DNA research. He felt, in addition, that the material submitted by Drs. Goldstein and Novick almost by innuendo suggests that the United States is violating the treaty. He said that RAC endorsement of the Goldstein-Novick amendment might be interpreted as RAC agreement with these innuendos. Dr. Mason said that if the Guidelines were to be amended to include some prohibition, he would prefer the George-Baltimore language to the Goldstein-Novick proposal. However, he did not feel the Guidelines should be used to attempt to resolve this issue. He warned that incorporating language prohibiting biological warfare into the Guidelines could inhibit possible future moves to make the Guidelines voluntary or abolish the Guidelines. He said that if it is felt that RAC should do anything, a RAC resolution on the topic, independent and separate from the Guidelines would be more appropriate. Dr. McKinney agreed; he opposed both the Goldstein-Novick proposal and the Baltimore motion. Mr. Daloz said that he supported the language in Mr. George's letter.

Dr. Ahmed quoted from Article I of the Convention:

> "Each...Party...undertakes never in any circumstance to develop, produce, stockpile, or otherwise acquire or retain:
>
> (1) Microbial or other biological agents or toxins, whatever their origin or method of production, of types and in quantities that have no justification for prophylactic, protective or other peaceful purposes;
>
> (2) Weapons, equipment, or means of delivery designed to use such agents or toxins for hostile purposes or in armed conflict."

Dr. Ahmed said that a key word, "research," was missing from the phrase "to develop, produce, stockpile, or otherwise acquire or retain." He suggested that while the word "develop" might encompass research, "develop" may also be strictly interpreted as an industrial activity or as a large development program. He said that the George language, consistent with the Convention, may not cover research; therefore, the Baltimore motion would not encompass the total concern. Dr. Ahmed then asked the DOD representative whether the Biological Weapons Convention applies to research activities.

Mr. Thornton recognized Dr. Robert Mikulak of the Arms Control and Disarmament Agency. Dr. Mikulak said he wished to make several points. He said the Arms Control and Disarmament Agency had no objection to the NIH incorporating language dealing with biological weapons into the Guidelines for Research Involving Recombinant DNA Molecules. The Convention includes provisions under which governments may pass additional legislation or regulations to implement the Convention in their own territory. The Arms Control and Disarmament Agency had, however, suggested language which the agency feels is more similar to the language of the Convention. Fewer problems of interpretation will arise with language similar to the Biological Weapons Convention than might arise from substantially different language. He noted that the language proposed by the Agency had been moved by Dr. Baltimore.

Dr. Mikulak said that the Arms Control and Disarmament Agency does not distinguish between offensive and defensive biological weapons. Both are biological weapons and, thus, prohibited by the treaty. The negotiated history of the Biological Weapons Convention makes absolutely clear that possession of biological weapons, even for defensive purposes, is prohibited; a party state is not permitted these weapons regardless of the stated intent. Dr. Mikulak said that concern had been expressed by Dr. Ahmed that Article I of the Convention might not prohibit research on biological weapons. He said that in his interpretation, the first Article of the

Convention is extremely broad; it prohibits not only developing, producing, and stockpiling, but uses the formulation "or otherwise acquire or retain." In his interpretation of that formulation, any activity for biological weapons purposes, including research, would be prohibited.

Mr. Thornton then recognized Dr. William Beisel of the Department of Defense, Department of the Army. Dr. Beisel said DOD currently is not involved in research on biological weapons. When the United States signed the Biological Weapons Convention, the entire research structure for the creation of such weapons was dismantled. Any weapons in storage at the Pine Bluff Arsenal in Arkansas were destroyed. The manufacturing plant at the Arsenal in Pine Bluff was turned over to the FDA to become the National Center for Toxicological Research. The large laboratory at Fort Detrick, in Frederick, Maryland, was turned over to the National Cancer Institute to become the Frederick Cancer Research Facility.

Dr. Beisel said the United States Army Medical Research Institute of Infectious Diseases (USAMRIID) at Fort Detrick is currently engaged in medical defensive research. The program is entirely unclassified and any individual can come and visit. The program focuses on diseases that could threaten U.S. troops or, secondarily, the U.S. population. He said the Centers for Disease Control (CDC) is officially responsible for defending the civilian population from a biological warfare attack. USAMRIID collaborates very closely with the CDC in that endeavor. Dr. Beisel said the USAMRIID program is attempting to develop vaccines or other prophylactic measures, and to develop methods for better, earlier, diagnosis. All of the research is of a public health nature. Dr. Beisel said vaccines developed by the USAMRIID program have on occasion been transmitted around the world and given to other governments.

Dr. McKinney noted that there are no prohibited experiments in the current Guidelines and said he opposed both the Goldstein-Novick proposal and Dr. Baltimore's motion.

Dr. Baltimore said that perhaps a resolution of the RAC would be adequate. He said that it could be misread as a lack of concern for the RAC to do nothing.

Dr. Nightingale thought it was necessary for RAC to issue some statement concerning biological weapons and recombinant DNA technology. What the statement is and how to make it needs to be discussed. One purpose of the Guidelines is to permit public participation in the formulation of policy. In this case, the policy exists so a statement from RAC would be an affirmation or endorsement of existing public policy. Such a statement within the content of the Guidelines would be appropriate. She said that a second function of the Guidelines is to protect the public; and, thus, insertion of a statement on biological weapons in the Guidelines is appropriate. She preferred that language be introduced into the Guidelines; language in the Guidelines would constitute a permanent record rather than a one time resolution. If such language were to be included in the Guidelines, she did not think the Guidelines would necessarily become hostage to "permanency" as suggested by Dr. Mason. She said she would prefer RAC issue a broad statement which avoided ambiguities about who is being defended or how. She suggested, in addition, that the section of the Guidelines dealing with the Federal Interagency Advisory Committee on Recombinant DNA Research be expanded; that Section should list the Interagency Committee membership (including DOD) and explicitly indicate that DOD, as well as the other members of the Committee, have agreed to abide by the NIH Guidelines for Research Involving Recombinant DNA Molecules.

Dr. Nightingale also noted that the Commission on Life Sciences of the National Academy of Sciences (NAS) has refused to conduct a study requested by the DOD via the Board on Army Science and Technology of the Commission on Engineering and Technical Systems. Most of the work in that study was to be classified and the NAS Commission on Life Sciences has established the principle that it will not do classified work.

Dr. Nightingale said the NAS Commission on Life Sciences was unwilling to conduct studies on biological warfare defense but agreed to cooperate with the Board of Army Science and Technology on a mycotoxin study. Mycotoxins were classified as chemicals. She asked Dr. Beisel to clarify his previous statement that they did no classified work. Dr. Baltimore asked Dr. Beisel to clarify how the medical defense program relates to classified work funded by DOD. Dr. Beisel explained that DOD funds three separate research areas: physical defense, medical defense, and intelligence gathering. The physical defense aspects involve protective clothing, decontamination, early warning devices, air sampling, etc. Some of these materials and processes are classified.

Dr. Berns, referring to the letter (tab 1076) of Dr. Krimsky, asked if DOD has more than one Institutional Biosafety Committee (IBC) registered with ORDA. Dr. Gartland replied that several IBCs at military installations are registered with ORDA: the Walter Reed Army Institute of Research and U.S. Army Medical Research Institute of Infectious Diseases, the Naval Medical Research Institute, and the Uniformed Services University of the Health Sciences. The Naval Biological Laboratories in California uses the IBC at the University of California, Berkeley.

Dr. Berns said that one person whom he greatly respected pointed out that RAC action could lead to the erroneous distinction that biological warfare employing recombinant DNA is worse than other biological warfare, and therefore, opposed the amendment.

Dr. Holmes agreed it was important to avoid statements conflicting with the Biological Weapons Convention. However, he viewed language added to the Guidelines concerning biological warfare as potentially clarifying the Biological Weapons Convention. He agreed that some of the Biological Weapons Convention language is vague. He suggested that any language developed by RAC should be clearer. He said he favors the language proposed by Mr. George, but suggested addition of the phrase "as potential biological weapons" after the word "toxins."

Dr. Gottesman said she was concerned with the question of how a biological weapon is distinguished from a chemical weapon. Some items, which would be defined by biologists as biological weapons, might be defined by others as chemical weapons. She suggested that any language added to the Guidelines might include some definitions of biological weapons. Dr. Gottesman suggested that language on biological weapons could logically be added at the very beginning of the Guidelines or at the beginning of Section III. Dr. Nightingale agreed; she suggested that the Guidelines might refer to the Biological Weapons Convention and endorse it in principle and then indicate that the NIH Guidelines deal only with recombinant DNA research.

Dr. Baltimore said that after listening to the discussion, he had concluded that RAC should not add language on biological weapons to the Guidelines. The treaty has been ratified by Congress and signed by the President. It is the law of the land. He suggested that RAC pass a resolution endorsing the treaty and indicating that recombinant DNA technology is covered by the Convention.

Dr. Mason called the question on Dr. Baltimore's previous motion as amended. Dr. Berns seconded the motion. Dr. McKinney said that before the vote was taken, Dr. Baltimore should indicate where in the Guidelines the language would be inserted. Mr. Thornton ruled that if Dr. Baltimore's motion was passed by the RAC, NIH staff would be given the responsibility for determining the appropriate place in the Guidelines to insert the language.

Mr. Thornton said that his ruling was subject to appeal by the RAC. No appeal was made. By a vote of thirteen in favor, six opposed, and one abstention, the question was called. Mr. Thornton then called the vote on Dr. Baltimore's motion, i.e., insertion into the Guidelines of the following language:

> "The use of recombinant DNA methodology for development of microbial or other biological agents, or toxins, of types or in quantities that have no justification for prophylatic, protective or other peaceful purposes, is prohibited."

By a vote of six in favor, twelve opposed, and two abstentions, the motion was defeated.

Dr. Holmes said he wished to present an alternative proposal. He said his opposition to Dr. Baltimore's motion was not so much against the intent as against the language which was phrased in a negative way. He moved adoption of the following language, either as a resolution to the Director or an amendment to the Guidelines:

> "Use of recombinant DNA methodology for development of microbial or other biological agents or toxins as biological or chemical weapons is prohibited, as specified by the 1972 Biological Weapons Convention."

Mr. Thornton said that Dr. Holmes should indicate whether the statement would be included in the Guidelines or sent as advice to the NIH Director. Dr. Holmes replied that he moved the language as an amendment to the Guidelines. Dr. McGarrity seconded the motion.

Dr. Martin then proposed a substitute motion in the form of a resolution not to be included in the Guidelines:

> "The Recombinant DNA Advisory Committee advises the Director, NIH, that the existing treaty of 1972 [Convention on the Prohibition of Development, Production, and Stockpiling of Bacteriological (Biological) and Toxin Weapons and on Their Destruction] includes the prohibition on the use of recombinant DNA methodology for development of microbial or other biological agents, or toxins, of types or in quantities that have no justification for prophylactic, protective or peaceful purposes."

Dr. Scandalios seconded the motion.

Dr. Ahmed moved to amend Dr. Martin's substitute motion by eliminating all of Dr. Martin's proposal and adding the following language as originally proposed by Drs. Novick and Goldstein to Section I of the Guidelines:

> "Construction of biological weapons by molecular cloning is prohibited."

The motion was seconded by Dr. Goldstein.

Dr. Baltimore characterized Dr. Ahmed's motion as dangerous in its assumptions. He felt Dr. Ahmed's motion implies that the Biological Weapons Convention is ambiguous. Dr. Baltimore felt that the treaty was very precisely written, with no indication of loopholes or ambiguities through which the methodologies of recombinant DNA can be used for the development of biological weaponry. He felt including the Goldstein-Novick language in the Guidelines could undermine the treaty obligations of the United States and raise the presumption that the use of recombinant DNA technology in developing biological weapons is permissible. Dr. McKinney called the question. Dr. Berns seconded. By a vote of nineteen in favor, one opposed, and no abstentions, the question was called.

The vote then occurred on the amendment to the substitute as offered by Dr. Ahmed. By a vote of two in favor, seventeen opposed, and one abstention, the RAC refused Dr. Ahmed's proposed amendment.

Mr. Thornton then called for discussion on Dr. Martin's substitute motion. Dr. Holmes said the major difference between Dr. Baltimore's earlier motion which the RAC had defeated and Dr. Martin's motion is that Dr. Baltimore's motion had involved insertion of text into the Guidelines and Dr. Martin's motion is a resolution to the Director. Dr. Holmes opposed Dr. Martin's motion; he said the language is vague and a RAC recommendation advisory to the Director is weaker than language added to the Guidelines. Mr. Mitchell supported Dr. Martin's proposal. He said the statement reveals the concern of the RAC, is an expression in the nature of a resolution, has impact, and is consistent with the Biological Weapons Convention.

Mr. Thornton then called the vote on Dr. Martin's substitute motion. By a vote of fourteen in favor, six opposed, and no abstentions, the substitute motion was adopted as the motion before the committee. Mr. Thornton then called the vote on the motion, as follows:

> "The Recombinant DNA Advisory Committee advises the Director, NIH, that the existing treaty of 1972 [Convention on the Prohibition of Development, Production, and Stockpiling of Bacteriological (Biological) and Toxin Weapons and on Their Destruction] includes the prohibition on the use of recombinant DNA methodology for development of microbial or other biological agents, or toxins, of types or in quantities that have no justification for prophylactic, protective or peaceful purposes."

By a vote of fifteen in favor, five opposed, and no abstentions, the RAC adopted the motion.

Dr. Ahmed requested that his vote against the motion be recorded. He said he voted against Dr. Martin's motion as he felt there were problems with it; nonetheless, he felt it is important to address the issue. He suggested that RAC address the question at future meetings. Dr. Goldstein also requested that his vote against the motion be recorded. He said he opposed the motion for the reasons stated by Dr. Ahmed and also because Dr. Martin's motion does not change the status quo.

Dr. Nightingale suggested that the Director might have the resolution printed as part of the Guidelines. Mr. Thornton said any decision to publish the resolution was at the discretion of the Director.

Dr. Goldstein asked if it was possible to vote on Dr. Holmes' motion. Mr. Thornton said that procedurally a motion to reconsider the vote on Dr. Martin's motion would be in order until the meeting is adjourned. No motion to reconsider was offered at that time.

IV. PROPOSED REVISION OF APPENDIX A, SUBLIST F

Dr. Friedman introduced the proposal (tab 1069) from Dr. Gary M. Dunny of the New York State College of Veterinary Medicine. Dr. Dunny requested that *Streptococcus agalactiae* be added to Appendix A, Sublist F. Dr. Dunny argued that *S. agalactiae* should be added to this sublist as it exchanges genetic information with other *Streptococcus* species included in Sublist F.

Dr. Gottesman noted that the current Guidelines specify P1 containment for Dr. Dunny's proposed experiments. She said that the data submitted by Dr. Dunny in support of this request are marginal; there is no evidence of chromosomal exchange. Dr. Friedman added that Dr. Dunny's data show only that an antibiotic resistance gene carried by a plasmid is expressed by the recipient species. Dr. Friedman then moved that Dr. Dunny's request to include S. agalactiae in Appendix A, Sublist F, be denied; he suggested that Dr. Dunny be informed that P1 conditions are indicated under the current Guidelines. Dr. Wensink seconded the motion. By a vote of twenty in favor, none opposed, and no abstentions, the motion to deny Dr. Dunny's request was carried.

V. PROPOSED REVISION OF THE GUIDELINES

Dr. Nightingale began discussion of the modifications (tabs 1071, 1072, 1074) to the Guidelines proposed by the Working Group on Revision of the Guidelines. She recalled to the committee that the RAC at its February 8-9, 1982, meeting recommended that NIH accept a proposed modification of the NIH Guidelines for Research Involving Recombinant DNA Molecules.

In recommending this modification to the NIH, the committee recommended that a working group be formed to further simply and modify the document. The NIH, following this recommendation, promulgated the Revised Guidelines on April 21, 1982. An ad hoc Working Group on Revision of the Guidelines was formed and convened for a meeting on April 19, 1982, to further modify the document promulated on April 21, 1982. Dr. Nightingale said the working group attempted to clarify and simplify, wherever possible, the structure and language of the Guidelines, to suggest changes appropriate in light of available data, and to recommend future activities in the area of guideline review and revision.

Dr. Nightingale then indicated four major proposed modifications offered by this working group. First, the working group had suggested the presentation of the Guidelines be rearranged primarily by placing the description of physical and biological containment into appendices. Second, the working group recommended that the RAC and NIH adopt for the Guidelines a revised version of the 1974 CDC Classification of Etiologic Agents on the Basis of Hazard. The working group also suggested that the RAC assume responsibility for regularly updating the listing. Dr. Nightingale explained that the original 1976 Guidelines used the Classification of Etiologic Agents on the Basis of Hazard, 4th Edition, July 1974, U.S. Department of Health, Education, and Welfare, Public Health Service, Center for Disease Control (CDC), as the reference source for classification of microorganisms for the purposes of the Guidelines. At the present time, the CDC and the NIH are engaged in an effort to revise this classification. The working group, however, felt that this revised version might not serve the purposes of the Guidelines as well as the original 1974 version as revised. Dr. Nightingale said this is the only proposal of the working group that received a letter of comment. Dr. Berns said he wished to reply to an issue raised by Dr. John Richardson of the CDC in a letter of June 10, 1982 (tab 1074), concerning the proposed revision of Appendix B for the purposes of the NIH Guidelines. Dr. Berns said the proposed revised classification would classify Rabies street virus as a Class 3 agent for all procedures.

Dr. Richardson suggested that a Class 2 designation was adequate. Dr. Berns said he had discussed the issue with Dr. Richardson, and they had agreed that a Class 3 specification for Rabies street virus was more appropriate for the purposes of the NIH Guidelines; investigators following the NIH Guidelines would more probably be using quantities of viruses greater than the quantities needed for diagnostic purposes. The CDC classification is based on use of diagnostic quantities.

Third, Dr. Nightingale said the working group had discussed at length the role and responsibilities of the IBCs. They noted that a greater burden had been placed on the IBCs by the April 21, 1982, revision of the Guidelines. The working group discussed whether RAC should collect information about IBC functions. One suggestion was that a questionnaire be sent to all IBCs. Mr. Mitchell commented that the IBCs have been delegated a great deal of responsibility, but RAC has little data on the actual functioning and effectiveness of the IBCs. He suggested that some mechanism of specific communication between RAC and the IBCs should be developed.

Fourth, Dr. Nightingale noted that the working group suggested an ongoing process of review and revision of the Guidelines; such a process should occur with some regular periodicity, perhaps once a year.

Mr. Thornton suggested that RAC proceed through the proposed revisions of the Guidelines section by section; amendments could then be offered in an orderly fashion. He requested a formal motion to adopt the proposed revised Guidelines as they appeared in the Federal Register of May 26, 1982 (tab 1072). Dr. Ahmed so moved, and Dr. Berns seconded the motion. Dr. Mason offered an amendment to commend the working group for its outstanding efforts in generating the proposed document. Dr. Ahmed accepted the amendment as did Dr. Berns.

Beginning with Section I of the Guidelines, Dr. Baltimore questioned the words "potentially harmful polynucleotide" in the second paragraph of Section I-B, Definition of Recombinant DNA Molecules. He asked how synthetic DNA segments could yield "potentially harmful polynucleotides" other than being translated to "potentially harmful polypeptides". Dr. Wensink suggested it might be a transposable element. It was agreed to leave the language as proposed.

Dr. Baltimore said that a "pharmacologically active agent" is equated with a toxin in Section I-B. He questioned that language. It was pointed out that the text says "e.g., a toxin or a pharmacologically active agent" and does not necessarily equate the two. Also, the text is identical with that in the current April 21, 1982, version of the Guidelines. Dr. Berns said the working group determined that proposals to clone genes for certain biologically active polypeptides should be carefully evaluated, as were proposals involving toxins. The language of Section III-A-1 and Appendix F have been modified to reflect this intent. Dr. Berns said these sections specify the LD50s that define "biologically active polypeptides." It was agreed to leave the language as proposed.

Dr. Nightingale then reviewed the proposed changes in Section III. She noted that a "caution" had been added to Section III-B-3. That caution is as follows:

> "CAUTION: Special care should be used in the evaluation of containment levels for experiments which are likely to either enhance the pathogenicity (e.g., insertion of a host oncogene) or to extend the host range (e.g., introduction of novel control elements) of viral vectors under conditions which permit a productive infection. In such cases, serious consideration should be given to raising physical containment by at least one level."

Dr. Nightingale said this is one instance where new information suggested that a caution be added. Dr. Ahmed asked to whom the caution was addressed. Dr. Berns replied that the caution is addressed primarily to the IBC. Dr. Ahmed asked if the phrase "consideration by the IBC" should be added. He felt the caution as proposed appeared parenthetical; the IBC should be cited more explicitly. Dr. Berns did not accept Dr. Ahmed's suggestion as he felt responsibility should be incumbent on both the investigator and the IBC. Dr. Ahmed withdrew the proposal.

Dr. Nightingale asked if Dr. Ahmed, as the maker of the motion, would agree to strike the work "viral" in Section III-B-2-a. The language reads in part:

> "Recombinant DNA experiments in which DNA from Class 4 agents is transferred into nonpathogenic prokaryotes or lower eukaryotes can be performed at P2 containment after demonstration that only a totally and irreversibly defective fraction of the agent's viral genome is present in a given recombinant."

Dr. Berns explained that currently all Class 4 agents classified in Appendix B are viruses. That situation might, however, change in the future, and deleting the word "viral" in Section III-B-2-a would provide greater flexibility. Dr. Ahmed agreed to delete the word "viral."

Dr. Gottesman noted that language from Sections III-B-2-a and III-B-2-b of the April 21, 1982, Guidelines had been combined by the working group into a new Section III-B-2-a. In so doing, the working group had moved experiments involving a totally and irreversibly defective fraction of Class 4 agents into Section III-B-2-a and delegated authority to the IBC to lower containment on experiments involving these agents.

Dr. Nightingale mentioned the inadvertent omission in Section III-B-4-a of language dealing with USDA permits for working with Class 5 agents and suggested suitable language be inserted analogous to that found at the end of Section III-B-2-b. Mr. Thornton asked if Dr. Ahmed would agree to insertion of such language in Section III-B-4-a. Dr. Ahmed agreed as did Dr. Berns.

Dr. Nightingale then referred to Section III-C, Experiments that Require IBC Notice Simultaneously with Initiation of Experiments. The first sentence of this section reads as follows:

> "Experiments not included in Section III-A, III-B, III-D, and subsections of these sections are to be considered in Section III-C."

She said the working group was concerned with the language of this section. They noted that non-exempt experiments which might merit more stringent review by RAC or by the IBC prior to initiation of the experiment might not be adequately described in Sections III-A and III-B and, thus, would automatically fall into Section III-C. Dr. Nightingale suggested that a reference be added at the end of the first paragraph of Section III-C drawing the reader's attention to the first two paragraphs of Section IV-A, which emphasizes the responsibility of the institution and those associated with it. Dr. Nightingale said the clause emphasizing institutional responsibility in Section IV-A ought to read:

> "Therefore, it is the responsibility of the Institution and those associated with it to adhere to the intent of the Guidelines as well as to their specifics."

The RAC agreed that the word "intent" should be substituted for the word "purpose" which was used in the version proposed by the working group. Dr. Ahmed agreed to add a reference to Section IV-A in Section III-C and to substitute the word "intent" for the word "purpose" in the language of Section IV-A. Dr. Berns agreed.

Dr. Baltimore questioned why low-risk oncogenic viruses had been classified in proposed Appendix B as Class 2 agents. He said most are not human pathogens at all, and many are innocuous. He felt that classifying low-risk oncogenic viruses as Class 1 agents and moderate-risk oncogenic viruses as Class 2 agents would be more reasonable. Dr. Berns did not agree completely; he felt some of the moderate-risk oncogenic viruses, such as Herpesvirus saimiri or EB virus, should be classified as Class 3 agents. Dr. Baltimore agreed that Herpesvirus saimiri might be classified as a Class 3 agent but felt Rous sarcoma virus should be classified as Class 1. Dr. Berns agreed that the list warranted closer looking at, but he did not feel that this RAC meeting was the appropriate time for such a virus by virus review. Dr. McKinney pointed out that P2 provides the investigator with physical protection that is desirable and necessary for working with these agents. He suggested low-risk oncogenic viruses should be used under Class 2 containment conditions. Dr. Baltimore noted that in the current Guidelines a listing is given in Appendix B of low-risk and moderate-risk oncogenic viruses, but no containment relative to the Guidelines is specified. The proposed revised Guidelines include the statements that low-risk oncogenic viruses "should be treated as Class 2 agents" and moderate-risk oncogenic viruses "should be treated as Class 3 agents." Therefore, this involves an increased stringency of the proposed revised Guidelines for these agents.

Dr. Brill questioned the inclusion of all Klebsiella strains as Class 2 agents in Appendix B. He said Klebsiella species are ubiquitous. Dr. Berns pointed out that Klebsiella was classified as Class 2 in the original 1974 edition of the Classification of Etiologic Agents; the working group had not changed its classification. Dr. Holmes said he could suggest several modifications to Appendix B: he agreed with Dr. Richardson that Schistosoma mansoni should be Class 2; the Psittacosis-Ornithosis-Trachoma group needs to be revised; consideration should be given to grouping Mycobacterium leprae with Mycobacterium tuberculosis. Mr. Thornton suggested that a working group review the Appendix B list and report to the RAC at its next meeting. The committee agreed.

Dr. Nightingale reviewed the proposed changes in Section IV, Roles and Responsibilities. These modifications include:

(1) in Section IV-B-2, language was inserted to the effect that the IBC's "responsibilities need not be restricted to recombinant DNA,"

(2) in Section IV-B-2-a, the requirement was deleted that 20 percent of the IBC membership not be affiliated with the institution (although the requirement was retained that at least two IBC members not be affiliated with the institution), and

(3) in Section IV-B-2-b, language recommending that "at least one member be a nondoctoral person from a laboratory technical staff" was modified to read "at least one member be from the laboratory technical staff."

Dr. Berns commented on the proposal to delete the word "nondoctoral". He said some members of the working group felt a "nondoctoral" technician with actual "hands-on" experience was most appropriate for this "slot" on the IBC.

Other members felt that anyone who had "hands on" experience and who was not a principal investigator (including technician, research associate, or post-doctoral fellow) was an appropriate representative of the laboratory technical staff. Following much discussion, the term "nondoctoral" had been deleted from the proposed revised Guidelines by the working group.

Dr. Ahmed questioned why the requirement was deleted that 20 percent of the IBC membership be non-affiliated with the Institution. Dr. Berns offered the example of an IBC just fulfilling the 20 percent specification, but wishing to add an additional specialist affiliated with the university. When this specialist was appointed, non-affiliated representation would fall below 20 percent, and the university would have to appoint another non-affiliated member. Dr. Berns said the working group felt the percentage of non-affiliated members was not critical as long as two non-affiliated members were present on the IBC. Dr. Ahmed pointed out that on an IBC composed of 20 members, with two non-affiliated members, non-affiliated representation would be 10 percent or half of the non-affiliated composition mandated under the current Guidelines. He said the failure to maintain this requirement troubled him. Dr. Mason pointed out that a five-membered IBC would have at least 40 percent of its membership non-affiliated. Dr. McKinney said he believed that the institution, which appoints members to the IBC, will respond to the intent of the Guidelines and appoint IBCs of an appropriate composition.

Moving to the next section, Dr. Nightingale called the attention of the RAC to Section IV-B-2-f. Section IV-B-2-f reads:

> "Institutions are encouraged to open IBC meetings to the public, whenever possible, consistent with protection of privacy and proprietary interests."

Dr. Nightingale said no modifications were suggested for this section but noted that one member of the working group, Ms. King, felt the issue of open meetings should be evaluated at some point in the future and that open meetings probably should eventually be required.

Dr. Nightingale finally noted the addition of proposed language to Section IV-D-4. The proposed language reads:

> "Note: Other Federal agencies which have adopted the NIH Guidelines may have the authority to terminate funding to their grantees should these grantees not comply with the NIH Guidelines."

She felt this statement is not sufficient and that the section should be expanded to include a description of the Federal Interagency Advisory Committee on Recombinant DNA Research and of its membership. Dr. Goldstein felt that some description of the Interagency Committee would be desirable. In particular, a statement that its members have agreed to abide by the NIH Guidelines should be included. Dr. Gottesman suggested that an Appendix, describing the Interagency Committee, its agency members, and a statement that these agencies have agreed to abide by the Guidelines, be added to the Guidelines. References would be made to this new Appendix at (1) Section IV-C-1-a-(4) which describes the Director's responsibility for maintaining this committee, and (2) under Section IV-D-4 in place of the "Note". Dr. Ahmed suggested the proposed Appendix should also describe how the Interagency Committee was formed, who it reports to, and what responsibilities member agencies have assumed with respect to the NIH Guidelines. Dr. Ahmed agreed to accept this amendment, as did Dr. Berns.

Dr. Goldstein said he still had concerns on the potential use of recombinant DNA technology for biological warfare. He noted that the Department of Defense (DOD) is a member of the Interagency Committee. He said that earlier in the meeting RAC heard of classified research conducted by DOD. However, several questions on this research had not been answered to Dr. Goldstein's satisfaction by the DOD representative. Dr. McCullough said that many DOD biomedical research projects are unclassified, but there are projects in defensive biological warfare techniques and processes that are classified. These projects might include aerosol detection devices, antibody identification devices, or air sampling processes. These are not weapons.

Dr. Goldstein asked if the motion made earlier in the meeting concerning the use of recombinant DNA technology for biological warfare might be reconsidered. Dr. Ahmed seconded. By a vote of five in favor, thirteen opposed, and no abstentions the RAC refused to reconsider the earlier motion.

Mr. Thornton called the attention of the RAC to Part D of tab 1072 which includes certain sections of the current Guidelines which the working group suggested deleting but which NIH staff felt should be retained. He said the version which Dr. Ahmed had moved includes these sections. If any member does not approve of the retention of any section, a specific motion to delete should be made. The sections to be retained are: (1) Section I-D-5 of Section I-D, General Definitions, which defines "Director, NIH," (2) Section IV-B-5-b and its subsections of IV-B-5, Principal Investigator, which deals with submissions by the principal investigator to the NIH, (3) Section IV-C-1-b-(1)-(a) and Section IV-C-1-b-(1)-(b) of Section IV-C-1-b, Specific Responsibilities of the Director, and (4) Section IV-C-1-b-(2) and its subsections which detail certain lesser actions which are the responsibility of the Director. No motion to delete any of these sections was made.

Dr. Brill returned to the issue of the classification of *Klebsiella* as a Class 2 agent in Appendix B. He suggested that the language in Appendix B which reads "*Klebsiella* - all species and all serotypes" be modified to read "*Klebsiella* - all strains known to originate from human and animal sources." Dr. Gottesman asked what an investigator would assume if he did not know the source of a strain. Dr. Brill replied that an investigator would assume that particular *Klebsiella* strain was a Class 1 agent. Dr. Gottesman pointed out that no new restrictions were being imposed on investigators working with *Klebsiella* by the proposed revised Guidelines. She questioned the appropriateness of modifying this language at this RAC meeting without data sufficient to formulate a reasonable motion. She felt a working group could examine the issue in greater detail. Dr. Ahmed agreed the issue should be referred to a working group; he felt insufficient information was available at the moment. Dr. McKinney said the Classification of Etiologic Agents states that "human etiologic agents" have been classified. Presumably, those strains of *Klebsiella* classified in proposed Appendix B are only the human pathogens. Dr. Tolin pointed out that *Klebsiella* appears in Sublist A of Appendix A and, therefore, many experiments involving *Klebsiella* will be totally exempt from the Guidelines.

Dr. Holmes suggested that the RAC might follow either of two options: (1) recommend Appendix B as proposed by the working group, or (2) retain Appendix B as it appears in the current Guidelines. He said he would suggest, as an amendment, that RAC retain Appendix B as it currently appears in the Guidelines. Dr. Berns disagreed; he said few substantive changes had been made in proposed Appendix B, and he would not accept Dr. Holmes' amendment. Dr. Holmes withdrew his amendment.

Mr. Thornton called the question on Dr. Ahmed's motion to recommend the proposed revised Guidelines, as amended. By a vote of eighteen in favor, none opposed, and no abstentions, the motion was accepted.

Dr. Nightingale moved that, as suggested by the Working Group on Revision of the Guidelines, a RAC Working Group be appointed to periodically review the Guidelines. By a vote of eighteen in favor, none opposed, and no abstentions, the motion was accepted.

Dr. Gottesman said that one issue discussed by the Working Group on Revision of the Guidelines was IBC functioning under the revised Guidelines. She suggested that a letter might be sent to the IBCs covering the following issues: are the IBCs experiencing problems with the revised Guidelines, do the IBCs disagree with RAC in terms of containment, are the Guidelines too stringent or too relaxed, does the IBC spend inappropriate amounts of time on any problem, how frequently do the committees meet, and does the committee fill other functions for the university, e.g., is the committee a general biosafety committee? If the committee is not a general biosafety committee, why not?

Dr. Gottesman said the effort would obviously be voluntary and the responses, therefore, would probably be somewhat biased; but the survey will at the minimum raise issues for discussion.

VI. FUTURE MEETING DATES

Dr. Gartland said the next meeting was scheduled for October 25, 1982. He assumed it would be a one day meeting.

VII. PRESENTATION OF CERTIFICATES OF SERVICE AND ADJOURNMENT

Mr. Thornton said that the June 28, 1982, meeting would be the last meeting for six RAC members as their terms of service would expire on June 30. The retiring members are Drs. Ahmed, Goldstein, Baltimore, Pinon, and Ms. King. Mr. Thornton said this meeting also was the last session of his term. He expressed his deep sense of friendship with many members of the Recombinant DNA Advisory Committee. He said he had learned much from the members of the committee. He expressed his thanks to the NIH staff for the invaluable support they had given. He also thanked Dr. Jim McCullough of the Congressional Research Service for his assistance over many years.

Certificates of service were then awarded to the retiring members. The meeting was adjourned at 4:40 p.m. on June 28, 1982.

Respectively submitted,

Elizabeth A. Milewski

Elizabeth A. Milewski, Ph.D.
Rapporteur

William J. Gartland Jr.

William J. Gartland, Jr., Ph.D.
Executive Secretary

I hereby certify that, to the best of my knowledge, the foregoing Minutes and Attachments are accurate and complete.

11-22-82
Date

Ray Thornton

Ray Thornton, J.D.
Chairman
Recombinant DNA Advisory Committee

RECOMBINANT DNA ADVISORY COMMITTEE

CHAIRMAN

THORNTON, Ray, J.D. (82)
President
Arkansas State University
State University, Arkansas 72467
501 972-2100

AHMED, Abdul Karim, Ph.D. (82)
Senior Staff Scientist
Natural Resources Defense Council, Inc.
122 East 42nd Street
New York, New York 10017
212 949-0049

BALTIMORE, David, Ph.D. (82)
Professor of Biology
Center for Cancer Research
Massachusetts Institute of Technology
Cambridge, Massachusetts 02139
617 253-6410

BERNS, Kenneth I., Ph.D., M.D. (83)
Chairman
Department of Immunology and Medical Microbiology
University of Florida College of Medicine
Gainesville, Florida 32610
904 392-3311

BRILL, Winston J., Ph.D. (83)
Vilas Research Professor
Department of Bacteriology
University of Wisconsin
Madison, Wisconsin 53706
608 262-3567

DALOZ, L. Albert (85)
R.F.D. 819
Hancock, NH 03449-0819
603 525-3788

FEDOROFF, Nina V., Ph.D. (84)
Staff Member
Department of Embryology
Carnegie Institution of Washington
115 West University Parkway
Baltimore, Maryland 21210
301 467-1414

FRIEDMAN, David, M.D. (85)
Professor of Microbiology
University of Michigan Medical School
Ann Arbor, Michigan 48109
313 763-3142

GOLDSTEIN, Richard, Ph.D. (82)
Associate Professor
Department of Microbiology and Molecular Genetics
Harvard Medical School
Boston, Massachusetts 02115
617 732-1911

HARRIS, Jean L., M.D. (83)
Vice-President
State Marketing Programs
Control Data Corporation, HQS-130
8100 East 34th Street
Minneapolis, Minnesota 55440
612 853-6996

HOLMES, King K., M.D., Ph.D. (84)
Professor of Medicine
Adj. Professor of Microbiology, Immunology, and Epidemiology
University of Washington
Seattle, Washington 98114
206 325-2997

KING, Patricia A., J.D. (82)
Associate Professor of Law
Georgetown University Law School
600 New Jersey Avenue, N.W.
Washington, D.C. 20001
202 624-8295

LANDY, Arthur, Ph.D. (85)
Professor of Medical Sciences
Brown University
Providence, Rhode Island 02912
401 863-2566

LEVINE, Myron M., M.D. (84)
Director
Center for Vaccine Development
Division of Infectious Diseases
University of Maryland
School of Medicine
Baltimore, Maryland 21201
301 528-7588

MAAS, Werner K., Ph.D. (83)
Professor
Department of Microbiology
New York University
School of Medicine
New York, New York 10016
212 340-5322

MARTIN, David W., Jr., M.D. (85)
Professor of Medicine and
Chief of Medical Genetics
University of California
Medical Center
San Francisco, California 94143
415 666-2524

MASON, James O., M.D., Dr. P.H. (83)
Executive Director
Utah State Department of Health
Post Office Box 2500
Salt Lake City, Utah 84113
801 533-6111

McGARRITY, Gerard J., Ph.D. (84)
Head
Department of Microbiolgy
Institute for Medical Research
Copewood Street
Camden, New Jersey 08103
609 966-7377

McKINNEY, Robert W., Ph.D. (84)
Chief, Occupational Safety
and Health Branch
Division of Safety
National Institutes of Health
Bethesda, Maryland 20205
301 496-2960

MITCHELL, Robert E. (85)
Attorney at Law
13915 San Antonio Drive
Norwalk, California 90650
213 863-8736

NIGHTINGALE, Elena O., Ph.D., M.D. (83)
Senior Program Officer
Institute of Medicine
National Academy of Sciences
Washington, D.C. 20418
202 334-2173

PINON, Ramon, Ph.D. (82)
Associate Professor
Department of Biology
B-022 Bonner Hall
University of California, San Diego
La Jolla, California 92093
714 452-2452

SAGINOR, Mark L., M.D. (85)
Director
Metabolic Research Medical Group, Inc.
2080 Century Park East
Los Angeles, California 90067
213 553-2345

SCANDALIOS, John G., Ph.D. (84)
Head
Department of Genetics
North Carolina State University
Raleigh, North Carolina 27650
919 737-2291

WENSINK, Pieter C., Ph.D. (85)
Associate Professor of Biochemistry
Brandeis University
Waltham, Massachusetts 02254
617 647-2421

EXECUTIVE SECRETARY

GARTLAND, William J., Jr., Ph.D.
Director, Office of Recombinant
DNA Activities
National Institute of Allergy
and Infectious Diseases
National Institutes of Health
Bethesda, Maryland 20205
301 496-6051

RECOMBINANT DNA ADVISORY COMMITTEE

NON-VOTING REPRESENTATIVES

CENTERS FOR DISEASE CONTROL

DOWDLE, Walter R., Ph.D.
Assistant Director for Science
Centers for Disease Control
Atlanta, Georgia 30333
404 329-3401

National Institute for Occupational Safety and Health (CDC)

LEMIN, Richard A.
Director
Division of Criteria Documents
and Standards Development
National Institute for Occupational
Safety and Health,
5600 Fishers Lane, Room 8A53
Rockville, Maryland 20857
301 443-3680

U.S. DEPARTMENT OF AGRICULTURE

TOLIN, Sue A., Ph.D.
Science and Education
Cooperative State Research Service
South Building, Room 6440
U.S. Department of Agriculture
Washington, D.C. 20250
202 447-5741

FULKERSON, John F., Ph.D. (ALT)
Science and Education Administration
Cooperative Research
U.S. Department of Agriculture
Washington, D.C. 20250
202 447-5741

U.S. DEPARTMENT OF COMMERCE

COX, John B.
Regulatory Analysis Division, Room 4512
Bureau of Industrial Economics
U.S. Department of Commerce
Washington, D.C. 20230
202 377-2565

U.S. DEPARTMENT OF ENERGY

DUDA, George, Ph.D.
Office of Health and
Environmental Research, EV-33
U.S. Department of Energy
Washington, D.C. 20545
202 353-3651

EDINGTON, Charles W., Ph.D. (ALT)
Deputy Director
Office of Health and Environmental
Research
U.S. Department of Energy
Washington, D.C. 20250
202 353-3251

U.S. DEPARTMENT OF THE INTERIOR

PIMENTEL, Mariano B., Ph.D.
Medical Director
U.S. Department of the Interior
Room 7045
18th & C Street, N.W.
Washington, D.C. 20240
202 343-2081

U.S. DEPARTMENT OF STATE

WALSH, William J., III
Biomedical Research Liason
and Health Affairs Officer
Oceans and International Environmental
and Scientific Affairs
U.S. Department of State
Washington, D.C. 20520
202 632-4824

U.S. DEPARTMENT OF TRANSPORTATION

CUSHMAC, George E., Ph.D.
Chemist
Research and Special Programs
Administration
U.S. Department of Transportation
Washington, D.C. 20590
202 426-2311

U.S. ENVIRONMENTAL PROTECTION AGENCY

LEVIN, Morris, Ph.D.
Director
Innovative Research Program (RD 675)
United States Environmental Protection Agency
Room 909 West Tower
401 M Street, S.W.
Washington, D.C. 20460
202 245-3025

FOOD AND DRUG ADMINISTRATION

National Center for Drugs & Biologics

MILLER, Henry I., M.D.
Medical Officer
National Center for Drugs & Biologics
Food and Drug Administration, Room 14B-04
5600 Fishers Lane
Rockville, Maryland 20857
301 443-3520

NATIONAL AERONAUTICS AND SPACE ADMINISTRATION

DeVINCENZI, Donald L., Ph.D.
Program Manager, Planetary Biology
Code SBL-3
National Aeronautics and Space Administration
Washington, D.C. 20546
202 755-3732

NATIONAL SCIENCE FOUNDATION

LEWIS, Herman W., Ph.D.
Senior Scientist for Recombinant DNA
Division of Physiology
Cellular and Molecular Biology
National Science Foundation
Washington, D.C. 20550
202 357-7647

HARRIMAN, Phillip, Ph.D. (ALT)
Executive Assistant
Directorate for Biological
Behavioral, and Social Sciences
Room 506
National Science Foundation
Washington, D.C. 20550
202 357-9854

U.S. VETERANS ADMINISTRATION

SCHULTZ, Jane S., Ph.D.
Geneticist
U.S. Veterans Administration
Medical Research Service - 151
2215 Fuller Road
Ann Arbor, Michigan 48105
313 769-7100 x696

BERMAN, Howard M. (ALT)
Health Scientist
Program Development and Review Division
U.S. Veterans Administration
810 Vermont Avenue, N.W.
Washington, D.C. 20420
202 389-5065

RECOMBINANT DNA ADVISORY COMMITTEE

LIAISON REPRESENTATIVES

JUENGST, Eric T. (Acting)
Program Specialist
Program of Science Technology
& Human Value
Mail Stop 104
National Endowment for the Humanities
Washington, D.C. 20506
202 724-0354

WEISS, Daniel L., M.D.
Division of Medical Sciences
National Academy of Sciences
2101 Constitution Avenue, N.W.
Washington, D.C. 20418
202 334-2227

IINO, Professor Tetsuo
Department of Biology
Faculty of Science
University of Tokyo
Hongo, Tokyo 113
Japan

DEPARTMENT OF HEALTH AND HUMAN SERVICES
PUBLIC HEALTH SERVICE
NATIONAL INSTITUTES OF HEALTH

RECOMBINANT DNA ADVISORY COMMITTEE
LARGE-SCALE REVIEW WORKING GROUP

MINUTES OF MEETING

JUNE 29, 1982

The Large-Scale Review Working Group was convened for its fourth meeting at 9:00 a.m. on June 29, 1982, in Building 1, Wilson Hall, at the National Institutes of Health, 9000 Rockville Pike, Bethesda, Maryland 20205. Drs. Kenneth Berns and Robert McKinney were co-chairmen.

Working Group members present for all or part of the meeting were:

Manuel Barbeito, NIH; Kenneth Berns, University of Florida (Co-chairman); James Mason, Utah State Department of Health; Robert McKinney, NIH, (Co-chairman); Elizabeth Milewski, NIH, (Executive Secretary); Henry Miller, National Center for Drugs and Biologics, FDA; John Richardson, Centers for Disease Control; and Sue Tolin, U.S. Department of Agriculture.

Other NIH staff present were:

Emmett Barkley, OD.

Others in attendance for all or part of the meeting were:

Charles Angevine, Beckman Instruments; Irene Brandt, Eli Lilly and Company; Maureen Chelius, Schering-Plough Corp.; Chia T. Chen, OSHA, U.S. Department of Labor; Frederic A. Eustis, III, Biogen, Inc.; Robert Fildes, Biogen, Inc.; John Galat, Schering-Plough Corp.; Parrish Galliher, Biogen, Inc.; Richard Geoghegan, E. I. Du Pont De Nemours & Company; Bruce Hamilton, Genex Corporation; Tim Henry, Health Industry Manufacturing Association; Tom M. Helscher, Monsanto Company; I. S. Johnson, Eli Lilly & Company; Judy Johnson, Library of Congress; M. J. Johnson, Pall Corporation; Chabi C. Kalita, Frederick Cancer Research Facility; Philip Landrigan, National Institute for Occupational Safety and Health; Herman Lewis, National Science Foundation; Asger Landlykke, Genex Corporation; D. S. Mabry, Pfizer, Inc.; James M. McCullough, Congressional Research Service; Al Muense, Beckman Instruments; William Muth, Eli Lilly & Company; Harvey Price, Industrial Biotechnology Association; Stephanie Soucek, National Institute for Occupational Safety and Health; Thaddeus T. Sze, Food and Drug Administration; and Dave Wareheim, SmithKline Beckman Corporation.

Dr. Berns, co-chairman, called the fourth meeting of the Large-Scale Review Working Group to order at 9:00 a.m. on June 29, 1982. Dr. Berns said he and his co-chairman, Dr. McKinney, had reviewed the minutes of the February 9, 1982 meeting. They had found the minutes to be complete and accurate. Dr. Mason moved approval of the minutes of the third meeting of the working group. The minutes were approved by a voice vote.

Medical Surveillance of Biotechnology Workers

Dr. Berns then introduced Dr. Landrigan of the National Institute for Occupational Safety and Health (NIOSH). Dr. Landrigan had presented to the working group, at the February 9, 1982 meeting, the document "Medical Surveillance of Biotechnology Workers: Report of the CDC/NIOSH, *Ad Hoc* Working Group on Medical Surveillance for Industrial Applications of Biotechnology."

Dr. Landrigan reviewed the history of the report. He said the CDC/NIOSH (Centers for Disease Control/National Institute for Occupational Safety and Health) working group had been asked to consider the strengths, limitations and nature of any medical surveillance program that might be developed for the medical monitoring of industrial workers engaged in industrial applications of recombinant DNA technologies. Dr. Landrigan said that as the CDC/NIOSH working group considered the issues, it became evident that medical surveillance had to be viewed as one of several layers of protection for industrial workers. The principal protection for industrial workers is provided by strict physical containment of the processes. Almost as important as strict physical containment is the development of good work practices, the development of worker training programs, and to the extent possible, the use of biologically attenuated organisms. After these protections are in place, the role of medical surveillance can be considered.

Dr. Landrigan said medical surveillance performs several functions. First, it serves as a check on the adequacy of other protection. Secondly, it is a defense against the unexpected; if unanticipated illness should occur, it facilitates the early detection and control of such illness.

Dr. Landrigan said the CDC/NIOSH working group report discusses in some detail the specific hazards medical surveillance might be directed against. These hazards may be classified in three categories. The first are microbial hazards; the hazards posed by colonization of the worker by recombinant DNA organisms. The CDC/NIOSH working group concluded that the likelihood of such an event is quite small, given that most organisms currently used are attenuated and that risk assessment information suggests an extremely small possibility of colonization by these organisms. The report cautions, however, that these assumptions should be reevaluated if more robust organisms are employed in industrial processes. The second class of potential hazard is exposure to biological products. Here, the CDC/NIOSH working group concluded, real risks exist. Risks from exposure to these products are probably not significantly different from exposure risks elsewhere in the pharmaceutical industry. Adverse affects and illnesses are observed in pharmaceutical manufacture workers exposed to biologically active products. As examples Dr. Landrigan mentioned the occurrance of gynecomastia in persons involved in the production of oral contraceptives, frequent nose bleeds in workers using ferrous sulfate, toxic hepatitis in people working with isopropanol and carbon tetrachloride, and nasal polyps in people involved in the production of menthol cold remedies. It is very clear that product exposure hazards exist in the pharmaceutical industry and that very strict containment of biologically active products has to be achieved at every stage of production. The third category of hazard is exposure to reagents used in the extraction and purification of the products. These hazards are not qualitatively or quantitatively different from hazards encountered in other sectors of the pharmaceutical or biotechnology industries.

Dr. Landrigan said the CDC/NIOSH report then outlines the components of a medical surveillance program for workers in biotechnology industries: (1) pre-employment examinations, which include collection of baseline serum samples, (2) periodic follow-up examinations, (3) provision for active follow-up of any illness which causes unexplained absences from work of 48 hours duration, and (4) conduct of epidemiological or other long term follow-up studies.

Dr. Landrigan said the report concludes with a statement on the limitations of medical surveillance: the likelihood is small that medical surveillance will detect any unexpected disease. Hopefully, that disease will not occur at all; strict containment and good work practices should prevent its occurrence. The report argues, however, that uncertainty, both social and medical, as to the unknown hazards of this new industry are sufficient to justify the development of medical surveillance programs.

Dr. Landrigan said the CDC/NIOSH report had been revised following the February 9, 1981 discussion of the document by the Large Scale Review Working Group, and suggestions offered by the working group were incorporated in the document. Dr. Landrigan said the scope of the report has been broadened beyond recombinant

DNA technology; now the report addresses medical surveillance in the biotechnology industry. He said the heart of the report and the specific recommendations are essentially unchanged, although some alterations have been made to reflect specific comments and criticisms. Dr. Landrigan called the committee's attention to the revised document (Attachment I).

Dr. Mason noted that the CDC/NIOSH report classified antibiotics as reagent hazards; he asked how antibiotics would be used as reagents. Dr. Landrigan said antibiotics are used to control the growth of the organisms in the fermentation vessels. He said antibiotics such as ampicillin can cause gastrointestinal distress.

Dr. Berns asked Dr. Landrigan to explain epidemiological studies. Dr. Landrigan replied that epidemiological studies of industrial workers usually are a tripartite effort by government, the industry and unions. In this instance, the industry bears initial primary responsibility. That responsibility would entail maintaining basic records, such as personnel records and records of specific exposures.

Dr. Berns, noting that Dr. Miller had criticized the first draft of the CDC/NIOSH report, asked Dr. Miller if he had any comments on this version. Dr. Miller said he found this version more acceptable than the first draft, but expressed a fundamental disagreement with the report's conclusions. He felt that the indiscriminate application of medical surveillance to the biotechnology industry is unlikely to be cost effective, and will be debilitating to industry. Dr. Berns questioned whether a pre-employment physical is standard practice in industry. Dr. Johnson of Eli Lilly and Company said that at Eli Lilly pre-employment physicals are common practice. They are available to all employees but mandatory for many; pre-employment physicals are mandatory for workers in production and research. Dr. Johnson said Eli Lilly viewed recombinant DNA technology as no different than other fermentation technologies; Eli Lilly therefore employs standard practice in medical surveillance. Dr. Fildes, vice-president of the Industrial Biotechnology Association (IBA), said IBA member companies have implemented a number of medical surveillance programs. Dr. Tolin stated her view that recombinant DNA technology should not be singled out for special medical surveillance programs.

Dr. Henry of the Health Industry Manufacturer's Association (HIMA) asked permission to comment. He said HIMA is a trade association representing 266 medical device and diagnostic product manufacturers. HIMA member companies will undoubtedly employ recombinant DNA technology at some time. HIMA believes that while the CDC/NIOSH report has thoughtfully considered the majority of pertinent issues, it does not arrive at a proper conclusion. HIMA believes that the report recommends medical surveillance on the basis of two weak arguments: (1) that medical surveillance affords a means for assessing the effectiveness of physical and biological containment, and (2) medical surveillance provides for early detection of unanticipated illness. Dr. Henry said these arguments are valid only if the processes involve organisms which produce some known disease. As the health hazards of exposure to altered microorganisms appear to be minimal, these arguments would not apply to the vast majority of recombinant DNA applications. By the time a recombinant DNA containing microorganism is used in large-scale production, it is a well characterized entity.

In addition, industrial applications of recombinant DNA organisms generally involve routine fermentations. Fermentation is not a new industry and most of the problem areas are known. Dr. Henry said HIMA has several questions about the proposed medical surveillance program: Who will pay for the exams and serum storage? How frequently should examinations occur? If surveyed groups will be small, how can long term epidemiological studies even be contemplated? Dr. Landrigan replied that the specifics of the CDC/NIOSH recommendation, physical examination, maintenance of serum samples, and retention of records, are innocuous. He thought reputable firms in the field currently follow these procedures and a few more as well: the bigger the company and the more sophisticated the technology the more likely medical surveillance programs are extant.

Dr. Mason said industrial health problems should be detected at the earliest possible moment. To that end, communication between industry, labor and government is necessary. Dr. Johnson said that industry has a responsibility to its employees, and he thought industry by and large met that responsibility. Industry has liability considerations which are a motivation to be very careful. He felt that although worker health is a serious issue, it is already reasonably well handled by the industry.

Dr. McKinney said medical surveillance is one method of assessing the effectiveness of containment. He said that in early stages of industrial development the methodology to assess whether infection or disease have occurred is not necessarily available. The means to assess the consequence of exposure to the technology must be considered and developed, and thus the necessity for medical surveillance programs must be evaluated.

Dr. Berns reminded the working group that RAC had charged the group with examining the potential utility and benefits of medical surveillance. In response to that mandate a report on medical surveillance has been generated and it would be appropriate for the working group to send that report to the RAC. Dr. Berns suggested that written comments to RAC concerning the report would be appropriate. Dr. Miller felt the CDC/NIOSH report would be more appropriately published elsewhere, rather than be discussed by the RAC. Dr. McKinney said the CDC/NIOSH report suggests prudent and reasonable medical surveillance practices for this industry. It does not suggest regulations. Dr. McKinney moved that the working group present the CDC/NIOSH report to the RAC, with the recommendation that the report be viewed as a framework against which specific medical surveillance programs could be designed. Dr. McKinney said it would be inappropriate to dictate precisely what should be done in each medical surveillance program.

Dr. Mason expressed concern that the CDC/NIOSH report may be too generic: he felt the fermentation industry in general (such as the beer industry) may not need to require pre-employment physicals; on the other hand companies producing hormones such as growth hormone or interferon might prudently implement medical surveillance programs.

Dr. Landrigan said medical surveillance is a very simple, largely passive means of detecting disease. He pointed out that medical surveillance had detected the major hazard of the brewing industry: hearing loss in workers in bottling plants where caps are slammed onto bottles at high decibels. Following the implementation of good hearing protection programs, the frequency of noise induced hearing loss is decreasing.

Dr. Berns said that if one assumes greater risk is associated with recombinant DNA or unanticipated unknown risk is possible, data on risk must be generated. To obtain such data, epidemiological studies would be performed. On the other hand if one believes there is no special risk, then the procedures already followed by industry are reasonable and these procedures are the basic suggestions of the CDC/NIOSH report. Dr. Berns then called the vote on Dr. McKinney's motion. By a vote of five in favor, one opposed, and two abstentions, Dr. McKinney's recommendation to forward the CDC/NIOSH report to the RAC was accepted.

Dr. Miller then moved the following resolution:

> "Recombinant DNA technology constitutes a very small subset of industrial microbiology. It affords no characteristics unique to itself likely to provide systematic or unique hazards, and, therefore, should not be subject to special scrutiny or treatment."

Dr. Berns called the vote on Dr. Miller's motion. On the first vote, three members of the working group supported the motion, three members were opposed, and one member abstained. The chairman then called a revote in which three members were in favor, three members were opposed and one member abstained. The chairman then broke the tie by voting in favor of the resolution. By a vote of four in favor, three opposed and one abstention the motion was accepted.

Dr. McKinney felt that while the working group should convey the idea that recombinant DNA technology may not entail any extraordinary hazard beyond those found in other fermentation technologies, it should be recognized that some hazards are associated with any technology. Dr. Mason said the CDC/NIOSH report was well done. He suggested that a preamble be added to the document.

This preamble would indicate that the IBC is responsible for assessing risks and initiating medical surveillance practices; the CDC/NIOSH document outlines a recommended approach for biotechnology medical surveillance when risk assessment makes such an approach prudent or when risk is unknown. Dr. Richardson supported Dr. Mason's proposal. Dr. Mason then offered a motion: that a preamble emphasizing IBC responsibility be added to the CDC/NIOSH report. By a vote of five in favor, none opposed and two abstentions the motion was accepted.

(Later in the meeting Dr. Landrigan read his version of a proposed preamble to the CDC/NIOSH report. Dr. Mason read his version of a proposed preamble. They agreed to discuss the preamble by telephone.)

Presentation by Eli Lilly and Company

Dr. Muth of Eli Lilly and Company said he would communicate some of Eli Lilly's experiences in producing human insulin using an *E. coli* K-12 host-vector system. Dr. Muth said the concerns and issues faced by the company have changed during Eli Lilly's involvement with recombinant DNA technology, although the primary aim of safely scaling up recombinant organism fermentations to commercial production has remained the same. Lilly's expertise in the fermentation industry dates back to the 1940's and primarily involves the use of *Streptomyces* and fungi for the manufacture of antibiotics. Although in recent years many technical changes have occurred in the age-old process of fermentation, the basic principles for fermentation of recombinant DNA organisms are essentially the same as those used since the 1940's for producing antibiotics. Several development projects using *Bacillus* and *E. coli* were Eli Lilly's principal prior experience in bacterial fermentations.

Dr. Muth then showed slides of some of the equipment employed in the fermentation process: closed stainless steel vessels, designed, built and tested to comply with pressure codes, modern computing instrumentation monitors, etc. Dr. Muth said antibiotic fermentors are designed primarily to exclude contaminating organisms. In compliance with the NIH Guidelines, these fermentors were adapted to contain the fermentation organisms as well as to exclude contaminators. Fermentor containment could be attained by altering standard antibiotic fermentors by (1) filtering or incinerating all exhaust gases, (2) installing proper agitator seals at the junction in the agitator shaft, (3) instituting proper sampling and inoculating procedures, and (4) chemically or thermally inactivating the fermentor contents prior to processing. Other aspects of the procedure requiring greater scrutiny were: (1) environmental containment monitoring, (2) development of detailed written procedural protocols, (3) training of fermentation personnel, and (4) validation of the complete system.

Dr. Muth said environmental containment monitoring is performed continuously and consists of microbiological sampling of the exhaust air systems after filtration, sampling of the operator environment, and integrity testing of the exhaust filter system. More than 5,000 environmental samples have been taken through May, 1982. No recombinant DNA containing organisms have been detected. Dr. Muth said the fermentation broth is tested after each chemical and thermal inactivation procedure. In addition the entire system was validated to show that the fermentation microbes had been inactivated. For example, when thermal sterilization was employed, the temperature at multiple points was measured throughout the fermentor and its processing lines. It was found that heat distribution within such complex systems is not as straightforward as it might appear. These studies led to changes in fermentor or piping designs. In addition to temperature measurements, validation was also concerned with the overall reproducibility of the inactivation processes. The interaction between the fermentor operator, the equipment, the computer, and the procedural protocol was observed to determine if these components complemented each other and insured inactivation reproducibility.

Dr. Muth said standard medical surveillance is available to all Eli Lilly employees, but is mandatory for all employees involved in any phase of recombinant DNA projects. It includes an annual physical examination, blood analysis, urinalysis, chest x-ray, height, weight, blood pressure measurements, general health questionnaire, an audiogram and an EKG. In addition, a baseline serum sample is prepared from each recombinant DNA worker and frozen in liquid nitrogen. Additional tests are required if an individual is exposed to a significant breach of containment, but a containment breach has never occurred. Operators must report all illnesses and are not allowed to work with viable organisms while on any type of antimicrobial therapy.

Dr. Muth then described Eli Lilly's first submission requesting exception to the 10 liter prohibition. He said the submission contained: (1) a description of the E. coli host and plasmid, (2) the design, test data, and validation results for 150 liter fermentors, (3) detailed operator protocols, and (4) risk assessment studies involving the feeding of recombinant organisms to germ-free animals. Also described was the method of chemical inactivation of the microbial population at the end of each fermentation run. The data were reviewed at the closed session of the June 1979 RAC meeting. On October 5, 1979, Eli Lilly received from the Director, Office of Recombinant DNA Activities, NIH, a letter stating that the Director, NIH, on the recommendation of the RAC, had approved the Eli Lilly request. Meanwhile Eli Lilly had completed construction of a 2,000 liter vessel. A request for permission to operate this equipment and for approval of a process to manufacture insulin via the fermentation of organisms producing proinsulin was made in March 1980. This request was approved by the Director, NIH, on the recommendation of the RAC and the 2,000 liter vessel began operation in May, 1981.

During 1979, Eli Lilly announced the capital expenditure of about $40 million for plant construction to manufacture biosynthetic human insulin. Fermentation plant design was patterned after the 2,000 liter system, with all of the containment features employed in the pilot plant installation preserved. This plant has been operating on a routine basis since mid-1981. Environmental monitoring has been an integral part of this operation since its inception. Eli Lilly now has over 16,000 hours of fermentation experience with the insulin producing E. coli host-vector systems and various pieces of fermentation equipment greater than 10 liters in volume. During this time Eli Lilly has had no breaches of containment nor detected any environmental contamination. All systems have functioned as designed and performed reliably.

Dr. Johnson said that many of the safety features Eli Lilly was currently employing were redundant. He said Eli Lilly had instituted many of these features because Lilly was the first company to apply recombinant DNA technology to production scale. He suggested many of these safety features could now be eliminated. In response Dr. McKinney invited representatives from industrial firms to submit recommendations or suggestions for modifying the "Physical Containment Recommendations for Large-Scale Uses of Organisms Containing Recombinant DNA Molecules." (Federal Register 45: 24968 (1980).)

Presentation of the Industrial Biotechnology Association

Dr. McKinney introduced Dr. Robert Fildes, vice-president of the Industrial Biotechnology Association (IBA) and president of Biogen, Inc. Dr. Fildes said the IBA is an international trade association of two dozen companies actively engaged in developing commercial products through biotechnology.

Dr. Fildes said compliance with the NIH Guidelines has become accepted industry practice. In addition the industry complies with the other extensive regulations to which it is subject. Currently government regulations governing biotechnology (other than the NIH Guidelines e.g., those of the EPA, OSHA, FDA, USDA) are comprehensive; industry, however, believes it can work under these regulations and safely produce effective products. Additional regulation would contribute little to public health and safety and would be duplicative and cumbersome from industry's point of view. Accordingly, the IBA believes that the present regulatory balance between the public and industry is proper, and should not be altered significantly.

The industry is beginning the transition from bench scale experiments to pilot plant operations. As part of that transition, industry has put into effect numerous practices which reflect concern with worker safety and the environment. Examples of industry practices among IBA members include:

- Use of physical and biological containment based on the NIH Guidelines;

- o Sterilization of wastes prior to disposal;
- o Challenge and validation of safety procedures;
- o Use of accounting systems for biologically active products consistent with good laboratory practices and good manufacturing practices;
- o Health monitoring programs; and
- o Careful design of procedures and equipment to minimize the possibility and effects of human error.

Dr. Fildes said some of these practices result from regulations to which industry is subject. Others result from compliance with the NIH Guidelines and from concern for worker and environmental safety. Finally, certain practices result from the knowledge gained from extensive experience in the fermentation of antibiotics and other biochemicals.

Dr. Fildes said experience has indicated that the present Physical Containment Recommendations for Large-Scale Uses of Organisms Containing Recombinant DNA Molecules are reasonable and workable, although quite stringent for work at the P1-LS level. The design requirements in the Recommendations are sensible and are consistent with other regulations relating to the manufacture of products for use with human subjects. While it has not yet been a problem for IBA members, potential difficulties may arise from the requirement in Section VII-B-2 of the Recommendations. This requirement specifies that all recombinant micro-organisms must be inactivated before the primary containment system is opened, and it may be very difficult in some processes to do so without compromising the product.

Dr. Fildes said the Institutional Biosafety Committee (IBC) plays a key role in the NIH Guidelines. IBA experience with IBCs has been favorable and IBA members believe that IBCs are the most appropriate entity for the detailed monitoring of large-scale procedures. The IBA strongly recommends their continued use. IBA members have generally found the IBCs to be useful and productive. For example, IBCs are valuable in assuring the community that independent review of experiments exists. Dr. Fildes said that while worldwide experience convinces IBA members that recombinant DNA research is safe, the IBCs will help establish an expanded data base to further demonstrate the safety of this work. In addition, IBCs bring together many different expertises and allow all safety issues to be addressed in a single forum within a company.

Dr. Fildes noted that most of the work being performed by IBA member companies is classified as exempt or P1. The IBA feels that a full-scale IBC review prior to initiation of an exempt large-scale experiment is not necessary, and recommends that exempt experiments should require only simultaneous notification of the IBC and not prior approval by the IBC. This approach is appropriate as the exempt classification means that the safety issue has been fully addressed. Moreover, large-scale experiments will be performed in a facility which has previously been approved by the IBC. Within the IBA there is significant sentiment for requiring only simultaneous IBC notice (as opposed to prior approval) for P1 experiments as well as for exempt experiments.

Many IBA members supplement IBC review with frequent monitoring by various other safety committees. These committees monitor the experiments on a day to day basis. At the same time, use of internal safety committees alleviate concerns about unnecessary disclosure of proprietary information; these concerns may be a problem with an IBC. The IBA believes that these internal safety committees are a good example of a useful addition to IBC review; an addition that can improve the overall monitoring process. General safety committees are industry practice now and, are useful not only to supplement IBC review but are also valuable in assessing and controlling safety risks of a more general nature. Such committees might typically review the use of flammable solvents, the design and safety of particular items of equipment, fire safety, emergency procedures and similar safety issues. Because of IBA views on the safety of recombinant DNA research per se, many IBA members see the conventional safety issues as the more significant ones to be assessed and controlled.

Dr. Fildes said the IBA has no problems with 10 liter volumes being the boundary between large and small scale experiments. The IBA does feel that 10 liters is an arbitrary boundary and certainly does not reflect industry practice. Most industrial pilot plant operations, for example, occur at the 250-3,000 liter size. As additional experience is accumulated with industrial applications, the IBA feels the committee will find it logically compelling to adjust the large-scale threshold upward.

Virtually all IBA members have instituted medical surveillance programs. Common to most of these programs are medical check-ups, storage of serum samples, and follow-up in cases of extended or serious illnesses. The IBCs are charged with reviewing medical monitoring programs as part of their responsibility under the Guidelines, and existing medical surveillance programs can be supplemented by the IBC for particular experiments. Thus, if any special requirements are appropriate for a particular procedure, the IBC can require special medical monitoring. The IBA thinks this approach is reasonable and recommends its continuance. Dr. Fildes said a number of IBA members question the need for any medical surveillance program directed specifically toward recombinant DNA experimentation since there is no evidence of hazards unique to recombinant DNA. Moreover, it is widely agreed that it is very difficult to run meaningful medical surveillance without knowing what is to be surveyed. Dr. Fildes pointed out that the proposed medical surveillance program would entail significant costs. A second important consideration is that employees must undergo mandatory medical procedures, an invasion of privacy which many find objectionable. In summary the IBA is currently not in favor of mandatory medical surveillance directed specifically at recombinant DNA work.

Finally, Dr. Fildes stressed the high value industry places on the type of dialogue that the Large Scale Review Working Group has formally initiated, as well as on the belief that direct benefits can be anticipated from its continuation and strengthening. In the next several years industrial applications of recombinant DNA research procedures and products will certainly increase. With its established scientific expertise, credibility, and record of demonstrated sensitivity to public interests, the RAC can and should reasonably contribute to identifying and exploring recombinant DNA issues particularly relevant to commercial applications. Such activity could complement the regulatory actions of various agencies (many of which currently have liaison representation on the RAC and Large Scale Review Working Group) and minimize the need for repetitive treatment of issues. Thus, without preempting any regulatory authority, the RAC would become a focal point for efficiently addressing recombinant DNA issues important to both science and commercial development. Under such a regime, industry's commitment to full compliance with RAC guidance would be expected to continue and be strengthened.

To move toward successful implementation of this role, the IBA offers two specific suggestions. First, both the Large Scale Review Working Group and the RAC itself would benefit by being better informed on what is occurring in industry. The IBA therefore suggests that an industry representative be placed on each body - without voting power but with responsibility to insure that industrial approaches and perspectives are taken into account on decisions affecting such interests. If the IBA was requested to do so, the IBA would be pleased to designate an expert with actual large scale recombinant DNA experience to serve in this role.

Secondly, the IBA believes that dialogue between the IBA and the Large Scale Review Working Group should continue periodically on a regular basis. The IBA has freely expressed views and concerns today. The IBA looks forward to continuing communication. In light of the working group responsibility to advise the RAC on scale-up matters, the IBA is confident that a regular channel of communication can be established which will promote understanding and respect for various points of view, which will sharpen issues that should be constructively addressed, and which will minimize undue strains on the NIH and the industrial community as compatible goals are pursued.

Dr. Johnson supported Dr. Fildes' comments on the possible appointment of an industrial expert as a liaison member to the RAC and/or to the Large Scale Review Working Group. He questioned the need, however, for any definition of large-scale under the Guidelines.

Dr. McKinney pointed out that industry is not obliged to comply with the NIH Guidelines. He said industry was to be complimented for the manner in which it complied voluntarily with the Guidelines and responded to the needs of the situation. Dr. Berns adjourned the meeting at 12:10 p.m.

Respectively submitted,

October 27, 1982
Date

Elizabeth Milewski
Elizabeth Milewski, Ph.D.
Executive Secretary

I hereby certify that, to the best of my knowledge, the foregoing Minutes are accurate and complete.

November 17, 1982
Date

Kenneth I. Berns
Kenneth I. Berns, Ph.D.
Co-Chairman
Large-Scale Review Working Group
of the Recombinant DNA Advisory Committee

October 27, 1982
Date

Robert W. McKinney
Robert W. McKinney, Ph.D.
Co-Chairman
Large Scale Review Working Group
of the Recombinant DNA Advisory Committee

Attachment I

June 14, 1982

MEDICAL SURVEILLANCE OF BIOTECHNOLOGY WORKERS: REPORT OF THE CDC/NIOSH *AD HOC* WORKING GROUP ON MEDICAL SURVEILLANCE FOR INDUSTRIAL APPLICATIONS OF BIOTECHNOLOGY

Philip J. Landrigan, M.D., M.Sc., Chairman
Mitchell L. Cohen, M.D.
Walter Dowdle, Ph.D.
Larry J. Elliott, B.S.
William E. Halperin, M.D.
J. Donald Millar, M.D.

From the Division of Surveillance, Hazard Evaluations and Field Studies, National Institute for Occupational Safety and Health, 4676 Columbia Parkway, Cincinnati, Ohio 45226.

SUMMARY

Planned industrial applications of biotechnologies resulting from advances in molecular genetics will increase potential exposures of skilled and unskilled workers to microorganisms containing recombinant deoxyribonucleic acid (DNA) and to their products. The health hazards of exposures to altered microorganisms appear minimal, given current use of highly attenuated microbial species. The hazards of occupational exposures to the biologically active products of those organisms appear, however, to be more substantial; product exposures in other sectors of the pharmaceutical industry have caused diseases such as gynecomastia, Cushing's syndrome, and toxic hepatitis. Sensitization to microbial peptides can produce occupational asthma.

Strict physical containment of recombined microorganisms and their products constitutes the primary defense against occupational exposures. Establishment of proper work practices and worker education programs is also of great importance. "Biological containment", achieved through the use of attenuated microbial species, provides a further defense. Medical surveillance of workers, although inherently limited in its ability to detect disease, affords a means for assessing the effectiveness of physical and biological containment and for early detection of unanticipated illness. Medical surveillance programs should be highly specific; they must evaluate the particular hazards which confront an occupational group. At a minimum, medical surveillance of biotechnology workers should include: (1) pre-employment examination with collection of baseline serum; (2) periodic follow-up; (3) evaluation of all illnesses causing 48 hours' absence from work; (4) epidemiologic studies; (5) periodic evaluation of data; and (6) regular communication of results to management and workers. Establishment of medical surveillance for workers in any newly developed industry constitutes prudent medical practice.

INTRODUCTION

The term "biotechnology" denotes the application of biological systems and organisms to technical and industrial processes.[1]

Microorganisms have for centuries been employed in such applications as the leavening of bread, the fermentation of beers and wines, and the ripening of cheese. Those traditional applications depended upon naturally occurring mutations to provide microbial strains with particular useful properties.

Modern biotechnology departs from its empirical forbears and is based on recent advances in molecular genetics and cell biology. Genetic manipulation, the systematic transfer of genetic material from one organism to another in order to alter the properties of the recipient organism, is the foundation of modern biotechnology. This technique of recombining molecules of deoxyribonucleic acid (DNA) to form recombinant DNA (rDNA) permits the planned development of microorganisms designed to produce specific chemical or biological products or to destroy particular toxic wastes.[2]

Biotechnologic applications are expected to find major use in the near future in the pharmaceutical, chemical, and food processing industries. In the next decade biotechnologic techniques will likely be employed in the production of enzymes, hormones, antibiotics, vaccines, diagnostic antigens, improved plant strains, and a wide variety of chemical feedstocks.[3] Several attractions of biotechnology are: (1) it is based largely on renewable resources and thus requires less input of energy than the petroleum-based chemical industry; (2) it will permit the production in pure form of sizeable quantities of certain enzymes and hormones which have heretofore been available only in minute amounts; (3) it may in certain instances permit production of biologically active molecules, such as viral vaccines, under safer working conditions than are afforded by traditional techniques.[1]

As the commercial applications of biotechnology are pursued, the number of persons engaged in such work will increase greatly. These persons will include not only professional staff, but also production workers, line supervisors, maintenance personnel, and janitors. The Congressional Office of Technology Assessment has estimated that by the year 2,000 as many as 80,000 to 200,000 workers may be employed in biotechnology applications.[4]

The Centers for Disease Control/National Institute for Occupational Safety and Health (CDC/NIOSH) Ad Hoc Working Group on Medical Surveillance for Industrial Applications of Biotechnology has considered the role that medical surveillance might play in the detection of any disease or dysfunction which might result from employment in industries utilizing biotechnologic applications. The Working Group recognizes that neither the existence, extent, nor severity of any health hazards which may be associated with biotechnological applications are known. The Group realizes further that the effectiveness of medical surveillance will inevitably be limited by such factors as the relatively small size of most groups under study, variability in individual exposures, potentially long induction-latency period from beginning of exposure to appearance of effects, and uncertainty as to the effects that may occur. Most importantly, the Group recognizes that medical surveillance can never replace the establishment of appropriate physical containment of recombined microorganisms and their products* and proper work practices as the primary defenses against occupational exposure and disease. Nevertheless, the Group has concluded that medical surveillance of workers engaged in commercial applications of biotechnologies can play a valuable auxiliary role in protecting worker health. Medical surveillance, in its essence, provides a means for evaluation of the effectiveness of physical and biological containment in protecting worker health. Also it is the most direct means for early identification of unsuspected adverse consequences of occupational exposure. It is therefore the opinion of the Working Group that the establishment of medical surveillance programs for biotechnology workers, as for workers in any new industry, constitutes prudent medical practice.

The Working Group considered three potential hazards of biotechnology in relation to medical surveillance: microbial hazards, product hazards and reagent hazards.

MICROBIAL HAZARDS

Under current working conditions, the health hazard of occupational exposure to genetically altered microorganisms appears to be slight.[6,7] Many

---

*The level of physical containment of microorganisms used in biotechnologic applications must be appropriate for their level of pathogenicity.[5]

microorganisms currently used in biotechnologic applications are debilitated, or "crippled" through genetic manipulation such that their ability to reproduce outside of a laboratory environment is severely curtailed. None of the organisms in current use have been shown to cause infection or disease in persons using biotechnologic techniques. Recent risk assessments suggest that the likelihood of infection by altered microorganisms is minimal.[6,7] Despite those reassurances, probabilistic arguments have been developed that workers engaged in industrial applications of biotechnologies may be colonized or infected by modified organisms.[8,9]

The primary defense against colonization or infection of biotechnology workers will be provided by strict physical containment of genetically altered organisms.[5] Development of proper work practices and educational programs for workers is also of great importance in reducing the likelihood of occupational exposures. In the development and capitalization of industrial biotechnologies, exposure control and worker protection should be given as great emphasis as process integrity and product development. Experience gained by NIOSH in other sectors of the chemical and pharmaceutical manufacturing industries indicates that preplanned maintenance is also a central aspect of exposure control; facilities for containment of altered organisms should periodically, in accordance with a strict timetable, be shut down for scheduled examination and repair. Procedures for evaluation of facilities and for validation of the integrity of physical containment should be developed at the outset as an integral component of facilities design.

A second defense against colonization or infection of biotechnology workers is provided by "biological containment". Such containment will be achieved through the continuing use of debilitated microorganisms. Any tendency toward reduction in levels of "biological containment" through the introduction to industry of more robust, less highly debilitated organisms should be approached with great caution and will require careful reassessment of potential health risks.

PRODUCT HAZARDS

Product hazards in biotechnology are not likely to differ qualitatively from those encountered in other sectors of the pharmaceutical and chemical industries; the fact that the molecules encountered in biotechnology are the products of bioorganisms rather than of synthetic catalysis will not alter their reactivity or toxicity. However, exposure to biologically active products constitutes a serious class of potential hazard throughout the chemical and pharmaceutical industries and biotechnologic applications are not likely to be exempt from such hazards.

Because of the physiologically reactive nature of many biological and pharmaceutical products, exposures to even minute quantities of some may cause medically significant effects. Occupational exposures to products in other sectors of the pharmaceutical industry have produced a spectrum of illnesses, including gynecomastia (in the manufacturing and packaging of estrogens),[10] Cushing's syndrome (in glucocorticoid manufacture),[11] nasal polyps (in production of menthol cough drops),[12] recurrent epistaxis (in compounding of ferrous sulfate), and toxic hepatitis (following exposure to isopropanol plus carbon tetrachloride).[13] The hazards of product exposure extend throughout the full manufacturing process from initial production to final packaging. Because of the biological activity of many of the products and by-products that will be encountered in biotechnologic applications, prevention of any resultant health hazards will, as elsewhere in the pharmaceutical industries, require extremely sophisticated engineering controls.

In addition to the specific hazards which may result from occupational exposures to particular products, workers in biotechnologic applications will also be at risk of sensitization to microbial proteins and peptides generated in the course of fermentation and extraction. A high frequency of sensitization to protein enzymes has been described previously among workers engaged in the commercial production of enzyme detergents.[14] Asthma is the most serious health consequence of such sensitization. Dermatitis and allergic rhinitis might also be expected to occur.

REAGENT HAZARDS

As in other sectors of the pharmaceutical and chemical industries, solvents and chemical reagents will be used extensively in the extraction, separation, and purification of the products produced in biotechnologic applications. Among the reagents which may be expected to be used in biotechnology are solvents (phenol, benzene, toluene, chloroform), buffers (sodium hydroxide, urea, ammonium hydroxide, magnesium chloride, potassium chloride), and antibiotics (chloramphenicol, tetracycline, ampicillin). Standard procedures for process enclosure, ventilation, and work practices, as well as adherence to OSHA standards and other appropriate guidelines will be required to protect biotechnology workers against those exposures.

PURPOSES OF MEDICAL SURVEILLANCE

Uncertainty provides the strongest argument for maintaining medical surveillance over workers engaged in industrial applications of biotechnology.[15] As is the case for any newly developed technology, there is a lack of information concerning the nature, or severity of any acute or chronic health hazards which might be associated with the industrial applications of biotechnology. Given that lack of knowledge, the CDC/NIOSH Working Group is of the opinion that medical surveillance of biotechnology workers constitutes prudent medical practice. Such surveillance should be aimed at the early detection of sentinel disease events.[16]

NATURE OF MEDICAL SURVEILLANCE

In its essence, medical surveillance of biotechnology workers consists of periodic evaluation; regular analysis of data; and regular communication of results to workers, management, and other interested parties.[17]

The components of a medical surveillance program for recombinant DNA workers which were considered by the Working Group are as follows:

a. preemployment examination and collection of baseline serum samples for storage;
b. periodic follow-up examination;
c. follow-up evaluation of all illnesses which cause absence from work of more than 48 hours' duration;
d. epidemiological and other longer term follow-up studies.

Preemployment Examinations - The purposes of preemployment examinations are (1) to establish a worker's health status prior to the start of work; (2) to provide baseline data for possible epidemiologic studies; (3) to identify conditions which may place a worker at heightened risk of work-related illness; and (4) to obtain data on such risk factors as tobacco, alcohol, and drug consumption. Fitness for employment in biotechnology must be established on an individual basis for each potential worker with any underlying medical condition. Among the conditions which may place a worker at heightened risk of acquiring occupational illness in biotechnology are the following:[18]

- conditions which impair the non-specific defenses against infection (chronic skin, respiratory tract, and bowel disease);
- impaired immune competence;
- immunosuppression (caused, for example, by steroids, radiation therapy, alkylating agents, or antimetabolites);
- long-term treatment with antibiotics;
- cancer;
- other chronic illnesses, such as chronic kidney disease, diabetes mellitus, or the collagen diseases;.

The collection and storage of frozen serum samples has become a widely accepted practice in the biotechnology industry. A serum sample is generally taken from each worker at the start of employment and, in some instances, periodically thereafter.[16] Such samples should be retained for at least the duration of a worker's active employment in biotechnology. Serology programs will be most cost-effective when they either assess specifically the development of antibodies against antigens associated with the organisms or products in a particular process or when they are simply stored in a bank and held at -70°C for future study or for reference in the event of illness.

Periodic Follow-up Examinations - Comprehensive periodic medical examinations are generally of little value in the detection of occupational disease. Any periodic examinations incorporated into a surveillance program must be specifically targeted toward evaluation of the particular hazards which may confront a particular group of workers. For example, studies of endocrine function might be devised for workers engaged in the production of peptide or steroid hormones, or appropriate evaluations of immune function undertaken for workers producing interferon or other immunochemicals.

Follow-up Evaluation of Illness - A biotechnology worker who develops illness or is absent from work for 48 hours without explanation should be actively evaluated. The importance of such active pursuit cannot be overemphasized. The evaluation of such illness should consider (a) whether the symptoms are in any way relatable to the microorganisms or products in the worker's place of employment, (b) whether an accident has occurred in the facility; and whether the ill worker was involved in the accident; and (c) whether any illnesses have occurred in co-workers.

Epidemiological and Other Long-Term Follow-up Studies - The likelihood that epidemiologic evaluations of biotechnology workers will in the near term produce useful results is slight, given the relatively small numbers of exposed workers and the long induction-latency periods which may need to elapse between beginning of exposure and appearance of disease. In the longer term, however, epidemiologic studies may be extremely useful as a health surveillance tool. Specific follow-up studies intended to evaluate specific outcomes will be the most cost-effective form of epidemiologic follow-up. Among the outcomes to be considered for long-term surveillance might be increases in cancer incidence or mortality rates, increased rates of endocrine disorders, and elevated rates of immunologic diseases. Surveillance might also be directed to the detection of adverse reproductive outcomes in the offspring of male or female workers. Many such studies might require the concommitant evaluation of appropriate control groups.

The necessary foundation for any long-term studies of biotechnology workers will be the indefinite maintenance of careful records on each worker by each institution or firm engaged in biotechnology. At a minimum, such records must include the name of each worker, personal identifying information including Social Security number, results of all physical examinations and special medical tests, a complete history of work experience (including information on areas of work, specific jobs, and specific organisms, processes, and products encountered), and a record of any illnesses or of any accidents in which the worker was involved.

LIMITATIONS OF MEDICAL SURVEILLANCE

The likelihood is small that a medical surveillance program for biotechnology workers will detect any illness caused by recombined organisms or by their products or reagents. Neither the nature nor the possible time of onset of any such illness is known. Further, such illnesses may appear in only one or a few workers. Nonetheless, the detection of any occupational illness caused by recombinant organisms or by their products will have important biological and public health consequences, and should be actively sought.[16]

CONCLUDING COMMENT

Medical surveillance of workers engaged in biotechnology will be no substitute for other mechanisms for the protection of workers in this industry. Physical containment of organisms and of their products will remain the first line of defense against occupational exposures.[5] Institution of proper work practices and of accurate and comprehensive educational programs for workers will continue to be of great importance. Biological containment, resulting from use of attenuated or debilitated organisms remains another important protection. There is however, uncertainty as to the possible health consequences of employment in the industries which are contemplating commercial application of biotechnology. Medical surveillance, with all of its shortcomings, provides a means for addressing that uncertainty.

References

1. Biotechnology: Report of a Joint Working Party. London: Her Majesty's Stationery Office, 1980.

2. Baxter JD: Recombinant DNA and medical progress. Hospital Practice, February 1980, pp. 57-67.

3. Fox JL: Genetic engineering industry emerges. Chem Eng News, 17 March 1980, pp. 15-23.

4. Centers for Disease Control: Occupational health assessments in the biotechnology industry. MMWR, in press.

5. Centers for Disease Control: Proposed Biosafety Guidelines for Microbiological and Biomedical Laboratories. Atlanta: Centers for Disease Control, 1981.

6. Levy SB, Marshall B, Rowse-Eagle D, Onderdonk A: Survival of Escherichia coli host-vector systems in the mammalian intestine. Science 209:391-394, 1980.

7. National Institutes of Health: Program to Reduce the Risks of Recombinant DNA Research: Proposed First Annual Update. Federal Register 45 (192): 61874-61878, 17 September 1980.

8. Rosenberg G, Simon L: Recombinant DNA: have recent experiments assessed all the risks? Nature 282:773-774, 1979.

9. Liberman DF, Kovacic SA: Biotype determinations for monitoring of EK 1 host strains used in recombinant DNA research. J Clin Microbiol 8:99-101, 1978.

10. Harrington JM, Stein GF, Rivera RV, deMorales AV: The occupational hazards of formulating oral contraceptives - a survey of plant employees. Arch Environ Health 33:12-14, 1978.

11. Newton RW, Browning MCK, Iqbal J, Piercy N, Adamson DG: Adrenocortical suppression in workers manufacturing synthetic glucocorticoids. Brit Med J 1:73-75, 1978.

12. National Institute for Occupational Safety and Health. Health Hazard Evaluation Report (HE 77-66-531): Sucrets Department, Merck, Sharpe, and Dohme, West Point, Pennsylvania. Cincinnati: NIOSH, October 1978.

13. Centers for Disease Control: Renal failure and hepatitis from inhaled carbon tetrachloride and isopropyl alcohol - Tennessee. MMWR 24:59-60, 1975.

14. Centers for Disease Control: Sensitization of Laundry-Products Workers to Proteolytic Bacterial Enzymes - New Jersey. MMWR 30:127-128, 1981.

15. National Cancer Institute, Office of Biohazard Safety: Medical Surveillance Programs - A Review with Recommendations. Bethesda: National Cancer Institute, July 1980.

16. Rutstein DD, Berenberg W, Chalmers TC, Child CG, Fishman AP, Perrin EB: Measuring the quality of medical care - a clinical method. New Engl J Med 294:582-588, 1976.

17. Langmuir AD: The surveillance of communicable diseases of national importance. New Engl J Med 268:182, 1963.

18. Medical Research Council, Genetic Manipulation Adivsory Group: GMAG Note No. 6 - Health Monitoring. London: Medical Research Council, March 1978.

health industry
manufacturers
association **hima**

1030 15th street, nw • washington, dc 20005-1598 • (202) 452-8240

July ~~21~~ 30, 1982

Dr. Elizabeth Milewski
Office of Recombinant DNA Activities
NIAID, National Institutes of Health
Building 31, Room 4A52
Bethesda, Maryland 20205

Dear Elizabeth:

Enclosed is a copy of the comments which I made at the Large-Scale Meeting. I hope that by using my text you will save the bother of removing all the "ands" and "ahhs" from the actual transcript.

I would appreciate it if you would check to see that my name is on, or is added to, the list of those who wish to receive notification of all RAC activities and updates on the Guidelines. I would also like to receive your excellent publication, the Recombinant DNA Technical Bulletin.

With best wishes.

Sincerely,

Tim

Timothy J. Henry, Ph.D.
Director, Biological Sciences

Enclosure

REMARKS OF DR. ROBERT A. FILDES

Chairman

Industrial Biotechnology Association
Committee on Industrial Applications and Scale-Up

June 29, 1982

Good morning ladies and gentlemen.

I am Robert A. Fildes, President of Biogen Inc., and Vice President of the Industrial Biotechnology Association. I am appearing before you this morning, with the gentlemen at my side, on behalf of the IBA's Committee on Industrial Applications and Scale-Up. With me today are:

Mr. Harvey Price, Executive Director of the IBA,
Mr. John Galat of Schering-Plough, Inc.,
Mr. Rick Eustis of Biogen Inc.,
Dr. Bruce Hamilton of Genex Corporation, and
Dr. Asger Langlykke of Genex Corporation.

The IBA is an international trade association presently consisting of two dozen companies actively engaged in developing commercial products utilizing biotechnology. A list of current IBA member companies is attached to this statement. Many new members are anticipated in the next several months. We are here today at your request to present information concerning commercial development associated with rDNA research that we already received a great deal of positive feed-back and requests for participation from HIMA member scientists.

I would now like to offer a few comments on the NIOSH/CDC proposal for medical surveillance of the Biotechnology Industry. HIMA believes that while the NIOSH/CDC proposal has thoughtfully considered the majority of the pertinent issues, it does not come to the proper conclusion. The proposal itself clearly documents several solid reasons why such a project should not be undertaken. To quote from the document, they are as follows: "The health hazards of exposure to altered micro-organisms appear minimal; ------ medical surveillance of workers is inherently limited in its ability to detect disease; ---- groups under study will be relatively small, ----- individual exposures will vary; -----potentially there will be long latent periods."

In spite of these negative factors, NIOSH recommended surveillance on the basis of two weak arguments. These are that medical surveillance (1) affords a means for assessing the effectiveness of physical and biological containment and (2) it provides for early detection of unanticipated illness. The first argument is valid only if the process involves organisms which produce some known disease, i.e., when there is something to measure. Yet NIOSH has also said that "the health hazards of exposure to altered micro-organisms appear to be minimal. Thus, the first argument for surveillance has no rationale

in the vast majority of R-DNA industrial applications. As far as detection of new illness is concerned, HIMA was led to conclude that since the risk in minimal, the population studied is small, and the exposures variable, therefore, the sensitivity and power of the system to detect illness is small. Waiting for an unknown disease to appear can be expensive and is potentially unrewarding.
It is also important to point out that industrial applications of R-DNA are generally routine fermentations. Fermentation is not a new industry and most of the areas where problems can occur are alrady known. To say that the use of R-DNA derived microorganisms poses a new hazard would negate what has been distilled out of the RAC's 7 year history. That is, in essence, that any hazard in a R-DNA experiment is no greater than that of the most hazardous parental organism. Further, that is true only in the early research stages. By the time that a R-DNA containing microorganism reaches large-scale production, it is a well characterized entity.

HIMA has several questions about specific components of the suggested surveillance program which should be answered before any final recommendations are put forth, such as: Who will pay for the exams and serum storage? How frequently should the exams occur? If groups will be small, how can long term epidemiological studies even be contemplated? Since each biotechnology project or company will be unique in terms of the organisms used and end products, how can NIOSH hope to pool all "biotechnology" industries for purposes of medical surveillance given the variable "risks"?

HIMA recommends that without any defined hazard or end point, any suggestions for blanket medical surveillance of the biotechnology industry is simply not justified. Singling out Biotechnology is completely unwarrented and without merit.

HIMA recognizes the roles that NIOSH and CDC are expected to play, but simply does not agree with the proposal's conclusion that blanket medical surveillance of the biotechnology industry is advisable.

HIMA Comments on the Revised Edition of the document
"Medical Surveillance of Biotechnology Workers:
Report of the CDC/NIOSH Ad Hoc Working Group on
Medical Surveillance for Industrial Applications of Biotechnology."

Presented at the Large-Scale Working Group meeting, June 29, 1982.

My name is Timothy Henry. I'm Director of Biological Sciences for the Health Industry Manufacturers Association. HIMA is a trade association that represents 266 medical device and diagnostic product manufacturers with some 570 operating divisions with names familiar to all of you. Last year these companies had aggregate sales of more than 10 billion dollars.

Biotechnology is an ever increasing factor in the plans of HIMA companies. Hybridoma technology has already had an important and positive impact upon these companies. Recombinant DNA technology has not yet had a similar impact upon our companies, but it is obvious to all of us in the industry that our members will undoubtedly be using R-DNA in their everyday lab work. HIMA has established two internal biotechnology interest groups -- one on hybridomas and one on R-DNA issues--and we hope that these committees soon will be able to offer cogent and helpful comments on issues before this working group or before RAC. The HIMA R-DNA committee was just formed and I have believe will supplement the information otherwise available to you. We will also attempt to answer questions that you may have and to assist you in identifying areas of questions and dialogue that can benefit from the continued association of our two groups. We hope that this dialogue will contribute to an enhancement of public acceptance of the biotechnology industry and the regulatory climate in which we operate. To that end I will discuss our members' practices in general terms in several particular areas of biotechnology commercialization.

Compliance with the NIH Guidelines has become accepted industry practice. In addition the industry has complied with the extensive other regulations to which it is subject. The present government regulations governing our work other than the NIH Guidelines are already comprehensive (e.g., those of the EPA, OSHA, FDA, U.S.D.A.), yet we believe that we can work under these regulations and safely produce effective products. Additional regulation would contribute little to public health and safety and would be duplicative and cumbersome from industry's point of view. Accordingly, we believe that the present regulatory balance has been properly struck between the public and industry, and should not be altered significantly.

1. Current Industry Practice.

One of the areas in which we think we could be most helpful to you is informing you as to current industry practices in the area of biotechnology. The industry is beginning to make the transition from bench scale experiments to pilot plant operations. As part of that transition the industry has put into effect numerous practices which reflect our concern with safety of workers and the environment. Examples of industry practices among our members include:

a. Use of physical and biological containment based on the NIH Guidelines;

b. Sterilization of wastes prior to disposal;

c. Challenge and validation of safety procedures;

d. Use of accounting systems for biologically active products consistent with Good Laboratory Practices and Good Manufacturing Practices;

e. Health monitoring programs; and

f. Careful design of procedures and equipment to minimize the possibility and effects of human error.

These are but a few of the areas in which we have instituted special controls. Many of these practices result from the regulations of the various agencies to which our industry is already subject. Others result from compliance with the NIH Guidelines and from our concern for worker and environmental safety. Finally, certain practices result from the knowledge we have gained from extensive experience in the fermentation of antibiotics and other biochemicals. These fermentations are very similar to the operations involved in fermentation of biotechnology products and provide an information base which we believe is very relevant to large-scale rDNA experiments. Many of our members have extensive experience in antibiotic and other large scale fermentation processes; others have employed as experts persons with extensive pharmaceutical experience in this area. Also, the IBA represents a forum in which significant aspects of industrial expertise can be shared among our members. It is our belief that the present industry standards represent a high level of care which exceeds that necessary for the kinds of experiments which are presently being carried out or contemplated at large-scale levels.

2. Problems with Present Large Scale Recommendations.

Our experience has indicated that the present Physical Containment Recommendations for Large-Scale Uses of Organisms Containing Recombinant DNA Molecules are reasonable and workable, although they are quite stringent for work at the P1-LS level. The design requirements in the Recommendations make sense to us and are consistent with other regulations relating to the manufacture of products for use with human subjects.

While it has not yet been a problem for IBA members, we believe there are potential difficulties arising from the requirement in Section VII-B-2 of the Recommendations that the primary containment system not be opened until all microorganisms are inactivated. To the extent that this requirement means that all recombinant microorganisms must be killed, it may be very difficult in some processes to do so without compromising the product. Killing the organism prior to opening the containment system is not pharmaceutical industry practice in certain fermentations such as those used for some antibiotics. While this situation does not call for a present solution, we wish to alert the Working Group as to its potential for causing difficulties as more fermentations move to the large-scale step.

3. IBC Review Has Proved Satisfactory.

The IBC plays a key role under the present NIH Guidelines. Our experience with IBCs has been favorable and we believe that they are the most appropriate entity for the detailed monitoring of large-scale work. We strongly recommend their continued use.

Our members have generally found the IBCs to be useful and productive. For example, IBCs are valuable in assuring the community that independent review of experiments does exist. While we are convinced by worldwide experience that rDNA research is safe, the IBCs will help establish an expanded data base which will further demonstrate the safety of this work. In addition, IBCs bring together many different expertises and allow all safety issues to be addressed in a single forum within a company.

Most of the work being performed by IBA members is classified as exempt or P1. We feel that a full-blown IBC review prior to initiation of an exempt large-scale experiment is not necessary. We recommend that exempt experiments require only simultaneous notification to the IBC and not prior approval of the IBC. This approach seems particularly appropriate because classification as exempt means that the issue of safety has already been addressed. Moreover, large-scale experiments will be performed in a facility which has previously been approved by the relevant IBC. Within the IBA there is significant sentiment for requiring only simultaneous IBC notice (as opposed to prior approval) for P1 experiments as well as for exempt experiments.

For your information many of our members supplement their IBC review with frequent monitoring through various kinds of safety committees. These committees are able to monitor the experiments on a day to day basis. At the same time internal safety committees obviate the concern for unnecessary disclosure of proprietary information which sometimes causes problems with an IBC. We believe that these safety committees are a good example of a useful addition to IBC review that can improve the overall process of monitoring.

General safety committees are industry practice now and, I believe, are useful not only to supplement the IBC review as indicated above but are also valuable in assessing and controlling safety risks of a more general nature. Such committees might typically review the use of flammable solvents, the design and safety of particular items of equipment, fire safety, emergency procedures and similar safety issues. Because of our view of the safety of rDNA research per se, many of us see the conventional safety issues as the more significant ones to be assessed and controlled.

4. <u>The 10 Liter Limit</u>.

Our membership has no problems with 10 liters as the boundary between large and small scale experiments. We do feel that 10 liters is an arbitrary boundary and certainly does not reflect industry practice. Most industrial pilot plant operations, for example, take place at the 250-3,000 liter size. As additional experience is accumulated with industrial applications, we think the committee will find it logically compelling to adjust the large-scale threshold upward.

5. <u>Medical Monitoring</u>.

Virtually all of our members have instituted medical surveillance programs. Common to most of these programs are medical check-ups, storage of serum samples and follow-ups in cases of extended or serious illnesses. Since the IBCs through the institutions are charged with the task of reviewing medical monitoring programs as part of their obligations under the Guidelines, these programs can be supplemented by the IBC in the case of particular experiments. Thus, if any special requirements are appropriate in the case of a particular experiment, the IBC can require a special program of medical monitoring. We think this approach is most reasonable and recommend its continuance.

A number of our members question the need for any medical surveillance program directed toward recombinant DNA experimentation specifically since there is no evidence of any hazard unique to rDNA experimentation. Moreover, it is widely agreed by health experts that it is very difficult to run meaningful medical surveillance without knowing what you are looking for. As the draft report on medical surveillance by CDC/NIOSH acknowledges, "comprehensive periodic medical examinations are generally of little value in the detection of occupational disease". Finally, we know that there are significant costs to these programs. Also important is the fact that we are forcing employees to undergo mandatory medical procedures, an intrusion on privacy which many find objectionable, in part because there is no obvious benefit. In summary we are presently not in favor of required medical surveillance directed specifically at rDNA work.

6. <u>Continuing RAC - Industry Dialogue</u>.

Finally, Mr. Chairman, I would like to stress from industry's point of view the high value that we place on the type of dialogue that your committee has formally initiated today, as well as our belief that direct benefits can be anticipated from its continuation and strengthening.

In the next several years industrial applications of rDNA research procedures and products will certainly grow. With its established scientific expertise, credibility and record of demonstrated sensitivity to public interests, the RAC can and should reasonably contribute to identifying and exploring rDNA issues particularly relevant to commercial use. Such activity could complement the regulatory actions of various agencies (many of which presently have liaison representation on the RAC and Large Scale Review Working Group) and minimize the need for repetitive treatment of issues. Thus, without preempting any regulatory authority, the RAC would become a focal point for efficiently addressing rDNA issues important to both science and commercial development. Under such a reasonable regime, industry's commitment to full compliance with RAC guidance would be expected to continue and be strengthened.

To move toward successful implementation of this role, we offer two specific suggestions. First, both the Large Scale Review Working Group and the RAC itself would benefit by being kept better informed on what is taking place in industry. We therefore suggest that an industry representative be placed on each body - without voting power but with responsibility to insure that industrial approaches and perspectives are taken into account on decisions affecting such interests. If we were requested to do so, IBA would be pleased to designate an expert with actual large scale rDNA experience to serve in this role.

Secondly, we believe that dialogue between the IBA and the Large Scale Review Working Group should continue periodically on a regular basis. We have freely expressed some of our committee's views and concerns to you today. We look forward to hearing whatever questions you may have. In light of your responsibility to advise the RAC on scale-up matters, we are confident that a regular channel of communication can be established which will promote understanding and respect for our various points of view, which will sharpen issues that should be constructively addressed and which will minimize undue strains on the NIH and industrial community as we pursue compatible goals.

Mr. Chairman, I appreciate the opportunity to have made this statement today, and my collegues and I would be pleased at this time to try to address any questions that you may have.

federal register

Friday
August 27, 1982

Part III

Department of Health and Human Services

National Institutes of Health

Recombinant DNA Research; Actions Under Guidelines

DEPARTMENT OF HEALTH AND HUMAN SERVICES

National Institutes of Health

Recombinant DNA Research; Actions Under Guidelines

AGENCY: National Institutes of Health, PHS, DHHS.

ACTION: Notice of actions under NIH Guidelines for Research Involving Recombinant DNA Molecules.

SUMMARY: This notice sets forth actions taken by the Director, National Institute of Allergy and Infectious Diseases, by authority of the Director, NIH, under the April 1982 Guidelines for Research Involving Recombinant DNA Molecules (47 FR 17180).

EFFECTIVE DATE: August 27, 1982.

FOR FURTHER INFORMATION CONTACT: Additional information can be obtained from Dr. William J. Gartland, Office of Recombinant DNA Activities (ORDA), National Institutes of Health, Bethesda, Maryland 20205 (301) 496-6051.

SUPPLEMENTARY INFORMATION: I am promulgating today a major action under the NIH Guidelines for Research Involving Recombinant DNA Molecules. This action involves a major revision of the Guidelines. In accordance with Section IV-E-1-b of the Guidelines, I find that this action complies with the Guidelines and presents no significant risk to health or the environment.

The structure of this announcement is as follows:

I. Background.
II. Draft Minutes of June 28, 1982, Meeting of the Recombinant DNA Advisory Committee (RAC).
III. Response of Director, NIAID, to the RAC Recommendations.
IV. Additional Changes.

Immediately following this announcement, there appears in separate section of the **Federal Register** the revised NIH Guidelines for Research Involving Recombinant DNA Molecules.

I. Background

The Recombinant DNA Advisory Committee (RAC) at its February 8-9, 1982 meeting, recommended that the National Institutes of Health (NIH) accept a proposed modification (46 FR 59734) of the NIH Guidelines for Research Involving Recombinant DNA Molecules. In supporting this modification, the RAC recommended that a working group be formed to simplify further and modify the document. On April 21, 1982, the NIH promulgated the revised Guidelines (47 FR 17180).

An *ad hoc* Working Group on Revision of the Guidelines was formed and convened for a meeting on April 19, 1982. The committee addressed several issues at this meeting. This first topic was an attempt to improve the "presentation" of the Guidelines. It was felt that most of Section II, which describes physical and biological containment standards, as well as shipping, should be moved to three separate new Appendices (G, H, and I). In addition, the section describing shipment (currently II-C) should be expanded to include further information on packaging and labeling. It was noted that the current Guidelines provide little concrete guidance for shipping materials; rather, they refer the reader to other sources.

Language describing "General Applicability" and "General Definitions" should be removed from Section IV and placed in Section I.

The working group discussed the question of whether the language of Section III-A-1 and Appendix F which refers to "toxins" also applies to other pharmacologically active molecules. A correspondent had questioned whether "pharmacologically active molecules" such as certain hormones should be treated as toxins. Pointing to Section I-B, second paragraph, which cites: "a toxin or a pharmacologically active agent," the working group agreed that the intent of the Guidelines is to cover these types of molecules and recommended that the language dealing with toxins in the Guidelines be amended to reflect that intent.

The working group discussed the issue of which document should be utilized to determine the pathogenic classification of an organism. The original 1976 Guidelines used the publication *Classification of Etiologic Agents on the Basis of Hazard*, 4th edition, July 1974; U.S. Department of Health, Education and Welfare, Public Health Service, Center for Disease Control, as the reference source for classification of microorganisms for the purposes of the Guidelines. All subsequent revisions of the Guidelines have also used this document. At the present time, the Centers for Disease Control (CDC) and the NIH are engaged in an effort to revise the *Classification of Etiologic Agents on the Basis of Hazard*. The working group felt, however, that this revised version might not serve the purposes of the Guidelines as well as the original 1974 version. Nonetheless, the working group noted that additional pathogens should be added to the classification in the Guidelines and that the classification should be updated regularly. It was also noted that some organisms might better be treated in a manner specific for the purposes of the Guidelines. The working group recommended, therefore, that the RAC and NIH adopt for the Guidelines a revised version of the 1974 CDC classification, and that the RAC should assume responsibility for regularly updating the listing. The working group recommended that (a) the following bacteria be added to the list of Class 2 bacterial agents:

Aeromonas hydrophila
Campylobacter fetus
Campylobacter jejuni
Edwardsiella tarda
Yersinia enterocolitica

and the listing for *Escherichia coli* be changed to refer to "all enteropathogenic, enterotoxigenic, enteroinvasive, and strains bearing Kl antigen;" (b) Vesicular stomatitis virus be listed as a Class 2 viral agent rather than a Class 3 viral agent; (c) Rabies street virus be classified as a Class 3 viral agent for all procedures; (d) Alastrim, Smallpox, and Whitepox should be listed as Class 5 viral agents rather than as Class 3 and Class 4 agents as the study of these viruses is restricted to a single national facility national facility (WHO Collaborating Center for Smallpox Research, Centers for Disease Control) and the language dealing with Poxviruses modified accordingly; (e) Viruses classified as low risk oncogenic viruses by the *National Cancer Institute Safety Standards for Research Involving Oncogenic Viruses* (October 1974, U.S. Department of Health, Education, and Welfare Publication Number (NIH) 75-790) should be classified as Class 2 agents for the purposes of the Guidelines; and (f) Moderate-risk oncogenic viruses should be classified as Class 3 agents for the purposes of the Guidelines. Furthermore, footnotes, references, and the title of Appendix B should be modified to reflect the status of a revised Appendix B.

The working group dealt with the issue of the composition of the Institutional Biosafety Committees (IBCs). A discussion arose as to the necessity of stating in current Section IV-D-2-a that not less than 20 percent of the membership of the IBC shall not be affiliated with the institution. It was felt that the 20 percent specification limits the flexibility of the university in appointing members to the IBC. The example was offered of an IBC fulfilling the 20 percent specification, but wishing to add an additional specialist affiliated with the university. However, non-affiliated representation would fall below 20 percent when this specialist is appointed and the university would have to appoint another non-affiliated member. The specification that at least two members shall not be affiliated with the institution should remain in the Guidelines to ensure community representation. It was felt that in a twenty member committee, two public members would provide adequate representation for the community. Members of the working group could not envisage IBCs larger than 20 members functioning smoothly. In addition, it was noted that ORDA reviews IBC membership for compliance and would be alert to cases in which an institution might attempt to dilute community representation by, for example, appointing a 50 member committee.

The working group also considered the language of current Section IV-D-2-b. A discussion ensued regarding representation on the IBC from the laboratory technical staff. If the term "nondoctoral" was deleted, postdoctoral associates might also be appointed to the IBC. Other members of the working group pointed out that technicians are, indeed, those most likely to be performing recombinant DNA experiments and those having the least "competitive" pressures exerted on them. Although technicians do experience certain types of pressures, many on the working group felt they would be among the best "watchpersons."

The working group also recommended a number of additional changes in the Guidelines. The recommendations of the working group, with minor modifications introduced by NIH staff were summarized in a **Federal Register** announcement on May 26, 1982 (47 FR 23110). The proposed revised Guidelines, incorporating the changes, were printed in their entirety in the same **Federal Register** announcement. Several additional proposed changes were also published for comment.

On June 28, 1982, the RAC reviewed the proposed revised Guidelines and the one letter of comment received on the proposed revisions. Part II of this announcement contains the draft minutes of the relevant portion of the June 28, 1982, RAC meeting. Part III gives the response of the Director, National Institute of Allergy and Infectious Diseases, to the RAC recommendations.

II. Draft Minutes of Relevant Portions of June 28, 1982, Meeting of the Recombinant DNA Advisory Committee

Dr. Nightingale began discussion of the modifications (tabs 1071, 1072, 1074) to the Guidelines proposed by the Working Group on Revision of the Guidelines. She recalled to the committee that the RAC at its February 8-9, 1982 meeting, recomended that the NIH accept a proposed modification of the NIH Guidelines for Research Involving Recombinant DNA Molecules. In recommending this modification to the NIH, the committee recommended that a working group be formed to further simplify and modify the document. The NIH, following this recommendation, promulgated the Revised Guidelines on April 21, 1982. An *ad hoc* Working Group on Revision of the Guidelines was formed and convened for a meeting on April 19, 1982, to further modify the document promulgated on April 21, 1982. Dr. Nightingale said the working group attempted to clarify and simplify, wherever possible, the structure and language of the Guidelines, to suggest changes appropriate in light of available data, and to recommend future activities in the area of guideline review and revision.

Dr. Nightingale then indicated four major proposed modifications offered by this working group. First, the working group had suggested the presentation of the Guidelines be rearranged primarily by placing the description of physical and biological containment into appendices. Second, the working group recommended that the RAC and NIH adopt for the Guidelines a revised version of the 1974 CDC *Classification of Etiologic Agents on the Basis of Hazard.* The working group also suggested that the RAC assume responsibility for regularly updating the listing. Dr. Nightingale explained that the original 1976 Guidelines used the *Classification of Etiologic Agents on the Basis of Hazard,* 4th Edition, July 1974, U.S. Department of Health, Education, and Welfare, Public Health Service, Center for disease Control (CDC), as the reference source for classification of microorganisms for the purposes of the Guidelines. At the present time, the CDC and the NIH are engaged in an effort to revise this classification. The working group, however, felt that this revised version might not serve the purposes of the Guidelines as well as the original 1974 version as revised. This is the only proposal of the working group that received a letter of comment, and Dr. Berns said he wished to reply to an issue raised by Dr. John Richardson of the CDC in a letter of June 10, 1982 (tab 1074), concerning the proposed revision of Appendix B for the purposes of the NIH Guidelines. Dr. Berns said the proposed revised classification would classify Rabies street virus as a Class 3 agent for all procedures. Dr. Richardson suggested that a Class 2 designation was adequate. Dr. Berns said he had discussed the issue with Dr. Richardson and they had agreed that a Class 3 specification for Rabies street virus was more appropriate for the purposes of the NIH Guidelines; investigators following the NIH Guidelines would more probably be using chemical quantities of viruses, rather than the quantities needed for diagnostic purposes on which the CDC classification was based.

Third, Dr. Nightingale said the working group had discussed at length the role and responsibilities of the IBCs. They noted that a greater burden had been placed on the IBCs by the April 21, 1982, revision of the Guidelines. The working group discussed whether RAC should collect information about IBC functions. One suggestion was that a questionnaire be sent to all IBCs.

Mr. Mitchell commented that the IBCs have been delegated a great deal of responsibility, but RAC has little data on the actual functioning and effectiveness of the IBCs. He suggested that some mechanism of specific communication between RAC and the IBCs should be developed.

Fourth, Dr. Nightingale noted that the working group suggested an ongoing process of review and revision of the Guidelines; such a process should occur with some regular periodicity, perhaps once a year.

Mr. Thornton suggested that RAC proceed through the proposed revisions of the Guidelines section by section; amendments could then be offered in an orderly fashion. He requested a formal motion to adopt the proposed revised Guidelines as they appeared in the **Federal Register** of May 26, 1982 (tab 1072). Dr. Ahmed so moved, and Dr. Berns seconded the motion. Dr. Mason offered an amendment to commend the working group for its outstanding efforts in generating the proposed document. Dr. Ahmed accepted the amendment as did Dr. Berns.

Beginning with Section I of the Guidelines, Dr. Baltimore questioned the words "potentially harmful polynucleotide" in the second paragraph of Section I-B, *Definition of Recombinant DNA Molecules.* He asked how synthetic DNA segments could yield "potentially harmful polynucleotides" other than being translated to "potentially harmful polypeptides". Dr. Wensink suggested it might be a transposable element. It was agreed to leave the language as proposed.

Dr. Baltimore said that a "pharmacologically active agent" is equated with a toxin in Section I-B. He questioned that language. It was pointed out that the text says "e.g., a toxin or a pharmacologically active agent" and does not necessarily equate the two. Also the text is identical with that in the current April 21, 1982 version of the Guidelines. Dr. Berns said the working group determined that proposals to clone genes for certain biologically active polypeptides should be carefully evaluated, as were proposals involving toxins. The language of Section III-A-1 and Appendix F have been modified to reflect this intent. Dr. Berns said these sections specify the LD50s that define "biologically active polypeptides." It was agreed to leave the language as proposed.

Dr. Nightingale then reviewed the proposed changes in Section III. She noted that a "caution" had been added to Section III-B-3. That caution is as follows:

CAUTION: Special care should be used in the evaluation of containment levels for experiments which are likely to either enhance the pathogenicity (e.g., insertion of a host oncogene) or to extend the host range (e.g., introduction of novel control elements) of viral vectors under conditions which permit a productive infection. In such cases, serious consideration should be given to raising physical containment by at least one level.

Dr. Nightingale said this is one instance where new information suggested that a caution be added. Dr. Ahmed asked to whom the caution was addressed. Dr. Berns replied that the caution is addressed primarily to the IBC. Dr. Ahmed asked if the phrase "consideration by the IBC" should be added. He felt the caution as proposed appeared parenthetical; the IBC should be cited more explicitly. Dr. Berns did not accept Dr. Ahmed's suggestion as he felt responsibility should be incumbent on both the investigator and the IBC. Dr. Ahmed withdrew the proposal.

Dr. Nightingale asked if Dr. Ahmed, as the maker of the motion, would agree to strike the work "viral" in Section III-B-2-a. The language reads in part:

* * * Recombinant DNA experiments in which DNA from Class 4 agents is transferred into nonpathogenic prokaryotes or lower eukaryotes can be performed at P2 containment after demonstration that only a totally and irreversibly defective fraction of the agent's viral genome is present in a given recombinant.

Dr. Berns explained that currently all Class 4 agents classified in Appendix B are viruses. That situation might, however, change in the future, and deleting the word "viral" in Section III-B-2-a would provide greater flexibility. Dr. Ahmed agreed to delete the word "viral."

Dr. Gottesman noted that language from Sections III-B-2-a and III-B-2-b of the April 21, 1982, Guidelines had been combined by the working group into a new Section III-B-2-a. In so doing, the working group had moved experiments involving a totally and irreversibly defective fraction of Class 4 agents into Section III-B-2-a, and delegated authority to the IBC to lower containment on experiments involving these agents.

Dr. Nightingale mentioned the inadvertment omission in Section III-B-4-a of language dealing with USDA permits for working with Class 5 agents, and suggested suitable language be inserted analogous to that found at the end of Section III-B-2-b. Mr. Thornton asked if Dr. Ahmed would agree to insertion of such language in Section III-B-4-a. Dr. Ahmed agreed as did Dr. Berns.

Dr. Nightingale then referred to Section III-C, *Experiments that Require IBC Notice Simultaneously with Initiation of Experiments*. The first sentence of this section reads as follows:

Experiments not included in Section III-A, III-B, III-D, and subsections of these sections are to be considered in Section III-C.

She said the working group was concerned with the language of this section. They noted that non-exempt experiments which might merit more stringent review by RAC or by the IBC prior to initiation of the experiment might not be adequately described in Sections III-A and III-B and, thus, would automatically fall into Section III-C. Dr. Nightingale suggested that a reference be added at the end of the first paragraph of Section III-C drawing the reader's attention to the first two paragraphs of Section IV-A, which emphasizes the responsibility of the institution and those associated with it. Dr. Nightingale said the clause emphasizing institutional responsibility in Section IV-A ought to read:

* * * Therefore, it is the responsibility of the Institution and those associated with it to adhere to the intent of the Guidelines as well as to their specifics.

The RAC agreed that the word "intent" should be substituted for the word "purpose" which was used in the version proposed by the working group. Dr. Ahmed agreed to add a reference to Section IV-A in Section III-C and to substitute the word "intent" for the word "purpose" in the language of Section IV-A. Dr. Berns agreed.

Dr. Baltimore questioned why low-risk oncogenic viruses had been classified in proposed Appendix B as Class 2 agents. He said most are not human pathogens at all, and many are extremely innocuous. He felt that classifying low-risk oncogenic viruses as Class 1 agents and moderate-risk oncogenic viruses as Class 2 agents would be more reasonable. Dr. Berns did not agree completely; he felt some of the moderate-risk oncogenic viruses, such as Herpesvirus saimiri or EB virus, should be classified as Class 3 agents. Dr. Baltimore agreed that Herpesvirus saimiri might be classified as a Class 3 agent but felt Rous sarcoma virus be classified as Class 1. Dr. Berns ageed that the list warranted closer looking at, but he did not feel that this RAC meeting was the appropriate time for such a virus by virus review. Dr. McKinney pointed out that P2 provides the investigator with physical protection that is desirable and necessary for working with these agents.

He suggested low-risk oncogenic viruses should be used under Class 2 containment conditions. Dr. Baltimore noted that in the current Guidelines a listing is given in Appendix B of low-risk and moderate-risk oncogenic viruses, but no containment relative to the Guidelines is specified. The proposed revised Guidelines include the new statements that low-risk oncogenic viruses "should be treated as Class 2 agents" and moderate-risk oncogenic viruses "should be treated as Class 3 agents." Therefore, this involves an increased stringency of the proposed revised Guidelines for these agents.

Dr. Brill questioned the inclusion of all *Klebsiella* strains as Class 2 agents in Appendix B. He said *Klebsiella* species are ubiquitous. Dr. Berns point out that *Klebsiella* was classified as Class 2 in the original 1974 edition of the *Classification of Etiologic Agents;* the working group had not changed its classification. Dr. Holmes said he could suggest several modifications to Appendix B: he agreed with Dr. Richardson that *Schistosoma mansoni* should be Class 2; the Psittacosis-Ornithosis-Trachoma group needs to be revised; consideration should be given to grouping *Mycobacterium leprae* with *Mycobacterium tuberculosis*. Mr. Thornton suggested in view of the number of specific concerns expressed concerning Appendix B that a working group review the list and report to the RAC at its next meeting. This was agreed to.

Dr. Nightingale reviewed the proposed changes in Section IV, *Roles and Responsibilities*. These modifications include:

(1) in Section IV-B-2, language was inserted to the effect that the IBC's

"responsibilities need not be restricted to recombinant DNA,"

(2) in Section IV-B-2-a, the requirement was deleted that 20 percent of the IBC membership not be affiliated with the institution (although the requirement was retained that at least 2 IBC members not be affiliated with the institution) and

(3) in Section IV-B-2-b, language recommending that "at least one member be a nondoctoral person from a laboratory technical staff" was modified to read "at least one member be from the laboratory technical staff."

Dr. Berns commented on the proposal to delete the word "nondoctoral". He said some members of the working group felt a "nondoctoral" technician with actual "hand-on" experience was most appropriate for this "slot" on the IBC. Others members felt that anyone who had "hand on" experience and who was not a principal investigator (including technician, research associate or post-doctoral fellow) was an appropriate representative of the laboratory technical staff. Following much discussion, the term "nondoctoral" had been deleted from the proposed revised Guidelines by the working group.

Dr. Ahmed questioned why the requirement was deleted that 20 percent of the IBC membership by non-affiliated with the institution. Dr. Berns offered the example of an IBC just fulfilling the 20 percent specification, but wishing to add an additional specialist affiliated with the university.

When this specialist was appointed, non-affiliated representation would fall below 20 percent, and the university would have to appoint another non-affiliated member. Dr. Berns said the working group felt the percentage of non-affiliated members was not critical as long as two non-affiliated members were present on the IBC. Dr. Ahmed pointed out that on an IBC composed of 20 members, with 2 non-affiliated members, non-affiliated representation would be 10 percent, or half of the non-affiliated composition mandated under the current Guidelines. He said the failure to maintain this requirement troubled him. Dr. Mason point out that a five-membered IBC would have at least 40 percent of its membership non-affiliated. Dr. McKinney said he believed that the institution, which appoints members to the IBC, will respond to the intent of the Guidelines and appoint IBCs of an appropriate composition.

Moving to the next section, Dr. Nightingale called the attention of the RAC to Section IV-B-2-f. Section IV-B-2-f reads:

Institutions are encouraged to open IBC meetings to the public whenever possible, consistent with protection of privacy and proprietary interests.

Dr. Nightingale said no modifications were suggested for this section, but noted that one member of the working group, Ms. King, felt the issue of open meetings should be evaluated at some point in the future, and that open meetings probably should eventually be required.

Dr. Nightingale finally noted the addition of proposed language to Section IV-D-4. The proposed language reads:

Note.—Other Federal agencies which have adopted the NIH Guidelines may have the authority to terminate funding to their grantees should these grantees not comply with the NIH Guidelines.

She felt this statement is not sufficient and that the section should be expanded to include a description of the Federal Interagency Advisory Committee on Recombinant DNA Research and of its membership. Dr. Goldstein felt that some description of the Interagency Committee, particularly a statement that its members have agreed to abide by the NIH Guidelines, would be desirable. Dr. Gottesman suggested that an Appendix, describing the Interagency Committee, its agency members, and a statement that these agencies have agreed to abide by the Guidelines, be added to the Guidelines. References would be made to this new Appendix at (1) Section IV-C-1-a-(4) which describes the Director's responsibility for maintaining this committee, and (2) under Section IV-D-4 in place of the "Note." Dr. Ahmed suggested the proposed Appendix should also describe how the Interagency Committee was formed, who it reports to, and what responsibilities member agencies have assumed with respect to the NIH Guidelines. Dr. Ahmed agreed to accept this amendment, as did Dr. Berns.

Dr. Goldstein said he still had concerns on the potential use of recombinant DNA technology for biological warfare. He noted that the Department of Defense (DoD) is a member of the Interagency Committee. He said that earlier in the meeting RAC heard of classified research conducted by DoD. However, several questions on this research had not been answered to Dr. Goldstein's satisfaction by the DoD representative. Dr. McCullough said that many DoD biomedical research projects are unclassified, but there are projects in defensive biological warfare techniques and processes that are classified. These projects might include aerosol detection devices, antibody identification devices, or air sampling processes. These are not weapons. Dr. Goldstein asked if the motion made earlier in the meeting concerning the use of recombinant DNA technology for biological warfare might be reconsidered. Dr. Ahmed seconded. By a vote of five in favor, thirteen opposed, and no abstentions the RAC, however, refused to reconsider the earlier motion.

Mr. Thorton called the attention of the RAC to Part D of tab 1072 which includes certain sections of the current Guidelines which the working group suggested deleting but which NIH staff felt should be retained. He said the version which Dr. Ahmed had moved includes these sections. If any member does not approve of the retention of any section, a specific motion to delete should be made. The sections to be retained are: (1) Section I-D-5 of Section I-D, *General Definitions*, which defines "Director, NIH," (2) Section IV-B-5-b and its subsections of IV-B-5, *Principal Investigator*, which deals with submissions by the principal investigator to the NIH, (3) Section IV-C-1-b-(1)-(a) and Section IV-C-1-b-(1)-(b) of Section IV-C-1-b, *Specific Responsibilities of the Director*, and (4) Section IV-C-1-b-(2) and its subsections which detail certain lesser actions which are the responsibility of the Director. No motion to delete any of these sections was made.

Dr. Brill returned to the issue of the classification of *Klebsiella* as a Class 2 agent in Appendix B. He suggested that the language in Appendix B which reads "*Klebsiella*—all species and all serotypes" be modified to read "*Klebsiella*—all strains known to originate from human and animal sources." Dr. Gottesman asked what an investigator would assume if he did not know the source of a strain. Dr. Brill replied that an investigator would assume that particular *Klebsiella* strain was a Class 1 agent. Dr. Gottesman pointed out that no new restrictions were being imposed on investigators working with *Klebsiella* by the proposed revised Guidelines. She questioned the appropriateness of modifying this language at this RAC meeting without data sufficient to formulate a reasonable motion. She felt a working group could examine the issue in greater detail. Dr. Ahmed agreed the issue should be referred to a working group; he felt insufficient information was available at the moment. Dr. McKinney said the *Classification of Etiologic Agents* states that "human etiologic agents" have been classified. Presumably, those strains of *Klebsiella* classified in proposed Appendix B are only the human pathogens. Dr. Tolin pointed out that *Klebsiella* appears in Sublist A of Appendix A, and therefore many experiments involving *Klebsiella* will be totally exempt from the Guidelines.

Dr. Holmes suggested that the RAC might follow either of two options: (1) Recommend Appendix B as proposed by the working group, or (2) retain Appendix B as it appears in the current Guidelines. He said he would suggest, as an amendment, that RAC retain Appendix B as it currently appears in the Guidelines. Dr. Berns disagreed; he said few substantive changes had been made in proposed Appendix B, and he would not accept Dr. Holmes' amendment. Dr. Holmes withdrew his amendment.

Mr. Thornton called the question on Dr. Ahmed's motion to recommend the proposed revised Guidelines, as amended. By a vote of eighteen in favor, none opposed, and no abstentions, the motion was accepted.

Response of Director, NIAID, to the RAC Recommendations

In this section, I will review the recommendations of the RAC on the proposed revised Guidelines. They were published for public comment in the **Federal Register** of May 26, 1982. Only one comment was received, from Dr. John Richardson, Director, Office of Biosafety, Centers for Disease Control. The comment dealt solely with Appendix B of the Guidelines and is discussed below under that heading.

The RAC at its June 28, 1982, meeting took the proposed revised Guidelines as they appeared in the **Federal Register** on May 26, 1982, as a starting point. They recommended a few additional changes which are discussed below, and then voted eighteen in favor, none opposed, and no abstentions to recommend this Guideline revision.

A. Parts I and II

The RAC recommended no changes in Parts I and II of the proposed revised Guidelines as published in the **Federal Register** of May 26, 1982 (47 FR 23110). I accept this recommendation.

B. Part III

In Section III–B–2–a, the RAC recommended deletion of the word "viral" in the second sentence which read as follows in the proposed revised Guidelines:

Recombinant DNA experiments in which DNA from Class 4 agents is transferred into nonpathogenic prokaryotes or lower eukaryotes can be performed at P2 containment after demonstration that only a totally irreversibly defective fraction of the agent's *viral* genome is present in a given recombinant. (Underlining added.)

The reason for the RAC's recommendation for deletion of the word "viral" is that although only viral agents are currently classified as Class 4 agents, removal of the specification of "viral" would allow for the possible introduction of different types of Class 4 agents in the future. I accept this recommendation.

At the end of Section III–B–4–a, the RAC recommended that language should be added regarding the requirement for a USDA permit for work with Class 5 agents. I accept this recommendation, and the following sentence has been added at the end of Section III–B–4–a:

A USDA permit is required for work with Class 5 agents [18,20].

At the end of the first paragraph of Section III–C, the RAC recommended that a reference should be added during the reader's attention to the policy statement in the first two paragraphs of Section IV–A. Section III–C deals with experiments not included in Sections III–A, III–B, or III–D. Concern had been raised that non-exempt experiments which might merit more stringent review by RAC or by the IBC prior to initiation of the experiment might not be adequately described in Sections III–A and III–B and, thus, would automatically fall into Section III–C. The working group members requested that the language of Section III–C be evaluated by the RAC in the hope that language might be developed to alert researchers and IBCs of this possibility. The first two paragraphs of the policy statement in Section IV–A state that the Guidelines cannot anticipate every possible situation, and that it is the responsibility of the institution to adhere to the intent of the Guidelines as well as to their specifics.

I accept the recommendation of the RAC that a reference to the first two paragraphs of Section IV–A be added to Section III–C. Accordingly, the following wording has been added at the end of the first paragraph of Section III–C:

(The reader should refer to the policy statement in the first two paragraphs of Section IV–A.)

Other than the changes discussed above, the RAC recommended adoption of Part III of the proposed revised Guidelines as published in the **Federal Register** of May 26, 1982 (47 FR 23110). I accept this recommendation.

C. Part IV

The RAC recommended changing the word "purpose" to "intent" in the last sentence of the second paragraph of Section IV–A to reflect more clearly the meaning of this sentence.

I accept this recommendation, and the last sentence of the second paragraph of Section IV–A has been modified to read as follows:

Therefore, *it is the responsibility of the Institution and those associated with it to adhere to the intent of the Guidelines as well as to their specifics.*

Under Section IV–B–2–a, I note that the RAC recommended accepting the proposal of the working group that the requirement for nonaffiliated membership on an Institutional Biosafety Committee (IBC) be changed to "at least two members" from the previous requirement for "at least two members (but not less than 20 percent of the membership of the committee)." I also note that in Section IV–B–2–b, dealing with recommendations for the composition of an IBC, the RAC recommended accepting the modification of item (iii) to read "at least one member be from the laboratory technical staff." The previous version read: "at least one member be a nondoctoral person from a laboratory technical staff." I accept these recommendations.

At the end of Section IV–C–1–a–(4), the RAC recommended addition of a reference to a new Appendix J (See discussion of Appendix J below). I accept this recommendation.

The RAC recommended deletion of the "Note" in Section IV–D–4 which had been proposed to read as follows:

Other Federal agencies which have adopted the NIH Guidelines may have the authority to terminate funding to their grantees should these grantees not comply with the NIH Guidelines.

Instead, the RAC recommended the addition of a new appendix (Appendix J) to the Guidelines which would have information about the Federal Interagency Advisory Committee on Recombinant DNA Research, and the insertion of a reference to Appendix J in place of the "Note." I accept this recommendation. A new Appendix J has been added to the Guidelines, and a reference to this appendix has been added under Section IV–D–4.

The working group had recommended deletion of several sections of Part IV of the Guidelines. These deletions were not incorporated into the proposed revised Guidelines as published in the **Federal Register** of May 26, 1982. NIH staff felt that retention of these sections would permit greater flexibility in interpreting and administering the Guidelines. Those sections which the working group suggested should be deleted but which NIH staff did not remove from the proposed revised Guidelines were cited in Section D of the **Federal Register** of May 26, 1982. At the RAC meeting, although specifically brought up, there was no motion to delete the above referenced material. Accordingly, these sections have been incorporated into the revised Guidelines.

Other than the changes discussed above, the RAC recommended adoption of Part IV of the proposed revised Guidelines as published in the **Federal Register** of May 26, 1982 (47 FR 23110). I accept this recommendation.

D. Parts V and VI

The RAC recommended no changes in Parts V and VI as proposed in the **Federal Register** of May 26, 1982 (47 FR 23110). I accept this recommendation.

E. Appendix A

The RAC recommended no changes in Appendix A as proposed in the **Federal Register** of May 26, 1982 (47 FR 23110). I accept this recommendation.

F. Appendix B

The working group had discussed which document should be utilized to determine the pathogenic classification of an organism. As noted earlier in this announcement, the original 1976 Guidelines used the publication *Classification of Etiologic Agents on the Basis of Hazard*, 4th Edition, July 1974; U.S. Department of Health, Education and Welfare, Public Health Service, Center for Disease Control, as the reference source for classification of microorganisms for the purposes of the Guidelines. All subsequent revisions of the Guidelines have also used this document. At the present time, the Centers for Disease Control (CDC) and the NIH are revising the *Classification of Etiologic Agents on the Basis of Hazard*. The working group felt, however, that this revised version might not serve the purposes of the Guidelines as well as the original 1974 version. Nonetheless, the working group noted that additional pathogens should be added to the classification in the Guidelines and that the classification should be updated regularly. It was also noted that some organisms might better be treated in a manner specific for the purposes of the Guidelines. The working group recommended, therefore that the RAC and NIH adopt for the Guidelines a revised version of the 1974 CDC classification, and that the RAC assume responsibility for regularly updating the listing.

I accept the recommendation that the RAC assume responsibility to update periodically a revised classification of microoganisms for the purposes of the NIH Guidelines for Research Involving Recombinant DNA Molecules. I have asked ORDA to designate a working group on classification of microorganisms to make its first report to the full committee at its next meeting.

The proposed revised classification developed by the working group on revisions was published in Appendix B of the proposed revised Guidelines in the **Federal Register** of May 26, 1982 (47 FR 23110).

The proposed revised classification was the only proposal of the working group which received a letter of comment. Dr. John Richardson, Director, Office of Biosafety, Centers for Disease Control (CDC) offered the following comments which were distributed to the RAC:

A. mallei is now *Pseudomonas mallei*
Diplococcus pneumoniae is now *Streptococcus pneumoniae*
Herellea vaginicola is now *Acinetobacter calcoaceticus*
Legionella pneumophila should be added to the list of Class 2 bacteria
Mima polymorpha—delete—same as *A. calcoaceticus*
Vibrio comma is now *Vibrio cholerae*
Vibrio fetus and *V. jejuni* are now *Campylobacter fetus* and *C. jejuni*, respectively.
Rabies virus—street virus should also be Class 2 (The only two recorded cases of laboratory-associated disease were due to a fixed and an attenuated strain, respectively)
Actinobacillus mallei is now *Pseudomonas mallei*
Schistosoma mansoni should be a Class 2 agent
Psittacoses-ornithoses-trachoma group should be redesignated *Chlamydia psittaci* and *C. trachomatis* and listed under Class 2 bacteria
Ebola fever virus should be added to the list of Class 4 viruses."

One member of the RAC, Dr. Berns, recommended that Rabies street virus be considered a Class 3 agent for the purposes of the Guidelines because although Rabies street virus could be classified as a Class 2 agent for work at diagnostic levels, larger than diagnostic levels will likely be used in experiments involving recombinant DNA techniques.

I accept Dr. Richardson's recommendations for amendment of the proposed classification of microorganisms in Appendix B, except that Rabies street virus will be classified as a Class 3 agent pending possible further consideration by the working group on classification of microorganisms.

Other specific changes in Appendix B were discussed at the RAC meeting in regard to *Klebsiella* and other organisms. The RAC recommended not adopting these further changes at this time, but rather awaiting the report of the working group on classification of microorganisms at a future RAC meeting.

In Appendix B of the proposed revised Guidelines, the working group had recommended that viruses classified as low risk oncogenic viruses by the *National Cancer Institute Safety Standards for Research Involving Oncogenic Viruses* (October 1974, U.S. Department of Health, Education, and Welfare Publication Number (NIH) 75-790) should be classified as Class 2 agents for the purposes of the Guidelines, and moderate-risk oncogenic viruses should be classified as Class 3 agents for the purposes of the Guidelines. One member of the RAC objected to the proposed classification of these viruses as being too stringent. He suggested that the low-risk oncogenic viruses should be put in Class 1, and the moderate-risk oncogenic viruses in Class 2. Because of differences of opinion about the appropriate classification for these viruses, because the proposed new designation of these agents as Class 2 and 3 would raise required containment vis-a-vis the current April 21, 1982, Guidelines (47 FR 17180), and because the working group on classification of microorganisms will be considering this issue and reporting back to the RAC at its next meeting, I am retaining for the present the status of these organisms as they appear in the April 21, 1982 Guidelines.

Other than the changes discussed above, the RAC recommended adoption of Appendix B of the proposed revised Guidelines as published in the **Federal Register** of May 26, 1982 (47 FR 23110). I accept this recommendation.

G. Appendices C through I

The RAC recommended no changes in Appendices C, D, E, F, G, H, and I as proposed in the **Federal Register** of May 26, 1982 (47 FR 23110). I accept these recommendations.

H. Appendix J

As noted in my review of Part IV of the Guidelines, I have accepted the recommendation of the RAC to add a new Appendix J to the Guidelines and to refer to this new appendix at two places in the text of Part IV. The new Appendix J provides information on the fucntions of the Federal Interagency Advisory Committee on Recombinant DNA Research, its membership, and a statement that the relevant Departments and Agencies have adopted the NIH

Guidelines for Research Involving Recombinant DNA Molecules for research which they conduct or support.

IV. Additional Changes

I am incorporating into the revised Guidelines published today the following additional changes:

A. Appendix E

1. Certification of chi-1776 (pBR325) as an EK2 host-vector system. Appendix E has been amended to indicate certification of *E. coli* K-12 strain chi-1776 with plasmid pBR325 as an EK2 host-vector system.

2. Decertification of certain *E. coli* K-12 strains. *E. coli* K-12 strains chi-1984, chi-2705, chi-2001, and chi-2263 have been decertified for use with certain lambda vectors. Reference to these strains have been deleted from Appendix E.

B. Appendix F

1. Section Appendix F-IV-E has been rewritten to update this Section. The new wording which has been incorporated reads as follows:

Appendix F-IV-E. Fragments F-1, F-2, and F-3 of the diphtheria toxin gene (tox) may be cloned in *E. coli* K-12 under P1 + EK1 containment conditions. Fragment F-1 and fragment F-2 both contain (i) some or all of the transcriptional control elements of *tox*, (ii) the signal peptide, and (iii) fragment A (the center responsible for ADP-ribosylation of elongation factor 2). Fragment F-3 codes for most of the non-toxic Fragment B of the toxin, and contains no sequences coding for any portion of the enzymatically-active fragment A moiety.

2. A new Section, Appendix F-IV-G, has been added to reflect a case-by-case decision under the Guidelines. The new section reads as follows:

Appendix F-IV-G. Genes from *Vibrio fluvialis, Vibrio mimicus* and non 0-1 *Vibrio cholerae*, specifying virulence factors for animals may be cloned under P1 + EK1 conditions. The virulence factors to be cloned will be selected by testing fluid induction in suckling mice and in Y-1 mouse adrenal cells.

Dated: August 18, 1982.

Richard M. Krause,

Director, National Institute of Allergy and Infectious Diseases, National Institutes of Health.

OMB's "Mandatory Information Requirements for Federal Assistance Program Announcements" (45 FR 39592) requires a statement concerning the official government programs contained in the *Catalog of Federal Domestic Assistance*. Normally NIH lists in its announcements the number and title of affected individual programs for the guidance of the public. Because the guidance in this notice covers not only virtually every NIH program but also essentially every federal research program in which DNA recombinant molecule techniques could be used, it has been determined to be not cost effective or in the public interest to attempt to list these programs. Such a list would likely require several additional pages. In addition, NIH could not be certain that every federal program would be included as many federal agencies, as well as private organizations, both national and international, have elected to follow the NIH Guidelines. In lieu of the individual program listing, NIH invites readers to direct questions to the information address above about whether individual programs listed in the *Catalog of Federal Domestic Assistance* are affected.

NIH programs are not covered by OMB Circular A-95 because they fit the description of "programs not considered appropriate" in Section 8-(b)-(4) and (5) of that Circular.

[FR Doc. 82-23305 Filed 8-26-82; 8:45 am]
BILLING CODE 4140-01-M

DEPARTMENT OF HEALTH & HUMAN SERVICES

Public Health Service
National Institutes of Health

Memorandum

Date July 15, 1982

From Director
National Institutes of Health

Subject Motion of the Recombinant DNA Advisory Committee on the 1972 Biological and Toxin Weapons Convention

To Executive Secretary
Recombinant DNA Advisory Committee

Thank you for transmitting to me the June 28 motion of the Recombinant DNA Advisory Committee (RAC) advising that the 1972 Biological and Toxin Weapons Convention includes the prohibition on the use of recombinant DNA methodology for development of microbial or other biological agents, or toxins, of types or in quantities that have no justification for prophylactic, protective, or other peaceful purposes. I appreciate the advice of the RAC on this important matter.

Please convey to the RAC members my sincere thanks for their diligent and important service to NIH, the scientific community, and the American public, in their continued oversight of the safety of recombinant DNA research.

James B. Wyngaarden, M.D.

SELECTED LETTERS AND DOCUMENTS RECEIVED IN THE PERIOD

NOVEMBER 1980 TO AUGUST 1982 RELEVANT TO THE

REVISION OF THE NIH GUIDELINES

THE PUBLIC HEALTH RESEARCH INSTITUTE
OF THE CITY OF NEW YORK, INC.

455 FIRST AVENUE, NEW YORK, N. Y. 10016
TEL. (212) 481-0746

November 25, 1980

Dr. William J. Gartland
Office of Recombinant DNA Activities (ORDA)
National Institutes of Health
Bethesda, Maryland 20205

Dear Bill:

In connection with Winston Brill's recent letter regarding lowering of containment for non-pathogenic pro- and lower eukaryotes, I would like to say that I concur but would prefer that the lowering be to P2 rather than P1 because of the large variety and number of organisms that will be affected.

Incidentally, I regret that I will be unable to attend the January 8-9 meeting.

With best wishes,

Richard Novick

RN:bc
cc: Dr. Winston Brill

STANFORD UNIVERSITY
STANFORD, CALIFORNIA 94305

DEPARTMENT OF BIOLOGICAL SCIENCES

December 18, 1980

Director
Office of Recombinant DNA Activities
Building 31, Room 4A 52
National Institutes of Health
Bethesda, Maryland 20205

Dear Sir:

Dr. Winston Brill has proposed that recombinant DNA experiments involving prokaryotes and lower eukaryotes nonpathogenic for man, animals, or plants, can be conducted under P1 containment. (Fed. Reg. Nov. 28. 1980)

I strongly support this proposal. It will greatly facilitate research, especially in lower eukaryotes such as Neurospora where present restrictions have made many important experiments impractical or underly laborious.

The proposal is consistant with a suggestion made by Dewitt Stettin in 1978, that conditions of containment appropriate for any recombinant DNA experiment are those which are dictated by the most virulent or dangerous organism entering into that experiment. Experience is now sufficient that this principle could well be substituted for the entire guidelines.

Sincerely yours,

David D. Perkins

David D. Perkins
Professor of Biology

DDP:dkh

STANFORD UNIVERSITY MEDICAL CENTER

DEPARTMENT OF GENETICS

December 19, 1980

Dr. William J. Gartland, Jr.
Executive Secretary
Recombinant Advisory Committee
Building 31, Room 4852
National Institutes of Health
Bethesda, MD 20205

Dear Dr. Gartland:

This letter is written in strong support of the proposal by Dr. Winston Brill that the Recombinant DNA Guidelines be amended to permit experiments involving non-pathogenic eukaryotes and lower prokaryotes to be carried out under P1 containment conditions.

During the more than six years that have elapsed since my colleagues and I first raised questions about the possible biohazardous consequences of certain types of recombinant DNA experiments, much experience and evidence has been accumulated to indicate that our concerns were unnecessary and unwarranted. At this point in time, there is no basis for requiring a level of containment for recombinant DNA experiments involving non-pathogenic prokaryotes and lower eukaryotes higher than is required for other work with the same organism. Thus, Dr. Brill's proposed amendment makes scientific sense, and it will help reduce impediments that still unnecesarily restrict current recombinant DNA work.

I strongly urge the approval of Dr. Brill's proposal.

Sincerely yours,

Stanley N. Cohen
Professor

SNC:ps

DEPARTMENT OF GENETICS, STANFORD UNIVERSITY SCHOOL OF MEDICINE, STANFORD, CALIFORNIA 94305 • (415) 497-5052

THE UNIVERSITY OF KANSAS MEDICAL CENTER
COLLEGE OF HEALTH SCIENCES AND HOSPITAL
RAINBOW BOULEVARD AT 39TH • KANSAS CITY, KANSAS 66103

SCHOOL OF MEDICINE
SCHOOL OF NURSING
SCHOOL OF ALLIED HEALTH
UNIVERSITY HOSPITAL

SCHOOL OF MEDICINE
DEPARTMENT OF MICROBIOLOGY
(913) 588-7010

December 22, 1980

Dr. William Gartland
Office of Recombinant DNA activities
National Institute of General Medical Science
National Institute of Health
Building 31, Room 4A52
Bethesda, Maryland 20014

Dear Dr. Gartland;

I should like to write in support of Dr. Winston Brill's proposal that all experiments with nonpathogenic procaryotes and lower eucaryotes be permitted under P-1 containment (Federal Register, November 28, 1980). My particular interest involves *Neurospora crassa*.

Experiments that we are now contemplating, involving the use of chimeric E coli/yeast plasmids in *Neurospora*, would require P-2 facility. Given the fact that *Neurospora* is a pathogen neither for man nor his crops; the expense and time delay involved in building a P-2 facility seems unjustified. I am sure that many people working with non-pathogenic lower eucaryotes are in a similar position. Relaxation of this overly stringent regulation would doubtless have a very beneficial effect on research with these organisms.

Sincerely,

John A. Kinsey

John A. Kinsey, Ph.D.
Microbiology

JAK:jlw

STANFORD UNIVERSITY, STANFORD, CALIFORNIA 94305
DEPARTMENT OF BIOLOGICAL SCIENCES

CHARLES YANOFSKY
MORRIS HERZSTEIN PROFESSOR
OF BIOLOGY

December 22, 1980

Director
Office of Recombinant DNA Activities
Building 31, Room 4A52
National Institutes of Health
Bethesda, Maryland 20205

Dear Sir or Madam:

I would like to express my approval of the proposal by Dr. Winston Brill, summarized on page 79386 of the Federal Register, Vol. 45, No. 231, Friday November 28, 1980. His proposal is realistic, based on our current information and experience of the past few years. The progress of recombinant DNA research will be hastened in this country if his proposal is adopted and unnecessary paper work and committee time will be avoided.

Yours truly,

Charles Yanofsky

CY:gm

STANFORD UNIVERSITY MEDICAL CENTER
STANFORD, CALIFORNIA 94305

DEPARTMENT OF BIOCHEMISTRY
STANFORD UNIVERSITY SCHOOL OF MEDICINE

Area Code 415
497-6161

December 23, 1980

Director
Office of Recombinant DNA Activities
Building 31, Room 4A52
National Institutes of Health
Bethesda, Maryland 20205

Dear Sir:

I support Winston Brill's proposal that all experiments with non-pathogenic lower pro- and eukaryotes be permitted under P1 containment.

Sincerely,

Ronald W. Davis

Ronald W. Davis
Professor of Biochemistry

RWD/ns

Duke University Medical Center
DURHAM, NORTH CAROLINA
27710

DEPARTMENT OF BIOCHEMISTRY

December 23, 1980

Director
Office of Recombinant DNA Activities
Building 31, Room 4A52
National Institutes of Health
Bethesda, Maryland 20205

Sir:

I would like to support Dr. Winston Brill's proposal that the Recombinant DNA Guidelines be amended to permit recombinant DNA experiments involving nonpathogenic prokaryotes and lower eukaryotes under P1 containment conditions. It would be helpful to eliminate impediments to recombinant DNA research using organisms such as Neurospora which offer practically no conceivable danger to man or to his environment. Many of us are convinced that organisms such as Neurospora, Yeast and other lower eukaryotes will provide host vector systems that are less likely to present a biological hazard than organisms that now can be handled under P1 conditions.

Yours,

Samson R. Gross
Professor of Genetics and Biochemistry

SRG:dh

Center for Health Sciences

Department of Physiological Chemistry
1215 Linden Drive
589 Medical Sciences Building
Madison, Wisconsin 53706
Telephone: (608) 262-1347

University of Wisconsin-Madison

December 23, 1980

Director
Office of Recombinant DNA Activities
Building 31, Room 4A52
National Institutes of Health
Bethesda, Maryland 20205

Dear Colleagues:

It has been called to my attention that the notices in the Federal Register, Vol. 45, No. 231 of November 28, 1980, include a proposal by Dr. Winston Brill that the Guidelines be amended to permit the use of P1 containment conditions for experiments involving non-pathogenic prokaryotes and lower eukaryotes.

I would like to state my support for this proposal, and urge that it be adopted. The need for higher levels of containment adds appreciably to the difficulty and cost of doing experiments and unnecessarily hampers progress in this important field.

Let me say that I think this proposal is timely - neither premature, nor past due. I was one of the "go slow" people when recombinant DNA work first emerged because I felt that a development of such great sweep and power might also have serious unforeseen possibilities for accident or mischief. I felt that we could afford to be very careful until there was more experience under our belt. This experience is now amply on hand, and any apprehensions I had have been put to rest.

A few developments have been especially reassuring. It now seems that the only thing revolutionary about recombinant DNA technology is to be able to make it happen at a time (now) and place (test tube) of our choosing; nature has in all likelihood been doing it for ages. Second, I have been impressed at how unlikely it is for an organism carrying foreign DNA to prosper in competition with highly attuned, wild organisms of the same species. (A friend of mine likens foreign DNA to a carburetor on a washing machine). My own experience is that I must keep my plasmid-carrying strains under selective pressure with antibiotics or they are outgrown by spontaneous variants which have lost the plasmid. Others tell me that they can quite reliably distinguish bacterial colonies carrying recombinant DNA plasmids from those carrying non-recombinant plasmids because recombinant colonies are considerably smaller due to their slower cell division. Finally, we now have more than five years of actual working with recombinant DNA in which no manipulated organism seems to have established itself at any time in the human, in domestic animals or plants, or in the wild.

In short, I think our original caution was prudent, but the grounds for apprehension have disappeared. I urge passage of Dr. Brill's proposal.

Sincerely,

Robert L Metzenberg

Robert L. Metzenberg
John Bascom Professor of
Physiological Chemistry

RLM/dch

UNIVERSITY OF CALIFORNIA, LOS ANGELES

BERKELEY • DAVIS • IRVINE • LOS ANGELES • RIVERSIDE • SAN DIEGO • SAN FRANCISCO SANTA BARBARA • SANTA CRUZ

OFFICE OF THE DEAN
SCHOOL OF MEDICINE
THE CENTER FOR THE HEALTH SCIENCES
LOS ANGELES, CALIFORNIA 90024

January 4, 1981

William J. Gartland, Jr., Ph.D.
Director, Office of Recombinant DNA Activities
Department of Health and Human Services
Public Health Service
National Institutes of Health
Bethesda, Maryland 20205

Dear Sir:

The recommendations submitted by the NIH-RAC, which appeared in the December 4 Federal Register, are very constructive and needed. I urge that these recommendations be approved.

Sincerely,

A. Frederick Rasmussen, Jr., M.D., Ph.D.
The Associate Dean

AFR:slp

UNIVERSITY OF WISCONSIN–MADISON

DEPARTMENT OF BACTERIOLOGY
1550 Linden Drive
Madison, Wisconsin 53706
Telephone: 608-262-2914

January 5, 1981

Dr. William Gartland
Office of Recombinant DNA Activities
Bldg. 31, National Institutes of Health
Bethesda, MD 20205

Dear Dr. Gartland:

There seems to be undue concern about the release of recombinant DNA-containing organisms into the environment. For most people working with recombinant DNA, there does not seem to be any need to release recombinant DNA-organisms outside of a contained laboratory or process facility; therefore, these people readily accept the restriction involving environment release. In the case of agricultural research, however, the benefits from recombinant DNA technology demand field experiments--experiments in which there is deliberate release of recombinant DNA-containing plants into the environment.

I am particularly concerned about the statement in the letter of November 20, 1981, by the Congressional Committee on Science and Technologies to the NIH. The Committee seems to be upset that the RAC may eliminate a specific provision in the current NIH Guidelines prohibiting the deliberate release into the environment of recombinant DNA organisms.

In the agricultural sciences, I predict that one of the first benefits of recombinant DNA experiments will be the design of crop plants that are resistant to pests such as bacteria, fungi, viruses, and insects. Such developments should have tremendous applications. One benefit of these breakthroughs will allow the farmer to become less dependent on chemical pesticides--a known danger to the consumer, and the farmer as well as to the worker in the pesticide industry. How do these proven dangers stack up against the imagined dangers that may exist by placing recombinant DNA organisms in experimental plants and in farmers' fields?

Most of the discussions regarding the potential dangers (believed, by most, to be quite small) of recombinant DNA have involved pathogenic microorganisms. It seems that when one thinks of recombinant DNA work with higher organisms, the potential dangers are even less. A collection of genes that render a plant resistant to a specific insect should not cause any particular problems to the farmers. A greater concern should be that countries not restricted to arbitrary rules that will present release of recombinant DNA organisms into the environment will be greater competitors of U.S. agriculture.

Dr. William Gartland
Page 2
January 5, 1981

The worry about recombinant DNA-modified plants posing any kind of hazard (for example--becoming an extraordinarily successful weed, for producing toxins that will kill all insects that land on it or will kill all birds that eat the seed) seems to be unnecessary.

A common response made by individuals who are upset about applications of the new technology is that we have not yet proven that there is absolutely no danger by growing recombinant DNA plants in the field. There is no way to be absolutely sure that no danger can exist in any technology--or, in fact, in anything that we do. However, dozens of plant scientists with USDA, university, or industrial affiliations, with whom I have spoken, believe that the potential dangers that may appear from field-grown recombinant DNA plants are less than the dangers caused by the introduction, by standard breeding, of genes from tropical wild corn into today's midwestern corn--a common current breeding practice. Breeding involves random introduction of genes--recombinant DNA technology is quite selective.

I hope that the opportunities for the consumer, the farmer, and the agricultural industry will not be stifled by rules which the experts deem to be unnecessary.

Sincerely yours,

Winston J. Brill
Vilas Research Professor of Bacteriology
Director of Research, Cetus Madison
Member, Recombinant DNA Advisory Committee

WJB:is
cc: Congressman Don Fuqua
Congressman Doug Walgren
Congressman Albert Gore

DEPARTMENT OF MICROBIOLOGY AND MOLECULAR GENETICS
HARVARD MEDICAL SCHOOL
25 SHATTUCK STREET
BOSTON, MASSACHUSETTS 02115

January 22, 1981

Dr. William Gartland, Jr.
Director
Office of Recombinant DNA Activities
NIAID
National Institutes of Health
Bethesda, Maryland 20205

Dear Bill:

I am writing in reference to the two alternative proposals for revision of the NIH guidelines for Recombinant DNA research which will come before the RAC at its February meeting.

Despite my sympathy for the rationale behind the Baltimore-Campbel proposal I believe it to be premature to do away with all mandatory aspects of the guidlines. Unexpected surprises still do arise as was seen by (i) the survival for longer than expected periods of time of the 'disabled' E. coli strains during testing with human subjects; (ii) higher than expected survival of 'disabled' E. coli in sewage treatment plant tests; (iii) the converting of E. coli K-12 into a pathogen through the cloning of a hemolysin determinant from the wild type strain (Portnoy & Falkow, 1981, J. Bacteriol. 148, 877); and (iv) the production of infectious polio virions from a cDNA copy (Racaniello & Baltimore, 1981, Science 214, 916). Other similar examples could be sited.

The alternative proposal by Susan Gottesman constructively deals with my concerns while still doing away with much of the undesirable red tape and delays previously associated with the guidelines. In particular, this modified but still mandatory version of the guidelines still covers what I believe to be areas of possible hazard: (i) the deliberate introduction of recombinant organisms into the environment (history records that the deliberate release of new organisms into an environment has sometimes been disastrous). Certainly in this area there should at least be the opportunity for public review and approval before such studies are carried out; (ii) the deliberate introduction of antibiotic resistance genes into organisms in which such genes are not normally found; (iii) the cloning of toxin genes (those specified in appendix G of the present guidelines). To this list I would also prefer to see something added with respect to cloning experiments which might produce a pathogenic virus (see above Racaniello & Baltimore article).

The Gottesman proposal appears to me to retain both NIH (ORDA) and local (IBC) oversight of recombinant DNA research in areas of legitimate scientific concern. It allows for efficient and uniform decisions to be made based on retention of national standards for the setting of containment levels. These aspects of the Gottesman proposal combined with the fact that it both lowers containment where appropriate and reduces much of the cumbersome paperwork make it appear far more desireable than the alternative Baltimore-Campbell proposal.

The Baltimore-Campbell proposal would eliminate all mandatory aspects of the NIH guidelines by replacing them with a 'voluntary' code of practices. This alternative would seem superficially to many scientists to expedite the pace of recombinant DNA studies by doing away with the time consuming procedures related to the functioning of the RAC and local IBCs. I do not believe that this in fact will be the result. Rather, haphazard illogical and nonuniform standards will be proposed by the governing bodies in the communities in which the research is being carried out.

The reality of the present situation is that the vast majority of experiments became exempt from the requirements of the NIH guidelines as of July 1981. The Gottesman proposal covering the remainder of these experiments is a responsible and reasonable document with requirements that will not be too cumbersome to either the experimenter, the IBCs, or the RAC.

Sincerely,

Richard Goldstein
Associate Professor

RG:jw

xxx 20205

March 5, 1981

Dr. Allan Campbell
Department of Biological Sciences
Stanford University
Stanford, CA 94305

Dear Allan:

I have just learned from Bernie Talbot that it is your expectation to introduce for discussion, at the next meeting of the Recombinant DNA Program Advisory Committee, a marked simplification of the Guidelines under which we currently operate. I should like to add my support, for what it is worth, to this notion - having felt for many years now that the hazard of over-regulation far exceeded the hazard of a monster chimera. I summarized my views in the talk which I gave to your Committee on the occasion of my resignation as Chairman. I enclose herewith a copy of my comments.

Sincerely yours,

DeWitt Stetten, Jr., M.D., Ph.D.
Senior Scientific Advisor, NIH
Building 16, Room 118
Bethesda, MD 20205

Gene, 3 (1978) 265—268 265
© Elsevier/North-Holland Biomedical Press, Amsterdam — Printed in The Netherlands

Invited Editorial

VALEDICTORY BY THE CHAIRMAN OF THE NIH RECOMBINANT DNA MOLECULE PROGRAM ADVISORY COMMITTEE*

I am taking a Chairman's prerogative to invade the printed agenda*. I should like at this time to share with you the reasons why I have felt impelled to resign my chairmanship of this Committee. Shortly after our last meeting of November 1977, I asked the Director, NIH, to accept my resignation and find a replacement for this chairmanship. He asked me to assist in the selection of a new Chairman and I have provided to him the names of candidates from which he is soon to make a choice. I am certain that you will be pleased with the name of my successor, and that the Committee will give the new Chairman the same devotion and industry which it has given to me.

There were, of course, personal reasons for my resignation. I am four years older than I was when I was first appointed, I fatigue more easily, and, as you are all aware, my visual acuity has continued to decrease until I am able to read only a very small fraction of the large amount of paper which passes over my desk in relation to this function. In addition, I have had a growing unhappiness with some of the directions which the recombinant DNA program has taken over the past four years. From my conversations with members of the Committee, I believe that this unhappiness is shared by some of you, and this may be a good opportunity to verbalize this discontent.

Prior to the Asilomar meeting of February 1975, I had had only modest contact with nucleic acids and with genetics. I had worked in the laboratory with lipids, polysaccharides, and proteins, but had never handled any nucleic acids. I had never worked on a genetic problem, and had certainly never engaged in microbiological research. Except for some briefing which I secured from members of the intramural NIH family, I came to Asilomar cold.

It has taken me several years to analyze and unscramble the experience of the Asilomar meeting. I now understand it more fully than I did at the time. It had many elements of a religious revival meeting. I heard several colleagues declaim against sin, I heard others admit to having sinned, and there was a general feeling that we should all go forth and sin no more. The imagery which was presented was surely vivid, but the data were scanty. I recall one scientist presenting information on the difficulty of colonizing the intestinal tract with *Escherichia coli* K-12, but his presentation was given little attention. We were all, in effect, led down to the river to be baptized and we all went willingly. I, for one, left the meeting enthralled. I had never been to a scientific meeting which had so excited me. On my return to Bethesda, I was asked to summarize

*Presented at the meeting of the Recombinant DNA Molecule Program Advisory Committee, April 28, 1978, NIH, Bethesda, Maryland.

the events at Asilomar before a meeting of the generally staid NIH Institute Directors and I believe I was able to transfer to them some of my excitement. Over the succeeding months, the Recombinant DNA Molecule Program Advisory Committee met and, by July 1975, it drafted a set of guidelines at Woods Hole, Massachusetts, which I at the time thought to be reasonably satisfactory. They did not conform to my prior notion of guidelines exactly, since they bordered on the encyclopedic. Nonetheless, I felt that we had successfully compromised most of the burning issues over which the Committee was initially strongly divided. When these guidelines were distributed, however, they elicited vigorous and often emotional responses, and among these responses there was one which I recall vividly. It charged our Committee with having violated the "spirit of Asilomar." At the time this expression did not catch my attention, but on consideration I was struck by the fact that despite the many, many meetings which I had attended at Atlantic City, I had never heard a reference to the "spirit of Atlantic City." This charge, in fact, pinpointed for me the notion that the experience at Asilomar was essentially a spiritual one rather than an intellectual one. It was, in the usual sense, not a scientific meeting at all. Whatever its purpose may have been in the minds of its initiators, a result was to fire the imagination, first, of the newspaper correspondents who were abundantly represented, and then of a substantial segment of the newspaper-reading public.

By December 1975, our Committee, meeting at La Jolla, again assembled a set of guidelines. Whereas up to that time I had insufficient confidence in my own judgment to hold a firm opinion on this issue, and found myself swayed by the views most recently presented, it was about the time of the La Jolla meeting that I began to wonder whether, indeed, any of the postulated hazards of recombinant DNA molecule technology were likely to materialize.

The La Jolla guidelines served as the basis for a discussion at a meeting of the NIH Director's Advisory Committee early in 1976, and this, in turn, was followed in July by the publication of the official NIH guidelines. In this last transformation, something happened which I found disturbing.

The mission of NIH is, I believe, very simply stated. It is to conduct and to support the very best biomedical research that it can find to conduct and support. Similarly, the mission of our Committee and of the guidelines which it drafted was to provide assurance that research in the area of recombinant DNA molecules would be conducted in such a fashion as not to jeopardize the laboratory, the community, or the environment. Both missions, it should be noted, are stated positively. It is the purpose both of NIH and of this Committee to encourage, to promote — not to forbid or to impede. The legal profession represented at the Director's Advisory Committee meeting was critical of the concept of guidelines, which in my judgement are designed to provide *guidance* to the investigator and to those who review his proposal. We were informed that what was needed was regulation, not guidance. This was exemplified by the recommendation that our instruction, written largely in the subjunctive mood (the investigator *should* . . .) be replaced by the more peremptory language of regulations (the investigator *shall* . . .). I recall arguing against such change in vain.

My reasons were very simple. It is my interpretation of the history of science and indeed of all culture that ***regulation is antithetical to creativity***, and creativity is the most important component of scientific advance. From this, it follows that the best regulation for the flowering of science is the least regulation — that is, the least regulation compatible with the needs of society. Furthermore, I feared and my fears were, I think, justified that regulation might lead to legislation with a specification of sanctions, i.e., punishment, for those who were in violation of the regulations. Whereas the so-called regulatory agencies of Government must from time to time adopt a punitive posture, this is, I believe, a poor posture for a research agency such as the National Institutes of Health.

Against what hazards were we proposing to draft regulations? With the passage of time, the hazards that had been pictured at Asilomar seemed to recede. Whereas a great number of positive and useful scientific results are being published based upon the technology of recombinant DNA molecules, to the best of my knowledge no adverse results have been noted. Indeed, I believe that there is at this time not one iota of acceptable evidence, i.e., data publishable in a scientific journal, to indicate that the recombinant DNA molecule technology has ever enhanced the pathogenicity or the toxigenicity of any microorganism. This, of course, does not mean that it never will do so, but it does cause one to wonder whether all of the present fuss is truly justified. It places the hazards in this area in the same category as those in many other areas for which we have no positive evidence. To clarify this point, let me offer you an analogy. Ever since the Middle Ages, it has been suspected that the ghosts of those who died by suicide are more menacing than ghosts in general. This anxiety, once implanted in the minds of the people, led to some interesting containment practices. The bodies of victims of suicide were excluded from traditional burial places, lest their ghosts pollute or otherwise disturb the more peaceful ghosts of those who died of natural causes. They were doomed to be buried in the crossroads, and in order to ensure that the ghosts not escape from the tomb, a stake was driven through the body of the victim into the underlying soil, thus pinning the ghost into its grave. This containment practice continued for many centuries and was ultimately abandoned only in the 18th century. Experience since that time has justified the conclusion — that the hazard which had earlier been postulated was either of very small magnitude or possibly nonexistent. We may yet prove to be wrong about the safety of unpinning the ghosts of suicide victims, but I should be surprised if this were so.

How long do we wait, in the absence of any positive evidence, before we decide that the hazards in a particular area of research are at a socially acceptable level? To this question I have no specific answer. Soon we may come to the conclusion that the manipulations of recombinant DNA technology do not of them selves add significantly to the dangers inherent in the conduct of microbiological research. Then we can replace our complex and, I repeat, encyclopedic guidelines by a very simple statement. This might take the following form: "The conditions of containment appropriate for any recombinant DNA experiment are those which are dictated by the most virulent or dangerous organism entering into that experiment." Is anything more really required?

I hope that none of you will construe any of my critical remarks as being personally directed. They are not. I have thoroughly enjoyed and been stimulated by my contacts with the many members of the Committee. I hope that I have established enduring friendships with many of you, and I shall certainly follow your further deliberations with great interest and concern. I should like particularly to express my appreciation to the several members of the NIH staff who have worked so hard and so loyally to keep this project afloat: Dr. Leon Jacobs who, from the beginning, has served as Co-Chairman of this Committee, Dr. Bernard Talbot, who has worked enormously hard and valiantly, Dr. William Gartland, Director of the Office of Recombinant DNA Activities, his small but energetic staff — Dr. Kamely and Dr. Goldberg. Then, there is Ms. Betty Butler, who not only made certain that all the paper flowed in the right directions but also nursed us through our several tortured meetings. To work with all of these people has been a very rewarding experience.

I wish you well in your future meetings.

DeWitt Stetten, Jr.

Deputy Director for Science
National Institutes of Health
Bethesda, MD 20014 (U.S.A.)

The Albany Medical College
of Union University
Albany, New York 12208

DEPARTMENT OF MICROBIOLOGY AND IMMUNOLOGY
THE NEIL HELLMAN MEDICAL RESEARCH BUILDING
(518) 445-5165

March 20, 1981

Dr. Elizabeth Milewski
Office of Recombinant DNA Activities
Building 31, Room 4A52
National Institutes of Health
Bethesda, Maryland 20205

Dear Dr. Milewski:

Dr. Donald Dean, director of the Bacillus Genetic Stock Center, has recently requested that the NIH Guidelines on utilization of Bacillus subtilis in recombinant DNA experiments be eased. The suggested changes on the use of asporogenic mutants, and redefining the physical containment levels for cloning DNA from CDC class 1 organisms and from other Bacilli into sporogenic B. subtilis strains seem to make a lot of sense. I would like to support Dr. Dean's request in the strongest terms.

Sincerely yours,

H. W. Taber

Harry W. Taber, Ph.D.
Professor of Microbiology
and Immunology

HWT:kc

Cornell University

Division of Biological Sciences

Section of Genetics & Development
Bradfield Hall
Ithaca, New York 14853
(607) 256-2100

23 March 1981

Dr. Elizabeth Milewski
Building 31, Room 4A52
ORDA-NIH
Bethesda, MD 20205

Dear Dr. Milewski:

I have recently seen a copy of the changes in NIH Guidelines for Bacillus subtilis recombinant DNA experiments proposed by Donald H. Dean.

I have worked with and studied Bacillus subtilis and its bacteriophages for the past fifteen years. On the basis of that experience, I fully approve of Dr. Dean's proposals.

Sincerely yours,

Stanley A. Zahler
Professor of Microbiology

sk
cc: D.H. Dean

SCHOOLS OF BASIC MEDICAL SCIENCES AND CLINICAL MEDICINE
UNIVERSITY OF ILLINOIS COLLEGE OF MEDICINE
190 Medical Sciences Building · 506 South Mathews · Urbana, Illinois 61801
(217) 333-9284

March 24, 1981

Dr. Elizabeth Milewski
Bldg. 31 Rm. 4A52
ORDA-NIH
Bethesda, MD 20205

Dear Dr. Milewski:

I am writing in support of efforts to certify Bacillus subtilis as a perfectly safe bacterium and to minimize restrictions of its use as a cloning vehicle. I have worked with B. subtilis for seven years, following an equal period of working with Escherichia coli. B. subtilis has proved to be entirely harmless, and we have had little difficulty with its surviving when it should not (e.g., surviving autoclaving and subsequently contaminating media). In fact, it dies easily (from lack of carbon/energy source of of oxygen). Its being an obligate aerobe and native to soil should make it especially fit as a cloning vehicle, in comparison with E. coli, which naturally inhabits intestines. The more the restrictions of its use are relaxed, the greater will be the tendency to shift from enteric bacteria to B. subtilis in cloning experiments, a desireable change. I urge you to remove all possible restrictions on its use in cloning experiments, and rely instead on standard (good) microbiological technique as customarily practiced by competent microbiologists and biochemists, for it will provide protection enough.

Yours sincerely,

George W. Ordal

George W. Ordal
Associate Professor of Biochemistry

TUFTS UNIVERSITY
School of Medicine

Department of Molecular Biology and Microbiology

March 24, 1981

Dr. Elizabeth Milewski
ORDA-NIH
Bldg. 31, Rm. 4A52
Bethesda, MD 20205

Dear Dr. Milewski:

I habe been informed by Dr. Donald H. Dean that he has requested specific changes in the NIH Guidelines for Recombinant DNA Research with respect to the use of Bacillus subtilis as a cloning system. I strongly endorse those specific changes as a means of bringing the B. subtilis system into greater use in recombinant DNA work.

Sincerely yours,

Abraham L. Sonenshein, Ph.D.
Associate Professor

ALS:ms

136 Harrison Avenue
Boston, Massachusetts 02111
617 956-6750

Cable FOODSCI

MASSACHUSETTS INSTITUTE OF TECHNOLOGY
Cambridge, Massachusetts 02139
U.S.A.

Department of Nutrition and Food Science

56-123

March 24, 1981

Dr. Elizabeth Milewski
Bldg. 31, Room 4A52
ORDA-NIH
Bethesda, MD 20205

Dear Dr. Milewski:

I would like to support the request of Dr. Donald H. Dean to ease the restrictions on using Bacillus subtilis for recombinant DNA experiments. This organism and its close relatives have been used widely in industry for both research and production. To my knowledge, its use has never led to medical problems and restriction of its use could result in the slowdown of medical progress.

Sincerely yours,

Arnold L. Demain

Arnold L. Demain

Syngenics, Inc.

March 25, 1981

Dr. Elizabeth Milewski
Building 31, Room 4A42
ORDA-NIH
Bethesda, MD 20205

Dear Dr. Milewski:

I am writing to you in support of Dr. Donald H. Dean's request for a reduction in the restriction imposed by the present NIH Guidelines involving the use of _B. subtilis_ for recombinant DNA research.

Dr. Dean's proposed changes are listed on page two of this communication.

I think that it is time to examine the present Guideline restrictions in the light of all available data. When this is done, _B. subtilis_ will be seen as a safe alternate host-vector system.

Sincerely yours,

John J. Donch
President

JJD/mpy

2904 Corvin Drive • Santa Clara • California 95051 • (408) 730-0843

Dr. Elizabeth Milewski
Page 2
March 25, 1981

Dr. Dean request the following changes:

1) Any Bacillus subtilis strain which does not revert to spore formation with a frequency greater than 10^{-7} can be used with indigenous vectors for cloning DNA from any non-prohibited source under conditions to be specified for E. coli K-12 and Saccharomyces cerevisae host vector systems.

2) Bacillus subtilis strains that do not carry an asporogenic mutation can be used with indigenous vectors for the cloning of DNA from CDC Class 1 organisms under P2 condition (Action Under the Guildlines, Appendix D).

3) Bacillus subtilis strains that do not carry an asporogenic mutation can be used with indigenous vectors for the cloning of DNA from any Bacillus sp. of CDC Class 1 under P1 conditions (Action Under the Guildlines, Appendix D).

STANFORD UNIVERSITY, STANFORD, CALIFORNIA 94305
DEPARTMENT OF BIOLOGICAL SCIENCES

CHARLES YANOFSKY
MORRIS HERZSTEIN PROFESSOR
OF BIOLOGY

April 6, 1981

Dr. William Gartland, Jr.
Office of Recombinant DNA Activities
National Institute of General Medical Sciences
National Institutes of Health
Building 31, Room 4A52
Bethesda, Maryland 20205

Dear Dr. Gartland:

I would like to register my support for section III, page 17995 of the Federal Register, Volume 46, No. 54, Friday, March 20, 1981.

I agree with all the statements in David Perkins' letter to you of February 1, 1981. Since Neurospora crassa is not a pest or pathogen, there is no justification for imposing more stringent containment conditions for research with Neurospora than for investigations with yeast or animal viruses. The current Guidelines are seriously hindering the use and development of Neurospora as a subject for recombinant DNA research.

I support also the more general recommendations of Drs. Campbell and Baltimore in the same issue of the Federal Register (page 17995). On the basis of the experience of scientists over the past five years it seems entirely appropriate to convert the Guidelines into a "Code of Standard Practice", and to reduce required containment levels as suggested by Campbell and Baltimore.

Sincerely yours,

Charles Yanofsky

CY:gm

UNIVERSITY OF CALIFORNIA, SAN FRANCISCO

BERKELEY • DAVIS • IRVINE • LOS ANGELES • RIVERSIDE • SAN DIEGO • SAN FRANCISCO SANTA BARBARA • SANTA CRUZ

SCHOOL OF MEDICINE
Department of Microbiology
and Immunology

SAN FRANCISCO, CALIFORNIA 94143

13 April 1981

Dr. William Gartland
Office of Recombinant DNA
National Institutes of
General Medical Sciences
Building 31, 4A52
Bethesda, Maryland 20205

Dear Dr. Gartland:

I am writing to offer enthusiastic support for the proposal to be put before the Recombinant DNA Advisory Committee by David Baltimore and Allan Campbell. Certainly in my own field of virology there has never been any reason to believe that recombinant DNA experiments were anymore dangerous than the viruses themselves; thus voluntary compliance with reasonable safety recommendations has always seemed preferable to the paper-laden system with which we are now burdened.

Yours,

Harold Varmus

Harold E. Varmus, M.D.
Professor

HEV:jm

McARDLE LABORATORY
FOR CANCER RESEARCH
DEPARTMENT OF ONCOLOGY
MEDICAL SCHOOL, UNIVERSITY OF WISCONSIN

April 14, 1981

Dr. William Gartland
Office of Recombinant DNA
National Institute of General
Medical Sciences
Building 31, 4A52
Bethesda, Maryland 20205

Dear Bill:

I would like to endorse strongly the proposal of Drs. A. Campbell and David Baltimore which would restore the true advisory nature of the NIH Guidelines and eliminate their mandatory and regulatory provisions [Federal Register 46 (1981) 17994-7]. There is very strong "grass-root" support for this proposal, which agrees with the present assessment that the hypothetical inadvertent risks, specifically due to use of the recombinant DNA technique, are not significant from the practical point of view. Also, the present imposition of unnecessary regulations, which are known to have adverse effects [see TIBS, 3 (1978) p. N243], is certainly not justified by these hypothetical risks.

It was nice to see you again in Reston.

Sincerely yours,

Waclaw Szybalski
Professor of Oncology

WS:mjg

450 North Randall Avenue, Madison, Wisconsin 53706
608-262-2177

DEPARTMENT OF HEALTH & HUMAN SERVICES

Public Health Service

National Institutes of Health
Bethesda, Maryland 20205

April 14, 1981

Dr. William Gartland
Office of Recombinant DNA
National Institute of General
Medical Sciences
Building 31, Room 4A52
NIH
Bethesda, MD 20205

Dear Dr. Gartland

I write in support of the proposal by Drs. David Baltimore and Allan Campbell to modify existing NIH Guidelines on Recombinant DNA Research. The proposal is based soundly write "....neither experimental evidence nor solid theoretical arguments have been advanced to support the position that recombinant DNA research poses any danger to human health or to the integrity of the natural environment". There is no question that this statement is valid. In view of this fact, reduction in regulatory activity in this area should be undertaken without delay.

Your sincerely,

Igor B. Dawid, Ph.D.
Chief, Developmental Biochemistry Section
Laboratory of Biochemistry

DUKE UNIVERSITY MEDICAL CENTER

Department of Microbiology
and Immunology
Office of the Chairman

April 14, 1981

Dr. William Gartland
Office of Recombinant DNA
National Institute of General
Medical Sciences
Building 31, 4A52
Bethesda, Maryland 20205

Dear Dr. Gartland:

I would like to support the proposal by Drs. Baltimore and Campbell to convert the NIH Guidelines for Recombinant DNA Research into a non-regulatory code of standard practices and to reduce the recommended containment levels for certain experiments.

Action on both parts of the proposal is overdue. No evidence has come to light during the past decade that the types of experiments covered by it pose any danger for mankind, and adherence to the present strict guidelines serves no purpose. Similarly, reduction of recommended containment levels is also justified, again on the grounds that ample experience has shown that no danger is posed by any of the experiments involved. I agree that constant reevaluation is desireable and indeed essential, and whenever areas of concern are perceived, they should be regulated. By the same token, when experience has shown that there is no danger, steps should be taken to modify directives that impede innovative research that is likely to yield tremendous benefits for mankind. In summary, I strongly support Baltimore and Campbell's proposal.

Sincerely yours,

Dr. W. K. Joklik
Chairman

WKJ/kge

cc: Dr. David Baltimore

Box 3020 • Durham, North Carolina 27710 • Telephone (919) 684-5138

THE ROCKEFELLER UNIVERSITY
1230 YORK AVENUE · NEW YORK, NEW YORK 10021

April 14, 1981

Dr. William Gartland
Office of Recombinant DNA
NIGMD, Bldg. 31, 4A52
National Institutes of Health
Bethesda, MD 20205

Dear Bill:

D. Baltimore and A. Campbell have brought to RAC a resolution whose purpose is to move the NIH Guidelines for Recombinant DNA Research to something more consonant with the scientific thought of the past four years.

There may still be come controversy over the genesis and wisdom of the actions taken which created the NIH Guidelines. Typical adjectives used run from foolish to self-serving to responsible. Be that as it may, there is no controversy over the fact that the Guidelines have outlived any usefulness they may have had. Recombinant DNA research has proven itself to be as safe as any other biological research. The evidence for this lies in myriads of successful experiments and the failure of many theoretical arguments, no matter how rigorously construed to prove otherwise.

It would be an important precedent for the N.I.H. to dismantle the unneeded regulatory structure. If scientists are ever again to attempt to cope with potential hazard, they must see that what they believed were temporary measures can be undone.

Yours sincerely,

Norton

Norton D. Zinder

CALIFORNIA INSTITUTE OF TECHNOLOGY

PASADENA, CALIFORNIA 91125

DIVISION OF BIOLOGY 156-29

April 15, 1981

Dr. William Gartland
Office of Recombinant DNA
National Institute of General Medical Sciences
Building 31, 4A52
Bethesda, MD 20205

Dear Dr. Gartland:

I am writing to express my interest in and approval of the proposal of Drs. Baltimore and Campbell (Federal Register 46, #54, pp. 17994-7 of 3/20/81) for further changes in NIH guidelines for recombinant DNA research. The reduction in recommended containment levels simply represents good laboratory practice in view of the experience that has been gained in the last five years. In addition, it seems particularly appropriate at this time of reduced financial support to eliminate regulatory provisions requiring a certain investment of time and money, and which have in any case applied only to research supported by NIH. If approved, this proposal would help to reduce red tape without jeopardizing either lab safety or scientific progress.

Yours,

Eric H. Davidson
Professor of Biology

EHD:rt

FRED HUTCHINSON CANCER RESEARCH CENTER

April 15, 1981

Dr. William Gartland
Office of Recombinant DNA
NIGMS, Bldg. 31, 4A52
Bethesda, Maryland 20205

Dear Dr. Gartland,

As you know, a proposal submitted by Drs. Allan Campbell and David Baltimore has recently appeared in the Federal Register (Friday, March 20, 1981 on pages 17994-7). The proposal is to convert the NIH guidelines to a non-regulatory code of standard practice and to reduce the containment levels for some experiments.

I think this is a reasonable proposal and strongly support it. It can be argued that the mandatory guidelines served a useful purpose in raising our level of consciousness about potential biohazards and the need to be cautious when entering new areas. But that function has by now been amply fulfilled. With over five years of experience behind us there is still no experimental or theoretical argument that recombinant DNA poses any significant dangers. Therefore, it makes no sense to continue spending government money to enforce regulations on a non-existant danger. There are plenty of real dangers that need more attention than they now receive.

Sincerely,

Ronald H. Reeder
Member and Program Head
Development Biology

The University of Chicago
Committee on Virology

Bernard Roizman, ScD.
Professor in the Departments of Microbiology
and Biophysics/Theoretical Biology

April 17, 1981

Dr. William Gartland
Office of Recombinant DNA
National Institute of General
Medical Sciences
Building 31, 4A52
Bethesda, MD 20205

Dear Dr. Gartland,

I am writing to support the Baltimore-Campbell proposal which appeared in the Federal Register Vol. 46, #54, 17994-7, 1981. The proposal makes scientific sense and will not compromise human health or the integrity of natural environment.

Sincerely yours,

Bernard Roizman

BR/pt

Kovler Viral Oncology Laboratories · 910 East 58th Street · Chicago, Illinois 60637 · (312) 947-1867

STANFORD UNIVERSITY MEDICAL CENTER
STANFORD, CALIFORNIA 94305

DEPARTMENT OF PATHOLOGY
DAVID KORN, M.D., PROFESSOR AND CHAIRMAN

STANFORD UNIVERSITY SCHOOL OF MEDICINE, L235
(415) 497-5252

April 17, 1981

Dr. William Gartland
Office of Recombinant DNA
National Institute of General Medical Sciences
Building 31, 4A52
Bethesda, Marvland 20205

Dear Dr. Gartland:

I am in favor of the proposal to convert NIH guidelines into a nonregulatory code of standard practices and to reduce the recommended containment levels for some experiments as published in the Federal Register, Friday, March 20, 1981 (pp 17994-7), vol. 46: paragraph 54.

Yours sincerely,

Irving L. Weissman, M.D.
Associate Professor of Pathology

ILW:jfm

DEPARTMENT OF HEALTH & HUMAN SERVICES

Public Health Service

National Institutes of Health
Bethesda, Maryland 20205

April 17, 1981

Dr. William Gartland
Office of Recombinant DNA
National Institute of General
Medical Sciences
Building 31, 4A52

Dear Dr. Gartland:

I would like to comment on the proposed modifications of the "NIH Guidelines for Research Involving Recombinant DNA Molecules" as suggested by David Baltimore and Allan Campbell and published in the Federal Register of Friday, March 20, 1981, on pages 17994-17997. Inevitably, the Baltimore-Campbell proposal must also be considered in the light of the alternative suggestions that emerged from the meeting of the Chairpersons of Institutional Biosafety Committees in November of 1980. Both of these proposals involve an attempt to bring the Guidelines into a state of consistency with present evaluations of the potential for hazard in recombinant DNA experiments. As I see that evaluation, there is widespread agreement that experiments involving E. coli K12 or S. cerevisiae host-vector systems will not generate harmful organisms. For other experimental systems the data are less firm, but there are no good scientific reasons to presume that significant problems are likely. For these reasons, continued surveillance of recombinant DNA experiments through complex registration and review requirements is unwarranted. Nevertheless, exemption of experiments from the Guidelines seems to me less desirable than inclusion in a set of standards as suggested by Baltimore and Campbell. The latter approach, if we can take adherence to the CDC Guidelines as an example, means that investigators will still consider new protocols from the point of view of possible difficulties and will have the pressure of peers and common standards to enforce caution. Therefore I conclude that the Baltimore-Campbell approach is more appropriate than option A or C. Option B is essentially similar to the Baltimore-Campbell proposal. I do not see any valid reason for requiring prior review or registration, including the special case of Class 3 agents and deliberate attempts to obtain expression of a eukaryote gene.

The above refers to that part of the Baltimore-Campbell proposal relevant to the administrative aspects of the Guidelines. The second part of their proposal constitutes a major change in the actual containment levels for a variety of experiments. In some instances a lowering of containment levels is clearly called for. However there are some experiments which I know too little about to comment upon. I urge that the RAC carefully consider the experimental classifications at this time and proceed to lower containment wherever appropriate. However, I should make it clear that regardless of the containment levels specified, I believe it is time to eliminate the regulatory aspects of the Guidelines. We have engaged, for almost a decade, in a thorough examination of questions about possible hazards. I, for one, am glad that we took the time to ask and seek answers. The Guidelines served important purposes during that period. However, that examination has consistently indicated that the initial concerns were unsupportable, and we should promptly bring the situation into realistic conformity with that conclusion.

Sincerely yours,

Maxine Singer

Maxine Singer

UNIVERSITY OF CALIFORNIA, SAN FRANCISCO

BERKELEY • DAVIS • IRVINE • LOS ANGELES • RIVERSIDE • SAN DIEGO • SAN FRANCISCO SANTA BARBARA • SANTA CRUZ

SCHOOL OF MEDICINE
DEPARTMENT OF BIOCHEMISTRY AND BIOPHYSICS

SAN FRANCISCO, CALIFORNIA 94143
(415) 666-4324

April 20, 1981

Dr. William Gartland
Office of Recombinant DNA
National Institute of General Medical Sciences
Building 31
4A52
Bethesda, Maryland 20205

Dear Dr. Gartland:

I would like to strongly recommend adoption of the proposal for changing the NIH Guidelines as published in the Federal Register of Friday, March 20, 1981 on pages 17994-7 (Vol. 46, #54). This proposal to convert the Guidelines into a non-regulatory code makes complete sense in terms of the past years experiences in showing lack of risk and brings recombinant DNA research into the same framework as other microbiological research.

Sincerely yours,

Howard M. Goodman

Howard M. Goodman
Professor of Biochemistry

HMG:bm

STANFORD UNIVERSITY MEDICAL CENTER

DEPARTMENT OF GENETICS

April 20, 1981

Dr. William Gartland
Office of Recombinant DNA
National Institute of General Medical Sciences
Building 31, 4A52
Bethesda, Maryland 20205

Dear Dr. Gartland:

I am writing to offer my strong support for the proposal to convert the NIH Guidelines into a non-regulating code of standard practice and to reduce the recommended containment level for some experiments, as put forth by Drs. David Baltimore and Allan Campbell and published in the Federal Register of Friday, March 20, 1981. I agree strongly with the justifications for this proposal provided by Drs. Baltimore and Campbell.

Sincerely yours,

Stanley N. Cohen
Professor

SNC:ps

DEPARTMENT OF GENETICS, STANFORD UNIVERSITY SCHOOL OF MEDICINE, STANFORD, CALIFORNIA 94305 • (415) 497-5052

UNIVERSITY OF CALIFORNIA, SAN FRANCISCO

BERKELEY • DAVIS • IRVINE • LOS ANGELES • RIVERSIDE • SAN DIEGO • SAN FRANCISCO SANTA BARBARA • SANTA CRUZ

SCHOOL OF MEDICINE
DEPARTMENT OF BIOCHEMISTRY AND BIOPHYSICS

SAN FRANCISCO, CALIFORNIA 94143
(415) 666-4324

22 April 1981

Dr. William Gartland
Office of Recombinant DNA
National Institute of General Medical Sciences
Building 31, 4A52
Bethesda, Maryland 20205

Dear Bill:

I wish to comment on the proposals by David Baltimore and Allan Campbell as outlined in the Federal Register of March 20, 1981 on pages 17994-7 (Vol 46, No. 54). In view of their general knowledge and experience, I believe these proposals are eminently reasonable. Of crucial importance is that the guidelines would now set standards and provide guidance rather than regulate the performance of experiments. This change would certainly aid research in this area without, in my view, compromising attention to possible health hazards.

Sincerely yours,

Bill

William J. Rutter
Professor and Chairman

kh

STANFORD UNIVERSITY MEDICAL CENTER
STANFORD, CALIFORNIA 94305

DEPARTMENT OF BIOCHEMISTRY
STANFORD UNIVERSITY SCHOOL OF MEDICINE

Area Code 415
497-6161

April 22, 1981

Dr. William Gartland, Head
Office of Recombinant DNA
NIGMS, Bldg. 31 4A52
Bethesda, MD 20205

Dear Bill,

I am writing to you regarding the proposed changes in The Guidelines for Recombinant DNA Research put forward by Drs. Baltimore and Campbell that appeared in the Federal Register of Friday, March 20, 1981 on pages 17994-7 (Vol. 46 #54). As I understand their recommendation it is 1) to convert the current NIH Guidelines for Recombinant DNA Research from mandatory regulations (for virtually all university and institute scientists) to a non-mandated, but recommended code of standard practices and 2) to reduce the recommended containment levels for certain experiments.

Lest there be any doubt about my views on this let me be quite direct. I strongly favor their suggestion and have done so for some time. Indeed, in a letter to Dave Baltimore of July 2, 1980, I said "I find it increasingly difficult to accept the maintenance of a non-trivial government bureaucracy to contend with the mythical possibility that recombinant DNA experimentation is hazardous. After all we have not imposed the same requirements on virus research or other 'potential hazardous' laboratory activities. In those instances, society and the government have accepted individual and institutional assurances for safe practices and culpability for negligence or deliberate violations. RAC has elected a strategy for evolutionary change in The Guidelines, but in my view, it has not been without paying a substantial price: the time and energy of ORDA, RAC members, institutional committee members and the scientists doing the research, as well as the expenditures to maintain ORDA, ORDA, RAC and the new layers of bureaucracy that have been spawned in the universities. I do believe it is time to seriously consider whether the ORDA-RAC format should continue . . . . I would favor its dissolution and replacement by something like the advisories put out by CDC in the field of pathogenic microorganisms and tumor virus research; that is, an effective and a relatively simple classification and advisory for handling pathogenic or potentially pathogenic organisms and viruses. Didn't that kind of advice serve us well for tumor viruses before recombinant DNA"?

I have no reason to change my views now. The present proposal seems eminently sensible and prudent. It transforms The Guidelines from regulations (which they were) to guidelines (which they should be). My own early concerns that some recombinant DNA experiments might carry risks have long been dissipated. The data, discussions and experience of the last six years have convinced me that our earlier concerns are no longer warranted. I now believe that there is more to fear from the intrusions of government in the conduct of scientific research than from recombinant DNA experiments themselves. Consequently, I welcome the changes put forward by Baltimore and Campbell and hope that RAC will approve them promptly.

With best wishes,

Sincerely,

Paul Berg

Paul Berg
Willson Professor of Biochemistry

c.c. Dr. David Baltimore
PB/hk

2677 Ellendale Place
Los Angeles, California 90007

May 5, 1981

Recombinant DNA Advisory Committee
Office of Recombinant DNA Activities
National Institutes of Health
Building 31, Room 4A52
Bethesda, Maryland 20205

Greetings:

It is contrary to canons of evidence and logic that the Committee is now considering deregulation of recombinant DNA activities.

Since the last weakening of the Guidelines, a protein thought to be implicated in Down's syndrome (mongolism)—human interferon—has been produced in three different microorganisms. Viral links to human cancer have been traced, and infectious pathogenic naked DNA has been identified. Scandals involving misuse of recombinant DNA technology have occurred at two campuses of the University of California.

Despite the evidence indicative of the need for increased caution, automated polynucleotide synthesizers have appeared on the market, greatly simplifying procedures for those who would abuse this technology. And genetic engineering firms have proliferated to a total capitalization of nearly $400 million.

Quite clearly, it will become increasingly easy for careless, hasty, subverted, subversive, or deranged scientists to sooner or later wreak major havoc to a major crop, livestock species, or humanity. Truly relevant safety studies have been only minimally attempted, and even these have shown equivocal results not conducive to reassurance. The 1918 influenza pandemic illustrated with 20,000,000 corpses that a pathogenic virus need not be "viable" in the longterm sense to be devastating in the short run.

It is time to substantially strengthen, not to weaken or discard, controls in this field. Members of the Committee should consider carefully how society and history might judge them in the not-too-distant future.

L. Douglas DeNike

L. Douglas DeNike, Ph.D.

UNIVERSITY OF WASHINGTON
SEATTLE, WASHINGTON 98195

Program in Social Management of Technology

May 8, 1981

Dr. Donald Fredrickson
Director
National Institutes of Health
Bethesda, MD 20205

Dear Dr. Fredrickson:

Proposals to weaken the application of the Recombinant DNA Guidelines are currently before you, and I am writing to ask that you not promulgate any of these changes until adequate risk assessment studies have been performed. I am referring to the RAC actions of April 23-24, 1981 to exempt experiments in the III-O category and to end the prohibition on experiments with genes coding for toxins. In addition, I have some comments on the proposal by Drs. Baltimore and Campbell to convert the Guidelines into a recommended code of practice.

As I wrote to Dr. John Nutter of NIAID on December 10, 1981, the NIH "Risk Assessment Program" is seriously flawed in two major respects. First, it is only concerned with physical/environmental/health risks and these are not the only ones presented by r-DNA work. In addition to ethical and political risks and considerations, recent violations of the Guidelines should make us sensitive to the risks of intentional misconduct, accidents, human fallibility, carelessness, arrogance. I suspect that the DNA "incidents" in the future (and surely these will occur) will be based on such human foibles at least as often as on the failure of technological equipment, etc. And yet, no work is being done to assess such risks and mitigate their adverse aspects. The recent OTA report on Applied Genetics was similarly facile in this regard.

Second, most of the NIH Risk program uses "evidence" from experiments not designed to evaluate risk at all. A scientific experiment cannot generally be said to prove a proposition which is not part of the initial hypothesis or, more importantly, which does not contribute to the research design. Can you imagine the scandal if NIH peer review sections approved funds for research where the experiments were designed and conducted for other objectives? Researchers do not make the necessary observations, perform relevant alterations to experimental conditions, collect requisite data or analyze the data from a risk perspective when their objective in carrying out an experiment is not risk analysis.

314 Guggenheim, FS-15 / Telephone: (206) 543-7029

Dr. Donald Fredrickson
Page 2
May 8, 1981

Thus, we cannot make any statements about the safety of III-0 experiments which would justify exempting them from the Guidelines. Thus, we cannot justify allowing work with genes coding for toxins in the absence of supporting risk assessment work.

Finally, the proposal by Drs. Baltimore and Campbell would continue an ill-advised trend. Over the past few years the Guidelines have been relentlessly watered-down, with responsibility for overseeing r-DNA work transferred from NIH to institutional biohazard committees. Most, if not virtually all, of these committees are woefully unprepared to handle these responsibilities. I speak from my 3 years experience on one of the better of them. IBCs do not have sufficient staff time (via the BSO or otherwise) to assure that what is going on in the laboratories actually reflects what is written in the Guidelines; for example, as you well know, NIH has only recently begun to consider a program to assess the structure and performances of IBCs. However, the IBCs have served as a useful screening device, and a forum for airing of local concerns, at minimal cost in either dollars or time. Thus, NIH should continue to require their existence and adequate functioning.

Thank you for your consideration of my views.

Very truly yours,

Philip Bereano

Philip L. Bereano
Associate Professor

PLB:ec

cc: Hon. Richard Schweiker, Secretary, U.S. Dept. of Health and Human Services, Washington DC 20014
Sen. Orrin Hatch, Chair, Committee on Labor and Human Resources, U.S. Senate, Washington DC 20510
Sen. Edward Kennedy, Committee on Labor and Human Resources, U.S. Senate, Washington DC 20510
Rep. Doug Walgren, Chair, Subc. on Science, Research and Technology, U.S. House of Rep. Washington, DC 20515
Rep. John Dingell, Chair, Committee on Energy and Commerce, U.S. House of Rep. Washington DC 20515

OSU

The Ohio State University

University Health Service
Division of
Environmental Health
and Safety
John W. Wilce Student
Health Center
1875 Millikin Road
Columbus, Ohio 43210
Phone 614 422-2112

May 14, 1981

Dr. William J. Gartland
Office of Recombinant DNA Activities
National Institute of Health
Bethesda, MD 20014

Dear Bill:

I have been reading in the popular press about some more relaxation of the NIH Guidelines on recombinant DNA work. I am particularly concerned about the experiments with genes which control bacterial toxins. Based on my past experience, I would suggest a cautious approach to this relaxation.

In the mid 1960's, staphylococcus enterotoxin was being investigated as a potential incapacitating agent in the biological warfare program. The protocol called for the propagation and purification of large amounts of the toxin. At Ft. Detrick, Maryland, and especially at the Directorate of Biological Operations in Pine Bluff, Arkansas, we found that many of our laboratory technicians developed an allergic state when we decreased some of our containment criteria. In some of the people the allergic reaction involved the eyes and in others the reaction was a severe respiratory distress. We had very few problems with classical enterotoxin intoxications, but we had many man-hours lost due to the allergic reactions. Staphylococcus enterotoxin is not classified as a lethal toxin but its reactivity as a hyperallergen created conditions in some individuals that were nearly lethal.

I am not certain that the enterotoxins and the allergen are the same chemical molecule, and I am not certain that all bacterial toxins are as potent as staph enterotoxin. Until the answers are known, I recommend against relaxation of the guidelines. I can visualize the sensitization of laboratory workers in a recombinant DNA laboratory and a shock expression from an incidental contact away from the laboratory.

Very truly yours,

E J Lazear

E. J. Lazear, Ph.D.
Biological Safety Officer

/lt

MEMORANDUM

DEPARTMENT OF HEALTH, EDUCATION, AND WELFARE
PUBLIC HEALTH SERVICE
NATIONAL INSTITUTES OF HEALTH

TO : Director, NIAID

DATE: JUN 22 1981

FROM : Director, NIH

SUBJECT: Delegation of Authorities Under the NIH Guidelines for Research Involving Recombinant DNA Molecules

The NIH Guidelines for Research Involving Recombinant DNA Molecules (Federal Register, Volume 45, pp. 77384-77409, November 21, 1980) specify in Section IV-C-8 that "'Director, NIH,' or 'Director' means the Director of the National Institutes of Health and any other officer or employee of NIH to whom authority has been delegated."

Previously, on July 12, 1979, I delegated to you certain specified authorities under the Guidelines. By this memorandum, I am hereby delegating to you all other responsibilities of the Director, NIH specified in the Guidelines. These are detailed in the subsections of Section IV-E-1 of the Guidelines, and include the Chairmanship of the Federal Interagency Advisory Committee on Recombinant DNA Research.

D. S. Fredrickson
Donald S. Fredrickson, M.D.

cc: Dr. Gartland
Dr. Talbot
Dr. Perpich

72 Jane Street
New York N Y 10014
(212) 675-7173

Coalition for Responsible Genetic Research

July 29, 1981

Dr. William Gartland
ORDA
National Institutes of Health
Bethesda, Md. 20014

Dear Dr. Gartland:

Our organization herewith submits comments on the Baltimore/Campbell proposal to downgrade the Recombinant DNA Guidelines from regulation to a recommended code of practice. Recent broad exemptions and elimination of prohibitions in recommended DNA research by the NIH make it especially impelling to maintain the guidelines as regulations.

The Baltimore/Campbell proposal would remove those mechanisms essential to the enforcement of the guidelines. Given the intensely competitive nature of the research and its development, this proposal would facilitate lower safety standards and less careful procedures. For some individuals and groups, regulation alone acts as a deterrent.

Under the Guidelines as regulation, the existence of Institutional Biosafety Committees is required with these committees responsible to the NIH. The IBC's exercise a measure of control over over the adequacy of safety procedures and the detection of hazards. They function, as well, as boards for the consideration of scientifically inadequate or improperly-conducted research. Linkage of IBC's with the NIH is of prime importance in maintenance of standards.

Industry has been complying with the NIH regulations voluntarily. Should "recommended standards" be substituted for the regulations, it is quite likely that industrial compliance will become meaningless: competitive pressures may well activate industry to take advantage of unregulated shortcuts to large-scale production. Historically, industrial self-policing has not been successful.

There are still many unanswered questions for this emerging technology (new host-vector systems, exchange of genetic material in the environment, etc.). Non-mandatory standards might convey a sense of "safeness" that would tend to close off the issue of potential risks. The optimum course of action should reasonably include risk assessment experimentation to keep pace with recombinant DNA research and development.

Further reason for mandatory Guidelines is the question of uniformity. Voluntary standards would be adopted as "required" by some institutions and not by others. The "patchwork" results might well create brain-drain situations; away from institutions which choose to be "more stringent". With competition among researchers as acute as it is, it seems not unlikely that the lowest common denominator of standards would ultimately prevail.

In view of the many contraindications to adopting the Baltimore/Campbell proposal, we strongly urge that the Guidelines remain as regulation.

FR;fh

Yours very truly,

Francine Simring
Executive Director

cc:

Richard Schweiker
Orrin Hatch
Edward Kennedy
Doug Walgren
John Dingell

WASHINGTON UNIVERSITY

ST. LOUIS, MISSOURI 63130

GRADUATE SCHOOL OF ARTS AND SCIENCES
OFFICE OF THE DEAN
314 / 889-6880

August 18, 1981

To: Dr. Elizabeth Milewski
Office of Recombinant DNA Activities
NIAID
Building 31, Room 4A52
National Institutes of Health
Bethesda, Maryland 20205

From: Luther S. Williams, Dean (LSW)
Graduate School of Arts and Sciences

I have reviewed the "document Evaluating Risks Associated with Recombinant DNA Research" - Proposed recommendation of the working group.

Overall, I am in agreement with this document as presented, especially the review of risk assessment data and reports of conferences addressing various aspects of presumed risks. The summary (recommendation S) on pages 35 and 36 are excellent statements of the salient items considered and the resulting conclusions.

My overall endorsement is for retention of the provisions of the Baltimore-Campbell Proposal with the important condition that the resulting guidelines are mandatory.

As my tenure on the RAC has ended, I shall not attend the September meeting.

31 August 1981

Thomas E. Malone, Acting Director
N ational Institutes of Health
Building 1, Room 124
Bethesda, Maryland 21015

Dear Mr. Malone:

It is with considerable concern that I write regarding the decisions of the National Institutes of Health which progressively weaken its modest controls for Recombinant DNA experiments. Instead of strengthening provisions for containment and for oversight by the NIH and local biohazards safety committees, the thrust has been to exempt increasing numbers and types of experiments. For example, in 1980 NIH's Recombinant Advisory Committee (RAC) reclassified as category III-O most work with E. Coli K-12 and Saccharomyces cerevisiae and determined that it could be done at the P1 level of physical containment, requiring registration only with the local biosafety committee, not with NIH. At its April 23-24, 1981 meeting, the RAC then exempted all experiments in the III-O category from the guidelines with the exception of large-scale work and experiments involving CDC class 3 agents.

Furthermore, RAC reclassified certain experiments with toxin genes at the same time. I understand, that one of the consultants who proposed this reclassification stressed that the risks from experiments with genes coding for toxins are unknown.

Such actions are most astonishing for scientists to take based, it appears, more on faith that nothing will go wrong -- the violations to date of the guidelines aside -- than on proper risk assessments studies along a range of present and projected experiments. It should be inconceivable for an organization of scientists such as NIH to preside over the steady dismantling of the guidelines before it has in hand a rich body of risk assessment information to support this position.

Additionally troublesome, particularly at a time when the commercialization of RDNA is growing, is the proposal by David Baltimore and Alan Campbell, members of the RAC, to move from mandatory guidelines to a recommended code of standard practice. If these are abolished, you are in effect creating a familiar situation wherein mandatory controls will follow lethal accidents or injury. This approach contradicts the whole idea of controls which is to prevent death or injury.

In contrast, by requiring safe practices in the uses of RDNA techniques and effective review and enforcement mechanisms, the NIH can show an authentic commitment both to high standards in research and the avoidance of harmful experiments. It does not have to repeat past mistakes and wait for human suffering to produce health and safety controls. The NIH can choose at the outset to put the health and safety of the whole society above special interests.

Thomas E. Malone
Acting Director
National Institutes of Health

31 August 1981
Page 2

It only seems fair that the burden of proof that RDNA research will not harm people's health or violate the integrity of the natural environment should fall on the shoulders of its practitioners and other supporters. It is they who have to earn the public's trust. The Baltimore and Campbell proposal which in effect says "trust us" is archaic in a world where the harmful sides of science and technology are all too visible. The public is rightly wary and should be respected for its concern.

In my view the proposal is a "thorough mistake", to borrow some apt words from Whitehead, especially when one observes the sometimes unseemly scramble for a piece of the action by universities and gene-slicing companies, and researchers in conflicts of interests which are bound to undermine not only public confidence but also the conduct of science itself.

These circumstances should dictate a move toward stricter standards and enforcement mechanisms which extend to the genetic engineering industry. However, if the Recombinant Advisory Committee accepts the proposal to replace mandatory guidelines with a code of standard practice, it is essential that the NIH lead a broad public discussion of this fundamental matter and that its decisions reflect the interests of all members of the society. By virtue of its present composition, the RAC's frame of reference remains too narrow to guide policy on RDNA research.

I look forward to hearing from you.

Sincerely,

Claire Nader

Suite 1013
1875 Connecticut Avenue, N.W.
Washington, D.C. 20009

Residential College
East Quadrangle

The University of Michigan
Ann Arbor, Michigan 48109
(313) 763-0176

September 2, 1981

Dr. William Gartland
ORDA
National Institutes of Health
Building 31, Room 4852
Bethesda, Maryland 20014

Dear Dr. Gartland:

I am opposed to the proposal from Eli Lilly & Co. (#1027 and #7, Federal Register, August 4, 1981). This proposal would exempt large-scale work involving E.coli K-12, Saccharamyces cerevisiae, Bacillus subtilis, and any other host-vector systems listed in Appendix C of the guidelines.

I have the following comments on Dr. Irving Johnson's justification of the proposal:

1. The statement that "the principle of the absence of increased risk with increased volume has been accepted by the RAC" is quite inaccurate, and not supported by the record. The claim is based on the decision of the RAC at its June 1980 meeting to delete a sentence in section I-D-6 of the guidelines which read as follows:

> "We differentiate between small- and large-scale experiments with organisms containing recombinant DNAs because the probability of escape from containment barriers normally increases with increasing scale."
> (Minutes, June 5-6, 1980, p.28-9)

The minutes of the meeting show that discussion of the proposal to delete this sentence was limited to the narrow issue of its accuracy. There is no indication that the decision was based on the far broader principle claimed by Dr. Johnson. Indeed, there is a strong indication that the committee did not accept that principle since it also voted to leave the full prohibition on large-scale work in place (p.29).

2. The fact that "no unforeseen difficulties have been encountered" when the industry has operated under controls involving prior review cannot be used to justify the claim that no problems will arise when controls are removed. Perhaps the genetic engineering industry has done so well because the controls were so effective; or perhaps it is because relatively little work has been undertaken; or perhaps it is because, as Dr. Johnson would claim, all the processes involved are safe. In fact, we do not know, because we do not have the social science or risk assessment data which might begin to give indications of the level of safety of large-scale genetic engineering.

3. The fact that the British Genetic Manipulation Advisory Group (GMAG) is to consider in late September a proposal from the Confederation of British Industry (CBI) to weaken the British controls for large-scale work should not be used to justify the Lilly proposal. By using a hypothetical decision in Britain to argue for a decision by the RAC to weaken controls in the U.S., Lilly is encouraging the two decision-making processes to move in a spiral, the end result of which could be seriously weakened controls in both countries. For a decision by the RAC to weaken oversight of industrial processes will place additional pressure on Britain and other countries to do likewise, lest they be left behind in the race for technological dominance in the genetic engineering field. (1)

In any case, it is not at all clear that GMAG will take the "positive action" which Dr. Johnson anticipates. My understanding is that there is no significant support for the CBI proposal, and strong criticism from some members of GMAG, particularly those who represent trade unions. So it seems unlikely that the proposal will be implemented. (2)

The RAC should also be aware that even if the CBI proposal were approved, large-scale work in Britain would still remain under regulation by the Health and Safety Executive (HSE). The CBI is not proposing that the HSE requirement that large-scale work be registered with the agency be removed. However, if the Lilly proposal is approved, no specific controls would apply in this country, and in particular, there would be no registration requirement. Consequently, it would be difficult to collect data on the extent and location of large-scale industrial processes, let alone exert any form of oversight.

4. No comparative studies of the risks of small- and large-scale work have been carried out, and any statements comparing these risks are developed against a background of very wide uncertainty. However, at least one study of the risks of large-scale work has been completed. This is the report of Dr. K.Sargeant and Dr. C.G.T.Evans of the Microbiological Research Establishment, Porton, U.K. commissioned by the Commission of European Communities and published in 1979.(3) The report does not play up the risks of large-scale work involving genetically manipulated organisms. It has been described as a "cool, non-scaremongering assessment."(4) Nevertheless, it points to several areas of concern, including the following:

a) "The new features presented by an expanding biotechnology today are the very large scale on which some micro-organisms are about to be grown for the first time, the very large number of people who will encounter these newly available micro-organisms or their products, and the possibility that the environment might be altered by their use or inadvertent release." (p.22)

b) Some of the special hazards of biotechnology rest on the possibility that the organisms thought to be in the fermenter are not what they are thought to be, or are not behaving in the way assumed. First, there may be phenotypic changes in which organisms adapt to changes in their environment with changes in their biochemical processes. Such changes might affect the virulence of organisms thought to be harmless. The authors point to the example of

Aspergillus flavus which produces aflatoxins in only trace amounts at 15 and 45 degrees centigrade, but at 35 degrees centigrade, produces 40 mg/kg (p.25).

Second, there might be genotypic variation or contamination with foreign organisms, particularly under conditions of continuous cultivation, where organisms are maintained through many thousands of generations: "If a contaminant arose which was able to maintain itself then no matter how carefully the original testing had been done, and irrespective of the purpose to which the product was to be put, no guarantee concerning either the safety of the process or the culture could be given. The situation is, in this respect, fundamentally different from farming with animals and plants, where much more precise control of the genotype is possible because one generation is cultivated at a time and alterations in genotype are, in any case, less frequent and much more obvious." (pp.34-5)

c) The discharge of live organisms into the environment might have ecological effects. For example, the continuous low-level discharge of antibiotic might create ideal conditions for the selection of resitant organisms. If contained on a plasmid, that genetic information "could then be passed by stages throughout the microbial world." (p.31) Another possible effect might be that "the discharge of live organisms to the environment could ... increase the food supply to the natural flora and fauna, or supply competition, which if successful, might change the natural balance with no predictable result." (p.31)

No doubt it is recognition of possibilities such as these which has led many scientists who have considered the hazards of small- and large-scale work work to conclude that large-scale work presents special types of problems which,at this stage in the development of the technology, require careful monitoring and control. I feel that that position is fully justified, and therefore support the continuation of the present system of prior review of large-scale proposals by the RAC.

Sincerely,

Susan Wright
Head, Science Program

Notes

1. On pressures in the genetic engineering field, see, e.g. the statement of Michael Ross of Genentech, Inc., quoted in the Wall Street Journal,8-28-81, p.28: "If you come out a year after someone else, forget it. You'll have 10% of the market, and he'll have 90%."

2. Letter of Donna Haber, Divisional Officer, Association of Scientific Technical and Managerial Staffs, London, and member, GMAG, 26th August 1981.

3. K.Sargeant and C.G.T.Evans, Hazards involved in the industrial use of micro-organisms: A study of the necessity, content and management principles of a possible Community action (Brussels: Commission of the European Communities, 1979).

4. Anthony Tucker, "The best of a nasty business," Guardian, 5-8-1980, p.22. See also Robert Walgate, " How safe will biobusiness be?" Nature, 1-10-80, pp.126-7.

DEPARTMENT OF HEALTH & HUMAN SERVICES

Public Health Service

National Institutes of Health
Bethesda, Maryland 20205

September 8, 1981

Dr. William Gartland
Office of Recombinant DNA Activities
Bldg. 31, Rm. 4A-52
Bethesda, MD 20205

Dear Dr. Gartland:

Thank you for sending me the proposal of the working group for revision of the Guidelines, dated August 21, 1981. Although I realize that there will be a formal request for public comment once the RAC adopts a recommendation, I would like now to make some comments on the document prepared the working group. Please transmit these comments to the RAC as they may wish to consider them during their discussions of the proposal.

I do not believe that the document does a convincing job of supporting the recommendations. This is not meant to indicate that I agree or disagree with the recommendations, but only to state that the arguments are not put forth as clearly as they might be. This results from the lengthy discussion of scarcely relevant issues and the very brief description of others.

To a large extent, the document has the tone of 1976, not 1981. The paragraph in the middle of page 5 (A. Basic Assumptions) is a good examples: these are not assumption but questions and the wording is not in concordance with sound scientific thinking. It never becomes clear why the newly proposed changes now make sense, as distinguished from changes previously adopted. For example, most experiments with E. coli K12 systems are already exempt from the Guidelines and any questions regarding those that are not exempt, or those involving alternative E. coli systems, turn on properties (such as ability to be established) relevant to many host-vector systems and on the nature of the recombinants (e.g., toxins, high expression systems, etc). The lengthy discussion of E. coli both in the text and the appendix seem out of place and do not help to focus on the present issues. On the other hand, the document addresses adequately neither the reasons for proposing to abandon the prohibitions nor the reasons for maintaining part IV essentially unaltered. The document should concentrate on the issues at hand and speak specifically to the proposed changes. Note too that the statement on the bottom of page 2 describing the recommendations as adopting the containment provisions of the Baltimore-Campbell proposal is incorrect: the containment provisions of the Baltimore-Campbell proposal did not, according to my copy, eliminate the prohibitions and further, they specified the use of biological containment.

The report makes a single brief recommendation regarding changes in part IV of the Guidelines. Yet the proposal on containment mandates corresponding changes in Part IV. Those sections of IV dealing with aspects of part III that would no longer exist (e.g., IV-D-3-f, IV-D-5-b) and with the prohibited experiments should be eliminated. Also, the recommendations make part II-D-1, II-D-2 and II-D-3 moot. If part of the motivation for the changes is to make the Guidelines more understandable and straightforward, irrelevant sections should be omitted.

There is a sense in which the recommendations appear inconsistent. This is perhaps best described by comparing them to the Baltimore-Campbell proposals. The latter represent a smaller change in containment than the proposal of the working group because the prohibitions were maintained and because biological containment remained a factor. On the other hand, the Baltimore-Campbell approach represented a larger change in regulation since the Guidelines became voluntary on a national basis, though not necessarily within an institution. The report of the working group deals with the scientific issues relevant to containment, but only very briefly with those relevant to regulatory mechanisms. Further, the statements about regulatory issues do not adequately support the recommendation to leave the extensive system of IBCs, RAC, ORDA, etc in place. The final report should deal explicitly with why changes in regulatory procedures are or are not recommended. Absent such discussion, the recommendations are mystifying and likely to engender additional skepticism in the scientific community. Clarifying the ambivalency, should entail dealing with one of the more difficult aspects of the present scene, namely, the public perception of scientific and technological risks. On the one hand, the available scientific evidence indicates that the initial questions about recombinant research have been answered to the effect that no serious potential for unique hazard exists. Yet, it is impossible to make an absolute statement; only the probability of risk can be described. The public, however, may remain anxious, to varying degrees, absent absolute assurances. If the recommendation to maintain the complex system of control is motivated by a concern for the anxieties of the public (a motivation that is not inappropriate if such anxieties exist) then I believe the report should so state. I offer the following possible wording for consideration and debate.

"The concerns about potential hazard that were raised when recombinant DNA experiments were first initiated need to be reevaluated in the light of present scientific evidence. That evidence, gathered over the last seven years, supports a conclusion that the likelihood of any untoward effects from these experiments is exceedingly low. Thus, the extensive and complex system of containment and control embodied in earlier versions of the Guidelines is no longer warranted, according to scientific evaluation. Nevertheless, the RAC recognizes that while scientific assessment can yield probabilities, it can never provide certainties. Accordingly, public concern about the experiments may remain and therefore some continuing evaluation and oversight is desirable."

Sincerely yours,

Maxine Singer

Maxine Singer, Ph.D.
Chief, Laboratory of Biochemistry
National Cancer Institute

Ray Thornton's Statement
September 10-11, 1981 NIH-RAC Meeting

I have a statement concerning our deliberations today. First, let me express my great confidence in Dick Krause, who has been delegated responsibility for receiving recommendations from this advisory committee. I have enjoyed many opportunities of working with him, and know his scientific and professional judgment will work to the benefit of the people affected by the actions of the National Institutes of Health.

At the same time, however, there can be no adequate statement as to how much we will all miss the wise counsel and leadership of Don Fredrickson as we continue to wrestle with the interaction of science and society. Don has a great gift of expressing clearly, as only an outstanding scientist could, his understanding of the continuing relationship between public policy and science.

Whenever either side of this relationship, the public or the scientific community, invades the province of the other or disregards the proper input of the other into decision making, the result is at best high levels of tension and frustration. At worst there may be attempts to regulate thought, as in laws regarding what theories may be taught; or just as bad, attempts to eliminate input from the public as to how scientific research should be conducted with public funds.

May I ask your indulgence as I cite the first few paragraphs of the statement I made in opening hearings on DNA research in Congress in 1977. This was at a time when legislation was being considered to prohibit or severely limit such research.

"True science always stands upon a frontier. It probes at the edges of our knowledge and our ignorance, and we accept its contributions as valuable, its continuation as a necessity. Perceived as a gradual extension of the sphere of knowledge, science is accepted and praised as both our benefactor and our servant.

"This is the science with which we are most comfortable, the science which explains how things work, which promises health, physical well-being, and material progress.

"But the boundaries of the physical and biological sciences are not so easily contained. From time to time we find or come upon a field of inquiry which fundamentally challenges our concepts of life and nature, which confronts us too directly for our collective comfort or convenience, and yet intrigues us too greatly to ignore.

"It is on this meeting ground of science and philosophy where man has made his greatest scientific advances. It is also here that science has caused its greatest strains upon our social, political, and religious institutions.

"When Galileo offered the theory that the Earth revolves around the Sun, it was bad enough to his contemporaries that he committed scientific error. It was worse that he committed heresy as well.

"Yet Galileo probed only the physical universe. As science has progressed and transformed our lives in so many ways, we have rejected many of the dogmas of an earlier day....

"... The scientific community often resolves its own conflicts more easily than our political community can even understand them....But the scientific community cannot ignore the concerns of its larger constituency, and Government cannot isolate itself from the science that it has encouraged and supported.

"Consideration of these questions brings us face to face with what I believe is one of the most fundamental issues before policymakers today: the issue of society interacting with science and the determination of the basic social responsibilities for the decision making process."

It has been a source of great personal satisfaction to me that my role as Chairman of the Science, Research, and Technology Subcommittee slowed the rush toward federal legislation, and eventually led to the acceptance by the Congress of guidelines promulgated by the NIH for the conduct of experiments funded by the public.

Except as required by local legislation, one who does not receive public money for the conduct of experiments is not affected in any way by such guidelines, unless by agreement such person accepts the guidelines on a voluntary basis. But I am unable to accept the suggestion that a person conducting research with public money stands entirely beyond the boundaries of public inquiry.

I believe the public has the right to say, and to ensure, that no public funds may be spent in an effort to construct drug resistant or toxigenic microorganisms. Certainly the public has the right to ensure that such microorganisms, if constructed, should not be released into the environment. Most would also agree that the public has the right to regulate under what conditions experiments with human subjects may be conducted.

There is, in summary, an ongoing vital connection between science and public policy.

Dr. Maxine Singer recognized this before the Congressional Committee and said:

> "Scientists today recognize their responsibility to the public that supports scientific work in the expectation that the results will have a significant positive impact on society. To describe the scientific community of the late twentieth century otherwise is to ignore or misunderstand the evidence. Dispute over the best way to exercise that responsibility must not be confused with a negation of it. The scientific community has accepted the counsel of ethicists, philosophers, and representatives of the public who have long troubled to point out this responsibility.
>
> "Scientists also accept the need to restrict certain laboratory practices in order to protect the safety and health of laboratory workers and the public. Further, we recognize the need to consider possible hazards before large scale activity is undertaken and before untoward events occur. But we differentiate between restrictions on hazardous or potentially hazardous activities and restrictions on intellectual freedom.

"For the future, scientists need to continue, together with federal and local governments, to evolve policies that offer protection from potential hazards and preserve opportunities for discovery and development of safe and desirable applications. Scientists must share their insights into the nature of living things with increasing numbers of people so that debate can be predicated on understanding rather than fear. In order to counteract the growing pessimism about the nature of knowledge, the proper separation of science from technology must be made and, in the continuing dialog, the distinct values and problems inherent in each must be carefully articulated. Finally if scientists commit themselves to their unique opportunities to serve as an early warning system, society can progress with prudence and caution as scientific knowledge grows."

In the Recombinant DNA Advisory Committee, an effort has been made to allow the public to have an input into recommendations which affect not only science, but the public as well, without unduly restricting the research which the public interest requires that we pursue.

The argument that guidelines for the conduct of publicly funded research are not needed because nothing more dangerous than now exists may be developed by this technology is beguiling, but false on two counts:

First, human experience has shown that any tool powerful enough to produce good results of sufficient importance to shake Wall Street and offer hope of treating diabetes is also powerful enough, wrongly used, to produce bad results of equal consequence.

Second, even accepting the assumption, with which I disagree, that nothing other than beneficial results may stem from this research, it does not follow that the public thereby loses its interest in having suitable guidelines for the expenditure of public funds.

Such guidelines might indeed need to be more carefully drawn, and perhaps should extend to all publicly funded research which may raise issues of the kind involved here.

Even if no additional increment of danger exists, it does not follow that dangerous or ethically or socially offensive experiments, with or without the technology involved here, should be conducted free of any guidelines except standards of good laboratory practices.

I am surprised to hear suggestions that because many of the unanswered questions relating to experiments in this field are political and social questions, that the guidelines have no further reason for existence. I doubt that the public will long remain aloof from decision making concerning the expenditure of public funds, whatever the purpose of those expenditures may be. If the possibility for interaction of science and public members as afforded by this committee is ended, some other mechanism for that input will be developed.

I believe the recommendation that the nature of the guidelines be downgraded to a simple statement of good laboratory practices, raises issues as serious - though opposite from - the ones considered by Congress several years ago.

In my view, the orderly progression of our recommendations to the Director, who has steadily eased the difficulties of performing experiments as rapidly as the consequences of that work may be evaluated, has been a useful example of the public working together with science to attain mutual goals.

I make this rather long statement in order to establish, for the record, my position with regard to the issue which the committee is considering, and to offer my views as to how we should proceed.

INSTITUTE OF MEDICINE
NATIONAL ACADEMY OF SCIENCES
2101 CONSTITUTION AVENUE WASHINGTON, D.C. 20418

September 24, 1981

Ray Thornton, J.D.
President
Arkansas State University
State University, Arkansas 72467

Dear Ray:

I am writing to follow up on the RAC meeting of September 10, 1981, and the action taken by RAC on the report of the subcommittee to review the guidelines.

I still support the basic thrust of the subcommittee's report. I was against making the guidelines totally voluntary and voted so. Once RAC voted to convert the guidelines to a voluntary code of standard practice, I did favor moving ahead with getting public comment on the matter. To this end, I strongly urge that ORDA place a notice in Science, JAMA, New England Journal of Medicine and Nature (as well as other publications you or others might think of) advising the readership of the proposal in question, of the issue of the Federal Register in which the proposal is published, of how to obtain that issue of the Federal Register, and urging comments to be sent in.

Even if publishing such notices delays the proceedings somewhat, in my view it is still necessary to do so. The broadening of solicitation of public comment is essential to proceeding responsibly. The Federal Register notice produces comment mostly from scientists with vested interest. We need their input but we also need to go beyond that.

I think the guidelines have served us well. Systematic, step-wise dismantlement would permit finding out what happens at each step. Your good statement of September 10 emphasizes that the public has an interest in having suitable guidelines for publicly funded research that raises issues such as recombinant DNA research does, and pehaps other kinds of research do or will. It is therefore imperative to be as informed as possible about the opinions of various publics (of scientists and non-scientists) before proceeding with changing to a voluntary code of standard practice and ceasing the required tracking of recombinant DNA research by IBC's.

If I can help in any way, please let me know.

Sincerely,

Elena

Elena O. Nightingale, M.D., Ph.D.
Senior Program Officer

cc: William Gartland, Jr., Ph.D.

Arkansas State University

OFFICE OF THE PRESIDENT
STATE UNIVERSITY, AR 72467
501/972-3030

October 2, 1981

Dr. Elena O. Nightingale
Senior Program Officer
Institute of Medicine
National Academy of Sciences
2101 Constitution Avenue
Washington, D.C. 20418

Dear Elena:

Thank you for your letter of September 24, 1981 regarding the committee action on relaxation of research guidelines.

I appreciate your views on the issue, as expressed through your vote, and I strongly agree that ORDA should place a notice in the publications you suggest. It is essential to have public comment from a broad base if we are to act responsibly and in the public interest.

Thank you for your support.

Sincerely,

Ray Thornton
President

RT:po

CC: William Gartland, Jr.

MASSACHUSETTS INSTITUTE OF TECHNOLOGY CAMBRIDGE, MASSACHUSETTS 02139
Center for Cancer Research Room E17-529B

November 19, 1981

Dr. William Gartland
Director, Office of Recombinant
DNA Activities
Building 31, Room 4A52
National Institutes of Health
Bethesda, Maryland 20205

Dear Dr. Gartland,

I am strongly in favor of the suggested revisions of the NIH guidelines. These revisions will be in the best interest of the public by increasing the rate of research and decreasing the bureaucracy of research. We now have extensive experience with DNA recombinant experiments and have no reason to anticipate they will yield unknown hazardous organisms, quite the contrary.

Sincerely yours,

Phillip A. Sharp
Professor

PAS/ms

COMMITTEE ON SCIENCE AND TECHNOLOGY
U.S. HOUSE OF REPRESENTATIVES
SUITE 2321 RAYBURN HOUSE OFFICE BUILDING
WASHINGTON, D.C. 20515
(202) 225-6371

November 20, 1981

Ray Thornton, Chairman
Recombinant Advisory Committee
National Institutes of Health
Bethesda, Maryland 20014

Dear Mr. Thornton: Ray

First, let us commend you and the other members of the NIH Recombinant DNA Advisory Committee for the excellent job the Committee has done under your fine leadership during the past four years. The responsible actions taken by the Committee stand as evidence that a broadly representative group from the scientific community and the lay public can effectively oversee the conduct of research in an area of high promise and arguable risk. We would like to commend the NIH, too, for its careful administration of the NIH Recombinant DNA guidelines.

We are writing to express some concerns that we have with regard to the recent proposal by the Committee to change the Guidelines to a voluntary code of standard practice. As we understand it, the changes in the Guidelines would accomplish the following:

(1) The Institutional Biosafety Committees would no longer be required to oversee proposals involving recombinant DNA.

(2) No longer would any type of recombinant DNA experiment be strictly prohibited. Rather, there would be only an admonition against two types of experiments: one, introducing drug resistance into organisms that would not naturally acquire it; and two, introducing the ability into organisms to manufacture several very lethal toxins.

(3) There would no longer be a specific provision prohibiting the deliberate release into the environment of recombinant DNA organisms.

(4) The Guidelines as they now exist would be no more than a voluntary code of standard laboratory practice with no mandated review of experiments by the Committee, and there would no longer be sanctions for scientists who exceed the bounds of safe experimentation.

It is our belief that some scientific experiments should require public review. The scientific community cannot isolate itself from the larger community that it serves and presume that an individual scientist is always capable of deciding that the degree of hazard associated with a particular experiment is acceptable to the public. Moreover, where public funds are spent, the expenditure of those funds carries with it an accountability to the public. Just as the public has a right to regulate the conditions under which human subjects are used in research, so does the public have the right to ensure that drug-resistant or toxigenic organisms are not constructed. Certainly, if such organisms are constructed the public must be assured through some form of open review that they are not released into the environment.

Scientists must accept (and we believe the majority do) the need to restrict certain hazardous laboratory practices to protect health and safety while realizing that these restrictions do not represent an infringement of their intellectual freedom. It would, we believe, be prudent for scientists to continue to share their insights with an increasing number of people. To do otherwise might invite a public reaction based on fear rather than on understanding.

Another concern that arises in this regard is that without reasonable Guidelines, the burgeoning industrial use of recombinant DNA technology would have no review. Up to now private firms have voluntarily submitted to review by the RAC. This voluntary compliance implies a consent to be governed and thus submission to the Guidelines then becomes non-voluntary, as we are sure you are aware.

If the Guidelines become only a voluntary code of standard practice, private firms will be more likely not to comply. The biotechnology industry is still too young for the inherent safety or hazard of the industry to be clear. Until the industry matures and this matter becomes clearer, we believe that a degree of caution should be exercised. The industry is very promising, however, and caution should be combined with encouragement, in our view.

Ray Thornton, Chairman
November 20, 1981
Page 3

We would request that you make the other members of the RAC aware of the concerns we have expressed. We would urge at the very least that the system of Institutional Biosafety Committees not be allowed to terminate. Perhaps these committees should be given some guidelines for action. It may be prudent to ask the individual IBC's to review any biologically hazardous experiment, whether or not it involves recombinant DNA.

We appreciate the opportunity to continue this discussion with you. We are confident that the Committee with yourself as Chairman will continue to act in the best interest of both the scientific and the non-scientific communities.

Sincerely,

DON FUQUA
Member of Congress

DOUG WALGREN
Member of Congress

ALBERT GORE
Member of Congress

UNIVERSITY OF MISSOURI-COLUMBIA

College of Agriculture
and School of Medicine

Biochemistry Department

M 121 Medical Sciences Building
Columbia, Missouri 65212
Telephone (314) 882-8795

November 25, 1981

Dr. William Gartland
Office of Recombinant DNA Activities
National Institutes of Health
Bethesda, MD 20205

Dear Dr. Gartland:

At its meeting on November 12, 1981, the University of Missouri Institutional Biosafety Committee discussed the proposal to change the NIH Guidelines to a voluntary code of practice status.

After some discussion, the IBC reached a consensus that the current practice does not impair research activities to a significant degree. Further, it was generally felt that the Guidelines had served the useful purpose of raising awareness levels to the problem of biological safety in general. This function would not be carried out as effectively by a purely voluntary mechanism. As new data on the benignity of rDNA procedures become available, further relaxation of the Guidelines will undoubtedly occur, but the very existence of a cumbersome procedure makes individual scientists more attuned to issues of laboratory safety.

Several members of the Committee also stated that some investigators still will require monitoring in the future, especially as some potentially hazardous applications (e.g., cloning toxin genes for vaccine production) are permitted. Therefore, keeping present IBC's in operation may be more effective in the long run than reestablishing committees to review certain protocols. The Committee therefore recommends that the Guidelines be adjusted as necessary, but not abolished completely, nor made purely voluntary.

Sincerely yours,

Francis J. Schmidt
Assistant Professor
Chair, University of Missouri IBC

FJS/cll

THE WISTAR INSTITUTE

THIRTY-SIXTH STREET AT SPRUCE

PHILADELPHIA, PA. 19104

HILARY KOPROWSKI, M.D.
DIRECTOR

PHONE: (215) 243-3700
CABLE ADDRESS: WISTARINST

December 23, 1981

Director
Office of Recombinant DNA Activities
Building 31, Room 4A52
National Institutes of Health
Bethesda, Maryland 20205

Dear Sir:

This letter is in response to the proposed revision of the NIH guidelines for research involving recombinant DNA. The members of our Institutional Biosafety Committee met to discuss the proposed revisions and we feel that we are in complete agreement with the spirit of these revisions. We feel, however, that it would be beneficial to include with these revisions a strong recommendation that each institution continue to have an internal review committee so that safety and responsibility in experimentation will be maintained.

The Wistar Institute had an internal committee before the guidelines required that we do so and will continue this practice in the future. We hope that other responsible institutes do the same.

Sincerely yours,

Peter Curtis /sb

Peter Curtis, Ph.D.
Chairman, Institutional
Biosafety Committee

/sb

STANFORD UNIVERSITY MEDICAL CENTER
STANFORD, CALIFORNIA 94305 • (415) 497-5715

STANFORD UNIVERSITY SCHOOL OF MEDICINE
Department of Medicine
Division of Infectious Diseases

December 29, 1981

Director, Office of Recombinant DNA Activities
National Institutes of Health
Building 31, Room 4 A 52
Bethesda, MD. 20205

Dear Sir:

I am writing to comment on the proposed revision of the NIH guidelines for research involving recombinant DNA molecules. I strongly support the RAC proposal that appeared in the Federal Register of 12-4-81. As a clinical specialist in infectious diseases and a researcher in animal virology, I have long felt that the risks of cloning eukaryotic (viral or cellular) DNAs in either prokaryotes or eukaryotes have been greatly exaggerated and that the NIH guidelines have been far too restrictive in this area. Some research has been unjustifiably slowed by the current regulations in my view. The new RAC proposals come much closer to an appropriate position in this area in my opinion.

Sincerely yours,

W.S. Robinson

William S. Robinson, M.D.
Professor of Medicine

Charles Weber
141 Mt. Horeb Road
Warren, New Jersey 07060

Dec. 29, 1981

Director, Office of recombinent DNA Activities
Building 31, Room 4A52
National Institutes of Health
Bethesda, Maryland 20205

Dear Sirs:

Making anything to do with recombinent genetics voluntary is similar to making stopping at a red light voluntary, only potentially much more ominous.

For scientists to speak of recombinent work as harmless because years of work have produced no bad illness is in the same category as a biologist defending his God given right to strew garbage around his yard, harbor pet rats, and run his sewage in an open channel, giving as a defense that he has been doing it for years and none of his family has come down with bubonic plague or cholera yet. Relatively he is right, but the recombinent researchers are not. The biologist can establish the status quo in one afternoon, should so many come to love rats that the plague threatens. The recombinent researchers not only never can, they can't even know if the status quo has been altered or to what end.

Some bizarre thing, like a disease turning all the wheat in the country bitter, would have a sensational impact. However, it would be virtually inconsequential compared to some of the horrer that could unfold, little more significant than the killer bee's invasion of South America or the rabbits that have found a happy home in Australia. The possibility that worries me is the introduction of some potent, or even innocuous gene where it was not before, which evolving for a long time could surface to plague our children a million years hence. There are chemical defense developements which almost certainly took tens of millions of years to evolve in termites.

We say that we must have the medical progress that recombinent work implies. Then,-disregarding decades of legitimate, reliable research, we fill our guts with fermented sugar, our lungs with poisonous smoke, our soils with lead and cadmium, and emasculate our food so badly that not even meal worms can survive on it. Then when the tottering gelatinous mass of protoplasm which results starts to creak and falter we say we absolutely must take desparate dangerous risks to develope magic elixers to shore it up. I don't buy it.

At least if the decision is to proceed, maintain regulatory safegaurds for all, especially industry. Then add one more layer of safety- use only organisms which must have water and can not live in or on animals, and perform all experiments in the middle of a desert.

Sincerely Yours,

Charles Weber

Charles Weber

STANFORD UNIVERSITY MEDICAL CENTER

DEPARTMENT OF GENETICS

December 29, 1981

Dr. William J. Gartland, Jr.
Director
Office of Recombinant DNA Activities
National Institute for Allergy and Infectious Diseases
National Institutes of Health
Bethesda, Maryland 20205

Dear Dr. Gartland:

This letter is written in support of the revision in the Recombinant DNA Guidelies proposed by Drs. David Baltimore and Allan Campbell. Since work in other areas with microorganisms that are known to be hazardous does not involve mandatory regulations, but rather involves voluntary adherence by investigators to a code of standard practice, it does not seem reasonable to require mandatory rules for research with recombinant DNA molecules --- which have shown no indication of presenting a special hazard. Surely, if a voluntary code of standard practice is sufficient to protect laboratory workers and the public from the effects of agents known to be hazardous, the same procedures should be adequate in the area of recombinant DNA research.

Mandatory guidelines seem to me to be a vestige from a time when it was believed that this area of research might present special hazards and that extraordinary precautions were necessary. At this point in time, all evidence indicates that a code of standard operating practices similar to that used by workers in other areas of microbiology is adequate protection.

I urge the adoption by the RAC of the proposal appearing in the Federal Register dated December 4, 1981.

Sincerely yours,

Stanley N. Cohen
Professor

SNC:ps

DEPARTMENT OF GENETICS, STANFORD UNIVERSITY SCHOOL OF MEDICINE, STANFORD, CALIFORNIA 94305 • (415) 497-5052

THE JOHNS HOPKINS UNIVERSITY
SCHOOL OF MEDICINE

DEPARTMENT OF MICROBIOLOGY

725 N. WOLFE STREET
BALTIMORE, MARYLAND 21205

December 31, 1981

Dr. William J. Gartland, Jr.
Director
Office of Recombinant DNA Activities
NIH
Building 31, Room 4A52
Bethesda, Maryland 20205

Dear Dr. Gartland:

I have examined the proposed revisions of the N.I.H. Guidelines for Research Involving Recombinant DNA Molecules that appears in the Federal Register of December 4, 1981. I am wholeheartedly in favor of their acceptance. The current guidelines, eventhough relaxed over previous versions, are still restrictive for my own research and for many other investigators whom I have talked to. In light of our increased knowledge regarding the high frequency of so-called illegitimate DNA exchanges in nature, catalyzed by viruses, plasmids, and transposable elements, and in view of the absence of dangerous products of recombinant work over the past few years, it seems prudent and safe to remove most of the remaining restrictions and administrative red tape.

I am strongly in favor of the RAC proposal and strongly oppose the Gottesman proposal.

Sincerely,

Hamilton O. Smith, M.D.
Professor, Department of
Molecular Biology &
Genetics

HOS:jo

Dr. William J. Gartland
Director
Office of Recombinant DNA Activities
National Institutes of Health
Building 31, Room 4A52
BETHESDA, MARYLAND 20205

This is in response to your Memorandum of December 18, 1981, inviting comments on two proposals for revision of the National Institutes of Health NIH Guidelines for Research Involving Recombinant DNA Molecules.

As a student of genetics, cytology, microbiology, infectious diseases and immunology for more than fifty (50) years, I recommend:

1. That all the restrictions imposed on Recombinant DNA and genetic engineering research and application be considered forever as most pitiful and wasteful examples of over-regulations and scares by those who failed to understand that this is only a continuation of genetic processes which began millions or billions of years ago and which have resulted in nothing worse than our poor stumbling humanity and our surrounding nature which is much more friendly than dangerous.

2. That all such drastic abuses of the freedom of our Scientists be forever banned by the most severe guidelines and limitations which can be developped and imposed.

3. That we do immediately whatever can be done to repair the damage to Research and compensate for the time lost and to facilitate progress in genetic engineering.

Thank you for this opportunity to comment.

Dr. Bernard LaSalle
6200 Westchester Park Drive, #1212
COLLEGE PARK, MD 20740

January 2, 1982

MASSACHUSETTS INSTITUTE OF TECHNOLOGY

CENTER FOR CANCER RESEARCH

77 MASSACHUSETTS AVENUE, CAMBRIDGE, MASSACHUSETTS 02139

January 4, 1982

Dr. William J. Gartland, Jr.
Department of Health & Human Services
Public Health Service
National Institutes of Health
Bethesda, Maryland 20205

Dear Dr. Gartland,

The NIH guidelines have served a useful role in reassuring the public that experiments using the new technology of recombinant DNA were proceeding with peer overview. Given the lack of appearance of any biohazard associated with these experiments over the past seven years and our current expectations of their benefits, I believe it is time to make the guidelines non-mandatory. Maintaining the guidelines, I.B. Committees and the associated paperwork is expensive. In addition, the equipment locked up in unuseable rooms as P3 laboratories is enormous. I see no justification for this cost in times of limited support for science.

The current NIH guidelines permit a vast range of experiments after obtaining approval. It is time to eliminate the costly bureaucracy and accept the December 4, 1981 revision proposed by the RAC committee. It was unfortuate that NIH assumed responsibility for the guidelines; it should relieve itself of this unnecessary burden now that it has a chance.

Sincerely yours,

Phillip A. Sharp
Professor

PAS/ms

THE JOHNS HOPKINS UNIVERSITY
SCHOOL OF MEDICINE

PARTMENT OF MICROBIOLOGY

725 N. WOLFE STREET
BALTIMORE, MARYLAND 21205

January 4, 1982

Dr. W.J. Gartland, Director
Office of Recombinant DNA Activities
National Institutes of Health
Building 31, Room 4A52
Bethesda, MD. 20205

Dear Dr. Gartland:

I strongly urge the adoption of the Dec. 4, 1981 Proposed Guidelines for Research Involving Recombinant DNA Molecules (Federal Register 46, 59,368). The risk assessment studies supported by the NIH were valuable. They showed that DNA of animal viruses is much safer in recombinant form in E. coli K-12 than in the original virus, since the ability of the recombinants to infect animals or humans is low or nonexistent. Therefore recombinant research should be encouraged as a means of understanding viral and other diseases and preventing them if possible (e.g., foot and mouth disease). Instead, recombinant research has been restricted by NIH Guidelines, slowed down, and subjected to a public stigma. Many millions of dollars have been wasted in reconstruction of laboratories to meet standards absurd even under 1978 or 1981 Guidelines, in printing of vast numbers of forms, and in loss of researchers' expensive time to innumerable meetings across the country to discuss hazards now recognized as fictitious (see Fed. Register 46, 59385).

Section III contains the statement, "No experiments should be performed which involve" introduction of new drug resistance to pathogens or transfer of genes for potent toxins. This should be sufficient to prevent harm from this research. No additional waste of time or of taxpayers' money should be required. In particular, the 12/7/81 proposal of S. Gottesman should not be approved. It does not even state the "new text" of containment for covered experiments.

Yours truly,

John F. Morrow

John F. Morrow, Ph.D.
Department of Molecular
Biology & Genetics

JFM:jo

UNIVERSITY OF VIRGINIA
SCHOOL OF MEDICINE
BOX 441
CHARLOTTESVILLE, VIRGINIA 22908

DEPARTMENT OF MICROBIOLOGY

January 4, 1982

William J. Gartland, Jr., Ph.D., Director
Office of Recombinant DNA Activities
Building 31, Room 4A52
National Institutes of Health
Bethesda, Maryland 20205

Dear Dr. Gartland:

I would like to go on record as strongly favoring the proposed revision by the Recombinant DNA Advisory Committee published in the Federal Register dated December 4, 1981 to the effect that

1. the Guidelines would cease to be mandatory,

2. Section III of the Guidelines would be greatly simplified and most experiments be done under P1 containment facilities,

3. the prohibition section (I-D) be eliminated except for I-D-2 and I-D-5.

This revision is long overdue and would greatly advance recombinant DNA technology without public risk. I congratulate you and the RAC and hope you proceed with these revisions forthwith.

Sincerely yours,

Robert R. Wagner

Robert R. Wagner, M.D.
Professor and Chairman

RRW:lrp

University of Illinois at Urbana-Champaign

Department of Microbiology
131 Burrill Hall
Urbana, Illinois 61801
(217) 333-1736

January 4, 1982

Director,
Office of Recombinant DNA Activities
National Institutes of Health
Building 31, Room 4A52,
Bethesda, MD 20205

Dear Sir:

I would like to take this opportunity to affirm my belief that the proposed revisions appearing in the Federal Register dated December 4, 1981 promulgated by the Recombinant DNA Advisory Committee be adopted without delay. Substantial experimental evidence dictates the wisdom of this decision.

I appreciate the opportunity to comment upon this important decision.

Sincerely yours,

Samuel Kaplan
Professor of Microbiology

SK:sb

STANFORD UNIVERSITY
STANFORD, CALIFORNIA 94305

DEPARTMENT OF BIOLOGICAL SCIENCES

4 January 1982

Dr. William Gartland
Director, Office of Recombinant DNA Activities
National Institutes of Health
Building 31, Room 4A52
Bethesda, Maryland 20205

RE: Proposed Revisions, NIH Guidelines

Dear Bill,

As you might expect, I prefer the "RAC Proposal: to the "Gottesman Proposal" and the "Gottesman Proposal" to the Current Guidelines. However, I am not entirely happy with the elimination from both proposals of any reference to large scale operations. As my views about large scale work are complicated, I will return to that subject at the end.

In considering the whole issue, I hope that RAC members will ask themselves, "Suppose that the Berg letter had never been written, the Asilomar Conference had never been held, and the NIH Guildelines did not yet exist. Could anyone justify introducing mandatory Guidelines at the present time, on the basis of rational concerns?" I can't imagine how.

Certainly, no one can deny the possibility that some day some artificial recombinant will harm somebody or something. But that fact by itself does not imply that a system of prior review is desirable unless we can see some way of anticipating the danger and identifying the culprit in advance. The typical RAC scenario, repeated may times during the last year I was a member, went something like this: Dr. X was to clone in bacterium Y, which is not an approved host. She submits data showing that bacterium Y (like all known natural species) is limited in its ability to spread, multiply and take over the natural world; and also that her laboratory strain (like other known laboratory strains) is at a competitive disadvantage to the wild strain, when tested in the wild. RAC reviews the data and grants a lowering of the required containment level. A lot of paper has been pushed, but has this really helped in identifying any potential hazards? "Dreaming the impossible dream" may be an admirable quest; but "predicting the unpredictable risk" is not a very practical charge for a committee. Yet RAC's mission has evolved more and more in that direction.

Now to large scale work and related matters: It is unfortunate that RAC's consensus on the desirability of a major reduction in regulation coincides with an explosive increase in the rate of industrial development of recombinant DNA technology. This certainly invites the interpretation by the public (or at least by journalists, who may register public opinion either present or future) that the reduction is contrived for the benefit of private economic interests. RAC might respond with a "go slow" approach, maintaining an image of caution by adopting a more conservative option such as the "Gottesman proposal." I do not favor such a response, which seems to say, "Since we can't think of anything sensible to do, let's do something silly so that at least we are taking some action that indicates some concern." I am sure these are not Susan's reasons for submitting her proposal; but if her proposal is adopted, I suspect it will be because it is perceived as setting the best pace for relaxation of the Guidelines, rather than because many people are convinced that it provides any protection from any danger. I remain convinced that honesty makes the best politics; and that if RAC sees no further need for regulation, it should say so.

To my mind, the question of RAC's responsibility with respect to industrial development has not yet been adequately addressed. I take it for granted that any technology practised on a sufficiently large scale, will have some undesirable side effects. That's been true of every other technology; why should recombinant DNA be different? Furthermore, the best time to think about minimizing any problems is when the technology is still emerging, before everything is set up and running.

Of course, the primary responsibility for monitoring emerging technologies does not rest with NIH or RAC, but with other agencies such as FDA, OSHA, EPA, CDC, etc. In the absence of any sign that recombinant DNA presents special hazards, RAC could justifiably opt to stay out of such matters. However, I believe that, as long as RAC continues to exist, it can serve a socially useful function by actively looking for potential problems and volunteering advice to those agencies as the occasion warrants. I would like to see such a function officially acknowledge by adding to the Guidelines as a RAC function something like "considering, and advising the Director NIH of, any potential problems connected with large scale production of organisms carrying recombinant DNA." The Director would then have the responsibliity of formally transmitting RAC's conclusions to other agencies as appropriate.

Something of this kind could provide what may be most needed in the years ahead -- someone to keep an eye on what is going on, and to suggest what safety testing may be needed in specific cases. I am sure that the representatives of industry will continue to push the notion that "If it's safe in small scale, it's safe in large scale." I consider their argument spurious for at least two reasons. First, the basis on which RAC has accepted that cloning in certain hosts such as _E. coli_ K-12 is quite safe is the improbability that a few bacteria that might escape could multiply extensively enough outside the laboratory to cause significant damage; for a large number of bacteria, that logic simply does not apply. Second, when we say something is safe, we mean only that there is no reason to expect danger. It would be impractical to test everything for unexpected hazards. It would be silly to require extensive safety testing on every clone that will be grown in 10 ml amounts in the laboratory; if there were any danger, the tests might be more hazardous than the experiment. However, if any organism is to be grown by the ton, it seems feasible to test it for unanticipated properties such as toxicity or allergenicity that might cause problems if not recognized in advance.

I think it would be unwise to assume that the regulatory agencies will be able to handle such matters adequately on their own. The current administration is unsympathetic toward regulation of industry, and the agencies risk emasculation by the Woodshedsman's budgetary axe.

In the Baltimore-Campbell proposal, the large scale limit was retained as a prohibition. My reason for favoring that course was that the issues I have mentioned above should be more fully aired and discussed before making any changes that might leave a vacuum in the surveillance of industrial development at this time.

To sum up, there are two actions I would like RAC to take: (1) approval of the RAC proposal for revision of the Guidelines; (2) a further addition to the Guidelines that would specify consideration of problems connected with production scale operation and advice to the appropriate regulatory agencies as proper RAC functions.

Sincerely yours,

Allan

Allan Campbell
Professor of Biological Sciences

AC:shm

THE JOHNS HOPKINS UNIVERSITY
SCHOOL OF MEDICINE

DEPARTMENT OF
MOLECULAR BIOLOGY AND GENETICS

725 N. WOLFE STREET
BALTIMORE, MARYLAND 21205

January 5, 1982

Dr. William J. Gartland, Jr.
Director
Office of Recombinant DNA Activities
National Institutes of Health
Building 31, Room 4A52
Bethesda, MD 20205

Dear Dr. Gartland:

I am responding to your memorandum of 18 December inviting comments on revision of the NIH Guidelines for Research Involving Recombinant DNA. After careful reading of the proposal by the RAC and that by Dr. Susan Gottesman, I strongly support the RAC proposal for making the guidelines voluntary and eliminating excessive administrative oversight. As I have argued on several prior occasions, it makes no sense to have more stringent requirements for research that carries only vague hypothetical risks than for experiments involving known pathogenic microbes. Voluntary guidelines have worked quite well for research involving pathogens and should work equally well for microbes containing recombinant DNA. Under voluntary guidelines the responsibility is with the individual investigator and his institution, as it should be. After several years of experience it is time to recognize that there is no scientific or social justification for retaining rules for recombinant DNA research that inhibit creativity and waste resources.

Sincerely,

Daniel Nathans
Professor and Director
Department of Molecular
Biology and Genetics

DN/lc

Apartado 315
1250 Escazu
Costa Rica
Jan. 5, 1982

Dr. William J. Gartland, Jr.
Office of Recombinant DNA Activities
National Institutes of Health
Building 31, Room 4A52
Bethesda, Maryland 20205
USA

Dear Sir:

I am happy to answer your request for comments on proposed revision of NIH Guidelines for Research involving Recombinant DNA Molecules. I am interested purely as a consumer, and as a private citizen who could be affected by possible dangers inherent in recombinant DNA activities.

I strongly support keeping the Guidelines just as they are. They should continue to be mandatory. None of the requirements should be eliminated. Section II of the Guidelines should remain as it is and not be simplified in any way. Experiments currently requiring P2 or P3 containment should continue as such. None of the prohibitions section (I-D) of the Guidelines should be eliminated.

I quote Dr. Sheldon Krimsky as my basic source for concern over the loosening of guidelines for recombinant DNA activities. I would like to see, on the contrary, strict guidelines imposed upon all private gene-research companies that are appearing literally all over the world. The guidelines, outside of NIH-funded research and certain other federally funded programs are not required. I think that they should be required everywhere!

Dr. Krimsky says: "The ability to reconstruct mocroorganisms with human, animal or plant genes is responsible for industrializing molecular genetics - in much the same way atomic fission and the synthesis of organic molecules gave rise to our nuclear and chemical industries. If the outlook for future applications of recombinant DNA technology is only partly accurate, it is reasonable to anticipate adverse side-effects. Although the nature and severity of these hazards cannot be predicted now, from our knowledge of similar technological revolutions, I believe the most serious risks could come from troublesome biological industrial effluent; occupational hazards; and unanticipated effects of biological agents purposely released into the environment."

"Overall, thesystem of controls for university reasarch has been successful. The decision-making process at the national level has been open, with participation from public interest advocates. It does not appear that the public faces special risks from recombinant DNA experiments carried out under the NIH guidelines (my note: AS THEY NOW EXIST) in research laboratories. But I have far less confidence in the safety of large scale commercial applications of the technology. Currently, there is no system of regulation for industry. Universities are under what in essence are mandatory controls (they can lose funding for failure to comply), but commercial institutions are covered under a voluntary compliance program. In the long run, it is not wise to have unenforceable recommendations for industrial scale genetic engineering."(My note: or for ANY genetic engineering!)

"The present regulatory structure for the university is appropriate. However, I think it would be a mistake to eliminate the guidelines and make them voluntary, as some have recently proposed. Several states and municipalities have passed laws that require the private sector to adhere structly to the NIH rules for gene splicing. For consistency, these laws cover both academic and commerical activities. There is no evidence that these laws have obstructed university research."

" I believe that industrial genetic engineering should be watched carefully by some independent body which can issue recommendations to the appropriate regulatory agencies. The federal government should help states develop a set of enforceable standards (perhaps under authority of the Resource ConservationnRecovery Act and the Occupational Safety and Health Act) to minimize expoxure of workers, the public, and the environment to industrial organisms. We should approach health and safety for this new technology in a preventive fashion - not because we know what the alternatives are, but because we don't know what they are. It would be truly gratifying to look back after thirty years of industrial gene splicing and applaud a remarkable safety record."

And as the Harvard Medical School Health Letter of August, 1981 expressed it: "But even when the guidelines (my note: the strict ones now in force) are given the forde of law, communities in which DNA work is going on remain edgy. People are demanding to know whether they should still fear the possible genetic mishaps that scientists themselves had qualms about only a few years ago. Recombinant DNA remains a controversial problem."

Very truly yours,

Jean P. Patterson

Jean P. Patterson

Cold Spring Harbor Laboratory

Cold Spring Harbor, New York 11724

January 5, 1982

Director, Office of Recombinant
DNA Activities
National Institutes of Health
Building 31, Room 4A52
Bethesda, Maryland 20205

Dear Dr. Gartland:

I heartily support the proposed revision of the NIH Guidelines for research involving recombinant DNA molecules. In particular, I support the revisions recommended by the recombinant DNA advisory committee. It is high time that these guidelines disappeared totally, and every step in that direction will be most welcome.

Yours sincerely,

R. J. Roberts

Richard J. Roberts

RJR/nd

EMORY UNIVERSITY SCHOOL OF MEDICINE
DEPARTMENT OF MICROBIOLOGY AND IMMUNOLOGY
502 Woodruff Memorial Building
Atlanta, Georgia 30322
January 5, 1982

Dr. William J. Gartland, Jr.
Director, Office of Recombinant DNA Activities
Department of Health and Human Services
Public Health Service
National Institutes of Health
Bethesda, Maryland 20205

Dear Dr. Gartland:

I am in favor of Annex C, completely abolishing the Guidelines, or, failing that, of the revision of the recombinant DNA guidelines proposed by RAC (Dec. 4, Federal Register) - which make adherence voluntary. The initial purpose of these guidelines was to make investigators conscious of potential hazards and appropriate containment. I believe that purpose has been effectively served. Since the initial promulgation of the guidelines, experiments have provided safety data that is reassuring and it seems appropriate at this time to relax the guidelines with this in mind. The guidelines were supposed to be an interim arrangement until data was available. It is now, and they should be eliminated. I have two specific comments to make which stem from my personal interests.

It has always seemed odd to me that the current system forces the investigator wishing to work with a bacterial pathogen whose genetics has not been studied much to first demonstrate that it can exchange genes with a suitable cloning host before cloning can proceed. Surely the preliminary in vivo experiment is at least as dangerous as the cloning experiment. These guidelines must certainly be delaying important research on pathogens.

I have a further concern about cloning of genes that are toxic for vertebrates since I believe the posture of the guidelines on this to be illogical. If an investigator wishes to work with a highly potent toxin having a very low LD_{50}, the investigator is certainly aware of the hazards and will take adequate precautions when handling the toxin. I submit that these are easier and therefore that such experiments are safer when the organism producing the toxin can be grown in a small volume. Cloning the toxin gene would permit this. For this reason, I believe it is actually safer to work with such toxins when their genes are cloned. Further-

Dr. William J. Gartland, Jr.
Page 2

more, if the gene is cloned out of the normal pathogenic host into a nonpathogenic strain unable to colonize people, that should add further to the safety. Thus, I see no logic for singling out toxins for special treatment in the guidelines or for dividing toxin experiments into classes dependent on LD_{50}. I therefore object to an "admonishment" against cloning of five particular toxin genes, (whatever "admonishment" means).

Sincerely yours,

June R. Scott

TUFTS UNIVERSITY
School of Medicine

Department of Molecular Biology and Microbiology

January 7, 1982

Dr. William J. Gartland
Office of Recombinant DNA Activities
NIAD, Building 31, Room 4A52
National Institutes of Health
Bethesda, Maryland 20205

Dear Dr. Gartland:

I have a problem in accepting the "Uniqueness Argument" presented as part of the discussion of risks associated with recombinant DNA research (Federal Register 46 [233] page 59386, 1981). In essence, this says that special precautions would be needed for recombinant DNA work only if "a unique organism, never found in Nature, might be constructed by recombinant DNA techniques." (my emphasis).

If I understand correctly, the notion is that a new pathogen that might be created by genetic engineers need be treated only as carefully as the pre-existing cognate pathogen. Fair enough, if all of Nature's experiments resulted in failure or in known organisms, but it does not follow that anything Nature has ever produced is *ipso facto* safe. It is not even true that the only dangerous organisms ever invented by Nature are modern pathogens. I would not like to meet the bacterial equivalent of a dinosaur.

There may be innumerable experiments that Nature has tried, rarely, which resulted in the death of humans (or other useful species), sometimes in isolated populations, sometimes for a limited time, but which haven't resulted in modern pathogens. In most cases such epidemics either pass unnoticed or remain unexplained or occurred before medicine was written down. Sometimes, as in the case of the late 15th century Syphilis before it became attenuated, we have an historical record of the problems that arose. It is a well-established principle that non-adapted pathogens can be too virulent for their hosts' and therefore for their own, survival. Organisms which became extinct in this way can hardly be called safe.

A second problem is this. It is not conceivable that Nature has tried all its experiments in every possible ecological circumstance. In any case, new combinations of environmental parameters are constantly being devised so that

136 Harrison Avenue
Boston, Massachusetts 02111
617 956-6750

organisms that once failed to survive might now find a more favorable habitat and pose a new danger to man or to his present environment.

The uniqueness argument may be moot as far as the present discussions go, but I would hope that this piece of illogic could be modified for any future discussions of the recombinant DNA.

Sincerely yours,

Mike Gill

D. Michael Gill, Ph.D.
Professor

DMG:ah

697 Hylan Boulevard
Staten Island, N.Y. 10305
January 7, 1982

Director
Office of Recombinant DNA Activities
Building 31 Room 4A52
National Institutes of Health
Bethesda, Maryland 20205

Dear Dr. Gartland;

Thank you for forwarding copies of the Federal Register published Dec. 4th 1981 and Dec. 7th 1981.

After serious consideration of both proposals for revision of the N.I.H. Guidelines for Recombinant DNA Research, the advantages of Dr. Gottesman's proposal, as published in the Federal Register vol. 46, No. 234 December 4, 1981, are apparent. Professionally, I must support Dr. Susan Gottesman in this matter.

Sincerely,
Mary Jane A. Ricciuti
Interested Citizen

THE INSTITUTE FOR CANCER RESEARCH

7701 BURHOLME AVENUE

FOX CHASE · PHILADELPHIA, PENNSYLVANIA 19111

(215) 342-1000 · CABLE ADDRESS: CANSEARCH

January 8, 1982

Dr. William J. Gartland, Jr.
Director
Office of Recombinant DNA Activities
National Institutes of Health
Building 31, Room 4A52
Bethesda, MD 20205

Dear Dr. Gartland:

I am writing to comment from the point of view of an IBC chairman on the relative merits of the two proposals to revise the DNA Guidelines described in the Federal Register of December 4 and 7, 1981, and summarized in your memorandum of December 18, 1981. I should like to point out some problems that might arise in attempting to implement the "Gottesman proposal".

This institute had had a staff committee on laboratory safety prior to the origin of concerns over recombinant DNA. Its influence with the staff and with the director stemmed from intellectual agreement that certain aspects of laboratory research involved real hazards and that our responsibilities to our colleagues or to the public required that safe handling practices be explored and developed and that appropriate safety guidelines be taught and observed. With the advent of the NIH Guidelines, this committee was modified, expanded, and institutionalized in order to bring it into compliance with what had become de facto federal regulations. This procedure found legitimacy and acceptance among our scientific colleagues only because there was at that time credible scientific concern over the safety of recombinant DNA research. All investigators did not give equal weight to these concerns but the views of those who counseled caution were acceded to. Staff cooperation with the IBC was excellent and outside members were glad to participate in our deliberations.

The following years saw a considerable expansion of recombinant DNA research at this institution, as at others, with concomitant increases in knowledge of both genetics and the process of infection that made it increasingly clear that the dangers of recombinant DNA research had been substantially overestimated. During this period, progressively more liberal guidelines came into use and the work and responsibility of the IBC was accordingly diminished. Most importantly, the intellectual basis for the IBC's authority had been correspondingly dissipated. As a result, respect for the IBC's function has decreased and colleagues are no longer as willing to serve as IBC members. As chairman, I now find it embarrassing to have to make demands on the time of our outside members (public health officials) to deal with matters that are essentially legalistic, rather than biological or medical.

Dr. William J. Gartland, Jr.
National Institutes of Health
January 8, 1982
Page Two

Should the "Gottesman proposal" be adopted, I can foresee a further erosion of the credibility of our IBC and thus of its ability to function. Even though it is apparently to be admitted that there is no intellectual basis for special restrictions concerning recombinant DNA, it is proposed to maintain in place a regulatory apparatus primarily for political reasons. Under such a system, I find it hard to see how I can persuade my colleagues to serve on the IBC or defend my own continued involvement. If, on the other hand, the DNA Guidelines were to be made voluntary, following the "RAC proposal", this problem would be far more easily resolved. The question of safety in recombinant DNA research would take its place beside other safety problems that have been handled without the establishment of pervasive bureaucracies. To sum up, the evolution of the recombinant DNA story has produced a climate in which the continuation of mandatory "guidelines" would fail to elicit the consent of the governed which is the fundamental precept of democratic governance, especially on matters of the general welfare.

I urge the committee to adopt the "RAC proposal" since it contains the elements required to deal with the future development of recombinant DNA research, and avoids the potential politicization of the guideline system that would be a logical outcome of the alternative proposal.

Sincerely yours,

Jerome J. Freed, Ph.D.
Chairman, Institute Biosafety Committee

JJF:ls

UNIVERSITY OF ILLINOIS AT CHICAGO CIRCLE
COLLEGE OF LIBERAL ARTS AND SCIENCES
DEPARTMENT OF BIOLOGICAL SCIENCES
BOX 4348, CHICAGO, ILLINOIS 60680
TELEPHONE: (312) 996-2211

UICC

Director
Office of Recombinant DNA Activities
National Institutes of Health
Building 31, Room 4A52
Bethesda, Maryland 20205

January 8, 1982

Dear Director:

I am glad to see that federal guidelines for research involving recombinant DNA molecules has eased significantly. This permits us all to get on to the business of our research more easily. However, I do feel that the complete elimation of these guidelines as described in the December 4, 1981 Federal Register would be unwise. Some form of mandatory control is required to lessen the chance of foolish risks. I favor the December 7, 1981 proposal that appeared as item 7 in the Federal Register.

Sincerely,

Susan W. Liebman

Susan W. Liebman
Associate Professor of Biological Sciences

Yale University

DEPARTMENT OF MOLECULAR BIOPHYSICS
AND BIOCHEMISTRY
P.O. Box 6666, 260 Whitney Ave.
New Haven, Connecticut 06511
(203) 43 6-3611

January 8, 1982

Dr. William Gartland, Jr.
Office of Recombinant DNA Activities
National Institutes of Health
Bethesda, Maryland 20205

Dear Dr. Gartland:

In this letter I would like to comment on the current proposal for a major revision of the Guidelines. Of the various proposals under consideration at present I would favor the Baltimore-Campbell proposal.

Yours sincerely,

Dieter Söll
Professor
Molecular Biophysics

DS:kam

UNIVERSITY OF ILLINOIS AT CHICAGO CIRCLE
COLLEGE OF LIBERAL ARTS AND SCIENCES
DEPARTMENT OF BIOLOGICAL SCIENCES
BOX 4348 CHICAGO ILLINOIS 60680
TELEPHONE (312) 996-2211

UICC

ombinant DNA Activities
tes of Health
4A52
ryland 20205

January 8, 1982

lad to see that federal o for research involving molecules has eased considerably. This permits us all the business of our research more easily. However, I the complete elimination of these guidelines as described 4, 1981 *Federal Register* would be unwise. Some form control is required to lessen the chance of favor the December 7, 1981 proposal that appeared as item *Register*.

Sincerely,

Susan W. Liebman

Susan W. Liebman
Associate Professor of Biological Sciences

Yale University

DEPARTMENT OF MOLECULAR BIOPHYSICS
AND BIOCHEMISTRY
P.O. Box 6666, 260 Whitney Ave.
New Haven, Connecticut 06511
(203) 436-3611

January 8, 1982

Dr. William Gartland, . .
Office of Recombinant [A Activities
National Institutes o. ealth
Bethesda, Maryland : :5

Dear Dr. Gartland:

In this letter ˜ ould like to comment on the current proposal for a major reision of the Guidelines. Of the various proposals un r consideration at present I would favor the Baltimore-C m ell proposal.

Yours sincerely,

Dieter Söll
Professor
Molecular Biophysics

DS:kam

Yale University

SCHOOL OF MEDICINE

333 Cedar Street
P.O. Box 3333
Department of Human Genetics
New Haven, Connecticut 06510

January 8, 1982

Dr. William Gartland, Jr.
Office of Recombinant DNA Activities
National Institutes of Health
Bethesda, MD 20205

Dear Bill:

At its meeting of December 17, 1981, Yale's Institutional Biosafety Committee voted unanimously to express its approval of the RAC proposal for relaxing the Recombinant DNA Guidelines, as summarized in Recombinant DNA Technical Bulletin, Vol. 4, No. 4, Dec., 1981.

In the Committee's view, recombinant DNA per se presents no hazard that is qualitatively different from the hazards associated with the pathogenicity of the hosts of vectors used. Hosts or vectors containing recombinant DNA should, therefore, be handled according to appropriate guidelines already in existence, such as the CDC guidelines for work with infectious organisms. When the pathogenicity of the host or vector will be predictably changed by virtue of the donor DNA it receives, the containment levels for handling it should be changed accordingly; our Committee believes that no special guidelines for recombinant DNA are needed.

We would appreciate your communicating this view to the RAC and to the Director of NIH.

Sincerely yours,

Edward A. Adelberg /JB

Edward A. Adelberg
Chairman

EAA/rjp

UNIVERSITY OF CALIFORNIA, SANTA CRUZ

BERKELEY • DAVIS • IRVINE • LOS ANGELES • RIVERSIDE • SAN DIEGO • SAN FRANCISCO | SANTA BARBARA • SANTA CRUZ

OFFICE OF THE CHANCELLOR | SANTA CRUZ, CALIFORNIA 95064

January 11, 1982

Director, Office of Recombinant DNA Activities
Building 31, Room 4A52
National Institute of Health
Bethesda, MD 20205

Re: Proposed Revisions of NIH Guidelines for Research Involving Recombinant DNA Molecules

Dear Sir:

The case for the proposed revision(s) of the Guidelines rests upon the arguments presented in the "Evaluation of the Risks Associated With Recombinant DNA Research" prepared by the Working Group in Revision of the Guidelines. This is a thoughtful document which attempts to set forth -- and to refute as to "extremely unlikely" -- the various putative scenarios of hazard from recombinant DNA experiments. The net result of this presentation is to dismiss the possibility of hazard from all recombinant DNA experiments except those involving known, very pathogenic agents (highly lethal toxins or highly dangerous pathogens), i.e., to dismiss the possibility of the creation of a novel pathogen, or of a more virulent form or a new mode of dissemination of an existing pathogen.

The arguments are plausible -- but in no instance are they quantitative. In no instance do they take into account the possibility of accident, of multiple and non-linear interactions, of evolutionary processes producing unexpected consequences in unplanned directions over a period of years.

I regard both proposed revisions (Federal Register, Dec. 4, Dec. 7) as too extreme, although of the two, the latter (presented by Dr. Susan Gottesman) is the preferrable.

I would suggest that the minimum provisions of a revised set of Guidelines should include that:

1) The Guidelines be mandatory, not voluntary;

2) Accordingly, there be penalties for non-compliance;

3) Institution Biohazard Committees of specified composition be retained with functions essentially as described in the Gottesman revision; and

4) Certain experiments continue, as before, to be prohibited (do we really wish to imply that incorporating the gene for botulinus toxin into *E. coli* or *B. subtilis* a minor prank?).

As an aside, I would like to respond to the section II A 3 a (Federal Register, Vol. 46, No. 233, Dec. 4, 1981, p. 59388) of the Annex B "Documents Prepared by Working Group on Revision of the Guidelines: Evaluation of Risks Associated With Recombinant DNA Research" to Recombinant DNA Research; Proposed Revised Guidelines, which cites certain articles which I wrote in 1975 and 1976. I am concerned that this section turns my argument "upside down." My point was that fertility barriers do normally exist between species (indeed, this is an important component of the definition of a species). These barriers undoubtedly were developed primarily to prevent "wasteful matings." But, because of the presence of these barriers in existence over hundreds of millions of years, we have had no information from which to predict the consequences, good or bad, of more-or-less random combinations of genetic material.

Thank you for the opportunity to comment on these proposed revisions.

Sincerely yours,

Robert L. Sinsheimer

Robert L. Sinsheimer
Chancellor

WRIGHT STATE

Wright State University
Dayton, Ohio 45435

School of Medicine
Office of the Dean
P.O. Box 927
Dayton, Ohio 45401
513/873-2933

January 11, 1982

William J. Gartland, Jr., Ph.D.
Director, Office of Recombinant
DNA Activities
National Institutes of Health
Building 31, Room 4A52
Bethesda, MD 20205

Dear Dr. Gartland:

Thank you for the opportunity to review and to comment on the two proposals for a major revision of the National Institutes of Health Guidelines for Research Involving Recombinant DNA Molecules. My colleagues and I find no major problems with either of the proposed revisions. We prefer the alternative appearing as item 7 in the Federal Register notice of December 7, 1981.

Cordially,

William D. Sawyer, MD

William D. Sawyer, M.D.
Dean, School of Medicine
Professor, Departments of Microbiology/
Immunology and Medicine

WDS:shw

THE PUBLIC HEALTH RESEARCH INSTITUTE
OF THE CITY OF NEW YORK, INC.
455 FIRST AVENUE, NEW YORK, N. Y. 10016
TEL. (212) 481-

January 11, 1982

Dr. William J. Gartland, Jr.
Dept. of Health & Human Services
Public Health Service
National Institutes of Health
Bethesda, MD 20205

Dear Bill:

This is in response to the alternative proposals currently under consideration for revision of the NIH Guidelines for Recombinant DNA Research. To put it very simply, I feel that the Baltimore-Campbell proposal to eliminate all mandatory aspects of the Guidelines and replace them with a voluntary code of practices is premature. I offer the following ideas in support of this position.

1) I agree that the chance of a significantly hazardous accident arising during any shotgun cloning experiment is sufficiently small to justify reduction to P1 containment of all such experiments, regardless of host, vector, etc.

2) Nevertheless, I am not sufficiently reassured regarding the possibility of hazardous outcomes in certain specific experiments to be willing to eliminate all mandatory controls. These experiments are the following: a) cloning experiments that are likely to result in the production of infectious pathogenic virusus (I note that it has recently been found that a cDNA copy of the poliovirus genome gives rise to infectious viruses upon introduction into mammalian cells (Racaniello and Baltimore, Science 214:916, 1981). b) The deliberate introduction of organisms containing cloned DNA into the environment. The ecological impact of unknown organisms in new habitats has so often been disastrous that I would not want to see this being done without at least the opportunity for public review and approval beforehand. c) The introduction of antibiotic resistance genes into organisms that do not naturally harbor such genes, where there is a possibility of therapeutic compromise as a consequence. d) Cloning experiments with toxins as described in appendix G of the extant Guidelines should continue to be regulated (I do not agree entirely with the provisions of appendix G, but that is another matter).

I feel that it is appropriate to point out here that it is probably incorrect to regard *E. coli* K12 as absolutely innocuous. On the one hand, it has been shown that K12 is capable of colonizing the mammalian gut under special circumstances (note that most wild strains of *E. coli* will not colonize the normal mammalian gut, primarily because they are unable to displace the resident strains; it is not obvious to me that K12 is any different in this respect). On the other hand, it has been shown that K12 can become significantly pathogenic under certain conditions. For example, a recent report by Portnoy and Falkow (J. Bacteriol. 148:877, 1981) describes the acquisition of mouse lethality by K12 as a consequence of receiving a cloned hemolysin determinant from a wild strain of E. coli.

In consideration of the above, I would be very pleased to see reduction to P1 containment of most of the currently regulated experiments but I would urge that the guidelines remain in effect with their present force for experiments such as those mentioned explicitly above.

Regards,

Richard P. Novick

RPN:cf

DEPARTMENT OF HEALTH AND HOSPITALS

DAVID L. ROSENBLOOM
Commissioner

818 HARRISON AVENUE
BOSTON, MASSACHUSETTS 02118

January 12, 1982

Director
Office of Recombinant DNA Activities
Building 31, Room 4A-52
National Institutes of Health
Bethesda, Maryland 20205

Dear Sir/Madam:

On behalf of the Boston Biohazards Committee, Department of Health and Hospitals, City of Boston, we wish to indicate our strong disagreement to the three current proposals for revision of existing guidelines for RDNA research (Baltimore-Campbell, RAC, and Gottesman) which appeared in the Federal Register of December 4, and 7, 1981.

We support the continued measured and reasonable improvement in the current guidelines, but we believe that the current proposals in their present form are not consistent with this aim.

Sincerely,

David L. Rosenbloom, Ph.D.
Commissioner

MILES

January 12, 1982

Gary A. Wilson, Ph. D.
Director
Microbiology Research
Biotechnology Group

Miles Laboratories, Inc.
P. O. Box 932
Elkhart, IN 46515
Phone (219) 262-7785
TWX 810-294-2259
Telex 258450

William J. Gartland, Jr., Ph.D.
Director, Office of Recombinant DNA Activities
Department of Health & Human Services
National Institutes of Health
Bethesda, Maryland 20205

Dear Bill,

I would like to comment on the proposed revision of the Recombinant DNA Guidelines that were published in the Federal Register, Friday, December 4, 1981 from the perspective of one who has been a principle investigator in the field, a member of the NIH IBC evaluation forum, a chairman of an IBC at a major university, and Director of Microbiology Research of a commercial institution. These comments do not reflect the official position of any of the groups with which I have had the pleasure to be associated, but rather an overall personal impression of one who has had to deal with the guidelines for the past 6 or 7 years, at both the Federal and the New York State level.

The scientists and concerned individuals at the Asilomar meeting are to be commended for the unprecedented steps they took in asking for a moratorium on potentially hazardous experiments until an assessment could be made of the risk. With a great deal of effort and good judgment, the NIH rapidly followed this meeting by carrying out their responsibility to establish guidelines so that individual researchers could apply the very elegant techniques of recombinant DNA to significant research projects. In my personal contacts, I have not encountered a scientist who ever believed that the experiments were as risky as originally conceived. While many expressed reservations of the potential hazards, no one that I know of in the field felt that the experiments or the products of recombinant DNA were so hazardous as to endanger the health and well being of themselves or members of their laboratories. Seven years of experience and hundreds of thousands of experiments, have not yielded any evidence to indicate that recombinant DNA technology is any more harmful then classical genetic experiments that have been conducted over the past eighty years. This lack of evidence of construction of dangerous life forms, is in sharp contrast to the wealth of knowledge that has been gained through the application of recombinant DNA technology. The ability to be able to proceed with the research in a cautious manner, reflects in no small measure, the fine job you, your staff and RAC have done over the years.

It is now time to take as bold a move as did those scientists at the Asilomar meeting. That move is to call a moratorium on the bureaucracy of recombinant DNA technology. The IBC's have over the last few years carried out their responsibilities in a conscientious and sincere manner but the time has come to dissolve these anachronisms. Believe me this statement is not easy to make after having served for two years as Chairman of the IBC at the University of Rochester and responsible for establishing a small bureaucracy to deal with recombinant DNA experiments. However, as most recombinant DNA experiments fall into the exempt category, the function of the IBC has become less meaningful. While some would embrace the proposal submitted by Dr. Susan Gottesman (Federal Register, December 7, 1981), I feel there is no need for retention of IBC's at local institutions.

If the RAC proposal of 12-4-81 were to be adopted, it is not clear to me what would be the fate of the NIH office of Recombinant DNA Activities. They have, over the years, with the help of RAC been so helpful in providing information on containment and good laboratory practice, that I would like to see them remain as an informational service providing up to date reviews and news that is normally published in the Recombinant DNA Technical Bulletin.

The guidelines should be changed to a voluntary code of standard practice. This code should be updated to reflect new discoveries by individuals in the field. It should not continue to be mandatory for institutions receiving NIH funding. The original purpose of the guidelines was to establish the potential risk of the experiments, not to distinguish between research under NIH funding or funded by a private sector. The past seven years have shown us that individual researchers are conscientious and have not applied recombinant DNA technology to make harmful microorganisms or products. If this were the aim of some malign individuals, retention of the IBC or mandatory compliance to the guidelines would not deter these individuals. It is time to take a bold step and remove the bureaucracy that has plagued recombinant DNA research. I enthusiastically endorse the RAC proposal and believe the revisions are necessary and timely.

Sincerely,

Gary A. Wilson

G. A. Wilson, Ph.D.

/pv

cc: R. J. Erickson
K. H. Meyer
W. Himmelsbach
F. E. Young

THE UNIVERSITY OF GEORGIA
OFFICE OF THE VICE PRESIDENT
FOR BUSINESS AND FINANCE
ATHENS, GEORGIA 30602

PHYSICAL PLANT DIVISION

January 12, 1982

Director, Office of Recombinant DNA Activities
National Institutes of Health
Building 31, Room 4A52
Bethesda, Maryland 20205

RE: Proposed Revisions to NIH Guidelines
for Recombinant DNA Research

Gentlemen:

I would urge that the RAC approve the Gottesman proposal (Federal Regulation 12/7/81) for revising the Guidelines for Recombinant DNA Research. In my opinion, the mandatory provision of the existing Guidelines requiring review by an I.B.C. was the key to this successful program, and I feel it is simply too soon to relax this requirement.

I would also ask genetic researchers to bear with the rest of the risk-related research community until we get our act together. Two years ago I pointed out that an important long range effect of the efforts of the entire genetic-related scientific community would be the establishment of a working model system for intelligent government-related self control in other risk-related areas of research in a university. During the evolution of recombinant DNA research here at the University of Georgia, especially during the writing of the "University's Standards for Conduct of Research Involving Biohazards" by our I.B.C., it became increasingly evident that risks involved in research with chemicals, radiation and other biohazards were certainly as serious, and infinitely more numerous, than those posed by Recombinant DNA Research. Thus, mandating an I.B.C. forced this and other universities to implement long-neglected but necessary safety programs. I am concerned that if this mandatory requirement is removed, entire safety programs will be jeopardized.

Very truly yours,

John M. Casey P.E.

John M. Casey, P.E.
Manager, Engineering Department
Physical Plant Division
Member - Biosafety Committee
University of Georgia

JMC:sm

SLOAN-KETTERING INSTITUTE *for* CANCER RESEARCH

DONALD S. WALKER LABORATORY, 145 BOSTON POST RD., RYE, N. Y. 10580 914-698-1100

January 12, 1982

Dr. William Gartland
Director, Office of Recombinant
DNA Activity
Bldg. 31, Rm. 4A52
National Institutes of Health
Bethesda, Maryland 20205

Dear Dr. Gartland and Members of the RAC:

The deliberate release of any man-made material into the environment ought to be regulated by law, since the environment belongs to everyone. This is particularly true if there is a potential for danger or if the specific long-range effects can only be guessed at. It is therefore irresponsible for the RAC and ORDA to appear to condone the release of any and all genetically engineered organisms. A strong recommendation for congressional action to control such emissions would make this action more socially responsible. It is not too soon to think about who will be to blame when a biological Agent Orange or PCB turns up - and it assuredly will turn up eventually. Biologists are no less error-prone than chemists and other human beings.

Yours sincerely,

Barbara H. Rosenberg

Barbara H. Rosenberg, Ph.D.
Associate Member, Sloan-Kettering Institute
Associate Professor of Biochemistry,
Graduate School of Medical Sciences
Cornell University

BHR/nc

PUBLIC AND SCIENTIFIC AFFAIRS BOARD

AMERICAN SOCIETY FOR MICROBIOLOGY

1913 I STREET, N.W.
WASHINGTON, D.C. 20006
TELEPHONE: CODE 202, 833-9680

12 January 1982

Dr. William J. Gartland
Director, Office of Recombinant DNA Activities
Building 31, Room 4A52
National Institutes of Health
Bethesda, Maryland 20205

Dear Dr. Gartland:

The Public and Scientific Affairs Board (PSAB) of the American Society for Microbiology (ASM) would like to submit the following comments on the proposed revisions of the NIH Guidelines for Research on Recombinant DNA which will be considered at the Recombinant DNA Advisory Committee meeting on February 8, 1982.

The Public and Scientific Affairs Board of ASM believes that there is need to streamline the guidelines for work with recombinant DNA. The present guidelines are cumbersome, in part overly restrictive, and do not take into account all the available information. We believe that simplifying them will result in greater use of safe procedures, and therefore, in greater safeguard of both microbiological workers, the community and the environment.

The debate in recent years has centered on the question of whether or not the introduction of foreign DNA into a host cell can result in an organism of greater pathogenicity than either the donor or the recipient. In other words, is the whole more dangerous than the sum of the parts? In the case of well characterized recipients, such as Escherichia coli, strain K-12, the answer is almost certainly no. Therefore, proper safety procedures for using such organisms are those that pertain to the donor of the recombined DNA. Proper procedures are not specific to recombinant DNA work but pertain to pathogenic agents in general. The key element in this consideration is that a considerable amount of information is available about Escherichia coli K-12 and a few other host organisms.

Our concern is for the fact that only sparse information is available for other host-vectors. With less characterized systems, new combinations may result in organisms of potentially increased pathogenicity than either the donor or the recipient. Thus, the introduction of genes for toxins of low potency in recipients that can colonize man, animals or plants, could result in potentially dangerous organisms. Analogous arguments can be made for certain drug resistance traits. On the other hand, we believe that, for a variety of reasons, risks are mainly to the workers in direct contact with the organisms and are not likely to result in danger to the community or the environment.

We are not only concerned with the paucity of information but also with the lack of mechanisms for its dissemination. Many workers using modern genetic technology are not versed in pathogenic microbiology and cannot be assumed to have proper training or access to up-to-date information.

In the light of these concerns, we believe that guidelines are necessary, and that they should continue to be revised in the light of new knowledge. Specifically, we believe the Recombinant DNA Advisory Committee (RAC) should continue to exist. It should be the principal resource for information gathering and for dispersal, and be available for consultation regarding individual cases. At present, it should continue to recommend suitable procedures for experiments dealing with potent toxins and the artificial introduction of resistance traits to clinically useful drugs.

Because we are of the opinion that the central concern is for the proper education of workers in the field, we recommend that local Institutional Biosafety Committees (IBC) take on a greater role in advising and regulating the activities within their institutions. Local control is more likely to be effective and appropriate to special conditions. We believe that individual institutions will be increasingly aware of their social obligations and liability, and will continue to devise bodies suitable to overview such activities.

Sincerely yours,

Harlyn O. Halvorson

H.O. Halvorson, Ph.D.
Chairman, Public and Scientific Affairs Board

M. Schaechter

Moselio Schaechter, Ph.D.
Chairman, Committee on Genetic, Molecular and Systematic Microbiology

EMBO EUROPEAN MOLECULAR BIOLOGY ORGANIZATION
Executive Secretary: Dr. John Tooze

EMBO European Molecular Biology Organization
Postfach 1022.40, D-6900 Heidelberg 1

Postfach 1022.40
6900 Heidelberg 1
Federal Republic of Germany

Dr. William J. Gartland Jr.
Director, Office of Recombinant
DNA Activities
National Institutes of Health
Building 31, Room 4A52
Bethesda, Md 20205
USA

13 January 1982

Dear Bill,

I am replying to your letter of December 18, 1981 in which you invite comments on proposals for a major revision of the National Institutes of Health Guidelines for Research Involving Recombinant DNA molecules.

In my opinion, the proposal published in the Federal Register of December 4, 1981 should be adopted. There seems to me to be no valid reason for mandatory regulation via guidelines of recombinant DNA research since there is no evidence that this activity is intrinsically hazardous. It is clear that anyone working with known dangerous organisms should take the necessary precautions mandated for those organisms but there is no reason for mandatory regulation of recombinant DNA work per se. A voluntary code of practice should be adequate and would, I believe, be respected.

That the guidelines desperately require simplification is self evident to anyone who tries to read and understand them. Finally, there is, I believe, no case for specific prohibitions because work with organisms that are included in the prohibitions is already covered by regulations etc. relating to the handling of dangerous organisms.

Since very many European countries either use the NIH guidelines or closely model national guidelines on them any decision taken by the NIH will have far reaching repercussions. I believe it is time to have the courage of our convictions and vote to convert the guidelines into a purely voluntary code of practice. This would endanger nothing, facilitate research and save a great deal of money.

Best regards,

John Tooze

McARDLE LABORATORY
FOR CANCER RESEARCH
DEPARTMENT OF ONCOLOGY
MEDICAL SCHOOL, UNIVERSITY OF WISCONSIN

January 13, 1982

To: William J. Gartland

From: Howard M. Temin Howard M Temin

Subject: Proposed Revisions of NIH Guidelines for Research Involving Recombinant DNA Molecules

Thank you for sending the Federal Registers of Dec. 4 and 7.

Philosophically, I am most in sympathy with the proposed guidelines in the Dec. 4 Federal Register. Certainly, in hindsight, such guidelines are all that should have been present when recombinant DNA work was just beginning.

However, now that we have had the history of the last years and the public concern about recombinant DNA, I question whether we can go back to essentially no regulation. I believe that we cannot and need some mechanism to protect in the future both the infant genetic engineering industry and academic work with recombinant DNA.

Therefore, I support a revision like that of Dr. Gottesman described in the Dec. 7 Federal Register. However, I think that more experiments should not require prior IBC approval, for example, section III-B-3-d should be moved to III-C, etc.

450 North Randall Avenue, Madison, Wisconsin 53706 608-262-2177

MCG

Medical College of Georgia
Augusta, Georgia 30912
Biological Safety
(404) 828-2663

January 15, 1982

Director
Office of Recombinant DNA Activities
Building 31, Room 4A52
National Institutes of Health
Bethesda, MD 20205

Dear Sir:

Having reviewed the recently proposed revisions in the NIH recombinant DNA Guidelines, I would like to make several comments. First, these NIH Guidelines have been amended on a rather frequent basis since they were initially developed. This no doubt has made life difficult for institutions which have sought to adopt these guidelines as the minimal standards for their Institutional Biosafety Committees (IBC's). However, it has been widely understood that NIH has made these changes as risk assessment data has become known and analyzed. This knowledge has been comforting and has made the revisions much easier to embrace.

Another point which I would like to make concerns the efficency with which investigators dealing with recombinant DNA molecules has been able to be conducted in accordance with these guidelines. I have only been the biological safety officer at this institution for a very short time, but I have found that recombinant DNA research has generally been accomplished smoothly and safely within the structure recommended by the guidelines. Nonetheless, I have encountered investigators who would not have included certain safety considerations into their planning had they not been required to do so by the campus IBC and by NIH in order to receive their funding. No doubt this same situation has occurred at other institutions as well.

Now I would like to link the previous two statements as they apply to the proposed revisions. The Recombinant DNA Advisory Committee (RAC) proposal would essentially take NIH out of the picture regarding the issuance of guidelines in this particular area of research. This action would be appropriate if all risk assessment determinations concerning recombinant DNA have been made. Although much more knowledge is now known than when these guidelines were originally drafted, some risk assessment research is still in progress and some has yet to be started. Under the RAC proposal, some institutions would automatically dismantle their IBC's and drop any sort of review of recombinant DNA research. Many responsible investigators would continue to engage in safety planning and analysis their work with recombinant molecules because they have had to do so for almost a decade and have incorporated this activity into their research routine. However, there would be researchers who would not take precautions in the area of safety which are not required of them. In addition, there is a chance that some of these people might conduct recombinant DNA investigations in some areas where the available knowledge is scant and the risk assessment work is still incomplete.

I feel that the RAC proposal is both sound and wise but not at this point in time. In light of the growing evidence that many manipulations of recombinant DNA molecules are indeed safe, further relaxation of the NIH Guidelines would be in order. Any proposal that retains even the most rudimentary structure for the review of recombinant DNA investigations would provide a means of ensuring that even the least conscientious investigators will implement the minimal containment precautions. With certain modifications, the Goffesman proposal could serve as a guide for most any institution should the RAC proposal be adopted, but, as previously stated, there would be institutions which would disolve their IBC's simply because it would no longer be required to ensure NIH funding.

So, the wise many must plan for the potential mistakes of the unwise few. Recombinant DNA technology is rapidly approaching the point where it can take its place in the laboratory as a safe research laboratory. However, until that point is reached, some sort of organized structure for the review of recombinant DNA research activities should still be required at institutions with researchers engaged in this type of work if they are to continue to receive NIH funding.

Sincerely,

William E. Homovec
Biological Safety Officer

WEH/lhj

INDIANA UNIVERSITY

DEPARTMENT OF BIOLOGY
Jordan Hall 138
Bloomington, Indiana 47405
(812) 337- 4431

15 January 1982

William J. Gartland, Jr., Ph.D.
Director, Office of Recombinant DNA activities
National Institutes of Health
Building 31, Room 4A52
Bethesda, MD 20205

Dear Dr. Gartland:

You have invited comment on the two proposals published in the Federal Register of December 4 concerning revision of the Guidelines for Recombinant DNA research.

At the meeting of IBC Chairmen a year or so ago, there was considerable discussion at the workshops, at the final plenary session, and among participants. I feel that the nearly unanimous opinion, held strongly by the members of the RAC with whom I talked, is in favor of making the Guidelines non-mandatory as described in the first of the two proposals.

I support this position.

Yours sincerely,

Dean Fraser
IBC Chairman

va

cc: Rollin Richmond
John Castellan

MONTGOMERY COUNTY HEALTH DEPARTMENT
Division of Disease Control
2000 Dennis Ave., Su. 206
Silver Spring, Md., 20902
681-5000

M E M O R A N D U M

January 18, 1982

TO: Director, Office of Recombinant DNA Activities
National Institutes of Health
Building 31, Room 4A52
Bethesda, Md., 20205

FROM: Eugene A. Rosenberger, M.D., Director
Division of Disease Control

SUBJ: Proposed Revisions of NIH Guidelines for Research Involving Recombinant DNA Molecules

REF: Your memo of December 18, 1981; subject as above.

The Montgomery County Health Department concurs with the proposed revisions developed by the Recombinant DNA Advisory Committee and published in the Federal Register dated December 4, 1981.

Under the revisions, it was noted that the National Institutes of Health Guidelines for Research Involving Recombinant DNA Molecules will become a voluntary code of good practice. In addition, it is understood that each institution conducting or sponsoring recombinant DNA research will have responsibility for monitoring its own activities in this area and that any unusual events would be reported to the Director, National Institutes of Health.

EAR/af
attachment
cc: Mrs. Ruth Spector, Montgomery County Council
Mr. Robert Carty, Acting Director, Health Dept.

Medical Research Council of Canada
Conseil de recherches médicales du Canada

18 January 1982

Dr. Bill Gartland
Director, ORDA
Building 31, Room 4A52
National Institute of Health
Bethesda MA 20205

Dear Bill,

Thank you for inviting my comments on the material published in the Federal Register on December 4 and 7 concerning the upcoming meeting of the RAC.

I see 3 major issues in any country's approach to guidelines:

The scientific validity of the matching of proposed containment for various experiments to the perceived risks;

the procedures used by an institution, be it federal or academic, to enforce the appropriate containment standards;

the legal effects of documents relating to safety.

All these three issues are central to the proposed revisions.

1. <u>The scientific validity of the Guidelines</u>

I support the thrust toward the principle that the containment required for recombinant DNA experiments shall be that determined by the most hazardous of the components of the system, with P1-HV1 basically the lowest level. This is generally where the Canadian Guidelines have been since mid 1980 (copy enclosed).

I have some comments on the two proposals:

Ottawa, Canada
K1A 0W9

...2

1) To my mind, neither of the new proposals seems to make it clear that HV1 is the lowest permitted level of biological containment. In the current Guidelines this was achieved by always talking of P1-EK1 etc. In the new, the only statement lies in section II - D-1, paragraph 2, and it is pretty weak; must one use HV1, or better? I believe this should be clarified, and HV1 should be required.

2) Why does the Working Group retain in the main text all the hoopla about HV2 and 3 when only HV2 is referred to and then only in Appendix G? Dr. Gottesman has also picked up this general point.

3) Why the prohibitions? Is it not more realistic to call them case-by-case on approval of the Director, NIH etc.? They are all judgement calls anyway. I agree in principle with Dr. Gottesman here.

4) The first sentence of para. 2 of section III (Working Group), including the footnote, seems too vague. Recommended by whom? And are all possible pathogens recommended by someone or other? I recognise the can of worms that this opens in view of the reluctance of the NIH and the RAC to start identifying containment levels for viruses and cells etc., but Dr. Gottesman and the Working Group has already broken the seal on the can and I think that it is necessary for the latter to be a bit more specific. We are a long way down that road in Canada, and it seems to be working, given our procedures.

2. Procedures

The specific point here relates to the recommendations on the existence of IBC's.

The Canadian MRC Biohazards Committee, which plays the RAC role in the Canadian context, and which has had a very different history from the RAC, has frequently discussed the issue of post-hoc responsibility as might be determined by the courts in the event of an accident. This issue had greater immediacy to our Guidelines than yours because ours cover known pathogens as well as conjectural ones. It was generally agreed that, in the event of actual harm arising from an accident, the courts would probably find the investigator and the institution responsible, probably in that order, and perhaps even if negligence was not proven, and would find the organisation that issued the standards responsible only in the extent that those standards could be shown to be negligent. An institution cannot exercise its responsibilities without some form of IBC. I understand from the first NIH meeting of the IBC Chairmen that many IBC's had taken responsibility of the whole range of biohazard problems in those institutions, and did not restrict themselves merely to recombinant DNA. I think that the existence of IBC's should be encouraged by the National Institutes of Health, and that the proposal to delete a requirement for them is too negative.

The process we use for our Guidelines is to have a simple statement with each grant application covered by the guidelines that the IBC has checked the facilities, and found them consistent with the proposed work. The Grants Committees and, if necessary, MRC staff, can comment on these. We have no prior authorization on an experiment by experiment basis (apart from case-by-case ones). The rest is up to the IBC and the investigator, thus putting primary responsibility where it should be.

3. <u>Legal Effect of Guidelines</u>

The issue here is voluntary or compulsory.

The problem in a voluntary approach is that it negates the likely result in the event of harm resulting from a laboratory accident where the research program receives NIH support but was not in compliance with NIH guidelines. A court would probably find fault with the investigator and institution because they did not adhere to a nationally recommended standard, compulsory or not, and might state that NIH did not act responsibly in not receiving assurance that its funds would be used in accord with its own guidelines. Parallels with human experimentation and the use of animals are obvious.

If the guidelines reflect a national approach to safety in the face of reasonably anticipated hazard, then why not express confidence in that judgement by requiring compliance as a condition of use of NIH funds? Other funding agencies can do what they like. The alleviation of bureaucratic nonsense is a matter at least as much of the procedures used as it is of the compulsory or voluntary nature of the NIH guidelines, which, in the last analysis, are likely to be seen as the national standards.

I look forward to hearing the results of the debate on February 8-9.

Best regards,

Francis

Francis Rolleston
Director, Special Programs

FSR/ct
Encl.

Hampshire College
Amherst, Massachusetts / 01002

IOOL OF NATURAL SCIENCE (413) 549-4600

January 18, 1982

Director, Office of Recombinant DNA Activities
Building 31, 4A52
National Institutes of Health
Bethesda, Maryland 20205

Dear Director:

I favor strongly the retention IBC oversight and current NIH compliance requirements as advocated by Dr. Gottesman (Fed. Reg. 46(234): pp. 59734 et seq.). These oversight and compliance requirements seem necessary to me for public safety, for public confidence in rDNA research, and for the recognition by scientists of the responsibilities they have to the rest of society.

The National Institutes of Health and other federal agencies dispensing grants of public monies must continue to be responsible to and responsive to society. The proposed change to "admonishments" is an abandonment of those responsibilities.

Thanks to the foresight of a few scientists,rDNA research was brought before society for conscious evaluation and regulation before any ill effects could harm individuals or damage the reputation of rDNA research with society. For the first time I know of,the implications, both good and bad, of a new technology have gotten wide debate before injury to society. Without the continuation of compliance requirements enforceable by the granting agencies, public confidence in the ability of our government to rule equitably will continue to decline.

Keep mandatory oversight, compliance, and enforcement in the guidelines and you will continue to earn the respect of the public you serve.

Cordially,

Lynn Miller

Lynn Miller,
Professor of Biology,
Natural Science,

LM/nao

ST. JUDE CHILDREN'S RESEARCH HOSPITAL
332 North Lauderdale, P.O. Box 318,
Memphis, Tennessee 38101
(901) 522-0300
Danny Thomas, *Founder*

19 January 1982

Dr. William J. Gartland, Jr.
Director, Office of Recombinant
DNA Activities
Building 31, Room 4A52
National Institutes of Health
Bethesda, Maryland 20205

Dear Dr. Gartland:

Thank you for sending copies of the proposed changes in NIH Guidelines for Recombinant DNA Research at my request.

Having read all of the material provided in the Federal Register of December 4 and 7, 1981, and in light of my other knowledge and experience, I conclude that Drs. Adelberg and Zinder have the correct position: there is no scientific justification for maintaining any Guidelines in force.

I don't believe that the social and political considerations that have been mentioned as justifications for maintaining this regulatory apparatus are worth worrying about. The news media and the public have forgotten about the hypothetical dangers of the new technology. That fad was blown so far out of proportion that it destroyed itself. Indeed, when no bad news materialized, the media took the opposite tack and have been overblowing the industrial potential of the technology.

I hope the Recombinant DNA Advisory Committee will express its confidence in the scientific process and in logical science policy and follow the lead of Drs. Adelberg and Zinder.

Sincerely,

David W. Kingsbury, M.D.
Member, Division of Virology

DWK/hmh

ROCHE INSTITUTE OF MOLECULAR BIOLOGY
Nutley, New Jersey 07110

January 19, 1982

Dr. William Gartland
Director of the Office of
Recombinant DNA
Dept. of Health & Human Services
National Institutes of Health
Bethesda, Md. 20205

Dear Dr. Gartland:

I am responding to your invitation for comments on the recent proposal for major revisions of the "National Institutes of Health Guidelines For Research Involving Recombinant DNA Molecules."

I would like to register my support for the recommendation of the NIH Recombinant DNA Advisory Committee (RAC). This proposal is based on careful consideration and analysis of the scientific evidence relevant to this topic which has been accumulated over the last several years. These analyses have been carefully documented in the point-by-point discussions published in the report of the Working Group on Revisions of the Guidelines. In contrast, the alternative proposal, which appears in Item 7 in the Federal Register notice of December 7, fails to provide any substantial justification for its recommendations.

I would like to congratulate NIH and the RAC for their timely and responsible action on this matter which is of great importance to the American public as well as to all of us in the scientific community.

Yours truly,

A. M. Skalka, Ph.D.
Department of Cell Biology

AMS:pcp

STANFORD UNIVERSITY
STANFORD, CALIFORNIA 94305-2493

DEPARTMENT OF BIOLOGICAL SCIENCES

January 19, 1982

Dr. William J. Gartland, Jr., Ph.D.
Director, Office of Recombinant DNA Activities
Building 31, Room 4A52
National Institutes of Health
Bethesda, MD 20205

Dear Dr. Gartland:

I have examined and compared the two current proposals for revising current NIH Guidelines (Fed. Reg. 12/4/81 and 12/7/81).

The Gottesman proposal represents a marked improvement over the current Guidelines, in liberalizing containment levels and review procedures. But it does not go far enough. I am convinced that the time is long overdue for the Guidelines to be made entirely nonmandatory.

In the absence of any demonstrated hazard, I see no justification for continuing to mandate the formal review procedures stipulated by the present Guidelines on the revisions proposed by Dr. Gottesman. I therefore strongly support the original RAC proposal.

Sincerely yours,

David D. Perkins

David D. Perkins
Professor of Biology

DDP/cml

UNIVERSITY OF WASHINGTON
SEATTLE, WASHINGTON 98195

Program in Social Management of Technology

January 19, 1982

Hon. Ray Thornton
Chair, Recombinant DNA Advisory Committee
ORDA, Bldg. 31, Room 4A52
National Institutes of Health
Bethesda, MD 20205

Dear Chairman Thornton

I appreciated the ability to chat with you during the AAAS meetings earlier this month, and as promised this letter contains my comments on the Baltimore-Campbell and Gottesman proposals regarding the status and nature of the r-DNA Guidelines which will be before the RAC at its upcoming meeting.

At the outset I will state my conclusion: I oppose the Baltimore-Campbell proposal because it relies on assumptions which I do not share (and believe are unwise) and evidence which is scanty.I favor continuation of the present Guidelines with their capacity for evolution; I would accept the Gottesman revisions as the "lesser-of-two-evils" but do not endorse them. Below I have organized my comments under four general headings: public policy considerations, risk considerations, problems of logical reasoning, problems of "conflict of interest." My experience with r-DNA issues grows out of my membership on the University of Washington IBC for 3 years, serving the U. S. Congress Office of Technology Assessment as a consultant on its applied Genetics Study, testifying before the special HEW panel which lead to the 1978 Revised Guidelines, and numerous appearances in public forums and media discussions of these issues.

(1) Public Policy Considerations

The mechanisms which have been set up to oversee r-DNA research are a novel experiment. They represent one of the few examples in which science (as distinct from technology -- although r-DNA activities share aspects of the latter as well) has been subject to explicit public scrutiny and regulation. They have involved the establishment of new institutional arrangements, the IBCs, with a potential for citizen participation. This was done in recognition of the extraordinary power of r-DNA work to transform aspects of our social milieu.

Even though the IBCs and RAC have been largely controlled by r-DNA researchers and associated scientists and administrators, there are many indications that their functioning has been salutory in regard to assuring high quality research which is socially responsible. They also offer the public (which has supported so much of this work with its dollars, bears the risks and any hazards which result, and will share in the benefits which materialize) at least some measure of input into the decision-making process and increased information about the activities which are being conducted. These mechanisms should be improved, not abandoned nor atrophied, and membership rotation should be accomplished so as to insure that individuals with a demonstrated track record of public interest activity sit on the IBCs and the RAC (unfortunately, the reverse has been occurring). How else is public confidence to be maintained in these areas? Certainly, the blandishments of self-interested scientists who are increasingly jockeying in the commercial r-DNA arena will not serve to allay public concerns.

The call for "voluntary compliance" has come to evidence a trade association mentality compatible neither with the public's rightful expectations nor the historical experience with self-regulation of commercial activities (which DNA surely is at this time). The assumption behind Baltimore-Campbell that self-regulation will protect the common weal is unlikely to prove valid.

The irony is, of course, that the overwhelming majority of r-DNA work is currently unregulated at the Federal level, after the successful campaigns by Drs. Rowe and Campbell, Singer, Adelberg, and others to greatly modify the 1978 Guidelines. The public in most communities requires greater regulation of its barbers that its r-DNA researchers, an absurdity I agree, but one not helped by the current proposals before the RAC.

The claim that adherence to the Guidelines is costly and cumbersome is a familiar argument, always advanced by special interests desiring to eliminate public accountability. Unfortunately, there is no indication in the Federal Register supporting materials that the only two studies of IBC composition and performance ever conducted (see testimony of Pfund to HEW panel, Sept. 1978; presentation by RAC, 1981) are being considered in evaluating proposals to abolish the IBCs. The second of these studies, in particular, indicates that the committees have performed well in many respects, not significantly hindered research progress, etc. Unfortunately, the promised NIH evaluation of IBCs has been postponed until after the Baltimore-Campbell proposal is decided; this is another example of an Alice-in-Wonderland logic which calls for "the verdict first, the evidence afterward."

(2) Risk Considerations

In general, risk considerations have been poorly understood in the continuing r-DNA policy discussions, and risk assessment often not appreciated at all. The materials produced by the RAC Working Group (46 Fed. Register 59385-90) are a better treatment than one has come to expect. A risk should be considered in terms of three essential aspects: the probability of its occurrence, the magnitude or severity of the hazard should it occur, and the distributional nature of the hazard (who bears the burden). There are four general categories of risk relevant to r-DNA work. The first is the unintentional abuse, which because of accident or general sloppiness, etc., results in an epidemic or environmental disaster. The second is intentional misuse, malfeasance, which is the application of the technology with malice and/or the training of persons who may use recombinant DNA techniques in such fashion. Third are the moral and ethical concerns, such as human interference with natural rules of evolution or whether specific experiments used to generate new knowledge are inherently immoral (in the same sense that some Nazi experiments which were evil did produce knowledge of utility). Finally, there are the political concerns, including our realization that access to new knowledge is very skewed and that economic interests play a disproportionate role in shaping the development of technological phenomenon. Related to this last category are the risks inherent in very competitive modes of scientific endeavor where struggles to be first with a new discovery (because of prestigious prizes and acclaim) have, as we shall see,led to the cutting of corners.

Whereas risk may be thought of as a generally objective measure of harm, the notion of safety should be understood as being subjective. Safety is the level of acceptable risk. Thus, safety depends on the notion of acceptability, and presumably involves issues of knowledge and acquiescence on the part of those subject to the probability of harm, for instance in the local communities.

Repeatedly over the past several years, scientists have minimized the risks in recombinant DNA research. We should understand that they are only considering those risks in the first category above, the technocratic view of risks. Other risks exist and need to be considered by NIH.

The NIH Risk Assessment Program has only been in operation for 2 years. Unfortunately, both the Final Plan of the Risk Assessment Program announced by NIH near the end of 1979, and the Update announced a year later in 1980, contain two main flaws.

1) The Final Plan ahd the Update state that "the vast majority of information relevant to recombinant DNA risk analysis has already come from research not primarily designed to provide information on risk" (emphasis added). The fact is that virtually none of this research was designed to provide risk information at all.Scientific experiment cannot generally be said to prove a proposition which is not part of the initial hypothesis or, more importantly, which does not contribute to the research design. Whatever the possibilities of this occurring fortuitously in a single experiment (and the probability is small), the likelihood is increasingly reduced as the number of experiments relied upon is multiplied. The researchers have not made the necessary observations, performed relevant alterations to the experimental conditions, collected pertinent data, analyzed the results from a risk perspective, etc. In my opinion the quoted sentence does not represent good scientific practice; to base policy on such a procedure could lead to significant negative consequences for the public.

2) The Final Plan and Update continue to proceed as if the only risks which are presented by r-DNA experimentation are scientific/physical/environmental/health ones. This is technocratic thinking in the extreme. Numerous commentators, myself included, have repeatedly over the past five years raised concerns about non-scientific risks. Yet the Update states "no risks of recombinant DNA research have been identified that are not inherent in the microbiological and biochemical methodology used in such research." What about risks of accidents, of human fallibility, or due to arrogance or carelessness? For example, did the violation of the Guidelines at the University of California, San Diego, occur because personnel in Dr. Kennedy's lab cloned the wrong virus by mistake? What might be the consequences of other mistakes in the future? Or was that California incident due to sabotage, as was first suggested (Science, Vol. 209, pp. 1101-2, 5 Sept. 1980)? What are the risks of sabotage (especially considering the often lax supervision of laboratory activities provided by IBCs and BSOs)? Or perhaps it was an intentional event (Science, Vol. 209, pp. 1494-95, 26 Sept. 1980)? Indeed, the risks of intentional "misuse" of this new technology of gene recombination are among the most important issues raised by the research, yet NIH refuses to acknowledge them, no less mount a program to assess and hopefully control them.

The NIH should be considering a "Non-Scientific Aspects" to its Risk Assessment Program. This should involve the talents of social scientists (sociologists, anthropologists, psychologists, public policy analysts working on risk assessment) and humanists (especially ethicists). This would require research activities particularly designed to probe issues such as those above.

None of the official r-DNA institutions have handled ethical and cultural issues well. This attitude is reflected in the OTA Report on Applied Genetics. The report's ten page chapter on risk (a rather slender treatment of the topic) contains only three sentences regarding ethical and moral concerns:

"the perceived risk associated with genetic engineering includes ethical and moral hazards as well as physical ones. It is important to recognize that these are part of the general topic of risk. To some, there is just as much risk to social values and structure as to human health and the environment. (For further discussion, see ch. 13)". (At p.207). Chapter 13 referred to, is nine pages long (in a report which is 331 pages in length) and is entitled "Genetics and Society". Less than one page of this chapter can be said to be devoted to ethical issues, and at least one third of that page is taken up by a long quotation from one religious philosopher favoring genetic engineering. The superficiality of this treatment, and its imbalance, are outrageous (there are numerous theologians urging caution , as well as ethical views which are not religiously based). But, as the report so candidly notes, "the present Guidelines are a comprehensive, flexible, and non-burdensome way of dealing with the physical risks associated with r-DNA while permitting the work to go forward. That is all they were ever intended to do." (p. 217) The Guidelines "do not address the admittedly uncertain, long-term cultural risks," (p. 217). Ethical risks and concerns relevant to recombinant techniques, have to do with the possibilities of intentional misuse; the inviolability of evolutionary boundaries; maldistributions of access to information and power; and the very nature of how risks are evaluated. These issues must be resolved before regulatory controls are abandoned.

In sum, I cannot agree with the conclusion offered by Drs. Baltimore and Campbell in support of their proposal that "since 1976, neither experimental evidence nor solid theoretical arguments have been advanced to support the position that recombinant DNA research poses any danger to human health or to the integrity of the natural environment" and that the hazards "appear to be non-existant." (46 Fed. Register 59382).

The fact that there have been so few known incidents is quite likely because of the Guideline's cautionary influences. Elimination of the Guideline procedures is thus logically likely to increase the probability that risks will turn into active hazards.

(3) Problems of Logical Reasoning

Proponents of r-DNA research have unfortunately often used fallacious logical arguments to support their positions on public policy issues. For example, there is the false syllogism that the combination of genetic materials from two species each of which is considered to be relatively harmless must itself be harmless. Certainly there are examples in other natural sciences (if not biology itself) in which synergistic effects or unexpected products have occurred. Since the host will occupy a different ecological niche from the donor, the expression of the foreign DNA in that environment may be harmful by itself. The specific argument that the product of introducing toxic genes into a host cannot be more pathogenic than the donor itself falls within this general category and is essentially unsupported by any body of experimental work; it is merely a nice mental construct.

Related to this logical problem is the inherent contradiction between the discussion of "natural exchange mechanisms" and evolutionary fitness (40 Fed. Register 59387, 59388-89) set forth by the RAC Working Group. Engineered genetic exchanges between species which do not do so in nature (say sea urchins and E. coli) can not be claimed to be harmless because nature must have weeded out such "monstrocities." There is no evidence at all that such matings occurred in the past and failed as "unfit". The concern over evolutionary implications logically means that only recombinations which have occurred in nature should be permitted in the laboratory or industrial establishment (perhaps to increase the volume of specimens, etc.). Contrary behavior must necessarily rest on an assumption that the evolutionary concern is false or trivial.

(4) Problems of "Conflict of Interest"

In the Working Group's summary of arguments it is stated that "most scientists now conclude, after almost a decade of experience, deliberate risk assessment experimentation, and theorizing, that the potential risks of recombinant DNA research have not materialized and most probably will not." (46 Fed. Register 59391). This statement is literally true -- most scientists do hold such a belief. I have attempted above to show why, however, I think the belief is ill-founded. We should be aware that most scientists have sociological and psychological reasons for so believing; for many this is merely a generalized "conflict of interest" reflecting their socialization into their profession and that profession's historical mores, but for others there is the more traditional basis (pecuniary, status and esteem) operating as a conflict.

Public interest in the accelerated commercialization of r-DNA work is very high. TV documentaries, AAAS sessions, etc. all indicate this. The norms and protocols of university communities are being severely stressed by the conflicting roles of the PI as benevolent scientist and as a principal in a commercial firm. The secrecy and competition thus engendered will also increase the probability of unexpected consequences and hazards materializing. At this time, abolishing the Guidelines and the units of local oversight would be sending exactly the wrong signals to the major actors and the general public. Until such time as commercial r-DNA work is regulated (and I believe it presents far greater risks and concerns than laboratory work), the current Guidelines at least provide some mechanisms for accountability over the academic-commercial intermix.

Finally, we have many examples of scientists intentionally using (or misusing) their knowledge for personal or political ends. This will undoubtedly happen in regard to r-DNA work. The Guidelines could (if NIH chooses to do so) provide a way to begin to deal with this issue, one which I consider serious and too long ignored. It's not that I expect legions of biological terrorists to spring up, but just as some ministers are sinners, so some scientists are non-altruistic.

I therefore urge the RAC to reject the Baltimore-Campbell proposal and any of its derivatives. Thank you for your attention to my views.

Very truly yours,

Philip L. Bereano
Associate Professor

PLB:blw

cc: Hon. Douglas Walgren, Chair, Subcommittee on Science, Research, and Technology, House Committee on Science and Technology

Hon. Albert Gore, Chair, House Subcommittee on Investigations and Oversight

Hon. Edward Kennedy, U. S. Senate

Boston University School of Public Health
School of Medicine
80 East Concord Street
Boston, Massachusetts 02118
(617) 247-6016

January 19, 1982

William Gartland, Ph.D.
Director
Office of Recombinant DNA Activities
National Institutes of Health
Building 31; 4A52
Bethesda, MD 20205

Dear Dr. Gartland:

I am writing to register my absolute disagreement with all three proposals (Baltimore-Campbell, RAC, and Gottesman) currently being considered for revising the guidelines regulating recombinant DNA research. The changes are hasty and are unwarranted given the state-of-the-art in risk assessment in this area. In particular the proposals allow almost any host-vestor system to be used, including wild-type E. coli. This is made to order for unintentional dissemination in the environment of organisms carrying recombinant DNA molecules. I simply cannot understand how any responsible proposal for revision could allow this at this time.

Like many others I support continued, measured, responsible revision and perhaps simplification of the guidelines. The current proposals do not fall into this category and are an absurdity.

Sincerely yours,

David Ozonoff, M.D., M.P.H.
Chief, Environmental Health Section

DO/scf

AMHERST COLLEGE
AMHERST • MASSACHUSETTS • 01002

Webster Center for Biological Sciences
Telephone: 413-542-2087
Secretary: 413-542-2314

20 Jan. 1982

Director
Office of Recombinant DNA Activities
Bldg 31, Rm 4A52, N.I.H.
Bethesda, MD 20205

I favor strongly the retention of IBC oversight and current N.I.H. compliance requirements as advocated by Dr. Gottesman. (Fed. Reg. 46(234): pp 59734 et seq.). These requirements are needed (1) for public safety, (2) for public confidence in rDNA research, and (3) for the recognition by scientists of the responsibilities that they have to everybody.

Sincerely yours,
Philip T. Ives, Ph.D.
Emeritus Research Associate
of The Faculty.

Member of the town's UMass
rDNA Biohazards Committee.

MEMORANDUM

DEPARTMENT OF HEALTH AND HUMAN SERVICES
PUBLIC HEALTH SERVICE
NATIONAL INSTITUTES OF HEALTH

TO :Director, Office of Recombinant DNA·Activities
National Institutes of Health
Building 31, Room 4A52
Bethesda, MD 20205

DATE: January 20, 1982

Thru: Director, NIDR/ Chief, LMI

FROM :Bruce M. Chassy, LMI/NIDR

SUBJECT: Proposed revisions of NIH guidelines for research involving recombinant DNA.

A careful review of the proposals described in the December 4th and December 7th Federal Registers has resulted in a distinct preference for the proposal described in the Dec. 4 Register. The major advantages seem to be:

1. The voluntary nature of the new guidelines. The past few years have demonstrated the research communities' awareness of potential biohazards and willingness to adhere to guidelines. Notice is taken of the virtual unenforceability of mandatory guidelines; guidelines, to be effective, rely on ethical compliance, whether voluntary or mandatory.

2. The downgrading of certain experiments from P_3 and P_2 to P_1 containment levels seems justified by the vast experience gained with recombinant DNA since the original guidelines were developed.

3. The principle of prior review should be abandoned. It is needlessly expensive and time-consuming given a properly designed set of guidelines.

4. Both prior review and the mandatory nature of the guidelines have required NIH to act as a Regulatory body. The Institute has responded very well and has established a clear course and policy that makes it unneccessary to require further direct control by NIH.

CITY OF CAMBRIDGE
DEPARTMENT OF HEALTH, HOSPITAL AND WELFARE
1493 CAMBRIDGE STREET CAMBRIDGE, MASSACHUSETTS 02139
Telephone 354-2020

January 21, 1982

Director, ORDA
Building 31, Room 4A52
National Institutes of Health
Bethesda, MD 20205

Re: Proposed changes in Guidelines
Federal Register of 12/4/81

Dear Sirs:

The Cambridge Biohazards Committee was established by local city ordinance in 1976-77, and has since that time reviewed recombinant DNA use in Cambridge, Massachusetts. Within the last two years we have reviewed in detail every change in the NIH Guidelines, reviewed in detail (and helped to revise) the local ordinance governing recombinant DNA use in this city, listened to extensive testimony from experts on large scale and small scale recombinant DNA use, inspected local laboratories using recombinant DNA, conducted a public hearing on recombinant DNA use, and testified before our city councillors on this issue. We have also had many extensive and detailed discussions with the Biological Safety officers of Harvard and MIT. Since we are local citizens not personally involved in recombinant DNA research, we think our comments on the recently proposed Guidelines can provide an unusual and useful perspective to the Federal Government as it considers these proposed revisions. Each of us has long experience in local civic affairs.

We recognize the need to simplify the Guidelines, particularly the specification of containment levels. We do not, however, think it is wise or necessary to abolish Institutional Biosafety Committees. We believe such committees provide a useful restraint on careless or overconfident researchers and an essential reassurance to local communities. The selection of appropriate containment levels for certain uses of recombinant DNA will remain complex, even with simplified Guidelines. Complex decisions are often improved by consultation with other thoughtful people. Secondly, whenever individuals use potential pathogens, or other potentially harmful materials for personal gain or financial reward, a conflict of interest can arise. In this situation, it is inadequate for the institution to leave responsibility for safety regulations entirely in the hands of individuals involved in the work. The potential conflict of interest is unreasonable, and is immediately obvious to the surrounding community even when it is not obvious to the institution or the individuals. For these reasons, we think Institutional Biosafety Committees should remain mandatory. For the same reasons, we support the continued requirement that such committees include at least two members who "represent the interests of the surrounding community." Such members give local communities a "window" through which to assess an industry's impact on local health and environment in a reasoned manner, and simply by their presence can provide a healthy balance to the deliberations of a safety committee.

We realize that in many institutions Biosafety Committees have had little work and will have even less if the Guidelines are further simplified. We believe, however, that IBC review is essential for recombinant DNA use involving disease-causing agents or the generation of toxins or pharmacologically-active substances. IBC's without such issues to review could either not meet, or could profitably direct their attention to the other potential biological hazards of their institution (radioactivity, toxic chemicals, etc.).

The other changes proposed in the December 4 Federal Register essentially abolish the present regulatory structure. Although the periodic revisions of the Guidelines have been moving slowly in this direction, we think such a marked acceleration of this trend is unreasonable. The well-intentioned mistakes of the general scientific and technical community on other issues have left many people in Cambridge (and perhaps elsewhere) cynical about scientists' abilities to extrapolate very far beyond their immediate past experience, particularly if the scientists' own self-interest is involved. For example, it seems unreasonable to us to have only an admonition against deliberate release into the environment of organisms containing recombinant genes for antibiotic resistance and harmful toxins. It also seems unreasonable to abolish the Guidelines for biological containment and at the same time make the Guidelines for physical containment mere recommendations. Finally, we think that elimination of the voluntary compliance program will leave institutions that use recombinant DNA without NIH funding in a peculiar position.

Our own perception is that the measured evolution of the Guidelines has been a model of the way new technologies can be introduced into densely populated areas with maximum safety and public reassurance. To abandon this process now would be a major error. We recognize that a continuation of the Guidelines is expensive. Abolition of the Guidelines (i.e., the December 4 RAC proposal) may, however, in the long run be even more expensive, by inviting multiple conflicting state and local regulations, or by inviting a backlash of mistrust and revulsion if public health hazards are eventually associated with the use of recombinant DNA in the future.

Sincerely yours,

Robert M. Neer, Chairman/bm

Cambridge Biohazards Committee

Robert M. Neer, M.D., Chairman
Melvin Chalfen, M.D., Commissioner of Health
Oliver E. Farnum
Elsa Stern
Zelia Kelleher

bkm

UNITED STATES DEPARTMENT OF AGRICULTURE
SCIENCE AND EDUCATION ADMINISTRATION

AGRICULTURAL RESEARCH
NATIONAL PROGRAM STAFF
BELTSVILLE, MARYLAND 20705

January 21, 1982

SUBJECT: Proposed Revisions of NIH Guidelines for Research Involving Recombinant DNA Molecules

TO: William J. Gartland, Director
Office of Recombinant DNA Activities
National Institutes of Health
Room 4A52, Building 31
Bethesda, Maryland 20205

The two proposals for a major revision of the NIH Guidelines for Research Involving Recombinant DNA Molecules, published in the Federal Register, December 4, 1981, and December 7, 1981, have been reviewed. Based on current scientific evidence, I recommend acceptance of the revision proposed by the Recombinant DNA Advisory Committee.

Thomas J. Army

THOMAS J. ARMY
Deputy Administrator
National Program Staff

The Commonwealth of Massachusetts

University of Massachusetts

Worcester 01605

MEDICAL CENTER
Department of Molecular Genetics
and Microbiology
55 Lake Avenue North

Telephone: (617) 356-2292

January 22, 1982

William J. Gartland, Jr., Ph.D.
Director, Office of Recombinant DNA Activities
Department of Health & Human Services
National Institutes of Health
Bethesda, Maryland 20205

Dear Dr. Gartland:

I am writing to support the proposal of the recombinant DNA advisory committee to modify the NIH guidelines so they would become a voluntary code of standard practice. I strongly urge that this proposal be adopted rather than the alternative proposal which appears as Item 7 in the Federal Register Notice of December 7, 1981. In 1974, a group of scientists set a precedent by asking that the consequences of a proposed experimental procedure be evaluated before experiments were conducted. The evaluation of these procedures has perhaps been more acrimonious than we might have hoped, but the process of evaluation has been an open one and has involved the collaboration of public, scientific and legislative bodies. Let us now set a new precedent. Now that we are convinced that the experiments present no legitimate danger to the public or to ourselves, let us dismantle a regulatory apparatus which is no longer necessary.

Sincerely yours,

Lydia Villa-Komaroff

Lydia Villa-Komaroff, Ph.D.
Assistant Professor

STANFORD UNIVERSITY MEDICAL CENTER
STANFORD, CALIFORNIA 94305

DEPARTMENT OF BIOCHEMISTRY
STANFORD UNIVERSITY SCHOOL OF MEDICINE

Area Code 415
497-6161

January 22, 1982

Dr. William J. Gartland
Department of Health and Human Services
National Institutes of Health
Bethesda, MD 20205

Dear Dr. Gartland,

I am writing in support of the RAC proposal to revise the NIH Guidelines for Recombinant DNA Research as set forth in the Federal Register of December 4, 1981.

I believe that the Guidelines for Recombinant DNA research are now dispensible. Based on the substantial amount of experience and experimentation with the recombinant DNA methodology during the last six years, there is widespread agreement that the risks that were once thought to be so plausible are actually remote or possibly nonexistent. If that judgement is indeed correct, and I know of no evidence to indicate otherwise, then it seems wasteful of effort and money, even counter-productive, to maintain the elaborate procedures and organizations that were setup to guard against the hypothetical threats. It has been my long-held view that the most beneficial feature of the Guidelines was their educational role; they highlighted the kind of concerns that were voiced and provided recommendations for workers in the field as to how safety considerations should be incorporated into their experimental designs and procedures. For that purpose referring to the revised Guidelines as a Guide (or Code) for Good Practice seems appropriate.

There is one minor point in the wording of the RAC proposal with which I differ. Emphasizing that the new recommendations are 'voluntary' places an unintended and unnecessary psychological focus on the change. I suspect that if the voluntary nature of the recommendations is emphasized, many will take that as an invitation to ignore them completely; after all who cares. But if the revised version makes strong recommendations and accompanying justifications for how such experiments should be carried out, there is a stronger liklihood that people would accept the recommendations as being reasonable. I prefer the approach the CDC uses, namely, to advise scientists of the concerns about certain organisms and make recommendations for how to work with various types of microbial pathogens and viruses. Voluntarism, while implicit, is deemphasized in favor of urging compliance.

I am strongly in favor of maintaining RAC but not necessarily ORDA except in so far as it serves a small staff function for RAC. RAC could well serve as an 'antenna' and 'intelligence' group in that their role would be to monitor progress and developments of recombinant DNA technology being alert to any developments that could bear on the issue of safety. RAC could be the trigger to initiate an appropriate response to any perceived or actual risk. I think that if RAC were constituted to provide such a 'watchguard' function and was responsible for responding to unanticipated developments, there might be less concern on the part of the public by what will be perceived as a drastic change in the regulations of this research.

Sincerely,

Paul Berg

PB/hk

123 COOLIDGE HILL
CAMBRIDGE, MASSACHUSETTS 02138

January 25, 1982

Office of Recombinant D N A Activities
N.I.H - Bldg 31; 4A52 - Bethesda.

Dear Sirs,

I am writing as a community member of the Harvard Biohazards Committee. As I do not have a scientific background I cannot comment on the scientific aspects of the recent regulations. However I was a member of the two Cambridge committees who studied the problems of D.N.A work being done in Cambridge, besides having been on the Cambridge City Council for twelve years. Politically speaking I feel it would be devastating to give up the Guideline as all our city regulations are based on compliance with the latest Guidelines. If independent guidelines were attempted at Cambridge request, the result would be chaos!

I also feel that the institutional and City committees are extremely important.

Sincerely yours -

Cornelia B. Wheeler

UNIVERSITY OF CALIFORNIA, LOS ANGELES UCLA

BERKELEY · DAVIS · IRVINE · LOS ANGELES · RIVERSIDE · SAN DIEGO · SAN FRANCISCO SANTA BARBARA · SANTA CRUZ

DEPARTMENT OF PATHOLOGY
UCLA SCHOOL OF MEDICINE
CENTER FOR THE HEALTH SCIENCES
LOS ANGELES, CALIFORNIA 90024

January 25, 1982

William J. Gartland, Jr., Ph.D.
Director, Office of Recombinant
DNA Activities
Building 31, Rm 4A52
National Institutes of Health
Bethesda, Maryland 20205

Dear Dr. Gartland:

I am strongly in favor of the proposed revision of the NIH Guidelines for Research Involving Recombinant DNA Molecules recommended by the Recombinant DNA Advisory Committee and published in the Federal Register, December 4, 1981. In my opinion, the vast majority of the experiments involving recombinant DNA have been shown to be safe. In addition, I believe that most institutions have shown that they are able to monitor laboratories and train laboratory workers to maintain reasonable biological safety. For these reasons, I believe that it would now be appropriate to make the Guidelines a voluntary code of standard practice.

Sincerely yours,

David D Porter

David D. Porter, M.D.
Professor of Pathology
Chairman, Institutional Biosafety Committee

DDP: shh

Hagedorn Research Laboratory
Niels Steensensvej 6 · DK-2820 Gentofte, Denmark · Tel. (1) 68 08 60

January 25, 1982

Director
Office of Recombinant DNA activities
National Institutes of Health
Building 31, Room 4A52
Bethesda
Maryland 20205
U.S.A.

Subject: Proposed Revision of NIH Guidelines for Research Involving Recombinant DNA Molecules

The revisions suggested by the Recombinant DNA Advisory Committee (RAC) with respect to simplifying the containment levels appear sound and advisable. We also agree that the Guidelines are most suitable as a standard for proper laboratory work.

It would, however, not be sensible to abandon the practice of having an Institutional Biosafety Committee (IBC) or an Institutional Review Board (IRB) made mandatory. Although Recombinant DNA research in the US is well advance it still has a lower volume in Europe. The responsibility of the scientists to keep the public informed and the sharing of responsibility for their activities would be best served by enforcing institutions to register planned experiments with the IRB/IBC.

It is likely that simply a revision of the guidelines will not alter the public opinion about Recombinant DNA activities. We believe that this aspect has not been properly dealt with in the revised guidelines, especially from the point of view that the NIH decision will certainly be guiding decisions in countries just now, perhaps less critically, entering this field of research.

It is our intention to report planned Recombinant DNA experiments to the IRB of the foundation Nordisk Insulinlaboratorium.

Sincerely yours,

Åke Lernmark, M.D.
Director of Research

Bruno Hansen, Chem.Eng., M.Sc.
Director of Research

UNIVERSITY OF ROCHESTER

ROCHESTER, NEW YORK 14627

VICE PRESIDENT
FOR CAMPUS AFFAIRS

26 January 1982

Dr. William J. Gartland
Director, Office of Recombinant DNA Activities
Building 31, Room 4A52
National Institutes of Health
Bethesda, Maryland 20205

Dear Dr. Gartland:

The University of Rochester supports the proposed revisions to the "NIH Guidelines for Research Involving Recombinant DNA Molecules" (the "Guidelines") proposed by the Recombinant DNA Advisory Committee (RAC) as published in the Federal Register, 4 December 1981, page 59368 et seq.

It has long been our philosophy that institutions such as universities should take all reasonable precautions in laboratory practices to protect the health and safety of the community as well as laboratory personnel. Such precautions should be taken not only with recombinant DNA procedures but also with procedures involving such matters as toxic agents, radiation and radioactive substances, pathogenic microorganisms and more familiar dangers such as electric shock, and fire. Self-regulation rather than mandatory federal regulations can and should be used to accomplish these ends.

One of the primary reasons for the development of the federal "Guidelines" was to prevent the unintentional construction of highly pathogenic and contagious microorganisms which could produce uncontrollable epidemics. The experience of numerous laboratory directors and scientists performing recombinant DNA research suggests that such presumed danger does not exist. In fact, with the approved vectors used in recombinant DNA procedures, the pathogenicity of artificially constructed microorganisms has proven to be far less than that of the naturally occurring host.

While we are in complete agreement that control of biological systems involving recombinant DNA should be at a level consistent with the appraised risk, we do not believe that the de facto regulation of recombinant DNA research, as represented by the current "Guidelines" or by the Gottesman Proposal (FR 12/7/81) is necessary to achieve adequate control. We believe that guidelines are highly desirable if they contain recommendations based on the best understanding at the time of issue of the mechanisms for attaining control. To this end the RAC has already provided valuable service and is undoubtedly the proper body for ongoing review and modification of any "Guidelines." Similarly, the "Laboratory Safety Monograph" has proved immensely valuable in providing investigators guidance in safe handling of hazardous materials, including many kinds that bear no relation to recombinant DNA.

We recognize that there are undoubtedly investigators who will feel that conformity to non-mandatory "Guidelines" could be a burden. Even now, except in States and localities which have explicit recombinant DNA legislation, the private sector is not subject to the "Guidelines" unless federal support is received. Our own experience has been that investigators tend to be over-conservative in performing such research, using P2 containment where P1 is allowed, for example. In part, this has reflected a desire for the technical control that better containment represents more than concern about the possible hazards.

It appears to us, however, that such "nonconformists" are in an extreme minority and that peer and other pressures will limit their propensity to follow less-than-adequate procedures. We already see evidence of this in relation to use of unregulated hazardous materials such as supertoxics and carcinogens where investigators following less than the norm for good laboratory practice are gently reminded by their colleagues of the need for improved management.

The "Guidelines" have also served a valuable function in establishing the concept of an Institutional Biosafety Committee (IBC), and it seems most likely that institutions will enlarge on the role of the IBC to include oversight of research with pathogens where recombinant DNA is not a factor. Our own IBC already has undertaken this to a limited extent.

In sum, we believe that non-mandatory "Guidelines" are highly desirable as being a focal point for knowledge on the safe handling of recombinant DNA molecules, their hosts and vectors. We do not believe that mandatory "Guidelines" significantly improve conformity to safe practices. We believe that investigators will comply voluntarily with the intent and content of non-mandatory "Guidelines" for the protection of themselves, their research, and the community.

We urge the adoption of the "Guidelines" proposed by the RAC.

Sincerely,

D. K. Hess

DKH:mgk

The University of Michigan
Medical School
Ann Arbor, Michigan 48109

Department of Microbiology and Immunology
6643 Medical Science Building II
Telephone (313) 763-3531

January 26, 1982.

Dr. William J. Gartland, Jr.
Director, Office of Recombinant DNA Activities
Building 31, Room 4A52
National Institutes of Health
Bethesda, Maryland 20205

Dear Dr. Gartland:

This letter is to comment on the two proposals for revision of the NIH Guidelines for Research Involving Recombinant DNA Molecules, referenced and summarized in your letter of December 18, 1981.

I have worked extensively, partly supported by a NIH contract, on problems of transfer of recombinant DNA molecules in E. coli-plasmid host-vector systems (partly summarized in ref. 1) and have discussed the potential hazards of such systems to the general population (2,3). Much the same reasoning I used there can also be applied to most other host-vector systems. For these reasons I concluded then - and would like to reaffirm now - that the early serious fears expressed by some concerning the hazards of experimentation with recombinant DNA were contradicted by the then known facts and concepts of microbial ecology and pathogenicity. They were therefore inappropriate from the outset as a basis for restricting this research. As is now well known, additional research, including my own, has consistently confirmed this viewpoint. I therefore can support the general intent of the current proposals to remove the bureaucratic burden of mandatory guidelines from all those research projects which must now submit to it simply because they happen to employ this technique.

I feel compelled to point out, however, that the above reasoning and research concerning the safety of recombinant DNA technology was based on the assumption that the hosts employed were of a kind which were unlikely to colonize man or the environment and that the vectors could not reasonably be expected to transfer to indigenous host microorganisms or host cells. As implied by Dr. Susan Gottesman's proposal, these statements certainly define the boundaries within which we can make informed judgements of safety. Beyond that, I know of no argument to allay the fears of those who may consider it dangerous to introduce genes that promote pathogenicity (especially those coding for toxins) into microorganisms which can colonize man or his environment or to introduce genes that may enhance pathogenicity (e.g. by specifying adhesins or metabolic traits such as iron chelation) into known pathogens. The results would be unpredictable. Nevertheless, someone like myself who is interested in microbial pathogenicity, must recognize this type of experimentation as a most powerful tool to study the mechanisms by which microorganisms produce disease and by which such diseases can be prevented or cured. In fact, I strongly suspect that many of today's problems in infections may not be solved without this type of experimentation, just as many others require (well supervised) experiments in human volunteers. For this reason, such experiments certainly should not be prohibited. On the other hand, the not unlikely consequence of enhanced pathogenicity for the resultant recombinants calls for certain safeguards.

I am therefore attracted to the intent of Dr. Gottesman's proposal of retaining a minimum of outside review and control of the type of experiments outlined in the preceding paragraph. I do not agree with all the concerns implied in Dr. Gottesman's proposal. For example, 500 liters of culture in a fermenter are probably less dangerous than 9 liters in a glass carboy in someone's laboratory. Nevertheless, I consider Dr. Gottesman's proposal to be the best-balanced approach yet to reconcile the often conflicting but nevertheless imperative needs of our society for aggressive research as well as for safety. Most of us will probably agree, on hindsight, that the recombinant DNA controversy was a lesson in what pitfalls to avoid in future conflicts of this nature. Part of the lesson is to avoid extremes, and that is what Dr. Gottesman's proposal tries to accomplish. I urge the RAC to adopt a final recommendation that embodies the basic philosophy expressed in her proposal.

Sincerely yours,

Rolf Freter, Ph.D.
Professor of Microbiology
and Immunology

RF/ew

References.

(1) Recomb. DNA Tech. Bull. 2 (2): 68-76 (1979).

(2) J. Infect. Dis. 137: 624-629 (1979).

(3) In: D. A. Jackson and S. P. Stitch (eds.): The Recombinant DNA Debate. Prentice - Hall (1979); pp. 155-172.

University of Illinois at Urbana-Champaign

Division of Environmental Health and Safety

333 McKinley Hospital
1109 South Lincoln Avenue
Urbana, Illinois 61801
(217) 333-2755

January 26, 1982

Dr. William J. Gartland, Jr.
Director
Office of Recombinant DNA Activities
National Institutes of Health
Building 31, Room 4A52
Bethesda, Maryland 20205

Dear Dr. Gartland:

The Subcommittee for Recombinant DNA Review of the University of Illinois at Urbana/Champaign (UIUC) endorses the proposed revisions to the NIH Recombinant DNA Guidelines published in the Federal Register dated December 4, 1981. The adoption of these revisions proposed by the RAC will, in effect, place recombinant DNA research in the same voluntary compliance status as that research which employs any etiologic agent. This action signifies that recombinant DNA research is no more hazardous (barring the stated NIH prohibitions) than research with the original source organism from which the recombinant DNA has been obtained. The Subcommittee agrees that recombinant DNA research should be conducted under a voluntary code of standard practice.

Reducing the recombinant DNA Guidelines from mandatory to voluntary compliance will not result in an end of UIUC surveillance of projects that pose any real or potential biological risk. UIUC monitored the use and disposal of biohazardous agents before the realization of recombinant DNA technology and the resultant mandatory NIH Recombinant DNA Guidelines. The adoption of this proposal will result in a reduction in paperwork, costs, and time needed to maintain regulatory compliance, not in the reduction of biohazard surveillance.

Sincerely,

Nelson S. Slavik

NSS:bw

Nelson S. Slavik, Ph.D.
Chairperson, Subcommittee for
Recombinant DNA Review

MASSACHUSETTS INSTITUTE OF TECHNOLOGY
COMMITTEE ON ASSESSMENT OF BIOHAZARDS

TELEPHONE: (617) 253-5360, 1740

77 MASSACHUSETTS AVENUE, 20B-238
CAMBRIDGE, MASSACHUSETTS 02139

26 January 1982

William J. Gartland, Jr., Ph.D.
Director, Office of Recombinant DNA Activities
National Institutes of Health
Building 31, Room 4A52
Bethesda, Maryland 20205

Dear Dr. Gartland:

This is in response to the request for comments on the proposed changes in the NIH Guidelines for Research Involving Recombinant DNA Molecules as published in the Federal Register, 4 December 1981 (Vol. 46, No. 233, pages 59368-59383).

We want to indicate our concern with the proposed change whereby the objective review beyond that of the principal investigator is essentially eliminated.

The exclusive dependence on determinations of appropriate containment by a principal investigator is, we feel, premature when the applications of recombinant technology are expanding rapidly with respect to the diversity of organisms being used and encompass virtually all fields of biological research.

We urge the Recombinant DNA Advisory Committee to preserve those mechanisms at both the institutional and national levels which ensure continuity in judgement in determining the appropriate containment requirements when new host vector systems are developed, or for other novel applications of this technology.

Respectfully,

Daniel F. Liberman

Daniel F. Liberman, Ph.D.
for the Committee on Assessment of Biohazards
Massachusetts Institute of Technology

HARVARD UNIVERSITY
THE BIOLOGICAL LABORATORIES

16 DIVINITY AVENUE
CAMBRIDGE, MASSACHUSETTS 02138

January 27, 1982

William J. Gartland, Jr.
Office of Recombinant DNA Activities
National Institutes of Health
Bldg. 31, Room 4A52
Bethesda, Md. 20205

Dear Dr. Gartland:

I have been out of close touch for a time with the recombinant DNA situation; but wish now to register strong objection to the Baltimore/Campbell proposal described in the Federal Register of Dec. 4, 1981, proposing that the NIH Guidelines be changed from mandatory to voluntary, and so modified as to make them weaker.

I have received a letter about these changes, discussing their impact, from Donna Smith at MIT and Terri Goldberg, Coordinator of the Science Resource Center. The letter is addressed to you, and I am thoroughly in accord with what it says.

One thing that bothers me particularly is that David Baltimore should still be in position to advise government on these matters without disclosing his by now deep conflict of interest. According to the Boston Globe of Dec. 10, 1981 he is now the second largest personal stockholder in Collaborative Genetics, which was to go public this month, with holdings valued at over $5 million.

Such conflict of interest in this field is deeply embarrassing and very widespread. It threatens to corrupt the entire relationship between academics and universities, and the public and government. The least that must be done about it is full disclosure. The entire concept of academic freedom is imperilled by it. University faculty members and administration must not be permitted any longer to advise the public and government on controversial issues without disclosing their personal interests — I mean money interests. The National Academy of Sciences and National Research Council has had to adopt such rules for members of its committees; and I should think that the government could do no less.

Sincerely,

George Wald

George Wald
Emeritus Professor of Biology; Nobel Laureate, 1967

Whom to believe? Who gains? Who loses?

Marshall Arisman

The Nuclear-Power-Truth Maze

New York Times
February 29, 1976

By George Wald

CAMBRIDGE, MASS.

ONE of the prevalent myths of our time is that Government policy is based on the best obtainable information — that if the Government knows which policy will most promote the public welfare it will adopt that policy, It is this belief that fosters the constant call for more research.

In fact, almost the opposite is true. A policy having been decided on—usually for economic or political reasons—the information is sought that will support it. That is, information follows policy, rather than the other way around.

As for the information itself, one needs to distinguish advocacy from judgment. Advocacy is what a lawyer does for his client in making a case. It is one-sided; presumably another, perhaps equally able advocate, prepares the other side. But judgment is something else. It must weigh both sides, one hopes impartially. There must at least be no overt bias. A judgment must be disinterested.

These are important considerations in the present public debate involving nuclear power. A bewildered and uneasy public is faced with highly technical problems, far beyond its capacity to evaluate. Hence it is forced to rely upon the opinions of experts. But then it is crucial whether those experts are advocates or judges.

One of the main factors that undermined public confidence in the United States Atomic Energy Commission was the realization that the main thrust of this public agency was to promote the nuclear-power industry and that it was willing to compromise on standards of safety to achieve this end.

It was largely the work of persons outside both Government and industry—indeed, opposed all the way by Government and industry—that eventually forced tighter safety standards and controls.

A bewildered public seeking expert and unbiased opinion hopes to find that in the universities. And rightly so. The entire insistence on academic freedom rests on the assumption that the universities are engaged in an objective and impartial search for truth.

One looks to them for both expertise and disinterestedness; but if one had to make a choice, disinterestedness is the more important. For experts are all about us; industry and Government employ large numbers of them. Disinterestedness is the rare and precious quantity.

I make so much of this because at present the public, trying to reach a position on nuclear power, finds professors on both sides. Whom is one to believe?

It needs to be understood that, as in so many other instances, those professors do not face a symmetrical situation. They must find their way in a heavily biased context.

One outcome, favoring the rapid spread of nuclear power, the relaxation of safety standards, the optimization of benefits and minimization of the risks involved—those views enlist large political and financial support, and are greeted with official approval, eager acceptance and wide publicity.

The other viewpoint, concerned as it is with troubling problems of power-plant safety, control of nuclear pollution, plutonium 239 as a source both of high toxicity and fission bombs, and the still wholly unresolved burden of nuclear-waste disposal that promises to remain a problem for hundreds of thousands of years—that opposition viewpoint offers no reward but its own conviction. It has no client, unless society at large becomes its client.

Early in 1975 a group of 32 "notable scientists," mainly physicists, issued a "Scientists' Statement on Energy Policy" that urged the rapid expansion of nuclear power as the only realistic solution of our coming energy needs. Recognizing potential dangers, it concluded that there exists no available alternative and that with proper care this expansion would involve benefits that far outweigh the risks.

Was this widely disseminated statement advocacy or judgment? One hopes the latter, since these are very distinguished scientists, widely respected by their colleagues. Twenty-six of them, including eleven Nobel Prize laureates, were identified only as professors in major universities.

HENCE, it was with some dismay that I read an analysis by a fellow academic physicist that showed that 14 of the 26 academic signers are members of the boards of directors of major United States corporations, including corporations directly and indirectly involved in energy production. I would not question the integrity of any of these persons; yet it must be recognized that such an affiliation in this connection does not *suggest*—it *defines* conflict of interest.

The only reprehensible element I would plead in the relationships themselves is in the failure to disclose them. Imagine the difference in impact had these academic signers listed themselves as directors of Exxon, Nuclear Systems, Iowa Electric Light and Power. Detroit Edison and the like!

The business of the energy industry is not to make energy but to make money. In pursuit of that single-minded purpose it continuously lobbies, infiltrates Federal agencies, funds candidates in both major parties, devotes many millions of dollars to "educational" propaganda, and does everything it can to avoid regulation.

We scientists are often asked whether it might be possible eventually to produce nuclear-power safely. That is a technical question, and the answer to it may well be *yes*. But that is the wrong way to ask the question. The real question we face is whether nuclear power can be produced safely *while maximizing profit*. The answer to that question is no.

We had a nice instance of the real situation at a news conference in Washington on Aug. 6, 1975, when the Union of Concerned Scientists presented to the Administration and Congress a petition signed by 2,300 scientists and engineers asking restraint on the further construction of nuclear-power plants until problems involving their safety were under better control.

ONE OF the speakers was Rear Adm. Ralph Weymouth, recently retired from the Navy. What had disturbed Admiral Weymouth was the great disparity between safety precautions observed by the Navy in its nuclear installations and those taken by the nuclear industry. The point is simple enough: The Navy operates without regard to profit, whereas the industry bends all its efforts to maximize profit, and regularly cuts corners to achieve that end.

Everyone is an idealist, not just you and your friends but all those on the other side. Just ask them, and they will tell you.

Having to find my way through a maze of frequently conflicting ideals, I finally adopted a rough rule of thumb: If the ideal costs something—in money, privilege, status—*that* makes it a little more credible. If, on the contrary, it pays off in any or all of those ways, then I fall back on the principle of scientific parsimony: If you have one explanation for a phenomenon there is no need to seek a second explanation.

Those of us who oppose nuclear power in its present forms have nothing to gain thereby but our share in the common good. Our opposition brings us into conflict with all the centers of power. It costs us our own money. It threatens rather than raises our professional status. Lately, three General Electric engineers and a Federal safety supervisor resigned their management jobs in nuclear-power installations. One gets no medals for such behavior, only opprobrium from Government and industry, only the lasting stigma of not being a team player.

Whom is one to believe? One cannot be sure. But it helps to know that those opposed to nuclear power have nothing to gain from their position but the public good, that they are indeed willing to pay for the privilege of speaking out.

George Wald, professor of biology at Harvard University, won the 1967 Nobel Prize in Physiology or Medicine.

UNIVERSITY OF CALIFORNIA, RIVERSIDE

BERKELEY • DAVIS • IRVINE • LOS ANGELES • RIVERSIDE • SAN DIEGO • SAN FRANCISCO SANTA BARBARA • SANTA CRUZ

TELEPHONE: (714) 787-5535

RESEARCH OFFICE
RIVERSIDE, CALIFORNIA 92521

January 27, 1982

Dr. William J. Gartland, Jr.
Director
Office of Recombinant DNA Activities
Building 31, Room 4A52
National Institutes of Health
Bethesda, Maryland 20205

Dear Dr. Gartland:

The Institutional Biohazards Committee at the University of California, Riverside, unanimously recommends adoption of the proposed Revised Guidelines for Recombinant DNA Research which appeared in the December 4, 1981, Federal Register (46 FR 59368). It is our Committee's belief that relaxation of the federal guidelines is based on careful study by RAC and ORDA and that public safety is not jeopardized.

Even if the December 4 guidelines are adopted, this campus will:

a) Continue to employ the existing guidelines as a voluntary code of standard practice;
b) retain the Institutional Biosafety Committee to serve as an advisory committee to certify proposed containment levels; and
c) take advantage of the simplified containment levels.

Thank you for the opportunity to comment on this important issue.

Sincerely,

Leland M. Shannon, Chairman
Institutional Biohazards Committee
Dean, Graduate Division and
Research Development

LMS:svs

cc: B. Cole

United States Department of Agriculture
Agricultural Research Service
North Central Region Northern Regional Research Center
1815 North University Street Peoria, Illinois 61604

January 27, 1982

Director, Office of
Recombinant DNA Activities
National Institutes of Health
Building 31, Room 4A52
Bethesda, MD 20205

Dear Sir:

Concerning the proposed revision of the NIH Guidelines on Recombinant DNA Research appearing in the December 4, 1981, Federal Register and the subsequent proposal published on December 7, 1981, the Northern Regional Research Center would prefer to have the Gottesman Proposal adopted in preference to the full RAC Committee proposal.

In the opinion of the Recombinant DNA research group at the Center and other interested individuals, the Guidelines function as a guide for good laboratory practices and act as a restraint, even on those who are not presently bound by the Guidelines. In our opinion, a relaxation of the Guidelines is necessary to promote and maintain interest and to advance knowledge in the field. We believe, however, this would best be achieved over a period of time, by degree, which is what we feel the Gottesman Proposal attempts to do.

Sincerely,

V. L. DAVISON
Safety Manager

UNIVERSITY OF CALIFORNIA, IRVINE

BERKELEY • DAVIS • IRVINE • LOS ANGELES • RIVERSIDE • SAN DIEGO • SAN FRANCISCO   SANTA BARBARA • SANTA CRUZ

OFFICE OF THE CHANCELLOR
IRVINE, CALIFORNIA 92717

January 28, 1982

Director
Office of Recombinant DNA Activities
National Institutes of Health
Building 31, Room 4A52
Bethesda, MD 20205

Dear Director,

In response to the proposals published in the December 4 and December 7, 1981 issues of the Federal Register, the University of California Irvine supports RAC's December 4, 1981 proposal, calling for the voluntary compliance of institutions with NIH guidelines with respect to research involving recombinant DNA molecules. If this proposal were adopted, however, this campus would retain an active Institutional Biosafety Committee which would continue to monitor such research on the campus in accordance with all applicable regulations and good scientific practices.

It would be expected that at the time that such a proposal became effective, the UC Irvine Institutional Biosafety Committee would design policies and procedures for the campus for local institutional monitoring and control.

Very truly yours,

Daniel G. Aldrich
Chancellor

UNIVERSITY OF CALIFORNIA, SAN DIEGO

BERKELEY • DAVIS • IRVINE • LOS ANGELES • RIVERSIDE • SAN DIEGO • SAN FRANCISCO   SANTA BARBARA • SANTA CRUZ

SCIENCE, TECHNOLOGY AND PUBLIC AFFAIRS

Q-060
LA JOLLA, CALIFORNIA 92093

January 28, 1982

Dr. William J. Gartland
Department of Health & Human Services
National Institutes of Health
Bethesda, Maryland 20205

Dear Bill:

I should like to comment briefly on the two proposals for revision of the NIH Guidelines that are on the RAC agenda for February 8-9, 1982.

The more drastic proposal made by RAC (Fed.Reg. 12/4/81) essentially terminates the quasi-regulatory role of NIH by transferring responsibility for "good practice" to local institutions who sponsor the research. The Gottesman proposal (Fed.Reg. 12/7/81), on the other hand, continues the gradual constriction of the quasi-regulated area while keeping central NIH responsibility intact. It is obvious that the "constriction curve" on which the Gottesman proposal and its antecedents lie projects toward the RAC proposal at some not-too-distant time. The difference between the two proposals thus reduces to the question whether the area remaining if the Gottesman proposal were to be adopted justifies continued quasi-regulation by NIH.

It is to be recalled that the NIH guidelines were conceived to cope with large uncertainty about possible risk entailed in certain projected RDNA experiments. In particular, attention came to focus on inadvertent pathogenic risk to investigators, supportive personnel and the general community. The shape of the "constriction curve" reflects rising confidence that the rationally estimated risk of such inadvertent effects is declining.

However, other areas of uncertainty that have had lesser attention have been repeatedly noted in the last several years. These include: 1) Risks of deliberate efforts to create and disseminate new pathogenic agents, as living organisms or their products; 2) Risks of scale-up, whether simply in amount of materials or in combination with other existing or new technologies; 3) Risks of deliberate dissemination into the environment of agents expected to yield benefits but conceivably yielding unanticipated dysbenefits; 4) Risks of effects broader than biological, ranging from social change to violation of accepted ethical principles. Estimates of risks in these areas have far less objective foundation than those relating to inadvertent pathogenic effects - because experience with them remains limited and because they have been less carefully addressed.

This suggests that the level of all remaining uncertainty is still substantial, i.e. that the constriction curve reflects welcome change primarily in only one area of uncertainty. No concerted mechanism for assessing the other areas has been created. There is ground for concern that adoption of the RAC proposal will be interpreted as a signal that all risk has been evaluated and brought to manageable levels. On the other hand, it is clear that the NIH, already stressed by an unusual and probably inappropriate regulatory burden, is not the ideal site for decision about the broader uncertainties. Moreover, the situation may indeed have reached the point where a continued regulatory operation for primarily NIH purposes has become superfluous and unnecessarily burdensome.

These considerations suggest an intermediate position between the two pending proposals. RAC has played a constructive role and is the single federal site where concerted public debate goes on about RDNA policy. Were RAC to couple adoption of the Gottesman proposal with a provisional endorsement of its own proposal as an objective to be achieved in a defined period, say three years, extrapolation of the constriction curve of NIH activity would be clearly delineated. Meanwhile, RAC might then also recommend that the intervening time be used to make best possible estimates of at least the first three areas of uncertainty enumerated above. In so doing NIH could enlist the support of other appropriate federal (the inter-agency committee) and non-federal agencies, with special attention to possible need for a continuing mechanism for further assessment and action.

Such recommendations would ensure that NIH does not abruptly and prematurely drop a responsibility it has honorably shouldered. Moreover, a mistaken conclusion that all uncertainty has been dissolved would be avoided and opportunity would be afforded to consider sound policy for many spin-off effects that are likely to generate controversy for some time to come.

Very best regards.

Sincerely yours,

Clifford Grobstein

CG:aw

THE UNIVERSITY OF GEORGIA
DEPARTMENT OF ENTOMOLOGY
ATHENS, GEORGIA 30602
U.S.A.

404.542.2816

January 28, 1982

Dr. William J. Gartland, Jr., Director
Office of Recombinant DNA Activities
National Institute of Health
Bethesda, MD 20205

Dear Dr. Gartland:

The University of Georgia Biosafety Committee would like to offer the following comments on the proposed changes in the NIH Guidelines for research involving recombinant DNA molecules. We believe the RAC proposal (Federal Register 12/4/81) goes too far in removing certain restrictions, and that the Gottesman proposal (Federal Register 12/7/81) is more restrictive than necessary. Of the two proposals, we support the RAC proposal, providing that the following additions are made:

1. retain the local Institutional Biosafety Committee;

2. require IBC approval prior to initiating any experiments involving the transfer of drug resistance or toxin genes to bacterial species in which they are not found in nature or the deliberate release to the environment of any organism containing recombinant DNA molecules;

3. require that the IBC notify the NIH of any IBC-approved project of the type described in #2 above.

Many institutions having a Biosafety Committee will retain it to evaluate experiments involving other types of hazards, i.e. human pathogens, oncogenic viruses, etc. Institutions, through their Biosafety Committee, will want to be informed about experiments being carried out within their jurisdiction that involve transfer of drug resistance or toxin genes, and especially the deliberate release of novel organisms, if for no other reason than to avoid the embarrasment of ignorance about such experiments should the public become alarmed by news of the initiation of one of these projects.

Our rationale for notifying the NIH is to insure that the RAC will always know what types of experiments related to transfer of drug resistance or toxin genes or the release of organisms are being carried out. It is conceivable that at some future time, the RAC may decide that a particular experiment poses a significant hazard and should be terminated.

Very truly yours,

Arden O. Lea, Chairman
University of Georgia
Biosafety Committee

AOL:ljs

HARVARD UNIVERSITY

DEPARTMENT OF CHEMISTRY

12 Oxford Street
Cambridge, Massachusetts 02138
U.S.A.

January 28, 1982

William Gartland, Ph.D.
Director
Office of Recombinant DNA Activities
National Institutes of Health
Building 31, 4A52
Bethesda, Maryland 20205

Dear Dr. Gartland:

The Institutional Biosafety Committee of Harvard University Faculty of Arts and Sciences met to discuss at some length the proposed revisions to the recombinant DNA guidelines. Although not quite unanimous, the majority of members voiced reservations concerning some of the changes being proposed. Of utmost concern was the speed with which the relaxation is being considered. We recognize the need for simplification and some relaxation of the guidelines and encourage their continued thoughtful evolution, as has occurred since 1978.

Aside from the above concerns, such significant changes will certainly present problems in communities which have implemented regulations governing recombinant DNA work. Most communities with such regulations have adopted existing NIH Guidelines as a framework for their own regulation. Consistency has been obtained, in large part, because local communities believe that the NIH has not taken lightly its responsibility with respect to the development and promulgation of their guidelines. In the absence of regulations which have been written with the advice of the scientific community and the public at large, we fear that the benefits of this new technology will not be forthcoming. We also feel that the concerns of the public regarding this research should not be underestimated at this time.

Finally it is this committees concern, that should these changes be adopted and local regulations not be altered, recombinant DNA research and development activities in Massachusetts would be conducted at a definite disadvantage compared to other regions. We urge a more careful relaxation of the guidelines than has been proposed.

Sincerely yours,

William N. Lipscomb, Ph.D.
Chairman - Committee on the Regulation of Hazardous Biological - Faculty of Arts and Sciences

Brigham and Women's Hospital
A Teaching Affiliate of Harvard Medical School
75 Francis Street, Boston, Massachusetts 02115
(617) 732-6803

January 28, 1982

William Gartland, Ph.D.
Director
Office of Recombinant DNA Activities
Building 31, 4A52
Bethesda, Maryland 20205

Dear Dr. Gartland:

The Institutional Biosafety Committee of Harvard Medical Area would like to register its concern about the proposed relaxation of the Guidelines for Recombinant DNA research. We are concerned primarily because in our work as a committee we have found it necessary to weight safety issues in individual protocols in this rapidly changing field, and we have the sense that some continuing uniform level of evaluation is still needed. We suggest that a deliberate and systematic phasing out of restrictions found to be unnecessary would make more sense than such an abrupt change as is being proposed by the Recombinant Advisory Committee.

In addition, a number of local communities throughout the country have enacted legislation to regulate this research. By in large the legislation defers to the NIH Guidelines for content. It has been possible for communities to accept these guidelines intact because of National Institutes of Health's reputation. It is our concern that the relaxation of the NIH Guidelines would lead some local communities to regulate this activity with different standards. The impact of such an occurrence could be devastating to the scientific community and the public in the long term.

We also see a potential problem with both proposals referencing the use of the CDC classification system as a guide for assessing the containment of recombinant DNA experiments. Acceptance of the revised CDC biosafety guidelines is certainly in question at this time. The ASM Public and Scientific Affairs Board has expressed the recommendation that laboratory safety should be left to the judgement and discretion of the investigator. It is our understanding that CDC will retract its most recent classification of etiologic agents. Does this not place the proposed NIH containment assessment scheme in trouble?

It is our committee's opinion that a relaxation such as the ones being proposed will create many problems. Such a change could have a significantly detrimental effect on recombinant DNA research and development activities in Massachusetts. We urge a more conservative approach at this time.

Sincerely yours,

Thomas O'Brien, M.D.
Chairman
Committee on the Regulation of
Hazardous Biological Agents -
Harvard Medical Area

Monsanto

Monsanto Company
800 N. Lindbergh Boulevard
St. Louis, Missouri 63166
Phone: (314) 694-1000

January 28, 1982

Director, Office of Recombinant
DNA Activities
Building 31, Room 4A52
National Institutes of Health
Bethesda, Md. 20205

Dear Sir:

Monsanto Company appreciates the opportunity of responding to the Request for Comments on "Recombinant DNA Research: Proposed Revised Guidelines" published by the National Institutes of Health (NIH) in the Federal Register, Friday, December 4, 1981, p. 59368 and Monday, December 7, 1981, p. 59734.

Monsanto Company is a major international supplier of chemicals, plastics, textile fibers and other products. As have many companies, Monsanto Company has an active biotechnology research program in which recombinant DNA techniques are used. We voluntarily comply with the NIH Guidelines on research involving recombinant DNA molecules and anticipate that we will continue. An Institutional Biosafety Committee (IBC) reviews projects for conformance with the Guidelines. In addition, a staff biosafety specialist provides consultation and oversight of all biotechnology programs.

Monsanto Company has a tradition of commitment to safety, health and environmental protection. Implementation of that commitment in our research laboratories has required the development of standard procedures, committees, professional staff, training programs, special facilities and an emergency response mechanism. Special policies and procedures have been adopted for the handling of biological systems.

Although the current and proposed approaches for the regulation of DNA experiments are acceptable to us, we believe a preferred approach would be to focus NIH expertise and experience on promoting the development of safety, health and environmental programs in all laboratories. Standard policies and procedures should be encouraged that clearly address the known hazards and utilize concensus standards relevant to the operations to be performed in each laboratory.

We urge the development by biologists and safety personnel of a concensus document of safe, healthful, environmentally acceptable and scientifically valid practices for research personnel handling all hazardous biological materials. One section of the document could deal with the potential hazards related to the use of recombinant DNA technology, including the use of toxin or drug-resistance genes and deliberate release to the environment of potentially hazardous altered organisms.

In summary, we encourage NIH to continue to urge all laboratories to maintain a program of safety, health, and environmental protection. We support the development of a concensus practice guide for the use by persons handling biological materials, including those using recombinant DNA techniques. Monsanto will continue to work towards safe laboratory practices in its own and other laboratories.

Sincerely,

Monte C. Throdahl

Monte C. Throdahl
Senior Vice President,
Environmental Policy Staff

MCT/lh

DEPARTMENT OF HEALTH & HUMAN SERVICES

Public Health Service

National Institutes of Health
Bethesda, Maryland 20205

January 28, 1982

Dr. William Gartland
Bldg. 31, Room 4A-52
NIH
Bethesda, MD 20205

Dear Bill:

I have studied the two published (Federal Register) proposals for revising the NIH Guidelines for Research Involving Recombinant DNA and have concluded that neither proposal adequately meets the current situation. This may be surprising since in April of 1981 I wrote to you in support of the Baltimore-Campbell proposal. However, the present version of that proposal differs in significant ways from the original version. In particular, the treatment of presently prohibited experiments is much more laissez-faire in the recent document and omits any reference to the deliberate release into the environment of any organism containing recombinant DNA, a point which, I believe, should be explicitly considered. Furthermore, reading the Gottesman proposal emphasized to me the value of offering investigators more detailed advice than provided by the very brief containment recommendations in Baltimore-Campbell. Nevertheless, I do still support the basic idea of the Baltimore-Cambell version, namely, that the Guidelines should at this time be advisory rather than regulatory.

As a result of this analysis I would like to propose a middle ground between the two published proposals. This takes the form of an advisory set of Guidelines based on the Gottesman proposal. In other words, the Gottesman proposal remains substantively intact, but is put in the form of recommendations or real Guidelines, rather than regulations. In my letter of last April I stated why regulations are no longer appropriate for recombinant DNA experiments. But I also indicated why a set of standard practices remains useful. My present suggestion is, I believe, consistent with my earlier arguments. Not only is a set of standard practices provided, but a framework is provided for continued monitoring of those experiments about which some question remains.

In order to give an explicit idea of my proposal I have gone through the Gottesman version as well as the present version of part IV of the existing Guidelines and written in suggested wording. Together, these essentially supply a complete revision. Copies of these "corrected" documents are appended. The suggested changes will need careful attention should my proposal be adopted. I am certain that I have not been thorough in making all the changes necessary to bring the documents into a form completely consistent with my proposal nor will my wording be accurate in all instances. Also, I have not considered what should be done with part VI although it probably should be eliminated for the reasons set forth in Baltimore-Campbell. Another issue that is not adequately addressed in my version is the expansion of the RACs advisory role into other areas of biological research.

The version I am submitting will, I believe, foster substantial "voluntary" attention to the central issue, namely, prudent approaches to new recombinant DNA experiments. It offers guidance to investigators in planning their experiments and urges on both investigators and institutions the need for consultation and review of novel studies. It emphasizes the fact that certain experiments remain questionable in many minds and should only proceed after extensive discussion with well-informed and responsible individuals under the aegis of the National Institutes of Health. I hope that the RAC will consider this proposal at its coming meeting.

Sincerely yours,

Maxine

Maxine Singer, Ph.D.
Chief, Laboratory of Biochemistry
National Cancer Institute

cc:
Bernard Talbot
Susan Gottesman
Ray Thornton
Paul Berg

HARVARD UNIVERSITY
THE BIOLOGICAL LABORATORIES

16 DIVINITY AVENUE
CAMBRIDGE, MASSACHUSETTS 02138

January 28, 1982

William J. Gartland, Jr., Director
Office of Recombinant DNA Activities
National Institutes of Health
Building 31 Room 4A52
Bethesda, MD 20205

Dear Dr. Gartland:

I want to register my opposition to the Baltimore/Campbell proposal described in the Federal Register of December 4, 1981, which would convert the NIH Guidelines to voluntary and would also weaken them in several respects.

I feel that this moment, when many new, small companies are still being formed and their standards of activity and mutual relationships are not at all clear, is not the correct time to weaken the Guidelines and lift their mandatory character.

Furthermore, I am very concerned over the serious conflict of interest that exists in having Dr. Baltimore being heavily involved in deregulation proceedings. Dr. Baltimore is treated as though he were speaking as a disinterested, academic scientist, when he, in fact, has a large financial interest in a commercial firm (Collaboratifve Genetics) that stands to profit from the deregulation he proposes.

To keep a modicum of confidence in the ethical conduct of the scientific community, it seems imperative that commercial connections be publically acknowledged and that all conflicts of interest of this sort be avoided.

For these and other reasons, I think that the Gottesman proposal is far preferable at this time.

Sincerely yours,

Ruth Hubbard

Ruth Hubbard
Professor of Biology

Residential College
East Quadrangle

The University of Michigan
Ann Arbor, Michigan 48109
(313) 763-0176

January 28, 1982

Hon. Ray Thornton
Chair, Recombinant DNA Advisory Committee
ORDA, Building 31, Room 4A52
National Institutes of Health
Bethesda, MD 20205

Dear Ray:

I strongly oppose the current proposals to weaken the NIH guidelines. Over the last three years, these controls have been drastically downgraded, particularly with respect to organisms designed to make products, organisms containing genes which code for toxins, and large-scale, industrial processes. In my view, the present need is to strengthen the guidelines, not weaken them further.

The conversion of the guidelines into a set of recommended practices without sanctions will be taken as a signal by the general public that the hazard issue has finally been laid to rest and by users, that safety prcautions need no longer be taken seriously. To encourage such misunderstandings to develop is irresponsible. The data on hazards of recombinant DNA technology is extremely poor; consequently, it is impossible to make any precise evaluation of the impacts on humans and on the environment from exposure to the broad range of organisms being developed in universities and private industry.

If the RAC further abandons its responsibilities to develop a policy that addresses the uncertainties surrounding hazard issues, it will become necessary for individual states to set their own standards, not only for private industry (which is not adequately covered by the NIH guidelines) but also for federally funded laboratories. I would much prefer to see the RAC carry out a full review of its policy of the last three years of progressively dismantling controls, and to decide to strengthen the guidelines, particularly in the areas I mention above, rather than to make state action necessary.

Sincerely,

Susan

Susan Wright
Head, Science Program, and
Member, Task Force on
Biotechnology, State of Michig

cc. Hon. Douglas Walgren
Hon. Albert Gore
Hon. Edward Kennedy

MASSACHUSETTS INSTITUTE OF TECHNOLOGY
77 MASSACHUSETTS AVENUE
CAMBRIDGE, MASSACHUSETTS 02139

DEPARTMENT OF BIOLOGY
16-531

January 29, 1982

PHONE: (617) 253-1000
253-4700

William Gartland, Director
Office of Recombinant DNA Activities
Building 31, Room 4A52
National Institutes of Health
Bethesda, Maryland 20205

Dear Bill:

I am writing to register my strong objection to the dismantling of the NIH Recombinant DNA Guidelines, as expressed in the Baltimore/Campbell Proposal, set forth in the Federal Register of 4 December 1981.

This proposal eliminates the mandatory nature of the guidelines for federally sponsored researchers, eliminates oversight by the National and Institutional DNA Committees, and removes all sanctions for violation of the Guidelines.

The Working Group Modification of the Baltimore/Campbell proposal, though maintaining some mandatory features, represents a major dilution and weakening of the guidelines, and should also be rejected by RAC.

In this period of rapid development and expansion of university and commercial applications of recombinant DNA technology, the nation needs the extension and broadening of the scope of the Guidelines, from just the federally sponsored research sector, to all genetic engineering applications. Despite the efforts invested by many RAC Members the proposed dismantling of the guidelines is scientifically and socially unsound, and would represent a failure of the RAC to carry out its public charge and trust.

The essentials of the Baltimore/Campbell proposals give the following signals to entrepreneurs in emerging industries: Outside of a very few proscribed experiments, any of a vast variety of modifications of organisms can be carried out without forethought, without special precautions, and without informing any agency of government of their nature;that there will be no sanctions if in fact irresponsible and dangerous procedures are enagaged in; and that no long term epidemiological, monitoring, risk assessment program need be put in place in parallel with the developing new technology. That is, anything goes.

The proposals now before the RAC

1) Rest on a fundamental logical fallacy in their development of regulatory approach.

2) Lack a meaningful scientific basis.

3) Violate major tenets of responsible occupational and environmental health practice.

4) Were developed without sufficient input from professionals in the area of public, occupational, and environmental health.

5) Represent a violation of basic notions of conflict of interest, in that members of the committee, via equity positions in emerging biotechnology corporations, stand to gain directly from this major alteration in regulatory process.

Below I expand briefly on each of these points:

Logical Fallacy

- The Baltimore/Campbell position, that "the time for Guidelines with attached ovesight procedures and penalties has passed" is based on an assessment of the potential risk associated with development in recombinant DNA technology. All of the risk assessment programs, for example those considered at the Falmouth and Pasadena Conferences, were based on the assumption of strict adherence to the existing guidelines. In particular, consideration of the risks associated with the introduction of foreign genes into micro-organiasms other than E. coli K12, or into wild type or disease causing strains of bacteria, were generally excluded.

- The conclusions with respect to limited risk referred only to operations carried out within the scope of the strict guidelines then in place and depended on adherence to the guidelines. However, these outcomes were then presented as evidence for minimal intrinsic risk, and as arguments that guidelines were not necessary. Each stage of the successive weakenings of the NIH guidelines have rested on the repetition of this fallacy.

- In summary the logic has been;

a) If the Guidelines are strictly followed, hazards are minimized.

b)Since the hazards are minimal,

c)There is no need for guidlines.

The above syllogism is false.

Risk Assessment

- The Federal Register of 4 December 1981 presents an "Evaluation of the Risks Associated ith Recombinant DNA Research" which attempts to provide scientific basis for the Baltimore/Campbell proposals. This document is somewhat unusual when compared with analogous Federal Register documentation providing background for the lead, cotton dust, carcinogen and other standards; rather than presenting clearly the biological and public health bases for concern, it reads more like an adversarial brief attempting to argue that the risks are minimal, rather than providing the scientific basis for identifying them when they do arise.

- For example, little emphasis or documentmentation is provided with respect to the profound and widespread role of plasmids in bacterial pathogenesis; the major problems in the control of hospital acquired infections; the fact that the plasmid transfer referred to in the text is in fact a major public health problem, due to transfers of plasmids coding for both antibiotic resistance and toxins. These fundamental factual bases for concern, though touched on, are not given appropriate prominence.

- The Document lays out three criteria requireds for generation of hazard by genetically modified micro-organisms: 1) uniqueness 2) establishment in some niche; 3) deleterious effects on humans or other hosts. It then points out that if any one were proved totally false, the basis for concern would be minimized. However, careful reading of the document makes clear that none of them have been proven false. In fact a much stronger case exists for likelihood of these three concerns than is made in the document. In fact with respect to the first, the technical arguments for the uniqueness and novelty of genetically modified organisms has been given enshrined in law through the Supreme Courts decision that genetically modified organisms can be patented,

- With respect to the second, the spread of organisms into new niches happens continually as a result of two interacting aspects of nature, the development of new niches (not mentioned in the report), and the radiation of existing organisms and newly evolved (or constructed) variants into these niches, or into existing but unoccupied niches.(For example, gypsy moths, chestnut blight,and antibiotic resistant bacteria in hospitals). The arguments based on Ecoli K12 are bascially irrelevant; the impact of these regulatory changes will be to accelerate the applications of genetic engineering technology and genetic exchange, between a great variety of organisms.Some of these, if allowed toenter the environment will either establish themselves, or transfer their genes to indigenous strains.

- With respect to the third, the literature of the last few years on microbial pathogenesis has clearly established that the introduction of a variety of genes - for colonization factors, toxins, antibiotic resistance, binding proteins, surface antigens, can increase the pathogenecity of the microbial strain for its host, or allow it to extend its host range.

Public Health Considerations

- Experiences with the organic chemical industry, with mining and extraction industtries, and with manufacturing and metalworking industries reveals clearly the long delays between the initiation of new industrial activities, and the discovery of the actual side effects on the human population. These lags derived in some cases from physiological delays between exposure to a disease-causing agent and disease, as with carcingoens, or from difficulties in identifying the etioogical agents of the disease, for example in Minamata disease.

- In no case has it been possible to fully predict the effects of the products of the new technolgoies on humans or the ecosystem.

- Recombinant DNA technology is less than ten years old. Its industrial applications have not even begun. Thus the course proposed by the Baltimore/Campbell proposals are singularly unwise and contrary to previous experience.The variety of living orgnaisms that can be generated through genetic modification of existing organisms is vastly greater than the variety of organic chemicals. Our experience of a vary narrow sector of microorganisms is clear; a subset of bacteria, viruses and fungi cause serious disease in humans. This is a major reason for our knwledge of them. To put foward the position that we can confidently predict the effects of all the great variety of modified microorganisms, many of which are not even conceptualized ,when we cannot even predict the pathogenicity of the existing organisms in the ecosystem without actual experimentation (for example, Legionella) is to deny the major body of public health experience.

Absence of Appropriate Expertise and Representation

- Though improvements have been made in recent appointments to the RAC, the data base for their deliberations,namely previous reports and discussions,were developed with minimal input from those with experience in occupational or environmental health, or industrial regulation. For example, representation from organized labor,particularly those sectors liable to be employed in the industries was minimal. Representation from organizations such as the American Public Health Association, Society for Occupational and Environmental Health, Sierra Club, Friends of the Earth, and other constituencies who have developed substantial technical expertise was also minimal.

- This is obvious in the absence throughout the RAC deliberations of reference to previous regulatory experience with pesticides,organics, heavy metals, carcinogens, or other health hazards associated with new technologies.The concrete experiences of attempts to predict risks before hand in other industries would suggest vastly greater caution than is called for in the Baltimore/Campbell proposals.

Conflict of Interest

- The Baltimore/Campbell proposal, if passed, will almost certainly be presented as a voluntary code for all rDNA activities, private and public, laboratory or industrial. Thus its actual character will be to weaken or eliminate the prospects for regulating emerging commercial activity.These porposals have certainly been looked on favorably by commercial interests and that sector of the scientific community that stands to profit from rapid commercial exploitation.

- If recent corporate prospectuses are correct, some members of RAC involved in the efforts to dismantle the guidelines have equity positions in corporations who stand to benefit from a relaxed regulatory climate. The Federal Register documents make no mention of this conflict.It was my understanding that members of government committees are not permitted to have investments in corporations they are charged with regulating.

In summary I recommend that both the original and the modified Baltimore/Campbell proposals be rejected. The existing Guidelines are administratively awkward and do need improvement. However, the character of the changes are the addition of health surveillance, systematic monitoring of unintentional releases o organisms, continuing risk assessment studies, and continued emphasis on trainng, enforcement of good procedures, and long term record keeping and oversight. With such procedures in place, the inconvenient emphasis on individual cases can be lessened.

The new genetic technologies have extraodinary social and econcomic potential. To realize the benefits we must learn from past mistakes, past technological arrogance and denial of problems, and be willing to invest in the safe procedure,assessment, and long term studies needed to minimize the negative side effects.

In not advancing these goals the current RAC proposals fail to protect the long term interests of the general public, the genetic engineering industry itself, and the scientific community.

Sincerely yours,

Jonathan King

Jonathan King
Professor of Biology

DEPARTMENT OF HEALTH & HUMAN SERVICES

Public Health Service

National Institutes of Health
Bethesda, Maryland 20205
Bldg. 7, Rm. 304

January 29, 1982

Dr. William J. Gartland, Jr.
Director, Office of Recombinant
DNA Activities
Building 31, Room 4A52
National Institutes of Health
Bethesda, Maryland 20205

Dear Bill:

This is to give my comments on the proposed changes in the NIH Guidelines presented in the Federal Register of December 4 and December 7, 1981.

First, I enthusiastically endorse the concept of reducing both the containment requirements and the administrative review. However, as to the means of achieving the reductions, I don't find either proposal to be fully satisfactory.

With regard to the Baltimore-Campbell proposal, I agree with making the great bulk of the guidelines a voluntary code of practice, but I would like to see retention of NIH's control over four categories of research that carry a clear potential of risk. These are 1) the drug resistance traits, 2) the highly potent polypeptide toxins, 3) deliberate release into the environment, and 4) virus-virus recombinants that could generate a nondefective virus with an expanded host range or tissue specificity. Numbers 1, 2, and 3 are the old prohibitions; they should not be prohibited (as would follow from the admonition in section III of the Baltimore-Campbell proposal) but should be done only after careful scrutiny.

With regard to nondefective virus-virus recombinants, I think there will be intensive investigation of the molecular basis of the exquisite species and tissue specificities of viral infections, using in vitro generated recombinants. This will be an exciting and important field, with implications not only for virus infections but also for cell regulation and control mechanisms. These experiments will by design generate novel viruses with expanded host ranges and increased ability to replicate in various cells or organs. I would like to be assured that such experiments are done with care, awareness, and external expert review.

I agree with the Gottesmann proposal to the extent that it maintains a residuum of NIH control and oversight, but I feel that the classification of experiments is still overly complex and that the use of the old CDC classification for deciding on containment conditions does not have a solid scientific basis.

In summary, I would like to see the regulatory aspects of the guidelines kept in place for a bare handful of experimental systems. This would serve two purposes: keeping the broadly acknowledged potential dangers under external scrutiny, and retaining the basic ORDA-RAC structure in place so that it can easily respond to future developments.

Sincerely yours,

Wallace P. Rowe, M.D.
Chief, Laboratory of Viral Diseases
National Institute of Allergy and Infectious Diseases

Lilly Research Laboratories
A Division of Eli Lilly and Company
307 East McCarty Street
Indianapolis, Indiana 46285

Irving S. Johnson, Ph.D.
Vice President

January 29, 1982

Dr. William J. Gartland, Jr., Director
Office of Recombinant DNA Activities
Building 39, Room 4A52
National Institutes of Health
Bethesda, Maryland 20205

Re: Recombinant DNA Research
Proposed Revised Guidelines for Research Involving
Recombinant DNA Molecules, 46 Fed. Reg. 59368
(December 4, 1981)

Dear Bill:

Eli Lilly and Company (Lilly) has been involved in recombinant DNA research and product development for several years. In addition to observing the 1974-76 moratorium on certain types of recombinant DNA research, Lilly scientists have voluntarily complied with the guidelines since their inception. Company representatives have regularly attended meetings of the NIH Recombinant DNA Advisory Committee, suggested certain modifications in the guidelines, and studied and commented on proposals advanced by others.

The proposed modifications in the guidelines might appear to impact primarily on NIH grantees and thus be considered to affect somewhat less directly, the non-NIH funded research laboratories that comply on a voluntary basis. We feel, however, that continuing unnecessary limitations on any significant part of the country's research endeavors adversely affects the entire research community. Furthermore, the obvious encouragement given to foreign practitioners of recombinant DNA technology by their respective governments places a responsibility on our Federal agencies to permit all U.S. laboratories, whether academic, government, or industrial to remain competitive in such efforts.

Anticipated public health and environmental risks in relation to recombinant DNA activities have not developed; increased inputs from experts in the fields of infectious disease etiology and pathology as well as risk assessment test results have indicated no more demonstrable hazard than that expected for the organisms from which the recombinant DNA is derived. Consequently, Lilly recommends that the current Baltimore/Campbell proposal and Dr. Gottesman's recommendations be given careful consideration.

As the company's experience with recombinant technology has progressed and both risk assessment and environmental monitoring data have accumulated (some from our own studies on host-vector systems for large scale use), we have come to view the constraints of the current NIH guidelines with some apprehension. It is now apparent that the broad background of four decades of experience in antibiotic fermentation is, indeed, applicable to large scale production of recombinant organisms and that the evidence of responsible conduct of that component of industry strongly supports the idea of converting the guidelines to a code of standard practice. Thus, philosophically, the status of this new technology would be returned to that which has been recognized as appropriate throughout more than a century of research on pathogenic bacteria and viruses. We view recombinant DNA experiments in this same light and conclude that formal controls over this activity do not serve a useful purpose. Although research may involve consideration of nearly all possible contingencies, it precludes certainty as to their occurrence; therefore, research in any scientific field always proceeds with some unknown elements of risk. However, by the time production status is achieved for a recombinant DNA or other product, those elements are no longer unknown, and the design and utilization of production facilities proceeds on the basis of better identified and tolerable risks, if any.

Company personnel have not explored the total cost of compliance with the guidelines for the past five years in detail, but it is readily apparent that compliance has involved hundreds of thousands of dollars spent on containment facilities for experiments which can now be conducted in an ordinary microbiological laboratory — plus several man-years of scientists' and other support personnel time spent in preparing, distributing, receiving, reading, and filing documents, conducting and participating in company and national meetings, all with concurrent travel and communications efforts. The Baltimore/Campbell proposal appears to embody a logical transition to decreased controls in this area.

We believe that responsible scientists in academic institutions and other organizations receiving NIH grants, can and will follow the guidelines on a voluntary basis. Should NIH receive information that a specific grantee is not conducting recombinant DNA research in a responsible manner, NIH can still exercise discretion or impose other sanctions with respect to grants to that organization. The proposed simplification of the guidelines with respect to containment levels is desirable as is the elimination of prohibitions in Section (I-D) of the guidelines.

Lilly also notes and appreciates the very thoughtful report submitted by Dr. Gottesman. Her recommendations contain several responsible suggestions for decreasing restrictions in the guidelines, which are not required for public health or laboratory safety. Although these merit careful consideration, we believe they could be improved - particularly with regard to minimizing the extensive bookkeeping and approval mechanisms that would still remain in place.

The Federal Register notice contains comments relative to industrial applications of recombinant DNA technology. In this regard, it should be noted that the report of the Commission of the European Communities entitled "Hazards Involved in the Industrial Use of Micro-organisms" states:

> (p. 27)
>
> "In practice, an industrial fermentation process is extremely unlikely to become contaminated with a highly pathogenic microorganism, because the environment inside an industrial fermenter is so different from that of the human body that pathogenicity confers no advantage upon the organism."
>
> (p. 36-38)
>
> "In discussion with firms involved in or intending exploitation of large scale biotechnology, we have been impressed by the well documented care that they have taken to ensure the wholesomeness of their products."....."The imposition of standards that are not measurable by available techniques, too-frequent changing of standards without adequate warning to the industry concerned, and the blind application to biotechnological products of standards more stringent than those applied to the traditional materials that they seek to replace, can impose an unwarranted burden on an industry already beset by restrictions and ill-founded suspicion."

It is Lilly's belief that industrial organizations involved in recombinant DNA technology have acted in a responsible manner. Such organizations have been and remain subject to a number of federal and state sanctions with respect to worker safety and environmental controls. In addition, at least insofar as the pharmaceutical industry is concerned, the initial products to be derived from recombinant DNA technology will be subject to the investigational new drug and new drug application review and approval procedures under Section 505 of the Federal Food, Drug, and Cosmetic Act. Consequently, any pharmaceutical products which become commercially available for health care will be reviewed for both safety and efficacy.

Because of a continuing, recognizable level of public interest in recombinant DNA technology, we also acknowledge the desirability of maintaining the RAC. New developments in the field gradually move us closer to the need for answers to ethical and philosophical questions about applications of the technology. Other new findings may point to problems not yet conceived. A periodic review of the field by the RAC would certainly be in order.

Further, with respect to long term safety considerations, it should be noted that representatives of federal agencies involved in environmental and public health matters participate in the activities of the RAC. Since both of the proposals under consideration would retain the RAC, the ad hoc representatives of various cabinet level and regulatory agencies would continue to serve. These individuals provide oversight, should safety concerns emerge.

It also appears desirable for local institutions to assume primary responsibility for safety considerations. In this regard, Lilly urges the RAC, should it adopt the Baltimore/Campbell proposal, to recommend:

1. the continuation of local Institutional Biosafety Committee activities in some form;

2. appropriate training in laboratory procedures and safety for research laboratory, development, and production personnel involved in recombinant DNA technology. Adequate scientific standards - such as the guidelines - whether mandatory or voluntary, become meaningful and effective only if local personnel are adequately trained and appropriate institutional procedures are followed; and

3. the issuing of a public statement pointing out the absence of any perceived need, on a scientific basis, for regulatory activity at the state or local level.

Finally, we acknowledge gratefully the astute study of the state of recombinant DNA technology and the critical evaluation of facts in the field which led Drs. Baltimore and Campbell to make this proposal.

We offer the above comments in a spirit of thoughtful concern with the hope that they may be of assistance to the committee in reaching a logical decision.

Very truly yours,

Irving S. Johnson

1199 National Union of Hospital and Health Care Employees a division of RWDSU/AFL-CIO
310 West 43rd Street, New York, N.Y. 10036 (212) 582-1890

January 29, 1982

Director
Office of Recombinant DNA Activities
National Institute of Health
Building 31, Room 4A52
Bethseda, Maryland 20205

Dear Sir/Madam:

Enclosed are comments on the proposed revisions of NIH Guidelines for Research Involving Recombinant DNA Molecules prepared by District 1199, National Union of Hospital and Health Care Employees. We regret that the early deadline for the receipt of comments did not enable us to comment specifically on the technical aspects of the proposals.

We hope you find these comments helpful in reevaluating the guidelines.

Very truly yours,

Laura Job
OSHA Coordinator

LJ/jw
coe: 1199
encl.

PROPOSED REVISIONS OF NIH GUIDELINES FOR

RESEARCH INVOLVING RECOMBINANT DNA MOLECULES

COMMENTS

Submitted by: Judith Berek
Vice President and Director of
Legislative and Professional Programs

Laura Job
Coordinator
Occupational Safety and Health Project

District 1199
National Union of Hospital and
Health Care Employees
RWDSU/AFL-CIO

January 29, 1982

District 1199, National Union of Hospital and Health Care Employees, represents over 120,000 health care employees nationally in service, maintenance, clerical, technical and professional classifications in health care institutions. Included in our membership are technicians, technologists, scientists, clerical workers, aides and housekeepers employed in laboratories engaged in recombinant DNA research. We wish to comment on the two proposed revisions of NIH Guidelines for Research Involving Recombinant DNA Molecules from both an occupational health and public health viewpoint.

1199 strongly opposed both the RAC and Gottesman Proposals. As health care workers we are well aware of the toll that new medical technology has taken on health care consumers and employees. The best example of this is the indiscriminate use of diagnostic and theraputic radiation. The use of fluoroscopy to monitor tuberculosis in the 1930's and 40's and the resulting increase in breast cancer taught us about the sensitivity of breast tissue to radiation. The widespread use of pelvimetry made clear the vulnerability of the fetus, as studies linked x-ray exposure in utero to increases in leukemia and genetic defects in those children. An increase in thyroid cancer has been related to the use of radiation therapy for enlarged thymus, tonsils, and adenoids in infants and children.

Pioneers in the field of radiology and their successors also suffered a much higher death rate from cancers and other diseases now known to be sensitive to radiation. Radiation technology is not unique. Whether it is the use of benzene in laboratories or DES during pregnancy the trend has been to develop and apply new technology without regulation, study the effects years later (after the effects have become tragically apparent), and then begin to regulate the technology.

District 1199 believes that the NIH Guidelines as they now exist are proof that we have learned the lesson that our experience with radiation, toxic substances and pharmecuticals teaches: that new and rapidly growing technology must be strictly regulated until it is proven safe. Any change in the present NIH guidelines that goes beyond administrative streamlining is premature. The absence of an epidemic due to recombinant DNA research does not indicate that the guidelines are unnecessarily severe. Actually this is

- more -

a very good argument for the guidelines' effectiveness. More important however, is our total ignorance of the long term effects of this research on both the public and on the research workers.

1199 members care daily for patients who have infections. Some of these infections are drug resistant, some spread throughout the hospital and infect other patients and employees; some infections such as influenza cannot be cured by medical science.... sometimes patients die of these infections. We should not risk adding newly synthesized and badly designed organisms to the human burden, as we do not yet have complete knowledge of, or control over those organisms which now assault us.

Research workers, having more proximity, would be at even greater risk of infection than the general public. Nothing is known about the long range effects of worker exposure to recombinant DNA molecules, and therefore long term epidemiological studies of these workers should be instituted.

For these reasons District 1199 strongly opposes any change in the NIH guidelines, and moreover, would like to see the present guidelines mandatory for industry as well as NIH fund recipients.

District 1199 regrets the absence of any labor representation on the Recombinant DNA Advisory Committee, and questions whether the scientific members on the committee's commercial interests in recombinant DNA technology have blinded them to the public welfare.

THE ROCKEFELLER UNIVERSITY
1230 YORK AVENUE · NEW YORK, NEW YORK 10021

January 29, 1982

Dr. William Gartland, Jr., Director
Office of Recombinant DNA Activities
National Institutes of Health
Bethesda, MD 20205

Dear Dr. Gartland:

I am writing in support of the proposal appearing in the December 4, 1981 Federal Register to 1) cease mandatory implementation of the Guidelines for experiments involving recombinant DNA, 2) simplify the Guidelines to the extent that most experiments now requiring P2 or P3 containment be recommended at P1, 3) eliminate the prohibitions section (I-D) of the current Guidelines.

Yours sincerely,

Michael W. Young

State University of New York at Buffalo

BIOSAFETY COMMITTEE

January 29, 1982

William J. Gartland, Jr., Ph.D., Director
Office of Recombinant DNA Activities
National Institutes of Health
Building 31, Room 4A52
Bethesda, Maryland 20205

Dear Dr. Gartland:

I am writing in response to the two main proposals presently being considered as a revision of the "NIH Guidelines for Research Involving Recombinant DNA Molecules". I have spoken with a few members of our Biosafety Committee and with physicians in the area who are experts in infectious diseases.

My feeling is that the RAC proposal may involve a greater change than is wise at the present time. The establishment of the local IBC and guidelines for conducting research with recombinant DNA have been useful. If a local institution is not required to have an IBC or a Biological Safety Officer there may be no one to review or supervise activities or to periodically remind individual investigators what a code of good practice should be. When guidelines are established, but not made mandatory, then less attention is given to them, more carelessness follows, and less concern will be devoted to avoiding and reporting accidents. I believe that guidelines for all microorganisms (as proposed by CDC) could be made mandatory by a local IBC as a useful safety regulation. This requirement would be more effective than a voluntary code of good practice.

My greatest concern about the RAC proposal involves the plan to eliminate prohibitions. The message that will come across at the local level is that the guidelines and all prohibitions have been abolished; the admonishments not to do experiments involving drug resistant traits and toxin genes will be lost and forgotten. At the very least these latter types of experiments should be highlighted, reviewed, approved and supervised by a local IBC, preferably with RAC review and NIH approval as stated in the Gottesman proposal.

In conclusion, I would favor the Gottesman proposal, particularly because of the statement on prohibitions (Section I-D) and secondly, to recognize the present need to continue mandatory guidelines and the local IBC.

Best wishes in your attempt to resolve these issues.

Sincerely yours,

Joseph H. Kite, Jr.

Joseph H. Kite, Jr., Ph.D.
Professor of Microbiology
Chairman of the University
Biosafety Committee

JHK:jlw

307 MICHAEL HALL BUFFALO, NEW YORK 14214 TEL. (716)831-3301

The University of Texas System Cancer Center
M. D. Anderson Hospital and Tumor Institute
Texas Medical Center • 6723 Bertner Avenue • Houston, Texas 77030

Office of the President

January 29, 1982

Director, Office of Recombinant
DNA Activities
Building 31, Room 4A52
National Institutes of Health
Bethesda, Maryland 20205

Dear Sirs:

The Subcommittee on Recombinant DNA of The University of Texas System Cancer Center has reviewed the two proposed Revised Guidelines for Recombinant DNA Research in the Federal Registers of December 4 and December 7, 1981. While the subcommittee sees no prospects of accidents associated with recombinant DNA research, we consider it prudent and timely to support the proposed guidelines of December 7, 1981 submitted by Dr. Susan Gottesman. These guidelines retain the Institutional Biosafety Committee to oversee certain experiments and NIH compliance required for others. We support a requirement for notification to the IBC of certain other recombinant DNA experiments as outlined in the Gottesman proposal.

Sincerely,

Harry D. Holmes, Ph.D.
Assistant to the President

HDH:bb

United States Department of Agriculture | Agricultural Research Service | Northeastern Region Plum Island Animal Disease Center | P.O. Box 848 Greenport, New York 11944

January 29, 1982

SUBJECT: Comments on Two Proposals Concerning Major Revision of NIH Guidelines for Research Involving Recombinant DNA Molecules

TO: Dr. William Gartland, Director
Office of Recombinant DNA Activities
NIH
Bldg. 31, Room 4A52
Bethesda, MD 20205

The two proposals were reviewed in detail by PIADC staff.

Our comments are summarized below:

1. We advise against adaption of the RAC proposal (Federal Register 12/4/81) and recommend adaption of the Gottesman proposal (Federal Register 12/7/81) with some modifications. Under 1-D prohibitions, we suggest that in addition to those items enclosed by brackets, ie, (drug resistance) that the following be added "and work with Class 4 and 5 agents".

2. General comment on III, Containment Levels. We are in agreement with the current containment levels as set forth by the proposed guidelines from CDC (Proposed Biosafety Guidelines for Microbiological and Biomedical Laboratories) and by the Arbovirus Committee (Am. J. Trop. Med. Hyg. 29: 1359-1381, 1980). Therefore, we suggest that the containment level for recombinant DNA research be that of the microorganism that is being worked with as defined in the above two references. Further, we recommend that the containment level for large scale production be one level above that for research and pilot "scale up" experiments.

3. Concerning Section IV, Roles and Responsibilities, we would suggest that the Gottesman proposal be modified as follows: Level 1 and 2 research work only be recorded with the local IBC; Level 3 work require prior approval of the local IBC and recorded with the NIH, ORDA. Finally, we recommend that work with Level 4 and 5 organisms and other work as noted in 1-D require prior approval of the local IBC and final approval of either the full RAC Committee or a subcommittee of the RAC set up for such purposes. Another safe guard would be a requirement of inspection of Level 4 facilities by an expert safety committee before approval of such work.

J. J. Callis
Director

cc:
J. H. Graves
H. L. Bachrach
D. M. Moore
J. S. Walker
G. Still

The Ohio State University

Graduate School
University Hall
230 North Oval Mall
Columbus, Ohio 43210
Phone 614 422-6031

January 29, 1982

Director
Office of Recombinant DNA Activities
Building 31, Room 4A52
National Institutes of Health
Bethesda, Maryland 20205

Dear Sir:

The Institutional Biosafety Committee of The Ohio State University has studied the "RAC Proposal" and the "Gottesman Proposal" for modification of the NIH Guidelines for Research Involving Recombinant DNA Molecules. By a vote of 9:1 of the members in attendance, the IBC voted approval of the RAC Proposal. Upon the recommendation of the IBC, The Ohio State University endorses the RAC Proposal and urges its final approval by the RAC and by the Director of the NIH.

If this modification of the NIH Guidelines goes into effect, The Ohio State University will disband its Institutional Biosafety Committee and handle safety considerations for recombinant DNA research by the same procedures used in other area of research.

Sincerely yours,

Timothy R. Donoghue
Associate Dean for Research

TRD/jl

THE UNIVERSITY OF MICHIGAN
LAW SCHOOL
HUTCHINS HALL
ANN ARBOR, MICHIGAN 48109

January 29, 1982

Dr. William J. Gartland, Jr.
Director, Office of Recombinant DNA Activities
National Institute of Health
Building 31, Room 4A52
Bethesda, Maryland 20205

Dear Dr. Gartland:

I would like to comment on the proposal of the Recombinant DNA Advisory Committee (RAC) to convert the current rDNA Guidelines to a voluntary code of standard practice and to eliminate prior approval by Institutional Biosafety Committees before experiments can be begun (or approval by NIH in other classes of experiments). I have followed the rDNA controversy closely since its early days. The original Guidelines appeared to be an acceptable balance between total prohibition of such research and the desire of at least some in the scientific community to proceed at full speed. The Guidelines represented a governmentally imposed norm, with regulatory teeth consisting of the sanction of refusal or withdrawal of funding, that was taken seriously by those engaged in research. I strenuously object to the attempt by the RAC to downgrade the Guidelines to the status of a moral code. Let me state my objection in the form of four propositions.

I. <u>The risks inherent in rDNA research are neither completely understood nor can they be dismissed as trivial</u>.

The Report of the Working Group on Revision of the Guidelines, while making a case for a scaling down of estimates of hazard with regard to certain assumptions regarding the "unique danger" of rDNA research, concludes that "a particular subject of experiments may still pose some possibility of risk . . . the possibility for improving the virulence, host range, or survivability of some pathogens does seem to exist." The Group asks how serious this risk is, suggesting that more risk assessment work is needed to confirm that these risks are real or not. Evidence that health and environment hazards of rDNA research are unfounded is still limited; the thrust toward dismantling the regulations seems to relate more to pressure to get on with the research in an exciting new scientific area, rather than to a rational assessment that new experiments on safety issues have resolved them favorably. The burden of proof as to safety should still be on the individual researcher, in

Dr. William J. Gartland, Jr.
January 29, 1982
Page two

the sense that experiments which he proposes are subject to external scrutiny both by IBCs and by NIH. These review procedures may not be completely satisfactory, but are certainly better than pure professional self-regulation.

II. The special nature of the risks of rDNA require a heavier regulatory burden than might be necessary in other areas.

The rDNA controversy poses problems of feared catas... he, with uncertainty as the dominant feature. The problem of uncertainty is intensified given the possibility tha... search into fundamental biological or physical sturctures may alter those structures in a way that does not normally occur in the natural environment. How then is this problem different from industrial production of toxic chemicals and airborne or waterborne effluent which may have long term health effects? The uncertainty involved may be equally pronounced as to carcinogenic or mutagenic effects or ecological damage. Radioactive materials pose unique half-life problems, requiring thousands of years in the cases of some materials to decay to a non-threatening level. Certain toxic chemicals likewise may not degrade, or may break down in pernicious and unpredictable ways. Both radioactive materials and toxic chemicals may enter the food chain or other ecological niches in ways which pose similar long term threats. With either type of hazard, however, the risk is enhanced because of the sheer volume of the hazardous substances produced as a byproduct of large scale commercial use and production. Production and use can therefore be reduced, stopped, or altered; regulatory measures to govern shipment and storage can be implemented; the source of the hazard, being traceable, can be pinpointed.

Research, such as biological research represented by the rDNA controversy, offers hazards of a different order of magnitude. The putative risks involve pathogens, altered organisms, changed immunological defenses. The source of these hazards can reproduce and mutate if an adaptive niche is available. The level of production required for self-sustaining growth requires only a single laboratory experiment, unlike toxic chemical byproducts, which are linked to commercial levels of production. Attention to research hazards is therefore best directed at the earliest stages of investigation.

This comparison suggests that hazards of rDNA research pose problems earlier, not being dependent upon volume production to generate a high level of risky byproducts. Second, regulatory approaches are needed at such an early stage. By the time a technology is in place, and a level of commercial production achieved, we have generally responded with a regulatory apparatus. The Environmental Protection Agency regulates toxic substances as well as industrial pollution; the Nuclear Regulatory Commission governs the hazards of nuclear power generation; OSHA regulates the workplace. Such regulation may be inadequate, but at least a mechanism to assess risks is in place. The same cannot be said for the regulation of scientific research at its inception. Recombinant DNA research and the biotechnology that has emerged from it command our attention because of scientific perceptions of the promise of the technique in uncovering areas of ignorance about human genetic structure, and the promise of profitable commercial applications. It is a paradigm case, like the development of nuclear research in the fifties, for hazards as part of the research itself, raising questions about the technique, its directions, and the effectiveness of scientific self-regulation when confronted with risky research.

Professional self-regulation, through a "voluntary code of standard practice," will be ineffective in controlling hazardous experiments.

A brief account of the status of the scientific enterprise as a profession will illustrate the limits of such self-regulation.

Science is a profession, sharing common features with law and medicine, such as a high educational requirement for entry; a monopolistic position with regard to the performance of certain functions; control of admission standards; and authority of professional bodies over member conduct and resulting hostility to lay involvement.

First, the profession specializes in the development and application of powerful knowledge, that is, knowledge considered vital to society's needs. The methods of science are formulated and accepted by the scientific community; the results of research are measured by criteria that the particular scientific specialty has developed. Science is thus a self-defined enterprise, rarely subject to external scrutiny. Extended specialized training in the corpus of knowledge of the profession is typical, and this socializing experience is longer and more encompassing than that of learners in other occupations.

Second, a system of monetary and psychic rewards exists, symbolic of achievement and therefore ends in themselves. Income and prestige increase as professionalism increases. Members strongly indentify with their profession, usually on a long-term basis and with little desire to leave it. Professionals are not uniquely motivated by altruism, although the institutional structure of the profession typically has an ideological commitment to serve society. Science in particular lacks a clear service orientation, such as law and medicine have, since the client or client group is not clearly delineated in science. While the work of most professionals is defined by the needs of a particular client, the cause for which a scientist works is more diffuse. The dominant idealogy of science is in fact that the scientist serves only the large goal of scientific truth in his pure research, a commitment to the value of advancing knowledge. In reality the motives of the scientist, like those of any professional, are a complex mixture of altruistic and egoistic behavior, with the ultimate goal the receipt of recognition of priority of discovery, with its attendant psychic and career benefits. The client group for the scientist is either a funding agency or scientific peers, in that the work performed and its success will be judged by peers and it is they who are being served in the sense by seeing unanswered questions resolved. Because of this lack of accountability to a specific client group, the informal code of scientists lacks prescriptions for how to conduct themselves with regard to either hazards arising out of research or harmful applications as outgrowths of a line of work.

Third, a profession possesses substantial autonomy and powers of self-control, gained either through professional associations which foster group consciousness and integration, protecting members from outside interference and imposition of standards, or through informal networks of collegial relationships. Typical traits include self-determination of educational standards; legislation affecting the profession shaped by the profession; and little lay evaluation and control, with norms of practice often more rigorous than legal controls. Autonomy may in fact be the core characteristic of a profession. If autonomy tests professional status, self-regulation is then the test of the autonomy of a professional grouping. Claims of autonomy are tested, in science as in medicine, by three claims. First, it is claimed that the knowledge and skill is special and laymen cannot evaluate it; second, professionals are responsible and can be trusted to work ethically without supervision; third, the profession can be trusted to take regulatory action if one of its members acts improperly.

Science can be distinguished from other professions by the intensely competive environment of research, as well as by its lack of a defined client group. In science, only one solution is available for a given problem. In business, markets can be expanded or new ones created; in law, no other lawyer is competing with the lawyer retained by the client to achieve a resolution of the client's problems. In science, no scientist has a monopoly on a line of research. As Gaston notes, "Competition in science is more like a race between runners in the same track and over the same distance at the same time."

Scientists in industry are usually seen as a professional subgroup. Since their incentives are more clearly determined by commitment to the industrial employer, their contribution to scientific knowledge is considered secondary to academic scientists, for reasons relating to the higher prestige of academic employment and the tension between employer demands and professional orientation in the industrial setting. Academic science has been seen as the paradigm for pure science, although it is apparent that most scientific areas have substantial and deepening industrial connections, and the great majority of scientists earn their living in technical work. Given the pressure to produce in an expanding field, recent evidence suggests that violations of scientific norms have occurred with increasing frequency in both academia and industry.

Originality is prized in science insofar as it demonstrates an important feature of the natural world for the first time. In crowded, "hot" fields, such as biology, competition tends to be particularly intense and tensions greater. With such intense competition, competitive behaviors may result that tend to evade, or violate, the norms of science, such as hasty publication, fraud or theft and secretiveness. The pirating of papers and falsification of data has become more visible in recent years, as major cases of cheating in the bio-medical area have emerged. Disruption of informal scientific etiquette may also occur as the result of intense pressures to achieve commercial applications of promising scientific techniques. As a scientific field becomes more competitive, with more at stake, there is no reason to trust professional self-regulation to adequately control either violations of the internal norms of good science, or violations of external norms (imposed through the Guidelines), addressing hazards.

III. The vacuum produced by the dismantling of the Guidelines may well be filled by state regulatory measures which will produce variant requirements from state to state.

Two recent examples of state legislation affecting rDNA research include N.Y. Public Health Law ss 3220-3223 (Supp. 1980-1981) which requires a certification procedure for the operation of laboratories engaged in such research, but bases its regulation upon the NIH Guidelines: "If the National Institutes of Health guidelines are revised, the commissioner shall revise the regulations for the conduct of recombinant DNA activity accordingly." Thus, if NIH downgrades its guidelines, New York will simply follow suit. Since the statute also preempts any local law or ordinance, it fails to present a significant regulatory threat. A second example is Maryland, in Maryland Anno Code art 43 ss 898-910 (1980). A license is required, and a Biohazards committee is to be apppointed to monitor licensed projects. The NIH Guidelines are used again as the baseline for regulation; however, sanctions are more elaborate including inspection of premises. These two examples make the point adequately, since the Maryland provision is more demanding than New York; in Maryland, it is not clear whether the downgrading of the NIH Guidelines will simply downgrade the state regulatory apparatus, as seems to be the case in New York.

IV. The existing regulatory structure should be left in place in order to force scientists to consider specific risks and to gain the benefit of outside assessments of the experiments proposed.

The current structure, utilizing the IBCs and NIH review processes, serves two essential functions. First it provides a "governor," a method by which potentially hazardous research can be temporarily stopped in order to allow more careful evaluation of risks, benefits, and future developments. The IBC review process compels a deliberate and explicit consideration of the area of uncertainty as to potential hazards of certain experiments, and should not be lightly dismissed in favor of self-regulation. Second, the IBC review process provides a method to counteract the bias of the investigator, who is understandably eager to proceed with his research in an area he has already identified as promising. If the IBC membership is properly constituted, with representation of viewpoints other than those of research scientists reflected in its membership, we would have a mechansim with some promise of evaluating the research in an objective fashion.

In summary, it is my opinion that the RAC proposal to dismantle the Guidelines and the review process would be a major mistake. Simplification of the Guidelines might well be useful, as proposed in the Alternative Proposal. But it is premature to conclude that an area of research as potentially hazardous as rDNA research should not be relegated to the control of the profession of science.

Sincerely yours,

Barry R. Furrow

Barry R. Furrow
Professor of Law (Visiting)

BRF/jhp

DEPARTMENT OF HEALTH & HUMAN SERVICES

Public Health Service

National Institutes of Health
Bethesda, Maryland 20205
Bldg. 2, Rm. 322

February 1, 1982

Dr. William Gartland, Director
Office of Recombinant DNA Activities
Building 31, Room 4A52
National Institutes of Health
Bethesda, Maryland 20205

Dear Dr. Gartland:

I want to comment on the two alternative proposed revisions of the NIH Recombinant DNA Guidelines that are now being considered. While decreased NIH supervision of large classes of non-hazardous experiments is certainly desirable, the RAC proposal goes rather too far, in my view, in the direction of removing controls. It would seem desirable to maintain some NIH oversight of experiments involving a degree of risk, as in Dr. Gottesman's suggested revision. My reasons are the following:

1. Although research to date has produced no evidence of hazard in recombinant DNA research, the class of experiments done so far has been quite limited. We know that random cloning of genomic segments is almost certainly safe, but we do not have the same assurance about deliberate attempts to make some types of animal virus recombinants or to clone toxin genes, for instance. Although the risks of such studies may be no worse than those which scientists in other areas regularly assess for themselves, the recombinant DNA field has a history that one cannot ignore. An accident in this area, especially against a background of recently dissolved Guidelines, could have social and political consequences of an entirely different scale than an ordinary laboratory accident.

2. If one accepts that there are still some risks, it woud seem wise to maintain a uniform nationwide mechanism for approval. Throwing all decisions back on the individual university or investigator would mean that the RAC's expertise in these matters would no longer be available, and many of its past deliberations would now have to be repeated with considerable effort at the local level, very likely with quite disparate decisions resulting. Since these are no primarily local issues, some uniformity is desirable. One would not want to encourage "forum-shopping" among recombinant DNA researchers.

In summary, while it is clearly appropriate to reduce or eliminate controls over many classes of experiments, the abolition of all NIH oversight appears premature.

Sincerely yours,

Martin Gellert

Martin Gellert
Laboratory of Molecular Biology
National Institute of Arthritis, Diabetes, and Digestive and Kidney Diseases

Genentech, Inc.
Genentech, Inc.
Genentech, Inc.
Genentech, Inc.
Genentech, Inc.

460 Point San Bruno Boulevard
South San Francisco, CA 94080
(415) 952-0123
TWX: 9103717168

February 1, 1982

Dr. William Gartland
Director, Office of Recombinant
DNA Activities
Building 31, Room 4A52
National Institutes of Health
Bethesda, Maryland 20205

Re: Notice of proposed revisions of the NIH Guidelines for Research Involving Recombinant DNA Molecules Fed. Reg. Vol. 46, No. 233, p.59368, December 4, 1981 and Fed. Reg. Vol. 46, No. 234, p.59734, December 7, 1981

Dear Mr. Gartland:

We are pleased to submit our comments on the proposed revisions of the NIH Guidelines published in the December 4 and December 7, 1981 issues of the Federal Register. Our detailed comments on specific sections of the proposals follow.

First, we would like to support the continuing evolution of the recombinant DNA guidelines as our body of knowledge concerning this technology increases. Both proposals are significant steps forward in this regard. We believe the guidelines have served and should continue to serve a useful purpose in assisting those involved with this technology to make informed judgements. As the guidelines have developed, there has been a healthy dialogue at the national level between people with differing points of view and therefor an open and realistic assessment of the potential risks of recombinant DNA technology has developed. The alternative to the attentiveness of the NIH could well be a patchwork of local and state regulations which might impede our national progress and do nothing to assure additional safety.

We believe Dr. Gottesman's proposal in general achieves these objectives, by setting reasonable standards for experiments for which sufficient information exists to do so and by assigning oversight responsibilities for certain experiments to the IBC and the NIH based on a rational assessment of potential hazard.

The portions of the Gottesman proposal for which we suggest clarification or revision are listed below with our comments.

Section I.B. Definition of Recombinant DNA Molecules

"Synthetic DNA segments likely to yield a potentially harmful polynucleotide or polypeptide (e.g. a toxin or a pharmacologically active agent) shall be considered as equivalent to their natural DNA counterpart."

Comment: We agree that the statement regarding synthetic DNA should be incorporated, however, we suggest rewording to clarify that not all pharmacologically active agents are harmful.

"Synthetic DNA segments likely to yield pharmacologically active agents or a potentially harmful polynucleotide or polypeptide (e.g. a toxin) shall be considered as equivalent to their natural DNA counterpart."

III.B.2. Experiments in Which DNA from CDC Class 2 or Class 3 Agents cloned in Nonpathogenic Prokaryotic or Lower Eukaryotic Host Vector Systems.

Comment: The title of this section should be expanded to include Class 4 and Class 5 agents since these two categories are discussed under this section in subpart III.B.2.b.

III.B.5. Experiments Involving More than 10 Liters of Culture

It is our belief that the 10 liter limit applied to the definition of large scale experiments is by necessity, arbitrary. It would seem however, that a definition based on total number of organisms per culture might be a more reasonable approach to establishing a limit

We suggest that the limit be based on the total number of organisms in any vessel of any size and recommend that the limit be set at 1×10^{14} cells. This corresponds to 10 liters of culture at a density of 1×10^{10} cells/ml.

Section III.C.2. Experiments Involving Formation of Recombinant DNA Molecules Containing No More than Two-Thirds of the Genome of Any Eukaryotic Virus

Comment: We question the selection of a certain size fraction of the viral genome as the only criteria for establishing containment levels. We recommend that "evidence that the genome is totally and irreversibly defective" be used as an alternate criteria as is done in sections III.B.2.a and III.B.2.b. Simlarly Sections III.B.2.a and III.B.2.b should include "no more than two-thirds of the genome of any eukaryotic virus" as an alternate criteria for reducing the containment level in these classifications of experiments.

Section IV.D.2. Membership and Procedures of the IBC
The Guidelines currently specify the membership of the IBC in terms of the number of non-affiliated members required, the number of nondoctoral members, etc.

We believe that the Guidelines should be revised to state only the expertise that is required and that this may be accomplished with members selected from within and/or outside of the Institution.

Section IV.E.2. Recombinant Advisory Committee
Because many commercial corporations have committed to comply with the Guidelines on a voluntary basis as evidenced by requests for exemptions to the 10 liter limit published in the Federal Register, we believe it is important that industry's viewpoint be represented on the RAC and suggest that the statement "Representatives from industry may serve as non-voting members" be added.

Again, we thank you for the opportunity to comment on the proposed revisions to the NIH guidelines.

Sincerely,

M J Ross

Dr. Michael Ross
Director, Protein Chemistry

MR:bs

INDUSTRIAL BIOTECHNOLOGY ASSOCIATION

February 1, 1982

Dr. William J. Gartland
Director
Office of Recombinant DNA Activities
Building 31, Room 4A52
National Institutes of Health
Bethesda, Maryland 20205

Re: Proposals to modify NIH's guidelines for research involving recombinant DNA molecules, 46 F.R.59368 (December 4, 1981) and 46 F.R.59734 (December 7, 1981)

Dear Dr. Gartland:

The comments set out below are submitted on behalf of the Board of Directors of the Industrial Biotechnology Association, Inc. (IBA). IBA is an association of industrial organizations actively involved in biotechnology programs. The association's purposes include promotion of commercial biotechnology and enhancement of its contributions to the public welfare, as well as cooperation with governmental agencies exercising responsibilities in the area of biotechnology. A list of IBA members as of February 1, 1982 is included with this letter.

We believe that the December 4 proposal by the RAC and the December 7 proposal by Dr. Susan Gottesman are each persuasive in some respects. Their best features should be combined to replace the present guidelines with a modernized version that will encourage variety and innovation to a greater extent, while retaining the confidence of both the scientific community and the general public.

The thrust of IBA's combined proposal is two-fold. First, we agree with the scientific judgments expressed in the RAC proposal to the effect that today's specific containment requirements are generally unduly conservative. Since the scientific community's self-initiated pause in the mid-1970's and formulation of the first version of the guidelines in 1976, much new recombinant DNA work has been performed in university and industrial laboratories

6110 Executive Boulevard, Rockville, MD 20852 (301) 984-9599 throughout the world. During this period, the accumulated scientific evidence has contributed substantially to our understanding that recombinant DNA research is not in fact a hazard to the public health or environment. Thus, while maintaining a reasonable degree of caution, and without deciding that the available evidence is conclusive, it makes sense today as a matter of public policy for government to focus on responsible ways to stimulate variety and innovation in recombinant DNA research and its applications. Identification and removal of unnecessary technical and economic impediments should receive a high priority.

Secondly, we believe that at the present juncture of recombinant DNA's evolution, the formal institutional structure of the RAC and IBC is both valuable and desirable to advise scientists and industry in decision-making concerning a few remaining areas of uncertainty, to serve as a focal point for public monitoring of recombinant DNA's continuing development, and to consider further guideline revisions. We regard this support, notwithstanding that it imposes some restrictions, as currently more of an aid for well-managed technological growth than an impediment.

We would note here that the guidelines' formulation and revision process has already produced substantial benefit. It has contributed to raising the level of sensitivity in the scientific and industrial communities to possible, particular hazards that might arise from biotechnology research and application -- a clearly desirable societal result even if, as it now appears, no credible hazards peculiar to recombinant DNA have been found. It has also put into place a federal guidance system which, while amenable to improvement, presently commands the confidence of the scientific community, since it allows guideline changes to occur as new evidence accumulates and safety-related judgments evolve; and also commands the confidence of the community beyond involved scientists, which can find comfort in an independent level of monitoring and review reflecting continued sensitivity to societal concerns.

The existing system is thus balanced in a way that, on the evidence that is available to us today, should neither be cast in concrete, nor cast aside too abruptly. The combined proposal that we recommend takes a middle ground between the Gottesman and RAC approaches, and promotes stability in recombinant DNA development. On the other hand, the Gottesman proposal, while recognizing the benefits of some continuing institutional guidance structure, is unduly conservative with respect to present expert scientific opinion. And the RAC proposal, while generally cogent with respect to scientific judgments, shows inadequate appreciation for the benefits of some continuing federal guidance as well as for a course of more moderate change as accumulated experience validates those scientific judgments.

We recommend consideration of a system that would modify the present guidelines with the following features:

1) Containment Guidelines - The heart of the RAC proposal, the simplified provisions of Section III, would be followed. The experiments for which there are admonitions, set out in III (a) and III (b) of the RAC proposal and which are presently prohibited, would instead be permitted only if approved on a case by case basis by NIH as indicated in item 4 below.

2) Prohibitions - Again following the RAC proposal, absolute prohibitions would be eliminated as inflexible and unnecessary. Formerly prohibited experiments would be possible under different sets of controls as indicated below.

3) Purpose; Roles and Responsibilities - Following the Gottesman proposal, the thrust of the original guidelines would remain unchanged, keeping them more than a voluntary code of good practice. Some significant procedural requirements would be retained. Formal institutional guidance, particularly via the IBC's, would continue to play a key role in technology development.

4) NIH Prior Approvals - As in the Gottesman proposal, certain highly sensitive experiments would require RAC review and NIH approval before being initiated. The two categories set out in Section III of the RAC proposal (i.e., experiments involving deliberate transfer of a drug resistance trait to microorganisms not known to acquire it naturally and deliberate formation of recombinant DNAs containing genes for the biosynthesis of toxins lethal for vertebrates at an LD_{50} of less than 100 nanograms per kilogram body weight) would be the sole classes of experiments requiring this ultimate precaution at the present time.

5) IBC Prior Approvals - As in the Gottesman proposal, large scale production would require IBC approval before initiation. However, the present 10 liter threshold for triggering this requirement is too cumbersome for current scale-up experiments, particularly industrial applications, as well as for many experiments that can now be performed with bench-top equipment. This threshold should be raised substantially.

6) IBC Monitoring and Record Keeping - As in the Gottesman proposal, experiments would generally be reported to the IBC as they are initiated. IBC's would thus continue their monitoring and record keeping functions, although approvals would not be necessary. Experiments neither exempt from the guidelines nor subject to approvals previously noted would be subject to this requirement. For example, experiments involving release of DNA organisms into the environment would fall into this category. While thorough monitoring of such activities remains prudent, further restrictions, except for those sensitive experiments previously noted, now seem unwarranted.

A few additional comments concerning IBA's recommendations are offered for your consideration.

First, IBA believes that industry is committed to continued adherence to the NIH guidelines as modified. Such responsible participation in recombinant DNA research and application has been an accepted tradition in the biotechnology industry, and continues to receive wide industry support. One significant reason for adherence to a uniform system of federal guidance and overseeing is our belief that such an approach is more compatible with commercial development and the benefits it brings to society than would be a system of varying local requirements. In its decisional process concerning this and future guideline revisions, NIH should solicit and weigh credible information on proposed changes from other cognizant governmental units.

Next, the combined modified guidelines that we recommend should contain a preface which expressly articulates the safety judgments that underlie the detailed decisions reached. This section should make explicit NIH's confidence in the safety of recombinant DNA activities today and the desirability of encouraging its development for the anticipated contribution to the public welfare. It should also indicate clearly that, when they were created, the guidelines were intended to be modified from time to time as experience accumulated; and that the decision reached in this instance was taken after careful consideration as well as after substantial opportunity for public input.

Additionally, we would emphasize that an effective IBC is the foundation of our proposed institutional guidance system. As in the past, it is anticipated that IBC's would make substantive contributions to ongoing activities at a minimal cost of bureaucratic requirements and delays. They are desirable from the standpoint of contributing to employee protection by heightening employee awareness of good laboratory practices; their monitoring activities assist in documenting safety records and compliance with the guidelines, as well as in identifying occasional problems which may profitably be addressed at the RAC/NIH level. Large scale industrial projects seeking approval would appropriately be handled by IBC's, since their consideration would provide adequate review with less chance of risking exposure of confidential and proprietary material than if the material were in the possession of the government.

The RAC, while reviewing fewer activities as a matter of course, would also continue to address itself to problem areas identified by IBC's, to guideline revisions as might appear appropriate, and to overseeing continued work in the recombinant DNA risk assessment area. In our view, it would continue to be a valuable resource in the federal guidance system.

Lastly, we would note briefly that we believe it time to reevaluate the 10 liter threshold for triggering review of scale-up applications. The 10 liter designation has a historical rather than a scientifically logical basis, and is outmoded in an era of growing industrial applications, in which the feasibility of large scale production will first be investigated with smaller fermentations. In IBA's proposal, prior IBC approval is required for large production scale processes, even though the DNA activity will obviously have been performed previously, and industry experience with scale-up of experiments is substantial. Moreover, other product regulatory requirements are likely to evolve. We therefore believe that the necessity of seeking repetitive approvals during scale-up is clearly undesirable, offering little discernible benefit and, as commercial applications become more prevalent, unreasonably increasing costs. Accordingly, we suggest that the approval threshold initially be raised to a level of at least the 200 - 250 liter range.

In conclusion, IBA appreciates the opportunity to comment on the proposed revision of the guidelines. We commend NIH for its thoughtful and considered approach to this task. We hope that our suggestions will be helpful in reaching a final decision, and we would be pleased to meet with NIH officials to discuss our position in greater detail, or to be of any further assistance in resolving the issues at hand.

Sincerely,

Harvey S. Price

Harvey S. Price
Executive Director

HSP/sr

Enclosure

January 31, 1981

IBA MEMBER COMPANIES

Agrigenetics Corporation
New York, New York

Alpha Therapeutics Corporation
Los Angeles, California

Applied Molecular Genetics, Inc.
Newbury Park, California

Biogen, Inc.
Cambridge, Massachusetts

Cetus Corporation
Berkeley, California

Clinical Assays
Division of Travenol Laboratories, Inc.
Cambridge, Massachusetts

Dow Chemical Company
Midland, Michigan

Genetics Institute
Boston, Massachusetts

Genex Corporation
Rockville, Maryland

Molecular Genetics, Inc.
Minnetonka, Minnesota

Procter & Gamble Company
Cinncinnati, Ohio

Schering-Plough Corporation
Kenilworth, New Jersey

SmithKline Corporation
Philadelphia, Pennsylvania

TRANSGENE
Paris, France

INSTITUTE OF MEDICINE
NATIONAL ACADEMY OF SCIENCES
2101 CONSTITUTION AVENUE WASHINGTON, D.C. 20418

February 1, 1982

Ray Thornton, J.D.
President
Arkansas State University
State University AR 72467

Dear Ray:

After attending the symposium at the recent AAAS meetings, studying the Baltimore-Campbell proposal (Federal Register, December 4, 1981) and the Gottesman proposal (Federal Register, December 7, 1981), and discussing these matters with colleagues in several relevant fields of science and public policy, I have come to the conclusion that, at least for now, we should retain the mandatory nature of the guidelines for recombinant DNA research, and the requirement for Institutional Biosafety Committees (IBC).

While almost all would agree that the probabilities of harm to workers or the public from recombinant DNA research are less--much less--than had been envisioned in 1975, it is not possible to assert that there is no risk at all, or that there are no unique features to risks from recombinant DNA research.

IBCs serve the necessary functions of monitoring research and providing a national communications network about research in the field. No other groups perform these functions. Requirement for IBC approval may slow some research, but, for the most part, recombinant DNA research is not seriously impaired by this.

About 15 percent of recombinant DNA research comes under the guidelines now. The guidelines could and should be simplified and revised further, and the Gottesman proposal takes us significantly in that direction. Soon we could move even further so that only a very small percent of recombinant DNA work would require special restrictions. These restrictions are felt particularly keenly by certain subsets of the population of recombinant DNA researchers, for example, those working with intact animal virus/animal cell systems, or those doing agricultural research and desiring to perform field experiments. Release of organisms with recombinant DNA into the environment is prohibited. The Baltimore-Campbell proposal would remove any restriction. The Gottesman proposal would require RAC review and NIH approval, not prohibition. The potential benefits of research with systems such as those mentioned above are great. We need to understand much more about host range and virulence of animal viruses, to develop new vaccines, and to develop crop plants that are resistant to destructive pests, etc. But it is in these areas of large potential benefit that even a small, unpredicted change (e.g. in host range of a virus) might produce a significant and different type of hazard than from other types of research. We should continue, I believe, to be responsibly conservative in these matters. The Gottesman proposal does just that. It would not be obstructive to the conduct of recombinant DNA research in these areas.

There are other areas of risk to be considered as well. The question of surveillance of large-volume experiments is one that needs further discussion before discarding it as insignificant. The deliberate misuse of recombinant DNA technologies for defensive or offensive reasons is a "scare scenario" that was discussed and discarded early in the debate. But recent trends in civil defense require reconsideration of such possibilities and the possible usefulness of mandatory guidelines in this context.

I believe we should continue to have a responsible process for guiding recombinant DNA research without undue restrictions. We should strive to reduce the complexity of the task while retaining the mechanism that has worked well so far. Since the problems have not all been resolved, this would be reassuring to the public and to the Congress, as well as scientifically valid.

The fundamental issue is to retain, until more is known, the guidelines and a process that responds to new information by appropriate revisions.

In the face of the enormous intensification of publicity about the possibilities for monetary rewards from recombinant DNA research, major abrupt change in the guidelines would appear to be an abandonment of all safeguards in the rush for commercial exploitation. This may be an unfair but plausible criticism.

My recommendation is to have a limited period of more relaxed regulations by supporting the Gottesman proposal now and immediately work to simplify the guidelines further as appropriate. Specific areas for further simplification can be discussed at the next meeting. Several come easily to mind.

The Gottesman proposal is a responsible next step in the process that started at Asilomar.

Sincerely,

Elena

Elena O. Nightingale, M.D., Ph.D.
Senior Program Officer

P.S. Our correspondence of last fall is attached. Were notices of the proposed actions published?

Enclosure

cc: RAC Members
William Gartland, Jr.

February 1, 1982

Dear RAC Member,

As many of you know, I have been involved with the revision of the NIH guidelines as a member of RAC, advisor to RAC, and chairman of the working group on revision of the guidelines. I oppose the RAC proposal, as published in the Federal Register (Dec. 4, 1981), and have submitted at alternate proposal (Federal Register, Dec. 7, 1981, item #7). I am writing to you now to explain my reasons for submitting this proposal and to ask you to seriously consider my alternative at the February RAC meeting.

My proposal contrasts with the RAC proposal in two major ways: (1) It retains IBCs and the non-voluntary nature of the guidelines and (2) It keeps containment levels somewhat higher than those proposed by RAC, and is more specific about what the containment levels for given experiments should be. My proposal, in common with the RAC proposal, does lower containment and procedures significantly from those found in the current guidelines, and simplifies the many categories in the current guidelines.

Why keep the IBCs and mandatory guidelines? In my mind, the relevant question at this stage is "Are there scientific grounds for continuing some control over the recombinant DNA field?" If, in fact, we believe that there is nothing about recombinant DNA experimentation which requires watching, the IBCs and mandatory adherance to guidelines become unnecessary. After a careful study of the issues (summarized in the document "Evaluation of the Risks Associated with Recombinant DNA Research" , Federal Register, Dec. 4, 1981, page 59385...), my own conclusion is that one cannot totally discount the possible risks. Apparently, most of the RAC agrees with me that experiments involving the cloning of toxin genes or indiscriminate rearrangements of antibiotic resistance genes should not be done without careful consideration and oversight, since even the RAC proposal admonishes people not to do these experiments.

Experiments which involve non-defective animal virus recombinants also cause concern. We do not yet understand enough about the biology of these viruses to always predict what determines host range and virulence. Currently, such animal virus recombinant DNA experiments are dealt with by NIH on a case-by-case basis, and then referred back to the IBCs for continuing oversight. My proposal suggests more general levels of containment, which would eliminate the need for investigators to come to NIH with their requests.

For these classes of experiments, and some others where we have little previous experience to guide our expectations, I believe that some expert group other than the principal investigator should be involved in assuring that appropriate procedures and containment practices are used. For the moment, at least, the IBCs seem to serve that role well. In addition, if there is a need for oversight, it seems quite appropriate that government-funded research should be expected to use the oversight mechanism, and that we make that expectation explicit. I have heard many discussions about the likelihood of IBCs remaining intact if the guidelines became voluntary; if we are agreed that this would be desirable, why are we so anxious to delete all mention of the IBCs from the guidelines?

Many of the arguments raised in the working group and in RAC depend on differences in interpretation of the statement that recombinant DNA is not uniquely dangerous. For some, this means that no danger is known or is likely to be found; for others, it means that equally hazardous experiments are being performed in fields other than recombinant DNA. I think that we all agree that some kinds of experiments outside the recombinant DNA field may pose dangers similar in scope to those posed by recombinant DNA. My response to this inconsistency, however, is not to lower our oversight of recombinant DNA to the lowest possible level, as RAC has proposed, but to realize that we may have built a good, workable system for overseeing research risks, that is worth perfecting.

My proposal is much more specific about containment levels than the RAC proposal. I have tried to use the same general principles which the RAC proposal urges the investigator to use: consider the pathogenicity of the host, and what, if any, effect the donor DNA might have. I have chosen to be more specific than either RAC or the working group recommendations. If we do require IBC oversight, as I am suggesting, I do not think that we do the IBCs any favor by removing all specific guidance. At the least, each IBC must then make a determination of the appropriate levels of containment for a given experiment. This seems an unnecessary waste of time; it is also likely to lead to inequities in the application of the guidelines in different parts of the country and in different institutions in the same cities. My proposal therefore sets a reasonable upper limit for containment, and allows the IBC latitude in lowering containment where appropriate.

In summary, I believe that research with recombinant DNA has not led to any clearly demonstrable risks, that many experiments are clearly not as dangerous as first suspected, and that some classes of experiments either still seem to pose problems or cannot yet be evaluated. We need a filter for catching these experiments and letting the others go on in as unencumbered a fashion as possible. Revisions of the guidelines over the last five years have done much to acheive this goal of focusing on some classes of experiments. In the process, the guidelines have become increasingly complex, and we have all become increasingly tired of dealing with the complexities. The RAC proposal has as its major advantage its appearance of simplicity, but we can at least approach that simplicity without sacrificing the useful oversight which the guidelines insure.

I would be happy to discuss my proposal with you in more detail, either in the next week by telephone (301-496-3524) or at the February RAC meeting. I look forward to seeing you there.

Sincerely,

Susan Gottesman

Susan Gottesman

UNIVERSITY OF WASHINGTON
SEATTLE, WASHINGTON 98195

Program in Social Management of Technology

2/1/82

Dear Bill -

I would appreciate, if it is possible, your correcting a fairly significant typo in the comment letter I addressed to Roy Thornton on the Baltimore-Campbell proposal.

P2, last ¶, line 6, in the parenthetical material there is a space after the word "by". Please insert "Dutton to the" at that place.

I just noticed this

Thanks — Phil Bereano

316 Guggenheim, FS-15 / Telephone: (206) 543-7029

Colorado State University
Fort Collins, Colorado
80523

Program Ethics and
Federal Regulations
Office of the Executive Secretary
303/491-7162

February 1, 1982

William J. Gartland, Jr., Director
Office of Recombinant DNA Activities
National Institutes of Health
Building 31, Room 4A52
Bethesda, Maryland 20205

Dear Dr. Gartland:

As executive secretary of the CSU Biohazard Committee, I have canvassed the scientific community regarding the two proposals for a major revision of the NIH Guidelines for Research Involving Recombinant DNA Molecules. One of our scientists strongly favors the revision in the Federal Register of December 4, 1981. He can do this with confidence because of the high standards of biosafety set at Colorado State University. From an ethical standpoint, however, I feel that this set of standards cannot be assumed to exist at all institutions. Bernard Rollin, Ph.D., the CSU Director of Bioethical Planning is also concerned with a progressive decline in biosafety standards that can result from the absence of federal regulations.

Dr. Rollin's statement is as follows: while it certainly makes sense to simplify requirements and eliminate bureaucracy, biosafety does not seem to be the best area in which to do this. Innocent persons are at risk and deserve, at the very least, the sort of safeguards which have hitherto been extant. The cost to researchers is a mild annoyance at worst; the benefit is some degree of extra care in using hazardous material and increased awareness of the social and ethical implications of science. To make guidelines voluntary is essentially to render them meaningless, as the history of the NIH Guidelines re laboratory animals has clearly shown. The December 7 proposal seems a reasonable compromise.

I concur completely with Dr. Rollin's statement.

Yours sincerely,

David H. Neil

David H. Neil, B.V.Sc., MRCVS
Executive Secretary

DHN:cr

Committee on Human Research • Animal Care Committee • Biohazard Committee
Painter Center for Laboratory Animals

Irwin D.J. Bross, Ph.D.
Director of Biostatistics
Roswell Park Memorial Institute
666 Elm Street
Buffalo, N.Y. 14263

February 1, 1982

William J. Gartland, Jr.
Director
Office of Recombinant DNA Activities
National Institute of Health
Building 31 Room 4A52
Bethesda, Maryland 20205

Dear Sir:

The Baltimore/Campbell proposal described in the Federal Register would eliminate any meaningful controls of Recombinant DNA Technology and would create a major hazard to the public health and safety.

I share the concerns outlined in the well reasoned letter from Donna Smith and Terri Goldberg and would support the Gottesman proposal. However, with the "gold rush" now on in biotechnology, I am afraid that the pressure for deregulation is overwhelming. A disgraceful chapter in American science that future historians will write is the complete failure of courage, will, and integrity of the U.S. scientists who capitulated to this pressure.

My purpose here is to note in the official record the personal liability of all persons, possibly including yourself, who implement the Baltimore/Campbell proposal. Sooner or later someone in the "gold rush" will take one shortcut too many and there will be human deaths and disabilities as a consequence of the deregulation of Recombinant DNA Technology.

<u>Before</u> the fact, let me note that due warning has been registered in this letter and that NIH has disregarded this warning. Therefore, all persons who implement the Baltimore/Campbell proposal will be personally liable for any civil and criminal penalties that may result from the public health hazards created by this proposal.

Very sincerely yours,

Irwin D.J. Bross, Ph.D.
Director of Biostatistics

IDJB/mak
Enc.

THE UNIVERSITY OF ROCHESTER

MEDICAL CENTER

SCHOOL OF MEDICINE AND DENTISTRY · SCHOOL OF NURSING
STRONG MEMORIAL HOSPITAL

601 ELMWOOD AVENUE
ROCHESTER, NEW YORK 14642
AREA CODE 716

Frank E. Young, M.D., Ph.D.
Dean, School of Medicine and Dentistry
Vice President for Health Affairs
(716) 275-3407

February 1, 1982

William J. Gartland, Jr., Ph.D.
Director
Office of Recombinant DNA Activities
National Institutes of General
Medical Sciences
Bethesda, Maryland 20014

Dear Bill:

I write to commend you on the farsighted action that was proposed by RAC in the Friday, December 4, 1981 issue of the Federal Register. Based on my experience in medical microbiology and my service on the RAC, I believe that the RAC proposal described in the Register is appropriate and sensible. I, therefore, support it. I believe that it has been highly appropriate that we take a cautious approach to recombinant DNA research and now that the concerns regarding hazards have been laid to rest, I believe this action is wholly warranted.

Thank you for your leadership.

Sincerely,

FEY:eb

cc: David Axelrod, M.D.
Glenn Haughie, M.D.

UNIVERSITY OF MINNESOTA
TWIN CITIES

Boynton Health Service
410 Church Street S.E.
Minneapolis, Minnesota 55455

February 1, 1982

Director, Office of Recombinant DNA Activities
National Institutes of Health
Building 31, Room 4A52
Bethesda, Maryland 20205

Dear Sir:

The University of Minnesota Institutional Biosafety Committee has reviewed the two proposals covering the major revision of the NIH Guidelines for Research Involving Recombinant DNA Molecules. The Committee unanimously favors the Gottesman proposal over the RAC proposal for the following reasons:

> The former retains certain prohibitions which we feel provide minimal safeguards and an element of protection against high risk experiments.
>
> The Gottesman proposal would greatly simplify the current guidelines, eliminating considerable confusion, while creating a much more usable guide for experimental scientists to follow.
>
> Recombinant DNA technology, as it relates to biotechnology, has fertilized the growth of a major new industry. The public is unusually aware of this growth and some still perceive it as creating an imminent danger to society.

The RAC proposal at the present time is both scientific and politically premature, and it should not be accepted.

Sincerely,

Dr. Patrick Cleary
Chairman

Institutional Biosafety Committee

PC:jb

UNIVERSITY OF CALIFORNIA, SAN FRANCISCO

BERKELEY • DAVIS • IRVINE • LOS ANGELES • RIVERSIDE • SAN DIEGO • SAN FRANCISCO — SANTA BARBARA • SANTA CRUZ

FRANCIS A. SOOY, M.D.
Chancellor

SHIRLEY CHATER
Vice Chancellor, Academic Affairs

Office of the Vice Chancellor, Academic Affairs
SAN FRANCISCO, CALIFORNIA 94143

February 1, 1982

Dr. William Gartland, Director
Office of Recombinant DNA Activities
National Institutes of Health
Building 31, Room 4A52
Bethesda, Maryland 20205

Dear Dr. Gartland:

RE: Proposed Recombinant DNA Guideline modifications

The UCSF Biosafety Committee has forwarded their comments to me concerning the several recombinant DNA guideline proposals being considered. As the Institutional Officer responsible for Biosafety issues on this campus, I am thus writing to you with this campus' opinion.

The Biosafety Committee acknowledged that the risk potential is viewed as being far less that originally thought. They thus applaud the containment downgrading proposed. As they feel that risk remains, they also endorse the restrictions that remain.

The important question is whether controls should be mandatory or voluntary. The Biosafety Committee feels strongly that whatever the federal action will be, every institution should maintain a strong review board. For reasons of consistency throughout the scientific world and across state lines and to forestall possible state legislative activities, it was agreed that mandatory controls would be preferable. In addition, the community members commented that "in an era when science is suspect in the community, evidence of institutional review is most important."

For the above reasons, the University of California, San Francisco endorses mandatory reviews as described in the "Gottesman Proposal" published on December 7, 1971.

Sincerely,

Shirley S. Chater
Vice Chancellor
Academic Affairs

EH

CC: Belle Cole
Karl Hittelman

William J. Gartland, Jr.
Director
Office of Recombinant DNA Activities
National Institute of Health
Building 31 Room 4A52
Bethesda, MD 20205

Dear Sir:

We are writing to register strong disapproval of the Baltimore/ Campbell proposal described in the Federal Register of December 4, 1981. This proposal would convert the NIH Guidelines from mandatory to voluntary and modifies the content to further weaken them.

Over the last six months, we have served as members of the Biotechnology Committee of the Massachusetts Public Health Association under the chair of Dr. David Ozonoff, writing a model ordinance for state and local communities. We have clearly examined the problems involved in assuring safe and long term development of biotechnology. We believe this proposal contravenes the last thirty years of experience in developing technology for maximal social benefit and minimal harm, and will not advance the productive development of recombinant DNA technology.

We support the Gottesman proposals to streamline the Guidelines but keep their mandatory character. Furthermore, we believe that broader legislation is needed to guide the rapidly developing commercial applications of rDNA technology.

We briefly summarize other reasons for our position.

1. Extensive experience in the chemical, manufacturing, and extraction industries reveal that the deleterious side effects to humans and the environment are frequently not detected until decades after the introduction of the technology into commercial use.

Recombinant DNA technology is only seven years old. It is only just now being tapped as a large scale production technology. None of the public health and epidemiological studies necessary to assess the long term side effects have been carried out. Thus, from the point of view of occupational and environmental health and ecosystem protection, we have no scientific basis for doing away with regulation at this juncture.

We note that even after they have been discovered, the fundamental nature of the deleterious action is not always understood, as in the case of asbestos and lung disease. It is naive to believe that the biomedical community understands the mechanism of disease causation so deeply that it can comfortably predict the absense of future problems.

2. Many of the key arguments on hazard derive from studies done under the assumption that manipulation would be limited to E. coli K12. For example, the Falmouth Conference explicitly excluded consideration of introduction of foreign DNA into organisms closer to wild strains, or other than E. coli. The current proposal opens up a variety of organisms to genetic manipulation in the absence of registration, notification, record keeping or health surveillance controls.

In addition, claims about the lack of nagative effects, not withstanding the lack of studies to identify such effects, might well be due to the efficacy of the present guidelines in preventing carelessness or release into the environment, rather than the lack of intrinsic survivability or hazard from genetically modified organisms.

Thus, much of the fundamental logic is profoundly flawed: under conditions of strong regulation there were no problems, therefore there is no need for regulations. This is akin to saying that since there have been no major nuclear reactor accidents under the Nuclear Regulatory Commission, we can do away with further oversight by the NRC.

3. Most of the activities, investigation, and discussion of the RAC over its history have focused on laboratory scale operations. However, the technology is rapidly expanding into commercial application with the attendant problems: large scale production and growth of the organisms; intentional introduction of modified organisms into the environment; selection for hardy rather than debilitated strains, workforces without training in pathogenic microbiology or even standard microbiology.

Since the existing guidelines set the standard for regulating commercial development, the dismantling of these guidelines represents the undercutting of the process of devising controls for commercial application and environmental uses before this use has been properly launched.

4. We are concerned over sharp conflicts of interest, not revealed in the Federal Register. For example, according to the Boston Globe of December 10, 1981, Professor Baltimore is the second largest private stockholder of Collaborative Genetics, which is to go public in January. His holdings would have a value of over $5,000,000. This information should have been made public, and in fact Professor Baltimore should have disqualified himself from the RAC deregulation proceedings.

The Gottesman proposal represents a far more reasonable course of action; the Guidelines would remain mandatory and provide a means for minimum controls and some caution without encumbering the development of the technology. The rapid progress of genetic engineering technology under relatively tight guidelines clearly points out that these guidelines have not retarded technological development unduly. The long term productive development of this technology requires the trust and cooperation of all sectors of our society; community, labor, environmentalists and church groups. This will require a government apparatus that will respond in a concerned and unbiased manner to oversee the future of rDNA

Sincerely,

Donna H Smith Technical Associate, MIT
Terri Goldberg, MPHA Recombinant DNA Conference Coordinator

Received in Office of Recombinant DNA Activities: February 3, 1982

THE UNIVERSITY OF MICHIGAN
ANN ARBOR, MICHIGAN 48109

C. G. Overberger
Vice-President for Research

February 4, 1982

Dr. William J. Gartland, Jr., Director
Office of Recombinant DNA Activities
Building 31, Room 4A52
National Institutes of Health
Bethesda, Maryland 20205

Dear Dr. Gartland:

I endorse the attached letter submitted to you by Dr. Rolf Freter, Professor of Microbiology and Chairman of the University of Michigan Committee C (Recombinant DNA Review Committee).

However, while endorsing the basic tenants of the Gottesman proposal to retain some oversight of federally-supported research on recombinant DNA, some compromise between the Gottesman and Baltimore/Campbell proposals to avoid some of the unnecessary restrictions of the former would seem appropriate. We will continue to perform our responsibilities on biological hazards.

Thank you for your continuing efforts on behalf of the scientific community to assure the public and government of the safety and the importance of properly performed genetic engineering research.

With kindest regards.

Sincerely,

Charles G. Overberger

CGO/mh
encl
cc: Alan Price
William Brockman

MRC
Medical Research Council

World Health Organization
Collaborating Centre for
Virus Reference and Research

MRC Common Cold Unit
Harvard Hospital,
Coombe Road,
Salisbury, Wilts,
SP2 8BW

telegrams Harvard, Salisbury
telephone Salisbury 22485

reference DAJT/RJL

Dr. William J. Gartland Jr.,
Department of Health and Human Services,
National Institutes of Health,
Bethesda,
Maryland 20205,
U.S.A.

11th February 1982

Dear Dr. Gartland

Thank you for your memorandum dated December 18th, which I have just received presumably due to postal delays.

What I have to say in reply to it is probably of only academic interest seeing that you will be considering the matter on February 8th and 9th. However you may be interested to know that on the whole I am in favour of the relaxations of the sort you outline. On the other hand I feel that as the administration and the social situations are rather different in the United Kingdom and the USA, it is not really for me to comment on the details of the changes which you propose to make. However, I do think that it is important to keep in being some sort of a structure for checking and advising scientists on procedures they may be planning or may have already undertaken. I would therefore not be happy with a system which abolished institutional bio-safety committees, or the responsibility of scientists to make their experiments known to them.

Similarly I think a central office where it would be possible to accumulate and concentrate experience, and expertise on the handling of difficult cases would continue to be an advantage. In practical terms it would probably also increase public confidence that the safety of recombinant DNA procedures was being taken seriously. I think it is important to maintain this responsible and cautious attitude towards the safety of laboratory work without impeding experiments. So I would be in favour wherever possible of avoiding a set up where more than a minority of procedures were only allowed after prior approval, since administrative delays might either hold up work or encourage people to disregard, not only that part of the system which was practically unworkable, but also the basic principles and philosophy of responsible scientific investigation.

If you should be any chance be interested in any other comments I may have do not hesitate to write.

Yours sincerely,

David Tyrrell

Dr. D.A.J. Tyrrell

February 19, 1982
65 Woolsley Avenue
Trumbull, Ct 06611

William Gartland, Director
Office of Recombinant DNA Activities
National Institutes of Health
9000 Rockville Pike
Bethesda, Md 20205

Dear Mr. Gartland,

I note in the Feb 17 issue of Chemical Week that you folks are reconsidering your position, giving in to some extant to the busy-bodies and other protesters, and are about to again clamp down on DNA and related research--by way of added regulations and impediments.

First, this whole controversy is stirred up by a bunch of activists who seek publicity, who look under the bed for terrorists every night and who are prime examples of "a little knowledge is a dangerous thing". They are in the same boat as the anti-floride people, the anti-nuclear, and all the others. In short, they have become the zero-progress pe ople. Many other examples abound.

Second, the "Frankenstein Monster" potential is much overrated, and researchers in the field are responsible people who are not likely to endanger us.

Third, much is to be gained from continued progress in this exciting field. You know this better than I--of the many promising lines now being pursued, and the many more possibilities open.

SO---please consider that for every such protester, there are thousands, perhaps millions, who are not worried. I am worried --but, not because of the DNA, etc potential dangers, but because of the poetntial government hampering of progress. You can tie them up in knows--witness the nuclear situation!

I suggest promoting legislation by Congress preventing any state or locality from going further than simply enforcing any existing federal guidelines. I feel national legislators and much less likely to cave in to stipid obstructionists than town councils or even state assemblies.

But--do nothing to hinder DNA research, please!

C W Hawley
Charles W. Hawley

Ph 203 268-3545

THE PUBLIC HEALTH RESEARCH INSTITUTE
OF THE CITY OF NEW YORK, INC.

455 FIRST AVENUE, NEW YORK, N. Y. 10016
TEL. (212) XXXXXX 578-0842

May 14, 1982

Dr. William J. Gartland, Jr., Director
Office of Recombinant DNA Activities
National Institute of General Medical Sciences
National Institutes of Health
Bethesda, Maryland 20205

Dear Dr. Gartland:

I am writing in strong support of the proposed amendment to section I-D of the NIH Guidelines, which would prohibit the construction of biological weapons by molecular cloning.

It has long been my conviction that the greatest potential for misuse of the new biology lies not in laboratory accident, or in the escape of hazardous material, but rather in the deliberate construction of biological weaponry. The potential of molecular cloning for biological weapons development is obvious, alarming, and not sufficiently appreciated by the public. The technology is not only powerful, but the required manipulations are relatively simple, inexpensive and easily conducted in clandestine fashion. These considerations suggest that we may be on the brink of a new arms race which may compound the suicidal dilemma already facing mankind in the nuclear age. This arms race would not be restricted to a few superpowers but would be accessible to the scientific personnel of many nations.

In this context, we as biologists face an awesome responsibility, perhaps greater than that faced by the community of physicists during W.W. II, because we have lived through the nuclear era and cannot pretend ignorance of the military consequences of our science. Our innocence was destroyed at Hiroshima. If we do not speak out now, history will surely condemn us.

Although the dangers are great, the opportunity for us to voice our warning is also great. A new realization has affected the peoples of all countries concerning the dangers of modern warfare. In this context an open stand by the biological community, and by RAC in particular, would likely have considerable impact on the public.

It is hoped that the adoption of the proposed amendment would bring pressure to bear on those scientists who might otherwise be tempted to cooperate in the development of biological weapons. It is also likely that members of Congress who are wavering on this issue would be influenced by adoption of the amendment.

Even if these arguments are rejected and it is believed that adoption of the amendment will have no strong and direct deterrent impact on misuse of recombinant

DNA technology, I would strongly urge adoption as a moral statement and in the interest of consistency. How can RAC not forbid the use of molecular cloning to develop biological weapons? Failure to do so would reduce all of RAC's previous deliberations to the level of absurdity. It would be ridiculous to debate the "dangers" of cloning Streptomyces fragments in B. subtilis and then refuse to prohibit weapons research.

Sincerely,

David Dubnau, Ph.D.
Member

DD:ah

UNIVERSITY OF CALIFORNIA, BERKELEY

BERKELEY • DAVIS • IRVINE • LOS ANGELES • RIVERSIDE • SAN DIEGO • SAN FRANCISCO • SANTA BARBARA • SANTA CRUZ

DEPARTMENT OF BIOCHEMISTRY BERKELEY, CALIFORNIA 94720

May 18, 1982

Dr. William S. Gartland
Executive Secretary
Recombinant DNA Advisory Committee
National Institutes of Health
Bethesda, Maryland 20205

Dear Dr. Gartland:

As a member of the Scientists' Committee on Chemical and Biological Warfare, I write in support of the Novick-Goldstein Amendment to the NIH Guidelines. This amendment, as I understand, is designed to prohibit construction of biological agents, including toxins, by the process of molecular cloning.

When President Nixon made his 1969 pledge to abandon preparation of biological weapons, members of our committee wrote to request verification of this salutary gesture by on site inspection. We never received a response to this request. Now there are allegations of use in wars abroad of biotoxins, and here at home there are rumors of military interest in development and production of agents by use of the new technology of molecular cloning. This would seem to be the time, prior to an irreversible military commitment, for decisive action from the bio-science community to prohibit this nefarious practice.

Sincerely,

J. B. Neilands
Professor of Biochemistry

JBN:pm
cc: R. Novick

The University of Alabama in Birmingham
Department of Microbiology

May 18, 1982

Dr. William Gartland, Jr.
Director
Office of Recombinant DNA Activities
National Institutes of Health
Room 4A52, Building 31
Bethesda, Maryland 20205

Dear Bill:

This is to indicate my approval for the adoption of an amendment to the NIH Guidelines to add a section I-D-7 on use of molecular cloning for the construction of biological weapons. This amendment to the Guidelines, although probably ineffectual, will be the right start and might subsequently lead to consideration by the United States Congress and United Nations and a more meaningful effective consideration of the issue by the world community.

Best regards.

Sincerely,

Roy Curtiss III

RCIII/pp

University Station / Birmingham, Alabama 35294

DEPARTMENT OF HEALTH & HUMAN SERVICES

Public Health Service

National Institutes of Health
Bethesda, Maryland 20205

May 21, 1982

Dr. William J. Gartland
Office of Recombinant DNA Activities, NIAID
Bldg. 31, Room 4A52
National Institutes of Health
Bethesda, Md. 20205

Dear Bill,

This is in response to the proposal by Drs' Novick and Goldstein which your office forwarded on May 10, 1982.

I am opposed to amendment of the current Guidelines to include the proposed language. Although the issue raised by the proponents of the amendment may be of personal concern to them as well as others, I do not consider it appropriate for action by the RAC. Rather the issue is one to be dealt with by the appropriate Branches of the Government charged with establishing national and international policy for the United States.

Therefore, I would suggest that persons who may have concerns about the issue raised by Drs.' Novick and Goldstein should communicate their concerns with appropriate officials of the Government.

Sincerely yours,

Robert W. McKinney

Robert W. McKinney, Ph.D.
Member, RAC

cc: Hon. Ray Thornton

DEPARTMENT OF MICROBIOLOGY AND MOLECULAR GENETICS
HARVARD MEDICAL SCHOOL
25 SHATTUCK STREET
BOSTON, MASSACHUSETTS 02115
617-732- 1920

May 25, 1982

Dr. William Gartland, Jr.
Office of Recombinant DNA
Activities
Bldg. 31, Rm. 4A52
N.I.H.
Bethesda, MD 20205

Dear Dr. Gartland,

I wish to offer my strong support for the amendment to the NIH guidelines on biological weapons proposed by Drs. Richard Novick and Richard Goldstein.

Sincerely yours,

Jonathan Beckwith

JB/am

MASSACHUSETTS INSTITUTE OF TECHNOLOGY CAMBRIDGE, MASSACHUSETTS 02139
Department of Biology Room 56-445 Tel. 617/253-7003

May 28, 1982

Dr. William Gartland
Office of Recombinant DNA Activities
NIAID - NIH
Bethesda, MD 20205

Dear Dr. Garland,

I am writing to express my emphatic support for the proposed amendment to the NIH Guidelines prohibiting the use of molecular cloning for the development of biological weapons. Such technology would represent a significant escalation in the application of scientific advances for destruction, and I urge the RAC to take a strong and explicit stand against it.

Yours sincerely,

Ethan Signer
Professor of Biology

hah
cc: Dr. Richard Novick

INSTITUTE OF MEDICINE
NATIONAL ACADEMY OF SCIENCES
2101 CONSTITUTION AVENUE WASHINGTON, D.C. 20418

May 28, 1982

William J. Gartland, Jr., Ph.D.
Office of Recombinant DNA Activities
NIAID/National Institutes of Health
Building 31, Room 4A52
Bethesda MD 20205

Dear Bill:

With reference to the Novick/Goldstein letter on use of molecular cloning for deliberate construction of biological weapons, I offer the following comment.

The military interest in recombinant DNA technologies for purposes of "defense" is a reality. I strongly endorse explicit prohibition of deliberate misuse of molecular cloning and any other biomedical technologies. That was one reason why I objected to making the guidelines voluntary (see attached letter of February 1, 1982, to Ray Thornton). There is, I believe, an interagency agreement to abide by the guidelines, and that includes the Department of Defense. Thus, while not the determining factor, non-compliance with the guidelines would, if nothing else, call attention to the fact that molecular cloning techniques were being used for biological warfare purposes.

I hope that RAC will discuss this issue at the next meeting so that an explicit prohibition to the construction of biological weapons by molecular cloning can be recommended.

Sincerely,

Elena

Elena O. Nightingale, M.D., Ph.D.
Senior Scholar-in-Residence

Attachment

ASSISTANT DIRECTOR
UNITED STATES ARMS CONTROL AND DISARMAMENT AGENCY

June 8, 1982

Dear Dr. Gartland:

ACDA Director Rostow has asked me to respond to your letter of May 19, 1982, which requested ACDA's comments on a proposal to amend the NIH Guidelines for Research Involving Recombinant DNA Molecules so as to introduce a prohibition against "the construction of biological weapons by molecular cloning."

We have no objection to the proposal, which is consistent with U. S. obligations under the 1972 Biological and Toxin Weapons Convention. As discussed below, we do, however, have suggestions for the precise formulation of the amendment to bring it more closely into line with the language of the Convention. This position has been coordinated with the Department of Defense and other interested agencies of the Executive Branch.

In your letter you requested comments on the statement (by those who proposed the amendment): "Laboratory research involving the construction of the organisms and the development of biological weapons for 'defensive' (e.g., deterrent) purposes would be excluded from the Biological Weapons Convention." The language and negotiating history of the Convention make clear that this statement is seriously mistaken.

Under Article I of the Convention, a Party "undertakes never in any circumstances to develop, produce, stockpile or otherwise acquire or retain:

"(1) Microbial or other biological agents, or toxins whatever their origin or method of production, of types and in quantities that have no justification for prophylactic, protective or other peaceful purposes;

William J. Gartland, Jr., Ph.D., Director
Office of Recombinant DNA Activities
National Institute of Allergy and Infectious Diseases
National Institutes of Health - Rm. 4A52, Bldg. 31
Bethesda, Maryland 20205

"(2) Weapons, equipment or means of delivery designed to use such agents or toxins for hostile purposes or in armed conflict."

The "Report of the Secretary of State" dated June 21, 1972, and transmitted to the Senate by the President on August 10, 1972 stipulates that:

"Article I provides that biological agents or toxins justified for purposes covered by the terms 'prophylactic' and 'protective' are not prohibited by this Convention. The word 'prophylactic' refers to activities related to the protection of the human body from the effects of organisms or substances to which an individual might be directly exposed. It encompasses medical activities such as diagnosis, therapy and immunization, and related research. The term 'protective' applies to the development of such equipment as decontamination systems, protective masks and clothing, air and water filtration systems, and detection and warning devices. Laboratory quantities of certain agents and toxins might well be required for research and testing in these areas. In order to avoid any possible ambiguity, it was made clear during the negotiation of this Convention that <u>the terms 'prophylactic' and 'protective' are not intended to convey any broader meaning which would in any way permit possession of biological agents or toxins for weapons purposes on the theory that such weapons were for defensive warfare, retaliation or deterrence</u>." <u>(emphasis added)</u>

The broad language of the Convention was intended to cover not only agents known at the time the Convention was negotiated, but also any that could later be developed through new scientific or technological developments. At the March 1980 Review Conference for the Convention, the Parties agreed that Article I had proved sufficiently comprehensive to have covered recent scientific and technological developments relevant to the Convention, including the development of recombinant DNA techniques.

As permitted by the Convention, the United States maintains an active program in biological defense against potential biological weapons which is restricted to medical defense matters such as vaccines, prophylaxis and therapy, and rapid identification of causative agents, and a smaller program in rapid detection technology to develop detection devices and systems to alert troops to adopt protective measures. In this program recombinant DNA techniques may be useful for the development of more effective vaccines of higher potency or of a more universal nature, of unique therapeutic drugs and biologics, and of more effective diagnostic reagents effective against a range of infectious diseases. This program does not, and will not, involve research to create and screen "new" organisms as potential biological warfare agents. Our research is, and will continue to be, limited to developing protective measures to recognized infectious diseases which pose a biological warfare hazard.

In view of the above--and to bring the formulation of the amendment as close as possible to the language of the Convention--we recommend that the amendment be modified to read:

> "The use of recombinant DNAs for development of microbial or other biological agents, or toxins, of types or in quantities that have no justification for prophylactic, protective or other peaceful purposes, is prohibited."

We appreciate your invitation to send an ACDA representative to the June 28 meeting of the Recombinant DNA Advisory Committee. I have asked Dr. Robert Mikulak of my staff to represent ACDA. If any questions arise, I suggest you contact Dr. Mikulak directly at 632-3422.

Sincerely yours,

James L. George

James L. George
Assistant Director
for Multilateral Affairs

HARVARD MEDICAL SCHOOL
DEPARTMENT OF ANATOMY

25 SHATTUCK STREET
BOSTON, MASSACHUSETTS 02115
TELEPHONE: (617) 732-1652

June 8, 1982

Dr. William Gartland, Jr.
Director
Office of Recombinant DNA Activities
Building 31, Room 4A52
National Institutes of Health
Bethesda, MD 20205

Dear Dr. Gartland:

I am writing to express my strong support of the Novick-Goldstein amendment of Section I-D entitled "I-D-7. The consruction of biological weapons by molecular cloning". The staggering power of this new technology for the construction of new forms of weaponry are as awesome as the current firepower of nuclear arsenals. I believe that we should learn from the current dilemma we now find ourselves in with respect to the nuclear arms race, and that we should take a strong positive step toward recognizing the potential future hazards of allowing the development of this technology, and limit our potential expansion into this area.

Our country is a world leader. We are responsible for our leadership role, and we should not set the precedent for developing this form of human destruction. I beg you to expend all possible effort in the consideration of this issue. I am grateful to you for your consideration and kindness.

Yours sincerely,

Daniel A. Goodenough
Professor of Anatomy

Department of the History of Science
Harvard University
Science Center 235, Cambridge, Mass. 02138
617-495-3741

June 8, 1982

Dr. William Gartland, Jr., Director
Office of Recombinant DNA Activities
Building 31, Room 4A52
National Institutes of Health
Bethesda, Maryland 20205

Dear Dr. Gartland:

I have heard from Drs. Richard Goldstein and Richard Novick that they are submitting a brief amendment to the NIH guidelines which would add to the list of prohibited activities the construction of biological weapons by molecular cloning.

Having followed the developments of molecular biology in general and recombinant DNA work in particular as a historian, I have been particularly sensitive to the manner in which guidelines have been developed for recombinant DNA work. With many others I've watched carefully the interaction between self-generated restrictions and imposed restrictions. I have been particularly concerned with the manner in which the science society interface has been handled and the means through which the scientific community has accepted responsibilities for the nature of its work. To see an important new area of science be developed for its military--indeed--disease and death-inflicting potentials would seem to me to be a particularly damaging step. One way of raising recognition of the dangers involved and indicating truly responsible, scientific and humane response would be to adopt for the guidelines the prohibitions against using this new field of molecular biology for biological warfare.

Thank you very much for your kind attention in this matter.

Sincerely yours,

Everett Mendelsohn
Professor of the History
of Science

EM/rk

DEPARTMENT OF THE ARMY
U.S. ARMY MEDICAL RESEARCH INSTITUTE OF INFECTIOUS DISEASES
FORT DETRICK, FREDERICK, MARYLAND 21701

IN REPLY REFER TO
SGRD-UIZ-C

9 June 1982

William J. Gartland, Jr., Ph.D.
Director
Office of Recombinant DNA Activities
National Institute of Allergy and
Infectious Diseases
National Institutes of Health
Building 31, Room 4A52
Bethesda, Maryland 20205

Dear Dr. Gartland:

Thank you for bringing this proposed amendment to my attention. I will plan to attend the RAC meeting on 28 June when this comes up for discussion. Prior to that time, however, you may wish to distribute to RAC members the following formal comment from my Agency.

DoD Statement

The DoD has no objection to the proposed amendment but believes it is unnecessary in view of the U.S. understanding of the terms of the Biological Weapon Convention (BWC) which already prohibits the use of recombinant DNA techniques for development of biological or toxin weapons.

The DoD position is to support and abide by the NIH Guidelines in full, in both its in-house, and contract funded research. This position would not change if the amendment was adopted.

There are, however, several items in the rationale for the proposal as developed by the authors which require correction so there is no misunderstanding. The statement that "the development prohibition is generally interpreted in military circles as applying only to the assembly of delivery vehicle" is false. The Department of Defense compliance with the BWC was clearly stated in a certification to the President in January 1976 by the Secretary of Defense that all programs were in full compliance with "prophylactic, protective, and other peaceful purposes" permitted by the Convention.

Further, the statement "the development of biological weapons for "defensive" (e.g., deterrent) purposes would be excluded" is also seriously mistaken as the position statement prepared by the Arms Control and Disarmament Agency (ACDA) points out. The Department has in earlier correspondence agreed to comply, both internally and through contract with established NIH Guidelines.

The military medical DoD interest in recombinant DNA technology is directly related to the development of means and methods for the prevention, diagnosis, or treatment of disease. Such interests are, or will be, targeted toward improved vaccines, new modalities of therapy or prophylaxis, and/or detection devices for a variety of organism identification and diagnostic purposes. Non-medical military interests cover areas of marine fouling problems; materials and polymer engineering; and fuels and lubricant potential, none of which have any relationship to biological weapons.

We agree with the proposed changes by ACDA to bring the proposal to the Guidelines into closer alignment with the Convention which is the basic instrument of national policy.

Sincerely,

William R. Beisel

WILLIAM R. BEISEL, M.D.
DoD Representative Federal Interagency
Advisory Committee on Recombinant DNA
Research

Institute of Molecular Biology
UNIVERSITY OF OREGON
Eugene, Oregon 97403

503/686-5151

June 11, 1982

Dr. William Gartland, Jr.
Director
Office of Recombinant DNA Activities
Building 31, Room 4A52
National Institutes of Health
Bethesda, Maryland 20205

Dear Dr. Gartland,

Drs. Richard Novick and Richard Goldstein have proposed an ammendment to Section I-D of the NIH Guidlines for Recombinant DNA Research. Their ammendment would prohibit under the Guidelines the construction of biological weapons by molecular cloning.

I strongly support the ammendment.

Sincerely yours,

Franklin W. Stahl

Franklin W. Stahl
Professor of Biology
Member, Institute of Molecular Biology

FWS:mc

TUFTS UNIVERSITY

Department of Urban and
Environmental Policy

June 11, 1982

Dr. William J. Gartland, Jr.
Executive Secretary
Recombinant DNA Advisory Committee
National Institutes of Health
Building 31
Bethesda, Maryland 20205

Dear Bill:

I strongly support the Goldstein-Novick amendment that the NIH Guidelines prohibit the construction of biological weapons by molecular cloning.

I have enclosed a segment of a paper entitled "Social Responsibility in an Age of Synthetic Biology: Beyond Biohazards" to be published in Environment. The section deals with biological weapons and recombinant DNA molecule technology. In the essay I conclude that there are three levels of social accountability over the use of rDNA for constructing biological weapons.

First, there is the Convention on the Prohibition of the Development, Production and Stockpiling of Bacteriological and Toxin Weapons which became effective in the US in March 1975. A United Nations review commission report issued in March 1980 concluded that biological materials constructed by rDNA techniques are covered by the Convention's articles. Second, there is a federal law (PL 93-608) requiring the Department of Defense to submit an annual report that explains expenditures in chemical and biological research programs. Third, there is an internal ruling by the Undersecretary of Defense that all rDNA activities funded by DOD will be conducted in compliance with the NIH Guidelines.

Unless the RAC continues to play a strong oversight role in the use of rDNA techniques that involve cloning toxigenic genes, genes that code for immunosuppressants or virulence factors the society will lose a critical area of oversight.

The Goldstein-Novick proposal provides an unambiguous statement of NIH's responsibility in this important area. Despite the DOD memoranda on the application of the rDNA Guidelines to work funded by the military, as of August 1981 ORDA's list of institutions that have registered IBCs included one of three military research centers that do biological research. The list included the US Army's chemical and biological research division at Frederick, Maryland, but did not include the Naval Bioscience Laboratory at Oakland, CA and the Walter Reed Army Institute of Research in Washington. If the DOD is serious about conforming to the Guidelines, it is curious that all the biological research centers would not be registered with ORDA and have appropriate IBCs.

Sincerely,

Sheldon Krimsky, Ph.D.
Assistant Professor

Medford, Massachusetts 02155
617 628-5000, extension 727

HARVARD MEDICAL SCHOOL
DEPARTMENT OF PATHOLOGY
25 SHATTUCK STREET
BOSTON, MASSACHUSETTS 02115

GEORGE TH. DIAMANDOPOULOS, M.D.
PROFESSOR OF PATHOLOGY

TEL. (617) 732-1964

June 14, 1982

Dr. William Gartland, Jr.
Director
Office of Recombinant DNA Activities
Building 31, Room 4A52
National Institutes of Health
Bethesda, Maryland 20205

Dear Doctor Gartland:

I wish to inform you that I support the proposed amendment "I-D-7. The construction of biological weapons by molecular cloning" to the N.I.H. guidelines.

Thank you for taking my wish into consideration.

Cordially,

George Th. Diamandopoulos, M.D.
Professor of Pathology

GThD:cmc

15 June, 1982

Dr. William Gartland, Jr., Director
Office of Recombinant DNA Activities
Building 31, Room 4A52
National Institutes of Health
Bethesda, Maryland, 20205

Dear Dr. Gartland:

I am writing this letter in support of the proposed amendment to the NIH Recombinant DNA Guidlines which would ament section I-D-7 by proscribing the "construction of biological weapons by molecular cloning."

I feel very strongly that the use of this technology to construct biological weaponry constitutes the most horrifying misuse of scientific knowledge that I can think of because of the effect its use might have and the manner in which it would be used. War in any form is an appallingly primitive and inhumae method of achieving ends, but the non-discriminating and unpredictable nature of biological warfare ranks second only to nuclear warfare in its disregard of the welfare of the planet we live on and depend upon for our very existence. The human race is (finally) becoming increasingly aware of the delicate balance of nature and the prppensity of man's (seemingly innocuous) tinkering to disrupt that balance. To deliberately construct an instrument which by its very nature is designed to affect a large segment of life seems to me to fly in the face of all that we have learned.

I realize that the mere adoption of this resolution by an advisory body will not deter the military as it is now constituted, but the act of debating the issues in a public forum may serve to inform the citizenry and generate sufficient public pressure to force a reconsideration.

Sincerely,

Janet Geisselsoder
1285 Montecito Ave. #36
Mountain View, CA. 94043

RUTGERS
THE STATE UNIVERSITY
OF NEW JERSEY

WAKSMAN INSTITUTE OF MICROBIOLOGY • BUSCH CAMPUS • NEW BRUNSWICK • NEW JERSEY 08903
MAILING ADDRESS: P.O. BOX 759 • PISCATAWAY • NEW JERSEY 08854

June 16, 1982

Dr. William Gartland Jr.

Director
Office of Recombinant DNA Activities
Building 31, Room 4A52
N.I.H.
Bethesda Md. 20205

Dear Dr. Gartland:

I have given some consideration to the recent proposal of Drs. Novick and Goldstein to discourage the use of recombinant DNA technology in the development of biological weapons by amending the NIH guidelines to prohibit it.

I agree that the development of biological weapons through cloning must be the most hazardous use of such techniques, and as long as the guidelines are to be preserved, this should be a prohibited activity. I have some concern that the guidelines may not be the proper place for this type of statement, and that the amendment they propose may adversely affect later discussions on the abolition of the guidelines. On balance, I support their view and their amendment.

Sincerely yours,

Michael Kent Showe

Michael Kent Showe

Visiting Professor

FRIENDS OF THE EARTH 72 Jane Street • New York, New York 10014 • (212) 675-5911

June 16, 1982

Dr. William Gartland, Jr.
Director
Office of Recombinant DNA Activities
Building 31, Room 4A52
National Institutes of Health
Bethesda, MD 20205

Dear Dr. Gartland,

I would like to express FOE's support of the amendment to place the development of biological weapons based on the use of recombinant DNA technology on the "prohibited" list in the recombinant DNA guidelines.

This request refers to the amendment co-authored by Dr. Richard Novick and Dr. Richard Goldstein.

The use of recombinant DNA technology for developing new weapons of biological warfare constitutes an egregious misuse of scientific knowledge.

Sincerely,

Andrea Gaines
Friends of the Earth

The University of Michigan

COLLEGE OF ENGINEERING
DEPARTMENT OF HUMANITIES

1079 EAST ENGINEERING BUILDING
ANN ARBOR, MICHIGAN 48109

(313) 764-1420

June 16, 1982

Dr. William Gartland, Jr.
Director
Office of Recombinant DNA Activities
Building 31, Room 4A52
National Institutes of Health
Bethesda, MD 20205

Dear Dr. Gartland:

I write in behalf of the Goldstein-Novick amendment prohibiting the development of biological weapons based on the use of recombinant DNA technology.

Although I am not a scientist, I was one of the organizers of the recombinant DNA teach-in organized here in 1976. And I have continued to follow the social, moral, and political issues associated with recombinant DNA technology since that time.

I am not so naive as to think that this amendment even if adopted will halt work on the development of recombinant DNA technology for military purposes. But much like the proposed freeze on nuclear weapons, this amendment will focus attention on the problem and, I would hope, foster realistic and effective consideration of the problem on an international level.

Sincerely,

Robert P. Weeks

Robert P. Weeks
Professor of Humanities

RPW:vlg

TUFTS UNIVERSITY
School of Medicine

Department of Molecular Biology and
Microbiology

June 16, 1982

Dr. William Gartland, Jr., Director
Office of Recombinant DNA Activities
Building 31, Room 4A52
National Institutes of Health
Bethesda, Maryland 20205

Dear Dr. Gartland:

I support the amendment to Section 1-D of the NIH Guidelines as follows:

1-D-7 -- The construction of biological weapons by molecular cloning.

Edward B. Goldberg
Professor

EBG:ah

136 Harrison Avenue
Boston, Massachusetts 02111
617 956-6750

Residential College
East Quadrangle

The University of Michigan
Ann Arbor, Michigan 48109
(313) 763-0176

June 16, 1982

Dr. William Gartland
Office of Recombinant DNA Activities
Building 31, Room 4A52
National Institutes of Health
Bethesda, MD 20205

Dear Bill:

I strongly support the amendment to prohibit the development of biological weapons submitted by Richard Novick and Richard Goldstein. It seems entirely appropriate that the RAC should address this issue and provide its advice to the NIH Director since the committee is charged with providing safeguards against the hazards of recombinant DNA technology. As Novick and Goldstein point out, the most serious biohazards will derive from the deliberate construction of biological weapons.

I would also like to know whether Department of Defense projects are registered with ORDA at this time. If so, could you provide the RAC and those on the ORDA mailing list with details of these projects (i.e. names of principle investigator and university; name of the division of the Department of Defense funding the project; amount funded; purpose of project; host-vector system).

Sincerely,

Susan Wright
Head, Science Program

HARVARD MEDICAL SCHOOL
MASSACHUSETTS GENERAL HOSPITAL

ARNOLD N. WEINBERG, M.D.
Professor of Medicine

INFECTIOUS DISEASE UNIT
MEDICAL SERVICES
Massachusetts General Hospital
Boston, Massachusetts 02114
726-3816

June 17, 1982

Dr. William Gartland, Jr.
Director
Office of Recombinant DNA Activities
Building 31, Room 4A52
National Institutes of Health
Bethesda, Maryland 20205

Dear Dr. Gartland:

I have become aware of the amendment to NIH Guidelines, prohibiting the construction of biological weapons by molecular cloning, offered by Drs Richard Goldstein and Richard Novick.

For all of the reasons that their arguments raise I can strongly endorse this amendment. I hope that your DNA Advisory Committee agrees with this stand and uses its considerable clout to add another safeguard to the recombinant DNA technology and politics.

Sincerely yours,

Arnold N. Weinberg, M.D.

ANW:ve

UNIVERSITY OF CALIFORNIA, SAN FRANCISCO

BERKELEY • DAVIS • IRVINE • LOS ANGELES • RIVERSIDE • SAN DIEGO • SAN FRANCISCO SANTA BARBARA • SANTA CRUZ

FRANCIS A. SOOY, M.D.
Chancellor
SHIRLEY CHATER
Vice Chancellor, Academic Affairs

Office of the Vice Chancellor, Academic Affairs
SAN FRANCISCO, CALIFORNIA 94143

June 18, 1982

Dr. William Gartland
Office of Recombinant DNA Activities
National Institutes of Health
Room 4A52, Building 31
Bethesda, MD 20205

Dear Dr. Gartland:

On behalf of the UCSF Biosafety Committee, I wish to express our support of the proposal of Drs. Richard P. Novick and Richard Goldstein to prohibit the construction of biological weapons by molecular cloning.

Karl J. Hittelman
Associate Vice Chancellor,
Academic Affairs

KJH/fo

cc: Vice Chancellor Shirley Chater
Dr. Keith Hadley
Ms. Erica Heath
Dr. Richard Novick
Dr. Richard Goldstein

The Commonwealth of Massachusetts
University of Massachusetts
Amherst 01003

Mailing Address:
ZOOLOGY DEPARTMENT
MORRILL SCIENCE CENTER

June 18, 1982

Dr. William Gartland, Jr.
Director
Office of Recombinant DNA Activities
Building 31, Room 4A52
National Institutes of Health
Bethesda, Maryland 20205

Dear Dr. Gartland,

This letter is in support of the ammendment to the NIH Recombinant DNA Guidelines that had been proposed by Drs. Richard Goldstein and Richard Novick: "1-D-7. The construction of biological weapons by molecular cloning".

It seems highly unlikely that viable pathogens or other noxious organisms will be accidently produced by recombinant DNA cloning procedures. On the other hand, if individuals specifically desired to alter the antigenic or antibiotic resistance properties of existing pathogens, confer pathogenic properties on benign organisms or to synthesize toxins, in vitro recombinant DNA procedures could be employed and, I expect, would be successful. If these applications of molecular cloning were directed at humans, domestic animals, crop plants or natural foliage, and wildlife, i.e. for the development of weapons for biological warfare, then they would be absolutely inconsistant with the intent and spirit of the NIH Recombinant DNA Guidelines.

Although there is an international treaty prohibiting the development of biological weapons, and there are statements in the existing Recombinant DNA Guidelines prohibiting some of the above described applications of molecular cloning, it is my feeling that a specific biological warfare ammendment remains warranted. There may well be biological weapons applications not covered by existing sanctions, and this issue is sufficiently grave that it should be raised in as many forums as possible.

In making the biological weapons ammendment to the NIH Guidelines, it should be clear that this sanction is not directed against the use of molecular cloning for the development of vaccines, antitoxins or therapeutic agents by the military or for the construction of organisms for the biological control of disease vectors or agricultural pests.

Dr. William Gartland, Jr.
June 18, 1982
Page 2.

I thank you for considering this letter.

Sincerely yours,

Bruce R. Levin
Professor

BRL:db

DEPARTMENT OF MEDICAL GENETICS

University of Toronto

June 18, 1982

Dr. William Gartland, Jr.
Director
Office of Recombinant DNA Activities
Building 31, Room 4A52
National Institutes of Health
Bethesda, Maryland
U.S.A. 20205

Dear Dr. Gartland,

I strongly support the amendment to section I-D submitted by Drs. Richard Goldstein and Richard Novick regarding "The Construction of Biological Weapons by Molecular Cloning".

I agree that the development of biological weapons based on the use of recombinant DNA technology should be prohibited.

Sincerely,

H. Murialdo, Ph.D.,
Associate Professor.

HM/jr

Telephone: (416) 978-7145 Faculty of Medicine Toronto Ontario M5S 1A8

DEPARTMENT OF STATE

Washington, D.C. 20520

BUREAU OF OCEANS AND INTERNATIONAL
ENVIRONMENTAL AND SCIENTIFIC AFFAIRS

June 18, 1982

Dr. William Gartland
Director, Office of Recombinant
DNA Activities
National Institutes of Health
Building 31, Room 4A52
Bethesda, Maryland 20014

Dear Bill:

This is to comment on the amendment to the National Institutes of Health (NIH) Guidelines on Recombinant DNA which has been proposed by Drs. Novick and Goldstein.

I have discussed the issue with Dr. Robert Mikulak of the Arms Control and Disarmament Agency and find myself in accord with that Agency's views as expressed in Dr. James L. George's letter to you of June 8, 1982. In addition to the views expressed in that letter and as a non-voting member of the Recombinant DNA Advisory Committee (RAC) I have some additional observations.

It has been my understanding that the purpose of the RAC is to advise the Director, NIH regarding safety aspects of experiments involving Recombinant DNA and of the NIH Guidelines. I believe that this issue introduces a political element into the RAC that is beyond the scope of its official mandate. Moreover, while there is no question about the propriety of members of the RAC expressing their opinion on this issue, the last paragraph on the first page of the rationale for the proposal gives me a great deal of concern. The description of the US military's interpretations of provisions in The 1972 Biological Weapons Convention is stated without substantiation or specific attribution. I believe that description is false.

If I am correct in my belief the issue should be clarified immediately before serious harm is done. This kind of lack of precision and correctness in these sensitive and complex matters is reprehensible. It can even be interpreted as belying the stated noble intent of the authors.

Unfortunately, I will not be able to attend the June 28 meeting. However, I would appreciate your communicating these views to the Committee as you think appropriate.

Sincerely,

Bill Walsh

William J. Walsh, III
Coordinator for Biomedical Research
and Health Affairs

UNIVERSITY OF CALIFORNIA, SAN FRANCISCO

BERKELEY • DAVIS • IRVINE • LOS ANGELES • RIVERSIDE • SAN DIEGO • SAN FRANCISCO — SANTA BARBARA • SANTA CRUZ

SCHOOL OF MEDICINE
DEPARTMENT OF PEDIATRICS
1421 HSW

SAN FRANCISCO, CALIFORNIA 94143

June 20, 1982

Dr. William Gartland, Jr.
Director
Office of Recombinant DNA Activities
Building 31, Room 4A52
National Institutes of Health
Bethesda, Maryland 20205

Dear Dr. Gartland:

I am writing to urge adoption of the proposed ammendment to the NIH Recombinant DNA Guidelines placing the development of biological weapons based on molecular cloning on the "prohibited" list. As a geneticist I am very aware of the potential utility of molecular cloning in the development of biological weapons. I believe that the use of molecular cloning for such purposes would represent one of the most dangerous, horrifying misuses of science imaginable -- increasing the dangers of biological warfare and eliminating the distinction between offensive and defensive weapons. Adoption of this Ammendment would put the scientific community on record in opposition to such research and would promote public recognition and debate concerning the dangers of such research.

Sincerely,

Jon Weil

Jon Weil, Ph.D.

MRC
Medical Research Council

Laboratory of Molecular Biology
Medical Research Council Centre
University Medical School
Hills Road, Cambridge CB2 2QH
England

telephone Cambridge (0223) 248011

telex - 81532

21st June 1982

Dr William Gartland, Jr
Office of Recombinant DNA Activities
Building 31, Room 4A52 - N I H
Bethesda, MD 20205

Dear Dr Gartland,

I would like to add my support to the proposed amendment, I-D-7, to the NIH Guidelines submitted by Drs Richard Novick and Richard Goldstein.

Yours sincerely,

F. Sanger

F. Sanger

UNIVERSITY OF WASHINGTON
SEATTLE, WASHINGTON 98195

School of Public Health and Community Medicine
Department of Environmental Health, SC-34

June 21, 1982

William J. Gartland, Ph.D.
Executive Director
Recombinant DNA Advisory Committee
National Institutes of Health
Building 31
Room 4A52
9000 Rockville Pike
Bethesda, Md. 20205

Dear Bill:

Many thanks for your continued mailings. As you can see, I am re-established in Seattle in my old position as Professor of Medicine and my new position as Chairman of this Department of Environmental Health.

I am writing to second the proposal from Novich and Goldstein that the RAC take an explicit position that the guidelines prohibit the use of molecular cloning or other genetic techniques for the development of biological weapons.

Wherever I speak about the public policy aspects of biotechnology and genetic engineering, there is usually a question about this matter. Our country and our scientific community should have a clear record.

Best wishes.

Sincerely yours,

Gil Omenn

GSO:vad

Gilbert S. Omenn, M.D., Ph.D.
Professor and Chairman
Environmental Health

72 Wendell Street
Cambridge, Massachusetts 02138

Dr. William Gartland, Jr.
Office of Recombinant DNA Activities
National Institutes of Health
Bethesda, Maryland 20205

21 June, 1982

Dear Dr. Gartland:

I am writing in support of the proposed amendment to section I-D of the NIH guidelines co-authored by Prof. Richard Goldstein and Dr. Richard Novick that would prohibit the use of molecular cloning for development of biological weapons. I support this amendment very strongly, especially at a time when biological weapons are becoming thinkable once again. Please, no more awful inventions for death.

Sincerely,

Alice Evans Tsen

Alice Evans Tsen

UNIVERSITY OF CALIFORNIA, BERKELEY

BERKELEY • DAVIS • IRVINE • LOS ANGELES • RIVERSIDE • SAN DIEGO • SAN FRANCISCO — SANTA BARBARA • SANTA CRUZ

VIRUS LABORATORY

22 June 82

BERKELEY, CALIFORNIA 94720

Dear Dr. Gartland:

I would like to support the amendment of Goldstein and Novick, outlawing the use of genetic engineering in biological warfare.

Sincerely,

Richard Calendar

Professor

Institutionen för mikrobiologisk genetik
Karolinska Institutet
104 01 Stockholm 60, Sweden

Stockholm 1982-06-22

Dr William Gartland Jr

Hereby we would like to state our support of the amendment "I-D-7. The construction of biological weapons by molecular cloning" to the NIH guidlines.

Anna Westöö   Elisabeth Ljungquist

COLUMBIA COLLEGE Columbia University in the City of New York | New York, N.Y. 10027
OFFICE OF THE DEAN
Hamilton Hall

June 23, 1982

Dr. William Gartland, Jr.
Director
Office of Recombinant DNA Activities
Building 31, Room 4A52
NATIONAL INSTITUTES OF HEALTH
Bethesda, MD 20205

Dear Dr. Gartland,

I support the enclosed amendment to the NIH-RDNA guidelines. I believe it accurately reflects the views of many of my colleagues, as well as my own personal view. I hope this amendment is given all possible consideration.

Sincerely,

Robert E. Pollack, PhD
Professor of Biological Sciences and
Dean-elect

REP:ms

Enc.

UNIVERSITY OF CALIFORNIA, BERKELEY

Cable: OFCSVCS TWX: 910-366-7114

BERKELEY • DAVIS • IRVINE • LOS ANGELES • RIVERSIDE • SAN DIEGO • SAN FRANCISCO | SANTA BARBARA • SANTA CRUZ

DEPARTMENT OF MOLECULAR BIOLOGY
WENDELL M. STANLEY HALL
BERKELEY, CALIFORNIA 94720

June 23, 1982

Dr. William Gartland, Jr.
Director
Office of Recombinant DNA Activities
Building 31, Room 4A52
National Institutes of Health
Bethesda, Maryland 20205

Dear Dr. Gartland:

I am writing to support the proposed amendment to the Recombinant DNA Guidelines prohibiting the construction of biological weapons by molecular cloning. I believe that this amendment will be an important force in deterring a dangerous misuse of recombinant DNA technology.

Sincerely,

Harrison Echols
Professor of Molecular Biology

HE:td

UNIVERSITY OF CALIFORNIA, SAN DIEGO

BERKELEY • DAVIS • IRVINE • LOS ANGELES • RIVERSIDE • SAN DIEGO • SAN FRANCISCO   SANTA BARBARA • SANTA CRUZ

PROGRAM IN SCIENCE, TECHNOLOGY
AND PUBLIC AFFAIRS

Q-060
LA JOLLA, CALIFORNIA 92093

June 23, 1982

Dr. William Gartland, Jr.
Director
Office of Recombinant DNA Activities
Building 31, Room 4A52
National Institutes of Health
Bethesda, Maryland 20205

Dear Bill:

I wish to record my strong support for the amendment to the NIH guidelines proposed by Richard Goldstein and Richard Novick. I agree entirely with their statement of rationale and further note that the matter is an excellent example of what the RAC can now usefully do to address important issues excluded from the Asilomar agenda and post-Asilomar policy making.

With very best regards,

Clifford Grobstein

CG:aw

Dr. William Gartland, Jr.
Director
Office of Recombinant DNA Activities
National Institutes of Health
Building 31, Room 4A52
Bethesda, MD 20205

June 23, 1982

Dr. Gartland:

I understand that Professor Richard Goldstein and Dr. Richard Novick have co-authored an amendment to section ID of the NIH guidelines, which would prohibit the use of molecular cloning for the development of biological warfare.

I am writing in support of this important amendment. I am sure that the majority of Americans, given the opportunity to understand recombinant DNA activities, would support stronger NIH guidelines than those which now exist, and would certainly support the proposed amendment.

Thank you,

Kate Cloud

Kate Cloud

UNIVERSITY OF CALIFORNIA, SAN DIEGO

BERKELEY • DAVIS • IRVINE • LOS ANGELES • RIVERSIDE • SAN DIEGO • SAN FRANCISCO SANTA BARBARA • SANTA CRUZ

DEPARTMENT OF BIOLOGY, B-022 LA JOLLA, CALIFORNIA 92093

June 23, 1982

Wm J. Gartland, Jr.
Program Administrator, Genetics Program
National Institute of General Medical Sciences
National Institutes of Health
Bldg. 4B, Room 922
Bethesda, Maryland 20014

Dear Bill,

It is my understanding that RAC is considering at its June 28-29, 1983 meeting the adoption of an amendment to the NIH guidelines that prohibits the application of recombinant DNA techniques to the development of biological weapons. As a former member of RAC and an active investigator in the area of recombinant DNA research, I fully support this amendment and urge every effort on your part to give this amendment full consideration by RAC and to bring to the attention of proper legislative bodies the views of the scientific community on this important issue.

Sincerely,

Don

Donald R. Helinski

an

STATE OF CONNECTICUT

DEPARTMENT OF HEALTH SERVICES

BUREAU OF HEALTH PROMOTION & DISEASE PREVENTION

June 23, 1982

Dr. William Gartland, Jr.
Director
Office of Recombinant DNA Activities
Building 31, Room 4A52
National Institutes of Health
Bethesda, Maryland 20205

Dear Dr. Gartland:

I would like to indicate my strong support for amendment I-D-7 to the NIH guidelines for recombinant DNA. I feel that the use of recombinant DNA experimentation for the purpose of developing organisms which could be used for "biologic warfare" is unacceptable both because of public health and humanitarian considerations. Any research which could be subsequently used for purposes of developing such weapons should be prohibited.

Thank you for your consideration of this matter.

Sincerely,

Stephen Havas, M.D.
Bureau Chief

e

Phone: 566-5911
79 Elm Street • Hartford, Connecticut 06115

UNIVERSITY OF CALIFORNIA, BERKELEY

BERKELEY • DAVIS • IRVINE • LOS ANGELES • RIVERSIDE • SAN DIEGO • SAN FRANCISCO | SANTA BARBARA • SANTA CRUZ

DEPARTMENT OF MICROBIOLOGY
AND IMMUNOLOGY

BERKELEY, CALIFORNIA 94720

June 23, 1982

Dr. William Gartland, Jr.
Director
Office of Recombinant DNA Activities
Building 31, Room 4A52
National Institutes of Health
Bethesda, MA 20205

Dear Dr. Gartland:

I am writing to urge support of the amendment of Drs. Richard Novick and Richard Goldstein which has been submitted to your office. I strongly feel it is essential that the use of molecular cloning for the development of biological weapons be explicitly prohibited.

Sincerely,

Claudia Henry

Claudia Henry
Associate Professor

CH:csl

Marine Biological Laboratory
WOODS HOLE, MASSACHUSETTS 02543

June 24/82

Dear Dr. Gartland,

I should like to express my strong support of the amendment to the NIH Guidelines for recombinant DNA activities, proposed by Dr. Richard Novick and Dr. Richard Goldstein.

Two or three years ago the Federation of American Scientists warned of the possibility that gene-splicing might be used to prepare new organisms for biological warfare. That possibility comes closer all the time.

It would be most important for the N.I.H. to do what it

can to thwart it.

Sincerely,

George Wald

Prof. George Wald
Biological Labs
Harvard University
Cambridge, Mass. 02138

TUFTS UNIVERSITY
School of Medicine
Department of Molecular Biology and Microbiology

June 24, 1982

Dr. William Gartland, Jr., Director
Office of Recombinant DNA Activities
Building 31, Room 4A52
National Institutes of Health
Bethesda, Maryland 20205

Dear Dr. Gartland:

I write in support of the Goldstein-Novick proposal to restrict the formation of biological weapons by molecular cloning. I hope the RAC looks favorably on the proposal, or a stronger version.

Recorded history shows us that nature has already invented poorly host-adapted pathogens which have been responsible for numerous violent epidemics. It must, therefore, be possible for man to re-create pathogens with similarly catastrophic potential from the modern (less virulent) descendants. It behooves us to restrain any desire to embark on such research.

Sincerely yours,

D. Michael Gill

D. Michael Gill, Ph.D.
Professor

DMG:ah

136 Harrison Avenue
Boston, Massachusetts 02111
617 956-6750

LESLEY COLLEGE

The Graduate School

June 24, 1982

Dr. Willima Gartland, Jr.
Director,
Office of REcombinant DNA Activities
Building 31, Room 4A52
National Institutes of Health
Bethesda, MD 20205

Dear Dr. Gartland:

I urge the REcombinant DNA Advisory Committee to adopt the ammendmend proposed by Drs. Novick and Goldstein that the development of biological weapons based on the use of recombinant DNA technology be placed on the prohibited list.

I believe that every effort must be made in every quarter to stress that reasonable people do not wish to see the proliferation of these weapons.

Although I am currently working outside the field of science, I spent a considerable portion of my academic life as a research biochemist and science educator. I am aware of the possible consequences of unprincipled scientific research.

Sincerely,

George E. Hein,
Professor

29 Everett Street Cambridge, MA 02238 (617) 868-9600

PHYSICIANS FOR SOCIAL RESPONSIBILITY

639 Massachusetts Avenue, Cambridge, MA 02139, (617) 491-2754

HELEN CALDICOTT, M.B., B.S.
President

July 7, 1982

Dr. William Gartland, Jr.
Director
Office of Recombinant DNA Activities
Building 31, Room 4A52
National Institutes of Health
Bethesda, MD 20205

Dear Dr. Gartland:

It has been brought to my notice that the military is considering using recombinant DNA technology for combative purposes. I find this absolutely repugnant and I think this was the worry of all the scientists who were concerned initially about DNA recombination.

I therefore recommend that the proposed amendment to the NIH guidelines Section I-D should be included. I enclose the amendment as follows.

Yours sincerely,

Helen Caldicott

Helen Caldicott, M.B., B.S.
President

HC/cjts

PROPOSED AMENDMENT TO THE NIH GUIDELINES

Section I-D shall be amended as follows:

"I-D-7. The construction of biological weapons by molecular cloning."

The rationale for this proposal is as follows:

The experience of many scientists throughout the world during the past seven or eight years has demonstrated that the original fears of catastrophic laboratory accidents involving novel microorganisms constructed by molecular cloning were largely unfounded.

Nevertheless, there remain grounds for concern in a few specific areas - three of which are correctly reflected in the currently operative version of the NIH guidelines. These three are: the transfer of clinically important antibiotic resistance to new species; the cloning of toxin determinants; and the deliberate release of recombinant organisms into the environment. A fourth area - one that is perhaps of greatest concern - has never been directly addressed by the RAC. This is the use of recombinant DNA technology for the development of new weapons of biological warfare.

The potential of molecular cloning in this area has been apparent from the start; indeed it was an important consideration in the minds of many of the scientists at the Asilomar Conference who were involved in the initial framing of the guidelines.

However, it was omitted from the guidelines, presumably because of the 1972 treaty prohibiting the "development, production and stockpiling" of biological weapons. This treaty seemed to provide at least some assurance of security; however, the "development" prohibition is generally interpreted in military circles as applying only to the assembly of delivery vehicles. Laboratory research involving the construction of the organisms and the development of biological weapons for "defensive" (e.g., deterrent) purposes would be excluded. It is noted that the treaty was adopted before the advent of molecular cloning and that subsequently much of the U.S. military apparatus for biological warfare research and development was publicly dismantled. Most recently, however, the obvious potential of molecular cloning has led to a substantial renewal of military interest.

It is our position that the use of molecular cloning for the deliberate construction of biological weapons is, per se, the most serious biohazard imaginable for this technology and that it constitutes an egregious misuse of scientific knowledge.

On the basis of these several considerations, it is proposed that the RAC adopt the above amendment explicitly prohibiting any use of molecular cloning for the development of biological weapons.

Against this proposal, it may seem that the extant regulations applying to the cloning of toxins, the transfer of resistance, and the dissemination of recombinant organisms thoroughly cover the possible use of cloning in biological warfare. In fact, the coverage under these provisions is grossly inadequate. On the one hand, it does not apply to agents of disease other than toxins; viruses, for example, have always been considered very attractive as biological weapons and their *a priori* attractiveness is enhanced substantially by the potential of molecular cloning. On the other hand, since the only militarily credible use of biological weapons involves surreptitious dissemination, the RAC prohibition against dissemination will certainly not inhibit the military forces of any country.

Admittedly, the adoption by the RAC of the proposed amendment will not directly interdict any military initiatives. It is nevertheless appropriate as an explicit public statement that could have several important effects. It will provide automatic public support for a refusal of the scientific community to participate in the development of biological weapons; it may convince governments that the 1972 prohibition should be construed as applying to laboratory research as well as to the means of delivery; and it may encourage individual governments and international bodies such as the UN, NATO, SEATO, Warsaw Pact signatories, the OAS, etc., to reaffirm these international prohibitions legislatively or by treaty.

Yale University

DEPARTMENT OF BIOLOGY

Kline Biology Tower
P.O. Box 6666
New Haven, Connecticut 06511

August 11, 1982

Dr. William Gartland
Executive Secretary
National Recombinant DNA Advisory Committee
NIH, Room 4A52, Bldg. 31
Bethesda, Maryland 20205

Dear Dr. Gartland:

I write you to register my opposition to the proposal that molecular cloning techniques be used in the development of biological weaponry. To me this constitutes an unwarranted and dangerous extension of the new biotechnology, which can only lead to a decreased security for the United States. I hope American scientists will see this point clearly and oppose all such trend.

Sincerely,

Arthur W. Galston

Arthur W. Galston
Professor of Biology

AWG:af

INDEX OF LETTERS AND DOCUMENTS

☆ U.S. GOVERNMENT PRINTING OFFICE: 1983-381-132:766

Lightning Source UK Ltd.
Milton Keynes UK
UKHW020645221118
332785UK00012B/1242/P

9 781528 040976